ULTIMATE MAJOR LEAGUE BASEB

DETROIT TIGERS

Michigan's Favorite Sports Team

By Roger Yoder

Images were courtesy of:

Front cover: Kevin Povenz. George Grantham Bain Collection: 19, 24, 50 (bot), 251, 320, 460. Baseball Digest: 213 (rgt), 336. Baseball Library: 26. Kristin Beat: Back (3). Bowman Gum: 62, 220 (rgt), 224. CBS Radio: 150 (top lft). Chicago Daily News: 34, 495. Detroit Free Press: 18, 266, 327, 448. Detroit Public Library (Ernie Harwell Collection): 7 (top, bot), 8, 9, 11, 12, 13, 14, 15, 17 (top, bot), 20, 21, 22, 23, 25, 27, 28 (top, bot), 29, 30, 31, 32, 36, 37, 38, 39 (top, bot), 40, 42, 43, 44, 45, 46, 47, 48, 49, 51, 52, 53, 54, 55, 57, 63, 65, 71, 75, 150 (bot), 151 (lft, mid, rgt), 155 (lft, mid, rgt), 165, 166, 167, 183 (bot), 194 (rgt), 195, 196 (lft, mid), 206, 208 (lft), 210 (lft), 213 (lft), 214 (lft), 217, 219, 220 (lft), 221 (lft), 222, 223, 225, 229, 230, 237, 241, 244, 250, 252, 255, 256, 257, 264, 268, 269, 270, 271, 272, 274, 277, 281, 283, 286, 289, 293, 295, 297, 298, 303, 304 (lft), 306, 309, 311, 313, 316, 318, 322, 324, 326, 331, 333, 337, 338 (lft), 346, 348, 354, 358, 366, 370, 387 (lft), 389, 392, 395, 398, 401, 404, 407, 408, 409, 413, 414, 415, 419, 424, 425, 430, 436, 437, 438, 440 (top), 449, 455, 462, 463, 469, 474, 478, 479, 482, 484, 485, 487, 492, 496, 497, 500, 508, 512, 520 (rgt), 525, 544, 545 (top), 546, 551 (1), 561. Detroit Tigers: 78, 83 (bot), 228, 282, 315 (rgt), 363, 368, 428, 441, 486, 518, 545 (bot). Heather Hall: 3. Hoover Family: 214 (rgt). Carl Horner: 502. C.J. Horner: 16. J.G. Howes Collection: 61 (bot). Jay Publishing: 69, 78, 218, 263, 314 (lft), 432 (lft), 447, 450, 503. Library of Congress & Photographs Division: 10, 16, 18, 19, 24, 26, 33, 34, 35, 41, 50 (bot), 56, 61 (bot), 70, 78. Major League Baseball: 50 (top), 73, 74, 81, 101, 105, 106, 109, 122, 127 (top, bot), 129, 132, 133, 136, 138, 139, 193, 197 (mid, rgt), 209 (rgt), 227, 232, 234, 242, 249, 254, 262, 278, 304 (mid), 307, 308 (top rgt, bot lft), 323, 328, 334, 335, 338 (rgt), 339, 342, 347, 356, 365, 371, 393, 396, 397, 405, 416, 417, 420, 422, 434, 439 (lft, top mid, bot mid, rgt), 442, 445, 452, 454, 458, 465, 471 (lft), 480, 498, 499, 514, 515, 516, 517. National Baseball Hall of Fame: 183 (top), 184 (all), 185 (all), 186 (all), 187 (all), 188 (all), 189 (all), 190 (all), 191 (all), 192 (all). National Photo Company Collection: 33, 41, 466. Sporting News: 10, 35. St. Louis Browns: 56, 243, 315)mid), 400. St. Louis Cardinals: 212. Topps Baseball Card Company: 58, 59, 60, 61 (top), 64, 66, 67, 68, 70, 72 (top, bot), 76, 77, 79, 80, 82, 83 (top), 84, 85, 86, 87, 88, 89, 90, 91, 92, 93, 94 (top, bot), 95, 96, 97, 98, 100, 102, 103, 104, 105 (top, bot), 107, 108, 110, 111, 112, 113, 114, 115, 116 (top, bot), 117, 118, 119, 120, 121, 123, 124, 125, 126, 128, 130, 131, 134, 135, 137, 150 (top rgt), 152 (lft, rgt), 194 (lft), 196 (rgt), 197 (lft), 201, 202, 207, 208 (rgt), 209 (lft), 210 (rgt), 211, 215 (lft, rgt), 216, 221 (rgt), 226, 231, 233, 235, 236, 238, 239, 240, 245, 246, 247, 248, 253, 258, 259, 260, 261, 265, 267, 273, 275, 276, 279, 280, 284, 285, 287, 288, 290, 291, 292, 294, 296, 299, 300, 301, 302, 304 (rgt), 305 (lft, mid, rgt), 308 (top lft, bot rgt), 310, 312, 314 (mid, rgt), 315)lft), 317, 319, 321, 325, 329, 330, 332, 340, 341, 343, 345, 349, 350, 351, 352, 353, 355, 357, 359, 360, 361, 362, 364, 367, 369, 372, 373, 374, 375, 376, 377, 378, 379, 381, 382, 383, 384, 385, 386, 387 (rgt), 388, 390, 391, 394, 399, 402, 403, 406, 410, 411, 412, 418, 421, 423, 426, 427, 429, 431, 432 (rgt), 433, 435, 440 (bot), 443, 444, 446, 451, 453, 456, 457, 459, 461, 464, 467, 468, 470, 471 (mid, rgt), 472, 473, 475, 476, 477, 481, 483, 488, 489, 490, 491, 493, 494, 501, 504, 505, 506, 507, 509, 510, 511, 513, 519, 520 (lft), 521, 522, 523, 524, 526, 527, 528, 545 (mid), 555 (2,3,4), 558, Back (2, 4). Mark-Richard Yoder: 6, Back (1). Roger Yoder: 168, 169, 170. Zeenut: 344.

First Edition

Published by Gatekeeper Press, 2167 Stringtown Rd., Suite 109, Grove City, OH 43123. 866-535-0913

Library of Congress Cataloging in Publication Data
Yoder, Roger L 1959-

Detroit Tigers: Michigan's Favorite Sports Team/by Roger Yoder

LCCN: 2021944131
ISBN 0-000000-00-0 (soft)

1. Detroit Tigers (Baseball team) – History. I. Title.
2. Sports
3. Michigan

Printed in the United States of America

DEDICATION

LANDON HALL

This book is dedicated in memory of Landon Hall. He died at the age of 12 on Wednesday, August 22, 2018. Landon had touched family and friends with his shining light. Although his life was short, he lived, loved, and laughed. Landon was going into the seventh grade at Addison Community Schools. He had a love for all sports and wore his favorite number two as a proud Panther in football, basketball, and baseball. Landon also enjoyed living on a lake where he could often be found fishing, swimming, and tubing with his friends. In addition to lake life, Landon also liked playing video games and jumping on the trampoline with his younger brothers. Landon was a kind and compassionate boy with a heart of gold. He always gave his all and never backed down from anything. Landon had the most amazing group of friends a boy could ask for and cherished them all. He was a friend to all and was willing to help anyone.

LIVE LIKE LANDON

ACKNOWLEDGEMENTS

This comprehensive history of the Detroit Tiger franchise could not have been possible without the gracious support from my wife Mercy, son Mark, daughter Caroline, relatives, and friends.

James and Vernia Grubb are my spiritual inspiration. Philippians 4:13: "I can do all this through him who gives me strength."

I thank Will and Heather Hall for their endorsement to dedicate this book in memory of their son Landon, a classmate of our daughter. May we never forget "*L Train*" and his short time with us.

Friends Ray Curran, David Johnson, and Kevin Way were steadfast with encouragement. Their optimism fueled those long days and nights when the project seemed insurmountable.

Kabayan Mike Price was a trusted advisor through the years. His advice and suggestions were instrumental to this book you will enjoy reading, "MARAMING SALAMAT PO".

The publishing experience can be overwhelming, although Rob Price and Eden Tuckman from Gatekeeper Press exhibited patience and understanding with this first-time author, thank you!

Former Tigers Jerry Don Gleaton, Walt Terrell and Dick Tracewski are baseball ambassadors. They provided insight on their time in Major League Baseball. Their background provided a trip down memory lane.

The Detroit Public Library, Library of Congress, Major League Baseball, and the Topps Baseball Card Company were sources for many of the images used. They have my admiration for all that they do.

Baseball is a game of statistics from the traditional to the sabermetrics of today. The background information was obtained from baseball-almanac.com, baseball-reference.com, mlb.com and Wikipedia.com.

I extend my appreciation to the team, broadcasters, media, and fans that have grown and nurtured a legacy for one of baseball's storied franchises. Let us all pass that Tiger tradition on to future generations.

CONTENTS

PREFACE

ROGER YODER

The Ultimate Major League Baseball book series brings you the Detroit Tigers: Michigan's favorite sports team. A book that chronicles the history of the Detroit Tiger MLB franchise, with almost 600 images. Relive the past through yearly reviews that recap each season month by month, including information on hitting, pitching, and defense. There are player and pitcher of the year selections, break out boxes for decade hitting and pitching leaders. Each decade has player and pitcher of the decade, with all-decade teams and pitching staffs presented. This book introduces the Most Effective Hitter (MEH) and Most Effective Pitcher (MEP) analytical evaluations. MEH considers offensive proficiency to compare players and teams from any era and level of play. MEP considers areas of pitching to determine the best on the mound. MEH was used to determine the Top-150 All-Time Tigers, Top-10 by position and five All-Time teams. The MEP comparison was utilized to determine the Top-50 All-Time Starters and Top-50 All-Time Relievers. The yearly and decade hitting and pitching leaders from 1901 through 2021 are included. The top 100 all-time hitting and pitching leaders by category are featured. Statistics from the traditional to the sabermetric data of today is provided for 102 offensive and 57 pitching categories. The yearly hitting leaders require a player to have played in 100 games or have 300 plate appearances, with all-time leaders requiring either 400 games played or 1,400 plate appearances. Pitching yearly leaders will have either started 15 games, appeared in 40 games, or had 140 innings pitched, with 40 games started or 195 games pitched for the all-time leader boards. All will be listed in cumulative categories as appropriate. I regret any errors discovered as you peruse this version of Tiger history. The Detroit Tigers: Michigan's favorite sports team would be a valuable addition to any library. Whether a casual fan or a savvy baseball enthusiast, you will enjoy many hours learning more about the storied Detroit Tiger MLB franchise.

OF * JIMMY BARRETT

Player of the Decade. Ty Cobb of Royston, Georgia, made his major-league debut on Wednesday, August 30, 1905, at the age of 18. He quickly became the game's premier player. The decade team leader in several categories, including slugging (.459), on-base plus slugging (.839), OPS+ (163), total average (.925), gross production average (.286), batting average (.337), BAbip (.365), secondary average (.266), total base average (1.7), bases produced average (2.3), sacrifice hits (65), and stolen bases (193), with a 25-game hit streak in 1906. The *"Georgia Peach"* led the American League three straight years for hits, runs batted in, hitting, slugging, OPS, OPS+, total bases, and offensive WAR, with 1907 (.350 BA, 5 HR, 119 RBI, 212 H, .468 SLG, .848 OPS, 167 OPS+, 283 TB, 53 SB, 6.5 oWAR), 1908 (.324 BA, 4 HR, 108 RBI, 188 H, .476 SLG, .844 OPS, 170 OPS+, 276 TB, 39 SB, 6.5 oWAR) and a Triple Crown in of 1909 (.377 BA, 9 HR, 107 RBI, .517 SLG, .947 OPS, 192 OPS+, 296 TB, 76 SB, 9.6 oWAR). Cobb was one of the few bright spots for the Tigers in the 1908 World Series loss (.368 BA, .400 OBP, .421 SLG, 4 RBI).

1900s

Year	W – L	Pct.	Pl
1901	74-61	.548	3
1902	52-83	.385	7
1903	65-71	.478	5
1904	62-90	.408	7
1905	79-74	.516	3
1906	71-78	.477	6
1907	92-58	.613	1
1908	90-63	.588	1
1909	**98-54**	**.645**	1
	683-632	.519	

All-Decade Team. Manager Hughie Jennings (280-175 .615) led team to the World Series 1907-1909. Pitcher Ed Summers (43-21 .672, 1.93 ERA) excelled in 1908 (24-12, 1.64 ERA). Catcher Boss Schmidt (.239 BA, 2 HR, 99 RBI) led team in defensive WAR (5.6). First baseman Claude Rossman (.280 BA, 2 HR, 179 RBI) hit .474 (.579 SLG) during the 1907 World Series. Second baseman Kid Gleason (.262 BA, 4 HR, 113 RBI) led decade for in-play percentage (87%) and strikeout ratio (0.03). Kid Elberfeld (.290 BA, 4 HR, 159 RBI) at short led the 1900s in AB/SO (31.9), BB/SO (3.7), strikeout ratio (0.03) and strikeout percentage (2.7%). Third baseman Doc Casey (.278 BA, 5 HR, 101 RBI) hit .283 and scored 105 runs in 1901. Left-fielder Sam Crawford (.304 BA, 31 HR, 300 RBI) led decade in games (1,038), plate appearances (4,423), at-bats (4,012), runs (562), hits (1,221), singles (866), doubles (210), triples (114), homers, oWAR (34.8), extra base hits (355), total bases (1,752), extra bases on long hits (531), percentage of hits for extra bases (29.1), stolen base runs created (963) and bases produced (2,177). Center-fielder Jimmy Barrett (.292 BA, 10 HR, 174 RBI) led team in on-base percentage (.382), walks (309) and walk percentage (11.7). Ty Cobb (.337 BA, 20 HR, 390 RBI) noted for his offense, led American League right-fielders in assists for 1907 (30), 1908 (23) and 1909 (21).

Pitcher of the Decade. Ed Summers (43-21 .672, 1.93 ERA) was one of the first knuckleball pitchers. He was the staff decade leader in winning percentage, balks (2), technical runs allowed (3.14), earned run average, ERA+ (127), FIP (2.30), DICE (3.14), WHIP (1.066), BB/9 (1.65), SO/BB (1.96), RA/9 (3.14), starter win percentage (.644) and dominant starter percentage (.344). The 23-year-old rookie led the 1908 staff in wins (24), ERA (1.64) Games (40), starts (32) games finished (8), innings (301), batters faced (1,195), ERA+ (145), WHIP (1.083) and BB/9 (1.6). He was 7-0 against Philadelphia in 1908, and won both games of a doubleheader on September 25, 7-2 in game one and a 1-0 10-inning game two shutout. Ed went 19-9 in 1909 leading Detroit in WHIP (1.047), BB/9 (1.7) and SO/W (2.06). Summers pitched 18 shutout innings facing visiting Washington on July 16. He could throw the knuckleball overhand, side-arm, underhanded and even pitched left-handed in the minors. The first Tiger rookie to start a postseason game, with his 1908 game four World Series start another highlight in team history.

P * ED SUMMERS

1900s Attendance

Year	Attn.	Avg.	Rk
1901	259,430	3,706	3
1902	189,469	2,828	6
1903	224,523	3,454	6
1904	177,796	2,251	7
1905	193,384	2,545	8
1906	174,043	2,231	7
1907	297,079	3,760	7
1908	436,199	5,592	5

All-Decade Pitchers. Summers went 15-5 on the road in 1908 and 12-2 at home in 1909. Bill Donovan (111-80 .581, 2.43 ERA) was the decade leader in shutouts (25), home runs (19), pitcher WAR (28.8), H/9 (7.77), SO/9 (4.56) and led league in 1903 for complete games (34) and win percentage (25-4 .862) in 1907. Ed Killian (95-71 .572, 2.34 ERA) led the staff in left on-base percentage (71.7), HR/9 (0.04), quality start percentage (.613), high quality start percentage (.583), games in relief (30) and relief wins (10). His best year came in 1907 (25-13 .658, 1.78 ERA). Ed Willett (37-26 .587, 2.51 ERA) led in relief losses (3) and was in top form for 1909 (21-10 .677, 2.34 ERA). George Mullin (157-134 .540, 2.66 ERA) led the Tigers in games (330), wins, losses, starts (298), games finished (30), complete games (258), shutouts (25), saves (6), quality starts (140), high quality starts (133), dominant starts (46), innings (2,592.1), hits (2,434), home runs (19), walks (833), strikeouts (1,091), hit by pitch (78), wild pitches (67), earned runs (765), runs (1,116), starter wins (147), starter losses (133), batters faced (10,636), no decisions (15), cheap wins (17), tough losses (39), relief wins (10), and relief win percentage (10-1 .909). Ed Siever (60-53 .531 2.61 ERA) had his best year in 1907 (18-11 .621, 2.16 ERA). Win Mercer (15-18 .455, 3.04 ERA) had four shutouts in 1902. Frank Kitson (35-43 .449 3.02 ERA) from Watson, Michigan completed all 28 of his starts in 1903. Roscoe Miller (29-25 .537, 3.18 ERA) led the decade in complete game percentage (.926), with a solid 1901 season (23-13 .639, 2.95 ERA). Joe Yeager (18-24 .429, 3.54 ERA) starred as a pitcher (12-11 .522, 2.61 ERA) and hitter (.296 BA) in 1901.

Hall of Fame outfielder Sam Crawford was the first to lead both the National and American leagues in home runs. His record of 309 career triples may never be challenged. He coached the University of Southern California 1924-1929 and was a Pacific Coast League umpire 1935-1938. Sam led his Wahoo, Nebraska high school football team to state titles in 1896 and 1897.

Team. Detroit was an inaugural member of the eight team American League, with MLB returning to the city after 13-years. The Tigers finished third for owner-manager George Stallings at 74-61 (.548), with 259,430 fans. Players went 5-1 in April including a 14-13 home win in their first game against Milwaukee on Thursday, April 25, with a 10-run Tiger ninth inning. Pop Dillon went 4-for-6 (4 2B, 5 RBI), Kid Gleason 3-for-6 (2 RBI), Kid Elberfeld (2 RBI), Ducky Holmes (2 RBI) and winning reliever Emil Frisk was 3-for-5 (RBI). Motown logged a 15-11 mark in May that included a 13-1 victory in Cleveland on Monday, May 20, behind Frisk (W 5-0, 9 IP, 1 ER) 2-for-5 (RBI), Doc Casey (4 R, 4 RBI), Elberfeld (2 RBI), Fritz Buelow (2 RBI) and Jimmy Barrett 3-for-5 (RBI). Detroit finished 10-14 in June with back-to-back home shutouts over Milwaukee 4-0 by Roscoe Miller (W 6-6, 9 IP, 0 ER, 7 H) on Friday, June 28 and 5-0 with Ed Siever (W 7-6, 9 IP, 0 ER, 4 H, 6 SO) the next day. The Bengals were 15-11 in July when Miller (W 7-6, 16 IP, 1 ER, 13 H) pitched a 7-5 16-inning complete game win at Milwaukee on Wednesday, July 3. The stars were Gleason 4-for-7 (RBI, 2 SB), Elberfeld 3-for-7 (2 RBI), Casey (2 RBI) and Sport McAllister (2 RBI). Players logged a 19-12 home win over Cleveland on Saturday, July 13. Nance went 6-for-6 (2 RBI), Gleason 3-for-5 (3 RBI), Davey Crockett 3-for-5 (3 RBI), Elberfeld 3-for-5 (2 RBI) and Miller (W 10-6, 9 IP). The team went 13-14 in August with a 12-1 win against Chicago at home on Friday, August 9, on the strength of a seven run sixth inning. Miller (W 17-7, 9 IP, 1 ER), Gleason 3-for-5 (HR, 3 RBI) and Holmes 3-for-5 starred. Several days later Motown defeated visiting Milwaukee 16-5 on Sunday, aided by Casey 4-for-5 (3 RBI), Elberfeld 3-for-5 (4 RBI), Holmes 3-for-5 (2 RBI, 2 SB) and Siever (W 11-11, 9 IP, 2 ER) with two RBI. Detroit closed 16-10 in September with a Siever (W 17-13, 8 IP, 0 ER) 2-for-4 (2 RBI) led a 21-0 shutout of Cleveland at home on Sunday, September 15. Home plate umpire Bill Hart called it after eight innings to allow the Blues to catch a train and was the most lopsided game in team history. Cleveland's Jack Bracken (L 3-7, 7 IP, 21 R, 24 H, 3 BB, CG) allowed 27 Tigers to reach base. McAllister went 3-for-5 (2 2B, HR, 7 RBI), Al Shaw 3-for-5 (4 R, 2 RBI), Barrett 2-for-3 (4 R, 2 RBI, 2 BB) and Buelow (2 RBI). The Bengals were 42-27 (.609) at home, 31-34 (.477) on the road, scored 741 runs and allowed 694. Miller completed his last 35 starts May 13-Sep 28.

1900s
Team Hitting

YEAR	AVG	HR	RBI	SB
1901	**.279**	**29**	**611**	204
1902	.251	22	488	130
1903	.268	12	451	128
1904	.231	11	431	112
1905	.243	13	421	129
1906	.242	10	427	206
1907	.266	11	551	196
1908	.263	19	520	165
1909	.267	19	521	**280**

UT * SPORT MCALLISTER

Offense. Detroit hit .279 BA, 742 R, .340 OBP, .370 SLG, .710 OPS, 1,730 TB and 93 OPS+, with MLB high in SH (135). Fritz Buelow (.225 BA, 2 HR, 29 RBI) caught, first baseman Pop Dillon (.288 BA, 1 HR, 42 RBI), Kid Gleason (.274 BA, 3 HR, 75 RBI) at second led the squad in games (135), at bats (547), triples (12), outs (412) and hit streak (25). Third baseman Doc Casey (.283 BA, 2 HR, 46 RBI) led the Tigers in hit by pitch (10), as Player of the Year shortstop Kid Elberfeld (.308 BA, 3 HR, 76 RBI) led the club in runs batted in, on-base percentage (.397), slugging (.428), OPS (.825), OPS+ (124), total average (.910), gross production average (.286), WAR (3.8), oWAR (4.0), batters run average (.166), batting average, BAbip (.303), secondary average (.306) and isolated power (.120). The leftfielder was Doc Nance (.280 BA, 3 HR, 66 RBI). The most effective hitter Jimmy Barrett (.293 BA, 4 HR, 65 RBI) at center led league in strikeouts (64) and team in games (135), plate appearances (630), runs (110), hits (159), singles (130), BAbip (.327), times on base (240), base runs (79), runs produced (171), runs created (79), bases produced (307) and walks (76). Ducky Holmes (.294 BA, 4 HR, 62 RBI) in right led squad in doubles (28), power/speed number (7.2), extra base hits (42), total bases (218) and steals (35). Sport McAllister (.301 BA, 3 HR, 57 RBI) led for in-play percentage (88%). Emil Frisk (.313 BA), Joe Yeager (.296 BA, 2 HR, 17 RBI) and Roscoe Miller (.208 BA, 14 RBI) led pitchers in hitting. The leading pinch-hitter was McAllister at .500 (2-4).

Pitching. The Tigers closed with a 3.30 ERA, 118 CG, eight SHO, 313 walks, 307 SO, 3.56 FIP, 1.381 WHIP, 10.1 H/9, 2.4 BB9, 2.3 SO/9 and led league in ERA+ (117), with youngest staff (25.3). The Pitcher of the Year and most effective pitcher Roscoe Miller (23-13, 2.95 ERA, 38 GM, 1 SV) led league in HR/9 (0.0) and was the staff leader in wins, win percentage (.639), starts (36), complete games (35), shutouts (3), innings (332), hits (339), walks (98), hit by pitch (13), batters faced (1,408), earned runs (109), runs (168), LOB% (62.86), pWAR (6.9), H/9 (9.2) and R/9 (4.6). Ed Siever (18-15, 3.24 ERA, 38 GM, 288.2 IP) led in games finished (5), homers (9), strikeouts (85) and SO/9 (2.7). Joe Yeager (12-11, 2.61 ERA, 1 SV) led in ERA, ERA+ (147) and WHIP (1.277). John Cronin (13-16, 3.89 ERA) led in wild pitches (5), FIP (3.44), DICE (3.51), BB9 (1.7) and SO/BB (1.48). Ed High (1-0, 3.50 ERA), Emil Frisk (5-4, 4.34 ERA) and Frank Owen (1-3, 4.34 ERA). Miller excelled June 25-September 4 (15-4 .789, 1.93 ERA), with nine straight wins during period of June 25-July 30 (9-0, 2.35 ERA).

1900s
Team Hitting

YEAR	OBP	SLG	OPS	OPS+
1901	**.340**	**.370**	**.710**	93
1902	.312	.320	.632	72
1903	.318	.351	.670	104
1904	.282	.292	.575	84
1905	.301	.311	.612	94
1906	.295	.306	.600	86
1907	.313	.335	.648	104
1908	.312	.347	.659	**111**
1909	.325	.342	.667	106

Defense. Detroit had a .930 fielding average and led the American League in assists (1,928), errors (410) and double plays (127). League leaders were pitchers Cronin in errors (12) and Siever in double plays (5), as Miller led in chances (136) and assists (112). Gleason led in assists (457) and errors (64) at second base. Casey in errors (58), double plays (25) and club in dWAR (1.0) at third. Shortstop Elberfeld led in chances (819), chances per game (6.8), putouts (332) and double plays (62). Outfielder Barrett led in assists (31) and chances per game (2.6). The team made a record 12 errors on Wednesday, May 1.

Righthander Roscoe Miller completed his last 35 starts May 13-September 28. The 24-year-old rookie pitched 10 innings or more five times (4-1 .800, 63.2 IP, 9 ER, .216 BA), with a 2-1 tough loss at Boston on Tuesday, August 27 (14.2 IP, 7 H, 0 ER).

1900s Games		
1.	Sam Crawford	1,038
2.	Matty McIntyre	712
3.	Charley O'Leary	691
4.	Germany Schaefer	626
5.	Ty Cobb	595
6.	Bill Coughlin	593
7.	Jimmy Barrett	589
8.	George Mullin	414
9.	Boss Schmidt	378
10.	Claude Rossman	373

Team. Detroit finished seventh for former National League umpire Frank Dwyer at 52-83 (.385), with 189,469 fans. The Tigers were 3-2 in April with a 11-3 victory at St. Louis on Tuesday, April 29, aided by Win Mercer (W 1-0, 9 IP, 2 ER, 5 H), Dick Harley 4-for-5 (2 RBI), Jimmy Barrett 3-for-5 (2 RBI), Ducky Homes (2 RBI) and Kid Elberfeld (2 RBI). Players registered a 13-12 record in May that included a five-game win streak starting on Sunday, May 11. The first-place Tigers prevailed during a seven-inning 19-11 slugfest versus Cleveland in Burns Park on Sunday, May 18. Detroit scored four runs in fourth, five in the fifth, sixth and seventh innings. Deacon McGuire was 2-for-3 (HR, 5 RBI), Joe Yeager 2-for-4 (5 RBI), Holmes 3-for-4 (3 RBI) and Fritz Buelow 3-for-4 (HR, 3 RBI). Motown went a horrific 36-69 (.343) for the rest of the season. The Bengals went 9-15 in June, as they won 11-2 over visiting Washington on Sunday, June 15. 21-year-old rookie George Mullin (W 3-2, 9 IP, 1 ER), Buelow 2-for-3 (3 RBI), Pop Dillon (2 RBI) and Barrett 3-for-5 led the way. Mercer (W 6-5, 9 IP, 0 ER, 3 H) tossed a three-hit 4-0 shutout over the Senators on Tuesday, with Elberfeld 3-for-4 (RBI) and Dillon 2-for-4 (2 RBI). The squad was 8-16 in July that included an 18-game hit streak by Barrett July 2-22 (.408 BA, .506 OBP). Mercer (W 9-6, 9 IP, 1 ER, 6 H) 2-for-3 (2 R, RBI) led a 6-1 home victory over St. Louis on Saturday, July 5. The club went 4-13 during 17 straight road games July 6-29. Ed Siever (9 IP, 0 ER, 5 H) threw a five-hit 8-0 shutout in Baltimore on Monday, July 21. Motown finished 8-20 during August, with a 1-15-1 record in a 17-game stretch August 10-26. Detroit won 10-2 in Baltimore on Friday, August 22, with Mullin (9 IP, 0 ER, 4 H) 1-for-3, Barrett (HR, 3 RBI), Sport McAllister (3 RBI) and Holmes 3-for-5 (RBI). Mullin excelled as a hitter August 22-September 26 (16-40, .400 BA, .460 OBP, .550 SLG, .410 BAbip). Players closed 11-18 in September, with a home doubleheader sweep of Washington 4-2 and 13-1 on Monday, September 1. Arch McCarthy (9 IP, 2 ER, 5 H) and Harley 3-for-4 (RBI) led game one, followed by Mullin (9 IP, 1 ER, 5 H) 2-for-5 (2 RBI), Doc Casey 4-for-5 (HR, 2 RBI), Pete LePine 2-for-5 (2 RBI), Buelow (2 RBI) and Barrett 3-for-5 in game two. Rookie Rube Kisinger (9 IP, 1 ER) out of Adrian College won 4-2 on Friday, September 26, with McAllister (2 RBI) and Yeager 3-for-4. The squad was 34-33 (.507) at home, 18-50 (.265) on the road and 0-10 in Philadelphia. The Tigers scored 566 runs while allowing 657.

MGR * FRANK DWYER

Offense. Detroit had a .251 BA, 566 R, .312 OBP, .320 SLG, .632 OPS, 1,484 TB and 72 OPS+. The catchers were Deacon McGuire (.227 BA, 2 HR, 23 RBI) and Fritz Buelow (.223 BA, 2 HR, 29 RBI). The trio of Pop Dillon (.206 BA, 22 RBI), Sport McAllister (.210 BA, 1 HR, 32 RBI) and Erve Beck (.296 BA, 2 HR, 22 RBI) manned first. The "*Kids*" were up the middle with Kid Gleason (.247 BA, HR, 38 RBI) at second and Kid Elberfeld (.260 BA, HR, 64 RBI) at short. Doc Casey (.273 BA, 3 HR, 55 RBI) at third led in at bats (520) and outs (387). Dick Harley (.281 BA, 2 HR, 44 RBI) in left led in triples (8) and HBP (12). The Player of the Year and most effective hitter was Jimmy Barrett (.303 BA, 4 HR, 44 RBI) at center who led in games (136), plate appearances (594), runs (93), hits (154), singles (125), doubles (19), on-base percentage (.397), slugging (.387), OPS (.784), OPS+ (114), total average (.848), base-out percentage (.850), gross production average (.276), WAR (3.1), oWAR (2.7), batters run average (.152), hitting, BAbip (.297), secondary average (.277), times on base (234), base runs (78), runs produced (133), runs created (78), power/speed number (6.9), extra base hits (29), extra bases on long hits (43), total bases (197), bases produced (295), steals (24), walks (74) and hitting streak (18). Ducky Holmes (.257 BA, 2 HR, 33 RBI) was in right-field. Joe Yeager (.242 BA, 1 HR, 23 RBI). George Mullin (.325 BA, .408 SLG, 11 RBI) led the pitchers.

1900s Runs		
1.	Sam Crawford	562
2.	Jimmy Barrett	383
3.	Matty McIntyre	372
4.	Ty Cobb	365
5.	Germany Schaefer	279
6.	Bill Coughlin	236
7.	Charley O'Leary	231
8.	Davy Jones	203
9.	Kid Elberfeld	175
10.	Doc Casey	174

Pitching. Motown recorded a 3.56 ERA, 116 CG, nine SHO, 370 walks, 245 SO, 105 ERA+, 3.52 FIP, 1.375 WHIP, 9.6 H/9, 2.8 BB/9, 1.9 SO/9 and led the league in saves (3). Detroit pitchers led a sweep of visiting Washington on Thursday, July 31, by a 9-1 score, followed by back-to-back 13-0 and 8-0 shutouts on Friday and Saturday. Pitcher of the Year Win Mercer (15-18, 3.04 ERA, 35 GM, 4 SHO, 282 H, 5 HR) led in wins, losses, win percentage (.455), starts (33), complete games (28), innings (281.2), HBP (10), LOB% (66.3), batters faced (1,170) and pWAR (6.1). The most effective pitcher was Ed Siever (8-11, 1.91 ERA, 4 SHO, 5.6 pWAR) that led MLB in HR/9 (0.0). He led the league for earned run average and ERA+ (195), with staff lead in FIP (2.83), DICE (3.16), WHIP (1.051), H/9 (7.9), BB/9 (1.5), SO/BB (1.13) and R/9 (3.5). George Mullin (13-16, 3.67 ERA, 35 GM, 282 H) led league in wild pitches (13) and club in walks (95), strikeouts (78), wild pitches (13), earned runs (106), runs (155) and SO/9 (2.7). Roscoe Miller (6-12, 3.69 ERA), Joe Yeager (6-12, 4.82 ERA, 5 HR), Arch McCarthy (2-7, 6.13 ERA) and Rube Kisinger (2-3, 3.12 ERA). Rookie Wish Egan (0-2, 2.86), a Michigan native from Evart, made his MLB debut.

Defense. Detroit committed 332 errors for a .943 fielding percentage, with a league leading 1,894 assists. The league leaders were catcher Buelow in errors (20), Gleason in putouts (320) and errors (42) at second base, centerfielder Barrett led all outfielders in chances (362) and putouts (326). Shortstop Elberfeld led his team in defensive WAR (1.1) for the 1902 season.

Jimmy Barrett excelled during the period of May 9-June 1 (19 GM, .400 BA, .494 OBP, .471 SLG, .422 BAbip), July 2-21 (17 GM, .418 BA, .513 OBP, .493 SLG, .444 BAbip). His other 1902 highlights included 18 three-hit games and 20 two-hit games.

The poor record for Detroit (52-83 .385) in 1902 was reflected in the team's statistics, as they scored the fewest runs (566) in the league, was sixth in ERA (3.56), and sixth in attendance with 189,469 at home games in Bennett Park and Burns Park.

Detroit Tigers 1903 American League

1900s Hits		
1.	Sam Crawford	1,221
2.	Ty Cobb	765
3.	Matty McIntyre	711
4.	Jimmy Barrett	660
5.	Germany Schaefer	558
6.	Charley O'Leary	521
7.	Bill Coughlin	500
8.	Claude Rossman	387
9.	Kid Elberfeld	305
10.	Davy Jones	300

Team. Detroit finished in fifth place under manager Ed Barrow with a 65-71 (.478) record playing before 224,523 fans at home. The Tigers opened the season at home with a 5-1 mark for April that included two dominant starts by Bill Donovan. Motown defeated visiting Cleveland 11-1 on Thursday, April 23, behind Donovan (W 1-0, 9 IP, 1 ER, 9 SO) 1-for-3 (RBI), Charlie Carr 4-for-4 (2 2B, 4 RBI) and Doc Gessler 2-for-3 (2 RBI). Donovan (W 2-0, 9 IP, 1 ER) won a 10-1 tilt with Chicago at Bennett Park on Wednesday, April 29, including Jimmy Barrett 5-for-5 (2 RBI, 2 SB) and four Tiger triples. Players registered a 12-16 record in May, as the Bengals destroyed Indian pitching 13-1 in Cleveland on Saturday, May 9 to end a six-game losing streak. Joe Yeager went 3-for-5, Kid Elberfeld 3-for-6 (2 RBI) and Donovan (W 3-1, 9 IP, 1 ER, 5 H, 9 SO) 2-for-4 to lead the way. The team was 9-2 during an 11-game stretch May 12-24 to move into first place, then lost six consecutive games to fall into sixth place. The squad went 9-12 in June with back-to-back shutout wins against Washington at home June 29-30. George Mullin (W 8-6, 9 IP, 0 ER, 4 H) blanked the Senators 3-0 on Monday. Frank Kitson (9 IP, 0 ER, 3 H) won 8-0 on Tuesday, with Sam Crawford 4-for-5 (2 3B, RBI, 2 SB), Herman Long 3-for-3 (2 2B, 2 RBI) and Fritz Buelow 3-for-4 (2 RBI). Players logged a 15-11 record in July, when the Tigers won 4-3 in 14-innings over Chicago at home on Friday, July 24. Carr went 3-for-7 (RBI) with pitchers Mullin (9 IP, 2 ER) and Rube Kisinger (W 3-1, 5 IP, 0 ER). The franchise had a record of 14-14 in August, with a doubleheader sweep of Philadelphia 3-0 and 5-4 at home on Thursday, August 20. Michiganders Kisinger (9 IP, 0 ER, 6 H) from Adrian and Kitson (W 13-10, 9 IP, 2 ER) from Watson, as Deacon McGuire was 2-for-3 (RBI) in game one and Crawford 4-for-5 (2 RBI) in game two. Detroit closed 10-17 in September with five straight doubleheaders September 6-14. The Bengals took a 7-3 decision in St. Louis on Saturday, September 5, with John Skopec (W 2-1, 9 IP, 2 ER), Crawford 3-for-3 (HR, 4 RBI) and Carr (2 RBI). The Tigers rolled to a 13-8 win in New York on Saturday, September 26. Crawford was 4-for-6 (4 RBI), Yeager (3 RBI), Carr (2 RBI) and Billy Lush with a 3-3-3-3 jackpot of 3-for-3 with three triples and three runs batted in. Detroit went 37-28 (.569) at home, 28-43 (.394) on the road, scored 567 runs and allowed 539.

MGR * ED BARROW

Offense. Detroit had a league low in doubles (162) and homers (12). The team finished with a .268 BA, .318 OBP, .351 SLG, .670 OPS, 1609 TB and 104 OPS+. The catcher was Deacon McGuire (.250 BA, 21 RBI). First baseman Charlie Carr (.281 BA, 23 2B, 2 HR, 79 RBI) led for in-play percentage (88%) and outs (407). Heinie Smith (.223 BA, HR, 22 RBI) manned second, with Joe Yeager (.256 BA, 43 RBI) at third and Sport McAllister (.260 BA, 22 RBI) played shortstop. Billy Lush led in left led MLB in sacrifice hits (34) and led his team in secondary average (.314). Centerfielder Jimmy Barrett (.315 BA, 2 HR, 31 RBI) led the league in walks (74) and led all Tigers in plate appearances (615), runs (95), singles (138), on-base percentage (.407), total average (.873), base-out percentage (.879), times on base (243), stolen bases (27), stolen base runs (8.1) and strikeouts (67). Player of the Year and the most effective hitter Sam Crawford (.335 BA, 23 2B, 4 HR, 89 RBI) in right led MLB in triples (25), as he led Motown in games (137), at bats (550), hits (184), doubles (23), runs batted in (89), slugging (.489), OPS (.855), OPS + (159), gross production average (.287), WAR (5.6), oWAR (5.4), batters run average (.171), batting average, BAbip (.360), base runs (87), runs produced (173), runs created (98), isolated power (.155), power/speed number (6.5), extra base hits (52), total bases (269), bases produced (312) and had the longest hitting streak (20). George Mullin (.278 BA, HR, 12 RBI) led the pitchers.

1900s Doubles		
1.	Sam Crawford	210
2.	Ty Cobb	118
3.	Matty McIntyre	94
4.	Germany Schaefer	75
5.	Charley O'Leary	74
6.	Claude Rossman	62
7.	Jimmy Barrett	59
8.	Bill Coughlin	56
9.	George Mullin	47
10.	Kid Elberfeld	43
	Ducky Holmes	43

Pitching. The Tigers recorded a 2.75 ERA, 123 CG, 15 SHO, 554 SO, 105 ERA+, 2.94 FIP, 1.258 WHIP, 8.8 H/9, 2.5 BB/9, and 4.2 SO/9. They led the league in walks (336) and HR/9 (0.1). Detroit had back-to-back shutouts in St. Louis 1-0 on Monday, September 7, and 3-0 at Cleveland on Friday, September 11. Pitcher of the Year George Mullin (19-15, 2.25 ERA, 4.9 pWAR) led the league in saves (2), walks (106) and staff in games (41), wins, win percentage (.559), starts (36), games finished (5), shutouts (6), innings (320.2), hits (284), walks (106), hit by pitch (8), earned runs (80), runs (128), earned run average, ERA+ (128). The most effective pitcher Bill Donovan (17-16, 2.29 ERA) led the league in complete games (34), as he completed all his starts. Bill led squad in wild pitches (7), strikeouts (187), LOB% (70.9), FIP (2.64), DICE (2.89), WHIP (1.114), pWAR (7.0), H/9 (7.2), SO/9 (5.5) and R/9 (3.0). Frank Kitson (15-16, 2.58 ERA) completed all 28 of his starts and led staff in homers (8), BB/9 (1.3) and SO/BB (2.68). Rube Kisinger (7-9, 2.96 ERA), rookie right-hander John Deering (3-4, 3.86 ERA), Mal Eason (2-5, 3.36 ERA), John Skopec (2-2, 3.43 ERA) and Harry Kane (0-2 8.50 ERA).

Defense. Detroit players committed 281 errors with a .950 fielding percentage/ Tiger league leaders were Mullin in pitcher chances (156), putouts (38) and assists (108). Catcher McGuire led in stolen bases (92). First baseman Carr led in assists (111). Center fielder Barrett led outfielders in assists (19). Carr and shortstop Kid Elberfeld led club in defensive War (0.4).

28-year-old pitcher Win Mercer (1902: 15-18, 3.04 ERA) was named manager for the 1903 season, although committed suicide in the Occidental Hotel in San Francisco on January 13, 1903, following a three-month western barnstorming tour.

Detroit chose 34-year-old Ed Barrow to manage in 1903. He had managed Toronto in Eastern League 1900-1902. The future Hall of Famer improved the club by 13 games, with seven new regulars that included pitcher Joe Yeager's move to third base.

1900s Triples	
1. Sam Crawford	114
2. Ty Cobb	49
Matty McIntyre	49
4. Jimmy Barrett	30
5. Germany Schaefer	25
6. Claude Rossman	24
7. Kid Elberfeld	20
8. Doc Casey	16
Kid Gleason	16
10. George Mullin	15

Team. Detroit finished in seventh under manager Ed Barrow (32-46) and Bobby Lowe (30-44) at 62-90 (.408), with a final attendance of 177,796. The Tigers were 6-6 after April that included an 8-2 win over visiting Chicago on Thursday, April 28, aided by Ed Killian (9 IP, 2 ER, 3 H) (2 RBI), Matty McIntyre 2-for-4 (3 RBI) and Bob Wood 2-for-3. Motown logged a 6-15 record in May, with a 5-4 loss to Washington at Columbia Park in Grand Rapids on Wednesday, May 25, with George Mullin (L 3-6, 8 IP, 3 ER) and Charlie Carr 3-for-3. Barrow resigned after 78 games due to disagreements with secretary-treasurer Frank Navin. 38-year-old second baseman Lowe was named player-manager for the rest of the season. Detroit was 11-13 during June, as the club fell 18-6 to Chicago at home on Monday, June 27. Pitchers Bill Donovan (5 IP, 9 R, 13 H, 2 BB) and Jesse Stovall (4 IP, 9 R, 11 H, 3 BB) allowed 31 White Sox hitters to reach base, with 24 hits, five walks and two hit batters. Motown finished 10-16 in July when they played 25 consecutive games on the road. Detroit swept a three-game set in Chicago July 3-4, as Mullin (W 11-8, 9 IP, 0 ER, 5 H) and Sam Crawford 3-for-4 (2B, 3B, SB) led a 4-0 shutout of the White Sox on Sunday. Players swept a doubleheader the next day 5-2 and 6-1. Carr (2 RBI) and Killian (9 IP, 2 ER, 6 SO) starred in game one, as Ed Gremminger 3-for-4 and Donovan (9 IP, 1 ER, 1 H) led the second victory on the Fourth of July. The Bengals were 14-13 in August that included a six-game winning streak thru Saturday, August 13. Killian (W 13-13, 9 IP, 1 ER) pitched a 12-1 win at Washington on Saturday, August 20. The offensive leaders were Charley O'Leary 3-for-5 (2 RBI), Bill Coughlin 3-for-5, Crawford 3-for-5, Lowe 3-for-5 and Charlie Hickman 1-for-3 (2 RBI, 2 SH). The squad went 11-21 in September including 10 doubleheaders. The players endured a 1-9 record during a 10-game stretch September 18-30, with the lone victory a Donovan (W 16-16, 9 IP, 0 ER, 3 H) and Jimmy Barrett 3-for-4 led 5-0 shutout of New York at home on Wednesday, September 28. Motown closed 4-6 in October when Charlie Jaeger (W 3-2, 9 IP, 0 ER, 5 H, 6 SO) and Rabbit Robinson 2-for-4 (2 RBI) led a 3-2 win versus visiting Washington on Monday, October 3. The game was completed in 1:25 with only 300 fans in Bennett Park. Detroit was 34-40 (.459) at home, 28-50 (.359) on the road, scored 505 runs and pitchers allowed 627.

1B * CHARLIE CARR

Offense. Detroit finished with a .231 BA, .282 OBP, .292 SLG, .575 OPS, 1556 TB, and 84 OPS+. Bob Wood (.246 BA, 1 HR, 17 RBI) and Lew Drill (.244 BA, 13 RBI) split the catching duties. Charlie Carr (.214 BA, 40 RBI) played at first, with second baseman Bobby Lowe (.208 BA, 40 RBI) the team leader for in-play percentage (88%). Ed Gremminger (.214 BA, HR, 28 RBI) was at third and Charley O'Leary (.213 BA, HR, 16 RBI at short. Leftfielder Matty McIntyre (.253 BA, 2 HR, 46 RBI) had a 17-game hit streak. Jimmy Barrett (.268 BA, 31 RBI) at center led MLB in games (162) and plate appearances (719). He led the league in walks (79), as he led his team in at bats (624), runs (83), hits (167), singles (152), on-base percentage (.353), gross production average (.234), WAR (3.1), oWAR (3.0), hitting, BAbip (.313), times on base (249), base runs (66), runs created (66), bases produced (281), strikeouts (91) and outs (465). Player of the Year and most effective hitter right-fielder Sam Crawford (.254 BA, 2 HR, 73 RBI) led the Bengals in doubles (22), triples (16), runs batted in, slugging (.361), OPS (.670), OPS+ (114), total average (.637), base-out percentage (.647), batters run average (.109), secondary average (.221), runs produced (120), isolated power (.107), power/speed number (3.6), extra base hits (40), total bases (203), stolen bases (20) and stolen base runs (6.0). Reserve Rabbit Robinson (.241 BA, 37 RBI). George Mullin (.290 BA, 8 RBI) led pitcher hitting and led the pinch-hitters at .333 (2-6).

1900s Home Runs	
1. Sam Crawford	31
2. Ty Cobb	20
3. Jimmy Barrett	10
4. Germany Schaefer	8
5. Ducky Holmes	6
6. Fritz Buelow	5
Doc Casey	5
8. Kid Elberfeld	4
Kid Gleason	4
Charles Hickman	4
Sport McAllister	4

Pitching. The team had a 2.77 ERA, 143 CG, 15 SHO, 433 walks, 556 SO, 92 ERA+, 2.84 FIP, 1.243 WHIP, 8.5 H/9, 2.7 BB/9, and 3.5 SO/9. Motown led the league in innings (1,430), walks (433), hit by pitch (69), batters faced (5,894) and homers per nine (0.1). Pitcher of the Year Bill Donovan (16-16, 2.46 ERA) led in win percentage (.500), wild pitches (11), hits per nine (7.7) and strikeouts per nine (4.2). The most effective pitcher Ed Killian (15-20, 2.44 ERA) led the staff in games finished (6), HBP (17), LOB% (70.7), FIP (2.67), DICE (3.25), WHIP (1.164), pWAR (4.5) and R/9 (3.2). George Mullin (17-23, 2.40 ERA) was league leader for walks (131), as he led Detroit in games (45), wins, losses, starts (44), complete games (42), shutouts (7), innings (382.1), hits (345), walks (131), strikeouts (161), earned runs (102), runs (154), earned run average and ERA+ (106). Frank Kitson (8-13, 3.07 ERA) led in homers (7), BB/9 (1.7) and SO/BB (1.82). Jesse Stovall (2-13, 4.42 ERA) had the league's worst pWAR (-2.5). Charlie Jaeger (3-3, 2.57 ERA) and rookie Bugs Raymond (0-1, 3.07 ERA). Killian and Mullin led MLB in HR/9 (0.0).

Defense. Detroit committed 273 errors for a .959 fielding percentage. The team was league leader in chances (6,738) and putouts (4,288). League leaders were Mullin in pitcher chances (204) and errors (13). Catchers Drill in errors (24) and double plays (11), as Buelow led in passed balls (14). Carr led in assists (121) at first. Outfielders Crawford led in double plays (8), with Barrett leading in chances (379), putouts (33) and assists (29). O'Leary at third led the Bengals in defensive WAR (0.8).

George Mullin had a good fastball and curveball, although would seek any advantage. He would try everything to distract hitters to include stalling, walking off the mound, messing with his belt, fixing his hat, retying his cleats, and talking to himself.

Mullin excelled during the periods of May 14-July 6 (12 CG, 9-3, 112 IP, 1.69 ERA, .222 BA, 4 SHO), July 22-August 30 (8 CG, 2-5, 73 IP, 1.36 ERA, .226 BA) with five tough losses, and for September 1-October 8 (8 CG, 4-4, 80.1 IP, 1.57 ERA, 3 SHO).

1900s Runs Batted In		
1.	Sam Crawford	567
2.	Ty Cobb	383
3.	Germany Schaefer	195
4.	Bill Coughlin	190
5.	Matty McIntyre	186
6.	Claude Rossman	179
7.	Jimmy Barrett	174
8.	Kid Elberfeld	159
9.	Charley O'Leary	147
10.	Charlie Carr	119

Team. Bill Armour led third place Detroit (79-74 .516), with 193,384 fans. The 35-year-old Armour had managed Cleveland (232-195, .543) the three previous years, including a Naps team that went 86-65 (.570) in 1904. The Tigers were 5-6 in April with a 5-0 shutout of visiting Cleveland on Wednesday, April 26, with Sam Crawford 4-for-4 (2 RBI) and Ed Killian (W 2-0, 9 IP, 0 ER, 5 H) 2-for-3 (RBI). Players recorded a 13-11 mark in May when Crawford was strong May 8-May 27 (.478 BA, .538 OBP, .609 SLG). Motown won 12-6 at home win over the New York Highlanders on Wednesday, May 24. The stars were Charley O'Leary (4 RBI), Crawford 2-for-3 (2 RBI), Charlie Hickman (2 RBI), Lew Drill (2 RBI) and reliever George Mullin (W 3-7, 3 IP, 0 ER, 1 H) 1-for-2 (2 RBI). Detroit was 11-13 in June when the Bengals played 20 of their 24 games on the road. Crawford homered in the fourth inning for a Bill Donovan (W 5-3, 9 IP, 0 ER, 4 H, 9 SO) 1-0 shutout win in Philadelphia on Tuesday, June 13. The franchise finished 14-13 in July including five consecutive wins by Killian July 11-August 1 (5-0, 37 IP, 1.70 ERA, 1 SHO). Detroit went 8-2 for a 10-game stretch July 13-22. Duff Cooley had three straight three-hit games July 21-22 versus Washington (9-for-14, .643 BA, .643 OBP, 1.000 SLG, .615 BAbip). The club went 11-17 in August as Crawford dominated the week of August 18-25 (.519 BA, .552 OBP, .667 SLG, .519 BAbip). Killian won five straight games again August 25-September 18 (5-0, 45 IP, 1.00 ERA, .222 BA, 3 SHO). Matty McIntyre excelled August 28-September 4 (.500 BA, .533 OBP, .607 SLG, .538 BAbip). Motown held on for an 5-3 win at home against New York on Wednesday, August 30, as 18-year-old rookie Ty Cobb hit a two-run double off future Hall of Famer Jack Chesbro in his first major league at-bat. The Tigers rebounded with a 21-11 record in September that included going 4-2 in back-to-back-to back doubleheaders September 4-6. Germany Schaefer was hitting .233 when he torched Cleveland pitching at home September 12-16 (4 GM, 9-for-16, .563 BA,.563 OBP, .813 SLG, .563 BAbip). Killian (W 22-13, 9 IP, 0 R, 3 H) drove in two during a three-hit 3-0 shutout in Cleveland on Monday, September 18, with Drill 3-for-3 and Chris Lindsay 3-for-4. Crawford found his niche September 23-29 (.520 BA, .613 OBP, .960 SLG, .520 BAbip). The Bengals won five consecutive games starting on Tuesday, September 26, as they moved from sixth place into third where they would finish the season. Players had a 4-3 record in October, with a 7-0 shutout at Cleveland on Thursday, October 5. Detroit logged a 45-30 (.600) record at home, including a 9-2 mark against St. Louis and were 34-44 (.436) in away games. Motown scored 512 runs as pitchers allowed opponents to score 602 times. That established a new record for the largest negative run differential for a winning team in major league baseball history.

P * ED KILLIAN

Offense. Detroit finished with a .243 BA, .302 OBP, .311 SLG, .613 OPS, 1546 TB and 94 OPS+. Lew Drill (.261 BA, 24 RBI) caught, as Chris Lindsay (.267 BA, 31 RBI) at first led for in-play percentage (88%). Germany Schaefer (.244 BA, 2 HR, 47 RBI) at second led in strikeouts (91) and outs (448). Bill Coughlin (.252 BA, 44 RBI) played third with Charley O'Leary (.213 BA, 33 RBI) at short. Matty McIntyre (.263 BA, 30 RBI) was in left and Duff Cooley (.247 BA, HR, 32 RBI) in center. Player of the Year and most effective hitter Sam Crawford (.297 BA, 6 HR, 75 RBI) in right led team in games (154), plate appearances (631), at bats (575), runs (73), hits (171), singles (117), doubles (38), triples (10), homers, runs batted in, on-base percentage (.357), slugging (.430), OPS (.786), OPS+ (149), total average (.797), base-out percentage (.799), gross production average (.268), WAR (5.3), oWAR (5.1), batters run average (.152), hitting, BAbip (307), secondary average (.257), times on base (224), base runs (83), runs produced (142), runs created (88), isolated power (.132), power/speed number (9.4), extra base hits (54), total bases (247), bases produced (319), steals (22), stolen bases runs (6.6), walks (50) and hitting streak (17). Ed Killian (.271 BA, 19 RBI) led all pitchers. Fred Payne at .429 (3-7) led Tiger pinch-hitters. Drill excelled the week of August 30-September 5 (8-for-12, .667 BA, .714 OBP, .667 SLG, .667 BAbip).

1900s On-Base Percentage		
1.	Jimmy Barrett	.382
2.	Ty Cobb	.380
3.	Kid Elberfeld	.376
4.	Sam Crawford	.351
5.	Davy Jones	.349
6.	Matty McIntyre	.340
7.	Doc Casey	.337
8.	Claude Rossman	.318
9.	Kid Gleason	.312
10.	George Mullin	.304

Pitching. Detroit recorded a 2.83 ERA, 124 CG, 17 SHO, 578 SO, 97 ERA+, 2.94 FIP, 1.261 WHIP, 8.2 H/9, 3.2 BB/9, and 3.9 SO/9, with league lead in walks (474) and homers per nine (0.1). Pitcher of the Year and most effective pitcher Ed Killian (23-14, 2.27 ERA, 7.6 H9) completed 33 starts without allowing a homer in 313.1 innings. He led MLB in HR/9 (0.0) and league for shutouts (8). Killian led staff in wins, win percentage (.622), HBP (13), LOB% (71.4), earned run average, ERA+ (120), WHIP (1.165), pWAR (7.2) and R/9 (3.1). George Mullin (21-21, 2.51 ERA, 4.3 SO/9) led the league in starts (41), complete games (35), innings (347.2), hits (303), runs (149), walks (138) and batters faced (1,428). He led staff in games (44), losses, homers (4), strikeouts (168), WP (6) and earned runs (97). Bill Donovan (18-15, 2.60 ERA, 7.6 H9, 4.3 SO/9) led in FIP (2.84) and DICE (3.32). Frank Kitson (12-14, 3.47 ERA) led in saves (1), BB/9 (2.3) and SO/BB (1.37). John Eubank (1-0, 2.08 ERA), George Disch (0-2, 2.64 ERA), Jimmy Wiggs (3-3, 3.27 ERA) and Eddie Cicotte (1-1, 3.50 ERA). Gene Ford (0-1, 5.66 ERA) led the staff in GF (6).

Defense. Detroit made 265 errors for a .957 fielding percentage. League leaders were catchers Clarke in passed balls (13) and Drill in steals allowed (105). Schaefer led in chances (829) and putouts (403) at second. Outfielders Crawford in fielding (.988) and Cooley in chances per game (2.5). Outfielder McIntyre and Coughlin at third led the club in defensive WAR (0.3).

Bill Donovan excelled May 26-June 25 (4-0, 38 IP, 2.13 ERA, 1.86 BA, .225 SLG, .220 BAbip) and August 24-September 18 (5-0, 45 IP, 2.00 ERA, .151 BA, .171 SLG, .178 BAbip). He dominated the St. Louis Browns (3 GM, 3-0, 1.64 ERA, .214 BA, 3 CG).

Detroit Tigers 1906 American League

1900s Slugging Percentage	
1. Ty Cobb	.459
2. Sam Crawford	.437
3. Kid Elberfeld	.380
4. Claude Rossman	.364
5. Jimmy Barrett	.358
6. Doc Casey	.355
7. Matty McIntyre	.339
8. Kid Gleason	.334
9. George Mullin	.333
10. Germany Schaefer	.316

Team. Detroit finished in sixth place under second-year manager Bill Armour with a 71-78 (.478) record and 174,043 fans. The team went 6-7 in April that included an Ed Siever (W 3-0, 10 IP, 1 R) 2-1 win at Chicago on Monday, April 30. Players were 12-10 in May, with an 8-3 win at Cleveland on Monday, May 7, when pitcher Bill Donovan (W 3-1, 9 IP, 3 ER) singled in the fifth inning, stole second, third and home to score, as the righthander scored two runs, had a triple and sacrifice hit in the game. George Mullin (9 IP, 2 R, 6 H) had a hit and two runs batted in during a 9-2 win over visiting Chicago on Thursday, May 3, as Sam Crawford went 4-for-5 (3 RBI). The Tigers had a 17-12 record in June, with 23 of 29 games played at home. The team reeled off six straight at home including a 13-4 win over Washington on Monday, June 4. Third baseman Bill Coughlin recorded a steal of second, third and home in the seventh inning. Players finished 11-15 in July when Siever (W 9-3, 9 IP, 2 R) won 3-2 in St. Louis on Sunday, July 1, with Crawford 2-for-3 and Chris Lindsay 3-for-4. Detroit finished 9-15 in August when Coughlin with a .226 average caught fire August 8-11 (5 GM, 10-for-20, .500 BA, .500 OBP, .600 SLG, .500 BAbip). Sam Thompson (2 RBI), Matty McIntyre 3-for-4, Fred Payne 2-for-3 (2 RBI) and Mullin (W 16-15, 9 IP, 1 R, 7 SO) 1-for-3 led a 5-1 home win against St. Louis on Friday, August 31. The Tigers were 14-15 in September with nine consecutive wins at home September 19-27. Motown swept a home double-header against Washington on Saturday, September 22, as Mullin won both games with rare back-to-back complete games on the same day. Mullin led the 5-3 win in game one (W 18-18, 9 IP, 3 R), followed by a 4-3 victory in game two (W 19-18, 9 IP, 3 R). Players closed the season 2-4 in October when Ed Killian (W 10-6, 9 IP, 1 R, 5 H) 2-for-4 (RBI) led 6-1 triumph in Chicago on Sunday, October 7. McIntyre went 4-for-5 and Germany Schaefer 2-for-3 with four stolen bases. Detroit went 42-34 (.553) at home and 29-44 (.397) on the road. Motown scored 518 runs, as their pitchers allowed opponents 598. 46-year-old Thompson, a future Hall of Famer had been out of baseball for eight years. He played for the Detroit Wolverines 1885-1888, with the 1887 championship year his best. Sam led the NL in at bats (545), hits (203), triples (23), runs batted in (166), average (.372), slugging (.565) and total bases (308).

OF * SAM THOMPSON

Offense. Detroit had a .242 BA, .295 OBP, .306 SLG, .600 OPS, 1507 TB and 86 OPS+. Fred Payne (.270 BA, 22 RBI), Jack Warner (.242 BA, 9 RBI) and rookie Boss Schmidt (.218 BA, 10 RBI) formed baseball's first known seasonal platoon at catcher. Chris Lindsay (.224 BA, 36 RBI) at first. Germany Schaefer (.238 BA, 2 HR, 43 RBI, 3.8 PSN, 31 SB, 9.3 SBR) at second led in strikeouts (57). Third baseman Bill Coughlin (.235 BA, 2 HR, 60 RBI, 3.8 PSN, 31 SB, 9.3 SBR) led in games (147) and outs (417), with Charley O'Leary (.219 BA, 2 HR, 41 RBI) playing short. Matty McIntyre (.260 BA, 39 RBI) in left led in secondary average (.256) and walks (56). Player of the Year 19-year-old centerfielder Ty Cobb (.316 BA, HR, 41 RBI) led in on-base percentage (.355), OPS (.749), OPS+ (132), total average (.759), base-out percentage (.772), gross production average (.258), batting average, BAbip (.353) and hitting streak (25). The most effective hitter Sam Crawford (.295 BA, 2 HR, 72 RBI) in right led team in plate appearances (610), at bats (563), runs (65), hits (166), singles (123), doubles (25), triples (16), runs batted in, slugging (.407), WAR (3.2), oWAR (3.6), batters run average (.137), in-play percentage (89%), times on base (205), base runs (72), runs produced (135), runs created (78), isolated power (.112), extra base hits (43), total bases (229) and bases produced (291). The fourth outfielder was Davy Jones (.260 BA, 23 RBI). George Mullin (.225 BA, 8 RBI) led all pitchers in hitting. Fred Payne led Bengal pinch-hitters at .429 (3-7).

1900s On-Base plus Slugging	
1. Ty Cobb	.459
2. Sam Crawford	.437
3. Kid Elberfeld	.380
4. Claude Rossman	.364
5. Jimmy Barrett	.358
6. Doc Casey	.355
7. Matty McIntyre	.339
8. Kid Gleason	.334
9. George Mullin	.333
10. Germany Schaefer	.316

Pitching. The Tigers recorded a 3.06 ERA, 128 CG, 7 SHO, 389 walks, 469 SO, 90 ERA+, 2.81 FIP, 1.339 WHIP, 9.4 H/9, 2.6 BB/9, and 3.2 SO/9. Detroit led league in hits allowed (1,398), hit by pitch (58), batters faced (5,578) and home runs per nine (0.1). The pitchers were their best in a three-game sweep of the Senators in Washington with back-to-back 4-0 shutout wins on Friday, May 11, and on Saturday, followed by a 3-1 Tiger win on Monday. Pitcher of the Year and most effective pitcher Ed Siever (14-11, 2.71 ERA) led staff in win percentage (.560), homers (5), earned run average, ERA+ (102), WHIP (1.280), BB/9 (1.8) and SO/BB (1.58). Red Donahue (9-15, 2.73 ERA) led the league in HR/9 (0.0) and squad in shutouts (3), FIP (2.51) and R/9 (3.6). George Mullin (21-18, 2.78 ERA) led league in runs (139), walks (108), batters faced (1,361) and staff in games (40), wins, losses, starts (40), complete games (35), innings (330) hits (315), strikeouts (123), earned runs (102), pWAR (4.7) and H/9 (8.6). Bill Donovan (9-15, 3.15 ERA) led in LOB% (70.8) and SO/9 (3.6). Ed Killian (10-6, 3.43 ERA) led in saves (2) and John Eubank (4-10, 3.53 ERA). Siever went undefeated in April (3 GM, 3-0 1.000, 28 IP, 5 R, 1.61 ERA, .233 BA).

Defense. Detroit committed 260 errors for a .959 fielding percentage. Tiger league leaders were pitchers Siever in fielding percentage (.986) and Mullin in assists (113). Warner led catchers in assists (136), with 79 of those as a Tiger. Schaefer at second led in total chances per game (6.3). Coughlin led third baseman in chances (482), putouts (188) and double plays (16). O'Leary at short led in putouts (326), errors (58) and total chances per game (6.2). Cobb led his team in dWAR (-0.4).

Ty Cobb hit .237 at class "C" Augusta in 1904 and had a .326 average for Augusta in 1905, as he earned his MLB debut that year. Cobb hit .316 for Motown in 1906 and was one of the American League's premier stars throughout his 24-year career.

Crawford sizzled June 26-July 11 (23-for-59, .390 BA, .419 OBP, .542 SLG, .390 BAbip), August 16-September 10 (32-for-81, .395 BA, .449 OBP, .556 SLG, .405 BAbip) and September 18-October 7 (23-for-56, .411 BA, .492 OBP, .625 SLG, .426 BAbip).

Detroit Tigers 1907 American League

1900s Pitching Wins	
1. George Mullin	157
2. Bill Donovan	112
3. Ed Killian	95
4. Ed Siever	60
5. Ed Summers	43
6. Ed Willett	37
7. Frank Kitson	35
8. Roscoe Miller	29
9. Joe Yeager	18
10. Win Mercer	15

Team. Detroit finished in first place under first year manager Hughie Jennings at 92-58 (.613), with 297,079 fans. The Tigers improved by 21 games under Jennings, with practically the same team that finished sixth in 1906. Motown lost the World Series to the Chicago Cubs four games to one. They went 8-5 in April when Ed Siever (9 IP, 0 ER, 2 H) threw a two-hit 3-0 home shutout of St. Louis on Wednesday, April 24, with Ty Cobb 3-for-4 and Germany Schaefer 3-for-4 (2 RBI). Motown was 12-9 in May, as Ed Killian excelled May 1-May 29 (5 GM, 4-0 , 38.0 IP, 2 ER, 0.47 ERA, .229 BA, .246 OBP, .244 SLG, .244 BAbip). Detroit crushed visiting Philadelphia 15-8 on Saturday, May 18, behind Cobb 4-for-6 (4 RBI). The Bengals scored six eight-inning runs for a 10-1 thrashing of visiting Washington on Thursday, May 23. Killian (W 5-2, 9 IP, 0 ER, 7 H), Davy Jones 2-for-3 (3 R, 2 SB), Sam Crawford (2 RBI), Claude Rossman (2 RBI), and Charley O'Leary (2 RBI) led the win. Their 12-12 record in June included a triple-play on consecutive days June 6-7. Detroit scored a 16-4 win in New York on Wednesday, June 12, as the Highlanders had 11 errors. The Bengals had a nine-run second inning, with Killian (8.2 IP, 1 R) the winner in long relief. Eight Tigers drove in runs, led by Jones (2 RBI), Coughlin (2 RBI), Crawford (2 RBI), Rossman (2 RBI), Red Downs (2 RBI) and Killian (2 RBI). Detroit was 19-9 in July when they endured a 13-2 home loss to the Senators on Wednesday, July 17. The club also logged a record of 19-9 in August, that included sweeping a five-game series at Washington August 2-5 to move into first place at 57-35 (.620). Crawford hit an inside-the-park homer during a 3-2 defeat of Walter Johnson making his MLB debut on Friday, August 2. Detroit finished 17-12 in September and 5-2 in October. The Bengals played to a 17-inning 9-9 tie in Philadelphia on Monday, September 30, as Donovan (17 IP, 9 R, 21 H, 3 BB, 11 SO) pitched all 17 innings facing 73 batters. The franchise swept a four-game series in Washington, including a 10-2 win on Wednesday, October 2. Cobb had an 11-game hit streak to end the season September 21-October 5 (11 GM, .500 BA, .509 OBP, .769 SLG, .522 BAbip), including five straight three-hit games September 30-October 3 (.615 BA, .630 OBP, .769 SLG, .652 BAbip). Motown went 18-4 versus the Senators including 10-1 at Washington. Detroit was 50-27 (.649) at home, including 10-1 over St. Louis and 42-31 (.575) during road games. The Bengals scored a league high, and a team record of 693 runs as their pitchers allowed opponents a mere 531.

P * BILL DONOVAN

Offense. Detroit had a .313 OBP, .648 OPS, 1745 TB, and 104 OPS+, as they led league in hitting (.266) and slugging (.336). Boss Schmidt (.244 BA, 23 RBI) caught, with Claude Rossman (.277 BA, 69 RBI) at first and Germany Schaefer (.258 BA, 1 HR, 32 RBI) at second. Bill Coughlin (.243 BA, 15 SB, 23 SH) manned third, with Charley O'Leary (.241 BA, 34 RBI) at short. Davy Jones (.273 BA, 27 RBI, 101 R) at left led club in secondary average (.256) and walks (60). Centerfielder Sam Crawford (.323 BA, 4 HR, 81 RBI) led the league in runs (102), isolated power (.137) and extra base hits (55). He led his team in doubles (34) and triples (17). Player of the Year and most effective hitter right-fielder Ty Cobb (.350 BA, 5 HR, 119 RBI) led MLB in hits (212), runs batted in, hitting and total bases (283). He led league for singles (165), slugging (.468), OPS (.848), OPS+ (167), total average (.919), oWAR (6.5), BAbip (.380), runs created (108), steals (53). Cobb led his team in plate appearances (642), at bats (605), on-base percentage (.380), base-out percentage (.921), gross production average (.288), WAR (6.8), batters run average (.175), times on base (241), base runs (95), runs produced (211), power/speed number (9.1), bases produced (356) and stolen base runs (14.7). Utility Red Downs (.219 BA, HR, 42 RBI). Ed Killian (.320 BA) and Bill Donovan (.266 BA, 19 RBI) led the pitchers. Pitcher George Mullin led pinch-hitters at .250 (5-20).

1900s Pitching Winning Percentage	
1. Ed Summers	.672
2. Ed Willett	.587
3. Bill Donovan	.583
4. Ed Killian	.572
5. George Mullin	.540
6. Roscoe Miller	.537
7. Ed Siever	.526
8. Win Mercer	.455
9. Frank Kitson	.449
10. Joe Yeager	.429

Pitching. The Tigers logged a 2.33 ERA, 120 CG, 15 SHO, 380 walks, 512 SO, 112 ERA+, 2.45 FIP, 1.212 WHIP, 8.4 H/9, 2.5 BB/9, and 3.4 SO/9, with league lead in pWAR (18.1). Pitcher of the Year Bill Donovan (25-4, 2.19 ERA) completed 27 of 28 starts, led MLB in win percentage (.862) and led team in wins, home runs (3), hits per nine innings (7.4) and strikeouts per nine innings (4.1). The most effective pitcher Ed Siever (18-11, 2.16 ERA) led league in HR/9 (0.0) and club in FIP (2.27), WHIP (1.121), BB/9 (1.7), strikeouts to walks (1.69) and runs allowed per nine innings (2.9).Ed Killian (25-13, 1.78 ERA) completed 29 of his 34 starts, led the league in LOB% (74.1) and staff in wins, games finished (8), earned run average, ERA+ (146) and pWAR (6.5). George Mullin (20-20, 2.59 ERA, 2.42 FIP) led MLB in hits (346), with league highs for runs (153) and earned runs (103). He led staff in HR/9 (0.025), games (46), losses, starts (42), complete games (35), shutouts (5), saves (3), innings (357.1), walks (106), strikeouts (146), hit by pitch (15) and wild pitches (6). John Eubank (3-3, 2.67 ERA) and Ed Willett (1-5, 3.70 ERA, 2.43 FIP). Killian was stellar during the period April 29-June 21 (10 GM, 7-2 .778, 76.1 IP, 1.53 ERA, .234 SLG, 2 SHO).

Defense. Motown had 265 errors for a .958 fielding average. League leaders included Schmidt in catcher errors (34), double plays (14) and caught stealing percentage (47%), O'Leary at short in putouts (353), outfielders Crawford and Jones for chances per game (2.4), as Cobb led in assists (30) and double plays (12). Schmidt and O'leary led the Tigers in dWAR (0.6).

Bill Donovan excelled at home (13-1), on the road (12-3), first half (9-1) and second half (16-3). He starred on no rest (2-0), on two days rest (5-0) and three days of rest (8-0). Bill dominated New York (6-0), Philadelphia (6-1) and Washington (3-0).

Ty Cobb had seven four-hit games of 4-for-6 (5 RBI) on May 18, 4-for-5 (4 R, 3 RBI) June 29, 4-for-5 July 8, 4-for-5 July 30, 4-for-5 (2 RBI) August 5, 4-for-5 (2 RBI) August 14 and 4-for-5 on October 1. Cobb recorded an additional 16 three-hit games.

1900s Pitching Games Started		
1.	George Mullin	298
2.	Bill Donovan	198
3.	Ed Killian	163
4.	Ed Siever	123
5.	Ed Summers	79
6.	Ed Willett	66
7.	Frank Kitson	64
8.	Roscoe Miller	54
9.	Joe Yeager	41
10.	Win Mercer	33

Team. First place Detroit finished 90-63 (.588) for Hughie Jennings, with 436,199 fans. The club lost for the second consecutive year to the Chicago Cubs in the world series four games to one. The Tigers stood at 3-9 in last place at the end of April. The club fell 12-8 to visiting Cleveland in 12 innings on Friday, April 17, as Germany Schaefer went 5-for-5 (2 RBI) and Ty Cobb 3-for-6 (4 RBI). Motown was 17-7 in May, including a 13-6 record in a stretch of 19 straight road games. 23-year-old rookie Ed Summers (W 5-2, 9 IP, 2 R, 2 BB, 8 SO), Sam Crawford (3 RBI), Boss Schmidt 3-for-4 (2 RBI) and Schaefer (2 RBI) led a 10-2 victory in Philadelphia on Thursday, May 28. George Mullin went 5-1 (.833) during May. Players finished 14-13 during June when Bill Donovan (W 5-0, 9 IP, 1 R, 3 H) went 1-for-3 and pitched a 6-1 gem at home against the White Sox on Tuesday, June 23. Detroit rolled to a 23-6 record in July, as the Bengals were 19-5 in 24 road games. Summers (W 12-7, 6 IP, 1 R) led a 21-2 massacre of the Athletics in Philadelphia on Friday, July 17, as 34 Tigers reached base, with 27 hits and seven walks. The 3-4-5 Motown hitters of Schaefer 4-for-5 (2 RBI), Crawford 4-for-5 (2 RBI) and Cobb 5-for-6 (5 RBI) were a combined 13-for-16 (.825 BA, 9 RBI). Other stars were Bill Coughlin 3-for-5, Red Downs 3-for-5 (2 RBI) and Claude Rossman 3-for-7 (3 RBI). Players logged a 11-13 mark in August that included an 18-1 blowout victory over Washington in Bennett Park on Saturday, August 8. Willett (W 12-3, 5 IP, 1 R) and George Winter (4 IP, 0 R) pitched for Detroit, as Burt Keeley (L 1-7, 18 R, 22 H, 3 BB) took the loss. Tigers on the prowl included Crawford 4-for-6, Rossman 3-for-5 (3 RBI), Coughlin 3-for-5 (2 RBI) and Willett 2-for-3 (2 RBI). The Bengals were 19-13 in September and 3-2 in October when Summers improved his record to 23-11 after he accomplished the rare feat of pitching two complete game wins in a doubleheader sweep of Philadelphia at home on Sunday, September 25. "Kickapoo Ed" won the first game 7-2 (9 IP, 2 R, 6 H) and then returned for a two-hit 1-0 shutout in the second game (10 IP, 0 R, 2 H, 6 SO). Donovan Pitched back-to-back shutouts of 6-0 (W 17-7, 9 IP, 0 ER, 7 H) over St. Louis at home on Sunday, October 3 and then a two-hit 7-0 (W 18-7, 9 IP, 0 ER, 2 H, 9 SO) gem in Chicago on Tuesday, as he pitched both games on two days of rest. Detroit won the season series with Washington (16-5 .762). The Tigers went 44-33 at home, including a 9-2 mark over Philadelphia, with a 46-30 (.605) mark on the road. Motown scored a league high 647 runs and allowed 547.

P * GEORGE WINTER

Offense. Detroit had a .312 OBP, .659 OPS, 1775 TB, and 110 OPS+, with league lead in doubles (199), hitting (.264) and slugging (.347). Catcher Boss Schmidt (.265 BA, HR, 38 RBI) led team for in-play percentage (87%). Claude Rossman (.294 BA, 2 HR, 71 RBI) was at first, Red Downs (.221 BA, HR, 35 RBI) at second and Bill Coughlin (.215 BA, 23 RBI) at third. Germany Schaefer (.259 BA, 3 HR, 52 RBI) at short led league in outs (476) and team in games (153), steals (40), stolen base runs (12.0) and strikeouts (75). Matty McIntyre (.295 BA, 28 RBI) at left led MLB in runs (105). He led league in plate appearances (678), singles (131) and times on base (258). Matty led Detroit for on-base percentage (.392) and walks (83). Sam Crawford (.311 BA, 7 HR, 80 RBI, 102 R) at center led the league in at bats (591), home runs (7) and power/speed number (9.5). Player of the Year and most effective hitter right-fielder Ty Cobb (.324 BA, 4 HR, 108 RBI) led MLB in triples (20, with league best for hits (188), doubles (36), runs batted in, slugging (.476), OPS (.844), OPS+ (170), total average (.906), oWAR (6.5), batting average, BAbip (.345), runs created (100), isolated power (.152), extra base hits (60) and total bases (276). Cobb led club in base-out percentage (.909), gross production average (.284), WAR (6.2), batters run average (.171), secondary average (.278), base runs (90), runs produced (192), bases produced (349) and hitting streak (15). George Mullin (.256 BA, HR, 8 RBI) led all Tiger pitchers in hitting. The leading pinch-hitter was Ira Thomas at .364 (4-11).

1900s Pitching Complete Games		
1.	George Mullin	258
2.	Bill Donovan	178
3.	Ed Killian	137
4.	Ed Siever	93
5.	Frank Kitson	68
6.	Roscoe Miller	50
7.	Ed Summers	47
	Ed Willett	47
9.	Joe Yeager	37
10.	Win Mercer	28

Pitching. The Tigers logged a 2.40 ERA, 15 SHO, walked 318, with 553 SO, 100 ERA+. The staff had a 2.23 FIP, 1.187 WHIP, 8.6 H/9, 2.1 BB/9, and 3.6 SO/9. Staff led league complete games (119), hits (1,313) and left on base (1,065). Pitcher of the Year knuckleballer Ed Summers (24-12, 1.64 ERA) led the major leagues in HBP (20). He led team in games (40), wins, starts, innings (301), balks (1), earned run average (1.64), ERA+ (145), WHIP (1.083) and BB/9 (1.6). The most effective pitcher Bill Donovan (18-7, 2.08 ERA) led in win percentage (.720), complete games (25), shutouts (6), strikeouts (141), FIP (1.78), DICE (2.67), pWAR (4.4), H/9 (7.8), SO/9 (5.2), SO/BB (2.66) and R/9 (2.9). Ed Willett (15-8, 18 CG) led in LOB% (75.0), Ed Killian (12-9, 2.99 ERA, 15 CG), George Mullin (17-13, 290.2 IP, 3.10 ERA, 26 CG) led MLB in earned runs (100), with staff lead for losses, hits (301), walks (71), wild pitches (12) and runs (142). Ed Siever (2-6, 3.50 ERA). George Winter (7 GM, 1-5, 1.60 ERA, 151 ERA+, .994 WHIP) and George Suggs (6 GM, 1-1, 1.67 ERA, 147 ERA+). Donovan excelled in October (2 GM, 2-0, 18 IP, 0 ER, 0.00 ERA, 14 SO, 2 SHO) to close the season.

Defense. The team made 307 errors for a .953 fielding average. League leaders were catcher Schmidt in chances per game (6.3), assists (184), errors (37), stolen bases allowed (115), caught stealing (129) and led Detroit in defensive WAR (0.8). Rossman led in assists (102) at first, as outfielders Cobb led in assists (23) and McIntyre in chances (354) and putouts (329).

Ed Summers excelled during the second half (21 GM, 13-5 .722, 163.1 IP, 29 BB, 1.065 WHIP), was a road warrior (22 GM, 15-5 .750, 163.1 IP, 23 BB, .226 BA, 0.961 WHIP) and dominated Philadelphia (7 GM, 7-0 1.000, 63 IP, .200 BA, 0.857 WHIP).

The Detroit Tigers (Ty Cobb .368 BA) hit a meager .203 in their World Series loss to the Cubs (2.60 ERA). The Bengals won game five 8-3 on a George Mullin complete game in Chicago, with the crowd of 6,210 the smallest in World Series history.

Detroit Tigers 1909 American League

1900s Pitching Earned Run Average		
1.	Ed Summers	1.93
2.	Bill Donovan	2.16
3.	Ed Killian	2.34
4.	Ed Willett	2.51
5.	Ed Siever	2.61
6.	George Mullin	2.66
7.	Frank Kitson	3.02
8.	Win Mercer	3.04
9.	Roscoe Miller	3.18
10.	Joe Yeager	3.54

Team. The pennant winner finished third under Hughie Jennings at 98-54 (.645), as Detroit lost the World Series for the third year in a row falling to Pittsburgh in seven games. The team set a new attendance record of 490,490. The team went 10-3 in April including a George Mullin (W 1-0, 9 IP, 0 ER, 1 H) one-hit 2-0 shutout over visiting Chicago on Wednesday, April 14. Ed Summers (W 2-0, 9 IP, 0 ER, 3 H) threw a 3-0 home shutout of Cleveland on Sunday, April 25, with Boss Schmidt 2-for-2. Players were 15-9 in May when Kid Speer (9.2 IP, 1 R) won his first MLB start 3-1 in 10-innings at St. Louis on Wednesday, May 5, with Claude Rossman (2 RBI). Mullin (W 6-0, 9 IP, 3 R) was 3-for-4 (3 R) in a 7-3 win over the Browns the next day. Motown rolled to a 16-5 victory over visiting New York on Tuesday, May 11, behind Ed Willett (6 IP, 1 R, 3 H) 1-for-2 (RBI), Oscar Stanage (3 RBI), Donie Bush 3-for-3 (3 R,2 RBI, 2 BB, 3 SB), Matty McIntyre 3-for-4 (2 RBI, 2 SB) and Ty Cobb (2 RBI). Detroit was 18-9 in June as Sam Crawford 4-for-5 (RBI), Charley O'Leary 2-for-3 (2 RBI, 2 SB), Germany Schaefer 2-for-3 (2 RBI) and George Suggs (9 IP, 1 R, 5 H) led an 8-1 home win versus St. Louis on Wednesday, June 23. The franchise finished 17-13 in July when the Tigers and Senators played a league record 18 scoreless innings in Detroit on Friday, July 16. Bush (3 SH) and Summers (18 IP, 0 ER, 7 H, 2 BB, 10 SO) starred for Motown. Willett (W 10-4, 9 IP, 0 R, 6 H) was 1-for-2, with a 1-0 shutout of St. Louis at home on Tuesday, June 22. The next day Ed Killian (9 IP, 0 ER) shut out visiting Boston 6-0, as Cobb was 3-for-4 (4 SB), Schmidt (2 SH) and Killian (2 SH). The club closed 17-9 for August with 14 straight wins August 19-September 2. Detroit had a 17-6 home win with New York on Friday, August 27, with a 10-run fourth inning. Stars were Willett (W 17-7, 6 IP, 0 ER, 1 H) 1-for-3 (3B), Cobb 4-for-5 (HR, 6 RBI), Jim Delahanty (4 RBI), Crawford 3-for-5 (HR, 3 RBI) and Davy Jones (2 RBI). Motown logged a 20-10 mark in September and 1-1 in October. Motown swept a doubleheader in Boston on Wednesday, September 29. Killian started and won both games winning 5-0 (W 10-9, 7 IP, 0 ER, 1 H) 1-for-3 (2 RBI), with Crawford (HR, 3 RBI) in game one, followed by an 8-3 game two win (W 11-9, 9 IP, 3 R), led by Crawford (4 RBI) and Cobb 2-for-3 (2 RBI). Bill Lelivelt (5 IP, 1 R) and Ralph Works (W 4-1, 4 IP, 0 R, 4 SO) pitched in a 3-1 win at Chicago on Sunday, October 2. The Bengals were 18-3 against St. Louis, 57-19 (.750) at home, and 41-35 (.539) on the road, scored a league high 666 runs and allowed 493.

P * RALPH WORKS

Offense. Detroit finished with a .325 OBP, .342 SLG, .667 OPS, 1742 TB, and 106 OPS+. The team led league in doubles (209), hitting (.267) and stolen bases (280). The catcher was Boss Schmidt (.209 BA, HR, 28 RBI), Claude Rossman (.261 BA, 39 RBI) was at first, with Germany Schaefer (.250 BA, 22 RBI) the second baseman. George Moriarty (.273 BA, HR, 39 RBI) played third. Shortstop Donie Bush (.273 BA, 33 RBI) led MLB in games (157, walks (88) and sacrifice hits (52). He led league for plate appearances (678) and runs (115), with club lead in strikeouts (74) and outs (439). Matty McIntyre (.244 BA, HR, 34 RBI) was in leftfield. Centerfielder Sam Crawford (.314 BA, 6 HR, 97 RBI) led the league in doubles (35) and extra base hits (55). He led his squad for at bats (589), triples (14), in-play percentage (83%) and hitting streak (23). Right-fielder, Triple Crown winner and Player of the Year Ty Cobb (.377 BA, 9 HR, 107 RBI) was the most effective hitter leading MLB in hits (216), homers (9), runs batted in, steals (76), hitting, on-base percentage (.431), slugging (.517), OPS (.947), OPS+ (192) and total bases (296. Cobb led league in runs (115), singles (164), total average (1.193), WAR (9.9), oWAR (9.6), BAbip (.399), secondary average (.356), times on base (270), runs created (127), power/speed number (16.1). He led Motown in base-out percentage (1.181), gross production average (.323), batters run average (.214), base runs (115), runs produced (213), isolated power (0.140), bases produced (420) and stolen base runs (22.8). George Mullin (.214 BA, 17 RBI) led pitchers in hitting. Detroit pinch-hitters hit a meager .135 when called upon.

1900s Pitching Innings Pitched		
1.	George Mullin	2,592.1
2.	Bill Donovan	1,746.1
3.	Ed Killian	1,462.2
4.	Ed Siever	1,036.0
5.	Frank Kitson	683.0
6.	Ed Summers	582.2
7.	Ed Willett	563.2
8.	Roscoe Miller	480.2
9.	Joe Yeager	348.2
10.	Win Mercer	281.2

Pitching. The Tigers recorded a 2.26 ERA, 16 SHO, walked 359, 528 SO and finished with an ERA+ of 112. The staff had a 2.49 FIP, 1.136 WHIP, 7.9 H/9, 2.3 BB/9, 3.3 SO/9, and led the league with 117 complete games. Pitcher of the Year and most effective pitcher George Mullin (29-8, 2.22 ERA) led MLB in wins, with league lead for win percentage (.784) and HR/9 (0.0). Mullin led staff in starts (35), complete games (29), innings (303.2), hits (258), walks (78), strikeouts (124), and pWAR (4.6). Ed Killian (11-9, 1.71 ERA, 4.0 WAR) led league in LOB% (78.6) and staff in earned run average ERA+ (148) and R/9 (2.3). Ed Summers (19-9, 2.24 ERA, 281.2 IP, 18 CG, 2.30 FIP, 4.0 WAR) led the squad FIP (3.08), WHIP (1.047), BB/9 (1.7), and SO/BB (2.06). Bill Donovan (8-7, 2.31 ERA), and Ed Willett (21-10, 2.34 ERA, 292.2 IP, 25 CG). The bullpen included 21-year-old Ralph Works (4-1, 1.97 ERA, 129 ERA+), George Suggs (1-3, 2.03 ERA, .992 WHIP, 126 ERA+) and rookie lefthander Kid Speer (4-4, 2.83 ERA).

Defense. Players committed 275 errors during the 1909 season for a .959 fielding percentage. Tiger league leaders were Summers in pitcher double plays (8) and Schmidt led all catches errors (20). Moriarty led the third basemen in fielding percentage (.939) and Bush led in shortstop chances (946), assists (567), errors (71) and his team in defensive WAR (2.2).

George Mullin started with a club record 11-0 (1.000), 16-4 (.800) in first half, 13-4 (.765) in second half, 15-2 (.882) at home and 14-6 (.700) on the road. Ty Cobb went 4-for-5 in games on May 12, May 24, August 27, September 22, and October 2.

Detroit recorded a franchise record 280 stolen bases in 1909. The leaders were Ty Cobb (76), Donie Bush (53), George Moriarty (34), Sam Crawford (30), Matty McIntyre (13), Davy Jones (12), Germany Schaefer (12), and Claude Rossman (10).

OWNER * FRANK NAVIN

Player of the Decade. Ty Cobb (.387 BA, 47 HR, 827 RBI) was Player of the Decade for the second consecutive decade. The decade leader in runs (1,049), hits (1,948), singles (1,427), doubles (313), triples (161), home runs (47), runs batted in (827), hit by pitch (46), on-base percentage (.456), slugging (.540), on-base plus slugging (.997), OPS+ (192), total average (1.232), gross production average (.340), offensive WAR (84.4), batting average (.387), BAbip (.408), secondary average (.365), times on base (2,596), extra base hits (521), extra bases on long hits (776), total bases (2,724), total base average (2.0), bases produced (3,902), bases produced average (2.9), stolen bases (576) and had a 40 game hitting streak in 1911. This Tiger was an absolute beast on the field of play, with nine batting titles and a .387 average during his 1,334 games. Cobb recorded 200 hits four times during the decade including 1911 (248 H, .419 BA), 1912 (226 H, .409 BA), 1915 (208 H, .369 BA) and the 1917 season (225 H, .383 BA).

1910s			
Year	W – L	Pct.	Pl
1910	86-68	.558	3
1911	89-65	.578	2
1912	69-84	.451	6
1913	66-87	.431	6
1914	80-73	.523	4
1915	**100-54**	**.649**	2
1916	87-67	.565	3
1917	78-75	.510	4
1918	55-71	.437	7
1919	80-60	.571	4
	790-704	.529	

All-Decade Team. Manager Hughie Jennings (790-704 .529) led Detroit to pair of second-place finishes in 1911 (89-65 .578) and 1915 (100-54 .649). Pitcher Harry Coveleski (69-43 .616, 2.34 ERA). Catcher Oscar Stanage (.232 BA, 8 HR, 290 RBI). First baseman George Burns (.266 BA, 15 HR, 222 RBI). Second Base Ralph Young (.231 BA, 3 HR, 158 RBI). Shortstop Donie Bush (.244 BA, 8 HR, 339 RBI) led the decade in games (1,449), plate appearances (6,597), at bats (5,462), walks (912) and walk percentage (13.8). Third baseman George Moriarty (.247 BA, 4 HR, 244 RBI). Leftfielder Bobby Veach (.304 BA, 21 HR, 643 RBI). Centerfielder Ty Cobb (.387 BA, 47 HR, 827 RBI) was an elite baseball player leading the Tigers in most hitting categories including runs (1,049), hits (1,948), singles (1,427), double (313), triples (161), home runs (47), runs batted in (827), HBP (46), on-base percentage (.456), slugging (.540), OPS (.997), oWAR (84.4), batters run average (.247), hitting, extra base hits (521), extra bases on long hits (776), total bases (2,724), total base percentage (2.04), bases produced (3,902), bases produced average (2.9), steals (576), caught stealing (113), stolen base runs (105.0) and stolen base runs created (2,072). Sam Crawford (.313 BA, 39 HR, 701 RBI) in right led for in-play percentage (83%) and at bats per run batted in (5.7).

MGR * HUGHIE JENNINGS

Pitcher of the Decade. Harry Coveleski (69-43 .616, 2.34) led the 1910s in technical runs allowed (3.39), earned run average, ERA+ (123), FIP (2.67), DICE (3.29), WHIP (1.131, BB/9 (2.37), RA/9 (3.39), quality start percentage (.704) and no decisions (25). The *"Giant Killer"* had three superb years 1914-1916 (65-36 .644). Coveleski's 1914 season (22-12 .647, 2.49 ERA, 112 ERA+, 303.1 IP) included a 14-4 mark at home. He won four complete games at home in June 1914 (4-0, 0.25 ERA, 3 SHO) and won seven straight in the month of July (7-0, 2.98 ERA) to reach 14-7. He finished 1915 (22-13 .629, 312.2 IP, 2.45 ERA, 124 ERA+) with a record of 6-2 (1.95 ERA, 0.896 WHIP) pitching on three days of rest and went 7-2 in July. Harry in 1916 (21-11 .656, 324.1 IP, 1.97 ERA, 145 ERA+) had a 1.051 WHIP and went 13-5 (.722) in home games. Other 1916 highlights included 6-2 (1.80 ERA) in June and 4-1 (0.98 ERA) in August. Coveleski was 13-0 (2.05 ERA, 132 IP) against Philadelphia (5-0 1914, 4-0 1915, 4-0 1916) during decade. He along with brothers Stan, John and Frank all played professional baseball.

1910s Attendance			
Year	Attn.	Avg.	Rk
1910	391,288	5,017	4
1911	484,988	6,381	4
1912	402,870	5,301	4
1913	398,502	5,243	5
1914	416,225	5,336	3
1915	476,105	6,183	3
1916	616,772	8,010	2
1917	457,289	6,017	3
1918	203,719	3,512	4
1919	**643,805**	**9,197**	1

All-Decade Pitchers. Pitcher of the Decade Coveleski was superb when starting on no rest (3-1 .750, .207 BA, .225 SLG, .235 BAbip). Bill Donovan (29-16 .644, 2.76 ERA) was his best in 1910 (17-7 .708, 2.44 ERA). Willie Mitchell (20-16 .556, 2.83 ERA) led the decade in left on-base percentage (71.0) and went 12-8 .600, 2.19 ERA in 1917. Hooks Dauss (126-92 .578, 2.85) was leader for games (269), wins, losses, starts (219), CG (156), SHO (16), SV (15), IP (1,869), hits (1,714), homers (25), walks (591), strikeouts (739), HBP (82), earned runs (592), runs (781), pWAR (21.3), starter wins (114), starter losses (84), batters faced (7,558), tough losses (43), relief losses (8), quality starts (148), high quality starts (145), dominant starts (49), and high quality start percentage (.662), with records of 24-13 in 1915, 19-12 in 1916 and 21-9 in 1919. Bernie Boland (67-47 .588, 3.01 ERA) was a solid starter in 1917 (16-11 .593, 2.68 ERA, 6 SV) and led staff in H/9 (7.68), games in relief (88), relief wins (13) and dominant start percentage (.273). Jean Dubuc (72-60 .545, 3.06 ERA) contributed a solid season in 1912 (17-10 .630, 2.77 ERA) and the leader with 48 wild pitches. Ed Summers (25-24 .510, 3.11 ERA) finished 13-12 .520 (2.53 ERA) in 1910. Howard Ehmke (30-26 .536, 3.09 ERA) was 17-10 .630, 3.18 ERA in 1919. George Mullin (52-45 .536, 3.11 ERA) became a 20-game winner during the 1910 campaign (21-12 .636, 2.87 ERA), as he led in shutouts (5) and complete game percentage (.804). Bill James (35-36 .493, 3.01 ERA) went 13-10 .565, 2.09 ERA in 1917 dominating the Boston Red Sox (4-0 1.000, 1.09 ERA, .193 BA, .200 BAbip).

The original "Yankee Killer" Harry Coveleski dominated New York in 1914 (3-2 .600, 46 IP, 1.96 ERA, .219 BA), 1915 (5-0 1.000, 48 IP, 1.50 ERA, .197 BA) and 1916 (4-1 .800, 64.1 IP, 1.26 ERA, .202 BA) for a combined mark of 12-3 .800, 1.53 ERA.

Boland's month of July 2018 (4-1 .800, 1.33 ERA, .180 BA) included dominant wins 7-0 at Washington on July 14 (9 IP, 5 H, 0 ER), 4-1 at New York on July 16 (9 IP, 3 H, 1 ER) with one day of rest and 2-1 over Philadelphia on July 26 (11 IP, 5 H, 1 ER).

Team. Detroit finished in third place for Hughie Jennings at 86-68 (.558), with 391,288 fans. Detroit went 8-4 in April, including a 6-2 record on the road. Ed Willett (9 IP, 0 ER, 5 H) pitched a 5-0 shutout in 1:31 at Cleveland on Thursday, April 21. The Bengals finished 15-12 in May with a 5-3 win in New York on Tuesday, May 10, aided by Davy Jones 4-for-5, Jim Delahanty 4-for-5 and George Mullin (W 5-1, 10 IP, 3 R). Willett (W 2-1, 9 IP, 0 ER, 2 H) and Donie Bush 3-for-3 (2 SB) led a 3-0 shutout at Chicago on Tuesday, May 3. George Mullin (9 IP 0 ER, 7 H) shutout the White Sox 4-0 the next day. The Tigers began an 11-game win streak on Saturday, May 28 that included a four-game series sweep in St. Louis May 29-31. Ed Summers (9 IP, 8 SO) 2-for-5 led a 13-4 victory over visiting St. Louis on Sunday, May 29, with Bush 5-for-6, Ty Cobb (HR, 4 RBI) and Boss Schmidt 3-for-4 (3 RBI). Detroit was 15-11 in June as they played 25 of their 26 games at home. Motown won 12-3 at home over Boston on Thursday, June 16, behind Cobb 3-for-5 (3 RBI), Oscar Stanage 2-for-3 (HR, 3 RBI), rookie Hack Simmons 3-for-5 (RBI) and Ed Killian (W 3-1, 9 IP, 3 R). The Bengals were 14-14 in July, as Willett (9 IP, 0 ER, 5 H) outdueled the great Walter Johnson (9 IP, 1 ER, 4 H) in a 1-0 home shutout of the Senators on Sunday, July 17. Players went 15-13 in August that included a Bill Donovan (W 11-4, 9 IP, 0 ER, 4 H) 2-for-3 led a 9-0 shutout in Boston on Saturday, August 20. George Moriarty (4 RBI) and Sam Crawford 3-for-4 (3 RBI) starred for Detroit. The Tigers closed 15-10 in September and 4-4 in October. Summers (9 IP, 3 R, 5 H) went 2-for-5 during a 15-3 blowout win in Cleveland on Saturday, September 10. Other stars were Jim Delahanty 3-for-3, Moriarty 4-for-6, Schmidt (2 RBI), Bush (2 RBI), Tom Jones (2 RBI), Schmidt (2 RBI) and Crawford 3-for-5. Motown took a 12-7 decision at St. Louis on Sunday, October 2, with Crawford 5-for-6, Cobb 4-for-5 (2 RBI), Jay Kirke 1-for-2 (2 SH, 2 RBI), Schmidt (2 RBI) and Tom Jones 3-for-5. Detroit was 46-31 (.597) at home, 40-37 (.519) on the road, scored 679 runs and pitchers allowed 584.

1910s
Team Hitting

YEAR	AVG	HR	RBI	SB
1910	.261	28	548	249
1911	**.292**	**30**	**657**	**276**
1912	.267	19	569	**276**
1913	.265	24	519	218
1914	.258	25	513	211
1915	.268	23	647	241
1916	.264	17	574	190
1917	.259	25	548	163
1918	.249	13	411	123
1919	.283	23	542	121

P * ED WILLETT

Offense. Detroit had a .261 BA, .329 OBP, .344 SLG, .674 OPS, 1735 TB and 105 OPS+. Oscar Stanage (.207 BA, 2 HR, 25 RBI) and Boss Schmidt (.259 BA, HR, 23 RBI) caught. Tom Jones (.255 BA, HR, 45 RBI) at first led in hit by the pitch (10). Jim Delahanty (.294 BA, 3 HR, 45 RBI) at second led in hit streak (18). George Moriarty (.251 BA, 2 HR, 60 RBI) was at third, Donie Bush (.262 BA, 3 HR, 34 RBI) at short led league in walks (78). Davy Jones (.265 BA, 24 RBI) played in left. Player of the Year and most effective hitter Ty Cobb (.382 BA, 8 HR, 91 RBI) at center led MLB in on-base percentage (.455), slugging (.549), OPS (1.004) and OPS+ (205). Cobb led league in runs (106), total average (1.312), WAR (10.6), BAbip (.410), secondary average (.421), isolated power (.167) and power/ speed number (14.2). He led club in hits (194), doubles (35), homers (8), base-out percentage (1.297), gross production average (.342), oWAR (9.7), batters run average (.241), hitting, times on base (262), base runs (119), runs created (127), extra base hits (56), total bases (279), bases produced (408), stolen bases (65) and stolen base runs (19.5). Right-fielder Sam Crawford (.289 BA, 5 HR, 120 RBI) led MLB in triples (19). He led team in games (154), plate appearances (650), at bats (588), in-play percentage (84%), runs produced (198) and outs (442).Outfielder Matty McIntyre (.236 BA, 25 RBI). George Mullin (.256 BA, HR, 11 RBI) led pitchers. Schmidt led Tiger pinch-hitters at .400 (2-5). Detroit went 9-3 for May 24-June 5 when Delahanty (.500 BA, .596 OBP, .516 SLG, .528 BAbip) excelled.

Pitching. The Tigers recorded a 2.82 ERA, 108 CG, 17 SHO, walked 460, 532 SO, and finished with an ERA+ of 93. The staff had a 3.02 FIP, 1.244 WHIP, 8.2 H/9, 3.0 BB/9, and 3.5 SO/9. Detroit pitchers had three straight shutouts of 1-0 over New York on Tuesday, July 26, 2-0 against Chicago on Thursday, July 28, and 1-0 versus Chicago on Friday, July 29. Pitcher of the Year George Mullin (21-12, 2.87 ERA) led the staff in wins, starts (32), complete games (27), shutouts (5), innings (289), hits (260), walks (102), earned runs (92), and runs (125). The most effective pitcher Bill Donovan (17-7, 20 CG, 2.44 ERA) led team in winning percentage (.708), strikeouts (107), fielding independent pitching (3.20), wins above replacement (3.3), strikeouts per nine innings (4.7), strikeouts to walks (1.75), runs allowed per nine innings (3.2), and complete game percentage (87%). Ed Willett (16-11) led team in earned run average (2.37), ERA+ (111), WHIP (1.110), and hits per nine innings (7.0). Ed Summers (13-12, 2.53 ERA, 18 CG) led Detroit in walks per nine innings (2.5). Ed Killian (4-3, 3.04 ERA), Sailor Stroud (5-9, 3.25 ERA) and Ralph Works (3-6, 3.57 ERA). Other contributors were Frank Browning (2-2, 2.57 ERA) and 22-year-old rookie left-hander Hub Pernoll (4-3, 2.96 ERA). Willet was spectacular July 17-September 12 (17 GM, 11-3, 115.1 IP, 82 H, .206 BA, .222 BAbip).

1910s
Team Hitting

YEAR	OBP	SLG	OPS	OPS+
1910	.329	.344	.673	105
1911	.355	**.388**	**.743**	103
1912	.343	.349	.691	100
1913	.336	.355	.691	103
1914	.336	.344	.681	102
1915	**.357**	.358	.715	110
1916	.337	.350	.687	103
1917	.328	.344	.672	105
1918	.325	.318	.642	98
1919	.346	.381	.727	106

Defense. The Tigers committed 288 errors during the 1910 season for a .956 fielding average. Shortstop Bush led the team in defensive wins above replacement (2.0) and was the league runner-up in chances (848), putouts (310) and assists (487).

Ty Cobb (.382 BA) lost the batting crown to Cleveland's Napoleon Lajoie (.383 BA) who went 8-for-8 during a final day double-header, as all eight were bunts not fielded by St. Louis. Cobb stole a base in five straight games twice June 4-8 and July 2-5.

Several Detroit Tiger pitchers held their own in the batter's box during the season including Ralph Works (.267 BA, 8-for-30) and George Mullin (.256 BA, 33-for-129) that scored 15 runs, with six doubles, two triples, 11 runs batted in and eight walks.

1910s Hitting Games		
1.	Donie Bush	1,450
2.	Ty Cobb	1,334
3.	Sam Crawford	1,076
4.	Bobby Veach	1,031
5.	Oscar Stanage	937
6.	Ossie Vitt	767
7.	George Moriarty	639
8.	Ralph Young	633
9.	Harry Heilmann	574
10.	George Burns	496

Team. Detroit finished second at 89-65 (.578) for Hughie Jennings with 484,988 fans. The Tigers were 13-2 in April, including 10-0 at home. George Mullin starred April 13-May 9 (6 GM, 6-0, 55 IP, 2.29 ERA). Ty Cobb (HR, 4 RBI) led a 7-6 victory over visiting St. Louis on Monday, April 24. Motown scored eight sixth inning runs the next day for an 11-9 win against the Browns, behind Sam Crawford 3-for-4 (4 RBI), Jim Delahanty (HR, 3 RBI) and pitcher Tex Covington 1-for-2 (2 RBI). Detroit defeated Cleveland 9-6 at home on Wednesday, April 26, with starter Ed Willett 2-for-2 (HR, 2 RBI), reliever Ralph Works (W 2-0, 4.2 IP, 0 ER, 2 H) and Del Gainer 3-for-3 (2 RBI). The team went 19-9 in May, when Works (W 5-0, 9 IP, 0 ER, 3 H), Crawford 3-for-4 (HR, 3 RBI) and Oscar Stanage (HR, 3 RBI) led a 10-0 home shutout of New York on Tuesday, May 9. Players finished 12-11 in June as Cobb dominated the first week of the month (6 GM, 8 R, 8 SB, 9 RBI, .654 BA, .679 OBP, .923 SLG, .654 BAbip), with four straight three-hit games June 1-5 in Washington, D.C. Delahanty recorded seven straight multi-hit games June 8-17 (16-for-29, .640 BA, .679 OBP, .840 SLG, .667 BAbip). Detroit prevailed 16-15 at home with Cleveland on Sunday, June 18, after trailing 13-1 for the largest comeback in team history. Cobb went 5-for-6 (5 RBI), Delahanty (3 RBI), Donie Bush (2 RBI) and Crawford (2 RBI). The squad was 18-10 in July when Crawford hit .600 (9-for-15) in three-games July 2-4. Delahanty drove in a run in nine straight games July 10-18 (14 RBI, .529 BA). The Tigers were 13-1 during July 4-18 to improve to 59-24 (.711). Delahanty was 5-for-5 (3B, HR, 4 RBI), Crawford (3 RBI), Charley O'Leary 3-for-4 (3 RBI), Cobb (2 RBI) and reliever Covington (W 6-1, 4.2 IP, 2 R, 2 H) to lead a 14-8 home win versus Philadelphia on Tuesday, July 11. Motown scored five runs in the second, third and fifth innings for a 16-7 win against visiting Boston on Tuesday, July 18. Cobb went 3-for-5 (4 RBI), Stanage (3 RBI) and George Moriarty 3-for-4 (2 RBI). The Bengals were 12-16 in August, with Cobb 3-for-3 (HR, 5 RBI) during a 13-6 win at Philadelphia on Tuesday, August 1. Cobb, Delahanty and Delos Drake executed a successful triple steal in the first inning of a 9-3 loss to visiting Boston on Friday, August 18. Detroit closed 13-12 in September and 2-5 in October. Players had a 1-0 home shut-out of Chicago 1-0 on Saturday, September 9, with a Drake-Bush-Gainer triple-play. Cobb had three steals in back-to-back 13-inning wins against the Indians of 2-1 (Bill Donovan W 8-8, 13 IP, 1 ER, 7 SO) at home on Sunday, September 10, and a Summers (W 10-7, 4 IP 0 ER) 9-6 win in Cleveland on Tuesday. Works (W 11-5, 9 IP, 0 ER, 3 H) led a 1-0 shutout at St. Louis on Saturday, October 7 with 66 fans at Sportsman's Park. The Bengals were 51-25 (.671) at home, 38-40 (.487) on the road, scored 831 runs and allowed 777.

1B * DEL GAINER

Offense. Detroit hit .292, .355 OBP, .388 SLG, .743 OPS, 2,056 TB and 103 OPS+. Oscar Stanage (.264 BA, 3 HR, 51 RBI) caught. Jim Delahanty (.339 BA, 3 HR, 94 RBI) at second led in hit by pitch (10). Charley O'Leary (.266 BA, 25 RBI) was at second and George Moriarty (.243 BA, HR, 60 RBI) on third. Shortstop Donie Bush (.232 BA, HR, 36 RBI) led the league in walks (98), outs (461) and plate appearances (701). Davy Jones (.273 BA, 19 RBI) and Delos Drake (.279 BA, HR, 36 RBI) manned left field. The MVP, Player of the Year, and most effective hitter Ty Cobb (.419 BA, 8 HR, 127 RBI) at center led MLB in WAR (10.7), runs (148), hits (248), doubles (47), runs batted in, steals (83), hitting, slugging (.620), OPS (1.086), OPS+ (196) and total bases (367). He led league for singles (169), triples (24), total average (1.459), oWAR (10.2), BAbip (.443), secondary average (.416), times on base (300), runs created (171), isolated power (.201) and extra base hits (79). Cobb led Detroit in home runs (8), on-base percentage (.466), base-out percentage (1.445), gross production average (.365), batters run average (.284), in-play percentage (83%), base runs (148), runs produced (266), power/speed number (14.6), total bases (367), bases produced (494), stolen base runs (24.9) and hitting streak (40). Sam Crawford (.378 BA, 7 HR, 115 RBI) played in right. George Mullin (.286 BA) led pitchers in hitting. Biff Schaller .353 (6-17) and Boss Schmidt .353 (6-17) were the leading Tiger pinch-hitters.

1910s Hitting Runs		
1.	Ty Cobb	1,051
2.	Donie Bush	958
3.	Sam Crawford	553
4.	Bobby Veach	516
5.	Ossie Vitt	417
6.	Ralph Young	262
7.	Harry Heilmann	247
8.	George Moriarty	229
9.	Oscar Stanage	219
10.	Davy Jones	209

Pitching. Motown logged a 3.73 ERA, 108 CG, eight SHO, 460 BB, 538 SO, 93 ERA+, 3.40 FIP, 1.423 WHIP, 9.8 H/9, 3.0 BB/9 and 3.5 SO/9. Detroit had back-to-back shutouts of 6-0 on Friday, April 14, and 2-0 the next day. Pitcher of the Year and most effective pitcher George Mullin (18-10, 3.07 ERA, 5.6 WAR) led in wins, starts (29), complete games (25), innings (234.1), homers (7), strikeouts (87), LOB% (71.1), earned run average, ERA+ (113),WHIP (1.306), pWAR (5.5), BB/9 (2.3) and R/9 (3.8). Bill Donovan (10-9, 3.31 ERA) led in H/9 (8.6) and SO/9 (4.3). Ed Summers (11-11, 3.66 ERA). Ed Willett (13-14, 3.66 ERA) led in games (38), losses, hits (261), walks (80), HBP (14), earned runs (94), and runs (136). Ralph Works (11-5, 3.87 ERA) led in win percentage (.688) and SHO (3). Ed Lafitte (11-8, 3.92) led in WP (8), Tex Covington (7-1, 4.09 ERA), Jack Lively (7-5, 4.59 ERA) and 20-year-old rookie Clarence Mitchell (1-0, 8.16 ERA). Mullin excelled August 26-October 4 (5-0, 47.1 IP, 1.33 ERA, 2 SHO).

Defense. Detroit made 318 errors for a .951 fielding percentage. Tiger league leaders were catcher Stanage in chances (852), putouts (599), assists (212), errors (41), stolen bases (166) and caught stealing (156). Shortstop Bush led in chances (1,003), total chances per game (6.7), putouts (372), assists (556) and errors (75). Outfielder Cobb led in chances (418), total chances per game (2.9), putouts (376) and double plays (10). Bush and Stanage led the team in defensive WAR (0.9).

Motown opened with a phenomenal 21-2 (.913) run, as they won their first 12 home games. Detroit went 12-1 during period of April 23-May 6 and 11-2 for July 2-15. Motown excelled during games on Mondays (16-6 .727) and Tuesdays (16-8 .667).

Detroit Tigers 1912 American League

1910s Hitting Hits	
1. Ty Cobb	1,948
2. Donie Bush	1,334
3. Sam Crawford	1,245
4. Bobby Veach	1,168
5. Oscar Stanage	697
6. Ossie Vitt	671
7. Harry Heilmann	575
8. George Moriarty	541
9. George Burns	467
10. Ralph Young	417

Team. Hughie Jennings led sixth place Detroit (69-84 .451), with 402,870 fans. The Tigers opened 6-9 in April, with Navin Field dedicated prior to the 6-5 win over Cleveland on Saturday, April 20, behind Jim Delahanty (3 RBI), Sam Crawford 3-for-5, and Ossie Vitt 3-for-5, as Ty Cobb stole home to score a run. The team was 14-11 in May as they scored a 16-5 home victory over St. Louis on Friday, May 3. Jean Dubuc (9 IP, 7 SO) went 2-for-4 (2 RBI), Donie Bush 2-for-4 (2 RBI), Delahanty (2 RBI), Del Gainer 3-for-5 (2 RBI) and 23-year-old rookie Jack Onslow 2-for-3 (2 RBI). Detroit lost 24-2 in Philadelphia on May 18, as future Hall-of-Famer Eddie Collins went 5-for-6 (4 R) with five steals for the Athletics. Detroit used replacements from Philadelphia and St. Joseph's College, with Ed Irwin 2-for-3 (2 3B) when regulars walked out in support of the suspended Cobb. Delahanty shined June 28-July 1 (10-for-15, .667 BA, .688 OBP, .733 SLG, .667 BAbip). The Bengals went 16-14 in July sweeping a doubleheader over visiting St. Louis on Thursday, July the Fourth. Cobb 3-for-3 (3 R, HR, 2 RBI), Crawford (2 RBI), George Moriarty (2 RBI) and Ed Willett (W 10-7, 9 IP) led a 9-3 game one win. Cobb stole second, third and home during the fifth inning. George Mullin (9 IP, 0 ER, 0 H) 3-for-4 celebrated his 32nd birthday with the team's first no-hitter 7-0 in game two. The Bengals scored six first inning runs in a Dubuc (W 9-4, 9 IP) 11-3 win at New York on Wednesday, July 10, as Cobb was 4-for-5, Vitt (2 RBI), Davy Jones (2 RBI) and Moriarty (2 RBI). Dubuc (W 10-4, 9 IP, 1 ER, 5 ER) tossed a 13-1 complete game win in Philadelphia on Wednesday, July 17, aided by Moriarty 4-for-4, Cobb 4-for-6, Baldy Louden (2 RBI) and rookie catcher Brad Kocher 2-for-4 (4 RBI) in his first major-league start. Cobb excelled July 14-20 (.639 BA, .649 OBP, 1.167 SLG, .618 BABIP), including 5-for-5 (2 HR, 5 RBI) during an 8-6 win at Philadelphia on Friday, July 19. The Tigers were 9-19 in August, as Dubuc (W 15-4, 9 IP, 0 ER, 2 H) went 2-for-4 (HR, 2 RBI) and Crawford (3 RBI) in a two-hit 7-0 shutout of visiting New York on Wednesday, August 7. Motown won 9-6 at Washington on Thursday, August 22. 19-year-old rookie first baseman Eddie Onslow went 4-for-5 (HR, 4 RBI) with a first inning grand slam. Reliever Willett (W 13-14, 5.2 IP, 3 H, 1 ER) was 1-for-3 to get the win. Detroit closed 12-11 in September and 0-4 in October, with a 1-9 mark in their last 10 games. 19-year-old rookie Charlie Wheatley (8 IP, 16 R, 21 H, 5 WP, 5 BB, 2 HBP) allowed 28 runners in a 16-5 loss at Cleveland, with Joe Jackson and Nap Lajoie a combined 7-for-7 (6 RBI) for the Indians on Friday, September 27. Players finished 37-39 (.487) at home, including 10-1 with New York, and 32-45 (.416) on the road. The Bengals scored 720 runs and allowed 777.

P * TEX COVINGTON

Offense. Detroit hit .267 BA, .343 OBP, .349 SLG, .691 OPS, 1,793 TB and 100 OPS+. Catcher Oscar Stanage (.261 BA, 41 RBI) led in strikeouts (55). George Moriarty (.248 BA, 54 RBI) was at first and Baldy Louden (.241 BA, HR, 36 RBI) at third. Donie Bush (.231 BA, 2 HR, 38 RBI) at short led league in walks (117) and team in secondary average (.337). Davy Jones (.294 BA, 24 RBI) was in left. Player of the Year and the most effective hitter centerfielder Ty Cobb (.409 BA, 7 HR, 83 RBI) led MLB in hits (226), caught steals (34), hitting, slugging (.584), OPS (1.040) and OPS+ (200). Cobb led league in hits singles (166) and BAbip (.424), with teams highs for runs (120), triples (23), homers, on-base percentage (.456), total average (1.102), base-out percentage (1.192), gross production average (.351), WAR (9.2), oWAR (8.9), batters run average (.262), in-play percentage (85%), times on base (274), base runs (130), runs produced (196), runs created (147), isolated power (.175), power/speed number (12.6), extra base hits (60), total bases (323), bases produced (427), steals (61) and hit streak (23). Sam Crawford (.325 BA, 4 HR, 109 RBI) in right led in games (149), plate appearances (647), at bats (581), runs batted in, stolen base runs (4.8) and outs (424). Jim Delahanty (.286 BA, 41 RBI). George Mullin (.278 BA, 12 RBI) led the pitchers. Hank Perry led pinch-hitters at .500 (3-6). Cobb dominated pitching June 23-August 4 (41 GM, .500 BA, .538 OBP, .786 SLG, .513 BAbip).

1910s Hitting Doubles	
1. Ty Cobb	313
2. Bobby Veach	216
3. Sam Crawford	192
4. Donie Bush	138
5. Harry Heilmann	100
6. Oscar Stanage	98
7. George Moriarty	92
8. George Burns	76
9. Ossie Vitt	75
10. Jim Delahanty	60

Pitching. The Tigers recorded a 3.77 ERA, 107 CG, seven SHO, 521 walks, 512 SO, 87 ERA+, 3.53 FIP, 1.433 WHIP, 9.5 H/9, 3.4 BB/9, and 3.4 SO/9. Motown led league in pitchers (20), HBP (61), WP (55), batters faced (5,774), HR/9 (0.1) and left on base (1,091). Pitcher of the Year Jean Dubuc (17-10, 2.77 ERA, 2 SHO) led in wins, win percentage (.630), SHO (2), walks (109), strikeouts (97), wild pitches (16), LOB% (68.7), earned run average, ERA+ (118), pWAR (4.4), hits per nine (7.8) and runs per nine (3.8). The most effective pitcher Ed Willett (17-15, 3.29 ERA) led in wins, starts (31), complete games (28), innings (284.1), hits (281), HBP (17), earned runs (104), runs (144) and WHIP (1.284). Joe Lake (9-11, 3.10 ERA) led in FIP (2.81), DICE (2.96), walks per nine (2.2), strikeouts per nine (4.8), and SO/BB (2.21). George Mullin (12-17, 3.54 ERA, 2 SHO, 3 HR) led in losses. Tex Covington (3-4, 4.12 ERA), and Ralph Works (5-10, 4.24 ERA). Others included Willie Jensen (1-2, 4.91 ERA), Bill Burns (1-4, 5.35 ERA), 19-year-old rookie Charlie Wheatley (1-4, 6.17 ERA) and 20-year-old rookie George Boehler (0-2, 6.47 ERA).

Defense. Detroit committed 337 errors for a .950 fielding percentage, as they led the American League in chances (6,758) and assists (2,283). Tiger league leaders were Stanage in catcher assists (168), double plays (14), passed balls (17) and stolen bases allowed (172). Bush led all shortstops in assists (547), chances per game (6.5) and the Bengals in defensive War (1.8).

Jean Dubuc won eight straight on the road May 11-July 25. He did not lose in July (8 GM, 7-0, 6 CG, 63 IP, .220 BA), with a one-hit 4-0 shutout at Chicago on Saturday, July 6. He won 10 straight decisions for a 16-4 record thru Sunday, August 11.

Ty Cobb (.409) won another batting title, as he made the news for attacking disabled fan Claude Lueker on Wednesday, May 15. He was suspended 10 games and fined $50 by league president Ban Johnson, as the incident led to the first players strike.

1910s Hitting Triples		
1.	Ty Cobb	161
2.	Sam Crawford	135
3.	Bobby Veach	92
4.	Donie Bush	60
5.	Harry Heilmann	44
6.	Ossie Vitt	40
7.	Oscar Stanage	28
8.	George Burns	24
9.	Marty Kavanaugh	19
	Ralph Young	19

Team. Detroit finished in sixth place under manager Hughie Jennings at 66-87 (.431), with an attendance of 398,502. The Tigers were 5-11 in April, that included a Jean Dubuc (9 IP, 0 ER, 3 H) 2-for-3 led 4-0 home shutout of St. Louis on Saturday, April 19 in a mere 1:23, with Hugh High 3-for-4 (2 RBI). Detroit went 12-16 in May with a nine-game losing streak thru Saturday, May 3. Ty Cobb went a phenomenal 10-for-12 (.833 BA, .889 OBP, 1.417 SLG, 2.306 OPS, .833 BAbip) for May 19-24. His extraordinary week raised his average to .508 for the season. The franchise swept a doubleheader at St. Louis on Sunday, May 25. Ed Willett (9 IP, 3 ER) 3-for-4 (2 RBI) and Cobb (2 RBI) led a game one 7-4 win. The Tigers took game two 8-6 behind rookies Bobby Veach 3-for-3 (3 RBI) and Henri Rondeau (2 RBI). The Tigers had a 11-17 record in June, as Marc Hall (9 IP, 0 ER, 4 H) pitched a 1-0 shutout gem at Chicago on Sunday, June 1. Hooks Dauss won twice during a series in Washington, D.C. First a 11-1 win (IP, 0 ER, 4 H, 6 SO) on Saturday, June 7, with Donie Bush 2-for-4 (HR, 3 RBI), Cobb (3 RBI), Sam Crawford (HR, 2 RBI), Michigan native Red McKee 3-for-4 (2 RBI) of Saginaw, and Ossie Vitt 3-for-3. Dauss (9 IP, 0 ER, 5 H, 6 SO) was 1-for-3 in a 11-0 shutout of the Senators on Wednesday, aided by Crawford (HR, 4 RBI), Cobb (HR, 3 RBI), McKee 3-for-4 (2 RBI) that featured a seven-run second inning. Detroit finished 13-15 in July as Crawford went 4-for-5 (5 RBI) and reliever Dubuc (5 IP, 0 ER) was 1-for-3 during a 9-8 home win against Philadelphia on Monday, July 14. Players were 13-12 in August with an Ed Willett (9 IP, 1 ER, 5 H, 7 SO) in a 7-1 victory over visiting Washington on Sunday, August 17, behind Oscar Stanage (3 RBI), Crawford (2 RBI) and Bush (4 BB). The Bengals logged a 10-14 mark in September and 2-2 in October. Detroit rolled to a 15-2 victory at Boston on Thursday, September 11 that included a seven-run eighth inning. Dauss (9 IP, 1 ER, 5 H) went 3-for-5 (4 RBI), Baldy Loudon (2 RBI), Crawford 3-for-5 (2 RBI), Veach 3-for-6 (2 RBI) and Eddie Onslow (2 RBI). Cobb logged six consecutive multi-hit games September 20-27 (.583 BA, .583 OBP, .792 SLG, .583 BAbip). 20-year-old rookie Michigander Wally Pipp from Grand Rapids went 2-for-4 (3 RBI) with two triples during a 7-5 victory over visiting Chicago on Saturday, October 4. Cobb was exceptional in games at home (.431 BA), and during May (.464 BA). Motown was 34-42 (.447) at home and 32-45 (.416) on the road. The Bengals scored 625 runs and allowed 716.

C * RED MCKEE

Offense. Detroit finished with a .265 BA, .336 OBP, .355 SLG, .691 OPS, 1,798 TB, with an OPS+ of 104. Oscar Stanage (.224 BA, 21 RBI) and 22-year-old rookie Red McKee (.283 BA, HR, 20 RBI) caught. Del Gainer (.267 BA, 2 HR, 25 RBI) was at first, Ossie Vitt (.240 BA, 2 HR, 33 RBI) at second base and George Moriarty (.239 BA, 30 RBI) at third. Shortstop Donie Bush (.251 BA, HR, 40 RBI) led MLB plate appearances (688). He led club in runs (98), walks (80) and outs (460). Bobby Veach (.269 BA, 64 RBI) played in left. Centerfielder Ty Cobb (.389 BA, 4 HR, 67 RBI) was the Player of the Year and most effective hitter. He led MLB in hitting, on-base percentage (.466) and OPS+ (194). Ty led the American League for total average (1.305), hitting, BAbip (.414), secondary average (.399). Cobb led his squad in singles (129), slugging (.534), OPS (1.000), base-out percentage (1.293), gross production average (.343), WAR (7.4), oWAR (7.6), batters run average (.243), base runs (102), steals (51), stolen base runs (15.3) and hitting streak (12). Right-fielder Sam Crawford (.317 BA, 9 HR, 83 RBI) led the MLB in triples (23 and total bases (298). He led league for at bats (609) and extra base hits (64), with team lead in games (153), hits (193), singles (129), doubles (32), homers, runs batted in, in-play percentage (85%), times on base (245), base runs (102), runs produced (152), runs created (110), isolated power (.172), power/speed number (10.6) and bases produced (363). Ed Willett (.283 BA, HR, 13 RBI) and Jean Dubuc (.267 BA, 2 HR, 11 RBI, .393 SLG) led the pitchers. The leading Tiger pinch-hitter was Hugh High at .263 (5-19).

1910s Hitting Home Runs		
1.	Ty Cobb	47
2.	Sam Crawford	39
3.	Harry Heilmann	22
4.	Bobby Veach	21
5.	George Burns	15
6.	Donie Bush	8
	Marty Kavanaugh	8
	Oscar Stanage	8
9.	Jim Delahanty	6
10.	Ira Flagstead	5

Pitching. The Tigers recorded a 3.38 ERA, 90 CG, four SHO, 504 walks, 468 SO, 86 ERA+ of 86, 3.21 FIP, 1.370 WHIP, 9.0 H/9, 3.3 BB/9, and 3.1 SO/9. The staff allowed leagues highs in runs per game (4.67), runs (715), earned runs (511), WP (46), batters faced (5,633) and left on base (1,022). Pitcher of the Year and most effective pitcher was 23-year-old rookie Hooks Dauss (13-12, 2.48 ERA, 22 CG) that led in win percentage (.520), shutouts (2), homers (4), strikeouts (107), hit by pitch (13), earned run average, ERA+ (118), FIP (3.10), DICE (3.55), WHIP (1.200), pWAR (3.4), hits per nine (7.5), walks per nine (3.3), strikeouts per nine (4.3), SO/BB (1.30) and runs per nine (4.0). Jean Dubuc (15-14, 2.89 ERA, 22 CG) led the league in WP (13), with team lead in games (36), wins, losses, innings (242.2) and walks (91). Ed Willett (13-14, 3.09 ERA) led the Tigers in losses, starts (30), hits (237), earned runs (83), runs (117), and walks per nine (3.3). Marc Hall (10-12, 3.27 ERA) led in LOB% (66.8). Joe Lake (8-7, 3.28 ERA), Carl Zamloch (1-6, 2.45 ERA), George Mullin (1-6, 2.75 ERA), Fred House (1-2, 5.20 ERA), Ralph Comstock (2-5, 5.37 ERA) and Al Klawitter (1-2, 5.91 ERA). Hall was exceptional for the period of May 23-June 15 (6 GM, 4-0, 31.2 IP, 0 HR, 1.14 ERA, .198 BA, .144 SLG). Dubuc and Willett led MLB in HR/9 (0.0).

Defense. Detroit led the league in assists (2,162) and errors (303) for a .954 fielding percentage. Tiger league leaders were Dubuc in pitcher chances (129), Gainer in chances per game (11.6) at first, as Bush at short led club in defensive WAR (0.9).

Sam Crawford registered four-hit games on Friday, April 11 (4-for-5, 2 R) at St. Louis; Thursday, June 5 (4-for-5, 2 RBI) at Philadelphia; Tuesday, June 17 (4-for-5, 2 RBI) at Boston; and Monday, July 14 (4-for-5, 5 RBI) at home against Philadelphia.

1910s Hitting Runs Batted In	
1. Ty Cobb	828
2. Sam Crawford	697
3. Bobby Veach	636
4. Donie Bush	330
5. Harry Heilmann	309
6. Oscar Stanage	283
7. George Moriarty	244
8. George Burns	220
9. Ossie Vitt	214
10. Jim Delahanty	180

Team. Detroit finished fourth for Hughie Jennings at 80-73 (.523) with 416,225 fans. The Tigers started the season 10-4 in April when 29-year-old Alex Main from Montrose, Michigan had a dominating MLB debut (3 GM, 3-0, 26 IP, 2 ER, 0.69 ERA, .218 SLG). The Tigers defeated visiting Cleveland 4-3 on Saturday, April 18, with reliever Main (W 1-0, 8 IP, 0 ER, 6 SO). Motown won 7-4 win versus Cleveland at home on Tuesday, April 21, with reliever Harry Coveleski (8 IP, 0 ER). Detroit went 13-13 in May, as the Tigers swept a series in New York. Coveleski (9 IP, 4 H, 0 ER) and Donie Bush 3-for-4 led a 4-0 shutout on Tuesday, May 12. Jean Dubuc (9 IP, 1 E, 2 H) and pinch-hitter Bobby Veach (2 RBI) starred in a 3-1 win on Thursday. Motown won 4-2 on Friday, with Hooks Dauss (9 IP, 1 ER, 5 H, 6 SO) on the mound. Sam Crawford 4-for-4 (3 RBI) and George Moriarty (2 RBI) powered an 8-5 triumph at Washington on Thursday, May 28. The Bengals were 16-14 in June with a Main (W 5-2, 5 IP, 0 ER, 3 H, 5 SO) 3-0 five inning gem over St. Louis at home on Friday, June 5. Coveleski had 34 consecutive scoreless innings June 7-24. Main pitched 30.1 straight innings without an earned run June 14-July 13. Coveleski won on consecutive days at home over Washington 3-2 (1.2 IP, 0 ER, 0 H) on Friday, June 19 and a dominant 1-0 shutout (9 IP, 0 ER, 4 H) the next day. Detroit was 10-16 in July with a Fourth of July 3-2 win against Cleveland at home by Main (W 6-4, 12 IP, 0 ER). Dubuc (13 IP, 2 ER) was 3-for-5 (2 RBI) during a 4-2 13-inning victory in Boston on Saturday, July 18. The Bengals and reliever Main (5 IP, 0 ER, 3 H) lost their next game 3-2 in 16 innings to the Red Sox on Monday. Boston hurlers Fritz Coumbe (8 IP, 0 ER) and Dutch Leonard (W 13-3, 0.85 ERA, 8 IP, 0 ER, 0 H, 9 SO) were superb. Players were 12-14 in August as Moriarty went 3-for-5 (4 RBI) in a 13-6 win at Cleveland on Sunday, August 16. The Tigers closed 17-11 in September and 2-1 in October. Pug Cavet (9 IP, 3 ER) and Ty Cobb 3-for-4 led a 13-4 home victory over St. Louis on Sunday, September 6. Players won eight straight games thru Wednesday, September 16. The team went 16-6 against both Chicago and Cleveland. Detroit finished 42-35 (.545) at home and 38-38 (.500) on the road. Motown scored 615 runs and allowed opponents 618. Coveleski went undefeated at home during June 7-September 18 (15 GM, 12-0 1.000, 114.1 IP, 17 ER, 1.34 ERA, .193 BA).

1B * GEORGE BURNS

Offense. Detroit logged a .258 BA, .336 OBP, .344 SLG, .681 OPS, 1,756 TB and 102 OPS+. The catcher Oscar Stanage (.193 BA, 25 RBI) led in strikeouts (58). George Burns (.291 BA, 5 HR, 57 RBI) at first led the league in hit by pitch (12), with team high 13-game hit streak. Marty Kavanagh (.248 BA, 4 HR, 35 RBI) was at second, as George Moriarty (.254 BA, HR, 40 RBI) at third led in stolen base runs (1.2). Shortstop Donie Bush (.252 BA, 32 RBI, 35 SB) led MLB in plate appearances (721) and walks (112), with league high in outs (482). Bush led Detroit in at bats (596), runs (97), singles (128) and times on base (265). Bobby Veach (.275 BA, HR, 72 RBI) at left led for in-play percentage (83%). Player of the Year and most effective hitter Ty Cobb (.368 BA, 2 HR, 57 RBI, 35 SB) at center led league in batting, on-base percentage (.466), slugging (.513) and OPS (.979). He led squad in OPS+ (190), total average (1.098), base-out percentage (1.166), gross production average (.338), batters run average (.235), BAbip (.389) and secondary average (.362). Right-fielder Sam Crawford (.314 BA, 8 HR, 104 RBI) led MLB in triples (26), led league in runs batted in and isolated power (.168). He led Motown in hits (183), homers, WAR (6.2), oWAR (6.7), base runs (104), runs produced (170), runs created (109), power/speed number (12.1), extra base hits (56), total bases (281) and bases produced (375). Harry Coveleski (.242 BA, 12 RBI) and Jean Dubuc (.226 BA, HR, 11 RBI) led the pitchers. Harry Heilmann at .273 (3-11) led pinch-hitters. 21-Year-old rookie Burns went a spectacular 10-for-14 August 3-8 (5 GM, .714 BA, .778 OBP, 1.143 SLG, 1.921 OPS, .769 BAbip).

1910s Hitting On-Base Percentage	
1. Ty Cobb	.457
2. Sam Crawford	.372
3. Bobby Veach	.368
4. Donie Bush	.355
5. Harry Heilmann	.348
6. Ossie Vitt	.324
7. George Burns	.313
8. George Moriarty	.306
9. Ralph Young	.288
10. Oscar Stanage	.283

Pitching. The Tigers recorded a 2.86 ERA, 81 CG, 13 SHO, 498 walks, 567 SO, 98 ERA+, 2.99 FIP, 1.263 WHIP, 8.2 H/9, 3.2 BB/9, and 3.6 SO/9. The staff led league in hit by pitch (65) and home runs per nine (0.1). Pitchers recorded a double-header sweep in Washington of 3-1 and 11-0 on Monday, August 24. Pitcher of the Year and the most effective pitcher Harry Coveleski (22-12, 2.49 ERA) led Motown in wins, win percentage (.647), starts (36), complete games (23), shutouts (5), innings (303.1), homers (4), walks (100), pWAR (5.4), hits per nine (7.4) and runs per nine (3.2). Hooks Dauss (19-15, 2.86 ERA, 302 IP) led MLB in HBP (18) and league in earned runs (96). Dauss led staff for HR/9 (0.089), games (45), losses, saves (3), hits (286), strikeouts (150), WP (8), runs allowed (126), FIP (3.10), DICE (3.18), SO/9 (4.5), and SO/BB (1.72). Ross Reynolds (5-3, 2.08 ERA). Pug Cavet (7-7, 2.44 ERA) led in games finished (13), earned run average, ERA+ (115) and WHIP (1.143). Alex Main (6-6, 2.67 ERA), Marc Hall (4-6, 2.69 ERA), Jean Dubuc (12-14, 3.46 ERA) and George Boehler (2-3, 3.57 ERA). Red Oldham (2-4, 3.38 ERA) led league in balks (3). Coveleski excelled June 4-July 8 (9 GM, 7-1, 61.1 IP, 1.17 ERA, .172 BA, .124 SLG, .181 BAbip) and July 27-September 6 (9 GM, 6-2, 70.2 IP, 1.40 ERA, .177 BA, .202 SLG, .195 BAbip).

Defense. Detroit committed 286 errors for a .958 fielding percentage, as they led league in chances (6,780) and assists (2,271). Tiger league leaders were Coveleski in pitcher chances (140) and assists (123). Catcher Stanage led in assists (190), errors (30), stolen bases (163), caught stealing (139) and caught stealing percentage (46%). Burns led in chances (1,688), chances per game (12.3), putouts (1,579) and errors (30) at first. Moriarty led in assists (312) at third. Bush led shortstops in chances (1,027), chances per game (6.5), putouts (425) and assists (544), as he led the Bengals in defensive WAR (2.4).

Ty Cobb hit .376 versus righthanders, .356 facing lefthanders, .376 on the road, 360 at home, .335 in the first half, and .395 during the second half. Cobb scorched pitchers from the Cleveland Indians (.448 BA) and Boston Red Sox (.434 BA).

1910s Hitting Slugging Percentage	
1. Ty Cobb	.541
2. Sam Crawford	.459
3. Bobby Veach	.424
4. Harry Heilmann	.412
5. George Burns	.362
6. George Moriarty	.308
7. Ossie Vitt	.302
8. Donie Bush	.296
9. Oscar Stanage	.291
10. Ralph Young	.280

Team. Detroit finished second under Hughie Jennings at 100-54 (.649), with 476,105 fans. Motown went 12-5 in April including 9-3 at home. Motown had a 10-run eighth inning during a Hooks Dauss (W 5-0, 9 IP, 1 ER, 4 H) 12-3 triumph of visiting St. Louis on Wednesday, April 28. Ty Cobb went 3-for-4 (4 R, 3B, 2 RBI), Sam Crawford 2-for-3 (3 3B, 2 RBI), Marty Kavanagh (3B, 2 RBI) and Red McKee (2 RBI). First year Tiger Bernie Boland (3-0, 30 IP, 1 ER, 0.30 ERA) set the franchise April earned run average record. The squad was 13-11 in May, with a Harry Coveleski (9 IP, 1 ER, 6 SO) 2-for-3 (2 2B, RBI) led 3-1 win over the Yankees at home on Wednesday, May 19. Detroit had nine stolen bases, as Cobb (3 BB) swiped four bases. The franchise finished 14-10 during June, including a 15-0 shutout win in Boston on Wednesday, June 9. Bobby Veach 4-for-5 (3 RBI), Kavanagh (2 3B, 3 RBI), Crawford (3 RBI), Cobb 3-for-5 (3 SB, 2 RBI), Ralph Young 3-for-5 (2 RBI) and Dauss (W 11-3, 6 IP, 0 ER, 3 H) led the way. Players lost a 7-6 13-inning decision in Philadelphia on Saturday, June 12, as reliever Bill Steen (8 IP, 1 ER) took the loss and Cobb had four steals. Detroit defeated St. Louis at home 4-2 on Wednesday, June 23, with Steen (9 IP, 0 ER, 9 SO) and Crawford 3-for-4 (2 RBI). Motown and Steen (9 IP, 2 ER) took a 7-2 win over Cleveland at home on Wednesday, June 30. Steen excelled as a Tiger in June (7 GM, 3-1, 1 SV, 39.2 IP, 1.59 ERA), with seven quality starts. Detroit went 18-10 in July that included a Coveleski (W 9-7, 7 IP, 0 ER, 3 H) 15-4 home win on Friday, July 9. They chased Boston starter Babe Ruth (L 7-5, .1 IP, 4 R, 2 H, 2 BB), with Kavanagh 2-for-3 (3 RBI), Crawford (3 RBI), Cobb (2 SB, 2 RBI), Veach (2 SB, 2 RBI) and George Burns (2 SB, 2 RBI). The squad rolled thru August at 23-7, with a spectacular 15-2 record for August 4-20. Players won back-to-back home doubleheaders against Cleveland by scores of 6-2 by Coveleski (W 16-10, 9 IP, 2 ER), Oscar Stanage 4-for-4 and Cobb (3 SB, 2 RBI) in the opener on Monday, August 16, as Bernie Boland (W 9-6, 9 IP, 0 ER, 1 H) led the 3-1 game two win. The next day Detroit won 10-3 with Jean Dubuc (W 16-9, 9 IP, 2 ER) and Cobb 4-for-5 (3 R, 3 SB, 2 2B), followed by a Red Oldham (9 IP, 3 ER) and Crawford (3 RBI) led 7-3 victory. First place Detroit (73-39 .652) beat visiting Philadelphia 11-1 on Friday, August 20, behind Bill James (9 IP, 0 ER), Veach (3 RBI) and Burns 3-for-5 (2 RBI). Players closed 18-11 in September and 2-0 in October. The club was 51-26 (.662) at home, including 10-1 over Chicago, and were 49-28 (.636) on the road. Motown scored 778 runs and their pitchers allowed 597.

OF * BOBBY VEACH

Offense. Detroit had a .268 BA, .357 OBP, .358 SLG, .715 OPS, 1,836 TB and 110 OPS+. Oscar Stanage (.223 BA, HR, 31 RBI) caught. George Burns (.253 BA, 5 HR, 50 RBI) at first led in homers (5) and strikeouts (51). Ralph Young (.243 BA, 31 RBI) was at second. Ossie Vitt (.250, HR, 48 RBI) at third led MLB in sacrifice hits (42). Shortstop Donie Bush (.228 BA, HR, 44 RBI) led AL in plate appearances (703) and team in outs (482). Bobby Veach (.313 BA, 3 HR, 112 RBI) at left led MLB in doubles (40). Player of the Year and most effective hitter Ty Cobb (.369 BA, 3 HR, 99 RBI) at center led MLB in runs (144), hits (208), steals (96), caught stealing (38), hitting, on-base percentage (.486), OPS (.973) and OPS+ (185). He led AL in singles (161), total average (1.267), WAR (9.5), oWAR (9.9), BAbip (.397), secondary average (.430), times on base (336), runs created (138) and total bases (274). Cobb led club in slugging (.487), total average (1.170), base-out percentage (1.261), gross production average (.340), batters run average (.233), base runs (138), runs produced (240) bases produced (488) and stolen base runs (6.0). Sam Crawford (.299 BA, 4 HR, 112 RBI) in right led league in triples (19) and extra base hits (54). He led team in at bats (612), in-play percentage (84%), power/speed number (6.9) and hit streak (19). Marty Kavanagh (.295 BA, 4 HR, 49 RBI) led pinch-hitters .500 (10-20). Jean Dubuc (.205 BA, 14 RBI) led pitchers. Crawford and Veach tied for AL lead in runs batted in (112).

1910s Hitting On-Base plus Slugging	
1. Ty Cobb	.998
2. Sam Crawford	.831
3. Bobby Veach	.792
4. Harry Heilmann	.760
5. George Burns	.675
6. Donie Bush	.651
7. Ossie Vitt	.626
8. George Moriarty	.614
9. Oscar Stanage	.574
10. Germany Schaefer	.568

Pitching. The Tigers recorded a 2.86 ERA, 86 CG, nine SHO, 492 walks, 550 SO, 106 ERA+, 2.92 FIP, 1.239 WHIP, 8.0 H/9, 3.1 BB/9, and 3.5 SO/9. Motown led league in saves (20) and innings (1,413.1). Pitcher of the Year Hooks Dauss (24-13, 2.50 ERA, 309.2 IP) led league in HR/9 (0.0) and staff in wins, losses, complete games (27), walks (115), LOB% (70.5), pWAR (5.5) and R/9 (3.3). The most effective pitcher Harry Coveleski (22-13, 2.45 ERA, 4 SV) led MLB in HBP (20), with league lead for games (50) and hits (271). He led staff in losses, starts (38), innings (312.2), strikeouts (150), runs (123), ERA, ERA+ (124), FIP (2.56), DICE (3.15), WHIP (1.145), BB/9 (2.5), SO/9 (4.3) and SO/BB (1.72). Bernie Boland (13-7, 3.11 ERA) led in win percentage (.650), games finished (16) and H/9 (7.4). Jean Dubuc (17-12, 3.21 ERA) led in SHO (5), homers (6), wild pitches (11) and earned runs (92). Bill James (7-3, 2.42 ERA), Bill Steen (5-1, 2.72 ERA, 4 SV), Red Oldham (3-0, 2.81 ERA, 4 SV) and Pug Cavet (4-2, 4.06 ERA).

Defense. Detroit had 258 errors for a .961 fielding average, as league leader in chances (6,656), putouts (4,228) and assists (2,170). Coveleski led pitchers in errors (11), Dauss in chances (153) and assists (137). Burns in chances per game (11.8) at first base and Young in errors (32) at second. Vitt led in fielding (.964), chances (534), chances per game (3.5), putouts (191), and assists (324) at third base, as he led his team in dWAR (1.7). Shortstop Bush led AL in chances (901) and assists (504).

Ty Cobb hit .369 to win his ninth-straight batting title, with hitting streaks of April 14-23 (10 GM, .469 BA), May 15-29 (12 GM, .550 BA), July 1-13 (13 GM, .458 BA), August 14-22 (10 GM, .486 BA) and for period September 5-24 (17 GM .412 BA).

"Road Warrior" Jean Dubuc (4-0, 1.22 ERA) won 1-0 at Philadelphia (9 IP, SHO) on August 4, 3-2 at Philadelphia (10 IP, 0 ER) on August 7, 5-3 at Chicago (9 IP, 3 ER) on August 14 and 10-3 at Cleveland (9 IP, 2 ER) on August 17 with two days of rest.

1910s Pitching Wins		
1.	Hooks Dauss	125
2.	Jean Dubuc	72
3.	Harry Coveleski	69
4.	Bernie Boland	67
5.	Ed Willett	59
6.	George Mullin	52
7.	Bill James	35
8.	Bill Donovan	31
9.	Howard Ehmke	30
10.	Ed Summers	25

Team. Detroit finished in third place with Hughie Jennings at 87-67 (.565) and had an attendance of 616,772. The Bengals were 9-6 in April, with an 8-1 record in nine games starting on Monday, April 17. Players won 6-5 over the Browns in St. Louis on Friday, April 28, when George Burns went 4-for-5 (2 RBI). Sam Crawford reached base five straight times as a pinch-hitter April 29-May 20. The Bengals were 9-16 in May that included a 16-2 win at Philadelphia on Tuesday, May 9, behind Ty Cobb (4 RBI), Harry Heilmann 3-for-5 (3 RBI), Burns (2 RBI, 2 SH). The long reliever Bernie Boland (SV 1, 6.2 IP, 1 ER, 3 H, SV) went 1-for-1 with three walks. The Tigers walked an MLB record 18 times. Motown finished 16-10 in June including two seven-game win streaks for a 14-1 mark during period of June 3-21. Newly acquired Earl Hamilton (9 IP, 0 ER) beat Philadelphia 8-2 at home on Sunday, June 18, with Oscar Stanage 3-for-4 (2 RBI) and Heilmann (2 RBI). Detroit was 18-15 in July with a 9-2 win in Philadelphia on Friday, July 7, behind Harry Coveleski (W 11-6, 9 IP, 2 ER) 3-for-5, Cobb 3-for-4 (HR, 2 RBI) and a Burns home run. The Tigers were 18-10 in August, as Boland (W 7-3, 9 IP, 0 ER) was 2-for-4, Cobb 4-for-5 (2 RBI) and Veach 3-for-4 (2 RBI) to lead a 9-0 home shutout of Philadelphia on Tuesday, August 8. Detroit swept a doubleheader in Washington 11-6 and 8-4 on Thursday, August 17. The game one 20-hit attack included a five-run 10th inning, as Donie Bush went 4-for-6 (3 RBI), Cobb 3-for-6 (3 RBI), Burns (2 RBI) and Veach 4-for-6. Game two leaders were Hooks Dauss (W 13-9, 6.2 IP, 2 ER) 2-for-3, Cobb 3-for-4 (3 RBI, 2 SB) and Burns (2 RBI). Detroit logged a 17-9 mark in September and 0-1 in October. Howard Ehmke (9 IP, 2 ER) won his first Tiger start 10-2 victory in Cleveland on Tuesday, September 12. Keys to the win were Cobb 4-for-5 (2 HR, 4 R, 4 RBI), Veach 4-for-5, Crawford 3-for-5 (2 RBI) and Heilmann (2 RBI). The first place Tigers (80-59 .576) won 4-1 the next day over visiting New York, with Coveleski (W 20-10, 7.1 IP, 1 ER, 5 H) 1-for-3, and Veach 3-for-4 (RBI). Detroit was 18-4 versus the last place Philadelphia Athletics, including 9-2 both at home and away. The team finished 49-28 at home, including a 14-4 mark at Navin Field in June, and 9-2 against Washington. The Bengals scored a league high 673 runs while their pitchers allowed 595 runs. The team stood 18-22 thru May and then meshed to go 69-45 (.605) thereafter.

P * BILL JAMES

Offense. Detroit finished with a .337 OBP, .687 OPS, 1,816 TB, and 103 OPS+. They led the American League in hitting (.264) and slugging percentage (.350). Oscar Stanage (.237 BA, 34 RBI) caught. George Burns (.286 BA, 4 HR, 73 RBI) at first led club in hitting streak (13). Second baseman Ralph Young (.263 BA, HR, 42 RBI, 153 GM). Ossie Vitt (.226 BA, 42 RBI, 153 GM) at third base led squad in plate appearances (705), at bats (597) and outs (494). Donie Bush (.225 BA, 33 RBI) was the shortstop. Bobby Veach (.306 BA, 3 HR, 89 RBI) was in left with team lead in doubles (33), triples (15), runs batted in, runs produced (178) and extra base hits (51). Centerfielder, Player of the Year, and most effective hitter Ty Cobb (.370 BA, 5 HR, 68 RBI) led MLB in runs (113) and steals (68). Cobb led the league in total average (1.134), oWAR (8.7), secondary average (.346) and runs created (125). He led his team in Hits (201), singles (155), home runs (5), on-base percentage (.451), slugging (.492), OPS (.943), OPS+ (178), WAR (8.0), batters run average (.217), hitting, BAbip (.393), times on base (281), base runs (118), power/speed number (9.3), total bases (267), bases produced (413), stolen base runs (6.0) and walks (78). Right-fielder Harry Heilmann (.282 BA, 2 HR, 77 RBI) led in isolated power (.129). Outfielder Sam Crawford (.286 BA, 47 RBI) led for in-play percentage (85%). George Cunningham (.268 BA) and Jean Dubuc (.256 BA, 9 RBI) led the pitchers. The best pinch-hitter was Crawford at .533 (8-15).

1910s Pitching Winning Percentage		
1.	Bill Donovan	.660
2.	Harry Coveleski	.616
3.	Bernie Boland	.588
4.	Hooks Dauss	.576
5.	Jean Dubuc	.545
6.	Howard Ehmke	.536
	George Mullin	.536
8.	Ed Willett	.522
9.	Ed Summers	.510
10.	Bill James	.493

Pitching. The Tigers had a 2.97 ERA, 81 CG, eight SHO, 578 walks, 531 SO, 97 ERA+, 3.04 FIP, 1.299 WHIP, 8.0 H/9, 3.7 BB/9, and 3.4 SO/9. The staff led league in hit by pitch (62), homers per nine (0.1) and runners left on base (1,116). Pitcher of the Year and most effective pitcher Harry Coveleski (21-11, 1.97 ERA) had one of his three shutouts in a 4-0 win (9 IP, 0 ER, 3 H) at Chicago on Wednesday, April 12. He also led in games (44), wins, win percentage (.656), starts (39), complete games (22), innings (324.1), hits (278), homers (6), strikeouts (108), runs (105), LOB% (71.9), earned run average, ERA+ (145), FIP (2.57), DICE (3.26), WHIP (1.051), pWAR (6.9), BB/9 (1.7), SO/BB (1.71) and R/9 (2.9). Jean Dubuc (10-10, 2.96 ERA) led in games finished (16) and hits per nine (7.1). Hooks Dauss (19-12, 3.21 ERA) led league in hit by pitch (16), with staff highs in losses, saves (4), walks (90), wild pitches (8) and earned runs (85). Rookie George Cunningham (7-10, 2.75 ERA) led in homers per nine (0.0). Willie Mitchell (7-5, 3.31 ERA) led in strikeouts per nine (4.2). Detroit native Bill James (8-12, 3.68 ERA), Earl Hamilton (1-2, 2.65 ERA), Howard Ehmke (3-1, 3.13 ERA) and Bernie Boland (10-3, 3.94 ERA).

Defense. Detroit committed 211 errors during the 1916 season with an .968 fielding percentage. Tigers leading the American League included pitcher Coveleski in assists (119), third baseman Vitt in fielding percentage (.964), chances (615), chances per game (4.1), putouts (208), assists (385) and double plays (32). Vitt led the franchise for defensive WAR (2.6).

Detroit had 19 hits during a 17-6 over St. Louis at home on Monday, May 29, with a nine run third inning. Jean Dubuc (8 IP, 3 ER) was 2-for-5 (RBI), Ty Cobb 4-for-6 (2B, 3B, 3 RBI), Bobby Veach 3-for-4 (3 RBI, 2 SH) and Harry Heilmann 3-for-4 (2 RBI).

Motown used numerous pinch-hitters in 1916 (31-for-127 .244 BA). Sam Crawford at .533 (8-15) led league with eight pinch-hits. Others in the pinch were Red McKee .333 (2-for-6), Harry Heilmann .313 (5-for-16) and George Burns .273 (3-for-11).

1910s Pitching Games Started		
1.	Hooks Dauss	219
2.	Jean Dubuc	130
3.	Harry Coveleski	125
4.	Ed Willett	113
5.	Bernie Boland	110
6.	George Mullin	97
7.	Bill James	71
8.	Howard Ehmke	60
9.	Ed Summers	48
10.	Bill Donovan	44

Team. Detroit finished fourth under Jennings at 78-75 (.510), with 457,289 fans. Players were 5-9 in April, as they lost 2-1 at Chicago in 14 innings on Saturday, April 28, with pitchers Harry Coveleski (7 IP, 1 ER) and Deacon Jones (6.1 IP, 0 ER, 3 H). Motown went 10-12 in May including a home doubleheader win over the Indians 4-1 and 9-1 on Wednesday, May 9. Howard Ehmke (9 IP, 1 ER, 3 H, 7 SO) and Ty Cobb (2 RBI) led the opener, with Harry Heilmann 4-for-4 (2 RBI), Sam Crawford (2 RBI), Tubby Spencer (2 RBI) and Jones (9 IP, 1 ER, 5 H) game two stars. Ehmke (12 IP, 1 ER, 5 H, 7 SO) defeated Boston at home on Sunday, May 13. Motown swept the tribe again in Cleveland on Wednesday, May 30, with a Bernie Boland (W 5-1, 9 IP, 0 ER) game one 4-1 win. Ehmke (9 IP, 1 ER, 5 H) won game two 5-1, aided by Bobby Veach 3-for-4 (3 RBI) and Heilmann 4-for-4 (2 RBI). Cobb reached base in 41 straight games including a 35-game hit streak May 31-July 5 (.464 BA, .516 OBP, .754 SLG). Players were 17-10 in June when Boland (W 6-1, 9 IP, 1 ER) 1-for-3 and Veach (HR, 2 RBI) guided a 6-4 win at New York on Tuesday, June 5, as Cobb was 5-for-5 (2 2B, 3B, RBI) to begin a stretch of eight straight multi-hit games June 5-16 (.613 BA, .647 OBP, 1.07 SLG, 1.744 OPS, .621 BABIP). Motown had a 1-0 shutout at Washington on Monday, June 18, behind Ben Dyer 2-for-4, Hooks Dauss (9 IP, 0 ER, 3 H) and Cobb (3 SB), with a mere 1,081 fans in Griffith Stadium. Detroit rolled to a 19-1 victory in St. Louis on Friday, June 29, with 19 hits and nine walks. The victory was led by Donie Bush 4-for-6 (4 R), Cobb 3-for-4 (3 R, 2 RBI), Veach (HR, 2 RBI), Oscar Stanage (2 RBI), Heilmann 3-for-5 (3 R, HR) and Coveleski (9 IP, 0 ER, 4 H) 2-for-5. The franchise was 20-14 in July with a 15-9 loss at St. Louis on Sunday, July 1, as Cobb was 3-for-5 and Crawford hit a two-run pinch-hit homer. Detroit went 13-15 in August, as pitchers threw back-to-back shutouts of 5-0 by Ehmke (9 IP, 0 ER, 5 H) 2-for-4 (RBI) and Cobb 3-for-4 (RBI) at Boston on Saturday, August 11. Willie Mitchell (9 IP, 0 ER, 5 H, 7 SO) won 8-0 the next day, as Cobb went 4-for-5 and Spencer 2-for-3 (2 RBI). Dauss (8 IP, 1 ER, 5 H) won 15-1 at Cleveland on Wednesday, August 29, with Cobb (4 RBI), Stanage (3 RBI), Ossie Vitt (2 RBI) and Heilmann (2 RBI). Players were 13-15 in September when they swept a doubleheader at Boston 5-2 and 1-0 on Wednesday, September 19. Bill James (W 12-9, 9 IP, 1 ER) won game one, followed by Dauss (W 16-13, 9 IP, 0 ER, 3 H). Cobb (HR, 3 RBI, 2 SB) powered an Ehmke (9 IP, 0 ER, 3 H) 4-0 shutout at Washington on Saturday, September 22. James (W 13-9, 9 IP, 2 ER) went 1-for-3 (RBI) in the 8-3 victory at Washington on Monday, with Cobb 4-for-4 (2 RBI) and four steals. Detroit closed 34-41 (.453) at home, 44-34 (.564) on the road, and 21-13 in blowout games. The Bengals scored 639 runs and allowed 577.

P * DEACON JONES

Offense. Detroit had a .328 OBP, .672 OPS, 1,750 TB, and 105 OPS+. Motown led the league in hitting (.259) and slugging (.344). Oscar Stanage (.205 BA, 30 RBI) caught, with George Burns (.226 BA, HR, 42 RBI) at first and Ralph Young (.231 BA, HR, 38 RBI) at second. Ossie Vitt (.254 BA, 45 RBI) manned third. Donie Bush (.281 BA, 23 RBI) at short led MLB in runs (112). He led team in plate appearances (673), walks (80) and outs (428). Bobby Veach (.319 BA, 8 HR, 110 RBI) in left led MLB in runs batted in (110). He led league for hit by pitch (9) and power/speed number (11.6), with club lead in games (154) and homers (8). Player of the Year Ty Cobb (.383 BA, 6 HR, 106 RBI) in center was the most effective hitter, as he led MLB in hits (225), doubles (44), triples (24), stolen bases (55), hitting, on-base percentage (.444), slugging (.570), OPS (1.014), OPS+ (209) and total bases (335). Cobb led league in at bats (588), runs (112), singles (151), total average (1.253), WAR (11.3), oWAR (10.6), BAbip (.400), secondary average (.384), times on base (290), runs created (148), isolated power (.187) and extra base hits (74). Ty led Detroit in base-out percentage (1.243), gross production average (.342), batters run average (.246), base runs (135), runs produced (207), bases produced (451), stolen base runs (16.5) and hitting streak (35). Harry Heilmann (.281 BA, 5 HR, 85 RBI) in right led in strikeouts (54). George Harper at .250 (4-16) led all Tiger pinch-hitters.

1910s Pitching Complete Games		
1.	Hooks Dauss	156
2.	Jean Dubuc	90
3.	Ed Willett	80
4.	George Mullin	78
5.	Harry Coveleski	68
6.	Bernie Boland	58
7.	Howard Ehmke	37
8.	Bill Donovan	35
9.	Ed Summers	32
10.	Bill James	29

Pitching. The Tigers recorded a 2.56 ERA, 20 SHO, 504 walks, 516 SO, 103 ERA+, 2.84 FIP, 1.227 WHIP, 7.8 H/9, 3.2 BB/9, and 3.3 SO/9. Staff led the league in hit by pitch (55), HR/9 (0.1) and left on base (1,106). The staff was superb September 19-28 (10 GM, 9-1, 1.01 ERA). Pitcher of the Year Bernie Boland (16-11, 2.68 ERA, 7.3 H/9) led the majors in homers per nine (0.0) and led team in saves (6). The most effective pitcher Willie Mitchell (12-8, 2.19 ERA) led in win percentage (.600), hit by pitch (13), FIP (2.49), DICE (3.23), WHIP (1.176), walks per nine (2.2), strikeouts per nine (3.9), and strikeouts to walks (1.74). Bill James (13-10, 2.09 ERA) led staff in walks (96), LOB% (74.6), earned run average, ERA+ (126), and pWAR (2.9). Hooks Dauss (17-14, 2.43 ERA) led in wins, starts (31), complete games (22), shutouts (6), innings (270.2), hits (243), strikeouts (102), WP (4), earned runs (73), and runs allowed (105). Harry Coveleski (4-6, 2.61 ERA). Howard Ehmke (10-15, 2.97 ERA) led in losses and strikeouts per nine (3.9). George Cunningham (2-7, 2.91 ERA, 7.3 H/9) led club in games (44) and games finished (25). Deacon Jones (4-4, 2.92 ERA). Mitchell and James led club in runs per nine (3.2).

Defense. Detroit committed 234 errors for a .964 fielding percentage. Tiger league leaders were Young in assists (449) at second base, outfielders Veach in errors (17) and Cobb in double plays (9). Stanage led the Bengals in defensive WAR (0.7).

Hooks Dauss was stellar at home July 6-19 (0.50 ERA, as he defeated Chicago 4-1 (9 IP, 0 ER) July 6, lost 1-0 (9 IP, 1 ER) to Boston on July 11, won 7-2 (9 IP, 1 ER) versus Philadelphia on July 15 and won 2-0 (9 IP, 0 ER, 3 H) over New York on July 19.

Detroit Tigers 1918 American League

1910s Pitching Earned Run Average		
1.	Harry Coveleski	2.34
2.	Hooks Dauss	2.85
3.	Bernie Boland	3.01
4.	Jean Dubuc	3.06
5.	Howard Ehmke	3.09
6.	George Mullin	3.11
7.	Ed Summers	3.11
8.	Ed Willett	3.12
9.	George Cunningham	3.13
10.	Ralph Works	3.95

Team. Detroit finished in seventh place under Hughie Jennings with a 55-71 (.437) record, with a paid attendance of 203,719. The Tigers were 2-4 in April, including a 3-2 tough loss by Bill James (12 IP, 2 ER, 7 SO) to Cleveland at home on Saturday, April 27. Motown finished 9-16 during May when they lost 19-3 at home to Chicago on Friday, May 3. The team lost seven consecutive games on the road from Saturday, May 11 thru Monday, May 20 to fall into last place. Detroit was at its best in June (16-15), including 5-2 on the road, with a five consecutive wins against the St. Louis Browns from Tuesday, June 18 thru Saturday, June 22. Ty Cobb reached base an amazing 41 games in a row June 17-July 31 (.484 BA, .529 OBP, .637 SLG). Bernie Boland (9 IP, 0 ER, 4 H) shutout Chicago 1-0 at home on Thursday, June 27, with Bobby Veach 2-for-2. Motown went 16-17 in July, as the Tigers won five straight road games thru Thursday, July 18, when the team outscored the Senators and Yankees 28-3. The starters completed all five games with a spectacular 0.60 earned run average during the stretch, with shutouts of 1-0 by Bill James (9 IP, 0 ER, 7 H) and Boland (9 IP, 0 ER, 5 H) 7-0 in the Nation's Capital. The Motor City defeated Philadelphia 2-1 at home on Friday, July 26, behind Boland (W 11-7, 11 IP, 1 ER). Rudy Kallio (9 IP, 0 ER, 6 H) and Marty Kavanagh 3-for-4 (3 RBI) led a 6-0 blanking of the visiting Athletics on Sunday, July 28. Detroit finished 9-18 in August, when they started the month losing four games being outscored 29-1. Opponents hit .345 with an 0.25 earned run average, as the Bengals hit a meager .165 with an unimpressive 6.75 earned run average. The Tigers edged Washington 7-6 in 18-innings at Navin Field on Sunday, August 4 to break the losing streak. The great Walter Johnson (L 18-12, 17.1 IP, 6 ER, 16 H) faced 75 hitters in the loss, as Deacon Jones (8 IP, 4 ER) and reliever Hooks Dauss (10 IP, 0 ER, 5 H, 6 SO) pitched for Detroit. The offense was led by Veach (3 RBI), Cobb 2-for-9 (RBI), Bob Jones (2 RBI) recorded three sacrifice hits and Donie Bush had two hits and four walks. Motown closed the season 3-1 in September. Ty Cobb had five multi-hit games in three days August 31-September 2 (.625 BA, 625 OBP, .708 SLG, .625 BABIP). The Bengals defeated Chicago 7-3 at home on Monday, September 2, behind 41-year-old Bill Donovan making his last MLB start (5 IP, 1 ER), Art Griggs 4-for-5 (2 RBI), Veach (2 RBI) and Cobb 3-for-5. Outfielders Cobb and Veach each pitched two innings. The Tigers had a record of 28-29 (.491) at home, including 8-2 against Chicago and 27-42 (.391) in away games. The team scored 476 times during the season as their pitchers would allow opponents 557 runs.

P * BERNIE BOLAND

Offense. Motown logged a .325 OBP, .318 SLG, .642 OPS, 1,355 TB and 98 OPS+. Archie Yelle (.174 BA, 8 RBI), Tubby Spencer (.219 BA, 10 RBI) and Oscar Stanage (.253 BA, HR, 16 RBI) caught. Harry Heilmann (.276 BA, 5 HR, 43 RBI) at first led in homers and power/speed number (7.2). Ralph Young (.188 BA, 21 RBI) played second. Third had Ossie Vitt (.240 BA, 17 RBI) and Bob Jones (.275 BA, 20 RBI) that led for in-play percentage (85%). Donie Bush (.234 BA, 26 RBI) at short led MLB in plate appearances (594) and squad in walks (79). Bobby Veach (.279 BA, 3 HR, 84 RBI) at left led MLB in runs batted and league in doubles (21). Player of the Year and most effective hitter Ty Cobb (.382 BA, 3 HR, 62 RBI) at center led MLB in hitting, on-base percentage (.440), slugging (.515), OPS (.955) and OPS+ (194). He led the league in triples (14), oWAR (6.7) and runs created (95). Cobb led his team in runs (81), hits (161), singles (125), total average (1.131), base-out percentage (1.126), gross production average (.327), WAR (6.5), batters run average (.222), BAbip (.398), times on base (204), base runs (89), runs produced (144), isolated power (.133), total bases (217), bases produced (292), steals (34), stolen base runs (10.2) and hit streak (21). George Harper (.242 BA, 16 RBI) was in right. Hooks Dauss (12 RBI) led the pitchers. George Cunningham led pinch-hitters at .375 (3-8). Stanage shined May 28-July 8 (9 GM, .464 BA, .500 OBP, .500 SLG, .520 BAbip). Cobb went on a 21-game hit streak June 29-July 17 (.558 BA, .591 OBP, .663 SLG, .566 BAbip).

1910s Pitching Innings Pitched		
1.	Hooks Dauss	1,869.0
2.	Jean Dubuc	1,145.0
3.	Harry Coveleski	1,023.1
4.	Bernie Boland	1,017.2
5.	Ed Willett	982.0
6.	George Mullin	801.2
7.	Howard Ehmke	492.0
8.	George Cunningham	477.0
9.	Ed Summers	416.1
10.	Ralph Works	410.0

Pitching. The Bengals had a 3.40 ERA, eight SHO, 437 walks, 374 SO, 78 ERA+, 2.91 FIP, 1.350 WHIP, 8.8 H/9, 3.4 BB/9, and 2.9 SO/9. The staff led league in pitchers (17), R/G (4.35), hits (1,130), earned runs (43), runs (557) and HR/9 (0.1). Pitcher of the Year Bernie Boland (14-10, 2.65 ERA) led league in HR/9 (0.0), as he led team in wins, win percentage (.583), shutouts (4), LOB% (72.7), earned run average, ERA+ (100), WHIP (1.191), pWAR (4.2), hits per nine (7.8) and runs per nine (3.0). The most effective pitcher Hooks Dauss (12-16, 3.15 ERA) led the league in earned runs (83), with club highs in games (33), losses, starts (26), complete games (21), saves (3), innings (249.2), hits (243), homers (3), strikeouts (73), hit by pitch (9), runs (105), FIP (2.61), DICE (3.38), BB/9 (2.1) and SO/BB (1.26). George Cunningham (6-7, 3.15 ERA) led in games finished (12). Rudy Kallio (8-14, 3.62 ERA) led his squad in walks (76), wild pitches (7) and strikeouts per nine (3.5). Cunningham and Kallio led MLB in HR/9 (0.0). Deacon Jones (3-2, 3.09 ERA). Rookie Eric Erickson excelled April 19-June 15 (9 GM, 4-3, 83.1 IP, 1.84 ERA) including a 2-2 tie at Washington on Friday, May 24 (16 IP, 1 ER, 12 SO). Boland shined for June 10-August 2 (13 GM, 9-2 .818, 9 CG, 4 SHO, 0.97 ERA, .177 BA, .149 SLG, .193 BAbip).

Defense. Detroit players committed 212 errors for a .960 fielding percentage. The lone Motor City league leader was Ralph Young who led all second basemen in errors (30). Third baseman Bob Jones led the Detroit franchise in defensive WAR (0.0).

World War I took a toll on the country and major-league baseball. The United States Secretary of War, Newton D. Baker, of Ohio, issued the unpopular orders to either work or fight. That edict would end the 1918 season prematurely on Labor Day.

1910s Pitching Earned Run Average

1.	Harry Coveleski	2.34
2.	Hooks Dauss	2.85
3.	Bernie Boland	3.01
4.	Jean Dubuc	3.06
5.	Howard Ehmke	3.09
6.	George Mullin	3.11
	Ed Summers	3.11
8.	Ed Willett	3.12
9.	George Cunningham	3.13
10.	Ralph Works	3.95

Team. Detroit finished fourth with manager Hughie Jennings at 80-60 (.571), with an attendance of 643,805. The team went 1-4 in April as Howard Ehmke (9 IP, 1 ER, 6 SO) won the season opener 4-2 at home against Cleveland on Friday, April 25. The Bengals were 12-12 in May that included an 8-2 10-game stretch when Ty Cobb was phenomenal May 19-May 31 (10 GM, .513 BA, .548 OBP, .769 SLG, .541 BAbip). The Tigers rolled to a 14-6 triumph in Cleveland on Friday, May 2, with Bobby Veach 4-for-4 (2 RBI), Bob Jones 3-for-4 (2 RBI), Harry Heilmann (2 RBI) and Ira Flagstead (2 RBI). Detroit was 17-10 in June including 11-0 in home games. The team swept a home series with Cleveland June 26-29 in Detroit. Bernie Boland (12 IP, 0 ER, 5 H) led a 1-0 shutout on Thursday, a 6-1 Hooks Dauss (9 IP, 1 ER, 5 H) win the next day, a Dutch Leonard (9 IP, 1 ER, 6 SO) 3-1 gem on Saturday and an Ehmke (9 IP, 0 ER, 1 H) 4-0 one-hit shutout on Sunday. Players finished 20-13 for July that included a 3-1 Slim Love (9 IP, 0 ER, 7 SO) dominant start win over visiting Washington on Friday, July 11. Players beat New York 13-2 at home on Tuesday, July 15. Ralph Young went 4-for-4 (4 RBI), Veach 3-for-5 (3 RBI), Cobb (2 RBI), Heilmann 3-for-4 (2 RBI) and Dauss (W 10-5, 9 IP, 2 ER). Newcomer Doc Ayers was impressive the month of July 21-August 20 (8 GM, 2-2, 45.1 IP, 1.19 ERA, .212 SLG), including a tough loss of 2-1 at Boston on Thursday, July 31 (11.2 IP, 1 ER). Detroit was their best at 18-9 in August. The club won 14-8 at Yankee Stadium on Saturday, August 2, led by Heilmann 4-for-5 (2 HR, 6 RBI), Veach (HR, 4 RBI), Cobb 4-for-5 (2 RBI) and reliever Ehmke (W 13-9, 6 IP, 2 ER, 3 H). Detroit went 14-2 during a 16-game stretch August 5-23. The team closed 12-12 in September, including a 16-inning 4-3 home win against Chicago on Tuesday, September 2. Ehmke (W 15-9, 16 IP, 0 ER) allowed three unearned runs, 24 runners on 17 hits and seven walks while facing 70 batters. Cobb excelled the period of September 2-17 (.529 BA, .607 OBP, .667 SLG, .551 BAbip), including a spectacular 7-for-10 (.700 BA) during three games September 13-17. The Tigers were 46-24 (.657) at home, including 9-1 against Philadelphia and 34-36 (.486) on the road. Motown scored 618 runs and allowed 578. Joe Pate (15-4 .789, 1.64 ERA and Paul Wahtel (21-14 .600, 2.40 ERA) were at class "B" Fort Worth.

C * EDDIE AINSMITH

Offense. Detroit had a .283 BA, .346 OBP, .727 OPS, 1,778 TB and 106 OPS+ and led the league in triples (84) and slugging (.381). The catcher was Eddie Ainsmith (.272 BA, 3 HR, 35 RBI), Harry Heilmann (.320 BA, 8 HR, 92 RBI) played first base and led the Bengals in home runs, power speed number (7.5), strikeouts (41) and hitting streak (21). Ralph Young (.211 BA, HR, 26 RBI) at second was the leader in outs (406) and Bob Jones (.260, HR, 52 RBI) played third. Shortstop Donie Bush (.244 BA, 33 RBI, 601 PA) led in walks (75). Player of the Year Bobby Veach (.355 BA, 3 HR, 97 RBI, 601 PA) in left led MLB in doubles (45) and triples (17). Bobby led team in at bats (538), runs batted in, slugging percentage (.519), WAR (6.7), runs produced (181), runs created (111), isolated power (.164), extra base hits (65), total bases (279) and bases produced (331). The most effective hitter Ty Cobb (.384 BA, HR, 67 RBI) at center led MLB in hitting, as he led club in runs (92), singles (141), on-base percentage (.428), OPS (.942), OPS+ (166), total average (1.052), base-out percentage (1.051), gross production average (.321), oWAR (6.1), batters run average (.216), BAbip (.400), in-play percentage (87%), times on base (230), base runs (101), stolen bases (28) and stolen base runs (8.4). Michigan native right-fielder Ira Flagstead (.331 BA, 5 HR, 47 RBI) from Montague, led team in secondary average (.293). Outfielder Chick Shorten (.315 BA, 26 RBI). Howard Ehmke (.253 BA) and Hooks Dauss (13 RBI) led the pitchers in hitting. The leading Tiger pinch-hitter was Ben Dyer at .375 (3-8). Cobb and Veach tied for MLB lead in hits (191).

1910s Pitching Innings Pitched

1.	Hooks Dauss	1,869.0
2.	Jean Dubuc	1,145.0
3.	Harry Coveleski	1,023.1
4.	Bernie Boland	1,017.2
5.	Ed Willett	982.0
6.	George Mullin	801.2
7.	Howard Ehmke	492.0
8.	George Cunningham	477.0
9.	Ed Summers	416.1
10.	Ralph Works	410.0

Pitching. The Tigers recorded a 3.30 ERA, 10 SHO, 436 walks, 428 SO, 97 ERA+, 3.30 FIP, 1.346 WHIP, 9.0 H/9, 3.1 BB/9, 3.1 SO/9, 85 complete games and led league in left on base (1,030). Pitcher of the Year Hooks Dauss (21-9) led the league in runs (125), as he led staff in wins, win percentage (.700), starts (32), complete games (22), innings (256.1), hits (262), homers (9), earned runs (101) and BB/9 (2.2). The most effective pitcher Dutch Leonard (14-13, 2.77 ERA) led in shutouts (4), strikeouts (102), hit by the pitch (7), earned run average, ERA+ (115), FIP (2.96), DICE (3.47), SO/9 (4.2) and SO/BB (1.57). Bernie Boland (14-16, 3.04 ERA) led in games (35), losses, LOB% (71.8), WHIP (1.245), pWAR (4.), H/9 (8.2) and R/9 (3.4). Howard Ehmke (17-10, 3.19 ERA) led major league baseball in walks (107). George Cunningham (1-1, 4.91 ERA) led in games finished (15). Others were Slim Love (6-4, 3.01 ERA), Willie Mitchell (1-2, 5.27 ERA), Rudy Kallio (0-0, 5.64 ERA) and Eric Erickson (0-2, 6.75 ERA). Doc Ayers stood 0-6 (2.89 ERA) with Washington when he was traded to Motown on Wednesday, June 25, as he finished 5-3 (2.69 ERA) for Detroit.

Defense. The players committed 205 errors for a .964 fielding percentage. The Tiger league leaders were Dauss in pitcher assists (101), with Ainsmith the leader for catcher errors (22) and stolen bases allowed (82), as he led Detroit in defensive WAR (0.3). Heilmann led American League first basemen in errors (31) and Bush led all shortstops in putouts with 290.

Discharged from the Navy in March, Howard Ehmke started on opening day. He logged the most innings during two home wins of 5-4 against Philadelphia on July 16 (W 11-7, 14 IP, 4 ER) and 4-3 over Chicago on September 2 (W 15-9, 16 IP, 0 ER).

Starting Tiger pitcher Howard Ehmke went 17-10 and hit .253 (23-91) in 1919, a year after missing the entire 2018 season while serving in the United States Armed Forces with the Navy during WWI after going 10-15 (2.97 ERA) in 1917 for Detroit.

Player of the Decade. Ty Cobb (.361 BA, 44 HR, 594 RBI) was the unprecedented Player of the Decade three times for the 1900s, 1910s and 1920s. The decade leader in on-base percentage (.435) and stolen bases (100). He was player-manager for Detroit 1921-1926. The 1921 team set the American League record with 1,724 hits for a .316 team average, as seven Tigers hit .300, with league leader Harry Heilmann (.394 BA), league runner-up Cobb (.389 BA), Bobby Veach (.338 BA), rookie Lu Blue (.308 BA), Johnny Bassler (.307 BA), Ira Flagstead (.305 BA), Bob Jones (.303 BA) and Ralph Young settling for a .299 average. Cobb, Heinie Manush and Harry Heilmann formed the only "Hall of Fame" outfield in history 1923-1926. Cobb had both speed and power traits as a player and received more votes for the first Hall of Fame class than Babe Ruth, Honus Wagner and 500-game winner Cy Young. His mark of 98.2 percent of votes stood for 56 years.

P * DUTCH LEONARD

1920s			
Year	W – L	Pct.	Pl
1920	61-93	.396	7
1921	71-82	.464	6
1922	79-75	.513	3
1923	83-71	.539	2
1924	**86-68**	**.558**	3
1925	81-73	.526	4
1926	79-75	.513	6
1927	82-71	.536	4
1928	68-86	.442	6
1929	70-84	.455	6
	760-778	.494	

All-Decade Team. Manager Ty Cobb (479-444 .519) led Detroit to a second-place finish in 1923 (83-71 .539). Pitcher Herman Pillette (34-32 .515, 3.42 ERA). Catcher Johnny Bassler (.308 BA, 1 HR, 313 RBI) led the 1920s decade in dWAR (5.0), AB/SO (30.7), walk percentage (15.2), walks per strikeouts (5.8), strikeout ratio (0.03) and strikeout percentage (2.6%). First baseman Lu Blue (.295 BA, 19 HR, 407 RBI). Second baseman Charlie Gehringer (.315 BA, 24 HR, 290 RBI). Shortstop Topper Rigney (.296 BA, 9 HR, 249 RBI). Third baseman Marty McManus (.280 BA, 35 HR, 232 RBI) led in percentage of hits for extra bases (34.8) and for pinch-hit average (.385). Leftfielder Heinie Manush (.321 BA, 38 HR, 345 RBI) led for being hit by the pitch (45). Centerfielder Ty Cobb (.361 BA, 44 HR, 594 RBI) led decade in on-base percentage (.435), stolen bases (100), caught stealing (75) and strikeout ratio (0.03). Right-fielder Harry Heilmann (.364 BA, 142 HR, 1,131 RBI) led the Tigers for games (1,417), plate appearances (6,121), (5,285), runs (962), hits (1,924), singles (1,284), doubles (397), triples (101), home runs (142), runs batted in (1,131), reached on error (57), slugging (.558), OPS (.991), oWAR (60.1), batters run average (.241), hitting, at bats per home run (37.2), at bats per run batted in (4.7), extra base hits (640), extra bases on long hits (1,025), total bases (2,949), total base percentage (2.08), bases produced (3,634), bases produced average (2.6), home run percentage (2.3%), home run average (16.12), stolen base runs created (2,019), walks (615) and for strikeouts (324).

Pitcher of the Decade. Herman Pillette (34-32 .515, 3.42 ERA) was the Detroit decade leader in left on-base percentage (67.4), earned run average, ERA+ (114), HR/9 (0.22), RA/9 (4.45), high quality start percentage (.539) and dominate start percentage (.184). He pitched a full year with Regina of Western Canada in 1920 (14-9, 2.25 ERA). His final game with Regina was a no-hit shutout against Moose Jaw. Herman dedicated the 1921 season (13-30, 326 IP, 55 GP) with Portland to prepare for a return to the major leagues. Desperate Detroit traded five players and $30,000 to the sad sack Beavers (51-134) in December to acquire Pillette and Sylvester Johnson (12-26). Pillette responded with his best year for the Tigers in 1922 (19-12 .613, 2.85 ERA), with four shutouts including three two-hitters, as he went 11-6 at home and was 9-3 in the first half.

P * RED OLDHAM

1920s Attendance			
Year	Attn.	Avg.	Rk
1920	579,650	7,431	4
1921	661,527	8,591	3
1922	861,206	11,184	2
1923	911,377	11,836	2
1924	**1,015,136**	**13,015**	2
1925	820,766	10,659	4
1926	711,914	8,789	4
1927	773,716	9,919	2
1928	474,323	6,160	4
1929	869,318	11,290	2

All-Decade Pitchers. Pillette's 1922 highlights were May (4-0 1.000, 1.74 ERA) and July (5-1 .833, 1.98 ERA). He went 12-5 (.706) pitching on two days of rest as a Tiger. Hooks Dauss (97-90 .519, 3.86 ERA) started in 1923 (21-13, .618, 3.62 ERA, 4 SHO) and led decade in games (269), wins, losses, complete games (89), saves (26), dominant starts (23), innings (1,521.2), hits (1,693), homers (62), runs (813), pitcher WAR (15.6), tough losses (27) and relief wins (29). Dutch Leonard (35-37 .486, 4.15 ERA) was decade leader for wild pitches (25), FIP (3.72), DICE (3.73), BB/9 (2.74), SO/9 (4.21) and SO/BB (1.53), with 1925 his best season (11-4 .733, 4.51 ERA). Rip Collins (44-40 .524, 3.94 ERA) led in quality start percentage (.824), WHIP (1.383) and starter win percentage (.526). His 1924 year (14-7 .667, 3.21 ERA) included May 26-July 1 (7-2 .778, 2.80 ERA, .227 BA). Earl Whitehill (87-78 .527, 4.10 ERA) led the 1920s in starts (191), shutouts (8) quality starts (86), high quality starts (79), walks (540), strikeouts (567), earned runs (654), starter wins (77), batters faced (6,299), no decisions (40), relief win Percentage (10-4 .714) and cheap wins (25). He was 9-3 in the first half and 5-0 1.000 (2.28 ERA) pitching on two days of rest in 1924 (17-9 .654, 3.86 ERA). Howard Ehmke (45-49 .479, 3.95 ERA) led in complete game percentage (.619) and hit by pitch (49). He stood 4-12 on July 16, then starred July 17-August 25 (9-1, 1.80 ERA). Ownie Carroll (37-37 .500, 3.92 ERA) started in 1928 (16-12 .571, 3.27 ERA), with shutouts facing Chicago at home of 3-0 on April 23 (9 IP, 5 H, 0 ER) and 6-0 on June 24 (9 IP, 7 H, 0 ER). Sam Gibson (28-29 .491, 4.06 ERA) in 1926 (12-9 .571, 3.48 ERA) excelled pitching at home (6-2 .750), in second half (10-3 .769, 2.52 ERA) and during September (5-0 1.000, 1,76 ERA). Ken Holloway (57-46 .553, 4.41 ERA) led the 1920s in games finished (82), games in relief (135) and relief win percentage (20-8 .714), with the 1924 (14-6 .700) and 1925 (13-4 .765) seasons his best. Red Oldham (29-40 .420, 4.25 ERA) had dominate home wins in 1922 of 5-1 against Washington on June 13 (9 IP, 1 ER) and 11-1 win over Philadelphia on July 31 (9 IP, 1 ER).

Pillette was stunning during July 15-22, 1922 (3-0, 0.33 ERA, .186 BA, .186 SLG, .209 BAbip), with a 2-0 shutout at Boston on July 15 (9 IP, 0 ER), 5-1 victory in New York July 19 (9 IP, 1 ER) and shutout the Yankees 2-0 (9 IP, 0 ER) on two days of rest.

1920s Team Hitting				
YEAR	AVG	HR	RBI	SB
1920	.270	30	561	76
1921	**.316**	58	793	95
1922	.306	54	735	78
1923	.300	41	739	87
1924	.298	35	769	100
1925	.302	50	798	97
1926	.291	36	717	88
1927	.289	51	765	**139**
1928	.279	62	686	113
1929	.299	**110**	**851**	95

Team. Detroit finished seventh for Hughie Jennings at 61-93 (.396), with 579,650 fans. Motown lost their first 13 games with an 0-11 record in April. Hooks Dauss (7 IP, 0 ER, 4 H) fell to 0-4 after losing to visiting St. Louis 2-0 on Thursday, April 29. The Bengals were 11-14 in May as Dutch Leonard (9 IP, 2 ER) was 2-for-3 during a 6-2 win in St. Louis on Sunday, May 30, aided by Bob Jones 3-for-5 (3 RBI) and Bobby Veach (HR, 2 RBI). The franchise had a June record of 10-18 that included Harry Heilmann 5-for-5 (2 RBI), Ty Cobb (2 RBI), Chick Shorten (2 RBI) and Eddie Ainsmith (2 RBI) leading a 11-10 victory in Cleveland on Tuesday, June 1. The team went 14-15 in July that included a 10-4 win in Boston on Tuesday, July 13, paced by Ira Flagstead 4-for-5 (3 R, 3 2B, 2 RBI). The Bengals swept a doubleheader at Washington on Tuesday, July 20. Players won 7-6 in 15-innings, with pitchers Red Oldham (9 IP, 6 ER) 2-for-4 (RBI) and Dauss (W 9-11, 6 IP, 3 H, 0 ER) 1-for-2, with Veach (2 RBI) hit by a pitch twice. Howard Ehmke (9 IP, 1 ER, 5 H), Ralph Young (2 RBI) and Donie Bush (2 RBI) led the game two 2-1 victory. Detroit outscored the Browns 21-8 at home on Sunday, July 25. The 22-hit performance was led by Oldham (9 IP, 3 ER) 3-for-5 (3 RBI), Ainsmith 4-for-5 (4 R, 4 RBI), Veach 4-for-6 (4 R, 2 RBI), Flagstead 3-for-5 (5 RBI) and Young (4 RBI). Motown scored seven runs in the first, five in the second and five runs in the third for a 17-5 lead. The Bengals were 13-15 in August, with Ehmke (9 IP, 0 ER, 3 H, 8 SO) 1-for-3 during a 1-0 shutout of visiting New York on Sunday, August 8. The game lasted a mere 1:13 to set an American League record. Motown won 11-9 at Yankee Stadium on Sunday, August 22, with Cobb 5-for-6 (2 RBI) and Heilmann 4-for-5 (2 RBI). The squad closed 11-18 in September and 2-2 in October. Detroit beat Boston 14-13 at home on Friday, September 17, when Veach was the first Tiger to hit for the cycle. He hit the imaginary 6-6-6 jackpot, 6-for-6 with six runs batted in. 19-year-old rookie right-hander John Bogart made his major-league debut with a quality start (6.2 IP, 3 H, 2 ER), as reliever Allen Conkwright (W 2-0, 3 IP, 0 ER) got the win. The Bengals went 32-46 (.410) at home, 29-47 (.380) on the road, scored 652 runs and allowed 832. Chick Shorten excelled the weeks of June 6-12 (.550 BA, .600 SLG) and September 19-25 (.632 BA, .789 SLG). 51-year-old Jennings resigned after the season. He had played 17 MLB seasons as a star shortstop (.311 BA) and managed for another 14 years with Detroit (1,131-972 .538). Hughie was a National Baseball Hall of Fame inductee in 1945, as was three of his players Ty Cobb (1936), Harry Heilmann (1951) and Sam Crawford (1957.

OF * CHICK SHORTEN

Offense. Detroit had a .270 BA, .334 OBP, .358 SLG, .693 OPS, 1,868 TB and 86 OPS+. Oscar Stanage (.231 BA, 17 RBI) and Eddie Ainsmith (.231 BA, HR, 19 RBI) caught, with Harry Heilmann (.308 BA, 9 HR, 89 RBI) at first. Ralph Young (.291 BA, 33 RBI) at second led in plate appearances (703), singles (146), times on base (260), walks (85) and outs (456). Babe Pinelli (.229 BA, 21 RBI) and Bob Jones (.249 BA, HR, 18 RBI) manned third. Shortstop Donie Bush (.263 BA, HR, 33 RBI, 15 SB) led MLB in sacrifice hits (48). Donie led Motown in stolen base runs (0.3) and strikeouts (32). Player of the Year Bobby Veach (.307 BA, 11 HR, 113 RBI) in left led for games (154), at bats (612), runs (92), hits (188), doubles (39), triples (15), homers, runs batted in, slugging percentage (.474), WAR (4.2), in-play percentage (86%), base runs (91), runs produced (194), runs created (102), isolated power (.167), power/speed number (11.0), extra base hits (65), total bases (290) and bases produced (337). The most effective hitter Ty Cobb (.334 BA, 2 HR, 63 RBI, 15 SB) at center led team in on-base percentage (.416), OPS (.867), OPS+ (132), total average (.875), base-out percentage (.911), gross production average (.300), oWAR (3.8), batters run average (.185), hitting, BAbip (.354), secondary average (.264) and hit streak (20). Ira Flagstead (.235 BA, 3 HR, 35 RBI) and Chick Shorten (.288 BA, HR, 40 RBI) played in right. Howard Ehmke (.238 BA, 5 RBI) led pitchers. The top pinch-hitters were Shorten at .333 (5-15) and Sammy Hale at .327 (17-52, HR, 6 RBI).

1920s Team Hitting				
YEAR	OBP	SLG	OPS	OPS+
1920	.334	.358	.693	86
1921	**.385**	.433	**.818**	**109**
1922	.373	.416	.788	108
1923	.377	.401	.778	106
1924	.374	.404	.779	102
1925	.380	.413	.793	103
1926	.366	.398	.765	99
1927	.363	.409	.772	99
1928	.340	.401	.742	92
1929	.360	**.453**	.813	108

Pitching. The Tigers recorded a 4.04 ERA, 74 CG, nine SHO, 561 walks, 93 ERA+, 3.82 FIP, 1.479 WHIP, 9.7 H/9, 3.6 BB/9, and 3.1 SO/9. Motown led the league in pitchers used (21), strikeouts (483), hit by pitch (56), and batters faced (5,857). Pitcher of the Year Howard Ehmke (15-18, 3.25 ERA, 19 QS) led in wins, win percentage (.455), starts (33), complete games (23), walks (124), HBP (13), LOB% (67.6), ERA, ERA+ (114), pWAR (4.2), H/9 (8.4), and R/9 (4.5). Hooks Dauss (13-21, 3.56 ERA, 19 QS) led in losses, innings (270.1), hits (308), homers (11), earned runs (107) and runs (158). The most effective pitcher Doc Ayers (7-14, 3.88 ERA, 3 SHO) led in games (46), strikeouts (103), FIP (3.14), DICE (3.39), BB/9 (2.7), SO/9 (4.4) and SO/BB (1.66). Dutch Leonard (10-17, 4.33 ERA, 3 SHO) led MLB in WP (13) and staff in WHIP (1.333). Red Oldham (8-13, 3.85 ERA). John Bogart (2-1, 3.04 ERA), Frank Okrie (1-2, 5.27 ERA), Allen Conkwright (2-1, 6.98 ERA) and Ernie Alten (0-1, 9.00 ERA). Class "B" Fort Worth had stars Bill Whitaker (24-6 .800), Joe Pate (26-8 .765, 314 IP, 0.987 WHIP), Dick Robertson (20-7 .741, 0.992 WHIP), and Paul Wachtel (26-10 .722, 308 IP).

Defense. Motown committed 229 errors for a .965 fielding average. Tiger league leaders were Dauss in pitcher assists (114), outfielders Heilmann in errors (19), Shorten in fielding (.989) and Veach in assists (26). Pinelli led Detroit in dWAR (0.5).

Hughie Jennings led the Detroit Tigers to American League pennants and World Series appearances during each of his first three years as manager. Pinch-hitter Sammy Hale led the American League in both pinch-hits (17) and pinch-hit at bats (52).

Detroit Tigers 1921 American League

1920s Hitting Games	
1. Harry Heilmann	1,417
2. Lu Blue	925
3. Ty Cobb	877
4. Johnny Bassler	767
5. Bob Fothergill	747
6. Heinie Manush	615
7. Bob Jones	606
8. Charlie Gehringer	578
9. Bobby Veach	573
10. Larry Woodall	548

Team. Detroit finished sixth for first year manager Ty Cobb at 71-82 (.464), with an attendance of 661,527. The Tigers went 6-7 in April with 27-year-old rookie Suds Sutherland (3-0, 0.59 ERA, .167 BA, .173 BAbip) rocking his MLB debut month. Hooks Dauss (9 IP, 3 ER), Ralph Young 4-for-4, Harry Heilmann 3-for-4 (HR, 3 RBI) and Cobb 3-for-4 powered a 7-3 victory in Chicago on Sunday, April 24. Motown was 18-15 in May with 28 games played at home. Red Oldham (9 IP, 0 ER, 4 H) 2-for-4 led a 9-0 shutout in St. Louis on Thursday, May 5, aided by Eddie Ainsmith 3-for-4 (2 RBI), Lu Blue 3-for-4, Cobb 3-for 5 (HR, 3 RBI) and Donie Bush (3 RBI). Motown defeated Chicago 11-1 at home on Thursday, May 26, with an eight-run first inning. Dauss (9 IP, 1 ER) went 2-for-3 (3 RBI) with Young (2 RBI), Bush (2 RBI) and Cobb (2 RBI) chipping in. Detroit went 10-14 in June, with a nine-game losing streak beginning on Saturday, June 11. The Bengals lost 13-8 in New York on Monday, June 13, when Babe Ruth (W 1-0, 5 IP, 3 ER) 2-for-3 (2 HR, 3 RBI) won his only start of the year. The club was 14-15 in July, as Heilmann slugged a 500-foot homer over the Navin Field centerfield wall during a 6-3 loss to Boston on Friday, July 8. Players won 2-1 over Philadelphia in 16-innings at home on Tuesday, July 12, behind Dutch Leonard (12 IP, 1 ER, 10 SO) 2-for 4 and Jim Middleton (W 4-3, 4 IP, 0 ER). Detroit prevailed 18-6 at Philadelphia on Friday, July 29, with Howard Ehmke (6 IP, 1 ER) 2-for-4, Ira Flagstead 4-for-5 (3 RBI), Cobb 3-for-4 (4 RBI), Johnny Bassler 3-for-4, Veach (HR, 2 RBI) and Heilmann 3-for-4 (HR, 3 RBI). The Tigers were 12-17 in August, with a 9-8 triumph in New York on Saturday, August 6, as Blue went 5-for-6 (2 RBI), and pitcher Oldham was 2-for-4 with a home run. Bert Cole (9 IP, 0 ER, 4 H) was 2-for-3 and Veach 4-for-4 (2 RBI) for a 10-0 home shutout of Boston on Friday, August 19, as Cobb went 3-for-5 collecting his 3,000th hit. The team closed 11-12 in September when rookie catcher Larry Woodall sizzled August 27-October 2 (16 GM, .419 BA, .457 OBP, .512 SLG, .474 BAbip). Detroit lost 5-4 in Cleveland on Wednesday, September 7, as Heilmann was 5-for-5 (2 RBI). Players lost 20-15 in Chicago on Friday, September 9, with Bob Jones 4-for-6, Veach (4 RBI), Heilmann (4 RBI), and Bassler (3 RBI), as Cobb 3-for-3 scored four runs. Motown went 37-40 (.481) at home and 34-42 (.447) on the road. The Tigers scored 887 runs, as pitchers allowed 852. Chick Shorten led American League pinch-hitters in hits (9) and at bats (37).

1B * LU BLUE

Offense. Detroit hit .316 to set the league record. The team had a .385 OBP, .433 SLG, .818 OPS, 2,365 TB and 109 OPS+. The catcher was Johnny Bassler (.307 BA, 56 RBI). Lu Blue (.308 BA, 33 2B, 11 3B, .416 OBP, .427 SLG, .843 OPS, 7.2 PSN) at first led club in games (153), plate appearances (709), walks (103) and strikeouts (47), with Ralph Young (.299 BA, 29 RBI) at second. Bob Jones (.303 BA, HR, 72 RBI) at third led for in-play percentage (85%). Donie Bush (.281 BA, 27 RBI) and Ira Flagstead (.305 BA, 31 RBI) played at short. Leftfielder Bobby Veach (.338 BA, 16 HR, 128 RBI, 43 2B) led in at bats (612) and outs (442). The most effective hitter was centerfielder Ty Cobb (.389 BA, 12 HR, 101 RBI, .352 GPA) that led in runs (124), triples (16), on-base percentage (.452), total average (1.132), base-out percentage (1.171), secondary average (.331), power/speed number (15.5) and steals (22). Player of the Year Harry Heilmann (.394 BA, 19 HR, 139 RBI, 43 2B, .352 GPA) in right led MLB in hits (237), as *"Slug"* led the league in hitting and BAbip (.399). He led his club in singles (161), homers (19), runs batted in, slugging (.606), OPS (1.051), OPS+ (167), WAR (6.8), oWAR (7.3), batters run average (.263), times on base (292), base runs (143), runs produced (234), runs created (162), isolated power (.213), extra base hits (76), total bases (365), bases produced (420) and hit streak (23). Howard Ehmke (.284 BA, 9 RBI) led pitchers in hitting. The top pinch-hitters were Flagstead .500 (2-4), and Woodall .381 (8-21, 4 RBI) who had four straight pinch-hits June 7-July 11. Class "A" Fort Forth had Clarence Kraft (212 H, 47 2B, 31 HR, .352 BA, 376 TB), and Cecil Coombs (.293 BA, 30 HR, 292 TB).

1920s Hitting Runs	
1. Harry Heilmann	962
2. Ty Cobb	672
3. Lu Blue	669
4. Charlie Gehringer	416
5. Heinie Manush	385
6. Bob Fothergill	367
7. Bobby Veach	343
8. Bob Jones	303
9. Fred Haney	264
10. Johnny Bassler	245

Pitching. Pitchers logged a 4.40 ERA, 72 CG, four SHO, 495 walks, 452 SO, 98 ERA+, 4.30 FIP, 1.536 WHIP, 10.6 H/9, 3.2 BB/9, and 2.9 SO/9. Staff led league in games finished (82), saves (16), hit by pitch (54), balks (7) and left on base (1,234). Pitcher of the Year and most effective pitcher Dutch Leonard (11-13, 3.75 ERA, 1 SHO, 15 HR) led league in SO/BB (1.90), with team lead in starts (32), innings (245), strikeouts (120), wild pitches (7), ERA, ERA+ (114), FIP (3.81), DICE (3.71), WHIP (1.371), pWAR (4.2), H/9 (10.0), BB/9 (2.3), strikeouts per nine (4.4), runs per nine (4.6) and quality starts (22). Red Oldham (11-14, 4.24 ERA, 1 SHO, 81 BB) led in games (40). Bert Cole (7-4, 4.27 ERA, 1 SHO), and Carl Holling (3-7, 4.30 ERA). Hooks Dauss (10-15, 4.33 ERA, 81 BB) led league in HBP (13), with staff highs for losses, complete games (16), hits (275), earned runs (112) and runs (141). Howard Ehmke (13-14, 4.54 ERA, 1 SHO, 15 HR, 81 BB) led league in hit by pitch (13). He was team leader in wins and win percentage (.481). Jim Middleton (6-11, 5.03 ERA) led in games finished (20). Suds Sutherland (6-2, 4.97 ERA). Lefthander Cole was superb during the period April 29-August 27 (9 GM, 4-0 1.000, 38.1 IP, 1.64 ERA, .199 SLG, 1 SV).

Defense. Detroit committed 231 errors for a .964 fielding average. League leaders were outfielder Veach in chances (416) and putouts (384). Jones led third basemen errors (27), and chances per game (3.9). He led Motown in defensive WAR (0.9).

Joe Pate (30-9 .769, 333 IP, 2.68 ERA), Richard Goodbred (8-3 .727, 3.08 ERA), Augie Johns (20-9 .690, 2.60 ERA), Paul Wachtel (23-12 .657, 317 IP, 2.98 ERA) and Bill Whitaker (23-16 .590, 311 IP, 2.43 ERA) were stars at class "A" Fort Worth.

The franchise set American League records in average (.316) and hits (1,724). Harry Heilmann (.394) edged Tiger teammate Ty Cobb (.389) for the batting title. Heilmann won four batting titles in 1921 (.394), 1923 (.403), 1925 (.393) and 1927 (.398).

1920s Hitting Hits	
1. Harry Heilmann	1,924
2. Ty Cobb	1,187
3. Lu Blue	1,002
4. Bob Fothergill	786
5. Charlie Gehringer	705
6. Bobby Veach	691
7. Johnny Bassler	690
8. Heinie Manush	674
9. Bob Jones	586
10. Jackie Tavener	490

Team. Detroit finished third for player manager Ty Cobb with a 79-75 (.513) record and 861,206 fans. The Tigers were 4-11 in April including a 15-7 victory over visiting Cleveland on Friday, April 21, aided by Harry Heilmann (5 RBI) and Bob Fothergill (4 RBI). They had a 16-11 record in May with a 9-7 loss to visiting Chicago on Sunday, May 7, despite the efforts of Cobb 5-for-5 (4 RBI) with three doubles. Motown fell 2-1 in 16-innings at St. Louis on Tuesday, May 30, as Red Oldham (14.1 IP, 1 ER) started. Detroit logged a 15-11 record in June when Johnny Bassler had five multi-hit games in a row June 2-7 (.588 BA, .611 OBP, .647 SLG). The Tigers went 15-3 during an 18-game stretch June 6-23. Herman Pillette (W 8-2, 9 IP, 0 ER, 2 H) and Heilmann (HR, 4 RBI) led an 8-0 shutout of visiting Washington on Sunday, June 11. Detroit won eight in a row June 13-20. The squad had a July record of 18-14, as Cobb recorded seven straight multi-hit games July 3-7 (.647 BA, .676 OBP, .882 SLG, .647 BAbip). The Tigers behind Cobb 5-for-5 (HR, 4 RBI), Danny Clark 3-for-4 (2 RBI and reliever Howard Ehmke (7 IP, 2 ER) 2-for-4 won 16-7 in Boston on Monday, July 17. Motown beat Philadelphia 13-2 at home on Saturday, July 29, with seven sacrifice hits. Pillette (W 13-4, 7 IP, 1 ER), Lu Blue 4-for-4 (4 R), Bobby Veach 4-for-4 (2 3B, RBI), Heilmann (4 RBI), Bob Jones 2-for-3 (HR, 3 RBI) and Cobb (2 RBI) led the way. The club finished 15-13 for August and won a home double-header over Boston 7-0 and 7-4 on Thursday, August 3. Pillette (W 14-4, 9 IP, 0 ER, 2 H) took the opener and reliever Ehmke (W 13-11, 8.2 IP, 0 ER, 4 H) won game two. Hooks Dauss (9 IP, 0 ER) shutout the Red Sox 7-0 the next day. Cobb had eight consecutive multi-hit games August 21-27. Detroit won 17-3 in Philadelphia on Tuesday, August 22, with a 17-hit attack led by Heilmann 4-for-6 (HR, 2 RBI), Veach (HR, 3 RBI) and George Cutshaw (4 RBI). Players closed 11-14 in September, as Fred Haney logged five straight multi-hit games September 4-8 (.579 BA, .636 OBP, .737 SLG, 1.373 OPS, .611 BABIP). Haney went 4-for-4 in an 8-6 loss at St. Louis on Tuesday, September 12. Reliver Oldham (5 IP, 1 ER) went 2-for-3 (2B, 3B, 5 RBI) and Haney (3 BB, 3B, 4 RBI) led a 11-5 win over Washington at home on Monday, September 18. Detroit was 17-5 versus New York, 43-34 (.558) at home, including 10-1 with Philadelphia. Motown went 36-41 (.468) on the road, including 9-2 at Yankee Stadium. The Bengals scored 828 runs and allowed opponents 791 runs.

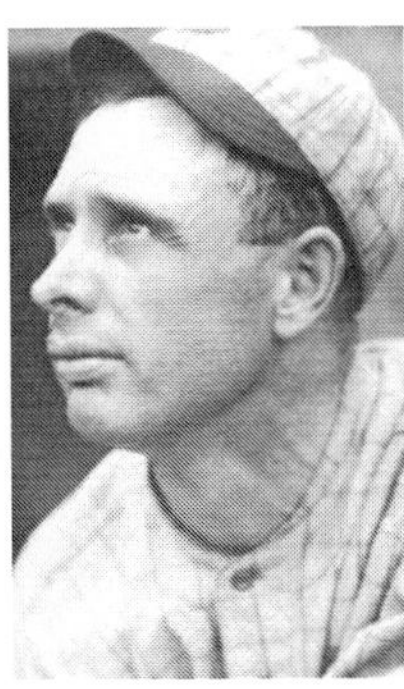
2B * GEORGE CUTSHAW

Offense. Detroit had a .306 BA, .373 OBP, .416 SLG, .788 OPS, 2,229 TB and 108 OPS+. Johnny Bassler (.323 BA, 41 RBI) caught. Lu Blue (.300 BA, 6 HR, 45 RBI) at first led in runs (131), walks (82) and strikeouts (48). George Cutshaw (.267 BA, 2 HR, 61 RBI) at second led for hit streak (18) and in-play percentage (88%). Bob Jones (.257 BA, 3 HR, 44 RBI) played third base. Shortstop Topper Rigney (.300 BA, 2 HR, 63 RBI) led league in games (155) and team in steals (17). Leftfielder Bobby Veach (.327 BA, 9 HR, 126 RBI) led league in games (155) and plate appearances (705). He led squad in at bats (618), runs batted in, runs produced (213), stolen base runs (2.1) and outs (453). Player of the Year Ty Cobb (.401 BA, 4 HR, 99 RBI) in center led in hits (211), singles (149), doubles (42), triples (16), on-base percentage (.462), OPS+ (169), gross production average (.349), WAR (6.7), oWAR (7.2), batting average, BAbip (.416), times on base (270), base runs (126), runs created (137), extra base hits (62), total bases (297) and bases produced (361). The most effective hitter Harry Heilmann (.356 BA, 21 HR, 92 RBI) in right led in homers, slugging (.598), OPS (1.030), OPS+ (169), total average (1.135), base-out percentage (1.143), batters run average (.253), secondary average (.378), isolated power (.242) and power/speed number (11.6). Red Oldham (.260 BA, 13 RBI) led pitchers, as Larry Woodall led pinch-hitters at .417 (5-12, 4 RBI). Cobb was extraordinary for July 3-31 (30 GM, .500 BA, .542 OBP, .700 SLG, .508 BAbip).

1920s Hitting Doubles	
1. Harry Heilmann	397
2. Ty Cobb	234
3. Lu Blue	176
4. Bob Fothergill	173
5. Bobby Veach	129
6. Heinie Manush	124
7. Charlie Gehringer	122
8. Johnny Bassler	98
9. Marty McManus	88
10. Bob Jones	87

Pitching. The Tigers recorded a 4.27 ERA, 67 CG, seven SHO, 473 walks, 461 SO, 91 ERA+, 4.13 FIP, 1.457 WHIP, 10.1 H/9, 3.1 BB/9, and 3.0 SO/9. Pitchers led league in HBP (84), batters faced (6,148) and left on base (1,196). Pitcher of the Year and most effective pitcher Herman Pillette (19-12, 2.85 ERA) led league in HR/9 (0.2), with staff highs in wins, win percentage (.613), starts (37), CG (18), shutouts (4), WP (6), LOB% (72.7), earned run average, ERA+ (136), WHIP (1.329), pWAR (5.8), H/9 (8.8), R/9 (3.6) and quality starts (22). Hooks Dauss (13-13, 4.20 ERA) led in FIP (3.60), DICE (3.59), BB/9 (2.4) and SO/BB (1.32). Howard Ehmke (17-17, 4.22 ERA) led the majors in hit by pitch (23) and league for earned runs (131). He led team in games (45), losses, innings (279.2), hits (299), walks (101), strikeouts (108), earned runs (131), runs (146) and SO/9 (3.5). Red Oldham (10-13, 4.67 ERA) led in homers (14). Syl Johnson (7-3, 3.71 ERA). Ole Olsen (7-6, 4.53 ERA), Bert Cole (1-6, 4.88 ERA), Roy Moore (0-0, 5.95 ERA) and Lil Stoner (4-4, 7.04). Pillette excelled for July 3-August 3 (6-1, 1.49 ERA, 72.2 IP, 3 SHO).

Defense. Detroit committed 192 errors for a .970 fielding percentage. The Bengals led the league in chances (6,375) and assists (2,016). Tiger league leaders were catcher Bassler in stolen bases allowed (73), Rigney led shortstops in errors (50). Jones led third basemen in fielding percentage (.962), and chances per game (3.7). He led his team in defensive WAR (0.9).

Johnny Bassler (121 GM, .323 BA) and Larry Woodall (50 GM, .341 BA) caught. Bassler excelled for the period May 30-July 7 (36 GM, .405 BA, .507 OBP, .416 BAbip). Woodall was impressive July 7-August 27 (24 GM, .403 BA, .442 OBP, .420 BAbip).

Class "A" Fort Worth had Clarence Kraft (.339 BA, 32 HR) at first, Tex Hoffman (.305 BA) at second, outfielder Ziggy Sears (.304 BA) and Art Phelan (.300 BA) at third. Several pitchers were Augie Johns (21-5 .808, 2.38 ERA), Paul Wachtel (26-7 .788, 2.44 ERA), Joe Pate 24-11 .686, 2.71 ERA), Sammy Ross (8-1 .889, 2.54 ERA) and Rich Goodbred (9-5 .643, 2.52 ERA).

1920s Hitting Triples	
1. Harry Heilmann	101
2. Ty Cobb	74
3. Lu Blue	66
4. Charlie Gehringer	63
5. Jackie Tavener	49
6. Bob Fothergill	44
Bobby Veach	44
8. Heinie Manush	42
9. Topper Rigney	29
10. Bob Jones	26

Team. Detroit finished second for Ty Cobb with an 83-71 (.539) record and attendance of 911,377. The Tigers were 8-5 in April, as Harry Heilmann went 4-for-5 (HR, 4 RBI) in an opening day 9-6 victory at St. Louis on Wednesday, April 18. The squad defeated the Browns 16-1 on Saturday, behind Topper Rigney 3-for-4 (4 RBI). Heilmann started the season with a 21-game hitting streak April 18-May 15 (.513 BA, .575 OBP, .763 SLG). The team went 11-16 in May including a 16-11 12-inning home loss to the Yankees on Monday, May 14, as New York scored eight runs in the twelfth inning. Detroit lost to Cleveland 17-4 at home on Friday, June 1, with a record of 12-12 during the month. Fred Haney hit .417 during June (24 GM, .481 OBP, .490 SLG) to raise his season average to .357. The team was 14-13 in July, as they recorded a 15-3 win in Cleveland led by Bert Cole (W 5-2, 9 IP 3 ER), Johnny Bassler 4-for-4 and Rigney (3 RBI). Motown swept a three-game series in Chicago July 24-25. The Tigers won a double-header 4-1 and 9-6 on Tuesday, July 24. Rigney 3-for-4 and Herman Pillette (9 IP, 1 ER) led the opener, as reliever Cole (W 6-3, 5 IP, 0 ER, 2 H) won the second game. Players were 16-10 in August that included a 5-4 13-inning victory over Washington at home on Sunday, August 26. Starter Cole (7 IP, 2 ER), reliever Pillette (W 13-15, 6 IP, 0 ER, 3 H), Heilmann 5-for-6 (HR, 2 RBI) and Lu Blue 4-for-7 led the win. The Tigers played at a 16-14 clip for September, as Cole (12 GM 7-2 .778, 2.95 ERA) factored in nearly a third of the decisions. Detroit won 14-4 over Chicago at home on Monday, September 3, with Cobb 3-for-4 and Bassler 4-for-5 (2 RBI), as Motown scored eight eighth inning runs. Cobb (3 GM, 8-for-11, .727 BA, .786 OBP, .909 SLG, 1.695 OPS, .727 BAbip) destroyed White Sox pitching September 3-4. Rookie Earl Whitehill excelled September 16-October 2 (5 GM, 1-0, 19 IP, 0.95 ERA, .068 BA, .167 OBP, .136 SLG, .067 BAbip). Motown played a doubleheader on six consecutive days starting on Monday, September 17. Cobb (6 GM, 7 RBI, .600 BA, .680 OBP, .900 SLG, .579 BAbip) excelled in the six-game three-day series Thursday thru Saturday at Boston. Pillette (9 IP, 1 ER, 5 H) defeated the visiting Indians 17-3 on Friday, September 28, as Heilmann 4-for-4 and Cobb each scored four runs. Players went 11-2 during their last 13 games of the season, including 6-1 in October. Detroit finished 45-32 (.584) at home and 38-39 (.494) on the road. The team scored 831 runs and pitchers allowed 741. Jack Calvo (208 H, .337 BA), Clarence Kraft (48 2B, 32 HR, .324 BA, 333 TB), Lil Stoner (27-11 .711, 2.65 ERA, 302 IP), Paul Wachtel (19-12 .613, 3.78 ERA), Joe Pate (23-15 .605, 2.91 ERA, 328 IP) and Augie Johns (18-12 .600, 2.74 ERA) were stars at class "A" Fort Worth.

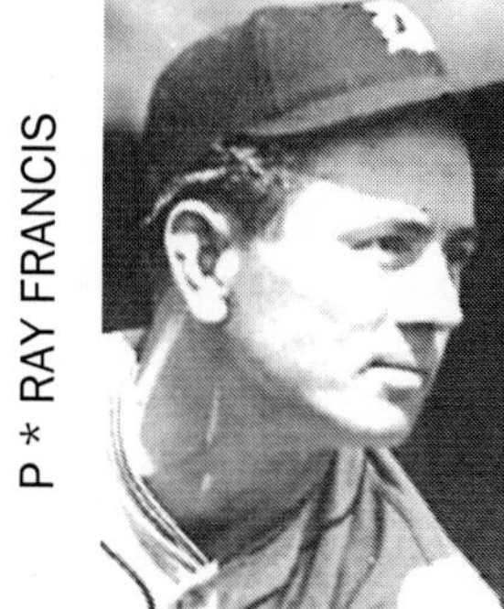

P * RAY FRANCIS

Offense. Detroit finished with a .300 BA, .377 OBP, .401 SLG, .778 OPS, 2,109 TB and 106 OPS+. Johnny Bassler (.298 BA, 49 RBI) caught. Lu Blue (.284 BA, HR, 46 RBI) at first led in walks (96). Second base was shared by Fred Haney (.282 BA, 4 HR, 67 RBI) the steals leader (13) and Del Pratt (.310 BA, 40 RBI, 1.2 SBR) that led for in-play percentage (84%). Bob Jones (.250 BA, HR, 40 RBI) played third and Topper Rigney (.315 BA, HR, 74 RBI, 11 3B) was at short. Leftfielder Heinie Manush (.334, 4 HR, 54 RBI) led MLB in hit by pitch (17). Ty Cobb (.340 BA, 6 HR, 88 RBI) manned center and led in games (145), plate appearances (648), at bats (556) and outs (399). Player of the Year and the most effective hitter Harry Heilmann (.403, 18 HR, 115 RBI, 11 3B) at right led league hitting, with team lead for runs (121), hits (211), singles (138), doubles (44), homers, runs batted in, on-base percentage (.481), slugging (.632), OPS (1.113), OPS+ (194), total average (1.288), base-out percentage (1.289), gross production average (.374), WAR (9.3), oWAR (8.9), batters run average (.292), BAbip (.414), secondary average (.374), times on base (290), base runs (144), runs produced (218), runs created (159), isolated power (.229), power/speed number (12.0), extra base hits (73), total bases (331), bases produced (414) and 21-game hitting streak. Bobby Veach (.321 BA, 2 HR, 39 RBI, 1.2 SBR) and Bob Fothergill (.315 BA, HR, 49 RBI). Earl Whitehill (.362 BA) and Hook Dauss (.231 BA, 13 RBI) led pitchers. The top pinch-hitters were Pratt at .571 (4-7), Woodall .571 (8-14), Veach .462 (6-13, 4 RBI) and Manush .429 (9-21, HR, 5 RBI).

1920s Hitting Home Runs	
1. Harry Heilmann	142
2. Ty Cobb	44
3. Heinie Manush	38
Bobby Veach	38
5. Marty McManus	35
6. Dale Alexander	25
7. Bob Fothergill	24
Charlie Gehringer	24
9. Lu Blue	19
10. Pinky Hargrave	13

Pitching. The Tigers had a 4.09 ERA, 61 CG, seven SHO, 449 walks, 447 SO, 95 ERA+, 3.93 FIP, 1.420 WHIP, 9.8 H/9, 2.9 BB/9, and 2.9 SO/9. The staff led league in games finished (94) and walks per nine (2.9). Pitcher of the Year and most effective pitcher Hooks Dauss (21-13, 3.62 ERA, 5 SV, 20 QS) led in wins, starts (39), complete games (22), shutouts (4), innings (316), hits (331), strikeouts (105), earned runs (127), runs (140), earned run average, ERA+ (110), FIP (3.49), DICE (3.55), pWAR (4.7), walks per nine innings (2.2) and runs per nine innings (4.0). Herman Pillette (14-19, 3.85 ERA, 20 QS) led MLB in losses and staff in walks (83). Syl Johnson (12-7, 3.98 ERA, 12 HR) led league in strikeouts per nine (4.7) and team in LOB% (69.6), WHIP (1.293), hits per nine (9.2) and in SO/BB (1.98). Bert Cole (13-5, 4.14 ERA, 5 SV) led in games (52), win percentage (.722) and games finished (26). Ken Holloway (11-10, 4.45 ERA, 12 HR), led in HBP (10). 24-year-old rookie left-hander Earl Whitehill (2-0, 2.73 ERA) impressed in his debut. Ray Francis (5-8, 4.42 ERA), Rip Collins (3-7, 4.87 ERA) and Ole Olsen (1-1, 6.31 ERA). Dauss opened 8-2 in April/May and then closed 9-3 in August/September.

Defense. Detroit made 200 errors for a .968 fielding average. League leaders were Pillette in pitcher errors (11), Blue in chances per game (11.3) at first and catcher Bassler in runners caught stealing (84), as Jones led the Bengals in dWAR (1.0).

The Tigers used five outfielders that combined for a .350 batting average. Harry Heilmann at .403, (194 OPS+, 44 2B, .632 SLG, 331 TB), Ty Cobb .340 (134 OPS+, 40 2B), Heinie Manush .334 (132 OPS+), Bobby Veach .321 and at Bob Fothergill .315.

1920s Hitting Runs Batted In		
1.	Harry Heilmann	1,133
2.	Ty Cobb	593
3.	Bob Fothergill	433
4.	Lu Blue	407
5.	Bobby Veach	406
6.	Heinie Manush	345
7.	Johnny Bassler	312
8.	Charlie Gehringer	290
9.	Topper Rigney	249
10.	Bob Jones	236

Team. Detroit finished third for Ty Cobb at 86-68 (.558), with 1,015,136 fans. The Tigers were 9-4 in April including 8-2 at home. Detroit finished 14-13 in May, as Ken Holloway had back-to-back 7-3 and 6-5 wins in New York on Saturday, May 24 (W 4-1, 9 IP, 3 ER) and on Sunday (w 5-1, 2 IP, 0 ER). Bert Cole (W 1-4, 8.2 IP, 1 ER) beat visiting St. Louis 5-4 on Tuesday, May 27, with a 2-0 shutout (W 2-4, 9 IP, 0 ER, 5 H) on two days rest in Cleveland on Friday, with two Del Pratt (2 RBI) sacrifice flies. Cobb torched the Indians May 31-June 1 (7-for-9, .778 BA, .800 OBP, 1.222 SLG, 2.022 OPS, .750 BAbip). The club finished 14-15 in June including a 10-6 victory in Cleveland on Sunday, June 1, as Cobb went 4-for-4 (HR, 4 RBI) and Lu Blue 3-for-5 (3 RBI). Detroit defeated Boston 10-4 at home on Sunday, June 15, behind Earl Whitehill (W 6-2, 9 IP, 4 ER) and Cobb 5-for-6. The Tigers were 18-11 in July, when Cobb went 4-for-4 (3 BB), Topper Rigney (3 SH) and six sacrifice hits during a 12-10 13-inning victory at Washington on July 10. Players were 10-1 on the road in July, including eight straight wins that began on Tuesday, July 15. Detroit outscored the Red Sox 42-14 to sweep a five-game series in Boston July 16-19. The Bengals won 18-1 on Saturday, July 19, on the strength of 21 hits and a 10-run second inning. Fred Haney at 5-for-6, Heinie Manush (4 RBI) and Larry Woodall 4-for-4 led the way. Bassler went 9-for-12 (.750 BA, .786 OBP, 1.167 SLG, 1.952 OPS, .727 BABIP) in New York July 21-24, including 5-for-5 in a 9-7 win over the Yankees on Monday. Holloway (W 9-2, 11 IP, 2 ER) pitching on two days of rest won 4-3 at home against Philadelphia on Tuesday, July 29. The team was 13-16 in August with a 7-2 victory at Yankee Stadium on Sunday, August 24. Manush 5-for-5 (3 RBI) and Dutch Leonard (9 IP, 2 ER) led the win before 50,000 fans. Motown went 18-9 in September, as Bassler had a 13-game hit streak September 1-20 (.476 BA, .532 OBP, .619 SLG, 16 RBI). Detroit beat visiting Cleveland 20-1 on Friday, September 5, as Holloway (W 11-5, 9 IP, 0 ER, 5 H) drove in two, Del Pratt 3-for-5 (4 RBI), Bassler (3 RBI), Heilmann (3 RBI), Rigney 3-for-4 (4 R, 3 RBI) and Frank O'Rourke (3 RBI). Detroit went 45-33 (.577) at home, and 41-35 (.539) on the road. The Bengals scored 849 runs and allowed 796 runs.

C * JOHNNY BASSLER

Offense. Detroit finished with a .298 BA, .374 OBP, .404 SLG, .779 OPS, 2,176 TB and 102 OPS+. Catcher Johnny Bassler (.346 BA, HR, 68 RBI) led in on-base percentage (.441) and hitting. Lu Blue (.311 BA, 2 HR, 53 RBI) was at first. Del Pratt (.303 BA, HR, 77 RBI) at second led in hit streak (19). Third had Fred Haney (.309 BA, HR, 30 RBI) and Bob Jones (.272 BA, 47 RBI) that led for in-play percentage (87%). Topper Rigney (.289 BA, 4 HR, 94 RBI) at short led in walks (102). Heinie Manush (.289 BA, 9 HR, 68 RBI) in leftfield led MLB for hit by pitch (16) and squad in stolen base runs (1.2). Centerfielder Ty Cobb (.338 BA, 4 HR, 79 RBI) led in games (155), plate appearances (727), at bats (625), runs (114), hits (211), singles (159), times on base (297), steals (23) and outs (443). Player of the Year and the most effective hitter Harry Heilmann (.346 BA, 10 HR, 114 RBI) in rightfield led MLB for doubles (45). He led Detroit in triples (16), homers, runs batted in, slugging (.533), OPS (.961), OPS+ (149), total average (1.042), base-out percentage (1.052), gross production average (.326), WAR (6.4), oWAR (6.2), batters run average (.218), hitting, BAbip (.360), secondary average (.339), base runs (123), runs produced (211), runs created (130), isolated power (.188), power/speed number (11.3), extra base hits (71), total bases (304), bases produced (395) and strikeouts (41). Bert Cole (.270 BA) led all pitchers. The leading pinch-hitters were Bassler at .600 (3-5, 3 RBI) and Al Wingo at .438 (7-16, HR, 9 RBI).

1920s Hitting On-Base Percentage		
1.	Ty Cobb	.435
2.	Harry Heilmann	.433
3.	Johnny Bassler	.420
4.	Al Wingo	.406
5.	Lu Blue	.403
6.	Topper Rigney	.389
7.	Bob Fothergill	.385
8.	Fred Haney	.383
9.	Charlie Gehringer	.380
10.	Heinie Manush	.379

Pitching. The Tigers recorded a 4.19 ERA, 60 CG, five SHO, 467 walks, 441 SO, 98 ERA+, 4.02 FIP, 1.472 WHIP, 10.2 H/9, 3.0 BB/9, and 2.8 SO/9. The squad led league in innings (1,394.2), BB/9 (3.0) and strikeouts to walks (0.94). Pitcher of the Year Earl Whitehill (17-9 3.86 ERA) led the majors in HBP (13), and staff in wins, starts (32), complete games (16), shutouts (2), innings (233), walks (79) and LOB% (66.6). The most effective pitcher Rip Collins (14-7, 3.21 ERA) led in strikeouts (75), WP (4), earned run average, ERA+ (128), FIP (3.64), DICE (3.60), WHIP (1.213), pWAR (3.5), H/9 (8.3), BB/9 (2.6), SO/9 (3.1), SO/BB (1.19), R/9 (4.1) and quality starts (17). Ken Holloway (14-6, 4.07 ERA) led in games (49), win percentage (.700) and games finished (22). Lil Stoner (11-10, 4.72 ERA) led in hits (271), homers (13), earned runs (113) and runs (130). Ed Wells (6-8, 4.06 ERA), Dutch Leonard (3-3, 4.56 ERA), Hooks Dauss (12-11, 4.59 ERA), Bert Cole (3-9, 4.69 ERA), Herman Pillette (1-1, 4.78 ERA), Syl Johnson (5-4, 4.93 ERA) and rookie Willie Ludolph (0-0, 4.76 ERA). Holloway went undefeated for the period of July 16-August 6 (5-0, 1.64 ERA, .186 BA, .221 SLG, .200 BAbip). Collins excelled pitching on three days of rest (5-1 .833, 2.65 ERA, .227 BA, .242 BAbip), with a 3-0 mark against Philadelphia.

Defense. Detroit committed 186 errors for a .971 fielding percentage, as they led the league in chances (6,418), putouts (4,199) and assists (2,033). League leaders were Blue in chances per game (11.1) at first and Rigney in fielding (.967) at short, as he led club in dWAR (1.0). Outfielders Cobb led in fielding (.986) and double plays (8) and Heilmann in assists (31).

Earl Whitehill was extraordinary pitching on two days of rest (5-0 1.000, 43,.1 IP, 2.28 ERA, 1 HR, 4 CG, 2 SHO). Whitehill was superb facing the Chicago White Sox (4-0 1.000, 30 IP, 1 CG) and the New York Yankees (5-1 .833, 51.2 IP, 4 CG) in 1924.

Clarence Kraft (203 H, 36 2B, 55 HR, .349 BA,.713 SLG, 414 TB) and Stump Edington (.335 BA) starred at class "A" Forth Worth. The Panthers had pitchers Ralph Head (15-3 .833, 2.38 ERA), Joe Pate (30-8 .789, 3.04 ERA), Augie Johns (12-5 .706, 3.53 ERA), Paul Wachtel (22-10 .688, 2.83 ERA), Jim Middleton (14-7 .667, 3.33 ERA) and Hank Hulvey (8-4 .667, 3.03 ERA).

1920s Hitting Slugging Percentage	
1. Harry Heilmann	.558
2. Ty Cobb	.517
3. Bob Fothergill	.486
4. Bobby Veach	.479
5. Heinie Manush	.475
6. Charlie Gehringer	.459
7. Marty McManus	.439
8. Al Wingo	.423
9. Lu Blue	.403
10. Topper Rigney	.393

Team. Detroit finished fourth for Ty Cobb at 81-73 (.526), with 820,766 fans. Motown went 4-11 in April, with a 1-9 mark for April 18-28. Harry Heilmann 3-for-5 (3 RBI), Hooks Dauss (W 1-0, 9 IP, 3 ER) and a five-run first inning led the Tigers to a 9-3 win over Chicago at home on Friday, April 17. The squad finished 14-15 in May, including a 14-8 win at St. Louis on Tuesday, May 5, as reliever Ed Wells (4.2 IP, 0 ER) got the save, and Cobb was 6-for-6 (4 R, 3 HR, 5 RBI), with an MLB record 16 total bases. Cobb went 3-for-6 (2 HR, 6 RBI) and Heilmann (2 HR, 2 RBI) the next day for a 11-4 victory against the Browns. Cobb hit .733 against Brown pitching May 4-6 (11-for-15, 5 HR, 12 RBI, .765 OBP, 1.800 SLG). Rookie Jackie Tavener had six straight multi-hit games May 29-June 2 (13-for-25, 6 RBI, .520 BA, .520 OBP, .600 SLG, .565 BAbip). The squad was 16-9 in June, with a 19-1 win in New York on Wednesday, June 17. Al Wingo (HR, 4 RBI) and Cobb (HR, 5 RBI) led with a record 13-run sixth inning. Detroit took a 7-4 victory in Cleveland on Monday, June 29, aided by Tavener 4-for-4 (2 RBI) and Dutch Leonard (W 8-3, 9 IP). The team was 15-14 in July when Frank O'Rourke shined July 1-20 (14 GM, 24-for-59, 13 RBI, .407 BA, .542 SLG). Dauss (W 9-5, 9 IP, 0 ER) threw a 5-0 home shutout of Boston on Wednesday, July 8, with Cobb 3-for-4 (2 RBI), and Heilmann 3-for-4 (HR). Rip Collins (9 IP, 2 ER) and Cobb 3-for-3 (3 RBI) powered a 5-2 home victory over Washington on Wednesday, July 15. The Bengals were 15-11 in August, when the club went 12-1 during the period of August 24-September 10. The offense took over at home with a 13-4 defeat of Washington on Monday, August 24, a 14-4 win over Boston on Tuesday with Fred Haney 4-for-4 (3 RBI), followed by an Earl Whitehill (9 IP, 2 ER) led 10-2 triumph of the Red Sox on Wednesday. Haney hit .560 for August 25-September 3. Detroit closed 15-12 in September, as Lil Stoner (9 IP, 1 ER) 2-for-4 led a 11-1 home win against St. Louis on Tuesday, September 8. Ken Holloway (W 10-3, 6 IP, 2 ER), Blue (4 RBI) and Johnny Bassler 3-for-3 aided the 12-9 victory at Washington on Thursday, September 17. Stoner (9 IP, 1 ER) drove in two runs in a 15-1 victory at Boston on Wednesday, September 23, with O'Rourke (4 RBI), Bassler (3 RBI) and Heilmann 4-for-5 (HR, 2 RBI). The team was 43-34 (.558) at home, 38-39 (.494) on the road, scored 903 runs and allowed 829. Class "A" Fort Worth featured Doc Smith (.363 BA), Ed Konetchy (.345 BA, 41 HR, 385 TB), Ziggy Sears (.321 BA, 301 TB), Cecil Davis (29 HR, 326 TB), Paul Wachtel (23-7 .767), Jim Walkup (19-7 .731), Augie Johns (20-8 .714) and Joe Pate (20-12 .625).

P * LIL STONER

Offense. Detroit finished with a .302 BA, .380 OBP, .413 SLG, .793 OPS, 2,218 TB and 103 OPS+. Johnny Bassler (.279 BA, 52 RBI) caught, as Lu Blue (.306, 3 HR, 94 RBI, 150 GM) at first led in stolen bases (19), stolen base runs (2.7), walks (83) and outs (408). Frank O'Rourke (.293 BA, 5 HR, 57 RBI) at second led in hit by the pitch (11). Fred Haney (.279 BA, 40 RBI) played third, as shortstop Jackie Tavener (.245 BA, 47 RBI) led in strikeouts (60). Al Wingo (.370 BA, 5 HR, 68 RBI, 151 OPS+) in left led in runs (104). Centerfielder and most effective hitter Ty Cobb (.378 BA, 12 HR, 102 RBI) led the league in OPS (1.066) and OPS+ (171). Cobb led his team for triples (12), on-base percentage (.468), slugging (.598), total average (1.206), base-out percentage (1.235), gross production average (.360), batters run average (.276), secondary average (.386), isolated power (.219) and power/speed number (12.5). Player of the Year Harry Heilmann (.393 BA, 13 HR, 134 RBI, 150 GM) in right had 65 multi-hit games, as he led MLB in times on base (293) and league in hitting. Heilmann led Detroit in Plate Appearances (664), at bats (573), hits (225), singles (161), homers, runs batted in, WAR (6.9), oWAR (7.1), BAbip (.398), base runs (137), runs produced (218), runs created (149), extra base hits (64), total bases (326), bases produced (399) and hit streak (20). Bob Fothergill (.353 BA) and Heinie Manush (.302 BA, 5 HR, 47 RBI) led for in-play percentage (81%). Lil Stoner (.291 BA, 8 RBI) led pitchers at the plate. The leading pinch-hitters were Fothergill at .500 (4-8, 6 RBI), Manush .429 (6-14) and Wingo at .333 (2-6, 3 RBI). Heilmann and O'Rourke led the team with 40 doubles.

1920s Hitting On-Base plus Slugging	
1. Harry Heilmann	.991
2. Ty Cobb	.952
3. Bob Fothergill	.871
4. Heinie Manush	.853
5. Bobby Veach	.853
6. Charlie Gehringer	.838
7. Al Wingo	.829
8. Lu Blue	.806
9. Johnny Bassler	.786
10. Marty McManus	.785

Pitching. The Tigers logged a 4.61 ERA, 65 CG, two SHO, 556 walks, 419 SO, 94 ERA+, 4.45 FIP, 1.545 WHIP, 10.3 H/9, 3.6 BB/9, and 2.7 SO/9, with the league lead in HBP (42) and cheap wins (22). Lil Stoner and Earl Whitehill led the league in cheap wins (5). Pitcher of the Year Dutch Leonard (11-4, 4.51 ERA, 3.1 BB/9) led in FIP (3.85), DICE (3.74), strikeouts per nine (4.7) and strikeouts to walks (1.51). The most effective pitcher Hooks Dauss (16-11, 3.16 ERA, 1 SHO) led in wins, losses, complete games (16), LOB% (69.6), earned run average, ERA+ (137), WHIP (1.417), WAR (4.0), hits per nine (9.4), runs per nine (4.3) and quality starts (16). Ken Holloway (13-4, 4.62 ERA) led in win percentage (.765). Earl Whitehill (11-11, 4.66 ERA, 1 SHO) led league in no decisions (11). He led the staff in losses, starts (33), innings (239.1), hits (267), homers (13), walks (88), strikeouts (83), HBP (10), earned runs (124) and runs (135). Jess Doyle (4-7, 5.93 ERA) led in games (45), games finished (34) and saves (8). Lil Stoner (10-9, 4.26 ERA, 3.1 BB/9), Rip Collins (6-11, 4.60 ERA) and Ed Wells (6-9, 6.18 ERA). Dauss was extraordinary for June 13-July 11 (6 GM, 6-0 1.000, 1.18 ERA, .187 BA, .188 BAbip).

Defense. Detroit committed 171 errors for a .973 fielding percentage. Tiger league leaders were O'Rourke in second basemen fielding percentage (.971) and Wingo in leftfielder double plays (8). Tavener led Detroit in defensive WAR (0.7).

Harry Heilmann led the league hitting (.393 BA) and runs batted in (134). He blazed a trail May 23-30 (18-for-28, .643 BA, .697 OBP, .786 SLG, .692 BAbip). Heilmann recorded eight four-hit games, including back-to-back efforts during a five-game series he dominated at Boston September 22-25, when he hit .684 (13-for-19, 2 HR, 11 RBI, .750 OBP, 1.053 SLG, .647 BAbip).

1920s Pitching Wins	
1. Hooks Dauss	97
2. Earl Whitehill	87
3. Ken Holloway	57
4. Lil Stoner	50
5. Howard Ehmke	45
6. Rip Collins	44
7. Ownie Carroll	37
8. Dutch Leonard	35
9. Herman Pillette	34
10. Red Oldham	29

Team. Sixth-place Detroit finished 79-75 (.513) for Ty Cobb, with 711,914 fans. The Tigers were 6-9 in April including a 5-3 home win over Cleveland on Friday, April 16, with Augie Johns (9 IP, 1 ER, 4 H) and Harry Heilmann (3 RBI). Motown finished 17-12 in May as pitcher Earl Whitehill was a perfect 6-0 during the month. Detroit rolled to a 14-7 win in Chicago on Wednesday, May 5, when Al Wingo was 3-for-5 (HR, 6 RBI). The Bengals scored a 14-10 victory at New York on Sunday, May 9, behind Ty Cobb 4-for-4 (2 HR, 4 RBI) and Johnny Neun 4-for-6. Johnny Bassler 4-for-5, Wingo 4-for-5 and Lil Stoner (9 IP, 2 ER) led a 9-2 win over visiting Chicago on Tuesday, May 25. Heinie Manush shined May 31-September 26 (109 GM, .400 BA, .434 OBP, .584 SLG). Motown went 14-13 in June logging an Ed Wells (9 IP, 0 ER, 5 H) 7-0 shutout at Cleveland on Wednesday, June 2, with Cobb 4-for-4. Players won seven straight games thru Sunday, June 27, as they swept a double-header with Cleveland on Saturday, June 26. The Tigers scored four first inning runs, as Wells (9 IP, 0 ER, 5 H) pitched a 5-0 shutout, followed by a Sam Gibson (9 IP, 2 ER) 7-2 victory aided by a five run Tiger eighth inning. Detroit had a 15-16 mark in July, with a Rip Collins (9 IP, 0 ER) 9-0 shutout in Boston on Friday, July 9, behind Frank O'Rourke 4-for-5. Collins (9 IP, 0 ER, 5 H), Manush 3-for-5 (2 RBI) and Lu Blue 3-for-5 led a 5-0 shutout in Philadelphia on Tuesday, July 20. Players were 15-11 in August, with an 11-4 victory at Boston on Wednesday, August 25, led by Gibson (9 IP, 0 ER), Heilmann 3-for-5 (HR, 4 RBI), Bob Fothergill 3-for-4 (3B, 2 RBI) and Manion 3-for-3. Motown recorded an 8-4 win in New York on Saturday, August 28, with reliever Stoner (W 7-5, 6 IP, 1 ER, 3 H), Fothergill 5-for-5 (2 RBI), and rookie Charlie Gehringer (2 RBI) from Fowlerville, Michigan. Detroit closed 12-14 in September with a 11-2 drubbing of Boston at home on Sunday, September 26. Manush was 4-for-5 (4 R) and Fothergill 5-for-5 (4 R, HR, 4 RBI) hit for the cycle. Players were 39-41 (.488) at home, and 40-34 (.541) on the road. The Tigers scored 793 runs as pitchers allowed 830. Class "A" Fort Worth had Ed Konetchy (.325 BA, 21 HR, 300 TB), and Ziggy Sears (.317 BA).

P * SAM GIBSON

Offense. Detroit had a .291 BA, .366 OBP, .398, .765 OPS, 2,116 TB and 99 OPS+. The catchers were Clyde Manion (.199 BA, 15 RBI), Johnny Bassler (.305 BA, 23 RBI) and Larry Woodall (.233 BA, 15 RBI). Lu Blue (.287 BA, HR, 52 RBI) at first led in secondary average (.352), steals (13) and walks (90). Charlie Gehringer (.277 BA, HR, 48 RBI) at second base led in triples (17), as Jack Warner (.251 BA, 34 RBI) played third. Jackie Tavener (.265 BA, HR, 58 RBI) at short led league in games (156). He led squad for plate appearances (614), at bats (532), strikeouts (53) and outs (426). Bob Fothergill (.367 BA, 3 HR, 73 RBI) in left led team in BAbip (.385) and in-play percentage (83%). Centerfielder Heinie Manush (.378 BA, 14 HR, 86 RBI) led MLB in hitting and BAbip (.382). He led Motown in runs (95), hits (188), singles (131), homers, slugging (.564), OPS (.985), OPS+ (154), isolated power (.187), power/speed number (12.3), total bases (281) and stolen base runs (0.3). Player of the Year and most effective hitter Harry Heilmann (.367 BA, 9 HR, 101 RBI) in right led in doubles (41), runs batted in, on-base percentage (.445), total average (1.040), base-out percentage (1.057), gross production average (.334), WAR (5.2), batters run average (.228), times on base (255), base runs (112), runs produced (182), runs created (119), extra base hits (58) and bases produced (341). Ty Cobb (.339 BA, 4 HR, 62 RBI) led in hit streak (21). Frank O'Rourke (.242 BA, HR, 41 RBI) and Al Wingo (.282 BA, HR, 45 RBI). Earl Whitehill (.253 BA, 10 RBI) led the pitchers. The leading Tiger pinch-hitters were Manush at .444 (4-9, 6 RBI), Cobb .429 (3-7, 3 RBI) and Blue .417 (5-12, 6 RBI). Heilmann and Manush tied for the team lead in oWAR (5.8).

1920s Pitching Winning Percentage	
1. Ken Holloway	.553
2. Earl Whitehill	.527
3. Rip Collins	.524
4. Hooks Dauss	.519
5. Herman Pillette	.515
6. Ownie Carroll	.500
7. Dutch Leonard	.493
8. Sam Gibson	.491
9. Howard Ehmke	.479
10. Lil Stoner	.463

Pitching. The Tigers recorded a 4.41 ERA, 57 CG, 10 SHO, 555 walks, 469 SO, 91 ERA+, 4.08 FIP, 1.524 WHIP, 10.1 H/9, 3.6 BB/9, and 3.0 SO/9, as the staff led league in innings (1,394.2), hits (1,570), HBP (46), balks (6), batters faced (6,183) and no decisions (42). Pitcher of the Year Sam Gibson (12-9, 3.48 ERA) led in win percentage (.571), complete games (16), LOB% (68.5), earned run average, ERA+ (116), pWAR (3.4), hits per nine (9.1) and runs per nine (4.3). The most effective pitcher Earl Whitehill (16-13, 3.99 ERA) led MLB in earned runs (112), with league lead for runs (136) and cheap wins (5). He led staff in wins, losses, starts (34), innings (252.1), hits (271), walks (79), strikeouts (109), HBP (8), FIP (3.45), DICE (3.53), WHIP (1.387), BB/9 (2.8), SO/9 (3.9), SO/BB (1.38) and quality starts (17). Ed Wells (12-10, 4.15 ERA) led league in shutouts (4). Lil Stoner (7-10, 5.47 ERA) led team in homers (11) and WP (6). Rip Collins (8-8, 2.73 ERA) led league in balks (3). Hooks Dauss (12-6, 4.20 ERA) led in games finished (23) and saves (9). Clyde Barfoot (1-2, 4.88 ERA), Ken Holloway (4-6, 5.12 ERA), Augie Johns (6-4, 5.35 ERA) and George Smith (1-2, 6.95 ERA). Jim Walkup (22-11 .667, 2.38 ERA) pitched at class "A" Fort Worth. Collins was spectacular during an undefeated stretch June 2-July 27 (10 GM, 4-0, 44.1 IP, 1.02 ERA, .203 BA, .223 BAbip).

Defense. The Bengals committed 197 errors for a .969 fielding percentage, as Detroit led the league in putouts (4,180). Tiger league leaders were pitchers Stoner in fielding percentage (1.000) and Wells in caught stealing percentage (77%). Tavener led all shortstops in double plays (92) and team in defensive WAR (0.5). Heilmann in right-field led for assists (18).

Several Tigers that excelled in limited roles were 39-year-old player/manager Ty Cobb (79 GM, .339 BA, 48 R, 62 RBI, .408 OBP, 138 OPS+), catcher Johnny Bassler (66 GM, .305 BA, 45 BB, .447 OBP) and Johnny Neun (97 GM, .298 BA) at first base.

Detroit used a record 17 pinch-hitters, with Bob Fothergill .667 (4-6), Lu Blue .417 (5-12), Heinie Manush .357 (5-14) and Ty Cobb .333 (6-18). First baseman Johnny Neun (.286 BA) led the American League in pinch-hits (12) and pinch-hit at bats (42).

1920s Pitching Games Started	
1. Earl Whitehill	191
2. Hooks Dauss	169
3. Lil Stoner	110
4. Rip Collins	102
5. Ken Holloway	98
6. Howard Ehmke	85
7. Dutch Leonard	84
8. Red Oldham	77
9. Herman Pillette	76
10. Ownie Carroll	73

Team. Detroit finished in fourth place led by first-year manager George Moriarty with an 82-71 (.536) record and 773,716 fans. Moriarty was an American League umpire 1917-1926 and the again 1929-1940 after two years of managing. The Tigers had a 6-6 record in April, as Bob Fothergill (HR, 3 RBI) and Earl Whitehill (9 IP, 0 ER, 4 H) led a 7-0 shutout of St. Louis at home on Wednesday, April 20. Players were 12-16 in May with a 17-11 win over visiting Boston on Monday, May 9, when Harry Heilmann was 4-for-5 (2 HR, 4 RBI), Jackie Tavener (3 RBI) and reliever George Smith went 2-for-3 (HR, 4 RBI) to get the win. First baseman Johnny Neun recorded a rare unassisted triple-play to end a Rip Collins (9 IP, 0 ER, 4 H) 1-0 shutout of Cleveland at home on Tuesday, May 31. Detroit went a combined 50-34 (.595) during the next three months. The Tigers finished 16-8 in June with five consecutive wins June 27-30. Detroit swept a doubleheader with visiting St. Louis on Tuesday, June 28, behind Pitchers Ownie Carroll (9 IP, 3 ER) 9-3 in the opener and then a 6-3 triumph by Collins (9 IP, 3 ER). The squad was 18-14 in July splitting a home doubleheader with New York on Saturday, July 9. The great Babe Ruth went 5-for-6 (2 2B, 2 HR, 7 RBI) with 13 total bases in a 19-7 Yankee game one win. Ruth would end the season with an MLB record of 60 home runs. Neun 5-for-5 (5 SB, 4 R, 3 RBI), Heilmann (SB, 3 RBI) and Johnny Bassler 3-for-3 (SB, 3 RBI) led the 14-4 game two win. Whitehill (9 IP, 3 ER, 6 SO) pitched on one day of rest and Jack Warner (HR, 2 RBI) led a 6-3 defeat of the Yankees on Sunday. Detroit logged an undefeated week at home July 17-23 (5-0). The Tigers went 16-12 in August including a 13-game home win streak thru Monday, August 22, when they won a double-header over New York 4-2 and 7-3. Sam Gibson (9 IP, 0 ER, 5 H) pitched game one, with reliever Smith (6 IP, 0 ER, 3 H, 4 SO) and Marty McManus (HR, 2 RBI) the stars in game two. Motown was 12-15 in September with 20 straight road games. The squad went 9-2 during an 11-game stretch through Monday, September 26 when Josh Billings (9 IP, 1 ER, 3 H) won 2-1 in Cleveland. Detroit was 2-0 in October with Heilmann 4-for-6 (2 2B, HR, 6 RBI) in a 11-5 home win over Cleveland on Sunday, October 2. The team finished 44-32 (.579) at home including 9-2 versus Boston and 38-39 (.494) in away games. Players scored 845 runs and pitchers allowed opponents 805.

P * JOSH BILLINGS

Offense. Detroit had an .289 BA, .363 OBP, .409 SLG, .772 OPS, 2,168 TB, and 99 OPS+. The team led the league in steals (139). Larry Woodall (.280 BA, 39 RBI) and Johnny Bassler (.285 BA, 24 RBI) caught, with Lu Blue (.260 BA, HR, 42 RBI) at first. Charlie Gehringer (.317 BA, 4 HR, 61 RBI) at second led with a 21-game hit streak. Jack Warner (.267 BA, HR, 45 RBI) at third led in stolen base runs (1.8) and strikeouts (45). Shortstop Jackie Tavener (.274 BA, 5 HR, 59 RBI) led in steals (19). Bob Fothergill (.359 BA, 9 HR, 114 RBI) was in left. Heinie Manush (.298 BA, 6 HR, 90 RBI) in center led in games (151), plate appearances (659), at bats (593), triples (18), in-play percentage (85%) and outs (439). Player of the Year and the most effective hitter Harry Heilmann (.398 BA, 14 HR, 120 RBI) in right led MLB hitting and BAbip (.394). He paced Motown in hits (201), doubles (50), homers, runs batted in, on-base percentage (.475), slugging (.616), OPS (1.091), OPS+ (180), WAR (7.2), oWAR (7.7), batters run average (.284), secondary average (.372), times on base (275), base runs (136), runs produced (212), runs created (148), isolated power (.218), power/speed number (12.3), extra base hits (73), total bases (311), bases produced (394) and walks (72). Marty McManus (.268 BA, 9 HR, 69 RBI). George Smith (.368 BA, 6 RBI) led pitchers. The best pinch-hitters were Gehringer at .375 (3-8) and Al Wingo (6 RBI). Class "A" Fort Worth featured Bill Sweeney (.343 BA), Eddie Moore (.329 BA), Dutch Holland (.313 BA) and Nolen Richardson (.313 BA).

1920s Pitching Complete Games	
1. Earl Whitehill	92
2. Hooks Dauss	89
3. Howard Ehmke	52
4. Lil Stoner	45
5. Ownie Carroll	40
6. Dutch Leonard	38
7. Ken Holloway	37
8. Rip Collins	34
9. Herman Pillette	33
10. Sam Gibson	32

Pitching. Motown recorded a 4.14 ERA, five SHO, 577 walks, 421 SO, 101 ERA+, 4.26 FIP, 1.527 WHIP, 10.0 H/9, 3.7 BB/9 and 2.7 SO/9. The staff led league in hit by pitch (47), balks (6), batters faced (6,165) and runners left on base (1,199). Pitcher of the Year and most effective pitcher Earl Whitehill (16-14, 3.36 ERA) led the league in walks (105) and balks (2). He led his team for games (41), wins, losses, starts (31), complete games (17), shutouts (3), innings (236), walks (105), strikeouts (95), hit by pitch (9), LOB% (69.9), earned run average, ERA+ (125), FIP (3.89), DICE (3.86), WHIP 1.453), pWAR (4.9), hits per nine innings (9.1), strikeouts to walks (0.90), runs per nine innings (4.2) and quality starts (17). Sam Gibson (11-12, 3.80 ERA, 6 WP) led in strikeouts per nine innings (3.7). Ownie Carroll (10-6, .3.98 ERA, 13 GF). Lil Stoner (10-13, 3.98 ERA, 6 WP) led in hits (251), earned runs (95), and runs (118). Ken Holloway (11-12, 4.07 ERA) led in saves (6), home runs (10) and BB/9 (3.0). Rip Collins (13-7, 4.69 ERA) led in winning percentage (.650). The pen had George Smith (4-1, .800, 3.91 ERA, 13 GF), 19-year-old rookie Josh Billings (5-4, 4.84 ERA), Don Hankins (2-0, 1.000, 6.33 ERA) and Ed Wells (0-1, 6.75 ERA).

Defense. Detroit committed 209 errors for a .967 fielding percentage. Motown led the league in double plays (173). League leaders were pitcher Gibson in caught stealing percentage (73%), Gehringer led in chances (769), chances per game (6.4), assists (438) and double plays (84) at second, as he led team in defensive WAR (0.9). Warner led in errors (24) at third base.

Earl Whitehill had his last nine appearances all on the road August 31-September 25 (9 GM, 4-2, 4 CG, 49 IP, 9 ER, 1.65 ERA, .207 BA, .207 SLG, .226 BAbip), including a 5-2 victory at Shibe Park in Philadelphia on Friday, September 9 (9 IP, 0 ER, 4 H).

Harry Heilmann was overwhelming August 20-24 (6 GM, 18-for-24 .750 BA, 2 HR, 8 RBI, .778 OBP, 1.208 SLG, 1.986 OPS, .727 BAbip). He had two five-hit games, six four-hit games, 16 three-hit games and 33 two-hit games for 57 multi-hit games.

1920s Pitching Earned Run Average		
1.	Herman Pillette	3.42
2.	Hooks Dauss	3.79
3.	Ownie Carroll	3.92
4.	Rip Collins	3.94
5.	Howard Ehmke	3.95
6.	Sam Gibson	4.06
7.	Earl Whitehill	4.10
8.	Dutch Leonard	4.15
9.	Red Oldham	4.25
10.	Ken Holloway	4.42

Team. Detroit (68-86 .442) finished sixth for manager George Moriarty with an attendance of 474,323. The Tigers were 7-13 in April when rookie Paul Easterling excelled April 16-20 (12-for-18 .667 BA, 3 HR, .667 OBP, 1.222 SLG, .750 BAbip). Reliever Elam Vangilder (5.1 IP, 1 ER) and Harry Rice 4-for-5 led a 10-inning 7-6 victory in Cleveland on Sunday, April 29. The Bengals finished 11-13 for May, as the squad lost seven straight games thru Thursday, May 17. Motown swept a four-game series in Cleveland beginning on Wednesday, May 30, with 4-3 triumph led by Chick Galloway 3-for-4 (HR, 2 RBI) and Earl Whitehill (9 IP, 3 ER). Detroit was 8-17 in June including a record of 1-9 for the period June 11-22, as the lone victory was an Ownie Carroll (9 IP, 1 ER, 3 H) 4-1 win at home against Washington on Saturday, June 16. Vangilder found his groove for the two months of June 21-August 21 (16 GM, 6-1 .857). The squad went 16-14 in July, with an unprecedented four consecutive doubleheaders beginning on the Fourth of July. The club swept a doubleheader 20-8 and 4-3 in 13-innings at Boston on Saturday, July 7. Rice went 3-for-5 (5 RBI, 3 SB), and Pinky Hargrave 3-for-5 (3 RBI) in the opener, as reliever Vangilder (7 IP, 0 ER) and Jackie Tavener (2 RBI) led the second game. The Bengals had a 16-14 mark in August, with a Vic Sorrell (9 IP, 1 ER) 5-3 win over Cleveland at home on Thursday, August 30. Detroit closed 10-15 in September when John Stone excelled for September 5-26 (14 GM, 16 RBI, .406 BA, .424 OBP, .656 SLG, .414 BAbip). Motown defeated visiting New York 19-10 on Saturday, September 29. The Tigers and Yankees combined for a nine-inning league record of 45 hits. Detroit had 27 hits, led by Charlie Gehringer 5-for-6, Bob Fothergill 4-for-5 (3 RBI), Marty McManus 4-for-6 (3 RBI), Hargrave 3-for-6 (3 RBI) and pitcher Vangilder 3-for-6 (HR, 3 RBI). The Tigers were 36-41 (.468) at home, including a 9-2 mark versus Boston, and 32-45 (.416) on the road. Detroit scored 744 runs, as their pitchers allowed opponents 804.

P * OWNIE CARROLL

Offense. Detroit finished with a .279 BA, .340 OBP, .401 SLG, .742 OPS, 2,123 TB, and 92 OPS+. The catchers were Pinky Hargrave (.275 BA, 10 HR, 63 RBI) and Larry Woodall (.210 BA, 13 RBI). Bill Sweeney (.252 BA, 19 RBI) at first led for in-play percentage (85%). Second baseman Charlie Gehringer (.320 BA, 6 HR, 74 RBI) led in games (154), plate appearances (691), at bats (603), runs (107), hits (193), singles (142), triples (16), on-base percentage (.395), WAR (4.5), oWAR (5.0), times on base (268), runs produced (175), bases produced (356), walks (69) and outs (432). Marty McManus (.288 BA, 8 HR, 73 RBI) played third. Jackie Tavener (.260 BA, 5 HR, 52 RBI) was the shortstop. Leftfielder Bob Fothergill (.317 BA, 3 HR, 63 RBI) led in stolen base runs (0.6). Centerfielder Harry Rice (.302 BA, 6 HR, 81 RBI) led in stolen bases (20). Player of the Year and most effective hitter Harry Heilmann (.328 BA, 14 HR, 107 RBI) at right led in doubles (38), home runs, runs batted in, slugging (.507), OPS (.897), OPS+ (.132), total average (.910), base-out percentage (.922), gross production average (.302), batters run average (.193), hitting, BAbip (.339), secondary average (.289), base runs (103), runs produced (176), runs created (110), isolated power (.179), extra base hits (62), total bases (283) and 21-game hitting streak. Rookie outfielders John Stone (26 GM, .354 BA, 2 HR, 21 RBI, 141 OPS+) and Paul Easterling (43 GM, .325 BA, 3 HR, 12 RBI) both had an impressive MLB debut. Sam Gibson (.286 BA, 6 RBI) and Josh Billings (.286 BA, 5 RBI) led the pitchers. Hargrave led Tiger pinch-hitters at .387 (12-31, HR, 11 RBI). Class "A" Fort Worth had stars Ralph Shinners (.363 BA), Red Rollings (.337 BA), Joe Banowitz (193 H, .334 BA, 54 2B), Hod Kibbie (.318 BA) and Eddie Moore (191 H, .306 BA). Heilmann and McManus led for power/speed number (9.3).

1920s Pitching Innings Pitched		
1.	Earl Whitehill	1,435.1
2.	Hooks Dauss	1,292.2
3.	Lil Stoner	984.1
4.	Ken Holloway	975.2
5.	Howard Ehmke	744.1
6.	Rip Collins	743.0
7.	Red Oldham	656.2
8.	Ownie Carroll	645.2
9.	Dutch Leonard	613.1
10.	Herman Pillette	562.2

Pitching. The Tigers logged a 4.32 ERA, five SHO, 567 walks, 451 SO, 96 ERA+, 4.12 FIP, 1.493 WHIP, 9.7 H/9, 3.7 BB/9, and 3.0 SO/9, with league lead in games finished (89) and walks (567). Pitcher of the Year and most effective pitcher Ownie Carroll (16-12, 3.27 ERA) led in wins, win percentage (.571), complete games (19), shutouts (2), innings (231), hits (219), walks (87), HBP (7), LOB% (69.9), earned run average, ERA+ (126), WHIP (1.325), pWAR (5.1), H/9 (8.5), BB/9 (3.4), R/9 (3.9) and quality starts (18). Elam Vangilder (11-10, 3.91 ERA, 21 GF) led in saves (5). Earl Whitehill (11-16, 4.31 ERA) led in losses, starts (30), strikeouts (93), earned runs (94), runs (131), FIP (3.70), DICE (3.79), strikeouts per nine (4.3) and strikeouts to walks (1.19). Rookie Vic Sorrell (8-11, 4.79 ERA) led league in homers (9). George Smith (1-1, 4.42 ERA, 21 GF) led in games (39). Others were 22-year-old rookie Phil Page (2-0, 2.45 ERA), Ken Holloway (4-8, 4.34 ERA), Sam Gibson (5-8, 5.42 ERA) and Charlie Sullivan (0-2, 6.57 ERA). Josh Billings (5-10, 5.12 ERA) had the league's worst pWAR (-1.1).

Defense. Detroit committed 216 errors for a .965 fielding average. Tiger league leaders were Carroll in pitcher pickoffs (4) and Gehringer in assists (507) at second base. Shortstop Tavener led in chances per game (5.7) and led his club in defensive WAR (0.4). Centerfielder Rice led all outfielders in errors (14) and Heilmann led league right-fielders in errors with seven.

The Bengals shutout the visiting Boston Red Sox 8-0 on Monday, September 24, with Sam Gibson (9 IP, 0 ER, 5 H) and John Stone 3-for-5 (3 RBI) leading the way. The game took a mere 1:30 with a new record low attendance of 404 at Navin Field.

Dale Alexander had a phenomenal season for the class "AA" International League Toronto Maple Leafs. He won the Triple Crown (.380 BA, 31 HR, 144 RBI), scored 155 runs, had 400 total bases and was league leader in doubles (49) and hits (236).

Team. Detroit finished sixth for Bucky Harris at 70-84 (.455) with 869,318 fans. The team started 6-9 in April with a 16-9 win at St. Louis on Sunday, April 29, led by Harry Heilmann 3-for-5 (4 RBI), rookie Dale Alexander (HR, 4 RBI) and pinch-hitter Bob Fothergill (2 RBI) doubled. Pitcher Earl Whitehill (9 IP, 9 ER, 14 H, 7 BB) went 3-for-5 (HR, 3 RBI) at the plate. Motown finished 18-12 in May that included a 13-7 win over visiting New York on Saturday, May 11, led by reliever George Smith (8.1 IP, 2 ER) 3-for-4 (2 RBI), Heilmann 4-for-5 (2 RBI), Alexander 3-for-5 (HR, 4 RBI), and Gehringer 3-for-5 (3 RBI). Fothergill excelled May 14-July 14 (47 GM, 39 RBI, .403 BA, .438 OBP, .729 SLG, .397 BAbip). The Bengals won six straight thru May 8. Detroit won a 21-inning 6-5 win in Chicago on Friday, May 24, as pitcher George Uhle (W 8-0, 20 IP, 5 ER, 17 H, 3 BB, 5 SO) went 4-for-9 at the plate. Detroit went 14-12 in June when Fothergill drove in runs at an alarming rate June 6-16 (9 GM, 2 HR, 17 RBI, .500 BA, .833 SLG). Players won 17-11 at Washington on Friday, June 7. The 23-hit attack was led by Charlie Gehringer 4-for-6 (3 2B, 7 RBI), Fothergill 4-for-6 (5 RBI) and Alexander 3-for-6 (HR, 2 RBI). Fothergill was spectacular June 7-18 (10 GM, 21-for-42 .500 BA, .500 OBP, .762 SLG, 1.262 OPS, .514 BAbip). The Tigers were 9-17 in July when Ownie Carroll (9 IP, 1 ER) tripled during a 4-1 win at Boston on Friday, July 26. The Team was 11-16 in August allowing a season high of runs during a 21-5 loss on the road at Washington on Monday, August 5. Detroit scored seven third inning runs on their way to a 17-13 home win over New York on Wednesday, August 14, during *"Charlie Gehringer Day."* Gehringer went 4-for-5 HR), Alexander 2-for-3 (4 RBI), Fothergill 2-for-4 (4 RBI), Heinie Schuble (3 RBI) and pinch-hitter Yats Wuestling 1-for-1 (2 RBI). The team closed 11-15 September and 1-3 for October. 23-year-old rookie Art Herring (W 1-0, 9 IP, 1 ER) had a dominant start in his MLB debut for a 2-1 victory in Boston on Thursday September 12. Earl Whitehill (9 IP, 3 ER), rookie catcher Ray Hayworth 4-for-5 (RBI) and Marty McManus 3-for-5 led a 6-3 victory in Chicago on Saturday, October 5, with a paltry 500 fans at Comiskey Park. Detroit went 38-39 (.494) at home and 32-45 (.416) on the road. Motown scored 926 runs while allowing 928. Class "A" Fort Worth had stars Joe Bonowitz (205 H, 43 2B, .359 BA, 310 TB), Eddie Moore (225 H, 31 2B, 30 3B, .335 BA, 322 TB), Karl Urban (202 H, .305 BA), Larmon Cox (47 2B, .304 BA), and pitcher Dick McCabe (8-3 .727).

1920s Pitching Walks		
1.	Earl Whitehill	540
2.	Hooks Dauss	397
3.	Lil Stoner	366
4.	Ken Holloway	338
5.	Howard Ehmke	306
6.	Ownie Carroll	274
7.	Rip Collins	240
8.	Red Oldham	231
9.	Sam Gibson	214
10.	Herman Pillette	192

MGR * BUCKY HARRIS

Offense. Detroit finished with a .360 OBP, .813 OPS, 2,531 TB, with an OPS+ of 108, and led league in doubles (339), triples (97), hitting (.299) and slugging (.453). Catching had Eddie Phillips (.235 BA, 2 HR, 21 RBI), Pinky Hargrave (.330 BA, 3 HR, 26 RBI) and Merv Shea (.290 BA, 3 HR, 24 RBI). The Player of the Year and most effective hitter was rookie Dale Alexander (.343 BA, 25 HR, 137 RBI) at first who led the league in games (155) and hits (215). He led his team in homers, runs batted in, slugging (.580), OPS (.977), base runs (128), runs created (144), isolated power (.236), extra base hits (83), total bases (363), strikeouts (63) and hit streak (16). Charlie Gehringer (.339 BA, 13 HR, 106 RBI) at second led league in games (155), plate appearances (717), runs (131), hits (215), doubles (45), Triples (19), power speed number (17.6) and steals (27), as he led squad in hits (215), singles (131), WAR (5.8), oWAR (6.9), times on base (285), runs produced (224), bases produced (428) and stolen base runs (2.1). Marty McManus (.280 BA, 18 HR, 90 RBI) was at third, with Heinie Schuble (.233 BA, 2 HR, 28 RBI) at short. Rookie Roy Johnson (.314 BA, 128 R, 10 HR, 69 RBI) in left led league for at bats (640) and doubles (45). He led Motown in walks (67) and outs (461). Centerfielder Harry Rice (.304 BA, 6 HR, 69 RBI). Harry Heilmann (.344 BA, 15 HR, 120 RBI) at right led in on-base percentage (.412), OPS (.977), OPS+ (149), total average (1.013), base-out percentage (1.032), gross production average (.327), batters run average (.226) and secondary average (.329). Outfielder Bob Fothergill (.354 BA, 6 HR, 62 RBI) led in batting average, BAbip (.354) and in-play percentage (89%). George Uhle (.343 BA, 13 RBI) and Emil Yde (.333 BA) led the pitchers. Yde at .412 (7-17) and Fothergill at .365 (19-52, 13 RBI) led pinch-hitters.

Pitching. The Tigers had a 4.96 ERA, five SHO, 646 walks, 467 SO, 87 ERA+, 4.63 FIP, 1.645 WHIP, 10.6 H/9, 4.2 BB/9, 3.0 SO/9, and 81 CG. The staff led league in innings (1,390.1), hits (1,641), earned runs (766), runs (928), walks (646), batters faced (6,345), left on base (1,248) and no decisions (34). Pitcher of the Year and most effective pitcher George Uhle (15-11, 4.08 ERA, 1 SHO) led in wins, win percentage (.577), CG (23), innings (249), hits (283), ERA, ERA+ (105), FIP (3.55), DICE (3.39), WHIP (1.369), pWAR (3.5), BB/9 (2.1), SO/BB (1.72), R/9 (5.1) and quality starts (15). Earl Whitehill (14-15, 4.62 ERA, 1 SHO) led in games (38), homers (16), strikeouts (103), H/9 (9.8) and SO/9 (3.8). Ownie Carroll (9-17, 4.63 ERA) led in losses, HBP (8) and LOB% (63.8). Vic Sorrell (14-15, 5.18 ERA, 1 SHO) led league in cheap wins (5) and club in starts (31), walks (106), earned runs (130), and runs (152). Lil Stoner (3-3, 5.26 ERA) led in saves (4). Emil Yde (7-3, 5.30 ERA) led in GF (16). Skinny Graham (1-3, 5.57 ERA) and Augie Prudhomme (1-6, 6.22 ERA). Class "A" Fort Worth had Jim Walkup (18-11 .621) and Dick Whitworth (16-12 .571).

1920s Pitching Strikeouts		
1.	Earl Whitehill	567
2.	Hooks Dauss	394
3.	Lil Stoner	296
4.	Dutch Leonard	287
5.	Howard Ehmke	274
6.	Ken Holloway	242
7.	Rip Collins	214
8.	Red Oldham	201
9.	Syl Johnson	182
10.	Sam Gibson	166

Defense. Detroit led the league in putouts (4,163) and errors (229) for a league low fielding average (.961). League leaders were Sorrell in pitcher fielding (1.000), and Alexander in first basemen errors (18), Gehringer at second led in fielding (.975), chances (928) and putouts (404). Johnson led all outfielders in chances (433), assists (25) and errors (31), as he led leftfielders in errors (22). Rice led centerfielders in errors (15). Hargrave and McManus led the team in defensive WAR (0.4).

Dale Alexander set the MLB record for hits by a rookie with 215. He was the first rookie to reach 200 hits. Detroit for the first time had three players with 100 runs batted in, with Alexander (137), Harry Heilmann (120) and Charlie Gehringer (106).

3B * MARV OWEN

Player of the Decade. Hank Greenberg (.323 BA, 206 HR, 851 RBI) led the decade in home runs, runs batted in, slugging (.617), on-base plus slugging (1.032), OPS+ (159), total average (1.149), gross production average (.341), BAbip (.339), secondary average (.454), total base average (2.3), bases produced average (3.0) and strikeouts (556). Greenberg recorded five superior seasons in 1934 (.339 BA, 63 2B, 26 HR, 139 RBI, 201 H, 156 OPS+, 356 TB, 6.3 WAR), 1935 MVP season (.328 BA, 16 3B, 36 HR, 168 RBI, 203 H, 170 OPS+, 389 TB, 7.7 WAR), 1937 (.337 BA, 14 3B, 40 HR, 184 RBI, 200 H, 172 OPS+, 397 TB, 7.5 WAR), 1938 (.315 BA, 58 HR, 147 RBI, 169 OPS+, 380 TB, 6.7 WAR) and 1939 (.312 BA, 42 2B, 33 HR, 113 RBI, 156 OPS+, 311 TB, 5.4 WAR). He finished top-six in MVP voting four times in the 1930s, 36.6 WAR and a star in 1934 World Series (.321 BA, 7 RBI). Hank led all 1939 first basemen in fielding average (.993).

1930s			
Year	W – L	Pct.	Pl
1930	75-79	.487	5
1931	61-93	.396	7
1932	76-75	.503	5
1933	75-79	.487	5
1934	**101-53**	**.656**	1
1935	93-58	.616	1
1936	83-71	.539	2
1937	89-65	.578	2
1938	84-70	.545	4
1939	81-73	.526	5
	818-716	.533	

All-Decade Team. Manager Mickey Cochrane (348-250 .582) won the pennant his first year in 1934 (101-53 .656), with the Tigers World Champions in 1935 (93-58 .616). Pitcher Firpo Marberry (31-17 .646, 3.81 ERA). Catcher Mickey Cochrane (.313 BA, 11 HR, 150 RBI) led in on-base percentage (.444), walk percentage (18.2%) and BB/SO (4.1). First baseman Hank Greenberg (.323 BA, 206 HR, 851 RBI). Second baseman Charlie Gehringer (.331 BA, 146 HR, 1,0003 RBI) led decade in games (1,434), plate appearances (6,497), at bats (5,629), runs (1,181), hits (1,865), singles (1,243), doubles (400), triples (76), runs batted in (1,003), hit by pitch (29), offensive WAR (58.3), AB/SO (26.9), bases produced (3,722), extra base hits (622), extra bases on long hits (990), caught stealing (52), stolen base runs created (2,100), walks (766), strikeout ratio (0.03) and strikeout percentage (3.2%). Shortstop Billy Rogell (.274 BA, 39 HR, 533 RBI) was leader in dWAR (13.0) and caught stealing (52). The Third baseman was Marv Owen (.278 BA, 25 HR, 423 RBI). Goose Goslin (.297 BA, 50 HR, 371 RBI) played in left, as Centerfielder Gee Walker (.317 BA, 61 HR, 469 RBI) led team for in-play percentage (84%), stolen bases (132), stolen base percentage (72.5%) and stolen base runs (9.6). John Stone (.303 BA, 41 HR, 323 RBI) was the All-Decade right-fielder.

P * ELDON AUKER

Pitcher of the Decade. Firpo Marberry (31-17 .646, 3.81 ERA) was the decade leader in win percentage, technical runs allowed (4.38), BB/9 (2.57) and RA/9 (4.38). He had a perfect 9-0 record pitching in relief during the 1930s. His best year as a Tiger was in 1933 (16-11 .593, 3.29 ERA, 131 ERA+), with a solid month of May 13-July 14 (10-2 .833, 3.05 ERA) that included a 7-1 victory over the Senators in Washington, D.C. on Tuesday, May 23 (9 IP, 3 H, 1 ER). Marberry was effective against St. Louis (3-0), Boston (4-1) and Cleveland (3-1) in 1933. The record setting closer started for Detroit in 1934 (15-5 .750, 4.57 ERA) that included a four-hit 12-0 home shutout of last place Chicago on Saturday, June 2 (9 IP, 4 H, 0 ER). The righthander enjoyed an impressive month of play August 7-September 8 (4-0, 1 SV, 1.17 ERA, .200 BA, .218 SLG). Several of his other 1934 highlights were 8-2 at home, 10-3 in first half, 7-0 pitching in relief (1.64 ERA, .226 BA), 4-0 against Philadelphia and 4-1 against the Chicago White Sox.

1930s Attendance			
Year	Attn.	Avg.	Rk
1930	649,450	8,326	3
1931	434,056	5,637	5
1932	397,157	5,092	4
1933	320,972	4,115	5
1934	919,161	11,490	1
1935	1,034,929	13,100	1
1936	875,948	11,376	2
1937	**1,072,276**	**13,926**	1
1938	799,557	10,121	2
1939	836,279	10,722	2

All-Decade Pitchers. Marberry pitched five games for Detroit in 1935 then umpired 96 games in the American League later in the season. Schoolboy Rowe (80-53 .602, 4.11 ERA) was decade leader for FIP (3.80), DICE (3.73), SO/BB (1.66), dominant start percentage (.210) and reliever win percentage (12-4 .750). Rowe was superb in 1934 (24-8 .750, 3.45 ERA). Tommy Bridges (150-102 .595, 3.76) led the decade in games (309), wins, losses, starts (266), complete games (156), shutouts (25), quality starts (137), high quality starts (130), dominant starts (48), innings (2,083), hits (2,015), home runs (138), walks (902), strikeouts (1,207), balks (7), hit by pitch (29), wild pitches (41), earned runs (870), runs (1,021), left on-base percentage (69.9), earned run average, pitcher WAR (35.4), H/9 (8.71), SO/9 (5.22), quality start percentage (.515), batters faced (9,033), cheap wins (36), and tough losses (24). George Uhle (29-30 .492, 3.84 ERA) was the decade leader in ERA+ (123), WHIP (1.293), complete game percentage (.629) and high-quality start percentage (.532). He went 7-3 (.700) during the second half of the 1931 season. Elden Auker (77-52 .597, 4.26 ERA) was solid in 1935 (18-7 .720, 3.83). Vic Sorrell (70-75 .483, 4.25) finished with decade highs for pickoffs (8) and no decisions (34). His best year was 1930 (16-11 .593, 3.86 ERA), when he was superb July 9-September 10 (9-2 .818, 2.83 ERA). Earl Whitehill (46-41 .529, 4.28) had his best season in 1930 (17-13 .567, 4.24 ERA). He stood 3-9 (6.98 ERA) thru June 26, then extraordinary June 27-August 23 (12 GM, 11-0 1.000, 100.1 IP, 2.15 ERA, .225 BA). General Crowder (25-14 .641, 4.76 ERA) was decade leader in starter win percentage (24-14 .632), with a record of 16-10 in 1935. Chief Hogsett (38-45 .458, 4.56 ERA) led the 1930s in games finished (129), saves (27), hit by pitch (29), HR/9 (0.50), games in relief (170), relief wins (24) and relief losses (24). Roxie Lawson (38-25 .603, 5.14 ERA) was his best in the 1937 season (18-7 .720, 5.26).

Pitcher George Uhle was a solid hitter in 1930 (.308 BA, .427 SLG, 21 RBI) and 4-for-4 on August 6. Tommy Bridges (66-32 .673) and Schoolboy Rowe (62-31 .667) dominated 1934-1936 (128-63 .670). Hooks Dauss left after walking the first batter on Saturday, September 29, 1923, as long reliever Earl Whitehill (W 1-0, 9 IP, 0 ER, 2 H) led a 3-0 win over visiting Cleveland.

YEAR	AVG	HR	RBI	SB
1930	.284	82	728	97
1931	.268	43	599	117
1932	.273	80	742	105
1933	.269	57	678	68
1934	**.300**	74	871	**125**
1935	.290	106	841	70
1936	**.300**	94	847	73
1937	.292	**150**	**872**	89
1938	.272	137	804	76
1939	.279	124	804	88

1930s Team Hitting

Team. Detroit finished fifth for manager Bucky Harris at 75-79 (.487), with an attendance of 649,450. Players went 5-10 in April that included a 6-3 win on opening day over St. Louis at home on April 15, behind George Uhle (6 IP, 3 ER) who homered and had two runs batted in. Marty McManus was on fire April 22-May 22 (28 GM, .424 BA, .525 OBP, .626 SLG, .415 BAbip). The Tigers were 13-14 in May with a 19-2 loss in Philadelphia on Thursday, May 1. Charlie Gehringer sizzled May 17-27 (10 GM, .512 BA, .553 OBP, .837 SLG, 1.390 OPS, .512 BAbip). The club won 16-11 in St. Louis on Tuesday, May 27. Gehringer 3-for-5, Harry Rice (HR, 4 RBI), Liz Funk (HR, 3 RBI) and Pinky Hargrave 4-for-5 (HR, 2 RBI) paced Detroit. The team was 11-17 in June when Dale Alexander (HR, 3 RBI) led a 6-0 shutout of Boston at home on Saturday, June 7, as Uhle was a double threat pitching (9 IP, 0 ER, 3 H) and hitting (2-for-3). Pitcher Uhle excelled as a hitter for over two months June 5-August 7 (28 GM, 22-for-53, .415 BA, .492 OBP, .566 SLG, .429 BAbip). Players were 19-15 in July when Waite Hoyt (9 IP, 1 ER), Roy Johnson 3-for-5 (2 RBI), John Stone 3-for-5 (2 RBI) and Alexander (2 RBI) powered a 11-1 home win over Cleveland on Friday, July 11. Detroit defeated visiting Washington 8-4 on Monday, July 14, as Alexander was 4-for-4 (5 RBI) and Uhle (W 9-8, 9 IP, 4 ER, 8 SO) went 3-for-4. The squad started Auguste with an -1 record and final monthly mark of (14-14). Gehringer was 4-for-6 (2 HR, 6 RBI) with a 12th-inning walk-off grand slam and 7-3 win over Chicago on Monday, August 4. Uhle (W 12-9, 9 IP, 1 ER, 4 H) went 4-for-4 (2B, RBI) in a 9-1 victory against visiting Cleveland on Wednesday, August 6. Vic Sorrell (W 13-8, 9 IP, 1 ER) and Paul Easterling (5 RBI) led a 15-1 win in Washington, D.C., on Sunday, August 17. The Tigers closed 13-9 in September when they played the last 20 games at home. The Bengals won a home doubleheader with New York on Saturday, September 13. Detroit had a five-run ninth inning for a 11-10 walk-off game one win, behind Bill Akers (2 HR, 4 RBI) and Frank Doljack (HR, 3 RBI). The Tigers were 45-33 (.577) at home and 30-46 (.395) on the road. The Bengals scored 783 runs as their pitchers allowed 833 runs. The class "A" Beaumont Exporters featured Ox Echardt (217 H, 55 2B, .379 BA, .534 SLG, 306 TB) and Heinie Schuble (.320 BA).

Offense. Detroit had a .284 BA, .344 OBP, .421 SLG, .764 OPS, 2,228 TB, and 91 OPS+. The catchers were Ray Hayworth (.278 BA, 22 RBI), Gene Desautels (190 BA, 9 RBI) and Pinky Hargrave (.285 BA, 5 HR, 18 RBI). Dale Alexander (.326 BA, 20 HR, 135 RBI) at first led league in games (154). He led team in homers, runs batted in, strikeouts (56) and hit streak (29). Player of the Year and most effective hitter Charlie Gehringer (.330 BA, 16 HR, 98 RBI) at second led MLB in caught stealing (15) and league in games (154). He led club in plate appearances (700), runs (144), hits (201), doubles (47), triples (15), on-base percentage (.404), slugging (.534), OPS (.938), OPS+ (134), total average (.958), base-out percentage (.993), gross production average (.315), oWAR (5.8), WAR (6.5), batters run average (.211), hitting, secondary average (.325), base runs (120), times on base (277), runs produced (226), runs created (132), isolated power (.205), extra base hits (78), power/speed number (17.4), total bases (326), bases produced (414), walks (69) and outs (437). Marty McManus (.320 BA, 9 HR, 89 RBI) at third led league in steals (23) and squad in stolen base runs (2.1). Mark Koenig (.240 BA, HR, 16 RBI) and Bill Akers (.279 BA, 9 HR, 40 RBI) were at short. John Stone (.311 BA, 3 HR, 56 RBI) in left led in BAbip (.346), with Liz Funk (.275 BA, 4 HR, 65 RBI) in center. Roy Johnson (.275 BA, 2 HR, 35 RBI) played in right and led all pinch-hitters at .286 (2-7). Whit Wyatt (.353 BA, HR, 9 RBI) and George Uhle (.308 BA, 2 HR, 21 RBI) led pitchers.

Pitching. The Tigers recorded a 4.70 ERA, 68 CG, four SHO, 574 SO, 102 ERA+, 4.82 FIP, 1.537 WHIP, 10.0 H/9, 3.8 BB/9, and 3.8 SO/9. Motown led league in walks (570) and hit by pitch (33). Pitcher of the Year Earl Whitehill (17-13, 4.24 ERA) led in wins, losses, starts (31), hits (248), earned runs (104), runs (139), FIP (4.18), DICE (3.68), home runs per nine (0.3), strikeouts per nine innings (4.4) and quality starts (17). The most effective pitcher George Uhle (12-12, 3.65 ERA) led in complete games (18), innings (239), home runs (18), strikeouts (117), LOB% (71.1), earned run average, ERA+ (131), WHIP (1.314), pWAR (6.2), hits per nine (9.0), BB/9 (2.8), SO/BB (1.56) and runs per nine (4.1). Vic Sorrell (16-11, 3.86 ERA) led in games (35), win percentage (.593) and shutouts (2). Chief Hogsett (9-8, 5.42 ERA) led league in hit by pitch (9). Charlie Sullivan (1-5, 6.53 ERA) led in games (40), games finished (18) and saves (5). Whit Wyatt (4-5, 3.57 ERA), Tommy Bridges (3-2, 4.06 ERA), Waite Hoyt (9-8, 4.78 ERA), Art Herring (3-3, 5.33 ERA) and Guy Cantrell (1-5, 5.66 ERA).

1930s Team Hitting

YEAR	OBP	SLG	OPS	OPS+
1930	.344	.421	.764	91
1931	.330	.371	.702	82
1932	.335	.401	.736	87
1933	.329	.380	.709	87
1934	.376	.424	.800	106
1935	.366	.435	.801	**110**
1936	**.377**	.431	.808	99
1937	.370	**.452**	**.822**	104
1938	.359	.411	.770	87
1939	.356	.426	.782	94

Defense. Detroit committed 188 errors for a .968 fielding percentage. Tiger league leaders were catcher Hayworth in passed balls (11), Alexander led the first basemen in errors (22) and double plays (132). Second baseman Gehringer led in fielding percentage (.979), as he led the Bengals in defensive WAR (1.1), McManus led the third basemen in fielding percentage (.966), putouts (152) and double plays (23). Johnson led all right fielders in assists (13), errors (15) and for double plays (5).

Dale Alexander led the league in runs batted in (135) driving in a run in eight straight games May 24-31 (3 HR, 11 RBI, .361 BA, .395 OBP, .611 SLG), with a 29-game hitting streak May 13-June 16 (29 GM, 6 HR, 40 RBI, .339 BA, .375 OBP, .579 SLG).

Vic Sorrell pitched two shutouts as he blanked the Red Sox 3-0 in Boston on Saturday, August 9 (W 12-7, 9 IP, 9 H, 0 ER, 3 SO) and then shutout the Athletics 4-0 at Navin Field in Detroit on Wednesday, September 10 (W 16-9, 9 IP, 4 H, 0 ER, 3 SO).

1930s Hitting Games		
1.	Charlie Gehringer	1,434
2.	Billy Rogell	1,207
3.	Pete Fox	904
4.	Hank Greenberg	882
5.	Gee Walker	794
6.	Marv Owen	792
7.	Ray Hayworth	632
8.	Jo-Jo White	630
9.	John Stone	567
10.	Goose Goslin	524

Team. Detroit finished seventh with Bucky Harris at 61-93 (.396) and an attendance of 434,056. The Tigers were 7-7 in April, with a 4-0 mark at home. John Stone pummeled pitching April 17-May 17 (25 GM, .404 BA, .465 OBP, .640 SLG, .400 BAbip). Tommy Bridges (9 IP, 0 ER, 4 H) and the Tigers shutout St. Louis 1-0 at home on Thursday, April 23. Detroit fell to 11-19 in May when Sone excelled May 1-5 (5 GM, 12-for-18, .667 BA, .700 OBP, .778 SLG, .667). The club endured two eight-game losing streaks for an 18-game stretch, with a mark of 2-16 (.111) that began Sunday, May 17. The Bengals won 4-2 in Chicago on Tuesday, May 26, as George Uhle (9 IP, 2 ER) pitched and was the hitting star with a homer and two RBIs. The Tigers fell to the New York Yankees 20-8 at home on Monday, May 18, when the pitchers allowed 19 hits and walked 15 hitters. Detroit went 8-17 in June, as they started the month 1-9. The lone win in that 10 games was a 1-0 11-inning complete game shutout by Uhle (11 IP, 0 ER, 5 H) at Washington on Friday, June 5. The club had a modest four-game win streak that began on Sunday, June 14. The squad slid to a 10-21 record in July, with Art Herring (9 IP, 3 ER) pitching a 12-3 win in Philadelphia on Tuesday, July 14, with Stone (HR, 3 RBI), Mark Koenig 3-for-5 (3 RBI) and Marty McManus 3-for 4. McManus was remarkable July 16-18 (3 GM, 10-for-12, .833 BA, .833 OBP, 1.000 SLG, 1.833 OPS, .833 BAbip). The Tigers had their best month in August (15-12), when Dale Alexander was 4-for-5 (2 RBI) and Earl Whitehill (9 IP, 1 ER) led the 7-1 triumph in Cleveland on Saturday, August 8. Players lost 7-5 in 16-innings to the visiting Yankees on Saturday, August 15, as Charlie Gehringer went 5-for-7. Chief Hogsett (7.2 IP, 4 ER) started for the Bengals and Uhle (8 IP, 3 ER) pitched in relief. Detroit closed 10-17 in September including a 3-0 Bridges (9 IP, 0 ER, 6 H) shutout at Boston on Thursday, September 10. The club went 36-41 (.468) in home games, with a meager record of 25-52 (.325) in games played on the road. The Tigers scored 651 runs as their pitchers would allow opponents 836 runs. Eddie Taylor (.300 BA), Whit Wyatt (11-3 .786, 1.51 ERA) and Tom Vaughn (11-6 .647, 2.91 ERA) starred for class "A" Beaumont.

P * GEORGE UHLE

Offense. Detroit had a .268 BA, .330 OBP, .371 SLG, .702 OPS, 2,015 TB and 82 OPS+. Ray Hayworth (.256 BA, 26 RBI) caught. Player of the Year Dale Alexander (.325 BA, 3 HR, 87 RBI) led the team in doubles (47), runs batted in, on-base percentage (.401), total average (.821), gross production average (.292), batters run average (.179), BAbip (.344) and runs produced (159) . Charlie Gehringer (.311, 4 HR, 53 RBI) manned second base and led in stolen base runs (1.5). Marty McManus (.271, 3 HR, 53 RBI) manned third, with Billy Rogell (.303 BA, 2 HR, 24 RBI) the shortstop. Leftfielder John Stone (.327 BA, 10 HR, 78 RBI) was the most effective hitter and led league in singles (142). He was Motown leader for hits (191), homers, slugging (.464), OPS (.852), OPS+ (120), base-out percentage (.844), WAR (3.4), oWAR (3.2), batters run average (.178), batting average, BAbip (.344), times on base (249), base runs (98), runs created (105) and 25-game hit streak. Hub Walker (.286 BA, 14 RBI) was in center. Right-fielder Roy Johnson (.279 BA, 8 HR, 54 RBI) led the league in triples (19), and outs (471). He led his team in games (151), plate appearances (698), runs (107),secondary average (.295), isolated power (.159), power/speed number (12.9), extra base hits (64), total bases (272), bases produced (377), steals (33), walks (72), and strikeouts (51). Key reserves were infielders Marv Owen (.223 BA, 3 HR, 39 RBI) and Mark Koenig (.253 BA, HR, 39 RBI). Rookie Gee Walker (.296 BA, HR, 28 RBI) made had an impressive MLB debut. George Uhle (.244 BA, 2 HR, 9 RBI) led pitchers. The leading pinch-hitters were Bill Akers at .400 (2-5), Gee Walker .375 (3-8, 3 RBI) and Uhle (5 RBI). Rookie Hub Walker scorched MLB pitching June 12-27 (.463 BA, .508 OBP, .593 SLG, .500 BAbip).

1930s Hitting Runs		
1.	Charlie Gehringer	1,179
2.	Hank Greenberg	701
3.	Billy Rogell	668
4.	Pete Fox	621
5.	Gee Walker	475
6.	Marv Owen	363
7.	Jo-Jo White	348
8.	Goose Goslin	346
9.	John Stone	338
10.	Roy Johnson	223

Pitching. The Tigers logged a 4.59 ERA, 86 CG, five SHO, 597 walks, 511 SO, 100 ERA+, 4.47 FIP, 1.550 WHIP, 10.1 H/9, 3.9 BB/9, and 3.3 SO/9, as they led league in walks (597) and wild pitches (26). Pitcher of the Year and most effective pitcher George Uhle (11-12, 3.50 ERA, 2 SHO, 2 SV) led in earned run average, ERA+ (130), FIP (3.96), DICE (3.84), WHIP (1.238), pWAR (5.6), H/9 (8.9), walks per nine (2.3), strikeouts to walks (1.29) and runs per nine (4.1). Earl Whitehill (13-16, 4.08 ERA) led MLB in homers (22), with staff lead for wins, losses, starts (34), complete games (22), innings (271.1), hits (287), walks (118), earned runs (123), runs (152), LOB% (68.0) and quality starts (16). Vic Sorrell (13-14, 4.15 ERA) led in wins, win percentage (.481) and HR/9 (0.3). Tommy Bridges (8-16, 4.99 ERA, 35 GM, 2 SHO) led league in wild pitches (9). He led staff in losses, strikeouts (105) and strikeouts per nine (5.5). Art Herring (7-13, 4.31 ERA) led league in HBP (8). Charlie Sullivan (3-2, 4.93 ERA) led in games finished (19). Waite Hoyt (3-8, 5.87 ERA) and Chief Hogsett (3-9, 5.93 ERA, 2 SV).

Defense. Detroit committed 221 errors for a .964 fielding average. Tiger league leaders were Uhle in pitcher fielding average (1.000), and Stone in left fielder double plays (5). Johnson led outfielders in assists (25), double plays (8) and right fielders in chances (352), putouts (313), assists (24) and double plays (8). McManus at third base led the Bengals for dWAR (0.5).

Dale Alexander had six consecutive multiple hit games during the period April 24-30 (.714 BA, .778 OBP, 1.143 SLG, 1.921 OPS, .700 BAbip). Dale raised his season batting average from .387 on Thursday, April 23 to .519 through Thursday, April 30.

John Stone (.327 BA, .388 OBP, .464 SLG) had hitting streaks of 11 games July 4-15 (.400 BA, 18-for-45), 23 games August 2-27 (.443 BA, 43-for-97) and nine games September 14-24 (.375 BA, 15-for-40). Stone recorded four four-hit games in 1931.

1930s Hitting Hits		
1.	Charlie Gehringer	1,865
2.	Billy Rogell	1,210
3.	Hank Greenberg	1,086
4.	Pete Fox	1,081
5.	Gee Walker	966
6.	Marv Owen	820
7.	John Stone	657
8.	Goose Goslin	582
9.	Ray Hayworth	524
10.	Jo-Jo White	475

Team. Detroit finished fifth for Bucky Harris at 76-75-2 (.503), with 397,157 fans. The Tigers were 10-5 in April, when Earl Whitehill (9 IP, 0 ER, 6 H) shutout the Browns 8-0 at home on Tuesday, April 19. Motown scored a 16-3 victory at Cleveland on Friday, April 22 with a six-run ninth inning. Whit Wyatt (W 3-0, 9 IP, 3 ER) 4-for-6 (HR, 2 RBI), Charlie Gehringer (4 RBI), Muddy Ruel (3 RBI), John Stone (HR, 2 RBI), Roy Johnson 4-for-6 and Gee Walker 4-for-6 led the way. The Bengals were 14-11 in May as a seven run seventh inning, Vic Sorrell (9 IP, 0 ER, 2 H) and Walker (4 RBI) led to a 11-0 shutout at Boston on Tuesday, May 10. They won a doubleheader in St. Louis on Monday, May 30, 17-9 with a 21-hit attack led by Gehringer 5-for-5 (HR, 5 RBI), John Stone (HR, 4 RBI) grand slam and Ray Hayworth 3-for-4 with a home run. Tommy Bridges (9 IP, 0 ER) and Walker 3-for-4 (2 RBI) led the game two 4-0 shutout. The team was 14-12 in June when Whitehill (W 5-1, 9 IP, 4 ER) pitched a 10-4 win over visiting Cleveland on Saturday, June 4, behind Jo-Jo White (3 RBI). Motown went 9-1 during a 10-game stretch thru Wednesday, June 29, when they won 13-4 at Cleveland. Gehringer (HR, 3 RBI), Earl Webb 3-for-5 (2 RBI) and Whitehill (W 7-4, 9 IP, 4 ER) went 3-for-4 (2 RBI). The squad had a 13-18 record in July that included Chief Hogsett (W 6-4, 9 IP, 2 ER) throwing a 3-2 victory at Washington on Tuesday, July 19. Players were 14-16 in August when Tommy Bridges (9 IP, 1 H, 7 SO, 0 BB) had a dominate start on Friday, August 5. He retired the first 26 Senators he faced during a 13-0 shutout. Motown scored seven fourth inning runs, with Gehringer 4-for-5 (2 RBI), Stone (3 RBI), Heinie Schuble (3 RBI), Webb (2 RBI) and Bridges 2-for-4 (2 RBI). The team closed 11-13 in September with a 14-inning 14-13 win versus visiting New York on Friday, September 9. Walker 5-for-8 and Gehringer (3 RBI) led Detroit, as *"The Iron Horse"* Lou Gehrig (HR, 8 RBI) drove in eight runs for New York. The Bengals were 16-6 against Boston, including 10-1 at home. The team went 42-34 (.553) at home and 34-41 (.453) on the road. Players scored 799 runs and allowed 787. Class "A" Beaumont had Pete Fox (.357 BA, .585 SLG), Hank Greenberg (39 HR), Paul Easterling (36 HR), Schoolboy Rowe (19-7 .731, 2.30 ERA), Dick Schultz (13-5 .722), Luke Hamlin (20-10 .667) and Orlin Collier (16-9 .640). Ignatius Walters hit a robust .400 at class "D" McCook in 1931. He excelled with Tiger affiliates in 1932 at class "B" Decatur (67 GM, .333 BA) and class "D" Moline (59 GM, .361 BA).

P * BUCK MARROW

Offense. Detroit finished with a .273 BA, .335 OBP, .401 SLG, .736 OPS, 2,170 TB and 87 OPS+. The lineup included catcher Ray Hayworth (.293 BA, 2 HR, 46 RBI). First baseman Harry Davis (.269 BA, 4 HR, 74 RBI) led in singles (110), triples (13) and outs (455). Player of the Year and most effective hitter Charlie Gehringer (.298 BA, 19 HR, 104 RBI) at second led in games (152), plate appearances (692), at bats (618), runs (112), hits (184), doubles (44), home runs (19), on-base percentage (.370), slugging (.497), OPS (.867), OPS+ (119), total average (.857), base-out percentage (.876), gross production average (.291), WAR (4.7), oWAR (4.4), batters run average (.183), secondary average (.311), times on base (255), base runs (106), runs produced (197), runs created (114), isolated power (.199), extra base hits (74), total bases (307), bases produced (384) and walks (68). Heinie Schuble (.271 BA, 5 HR, 51 RBI) manned third, with Billy Rogell (.271 BA, 9 HR, 60 RBI) at short. Leftfielder John Stone (.297 BA, 17 HR, 109 RBI) led in runs batted in. Gee Walker (.323 BA, 8 HR, 76 RBI) played in centerfield, as he led in batting average, BAbip (.339), in-play percentage (87%), power/speed number (12.6), stolen bases (30) and stolen base runs (5.4). The right-fielder was Earl Webb (.287 BA, 3 HR, 51 RBI). Roy Johnson was traded to Boston on June 13, as his combined 1932 season totals led the American League for power/speed number (16.5). Chief Hogsett (.246 BA, 2 HR, 5 RBI) and Earl Whitehill (.244 BA, 7 RBI) led pitchers in hitting. The leading Tiger pinch-hitters were Billy Rhiel at .480 (12-25) and Jo-Jo White at .375 (9-24).

1930s Hitting Doubles		
1.	Charlie Gehringer	400
2.	Hank Greenberg	262
3.	Billy Rogell	227
4.	Gee Walker	216
5.	Pete Fox	205
6.	Marv Owen	135
7.	John Stone	125
8.	Goose Goslin	116
9.	Ray Hayworth	90
10.	Mickey Cochrane	83

Pitching. Motown had a 4.30 ERA, 67 CG, nine SHO, 592 walks, 521 SO, 110 ERA+, 4.47 FIP, 1.477 WHIP, 9.4 H/9, 3.9 BB/9, and 3.4 SO/9, with league lead for hit by pitch (31). Pitcher of the Year Earl Whitehill (16-12, 4.54 ERA, 31 GS, 5 HBP) led in wins, win percentage (.571), complete games (17), innings (244), hits (255), homers (17), earned runs (123) and runs (136). The most effective pitcher Vic Sorrell (14-14, 4.03 ERA, 31 GS, 0.4 HR/9) led in losses, FIP (3.94), DICE (3.92) and quality starts (16). Tommy Bridges (14-12, 3.36 ERA, 6 WP) led MLB in shutouts (4), as he led his team in walks (119), strikeouts (108), LOB% (72.5), earned run average, ERA+ (140), pWAR (4.5), H/9 (7.8), SO/9 (4.8) and R/9 (4.3). Chief Hogsett (11-9, 3.54 ERA, 5 HBP, 0.4 HR/9) led in games (47), games finished (27) and saves (7). Whit Wyatt (9-13, 5.03 ERA, 6 WP). George Uhle (6-6, 4.48 ERA) led in WHIP (1.323), walks per nine (2.6) and SO/BB (1.21). Art Herring (1-2, 5.24 ERA), 22-year-old rookie Buck Marrow (2-5, 4.81 ERA) and rookie Izzy Goldstein (3-2, 4.47 ERA) for his only year in the show. Tommy Bridges was superb for period of August 5-14 (3-0, 0.67 ERA, 27 IP, 3 CG, 2 SHO), with a 13-0 home shutout of Washington on Friday, August 5 (9 IP, 0 ER, 1 H, 7 SO) and a 3-0 shutout at Cleveland on Sunday, August 14 (9 IP, 0 ER, 5 H).

Defense. Detroit committed 186 errors for a .969 fielding percentage. The lone Tiger American League leader was Gehringer in putouts (396), errors (30) and double plays (110) at second base. Shortstop Rogell led the Bengals in defensive WAR (1.4).

Earl Whitehill starred for sparce crowds including a 4-3 win at St. Louis with 500 at Sportsman Park on Saturday, April 30 (W 3-0, 9 IP, 2 ER), 8-3 win over visiting Washington at home before 500 on Wednesday, September 14 (W 14-12, 9 IP, 3 ER) and a 12-0 shutout of the Browns at home on Friday, September 23 (W 16-12, 9 IP, 0 ER, 3 H) with a mere 600 at Navin Field.

1930s Hitting Triples	
1. Charlie Gehringer	76
2. Billy Rogell	64
3. Hank Greenberg	53
4. Pete Fox	48
5. John Stone	45
6. Marv Owen	38
7. Roy Johnson	34
Marty McManus	34
9. Jo-Jo White	33
10. Gee Walker	32

Team. Detroit finished in fifth at 75-79 (.539) under Bucky Harris (73-79) and Del Baker (2-0), with 320,972 fans. The team went 8-8 in April including a three-game sweep of St. Louis at home. Billy Rogell 4-for-4 and Firpo Marberry (9 IP, 1 ER) led a 5-1 win on Saturday, April 22, with a Tommy Bridges (9 IP, 0 ER, 1 H, 6 SO) 2-0 shutout on Sunday, followed by a Carl Fischer (8.2 IP, 2 ER) led 4-3 victory on Monday. The Tigers were 8-15 in May, as they endured a record of 2-9 for a two-week stretch thru Monday, May 22. Ray Hayworth (HR, 2 RBI), Rogell (2 RBI) and Pete Fox 4-for-6, along with rookies Hank Greenberg (HR, 2 RBI) and Schoolboy Rowe (9 IP, 1 ER, 8 SO) rolled to a 10-1 victory in Philadelphia on Friday, May 26. Players were 17-14 in June including a 16-4 home victory against Boston on Saturday, June 24, led by John Stone (HR, 4 RBI), Marv Owen 3-for-5 (HR, 5 RBI, 4 R) and pitcher Vic Frazier (9 IP, 4 ER) went 3-for-4. Gee Walker hit .400 for the period June 24-July 4 (9 GM, .400 BA, .415 OBP, .575 SLG, .500 BAbip). Detroit was 14-14 in July, with 24 of the 28 games on the road. Vic Sorrell (10.2 IP, 1 ER) lost 1-0 11-inning heartbreaker at Boston on Wednesday, July 12. Gehringer was exemplary during July 21-August 22 (31 GM, .429 BA, .469 OBP, .602 SLG, .429 BAbip). The squad had a 16-15 mark in in August including a 13-inning 15-6 home loss to Cleveland on Saturday, August 5, as the Indians had a nine-run thirteenth inning, with Tiger Hayworth 5-for-6. Sorrell (W 8-11, 17 IP, 3 ER, 17 H, 4 BB, 5 SO) went the distance facing 70 batters in a 17-inning 6-5 victory in Chicago on Sunday, August 13. Greenberg went 4-for-8 (2 RBI) with three doubles. The club closed 11-13 in September and 1-0 in October, with six straight wins to end the season. Rookie Elden Auker (9 IP, 3 ER) won 10-3 at Philadelphia on Thursday, September 21, behind Fox (3 RBI), Harry Davis (3 RBI), Stone 3-for-5 (HR, 2 RBI) and Gehringer 3-for-4 (RBI). Auker (9 IP, 0 ER, 4 H) then shutout Cleveland 3-0 at home on Saturday, September 30. Motown was 43-35 (.551) at home, including 6-0 in September and 32-44 (.421) on the road. Detroit scored 722 runs while allowing 733. Class "AA" Toronto had Ike Boone (.357 BA), Ralph Birkofer (16-8 .667) and Luke Hamlin (21-13 .618). Elden Auker (16-10 .615, 2.50 ERA) pitched at class "A" Beaumont.

P * VIC FRAZIER

Offense. Detroit finished with a .269 BA, .329 OBP, .380 SLG, .709 OPS, 2,089 TB, with an OPS+ of 87. Ray Hayworth (.245 BA, HR, 45 RBI) was the catcher. Hank Greenberg (.301 BA, 12 HR, 85 RBI) played first base and led in slugging (.468), BAbip (.343), secondary average (.278), isolated power (.167) and strikeouts (78). Player of the Year and the most effective hitter Charlie Gehringer (.325 BA, 12 HR, 108 RBI) at second base led the team for plate appearances (705), at bats (628), runs (104), hits (204), singles (144), doubles (42), runs batted in, on-base percentage (.393), slugging (.468), OPS (.862), OPS+ (126), total average (.855), base-out percentage (.866), gross production average (.294), WAR (7.2), oWAR (5.4), batters run average (.183), batting average, times on base (275), base runs (109), runs produced (200), runs created (116), extra base hits (60), total bases (294), bases produced (367) and outs (434). Marv Owen (.262 BA, 2 HR, 64 RBI) was at third. Shortstop Billy Rogell (.295 BA, 57 RBI) led in doubles (42) and walks (79). Gee Walker (.280 BA, 9 HR, 63 RBI) in left led for power/speed number (13.4), steals (26) and stolen bases runs (2.4). Centerfielder Pete Fox (.288 BA, 7 HR, 58 RBI) led in triples (13), in-play percentage (87%) and 18-game hit streak. John Stone (.280 BA, 11 HR, 80 RBI) manned right-field. Schoolboy Rowe (.220 BA, 6 RBI) led the pitchers. The top pinch-hitters were Heinie Schuble at .500 (4-8) and Jo-Jo White .435 (10-23, 8 RBI). Gehringer and Rogell both tied for the MLB lead in games played (155). Gehringer and Greenberg led team in homers (12).

1930s Hitting Home Runs	
1. Hank Greenberg	206
2. Charlie Gehringer	146
3. Rudy York	88
4. Gee Walker	61
5. Pete Fox	54
6. Goose Goslin	50
7. John Stone	41
8. Billy Rogell	39
9. Marv Owen	25
10. Dale Alexander	23

Pitching. The Tigers had a 3.95 ERA, 69 CG, six SHO, 561 walks, 575 SO, 109 ERA+, 4.01 FIP, 1.413 WHIP, 3.6 BB/9, and 3.7 SO/9. Staff led league in innings (1,398), balks (6) and H/9 (9.1). Pitcher of the Year and most effective pitcher Firpo Marberry (16-11, 3.29 ERA) led league in WHIP (1.229), as he led his team in games (37), wins, starts (32), innings (238.1), LOB% (71.1), pWAR (5.3) and R/9 (3.7). Tommy Bridges (14-12, 3.09 ERA) led league in hit by pitch (6), and H/9 (7.4). Bridges led staff in complete games (17), shutouts (2), walks (110), strikeouts (120), earned run average, ERA+ (139), H/9 (7.4) and quality starts (18). Carl Fischer (11-15, 3.55 ERA) led league in homers per nine (0.2). Vic Sorrell (11-15, 3.79 ERA) led in hits (233), homers (18), earned runs (98) and runs (112). Schoolboy Rowe (7-4, 3.58 ERA) led in win percentage (.636), FIP (3.10), DICE (3.3), SO/9 (5.5) and SO/BB (2.42). Chief Hogsett (6-10, 4.50 ERA) led MLB in games finished (34), as he led staff for games (45) and saves (9). Art Herring (1-2, 3.84 ERA), Whit Wyatt (0-1, 4.24 ERA), Elden Auker (3-3, 5.24 ERA) and Vic Frazier (5-5, 6.64 ERA).

Defense. Detroit committed 178 errors for a .971 fielding percentage. The Bengals led the league for putouts (4,193) and double plays (167). Tigers leading the league included second baseman Gehringer in chances (917), assists (542) and double plays (111), as Rogell led in chances (903), putouts (326), and double plays (116) at shortstop. Walker led all American League leftfielders in errors (14) and double plays (4). Gehringer and Rogell tied for the team lead in defensive War (2.3).

Hank Greenberg was in the minors at Raleigh/Hartford in 1930 (.303 BA, 27 2B, 16 3B, 21 HR), Evansville/Beaumont in 1931 (.317 BA, 41 2B, 10 3B, 15 HR) and Beaumont in 1932 (.290 BA, 31 2B, 11 3B, 39 HR) to earn a spot in the 1933 Tiger lineup.

Gehringer was 4-for-5 in a 10-9 win over Washington on Sunday, May 7; 4-for-5 (1 HR, 4 RBI) in an 8-7 win at Cleveland on Monday, June 5; 4-for-5 in a 11-7 loss at New York Sunday, July 9, and 4-for-6 in a 12-8 win at Washington Sunday, July 23.

1930s Hitting Runs Batted In	
1. Charlie Gehringer	1,003
2. Hank Greenberg	853
3. Billy Rogell	532
4. Gee Walker	468
5. Pete Fox	445
6. Marv Owen	421
7. Goose Goslin	369
8. John Stone	320
9. Rudy York	298
10. Ray Hayworth	228

Team. Detroit won the pennant for Mickey Cochrane at 101-53 (.656), with 919,161 fans. The Tigers lost the World Series in seven games to the St. Louis Cardinals, as former Tiger George Moriarty was an umpire. They were 6-4 in April, as Carl Fischer (9 IP, 5 H, 0 ER, 6 SO) had a 4-0 shutout at Cleveland on Friday, April 20. Detroit had a 15-14 record in May including a 14-4 loss on Sunday, May 6, as the Red Sox scored 12 runs in the fourth. Firpo Marberry tied an MLB record by serving up four straight triples. Vic Sorrell (9 IP, 0 ER, 2 H) had a 5-0 shutout at Washington on Monday, May 14. Detroit was 19-8 in June when Billy Rogell (5 RBI), Charlie Gehringer 4-for-5 (3 RBI) and Marberry (W 7-2, 9 IP, 0 ER, 4 H) 1-for-4 (2 RBI) led a 12-0 shutout in Chicago on Saturday, June 2. Cochrane (HR, 3 RBI) and Gehringer (HR, 3 RBI) paced a 11-2 win on Sunday. Sorrell (9 IP, 2 ER), Gehringer 4-for-5 (3 R, 6 RBI) and Hank Greenberg 3-for-5 (HR, 4 RBI) led a 20-2 home win over Cleveland on Tuesday, with 21 hits and a nine-run fourth inning. The players were 20-11 in July, including a 4-2 home loss to New York on Friday, July 13, when Babe Ruth hit his 700th home. Players were 23-6 (.793) in August when they were 9-0 at home and won 14 straight games. Elden Auker (W 9-4, 9 IP, 0 ER, 4 H) threw a 3-0 shutout at Cleveland on Thursday, August 2. Detroit swept visiting Chicago the weekend of August 3-5, Schoolboy Rowe (W 15-4, 7 IP, 0 ER, 1 H) pitched a 14-0 shutout and was 3-for-4 (2 RBI) on Friday. Red Phillips (9 IP, 4 ER) won 16-4 on Saturday led by Greenberg (HR, 4 RBI), with a Tommy Bridges (W 14-6, 9 IP 0 ER, 6 H) 7-0 shutout on Sunday. Marberry was effective for the month of August 7-September 8 (4-0, 1.17 ERA, .200 BA, .218 SLG). The team closed 18-10 in September, with a 15-1 Fischer (7 IP, 1 ER) win at St. Louis on Saturday, September 22, as Goslin was 5-for-5 (RBI) and Gehringer 3-for-5 (4 RBI). Detroit had a 11-run seventh inning. Gehringer (3B, 1B, 3 RBI) starred in the inning. The Tigers were 17-5 against Chicago, 54-26 (.675) at home, and 47-27 (.635) on the road. Motown scored a team record 958 runs and allowed 708, as the eight position starters averaged 103 runs. Claude Capps (47-for-107, .439 BA, .738 SLG) was exceptional for class "D" Charleroi.

P * SCHOOLBOY ROWE

Offense. Detroit had a .376 OBP, .424 SLG, .800 OPS, 2,320 TB, and 106 OPS+. Motown led the league in batting average (.300), runs (958), doubles (349) and stolen bases (124). Most Valuable Player Mickey Cochrane (.320 BA, 2 HR, 75 RBI) was the catcher. First baseman, Player of the Year, and most effective hitter Hank Greenberg (.339 BA, 26 HR, 139 RBI) led MLB in extra base hits (96), with league high for doubles (63) and BAbip (.369). *"Hammerin' Hank"* led the Tigers in home runs, runs batted in, slugging (.600), OPS (1.005), OPS+ (156), total average (1.071), base-out percentage (1.081), gross production average (.332), batters run average (.239), secondary average (.374), runs created (144), isolated power (.261), power/speed number (13.4), total bases (356), bases produced (428) and strikeouts (93). Second baseman Charlie Gehringer (.356 BA, 11 HR, 127 RBI) led MLB in runs (135) and league in hits (214). *"The Mechanical Man"* led Motown in singles (146), on-base percentage (.450), gross production average (.332), WAR (8.4), oWAR (7.5), batting average, times on base (316), base runs (137), runs produced (251) and walks (99). Marv Owen (.317 BA, 8 HR, 98 RBI) at third led his team in triples (9). Billy Rogell (.296 BA, 3 HR, 99 RBI) was the shortstop. Left-fielder Goose Goslin (.305 BA, 13 HR, 100 RBI) led in at bats (614), outs (436) and 30-game hit streak. Jo-Jo White (.313 BA 43 RBI) at center led in steals (28) and stolen base runs (4.8). Pete Fox (.285 BA, 2 HR, 44 RBI) was in right. Outfielder Gee Walker (.300 BA, 6 HR, 40 RBI) led Motown for in-play percentage (86%). Schoolboy Rowe (.303 BA, 2 HR, 22 RBI) led pitchers in batting. The best Tiger pinch-hitter was Walker at .294 (5-17). Gehringer, Owen and Rogell were tied for MLB lead in games (154).

1930s Hitting On-Base Percentage	
1. Hank Greenberg	.415
2. Charlie Gehringer	.409
3. Goose Goslin	.376
4. John Stone	.364
5. Jo-Jo White	.363
6. Billy Rogell	.362
7. Pete Fox	.353
8. Gee Walker	.351
9. Roy Johnson	.343
10. Marv Owen	.342

Pitching. The team logged a 4.06 ERA, 74 CG, 488 walks, 640 SO, 108 ERA+, 4.10 FIP, 1.426 WHIP, 9.6 H/9, and 4.2 SO/9. The staff led league in wins (101), win percentage (.656), shutouts (13), walks per nine (3.2), strikeouts to walks (1.31), no decisions (39) and cheap wins (21). Pitcher of the Year and most effective pitcher Schoolboy Rowe (24-8, 3.45 ERA, 3 SHO) led league in strikeouts to walks (1.84), as he led his staff in games (45), wins, hits (259), FIP (3.51), DICE (3.39), WHIP (1.278), pWAR (5.8), SO/9 (5.0), SO/BB (1.84) and R/9 (3.7). Elden Auker (15-7, 3.42 ERA) led in earned run average, ERA+ (128) and walks per nine (2.5). Tommy Bridges (22-11, 3.67 ERA, 3 SHO, 3 SV) led league in starts (35). He led club in losses, complete games (23), innings (275), homers (16), walks (104), strikeouts (151), earned runs (112), runs (117), LOB% (71.6), H/9 (8.1) and quality starts (19). Chief Hogsett (3-2, 4.29 ERA, 3 SV) led in games finished (19). Firpo Marberry (15-5, 4.57 ERA). General Crowder (5-1, 4.19 ERA), Carl Fischer (6-4, 4.36 ERA), Vic Sorrell (6-9, 4.79 ERA) and Luke Hamlin (2-3, 5.38 ERA). Class "A" Beaumont had stars Red Phillips (15-5 .750, 2.18 ERA) and Steve Larkin (11-6 .647, 2.57 ERA).

Defense. Detroit made 156 errors for a .974 fielding average. League leaders were pitchers Crowder and Rowe in fielding (1.000), Gehringer in fielding (.981) and assists (516) at second. Owen led in putouts (202) at third base. Rogell led in assists (518) at short, as he led his team in dWAR (2.2). Fox led outfielders in double plays (4) and right-fielders in double plays (3).

Babe Ruth went to Hawaii rather than discuss managing Detroit. Owner Frank Navin then traded a player and $100,000 to Philadelphia for catcher Mickey Cochrane. He as player/manager was the 1934 American League MVP. Schoolboy Rowe won 16 consecutive decisions to tie the MLB record held by superstars Walter Johnson, "Smoky" Joe Wood, and "Lefty" Grove.

1930s Hitting Slugging Percentage	
1. Hank Greenberg	.617
2. Charlie Gehringer	.507
3. Gee Walker	.469
4. John Stone	.460
5. Goose Goslin	.456
6. Pete Fox	.433
7. Roy Johnson	.420
8. Billy Rogell	.381
9. Marv Owen	.374
10. Jo-Jo White	.344

Team. Motown finished first at 93-58 (.616) for Mickey Cochrane, with an attendance of 1,034,929. Detroit won the pennant and defeated the Cubs 4-2 in the World Series. The squad was 5-9 in April as Tommy Bridges (9 IP, 0 ER, 7 SO) threw a 18-0 shutout in St. Louis on Monday, April 29, behind Hank Greenberg (HR, 4 RBI) and Goose Goslin (HR, 3 RBI). Players went 15-8 in May that included a 16-6 win at Washington. Billy Rogell went 4-for-5, Pete Fox 4-for-6 and Ray Hayworth (4 RBI), as 26 Tigers reached base. Players were 18-12 in June with a 10-game win streak. The squad won a doubleheader in St. Louis on Sunday, June 30. The Bengals scored eight first inning runs in a 18-1 Schoolboy Rowe (9 IP, 1 ER) game one victory led by Pete Fox 3-for-5 (6 RBI). Fox then was 5-for-6 (HR, 3 RBI) in the 11-6 victory to follow. The Tigers had recorded back-to-back 19-hit games. Detroit had a 20-8 record in July that included a General Crowder (W 11-6, 9 IP, 0 ER, 4 H) 4-0 shutout in New York on Wednesday, July 24. The Tigers were 23-7 in August as Rowe (W 13-9, 9 IP, 2 ER) went 5-for-5 (3 R, 2B, 3B, 4 RBI) during a 18-2 thrashing of visiting Washington on Wednesday, August 14. Greenberg (3 RBI), Goslin (3 RBI), Cochrane (2 RBI) and Rogell (2 RBI) victimized Senators Bobo Newsom (2 IP, 8 ER, 6 H, 2 BB) and Jim Hayes (2 IP, 7 ER, 6 H, 3 BB). Elden Auker (W 14-5, 9 IP, 3 ER) and Greenberg 3-for-5 (HR, 5 RBI) led a 13-3 victory at St. Louis on Thursday, August 29. Players closed 12-14 in September with a 15-1 win in Philadelphia on Saturday, September 7, with Auker (W 16-5, 9 IP, 1 ER, 2 H) and Charlie Gehringer 4-for-6 (5 RBI). Motown went 17-5 (.773) versus St. Louis, with an amazing 38-14 (.731) mark in blowout games. Players were 53-25 (.679) at home, 40-33 (.548) on the road, scored 919 runs and allowed 665. Class "AA" Portland featured Moose Clabaugh (.342 BA, 56 2B, 311 TB), Nino Bongiovanni (.338 BA, 244 H, 303 TB), Gil English (.327 BA, 221 H), Chester Wilburn (.317 BA, 225 H) and Bill Cissell (.316 BA, 204 H). Class "A" Beaumont had stars Al Vincent (.312 BA), Bud Bates (.308 BA), Rudy York, .301 BA, 32 HR, .572 SLG), Red Phillips (20-11 .645, 2.80 ERA), Pat McLaughlin (14-9 .609, 3.23 ERA) and George Gill (16-11 .593, 3.13 ERA).

P * GENERAL CROWDER

Offense. Detroit finished with a .290 BA, .366 OBP, .435 SLG, .801 OPS, 2,358 TB, and 110 OPS+. Catcher Mickey Cochrane (.319 BA, 5 HR, 46 RBI) led in on-base percentage (.452) and walks (96). Most Valuable Player, Player of the Year, and most effective hitter Hank Greenberg (.328 BA, 36 HR, 168 RBI) at first base led MLB in Homers, runs batted in, total bases (389, extra base hits (98) and runs created (159. Hank led the league in isolated power (.300). He led his team in games (152), plate appearances (710), at bats (619), hits (203), doubles (46), triples (16), slugging (.628), OPS (1.039), OPS+ (170), total average (1.138), base-out percentage (1.144), gross production average (.342), oWAR (7.3), batters run average (.257), BAbip (.339), times on base (290), base runs (144), runs produced (252), bases produced (480) and strikeouts (91). Second baseman Charlie Gehringer (.330 BA, 19 HR, 108 RBI) led in runs (123), singles (142), WAR (7.8), batting average and outs (430). Marv Owen (.263 BA, 2 HR, 72 RBI) played at third, with Billy Rogell (.275 BA, 6 HR, 74 RBI) at short and Goose Goslin (.292 BA, 9 HR, 111 RBI) in left. Jo-Jo White (.240 BA, 2 HR, 33 RBI) at center led in steals (19). Pete Fox (.321 BA, 15 HR, 72 RBI) in right led team in power/speed number (14.5), stolen base runs (1.8) and hitting streak (29). Gee Walker (.301 BA, 7 HR, 56 RBI) was a reserve. Schoolboy Rowe (.312 BA, 3 HR, 28 RBI) led pitchers, as he terrified fellow pitchers August 4-September 21 (12 GM, 3 HR, 13 RBI, .444 BA, .459 OBP, .806 SLG, .464 BAbip). The top pinch-hitters were Fox at .600 (3-5) and Gee Walker .538 (7-13).

1930s Hitting On-Base plus Slugging	
1. Hank Greenberg	1.032
2. Charlie Gehringer	.916
3. Goose Goslin	.832
4. John Stone	.823
5. Gee Walker	.820
6. Pete Fox	.786
7. Roy Johnson	.763
8. Billy Rogell	.742
9. Marv Owen	.717
10. Jo-Jo White	.707

Pitching. The Tigers recorded a 3.82 ERA, 522 walks, 584 SO, 109 ERA+, 4.16 FIP, 1.438 WHIP, 9.5 H/9, 3.4 BB/9, and 3.9 SO/9, with league lead for wins, win percentage, complete games (87), shutouts (16), HBP (30), balks (4) and in quality starts (87). Detroit had consecutive home shutouts of 7-0 against New York on Friday, June 21 and 7-0 over Washington the next day. Pitcher of the Year Tommy Bridges (21-10, 3.51 ERA) led league in homers (22), strikeouts (163) and quality starts' (21). He led staff in wins, CG (23), hits (277), walks (113), wild pitches (5), runs (129), earned run average, ERA+ (118) and SO/9 (5.3). The most effective pitcher Schoolboy Rowe (19-13, 3.69 ERA) led MLB in shutouts (6), SO/BB (2.06). He led his staff in games (42), losses, innings (275.2), FIP (3.32), DICE (3.26), WHIP (1.233), pWAR (3.7), H/9 (8.9), HR/9 (0.4), BB/9 (2.2) and SO/BB (2.06). Eldon Auker (18-7, 3.83 ERA) led league in win percentage (.720) and staff in LOB% (74.4). General Crowder (16-10, 4.26 ERA) led in earned runs (114). Chief Hogsett (6-6, 3.54 ERA) led MLB in games finished (30) and team in saves (5). Roxie Lawson (3-2, 1.58 ERA), Joe Sullivan (6-6, 3.51 ERA) and Vic Sorrell (4-3, 4.03 ERA). Rowe excelled during period of July 31-September 9 (8-1 .899, 66 IP, 1.77 ERA, .207 BA, 7 CG, 3 SHO).

Defense. Detroit led league in fielding average (.979) with 126 errors. League leaders were Crowder and Auker in pitcher fielding (1.000), Greenberg in assists (99) at first, Gehringer in fielding average (.985) and assists (489) at second. Rogell in fielding average (.971), double plays (104) and team defensive WAR (2.7) at short. Fox led in fielding average (.991) in right.

Michigander Frank Navin from Lenawee County served the Franchise from 1902 to his death on Wednesday, November 13, 1935. He was instrumental in acquiring future Hall of Famers and realized his dream, with the 1935 World Championship.

MVP Hank Greenberg (120 R, 46 2B, 16 3B, 36 HR, 168 RBI, .328 BA, .411 OBP, .628 SLG, 389 TB, 170 OPS+) had one of the best seasons ever. He had a sequential five-game runs batted in streak of 0 RBI, 1 RBI, 2 RBI, 3 RBI and 4 RBI for June 20-23.

1930s Pitching Wins		
1.	Tommy Bridges	150
2.	Schoolboy Rowe	80
3.	Eldon Auker	77
4.	Vic Sorrell	57
5.	Earl Whitehill	46
6.	Chief Hogsett	38
	Roxie Lawson	38
8.	Firpo Marberry	31
9.	George Uhle	29
10.	General Crowder	25

Team. Detroit finished second at 83-71 (.539) under managers Mickey Cochrane (65-55) and Del Baker (18-16), with 875,948 fans. Charlie Gehringer started the season strong April 14-May 4 (16 GM, 14 RBI, .408 BA, .648 SLG), as the club went 7-6 in April. Elden Auker (9 IP, 0 ER, 6 H) and Hank Greenberg (4 RBI) led a 10-0 shutout at St. Louis on Thursday, April 23. Players were 16-15 in May, as Motown edged New York 10-9 at home on Thursday, May 21, behind Gehringer 4-for-6, Goose Goslin 4-for-6, Marv Owen 3-for-4 (3 RBI) and Chad Kimsey (4 IP, 0 ER). Pitcher Auker was 3-for-4 (4 RBI) at the plate during a 13-10 win at Cleveland the next day. The Bengals were 13-11 in June including a 18-9 win aided by a 10-run third inning at Philadelphia on Thursday, June 4, as Cochrane had a grand slam homer and Gehringer went 3-for-4 (6 RBI). Gee Walker excelled June 21-July 9 (14 GM, 29 RBI, .463 BA, .687 SLG) and Gehringer June 24-July 22 (25 GM, 25 RBI, .410 BA, .690 SLG). Detroit went 8-2 in a 10-game stretch June 23-July 4 led by Al Simmons (10 GM, 3 HR, 16 RBI, .500 BA, .571 OBP, .857 SLG, .486 BAbip). The squad had a 16-14 July mark with a 25-hit attack during a 21-6 Tommy Bridges (W 9-5) led victory at Chicago on Wednesday, July 1. Gehringer was 4-for-6 (3 RBI), Goslin 4-for-6 and Walker 4-for-7 (HR, 7 RBI). The Tigers were 16-16 in August with a 13-4 home win against Washington on Saturday, August 1, with Simmons 4-for-5 (4 R, 2 HR, 5 RBI) and Ray Hayworth 3-for-4 (HR, 3 RBI). Walker went 5-for-5 at Boston during a Schoolboy Rowe (W 15-7, 9 IP, 0 ER, 2 H) 5-0 shut out on Tuesday, August 25. Detroit closed 15-9 in September that included nine straight wins. The Bengals won a home doubleheader versus St. Louis 12-0 and 14-0 on Tuesday, September 22. Auker (9 IP, 0 ER, 5 H), Simmons 3-for-5 (HR, 5 RBI) and Birdie Tebbetts 3-for-5 (HR) led game one, followed by a Bridges (W 23-10, 9 IP, 0 ER, 3 H) gem aided by Pete Fox (5 RBI). The team was 44-33 (.571) at home and 39-38 (.506) on the road. Motown scored 921 runs and allowed 871. Class "D" Alexandria manager Art Phelan led stars Cecil Dunn (219 H, 45 2B, 13 3B, 47 HR, .378 BA, .744 SLG, 431 TB), James Morris (16-3 .842), Quinn Lee (22-5 .815), and Bob Harris (18-7 .720). Class "D" Tiffin featured Jack Suydam (23 HR, .385 BA, .683 SLG), Zeke Clementi (37 HR, .377 BA, .798 SLG.) and Edward Bastien (18-8 .692). Louis Batterson of Ann Arbor, Michigan, hit a prodigious .429 (21-for-49) during a 13-game stretch for class "B" Augusta.

1B * JACK BURNS

Offense. Detroit had a .291 BA, .366 OBP, .398, .765 OPS, 2,116 TB and 99 OPS+. Ray Hayworth (.240 BA, HR, 30 RBI) caught, Jack Burns (.283 BA, 4 HR, 63 RBI) was at first. Player of the Year and the most effective hitter Charlie Gehringer (.354 BA, 15 HR, 116 RBI) at second led the league in doubles (60). He led Motown in plate appearances (731), at bats (641), runs (144), hits (227), triples (12), on-base percentage (.431), slugging (.555), OPS (.987), OPS+ (142), total average (1.075), base-out percentage (1.077), gross production average (.333), WAR (7.4), oWAR (6.9), batters run average (.239), hitting, times on base (314), base runs (142), runs produced (245), runs created (154), extra base hits (87), total bases (356) and bases produced (443). Marv Owen (.295 BA, 9 HR, 105 RBI) manned third, as shortstop Billy Rogell (.274 BA, 6 HR, 68 RBI) led in outs (441). Goose Goslin (.315 BA, 24 HR, 125 RBI) in left led in homers, runs batted in, secondary average (.378), isolated power (.212), power/speed number (17.7), stolen base runs (1.8), walks (85) and strikeouts (50). Centerfielder Al Simmons (.327 BA, 13 HR, 112 RBI). Right-fielder Gee Walker (.353 BA, 12 HR, 93 RBI) led in BAbip (.358), in-play percentage (86%) and steals (17). Pete Fox (.305 BA, 4 HR, 26 RBI). Elden Auker (.308 BA, 15 RBI) and Red Phillips (.303 BA) led pitchers. Jo-Jo White .357 (10-28, 5 RBI) led pinch-hitters.

1930s Pitching Winning Percentage		
1.	Eldon Auker	.647
2.	Roxie Lawson	.603
3.	Schoolboy Rowe	.602
4.	Tommy Bridges	.595
5.	Slick Coffman	.565
6.	Earl Whitehill	.529
7.	George Uhle	.492
8.	Vic Sorrell	.483
9.	Chief Hogsett	.458
10.	Art Herring	.375

Pitching. The Tigers recorded a 5.00 ERA, 76 CG, 562 walks, 526 SO, 99 ERA+, 4.73 FIP, 1.566 WHIP, 10.4 H/9, 3.7 BB/9, and 3.5 SO/9, with a league lead in SHO (13). Pitcher of the Year Tommy Bridges (23-11, 3.60 ERA) led MLB in starts (38), with league lead in wins, strikeouts (175) and quality starts (20). Tommy led Detroit in win percentage (.676), complete games (26), shutouts (5), innings (294.2), hits (289), homers (21), walks (115), hit by pitch (5), wild pitches (6), runs (141), LOB% (70.6), earned run average, ERA+ (137), pWAR (6.4), hits per nine (8.8), SO/9 (5.3) and runs per nine (4.3). The most effective pitcher Schoolboy Rowe (19-10, 4.51 ERA, 41 GM) led in earned runs (123), FIP (3.93), DICE (3.66), WHIP (1.345), BB/9 (2.3) and SO/BB (1.80). Eldon Auker (13-16, 4.89 ERA) led league in tough loses (5), with staff lead in losses and HR/9 (0.5). Chad Kimsey (2-3, 4.85 ERA, 3 SV) led in games finished (17). Vic Sorrell (6-7, 5.28 ERA, 3 SV), Jake Wade (4-5, 5.29 ERA), Roxie Lawson (8-6, 5.48 ERA, 41 GM, 3 SV), Red Phillips (2-4, 6.49 ERA), Joe Sullivan (2-5, 6.78 ERA) and General Crowder (4-3, 8.39 ERA).

Defense. Players committed a league low 154 errors for a .974 fielding average. League leaders were pitchers Bridges in putouts (19), Hogsett in errors (6), Auker in assists (60) and double plays (7). Gehringer led in chances (946), chances per game (6.1), assists (524), errors (25), double plays (116) and fielding average (.974) at second. Owen in third led in base putouts (190) and double plays (28), Rogell in fielding average (.965) at short, as he led team in dWAR (1.5). Simmons led outfielders in fielding average (.986) in center and Walker led the league in assists (14) and double plays (5) in right field.

The duo of Al Simmons (7 GM, 2 HR, 9 RBI, 18-for-29, .621 BA, .656 OBP, .966 SLG, 1.622 OPS, .615 BAbip) and Gee Walker (8 GM, 2 HR, 11 RBI, 21-for-37, .568 BA, .600 OBP, .946 SLG, 1.546 OPS, .576 BAbip) dominated for the period August 1-8.

19-year-old Barney McCosky (19 3B, .400 BA, .614 SLG) of Detroit Southwestern High School shined in his pro debut at Class "C" Charleston. Teammates included Ralph Hodgin (41 2B, .337 BA), Ignatius Walters (.336 BA), and Stan Corbett (20-9 .690).

Detroit Tigers 1937 American League

1930s Pitching Games Started		
1.	Tommy Bridges	266
2.	Eldon Auker	136
3.	Vic Sorrell	130
4.	Schoolboy Rowe	119
5.	Earl Whitehill	96
6.	George Uhle	62
7.	Roxie Lawson	60
8.	Firpo Marberry	53
9.	General Crowder	48
10.	Chief Hogsett	46

Team. Detroit had a second-place finish at 89-65-1 (.578) under Mickey Cochrane (42-33-1), Del Baker (41-23), and Cy Perkins (6-9), with an attendance of 1,072,276. The Tigers were 4-2 in April, as they opened with an Elden Auker (9 IP, 2 ER) 4-3 win over visiting Cleveland on Tuesday, April 20, as Gee Walker went 4-for-4 and hit for the cycle. Players were 16-15 in May when Hank Greenberg (HR, 4 RBI) hit a homer to centerfield that left Fenway Park during an 11-9 loss on Saturday, May 22. The Bengals defeated the visiting Browns 18-3 on Sunday, May 30, as Walker was 4-for-6 (2 HR, 7 RBI) and Greenberg 5-for-5 (2 HR, 5 RBI, 4 R). Detroit was 15-10 in June with a 9-8 win in 15-innings at Washington on Tuesday, June 15, as reliver Boots Poffenberger (6.1 IP, 0 ER, 3 H) got the win and was 1-for-3 at the plate. The squad had a 16-10 record in July, as Tommy Bridges (W 10-3, 9 IP, 0 ER, 5 H, 6 SO) shutout Washington 6-0 at home on Saturday, July 17, with Charlie Gehringer (HR, 3 RBI). The Tigers were 19-12 in August when Gehringer thoroughly dominated pitching the week of August 8-14 (17-for-26, 14 R, 4 HR, 15 RBI, 9 BB, .654 BA, .743 OBP, 1.231 SLG, .591 BAbip). Motown won a home series over St. Louis, with a 7-6 win on Friday, August 13, and swept a double-header the next day. Auker (9 IP, 1 ER, 4 H) went 2-for-4 (2 HR, 5 RBI, SH) to lead a 16-1 game one rout, with help from Walker 4-for-5, Pete Fox 4-for-6 and Billy Rogell (3 RBI). Poffenberger (W 8-2, 9 IP) went 2-for-4 (RBI) to win game two 20-7, as the 22-hit attack was led by Gehringer 5-for-5 (2 HR, 6 RBI), Walker 3-for-5 (HR, 4 RBI), Goose Goslin (HR, 3 RBI), rookie Rudy York (HR, 2 RBI), and Fox 3-for-5 (HR). The 36 runs in a doubleheader set an MLB record, as Gehringer went 7-for-8 on the day. The Tigers defeated Washington 12-3 at home on Tuesday, August 31, as Roxie Lawson (W 17-4, 9 IP, 2 ER), York 4-for-4 (2 HR, 7 RBI) and Fox (HR, 2 RBI) starred. The team closed 17-15 in September with George Gill dominating September 2-28 (7 GM, 6-0 1.000, 2.13 ERA, .235 BA). Gill (W 11-3, 9 IP, 0 ER, 5 H) won 6-1 in St. Louis on Tuesday, September 28, with Greenberg (2 RBI) and Marv Owen (2 RBI). Players were 2-1 in October when Jake Wade (9 IP, 0 ER, 1 H, 4 BB, 7 SO) pitched a one-hit 1-0 shutout of Cleveland at home on Sunday, October 3, as Indian righthander Johnny Allen (15-1) lost his bid for an undefeated record. The franchise went 16-6 versus Washington, 49-28 (.636) at home and 40-37 (.519) in road games. Detroit scored 935 runs and they allowed 841.

OF * GEE WALKER

Offense. Detroit had a .370 OBP, .452 SLG, .822 OPS, 2,494 TB, and 104 OPS+, with league high average (.292). Catcher Rudy York (.307 BA, 35 HR, 101 RBI) led MLB in AB/HR (10.7) and team for isolated power (.344). Player of the Year Hank Greenberg (.337 BA, 40 HR, 184 RBI) at first led MLB in runs batted, extra base hits (103) and runs created (172), He led league qualifiers in isolated power (.332). Hank led club for games (154), plate appearances (701), at bats (594), runs (137), doubles (49), triples (14), home runs, slugging (.668), OPS (1.105 OPS), OPS+ (172), WAR (7.7), oWAR (7.6), batters run average (.291), secondary average (.512), times on base (305), base runs (155), runs produced (281), runs created (173), total bases (397), bases produced (507), walks (102) and strikeouts (101). Most Valuable Player Charlie Gehringer (.371 BA, 14 HR, 96 RBI) at second led league in hitting (.371), BAbip (.371). He led team in singles (154) and on-base percentage (.458). Marv Owen (.288 BA, HR, 45 RBI) at third led for in-play percentage (84%), Billy Rogell (.276 BA, 8 HR, 64 RBI) at short. Leftfielder Gee Walker (.335 BA, 18 HR, 113 RBI) led MLB in power/speed number (20.2), with squad lead for at bats (635), hits (213), stolen bases (23), stolen base runs (2.7) and hitting streak (27). Jo-Jo White (.246 BA, 21 RBI) was in center. Pete Fox (.331 BA, 12 HR, 82 RBI) in right led for in-play percentage (84%) and outs (438). Roxie Lawson (.259 BA, 6 RBI) led the pitchers. White at .400 (2-5) and Goslin (2 HR, 6 RBI) led Tiger pinch-hitters.

1930s Pitching Complete Games		
1.	Tommy Bridges	156
2.	Schoolboy Rowe	77
3.	Eldon Auker	70
4.	Vic Sorrell	55
	Earl Whitehill	55
6.	George Uhle	39
7.	Roxie Lawson	27
8.	Firpo Marberry	22
9.	Bobo Newsom	21
10.	General Crowder	20

Pitching. The Tigers recorded a 4.87 ERA, six SHO, 635 walks, 485 SO, 96 ERA+, 4.73 FIP, 1.565 WHIP, 9.9 H/9, 4.1 BB/9, and 3.2 SO/9. Motown led league in balks (4) and no decisions (39). Pitcher of the Year and most effective pitcher Eldon Auker (17-9, 3.88 ERA, 0.5 HR/9) led in games (39), starts (32), complete games (19), innings (252.2), HBP (6), ERA, ERA+ (120), WHIP (1.373), pWAR (4.3), runs per nine (4.5) and quality starts (18). Tommy Bridges (15-12, 4.07 ERA) led in losses, shutouts (3), hits (267), strikeouts (138), LOB% (68.2), FIP (3.88), DICE (3.82), walks per nine (3.3), strikeouts per nine (5.1) and SO/BB (1.52). Slick Coffman (7-5, 4.65 ERA) led league in balks (2). Roxie Lawson (18-7, 5.26 ERA) led in wins, win percentage (.720), homers (17), walks (115), wild pitches (6), earned runs (127) and runs (141). Jake Wade (7-10, 5.39 ERA) led league in no decisions (9) and club in hits per nine (8.7). George Gill (11-4, 4.51 ERA) led in games finished (18). Jack Russell (2-5, 7.59 ERA) led in saves (4). Boots Poffenberger (10-5, 4.65 ERA, 0.5 HR/9), Pat McLaughlin (0-2, 6.34 ERA) and Schoolboy Rowe (1-4, 8.62 ERA).

Defense. Detroit led the league in fewest errors (147) and in fielding percentage (.976). Tiger league leaders were pitchers Wade in fielding (1.000), Lawson in putouts (16), Auker in pitcher chances (90) and assists (72). York led in catcher passed balls (12), Greenberg in chances (1,592) and putouts (1,477) at first base, as Gehringer led second baseman in fielding percentage (.986) and team in defensive WAR (1.1). Owen led in fielding (.970) at third and Rogell in fielding (.968) at short.

Catcher Rudy York (30 GM, .363 BA, .429 OBP, .920 SLG, 1.329 OPS) had a historic month of August. His 18 homers broke Babe Ruth's record of 17 set back in September of 1927 and his 50 RBIs broke Lou Gehrig's record of 48 set in August 1935.

Babe Herman (.348 BA) and Alta Cohen (15-7 .682) played for class "AA" Toledo. Ed Hall (.333 BA) and Fred Frink (.323 BA) were stars at class "A" Sioux City. Class "A1" Beaumont featured Michigan native Barney McCosky (.318 BA) from Detroit.

1930s Pitching Earned Run Average	
1. Tommy Bridges	3.76
2. George Uhle	3.84
3. Schoolboy Rowe	4.11
4. Eldon Auker	4.26
5. Vic Sorrell	4.27
6. Earl Whitehill	4.28
7. Art Herring	4.53
8. Chief Hogsett	4.56
9. Roxie Lawson	5.14
10. Slick Coffman	5.38

Team. Detroit finished fourth for Mickey Cochrane (47-51) and Del Baker (37-19 .661) at 84-70 (.545), with an attendance of 799,557. The Tigers were 5-6 in April when Chet Laabs (HR, 5 RBI) and Vern Kennedy (9 IP, 1 ER) were instrumental in a 10-1 win in St. Louis on Monday, April 25. The club was 13-12 in May, as Rudy York (HR, 5 RBI) led a 13-7 home win of Washington on Monday, May 16. The squad went 15-15 in June including a 18-12 victory at Washington on Sunday, June 12. Charlie Gehringer went 4-for-6 (HR, 3 RBI), and York (HR, 3 RBI), with a 10 run Tiger sixth inning. The 13-13 mark in July included an Elden Auker (9 IP, 0 ER, 4 H) 4-0 home shutout of Chicago on Saturday, July 9, aided by Hank Greenberg 3-for-3 (2 HR, 3 RBI). The Tigers were 8-0 for the week of Sunday, July 24, as Greenberg (.571 OBP, 1.483 SLG, 2.054 OPS, 9 HR, 21 RBI, 11 R, 6 BB) hit .483 for the week, with his ninth homer tying Babe Ruth's record set in 1930. Greenberg (2 HR, 2 RBI) powered a 6-5 home win against Washington on Tuesday, July 26, with 68,000 fans at Briggs Stadium. Auker (9 IP, 1 ER) and Greenberg 3-for-4 (2 HR, 4 RBI) led the 9-2 win versus Philadelphia at home on Friday, July 29. Detroit had a record of 16-14 in August including a Greenberg (2 HR, 5 RBI) walk-off homer for reliever Jake Wade (5 IP, 0 ER, 1 H) who defeated the Browns 8-7 on Friday, August 19. The Bengals were 20-9 in September and 2-1 in October, with a Boots Poffenberger (5 IP, 0 ER, 3 H) and Gehringer (HR, 2 RBI) led 3-0 five-inning home shutout of Philadelphia on Wednesday, September 21. Detroit beat visiting St. Louis 10-2 in seven innings on Tuesday, September 27, behind Slick Coffman (7 IP, 2 ER), Gehringer (HR, 3 RBI), and Dixie Walker 3-for-4, as Greenberg's (2 HR, 4 RBI) 58th homer set the MLB record for righthanders. George Gill (W 12-9, 9 IP, 0 ER) shutout the Browns 12-0 the next day, aided by Birdie Tebbetts 3-for-5 (HR, 4 RBI). Harry Eisenstat (W 9-6, 9 IP, 1 ER) outdueled future Hall of Famer Bob Feller (9 IP, 4 ER, 18 SO) for a 4-1 win in Cleveland on Sunday, October 2. The Tigers were 48-31 (.608) at home including 9-2 versus Boston, and 36-39 (.480) on the road. Detroit scored 744 runs and allowed 804. Class "AA" Toledo had stars Chet Morgan (.357 BA), Homer Peel (.327 BA), Michigander Benny McCoy (.309 BA, 300 TB) of Jenison, Fred Johnson (12-4 .750) and Johnny Johnson (7-2 .778).

CF * CHET MORGAN

Offense. Detroit had a .272 BA, .359 OBP, .411 SLG, .770 OPS, 2,168 TB, and 87 OPS+. Catcher Rudy York (.298 BA, 33 HR, 127 RBI) hit four grand slam homers. Player of the Year and most effective hitter Hank Greenberg (.315 BA, 58 HR, 147 RBI) at first led MLB in runs (143), homers, walks (119) and AB/HR (9.6). Greenberg led the league in secondary average (.586) and isolated power (.369). Hank led the Tigers in runs batted in, on-base percentage (.438), slugging (.683), OPS (1.122), OPS+ (169), total average (1.306), base-out percentage (1.316), gross production average (.368), WAR (7.0), oWAR (6.9), batters run average (.298), hitting, times on base (297), base runs (152), runs produced (232), runs created (166), extra base hits (85), total bases (380), and bases produced (506). Second baseman Charlie Gehringer (.306 BA, 20 HR, 107 RBI) led MLB in power/speed number (16.5). He led team for plate appearances (689) and stolen base runs (3.6). Don Ross (.260 BA, HR, 30 RBI) was at third and Billy Rogell (.259 BA, 3 HR, 55 RBI) at short. Dixie Walker (.308, 6 HR, 43 RBI) in left led in BAbip (.322). Chet Morgan (.284 BA, 27 RBI) in center led for in-play percentage (88%). Pete Fox (.293 BA, 7 HR, 96 RBI) in right led for at bats (634), hits (186), singles (134), doubles (35), triples (10), steals (16) and outs (463). Mark Christman (.248 BA, HR, 44 RBI), Jo-Jo White (.262 BA, 15 RBI) and Chet Laabs (.237 BA, 7 HR, 37 RBI) were reserves. Vern Kennedy (.291 BA, 8 RBI) led the pitchers. The leading pinch-hitters were Laabs at .375 (2-7) and Birdie Tebbetts at .375 (2-7). Greenberg's 58 homers tied the league record of 58 set by Jimmy Foxx in 1932. Greenberg and Gehringer led with 13-game hitting streaks.

1930s Pitching Innings Pitched	
1. Tommy Bridges	2,083.0
2. Schoolboy Rowe	1,126.2
3. Eldon Auker	1,083.2
4. Vic Sorrell	1,029.2
5. Earl Whitehill	736.0
6. Chief Hogsett	703.1
7. George Uhle	579.1
8. Roxie Lawson	539.2
9. Firpo Marberry	413.0
10. General Crowder	351.2

Pitching. Motown logged a 4.79 ERA, three SHO, 608 walks, 435 SO, 106 ERA+, 4.72 FIP, 1.587 WHIP, 10.2 H/9, 4.1 BB/9 and 2.9 SO/9. Pitcher of the Year and most effective pitcher Tommy Bridges (13-9, 4.59 ERA, 13 CG) led in wins, win percentage (.591), strikeouts (101), FIP (3.98), DICE (4.06), H/9 (10.2), SO/9 (6.0) and SO/BB (1.74). George Gill (12-9, 4.12 ERA, 13 CG, 1 SHO) led in homers (15), LOB% (73.0), ERA, ERA+ (124), WHIP (1.494), pWAR (3.7), BB/9 (2.7), R/9 (4.5) and quality starts (12). Vern Kennedy (12-9, 5.06 ERA) led league in balks (2). He led staff in starts (26), innings (190.1), hits (215), walks (113), WP (7), earned runs (107), runs (123) and H/9 (10.2). Eldon Auker (11-10, 5.27 ERA, 1 SHO) led in losses, HBP (5) and WHIP (1.494). Roxie Lawson (8-9, 5.46 ERA) and Al Benton (5-3, 3.30 ERA). Harry Eisenstat (9-6, 3.73 ERA) led in GF (17) and saves (4). Slick Coffman (4-4, 6.02 ERA) led in games (39). Jake Wade (3-2, 6.56 ERA). Bridges shined June 5-20 (3-0, 20.1 IP, 0.89 ERA, .167 SLG, .181 BA). Texas League MVP Dizzy Trout (23-8 .742, 2.40 ERA) was at Beaumont and class "AA" Toledo. Boots Poffenberger was at Toledo (8-3 .727), with his MLB debut for Detroit (6-7, 4.82 ERA, 1 SHO).

Defense. Detroit committed 147 errors for league best fielding percentage (.976). Tiger league leaders were catcher York in fielding percentage (.990) and passed balls (10), Greenberg in chances (1,618), putouts (1,484) and assists (120) at first base. Gehringer led in chances (869), putouts (393) and assists (455) at second base. Fox led all outfielders in fielding percentage (.994) and right fielders in fielding percentage(.993). Rogell led his team in defensive War (1.3) as a shortstop.

Greenberg hit 58 home runs chasing Babe Ruth's major-league record of 60. He set the record of 11 multi-homer games in 1938. Hank hit four straight homers against Washington at home, with two on Tuesday July 26 and two the following day.

1930s Pitching Walks	
1. Tommy Bridges	902
2. Vic Sorrell	403
3. Eldon Auker	378
4. Schoolboy Rowe	325
5. Roxie Lawson	316
6. Earl Whitehill	291
7. Chief Hogsett	287
8. Jake Wade	207
9. George Uhle	166
10. Whit Wyatt	158

Team. Detroit finished in fifth place for Del Baker at 81-73-1 (.526), with 836,279 fans. The team went 6-5 in April when Hank Greenberg hit a 14th-inning walk-off homer for an 8-7 win over Chicago at home on Thursday, April 20, with pitchers Al Benton (7 IP, 4 ER) and Roxie Lawson (7 IP, 1 ER). Motown beat visiting Cleveland 14-1 on Sunday, April 20, aided by Tommy Bridges 2-for-4 (9 IP, 1 ER, 8 SO), Charlie Gehringer 4-for-5 (HR, 5 RBI), Greenberg 3-for-4 (2 RBI), and Dixie Walker 4-for-5 that scored five runs. Detroit had a 10-17 record in May, as the Bengals defeated visiting St. Louis 12-5 on Saturday, May 27, led by Beau Bell 3-for-5 (3 RBI) and Gehringer 4-for-5 (HR, 5 RBI) who hit for the cycle. The Tigers were 18-8 in June that included nine straight wins June 8-16. 22-year-old rookie Barney McCosky and Earl Averill started the game with back-to-back homers during a 6-5 loss in Philadelphia on Thursday, June 22. The squad went 14-16 in July that included Greenberg going 9-for-12 July 20-22 (.750 BA, .750 OBP, 1.000 SLG, .800 BAbip). The Bengals won a double-header in Philadelphia 14-0 and 5-3 on Sunday, July 30. Bobo Newsom (9 IP, 0 ER, 5 H, 8 SO), Greenberg 4-for-4 (HR, 4 R), Pinky Higgins (HR, 4 RBI) and Frank Croucher (HR, 3 RBI) led game one, followed by Fred Hutchinson (7.1 IP, 3 ER) in game two. Detroit finished 17-12 in August when Gehringer from Fowler High School excelled during the period of August 15-25 (13-for-21, 4 HR, 10 RBI, .619 BA, .636 OBP, 1.286 SLG, 1.922 OPS, .529 BAbip). The Bengals defeated Washington 8-1 at home on Thursday, August 24, with Gehringer 4-for-5 (2 RBI) and Dizzy Trout (9 IP, 1 ER). Motown closed 15-14 in September and 1-1 in October, with a 14-10 victory over the Red Sox at home on Friday, September 1, led by Higgins (2 HR, 4 RBI) and Birdie Tebbetts (HR, 4 RBI). Reliever Bud Thomas (W 7-0, 6 IP, 1 ER, 3 H), Greenberg 2-for-2 (2 BB, 2 R) and Roy Cullenbine (3 RBI) assisted in a 5-4 win in St. Louis on Tuesday, September 26. Motown was 42-35 (.545) at home, 39-38 (.506) on the road, scored 849 runs and allowed 762. John Zapor (.349 BA), Steve Rachunok (22-6 .786, 2.15 ERA) and Ed Weiland (18-9 .667, 2.68 ERA) were at class "C" Henderson. Class "C" Hot Springs had stars Steve Carter (.369 BA), Cyril Pfeifer (.358 BA) and Al Gardella (32 HR).

P * BUD THOMAS

Offense. Detroit finished with a .279 BA, .356 OBP,426, 782 OPS, 2,270 TB and 94 OPS+. Catcher Birdie Tebbetts (.261 BA, 4 HR, 53 RBI) led for in-play percentage (84%). Player of the Year and most effective hitter Hank Greenberg (.312 BA, 33 HR, 113 RBI) at first base led the league in strikeouts (95). Greenberg led Motown in doubles (42), home runs, runs batted in, slugging (.622), OPS (1.042), OPS+ (156), total average (1.152), base-out percentage (1.156), gross production average (.344), WAR (5.5), batters run average (.256), BAbip (.331), secondary average (.502), base runs (121), runs produced (191), runs created (131), isolated power (.310), power/speed number (12.9), extra base hits (82), total bases (311), bases produced (410), walks (91) and strikeouts (95). Second baseman Charlie Gehringer (.325 BA, 16 HR, 86 RBI) led in on-base percentage (.423), and average. Pinky Higgins (.276 BA, 8 HR, 76 RBI) at third led in hit streak (16). Frank Croucher (.269 BA, 5 HR, 40 RBI) was at short, with Earl Averill (.262 BA, 10 HR, 58 RBI) in left. Centerfielder Barney McCosky (.311 BA, 4 HR, 58 RBI) led in games (147), plate appearances (692), at bats (611), runs (120), hits (190), triples (14), BAbip (.331), times on base (262), stolen base runs (3.6) and outs (441). Right-fielder Pete Fox (.295 BA, 7 HR, 66 RBI) led for in-play percentage (84%) and steals (23). Rudy York (.307 BA, 20 HR, 68 RBI) was a valuable utilityman. Fred Hutchinson (.382 BA, 6 RBI) led the pitchers in hitting. The top pinch-hitters were Red Kress at .800 (4-5), Gehringer .375 (3-8) and York (HR, 8 RBI). Michigander Benny McCoy of Grandville High School played at class "AA" Toledo (.323 BA), with his MLB debut for the Tigers (.323 BA).

1930s Pitching Strikeouts	
1. Tommy Bridges	1,207
2. Schoolboy Rowe	540
3. Vic Sorrell	372
4. Eldon Auker	351
5. Earl Whitehill	271
6. Chief Hogsett	259
7. George Uhle	232
8. Roxie Lawson	167
Whit Wyatt	167
10. Bobo Newsom	164

Pitching. The team had a 4.29 ERA, seven SHO, 574 walks, 114 ERA+, 4.33 FIP, 1.466 WHIP, 9.4 H/9, and 3.8 BB/9. The staff led league in strikeouts (633) and SO/9 (4.2). Pitcher of the Year and most effective pitcher Tommy Bridges (17-7, 3.50 ERA) led in win percentage (.708), HBP (6), FIP (3.41), DICE (3.43), WHIP (1.247), BB/9 (2.8) and SO/BB (2.11). Bobo Newsom (17-10, 3.37 ERA) was 20-11 overall, as he led MLB in starts (37). Bobo led league in complete games (24) and batters faced (1,261), with staff lead in wins, starts (31), CG (21), SHO (3), innings (246), hits (222), walks (104), strikeouts (164), earned runs (92), LOB% (73.9), ERA, ERA+ (144), pWAR (7.2), H/9 (8.1), SO/9 (6.0), R/9 (3.7) and quality starts (19). Dizzy Trout (9-10, 3.61 ERA) led league in HR/9 (0.3). Schoolboy Rowe (10-12, 4.99 ERA) led in losses, homers (17) and runs (113). Al Benton (6-8, 4.56 ERA) led in games (37), GF (18) and saves (5). Archie McKain (5-6, 3.68 ERA) and Vern Kennedy (0-3, 6.43 ERA). Bud Thomas (7-0, 4.18 ERA) closed the season in style September 8-October 1 (2-0, 12.2 IP, 0.71 ERA, .186 BA, .200 OBP, .140 SLG, .175 BAbip). Dave Read (13-5 .722) was at class "D" Fulton, with Johnny Sain (18-10 .643) assigned to class "D" Newport.

Defense. Detroit committed 198 errors for a .967 fielding average. League leaders were Gill in pitcher putouts (25), as Tebbetts led catchers in assists (64), errors (16), caught stealing (34), and caught stealing percentage (48%). He led the Tigers in dWAR (0.8). Greenberg led in fielding (.993) at first, Gehringer in fielding (.977) at second, McCosky led outfielders in putouts (428) and centerfielders in fielding (.986), chances (414) and putouts (401). Fox led right fielders in fielding (.967).

Charlie Gehringer 4-for-5 (5 RBI) hit for the cycle on Saturday, May 27, with hits in the unlikely order of single-double-triple-home run. He had four-hit games of 4-for-5 (HR, 5 RBI) on Sunday, April 30, and then 4-for-5 (2 RBI) on Thursday, August 24.

Pitcher Tommy Bridges (2.1 IP, 0 ER, 2 H, 3 SO) earned the win in his fifth All-Star game appearance. The American League won 3-1 over the National League on Tuesday, July 11 at Yankee Stadium in the Bronx, New York, with 62,892 in attendance.

OF * HANK GREENBERG

Player of the Decade. Hank Greenberg (.308 BA, 100 HR, 349 RBI) led in slugging (.613), on-base plus slugging (1.018), OPS+ 165), total average (1.084), gross production average (.335), secondary average (.472), total base average (2.3) and bases produced average (2.0). The first MVP at different positions (1935-1B, 1940-LF). The 1940 MVP (.340 BA, 50 2B, 41 HR, 150 RBI, 171 OPS+, 385 TB) was a World Series star (.357 BA, HR, 6 RBI) facing Cincinnati. Hank led left fielders in putouts (246), assists (13) and errors (13) in 1940. Greenberg missed five seasons due to WWII service. He returned in 1945 (78 GM, .311 BA, 13 HR, 60 RBI, 166 OPS+) to lead Detroit to the pennant and World Series Championship (.304 BA, 2 HR, 7 RBI, .696 SLG) against the Chicago Cubs. The first major-league player to hit 25 homers in both leagues. He was general Manager of the Cleveland Indians 1950-1957 and the Chicago White Sox 1959-1961.

1940s

Year	W – L	Pct.	Pl
1940	90-64	.584	1
1941	75-79	.487	4
1942	73-81	.474	5
1943	78-76	.506	5
1944	88-66	.571	2
1945	88-65	.575	1
1946	**92-62**	**.597**	2
1947	85-69	.552	2
1948	78-76	.506	5
1949	87-67	.565	4
	834-705	.542	

All-Decade Team. Manager Steve O'Neill (509-414 .551) led Detroit to the World Championship in 1945 (88-65 .575). Pitcher Hal Newhouser (170-118 .590, 2.84 ERA). Catcher Birdie Tebbetts (.262 BA, 8 HR, 156 RBI) had his best year in 1940 (.296 BA, 4 HR, 46 RBI). He led catchers that year in assists (89), double plays (10) and runners caught stealing (41). First baseman Rudy York (.275 BA, 151 HR, 638 RBI) led in games (924), plate appearances (3,995), at bats (3,504), runs (514), hits (962), doubles (175), home runs (151), runs batted in (638), offensive WAR (16.9), extra base hits (362), extra bases on long hits (700), total bases (1,662), bases produced (2,153), walks (466) and strikeouts (493). Second baseman Eddie Mayo (.265 BA, 23 HR, 229 RBI) led for defensive WAR (5.0), as he led the league in fielding at third base in 1943 (.976) and then at second base in 1945 (.980). Shortstop Eddie Lake (.230 BA, 23 HR, 110 RBI) led in walk percentage (17.0) and was the league leader in power/speed number in 1946 (10.4) and 1947 (11.5). Third baseman George Kell (.325 BA, 14 HR, 237 RBI) led for batting average, BAbip (.330) and strikeout percentage (2.7). Kell's 1949 season (.343 BA, 3 HR, 59 RBI) is remembered for him edging Ted Williams (.343 BA, 43 HR, 159 RBI, 191 OPS+) for the batting title (.34291 to .34276) denying Williams his third Triple Crown as the MVP led the league in home runs and runs batted in. The decade outfielders were Hank Greenberg (.308 BA, 100 HR, 349 RBI) the back-to-back Player of the Decade; Roy Cullenbine (.273 BA, 66 HR, 227 RBI) led in on-base percentage (.419), with 1946 (.335 BA, 15 HR, 56 RBI, 175 OPS+) his top campaign; and Dick Wakefield (.293 BA, 56 HR, 314 RBI) that became an MLB star in 1943 (.316 BA, 7 HR, 79 RBI, 200 H) and 1944 (78 GM, .355 BA, 12 HR, 53 RBI, 190 OPS+).

GM* BILLY EVANS

Pitcher of the Decade. Hal Newhouser (170-118 .590, 2.84 ERA) led Tiger decade hurlers in games (377) wins, win percentage, starts (305), complete games (181), shutouts (31), quality starts (201), high quality starts (189), dominant starts (79), innings (2,453.1), hits (2,127), home runs (84), walks (1,068), strikeouts (1,579), balks (6), wild pitches (52), earned runs (774), runs (927), technical runs allowed (3.40), left on-base percentage (73.8), earned run average, ERA+ (138), FIP (3.01), DICE (3.48), pitcher WAR (54.1), H/9 (7.8), HR/9 (0.31), RA/9 (3.4), batters faced (10,360), pickoffs (15), no decisions (35), cheap wins (21), tough losses (44), complete game percentage (.593), quality start percentage (.659), high quality start percentage (.620) and dominate start percentage (.259). Newhouser was MVP for 1944 (29-9 .763, 2.22 ERA), with identical 13-5 marks at home and in first half, 16-4 records on the road and in the second half. The 1945 MVP (25-9 .735, 1.81 ERA) finished 14-2 at home, 12-3 in second half and 7-0 (1.22 ERA) in June, with an impressive 18-2 record in games started on three day's rest. The 1946 MVP runner-up (26-9 .743, 1.94 ERA) went 16-3 in the first half, with a combined 12-2 in June and July. Hal went 6-1 (1.88 ERA) in September/October of 1948 and was 6-1 pitching during June games of the 1949 season.

1940s
Attendance

Year	Attn.	Avg.	Rk
1940	1,112,693	14,085	1
1941	684,915	8,895	4
1942	580,087	7,534	3
1943	606,287	7,773	2
1944	923,176	11,836	1
1945	1,280,341	16,847	1
1946	1,722,590	21,805	2
1947	1,398,093	17,476	4
1948	1,743,035	22,637	3
1949	**1,821,204**	**23,349**	3

All-Decade Pitchers. Newhouser finished 21-12 in 1948 and 18-11 in 1949. Tommy Bridges (44-36 .550, 3.05 ERA) was his best in 1943 (12-7 .632, 2.39 ERA). Virgil Trucks (87-63 .580, 3.29 ERA) led in relief win percentage (13-7 .650) and was an All-Star in 1949 (19-11 .633, 2.81 ERA, 6 SHO). Dizzy Trout (129-119 .520, 3.01 ERA) led for losses, games finished (93), balks (6), hit by pitch (21), and relief wins (19), with a splendid 1943 (20-12 .625) and 1944 (27-14 .659. Fred Hutchinson (63-46 .578, 3.56 ERA) led the decade in home runs (84), WHIP (1.231), BB/9 (2.50) and SO/BB (1.70), with a respectable 1949 (15-7 .682, 2.96 ERA, 141 ERA+, 161 WHIP). Bobo Newsom (33-25 .569, 3.69 ERA) led in SO/9 (5.93), with an AL best 168 ERA+ in 1940 (21-5 .808, 2.83 ERA). Detroit native Ted Gray (16-14 .533, 3.91 ERA) had a decade best 7.80 H/9, with a combined 12-4 record at home in 1948 and 1949. Al Benton (60-53 .531, 3.30 ERA) led decade in saves (40), games in relief (140) and relief losses (19). He was an All-Star in 1941 (15-6 .714, 2.97 ERA, 153 ERA+). Hal White (27-31 .466, 3.52 ERA) starred as a rookie August 9-September 1, 1942 (4-0, 1.24 ERA, .180 BA, .204 BAbip). Stubby Overmire (47-45 .511, 3.92 ERA) a native of Moline, Michigan was superb in 1947 (11-5 .688, 3.77 ERA).

Tommy Bridges was superior in 1943: May 15-September 4 (11-1 .917, 135 IP, 8 CG, 2.13 ERA, .213 BA, 2 SHO), at home (8-3 .727, 1.65 ERA, .196 BA, .231 BAbip), first half (6-2 .750, 1.95 ERA, .205 BA), in July (4-0 .800, 1.08 ERA, .197 BA), and August 4-1 .800, 2.41 ERA, .224 BA, .222 BAbip). Former Tiger Rudy York hit two grand slam homers July 27 (2 HR, 10 RBI).

Detroit Tigers 1940 American League

1940s Team Hitting				
YEAR	AVG	HR	RBI	SB
1940	**.286**	**134**	**829**	**66**
1941	.263	81	637	43
1942	.246	76	547	39
1943	.261	77	572	40
1944	.263	60	591	61
1945	.256	77	588	60
1946	.258	108	644	65
1947	.258	103	662	52
1948	.267	78	661	22
1949	.267	88	707	39

Team. Detroit won the pennant under Del Baker at 90-64 (.584), with an attendance of 1,112,693 to crack the one-million mark. Players lost the World Series to Cincinnati in seven games. The squad was 6-5 in April as Cotton Pippen (8.1 IP, 3 ER) led a 4-3 defeat of visiting Cleveland on Monday, April 29. Motown went 14-10 during May including a 10-7 home win over Boston on Monday, May 20, with Pinky Higgins 3-for-5 (3 HR, 7 RBI) hitting three consecutive homers. The Bengals won a home doubleheader on Thursday, May 30, as Tommy Bridges (9 IP, 1 ER) won 2-1. Hometown hero Barney McCosky from Detroit went 5-for-5, Hank Greenberg 3-for-3 (3 RBI) and Rudy York 3-for-4 (HR, 4 RBI) to lead the 15-6 game two win. The Tigers were 18-10 in June when the squad defeated the visiting Yankees 9-2 on Sunday, June 23, behind Bobo Newsom (W 9-1, 9 IP, 2 ER), Higgins 4-for-4 and York 3-for-4 (3B, HR, 4 RBI). The Bengals had a 19-13 record in July drawing 56,272 fans for a doubleheader split with Cleveland on Thursday, July 4. The team went 15-15 in August, with a 12-1 victory in Boston on Saturday, August 24, when York went 4-for-6 (5 RBI). Detroit closed 18-11 in September including 17-5 in home games. The team won a home doubleheader over Chicago on Wednesday, September 25. Newsom (W 20-4, 2 IP, 0 ER) won game one 10-9 with McCosky 4-for-6 and Pete Fox (3 RBI). Newsom (W 21-4, 9 IP, 2 ER, 7 SO) returned to win game two 3-2. Players clinched the pennant on Friday with a Floyd Giebell (9 IP, 0 ER, 6 H, 6 SO) 2-0 shutout in Cleveland. The Bengals won the season series over St. Louis 18-4, including 10-1 at home. Detroit went 50-29 (.633) at home and 40-35 (.533) in away games. Motown led the league with 888 runs scored while allowing opponents 717 runs. Hal White (16-4 .800, 2.43 ERA), Fred Hutchinson (7-3, 2.49 ERA) and Clyde McCullough (.324 BA, 27 HR) starred at class "AA" Buffalo. Joe Wood (.345 BA), Moon Mullen (.340 BA), James Steger (14-4 .778, 2.55 ERA), Bob Gillespie (18-9 .667) and Frank Masters (15-9 .625, 2.62 ERA) were assigned to class "C" Henderson.

C * BILLY SULLIVAN

Offense. Detroit had 312 doubles, .366 OBP, .442 SLG, .808 OPS, 2,393 TB, and 101 OPS+, with league best .286 average. The catchers were Birdie Tebbetts (.296 BA, 4 HR, 46 RBI) the in-play percentage (87%) leader and Billy Sullivan (.309 BA, 3 HR, 41 RBI). Rudy York (.316 BA, 33 HR, 134 RBI) at first led league in games (155). He led club in plate appearances (686) and strikeouts (88). Charlie Gehringer (.313 BA, 10 HR, 81 RBI) at second led in stolen base runs (3.0) and walks (101). Pinky Higgins (.271 BA, 13 HR, 76 RBI) was at third. Dick Bartell (.233 BA, 7 HR, 53 RBI) at short led in outs (429). The MVP, Player of the Year, and most effective hitter Hank Greenberg (.340 BA, 41 HR, 150 RBI) in left led MLB for doubles (50), runs batted in, slugging (.670), OPS (1.103), total bases (384), extra base hits (99) and runs created (166). Hank led league for homers, total average (1.215), oWAR (7.2), secondary average (.497) and isolated power (.330). He led team in runs (129), on-base percentage (.433), OPS+ (171), base-out percentage (1.221), gross production average (.363), WAR (7.1), batters run average (.289), times on base (289), base runs (149), runs produced (238), power/speed number (10.5), bases produced (483) and hit streak (18). Barney McCosky (.340 BA, 4 HR, 57 RBI) at center led MLB in hits (200) and triples (19). He led team in at bats (589), singles (138), BAbip (.360) and steals (13). Pete Fox (.289, 5 HR, 48 RBI) and Bruce Campbell (.283 BA, 8 HR, 44 RBI) manned right. Lynn Nelson (.348 BA), Schoolboy Rowe (.269 BA, 18 RBI) and Bobo Newsom (16 RBI) led the pitchers. Red Kress at .600 (3-5), Sullivan .417 (5-12, 2 HR, 3 RBI), Lynn Nelson .364 (4-11), and Earl Averill at .313 (10-32, 7 RBI) led pinch-hitters.

1940s Team Hitting				
YEAR	OBP	SLG	OPS	OPS+
1940	**.366**	**.442**	**.808**	**101**
1941	.340	.375	.714	81
1942	.314	.344	.658	79
1943	.324	.359	.683	94
1944	.332	.354	.687	92
1945	.324	.361	.684	93
1946	.338	.374	.712	93
1947	.353	.377	.730	100
1948	.353	.375	.728	91
1949	.361	.378	.739	95

Pitching. The Tigers had a 4.01 ERA, 59 CG, nine SHO, 570 walks, 118 ERA+, 3.98 FIP, 1.451 WHIP, 9.3 H/9, and 3.7 BB/9. Pitchers led league in in saves (23), strikeouts (752), balks (5), pWAR (24.6) and SO/9 (4.9) Pitcher of the Year and most effective pitcher Bobo Newsom (21-5, 2.83 ERA) led the majors in ERA+ (168), with league lead for balks (2) and no decisions (10). He led his team in wins, starts (34), complete games (20), shutouts (3), innings (264), hits (235), homers (19), walks (100), strikeouts (164), earned runs (83), runs (110), ERA, pWAR (7.4), SO/BB (1.64) and quality starts (21). Newsome was 13-3 at home and 8-2 on the road, 12-1 in first half and 9-4 in second half. Tommy Bridges (12-9, 3.37 ERA) led in wild pitches (5), FIP (3.55), DICE (3.71), H/9 (7.8) and SO/9(6.1). Schoolboy Rowe (16-3, 3.46 ERA) led league in win percentage (.842), as he led staff in LOB% (75.6), WHIP (1.260), walks per nine (2.3) and R/9 (3.6). Johnny Gorsica (7-7, 4.33 ERA) led in HBP (4). Al Benton (6-10, 4.42) led MLB in saves (17), with team lead in games (42), losses and games finished (35). Hal Newhouser (9-9, 4.86 ERA), Fred Hutchinson (3-7, 5.68 ERA), Archie McKain (5-0, 2.82 ERA), Dizzy Trout (3-7, 4.47 ERA) and Tom Seats (2-2, 4.69 ERA).

Defense. Detroit committed 194 errors for a .968 fielding percentage. Tiger league leaders were Rowe in pitcher fielding percentage (1.000), Gorsica in errors (4) and Newsom and Rowe in caught stealing (100%). Tebbetts led in catcher chances per game (6.3), assists (89), errors (17), double plays (10), and caught stealing (41). He led the Bengals for defensive WAR (1.0). Greenberg led all outfielders in errors (15), as he led the leftfielders in chances (326), putouts (297), and assists (14).

Hank Greenberg reached base in 32 straight games May 5-June 19 (10 HR, 33 RBI, .369 BA, .431 OBP, .762 SLG). He played in back-to-back doubleheaders September 18-19 (4 HR, 12 RBI, .583 BA, .737 OBP, 1.833 SLG) versus Philadelphia at home.

First baseman Rudy York drove in a run during 12 straight games September 11-20 (6 HR, 28 RBI, .531 BA, .566 OBP, 1.041 SLG). He had six straight games with multiple runs batted in September 17-20 (4 HR, 18 RBI, .542 BA, .577 OBP, 1.208 SLG).

1940s Hitting Games		
1.	Rudy York	924
2.	Pinky Higgins	725
3.	Doc Cramer	720
4.	Dick Wakefield	632
5.	Eddie Mayo	587
6.	Jimmy Outlaw	532
7.	Pat Mullin	509
8.	Bob Swift	501
9.	George Kell	483
10.	Hoot Evers	479

Team. Detroit finished fourth for Del Baker at 75-79 (.396), with an attendance of 684,915. The squad started 6-7 in April that included a 12-8 win over visiting Boston on Wednesday, April 30. Frank Croucher went 3-for-5, Rudy York 3-for-5 (HR, 5 RBI), Bruce Campbell 3-for-4 and Birdie Tebbetts 3-for-4 (3 RBI). The Tigers were 17-13 in May when Schoolboy Rowe (9 IP, 1 ER) led a 15-1 victory against Philadelphia at home on Friday, May 2, behind Charlie Gehringer 4-for-5 (3 RBI) and Billy Sullivan (HR, 3 RBI). Detroit had a record of 12-16 in June, as they were 9-2 June 7-19. Bobo Newsom (9 IP, 2 ER, 9 SO) led a 5-2 win against visiting Philadelphia on Wednesday, June 11. The team had a 10-19 July record, with the All-Star game at Briggs Stadium on July 8. The game drew 54,674 fans, as former Tiger Babe Pinelli was an umpire, with Detroiters Ty Tyson (WWJ) and Harry Heilmann (WXYZ) on radio. The Bengals lost 12-6 to New York at home on Sunday, July 20 during a 4:05 17-inning marathon. Tiger reliever Al Benton (L 6-2, 11.2 IP, 7 ER, 11 H) faced 49 batters in 11 plus innings, as Gehringer went 3-for-4 and walked four times. Players were 17-14 in August including a 11-2 win for Benton (9 IP, 2 ER) at Cleveland on Wednesday, August 6. Benton became the only player to have two sacrifice hits in the same inning, accomplishing the feat during the third inning, as Barney McCosky had four RBIs. Rip Radcliff torched pitching during the six-week period of August 16-September 27 (32 GM, .400 BA, .434 OBP, .504 SLG, .412 BAbip). Detroit closed 13-10 in September with wins of 9-5 and 16-8 to sweep a double-header with St. Louis at home on Monday, September 1. Detroit won game one on the strength of Rudy York 4-for-5 (3 HR, 5 RBI), Pinky Higgins 3-for-5 (HR) and Benton (W 10-6). Players rallied from a 7-0 deficit in game two to win, with a nine-run sixth inning. McCosky 2-for-4 (HR, 4 RBI), Dutch Meyer 3-for-5 (4 RBI) and Campbell (HR, 3 RBI) led the Tiger 20-hit attack, as reliever Gorsica (7.1 IP, 1 ER) got the win. The Bengals were 43-34 (.558) at home, and 32-45 (.416) on the road. Players scored 686 runs and allowed 743. Pitcher Fred Hutchinson (26-7, 2.44 ERA, 31 CG) hit .392 (58-for-148) for class "AA" Buffalo. Class "AA" San Francisco featured Nanny Fernandez (.327 BA, 46 2B, 19 HR, 129 RBI, 366 TB), Ted Jennings (.326 BA), Larry Jensen (16-10, 2.80 ERA) and Sam Gibson (13-7, 3.31 ERA). Sal Maglie (20-15, 2.67 ERA) and Michigander John M. Williams (.286 BA) from North Adams high school and Hillsdale College were with class "A" Elmira.

Offense. Detroit had a .268 BA, .330 OBP, .371 SLG, .702 OPS, 2,015 TB and 82 OPS+. Birdie Tebbetts (.284 BA, 2 HR, 47 RBI) was the catcher. Player of the Year Rudy York (.259 BA, 27 HR, 111 RBI) at first led in games (155), plate appearances (687), at bats (590), runs (91), doubles (29), home runs, runs batted in, secondary average (.356), times on base (246), base runs (96), runs produced (175), runs created (97), isolated power (.197), extra base hits (59), total bases (269), bases produced (364), strikeouts (88) and outs (458). Charlie Gehringer (.220 BA, 3 HR, 46 RBI) at second led in walks (95). Third baseman Pinky Higgins (.298 BA, 11 HR, 73 RBI) led the Tigers in hits (161) and power/speed number (6.9). Frank Croucher (.254 BA, 2 HR, 39 RBI) at short led in stolen base runs (0.6). Rip Radcliff (.317 BA, 3 HR, 40 RBI) in left led for in-play percentage (90%) and hitting streak (20). The most effective hitter Barney McCosky (.324 BA, 3 HR, 55 RBI) at center led squad in singles (124), on-base percentage (.401), OPS (.827), OPS+ (110), total average (.816), base-out percentage (.828), gross production average (.287), WAR (3.2), oWAR (2.7), batters run average (.169), batting average, BAbip (.343), stolen bases (8) and stolen base runs (0.6). Bruce Campbell (.275 BA, 15 HR, 93 RBI) in right led in triples (10) and slugging (.457). Pat Mullin (54 GM, 42 R, .345 BA, .509 SLG, 130 OPS+) made his MLB debut. Johnny Gorsica (.298 BA) and Schoolboy Rowe (.273 BA, HR, 12 RBI) led pitchers. The leading Detroit pinch-hitters were McCosky at 1.000 (3-3, 2 RBI), Rowe at .500 (3-6, 3 RBI), and Campbell at .500 (2-4).

1940s Hitting Runs		
1.	Rudy York	515
2.	Dick Wakefield	334
3.	Doc Cramer	329
4.	Eddie Lake	290
5.	Barney McCosky	289
6.	George Kell	286
7.	Pat Mullin	284
8.	Hank Greenberg	279
9.	Pinky Higgins	278
10.	Eddie Mayo	269

Pitching. The team logged a 4.18 ERA, 52 CG, seven SHO, 645 walks, 109 ERA+, 3.84 FIP, 1.479 WHIP, 9.1 H/9, and 4.2 BB/9. Detroit led league in strikeouts (697), FIP (3.84), SO/9 (4.5), SO/BB (1.08), pWAR (23.1) and no decisions (34). Pitcher of the Year Al Benton (15-6, 2.97 ERA) led in wins, win percentage (.714), GF (19), saves (7), LOB% (73.9), ERA, ERA+ (153), WHIP (1.237), pWAR (5.5), H/9 (7.4) and R/9 (3.6). The most effective pitcher was Tommy Bridges (9-12, 3.41 ERA). Johnny Gorsica (9-11, 4.47 ERA) led in BB/9 (2.9). Bobo Newsom (12-20, 4.60 ERA) led MLB in losses, and was league leader for games (43), starts (36), complete games (12), SHO (2), innings (250.1), hits (265), homers (15), strikeouts (175), HBP (3), earned runs (128), runs (140), FIP (3.89), DICE (3.83), SO/9 (6.3), SO/BB (1.48) and quality starts (17). Hal Newhouser (9-11, 4.79 ERA) led league in no decisions (8), with team lead for walks (137) and HR/9 (0.3). Dizzy Trout (9-9, 3.74 ERA), Schoolboy Rowe (8-6, 4.14 ERA), Bud Thomas (1-3, 4.21 ERA), and Archie McKain (2-1, 5.02 ERA), with 24-year-old rookie Hal Manders (1-0, 2.35 ERA).

Defense. Detroit committed 186 errors for a .969 fielding percentage. Tiger league leaders were Newhouser in pitcher fielding percentage (1.000), Tebbetts in catcher total chances per game (5.7), assists (83), and caught stealing (34). Birdie led the club in dWAR (0.7). York at first led in errors (21), as Gehringer led second basemen in fielding percentage (.982).

Al Benton was an All-Star selection at the break (20 GM, 6-1 .857, 1.98 ERA, .184 BA, .204 BAbip, 6 SV). Michigander Johnny Lipon from Detroit Chadsey High School led the Michigan State League in hits (176), home runs (35) and runs batted in (115).

The Tigers signed 20-year-old University of Michigan star Dick Wakefield on Saturday, June 21, for $52,000 and a Ford Lincoln. He was at class "B" Winston-Salem (55 GM, .300 BA, .507 SLG), with his MLB debut for Detroit on Thursday, June 26.

1940s Hitting Hits	
1. Rudy York	962
2. Pinky Higgins	768
3. Doc Cramer	743
4. Dick Wakefield	624
5. George Kell	621
6. Eddie Mayo	586
7. Barney McCosky	554
8. Hoot Evers	517
9. Pat Mullin	472
10. Hank Greenberg	442

Team. Detroit finished fifth with Del Baker at 73-81 (.474), with an attendance of 580,087. The Team started 11-7 in April, including 7-1 in home games, with a Hal White (9 IP, 0 ER, 5 H) 9-0 shutout of the visiting White Sox on Thursday, April 23. The Tigers went 15-15 in May, as White (9 IP, 0 ER) shutout the White Sox again 14-0 in Chicago on Sunday, May 24, as Rip Radcliff went 4-for-4 (4 RBI) and Pinky Higgins 2-for-4 (5 RBI). The players scored a 14-3 home win against Cleveland on Friday, May 29, led by Birdie Tebbetts 3-for-5 (3 RBI) and White (9 IP, 3 ER, 6 SO). Detroit had a record of 15-13 June that included an 8-7 victory in Philadelphia on Thursday, June 4, as Don Ross (HR, 3 RBI) and Tebbetts (2 RBI) had clutch pinch-hits. The squad fell to 8-19 in July, as Hal Newhouser (9 IP, 1 ER, 3 H, 10 SO) led a 5-1 triumph in Cleveland on Friday, July 3. Virgil Trucks dominated hitters July 26-August 30 (5-1, 53 IP, 1.36 ERA, .203 BA, .223 SLG, .223 BAbip) including a 1-0 shutout at Philadelphia in 1:45 on Wednesday, August 26 (W 12-6, 9 IP, 0 ER). The club was 15-14 in August, when the Bengals defeated Boston at home 8-4 on Sunday, August 2, behind Dizzy Trout (9 IP, 4 ER) 2-for-4 (HR, 3 RBI), Pinky Higgins (HR, 2 RBI) and Billy Hitchcock (2 RBI). The Bengals prevailed 4-2 in Cleveland on Wednesday, August 12, with winning reliver Roy Henshaw (7 IP, 0 ER, 4 H), Barney McCosky 4-for-4 and York 3-for-4 (HR, 2 RBI). McCosky was astonishing at Washington August 28-29 (6-for-8, 4 BB, .750 BA, .833 OBP, 1.000 SLG, .750 BAbip). Detroit closed 9-13 in September when Ross went 3-for-4 (4 RBI), Rudy York 2-for-4 (2 RBI) and White (9 IP, 0 ER, 4 H) shutout the Senators at home on Sunday, September 13. Tommy Bridges (W 9-6, 9 IP, 7 SO), McCosky 3-for-4 (HR, 2 RBI) and Doc Cramer 3-for-4 directed a 6-4 home win against Chicago on Monday, September, with a mere 879 fans at Briggs Stadium. Motown closed 43-34 (.558) at home, including 8-3 against Chicago and Cleveland. The Bengals were 30-47 (.390) on the road. The team scored 589 runs and allowed 587. Dick Wakefield (.35 BA, 44 2B) was at class "A1" Beaumont, with Johnny Welaj (.309 BA, 30 SB), Mickey Rocco (23 HR, 82 RBI), Dutch Meyer (20 HR, 89 RBI) and Andy Sierra (17-11 .607, 3 SHO) at class "AA" Buffalo.

P * TOMMY BRIDGES

Offense. Detroit had a .314 OBP, .344 SLG, .658 OPS, 1,832 TB, and 79 OPS+. With a league low .246 average. The catcher was Birdie Tebbetts (.247 BA, HR, 27 RBI). The Player of the Year first baseman Rudy York (.260 BA, 21 HR, 90 RBI) led Motown in runs (81), home runs, runs batted in, WAR (3.0), secondary average (.295), runs produced (150), isolated power (.168), extra base hits (51), total bases (247), walks (73) and strikeouts (71). Jimmy Bloodworth (.242 BA, 13 HR, 57 RBI) played at second, as Pinky Higgins (.267 BA) at third base led in doubles (34) and oWAR (2.4). Shortstop Billy Hitchcock (.211 BA, 29 RBI). leftfielder Barney McCosky (.293 BA, 7 HR, 50 RBI) was the most effective hitter leading in games (154), hits (176), triples (11), on-base percentage (.365), gross production average (.267), batting average, BAbip (.304), times on base (244), base runs (88), runs created (90), power/speed number (8.6), total bases (247), bases produced (326), stolen bases (11), stolen base runs (0.3) and with a 15-game hitting streak. Doc Cramer (.263 BA, 43 RBI) in center led MLB for at bats (630), with team highs in plate appearances (682), singles (136), in-play percentage (90%) and outs (489). Ned Harris (.271 BA, 9 HR, 45 RBI) at right led in slugging (.430), OPS (.781), OPS+ (112), total average (.737), base-out percentage (.752) and batters run average (.150). Dizzy Trout (.213 BA, HR, 7 RBI) led pitchers in hitting. The leading Tiger pinch-hitters were Harris at .429 (6-14, 2 HR, 3 RBI) and Don Ross at .313 (5-16, 3 RBI).

1940s Hitting Doubles	
1. Rudy York	175
2. Pinky Higgins	141
3. George Kell	110
4. Hank Greenberg	104
5. Dick Wakefield	102
6. Eddie Mayo	99
7. Barney McCosky	97
8. Doc Cramer	96
9. Hoot Evers	86
10. Pat Mullin	76

Pitching. Motown recorded a 3.13 ERA, 65 CG, 12 SHO, 598 walks, 3.35 FIP, 1.371 WHIP, 8.5 H/9, and 3.8 BB/9. Pitcher led the American League in starts (156), strikeouts (671), ERA+ (127), pWAR (26.9), SO/9 (4.3), left on base (1,254), no decisions (31), tough losses (33), and youngest age (27.1). Pitcher of the Year and most effective pitcher Virgil Trucks (14-8, 2.74 ERA) led MLB in home runs per nine (0.161). He led staff in wins and win percentage (.636). Hal Newhouser (8-14, 2.45 ERA) led league in hits per nine (6.7). Hal led staff in games (38), saves (5), walks (114), earned run average and ERA+ (162). Tommy Bridges (9-7, 2.74 ERA) led his team in FIP (2.87), DICE (3.45), WHIP (1.293), BB/9 (3.2) and strikeouts to walks (1.59). Al Benton (7-13, 2.90 ERA) led MLB for no decisions (11), with club lead in starts (30), innings (226.2), strikeouts (110), pWAR (5.6) and quality starts (20). 23-year-old rookie Hal White (12-12, 2.91 ERA) led in shutouts (4), HBP (5), LOB% (75.4) and runs per nine (3.3). Dizzy Trout (12-18, 3.43 ERA) led league in WP (8). He led staff for losses, complete games (13), hits (214), home runs (15), earned runs (85) and runs (98). Hal Manders (2-0, 4.09 ERA), Roy Henshaw (2-4, 4.09 ERA), Johnny Gorsica (3-2, 4.75 ERA), Jack Wilson (0-0, 4.85 ERA) and Charlie Fuchs (3-3, 6.63 ERA). Bridges and Newhouser led American League in SO/9 (5.0).

Defense. Detroit committed 194 errors for a .969 fielding percentage and led the league in chances (6,195). Tiger league leaders were Tebbetts in catcher chances (527), chances per game (5.4), putouts (446) and in errors (12). York led first basemen in assists (146), Harris led right fielders in errors (10), with Bloodworth leading the Bengals in defensive WAR (1.1).

Outfielder Barney McCosky had several notable hitting streaks during the 1942 season, including 11-games May 21-30 (.381 BA), 11-games July 1-12 (.327 BA), 15-games July 25-August 9 (.393 BA) and 11-games August 26-September 6 (.409 BA).

Al Benton was an All-Star game selectee, after going 6-5 (2.43 ERA) during first half. The American League prevailed 3-1 at the Polo Grounds in New York on July 6, as Benton had a five-inning save. He then went 1-8 (3.53 ERA) in the second half.

1943

1940s Hitting Triples		
1.	Barney McCosky	38
2.	Rudy York	36
3.	Pat Mullin	32
4.	Doc Cramer	29
	Dick Wakefield	29
6.	George Kell	26
7.	Hoot Evers	21
8.	Vic Wertz	19
9.	Hank Greenberg	16
10.	Joe Hoover	15

Team. Detroit finished fifth for Steve O'Neill at 78-76 (.506), with an attendance of 320,972. The club logged a 4-3 mark in April including a Virgil Trucks (9 IP, 0 ER, 4 H) 4-0 shutout at Cleveland on Thursday, April 22, as Doc Cramer went 5-for-5. Stubby Overmire (9 IP, 0 ER, 5 H, 6 SO) and Paul Richards (2 BB, 2 RBI) led a 4-1 triumph in Cleveland on Sunday, April 25. Players were 12-13 in May with a 4-1 11-inning win at Chicago on May 9, led by Dizzy Trout (11 IP, 1 ER) that was 4-for-5 at the plate. Trout (W 4-1, 9 IP, 0 ER, 2 H) threw a two-hit 4-0 of visiting Boston on Saturday, May 22, as Jimmy Bloodworth went 3-for-4 (4 RBI). The Tigers were 11-14 in June when Dick Wakefield (HR, 3 RBI) and Rudy York was 3-for-4 (2 HR, 4 RBI) to lead a 9-5 triumph in St. Louis on Sunday, June 27. The Bengals were 19-14 in July that included 10-9 win at home versus New York on Saturday, July 3, after trailing 9-3. The offense was led by Prince Oana 2-for-3 (HR, 3 RBI), York (2 RBI), Jimmy Bloodworth (2 RBI), and Rip Radcliff with a two-run pin-hit. with a Tommy Bridges (12 IP, 2 ER) 16-inning 4-3 home win over Washington on Tuesday, July 6. The squad had a 17-14 mark in August, as they won a doubleheader over New York at home on Sunday, August 22. Trout (W 15-9, 9 IP, 0 ER) threw a 12-0 shutout with Wakefield (HR, 3 RBI). Bridges (W 11-3, 9 IP, 3 ER) won game two 8-3, with 58,404 fans. Players won a doubleheader in St. Louis on Sunday, August 29. Trucks (W 13-7, 9 IP, 9 SO) had a 15-5 victory behind Joe Wood 2-for-2 (HR, 4 RBI), followed by a 4-2 win by Bridges (W 12-3, 9 IP, 2 ER, 7 SO). Motown closed 13-18 in September and 2-0 in October. Trout (W 20-12, 9 IP, 1 ER) won 4-1 at Washington on Sunday, October 3. Detroit was 45-32 (.584) at home, 33-44 (.429) on the road, scored 632 runs and allowed 560. The class "B" Hagerstown Owls (83-57 .593) were led by 27-year-old player manager Bob Maier (118 R, 214 H, 52 2B, 116 RBI, .363 BA, 311 TB), Thomas Davis (114 R, .345 BA, 104 RBI), George D'addario (110 R, 41 2B, 15 3B, .337 BA, 99 RBI), and Pat Riley (105 R, .320 BA, 104 RBI).

1B * RUDY YORK

Offense. Detroit finished with a .329 OBP, .380 SLG, .709 OPS, 2,089 TB, and 87 OPS+, with a league best .261 average. Paul Richards (.220 BA, 5 HR, 33 RBI) caught. Player of the Year and most effective hitter Rudy York (.271 BA, 34 HR, 118 RBI) at first led MLB in home runs, as he led AL in games (155), runs batted in, slugging (.527), runs created (109), isolated power (.256), total bases (301) and extra base hits (67). York led Motown in triples (11), OPS (.893), OPS+ (152), total average (.871), base-out percentage (.884), gross production average (.296), WAR (6.3), oWAR (5.2), batters run average (.191), secondary average (.403), base runs (106), runs produced (174), power/speed number (8.7), bases produced (390) and walks (84). Jimmy Bloodworth (.241 BA, 6 HR, 52 RBI) at second led MLB in double plays grounded into (29), with Pinky Higgins (.277 BA, 10 HR, 84 RBI) at third. Joe Hoover (.243 BA, 4 HR, 38 RBI) in left led league in sacrifice hits (28) and outs (478), with team lead for steals (6) and strikeouts (101). Leftfielder Dick Wakefield (.316 BA, 7 HR, 79 RBI) led MLB in at bats (633). He led AL for games (155), plate appearances (697), hits (200) and doubles (38). Dick led Detroit in runs (91), on-base percentage (.377), hitting, BAbip (.341), times on base (262) and hit streak (21). Doc Cramer (.300 BA, HR, 43 RBI) in center led league in singles (159) and in-play percentage (91%), as Ned Harris (.254 BA, 6 HR, 32 RBI) in right led in steals (6). Prince Oana (.385 BA, HR, 7 RBI) led pitchers. The leading pinch-hitters were Oana at .333 (3-9, 4 RBI) and Harris .308 (4-13). Edward Kobesky (.259 BA, 18 HR, 88 RBI) and Rufe Gentry (20-16, 2.65 ERA, 27 CG, 7 SHO) were at class "AA" Buffalo.

1940s Hitting Home Runs		
1.	Rudy York	151
2.	Hank Greenberg	100
3.	Pat Mullin	58
4.	Roy Cullenbine	57
5.	Dick Wakefield	56
6.	Pinky Higgins	52
7.	Vic Wertz	33
8.	Hoot Evers	31
9.	Jimmy Bloodworth	24
10.	Eddie Lake	23

Pitching. The Tigers recorded a 3.00 ERA, 67 CG, 549 walks, 1.257 WHIP, 3.5 BB/9, and 4.5 SO/9, as staff led league in starts (155), shutouts (18), strikeouts (706), ERA+ (96), FIP (3.08), pWAR (18.5), H/9 (7.8), HR/9 (0.3), SO/9 (4.5) and no decisions (10), with the youngest staff (26.9). Pitcher of the Year Dizzy Trout (20-12, 2.48 ERA) led MLB in WAR (10.9). He led league in wins (20) and shutouts (5). Dizzy led staff in games (44), starts (30), complete games (18), saves (6), innings (246.2), hits (204), wild pitches (6), earned runs (68), pWAR (5.0), H/9 (7.4) and quality starts (21). The most effective pitcher Tommy Bridges (12-7, 2.39 ERA) led in win percentage (.632), LOB% (78.6), earned run average, ERA+ (146), FIP (2.68), DICE (3.27) and R/9 (2.7). Virgil Trucks (16-10, 2.84 ERA) led league in cheap wins (5). He led club in homers (11), WHIP (1.095) and SO/BB (2.27). Hal Newhouser (8-17, 3.04 ERA) led league in walks (111), HR/9 (0.1) and tough losses (9). He led team in losses, strikeouts (144), runs (88) and SO/9 (6.6). Stubby Overmire (7-6, 3.18 ERA) led in BB/9 (2.3). Johnny Gorsica (4-5, 3.36 ERA) led in GF (18). Hal White (7-12, 3.39 ERA) and Roy Henshaw (0-2, 3.79 ERA). Class "B" Hagerstown had William Angstadt (17-7 .708, 3.19 ERA, 2 SHO) and Charley Miller (20-14 .588, 3.63 ERA, 26 CG, 2 SHO).

Defense. Detroit made 177 errors for a .971 fielding average. League leaders were pitchers Trucks and Bridges in fielding (1.000), Trout in chances (91), assists (67), and errors (4). Newhouser led in pickoffs (3), catcher Richards in fielding (.986), chances (632), chances per game (6.3), putouts (537), double plays (12), caught stealing (55), and caught stealing percentage (60%), as he led club in dWAR (2.0). York led in assists (149) at first, Higgins in errors (26) at third, Hoover in errors (41) at short. Wakefield led leftfielders in errors (11), Cramer in center led for fielding (.985) and in double plays (3).

Dick Wakefield was the 1942 Texas League MVP at Beaumont (149 GM, .345 BA, 44 2B, 277 TB). He joined Detroit for 1943, with a 21-game hit streak April 25-May 23. He went 4-for-5 on Saturday, June 19 and was 4-for-5 on Thursday, August 19.

Tommy Bridges threw back-to-back shutouts of 9-0 (W 6-2, 3 H, 3 SO) against Philadelphia in Detroit on Sunday, July 11, and then a 3-0 (W 7-2, 4 H, 11 SO) win in Chicago on Saturday, July 17, lowering his earned run average to a spectacular 1.71.

1940s Hitting Runs Batted In		
1.	Rudy York	638
2.	Pinky Higgins	396
3.	Hank Greenberg	349
4.	Dick Wakefield	314
5.	Hoot Evers	275
6.	Pat Mullin	259
7.	Vic Wertz	244
8.	Doc Cramer	243
9.	George Kell	237
10.	Eddie Mayo	229

Team. Detroit finished in second place for Steve O'Neill at 88-66 (.571), with an attendance of 923,176. The Tigers were 4-7 in April when Rudy York had a home run for hit number 1,000 during a 3-1 loss to visiting St. Louis on Wednesday, April 19. Players went 17-13 in May that included a 4-2 win at Yankee Stadium on Wednesday, May 10, as Trout (9 IP, 2 ER) pitched and went 3-for-4 at the plate. Detroit scored a 15-2 home win over Washington on Sunday, May 28, behind Pinky Higgins 4-for-4 and Jimmy Outlaw (5 RBI). The team finished 10-16 in June including a 16-inning 4-3 victory against New York at home on Thursday, June 1. Detroit had a 17-14 record in July, with a nine-game win-streak that began with a Hal Newhouser (W 16-6, 9 IP, 8 SO) 13-7 home win against New York on Sunday, July 30, as Dick Wakefield went 3-for-5 (HR, 4 RBI). The squad finished 19-8 for August, when Newhouser (W 20-7, 9 IP, 0 ER, 6 SO) threw a 3-0 shutout on Friday, August 18. Detroit fell 17-2 to St. Louis at home on Sunday, August 27, when 23 Browns reached base. Trout (W 22-9, 9 IP, 0 ER) pitched a 7-0 shutout at home against Chicago on Tuesday, August 29 and was 3-for-4 (HR, 5 RBI) as a hitter. The club closed 21-7 in September and 0-1 in October, as Wakefield was exemplary the three weeks of September 8-29 (33-for-64, .516 BA, .613 OBP, .781 SLG, .537 BAbip). including a 6-0 home shutout of Philadelphia on Tuesday, September 26, as Trout (W 27-12, 9 IP, 0 ER, 6 H) did not record a walk or strikeout. Detroit went 17-5 against the Senators, including 9-2 in Washington, D.C. The Bengals were 43-34 (.558) at home including 9-2 with New York, 45-32 (.584) on the road, scored 658 runs and allowed 581. All-Star pitchers Newhouser and Trout were a combined (56-23 .709), as Motown went 61-33 .649 in their appearances. Future manager Mayo Smith (.340 BA, 149 BB, 123 R), Edward Kobesky (.328 BA, 26 HR, 129 RBI), Otto Denning (.288 BA, 21 HR, 99 RBI) and Mike Roscoe (16-10, 3.43 ERA) were at "AA" Buffalo.

P * DIZZY TROUT

Offense. Detroit had a .263 BA, .332 OBP, .354 SLG, .687 OPS, 1,893 TB, and 92 OPS+. Bob Swift (.255 BA, HR, 19 RBI) split catching with Paul Richards (.237 BA, 3 HR, 37 RBI) the leader in stolen base runs (0.6). Player of the Year Rudy York (.276 BA, 18 HR, 98 RBI) at first led in home runs, runs batted in, base runs (87), runs produced (156), runs created (90), power/speed number (7.8), extra base hits (52), total bases (256), bases produced (329) and strikeouts (73). Eddie Mayo (.249 BA, 5 HR, 63 RBI) at second led league in sacrifice hits (28) and outs (509), as he led club for games (154), plate appearances (696), at bats (607) and steals (9). Pinky Higgins (.297 BA, 7 HR, 76 RBI) at third led in runs (79), doubles (32), WAR (4.0), times on base (246), base runs (87) and walks (81). Joe Hoover (.236 BA, 29 RBI) played at short. Dick Wakefield (78 GM, .355 BA, 12 HR, 53 RBI, 55 BB) and Jimmy Outlaw (.273 BA, 3 HR, 57 RBI) were in left field. The most effective hitter Wakefield got a 90-day leave from the Navy. He led for on-base percentage (.464), slugging (.576), OPS (1.040), OPS+ (190), total average (1.162), base-out percentage (1.173), gross production average (.353), oWAR (4.2), batters run average (.267), hitting, BAbip (.366), secondary average (.420) and isolated power (.221). Doc Cramer (.292 BA, 2 HR, 42 RBI) in center led for hits (169), singles (138), triples (9), in-play percentage (89%) and hit streak (18). 40-year-old rookie Chuck Hostetler (.298 BA, 0 HR, 20 RBI) and Outlaw shared right. Dizzy Trout (.271 BA, 5 HR, 24 RBI) and Boom-Boom Beck (.318 BA) led the pitchers. Al Unser at 1.000 (2-2, HR, 5 RBI) led the Tiger pinch-hitters.

1940s Hitting On-Base Percentage		
1.	Roy Cullenbine	.419
2.	Hank Greenberg	.405
3.	Charlie Gehringer	.397
4.	Dick Wakefield	.396
5.	George Kell	.390
6.	Barney McCosky	.387
7.	Hoot Evers	.374
8.	Vic Wertz	.368
9.	Pinky Higgins	.366
10.	Eddie Lake	.365

Pitching. The Tigers had 452 walks, 568 SO, 1.304 WHIP, 8.8 H/9, and 2.9 BB/9, as the staff led league in starts (156), CG (87), SHO (20), balks (5), ERA (3.09), ERA+ (115), FIP (3.11), HR/9 (0.3), SO/9 (3.7) and for quality starts (101), with the youngest staff (27.1). The MVP, Pitcher of the Year, and most effective pitcher Hal Newhouser (29-9, 2.22 ERA) led MLB in wins and strikeouts (187). He led league in balks (2), SO/9 (5.4), and starts (25). Hal led team in win percentage (.763), FIP (3.13), DICE (3.04), H/9 (7.6) SO/BB (1.83). Dizzy Trout (27-14, 2.12 ERA, 104 R,) led MLB in WAR (10.9), pWAR (9.3), ERA, Innings (352.1), complete games (33), SHO (7), hits (314), batters faced (1,421), ERA+ (167) and quality starts (31). He led league for starts (40) and tough losses (7). Trout led staff in games (49), LOB% (76.5) and WHIP (1.127). Stubby Overmire (11-11, 3.07 ERA) led league in HR/9 (0.1). Johnny Gorsica (6-14, 4.11 ERA) led in saves (4). Rufe Gentry (12-14, 4.24 ERA, 104 R) led league in BB (108) and club in earned runs (96). Boom-Boom Beck (1-2, 3.89 ERA) led in GF (15). Jake Mooty (0-0, 4.45 ERA) and Joe Orrell (2-1, 2.42 ERA). Trout and Gentry led club in homers (9) and runs (104). Newhouser went 9-1 pitching on two or less days of rest as Trout was 8-1 (1.71 ERA) pitching on three days of rest.

Defense. Detroit had 190 errors for a .970 fielding average and led league in assists (1,952). League leaders were Trout in pitcher chances (119), assists (94), errors (4) and double plays (8). Catcher Richards led in chances per game (5.4), double plays (13) and caught stealing (63%). York led in errors (17) and double plays (163) at first. Mayo led in double plays (120) at second and team leader in dWAR (2.4), Higgins led in errors (22) at third and Hoover in chances per game (6.0) at short.

Hal Newhouser was consistent at home (13-5, 2.22 ERA) and away (16-4, 2.27 ERA). He was superb April 21-May 11 (3-2, 0.80 ERA, .180 BA, 1 SHO), May 13-June 12 (4-1, 1.04 ERA, .188 BA) and for August 27-Septembe 20 (6-0, 1.33 ERA, 2 SHO).

Dizzy Trout excelled at home (15-8, 2.02 ERA), on the road (12-6, 2.23 ERA), the periods of May 4-June 10 (9 GM, 6-1, 0.84 ERA, .230 BA), July 29-August 16 (6 GM, 6-0, 1.15 ERA, 1 SHO) and August 21-September 9 (5 GM, 4-1, 0.72 ERA, 3 SHO).

1940s Hitting Slugging Percentage		
1.	Hank Greenberg	.613
2.	Rudy York	.474
3.	Roy Cullenbine	.462
4.	Pat Mullin	.461
5.	Dick Wakefield	.447
6.	Vic Wertz	.437
7.	Barney McCosky	.435
8.	George Kell	.431
9.	Hoot Evers	.425
10.	Pinky Higgins	.404

Team. Steve O'Neill managed the first place Tigers (88-65-2 .575), with 1,280,341 fans. The pennant winners won the World Series in seven games over the Cubs. Teams held spring training in Indiana due to the war. Les Mueller in his first game since 1941 due to WWII allowed a single to one-armed Pete Gray at St. Louis on Tuesday, April 17, as the Tigers were 6-3 in April. Motown went 13-9 in May with a home doubleheader sweep of St. Louis on Sunday, May 6, with shutouts of 3-0 by Hal Newhouser (9 IP, 0 ER, 1 H) and 1-0 by Al Benton (9 IP, 0 ER, 6 SO). Newhouser excelled May 12-July 2 (10-1 .909, 11 CG, 101.2 IP, 1.24 ERA, .207 BA, 2 SHO). The squad was 18-12 in June when Newhouser (W 10-4, 9 IP, 0 ER, 5 H) went 2-for-4 (3 RBI) during a 5-0 shutout versus Cleveland at home on Wednesday, June 20. Detroit finished 14-12 in July that included a 24-inning 1-1 tie in 4:48 at Philadelphia called for darkness on Saturday, July 21. Mueller (19.2 IP, 0 ER) faced 74 hitters, as no one since had an outing that long. Irv Hall of the Athletics went 2-for-11. The Tigers finished 18-17 in August with an 9-6 win against visiting New York on Sunday, August 12, as reliever Jim Tobin (3 IP, 0 ER) hit an eleventh-inning three-run walk off homer. Red Borom went 5-for-6 (2 RBI) during a 15-4 triumph the next day. Motown closed 19-12 in September, as reliever Newhouser (W 25-9, 2.2 IP, 5 SO) won the pennant clincher 6-3 at St. Louis on Sunday, September 30, with a Greenberg ninth-inning grand slam. Detroit was 50-26 (.658) at home, 38-39 (.494) on the road, scored 633 runs and allowed 565. Class "AA" Buffalo had stars John McHale (92 GM, .313 BA, 22 HR, 75 RBI) from Detroit Catholic Central High School, and Ed Mierkowicz (.303 BA, 21 HR, 94 RBI) with Ed Boland (.301 BA, 23 HR, 111 RBI).

P * GEORGE CASTER

Offense. Detroit logged a .256 BA, .324 OBP, .361 SLG, .684 OPS, 1,897 TB, and 93 OPS+. Motown led the league in doubles (227). Bob Swift (.233 BA, 24 RBI) and Paul Richards (.256 BA, 3 HR, 32 RBI) caught. Rudy York (.264 BA, 18 HR, 87 RBI) at first led MLB in games (155) and GIDP (23). He led team in plate appearances (655), at bats (595), hits (157), power/speed number (9.0), total bases (246), strikeouts (85) and outs (467). The Sporting News MVP Eddie Mayo (.285 BA, 10 HR, 54 RBI) was at second, and Bob Maier (.263 BA, HR, 34 RBI) manned third. Skeeter Webb (.199 BA, 21 RBI) at short led in steals (8). Left had Jimmy Outlaw (.271 BA, 34 RBI) and the most effective hitter Hank Greenberg (78 GM, .311 BA, 13 HR, 60 RBI). Hank led for on-base percentage (.404), slugging (.544), OPS (.948), OPS+ (166), total average (.974), base-out percentage (.980), gross production average (.318), batters run average (.220), hitting, BAbip (.327), secondary average (.396), isolated power (.233) and 15-game hit streak. Centerfielder Doc Cramer (.275 BA, 6 HR, 58 RBI) led in singles (113), triples (8) and in-play percentage (87%). Player of the Year Roy Cullenbine (.277 BA, 18 HR, 93 RBI) in right led league for walks (113), 102 with Detroit, and secondary average (.386) .373 with Motown. He led his team in runs (80), doubles (27), runs batted in, oWAR (4.5), times on base (250), base runs (95), runs produced (155), runs created (94), extra base hits (50), bases produced (340) and stolen base runs (0.6). Hal Newhouser (.257 BA, 17 RBI) led the pitchers. The leading pinch-hitters were Greenberg at .400 (2-5, 3 RBI), Mayo .333 (2-6) and pitcher Zeb Eaton (2 HR, 6 RBI).

1940s Hitting On-Base plus Slugging		
1.	Hank Greenberg	1.018
2.	Roy Cullenbine	.882
3.	Dick Wakefield	.843
4.	Rudy York	.835
5.	Pat Mullin	.825
6.	George Kell	.822
	Barney McCosky	.822
8.	Vic Wertz	.805
9.	Hoot Evers	.799
10.	Pinky Higgins	.770

Pitching. The Tigers had a 2.99 ERA, 78 CG, 538 walks, 3.35 FIP, 1.322 WHIP, 8.4 H/9, and 3.5 BB/9. The staff led league in win percentage (.575), shutouts (19), saves (16), strikeouts (588), balks (5), ERA+ (119), HR/9 (0.3) and SO/9 (3.8). The Most Valuable Player, Pitcher of the Year, and most effective pitcher Hal Newhouser (25-9, 1.81 ERA) led MLB for WAR (12.2), pWAR (11.3), earned run average, wins, FIP (2.45), innings (313.1), strikeouts (212), starts (36), complete games (29), shoutouts (8), wild pitches (10), batters faced (1,261), ERA+ (195), H/9 (6.9), SO/9 (6.1) and quality starts (31). He led league for win percentage (.735), LOB% (80.7) and HR/9 (0.1). *"Prince Hal"* led staff in win percentage in his starts (26-10, .722), walks (110), DICE (2.91), WHIP (1.114), SO/BB (1.93) and R/9 (2.1). Dizzy Trout (18-15, 3.14 ERA, 8 HR) led in games (41), losses, hits (252), earned runs (86) and runs (108). Stubby Overmire (9-9, 3.88 ERA) led in saves (4), HBP (3) and BB/9 (2.3). George Caster (5-1, 3.86 ERA) led in games finished (10). Al Benton (13-8, 2.02 ERA), Les Mueller (6-8, 3.68 ERA, 8 HR), Joe Orrell (2-3, 3.00 ERA), Jim Tobin (4-5, 3.55 ERA), Zeb Eaton (4-2, 4.05 ERA) and Walter Wilson (1-3, 4.61 ERA). 17-year-old rookie Art Houtteman (0-2, 5.33 ERA) from Detroit Catholic Central High School made his MLB debut. Newhouser dominated opposing hitters during the period September 2-29 (6 GM, 3-1, 0.98 ERA, .205 BA, .228 SLG, 3 SHO).

Defense. Detroit had 158 errors for a .975 fielding average. League leaders were Newhouser in pitcher fielding (1.000), York in putouts (1,464), errors (19) and chances (1,596) at first, as he tied the record of 34 chances at Philadelphia on July 21. Mayo led in fielding average (.980) at second and led club in dWAR (2.1). Outfielders Cramer led in fielding average (.991), Outlaw in double plays (6) and double plays (5) in left, Cullenbine in chances (356), assists (23) and right fielders in assists (19) and double plays (3). Swift played 24 errorless innings as catcher in a game on Saturday, July 21, as that tied the record.

Newhouser was 14-2 (1.41 ERA) at home, 11-7 (2.26 ERA) away, 13-6 (1.66 ERA) in first half and 12-3 (1.98 ERA) in second half. He dominated right-handed hitters (.212 BA, .273 OBP, .267 SLG) and left-handed batters (.219 BA, .295 OBP, .273 SLG).

The Army discharged Greenberg on July 1 and hit a homer in his first game on July 4. He had a pinch-hit two-run walk-off single in a 9-8 win over Boston the next day. Hank shined the week of July 24-30 (8 GM, 9 HR, 21 RBI, .483 BA, 1.483 SLG).

1940s Pitching Wins		
1.	Hal Newhouser	170
2.	Dizzy Trout	129
3.	Virgil Trucks	87
4.	Fred Hutchinson	63
5.	Al Benton	60
6.	Stubby Overmire	47
7.	Tommy Bridges	44
8.	Johnny Gorsica	37
9.	Bobo Newsom	33
10.	Hal White	27

Team. Steve O'Neill led Detroit (92-62-1 .597) to second place, with 1,722,590 fans. The club had a 7-5 record in April when Dick Wakefield went 3-for-4 (5 RBI) and Hal Newhouser (9 IP, 0 ER, 2 H, 7 SO) tossed a two-hit 7-0 shutout in Cleveland on Saturday, April 20. Players were 15-14 in May that included a 3-1 win facing Boston at home on Sunday, May 19, to salvage a doubleheader split. Motown was led by Newhouser (W 6-1, 9 IP, 0 ER, 4 H, 9 SO), Hank Greenberg (HR), and back-to-back sixth-inning home runs by Jimmy Outlaw and Wakefield. The team went 14-11 in June defeating Boston 16-2 at home on Wednesday, June 26, behind Newhouser (W 13-3, 9 IP, 1 ER, 10 SO) 2-for-5 (HR, 4 RBI), Greenberg (4 RBI) and Birdie Tebbetts (3 RBI). Detroit had a 20-10 mark in July, with a double-header win at New York on Sunday, July 14, 5-1 by Newhouser (W 17-3, 9 IP, 0 ER, 3 H, 9 SO) and 6-3 by Stubby Overmire (9 IP, 3 ER, 5 H, 7 SO). Fred Hutchinson (9 IP, 0 ER, 2 H, 9 SO) went 2-for-3 during a 2-0 shutout on Monday for a series sweep. The Tigers were 15-13 in August, when Dizzy Trout (9 IP, 0 ER, 3 H) outdueled Bob Feller (8 IP 1 ER, 3 H) for a 1-0 shutout at Cleveland on Tuesday, August 13, with 65,765 fans. Trout (W 11-12, 9 IP, 0 ER) threw a 5-0 shutout at Washington on Friday, August 23, aided by Wakefield 3-for-4 (3B, HR, 2 RBI). Newhouser (W 23-6, 9 IP, 3 ER, 10 SO) had a 11-3 win in St. Louis on Saturday, August 31, with Skeeter Webb 4-for-6 (3 RBI), and Wakefield 3-for-5 (3 R, 3 RBI). The squad closed 21-9 in September with a 16-inning 4-3 loss at Chicago on Tuesday, September 3, when Virgil Trucks (15.1 IP, 3 ER) faced 56 batters. Detroit won 10 straight games September 16-24. Motown won 15-1 at Cleveland on Friday, September 20, behind Hutchinson (7 IP, 1 ER, 6 SO), George Kell 6-for-7 (4 R, 3 RBI), and Wakefield (HR, 5 RBI). Trout pitched (9 IP, 1 ER, 5 H, 6 SO) and hit (HR, 3 RBI) his way to a 10-1 win over visiting St. Louis on Tuesday, September 24, as Greenberg went 3-for-4 (2 HR, 4 RBI). Lou Kretlow (9 IP, 3 ER) was 2-for-4 (RBI) and Greenberg 3-for-4 (2 HR) to pace the 6-3 home victory against St. Louis on Thursday. The team was 48-30 (.615) at home including 10-1 with Philadelphia, 44-32 (.579) on the road with a 10-1 mark in Cleveland. Detroit scored 704 runs and allowed 567. Class "A" Williamsport had Ernest Sills (9-3 .750, 3.18 ERA), with Prince Oana (24-10 .706, 2.54 ERA) at class "A" Dallas. Class "AAA" Buffalo had Vic Wertz (.301 BA, 19 HR, 91 RBI), Detroiter John McHale (25 HR, 94 RBI) and Hal Manders (10-4 .714).

P * HAL NEWHOUSER

Offense. Detroit finished with a .258 BA, .338 OBP, .374 SLG, .712 OPS, 1,991 TB and 93 OPS+. Birdie Tebbetts (.243 BA, HR, 34 RBI) caught. Player of the Year and most effective hitter Hank Greenberg (.277 BA, 44 HR, 127 RBI) at first led MLB in homers and AB/HR (11.9). Hank led league for runs batted in and isolated power (.327), with team lead for doubles (29), slugging (.604), WAR (6.5), oWAR (5.8), secondary average (.488), base runs (110), runs produced (173), runs created (118), extra base hits (78), total bases (316), bases produced (401) and strikeouts (88). Jimmy Bloodworth (.245 BA, 5 HR, 36 RBI) was at second. George Kell (.327 BA, 4 HR, 41 RBI) at third led in triples (9) and in-play percentage (87%)). Shortstop Eddie Lake (.254 BA, 8 HR, 31 RBI) led MLB in plate appearances (705) and outs (464). He led the league in games (155) and power/speed number (10.4), as he led team in at bats (587), runs (105), hits (149), singles (116), times on base (256), steals (15) and walks (103). Dick Wakefield (.268 BA, 12 HR, 59 RBI) was in leftfield. Centerfielder Hoot Evers (.266 BA), 4 HR, 33 RBI) led in stolen base runs (1.5). Roy Cullenbine (.335 BA, 15 HR, 56 RBI) in rightfield led the Bengals in on-base percentage (.477), OPS (1.014), OPS+ (175), total average (1.202), base-out percentage (1.200), gross production average (.349), batters run average (.255), hitting, and BAbip (.347). Fred Hutchinson (.315 BA, 13 RBI) led pitchers, and was the best pinch-hitter at .400 (2-5). Kell and Cullenbine had 14-game hitting streaks.

1940s Pitching Winning Percentage		
1.	Hal Newhouser	.590
2.	Fred Hutchinson	.578
3.	Bobo Newsom	.569
4.	Tommy Bridges	.550
5.	Al Benton	.531
6.	Dizzy Trout	.520
7.	Stubby Overmire	.511
8.	Johnny Gorsica	.487
9.	Hal White	.466
10.	Art Houtteman	.436

Pitching. Motown had a 3.22 ERA, 99 ERA+, 4.73 FIP, 1.566 WHIP, 10.4 H/9, 3.7 BB/9, and 3.5 SO/9, as the staff led league in complete games (94), SHO (17), BB (497), strikeouts (896) and pWAR (22.6). Pitcher of the Year and most effective pitcher Hal Newhouser (26-9, 1.94 ERA) led MLB in ERA, wins, FIP (1.97), WHIP (1.069), H/9 (6.612), SO/9 (8.457) and ERA+ (190), with league lead for win percentage (.743). He led Motown for starts (34), complete games (29), SHO (6), innings (292.2), walks (98), strikeouts (275), WP (8), LOB% (79.0), DICE (2.58), pWAR (9.6), HR/9 (0.3), SO/BB (2.81), R/9 (2.4) and quality starts (26). Dizzy Trout (17-13, 2.35 ERA) led in games (38), losses and hits (244). Fred Hutchinson (14-11, 3.09 ERA). Virgil Trucks (14-9, 3.23 ERA) led MLB in homers (23) and league in no decisions (8). He led club in earned runs (85) and runs (94). George Caster (2-1, 5.66 ERA) led in GF (19) and saves (5). Al Benton (11-7, 3.65 ERA), Stubby Overmire (5-7, 4.62 ERA) and Hal White (1-1, 5.60 ERA). Newhouser shined June 24-July 14 (5-0, 46 IP, 42 SO, 0.39 ERA, .148 BA, .220 OBP, .198 SLG, .186 BAbip).

Defense. Detroit committed 155 errors for a .974 fielding average. They led league in putouts (4,199). Tiger league leaders were Trout in pitcher chances (86) and assists (64), Greenberg in errors (15) and chances per game (9.9) at first. Kell at third led in chances (415), chances per game (3.0), putouts (141), assists (267), double plays (27) and fielding percentage (.983).

Detroit native Hal Newhouser of Wilbur Wright High School began his career 1939-1943 at 34-52 .395 (3.69 ERA, 112 ERA+) and then became the best MLB pitcher 1944-1946 at 80-27 .748 (1.99 ERA, 180 ERA+), as an All-Star and MVP 1944-1945.

Hank Greenberg led the league in homers and RBIs for his last two full seasons as a Tiger (1940: 41 HR, 150 RBI and 1946: 44 HR, 127 RBI). He was sold to Pittsburgh for $75,000 on January 18, 1947. The first MLB player to earn $100,000 per year.

1940s Pitching Games Started		
1.	Hal Newhouser	305
2.	Dizzy Trout	239
3.	Virgil Trucks	159
4.	Fred Hutchinson	110
5.	Stubby Overmire	103
6.	Al Benton	100
7.	Tommy Bridges	96
8.	Bobo Newsom	70
9.	Johnny Gorsica	64
10.	Art Houtteman	55
	Hal White	55

Team. Detroit finished second for Steve O'Neill at 85-69 (.552), with 1,398,093 fans. Motown was 6-6- in April, when Hal Newhouser (9 IP, 0 ER, 4 H) threw a 4-0 shutout in St. Louis on Tuesday, April 15. The club went 18-8 in May with a Dizzy Trout (W 4-1, 13.1 IP, 2 ER) led 14-inning 4-2 win in Philadelphia on Thursday, May 15. George Kell was superb May 18-June 15 (34-for-82, .415 BA, .598 SLG). Motown fell 8-3 to visiting St. Louis on Friday, May 30, with native Detroiter John McHale 2-for-4 (2 R, 2 HR, 3 RBI), and 56,367 fans at Briggs Stadium. The Bengals were 8-17 in June, as Newhouser (9 IP, 0 ER, 4 H) shutout Boston 5-0 at home on Sunday, June 8. Detroit lost 10 straight thru Monday, June 23. Players had a 17-12 record in July when Eddie Mayo excelled July 12-August 10 (41-for-101, .406 BA, .545 SLG). Fred Hutchinson (W 8-3, 9 IP, 0 ER, 2 H, 8 SO) went 3-for-4 (2 RBI) in an 8-0 home shutout to end the 19-game win streak of first place New York on Friday, July 18, with Dick Wakefield 3-for-4 (RBI), Mayo 3-for-4 and Hoot Evers 3-for-5 (2 RBI). Detroit swept a twinbill over New York at home on Sunday, July 20, with a franchise record crowd of 58,369. Newhouser (9 IP, 1 ER, 3 H) won 4-1, followed by an 11-inning 12-11 victory aided by Roy Cullenbine (4 BB, HR, 3 RBI). The club finished 20-17 in August that included a stellar week for Kell of August 3-9 (10-for-15, .714 BA, .733 OBP, 1.143 SLG, .692 BAbip). Motown won 5-4 in St. Louis on Friday, August 29, as Hutchinson (9 IP, 3 ER, 8 SO) was 2-for-4, with a third-inning triple and then he stole home. The team closed 16-9 in September, as Motown swept a double-header 16-6 and 8-4 over the Senators in Washington on Sunday, September 14. The game one 20-hit attack was led by 22-year-old rookie Vic Wertz 4-for-5 (HR, 4 RBI) hit for the cycle and scored five runs, Evers 4-for-5 (HR, 3 RBI), Kell 4-for-5 (3 RBI), Pat Mullin (3 RBI) and Hal Wagner (2 RBI). Motown was 46-31 (.597) at home, 39-38 (.506) on the road, scored 714 runs and allowed 642. Class "C" Lubbock had a star-studded lineup of Bill Serena (57 HR, 190 RBI, .374 BA, 140 BB, 421 TB), Jackie Sullivan (20 HR, 120 RBI, .355 BA), Zeke Wilemon (13 HR, 96 RBI, .339 BA), Virgil Richardson (29 HR, 113 RBI, .337 BA, 92 BB), Frank Alexander (.329 BA), Pat Rooney (.328 BA), Clem Cola (24 HR, 91 RI, .326 BA, 92 BB), Mike Dooley (19 HR, 102 RBI, .316 BA), and Jack Cerin (18 HR, 101 RBI, .297 BA). Former Tiger Michigander Frank Secoury (.295 BA) of Port Huron closed his career with class "AA" Dallas. He then umpired in the Texas League 1949-1951 and National League 1952-1970.

C * BOB SWIFT

Offense. Detroit had a .258 BA, .353 OBP, .377 SLG, .730 OPS, 1,990 TB and 100 OPS+, as they led the American League in doubles (234). Bob Swift (.251 BA, HR, 21 RBI) and Hal Wagner (.288 BA, 5 HR, 33 RBI) caught. The most effective hitter Roy Cullenbine (.224 BA, 24 HR, 78 RBI) at first led in home runs, total average (.898), base-out percentage (.905), WAR (4.3), secondary average (.496), bases produced (336) and walks (137). Eddie Mayo (279 BA, 6 HR, 48 RBI) at second led with a 20-game hitting streak. Player of the Year George Kell (.320 BA, 5 HR, 93 RBI) at third led in hits (188), singles (149), doubles (29), runs batted in, hitting, in-play percentage (86%), times on base (252), base runs (90), runs produced (163), runs created (94) and total bases (242). Eddie Lake (.211 BA) at short led MLB in games (158) and plate appearances (732), with league lead for power/speed number (11.5) and outs (508). He led team in runs (96), triples (6), and steals (11). Dick Wakefield (.283 BA, 8 HR, 51 RBI) in left led in on-base percentage (.412), OPS+ (127), gross production average (.289) and batters run average (.170). Hoot Evers (.296 BA, 10 HR, 67 RBI) played centerfield. Pat Mullin (.256 BA, 15 HR, 62 RBI) in right led in triples (6), slugging (.470), OPS (.829), isolated power (.214), extra base hits (49) and strikeouts (66). Outfielder Vic Wertz (.288 BA, 6 HR, 44 RBI) led in BAbip (.345), stolen base runs (0.6) and strikeouts (66). Fred Hutchinson (.302 BA, 2 HR, 15 RBI) and Art Houtteman (.300 BA, 3 RBI) led the pitchers. The leading pinch-hitters were Mullin at .375 (2-7), Wakefield .375 (2-7), Hutchinson .313 (5-16) and Doc Cramer (6 RBI).

1940s Pitching Complete Games		
1.	Hal Newhouser	181
2.	Dizzy Trout	132
3.	Virgil Trucks	65
4.	Fred Hutchinson	59
5.	Tommy Bridges	44
6.	Al Benton	38
	Stubby Overmire	38
8.	Bobo Newsom	32
9.	Art Houtteman	24
10.	Johnny Gorsica	22

Pitching. The Tigers recorded a 3.57 ERA, 531 walks, 648 SO, 106 ERA+, 1.368 WHIP, 8.9 H/9, and 4.2 SO/9. Pitchers led league in starts (158), CG (77), SHO (15), FIP (3.48), pWAR (15.1), BB/9 (3.4), SO/BB (1.22) and quality starts (94). Pitcher of the Year Fred Hutchinson (18-10, 3.03 ERA, 3 SHO, 14 HR) led the league in BB/9 (2.5) and SO/BB (1.85). *"Hutch"* led Detroit in wins and WHIP (1.238). The most effective pitcher Hal Newhouser (17-17, 2.87 ERA, 3 SHO, 91 ER, 105 R, 0.3 HR/9) led MLB in hits (268), wild pitches (11), tough losses (9) and complete games (24). He led league in losses, with staff lead in games (40), starts (36), innings (285), walks (110), strikeouts (176), LOB% (74.9), ERA, ERA+ (132), FIP (2.85), DICE (3.35), pWAR (5.8), H/9 (8.5), SO/9 (5.6), R/9 (3.3) and quality starts (26). Dizzy Trout (10-11, 3.48 ERA, 0.3 HR/9). Virgil Trucks (10-12, 4.53 ERA, 14 HR, 91 ER, 105 R). Stubby Overmire (11-5, 3.77 ERA) led in win percentage (.688). Johnny Gorsica (2-0, 3.75 ERA) led in GF (16). Al Benton (6-7, 4.40 ERA) led in saves (7). Art Houtteman (7-2, 3.42 ERA) and Hal White (4-5, 3.61 ERA).

Defense. Detroit committed 155 errors (.975). Tiger league leaders were Tebbetts in catcher errors (10) and Cullenbine in first basemen assists (139). Kell led in third basemen chances (520), chances per game (3.4), assists (333), and errors (20), with team lead for dWAR (0.7). Lake led in errors (43) at short, as leftfielder Wakefield led all outfielders in errors (11).

First-place class "C" Lubbock (99-41 .707) averaged 8.9 runs, led by Bill Serena (183), 29-year-old player/manager Jackie Sullivan (140), Jack Cerin (126), Pat Rooney (116), Mike Dooley (114), and Virgil Richardson (107). The staff had Paul Hinrichs (18-5 .783), Leonard Heinz (20-6 .769), Girard Ahrens (13-4 .765), Royce Mills (13-6 .684), and Fay Rosson (19-11 .633).

1940s Pitching Earned Run Average		
1.	Hal Newhouser	2.84
2.	Dizzy Trout	3.01
3.	Tommy Bridges	3.05
4.	Al Benton	3.30
5.	Fred Hutchinson	3.56
6.	Bobo Newsom	3.69
7.	Hal White	3.81
8.	Stubby Overmire	3.92
9.	Art Houtteman	4.11
10.	Johnny Gorsica	4.18

Team. Detroit finished in fifth for Steve O'Neill at 78-76 (.506), with a record attendance of 1,743,035. The Tigers were 4-7 in April with a three-game series sweep in Chicago to open the season. The Bengals were 15-13 in May when Virgil Trucks (8.1 IP, 1 ER, 6 SO) started a 4-1 win at Washington, D.C. on Tuesday, May 11, with Vic Wertz (4 RBI) hitting two triples. The squad had a 10-14 mark in June that included a 6-2 triumph at Yankee Stadium on Thursday, June 3, as Detroit had a four-run eleventh inning. Hal Newhouser (11 IP, 2 ER), Pat Mullin 3-for-4, Wertz (HR) and Hoot Evers (HR) led the way. Detroit lost 7-4 to New York the next day, as the crowd of 64,261 watched Tiger pinch-hitter Dick Wakefield tie the score 4-4 on a three-run home run in the seventh inning. Newhouser dominated for the three-weeks of June 30-July 21 (6 GM, 5-0, 35.1 IP, 0.76 ERA, .190 BA, .119 SLG). Players were 17-14 in July that included seven straight wins. Fred Hutchinson (9 IP, 2 ER, 6 SO) beat visiting Philadelphia 17-2 on Friday, July 30, as Bob Swift went 3-for-4 (5 RBI), George Kell (HR, 4 RBI), Wakefield (3 RBI) and Wertz (HR, 2 RBI). The club had an August record of 13-13. Motown lost 6-2 to the first-place Indians on Monday, August 9, with a night attendance record of 56,586 at Briggs Stadium. Detroit split a doubleheader in New York on Sunday, August 29. Johnny Lipon was 3-for-5 in the 9-6 game one win, followed by a 11-10 loss, as the Tigers scored five runs in the sixth and seventh innings to take the lead after trailing 9-0. They were led by Lipon 4-for-5, Evers 4-for-5 (HR, 3 RBI), Jimmy Outlaw (4 RBI) and Mullin 3-for-4 (HR, 3 RBI). The team closed 17-14 in September and 2-1 in October. Lipon went 4-for-5 in a 13-inning 3-2 victory at Cleveland on Thursday, September 9. Newhouser (W 21-12, 9 IP, 1 ER, 5 H) and Wertz 3-for-4 (3 2B, 3 RBI) aided a 7-1 win in Cleveland on Sunday, October 3, with 74,181 fans. The club was an identical 39-38 (.506) at home and away. Players scored 700 runs and allowed 726. Coaker Triplett (.353 BA, 19 HR, 83 RBI) and Johnny Groth (.340 BA, 30 HR, 97 RBI) were exemplary players for class "AAA" Buffalo.

SS * JOHNNY LIPON

Offense. Detroit finished with a .267 BA, .353 OBP, .375 SLG, .728 OPS, 1,965 TB, and 91 OPS+. The catcher was Bob Swift (.223 BA, 4 HR, 33 RBI). Sam Vico (.267 BA, 8 HR, 58 RBI) at first led in games (144), and outs (424). Eddie Mayo (.249 BA, 2 HR, 42 RBI) manned second base. George Kell (.304 BA, 2 HR, 44 RBI) at third led for in-play percentage (85%). Johnny Lipon (.290 BA, 5 HR, 52 RBI) played shortstop and led in steals (4), with Vic Wertz (.248 BA, 7 HR, 67 RBI) in left field. Player of the Year centerfielder Hoot Evers (.314 BA, 10 HR, 103 RBI) led in plate appearances (606), at bats (538), hits (169), singles (120), doubles (33), runs batted in, batting average, BAbip (.320), runs produced (174) and power/speed number (4.6). The most effective hitter right-fielder Pat Mullin (.288 BA) led in runs (91), triples (11), home runs, slugging (.504), OPS (.889), OPS+ (132), WAR (3.5), oWAR (3.5), batters run average (.194), base runs (93), runs created (96), isolated power (.216), extra base hits (50), total bases (250), bases produced (328), and walks (77). Outfielder Dick Wakefield (.276 BA, 11 HR, 53 RBI) led in on-base percentage (.406), total average (.921), base-out percentage (.925), gross production average (.301) and secondary average (.410). Neil Berry (.266 BA, 16 RBI). Fred Hutchinson (.205 BA, HR, 12 RBI) led pitchers. The leading pinch-hitters were Jimmy Outlaw at .417 (5-12, 3 RBI) and Dick Wakefield at .400 (8-20, 3 HR, 10 RBI). Kell, Mayo, Mullin and Vico had 12-game hit streaks. The first-place class "A" Flint Arrows (89-49 .645) had George Lerchen (110 R, .337 BA) of Detroit Western High School, Ken Rogers (9-2 .818, 3.28 ERA), Dick Marlowe (12-5 .706, 3.16 ERA), Norman Scott (12-5 .706) and Alex Nedelco (16-7 .696, 2.08 ERA).

1940s Pitching Innings Pitched		
1.	Hal Newhouser	2,453.1
2.	Dizzy Trout	2,026.1
3.	Al Benton	973.1
4.	Fred Hutchinson	912.1
5.	Stubby Overmire	830.2
6.	Tommy Bridges	743.1
7.	Johnny Gorsica	723.2
8.	Hal White	527.1
9.	Bobo Newsom	514.1
10.	Art Houtteman	512.0

Pitching. The Tigers had a 4.79 ERA, 589 walks, three SHO, 106 ERA+, 4.72 FIP, 1.587 WHIP, 10.2 H/9, with league lead in strikeouts (678), FIP (3.86), BB/9 (3.8), strikeouts per nine (4.4) and strikeouts to walks (1.15). Pitcher of the Year and most effective pitcher Hal Newhouser (21-12, 3.01 ERA, 2 SHO) led the league in wins, FIP (3.19), home runs per nine (0.3) and team in win percentage (.636), starts (35), complete games (19), innings (272.1), hits (249), walks (99), strikeouts (143), LOB% (71.6), earned run average, ERA+ (145), DICE (3.53), pWAR (6.5), runs per nine (3.6) and quality starts (22). Dizzy Trout (10-14, 3.43 ERA, 2 SHO) led league in home runs per nine (0.3). Virgil Trucks (14-13, 3.78 ERA, 43 GM) led in wild pitches (7), hits per nine (8.1) and strikeouts per nine (5.2). Fred Hutchinson (13-11, 4.32 ERA) led league in home runs (32), WHIP (1.226), walks per nine (2.0), strikeouts to walks (1.92) and team in earned runs (106) and runs (119). Art Houtteman (2-16, 4.66 ERA, 43 GM) led in losses and saves (10). Stubby Overmire (3-4, 5.97 ERA) led in games finished (16). Ted Gray (6-2, 4.22 ERA), Al Benton (2-2, 5.68 ERA), Hal White (2-1, 6.12 ERA) and Detroit native 21-year-old rookie Billy Pierce (3-0, 6.34 ERA). Saul Rogovin (13-7) pitched for the class "AAA" Buffalo Bisons.

Defense. Players committed 155 errors (.974). League leaders were pitchers Hutchinson and Trucks in fielding (1.000), Swift in catcher passed balls (10), Mullin in right fielder chances (245) and putouts (231), as Lipon led club in defensive WAR (0.7).

Bruce Blanchard (.327 BA) and Joe Ginsberg (.326 BA) played for class "A" Williamsport, with Wayne Blackburn (.326 BA) at class "AA" Little Rock. Hillis Layne (.342 BA, 80 RBI) and Earl Rapp (.298 BA, 17 HR, 96 RBI) were stars at class "AAA" Seattle.

Detroit was the last team in the league to play a night game when they beat Philadelphia 4-1 on Tuesday, June 15, 1948, in front of 54,480 fans. The game featured Hal Newhouser (W 8-4, 9 IP, 1 ER, 2 H) facing future Tiger Joe H. Coleman (L 7-3).

1940s Pitching Walks	
1. Hal Newhouser	1,068
2. Dizzy Trout	746
3. Al Benton	403
4. Tommy Bridges	390
5. Hal White	251
6. Fred Hutchinson	248
7. Johnny Gorsica	247
8. Stubby Overmire	234
9. Bobo Newsom	218
10. Ted Gray	180

Team. Detroit finished for Red Rolfe at 87-67 (.565), with 1,821,204 fans. The Tigers were 6-5 in April, as George Kell had five straight multi-hit games April 23-28 (.522 BA, .560 OBP, .609 SLG). Motown won a doubleheader in Chicago on Tuesday, April 26. Vic Wertz (HR, 3 RBI) and Virgil Trucks (W 2-0, 7 IP, 2 ER) led a 6-2 game one win, followed by a 7-5 triumph behind Aaron Robinson (HR, 4 RBI). The Bengals went 14-14 during May when Kell torched Browns pitching May 13-15 (.600 BA .600 OBP, .850 SLG), including a 4-for-5 effort on Sunday, May 15. Motown lost 15-7 at Philadelphia on Saturday, May 21, after leading 7-0. Detroit closed 18-12 for June, with a Virgil Trucks (W 8-3, 11 IP, 3 H, 2 ER) 3-2 victory at home over New York on Wednesday, June 8, with 54,919 fans, as the Tigers took 13 walks. Fred Hutchinson (9 IP, 0 ER) and Hoot Evers (3 RBI) led a 7-0 shutout at Washington on Sunday, June 19. Pat Mullin 4-for-4 (3 HR, 5 RBI) and Wertz 4-for-5 (3 2B, 4 RBI) paced a 12-4 win at Yankee Stadium on Sunday, June 26, with a crowd of 62,382. Tommy Bridges won the All-Star game, as the American League won 3-1 on Tuesday, July 11, with 62,892 fans in the Bronx. Players were 16-15 in July with a 13-7 win in Washington on Thursday, July 28, with a mere 1,485 fans. Dizzy Trout (HR, 4 RBI) got the decision and hit a grand slam, as Detroit scored seven ninth inning runs. The team swept a doubleheader at Philadelphia 3-0 and 6-0 on Sunday, July 31, with shutouts by Ted Gray (9 IP, 0 ER) and Hutchinson (W 8-4, 9 IP, 0 ER, 5 H). The Motor city finished 8-12 in August, as Wertz (2 HR, 6 RBI) and Art Houtteman (W 11-7, 9 IP, 2 ER) aided a 13-2 win against visiting New York on Wednesday, August 24. The Bengals were 15-7 in September winning their first 10 games of the month. Houttemann (W 13-7, 9 IP, 0 ER) went 2-for-4 and pitched a 7-0 shutout of Boston at home on Thursday, September 1, with Wertz 4-for-5 (2 RBI) and Mullin 3-for-4. Trucks (W 16-10, 9 IP, 0 ER), Wertz (3 RBI) and Kell (3 RBI) led an 8-0 shutout of visiting Chicago the next day. Detroit dominated the Washington Senators (18-4 .818), were 50-27 (.649) at home, and 37-40 (.481) on the road. The Bengals scored 751 runs and allowed 655. Minor league stars included Kenneth Humphrey (.334 BA) at class "AA" Williamsport, Hal Simpson (.345 BA, 28 HR, 319 TB) at class "AA" Little Rock, and Bill Butland (9-3) with class "AAA" Toledo. Carl Linhart (.311 BA, 23 HR, 114 RB) and Eddie Neville (25-10 .714, 2.59 ERA, 25 CG, 8 SHO) were stars at class "B" Durham.

CF * JOHNNY GROTH

Offense. Detroit logged a .267 BA, .361 OBP, .378 SLG, .739 OPS, 1,986 TB and 95 OPS+. Catcher Aaron Robinson (.269 BA, 13 HR, 56 RBI) led in secondary average (.369). Paul Campbell (.278 BA, 3 HR, 30 RBI) was at first, as Neil Berry (.237 BA, 18 RBI) manned second. The most effective hitter George Kell (.343 BA, 3 HR, 59 RBI) at third led MLB in hitting and the league for BAbip (.348). Kell led club in runs (97), doubles (38), triples (9), on-base percentage (.424), OPS (.892), OPS+ (.136), total average (.877), base-out percentage (.895), gross production average (.308), WAR (4.8), oWAR (4.6), batters run average (.193), and hitting streak (20). Johnny Lipon (.251 BA, 3 HR, 59 RBI) played short. Hoot Evers (.303 BA, 7 HR, 72 RBI) in left led for power/speed number (6.5). Centerfielder Johnny Groth (.293 BA, 11 HR, 73 RBI) led for slugging (.471). Player of the Year Vic Wertz (.304 BA, 20 HR, 133 RBI) in right led league in games (155), with team highs for plate appearances (695), at bats (608), hits (185), homers, runs batted in, times on base (265), base runs (105), runs produced (209), runs created (109), extra base hits (52), total bases (283), bases produced (365), walks (80), strikeouts (61) and outs (452). Infielders Eddie Lake (.196 BA, HR, 15 RBI) and Don Kolloway (.294 BA, 2 HR, 47 RBI) that led for in-play percentage (85%). Outfielder Pat Mullin (.268 BA, 12 HR, 59 RBI) led in isolated power (.181). Fred Hutchinson (.247 BA, 7 RBI) and Art Houtteman (.244 BA, 7 RBI) led pitchers. Campbell led all pinch-hitters at .625 (5-8, HR).

1940s Pitching Strikeouts	
1. Hal Newhouser	1,579
2. Dizzy Trout	930
3. Tommy Bridges	467
4. Fred Hutchinson	429
5. Al Benton	410
6. Bobo Newsom	339
7. Johnny Gorsica	272
8. Stubby Overmire	231
9. Art Houtteman	228
10. Hal White	219

Pitching. The team had a 3.77 ERA, 628 walks, 631 SO, 111 ERA+, 3.95 FIP, 1.411 WHIP, 8.6 H/9, 4.1 BB/9, and 4.1 SO/9, as staff led league in SHO (19), innings (1,393.2) and SO/BB (1.0). Pitcher of the Year Virgil Trucks (19-11, 2.81 ERA) led MLB in shutouts (6) and strikeouts (153). He led staff in games (41), wins, losses, saves (4), walks (124), earned run average, ERA+ (148), pWAR (6.9), hits per nine (6.8), strikeouts per nine (5.0) and runs per nine (3.1). Fred Hutchinson (15-7, 2.96 ERA) led league in WHIP (1.161), walks per nine (2.5) and staff in win percentage (.682) and LOB% (77.0). Hal Newhouser (18-11, 3.36 ERA) led league in hits (277) and earned runs (109). He led club in starts (35), complete games (22), innings (292), runs (118), FIP (3.51), DICE (4.00) and quality starts (21). Detroit native Ted Gray (10-10, 3.51 ERA) led in wild pitches (7). Art Houtteman (15-10, 3.71 ERA) led in strikeouts to walks (1.44). Dizzy Trout (3-6, 4.40 ERA) led in games finished (24). Others were Stubby Overmire (1-3, 9.87 ERA), Marlin Stuart (0-2, 9.10 ERA), Marv Grissom (2-4, 6.41 ERA) and Lou Kretlow (3-2, 6.16 ERA).

Defense. The Bengals committed 132 errors for a .978 fielding percentage and led the league in putouts (4,170). Tiger league leaders were pitchers Gray in fielding (1.000), Garver in errors (5) and Houtteman in double plays (7). Groth led centerfielders in double plays (3) and Wertz in right-fielder double plays (5), as Lipon led the team in defensive WAR (1.1).

Class "AAA" Buffalo featured Bob Hooper (19-3 .864), Saul Rogovin (16-6 .727), Coaker Triplett (.322 BA, 22 HR, 102 RBI), Gene Markland (.305 BA, 25 HR, 90 RBI, 142 R), Ray Coleman (.295 BA, 23 HR, 113 RBI) and George Byam (19 HR, 106 RBI).

Trucks had 25.2 scoreless innings June 8-23 (5 GM, 3-0, 0.00 ERA, .096 BA, 100.0 LOB%, 2 SHO). Virgil was spectacular again during period of August 30-September 30 (5 GM, 4-0, 36 IP, 1 ER, 0.25 ERA, .169 BA, .223 OBP, .185 SLG, .200 BAbip, 3 SHO).

MGR * RED ROLFE

Player of the Decade. Al Kaline (.311 BA, 125 HR, 544 RBI) was decade leader in home runs (125), runs batted in (544), defensive WAR (5.9), extra bases on long hits (599), stolen bases (51) and walks (344). Kaline entered the lineup as a 19-year-old rookie in 1954 that included a blazing August (.416 BA, .468 BAbip) and second half (.315 BA). He excelled during the first half of 1955 (.371 BA, 19 HR, 67 RBI) to be an All-Star. His best year of 1955 (.340 BA, 27 HR, 102 RBI, 162 OPS+) had him the league leader in hits (200), average, and total bases (321). Kaline followed that as an All-Star in 1956 (.314 BA, 27 HR, 128 RBI, 327 TB, 139 OPS+). Al was the league leader in slugging (.530) and OPS (.940) in 1959 season (.327 BA, 27 HR, 94 RBI, 151 OPS+). Mr. Tiger reached base in 55 straight games July 26-September 21, 1956 (76-for-209, .364 BA, 10 HR, 54 RBI, .456 OBP, .612 SLG, 1.068 OPS). Kaline went 9-for-13 against Chicago July 7-8, 1958 (.692 BA, 2 HR, 10 RBI, .714 OBP, 1.308 SLG, 2.022 OPS, .636 BAbip). He excelled with the bases loaded (.358 BA, 67 R, 61 RBI) and in games at Fenway Park at in Boston (64-for-213 .300 BA, 9 HR, 31 RBI).

1950s			
Year	W – L	Pct.	Pl
1950	**95-59**	**.617**	2
1951	73-81	.474	5
1952	50-104	.325	8
1953	60-94	.390	6
1954	68-86	.442	5
1955	79-75	.513	5
1956	82-72	.532	5
1957	78-76	.506	4
1958	77-77	.500	5
1959	76-78	.494	4
	738-802	.479	

All-Decade Team. Manager Red Rolfe (278-256 .521) led Motown to a spectacular 1950 (95-59 .617) campaign good for second place, including 17-5 (.773) against both Philadelphia and St. Louis. Pitcher Frank Lary (79-69 .534, 3.32 ERA) went 21-6 against New York during the decade. Catcher Red Wilson (.267 BA, 21 HR, 154 RBI) led the league in range factor in 1958 (6.76) and 1959 (6.93). First baseman Walt Dropo (.266 BA, 40 HR, 210 RBI) played 152 games in 1953 (.248 BA, 13 HR, 96 RBI) when he led the league in assists (127). Second baseman Jerry Priddy (.267 BA, 26 HR, 176 RBI) joined Detroit in 1950 (.277 BA, 13 HR, 75 RBI, 104 R, 729 PA). Shortstop Harvey Kuenn (.314 BA, 53 HR, 423 RBI) led the 1950s in games (1,049), plate appearances (4,750), at-bats (4,372), runs (619), hits (1,372), singles (1,032), doubles (244), triples (43), oWAR (25.5), in-play percentage (87.2), times on base (1,702), extra base hits (340), total bases (1,861), bases produced (2,234), steals (51), with a 22-game hit streak in 1959. The 1953 Rookie of the Year (.308 BA, 2 HR, 48 RBI, 209 H, 731 PA). Third baseman Ray Boone (.291 BA, 105 HR, 460 RBI) was a solid Tiger in 1953 (.312 BA, 22 HR, 93 RBI, 157 OPS+), 1954 (.295 BA, 20 HR, 85 RBI), 1955 (.284 BA, 20 HR, 116 RBI) and 1956 (.308 BA, 25 HR, 81 RBI). Left fielder Charlie Maxwell (.281 BA, 103 HR, 347 RBI) from Lawton, Michigan led in strikeouts (323) and became an All-Star in 1956 (.326 BA, 28 HR, 87 RBI). Center fielder Al Kaline (.311 BA, 125 HR, 544 RBI) finished the MVP voting second in 1955 and third the following year. Right-fielder Vic Wertz (.286 BA, 71 HR, 268 RBI) returned to All-Star form for the 1951 (.285 BA, 27 HR, 94 RBI) season.

TV * VAN PATRICK

Pitcher of the Decade. Frank Lary (79-69 .534, 3.32 ERA) led the 1950s in wins, complete games (78), quality starts (102), high quality starts (91), dominate starts (36), hit by pitch (53), intentional walks (24), technical runs allowed (3.79), earned run average, ERA+ (121), pWAR (20.0), runs per nine (3.79), quality start percentage (.600), dominant start percentage (.212), pickoffs (7) and tough losses (27). Lary starred in 1956 (21-13 .618, 3.15 ERA) when he stood 10-12 and then was stellar August 8-September 29 (13 GM, 11-1 .917, 1 SV, 1.00 ERA, .191 BA, .223 BAbip), including eight straight wins. His 1959 (17-10 .630, 3.55 ERA) season was another solid campaign, with a league best BB/SO (2.98). Lary became the *"Yankee Killer"* 1956-1959 (19-5 .792) including 1956 (5-1 .833, 2.89 ERA), 1957 (2-2), 1958 (7-1 .875, 1.86 ERA, .204 BA) and 1959 (5-1 .833, 3.16 ERA).

1950s Attendance			
Year	Attn.	Avg.	Rk
1950	**1,951,474**	**24,092**	2
1951	1,132,641	14,710	5
1952	1,026,846	13,336	5
1953	884,658	11,198	5
1954	1,079,847	14,024	4
1955	1,181,838	15,349	5
1956	1,051,182	13,477	3
1957	1,272,346	16,524	2
1958	1,098,924	14,272	2
1959	1,221,221	15,860	4

All-Decade Pitchers. Lary was phenomenal in September 1956 (7-0 1.000, 0.86 ERA, .175 BA, .203 SLG, .209 BAbip, 7 CG). Jim Bunning (59-39 .602, 3.55 ERA) led the decade in balks (5), LOB% (77.4), H/9 (7.88), SO/9 (6.75) and SO/BB (2.21), with 1957 (20-8 .714, 2.69 ERA) his best year. Paul Foytack (58-52 .527, 3.87 ERA) led in wild pitches (25) and 14-11 (3.14 ERA) in 1957. Ned Garver (38-40 .487, 3.68 ERA) led for complete game percentage (.500), with five straight complete game wins in July of 1955. Billy Hoeft (74-78 .487, 4.02 ERA) was decade leader in games (239), losses, starts (176), shutouts (16), innings (1,324.2), hits (1,331), homers (129), walks (481), strikeouts (783), earned runs (591), runs (634), batters faced (5,693), no decisions (34), cheap wins (13). He was an All-Star in 1955 (16-7 .696, 2.99 ERA, 7 SHO). Fred Hutchinson (29-19 .604, 3.78 ERA) led in win percentage, FIP (3.46), DICE (3.94), BB/9 (1.62), high quality start percentage (.533) and relief win percentage (10-1 .909). His best year was 1950 (17-8 .680, 3.96 ERA). Detroiter Steve Gromek (45-41 .523, 3.77 ERA) was his best in 1954 (18-16 .529, 2.74 ERA, 136 ERA+). Dizzy Trout (23-24 .489, 3.99 ERA) had a league best FIP (3.67) in 1950 (13-5 .722, 3.75 ERA). Al Aber (22-24 .478, 4.12 ERA) led in games finished (74), saves (14), games in relief (129), relief wins (15) and holds (9). Ray Herbert (12-14 .462, 5.09 ERA) from Detroit led squad in HR/9 (0.52) and stood 4-0 (1.42 ERA, 301 ERA+) to start the 1951 season when he was ordered to military service.

20-year-old Billy Hoeft pitched a 4-2 home win over Chicago on Monday, September 7, 1953. The left-hander made history with an immaculate inning, striking out Jim Rivera, Mike Fornieles and Chico Carrasquel on nine pitches in the seventh inning.

Jim Bunning was the first in MLB history to throw a no-hitter in both leagues (AL: Detroit 7-20-1957, NL: Philadelphia 6-21-1964), win 100 games in both leagues (AL: 118, NL: 106) and register 1,000 strikeouts in both leagues (AL: 1,406, NL: 1,449).

Team. Detroit finished second for Red Rolfe at 95-59 (.617), with an attendance of 1,951,474. The club went 6-3 in April including a Vic Wertz (4-for-5) led 5-2 win in St. Louis 5-2 on Tuesday, April 25. The Bengals were 16-9 in May with a 10-2 mark on the road. Virgil Trucks (11 IP, 0 ER, 5 H, 7 SO) pitched a 1-0 11-inning shutout over visiting St. Louis on Saturday, May 13. The squad had a record of 16-3 for May 30-June 18. Motown was 21-9 in June when they won 16-5 in Philadelphia on Friday, June 2, as George Kell was 4-for-7 (3 RBI) hitting for the cycle and pitcher Fred Hutchinson (3 RBI) went 4-for-6. The Tigers scored a 18-8 victory in Boston on Saturday, June 10, behind Jerry Priddy 4-for-5, Johnny Groth 5-for-6 (4 RBI) and Wertz (HR, 3 RBI). Players defeated the Red Sox 9-6 in 14-innings the next day, as Ted Gray (W 6-2, 9 IP, 0 ER, 4 H, 5 SO) won in long relief. Detroit went 16-13 in July with Kell 3-for-4 (HR, 2 RBI) during a 5-3 loss in Cleveland on Friday, July 2, with 78,187 fans. The Tigers were 18-13 in August, as Hal White (9 IP, 0 ER, 2 H) went 1-for-3 (RBI) during a 4-0 shutout of New York at home on August 2. Dizzy Trout (W 8-2, 9 IP, 0 ER) was 1-for-3 (RBI) pitching a 4-0 shutout over visiting Washington on Sunday, August 6. The first-place Tigers (71-38) beat St. Louis (38-71) 6-0 during an Art Houtteman (W 16-9, 9 IP, 0 ER, 1 H) one-hit home shutout, aided by Groth 3-for-4 (HR, 3 RBI). The team closed 18-11 in September when Hoot Evers (6 RBI) hit for the cycle during a 13-13 10-inning home tie with Cleveland on Thursday, September 7. Charlie Keller had been a pinch-hitter (43 GM, 9-43, 10 RBI, .290 BA, .488 OBP, .516 SLG) all season through September 18. Keller was given a start in left and went 4-for-5 (2 HR, 5 RBI), behind Pat Mullin (HR, 2 RBI) and Houtteman (W 19-11, 9 IP, 4 ER) 3-for 5 (2 RBI) for a 12-4 win at home against Philadelphia on Tuesday, September 19. Groth, Kell and Priddy led the major leagues in games (157). Motown was 50-30 (.625) at home, 45-29 (.608) on the road, scored 837 runs and allowed 713. 20-year-old Frank Lary (9-2 .818, 2.25 ERA) played at the class "D" level with Jamestown and Thomasville.

1950s
Team Hitting

YEAR	AVG	HR	RBI	SB
1950	**.282**	114	**788**	23
1951	.265	104	636	37
1952	.243	103	529	27
1953	.266	108	660	30
1954	.258	90	552	48
1955	.266	130	724	41
1956	.279	150	745	43
1957	.257	116	574	36
1958	.266	109	611	48
1959	.258	**160**	665	34

P * ART HOUTTEMAN

Offense. Detroit had a .282 BA, .369 OBP, .417 SLG, .786 OPS, 2,245 TB and 98 OPS+. Aaron Robinson (.226 BA, 9 HR, 37 RBI) was the catcher. Don Kolloway (.289 BA, 6 HR, 62 RBI) at first led for in-play percentage (86%). Jerry Priddy (.277 BA, 13 HR, 75 RBI) at second led in plate appearances (729), walks (95), strikeouts (95) and outs (489). Third baseman George Kell (.340 BA, 8 HR, 101 RBI) led major league baseball in hits (218) and doubles (56), as he was league leader for at bats (641) and runs created (124). Kell led the Bengals in runs (114), singles (148), WAR (4.9), oWAR (4.6), hitting, BAbip (.341), times on base (285), base runs (117), runs produced (207), extra base hits (70), total bases (310) and hitting streak (20). Shortstop Johnny Lipon (.293 BA, 2 HR, 63 RBI) led in steals (9). Hoot Evers (.323 BA, 21 HR, 103 RBI) in left led league in triples (11). He led club for slugging (.551), OPS (.959), OPS+ (141), batters run average (.221), isolated power (.228) and power/speed number (8.1). Johnny Groth (.306 BA, 12 HR, 85 RBI) in center led for walks (95). Player of the Year and most effective hitter Vic Wertz (.308 BA, 27 HR, 123 RBI) at right field led in home runs, runs batted in, total average (.978), base-out percentage (.980), secondary average (.386) and bases produced (389). Reserves Dick Kryhoski (.219 BA, 4 HR, 19 RBI), Pat Mullin (.218 BA, 6 HR, 23 RBI) and Bob Swift (.227 BA, 2 HR, 9 RBI). Fred Hutchinson (.326 BA, 20 RBI) led pitchers in hitting. The best pinch-hitters were Robinson at .800 (4-5, HR, 3 RBI) and Keller .345 (10-29, 11 RBI).

Pitching. The Tigers had a .4.12 ERA, nine SHO, 553 walks, 576 SO, 114 ERA+, 4.31 FIP, 1.419 WHIP, 9.2 H/9 and 3.7 SO/9, with league best for CG (72), innings (1,407.1), homers (141), pWAR (16.7), BB/9 (3.5) and SO/BB (1.04). Pitcher of the Year Art Houtteman (19-12, 3.54 ERA) of Detroit led American League in shutouts (4), homers (29) and LOB% (77.9). He led staff in wins, starts (34), complete games (21), innings (274.2), walks (99), HBP (8), earned runs (108), earned run average, ERA+ (132), WHIP (1.296), pWAR (6.0), H/9 (8.4) and R/9 (3.7). The most effective pitcher Dizzy Trout (13-5, 3.75 ERA) led in win percentage (.722), HR/9 (0.6). Fred Hutchinson (17-8, 3.96 ERA) led the league in BB/9 (1.9), SO/BB (1.48), with team lead for hits (269) and runs (119). Hal Newhouser (15-13, 4.34 ERA) led in losses. Ted Gray (10-7, 4.40) led in strikeouts (102) and SO/9 (6.1). Hal White (9-6, 4.54 ERA) led in games (42). Paul Calvert (2-2, 6.31 ERA) finished 19 games. Hank Borowy (1-1, 3.31 ERA), Virgil Trucks (3-1, 3.54 ERA), Saul Rogovin (2-1, 4.50 ERA) and Marlin Stuart (3-1, 5.56 ERA). Hutchinson and Trout tied as league leader in FIP (3.67).

1950s
Team Hitting

YEAR	OBP	SLG	OPS	OPS+
1950	**.369**	.417	**.786**	98
1951	.337	.380	.717	94
1952	.318	.352	.670	86
1953	.331	.387	.718	95
1954	.322	.367	.688	90
1955	.344	.394	.739	101
1956	.356	**.420**	.776	**104**
1957	.323	.378	.701	89
1958	.326	.389	.715	91
1959	.335	.400	.735	97

Defense. Detroit made 120 Errors and led the league in fielding (.981), chances (6,211), putouts (4,215) and assists (1,876). Al leaders were pitchers Trout in fielding (1.000), Houtteman in caught stealing (89%) and pickoffs (4). Kolloway in chances per game (10.0) at first. Second baseman Priddy led MLB in dWAR (2.7, the league leader for chances (1,001), chances per game (6.4), assists (542) and double plays (150). Kell in fielding (.982) at third, Lipon at short in chances (789), chances per game (5.4), assists (483), errors (33) and double plays (126). Evers led outfielders in fielding (.997) and leftfielders in chances (336), putouts (321) and double plays (3). Wertz led league all right-fielders in chances (298), putouts (283) and errors (10).

Manager Kenneth Holtcamp of class "D" Richmond (80-58 .580) had a stellar staff that featured star pitchers Billy Hoeft (10-1 .909, 1.71 ERA, 0.968 WHIP), Dan Searle (13-3 .813, 2.12 ERA, 1.052 WHIP), and Donald Coppage (22-6 .786, 2.53 ERA).

Class "C" Butler had Joseph Pendleton (.345 BA) and Paul Foytack (18-6 .750), Ernie Funk (22-6 .786) at class "A" Flint, Pat Haggerty (.346 BA) for class "AA" Little Rock, with Joe Ginsberg (.336 BA) and Marlin Stuart (9-3 .750) at class "AAA" Toledo.

1950s Hitting Games	
1. Harvey Kuenn	1,049
2. Al Kaline	904
3. Johnny Groth	700
4. Ray Boone	683
5. Frank Bolling	646
6. Charlie Maxwell	610
7. Bill Tuttle	581
8. Jerry Priddy	451
9. Red Wilson	440
10. Frank House	439

Team. Detroit finished fifth for Red Rolfe at 73-81 (.474), with 1,132.641 fans. Detroit was 3-5 in April, with a 7-4 home win over St. Louis on Monday, April 23, when Pat Mullin (HR, 3 RBI) hit a three-run pinch-hit homer in the fifth to tie the score, and Vic Wertz (HR, 3 RBI) hit a three-run walk-off home run, as 23-year-old rookie Joe Ginsberg was 3-for-3 and homered. The Bengals logged a 14-15 record in May including 12-3 for the period May 4-20. Pitcher Hal Newhouser (9 IP, 4 ER) was 2-for-3 (RBI) at the plate during an 8-4 home win over Boston on Friday, May 4, with Dick Kryhoski 4-for-4 (3 RBI) and Jerry Priddy (3 RBI). Motown won 12-4 at Washington on Tuesday, May 15, led by Bud Souchock 2-for-2 (HR, 4 RBI), Mullin 3-for-3 (3 RBI), and Wertz 3-for-3, as Newhouser (9 IP, 4 ER) had two sacrifice hits. Detroit endured a 1-12 stretch during May 21-June 3. Fred Hutchinson struggled for the first two months April-May (2-2, 30.1 IP, 5 BB, 5.64 ERA, .357 BA, .364 BAbip) then excelled for six weeks June 1-July 14 (5-1, 53 IP, 5 BB, 1.70 ERA, .222 BA, .233 BAbip). The team played to a 14-12 mark in June that included 8-1 mark for games played June 3-12. Gene Bearden (9 IP, 0 ER, 4 H) shutout visiting Washington 4-0 on Tuesday, June 5, with George Kell 4-for-4. The squad was 12-18 in July when Bob Cain (9 IP, 3 ER, 5 H, 6 SO) pitched a 13-3 home victory against Cleveland on Saturday, July 7. The 20-hit Tiger attack was led by hometown hero Ginsberg 4-for-5 (HR, 5 RBI) from Detroit Cooley High School, Johnny Groth (3 RBI), Kryhoski 3-for-5, and Hoot Evers 5-for-5 with five runs scored. The City of Detroit celebrated its 250th anniversary as host for the All-Star game on Tuesday, July 10. Motown fell 10-9 in 10-innings to first place Boston at home on Sunday, July 22, behind Kryhoski (4 RBI), Charlie Keller 3-for-4 (HR, 2 RBI) and Groth 3-for-5. Players were 16-19 in August with Cain (8.1 IP, 0 ER) walking 3'7" Eddie Gaedel of the Browns in his lone MLB at bat during a 6-2 Tiger win in St. Louis on Sunday, August 19. Motown closed 14-12 in September with a 2-1 14-inning win in Chicago on Friday, September 7, when Virgil Trucks (14 IP, 0 ER, 5 H, 7 SO) faced 50 batters and Groth went 4-for-6. Detroit finished 36-41 (.558) at home, and 37-40 (.416) on the road. Detroit scored 685 runs as pitchers allowed opponents 741.

1B * DICK KRYHOSKI

Offense. Detroit had a .265 BA, .337 OBP, .380 SLG, .717 OPS, 2,026 TB and 94 OPS+. Joe Ginsberg (.260 BA, 8 HR, 37 RBI) caught. Dick Kryhoski (.287 BA, 12 HR, 57 RBI) at first led in hit streak (13). Jerry Priddy (.260 BA, 8 HR, 57 RBI) at second led league in games (154). He led club in triples (6), strikeouts (73) and outs (465). George Kell (.319 BA, 2 HR, 59 RBI) at third led league in hits (191), singles (150), and doubles (36), with team lead for plate appearances (674), at bats (598), runs (92), on-base percentage (.386), oWAR (3.8), hitting, BAbip (.327), in-play percentage (86%), times on base (256), steals (10) and stolen base runs (1.2). Shortstop Johnny Lipon (.265 BA, 38 RBI). Hoot Evers (.224 BA, 11 HR, 46 RBI) in left led in power/speed number (6.9), with Johnny Groth (.299 BA, 3 HR, 49 RBI) in center. Player of the Year and most effective hitter Vic Wertz (.285 BA, 27 HR, 94 RBI) in right in homers, runs batted in, slugging (.511), OPS (.894), OPS+ (140), total average (.888), base-out percentage (.896), gross production average (.300), WAR (4.4), batters run average (.195), secondary average (.375), base runs (94), runs produced (153), runs created (98), isolated power (.226), extra base hits (55), total bases (256), bases produced (334) and walks (78). Pat Mullin (.281 BA, 12 HR, 51 RBI) led in triples (6). Hal Newhouser (.310 BA) led pitchers. The top pinch-hitters were Kryhoski at .400 (4-10) and Charlie Keller (HR, 13 RBI).

1950s Hitting Runs	
1. Harvey Kuenn	620
2. Al Kaline	521
3. Ray Boone	351
4. Charlie Maxwell	327
5. Frank Bolling	318
6. Johnny Groth	299
7. Bill Tuttle	278
8. Vic Wertz	231
9. Jerry Priddy	228
10. George Kell	217

Pitching. The Tigers recorded a 4.29 ERA, 51 CG, seven SHO, 602 walks, 597 SO, 97 ERA+, 3.98 FIP, 1.436 WHIP, 9.0 H/9, 3.9 BB/9, and 3.9 SO/9. The staff led league in HBP (40), WP (40), tough losses (24) and no decisions (36), with Ted Gray and Dizzy Trout leading the AL in losses. Pitcher of the Year Virgil Trucks (13-8, 4.33 ERA) led in wins (13), win percentage (.619) and WP (6). The most effective pitcher Fred Hutchinson (10-10, 3.68 ERA, 9 CG) led MLB in BB/9 (1.3) and league in SO/BB (1.96). He led staff for SHO (2), hits (204), earned run average, ERA+ (113), FIP (3.21), DICE (3.66), WHIP (1.227), pWAR (3.2) and R/9 (4.0). Trout (9-14, 4.04 ERA) led in games (42) and saves (5). Gray (7-14, 4.06 ERA, 9 CG) led league in no decisions (8), and tough losses (6). Ted led team in starts (28), innings (197.1), homers (17), walks (95), strikeouts (131), earned runs (89), runs (103), SO/9 (6.0) and quality starts (14). Marlin Stuart (4-6, 3.77 ERA) led in LOB% (74.3). Hal Newhouser (6-6, 3.92 ERA) of Detroit and 21-year-old righthander Ray Herbert (4-0, 1.42 ERA, 301 ERA+) of Detroit Catholic High School. Saul Rogovin (1-1, 5.25 ERA, 81 ERA+) dealt to Chicago for Bob Cain on 15 May led MLB in ERA (2.78) and ERA+ (146). Cain (11-10, 4.70 ERA) led staff in HBP (11), and Hal White (3-4, 4.74 ERA) led in games finished (19). Gene Bearden (3-4, 4.33 ERA), and Hank Borowy (2-2, 6.95 ERA). Cain and Trout led in H/9 (8.1), as Trucks and Hutchinson led for HR/9 (0.5).

Defense. Detroit made 163 errors for a .974) fielding average and led league in chances (6,156). League leaders were catcher Ginsberg in steals (47), Priddy in chances (918), putouts (437), assists (463), double plays (118) at second and team leader in dWAR (0.5), Kell in chances (505), chances per game (3.4), assists (310) and double plays (34) at third. Lipon led in errors (33) at short, as Groth at center in outfielder fielding (.993), with Wertz in right leading in chances (262) and putouts (251).

Bubba Phillips (.335 BA) and Jack Cerin (.328 BA) played at class "A" Williamsport. Al Yaylian (16-5 .762) and Verne Williams (12-5 .706) were at class "AA" Little Rock. Russ Sullivan (.341 BA, 11 HR, 88 RBI) and Monk Poole (13-7 .650) at "AAA" Toledo.

The Tigers lost their best pitcher Art Houtteman (19-12) after the 1951 season when he was drafted during the winter for the Korean War. Then Detroit lost Ray Herbert (4-0, 1.42 ERA, 301 ERA+) who was drafted on Wednesday, May 16, 1951.

Team. Detroit (50-104 .325) finished last under Red Rolfe (23-49) and Fred Hutchinson (27-55), with 1,026,846 fans. Charlie Gehringer served the club as general manager. Players lost their first eight games and went 2-9 in April. Vic Wertz (HR, 3 RBI), Joe Ginsberg (HR, 3 RBI) and Art Houtteman (9 IP, 0 ER, 1 H) led a 13-0 one-hit shutout of Cleveland at home on Saturday, April 26. Ted Gray (9 IP, 0 ER, 7 SO) and Pat Mullin 3-for-4 shutout the Indians the next day 1-0. Motown had a 10-16 record in May, as they lost to Chicago at home 8-5 in 16 innings on Friday, May 9, with George Kell 4-for-7, Mullin 4-for-7 and starter Virgil Trucks (8.1 IP, 3 ER). Trucks (9 IP, 0 ER, 0 H, 7 SO) won a no-hitter 1-0 over Washington at home on Thursday, May 15, as Wertz went 2-for 3 with a two-out ninth inning walk-off homer. Detroit was 10-21 in June when Trucks (9 IP, 0 ER, 6 H, 7 SO) threw a 7-1 home win versus Boston on Tuesday, June 24, aided by Johnny Pesky (HR, 2 RBI), Jerry Priddy 3-for-4 (HR) and Walt Dropo 3-for-4. The Tigers were 13-19 in July with an 8-2 triumph in New York on Monday, July 14, behind Dropo 5-for-5 (2 RBI). The squad went 8-22 in August including a 4-15 record on the road. 46-year-old Satchel Paige (12 IP, 0 ER, 9 SO) of the Browns outdueled Trucks (9 IP, 0 ER, 9 SO) for a 1-0 shutout in Motown on Wednesday, August 6. Trucks (9 IP, 0 ER, 0 H, 1 BB, 8 SO) threw a 1-0 no-hitter at New York on Monday, August 25. That was his fifth game of at least nine innings without allowing an earned run and sixth dominate start. Hal Newhouser (9 IP, 1 ER) led a 4-1 win over Cleveland at home on Thursday, August 28, with 53,988 fans. The Bengals were paced by Matt Batts 3-for-4, and Cliff Mapes (HR, 2 RBI). Detroit went 7-17 in September, as 29-year-old rookie Russ Sullivan was extraordinary September 9-15 (10-for-19 .526 BA, .526 OBP, .789 SLG, .563 BAbip). Motown scored a 5-4 win over visiting Washington on Monday, September 15, behind Bill Wight (6 IP, 0 ER, 5 SO), 19-year-old rookie Harvey Kuenn 4-for-5 (2 RBI) and Sullivan 3-for-4, with a meager 1,239 fans. 27-year-old rookie Wayne McLeland set an MLB record for most career appearances (10) without recording a strikeout. The Bengals closed 32-45 (.558) at home, and 18-59 (.390) on the road. The Tigers scored 557 runs while allowing a league high of 738 runs. Paul Campbell (.318 BA) was at class "A" Williamsport.

1950s Hitting Hits		
1.	Harvey Kuenn	1,372
2.	Al Kaline	1,047
3.	Ray Boone	723
4.	Johnny Groth	647
5.	Frank Bolling	625
6.	Charlie Maxwell	566
	Bill Tuttle	566
8.	George Kell	454
9.	Jerry Priddy	448
10.	Vic Wertz	385

1B * WALT DROPO

Offense. Detroit had a .243 BA, .318 OBP, .352 SLG, .670 OPS, 1,851 TB and 86 OPS+. The lineup featured catcher Joe Ginsberg (.221 BA, 6 HR, 36 RBI) that led squad in walks (51). Player of the Year first baseman Walt Dropo (.279 BA, 23 HR, 70 RBI) led in runs (56), homers, runs batted in, base runs (65), runs produced (103), runs created (70), power/speed number (3.7), extra base hits (43), total bases (220), bases produced (248), and strikeouts (63). Jerry Priddy (.283 BA, 4 HR, 20 RBI) at second base led in on-base percentage (.379), oWAR (2.2) and BAbip (.305), Fred Hatfield (.236 BA, 2 HR, 25 RBI) manned third base and Neil Berry (.228 BA, 13 RBI) was the shortstop, with Pat Mullin (.251 BA, 7 HR, 35 RBI) in leftfield. Centerfielder Johnny Groth (.284 BA, 4 HR, 51 RBI) led in games (141), plate appearances (580), at bats (524), runs (56), hits (149), singles (121), doubles (22), hitting, in-play percentage (83%), times on base (200), runs produced (103), walks (51), and outs (401). The most effective hitter right-fielder Vic Wertz (.246 BA, 17 HR, 51 RBI) led Detroit in slugging (.498), OPS (.851), OPS+ (135), total average (.860), base-out percentage (.860), gross production average (.283), WAR (2.2), batters run average (.176), secondary average (.418), isolated power (.253) and stolen base runs (0.3). Reserves included Bud Souchock (.249 BA, 13 HR, 45 RBI) from Kalamazoo and Cliff Mapes (.197 BA, 9 HR, 23 RBI). Jim Delsing excelled September 14-20 (.500 BA, .600 OBP, .688 SLG, .467 BAbip). The leading Tiger pinch-hitters were Don Kolloway at .300 (6-20, 2 HR, 8 RBI) and Souchock at .300 (6-20, HR, 8 RBI). Dropo and Groth had 11-game hitting streaks. Frank Carswell (.344 BA, 30 HR, 101 RBI, 300 TB) was spectacular for the class "AAA" Buffalo Bisons.

Pitching. The team had a 4.25 ERA, 51 CG, 10 SHO, 591 walks, 702 SO, 89 ERA+, 3.75 FIP, 1.430 WHIP, 9.0 H/9, 3.8 BB/9, and 4.6 SO/9, as pitchers led league in earned runs (656), runs (738), balks (4), wild pitches (37) and tough losses (32). Pitcher of the Year Hal Newhouser (9-9, 3.74 ERA) led in winning percentage (.500), earned run average (3.74), ERA+ (101), WHIP (1.266) and R/9 (4.2). The most effective pitcher Virgil Trucks (5-19, 3.97 ERA, 3 SHO) led league for losses in starts (23) and led his staff in hit by pitch (7), FIP (3.23), DICE (3.84), pWAR (1.9) and SO/9 (5.9). Ted Gray (12-17, 4.14 ERA) led in wins, starts (32), complete games (13), innings (224), homers (21), walks (101), strikeouts (138), runs (118), H/9 (8.5) and quality starts (19). Art Houtteman (8-20, 4.36 ERA) led in losses, hits (218), earned runs (107), BB/9 (2.6) and SO/BB (1.68). Bill Wight (5-9, 3.88 ERA, 3 SHO) led in LOB% (71.2) and HR/9 (0.4). Hal White (1-8, 3.69 ERA) led his staff in games (41), games finished (31) and saves (5). Marlin Stuart (3-2, 4.93 ERA) and Dick Littlefield (0-3, 4.34 ERA). 19-year-old Billy Hoeft (2-7, 4.32 ERA) made his MLB debut on Friday, April 18.

1950s Hitting Doubles		
1.	Harvey Kuenn	244
2.	Red Wilson	170
3.	Al Kaline	156
4.	Johnny Groth	122
5.	Frank Bolling	106
6.	Ray Boone	100
	George Kell	100
8.	Jerry Priddy	77
	Bill Tuttle	77
10.	Vic Wertz	76

Defense. Detroit made 152 errors for a .975 fielding average. Tigers leading the league were Ginsberg in catcher wild pitches (19) and Dropo in first basemen chances (1,437). Hatfield led third basemen in assists (276), fielding average (.971) and team in defensive WAR (0.5). Lipon led shortstops in fielding average (.981), as Groth led all centerfielders in assists (14).

Walt Dropo starred July 14-22 (10 GM, .571 BA, .591 OBP, .833 SLG, 13 RBI), with a record 12 straight hits and red hot 13-for-14 July 14-15 (.929 BA, .929 OBP, 1.143 SLG, .929 BAbip), with 5-for-5 on Monday and 8-for-9 in a Tuesday doubleheader.

Harvey Kuenn played 63 games at class "B" Davenport (.340 BA) of the Illinois-Indiana-Iowa League. He was 2-for-5 in his MLB debut at home versus Chicago on Saturday, September 6, an 11-inning 4-3 loss. Kuenn hit .325 in 19 games for Detroit.

1950s Hitting Triples		
1.	Harvey Kuenn	43
2.	Al Kaline	34
3.	Ray Boone	30
4.	Bill Tuttle	23
5.	Frank Bolling	22
6.	Johnny Groth	19
7.	Jerry Priddy	17
8.	Hoot Evers	13
9.	Charlie Maxwell	13
10.	Four Players	11

Team. Sixth-place Detroit (60-94 .390) drew 884,658 fans for manager Fred Hutchinson. 22-year-old rookie shortstop Harvey Kuenn opened with a 10-game hit streak April 14-24 (.413 BA). Motown went 2-13 in April, as Jim Delsing (2 HR, 4 RBI) and reliever Dave Madison (6.2 IP, 1 ER) led a 6-5 home win over Cleveland on Friday, April 17. The Bengals were 8-18 in May including an 8-4 home win facing Washington on Wednesday, May 6, as Ned Garver (9 IP, 4 ER) hit a two-run homer. Rookie Michigander Don Lund from Detroit Southeastern High School went 4-for-5 (2 RBI) in a 9-8 loss at Yankee Stadium on Wednesday, May 20. The club had a 10-18 June record that included a 17-1 loss in Boston on Wednesday, June 17. The Red Sox returned for a 23-3 triumph the next day, with a league record 17-run seventh inning. 23 hitters went to bat, including Gene Stephens an unprecedented 3-for-3 in the inning. Kuenn excelled June 18-30 (10 GM, .512 BA, .565 OBP, .683 SLG, .513 BAbip). 18-year-old free agent Al Kaline, a four-year All-State selectee for Baltimore Southern High School was signed on Friday, June 19. The Bengals were 15-15 in July when Ray Boone drove in a run during eight straight games during July 3-8. He his stride for the period of July 5-6 (3 GM, 2 HR, 6 RBI, 9-for-12 .750 BA, .786 OBP, 1.500 SLG, .757 BAbip). Ralph Branca (9 IP, 1 ER) led a 13-3 over Philadelphia at home on Sunday, July 19, with Boone (HR, 4 RBI), Don Lund (HR, 3 RBI) and Walt Dropo (HR, 2 RBI). The team finished 13-19 in August that included a Garver (9 IP, 1 ER) 2-1 victory in Boston on Sunday, August 2. Garver (11 IP, 1 ER, 5 H) pitched a 2-1 win at Chicago on Saturday, August 22. Motown won a home doubleheader versus Philadelphia on Sunday, August 30, with a 10-1 win by Steve Gromek (9 IP, 1 ER) followed by a Al Aber (8 IP, 1 ER, 6 SO) 9-1 triumph aided by Bob Nieman 3-for-4 (HR, 3 RBI) and Dropo (3 RBI). Motown closed 12-11 in September when Billy Hoeft (9 IP, 2 ER, 7 SO) won 4-2 over Chicago at home on Monday, September 7. He was the first Tiger with an immaculate inning by striking out the side in the seventh on nine pitches. Replacement outfielder Kaline hit a homer in his debut in Cleveland on Saturday, September 26. Players were 30-47 (.390) both at home and away, scored 695 runs and allowed 923.

2B * JOHNNY PESKY

Offense. Detroit logged a .266 BA, .331 OBP, .387 SLG, .718 OPS, 2,150 TB and 95 OPS+, as they led league with 259 doubles. Matt Batts (.278 BA, 6 HR, 42 RBI) was the catcher. Walt Dropo (.248 BA, 13 HR, 96 RBI) at first base led in runs batted in, runs produced (144), stolen base runs (0.6) and strikeouts (69). Johnny Pesky (.292 BA, 2 HR, 24 RBI) was at second base. Player of the Year and most effective hitter Ray Boone (.312 BA, 22 HR, 93 RBI) at third base led Motown in home runs, on-base percentage (.395), slugging (.556), OPS (.951), OPS+ (156), total average (.985), base-out percentage (.989), gross production average (.317), WAR (4.6), oWAR (5.1), batters run average (.217), batting average, secondary average (.371), runs produced (144) and isolated power (.244). All-Star shortstop Harvey Kuenn (.308 BA, 2 HR, 48 RBI) led MLB in plate appearances (731), at bats (679), hits (209) and outs (486). The Rookie of the Year led league in singles (167). Kuenn led the Bengals for runs (94), doubles (33), triples (7), BAbip (.320), in-play percentage (88%), times on base (260), base runs (88), runs created (93), total bases (262), bases produced (312), stolen bases (6) and had a 15-game hit streak. Bob Nieman (.281 BA, 15 HR, 69 RBI) in left field led in extra base hits (52). Centerfielder Jim Delsing (.288 BA, 11 HR, 62 RBI) led in walks (66). Don Lund (.257 BA, 9 HR, 47 RBI) in right led for power/speed number (4.5). Outfielder Bud Souchock (.302 BA, 11 HR, 46 RBI) and infielder Fred Hatfield (.254 BA, 3 HR, 19 RBI) were key reserves. Ted Gray (.230 BA, 7 RBI) led pitchers in hitting. The leading Tiger pinch-hitters were Pesky at .387 (12-31), Hatfield .368 (7-19), Batts .333 (4-12), Frank Carswell at .333 (4-12) and Pat Mullin (HR, 9 RBI).

1950s Hitting Home Runs		
1.	Al Kaline	125
2.	Ray Boone	105
3.	Charlie Maxwell	103
4.	Vic Wertz	71
5.	Frank Bolling	55
6.	Harvey Kuenn	53
7.	Frank House	42
8.	Walt Dropo	40
9.	Steve Souchock	38
10.	Bill Tuttle	35

Pitching. The Tigers had a 5.25 ERA, 50 CG, two SHO, 585 walks, 645 SO, 77 ERA+, 4.42 FIP, 1.567 WHIP, 10.4 H/9, 3.7 BB/9 and 4.1 SO/9. Motown league for youngest staff (26.7), starts (158), innings (1,415), hits (1,633), earned runs (826), runs (923), homers (154) and batters faced (6,351). Pitcher of the Year and most effective pitcher Ned Garver (11-11, 4.45 ERA) led in wins, win percentage (.500), complete games (13), innings (198.1), hits (228), wild pitches (4), ERA, ERA+ (91), FIP (3.97), DICE (4.38), pWAR (2.3), homers per nine (0.7) and runs per nine (4.9). Ted Gray (10-15, 4.60 ERA) led league in homers (25) and tough losses (6) and team in losses, starts (28), walks (76), strikeouts (115), WHIP (1.375), hits per nine (8.5), strikeouts per nine (5.9) and quality starts (13). Billy Hoeft (9-14, 4.83 ERA) led in earned runs (106) and runs (113). Steve Gromek (6-8, 4.51 ERA, 1 SHO) led in HBP (8), LOB% (70.8) and SO/BB (1.64). Ralph Branca (4-7, 4.15 ERA), Al Aber (4-3, 4.46 ERA), Art Houtteman (2-6, 5.90 ERA, 1 SHO) and Hal Newhouser (0-1, 7.06 ERA). Ray Herbert (4-6, 5.24) lead in games (43), games finished (22) and saves (6). Hal Erickson (0-1, 4,73 ERA), Dick Marlowe (6-7, 5.26 ERA) and 17-year-old rookie Bob Miller (1-2, 5.94 ERA). Dave Madison (3-4, 6.82 ERA), Bill Wight (0-3, 8.88 ERA) and Dick Weik (0-1, 13.97 ERA). Hoeft and Gromek led for BB/9 (2.6)

Defense. Detroit made 135 errors for a .978 fielding percentage and led league in chances (6,119) and putouts (4,242). Tiger league leaders were pitcher Gray in runners caught stealing (13), Dropo in first basemen assists (127), Kuenn in shortstop putouts (308) and Delsing in centerfielder fielding (.992). Reserve third baseman Hatfield led team in defensive War (0.1).

Ray Boone (101 GM, .312, 22 HR, 93 RBI) was traded to Detroit. He tied an MLB record with four grand slams in a year. He hit two slams with Cleveland on May 10 and May 24, with two for Motown on July 19 and August 2. Class "AA" Little Rock had Ralph Atkins (34 HR, 100 RBI), with Milt Jordan (12-1 .923, 3.11 ERA) and Frank Lary (17-11 .607) at class "AAA" Buffalo.

1950s Hitting Runs Batted In		
1.	Al Kaline	544
2.	Ray Boone	460
3.	Harvey Kuenn	423
4.	Charlie Maxwell	347
5.	Johnny Groth	295
6.	Vic Wertz	268
7.	Frank Bolling	253
8.	Bill Tuttle	250
9.	Walt Dropo	210
10.	George Kell	177

Team. Detroit finished in fifth place for manager Fred Hutchinson at 68-86 (.442), with 1,079,847 fans. The Tigers were 7-4 in April when Ned Garver (9 IP, 0 ER, 5 H) threw a 1-0 shutout in Baltimore on Saturday, April 17. Steve Gromek (9 IP, 3 ER) and Walt Dropo 3-for-5 (3 RBI) led an 8-3 victory on Sunday. The Bengals were 13-13 in May winning a doubleheader at home over Boston on Sunday, May 16, despite Ted Williams going 8-for-9 (2 HR, 9 RBI) in his return from an injury. Detroit won game one 7-6, then Gromek (W 6-1, 1 IP, 0 ER) won the 14-inning game two 8-8. Gromek (W 7-1, 9 IP, 3 ER, 7 SO) won 8-3 on Tuesday facing Philadelphia on one day of rest. Motown had a 11-20 mark in June with a 16-5 win at Philadelphia on Friday, June 11, aided by six homers and a six-run seventh inning. Ray Boone was 3-for-4 (2 HR, 6 RBI), Al Kaline (HR, 4 RBI), and reliever Ray Herbert (4.2 IP, 0 ER, 1 H) went 1-for-3 (HR, 2 RBI) for the win. The squad went 14-18 in July when Boone mired in a week-long slump July 1-7 (1-for-23 .043 BA, .000 BAbip) caught fire July 8-10 (3 GM, 8-for-9 .889 BA, .900 OBP, 1.333 SLG, 1.000 BAbip). Motown took a 10-2 home win against Philadelphia on Wednesday, July 28, behind Bud Souchock (2 HR, 6 RBI), Bill Tuttle 3-for-3 and Al Aber (9 IP, 2 ER, 7 SO). Detroit went 12-18 in August, with a Garver (W 10-7, 9 IP, 0 ER, 5 H, 6 SO) 4-0 shutout of Cleveland at home on Tuesday, August 10. The Bengals lost 1-0 in 16-innings at Chicago on Friday, August 13, as Aber (15.1 IP, 1 ER, 8 SO) took the tough loss. The club closed 11-13 in September, as Garver (W 13-9, 9 IP, 1 ER, 4 H) won 9-1 at Chicago on Monday, September 6. Players had a 9-4 (.692) record in extra-inning games. Detroit won the season series with Baltimore 14-8 (.636), including 8-3 at home. The Tigers were 35-42 (.455) at home, and 33-44 (.429) on the road. Motown scored 584 runs and allowed 664 runs. Michigander Ron Witucki (87 GM, 126-for-315, 90 RBI) of Bay City hit a dazzling .400 at class "D" Jamestown. Class "A" Wilkes-Barre had Ben Cardoni (8-2 .800, 2.44 ERA), Duke Maas (11-3 .786, 1.10 ERA) and Frank Logan (10-3 .769, 2.51 ERA). Russ Sullivan (.333 BA) was at class "AA" Little Rock. Class "AAA" Buffalo had Frank Carswell (.318 BA, 16 HR, 87 RBI) and Ron Northey (.308 BA, 25 HR, 85 RBI).

C * MATT BATTS

Offense. Detroit had a .258 BA, .322 OBP, .367 SLG, .688 OPS, 1,918 TB, and 90 OPS+. The catcher was Frank House (.250 BA, 9 HR, 38 RBI). Walt Dropo (.281 BA, 4 HR, 44 RBI) at first led in BAbip (.308), with Frank Bolling (.236 BA, 6 HR, 38 RBI) at second. Player of the Year and most effective hitter Ray Boone (.295 BA, 20 HR, 85 RBI) at third led in homers, runs batted in, on-base percentage (.376), slugging (.466), OPS (.842), OPS+ (131), total average (.814), base-out percentage (.822), gross production average (.286), WAR (4.4), oWAR (4.1), batters run average (.175), secondary average (.306), times on base (233), base runs (92), runs produced (140), runs created (95), isolated power (.171), power/speed number (6.7), extra base hits (46), bases produced (328) and walks (71). Shortstop Harvey Kuenn (.306 BA, 5 HR, 48 RBI) led MLB in games (155), at bats (656) and outs (493). He led the league in hits (201), with team lead for plate appearances (696), runs (81), singles (162), doubles (28), hitting, in-play percentage (92%), total bases (256) and steals (9). Jim Delsing (.248 BA, 6 HR, 38 RBI) was in left. Centerfielder Bill Tuttle (.266 BA, 7 HR, 58 RBI) led in triples (11). 19-year-old rookie right-fielder Al Kaline (.276 BA, 4 HR, 43 RBI) led in stolen bases (9). Billy Hoeft (6 RBI) led pitchers in hitting. The top pinch-hitters were Matt Batts at .400 (2-5, 3 RBI), Delsing .385 (5-13, HR, 4 RBI) and Bob Nieman at .308 (8-26). House and Kuenn had 14-game hitting streaks. House and Boone tied for stolen base runs lead (0.0). Tom Sarna hit an astounding .372 for class "C" Idaho Falls, with William Hoffer (.319 BA) playing at class "B" Durham.

1950s Hitting On-Base Percentage		
1.	George Kell	.391
2.	Vic Wertz	.387
3.	Charlie Maxwell	.377
4.	Al Kaline	.374
5.	Ray Boone	.372
6.	Johnny Groth	.370
7.	Harvey Kuenn	.360
8.	Hoot Evers	.356
9.	Jerry Priddy	.355
10.	Johnny Lipon	.353

Pitching. Motown logged a 3.81 ERA, 58 CG, 13 SHO, 506 walks, 603 SO, 98 ERA+, 4.00 FIP, 1.360 WHIP, 8.9 H/9, 3.3 BB/9, and 3.9 SO/9, with league lead for youngest staff (27.2). Pitcher of the Year Steve Gromek (18-16, 2.74 ERA, 4 SHO) led the majors in hit by pitch (12) and tough losses (8). He led the league for LOB% (81.9) and pWAR (5.0). Gromek led his staff in wins, losses, complete games (17), innings (252.2), hits (236), home runs (26), earned run average, ERA+ (136), BB/9 (2.0), R/9 (3.0) and quality starts (24). The most effective pitcher Ned Garver (14-11, 2.81 ERA) led in win percentage (.560), WHIP (1.129) and hits per nine (7.9). George Zuverink (9-13, 3.59 ERA) led in saves (4). Billy Hoeft (7-15, 4.58 ERA, 4 SHO, 3 WP, 93 R) led in strikeouts (114), earned runs (89), strikeouts per nine (5.9) and SO/BB (1.93). Al Aber (5-11, 3.97 ERA) led in FIP (3.40), DICE (4.00) and HR/9 (0.6). Bob Miller (1-1, 2.45 ERA) led in games finished (22). Ray Herbert (3-6, 5.87 ERA, 3 WP) led in games (42). Dick Marlowe (5-4, 4.18 ERA), Ted Gray (3-5, 5.38 ERA) and Ralph Branca (3-3, 5.76 ERA). Gromek and Garver led in starts (32). Garver and Zuverink led in walks (62) and runs (93). Class "AAA" Buffalo had pitcher Frank Lary (15-11, 3.39 ERA).

Defense. Detroit made 128 errors (.979). Tiger league leaders were Dropo in fielding average (.996) at first base and Boone in putouts (170) at third base. Kuenn at short led in in chances (818), putouts (294) and assists (496), as he led club in dWAR (1.7). Delsing led left fielders in fielding (.995). Kaline led the right fielders in chances (305), putouts (280) and assists (16).

Hometown star Steve Gromek from Hamtramck, Michigan, a St. Ladislaus High School graduate, was traded to the Bengals in 1953. The righthander started 1954 in style April 13-May 13 (5-0, 5 CG, 47 IP, 1.72 ERA, .202 BA, .228 OBP, .203 BAbip).

Harvey Kuenn went 4-for-5 (4 RBI) on June 8 in New York, 4-for-5 against Philadelphia at home July 29, 4-for-5 at Cleveland August 19, 4-for-5 versus Philadelphia at home September 10 and then 5-for-5 at home facing Cleveland on September 19.

Team. Detroit finished fifth for Bucky Harris at 79-75 (.513), with an attendance of 1,181,838. The Team went 10-5 in April that included a 16-0 Steve Gromek (9 IP, 0 ER) home shutout of Kansas City on Sunday, April 17, as Al Kaline was 4-for-5 (3 HR, 6 RBI), with two homers in the sixth inning. The Tigers were 9-2 during April 16-30 and had a mark of 12-15 in May. Detroiter Billy Hoeft (W 4-2, 9 IP, 0 ER, 6 H, 7 SO) shutout Chicago 1-0 at home on Friday, May 27. Players were 16-11 in June when they scored a 18-7 victory in Washington on Friday, June 24. The offense was led by Bill Tuttle 3-for-5 (HR, 4 RBI), Kaline 3-for-5, Ray Boone (3 RBI), Frank House (HR, 3 RBI) and Earl Torgeson with four walks. Detroit was 17-16 in July that included a six consecutive losses thru the Fourth of July holiday. The club beat visiting Baltimore 12-4 on Tuesday, July 19. Pitcher Babe Birrer (SV 2, 4 IP, 0 ER, 3 H) went 2-for-2 (2 HR, 6 RBI) with two three-run homers. The club was 12-18 in August including a Harvey Kuenn 4-for-6 led 13-10 win at Washington on Tuesday, August 2. Frank Lary (9 IP, 0 ER, 2 H) shutout the Senators 3-0 the next day. Hoeft (W 12-6, 9 IP, 0 ER, 2 H) shutout Cleveland 7-0 in Motown on Tuesday, August 16, behind Tuttle 3-for-4 (HR, 4 RBI) and House 3-for-4 (HR, 3 RBI). Hoeft had seven straight complete games for the month of August 11-September 11 (5-2, 1.62 ERA, 61 IP, .186 BA, .253 OBP, .260 SLG, .196 BAbip). Detroit closed 12-10 in September, as pitcher Ned Garver (W 12-13, 9 IP, 1 ER) went 2-for-4 at the plate, with a home run and scored three runs to lead a 17-1 ambush in Kansas City on Sunday, September 4. Boone 3-for-4 (HR, 5 RBI), Tuttle 3-for-5 (2 RBI), Kuenn (2 RBI) and Bubba Phillips (2 RBI) paced the victory. 20-year-old Kaline (.340 BA) became the youngest batting champion in league history. Motown went 17-5 versus Washington, 46-31 (.597) at home, 33-44 (.429) on the road, scored a league high 775 runs and allowed 658. Class "A" Augusta featured Bill Furlong (7-2 .778), William Hoffer (.311 BA) and Tom Sarna (.305 BA, 18 HR).

1950s Hitting Slugging Percentage

	Player	SLG
1.	Vic Wertz	.517
2.	Bud Souchock	.492
3.	Al Kaline	.489
4.	Ray Boone	.482
	Charlie Maxwell	.482
6.	Hoot Evers	.455
7.	George Kell	.435
	Pat Mullin	.435
9.	Harvey Kuenn	.426
10.	Johnny Groth	.409

P * BABE BIRRER

Offense. Detroit logged a .266 BA, .344 OBP, .394 SLG, .739 OPS, 2,084 TB and 101 OPS+. Frank House (.259 BA, 15 HR, 53 RBI) and Red Wilson (.220 BA, 2 HR, 17 RBI) caught. Earl Torgeson (.283 BA, 9 HR, 50 RBI) at first led in secondary average (.363), steals (9) and stolen base runs (2.7). Fred Hatfield (.232 BA, 8 HR, 33 RBI) and Harry Malmberg (.216 BA, 19 RBI) were at second. Ray Boone (.284 BA, 20 HR, 116 RBI, 15 HS) at third led league in runs batted in. Harvey Kuenn (.306 BA, 8 HR, 62 RBI) at short led MLB in doubles (38) and team for in-play percentage (89%). Jim Delsing (.239 BA, 10 HR, 60 RBI) played in left. Bill Tuttle (.279, 14 HR, 78 RBI) at center led MLB in games (154) and double plays grounded into (25), as he led the league for outs (481) and team in plate appearances (698). Player of the Year and All-Star Al Kaline (.340 BA, 27 HR, 102 RBI, 15 HS) in right led MLB in hitting and hits (200). Al was league leader for BAbip (.339) and total bases (321). He led team in runs (121), singles (141), triples (8), homers, on-base percentage (.421), slugging (.546), OPS (.967), OPS+ (162), total average (.993), base-out percentage (1.012), gross production average (.326), WAR (8.2), oWAR (7.1), batters run average (.230), times on base (287), base runs (126), runs produced (196), runs created (135), isolated power (.206), power/speed number (9.8), extra base hits (59), bases produced (409), walks (82) and strikeouts (57). Ned Garver (.224 BA, HR, 13 RBI) led pitchers. The leading pinch-hitters were Jack Phillips at .444 (8-18, 4 RBI), Earl Torgeson .375 (3-8, HR, 6 RBI) and Ferris Fain at .333 (3-9).

Pitching. The Tigers had a 3.79 ERA, 517 walks, 629 SO, 103 ERA+, 3.84 FIP, 1.375 WHIP, 9.0 H/9, 3.4 BB/9, and 4.1 SO/9. The staff led league for complete games (66). Pitcher of the Year Billy Hoeft (16-7, 2.99 ERA) led MLB in shutouts (7), with staff lead for wins, win percentage (.696), complete games (17), strikeouts (133), LOB% (78.8), earned run average, ERA+ (130), FIP (3.27), DICE (3.86), WHIP (1.191), pWAR (5.0), hits per nine (7.7), strikeouts per nine (5.4) and runs per nine (3.1). Frank Lary (14-15, 3.10 ERA) led MLB in homers per nine (0.383) and tough losses (10). Lary led his club in innings (235), walks (89), wild pitches (7) and quality starts (22). Ned Garver (12-16, 3.98 ERA) led the league in hits (251), earned runs (102), and runs (115). Garver led the staff in losses and starts (32). Steve Gromek (13-10, 3.98 ERA) led league in walks per nine (1.8) and team in homers (26), HBP (9) and strikeouts to walks (1.97). Joe Coleman (2-1, 3.20 ERA, 3 SV), and Leo Cristante (0-1, 3.19 ERA). Al Aber (6-3, 3.38 ERA, 3 SV) led in games (39) and GF (22). Babe Birrer (4-3, 4.15 ERA, 3 SV) and Duke Maas (5-6, 4.88 ERA) from Utica, Michigan. Paul Foytack (0-1, 5.26 ERA), rookie Jim Bunning (3-5, 6.35 ERA) and George Zuverink (0-5, 6.99 ERA). Class "A" Augusta had Bob Miller (8-2 .800, 1.73 ERA) and Bob Shaw (9-4 .692, 3.14 ERA).

1950s Hitting On-Base plus Slugging

	Player	OPS
1.	Vic Wertz	.904
2.	Al Kaline	.863
3.	Charlie Maxwell	.859
4.	Ray Boone	.854
5.	George Kell	.826
6.	Hoot Evers	.811
7.	Bud Souchock	.803
8.	Harvey Kuenn	.786
9.	Pat Mullin	.781
10.	Johnny Groth	.779

Defense. Detroit committed 139 errors for .976 fielding percentage. Tiger league leaders were Hoeft in pitcher fielding percentage (1.000), and Lary in caught stealing (12). Catcher House led the Bengals in dWAR (0.7). Leftfielder Delsing led in fielding (.995). Tuttle led outfielders in chances (461), and putouts (442), as he led centerfielders in chances (460), chances per game (3.0), putouts (441), assists (12) and errors (7). Kaline led all right fielders in chances (327) and in putouts (306).

Gene Hummer from Detroit, served as a ball boy in 1955 at the age of 16 and then was bat boy in 1956 as a 17-year-old. His experiences with the Detroit Tigers are detailed in the "Gene Hummer Bat Boy" book by Steven Cranford published in 2012.

Ray Boone led team with a 15-game hitting streak July 6-23 (.462 OBP, .712 SLG), as he was an RBI machine July 10-23 (10 GM, 5 HR, 19 RBI). His stellar games in 1955 included 2-for-5 (HR, 4 RBI) on April 24, 3-for-4 (5 RBI) on July 10, 3-for-4 (HR, 4 RBI) on July 17, 3-for-4 (2 HR, 4 RBI) on July 22, 4-for-6 (4 RBI) on July 26, and a 3-for-4 (HR, 5 RBI) effort on September 4.

1950s Pitching Wins		
1.	Frank Lary	79
2.	Billy Hoeft	74
3.	Paul Foytack	60
4.	Jim Bunning	59
5.	Steve Gromek	45
6.	Ted Gray	42
7.	Ned Garver	38
8.	Hal Newhouser	30
9.	Art Houtteman	29
10.	Virgil Trucks	27

Team. Detroit finished fifth for Bucky Harris at 82-72 (.532), with 1,051,182 fans. The Tigers went 4-6 in April with a Billy Hoeft (W 1-0, 10 IP, 0 ER) 1-0 home win against Cleveland on Sunday, April 29. Bill Tuttle hit a 10th-inning walk-off home run off loser Herb Score (9.2 IP, 1 ER, 3 H, 13 SO). Players were 14-15 in May with a seven-game win streak. Pitcher Paul Foytack (W 4-2, 9 IP, 3 ER) went 3-for-5 (5 RBI) to lead a 11-3 win at Kansas City on Wednesday, May 30. The Squad was 12-15 in June, as Detroit endured a 10-game losing streak thru Wednesday, June 27. Red Wilson (HR, 5 RBI), Al Kaline 4-for-6 (HR, 2 RBI), Tuttle 3-for-5 (2 RBI) and Foytack (9 IP, 2 ER, 6 SO) led a 14-2 win versus visiting Kansas City on Saturday, June 30. The club went 15-17 in July when Kaline dominated the week of July 7-14 (3 HR, 14 RBI, .577 BA, .586 OBP, 1.000 SLG, .500 BAbip), as he drove in a run in six straight games. Detroit swept a double-header at Chicago 17-5 and 8-6 on Sunday, July 8. The Bengals had an eight-run third inning of game one, as Tuttle was 4-for-5, Kaline 3-for-5 (HR, 5 RBI). Harvey Kuenn went 4-for-5 in game two. Foytack (9 IP, 15 SO) set the strikeout record during a 6-5 loss to visiting Washington on Saturday, July 28, as Kaline 4-for-5 and Frank House 4-for-5 (2 RBI) were a combined 8-for-10. Detroit was 17-12 in August, with a 18-3 home loss to Boston on Thursday, August 2, when Jackie Jensen went 3-for-5 (HR, 9 RBI) for the Red Sox. The Tigers logged a 6-4 15-inning victory in 4:32 at Cleveland on Tuesday, August 14. Motown closed 20-7 in September when Frank Lary (7-0, 0.86 ERA, .175 BA, .203 SLG, .209 BAbip) dominated. Lary (W 16-13, 9 IP, 0 ER, 4 H) threw a 6-0 shutout at Kansas City on Thursday, September 6, with Ray Boone (HR, 2 RBI) and Michigander Charlie Maxwell (HR, 2 RBI) of Lawton. Lary (W 17-13, 9 IP, 0 ER, 2 H) shutout Washington 12-0 at home on Tuesday, September 11, paced by Boone (HR, 2 RBI). Motown scored nine fourth inning runs, with 14 Tigers batting, as Frank Bolling had a single and triple during the inning. The Bengals registered an 8-4 victory at Cleveland on Sunday, September 30, when Hoeft (W 20-14, 4 IP, 2 ER, 4 SO) won his 20th game of the year. Detroit went 37-40 (.481) at home and 45-32 (.584) on the road including 10-1 in Kansas City. Motown scored 789 runs and allowed 699.

P * PAUL FOYTACK

Offense. Detroit had a .356 OBP, .420 SLG, .776 OPS, 1,991 TB, and 93 OPS+, with a league high batting average (.279 BA). The catchers were Frank House (.240 BA, 10 HR, 44 RBI) the in-play percentage (85%) leader and Red Wilson (.289 BA, 7 HR, 38 RBI). Earl Torgeson (.264 BA, 12 HR, 42 RBI) at first led in secondary average (.412). Second baseman Frank Bolling (.281 BA, 7 HR, 45 RBI). Ray Boone (.308 BA, 25 HR, 81 RBI) at third led with a 16-game hit streak. Shortstop Harvey Kuenn (.332 BA, 12 HR, 88 RBI, 32 2B, .333 BAbip) led the league in hits (196), with team lead in singles (145), hitting and stolen bases (9). The most effective hitter was left-fielder Charlie Maxwell (.326 BA, 28 HR, 87 RBI, .333 BAbip) that led in runs (97), homers, on-base percentage (.414), slugging (.534), OPS (.948) and OPS+ (148), total average (1.015), base-out percentage (1.017), gross production average (.320), batters run average (.220), walks (79) and strikeouts (74). Centerfielder Bill Tuttle (.253 BA, 9 HR, 65 RBI). Player of the Year right-fielder Al Kaline (.314 BA, 27 HR, 128 RBI, 32 2B) led in games (153), plate appearances (693), at bats (617), triples (10), runs batted in, WAR (6.5), oWAR (5.3), times on base (265), base runs (117), runs produced (197), runs created (125), isolated power (.216), power/speed number (11.1), extra base hits (69), total bases (327), bases produced (404), stolen base runs (1.5) and outs (439). Jim Bunning .333 (6-18) and Al Aber .300 (3-10) led the pitchers. The leading pinch-hitters were Maxwell at .571 (4-7, 4 RBI), Jim Small .500 (7-14), Torgeson .370 (10-27, HR, 3 RBI), House .333 (3-9, 2 HR, 6 RBI) and Jack Phillips .333 (3-9).

1950s Pitching Winning Percentage		
1.	Jim Bunning	.602
2.	Frank Lary	.534
3.	Steve Gromek	.523
4.	Hal Newhouser	.508
5.	Paul Foytack	.488
6.	Ned Garver	.487
	Billy Hoeft	.487
8.	Virgil Trucks	.450
9.	Art Houtteman	.433
10.	Ted Gray	.420

Pitching. The Tigers recorded a 4.06 ERA, 62 CG, nine SHO, 655 walks, 788 SO, 103 ERA+, 4.07 FIP, 1.482 WHIP, 9.1 H/9, 4.3 BB/9, and 5.1 SO/9, as staff led league for starts (155), intentional walks (49), hit by pitch (44), left on base (1,250) and cheap wins (15). Pitcher of the Year and most effective pitcher Frank Lary (21-13, 3.15 ERA) led the majors in HBP (12). He led staff for wins, win percentage (.618), starts (38), complete games (20), innings (294), hits (289), LOB% (77.4), earned run average, ERA+ (132), FIP (3.44), DICE (4.07), WHIP (1.378), pWAR (6.3), HR/9 (0.6), BB/9 (3.6), R/9 (3.6), team wins in his starts (24) and quality starts (24). Paul Foytack (15-13, 3.59 ERA) led MLB in walks (142), with staff lead for games (43), homers (24), strikeouts (184), wild pitches (8), H/9 (7.4) and SO/9 (6.5). Billy Hoeft (20-14, 4.06 ERA) led the league in cheap wins (5). He led club in losses, shutouts (4), earned runs (112), runs (127) and So/BB (1.65). Al Aber (4-4, 3.43 ERA) led in games finished (28) and saves (7). Jim Bunning (5-1, 3.71 ERA), Virgil Trucks (6-5, 3.83 ERA), Walt Masterson (1-1, 4.17 ERA), Steve Gromek (8-6, 4.28 ERA) and Duke Maas (0-7, 6.54 ERA). Hoeft won five straight starts during May 24-June 16 (5 GM, 5-0, 2.37 ERA, .221 BA).

Defense. Motown had 140 errors (.976), with Tiger league leaders Kuenn in fielding (.968) at short, and team in dWAR (0.8). Maxwell led in fielding (.986) and assists (10) at left. Centerfielder Tuttle in assists (13) and errors (9), as Kaline led outfielders in assists (18). He led right-fielders in fielding (.984), total chances (322), putouts (303), assists (14) and double plays (4).

Pitchers excelling in the minors were John Tsitouris (13-6 .684, 1.51 ERA), Bob Bruce (9-3 .750, 1.71 ERA) and Don Lee (7-3 .700, 2.51 ERA) at class "A" Augusta. Hal Woodeshick (12-5 .706, 2.75 ERA) pitched for the class "AAA" Charleston Senators.

Maxwell went 4-for-6 on May 5, had four straight multi-RBI games May 8-12 (4 HR, 8 RBI), was 3-for-4 (2 HR, 4 RBI) on June 29, walked in six straight games July 6-13, 4-for-5 effort on August 3 and excelled September 23-25 (3 HR, 9 RBI, 1.154 SLG).

1950s Pitching Games Started	
1. Billy Hoeft	176
2. Frank Lary	170
3. Paul Foytack	144
4. Ted Gray	119
5. Jim Bunning	110
6. Ned Garver	94
7. Steve Gromek	88
8. Art Houtteman	71
9. Virgil Trucks	70
10. Hal Newhouser	67

Team. Manager Jack Tighe led Motown (78-76 .506) to fourth place, with 1,272,346 fans in attendance. The club was 5-8 in April including a Frank Lary (9 IP, 0 ER, 6 SO) 7-0 home shutout of the Indians on Saturday, April 20. Reliever Duke Maas (6 IP, 0 ER, 3 H) completed a 5-0 shutout at Cleveland on Friday, April 26, aided by Al Kaline 3-for-4 (2 2B, HR, 4 RBI). Detroit was 16-12 in May with a 11-3 win over visiting Washington on Wednesday, May 8, led by Charlie Maxwell 2-for-3 (HR, 3 RBI) and Jim Bunning (SV 1, 4 IP, 0 ER, 0 H, 4 SO). Players were 14-15 in June including a 3-1 triumph in Chicago on Sunday, June 2, with Kaline 4-for-4, Frank House 3-for-3 (2 RBI) and Bunning (W 4-1, 8.1 IP, 1 ER, 6 SO). Motown had a 9-4 home win versus New York on Monday, June 10, paced by Maxwell 2-for-3 (2 HR, 5 RBI), Kaline (HR, 2 RBI), Harvey Kuenn 2-for-3 (HR) and Lary (7 IP, 2 ER, 5 SO). Paul Foytack (W 8-4, 12.2 IP, 1 ER, 5 H) pitched a 2-1 victory in Baltimore on Saturday, June 22. Detroit finished 14-14 in July, as they swept a home double-header with Baltimore 10-6 and 7-6 on Sunday, July 14. Billy Hoeft (9 IP, 2 ER) went 3-for-4 (2 HR, 3 RBI), Bill Tuttle 4-for-5, Kuenn 3-for-5 and Frank Bolling 3-for-5 in the first game, followed by a Red Wilson game-winning walk-off tenth inning single in game two. Motown went 15-16 in August that included a 17-inning 4-3 loss in 4:24 at Washington on Saturday, August 3, as starter Hoeft (7 IP, 1 ER, 7 H) and reliever Harry Byrd (7 IP, 1 ER, 3 H) pitched seven innings. Players won 13-4 versus Washington at home on Friday, August 23, led by Kaline (HR, 5 RBI) and Maxwell (HR, 3 RBI). Detroit closed 14-11 in September with a 6-1 win at Cleveland. Dave Philley (HR, 3 RBI) and Kaline (HR, 2 RBI) supported Bunning (W 16-7, 9 IP, 1 ER, 3 H). The Tigers had a 10-2 record for the period of September 2-15. The Bengals took a 12-2 victory at Washington on Wednesday, September 11, behind Lary (9 IP, 2 ER), Ray Boone (3 RBI) and Frank House (HR, 3 RBI). Motown fell 5-4 in Cleveland on Monday, September 23, as Kaline went 3-for-4 (2 RBI) with three steals. Foytack (W 14-10, 6.1 IP, 2 ER) won 3-2 on the road with a mere 957 fans in Comiskey Park on Thursday, September 26. Detroit was 45-32 (.584) at home, 33-44 (.429) in away games, as they scored and allowed 614 runs. 20-year-old Michigan native Bob Duncan (.283 BA) from North Adams High School played at class "D" Montgomery.

C * FRANK HOUSE

Offense. Detroit had a .257 BA, .323 OBP, .378 SLG, .701 OPS, 2,022 TB and 89 OPS+. Frank House (.259 BA, 7 HR, 36 RBI) was the catcher. Ray Boone (.273 BA, 12 HR, 65 RBI) at first led in stolen base runs (-0.3), second baseman Frank Bolling (.259 BA, 15 HR, 40 RBI) led in triples (6) and hitting streak (18). Reno Bertoia (.275 BA, 4 HR, 28 RBI) at third base led in BAbip (.309). Shortstop Harvey Kuenn (.277 BA, 9 HR, 44 RBI) led in games (151), plate appearances (679), at bats (624), hits (173), singles (128), doubles (30), triples (6), in-play percentage (87%), times on base (220) and outs (482). The most effective hitter Charlie Maxwell (.276 BA, 24 HR, 82 RBI) in left field led in homers (24), on-base percentage (.377), slugging (.482), OPS (.858), OPS+ (131), total average (.876), base-out percentage (.884), gross production average (.290), oWAR (3.7), batters run average (.180), secondary average (.362), isolated power (.205), stolen base runs (-0.3), walks (76) and strikeouts (84). Bill Tuttle (.251 BA, 5 HR, 47 RBI) patrolled center. Player of the Year Al Kaline (.295 BA, 23 HR, 90 RBI) in right-field led in runs (83), runs batted in, WAR (5.5), hitting, base runs (88), runs produced (150), runs created (95), power/speed number (14.9), extra base hits (56), total bases (276), bases produced (330) and stolen bases (11). Lou Sleater (.250 BA, 3 HR, 7 RBI) and Billy Hoeft (3 HR, 10 RBI) led pitchers. The top pinch-hitters were Maxwell at 1.000 (3-3), Bill Taylor .500 (2-4), Dave Philley .400 (10-25, 4 RBI) and Jack Dittmer at .333 (4-12).

1950s Pitching Complete Games	
1. Frank Lary	78
2. Billy Hoeft	71
3. Paul Foytack	52
4. Ned Garver	47
5. Ted Gray	39
6. Jim Bunning	38
7. Steve Gromek	35
8. Art Houtteman	34
9. Hal Newhouser	30
10. Virgil Trucks	28

Pitching. The club recorded a 3.56 ERA, seven SHO, 505 walks, 756 SO, 109 ERA+, 3.90 FIP, 1.294 WHIP, 8.4 H/9, 3.2 BB/9 and 4.8 SO/9. The staff led league in innings (1,417.2) and hit by pitch (43). Pitcher of the Year and most effective pitcher Jim Bunning (20-8, 2.69 ERA, 45 GM) led the league in wins, innings (267.1), and LOB% (82.1). He led the team for winning percentage (.714), complete games (14), homers (33), strikeouts (182), ERA, ERA+ (144), WHIP (1.070), pWAR (6.3), H/9 (7.2), BB/9 (2.4), SO/9 (6.1), SO/BB (2.53), R/9 (3.1) and quality starts (19). Paul Foytack (14-11, 3.14 ERA, 5 WP) led in walks (104) and wild pitches (5). Duke Maas (10-14, 3.28 ERA, 45 GM, 2 SHO) led in saves (6). Billy Hoeft (9-11, 3.48 ERA) led in FIP (3.40) and DICE (3.94). Frank Lary (11-16, 3.98 ERA, 2 SHO, 5 WP) led MLB in hit by pitch (12). He led Motown in losses, starts (35), hits (250), earned runs (105), and runs (111). Lou Sleater (3-3, 3.76 ERA) led in games finished (19). Joe Presko (1-1, 1.64 ERA), Jim Stump (1-0, 2.03 ERA), Harry Byrd (4-3, 3.36 ERA), Don Lee (1-3, 4.66 ERA), Steve Gromek (0-1, 6.08) and Al Aber (3-3, 6.81 ERA). Class "C" Idaho Falls featured star pitchers Howie Koplitz (14-4 .778, 3.34 ERA) and Bob Dustal (13-5 .722, 3.16 ERA).

Defense. Detroit committed 121 errors (.980) and led league in putouts (4,244). League leaders were Bunning in pitcher fielding (1.000), Bolling in errors (16) at second and shortstop Kuenn in errors (27). Maxwell led in outfield fielding (.997) and leftfielders in chances (328) and putouts (321). Kaline led all the right-fielders in fielding (.993) and team in dWAR (1.4).

First-place class "A" Augusta (98-56 .636) had star pitchers Ron Rozman (15-1 .938, 1.64 ERA), William Mitchell (9-1 .900, 2.18 ERA) and Richard Duffy (8-2 .800, 1.53 ERA). James Atkins (14-5 .737, 2.86 ERA) was assigned to class "AA" Birmingham.

Walter O. Briggs Sr. was part owner 1919-1934, sole owner 1935-1952 and son Spike the owner 1952-1956. They employed Hall of Famers in Ty Cobb, Harry Heilmann, Charlie Gehringer, Hank Greenberg, Hal Newhouser, George Kell and Al Kaline.

1950s Pitching Earned Run Average		
1.	Frank Lary	3.32
2.	Jim Bunning	3.55
3.	Ned Garver	3.68
4.	Steve Gromek	3.77
5.	Virgil Trucks	4.01
6.	Billy Hoeft	4.02
7.	Paul Foytack	4.07
8.	Art Houtteman	4.15
9.	Hal Newhouser	4.19
10.	Ted Gray	4.38

Team. **Detroit finished** fifth for managers Jack Tighe (21-28) and Bill Norman (56-49) at 77-77 (.500), with 1,098,924 fans. The Tigers were 8-7 in April, with a 9-1 home win over Cleveland on Saturday, April 19, with Paul Foytack (9 IP, 0 ER, 6 H, 7 SO), and Harvey Kuenn 3-for-5 (HR, 3 RBI). Motown went 11-16 in May that included a 4-2 win against visiting Boston on Wednesday, May 28. Gail Harris (HR, 2 RBI) had a pinch-hit walk-off two-run homer, with Billy Martin (2 RBI) and Frank Lary (9 IP, 2 ER). Players were 15-11 in June, when Ozzie Virgil broke the team's color-barrier during a 11-2 victory at Washington on Friday, June 6, aided by Red Wilson 3-for-4, Johnny Groth 3-for-5 (HR, 2 RBI), Gus Zernial (HR, 2 RBI) and Billy Hoeft (9 IP, 2 ER, 4 H) 2-for-3. Players won a twinbill in Boston on Wednesday, June 11, 7-0 with Lary (9 IP, 0 ER, 5 H) 2-for-4 (3 RBI) and 9-3 behind Jim Bunning (8.2 IP, 2 ER, 12 SO) and Martin (2 HR, 5 RBI). Lary (9 IP, 0 ER, 4 H, 6 SO) and Bunning (9 IP, 0 ER, 5 H, 8 SO) logged shutouts of 2-0 and 3-0 in New York on Sunday, June 15. Detroit won 9-2 over Washington at home on Tuesday, June 17, behind Frank Bolling 4-for-6 (HR, 2 RBI), Kaline (HR, 3 RBI) and Virgil 5-for-5 in his first Tiger home game. Motown had a 12-18 mark in July, with a Bunning (9 IP 0 ER, 0 H, 12 SO) 3-0 no-hitter in Boston on Sunday, July 20. The club was 15-14 in August with a 7-1 win at Washington on Wednesday, August 20, led by Kaline (2 HR, 6 RBI) and Lary (9 IP, 0 ER, 8 SO). The club closed 16-11 in September when Kaline reached base in eight straight at bats September 7-10 (3 GM, 6-for-6, 2 BB, 1.000 BA, 1.000 OBP, 1.000 SLG, 1.000 BAbip). The Bengals logged a 13-2 home win over Baltimore on Saturday, September 13, with Bunning (9 IP, 2 ER, 6 H, 11 SO), Harris 3-for-5 (2 HR, 4 RBI), Kuenn 3-for-5 (2 RBI), Coot Veal (2 RBI) and Wilson 3-for-4 (2 RBI). Motown was 43-34 (.558) at home, 34-43 (.442) on the road, scored 659 runs and allowed 606. Bobo Osborne (19 HR, 97 RBI) was at class "AAA" Charleston, with Bob Thorpe (.324 BA, 23 HR) playing at class "AA" Birmingham.

P * AL CICOTTE

Offense. Detroit had a .267 BA, .353 OBP, .375 SLG, .728 OPS, 1,965 TB and 91 OPS+. Catcher Red Wilson (.299 BA, 3 HR, 29 RBI) led in steals (10) and stolen base runs (3.0). Gail Harris (.273 BA, 20 HR, 82 RBI) at first led in triples (8), homers and isolated power (.208). Frank Bolling (.269 BA, 14 HR, 75 RBI) at second led MLB in sacrifice flies (9). He led team for games (154), plate appearances (681), at bats (610), runs (91) and outs (472). Reno Bertoia (.233 BA, 6 HR, 27 RBI) manned third base. Shortstop Billy Martin (.255 BA, 7 HR, 42 RBI) led in strikeouts (62). Charlie Maxwell (.272 BA, 13 HR, 65 RBI) at left led in secondary average (.327) and walks (64). Centerfielder Harvey Kuenn (.319 BA, 8 HR, 54 RBI) led MLB in doubles (39), as he led Motown in hits (179), singles (129), hitting, BAbip (.327), in-play percentage (84%) and times on base (230). Player of the Year and most effective hitter Al Kaline (.313 BA, 16 HR, 85 RBI) in right led for runs batted in, on-base percentage (.374), slugging (.490), OPS (.864), OPS+ (130), total average (.823), base-out percentage (.836), gross production average (.291), WAR (6.5), oWAR (3.6), batters run average (.182), base runs (93), runs produced (153), runs created (100), power/speed number (9.7), extra base hits (57), total bases (266), bases produced (327) and hitting streak (18). Billy Hoeft (.273 BA, 5 RBI) led the pitchers. The leading pinch-hitters were Bill Taylor at .500 (3-6), Gus Zernial .395 (15-38, 3 HR, 12 RBI), Johnny Groth .375 (6-16, 3 RBI), Tito Francona .364 (8-22, 4 RBI) and Gail Harris at .357 (5-14, HR). Outfielder George Alusik (.325 BA, 18 HR, 88 RBI) played for class "A" Augusta.

1950s Pitching Innings Pitched		
1.	Billy Hoeft	1,324.2
2.	Frank Lary	1,253.2
3.	Paul Foytack	1,094.1
4.	Jim Bunning	841.0
5.	Ted Gray	818.2
6.	Steve Gromek	724.0
7.	Ned Garver	702.0
8.	Art Houtteman	564.1
9.	Virgil Trucks	519.0
10.	Hal Newhouser	485.2

Pitching. Pitchers logged a 3.59 ERA, eight SHO, 437 walks, 3.63 FIP, 1.275 WHIP, 8.6 H/9, and 2.9 BB/9, as they led league in complete games (59), strikeouts (797), ERA+ (113) and SO/9 (5.3). Pitcher of the Year and most effective pitcher Frank Lary (16-15, 2.90 ERA, 34 GS, 3 SHO) led the major leagues in pWAR (6.7). He led league for complete games (19), innings (260.1), and hit by pitch (12). Lary led staff for wins, losses, hits (249), LOB% (79.1), earned run average, ERA+ (139), FIP (3.39), DICE (3.91), walks per nine (2.4), runs per nine (3.1) and quality starts (21). Paul Foytack (15-13, 3.44 ERA, 7.7 H/9) led in earned runs (88), runs (98) and WHIP (1.196). Jim Bunning (14-12, 3.52 ERA, 34 GS, 3 SHO, 7.7 H/9) led the league in balks (3), with club lead in win percentage (.538), homers (28), walks (79), strikeouts (177), wild pitches (5), strikeouts per nine (7.3) and strikeouts to walks (2.24). Herb Moford (4-9, 3.61 ERA), George Susce (4-3, 3.67 ERA) and Billy Hoeft (10-9, 4.15 ERA). Hank Aguirre (3-4, 3.75 ERA) led in games (44), games finished (16) and saves (5). Tom Morgan (2-5, 3.16 ERA), Al Cicotte (3-1, 3.56 ERA) and Bill Fisher (2-4, 7.63 ERA). Class "A" Augusta featured star Wyman Carey (8-1 .889, 2.56 ERA).

Defense. Detroit led league in fewest errors (106) and fielding average (.982). League leaders were pitchers Lary in putouts (20), Bunning and Foytack in fielding average (1.000). Wilson led in catcher fielding (.992) and Harris in errors (15) at first. Bolling led in fielding average (.985) and assists (445) at second. Kuenn led outfielders in chances (373), chances per game (2.7), and putouts (358), as he led centerfielders in chances (370) and putouts (355). Kaline led outfielders in fielding (.994) and assists (23). He led right-fielders in fielding (.994), chances (335), and assists (22), as "Mr. Tiger" led team in dWAR (2.2).

The "Yankee Killer" Frank Lary went 7-1 against New York (1.86 ERA, 67.2 IP, 6 CG, 2 SHO) in 1958. He was consistent versus the Bronx Bombers at home (3-1, 1.91 ERA, 33 IP, 3 CG, 1 SHO) and in Yankee Stadium (4-0, 1.82 ERA, 34.2 IP, 3 CG, 1 SHO).

Bill Harrington (20-7 .741, 2.99 ERA), Joe Grzenda (16-7 .696, 3.19 ERA) and Phil Regan (15-8 .652) were stars for first-place class "AA" Birmingham (91-62 .595) in the Southern Association, where Michigander Lee Weyer of Imlay City was an umpire.

1950s Pitching Walks	
1. Paul Foytack	481
Billy Hoeft	481
3. Ted Gray	400
4. Frank Lary	394
5. Jim Bunning	286
6. Virgil Trucks	241
7. Ned Garver	211
8. Art Houtteman	193
9. Steve Gromek	190
10. Dizzy Trout	158

Team. Detroit finished fourth with Bill Norman (2-15) and Jimmy Dykes (74-63) at 76-78 (.494), with an attendance of 1,221,221. Motown was hit hard when Hall of Famer Mel Ott, a popular Tiger radio and television broadcaster died on Friday, November 21, 1958. The National League established the Mel Ott Award for the home run champion in 1959. Motown was 2-13 in April when Al Kaline went 4-for-4 and Eddie Yost (HR, 2 RBI) led a 5-2 win at Chicago on Saturday, April 18. The Bengals were 18-10 in May that included four consecutive homers by Charlie Maxwell during a Sunday, May 3 doubleheader. Frank Bolling and Maxwell (HR, 2 RBI) led a 4-2 triumph in the opener. Maxwell was 3-for-3 (3 HR, 6 RBI) in the 8-4 game two victory on Dykes first day as manager. The squad lost 17-6 at home to Boston on Wednesday, May 6, despite Kaline 2-for-3 (2 HR, 4 RBI) and Lou Berberet 3-for-4 (HR, 2 RBI). Detroit won 14-2 in Boston on Monday, May 18, aided by Jim Bunning (9 IP, 2 ER) 4-for-4 (3B, HR, 5 RBI), Maxwell (HR, 3 RBI), Kaline (HR, 3 RBI) and Bolling 3-for-4 (HR). Kuenn finished 6-for-9 during a doubleheader at Cleveland to raise his average to .400 on Sunday, May 24. The team logged a 18-13, as Ray Narleski won three games during a 10-2 12-game stretch during June 5-15. Paul Foytack (9 IP, 2 ER), Gus Zernial (2 HR, 5 RBI), Wilson (HR, 3 RBI) and Kaline (HR, 2 RBI) powered a 12-2 win versus the Orioles at home on Saturday, June 27. Players were 12-18 in July including a 2-13 mark for July 3-18. Detroit defeated visiting Washington 11-2 on Thursday, July 23 behind Wilson (4 RBI), Kuenn 4-for-4 (4 R, 3 RBI) and Kaline 4-for-5 (2 RBI). The Bengals were 15-11 in August when Bunning (1 IP, 0 ER, 0 H, 3 SO) became the second Tiger with an immaculate inning, striking out the side in the ninth on nine pitches during a 5-4 home loss to Boston on Sunday, August 2. Yost 3-for-3 (HR, 4 RBI), Kuenn 5-for-5 and Frank Lary (W 16-8, 7.2 IP) led a 9-5 win over Baltimore at home on Sunday, August 23. Wilson (HR, 2 RBI) and pitcher Don Mossi (9 IP, 0 ER, 3 H, 8 SO) 2-for-4 (HR) led a 5-0 shutout in Kansas City on Sunday, August 30. The Tigers closed September 11-13, with a Bunning (W 16-11, 9 IP, 1 ER, 3 H, 9 SO) 3-1 win at Boston on Wednesday, September 9. The team went 32-14 (.696) in the first 46 games under Dykes. The club was 41-36 (.532) at home, 35-42 (.455) on the road, scored 712 runs and allowed 732 runs.

C * LOU BERBERET

Offense. Detroit finished with a .258 BA, .335 OBP, .400 SLG, .735 OPS, 2,082 TB, and 97 OPS+. Lou Berberet (.216 BA, 13 HR, 44 RBI) caught, with Gail Harris (.221 BA, 9 HR, 39 RBI) at first base and Frank Bolling (.266 BA, 13 HR, 55 RBI) at second. Eddie Yost (.278 BA, 21 HR, 60 RBI) at third led MLB in times on base (292) and walks (135). "*The Walking Man*" led league in runs (115), on-base percentage (.435) and total average (.997). Yost led Motown in games (148), plate appearances (675), total average (.992), base-out percentage (.997), secondary average (.430) bases produced (371) and stolen base runs (1.5). Rocky Bridges (.268 BA, 3 HR, 35 RBI) manned short. Leftfielder Charlie Maxwell (.251 BA, 31 HR, 95 RBI) led in homers, runs batted in and isolated power (.210), strikeouts (91) and outs (405). Player of the Year and most effective hitter Al Kaline (.327 BA, 27 HR, 94 RBI) at center led the league in slugging (.530), OPS (.940) and OPS+ (151). He led squad in WAR (6.0), batters run average (.217), power/speed number (14.6) and steals (10). Harvey Kuenn (.353 BA, 9 HR, 71 RBI) at right led the league in hits (198), doubles (42), hitting, BAbip (.364) and runs created (117). He led club in at bats (561), triples (7), in-play percentage (84%), base runs (105), runs produced (161), runs created (113), extra base hits (58), total bases (281) and hit streak (22). Catcher Red Wilson (.263 BA, 4 HR, 35 RBI). Jerry Davie (.400 BA, 2 RBI) and Tom Morgan (.391 BA, 2 HR, 4 RBI) led pitchers. The top pinch-hitters were Maxwell at .375 (3-8, HR, 5 RBI) and Johnny Groth at .308 (4-13, HR, 5 RBI). Kaline, Kuenn and Yost led team in oWAR (5.4).

1950s Pitching Strikeouts	
1. Billy Hoeft	783
2. Frank Lary	643
3. Jim Bunning	631
4. Paul Foytack	630
5. Ted Gray	515
6. Steve Gromek	309
7. Virgil Trucks	286
8. Ned Garver	254
9. Art Houtteman	225
10. Dizzy Trout	197

Pitching. The team had a 4.20 ERA, 53 CG, nine SHO, 432 walks, 829 SO, 97 ERA+, 4.07 FIP, 1.293 WHIP, and 8.8 H/9. Pitchers led league in homers (177), BB/9 (2.9), SO/9 (5.5) and SO/BB (1.9). Pitcher of the Year and most effective pitcher Don Mossi (17-9, 3.36 ERA, 3 SHO) led in win percentage (.654), complete games (15), earned run average, ERA+ (121), FIP (3.27), DICE (3.73), WHIP 1.136), pWAR (4.1), R/9 (3.6) and quality starts (20). Frank Lary (17-10, 3.55 ERA, 3 SHO) led league in SO/BB (2.98). Jim Bunning (17-13, 3.89 ERA) led the league in home runs (37) and strikeouts (201), as he led staff in innings (249.2), walks (75), LOB% (76.7), H/9 (7.9) and SO/9 (7.2). Paul Foytack (14-14, 4.64 ERA, 240.1 IP) led league in starts (37), earned runs (124), runs (137) and team losses in starts (21). He led his team in losses, hits (239) and WP (6). Closer Tom Morgan (1-4, 3.98 ERA) led in games (46), games finished (22) and saves (9). Pete Burnside (1-3, 3.77 ERA), Dave Sisler (1-3, 4.01 ERA) and Ray Narleski (4-12, 5.78). Bunning, Lary and Mossi led in wins (17). Mossi and Lary led for BB/9 (1.9). Lary and Bunning led in HBP (11). Mossi went undefeated for August 25-September 27 (6 GM, 6-0, 50 IP, 2.16 ERA, .184 BA, .232 OBP, .274 SLG, .215 BAbip).

Defense. Detroit committed a league low 124 errors (.978). Yost led in fielding (.962) and putouts (168) at third base. Maxwell led leftfielders in fielding (.987), Kuenn for fielding (.990) in right. Bolling at second base led team for dWAR (1.6).

Class "A' Knoxville had pitcher Jim Proctor (15-5 .750, 2.19 ERA). Gordon Seyfried (14-7 .667, 3.26 ERA), with Michigan natives Ron Witucki (.373 BA) from Bay City and Phil Regan (10-5 .667, 2.94 ERA) of Otsego played for class "AA" Birmingham.

Bill Freehan grew up in Royal Oak and was a 1959 graduate of Bishop Barry High School in St. Petersburg, Florida. Freehan, George Cook of Detroit Cody High School and Willie Horton out of Detroit Northwestern High School were highly rated catchers. Horton and Freehan would play for the Detroit Lundquist team that won the 1960 National Sandlot Championship.

Detroit Tigers 1960s American League

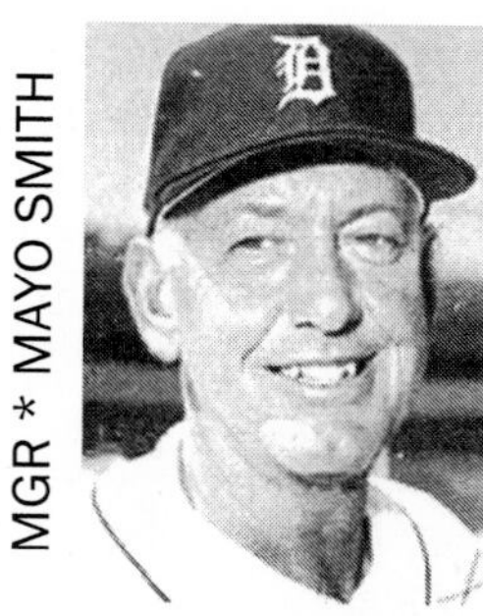
MGR * MAYO SMITH

Player of the Decade. Al Kaline (.296 BA, 210 HR, 772 RBI) was the back-to-back Player of the Decade (1950s and 1960s). Kaline was decade leader in runs (811), hits (1,399), singles (911), doubles (247), on-base percentage (.381), OPS+ (145), gross production average (.295), offensive WAR (43.6), batting average (.296), extra base hits (488) and 22-game hit streak in 1961. His highlights included August 27-September 2, 1960 (16-for-29 .552 BA, .606 OBP, .690 SLG, .615 BAbip) and July 17-23, 1961 (13-for-26 .500 BA, .606 OBP, .731 SLG, .545 BAbip), as he drove in a run during six straight games during April 26-May 2, 1962 (.414 BA, 4 HR, 11 RBI, .433 OBP, .966 SLG). Other notable periods were for June 7-13, 1963 (15-for-29 .517 BA, 6 HR, 13 RBI, .548 OBP, 1.241 SLG, 1.790 OPS, .409 BAbip), June 3-9, 1964 (16-for-27 .593, .645 OBP, .815 SLG, 1.460 OPS, .625 BAbip). He was blazing hot in a series at California June 7-9, 1965 (7-for-9 .778 BA, 3 HR, 5 RBI, .818 OBP, 2.000 SLG, .667 BAbip), May 10-12, 1968, at Washington (7-for-10 .700 BA, HR, 8 RBI, .769 OBP, 1.200 SLG, .667 BAbip) and at Cleveland for July 19-20, 1969 (9-for-14 .643 BA, .667 OBP, .643 SLG, .750 BAbip).

1960s			
Year	W – L	Pct.	Pl
1960	71-83	.461	6
1961	101-61	.623	2
1962	85-76	.528	4
1963	79-83	.488	5
1964	85-77	.525	4
1965	89-73	.549	4
1966	88-74	.543	3
1967	91-71	.562	2
1968	**103-59**	**.636**	1
1969	90-72	.556	2
	882-729	.547	

All-Decade Team. Manager Mayo Smith (363-285 .560) enjoyed immediate success with a second-place finish in 1967 (91-71 .562), World Championship in 1968 (103-59 .636), followed with runner-up finish in 1969 (90-72 .556). Pitcher Denny McLain (114-57 .667, 3.04 ERA). Catcher Bill Freehan (.262 BA, 110 HR, 416 RBI) led the 1960s in hit by pitch (11) and defensive WAR (6.4). First baseman Norm Cash (.275 BA, 278 HR, 831 RBI) led the decade in games (1,442), plate appearances (5,708), at bats (4,819), homers (278), runs batted in (831), on-base plus slugging (.878), total average (.905), gross production average (.295), secondary average (.387), times on base (2,162), extra bases on long hits (1,075), total bases (2,401), bases produced (3,218), walk percentage (13.6) and strikeouts (770). Second baseman Jake Wood (.251 BA, 35 HR, 167 RBI) led for BAbip (.293) and stolen bases (79). Shortstop Dick McAuliffe (.255 BA, 142 HR, 487 RBI) led team in triples (59). Third baseman Don Wert (.247 BA, 71 HR, 330 RBI). Left fielder Willie Horton (.269 BA, 141 HR, 461 RBI). Centerfielder Al Kaline (.296 BA, 210 HR, 772 RBI) had superior seasons in 1962 (.304 BA, 29 HR, 94 RBI, 152 OPS+), 1963 (.312 BA, 27 HR, 101 RBI, 144 OPS+), 1966 (.288 BA, 29 HR, 88 RBI, 161 OPS+) and 1967 (.308 BA, 25 HR, 78 RBI, 176 OPS+). Right fielder Rocky Colavito (.271 BA, 139 HR, 430 RBI) was decade leader for slugging (.501), total base average (1.9) and bases produced average (2.4).

P* DENNY MCLAIN

Pitcher of the Decade. Denny McLain (114-57 .667, 3.04 ERA) led the decade in wins, complete games (93), shutouts (26), quality starts (134), high quality starts (123), dominate starts (49), homers (176), WHIP (1.094), pWAR (22.1), quality start percentage (.654), high quality start percentage (.600), dominate start percentage (.239), complete game percentage (.454), starter win percentage (.669) and cheap wins (14). He became staff leader in 1965 (16-6 .727, 2.61 ERA, 192 SO, 4 SHO) and 1966 (20-14 .588, 3.92 ERA, 192 SO, 4 SHO). He stood 25-3 in 1968 after the period June 13-August 16 (16-1 .941, 1.62 ERA, .184 BA, .239 OBP, .287 SLG, .217 BAbip), that included 32 innings without allowing an earned July 23-August 8. McLain won the Cy Young in 1968 (31-6 .838, 1.96 ERA, 280 SO, 6 SHO) and 1969 (24-9 .727, 2.80 ERA, 9 SHO). The decade had him at 15-2 (.882) versus Kansas City/Oakland and 15-4 (.789) over Minnesota.

1960s Attendance			
Year	Attn.	Avg.	Rk
1960	1,167,669	15,165	4
1961	1,600,710	19,521	2
1962	1,207,881	14,730	3
1963	821,952	10,148	6
1964	816,139	9,953	6
1965	1,029,645	12,712	4
1966	1,124,293	13,880	5
1967	1,447,143	17,648	3
1968	**2,031,847**	**25,085**	1
1969	1,577,481	19,475	2

All-Decade Pitchers. Chicago native Denny McLain dominated the White Sox during a one-hit 1-0 shutout at Comiskey Park (9 IP, 1 H, 0 ER) on May 6, 1966. Earl Wilson (60-39 .606) went 13-6 (.684, 2.59 ERA) after a June 1966 trade to Detroit, followed in 1967 (22-11 .667). Mickey Lolich (102-74 .580, 3.46 ERA) led the 1960s in losses, starts (219), innings (1,528.1), hits (1,318), walks (518), strikeouts (1,336), HBP (60), intentional walks (27), wild pitches (53), earned runs (587), runs (640), FIP (3.13), DICE (3.62), SO/9 (7.87), batters faced (6,375), pickoffs (19), no decisions (54), cheap wins (14), tough losses (24). He was an All-Star in 1969 (19-11 .633, 3.14 ERA, 271 SO). Jim Bunning (59-48 .551, 3.36 ERA) was an All-Star in 1962 (19-10 .655, 3.59 ERA). Don Mossi (42-35 .545, 3.53 ERA) led the decade in BB/9 (1.69) and SO/BB (2.99). He stood 14-3 thru August of 1961. Michigander Fred Gladding (26-11 .703, 2.70 ERA) from Flat Rock led for win percentage, earned run average, technical runs allowed (2.96), left on-base percentage (81.2), HR/9 (0.72), RA/9 (2.96), games in relief (216) and relief wins (26). He was flawless to start 1967 season during April 11-June 3 (13 GM, 1-0, 10 SV, 0.00 ERA, .156 BA, .156 SLG, .222 BAbip). Terry Fox (26-17 .605, 2.77 ERA) led the decade for games finished (128), saves (55), ERA+ (137), relief wins (26) and relief losses (17). Hank Aguirre (61-60 .504, 3.26 ERA) led in games (287), and balks (7). He was solid in 1962 (16-8 .667, 2.21 ERA). Pat Dobson (11-20 .355, 3.06 ERA) led Detroit during in H/9 (7.31) and dominant during August 12-October 1, 1967 (10 GM, 1-0, 0.48 ERA, .150 BA, .217 SLG, .163 BAbip).

Pitcher Denny McLain earned the Cy Young Award in 1968 and 1969, the American League MVP Award in 1968 when the Tigers won their first World series since 1945, as the 24-year-old righthander was baseball's first 30-game winner since 1934.

Mickey Lolich led the American League with six shutouts in 1967, as the Tigers fell one game short of winning the American League Pennant despite the superlative efforts of Lolich in his last 11 starts (9-1 .900, 1.33 ERA, 87.2 IP, 50 H, 18 BB, 81 SO).

Detroit Tigers 1960 American League

Team. Detroit finished sixth (71-83 .461) under managers Jimmy Dykes (44-52 .458), Billy Hitchcock (1-0 1.000), and Joe Gordon (26-31 .456) with 1,167,669 fans. The Bengals traded Don Demeter to Cleveland on April 12 for Norm Cash and then traded batting champion Harvey Kuenn to the Indians on April 17 for home run champion Rocky Colavito. The team went 5-4 in April, as they had a 10-game losing streak from Tuesday, April 26 thru Saturday, May 7. The Tigers had a 12-14 month of May that included a two-game series sweep in Washington, with a Don Mossi (9 IP, 0 ER, 3 H, 7 SO) 1-0 shutout on Tuesday, May 10, and then a Frank Lary (9 IP, 0 ER, 5 H, 7 SO) 1-0 shutout the next day. The squad lost 11-7 in Boston on Thursday, June 30 to finish the month at 15-16 (.484). The club was 12-15 in July, including a 12-10 victory in Kansas City on Sunday, July 10, when Colavito went 3-for-5 (2 HR, 6 RBI). Players swept a home doubleheader the next Sunday with New York 12-2 in game one led by Cash (HR, 4 RBI), Colavito (HR, 3 RBI) and Chico Fernandez (3 RBI). The Bengals took game two 3-2. Detroit logged a 15-18 mark in August that included a Hank Aguirre (W 4-2, 6 IP, 0 ER, 1 H, 9 SO) 12-2 win at Yankee Stadium on Wednesday, August 3, as Cash 2-for-2 (3 BB, 3 RBI, HBP) reached base six times. Later that day Dykes and coach Luke Appling were traded to Cleveland for Gordon and coach Jo-Jo White in the only manager for manager trade. The team closed 11-15 in September and 1-1 in October when Jim Bunning (9 IP, 0 ER, 3 H) beat Early Wynn (8 IP, 1 ER, 4 H) 2-0 at Chicago on Tuesday, September 27, in a duel of future Hall of Famers. Bob Bruce (7.2 IP, 2 ER) led a 6-4 victory in Kansas City on Saturday, October 1, with Fernandez 3-for-5 (4 RBI), Al Kaline 4-for-5 and Harry Chiti 3-for-4. The Tigers were 40-37 (.519) at home, 31-46 (.403) on the road, scored 633 runs and allowed 644. Class "AA" Birmingham featured Stan Palys (.370 BA, 200 H, 101 R, 28 HR, 116 RBI, 353 TB) and Ron Nischwitz (14-7 .667, 2.31 ERA, 4 SHO). The class "AA" Victoria Rosebuds had Jim Raugh (11-4 .733, 3.33 ERA) and Kal Segrist (.325 BA, 21 HR, 93 RBI).

1960s Team Hitting

YEAR	AVG	HR	RBI	SB
1960	.239	150	601	66
1961	**.266**	180	**779**	**98**
1962	.248	**209**	719	69
1963	.252	148	648	73
1964	.253	157	658	60
1965	.238	162	634	57
1966	.251	179	682	41
1967	.243	152	618	37
1968	.235	185	639	26
1969	.242	182	649	35

P * DAVE SISLER

Offense. Detroit had a .239 BA, .324 OBP, .375 SLG, .698 OPS, 1,949 TB and 86 OPS+. The lineup had catcher Lou Berberet (.194 BA, 5 HR, 23 RBI). First baseman Norm Cash (.286 BA, 18 HR, 63 RBI) led in slugging (.501), OPS (.903), OPS+ (140), total average (.984), base-out percentage (.992), gross production average (.306), WAR (2.9), batters run average (.202), batting average, BAbip (.295) and secondary average (.405). Frank Bolling (.254 BA, 9 HR, 59 RBI) at second led for in-play percentage (82%). Eddie Yost (.260 BA, 14 HR, 47 RBI) at third led MLB in walks (125). He led the league for on-base percentage (.414) and times on base (262). Yost led the Bengals in plate appearances (636), runs (78), oWAR (3.8), base runs (88) and bases produced (328). Chico Fernandez (.241 BA, 4 HR, 35 RBI) manned short, as leftfielder Charlie Maxwell (.237 BA, 24 HR, 81 RBI) led in triples (5). The most effective hitter Al Kaline (.278 BA, 15 HR, 68 RBI) at center led in games (147), hits (153), singles (105), doubles (29), runs produced (130), runs created (83), power/speed number (16.8), and steals (19). Player of the Year Rocky Colavito (.249 BA, 35 HR, 87 RBI) in right led for at bats (555), homers, runs batted in, runs created (83), isolated power (.225), extra base hits (54), total bases (263), strikeouts (80), and outs (444). Steve Bilko (.207 BA, 9 HR, 25 RBI), Neil Chrisley (.255 BA, 5 HR, 24 RBI) and Ozzie Virgil (.227 BA, 3 HR, 13 RBI) were reserves. Frank Lary (.183 BA, 2 HR, 13 RBI) led pitchers in hitting. The best Tiger pinch-hitters were Johnny Groth at .500 (4-8), Kaine .500 (2-4) and Cash at .391 (9-23, 3 HR, 9 RBI). Kaline and Colavito had 12-game hitting streaks.

Pitching. Motown had a 3.64 ERA, 40 CG, seven SHO, 474 walks, 3.77 FIP, and 8.6 H/9, with league lead for innings (1,405.2), strikeouts (824), balks (5), HBP (47), ERA+ (110), FIP (3.77), WHIP (1.288), pWAR (20.6), BB/9 (3.0), SO/9 (5.3), SO/W (1.74), tough losses (27) and quality starts (87). Pitcher of the Year Frank Lary (15-15, 3.51 ERA) led MLB in hit by pitch (19). He led league in starts (36), CG (15), innings (274.1) and hits (262). Lary led his staff in wins, losses, homers (25), WP (8), earned runs (107) and runs (125). The most effective pitcher Jim Bunning (11-14, 2.79 ERA) led league in strikeouts (201), FIP (2.86), pWAR (6.6), SO/9 (7.2), SO/BB (3.4), and quality starts (23). He led club in SHO (3), walks (64), ERA, ERA+ (143), DICE (3.33), WHIP (1.115), H/9 (7.8), HR/9 (0.7) and R/9 (3.3). Don Mossi (9-8, 3.47 ERA) led in win percentage (.529) and BB/9 (1.8). Pete Burnside (7-7, 4.28 ERA) led league in balks (2). Dave Sisler (7-5, 2.48 ERA) led squad in games (41) and games finished (19). Hank Aguirre (5-3, 2.85 ERA) led in saves (10). Bill Fischer (5-3, 3.44 ERA), Bob Bruce (4-7, 3.74 ERA), Phil Regan (0-4, 4.50 ERA) and Paul Foytack (2-11, 6.14 ERA).

1960s Team Hitting

YEAR	OBP	SLG	OPS	OPS+
1960	.324	.375	.698	86
1961	**.347**	**.421**	**.768**	102
1962	.330	.411	.740	95
1963	.327	.382	.708	96
1964	.319	.395	.714	96
1965	.312	.374	.686	94
1966	.321	.406	.727	105
1967	.325	.376	.702	105
1968	.307	.385	.692	**107**
1969	.316	.387	.703	92

Defense. Detroit committed 138 errors for a .977 fielding average and led the American League in putouts (4,220). Tiger league leaders were pitchers Bunning and Mossi in fielding percentage (1.000). Yost led third basemen in errors (26). Fernandez led shortstops in errors (34) and the Bengals in defensive WAR (1.3). Leftfielder Maxwell led all outfielders in fielding percentage (.996). Colavito led all outfielders in double plays (5) and right-fielders in putouts (272) and assists (9).

All-Star pitcher Jim Bunning had the White Sox number at Chicago in September (2-0, 0.64 ERA,14 IP, 1 ER, 5 H, 2 BB, 3 SO), with a 6-4 Tiger win on Sunday, September 4 (5 IP, 1 ER) and a 3-hit 2-0 shutout on Tuesday, September 27 (9 IP, 0 ER, 3 H).

Bobo Osborne (.342 BA, 34 HR, 119 RBI), George Alusik (.329 BA, 26 HR, 106 RBI) and Steve Boros (.317 BA, 30 HR, 119 RBI) were at "AAA" Denver, with Purnal Goldy (.342 BA, 20 HR, 106 RBI) and Leo Smith (.301 BA, 16 HR, 111 RBI) at "A" Knoxville.

1960s Hitting Games	
1. Norm Cash	1,442
2. Al Kaline	1,322
3. Dick McAuliffe	1,154
4. Bill Freehan	967
5. Don Wert	962
6. Willie Horton	735
7. Jim Northrup	654
8. Rocky Colavito	629
9. Jake Wood	592
10. Mickey Stanley	573

Team. Bob Scheffing led second-place Detroit (101-61 .623), with 1,600,710 fans. The club went 10-4 in April when Frank Lary (9 IP, 0 ER, 1 H) was 2-for-4 (RBI) and shutout Chicago 7-0 at home on Friday, April 14. Don Mossi (W 2-0, 9 IP, 1 ER, 9 SO) and Rocky Colavito (HR, 3 RBI) paced a 9-1 win over visiting Los Angeles on Friday, April 21. The team was 19-12 in May when Phil Regan (W 4-0, 9 IP, 1 ER) led a 9-1 victory in Baltimore on Wednesday, May 17. Norm Cash, Steve Boros of Flint Northern High School and Dick Brown hit back-to-back-to-back ninth-inning homers for a 5-2 win at Minnesota on Tuesday, May 23. Players were 19-10 in June when Jim Bunning (9 IP, 0 ER, 4 H, 6 SO) shutout Minnesota 2-0 at home on Friday, June 2. Motown lost 7-4 to visiting Washington on Sunday, June 11, as the second homer by Cash was the first by a Tiger to clear the right-field roof. Colavito went 4-for-5 in a 6-5 12-inning triumph in Baltimore on Friday, June 30. Detroit closed 16-12 in July taking a twinbill at home over the Angels on Sunday, July 9, 1-0 by Lary (W 13-4, 9 IP, 0 ER, 3 H, 10 SO) and 6-3 behind Bunning (W 9-6, 8.1 IP, 3 ER, 10 SO). Detroit swept a home doubleheader over Kansas City on July 16. Mossi (W 10-2, 9 IP, 1 ER) 1-for-3 (HR, 2 RBI) and Cash (3 RBI) won 11-1, followed by an 8-3 win with Colavito (2 HR, 5 RBI), Cash (HR, 2 RBI) and Regan (W 9-4, 9 IP, 3 ER). Motown won 17-14 at Kansas City on Sunday, July 23 with Cash 4-for-5 (5 RBI), Colavito (4 RBI) and Frank House (3 RBI), with a nine-inning record time of 3:54. The club had a 22-9 record for August, with a 17-3 win at Minnesota on Saturday, August 12. Chico Fernandez was 4-for-6 (5 RBI), Cash (HR, 4 RBI) and Colavito 4-for-5 (3 RBI). Colavito hit four homers during a twinbill at Washington on Sunday, August 27. Mossi (W 14-3, 8.2 IP, 1 ER) won 7-4, followed by a Foytack (9 IP, 1 ER) 10-1 win, with Colavito 3-for-5 (3 HR, 6 RBI). Players were 14-14 in September and 1-0 in October. Mossi (L 14-4, 8.2 IP, 1 ER, 7 SO) lost a dominate start 1-0 on Friday, September 1, with 65,566 fans at Yankee Stadium. The Bengals logged an 8-3 win at Minnesota on Sunday, October 1, with 19-year-old rookie Bill Freehan 2-for-4 (2 RBI). Detroit was 50-31 (.617) at home, 51-30 (.630) on the road, scored 841 runs and allowed 671.

OF * ROCKY COLAVITO

Offense. Detroit had a .347 OBP, .421 SLG, .768 OPS, 2,342 TB, and 102 OPS+, as team led league in hitting (.266) and runs (841). Dick Brown (.266 BA, 16 HR, 45 RBI) caught. Player of the Year and most effective hitter Norm Cash (.361 BA, 41 HR, 132 RBI) at first led MLB in hitting, on-base percentage (.487), OPS (1.148), times on base (326) and runs created (178). He led league in hits (193), BAbip (.370) and IBB (19), with team lead for slugging (.662), OPS+ (201), total average (1.358), base-out percentage (1.368), gross production average (.384), WAR (9.2), oWAR (8.5), batters run average (.321), secondary average (.544), base runs (159), isolated power (.301), total bases (354), bases produced (489) and walks (124). Jake Wood (.258 BA, 11 HR, 69 RBI) at second led MLB in triples (14) and strikeouts (141), with team high in plate appearances (731), at bats (663), singles (129), steals (30), stolen base runs (3.6) and outs (515). Steve Boros (.270 BA, 5 HR, 62 RBI) was at third. Rocky Colavito (.290 BA, 45 HR, 140 RBI) at left led MLB in games (163). Rocky led the club in runs (129), homers, runs batted in, runs produced (224) and extra base hits (77). Billy Bruton (.257 BA, 17 HR, 63 RBI) at center led in power/speed number (19.2). Al Kaline (.324 BA, 19 HR, 82 RBI) at right led MLB in doubles (41), with team lead for stolen base runs (3.6) and hit streak (22). Dick McAuliffe (.256 BA, 6 HR, 33 RBI). Frank Lary (.231 BA, HR, 5 RBI) led pitchers. The top pinch-hitters were Kaline .600 (3-5, 4 RBI), Bubba Morton .297 (11-37, 9 RBI) and Charlie Maxwell (3 HR, 9 RBI). Cash (9-for-11 .818 BA, .875 OBP, 1.091 SLG, .800 BAbip) mashed during a four-game home sweep of Boston August 18-20.

1960s Hitting Runs	
1. Al Kaline	811
2. Norm Cash	779
3. Dick McAuliffe	630
4. Bill Freehan	399
5. Don Wert	381
6. Rocky Colavito	377
7. Willie Horton	334
8. Billy Bruton	315
9. Jim Northrup	292
10. Jake Wood	278

Pitching. Motown logged a 3.55 ERA, 10 SHO, 836 SO, 116 ERA+, 3.97 FIP, 1.283 WHIP, 8.7 H/9, and 5.2 SO/9, as staff led league in walks (469), BB/9 (2.9) and SO/BB (1.78). Pitcher of the Year Frank Lary (23-9, 3.24 ERA, 4 SHO) led MLB in CG (22) and quality starts (25), as he led club in wins, win percentage (.719), innings (275.1), hits (252), WP (6), earned runs (99) runs (117) and pWAR (4-3). The most effective pitcher Jim Bunning (17-11, 3.19 ERA, 4 SHO) led in losses, starts (37), walks (71), strikeouts (194), HBP (9), FIP (3.23), DICE (3.66), WHIP (1.131), H/9 (7.8) and SO/9 (6.5). Don Mossi (15-7, 2.96 ERA) led MLB in SO/BB (2.915), and league in BB/9 (1.8). "*Ears*" led staff in homers (29), LOB% (76.8), ERA, ERA+ (139) and R/9 (3.6). Terry Fox (5-2, 1.41 ERA) led in GF (25) and saves (12). Hank Aguirre (4-4, 3.25 ERA) led in games (45). Ron Kline (5-3, 2.72 ERA), Paul Foytack (11-10, 3.93 ERA), Bob Bruce (1-2, 4.43 ERA), Bill Fischer (3-2, 5.01 ERA) and Phil Regan (10-7, 5.25 ERA). Terry Fox excelled May 29-July 6 (2-0, 4 SV, 17 IP, 0.00 ERA, .155 BA, .194 OBP). Minor League Player of the Year and Southern Association MVP Howie Koplitz was at class "AA" Birmingham (23-3 .885, 2.11 ERA, 3 SHO) and Detroit (2-0, 2.25 ERA) for a combined 25-3 (.893).

Defense. Detroit committed 146 errors for a .976 fielding percentage. Tiger league leaders were pitchers Bunning in runners caught stealing (11), Foytack in fielding percentage (1.000), Mossi in double plays (8), Lary in total chances (88) and putouts (32). Brown led the catchers in caught stealing percentage (56%), Cash led in chances (1,369) and putouts (1,231) at first base. Wood led in errors (25) at second base, Colavito in outfielder assists (16) and leftfielder chances (323), putouts (301) and assists (14). Bruton led outfielders in chances (419) and putouts (406), as Kaline led the team in defensive WAR (2.3).

All-Star Norm Cash dominated May 4-June 27 (55 GM, 20 HR, 50 RBI, .404 BA, .515 OBP, .781 SLG) and August 18-September 14 (26 GM, .402 BA, .514 OBP, .644 SLG, .455 BAbip). Cash led a twin-bill sweep at Kansas City on July 23 (6-for-8, HR, 8 RBI).

Herb Plews (.372 BA), Purnal Goldy (.351 BA), Stan Palys (.333 BA, 114 RBI) and Legrant Scott (.314 BA, 128 R) were at "AA" Birmingham, as Dick McAuliffe (.353 BA), Don Wert (.328 BA) and Jimmy McDaniel (30 HR, 114 RBI) played at "AAA" Denver.

1960s Hitting Hits	
1. Al Kaline	1,399
2. Norm Cash	1,326
3. Dick McAuliffe	1,056
4. Bill Freehan	865
5. Don Wert	848
6. Willie Horton	694
7. Rocky Colavito	633
8. Jim Northrup	604
9. Billy Bruton	525
10. Jake Wood	467

Team. Detroit placed fourth for Bob Scheffing at 85-76 (.528), with 1,207,881 fans. The team went 8-6 in April when Jim Bunning (9 IP, 2 ER) led a 9-2 win over Washington at home on Tuesday, April 17, aided by Billy Bruton (HR, 4 RBI), Al Kaline (HR, 2 RBI), and Dick Brown 3-for-4 (HR, 2 RBI). Bruton (3 RBI), Kaline (3 RBI) and Rocky Colavito (3 RBI) paced a 13-4 home win against Los Angeles on Friday, April 27. Players were 16-13 in May, with a 10-2 12-game stretch that included an 8-6 win at Cleveland on Sunday, May 20, behind Cash (HR, 2 RBI) and Kaline 4-for-5 (2 HR, 3 RBI). Closer Terry Fox was perfect May 31-July3 (12 GM, 20 IP, 0.00 ERA, .222 BA, .222 SLG). The Squad was 13-17 in June including a dreadful seven-game losing streak. The Tigers lost 9-7 during a 22-inning seven-hour game on Sunday, June 24, when Colavito went 7-for-10. Hank Aguirre (W-6-2, 9 IP, 0 ER, 3 H, 1 BB, 11 SO) threw a 3-hit 1-0 shutout at Baltimore on Friday, June 29. The Bengals were 12-15 in July, as Sam Jones (9 IP, 1 ER, 6 H, 10 SO) continued his neck cancer recovery. He led a 2-1 home win over Chicago on Monday, July 2. Colavito 3-for-5 (3 HR, 5 RBI) hit three straight homers in a 7-6 loss in at Cleveland on Thursday, July 5. Detroit won 10-3 in Kansas City on Friday, July 20 with six homers. Several leading the way were Bruton 4-for-5 (3 RBI), Cash (2 HR, 3 RBI), and Chico Fernandez (2 RBI). The Tigers were 18-15 in August, as Steve Boros had a mythical 3-3-3-3 jackpot (3-for-3, 3 HR, 3 RBI) slugging three straight homers in a 6-5 loss at Cleveland on Monday, August 6. Colavito (2 HR, 6 RBI) and Aguirre (W 9-5, 9 IP, 1 ER, 7 SO) powered a 7-2 victory at Yankee Stadium on Saturday, August 11. Detroit defeated visiting Baltimore 13-10 on Tuesday, August 14, with Kaline (HR, 6 RBI) and Bruton (4 RBI). Motown defeated Washington 11-1 at home on Friday, August 24, with Phil Regan (9 IP, 1 ER), Boros (HR, 4 RBI), Bruton (HR, 3 RBI) and Colavito (HR, 3 RBI). The club closed 18-10 in September when Bunning (W 17-8, 9 IP, 9 SO) defeated visiting Boston 14-6 on Thursday, September 13, behind Fernandez (HR, 4 RBI), Kaline (HR, 3 RBI), Colavito (HR, 3 RBI), Cash (HR, 2 RBI) and Brown 3-for-4. Aguirre (W 16-8, 9 IP, 1 ER, 6 SO) had a 3-2 home win over Kansas City on Saturday, September 29, with a Bubba Morton walk-off single and McAuliffe 3-for-4. Motown finished 16-2 (.889) facing Baltimore. Detroit was 49-33 (.598) at home, with 9-2 records against Kansas City and Washington, 36-43 (.456) on the road, scored 758 runs and allowed 692.

P * HANK AGUIRRE

Offense. Detroit had a .248 BA, .330 OBP, .411 SLG, .740 OPS, 2,242 TB, and 95 OPS+, with league lead in homers (209). Catcher Dick Brown (.241 BA, 12 HR, 40 RBI) led for in-play percentage (77%). Norm Cash (.243 BA, 39 HR, 89 RBI) at first led MLB in HBP (13). He led team in runs (94), homers, on-base percentage (.382), secondary average (.481), walks (104) and strikeouts (82). Second was manned by Dick McAuliffe (.263 BA, 12 HR, 63 RBI) and Jake Wood (.226 BA, 8 HR, 30 RBI) that led in steals (24) and stolen base runs (5.4). Steve Boros (.228 BA, .407 SLG) was at third, with Chico Fernandez (.249 BA, 20 HR, 59 RBI) the shortstop. Player of the Year Rocky Colavito (.273 BA, 37 HR, 112 RBI) in left led the league in total bases (309), with club lead in games (161), plate appearances (701), at bats (601), hits (164), doubles (30), runs batted in, WAR (5.7), oWAR (4.1), times on base (262), base runs (112), runs produced (165), runs created (115), bases produced (407) and outs (463). Billy Bruton (.278 BA, 16 HR, 78 RBI) at center led in singles (108), BAbip (.291), power/speed number (14.9) and hitting streak (14). The most effective hitter Al Kaline (.304 BA, 29 HR, 94 RBI) at right led in triples (6), slugging (.593), OPS (.969), OPS+ (152), total average (.980), base-out percentage (.980), gross production average (.317), batters run average (.222), hitting and isolated power (.289). Jim Bunning (.242 BA, HR, 5 RBI) led pitchers, with Vic Wertz the top pinch-hitter at .321 (17-53, 3 HR, 14 RBI). Cash cleared the Tiger Stadium right-field roof on May 11, July 27, and July 29.

1960s Hitting Doubles	
1. Al Kaline	247
2. Norm Cash	175
3. Dick McAuliffe	147
4. Bill Freehan	126
5. Jim Northrup	115
Don Wert	115
7. Rocky Colavito	107
8. Willie Horton	102
9. Billy Bruton	74
10. Mickey Stanley	72

Pitching. The Tigers recorded a 4.25 ERA, 51 CG, 10 SHO, 591 walks, 702 SO, 89 ERA+, 3.75 FIP, 1.430 WHIP, 9.0 H/9, 3.8 BB/9, and 4.6 SO/9, with league lead in pWAR (22.0). Pitcher of the Year and most effective pitcher Hank Aguirre (16-8, 2.21 ERA, 2 SHO, 18 QS) led MLB in earned run average, pWAR (7.4) and ERA+ (185). He led the league in FIP (2.99), WHIP (1.051) and H/9 (6.8). "*Mex*" led his staff in win percentage (.667), LOB% (77.7), HR/9 (0.6), SO/9 (6.5) and R/9 (2.8). Jim Bunning (19-10, 3.59 ERA, 2 SHO, 18 QS) led league in hits (262), with club lead for wins, starts (35), complete games (12), innings (258), home runs (28), walks (74), strikeouts (184), hit by pitch (13), earned runs (103), and runs (112). Don Mossi (11-13, 4.19 ERA) led in losses, BB/9 (1.8) and SO/BB (3.36). Paul Foytack (10-7, 4.39 ERA) led league in balks (2) and squad in wild pitches (5). Terry Fox (3-1, 1.71 ERA) led in GF (28) and saves (16). Ron Nischwitz (4-5, 3.90 ERA) led in games (48). Sam Jones (2-4, 3.65 ERA), Phil Regan (11-9, 4.04), Ron Kline (3-6, 4.31), Jerry Casale (1-2, 4.66 ERA), Howie Koplitz (3-0, 5.26 ERA) and Frank Lary (2-6, 5.74).

Defense. Motown had 156 errors (.974). League leaders were pitchers Bunning, Foytack, Mossi and Regan in fielding (1.000). Wood in errors (20) at second, Colavito in left for fielding (.992), chances (372), and putouts (359). He led club in dWAR (0.9). Bruton led in errors (7) at center and led all outfielders in chances (408), chances per game (2.8), and putouts (396).

Relief pitcher Terry Fox (83 GM, 8-3 .727, 1.56 ERA, 28 SV, 264 ERA+) enjoyed the best back-to-back seasons for a closer in franchise history with 1961 (39 GM, 5-2, 1.41 ERA, 12 SV, 292 ERA+) and in 1962 (44 GM, 3-1, 1.71 ERA, 16 SV, 241 ERA+).

Michigander Jim Northrup (.324 BA) from Breckenridge won a batting title at class "C" Duluth-Superior. Chico Salmon (.330 BA), and Joel McDaniel (15-5 .750) were at class "A" Knoxville. Frank Kostro (.321 BA, 97 RBI) starred for class "AAA" Denver.

Detroit Tigers 1963 American League

1960s Hitting Triples	
1. Dick McAuliffe	59
2. Norm Cash	33
3. Al Kaline	31
4. Jim Northrup	27
5. Jake Wood	26
6. Billy Bruton	23
7. Willie Horton	18
8. Bill Freehan	16
9. Gates Brown	15
Don Wert	15

Team. Detroit finished sixth for Bob Scheffing (24-36 .400) and Chuck Dressen (55-47 .539) at 79-83 (.488), with 821,952 fans. The club was 8-10 in April including a 4-3 15-inning loss at Boston on Saturday, April 20, as Jim Bunning (12 IP, 1 ER, 10 SO) pitched. Motown beat Los Angeles 4-3 at home on Wednesday, April 24 in 15 innings, aided by Al Kaline (HR, 3 RBI) and Bunning (7 IP, 2 ER, 3 H, 6 SO). The Tigers were 11-16 in May with a 14-0 home win over Cleveland on Friday, May 10, when Michigan native Phil Regan (9 IP, 0 ER, 3 H, 1 BB, 7 SO) from Wayland High School had his lone MLB shutout and homer, as Dick McAuliffe (HR, 6 RBI) and Rocky Colavito homered. Colavito hit his 250th homer in a 7-5 loss at Washington on Saturday, May 18. Players had a 10-19 record in June, with a 6-1 at home win over Boston on Monday, June 10, behind Bill Faul (9 IP, 1 ER, 3 H), and Jake Wood 3-for-5, as Kaline (2 HR, 4 RBI) hit his 200th homer. Dressen took over on Tuesday, June 18, after Scheffing was fired. Gates Brown hit a homer in his first major-league at bat in Boston the next day. Detroit had a 14-14 mark in July, as Hank Aguirre (9 IP, 1 ER, 5 H) led a 9-1 home win against Baltimore on Wednesday, July 17, with a Gus Triandos eighth-inning grand slam. A feeling of déjà vu gripped Tiger Stadium fans, as Aguirre (9 IP, 1 ER, 6 SO) pitched a matching one-run complete game during his next outing, a 5-1 victory over Chicago at home on Tuesday, July 23, with an eighth-inning Norm Cash grand slam. The team had a record of 22-8 in August when Kaline (HR, 4 RBI) went 3-for-3 in a 5-4 home win over Boston on Wednesday, August 7, with their MLB record 12th straight errorless game. Players were 11-1 August 17-29 that included a 17-2 home victory over Kansas City on Friday August 23, paced by Cash (2 HR, 4 RBI), Don Wert (HR, 3 RBI), and Frank Lary (9 IP, 2 ER) drove in two runs. The Tigers were 14-16 in September, with a Bunning (9 IP, 2 ER, 7 SO) 3-2 win over visiting New York on Tuesday, September 3, with a George Smith 15th-inning walk-off single. 19-year-old righthander Denny McLain (9 IP, 1 ER, 8 SO) won his MLB debut 4-3 over his hometown White Sox at home on Saturday, September 21, when he picked off two runners and became the sixth teenage pitcher to hit a homer. Wert homered for a 1-0 Bunning (9 IP, 0 ER, 8 SO) win over visiting Washington on Tuesday. Bunning starred during his last month as a Tiger (2-0, 43 IP, 1.26 ERA). Detroit was 47-34 (.580) at home including 8-1 versus Kansas City, 32-49 (.395) on the road, scored 700 runs and allowed 703. Willie Horton of Detroit Northwestern High School hit .333 at class "AA" Knoxville. He then had a pinch-hit single during his MLB debut on Tuesday, September 10.

P * PHIL REGAN

Offense. Detroit logged a .266 BA, .331 OBP, .387 SLG, .718 OPS, 2,150 TB, and 95 OPS+, with league high 259 doubles. Gus Triandos (.239 BA, 14 HR, 41 RBI) and rookie Bill Freehan (.243 BA, 9 HR, 36 RBI) split the catching. First baseman Norm Cash (.270 BA, 26 HR, 79 RBI) led in on-base percentage (.386), total average (.876), base-out percentage (.886), secondary average (.379), isolated power (.201) and walks (89). Jake Wood (.271 BA, 11 HR, 27 RBI) at second led in stolen bases (18), power/speed number (13.7), and stolen base runs (2.4). Bubba Phillips (.246 BA, 5 HR, 46 RBI) at third led for in-play percentage (85%), with Dick McAuliffe (.262 BA, 13 HR, 61 RBI) at short. Rocky Colavito (.271 BA, 22 HR, 91 RBI) in left led league in plate appearances (692). He led team in games (160), at bats (597), runs (91), doubles (29), times on base (247), bases produced (345), strikeouts (78) and outs (463). Billy Bruton (.256 BA, 8 HR, 489 RBI) in center led in triples (8). Player of the Year and most effective hitter Al Kaline (.312 BA, 27 HR, 101 RBI) in right-field led for hits (172), singles (118), homers, runs batted in, slugging (.514), OPS (.889), OPS+ (144), gross production average (.297), WAR (5.4), oWAR (5.2), batters run average (.192), hitting, BAbip (.302), base runs (98), runs produced (163), runs created (106), isolated power (.201), extra base hits (54), total bases (283) and 16-game hitting streak. Frank Lary (.229 BA, 6 RBI) led pitchers. The leading Bengal pinch-hitters were Willie Horton at .600 (3-5, HR, 3 RBI), Kaline at .600 (3-5) and Bruton at .500 (6-12, 5 RBI).

1960s Hitting Home Runs	
1. Norm Cash	278
2. Al Kaline	210
3. Dick McAuliffe	142
4. Willie Horton	141
5. Rocky Colavito	139
6. Bill Freehan	110
7. Jim Northrup	74
8. Don Wert	71
9. Billy Bruton	46
10. Don Demeter	43

Pitching. The Tigers had a 3.90 ERA, 42 CG, six SHO, 477 walks, 930 SO, 96 ERA+, 4.02 FIP, 1.294 WHIP, 8.7 H/9, 2.9 BB/9 and 5.7 SO/9. Pitcher of the Year Phil Regan (15-9, 3.86 ERA) led in wins, win percentage (.625), and went 13-3 (.813) after Dressen became manager. The most effective pitcher Mickey Lolich (5-9, 3.55 ERA) led in WP (8), ERA, ERA+ (105), FIP (3.49), DICE (4.01) and HR/9 (0.8). Hank Aguirre (14-15, 3.67 ERA) led in losses, CG (14), SHO (3), HBP (8), LOB% (76.8%), pWAR (2.9) and R/9 (3.8). Jim Bunning (12-13, 3.88 ERA) led MLB in homers (38) and league for runs (119). He led staff in starts (35), innings (248.1), hits (245), walks (69), strikeouts (196), earned runs (107), runs (119), SO/9 (7.1) and SO/BB (2.84). Don Mossi (7-7, 3.74 ERA) led in WHIP (1.035), H/9 (8.1) and BB/9 (1.2). Bill Faul (5-6, 4.64 ERA) led league in balks (3). Terry Fox (8-6, 3.59 ERA) led in games (46), GF (29) and saves (11). Fred Gladding (1-1, 1.98 ERA), Frank Lary (4-9, 3.27 ERA), Bob Anderson (3-1, 3.30 ERA) and Tom Sturdivant (1-2, 3.76 ERA). Class "AAA" Syracuse had Willie Smith (14-2 .875, 2.11 ERA, 4 SHO), Alan Koch (11-2 .846, 3.36 ERA) and Bob Dustal (11-6 .647, 2.98 ERA). Fritz Fisher (10-6 .625, 2.97 ERA) was at class "AA" Knoxville, with Robert Laton (12-4, 3.02 ERA) at class "A" Thomasville. John Gregory (9-4 .692, 2.37 ERA) was assigned to class "A" Lakeland.

Defense. The Bengals committed 113 errors (.981). League leaders were Triandos in catcher fielding (.998) and passed balls (14), Colavito for fielding (.993) in left, Kaline for fielding (.992) in right. Catcher Freehan led Detroit in defensive WAR (0.6).

The Sporting News Player of the Year Al Kaline hit .415 with men on base, .412 with bases loaded, .400 in extra innings and .398 with runners in scoring position. He went 4-for-7 (2 HR, 4 RBI) in an 8-6 win at Minnesota on Thursday, September 19.

Denny McLain was a combined 18-6 (.750) at class "AA" Knoxville (5-4 .556, 3.51 ERA) and class "A" Duluth-Superior (13-2 .867, 2.55 ERA), with his MLB debut in September. Ken Avery (13-4) and Pat Jarvis (14-6) also pitched for Duluth-Superior.

1960s Hitting Runs Batted In		
1.	Norm Cash	830
2.	Al Kaline	773
3.	Dick McAuliffe	488
4.	Willie Horton	461
5.	Rocky Colavito	430
6.	Bill Freehan	416
7.	Don Wert	331
8.	Jim Northrup	291
9.	Billy Bruton	218
10.	Mickey Stanley	187

Team. Detroit finished fourth under Chuck Dressen at 85-77 (.525), with an attendance of 816,139. The team was 7-6 in April, with a Mickey Lolich (9 IP, 0 ER, 3 H, 7 SO) 5-0 shutout in Minnesota on Friday, April 24, as Jerry Lumpe went 3-for-5 (3 RBI). The squad finished 11-18 in May when Lolich (9 IP, 2 ER, 3 H) led a 7-2 win over New York at home on Tuesday, May 12, behind Don Wert 3-for-4 and Willie Horton (2 3B, 2 RBI). The squad went 14-14 in June, as "*Mr. Tiger*" Al Kaline hit .593 for the week of June 3-9 (7 GM, 16-for-27, .645 OBP, .815 SLG, .625 BAbip). The Bengals beat visiting Minnesota 16-1 on Tuesday, June 9, as Detroit leading 8-1 then scored eight seventh inning runs. Kaline was 3-for-5, Don Demeter 3-for-5 (2 HR, 5 RBI) and Bill Freehan 3-for-4 (HR, 4 RBI). Freehan went 5-for-5 in a 5-4 loss in New York on Saturday, June 27. Motown had a record of 18-17 in July when they split a doubleheader with Boston at home on Friday, July 10. The Bengals lost 7-6 with Dick McAuliffe 3-for-4 (2 HR, 4 RBI), followed by an 8-3 victory, as McAuliffe was 2-for-3 (HR, 3 RBI). He went 5-for-7 (3 HR, 7 RBI) on the day. Kaline homered in four straight games July 22-24 (1.167 SLG), with an eight-game RBI streak July 22-July 28 (4 HR, 13 RBI, .424 BA, .970 SLG). The Tigers were 20-10 in August with a seven-game win streak that began on Tuesday, August 4. Detroit lost to the Angels 4-3 at home on Thursday, August 20, before 2,173 fans, the smallest night crowd in team history. The club closed 13-10 in September including a sweep in Washington during the weekend of Friday, September 4. Dave Wickersham (W 17-10, 8 IP, 0 ER, 3 H) won 1-0 on Friday, a Lolich (W 15-7, 9 IP, 0 ER, 4 H, 7 SO) 4-0 shutout on Saturday, as Wert was 3-for-4. Detroit won 9-3 on Sunday, led by Demeter 3-for-5 (HR, 5 RBI), George Thomas 3-for-4 (HR) and Hank Aguirre (7 IP, 2 ER, 5 SO). Bill Roman out of Detroit Cooley High School had a memorable MLB debut, with a pinch-hit home run during a 11-8 loss in Yankee Stadium on Wednesday, September 30. Detroit went 46-35 (.568) at home, 39-42 (.481) on the road, scored 699 runs and allowed 678. Class "A" Jamestown had Jim Mooring (90 GM, .377 BA, 22 HR, 89 RBI, .637 SLG). Class "AAA" Syracuse had Mack Jones (109 R, .317 BA, 18 3B, 39 HR, 102 RBI, .630 SLG, 336 TB), along with Michiganders Willie Horton (.288 BA, 28 HR, 99 RBI) out of Detroit and Jim Northrup (.312 BA, 13 3B, 18 HR, 92 RBI) from Breckenridge and Alma College.

P * DAVE WICKERSHAM

Offense. Detroit had a .253 BA, .319 OBP, .395 SLG, .714 OPS, 2,178 TB, and 96 OPS+ of 96, as the Tigers led the league in triples (57). Player of the Year catcher Bill Freehan (.300 BA, 18 HR, 80 RBI) led in triples (8), oWAR (4.6), hitting and runs produced (131). Norm Cash (.257 BA, 23 HR, 83 RBI) at first base led in runs batted in and secondary average (.344). Second baseman Jerry Lumpe (.256 BA, 6 HR, 46 RBI) led team in plate appearances (688), at bats (624), hits (160), singles (127), in-play percentage (82%) and outs (489). Don Wert (.257 BA, 9 HR, 55 RBI) manned third. Shortstop Dick McAuliffe (.241 BA, 24 HR, 66 RBI) led in games (162), runs (85), homers, walks (77) and strikeouts (96). Leftfielder Gates Brown (.272 BA, 15 HR, 54 RBI) led in power/speed number (12.7). Billy Bruton (.277 BA, 5 HR, 33 RBI) led in BAbip (.324), steals (14) and stolen base runs (1.2), as he split centerfield with George Thomas (.86 BA, 12 HR, 44 RBI). The most effective hitter was right-fielder Al Kaline (.293 BA, 17 HR, 68 RBI) that in doubles (31), on-base percentage (.383), slugging (.469), OPS (.851), OPS+ (134), total average (.852), base-out percentage (.856), gross production average (.289), WAR (5.6), batters run average (.179), times on base (232), base runs (91), runs created (94), extra base hits (53), total bases (246), bases produced (325) and 14-game hitting streak. Don Demeter (.256 BA, 22 HR, 80 RBI) and Jake Wood (.232 BA, 1 HR, 7 RBI) were utility players. Phil Regan (.317 BA) led the pitchers. Thomas at .353 (6-17, HR, 3 RBI) led Tiger pinch-hitters. Demeter destroyed Minnesota pitching June 8-9, with 6-for-9 (2 GM, 3 HR, 9 RBI, .667 BA, .700 OBP, 1.667 SLG, .600 BAbip).

1960s Hitting On-Base Percentage		
1.	Al Kaline	.381
2.	Norm Cash	.380
3.	Rocky Colavito	.364
4.	Steve Boros	.358
5.	Dick McAuliffe	.348
6.	Bill Freehan	.343
7.	Billy Bruton	.336
8.	Willie Horton	.334
9.	Jim Northrup	.326
10.	Gates Brown	.324

Pitching. Motown logged a 3.84, 35 CG, nine SHO, 536 walks, 993 SO, 96 ERA+, 3.92 FIP, 1.293 WHIP, 8.3 H/9, 3.3 BB/9 and 6.2 SO/9. Pitcher of the Year and most effective pitcher Mickey Lolich (18-9, 3.26 ERA) led league in shutouts (6) and team in games (44), win percentage (.667), complete games (12), shutouts (6), strikeouts (192), wild pitches (7), LOB% (77.4), earned run average, ERA+ (113), FIP (3.30), DICE (3.69), WHIP (1.121), pWAR (3.6), BB/9 (2.5), SO/9 (7.4), SO/BB (3.00) and R/9 (3.4). Wickersham (19-12, 3.44 ERA) led in wins, losses, starts (36), innings (254), hits (224), homers (28), walks (81), HBP (12), earned runs (97), runs (108) and quality starts (24). Hank Aguirre (5-10, 3.79 ERA) led in H/9 (7.5). Joe Sparma (5-6, 3.00 ERA), Denny McLain (4-5, 4.05 ERA) and Phil Regan (5-10, 5.03 ERA). Larry Sherry (7-5, 3.66 ERA) led in games finished (24) and saves (11). Fred Gladding (7-4, 3.07 ERA), Terry Fox (4-3, 3.39 ERA), Ed Rakow (8-9, 3.72) and Julio Navarro (2-1, 3.95 ERA). Class "A" Jamestown featured John Skulley (9-2, .818). Earl Griffin (9-1 .900, 1.50 ERA) was assigned to class "A" Lakeland, with Fritz Fisher (9-3 .750, 2.82 ERA) at class "AA" Knoxville. Bill Faul (11-1 .917) excelled for class "AAA" Syracuse.

Defense. The team committed 111 errors (.982). League leaders were Regan in pitcher fielding (1.000), catcher Freehan in runners caught stealing (54%) and team dWAR (1.7), Cash in fielding (.997) at first and McAuliffe in errors (32) at shortstop.

Lolich excelled July 1-September 10 (9-1, 1.63 ERA, .176 BA, .238 OBP, .211 BAbip). He had three shutouts in a row September 1-9, with a 30.2 consecutive scoreless innings streak September 1-12 (3-0, .144 BA, 0.652 WHIP, 4.4 H/9, 1.5 BB/9, 8.8 SO/9).

University of Michigan All-American Bill Freehan set the Big Ten Conference batting record of .585 in 1961. He had 49 multi-hit games as an All-Star for Detroit in 1964. He had a 10-game hitting streak August 7-16 (4 HR, 9 RBI, .439 BA, .829 SLG).

1960s Hitting Slugging Percentage	
1. Rocky Colavito	.501
2. Norm Cash	.498
3. Al Kaline	.494
4. Willie Horton	.486
5. Don Demeter	.456
6. Gates Brown	.443
7. Jim Northrup	.439
8. Dick McAuliffe	.422
9. Charlie Maxwell	.416
10. Bill Freehan	.410

Team. Bob Swift (24-18 .571) and Chuck Dressen (65-55 .542) led Detroit (89-73 .549) to fourth with 1,029,645 fans. The team went 8-4 in April as Al Kaline (5 RBI) led a 11-4 win at Kansas City on Tuesday, April 13. The squad was 17-15 in May, as 22-year-old rookie Willie Horton had a five-game multi-hit streak May 11-15 (15-for-22, .682 BA, 6 HR, 16 RBI, .680 OBP, 1.591 SLG, .643 BAbip), with back-to-back games of two homers and five runs batted in. Motown won 13-3 at Washington on Thursday, May 13, behind Hank Aguirre (W 4-0, 9 IP, 2 ER, 7 SO), Horton 3-for-4 (2 HR, 5 RBI), and Don Demeter (HR, 4 RBI). Bill Freehan (2 HR, 5 RBI) led an 8-3 win at Chicago on Monday, May 24. Joe Sparma (9 IP, 1 ER, 5 H, 9 SO) 1-for-3 (2 RBI) sparked a 4-1 home win over New York on Thursday, May 27. Aguirre (9 IP, 0 ER, 2 H) beat Cleveland 1-0 the next day, followed by a 10-inning 1-0 home shutout of Cleveland by Mickey Lolich (10 IP, 0 ER, 2 H) on Saturday. The squad was 14-12 in June with eight straight home wins. 50,383 fans watched on Sunday, June 13, as Aguirre (W 7-2, 8 IP, 4 ER, 7 SO) with a .076 career average hit a single to score the winning run in a 5-4 home win over Minnesota. Horton (HR, 3 RBI) and Denny McLain (6.2 IP, 2 ER, 14 SO) with a Tiger relief record of 14 strikeouts led a 6-5 win over Boston at home on Tuesday. Players beat Boston 9-4 the next day, aided by Horton 3-for-4 (HR, 5 RBI) and a Demeter two-run pinch-hit single. Detroit was 17-12 in July with a McLain (W 8-3, 9 IP, 1 ER, 3 H, 12 SO) 2-1 home win of Cleveland on Wednesday, July 21. Motown won 13-2 at home over Chicago on Sunday, July 25, paced by Jerry Lumpe (HR, 3 RBI), Norm Cash (2 HR, 4 RBI) and Dick McAuliffe (HR, 4 RBI). The Tigers were 17-16 in August when they beat Kansas City 11-1 at home on Thursday, August 12, with Aguirre (9 IP, 1 ER, 4 H, 11 SO) and Demeter 3-for-4 (HR, 7 RBI). Motown closed 14-13 in September and 2-1 in October. Sparma (W 12-6, 7 IP, 0 ER, 9 SO) and Don Wert 2-for-3 (2 BB, HR, 4 RBI) won 5-4 in Minnesota on Thursday, September 2. Phil Regan (9 IP, 2 ER), Wert 3-for-4 (HR, 3 RBI), and Cash (HR, 3 RBI) led a 11-2 home win over Washington on Sunday, September 5. The Bengals went 13-5 (.722) with Kansas City. Detroit was 47-34 (.580) at home, 42-39 (.519) on the road, scored 680 runs and allowed 602.

P * FRED GLADDING

Offense. Detroit finished with a .238 BA, .312 OBP, .374 SLG, .686 OPS, 2,008 TB and 94 OPS+. Bill Freehan (.234 BA, 10 HR, 43 RBI) was the catcher. Comeback Player of the Year and most effective hitter Norm Cash (.266 BA, 30 HR, 83 RBI) at first led league in secondary average (.411), and isolated power (.246). He led team in doubles (23), homers, slugging (.512), OPS (.883), OPS+ (148), base-out percentage (.912), gross production average (.295), WAR (5.4), oWAR (4.2), batters run average (.190), base runs (87), runs created (89), power/speed number (10.0), extra base hits (54), bases produced (322), walks (77) and hit streak (14). Jerry Lumpe (.257 BA, 4 HR, 39 RBI) at second led for in-play percentage (81%), steals (7) and stolen base runs (2.1). Tiger of the Year Don Wert (.261 BA, 12 HR, 53 RBI) at third led the league in games (162), with club lead in plate appearances (697), at bats (609), runs (81), hits (159), singles (123), times on base (235) and outs (483). Shortstop Dick McAuliffe (.260 BA, 15 HR, 53 RBI) led in triples (6). Player of the Year left-fielder Willie Horton (.273 BA, 29 HR, 104 RBI) led in runs batted in, runs produced (144), total bases (251) and strikeouts (101). Don Demeter (.278 BA, 16 HR, 58 RBI) at center led in BAbip (.296). Right-fielder Al Kaline (.281 BA, 18 HR, 72 RBI) led in on-base percentage (.388), total average (.899) and hitting. Joe Sparma (.135 BA, 3 RBI) led pitchers in hitting. The leading pinch-hitters were Demeter at .400 (6-15, 3 RBI), Kaline .364 (4-11), Jake Wood .360 (9-25) and Gates "*Gator*" Brown (HR, 7 RBI).

1960s Hitting On-Base plus Slugging	
1. Norm Cash	.878
2. Al Kaline	.875
3. Rocky Colavito	.865
4. Willie Horton	.820
5. Dick McAuliffe	.770
6. Gates Brown	.767
7. Jim Northrup	.765
8. Don Demeter	.755
9. Bill Freehan	.753
10. Steve Boros	.742

Pitching. The Tigers had a 3.35 ERA, 12 SHO, 509 walks, 1,069 SO, 105 ERA+, 3.42 FIP, 1.232 WHIP, 7.9 H/9, 3.1 BB/9, and 6.6 SO/9. The staff led league in complete games (45). Pitcher of the Year and most effective pitcher Denny McLain (16-6, 2.61 ERA) led league in LOB% (81.3), with club lead for wins, win percentage (.727), complete games (13), shutouts (4), homers (25), earned run average, ERA+ (134), WHIP (1.071), pWAR (4.6), H/9 (7.1), BB/9 (2.5) and R/9 (3.0). Joe Sparma (13-8, 3.18 ERA, 7 WP) led in walks (75). Mickey Lolich (15-9, 3.44 ERA, 7 WP) led the majors in HBP (12). He led staff for starts (37), innings (243.2), hits (216), strikeouts (226), earned runs (93), runs (103), FIP (2.92), DICE (3.41), SO/9 (8.3) and SO/BB (3.14). Hank Aguirre (14-10, 3.59 ERA). Dave Wickersham (9-14, 3.78 ERA) led in losses and home runs per nine (0.6). Terry Fox (6-4, 2.78 ERA) led in saves (10). Michigander Fred Gladding (6-2, 2.83 ERA) from Flat Rock led in games (46). Orlando Pena (4-6, 2.51 ERA), Ron Nischwitz (1-0, 2.78 ERA), Larry Sherry (3-6, 3.10 ERA), Julio Navarro (0-2, 4.20 ERA) and Phil Regan (1-5, 5.05 ERA). McLain dominated for the June 8-October 2 (23 GM, 15-3 .833, 2.11 ERA, .203 BA, .235 BAbip).

Defense. Motown had 116 errors (.981). League leaders were Sparma in pitcher errors (6), Freehan in catcher fielding (.996), chances (926), chances per game (7.2), putouts (865) and tied MLB record of 19 putouts on Tuesday, June 15. Cash led in assists (97) at first, Wert at third in fielding (.976), chances (506) and club in dWAR (1.4). Horton in left led for fielding (.991).

The class "A" level had Chris Barkulis (.335 BA) at Duluth-Superior, John Skulley (16-6 .727, 2.13 ERA) at Daytona Beach and Jack DiLuro (12-7 .632, 2.64 ERA, 5 SHO) at Rocky Mount. Fritz Fisher (14-6 .700, 2.37 ERA) was at class "AA" Montgomery.

McLain went 10-2 at home and won eight straight 12-July 25 (8-0 1.000, 1.97 ERA, .186 BA, .224 BAbip). He relieved Dave Wickersham in a 6-5 home win over Boston on Tuesday, June 15 and struck out the first seven batters to set a major-league record. Denny closed the season in style for September 18-October 2 (4 GM, 4-0, 30 IP, 31 SO, 0.90 ERA, .178 BA, .219 BAbip).

1960s Pitching Wins	
1. Denny McLain	114
2. Mickey Lolich	102
3. Hank Aguirre	61
4. Earl Wilson	60
5. Jim Bunning	59
6. Joe Sparma	52
7. Frank Lary	44
8. Don Mossi	42
Phil Regan	42
10. Dave Wickersham	40

Team. Third-place Detroit (88-74 .543) played for managers Chuck Dressen (16-10 .615), Bob Swift (32-25 .561) and Frank Skaff (40-39 .506), with an attendance of 1,124,293. The team was 10-6 in April including an 8-3 home win over Washington on Friday, April 15, led by Orlando Pena (5 IP, 0 ER, 2 H, 4 SO) and a Dick McAuliffe (HR, 4 RBI) grand slam. The squad went 13-12 in May, as Denny McLain (9 IP, 0 ER, 1 H) pitched a 1-0 shutout at Chicago on Friday, May 6, as J.C. Martin hitting .182 got the lone White Sox hit. Dressen suffered his second heart attack in two years on May 16, with third base coach Swift taking over. The squad was 21-9 in June, including a 20-hit 16-4 triumph in Boston on Thursday, June 16. McLain (W 10-3, 9 IP, 3 ER) was 2-for-4 (RBI), with McAuliffe (HR, 3 RBI), Al Kaline 4-for-4, Gates Brown (HR), Jim Northrup 4-for-5 (2 RBI), Willie Horton 3-for-6 (HR, 6 RBI) and Bill Freehan (HR). Dave Wickersham (W 4-0, 9 IP, 1 ER, 5 H) and McAuliffe 3-for-3 with two homers paced a 2-1 victory on Sunday, June 19, with 61,071 fans in Yankee Stadium. Swift managed to the All-Star break when he was diagnosed with lung cancer and replaced by Skaff. McLain (13-4, 3.09 ERA, .182 BA, .183 BAbip) started the All-Star game in St. Louis on Tuesday, July 12. Detroit was 11-20 in July that included 8-5 win over visiting Baltimore on Friday, July 15, with Bill Monbouquette (4 IP, 0 E, 0 H), Northrup 3-for-5 (2 RBI) and pitcher Earl Wilson hit a pinch-hit walk-off homer in the thirteenth inning. The Tigers were 16-14 in August, as Dressen died on August 10. Don Wert had five straight multi-hit games August 9-14 (2 HR, 8 RBI, .571 BA, .625 OBP, 1.048 SLG, .566 BAbip). Wilson (W 6-3, 9 IP, 1 ER, 4 H) went 3-for-4 (HR, 5 RBI), with Norm Cash 3-for-3 (3 BB) during a 13-1 win at Boston on Saturday, August 13. Motown beat visiting Chicago 8-0 on Thursday, August 25, led by McLain (W 15-11, 9 IP, 0 ER, 2 H, 9 SO) and McAuliffe (HR, 3 RBI). McLain (W 16-11, 9 IP, 3 ER, 11 SO) threw 229 pitches on three days of rest in a 6-3 win over Dave McNally (L 12-4, 9 SO) at Baltimore on Monday, August 29, as Horton went 3-for-5 (2 HR, 5 RBI). The club closed 17-11 in September and 0-2 in October. Johnny Podres (9 IP, 0 ER, 5 H) shutout visiting California 7-0 on Thursday, September 22. Mayo Smith was named manager on October 3 to become the team's fourth manager in five-months. Swift died on Monday, October 17. Motown was 42-39 (.519) at home and 46-35 (.568) in away games. Motown scored 719 runs and allowed 698.

P * EARL WILSON

Offense. Detroit had a .251 BA, .321 OBP, .406 SLG, .727 OPS, 2,234 TB, and 105 OPS+. The club led league in homers (179). Catcher Bill Freehan (.234 BA, 12 HR, 46 RBI) led in stolen base runs (0.3). Player of the Year Norm Cash (.279, 32 HR, 93 RBI) at first base led in games (160), plate appearances (682), at bats (603), runs (98), hits (168), homers, times on base (238), base runs (97), runs produced (159), runs created (101), total bases (288), bases produced (356) and outs (457). Jerry Lumpe (.231 BA, HR, 26 RBI) at second led for in-play percentage (82%). Don Wert (.268 BA, 11 HR, 70 RBI) at third base led in singles (117) and steals (6). Dick McAuliffe (.274 BA, 23 HR, 56 RBI) led in triples (8), WAR (6.0), BAbip (.288) and hitting streak (11), as he split the shortstop position with Ray Oyler (.171 BA, 1 HR, 9 RBI). Willie Horton (.262 BA, 27 HR, 100 RBI) in left led for runs batted in and strikeouts (103). The most effective hitter Al Kaline (.288 BA, 29 HR, 88 RBI) led in doubles (29), on-base percentage (.392), slugging (.534), OPS (.927), OPS+ (161), total average (.969), base-out percentage (.983), gross production average (.310), batters run average (.209), hitting, secondary average (.415), isolated power (.246), power/speed number (8.5), extra base hits (59) and walks (81). Kaline shared centerfield with Mickey Stanley (.289, 3 HR, 19 RBI). Jim Northrup (.265 BA, 16 HR, 58 RBI) was in right-field. Earl Wilson (.234 BA, 5 HR, 17 RBI) led the pitchers. The top pinch-hitters were Northrup at .400 (4-10, HR, 3 RBI), Stanley .333 (3-9) and the "*Gator*" (2 HR, 9 RBI).

1960s Pitching Winning Percentage	
1. Denny McLain	.667
2. Earl Wilson	.606
3. Mickey Lolich	.580
4. Jim Bunning	.551
5. Don Mossi	.545
6. Dave Wickersham	.541
7. Frank Lary	.518
8. Hank Aguirre	.504
9. Joe Sparma	.495
10. Phil Regan	.488

Pitching. Motown recorded a 3.85 ERA, 36 CG, nine SHO, 520 walks, 1,026 SO, 91 ERA+, 3.94 FIP, 1.290 WHIP, 8.4 H/9, 3.2 BB/9, and 6.3 SO/9, as the Tigers led league in homers (185), HBP (42) and cheap wins (14). Pitcher of the Year and most effective pitcher Earl Wilson (13-6, 2.59 ERA) acquired from Boston on June 14, led league in pWAR (5.9), with staff lead in win percentage (.684), LOB% (81.7), earned run average, ERA+ (134), FIP (2.97), DICE (3.42), WHIP (1.004), pWAR (4.5), H/9 (6.9), BB/9 (2.1), SO/BB (3.50) and runs per nine (2.7). Denny McLain (20-14, 3.92 ERA) led MLB in home runs (42), with league lead for earned runs (115) and runs (120). McLain led staff in wins, starts (38), complete games (14), shutouts (4), innings (264.1), hits (205), walks (104), strikeouts (192) and quality starts' (23). Mickey Lolich (14-14, 4.77 ERA) led league in cheap wins (5) and led club in strikeouts per nine (7.6). Dave Wickersham (8-3, 3.20 ERA). Orlando Pena (4-2, 3.08 ERA). Larry Sherry (8-5, 3.82 ERA) led in games (55), games finished (39) and saves (20). Fred Gladding (5-0, 3.28 ERA), Johnny Podres (4-5, 3.43 ERA), Hank Aguirre (3-9, 3.82 ERA), Bill Monbouquette (7-8, 4.73 ERA) and Joe Sparma (2-7, 5.30 ERA).

Defense. Team made 120 errors (.980). League leaders were pitchers McLain in fielding (1.000), Wilson in putouts (34), errors (5), catcher Freehan in fielding (.996), chances (958), chances per game (7.3), and putouts (898), Cash in assists (114) and errors (17) at first. Lumpe led in fielding (.991) at second and club in dWAR (1.2), as Kaline led outfielder fielding (.993).

The Tiger of the Year and Player of the Year Al Kaline recorded three four-hit games, including 4-for-4 at Boston on Thursday, June 16, 4-for-5 against the California Angels at home on Monday, July 4 and 4-for-5 at Washington on Monday, August 8.

James Olms (9-4 .692, 1.82 ERA) and Norm McRae (10-5 .667, 2.83) were at class "A" Daytona Beach. Mike Marshall (11-7 .611, 2.33 ERA), a former MSU Spartan pitched at class "AA" Montgomery. Jim Rooker was 22-12 (.647) overall in the minors.

1960s Pitching Games Started		
1.	Mickey Lolich	219
2.	Denny McLain	205
3.	Jim Bunning	141
4.	Joe Sparma	136
5.	Hank Aguirre	135
6.	Earl Wilson	129
7.	Frank Lary	104
8.	Phil Regan	101
9.	Don Mossi	99
10.	Dave Wickersham	81

Team. Mayo Smith led second place Detroit (91-71 .562), with 1,447,143 fans. The squad was 10-6 in April when no hit in Baltimore, as Earl Wilson (8 IP, 1 ER, 2 H) won 2-1 on Sunday, April 30. The squad went 16-9 in May, with a 10-8 win in Boston on Saturday, May 13, led by Jim Northrup 4-for-5 and Willie Horton 3-for-4 for their seventh straight victory, with a six run ninth that included a Bill Freehan three-run shot Wilson pinch-hit two-run homer. Northrup (HR, 5 RBI) paced a 9-3 win over Boston at home on Thursday, May 25. Players were 12-18 in June when they won 15-10 at Minnesota on Tuesday, June 13, with a 10-run sixth inning that included a Jim Price pinch-hit two run single, and Dave Wickersham (4 IP, 0 ER) save. Motown lost 6-5 in 19-innings to Kansas City in 5:40 home on Saturday, June 17, as five Tiger pitchers faced 84 batters. 24-year-old rookie Mike Marshall was stunning in June (10 GM, 20.1 IP, 2 ER, 0.89 ERA, 2 SV) and July (11 GM, 20 IP, 1 ER, 0.45 ERA, 8 SV). Detroit was 15-12 in July that included a 11-4 home win versus New York on Saturday, July 22, behind Horton (HR, 3 RBI) and Norm Cash 4-for-5 (HR, 5 RBI) with an eighth inning grand slam. Players were 21-14 in August when Mickey Lolich (3-0, 0.87 ERA, 2 SHO) and John Hiller (3-0, 0.80 ERA, 2 SHO, 3 SV) went undefeated. Four pinch-hitters struck out to tie an MLB record in a 11-5 loss at Cleveland on Friday, August 4. Ray Oyler (HR, 3 RBI) led a 3-2 home win over Baltimore on Sunday, August 13. Al Kaline hit his 300th home run in a 4-2 win against Cleveland on Sunday August 20. Joe Sparma (W 13-6, 9 IP, 0 ER, 4 H) shutout Minnesota 10-0 at home on Wednesday, August 23, led by Dick Tracewski 4-for-5 (3B, 3 RBI), Horton 2-for-2 (BB, HR) and Oyler 2-for-3 (2 BB). The club closed 16-11 in September and 1-1 in October. Wilson (W 19-10, 5.1 IP, 0 ER, 2 H) and Fred Lasher (SV 4, 3.2 IP, 0 ER, 6 SO) led a 5-0 shutout in Minnesota on Sunday, September 3. Sparma (W 14-8, 9 IP, 0 ER, 2 H, 8 SO) shutout Kansas City 4-0 at home on Tuesday, September 5. The next day Detroit won a home doubleheader, behind Kaline (3 RBI) and Eddie Mathews (2 HR, 3 RBI) 8-5 in game one, followed by Wilson (W 20-10, 9 IP, 3 ER) with a two-run homer for a 6-3 win. Players were 52-29 (.642) at home, 39-42 (.481) on the road, scored 683 runs and allowed 587. Wilson was superb June 28-August 29 (10-2 .833, 2.58 ERA, .182 BA, .201 BAbip). Class "A" Statesville had Hector Soto (.337 BA) and Joseph Brauer (17-7 .708, 2.48 ERA). Lenny Green (.329 BA) of Detroit Pershing High School was at class "AAA" Toledo, as Lasher was exceptional for Tiger affiliates (44 GM, 10-2 .833, 0.64 ERA).

P * MIKE MARSHALL

Offense. Detroit had a .243 BA, .325 OBP, .376 SLG, .702 OPS, 2,035 TB and 105 OPS+. Tiger of the Year catcher Bill Freehan (.282 BA, 20 HR, 74 RBI) led MLB in HBP (20). He led club in games (155) and hits (146). Norm Cash (.242 BA, 22 HR, 72 RBI) was at first. Dick McAuliffe (.239 BA, 22 HR, 65 RBI) at second led in plate appearances (675), at bats (557), triples (7), times on base (245), bases produced (340), walks (105), strikeouts (118), outs (437) and hit streak (14). Don Wert (.257 BA, 6 HR, 40 RBI) at third led in singles (106) and in-play percentage (79%). Shortstop Ray Oyler (.207 BA, HR, 29 RBI). Leftfielder Willie Horton (.274 BA, 19 HR, 67 RBI). Center had Mickey Stanley (.210 BA, 7 HR, 24 RBI) that led in steals (9) and Jim Northrup (.271 BA, 10 HR, 61 RBI) the BAbip (.308) leader. Player of the Year and most effective hitter Al Kaline (.308 BA, 25 HR, 78 RBI) at right led in runs (94), doubles (28), homers, runs batted in, on-base percentage (.411), slugging (.541), OPS (.952), OPS+ (176), total average (1.009), base-out percentage (1.015), gross production average (.320), WAR (7.5), oWAR (6.6), batters run average (.222), hitting, secondary average (.428), base runs (99), runs produced (147), runs created (102), isolated power (.234), power/speed number (12.1), extra base hits (55) and total bases (248). Jerry Lumpe (.232 BA, 4 HR, 17 RBI) and Dick Tracewski (.280 BA, 1 HR, 8 RBI). Earl Wilson (.185 BA, 4 HR, 15 RBI) led the pitchers, as Tracewski led all pinch-hitters at .300 (3-10).

1960s Pitching Complete Games	
1. Denny McLain	93
2. Mickey Lolich	62
3. Frank Lary	45
4. Hank Aguirre	41
5. Jim Bunning	40
6. Earl Wilson	35
7. Don Mossi	32
8. Joe Sparma	30
9. Dave Wickersham	22
10. Phil Regan	20

Pitching. The Tigers had a 3.32 ERA, 46 CG, 16 SHO, 472 walks, 1,038 SO, 99 ERA+, 3.52 FIP, 1.179 WHIP, 7.7 H/9, 2.9 BB/9, and 6.5 SO/9, as they led league in homers (151). Pitcher of the Year Earl Wilson (22-11, 3.27 ERA) led MLB in wins, as he led staff for win percentage (.667), starts (38), complete games (12), innings (264), hits (216), walks (92), strikeouts (184), wild pitches (8) and LOB% (79.0). The most effective pitcher Mickey Lolich (14-13, 3.04 ERA) led the major leagues in SHO (6), with Tiger lead for earned run average, ERA+ (107), FIP (2.65), DICE (3.11), WHIP (1.083), pWAR (2.7), H/9 (7.3), BB/9 (2.5), SO/9 (7.7), SO/BB (3.11) and R/9 (3.1). Joe Sparma (16-9, 3.76 ERA) led staff in HBP (8). Denny McLain (17-16, 3.79 ERA) led MLB in homers (35). He led his team in losses, earned runs (99), and runs (110). Fred Gladding (6-4, 1.99 ERA) led in games (42), games finished (25) and saves (12). Michigander Mike Marshall (1-3, 1.98 ERA) of Adrian High School, Hank Aguirre (0-1, 2.40 ERA), John Hiller (4-3, 2.63 ERA), Dave Wickersham (4-5, 2.74 ERA), Pat Dobson (1-2, 2.92 ERA), Johnny Podres (3-1, 3.84 ERA). Class "AA" Montgomery had pitchers Bob Reed (11-6 .647, 2.35 ERA, 4 SHO) and Dick Drago (15-10 .600, 2.41 ERA, 4 SHO).

Defense. Detroit committed 132 errors (.978). Tiger league leaders were Wilson in pitcher fielding (1.000) and pickoffs (6), Freehan in catcher fielding (.992), chances (1,021), putouts (950) and steals (59), Cash in fielding (.995) and assists (112) at first base. McAuliffe in errors (21) at second, Kaline in right-field errors (6). Shortstop Oyler led team in defensive WAR (2.7).

Wilson shined at home (13-2 .867), second half (12-4 .750), facing Baltimore (4-0), Chicago (3-0), Kansas City (3-0) and Boston (3-0). Lolich had a September to remember (6-1, 58.1 IP, 1.54 ERA, .163 BA, .209 OBP, .197 SLG, .215 BAbip, 3 SHO).

Hiller started in the minors (24 GM, 9-3, 2.73 ERA) then in Detroit (23 GM, 4-3, 2.63 ERA), as he set the franchise rookie record of 28⅔ consecutive scoreless innings. John excelled in August (8 GM, 3-0, 0.80 ERA, .192 BA, .205 OBP, 3 SV, 2 SHO).

1960s Pitching Earned Run Average	
1. Hank Aguirre	2.74
2. Denny McLain	3.04
Earl Wilson	3.04
4. Jim Bunning	3.36
5. Dave Wickersham	3.40
6. Mickey Lolich	3.46
7. Don Mossi	3.53
8. Frank Lary	3.70
9. Joe Sparma	3.83
10. Phil Regan	4.50

Team. Mayo Smith led Detroit (103-59 .636) to the pennant, with 2,031,847 fans. Motown won the World Series over St. Louis in seven games. The team was 12-5 in April as Denny McLain (9 IP, 0 ER, 5 H), Dick McAuliffe (HR, 3 RBI) and Ray Oyler 3-for-4 led a 7-0 shutout in New York on Saturday, April 27. Players were 16-11 in May when McLain (W 5-0, 9 IP, 1 ER) and Al Kaline 3-for-4 (HR, 6 RBI) guided a 12-1 win at Washington on Friday, May 10. The team went 20-11 in June including a McLain (W 13-2, 9 IP, 3 ER, 8 SO) 14-3 triumph at Cleveland on Monday, June 24, with Northrup's (2 HR, 8 RBI) two grand slams, Jim Price (HR, 2 RBI) and Bill Freehan (2 RBI). Detroit had a 17-12 July record, with a 13-10 home win over California on the Fourth of July. The fireworks included nine home runs, six by Detroit. Northrup (2 HR, 5 RBI), and Norm Cash (2 HR, 3 RBI) led the way. Freehan (3 HR, 6 RBI) aided an 8-5 home win with Oakland the next day. McLain (W 20-3, 9 IP, 0 ER, 3 H) went 2-for-4 in a 9-0 shutout at Baltimore on Saturday, July 27, behind Horton (2 HR, 4 RBI) and Cash 4-for-5. The squad was 20-12 during August, as new reliever Don McMahon excelled in August (14 GM, 2-0, 23.2 IP, 21 SO, 0.38 ERA, .165 BA, .230 OBP, .228 SLG, .207 BAbip). Players won a home doubleheader versus Cleveland on Tuesday, August 6, with a 2-1 17-inning win on a Dick Tracewski walk-off single in game one. Starter John Hiller (8 IP, 1 ER, 4 H, 6 SO) struck out the first six Indians for an MLB record. Kaline had a sixth-inning two-run pinch-hit double for a 5-2 game two victory. Mickey Lolich stood 7-7 on August 6, then finished the season strong (10-2 .833, 2.08 ERA, .170 BA, .237 SLG, .234 BAbip). Detroit won a home doubleheader on Sunday, August 11, 5-4 in 14 innings, with a pinch-hit walk-off homer by Gates Brown. The "*Gator*" had a walk-off single for a game two 6-5 win. Motown won 10-9 in 11-innings at Boston on Saturday, August 17, with reliever McMahon (4 IP, 1 ER, 3 SO) and Cash 5-for-6 (HR, 5 RBI). The team played a 3-3 19-inning tie in New York on Friday, August 23, with Tiger reliever Hiller (9 IP, 0 ER, 4 H) facing 37 hitters. Earl Wilson (9 IP, 1 ER, 4 H, 9 SO) went 2-for-4 (HR, 4 RBI) in a 9-1 victory over visiting Baltimore on Friday, August 30, with 53,575 fans. Detroit was 18-8 in September when McLain (W 30-5, 9 IP, 10 SO) recorded his 30th win in a 5-4 home win facing Oakland on Saturday, September 14. Northrup hit five grand slam home runs in 1968. Motown went 34-15 (.694) versus lefthanders, 22-7 (.759) in blowouts, 56-25 (.691) at home, and 47-34 on the road (.580). Detroit scored 671 runs and allowed 492 runs.

OF * WILLIE HORTON

Offense. Detroit had a .235 BA, .307 OBP, .692 OPS, 2,115 TB, and 107 OPS, with league lead in homers (185) and slugging (.385). Catcher Bill Freehan (.263 BA, 25 HR, 84 RBI) led in games (155), WAR (6.9) and oWAR (6.6). Norm Cash (.263 BA, 25 HR, 63 RBI) was at first. Dick McAuliffe (.249 BA, 16 HR, 56 RBI) at second led league in runs (95). He led club in plate appearances (658), triples (10), times on base (226), power/speed number (10.7), steals (8) and walks (82). Don Wert (.200 BA, 12 HR, 37 RBI) was at third. Tommy Matchick (.203 BA, 3 HR, 14 RBI), Dick Tracewski (.156 BA, 4 HR, 15 RBI) and Ray Oyler (.135 BA, HR, 12 RBI) were at short. Player of the Year and most effective hitter Willie Horton (.285 BA, 36 HR, 85 RBI) at left led in homers, slugging (.543), OPS (.895), OPS+ (165), total average (.867), base-out percentage (.878), gross production average (.294), batters run average (.191), secondary average (.348), base runs (90), runs created (98), isolated power (.258), extra base hits (58), total bases (278), bases produced (327), strikeouts (110) and hit streak (14). Mickey Stanley (.259 BA, 11 HR, 60 RBI) at center led MLB in GIDP (22). He led club for at bats (583), singles (118), in-play percentage (81%) and outs (469). Jim Northrup (.264 BA, 21 HR, 90 RBI) at right led in hits (153), doubles (29), runs batted in and runs produced (145). Al Kaline (.287 BA, 10 HR, 52 RBI) led in on-base percentage (.392) and BAbip (.299). Earl Wilson (.227 BA, 7 HR, 17 RBI) led pitchers. Several pinch-hitters were Kaline at .500 (5-10, HR, 5 RBI), Gates Brown .450 (18-40, 3 HR, 7 RBI) and Matchick .385 (5-13).

1960s Pitching Innings Pitched	
1. Mickey Lolich	1,528.1
2. Denny McLain	1,501.2
3. Hank Aguirre	1,315.0
4. Jim Bunning	1,026.1
5. Earl Wilson	866.1
6. Joe Sparma	836.1
7. Frank Lary	755.0
8. Phil Regan	746.2
9. Don Mossi	701.2
10. D. Wickersham	675.1

Pitching. Detroit had a 2.71 ERA, 16 SHO, 486 walks, 1,115 SO, 111 ERA+, 3.06 FIP, 1.118 WHIP, 7.1 H/9, 2.9 BB/9, and 6.7 SO/9. Pitchers led league for CG (59) and innings (1,489.2). MVP, Cy Young Award, Player of the Year, Tiger of the Year, and most effective pitcher Denny McLain (31-6, 1.96 ERA) led MLB in wins, win percentage (.838), starts (41), quality starts (35), innings (336) and homers (31). He led league in complete games (28), as he led staff in SHO (6), hits (241), strikeouts (280), runs (86), LOB% (84.0), ERA, ERA+ (154), FIP (2.53), DICE (3.15), WHIP (0.905), pWAR (7.4), H/9 (6.5), BB/9 (1.7), SO/BB (4.44) and R/9 (2.3). Denny went 17-2 on the road and was 6-0 versus Minnesota. Earl Wilson (13-12, 2.85 ERA) led in losses and WP (7). Mickey Lolich (17-9, 3.19 ERA) led in HBP (11), earned runs (78) and SO/9 (8.1). Lolich was the World Series MVP (3-0, 1.67 ERA, .206 BA). Joe Sparma (10-10, 3.70 ERA) led AL in no decisions (12). He led team in walks (77) and HR/9 (0.7). Rookie Daryl Patterson (2-3, 2.12 ERA, 7 SV) led in GF (22). Pat Dobson (5-8, 2.66 ERA, 7 SV) led in games (47). Don McMahon (3-1, 2.02 ERA), John Wyatt (1-0, 2.37 ERA), John Hiller (9-6, 2.39 ERA), Fred Lasher (5-1, 3.33 ERA) and Jon Warden (4-1, 3.62 ERA). Class "A" Lakeland had Joseph Brauer (9-0, 2.10 ERA) and Matthew Hoar (8-3, 1.26 ERA, 4 SHO), with Nicholas Ross (7-2, 4.02 ERA) of Dearborn Divine Child High School at class "A" Rocky Mount.

Defense. Detroit had 105 errors, as they led league in fielding (.983) and putouts (4,463). League leaders were McLain in pitcher chances (77), and putouts (36), Freehan in catcher chances (1,050), putouts (971), double plays (15), steals (66) and caught stealing (38). Stanley led in outfielder fielding (1.000), as right-fielder Northrup led the team for defensive WAR (1.4).

Class "AAA" Toledo featured pitchers Fred Scherman (8-2 .800, 1.76 ERA), Jim Rooker (14-8 .636, 2.61 ERA), Michigan State University product Mike Marshall (15-9 .625, 2.94 ERA) and Dick Drago (15-8 .652, 3.36 ERA) from the University of Detroit.

1960s Pitching Walks	
1. Mickey Lolich	518
2. Denny McLain	422
3. Joe Sparma	411
4. Hank Aguirre	363
5. Jim Bunning	278
6. Earl Wilson	264
7. Phil Regan	258
8. Dave Wickersham	229
9. Paul Foytack	199
10. Frank Lary	185

Team. Detroit finished second at 90-72 (.556) for Mayo Smith with an attendance of 1,577,481 in the Eastern Division. The Tigers were 10-10 in April including a 12-3 home win against Cleveland on Thursday, April 10, when Bill Freehan went 3-for-5 (2 HR, 5 RBI). The squad had a 15-8 record in May as Mickey Stanley (HR, 4 RBI) led a 6-3 home win over California on Friday, May 23, and Mickey Lolich (W 6-1, 9 IP, 3 ER, 4 H, 16 SO) set the franchise record with 16 strikeouts. Joe Sparma (9 IP, 0 ER, 1 H, 8 SO) lost his no-hitter in the ninth inning of a 3-2 win at Seattle on Saturday, May 31. The team went 14-14 in June as Lolich (9 IP, 1 ER, 4 H, 16 SO) tied his record of 16 strikeouts during a 10-inning 3-2 loss to Seattle at home on June 9. Detroit had a July record of 17-13 that included a 15-3 home win over Cleveland on Saturday, July 12, behind Lolich (W 12-2, 9 IP, 3 ER, 10 SO), Norm Cash 3-for-3 (3 RBI), Jim Northrup 3-for-4 (3 RBI), Jim Price (HR, 5 RBI, 2 SF) and Don Wert 4-for-5 (2 HR, 2 RBI). The Bengals were 21-9 in August with a 6-2 win over visiting Chicago on Sunday, August 3, aided by Price 2-for-3 (HR) and Willie Horton's (HR, 4 RBI) ninth inning walk-off grand slam. Northrup was 6-for-6 (2 HR, 3 RBI) and Cash (HR, 2 RBI) hit a two-run walk-off homer for the 5-3 13-inning win over Oakland on Thursday, August 28. Horton hit .500 for the week of August 28-September 3 (8 GM, 8 HR, 14 RBI, .533 OBP, 1.393 SLG), including a homer in five straight games. The club closed September 13-17 and 0-1 in October, as reliever Tom Timmerman (6 IP, 0 ER, 2 H) pitched during a 14-inning 6-5 home loss to Baltimore 6-5 on Sunday, September 7. Lolich (W 19-10, 9 IP, 3 ER, 7 SO) won 10-3 at Boston on September 28, followed by a 2-1 loss in Baltimore (9 IP, 2 ER) on two days of rest. Players went 10-2 (.833) against Seattle. The team was 46-35 (.568) at home, 44-37 (.543) on the road, scored 701 runs and allowed 601. Class "AAA" Toledo had Ike Brown (64-for-180 .356 BA), Tom Timmermann (9-2 .818, 2.41 ERA), Michiganders Gary Taylor (12-5 .706) from Detroit and Dave Campbell (38-for-89 .427 BA) from Manistee. John Young (.325 BA, 26 SB) was at class "A" Lakeland. Class "A-" Batavia had stars Jack Wosman (65-for-170 .382 BA), and Ronald Thomas (6-2 .750, 1.75 ERA, 11 SV).

P * PAT DOBSON

Offense. Detroit had a .242 BA, .316 OBP, .387 SLG, .703 OPS, 2,108 TB and 92 OPS+. Bill Freehan (.262 BA, 16 HR, 49 RBI) was the catcher. Norm Cash (.280 BA, 22 HR, 74 RBI) at first base led in runs (81), runs produced (133) and walks (63). Dick McAuliffe (.262 BA, 11 HR, 33 RBI) at second led in on-base percentage (.369) and secondary average (.358). Don Wert (.225 BA, 14 HR, 50 RBI) was at third. Michigan native Tom Tresh (.224 BA, 13 HR, 37 RBI) of Allen Park High School played at short. Player of the Year left-fielder Willie Horton (.262 BA, 28 HR, 91 RBI) led in homers, runs batted in and strikeouts (93). The most effective hitter Jim Northrup (.295, 25 HR, 66 RBI) at center led in hits (160), singles (99), doubles (31), slugging (.508), OPS (.866), OPS+ (136), total average (.847), base-out percentage (.854), gross production average (.288), WAR (5.0), oWAR (4.4), batters run average (.182), hitting, BAbip (.308), times on base (215), base runs (92), runs created (99), isolated power (.214), extra base hits (61), total bases (276), bases produced (332) and had a 13-game hitting streak. Al Kaline (.272 BA, 21 HR, 69 RBI) in right won the Hutch Award. Outfielder Mickey Stanley (.235 BA, 16 HR, 70 RBI) led in games (149), plate appearances (651), at bats (592), in-play percentage (80%), power/speed number (10.7), stolen bases (8) and outs (476). Tommy Matchick (.242 BA, 32 RBI) led in stolen base runs (0.9) and was the leading Tiger pinch-hitter at .500 (8-16). John Hiller (.286 BA) led the pitchers in hitting, as Robert Cole (61-for-167 .365 BA) played with Bristol.

1960s Pitching Strikeouts	
1. Mickey Lolich	1,336
2. Denny McLain	1,098
3. Jim Bunning	775
4. Hank Aguirre	714
5. Earl Wilson	635
6. Joe Sparma	563
7. Phil Regan	414
8. Dave Wickersham	410
9. Don Mossi	395
10. Frank Lary	388

Pitching. The team had a 3.31 ERA, 586 walks, 113 ERA+, 3.51 FIP, 1.262 WHIP, 7.7 H/9, and 3.6 BB/9. Staff led league for CG (55), shutouts (20), strikeouts (1,032) and SO/9 (6.4). Cy Young Award winner, Pitcher of the Year, Tiger of the Year, and most effective pitcher Denny McLain (24-9, 2.80 ERA) led MLB in shutouts (9), as he led league for wins, starts (41), innings (325), hits (288) and batters faced (1,304). McLain led staff in win percentage (.727), CG (23), homers (25), earned runs (101), LOB% (78.4), earned run average, ERA+ (134), WHIP (1.092), pWAR (8.1), BB/9 (1.9), SO/BB (2.70), R/9 (2.9) and quality starts (28). Mickey Lolich (19-11, 3.14 ERA) led in losses, walks (122), strikeouts (271), HBP (14), WP (14), runs (111) and SO/9 (8.7). Earl Wilson (12-10, 3.31 ERA), Tiger Rookie of the Year Mike Kilkenny (8-6, 3.37 ERA) and Joe Sparma (6-8, 4.76 ERA). Pat Dobson (5-10, 3.60 ERA) led in games (49) and GF (22). Don McMahon (3-5, 3.89 ERA) led in saves (11). Tom Timmermann (4-3, 2.75 ERA), Fred Lasher (2-1, 3.07 ERA) and John Hiller (4-4, 3.99 ERA). John Gregory (11-2 .846, 1.89 ERA) was with class "AA" Montgomery. Jerome Donahue (10-1 .909, 1.89 ERA) and Phil Meeler (1.50 ERA, 28 SV) were at class "A" Rocky Mount.

Defense. Tiger players committed 130 errors for a .979 fielding average. League leaders were pitchers Lolich and McLain in stolen bases (24), Lolich in pickoffs (7), catcher Freehan in fielding (.992), chances (877), total chances per game (7.3), putouts (821) and stolen bases (69). Leftfielder Horton led in errors (7), with his 11 putouts on Friday, July 18, tying the American League record. Right-fielder Kaline led in double plays (4) as infielder Matchick led team in defensive WAR (0.9).

Mickey Lolich did not lose for two-months May 7-July 7 (11 GM, 9-0, 2.09 ERA, 86 IP, 97 SO, .185 BA, .259 OBP, .273 SLG, .251 BAbip), with a club record 16 strikeouts on May 23 against California and then fanned 16 again on June 9 versus Seattle.

Mayo Smith fired popular pitching coach Johnny Sain on Sunday, August 10. Denny McLain (65-28 .699, 2.70 ERA, 18 SHO, two Cy Young Awards) and Mickey Lolich (46-27 .630, 3.02 ERA, 11 SHO) prospered under his pitching tutelage 1967-1969.

MGR * BILLY MARTIN

Player of the Decade. Steve Kemp (.283 BA, 59 HR, 272 RBI) was the decade leader for gross production average (.280), as he denied runner-up Al Kaline a chance to be Player of the Decade for the third time. Detroit finished sixth in 1975 (57-102) receiving the first draft choice in 1976. Kemp (.283 BA, 59 HR, 272 RBI) was selected first out of the University of Southern California in the January 1976 MLB draft. He spent 1976 in the minors (.328 BA, 19 HR, 81 RBI) and was ready for the show. Kemp solidified left field for Detroit as a rookie in 1977 (.257 BA, 18 HR, 88 RBI), that included the week of May 16-22 (10-for-20, .500 BA, .565 OBP, .700 SLG). Steve was a stellar performer April 7-May 27, 1979 (37 GM, 8 HR, 33 RBI, .403 BA, .487 OBP, .657 SLG, .426 BAbip), as he earned his only All-Star appearance. His best year was in 1979 (.318 BA, 26 HR, 105 RBI, 149 OPS+) when he hit .420 during 38-day games (14 HR, 40 RBI).

1970s			
Year	W – L	Pct.	Pl
1970	79-83	.488	4
1971	**91-71**	**.562**	2
1972	86-70	.551	1
1973	85-77	.525	3
1974	72-90	.444	6
1975	57-102	.358	6
1976	74-87	.460	5
1977	74-88	.457	4
1978	86-76	.531	5
1979	85-76	.528	5
	789-820	.490	

All-Decade Team. Manager Billy Martin (248-204 .549), a former Tiger second baseman in 1958, led Detroit to an Eastern Division Crown in 1972 (86-70 .551). Pitcher Mickey Lolich (105-101 .510, 3.45 ERA). Catcher Bill Freehan (.262 BA, 90 HR, 342 RBI) led in HBP (42). Norm Cash (.263 BA, 95 HR, 257 RBI) at first led decade in slugging (.469), on-base plus slugging (.828), OPS+ (132), total average (.823) and secondary average (.344). Second baseman Dick McAuliffe (.236 BA, 50 HR, 184 RBI) led for walk percentage (12.8). Shortstop Eddie Brinkman (.222 BA, 28 HR, 180 RBI) led MLB in fielding for 1972 (.990), with a record 72 straight errorless games. *"Steady Eddie"* led Class "AA" Montgomery to the Southern League Title in 1977 (86-51 .628), when he mentored league MVP Alan Trammell (.291 BA, 19 3B). Aurelio Rodriguez (.239 BA, 85 HR, 423 RBI) at third was decade leader for games (1,241), plate appearances (4,649), at bats (4,352), hits (1,040), doubles (193), dWAR (8.6), times on base (1,261), extra base hits (309), extra bases on long hits (510), total bases (1,550), and SH (52). Steve Kemp at left hit .500 (5-for-10) in 1979 with the bases loaded. Centerfielder Ron LeFlore (.297 BA, 51 HR, 265 RBI) led team in runs (532), singles (755), triples (38), oWAR (21.4), hitting, BAbip (.353), run scoring percentage (40.6), total base average (1.7), bases produced (1,870), bases produced average (2.4), steals (294), and strikeouts (628). LeFlore started 1976 with a 30-game hit streak April 17-May 27 (.392 BA, .432 OBP, .554 SLG, .476 BAbip). Right fielder Al Kaline (.278 BA, 64 HR, 266 RBI) carried the Tigers to the 1972 Eastern Division Title during his last 10 games September 21-October 3 (21-for-41 .512 BA, 4 HR, 8 RBI, .523 OBP, .878 SLG, 1.401 OPS, .486 BAbip). DH Rusty Staub (.277 BA, 70 HR, 358 RBI) was an All-Star in 1976 (.299 BA, 15 HR, 96 RBI, 137 OPS+).

P * LES CAIN

Pitcher of the Decade. Mickey Lolich (105-101 .510, 3.45 ERA) led decade in wins, losses, starts (240), complete games (128), shutouts (18), quality starts (148), high quality starts (140), dominant starts (51), innings (1,833.1), hits (1,775), home runs (184), strikeouts (1,343), wild pitches (56), earned runs (702), runs (775), pWAR (32.6), SO/BB (2.71), batters faced (7,605), pickoffs (33) and tough losses (38). He was a 20-game winner in 1971 (25-14 .641, 2.92 ERA, 29 CG, 376 IP, 308 SO, 4 SHO) and in 1972 (22-14 .611, 2.50 ERA, 23 CG, 327.1 IP, 250 SO, 4 SHO). Mickey pitched his final shutout as a Tiger during a 1-0 home win over Boston on Friday, April 25, 1975 (9 IP, 0 ER, 4 H). Lolich and Bill Freehan formed the top pitcher-catcher battery in MLB history, with 324 games. Their first game together was on Tuesday, May 21, 1963 (L 0-1, 6 IP, 3 ER, 7 SO) and last on Monday, September 8, 1975 (L 11-17, 8 IP, 1 ER, 7 SO). Mickey is the all-time Tiger leader in many categories several of which were for starts (459), shutouts (39) and strikeouts (2,659).

1970s Attendance			
Year	Attn.	Avg.	Rk
1970	1,501,293	18,534	2
1971	1,591,073	19,643	2
1972	**1,892,386**	**24,261**	1
1973	1,724,146	21,286	1
1974	1,243,080	15,347	3
1975	1,058,836	13,347	6
1976	1,467,020	18,338	4
1977	1,359,856	16,788	7
1978	1,714,893	21,172	5
1979	1,630,929	20,387	7

All-Decade Pitchers. Mark Fidrych (27-16 .628, 2.79 ERA) was the decade leader in FIP (3.54), DICE (3.54), WHIP (1.090) and RA/9 (3.1). Fidrych dominated the first half of his rookie 1976 season (9-2 .818, 1.78 ERA, .218 BA, .234 BAbip) starting the All-Star game. He closed 1976 (19-9 .679, 2.34 ERA, 24 CG, 4 SHO, 159 ERA+) as Rookie of the Year. Dave Rozema (28-23 .549, 3.19 ERA) led decade in BB/9 (1.80), with rookie season of 1977 (15-7 .682, 3.09 ERA, 139 ERA+) his best. Jack Morris (21-13 .618, 3.66 ERA) excelled in 1979 (17-7 .708, 3.28 ERA) at his best in home games (13 GM, 9-3 .750, 2.32 ERA, .220 BA). Milt Wilcox (31-24 .564, 3.96 ERA) was a phenomenal 19-3 .864 during the decade for July (8-1 .889) and August (11-2 .846). Joe Coleman (88-73 .547, 3.82 ERA) was decade leader in walks (576), hit by pitch (52), wild pitches (56), no decisions (35), and cheap wins (18). He had success in 1971 (20-9 .690) and 1973 (23-15 .605). Les Cain (22-19 .537, 4.05 ERA) was a 22-year-old rookie in 1970 (12-7 .632, 3.84 ERA) that included the period May 13-August 28 (11-2 .846), with dominant start in a 7-1 win at California on August 16 (9 IP, 4 H, 1 ER, 10 SO). John Hiller (69-63 .523, 2.74 ERA) was decade leader in games (426), games finished (321), saves (115), intentional walks (64), SO/9 (8.02), games in relief (409), relief wins (63) and relief losses (53). He was splendid in 1973 (10-5 .667, 1.44 ERA, 38 SV, 283 ERA+) and became an All-Star in 1974 (17-14 .548, 2.64 ERA, 13 SV). Tom Timmermann (22-24 .478, 3.49 ERA) recorded 27 saves in 1970 when he held righthanded hitters to a .195 average. Fred Scherman (24-15 .615, 3.35 ERA) led in holds (8). He held lefthanded hitters to a .185 average during his 1971 season (11-6 .647, 2.71 ERA, 20 SV).

The Tigers double-play combination of second baseman Lou Whitaker (1976 Florida State League MVP) and shortstop Alan Trammell (1977 Southern League MVP) would play a major-league record of 1,918 games together from 1977 through 1995.

Team. Detroit (79-83 .488) finished fourth for Mayo Smith, with 1,501,293 fans. The team was 12-16 in April when Mickey Lolich (9 IP, 0 ER, 10 SO) threw an opening day 5-0 shutout at Washington on Monday, April 6, with Cesar Gutierrez 3-for-5 (2 RBI). Motown won eight straight games April 12-24. Al Kaline went 5-for-5, Bill Freehan 2-for-3 (HR, 3 RBI) and reliever John Hiller (5.2 IP, 1 ER) led an 8-6 win in Minnesota on Friday, April 24. The Bengals were 9-17 in May as rookie Les Cain went undefeated May 13-July 13 (12 GM, 8-0, 3.30 ERA). Detroit won back-to-back walk-off wins over the Yankees, with a Freehan ninth-inning home run to centerfield for a 4-3 Cain (9 IP, 3 ER, 6 SO) victory on Monday, May 25. Earl Wilson (9 IP, 0 ER, 4 H, 7 SO) shutout New York 3-0 the next day, aided by a dramatic Willie Horton three-run ninth-inning homer. The Tigers went 17-10 in June with an 8-3 win over Milwaukee at home paced by Horton (3 HR, 7 RBI) on June 9. The Tigers won 9-8 in a 12-inning game at Cleveland on Sunday, June 21, aided by Jim Northrup (2 HR, 5 RBI) and Gutierrez with a .218 average went 7-for-7. Cain (9-2 .818) was an All-Star snub. Detroit went 19-12 in July with a 5-2 win in Minnesota on Tuesday, July 21, with Dick McAuliffe 4-for-5. Motown had a 12-18 mark in August, as Cain (W 11-4, 9 IP, 1 ER, 10 SO) led a 7-1 win on Sunday, August 16. Lolich (8 IP, 0 ER, 2 H, 14 SO) shutout Milwaukee 1-0 at home on Sunday, August 23. the squad closed September 9-20 and 1-0 in October, with a 10-1 loss in Boston on Wednesday, September 2, as Gene Lamont hit a third-inning homer in his first MLB at bat. Hiller (9 IP, 0 ER, 2 H, 11 SO) shutout Cleveland 1-0 at home on Thursday, October 1. He struck out seven straight to tie the league record. Hiller suffered three heart attacks on Monday, January 11, 1971. The Bengals were 42-39 (.519) at home, 37-44 (.457) on the road, scored 666 runs and allowed 731. Cain had 156 strikeouts for the franchise rookie record. Joe Staton (.346 BA, 42 SB) was at class "A" Lakeland. Michael Fremuth (6-1 .857, 1.31 ERA) and Dan Bootcheck (13-8 .619, 1.92 ERA, 5 SHO) pitched at class "A" Rocky Mount, with future MLB umpire Michigander Frederick Spenn of Monroe working in the Carolina League.

1970s Team Hitting

YEAR	AVG	HR	RBI	SB
1970	.238	148	619	29
1971	.254	**179**	652	35
1972	.237	122	531	17
1973	.254	157	592	28
1974	.247	131	579	67
1975	.249	125	546	63
1976	.257	101	566	107
1977	.264	166	676	60
1978	**.271**	129	666	90
1979	.269	164	**729**	**176**

P * TOM TIMMERMANN

Offense. Detroit had a .238 BA, .322 OBP, .374 SLG, .696 OPS, 2,009 TB and 91 OPS+. Catcher Bill Freehan (.241 BA, 16 HR, 52 RBI). Norm Cash (.259 BA, 15 HR, 53 RBI) at first led in on-base percentage (.383), total average (.821), base-out percentage (.828) and secondary average (.373). Dick McAuliffe (.234 BA, 12 HR, 50 RBI) at second led in games (146), plate appearances (639), oWAR (3.2), times on base (228) and walks (101). Don Wert (.218 BA, 6 HR, 33 RBI) was at third base. Shortstop Cesar Gutierrez (.243 BA, 22 RBI) led for in-play percentage (84%). Player of the Year and most effective hitter Willie Horton (.305 BA, 17 HR, 69 RBI) in left led for slugging (.501), OPS (.855), OPS+ (133), gross production average (.285), batters run average (.177), hitting, BAbip (.306), isolated power (.197) and hitting streak (16). Mickey Stanley (.252 BA, 13 HR, 47 RBI) at center led in at bats (568), runs (83), hits (143), singles (98), triples (11), power/speed number (11.3), stolen bases (10), stolen base runs (2.4) and outs (455). The right-fielders were Al Kaline (.278 BA, 16 HR, 71 RBI) that led in doubles (24), WAR (3.2), oWAR (3.2), base runs (80) and runs created (79), and Jim Northrup (.262 BA, 24 HR, 80 RBI) led in homers, runs batted in, runs produced (127), runs created (79), extra base hits (48), total bases (231), bases produced (292) and strikeouts (68). Elliott Maddox (.248 BA, 3 HR, 24 RBI) was the Tiger Rookie of the Year. Les Cain (.162 BA, HR, 9 RBI) led pitchers. The top pinch-hitters were Gates Brown (HR, 13 RBI), Dalton Jones at .379 (11-29, 7 RBI), Norm Cash .353 (6-17, HR, 4 RBI) and Ike Brown .333 (7-21, 3 RBI).

Pitching. The Tigers had a 4.09 ERA, 33 CG, seven SHO, 623 walks, 1,045 SO, 92 ERA+, 3.93 FIP, 1.427 WHIP, 9.0 H/9, 3.9 BB/9, and 6.5 SO/9, as staff led league in batters faced (6,319) and left on base (1,246). Pitcher of the Year Les Cain (12-7, 3.84 ERA) led in win percentage (.632), HBP (7), H/9 (8.3) and SO/9 (7.8). The most effective pitcher Mickey Lolich (14-19, 3.80 ERA) led MLB in losses and league in earned runs (115). He led staff in wins, starts (39), complete games (13), SHO (3), IP (227.2), hits (272), walks (109), strikeouts (230), wild pitches (14), runs (125), LOB% (75.0), ERA, ERA+ (99), pWAR (4.5), SO/BB (2.11), R/9 (4.1) and QS (24). Joe Niekro (12-13, 4.06 ERA) led in homers (28). Earl Wilson (4-6, 4.41 ERA) led in WHIP (1.240). Denny McLain (3-5, 4.63 ERA) and Mike Kilkenny (7-6, 5.16 ERA). Tiger of the Year Tom Timmermann (6-7, 4.11 ERA) led in games (61), GF (43), SV (27), FIP (3.21) and DICE (3.57). John Hiller (6-6, 3.03 ERA), Fred Scherman (4-4, 3.23 ERA), Daryl Patterson (7-1, 4.85 ERA) and Bob Reed (2-4, 4.86 ERA). Class "AA" Montgomery had Lerrin LaGrow (11-4 .733, 2.10 ERA) and Charles Swanson (12-5 .706, 1.88 ERA). Arthur Clifford (9-1 .900, 0.91 ERA) and Mitchell Angelier (9-3 .750, 1.60 ERA) were at class "A" Lakeland.

1970s Team Hitting

YEAR	OBP	SLG	OPS	OPS+
1970	.322	.374	.696	91
1971	.325	.405	.730	102
1972	.305	.356	.661	94
1973	.320	.390	.710	95
1974	.303	.366	.669	91
1975	.301	.366	.666	86
1976	.315	.365	.680	97
1977	.318	.410	.728	94
1978	**.339**	.392	.730	103
1979	**.339**	**.415**	**.754**	100

Defense. Players made 133 errors for a .978 fielding average. The Tiger league leaders were pitcher Lolich in caught stealing (16) and pickoffs (13), catcher Freehan in fielding average (.997), as he led Detroit in dWAR (1.2). Centerfielder Stanley led American League outfielders in fielding average (1.000). Second baseman McAuliffe recorded 11 assists on Sunday, May 3.

Detroit took a doubleheader at Cleveland 7-2 and 9-8 in 12 innings on Tuesday, June 21. Shortstop Cesar Gutierrez scored three runs and set a major-league record by going 7-for-7 at the plate during game two of the doubleheader with the Indians.

22-year-old Elliott Maddox from the University of Michigan shined September 23-October 1 (10-for-16 .625 BA, .625 OBP, .750 SLG, .714 BAbip). He went 4-for-4 in a 7-4 loss on Thursday, September 24 at Baltimore, with a paltry crowd of 3,069.

Detroit Tigers 1971 American League

1970s Hitting Games		
1.	Aurelio Rodriguez	1,241
2.	Mickey Stanley	943
3.	Bill Freehan	807
4.	Ron LeFlore	787
5.	Willie Horton	780
6.	Eddie Brinkman	630
7.	Jim Northrup	625
8.	Al Kaline	608
9.	Jason Thompson	579
10.	Norm Cash	576

Team. Detroit (91-71 .562) closed second for Billy Martin, with 1,591,073 fans. The Bengals were 10-10 in April including a record home opening crowd of 54,089 in a Mickey Lolich (W 1-0, 9 IP, 2 ER, 8 SO) 8-2 win over Cleveland on Tuesday, April 6. Willie Horton went 5-for-6 (2 HR, 6 RBI) in a 10-inning 10-9 win over Boston at home on Saturday, April 17. The squad finished 16-12 in May as 53,337 fans watched players win a home doubleheader against Washington on Sunday, May 23. Lolich (W 7-3, 9 IP, 0 ER, 4 H, 10 SO), Al Kaline (HR, 3 RBI) and Norm Cash (HR, 2 RBI) led the 5-0 game one win. The game two 11-0 victory had Cash 3-for-4 (2 HR, 5 RBI), Dalton Jones 2-for-2 (HR) and Les Cain (W 1-0, 6 IP, 0 ER, 3 H, 6 SO). The squad went 16-13 in June losing 15-6 in Baltimore on Tuesday, June 29, with Jim Northrup (2 HR, 4 RBI). Detroit had a record of 13-15 in July, as Cash (2 HR, 6 RBI) and Lolich (W 13-6, 9 IP, 2 ER) powered a 12-7 win against visiting New York on Tuesday, July 6. Lolich (W 16-7, 11 IP, 2 ER, 10 SO) pitched an 11-inning 5-4 home win against Kansas City on Tuesday, July 27. Motown lost to visiting California 3-2 on Saturday, July 31, with Lolich (L 16-8, 12 IP, 3 ER, 14 SO) and Horton (2 HR). Players were 17-12 in August, as Dick McAuliffe was 3-for-4 (HR, 6 RBI) during a 12-8 win at Boston on Saturday, August 7. Detroit lost 12-11 to the Red Sox on Monday, with Bill Freehan 3-for-4 (3 HR, 3 RBI) and Horton 3-for-4 (2 HR, 5 RBI). The Tigers won 12-3 in Milwaukee on Tuesday, August 10, behind McAuliffe (HR, 3 RBI), Cash (HR, 3 RBI) and Freehan (HR, 3 RBI). The club went 19-9 in September with Northrup 5-for-5 (2 HR) during a 3-2 11-inning victory at Washington on Tuesday, September 7, with pitchers Joe Coleman (9 IP, 2 ER, 8 SO) and Fred Scherman (W 9-6, 2 IP, 0 ER, 0 H, 2 SO). Reliever Tom Timmermann (5.1 IP, 0 ER, 1 H) and Tony Taylor 4-for-4 (HR) led a 3-2 over visiting Boston on Sunday, September 12. Detroit went 10-2 (.833) versus Milwaukee, 54-27 (.667) at home and 37-44 (.457) on the road. The Bengals scored 701 runs and their pitchers allowed 645. Michael Dwyer (49 GM, 2.05 ERA, 9 SV) played with class "A" Rocky Mount.

UT * IKE BROWN

Offense. Detroit had a .254 BA, .325 OBP, 730 OPS, 2,226 TB, and 102 OPS+, with league high for homers (179) and SLG (.405). Catcher Bill Freehan (.277 BA, 21 HR, 71 RBI) led in WAR (4.3) and oWAR (4.1). Comeback Player of the Year, Player of the Year, and most effective hitter Norm Cash (.283 BA, 32 HR, 91 RBI) at first led league in isolated power (.248), as he led team in homers, runs batted in, slugging (.531), OPS (.903), OPS+ (149), total average (.933), base-out percentage (.934), batters run average (.197), secondary average (.381), base runs (83), runs produced (131), runs created (89) and bases produced (300). Dick McAuliffe (.208 BA, 18 HR, 57 RBI) at second led in stolen base runs (0.6). Aurelio Rodriguez (.253 BA, 15 HR, 39 RBI) at third led in plate appearances (639), at bats (604), hits (153), singles (101), doubles (30), triples (7), extra base hits (52), total bases (242), strikeouts (93) and outs (476). Shortstop Eddie Brinkman (.228 BA, HR, 37 RBI). Willie Horton (.289 BA, 22 HR, 72 RBI) in left led in hit streak (15). Mickey Stanley (.292 BA, 7 HR, 41 RBI) at center led in BAbip (.311) and in-play percentage (82%). Al Kaline (.294 BA, 15 HR, 54 RBI) in right led in on-base percentage (.416), gross production average (.303), hitting, times on base (208) and walks (82). Jim Northrup (.270 BA, 16 HR, 71 RBI) led in power/speed number (9.7) and steals (7). Gates Brown (.338 BA, 11 HR, 29 RBI), Ike Brown (.255 BA, 8 HR, 19 RBI), Tony Taylor (.287 BA, 3 HR, 19 RBI) and Dalton Jones (.254 BA, 5 HR, 11 RBI). Fred Scherman (.208 BA, 4 RBI) led pitchers. The best pinch-hitters were Mickey Stanley at .500 (3-6), Tony Taylor .400 (4-10, 5 RBI), Jim Northrup .357 (5-14), Gates Brown .346 (9-26, 2 HR, 5 RBI), Cesar Gutierrez .333 (3-9), Ike Brown .316 (6-19, 2 HR, 6 RBI) and Kevin Collins at .300 (9-30, HR).

1970s Hitting Runs		
1.	Ron LeFlore	532
2.	Aurelio Rodriguez	417
3.	Mickey Stanley	397
4.	Willie Horton	337
5.	Bill Freehan	307
6.	Al Kaline	290
7.	Jim Northrup	279
8.	Jason Thompson	269
9.	Rusty Staub	264
10.	Norm Cash	249

Pitching. Detroit had a 3.63 ERA, 53 CG, eight SHO, 609 walks, 100 ERA+, 3.55 FIP, 1.338 WHIP, 8.3 H/9 and 3.7 BB/9, as the staff led the league in strikeouts (1,000), hit by pitch (49) and SO/9 (6.1). Pitcher of the Year, Tiger of the Year, and most effective pitcher Mickey Lolich (25-14, 2.92 ERA, 7.4 SO/9) led MLB in wins, innings (376), strikeouts (308), starts (45), hits (336) and batters faced (1,538). Mickey led league for complete games (29), with staff lead in losses, shutouts (4), homers (36), earned runs (122), runs (133), WHIP (1.138), pWAR (8.5), BB/9 (2.2), SO/BB (3.35) and quality starts (31). Joe Coleman (20-9, 3.15 ERA, 7.4 SO/9) led league in HR/9 (0.5) and club in win percentage (.690), walks (96), FIP (2.65), DICE (3.20). Dean Chance (4-6, 3.51 ERA), Les Cain (10-9, 4.35 ERA), Joe Niekro (6-7, 4.49 ERA) and Mike Kilkenny (4-5, 5.00 ERA). Fred Scherman (11-6, 2.71 ERA) led in games (69), games finished (40), saves (20), LOB% (82.6), earned run average, ERA+ (134), H/9 (7.2) and R/9 (3.0). Ron Perranoski (0-1, 2.50 ERA), Tom Timmermann (7-6, 3.86 ERA), Bill Denehy (0-3, 4.22 ERA), Bill Gilbreth (2-1, 4.80 ERA) and Bill Zepp (1-1, 5.12 ERA). Class "AAA" Toledo had star Chuck Seelbach (12-2 .857). Class "AA" Montgomery featured Jack Whillock (5-2 .714, 1.19 ERA, 15 SV), with Steve Grilli (5-0 1.000, 1.98 ERA) playing for class "A" Lakeland. Lolich became just the second 25-game winner in American League history to not garner the Cy Young Award.

Defense. Detroit committed the fewest errors (106) to lead league in fielding average (.983) and division in putouts (4,395). League leaders were Chance in pitcher errors (6), Freehan in catcher chances (966), putouts (912) and stolen bases (67). Brinkman led in assists (513) at short and team in defensive WAR (1.8). Right-fielder Kaline led outfielders in fielding (1.000).

Achievements for Lolich were the most complete games in 25 years, most innings since 1904, team record 308 strikeouts, 14 strikeouts in back-to-back games on July 31 and August 4, with back-to-back shutouts on September 2 and September 6.

1970s Hitting Hits	
1. Aurelio Rodriguez	1,040
2. Ron LeFlore	970
3. Willie Horton	796
4. Mickey Stanley	784
5. Bill Freehan	726
6. Rusty Staub	582
7. Jim Northrup	580
8. Al Kaline	561
9. Jason Thompson	538
10. Norm Cash	467

Team. Detroit won the Eastern Division under Billy Martin at 86-70 (.551), with a league best attendance of 1,892,386. The franchise lost the league championship series to Oakland in five games. The club was 7-4 in April, as they defeated Chicago on a Tom Timmermann (9 IP, 0 ER, 3 H) 12-0 shutout aided by Eddie Brinkman 3-for-4 (4 RBI) and Norm Cash 3-for-5 (HR, 4 RBI) on Friday, April 28. The team went 14-12 in May with a 5-4 10-inning win at Cleveland on Wednesday, May 31. The Bengals went 15-12 in June, with a Joe Coleman (9 IP, 0 ER, 3 H, 10 SO) 3-0 win at California on Friday, June 16, with home runs by Dick McAuliffe and Mickey Stanley. The Bengals squeaked out a 2-1 victory in Baltimore on Saturday, June 24, behind Coleman (11 IP, 1 ER, 4 H, 11 SO). Consecutive homers by Aurelio Rodriguez, Al Kaline and Willie Horton scored four first inning runs in a 5-2 win at home over New York on Tuesday, June 27, as Lolich (W 12-5, 9 IP, 2 ER, 9 SO) pitched on two days of rest. Detroit went 19-12 in July, that included a mid-month 14-game stretch of 12-2. The team played to a 12-18 record in August, including a doubleheader split in New York on Wednesday, August 9, when Woodie Fryman (9 IP, 0 ER, 6 H) won a 6-0 shutout in his American League and Tiger debut during game one. Motown rolled into Minnesota and swept three 11-inning games the weekend of Saturday, August 26. The squad closed 16-11 in September and 3-1 in October including a three-game weekend sweep in Milwaukee starting on Friday, September 29, with a 12-5 win as Jim Northrup went 4-for-4 (5 RBI), 13-4 the next day with Kaline 4-for-5 (HR), and a John Hiller (9 IP, 1 ER, 5 H) 5-1 triumph on Sunday. Lolich (W 22-12, 9 IP, 15 led a 4-1 home win over Boston on Monday, October 2. Detroit went 44-34 (.564) at home, 36-43 (.456) on the road, scored 558 runs and allowed 514. Dave Lemanczyk (7-1 .875, 1.77 ERA) and Joe McIlvaine (43 GM, 9-6 .600, 1.57 ERA) played for class "A" Lakeland, with Fred Bruntrager (10-5 .667, 1.67 ERA) at class "A" Clinton.

C * DUKE SIMS

Offense. Detroit had a .248 BA, .330 OBP, .411 SLG, .740 OPS, 2,242 TB and 95 OPS+, with a league high 209 homers. Catcher Bill Freehan (.262, 10 HR, 56 RBI) led in on-base percentage (.354), WAR (4.2), oWAR (4.2), hitting, and hit streak (13). Player of the Year and most effective hitter Norm Cash (.259 BA, 22 HR, 61 RBI) at first led in homers, runs batted in, secondary average (.295), base runs (64), runs created (66), isolated power (.186) and bases produced (246). Dick McAuliffe (.240 BA, 8 HR, 30 RBI) at second led in walks (59). Third baseman Aurelio Rodriguez (.236 BA, 13 HR, 56 RBI) led in plate appearances (639), at bats (601), runs (65), hits (142), singles (101), doubles (23), times on base (172), runs produced (102), extra base hits (41), total bases (214), strikeouts (104) and outs (484). Tiger of the Year Eddie Brinkman (.203 BA, 6 HR, 49 RBI) at short led the league in games (156) and for in-play percentage (82%). Willie Horton (.231 BA, 11 HR, 36 RBI) was the leftfielder. Mickey Stanley (.234 BA, 14 HR, 55 RBI) at center led in triples (6). Right-fielder Al Kaline (.313 BA, 10 HR, 32 RBI). Outfielder Jim Northrup (.261, 8 HR, 42 RBI) led in power/speed number (5.3). Reserves Tony Taylor (.303 BA, HR, 20 RBI), Ike Brown (.250 BA, 2 HR, 10 RBI) and Gates Brown (.230 BA, 10 HR, 31 RBI). Deadline acquisition Duke Sims (.316 BA, 4 HR, 19 RBI) was a key down the stretch. Joe Niekro (.250 BA) led the pitchers. Key pinch-hitters were Stanley at .600 (3-5), Kaline .417 (10-24), Freehan .375 (3-8), Paul Jata .333 (4-12) and Taylor at .300 (6-20). Class "AA" Montgomery had Murray Robinson (28 HR, 94 RBI), with Dan Meyer (93-for-235, 14 HR, 46 RBI, .396 BA, .672 SLG) at Bristol.

1970s Hitting Doubles	
1. Aurelio Rodriguez	193
2. Mickey Stanley	129
3. Ron LeFlore	126
4. Bill Freehan	115
5. Willie Horton	109
6. Rusty Staub	104
7. Al Kaline	95
8. Jim Northrup	89
9. Jason Thompson	77
10. Steve Kemp	73

Pitching. The Tigers had a 2.96 ERA, 46 CG, 11 SHO, 465 walks, 952 SO, 108 ERA+, 3.08 FIP, 1.208 WHIP, 7.9 H/9, 3.0 BB/9, and 6.2 SO/9, as staff led league in pitchers (20). Pitcher of the Year and most effective pitcher Mickey Lolich (22-14, 2.50 ERA) led in wins, starts (41), complete games (23), shutouts (4), innings (327.1), hits (282), home runs (29), strikeouts (250), hit by pitch (11), earned runs (91), runs (100), LOB% (81.8), earned run average, ERA+ (127), FIP (2.80), DICE (3.40), pWAR (7.4), BB/9 (2.0), SO/BB (3.38), R/9 (2.7) and quality starts (32). Joe Coleman (19-14, 2.80, 280 IP) led in walks (110), wild pitches (9), H/9 (6.9) and SO/9 (7.1). Woodie Fryman (10-3, 2.06 ERA) led in win percentage (.769) and team win percentage in his starts (.786). Tiger Rookie of the Year Chuck Seelbach (9-8, 2.89 ERA, 0.5 HR/9) led in games (61), games finished (34) and saves (14). Other relievers were Lerrin LaGrow (0-1, 1.32 ERA), Chris Zachary (1-1, 1.41 ERA), John Hiller (1-2, 2.03 ERA), Tom Timmermann (8-10, 2.89 ERA), Bill Slayback (5-6, 3.20), Fred Scherman (7-3, 3.64 ERA, 0.5 HR/9) and Joe Niekro (3-2, 3.83 ERA). Niekro threw a no-hitter for class "AAA" Toledo versus Tidewater. Toledo had Bill Gilbreath (56 GM, 5-3 .625, 1.92 ERA, 14 SV). Class "AA" Montgomery had stars Dan Fife (14-7 .667, 3.10 ERA) of Clarkston High School, Steve Grilli (11-3 .786, 1.72 ERA), Jerome Donahue (1.92 ERA, 13 SV), and Dan Bootcheck (12-6 .667, 2.92 ERA).

Defense. Detroit committed a league low 96 errors for a .984 fielding average. Tiger league leaders were catcher Freehan in stolen bases (57), Rodriguez in chances (514), putouts (150), assists (348) and chances per game (3.4) at third. Shortstop Brinkman led in fielding (.990), as he went 72 consecutive games without an error and led the team in defensive WAR (1.9).

Al Kaline finished the season with a 10-game hitting streak September 21-October 3 (.512 BA, 4 HR, 8 RBI, 15 R, .523 OBP, .878 SLG, 1.401 OPS, .486 BAbip), as the club went 8-2 in those games on their way to the team's first Eastern Division title.

Late season waiver pick-ups in pitcher Woodie Fryman (10-3, 2.06 ERA, 154 ERA+) from Philadelphia on August 2 and catcher Duke Sims (.316 BA, 168 OPS+) from Los Angeles on August 4 were crucial during the Bengals drive for Eastern Division title.

1970s Hitting Triples	
1. Ron LeFlore	38
2. Mickey Stanley	34
3. Aurelio Rodriguez	31
4. Bill Freehan	19
5. Jim Northrup	15
Lou Whitaker	15
7. Willie Horton	13
8. Steve Kemp	11
Dick McAuliffe	11
10. Four Players	10

Team. Detroit finished third for Billy Martin (71-63) and Joe Schultz (14-14) at 85-77 (.525), with an attendance of 1,724,146. The club was 10-10 in April when the start of season was delayed due to a player strike. All-Star Willie Horton of Detroit Northwestern High School was 4-for-4 in 7-1 win at Boston on Wednesday, April 18. Joe Coleman (W 5-1, 9 IP, 0 ER) led a 6-1 win over visiting Kansas City on Sunday, April 29. The Bengals were 15-11 in May as Jim Perry shined May 4-June 5 (8 GM, 5-1, 51.2 IP, 2.26 ERA, .240 BA, .278 OBP). Perry (11 IP, 0 ER, 5 H) started a 13-inning 1-0 win over Oakland at home on Friday, May 25. The team went 12-17 in June, as Mickey Lolich (9 IP, 1 ER, 7 SO) and Dick McAuliffe (HR, 5 RBI) led an 8-2 win in Minnesota on Sunday, June 3. Detroit had a 19-10 record in July when Lolich (9 IP, 0 ER, 4 H) won a home 1-0 shutout over visiting Baltimore on July 1, with two days of rest. Motown and Jim Perry won 5-4 at Cleveland with Gaylord Perry on Tuesday, July 3, in the first brother match-up in league history. Jim Northrup was 3-for-4 (2 HR, 8 RBI), Horton (3 RBI) and Perry (7 IP, 2 ER) in a 14-2 victory against Texas at home on Wednesday, July 11. Detroit beat Kansas City 14-4 at home on Wednesday, July 18, behind McAuliffe 3-for-4 (HR, 4 RBI), Gates Brown (HR, 3 RBI), Duke Sims 3-for-4 (HR, 2 RBI), Mickey Stanley (HR, 2 RBI) and Coleman (W 15-8, 9 IP, 3 ER). Brown went 4-for-4 in a 4-3 loss in Texas on Sunday, July 22, as reliever John Hiller (8.1 IP, 1 ER, 5 H, 10 SO) faced 32 batters on one day of rest. Frank Howard was exceptional for July 26-29 (4 GM, 4 HR, 8 RBI, .429 BA, .429 OBP, 1.286 SLG). The Bengals were 15-16 in August with a 9-1 stretch thru Friday, August 3. The team closed 14-13 in September, as Northrup hit two homers and Coleman (W 22-15, 9 IP, 0 ER, 6 SO) had a one-hit 3-0 home shutout of Boston on Sunday, September 23. Detroit went 15-3 with Boston (.833). Players were 47-34 (.580) at home, 38-43 (.469) on the road, scored 642 runs and allowed 674. Detroiter Art James (48 SB) played for class "A" Clinton.

P * JIM PERRY

Offense. Detroit had a .254 BA, .320 OBP, .390 SLG, .710 OPS, 2,148 TB and 95 OPS+. Bill Freehan (.234 BA, 6 HR, 29 RBI) and Duke Sims (.242 BA, 8 HR, 30 RBI) caught. Norm Cash (.262 BA, 19 HR, 40 RBI) at first led in homers, total average (.828), base-out percentage (.830), secondary average (.342) and isolated power (.209). Dick McAuliffe (.274 BA, 12 HR, 47 RBI) led in on-base percentage (.366) and WAR (2.6), as he split second base with Tony Taylor (.229 BA, 5 HR, 24 RBI, 80% IPP) that led for power/speed number (6.4) and steals (9). Aurelio Rodriguez (.222 BA, 9 HR, 58 RBI) at third led in doubles (27), runs batted in and strikeouts (85). Shortstop Eddie Brinkman (.237 BA, 7 HR, 40 RBI) led league in games (162). Player of the Year and most effective hitter Willie Horton (.316 BA, 17 HR, 53 RBI) at left led in slugging (.501), OPS (.863), OPS+ (136), gross production average (.288), oWAR (2.8), batters run average (.181), hitting, BAbip (.334), runs created (75) and hitting streak (15). Centerfielder Mickey Stanley (.244 BA, 17 HR, 57 RBI, 80% IPP) led for plate appearances (661), at bats (602), runs (81), hits (147), times on base (195), base runs (68), runs produced (121), extra base hits (45), total bases (231), bases produced (279) and outs (481). Jim Northrup (.307 BA, 12 HR, 44 RBI) in right led in triples (7) and on-base percentage (.366). The designated hitters were Gates Brown (.236 BA, 12 HR, 50 RBI) that led in walks (52) and Frank Howard (.256 BA, 12 HR, 29 RBI) who led pinch-hitters (3 HR, 4 RBI). Al Kaline (.255 BA, 10 HR, 45 RBI) led in stolen base runs (0.6). Outfielder Dick Sharon (.242 BA, 7 HR, 16 RBI) was Tiger Rookie of the Year.

1970s Hitting Home Runs	
1. Willie Horton	121
2. Norm Cash	95
3. Jason Thompson	94
4. Bill Freehan	90
5. Aurelio Rodriguez	85
6. Mickey Stanley	77
7. Jim Northrup	71
8. Rusty Staub	70
9. Al Kaline	.64
10. Steve Kemp	59

Pitching. Pitchers had a 3.90 ERA, 39 CG, six SHO, 493 walks, 911 SO, 104 ERA+, 3.77 FIP, 1.355 WHIP, 9.1 H/9, 3.1 BB/9, and 5.7 SO/9. The staff led league in saves (46) and SO/W (1.85). Pitcher of the Year, Comeback Player of the Year, Fireman of the Year, Hutch Award winner, Tiger of the Year, and most effective pitcher John Hiller (10-5, 1.44 ERA) led MLB with a record 38 saves. He led the league in games (65) and GF (60). Hiller led staff for win percentage (.667), LOB% (90.5), earned run average, ERA+ (283), FIP (2.25), DICE (2.68), WHIP (1.021), pWAR (7.9), H/9 (6.4), HR/9 (0.5), BB/9 (2.8), SO/9 (8.9), SO/BB (3.18) and R/9 (1.5). Joe Coleman (23-15, 3.53 ERA) led league in HBP (10), with club lead for wins and walks (93). Mickey Lolich (16-15, 3.82 ERA) led league in no decisions (11), with Tiger highs in starts (42), complete games (17), shutouts (3), innings (308.2), hits (315), homers (35), strikeouts (214), wild pitches (12), earned runs (131) and runs (143). Jim Perry (14-13, 4.03 ERA), Woodie Fryman (6-13, 5.36 ERA), Bob Miller (4-2, 3.43 ERA), Fred Scherman (2-2, 4.23 ERA), Lerrin LaGrow (1-5, 4.33 ERA), Mike Strahler (4-5, 4.37 ERA) and Ed Farmer (3-0, 5.00 ERA). Charles Swanson (10-4, 2.02 ERA, 6 SHO) and Tom Makowski (8-1, 3.04 ERA) were at class "AA" Montgomery. James Murray (11-5, 4 SHO) with class "A" Clinton and George Cappuzzello (9-5, 2.85 ERA) at class "A" Anderson. Class "A" Lakeland had star pitchers Gene Pentz (12-5, 2.66 ERA), Michael Dwyer (48 GM, 1.54 ERA, 21 SV) and Larry Ike (2.32 ERA, 7 SHO) from Grand Rapids Ottawa Hills High School.

Defense. Detroit had a league low 112 errors (.982). Tiger league leaders were pitcher Lolich in runners caught stealing (19), Freehan in catcher fielding (.995) and team leader in defensive WAR (1.9), Rodriguez in fielding (.971) at third, left fielder Horton in outfield errors (10). Stanley led in fielding (.993) at center, tying league record with 11 putouts on Friday, July 13.

John Hiller had amazing stretches of May 14-July 9, (22 GM, 3-0, 15 SV, 35.1 IP, 35 SO, 0.25 ERA, .161 BA, .228 OBP, .185 SLG, .222 BAbip) and August 3-September 29 (22 GM, 3-2, 15 SV, 48.1 IP, 49 SO, 0.93 ERA, .218 BA). The two periods had similarities with 22 games each, 15 saves each, and the Tigers went 18-4 during each of the periods and 36-8 (.818) overall.

1970s Hitting Runs Batted In		
1.	Willie Horton	425
2.	Aurelio Rodriguez	423
3.	Rusty Staub	358
4.	Bill Freehan	342
5.	Jason Thompson	334
6.	Mickey Stanley	313
7.	Jim Northrup	279
8.	Steve Kemp	272
9.	Al Kaline	266
10.	Ron LeFlore	265

Team. The "*Major*" Ralph Houk led last place Detroit (72-90 .444), with 816,139 fans. The squad went 9-10 in April, as John Hiller (3-0, 25.1 IP, 0.36 ERA, 1 ER, 20 SO, 3 SV) had the club's second-best April earned run average in history. Players finished 13-14 in May with a 5-2 win in New York on Tuesday, May 14, led by Mickey Lolich (9 IP, 2 ER, 3 H) and Aurelio Rodriguez 4-for-5. Lolich (9 IP, 1 ER, 5 H, 11 SO) pitched a 2-1 win over visiting Cleveland on Sunday, May 26. The had a 16-12 mark in June, as Bill Freehan went 4-for-4 and Woodie Fryman (7.1 IP, 0 ER, 4 H, 8 SO) starred in a 2-0 victory in Anaheim on Sunday, June 2. The Bengals finished 11-17 including 2-14 during a 16-game stretch. Hiller (W 11-5) and Jim Northrup 3-for-4 (2 HR, 5 RBI) led an 8-6 win over New York at home on Wednesday, July 3. Fryman (9 IP, 2 ER) led an 8-2 win in Kansas City on Saturday, July 13, aided by Marv Lane 4-for-4 (2 R, 2 RBI, 2 SB) of Detroit Pershing High School. Players lost 2-1 in 14 innings to the Royals on Sunday, with Joe Coleman (7 IP, 1 ER, 4 H, 9 SO) and Hiller (6 IP, 0 ER, 4 H). Hiller dominated the period of July 28-August 27 (11 GM, 4-2, 33.1 IP, 33 SO, 0.81 ERA, .165 BA, .193 SLG). Motown was 13-17 in August, as Fryman (9 IP, 0 ER, 10 SO) pitched a one-hit 2-0 shutout at Milwaukee on Thursday, August 1, as Ron LeFlore made his MLB debut. Detroit fell 4-3 in 14 innings at Texas on Friday, August 9, as Hiller (L 13-8, 5.1 IP, 1 ER, 2 H) issued 11 walks. Lolich (W 15-14, 11 IP, 0 ER) outdueled Nolan Ryan (L 16-13, 11 IP, 1 ER, 4 H, 19 SO), as each faced 41 batters in a 1-0 Tiger shutout in Anaheim on Tuesday, August 20. The Tigers were 10-18 in September and 0-2 in October, when they won 11-3 in New York on Sunday, September 8, behind Freehan 4-for-5 (HR, 7 RBI) and Al Kaline (3 RBI). Hiller (W 17-10, 3 IP, 0 ER, 1 H) set the league record for relief wins during a 9-7 home victory over Milwaukee on Thursday, September 12. Kaline hit his team record 399th homer in Boston on Wednesday, September 18, with his 3,000th hit coming in his hometown of Baltimore on Tuesday, September 24. The Bengals were 36-45 (.444) at home and away, scored 620 runs and allowed 768.

MGR * RALPH HOUK

Offense. Detroit had a .247 BA, .303 OBP, .366 SLG, .669 OPS, 2,038 TB and 91 OPS+. Gerry Moses (.237 BA, 4 HR, 19 RBI) was catcher. Player of the Year and most effective hitter Bill Freehan (.297 BA, 18 HR, 60 RBI) at first led in triples (5), home runs, on-base percentage (.361), slugging (.479), OPS (.840), OPS+ (139), total average (.806), base-out percentage (.812), gross production average (.282), WAR (4.1), oWAR (4.1), batters run average (.171), batting, BAbip (.295), secondary average (.281), runs created (77) and isolated power (.182). Gary Sutherland (.254 BA, 5 HR, 49 RBI) at second led league in outs (489. He led Motown in plate appearances (652), at bats (619), hits (157), singles (131), in-play percentage (89%) and hit streak (15). Aurelio Rodriguez (.222 BA, 5 HR, 49 RBI, 0.6 SBR) at third led in games (159) and triples (5). Shortstop Eddie Brinkman (.221 BA, 14 HR, 54 RBI) and Willie Horton (.298 BA, 15 HR, 47 RBI) in left. Mickey Stanley (.221 BA, 8 HR, 34 RBI) in center led in power/speed number (6.2), with Jim Northrup (.237 BA, 11 HR, 42 RBI) in right. Tiger of the Year designated hitter Al Kaline (.262 BA, 13 HR, 64 RBI) led in runs (71), doubles (28), runs batted in, times on base (212), base runs (73), runs produced (122), extra base hits (43), total bases (217), bases produced (284), walks (65) and strikeouts (75). "*Mr. Tiger*" retired after a stellar 22-year MLB career with Detroit. Tiger Rookie of the Year Ron LeFlore (.260 BA, 2 HR, 13 RBI) led in steals (23). The best pinch-hitters were Horton at .500 (3-6, 4 RBI), Marv Lane .500 (3-6), Norm Cash .333 (3-9) and Gates Brown at .302 (16-53, 3 HR, 11 RBI). Bryan Lambe (.341 BA) was extraordinary playing at class "AA" Montgomery.

1970s Hitting On-Base Percentage		
1.	Steve Kemp	.376
	Lou Whitaker	.376
3.	Al Kaline	.370
4.	Norm Cash	.362
5.	Rusty Staub	.358
6.	Ron LeFlore	.350
7.	Jason Thompson	.349
8.	Willie Horton	.341
	Jim Northrup	.341
10.	Three Players	.339

Pitching. Detroit had a 4.16 ERA, 54 CG, six SHO, 621 walks, 869 SO, 91 ERA+, 4.06 FIP, 1.418 WHIP, 8.9 H/9, 3.8 BB/9, and 5.4 SO/9. Pitchers led league in homers (148), IBB (69), wild pitches (58), earned runs (673), runs (768), runs per game (4.74) and no decisions (38). Pitcher of the Year and most effective pitcher John Hiller (17-14, 2.64 ERA, 1.260 WHIP, 7.6 H/9) led the league for IBB (19). Hiller led his staff for games (59), wins, win percentage (.548), saves (13), LOB% (79.2), earned run average, ERA+ (143), FIP (2.96), DICE (3.38), pWAR (4.1), HR/9 (0.6), SO/9 (8.0) and R/9 (3.1). Mickey Lolich (16-21, 4.15 ERA, 1.260 WHIP) led MLB in home runs (38) and earned runs (142). He led league in losses, with staff lead in CG (27), SHO (3), innings (308), hits (310), strikeouts (202), earned runs (142), BB/9 (2.3) and SO/BB (2.59). Joe Coleman (14-12, 4.32 ERA) led league in runs (160) and HBP (12). He led staff in walks (158), wild pitches (13) and quality starts (20). Lerrin LaGrow (8-19, 4.66 ERA), Woodie Fryman (6-9, 4.32 ERA, 7.6 H/9) and Dave Lemanczyk (2-1, 4.00 ERA). Fred Holdsworth (0-3, 4.29 ERA), Jim Ray (1-3, 4.47 ERA), Bill Slayback (1-3, 4.77 ERA) and Luke Walker (5-5, 4.99 ERA). Vern Ruhle (20-5 .800) was a 20-game winner with class "AA" Montgomery (5-0), class "AAA" Evansville (13-5) and MLB Detroit (2-0).

Defense. Detroit committed 158 errors for a .975 fielding percentage and led division in defensive efficiency (.698). Tiger league leaders were pitchers Fryman in fielding percentage (1.000), Coleman in stolen bases (46) and Lolich in caught stealing (32). LeFlore in center led all outfielders in errors (11). Shortstop Brinkman led the Bengals in defensive WAR (2.0).

Michigan native Ron LeFlore from Detroit was signed out of the Michigan State Prison in Jackson to play 32 games at class "A" Clinton in 1973. He started 1974 with class "A" Lakeland (.339 BA, 42 SB) and had his major-league debut on August 1.

Fred Strike (10-4 .714, 2.97 ERA) was at class "AA" Montgomery, with Greg Kuhl (1.32 ERA, 6 SV) at class "A" Clinton. Bob Sykes (11-0 1.000, 1.07 ERA, 6 SHO), Mark Fidrych (3-0 1.000, 2.38 ERA, 7 SV) and Tim Corcoran (.370 BA) starred at Bristol.

1970s Hitting Slugging Percentage	
1. Norm Cash	.469
2. Willie Horton	.458
3. Steve Kemp	.450
4. Ben Oglivie	.444
Lance Parrish	.444
6. John Wockenfuss	.442
7. Jason Thompson	.441
8. Rusty Staub	.434
9. Jim Northrup	.420
10. Bill Freehan	.414

Team. Ralph Houk led Last-place Detroit (57-102 .358), with 1,058,836 fans. The team went 10-6 in April as Nate Colbert (HR, 3 RBI) and Willie Horton (HR, 2 RBI) led a 5-3 win at New York on Friday, April 11. Colbert (HR, 4 RBI) hit a grand slam during a 7-2 win over the Yankees the next day. 24-year-old rookie Leon Roberts from Portage Northern High School started with a 17-game hitting streak April 13-May 16 (.383 BA, .431 OBP, .650 SLG, .408 BAbip), as he reached base in his first 24 games of the season. The Bengals were 9-15 in May with a 17-3 loss at Milwaukee on Thursday, May 1, as the Brewers were led by future Hall of Famers 41-year-old Hank Aaron 4-for-4 (2 RBI) and 19-year-old Robin Yount (HR, 4 RBI). Motown had an 8-24 mark in June, with a 11-2 triumph in Oakland on Friday, June 6, behind Mickey Lolich (W 7-3, 6 IP, 2 ER) and Horton 3-for-5 (HR, 4 RBI). Detroit was 19-14 in July, with a 14-3 (.823) 17 game stretch July 3-20, that included nine consecutive wins July 3-10 when Horton excelled (9 GM, 19-for-33 .576 BA, .579 OBP, .667 SLG, .563 BAbip). Lerrin LaGrow (9 IP, 1 ER), Mickey Stanley 3-for-4 and Aurelio Rodriguez (4 RBI) directed a 9-1 victory in Chicago on Thursday, July 17. The Bengals lost a team record 19 straight games July 29-August 15. Ray Bare (9 IP, 0 ER, 2 H, 6 SO) pitched a two-hit 8-0 shutout in California on Saturday, August 16, aided by Bill Freehan 4-for-5 (3 RBI) and Tom Veryzer (3 RBI). The players were 6-22 in August that included an 8-7 loss in Boston on Monday, August 1, with Horton 3-for-5 (2 HR, 5 RBI) and Freehan 3-for-5 (2 HR, 2 RBI). Detroit scratched out a 6-5 12-inning victory at Minnesota on Saturday, August 23, paced by Horton (HR, 2 RBI), Rodriguez (2 HR, 2 RBI), and Veryzer 3-for-4 (HR). The Tigers closed 5-21 in September, as Vern Ruhle (9 IP, 2 ER) led a 11-2 triumph at Cleveland on Friday, September 5, with 23-year-old rookie Dan Meyer (3 RBI), Horton 3-for-5 (2 HR, 4 RBI) and Veryzer 3-for-4. Motown was 31-49 (.388) at home, 26-53 (.329) on the road, scored a league low 570 runs and allowed 786. Jason Thompson (.324 BA) and Mike Ibarquen (6-1, .857, 2.61 ERA) were at class "AA" Montgomery.

OF* MICKEY STANLEY

Offense. Detroit had a .249 BA, .301 OBP, .366 SLG, .666 OPS, 1,962 TB and 86 OPS+. The catcher was Bill Freehan (.246 BA, 14 HR, 47 RBI) that led in oWAR (1.9), secondary average (.232), isolated power (.152) and stolen base runs (0.6). First base was manned by Jack Pierce (.235 BA, 8 HR, 22 RBI), Nate Colbert (.147 BA, 4 HR, 18 RBI) and Dan Meyer (.236 BA, 8 HR, 47 RBI) who led squad for in-play percentage (87%) and stolen base runs (0.6). Gary Sutherland (.258 BA, 6 HR, 39 RBI) at second led in on-base percentage (.321) and walks (45), as third baseman Aurelio Rodriguez (.245 BA, 13 HR, 60 RBI) led in doubles (20), triples (6), WAR (1.9) and extra base hits (39), with the shortstop Tom Veryzer (.252 BA, 5 HR, 48 RBI). Ben Oglivie (.286 BA, 9 HR, 36 RBI) was in left and led in base-out percentage (.664) and batting average. Ron LeFlore (.258 BA, 8 HR, 37 RBI) in center led in runs (66), triples (6), BAbip (.331), power/speed number (12.4), stolen bases (28) and strikeouts (139). Michigan native Leon Roberts (.257 BA, 10 HR, 38 RBI) from Vicksburg and the University of Michigan in right led for hitting streak (17). Player of the Year, Tiger of the Year and most effective hitter Willie Horton (.275 BA, 25 HR, 92 RBI) as designated hitter led in games (159), plate appearances (667), at bats (615), hits (169), singles (130), homers, runs batted in, slugging (.421), OPS (.740), OPS+ (106), total average (.648), gross production average (.249), batters runs average (.134), times on base (213), base runs (80), runs produced (129), runs created (83), extra base hits (39), total bases (259), bases produced (304) and outs (474). Grand Rapids native Mickey Stanley (.256 BA, 3 HR, 19 RBI). The top pinch-hitters were Stanley at .500 (2-4) and second baseman John Knox .400 (2-5).

1970s Hitting On-Base plus Slugging	
1. Norm Cash	.831
2. Steve Kemp	.826
3. Willie Horton	.799
4. Rusty Staub	.792
5. Jason Thompson	.790
6. Ben Oglivie	.773
7. Jim Northrup	.761
8. Ron LeFlore	.756
9. Bill Freehan	.753
10. Al Kaline	.751

Pitching. The team logged a 4.27 ERA, 52 CG, eight SHO, 533 walks, 787 SO, 93 ERA+, 3.95 FIP, 1.453 WHIP, 9.6 H/9, 3.4 BB/9, and 5.1 SO/9, as pitchers led league in hits (1,496). Pitcher of the Year and Tiger Rookie of the Year Michigander Vern Ruhle (11-12, 4.03 ERA) of Coleman, led in win percentage (.478), SHO (3) and H/9 (9.4). The most effective pitcher Mickey Lolich (12-18, 3.78 ERA) led in wins, starts (32), complete games (19), innings (240.2), hits (260), SO (139), LOB% (68.9), ERA, ERA+ (105), FIP (3.26), DICE (3.67), WHIP (1.346), pWAR (4.0), HR/9 (0.7), BB/9 (2.4), SO/BB (2.17), R/9 (4.5) and quality starts (19). Joe Coleman (10-18, 5.55 ERA) led in homers (27), walks (85), HBP (9), wild pitches (15), earned runs (124), runs (137) and SO/9 (5.6). Lerrin LaGrow (7-14, 4.38 ERA) and Ray Bare (8-13, 4.48 ERA). John Hiller (2-3, 2.17 ERA, 185 ERA+) led in games finished (34) and saves (14). Dave Lemanczyk (2-7, 4.46 ERA), Tom Walker (3-8, 4.45 ERA), Fernando Arroyo (2-1, 4.56 ERA) and Bob Reynolds (0-2, 4.67 ERA). Class "AAA" Evansville had Steve Grilli (11-4 .733, 3.00 ERA, 12 SV) and Ike Brookens (7-3 .700, 1.67 ERA, 11 SV). Steve Trella (1.76 ERA, 5 SHO) and Dave Rozema (14-5 .737, 2.09 ERA, 5 SHO) were with class "A" Clinton.

Defense. Detroit had 173 errors for a .972 fielding average and the worst defensive efficiency (.683. League leaders were Lolich in pitcher fielding (1.000), Freehan in catcher fielding (.991), Rodriguez at third led in chances (536), total chances per game (3.5) and led the Bengals in dWAR (1.2), Meyer led for errors (7) in left. LeFlore led centerfielders in assists (12).

John Hiller was flawless to start and end his 1975 season during April 10-May 10 (1-0, 4 SV, 14.1 IP, 19 SO, 0.00 ERA, .143 BA, .143 SLG, .233 BAbip, 12.2 SO/9) and then June 28-July 25 (5 SV, 18.1 IP, 25 SO, 0.00 ERA, .159 BA, .206 SLG, 12.4 SO/9).

Detroit traded for All-Star Nate Colbert who had averaged 31 home runs and 90 runs batted in during his previous four years with San Diego. Colbert stumbled out of the gate (45 GM, .173 BA, .231 OBP, .276 SLG, 41 OPS+) and was sold to Montreal.

Team. Detroit (75-78 .460) closed fifth for Ralph Houk, with 1,467,020 fans. Motown was 7-6 in April, with Willie Horton named Player of the Month (13 GM, 5 HR, 18 RBI, .388 BA, .464 OBP, .735 SLG). Ron LeFlore reeled off a career best 30-game hit streak during April 17-May 27 (51-for-130, .392 BA, .554 SLG). Horton drove in a run during 10 straight games April 18-May 1. The Bengals won 10-2 at home against Oakland on Tuesday, April 27, led by Jason Thompson 4-for-5, Rusty Staub (HR, 4 RBI) and Joe Coleman (6.1 IP, 2 ER, 5 SO). Dave Roberts (9 IP, 0 ER, 2 H) won 8-1 the next day. Motown went 10-17 in May as LeFlore was the Player of the Month (45-for-113, .398 BA, .575 SLG). Michigan native Vern Ruhle (9 IP, 1 ER, 5 H) of Coleman High School led a 10-1 win in Chicago on Saturday, May 1, with Thompson 3-for-4 (HR, 3 RBI) and LeFlore (4 SB). Mark Fidrych (9 IP, 1 ER, 2 H) won his first major league start 2-1 at home over Cleveland on Saturday, May 15. Fidrych (11 IP, 4 ER, 8 SO) faced 47 hitters in a 5-4 victory over visiting Milwaukee on Monday, May 31. John Hiller won both games of a doubleheader on Tuesday 8-7 and 6-5. Reliever Steve Grilli (6 IP, 1 ER, 3 H) pitched in game one and Dan Meyer was 4-for-5 in game two. The squad was 17-12 in June when Fidrych was Pitcher of the Month (6 GM, 6-0, 1.99 ERA, .226 BA). Hiller shined June 4-July 2 (10 GM, 2-0, 22.1 IP, 1.21 ERA, .145 BA, .211 SLG, .213 BAbip). Fidrych (W 8-1, 9 IP, 1 ER) beat visiting New York 5-1 in the ABC Monday Night Game of the Week on June 28. Motown was 14-16 in July as Fidrych (W 9-1, 9 IP, 0 ER, 4 H) shutout Baltimore 4-0 on Saturday, July 3. The "Bird" started the All-Star game on July 13, followed by a (W 10-2, 11 IP, 0 ER, 6 SO) 1-0 shutout of Oakland at home on Friday, July 16. Hiller (W 10-4, 2.2 IP, 0 ER) led a 13-inning 4-3 win at Milwaukee the next day, with Ben Oglivie 4-for-6. Roberts (9 IP, 0 ER, 5 H) threw a 1-0 shutout in Milwaukee on Wednesday, July 28. The club went 13-18 in August including a Bill Freehan (4 RBI) led 15-5 home win over Cleveland on Sunday, August 8. Freehan went 3-for-3 (3 RBI) with his 200th homer in a 12-7 home loss to Chicago on Tuesday, August 24. Players closed 10-18 in September and 3-0 in October, as Hiller (W 12-8, 9 IP, 0 ER, 4 H, 7 SO) logged a 5-0 shutout in Milwaukee on Friday, October 1. Detroit finished 36-44 (.450) at home, and 38-43 (.469) on the road. Motown scored 609 runs and allowed 709.

1970s Pitching Wins	
1. Mickey Lolich	105
2. Joe Coleman	88
3. John Hiller	69
4. Milt Wilcox	31
5. Dave Rozema	28
6. Mark Fidrych	27
7. Jack Billingham	25
Vern Ruhle	25
9. Fred Scherman	24
10. Les Cain	22
Woodie Fryman	22

P * MARK FIDRYCH

Offense. Detroit had a .251 BA, .321 OBP, .406 SLG, .727 OPS, 2,234 TB and 105 OPS+. The catchers were Bill Freehan (.270 BA, 5 HR, 27 RBI), Bruce Kimm (.263 BA, 1 HR, 6 RBI) and John Wockenfuss (.222 BA, 3 HR, 10 RBI). Jason Thompson (.218 BA, 17 HR, 54 RBI) at first led in homers and secondary average (.318). Pedro Garcia (.198 BA, 3 HR, 20 RBI) was at second, Aurelio Rodriguez (.240 BA, 8 HR, 50 RBI) at third, with Tom Veryzer (.234 BA, HR, 25 RBI) the shortstop. Alex Johnson (.268 BA, 6 HR, 45 RBI) was in left. The most effective hitter All-Star Ron LeFlore (.316 BA, 4 HR, 39 RBI) at center led league in BAbip (.391). He led team in runs (93), singles (137), triples (8), base-out percentage (.829), WAR (5.3), oWAR (5.6), hitting, steals (58), stolen base runs (5.4), strikeouts (111) and hit streak (30). Player of the Year Rusty Staub (.299 BA, 15 HR, 96 RBI) at right led league in games (161). He led club in plate appearances (690), at bats (589), hits (176), doubles (28), runs batted in, on-base percentage (.386), OPS (.818), OPS+ (137), total average (.794), gross production average (.282), batters run average (.167), times on base (266), base runs (97), runs produced (154), runs created (98), extra base hits (46), total bases (255), bases produced (341), walks (83) and outs (448). Designated hitter Willie Horton (.262 BA, 14 HR, 56 RBI). Ben Oglivie (.285, 15 HR, 47 RBI) led in slugging (.492), isolated power (.207) and power/speed number (11.3). Dan Meyer (.252 BA, 2 HR, 16 RBI) led for in-play percentage (86%). Top pinch-hitters were Mickey Stanley at .316 (6-19, 4 RBI), Johnson .313 (5-16) and Oglivie (3 HR, 9 RBI). Johnson of Detroit Northwestern High School had five straight multi-hit games April 27-May 4 (.440 BA, .560 SLG) and ruled the week of May 22-28 (.517 BA, .828 SLG). Staub walked in six straight games May 17-23.

Pitching. Motown had a 3.87 ERA, 55 CG, 12 SHO, 550 walks, 738 SO, 96 ERA+, 3.73 FIP, 1.381 WHIP, 9.0 H/9, 3.5 BB/9 and 4.6 SO/9. All-Star, American League Rookie of the Year, Pitcher of the Year, Tiger of the Year, Tiger Rookie of the Year, and most effective pitcher Mark Fidrych (19-9, 2.34 ERA, 4 SHO) led MLB in pWAR (9.6), ERA and ERA+ (159), with league lead for CG (24). "*The Bird*" led staff in wins, win percentage (.679), FIP (3.15), DICE (3.52), WHIP (1.079), HR/9 (0.4), BB/9 (1.9), SO/BB (1.83), R/9 (2.7) and quality starts (23). Vern Ruhle (9-12, 3.92 ERA) led in homers (19). Dave Roberts (16-17, 4.00 ERA, 4 SHO) led in losses, starts (36), innings (252), hits (254), earned runs (112) and runs (122). Ray Bare (7-8, 4.63 ERA), Joe Coleman (2-5, 4.86 ERA) and Dave Lemanczyk (4-6, 5.09). John Hiller (12-8, 2.38 ERA) led in games (56), GF (46), saves (13), walks (67), strikeouts (117), LOB% (82.1), H/9 (6.9) and SO/9 (8.7). Bill Laxton (0-5, 4.09 ERA) led in HBP (6). Jim Crawford (1-8, 4.53 ERA) led in wild pitches (7). Steve Grilli (3-1, 4.64 ERA). Class "AA" Montgomery had Dennis DeBarr (11-2 .846, 2.36 ERA, 10 SV), Dave Rozema (12-4 .750, 1.57 ERA, 4 SHO) and Frank Harris (12-4 .750, 2.72 ERA). Bristol had Roger Weaver (6-2 .750, 1.43 ERA) and Mike Burns (7-3 .700, 2.78 ERA) from Jackson Northwest High School.

1970s Pitching Winning Percentage	
1. Mark Fidrych	.628
2. Jack Billingham	.625
3. Milt Wilcox	.564
4. Dave Rozema	.549
5. Joe Coleman	.547
6. John Hiller	.523
7. Mickey Lolich	.510
8. Joe Niekro	.488
9. Tom Timmermann	.478
10. Woodie Fryman	.468

Defense. The Bengals led the division in chances (6,423), errors (168) and led the league in assists (1,961). Tiger league leaders were pitchers Bare, Fidrych and Ruhle in fielding (1.000), Roberts in double plays (6) and Fidrych in assists (59). Thompson led in chances per game (10.7) at first and Rodriguez led in fielding (.978) at third with a Gold Glove. Johnson led in errors (8) at left and LeFlore in center led outfielders in errors (11). Catcher Kimm led the club for defensive WAR (0.9).

Steve Kemp (66-for-171 .386 BA) was at class "AAA" Evansville. Class "A" Lakeland had Mel Jackson (48 SB), Lou Whitaker (48 SB), Pat Underwood (6-2 .750, 2.22 ERA), John Murphy (11-5 .688, 2.46 ERA) and Dana McManus (9-5 .643, 2.73 ERA).

1970s Pitching Games Started	
1. Mickey Lolich	240
2. Joe Coleman	201
3. Vern Ruhle	76
4. Dave Rozema	72
5. Milt Wilcox	69
6. Woodie Fryman	65
7. Lerrin LaGrow	63
8. Les Cain	60
9. Dave Roberts	58
10. Joe Niekro	56

Team. Detroit finished in fourth led by Ralph Houk at 74-88 (.457), with an attendance of 1,359,856. The club was 8-12 in April when 20-year-old rookie Dave Rozema (9 IP, 0 ER, 4 H) from Grand Rapids Christian High School had an 8-0 shutout in Boston on April 21, with Jason Thompson (HR, 4 RBI). The team scored seven third inning runs with a Thompson grand slam in a 10-9 home win on Wednesday, April 27. Players were 10-14 in May, as Rozema (9 IP, 3 ER) logged a 14-3 win in Chicago on Sunday, May 22, aided by Steve Kemp 3-for-4 (4 R), Thompson 3-for-5 (HR, 5 RBI), Tim Corcoran 3-for-4 (2 RBI) and Milt May (3 RBI). The Tigers were 16-12 in June when Mark Fidrych excelled June 2-July 3 (6 GM, 6-0, 1.33 ERA, 54 IP, 5 BB, 35 SO, .221 BA, .241 OBP, .272 SLG, .261 BAbip), including a 2-1 win versus New York on Monday, June 20 (9 IP, 1 ER, 3 H, 9 SO), with 47,236 fans at Tiger Stadium. Detroit went 12-17 in July that included a Rozema (W 8-4, 9 IP, 2 ER) 11-3 win in Toronto on Saturday, July 16, paced by Rusty Staub 3-for-5, Thompson (HR, 4 RBI), Aurelio Rodriguez (HR, 3 RBI) and May 3-for-5 (HR, 2 RBI). The squad went 17-12 in August including a 13-1 home win over Seattle on Monday, August 15, behind May 2-for-3 (HR, 5 RBI) and Bob Sykes (9 IP, 1 ER). Thompson hit a pitch out of Tiger Stadium during a 5-4 loss to New York on Thursday, August 18. The team closed 10-20 in September and 1-1 in October, as 21-year-old rookie catcher Lance Parrish went 3-for-4 (HR, 4 RBI) and scored four runs in a 12-5 home win with Baltimore on Wednesday, September 7. Thompson cleared the roof with a fourth inning shot in a 9-4 loss to New York on Saturday, September 17. Motown was 39-42 (.481) at home and 35-46 (.432) on the road. Players scored 714 runs and allowed 751. Class "AAA" Evansville had stars Tim Corcoran (.346 BA, .625 SLG), Bob Adams (.330 BA) and Parrish (25 HR, 90 RBI). Speedster Mel Jackson (43 SB) was with first-place class "A" Lakeland (85-53 .616). Joe Rothwell (.350 BA) and Clifton Wilder (.346 BA) played with Bristol.

DH * RUSTY STAUB

Offense. Detroit had a .264 BA, .318 OBP, .410 SLG, .728 OPS, 2,296 TB, and 94 OPS+. Catcher Milt May (.249 BA, 12 HR, 46 RBI). Player of the Year Jason Thompson (.270 BA, 31 HR, 105 RBI) at first led in homers, runs batted in, slugging (.487), total average (.808), WAR (3.9), secondary average (.340), isolated power (.217), extra base hits (60) and walks (73). Tito Fuentes (.309 BA, 5 HR, 51 RBI, 82% IPP) at second led in singles (156) and triples (10). Aurelio Rodriguez (.219 BA, 10 HR, 32 RBI) and Phil Mankowski (.276 BA, 3 HR, 27 RBI) manned third base. Tom Veryzer (.197 BA, 2 HR, 28 RBI) was at short. Left-fielder Steve Kemp (.257 BA, 18 HR, 88 RBI). Tiger of the Year and most effective hitter centerfielder Ron LeFlore (.325 BA, 16 HR, 57 RBI) led in plate appearances (698), at bats (652), runs (100), hits (212), singles (156), triples (10), on-base percentage (.363), OPS (.838), OPS+ (123), base-out percentage (.832), gross production average (.282), oWAR (4.8), batter run average (.172), hitting, BAbip (.378), times on base (253), base runs (101), runs created (113), power/speed number (22.7), total bases (310), bases produced (386), stolen bases (39), stolen base runs (0.3), strikeouts (171) and hitting streak (17). Ben Oglivie (.262 BA, 21 HR, 61 RBI) was in right field. The designated hitter Rusty Staub (.278 BA, 22 HR, 101 RBI) led MLB in GIDP (27), as *"Le Grand Orange"* led club in doubles (34), runs produced (163) and outs (490). John Wockenfuss (.274 BA, 9 HR, 25 RBI) and outfielder Mickey Stanley (.230 BA, 8 HR, 23 RBI). The leading Tiger pinch-hitters were LeFlore at .667 (2-3, HR), May .400 (2-5, HR), Bob Adams .333 (4-12, HR), Oglivie .333 (4-12) and Tim Corcoran at .313 (10-32, HR, 4 RBI). Thompson and Staub led in games played (158). 19-year-old rookie and future Hall of Famer Alan Trammell had a successful MLB debut on Friday, September 9, with a 2-for-3 effort.

1970s Pitching Complete Games	
1. Mickey Lolich	128
2. Joe Coleman	56
3. Mark Fidrych	33
4. Dave Rozema	31
5. Milt Wilcox	24
6. Dave Roberts	23
7. Lerrin LaGrow	18
8. Vern Ruhle	14
9. Jack Billingham	12
Jack Morris	12

Pitching. Team had a 4.13 ERA, 44 CG, three SHO, 470 walks, 784 SO, 104 ERA+, 4.12 FIP, 1.370 WHIP, 9.4 H/9, 2.9 BB/9 and 4.8 SO/9. Rookie Pitcher of the Year, Pitcher of the Year, Tiger Rookie of the Year, and most effective pitcher Dave Rozema (15-7, 3.09 ERA) led the league in BB/9 (1.4). He led staff for wins, winning (.682), complete games (16), innings (218.1), homers (25), HBP (7), LOB% (77.2), earned run average, ERA+ (139), FIP (3.95), DICE (4.21), WHIP (1.173), pWAR (5.6), H/9 (9.2), SO/BB (2.71), R/9 (3.6) and quality starts (18). Fernando Arroyo (8-18, 4.17 ERA, 28 GS) led in losses, hits (227), earned runs (97), runs (102). Bob Sykes (5-7, 4.41 ERA) led in SO/9 (3.9). Mark Fidrych (6-4, 2.89 ERA), Dave Roberts (4-10, 5.15 ERA) and Vern Ruhle (3-5, 5.70 ERA) from Olivet College. Steve Foucault (7-7, 3.15 ERA) led in games finished (34) and saves (13). John Hiller (8-14, 3.56 ERA, 6 WP) led in games (45), walks (61), strikeouts (115) and IBB (8). Jim Crawford (7-8, 4.79 ERA, 6 WP) and Steve Grilli (1-2, 4.83). Milt Wilcox was at class "AAA" Evansville (9-4, 2.44 ERA) and the Tigers (6-2, 3.64 ERA). Class "A" Lakeland had Mike Chris (18-5 .783, 2.01 ERA) and Larry Corr (7-2, 2.29 ERA), with Charles Irving (9-1 .900, 2.81 ERA) at Bristol.

Defense. Detroit committed 142 errors (.978), led the league in chances (6,446), assists (1,933) and division in putouts (4,371). League leaders were May in catcher double plays (12), as he led team in dWAR (1.3), Thompson led in chances (1,712), putouts (1,599) and chances per game (10.8) at first. Second baseman Fuentes led in chances (864), putouts (379), errors (26), double plays (115), chances per game (5.7) and innings played (1,327). LeFlore led centerfielders in assists (12).

Ron LeFlore scorched pitching during the periods of June 25-July 12 (32-for-80, .400 BA), and August 4-20 (33-for-75, .440 BA). He had 16 multi-hit games in July for team record that included four three-hit games, with another 12 two-hit games.

First-place class "AA" Montgomery (86-51 .628) had Dave Stegman (.345 BA), Pat Underwood (9-2 .818, 2 SHO), Gary Christenson (13-4 .765, 3.14 ERA, 3 SHO), John Murphy (9-3 .750) and Mike Burns (11-5 .688, 3 SHO) from Jackson, Michigan.

1970s Pitching Earned Run Average	
1. John Hiller	2.74
2. Dave Rozema	3.19
3. Mickey Lolich	3.45
4. Tom Timmermann	3.49
5. Jack Billingham	3.63
6. Joe Coleman	3.82
7. Vern Ruhle	4.12
8. Woodie Fryman	4.13
9. Joe Niekro	4.17
10. Dave Roberts	4.39

Team. Manager Ralph Houk led Detroit (86-76 .531) to a fifth-place finish, with 1,714,893 fans. The squad was 13-5 in April when a Tiger Stadium crowd of 52,528 witnessed a Mark Fidrych (9 IP, 2 ER) 6-2 win over Toronto on Friday, April 7. Rusty Staub dominated the week of April 17-25 (6 GM, 2 HR, 13 RBI, .400 BA, .680 SLG). Jack Billingham (9 IP, 1 ER, 3 H) led a 4-1 win at Chicago on Monday, April 24. Staub reached base in 31 consecutive games April 28-May 31. Players were 13-15 in May, as Bob Sykes shutout the Athletics twice, 6-0 in Oakland on Saturday, May 6 (9 IP, 0 ER, 4 H, 9 SO) and then 15-0 at home on Sunday, May 14 (9 IP, 0 ER, 4 H). The Bengals defeated Seattle 4-2 in 16 innings at home on Tuesday, May 16, behind Lance Parrish (HR, 2 RBI), Milt Wilcox (6.1 IP, 2 ER, 3 H) and John Hiller (6.2 IP, 0 ER, 3 H, 5 SO). The franchise went 10-18 in June with an 8-1 triumph in Milwaukee on Wednesday, June 7, aided by Steve Kemp 3-for-4, Staub (HR, 4 RBI) and Jim Slaton (W 6-2, 9 IP, 1 ER, 5 H). Detroit had a record of 19-11 in July as Staub excelled July 1-7 (8 GM, 14 RBI, .412 BA, .462 OBP, .647 SLG). Motown won 12-7 in Texas on Friday, July 7, as Ron LeFlore was 4-for-5, Staub 3-for-5 (4 RBI) and 20-year-old rookie shortstop Alan Trammell 5-for-6 (2 RBI). 21-year-old rookie Lou Whitaker (HR, 2 RBI) hit an upper deck walk-off homer for a 4-3 win against Seattle on Friday, July 28. The Tigers had a 9-2 mark at home during a 11-game stretch in July. The team was 18-10 in August including a 7-1 win over visiting Chicago on Friday, August 4, with Parrish 3-for-4 (HR) and Kip Young (9 IP, 1 ER, 6 SO). Steve Dillard 3-for-5 and Slaton (9 IP, 2 ER) guided a 7-3 win at Minnesota on Tuesday, August 22, as Leflore set a league record with his 27th consecutive stolen base. The club closed 13-16 in September and 0-1 in October. Billingham (W 15-6, 9 IP, 2 ER) and Kemp (HR, 3 RBI) led a 6-2 win in Kansas City on Friday, September 1. Detroit was 47-34 (.580) at home, 39-42 (.481) on the road, scored 714 runs and pitchers allowed 653.

P * JIM SLATON

Offense. Motown logged a .271 BA, .339 OBP, .392 SLG, .730 OPS, 2,193 TB and 103 OPS+. There was a catching duo of Milt May (.250 BA, 10 HR, 37 RBI) and Lance Parrish (.219 BA, 14 HR, 41 RBI) that led in isolated power (.205). The most effective hitter Jason Thompson (.287 BA, 26 HR, 96 RBI) at first base led in home runs, slugging (.472), OPS (.836), OPS+ (.131), total average (.817), gross production average (.282), WAR (5.6), batters run average (.171), secondary average (.311), base runs (98), runs created and (101). Rookie of the Year and Tiger Rookie of the Year second baseman Lou Whitaker (.285 BA, 3 HR, 58 RBI) led squad in triples (7). Aurelio Rodriguez (.265 BA, 7 HR, 43 RBI) and Phil Mankowski (.275 BA, 4 HR, 20 RBI) manned third base, with rookie Alan Trammell (.268 BA, 2 HR, 34 RBI) at short. Left fielder Steve Kemp (.277 BA, 15 HR, 79 RBI) led in on-base percentage (.379) and walks (97). Tiger of the Year centerfielder Ron LeFlore (.297 BA, 12 HR, 62 RBI) led MLB in runs (126) and singles (153). He led league for steals (68), with club lead in plate appearances (741), at bats (666), hits (198), base-out percentage (.824), oWAR (5.2), hitting, BAbip (.335), times on base (267), runs produced (176), power/speed number (20.4), bases produced (403), stolen base runs (10.8), strikeouts (104) and hit streak (27). Tim Corcoran (.265 BA, HR, 27 RBI) was in right. Player of the Year designated hitter Rusty Staub (.273 BA, 24 HR, 121 RBI) led in games (162), runs batted in, extra base hits (55), total bases (279) and outs (505). The leading pinch-hitters were Whitaker at .500 (3-6), John Wockenfuss .353 (6-17) and Rodriguez at .350 (7-20, HR). LeFlore and Staub led in doubles (30).

1970s Pitching Innings Pitched	
1. Mickey Lolich	1,833.2
2. Joe Coleman	1,407.2
3. John Hiller	911.0
4. Dave Rozema	525.0
5. Milt Wilcox	518.0
6. Vern Ruhle	489.0
7. Lerrin LaGrow	474.1
8. Woodie Fryman	425.0
9. Joe Niekro	382.1
10. Dave Roberts	381.1

Pitching. Detroit had a 3.64 ERA, 60 CG, 12 SHO, 503 walks, 684 SO, 105 ERA+, 3.96 FIP, 1.335 WHIP, 8.9 H/9, 3.1 BB/9 and 4.2 SO/9. Pitcher of the Year and most effective pitcher John Hiller (9-4, 2.34 ERA) led in games (51), win percentage (.692), games finished (46), saves (15), LOB% (79.5), earned run average, ERA+ (165), FIP (2.96), DICE (3.38), WHIP (1.072), H/9 (6.2), HR/9 (0.6), SO/9 (7.2), SO/BB (2.11) and R/9 (2.6). Dave Rozema (9-12, 3.14 ERA, 16 QS) led in pWAR (4.0) and BB/9 (1.8). Milt Wilcox (13-12, 3.76 ERA) led in complete games (16) and strikeouts (132). Jack Billingham (15-8, 3.88 ERA, 16 QS) led in shutouts (4). Jim Slaton (17-11, 4.12 ERA, 16 QS) led in wins, starts (34), innings (233.2), hits (235), home runs (27), walks (85), wild pitches (10), earned runs (107) and runs (117). Bob Sykes (6-6, 3.94 ERA), Steve Foucault (2-4, 3.13 ERA) and Jim Crawford (2-3, 4.35 ERA). Rookie righthanders Kip Young (6-7, 2.81 ERA), Jack Morris (3-5, 4.33 ERA) and Steve Baker (2-4, 4.55 ERA). The class "AAA" Evansville Triplets had Baker (8-1 .889, 3.21 ERA), Sheldon Burnside (14-5 .737, 3.52 ERA) and Kip Young (11-3 .786, 3.02 ERA), with Ralph Treuel (12-6, 3.18 ERA, 4 SHO) at class "AA" Montgomery.

Defense. Detroit committed 118 errors (.981) and led league in double plays (177). League leaders were pitchers Rozema in fielding (1.000) and Slaton in double plays (6), Thompson in double plays (153) and chances per game (10.6) at first base, Rodriguez in fielding (.987) at third, Kemp in leftfielder chances (344) and putouts (325). LeFlore led outfielders in chances (457), putouts (438), errors (11) and double plays (4) in centerfield. Shortstop Trammell led the club in defensive WAR (1.7).

Jack Billingham was 5-0 in July as he pitched like his Hall-of-Fame cousin Christy Mathewson in back-to-back shutouts of the California Angels 4-0 in Anaheim on Sunday, July 16 (W 8-5, 9 IP, 0 ER) and 5-0 at home on Friday, July 21 (W 9-5, 9 IP, 0 ER).

Ron LeFlore recorded four four-hit games, as Rusty Staub had a five-RBI game. Class "A" Lakeland had Raphael Hampton (.337 BA), Joseph Janton (11-6, 3.02 ERA, 4 SHO) and 19-year-old Dave Steffen (9-4 .692, 0.87 ERA) from Dearborn, Michigan.

1970s Pitching Walks	
1. Joe Coleman	576
2. Mickey Lolich	496
3. John Hiller	414
4. Les Cain	205
5. Lerrin LaGrow	181
6. Milt Wilcox	178
7. Woodie Fryman	162
8. Fred Scherman	160
9. Vern Ruhle	145
10. Jack Morris	131

Team. Detroit finished in fifth place under managers Less Moss (27-26), Dick Tracewski (2-0) and Sparky Anderson (56-50) at 85-76 (.528), with 1,630,929 fans. The team went 7-9 in April, as Dave Rozema (9 IP, 1 ER, 3 H) had a dominant start during a 4-1 win over Toronto at home on Sunday, April 22. Motown logged a 15-12 mark in May, that included a Rozema (9 IP, 1 ER) and Alan Trammell 3-for-4 (5 RBI) led 10-3 home win against Baltimore on Sunday, May 27. Detroit won six straight games thru Thursday, May 31. Jack Billingham (8 GM, 32.2 IP, 1.65 ERA, .229 BA, .283 OBP, .253 BABIP) pitched well in May with a 4-1 record. The Bengals were 13-16 in June as Ron LeFlore went 4-for-5 with three stolen bases in a 9-3 win at Oakland on Saturday, June 2. Rozema (9 IP, 0 ER, 5 H) shutout the Athletics 2-0 on Sunday. Detroit won 10-4 at Boston on Tuesday, June 19, behind Lance Parrish 3-for-5 (HR, 4 RBI). Players were 18-13 in July winning 14-5 in Chicago on Sunday, July 15, when outfielder Steve Kemp went 5-for-6. John Wockenfuss homered in three straight games July 25-30, the first two in consecutive games as a pinch-hitter. The Tigers finished 20-12 during August, as Mike Chris (W 1-0, 6 IP, 2 ER, 2 H) no-hit visiting Kansas City for six innings in his first major league start on Saturday, August 4. Motown split a doubleheader with Texas at home on Wednesday, August 8. The Rangers won 16-9 in game one, as Champ Summers was 2-for-3 (HR, 5 RBI) for Detroit. The Bengals took the nightcap 10-4 behind Lynn Jones 3-for-5 (HR, 2 RBI), Bruce Robbins (6.2 IP, 2 ER, 1 H) and Wockenfuss 3-for-4 (2 HR, 5 RBI) with a grand slam home run. Players edged Seattle 4-3 at home on Sunday August 26, paced by Kemp 4-for-5 (2 HR, 3 RBI) and Aurelio Lopez (W 7-3, 3 IP, 0 ER, 1 H, 3 SO). The club closed 12-14 in September, as LeFlore 3-for-3, Jason Thompson (HR, 4 RBI) and Rozema (5 IP, 0 ER, 5 SO) led a 14-1 win over Cleveland at home on Tuesday, September 11. Jack Morris (W 15-7, 9 IP, 0 ER, 4 H, 7 SO) and Lou Whitaker 3-for-3 powered a 5-0 triumph over the visiting Orioles on Wednesday, September 19. LeFlore swiped four bases in a Lopez (W 10-1, 2 IP, 0 ER, 3 SO) 3-2 win at Boston on Sunday, September 23. The team was 46-34 (.575) at home and 39-42 (.481) on the road. The Bengals scored 770 runs, as pitchers allowed opponents 738.

OF * LYNN JONES

Offense. Detroit had a .269 BA, .339 OBP, .415 SLG, .754 OPS, 2,229 TB and 100 OPS+. Catcher Lance Parrish (.276 BA, 19 HR, 65 RBI) led in doubles (26) and strikeouts (105). Jason Thompson (.246 BA, 20 HR, 79 RBI) at first led in walks (70). Lou Whitaker (.286 BA, 3 HR, 42 RBI) at second led in WAR (4.5) and walks (78). Aurelio Rodriguez (.254 BA, 5 HR, 36 RBI) at third led for in-play percentage (83%), with Alan Trammell (.276 BA, 6 HR, 50 RBI) at short. Player of the Year, Tiger of the Year and most effective hitter Steve Kemp (.318 BA, 26 HR, 105 RBI) in left led in doubles (26), homers, runs batted in, on-base percentage (.398), slugging (.543), OPS (.941), OPS+ (149), total average (.949), base-out percentage (.967), gross production average (.315), oWAR (4.5), batters run average (.215), batting, secondary average (.361), base runs (100), runs produced (167), runs created (106), isolated power (.224), extra base hits (55) and bases (266). Ron LeFlore (.300 BA, 9 HR, 57 RBI) at center led in games (148), plate appearances (654), at bats (600), runs (110), hits (180), singles (139), triples (10), BAbip (.343), times on base (232), power/speed number (16.1), bases produced (379), stolen bases (78), stolen base runs (15.0), outs (452) and hitting streak (15). Jerry Morales (.211 BA, 14 HR, 56 RBI) was in right, with designated hitter Rusty Staub (.236 BA, 9 HR, 40 RBI). Tiger Rookie of the Year Lynn Jones (.296 BA, 4 HR, 26 RBI), Champ Summers (.313 BA, 20 HR, 51 RBI) and John Wockenfuss (.264 BA, 15 HR, 46 RBI). Summers .308 (4-13, 2 HR, 4 RBI) and Wockenfuss (2 HR, 5 RBI) led pinch-hitters. Tim Corcoran (.338 BA) and Rick Peters (.320 BA, 30 SB) were at class "AAA" Evansville. Rick Leach (.304 BA) from the University of Michigan was assigned to the class "A" Lakeland Tigers.

1970s Pitching Strikeouts	
1. Mickey Lolich	1,343
2. Joe Coleman	1,000
3. John Hiller	812
4. Milt Wilcox	323
5. Les Cain	290
6. Woodie Fryman	283
7. Lerrin LaGrow	209
Tom Timmermann	209
9. Vern Ruhle	192
10. Jack Morris	189

Pitching. The team had a 4.27 ERA, 25 CG, two SHO, 547 walks, 802 SO, 102 ERA+, 4.38 FIP, 1.388 WHIP, 9.0 H/9, and 3.5 BB/9, as they led league in homers (167), SO/9 (5.1) and no decisions (49). Pitcher of the Year Jack Morris (17-7, 3.28 ERA) led in wins, win percentage (.708), complete games (9), innings (197.2), home runs (19), strikeouts (113), wild pitches (9), pWAR (5.8) and quality starts (18). The most effective pitcher Aurelio Lopez (10-5, 2.41 ERA) led in games (61), games finished (49), saves (21), LOB% (84.7), ERA, ERA+ (181), FIP (3.57), DICE (3.83), WHIP (1.150), H/9 (6.7), SO/9 (7.5) and R/9 (2.6). Jack Billingham (10-7, 3.30 ERA) led in HR/9 (0.7). Milt Wilcox (12-10, 4.35 ERA) led team in losses, starts (29), hits (201), walks (73), hit by pitch (11), earned runs (95), and runs (105). Pat Underwood (6-4, 4.59 ERA) BB/9 (2.1) and SO/BB (2.86). Dave Rozema (4-4, 3.51 ERA), Bruce Robbins (3-3, 3.91 ERA), Dan Petry (6-5, 3.95 ERA), Kip Young (2-2, 6.39 ERA), Steve Baker (1-7, 6.64 ERA), Mike Chris (3-3, 6.92 ERA), Dave Tobik (3-5, 4.33 ERA), and John Hiller (4-7, 5.22 ERA, 9 SV).

Defense. Detroit led the American League in fielding percentage (.981), as they committed the fewest errors (120). Tiger league leaders were Wilcox in pitcher fielding percentage (1.000) and double plays (7). Parrish led all the catchers in passed balls (21) and led the Bengals for defensive WAR (1.8). Leftfielder Kemp the league in assists (12) and double plays with two.

Champ Summers struggled in the National League with Cincinnati 1977-79 (99 GM, .199 BA, .310 OBP, .345 SLG, .655 OPS, 78 OPS+) and excelled in American League for Detroit for 1979 (90 GM, .313 BA, .414 OBP, .614 SLG, 1.028 OPS, 171 OPS+).

Aurelio Lopez shined June 24-August 29 (5-2, 16 SV, 1.27 ERA). Class "AAA" Evansville had Dave Tobik (4-0, 0.47 ERA, 9 SV) and Roger Weaver (8-2). Bruce Robbins (7-1 .875, 2.97 ERA) and Larry Corr (6-3, 1.98 ERA) was at class "AA" Montgomery.

OF/DH * KIRK GIBSON

Player of the Decade. Kirk Gibson (.276 BA, 149 HR, 494 RBI) led his Detroit Tigers during the decade in slugging (.482), on-base plus slugging (.838), total average (.885), BAbip (.310), bases produced average (2.4) and strikeouts (710). Gibson reached base in 33 consecutive games August 12-September 18 of 1981 (.391 BA, .431 OBP, .586 SLG, .447 BAbip) and finished the strike-shortened season with a .328 batting average. He enjoyed four solid seasons in 1984 (92 R, 27 HR, 91 RBI, 29 SB), 1985 (96 R, 29 HR, 97 RBI, 30 SB, 301 TB), 1986 (28 HR, 86 RBI, 34 SB) and 1987 (95 R, 24 HR, 79 RBI, 31 SB). His decade highlights included a 5-for-6 (HR, 2 RBI) effort in a 4-2 home win over Minnesota on Friday, May 14, 1982, and a 14-game hit streak August 14-28, 1984 (20 R, 4 HR, 12 RBI, .442 BA, .525 OBP, .827 SLG, 1.352 OPS, .475 BAbip). Kirk walked three times in a game on five occasions in 1985. Gibson was 4-for-4 (2 R, 2 HR, 5 RBI) in a 6-5 victory on Monday, April 7 over the visiting Boston Red Sox to open 1986. Gibson went 2-for-4 (3 RBI, 3 SB) with three Runs batted in and three steals during a 9-4 win in Oakland on Friday, September 5, 1986.

1980s

Year	W – L	Pct.	Pl
1980	84-78	.519	4
1981	60-49	.550	3
1982	83-79	.512	4
1983	92-70	.568	2
1984	**104-58**	**.642**	1
1985	84-77	.522	3
1986	87-75	.537	3
1987	98-64	.605	1
1988	88-74	.543	2
1989	59-103	.364	7
	839-727	.536	

All-Decade Team. Manager Sparky Anderson (839-727 .536) led Motown to first place finishes in 1984 (104-58 .642) and 1987 (98-64 .605), with second place teams in 1983 (92-70 .568) and 1988 (88-74 .543). Pitcher Jack Morris (162-119 .577, 3.66 ERA). Catcher Lance Parrish (.266 BA, 176 HR, 587 RBI) was a six-time Tiger All-Star, with five Silver Slugger Awards and three Gold Gloves. First baseman Dave Bergman (.262 BA, 29 HR, 154 RBI) excelled as a pinch-hitter in 1984 (.304 BA, HR, 7 RBI). Second baseman Lou Whitaker (.275 BA, 143 HR, 619 RBI) became an All-Star for the first of five straight years in 1983 (.320 BA, 12 HR, 72 RBI, 40 2B, 94 R, 294 TB). All-Star Shortstop Alan Trammell (.290 BA, 130 HR, 637 RBI) was MVP runner-up in 1987 (.343 BA, 28 HR, 105 RBI, 109 R, 21 SB, 329 TB, 155 OPS+), with five Gold Gloves in the 1980s. Third baseman Tom Brookens (.245 BA, 62 HR, 376 RBI) was 5-for-5 (3B, HR, 2 RBI, SB) and started a 5-4-3 triple play in an 8-6 win at Milwaukee on Wednesday, August 20, 1980. Larry Herndon (.278 BA, 83 HR, 364 RBI) in left had career years in 1982 (.292 BA, 23 HR, 88 RBI) and 1983 (.302 BA, 20 HR, 92 RBI). Centerfielder Chet Lemon (.263 BA, 137 HR, 504 RBI) was an All-Star in 1984 (.287 BA, 20 HR, 76 RBI) when he led league in fielding (.995). Right fielder Kirk Gibson (.276 BA, 149 HR, 495 RBI) led league in 1984 for power/speed number (28.0) and was the ALCS MVP during the three-game sweep of Kansas City (.417 BA, .500 OBP, .750 SLG). Designated hitter Darrell Evans (.238 BA, 141 HR, 405 RBI) was first to hit 40 homers in both leagues for Atlanta in 1973 (41 HR, 104 RBI) and Detroit in 1985 (40 HR, 94 RBI), with 1987 (34 HR, 99 RBI) a good season.

P * JACK MORRIS

Pitcher of the Decade. Jack Morris (162-119 .577, 3.66 ERA) led the 1980s MLB pitchers in starts, complete games, innings, and wins. The Bengal decade leader in wins, losses, starts (332), complete games (133), shutouts (20), quality starts (199), high quality starts (183), dominant starts (60), innings (2,443.2), hits (2,212), homers (264), walks (858), strikeouts (1,629), balks (20), intentional walks (66), wild pitches (124), earned runs (995), runs (1,085), pWAR (30.3), batters faced (10,208), cheap wins (28), tough losses (43) and complete game percentage (.401). He finished third in Cy Young voting in 1981 (14-7 .667, 3.05 ERA) as he led league in wins and 1983 (20-13 .606, 3.34 ERA) when league leader for innings (293.2) and 232 strikeouts. His best year was 1986 (21-8 .724, 3.27 ERA) with a league high six shutouts. He threw three consecutive shutouts of 7-0 on July 9 at Minnesota (9 IP, 6 H, 4 SO), 5-0 on July 13 in Kansas City (9 IP, 4 H, 12 SO) and then 5-0 at home on July 18 over the Texas Rangers (9 IP, 2 H, 11 SO).

1980s Attendance

Year	Attn.	Avg.	Rk
1980	1,785,293	21,772	7
1981	1,149,144	20,894	5
1982	1,636,058	20,198	7
1983	1,829,636	22,588	8
1984	**2,704,794**	**32,985**	1
1985	2,286,609	28,230	3
1986	1,899,437	23,450	7
1987	2,061,830	25,455	7
1988	2,081,162	25,693	8

All-Decade Pitchers. Morris was flawless July 5-August 1 of 1986 (5-0, 42 P, 1 ER, 6 BB, 39 SO, 0.21 ERA, .153 BA, .185 OBP, .208 BAbip). Frank Tanana (61-51 .545, 3.87 ERA) led in pickoffs (16), with 1985 (10-7 .588, 3.34 ERA) his best as a Tiger. Dan Petry (101-76 .571, 3.74 ERA) led the 1980s in hit by pitch (33), pickoffs (16) and no decisions (56), with 1983 (19-11 .633, 3.92 ERA) and 1984 (18-8 .692, 3.24) his top seasons. Milt Wilcox (66-51 .564, 3.89 ERA) finished 1984 (17-8 .680, 4.00 ERA) as his seventh straight year with at least 10 wins. Doyle Alexander (29-29 .500, 3.91 ERA) started 1987 with Atlanta (5-10, 4.13 ERA) and traded to Detroit (9-0, 1.52 ERA, 279 ERA+). Dave Rozema (29-23 .558, 3.58 ERA) from Grand Rapids led for BB/9 (2.39) and a combined 11-3 (.786) for 1982-1983. Juan Berenguer (25-21 .543, 3.87 ERA) started in 1983 (9-5 .643, 3.14 ERA). Mike Henneman (31-13 .705, 2.85 ERA) led the 1980s in win percentage (.705), FIP (3.48), DICE (3.68) and holds (13), with three superb seasons to begin his MLB career of 1987 (11-3 .786), 1988 (9-6 .600), and 1989 (11-4 .733). Willie Hernandez (36-31 .537, 2.98 ERA) led in games (358), games finished (279), saves (120), WHIP (1.121), SO/9 (7.15) and SO/BB (2.78). He was an All-Star, MVP, and Cy Young Award winner in 1984 (9-3 .750, 1.92 ERA, 32 SV, 204 ERA+, 2.58 FIP, 0.941 WHIP). The Detroit franchise logged an 63-17 (.788) record in games Hernandez appeared in during 1984. Aurelio Lopez (43-25 .632, 3.62 ERA) starred in 1980 (13-6 .684, 3.77 ERA, 21 SV) and 1984 (10-1 .909, 2.94 ERA).

Tom Monaghan grew up in a Jackson orphanage, served in the Marines and the founder of Domino's Pizza. His first year as owner was memorable with the 1984 first-place Tigers (104-58 .642), World Title, and home attendance record of 2,704,794.

1980s Team Hitting				
YEAR	AVG	HR	RBI	SB
1980	.273	143	767	75
1981	.256	65	403	61
1982	.266	177	684	93
1983	**.274**	156	749	93
1984	.271	187	788	106
1985	.253	202	703	75
1986	.263	198	751	**138**
1987	.272	**225**	**840**	106
1988	.250	143	650	87
1989	.242	116	564	103

Team. Detroit finished fifth for Sparky Anderson at 84-78 (.519), with an attendance of 1,785,293. The Tigers were 7-11 in April when Jack Morris (9 IP, 0 ER, 3 H) led a 5-1 win at Kansas City on Thursday, April 10. Steve Kemp (2 HR, 4 RBI) powered an 8-6 win over the Royals at home on Saturday, April 19. Players were 12-14 in May as Kirk Gibson went 3-for-3 (HR) and Milt Wilcox (9 IP, 0 ER, 4 H) threw a 4-0 shutout in Oakland on Sunday, May 4. Dan Petry (9 IP, 0 ER, 4 H, 7 SO) recorded a 4-0 shutout in Anaheim on Sunday, May 11. The club went 19-6 in June that included a Wilcox (W 8-2, 9 IP, 0 ER, 5 H) 8-2 gem facing visiting Seattle on Monday, June 4, aided by John Wockenfuss 2-for-3 (HR, 3 RBI). The Bengals won 13-3 in Cleveland on Wednesday, June 25, as Wilcox (W 8-4, 9 IP, 2 ER) recorded his sixth consecutive complete game win, with Kemp 3-for-5 (3 RBI). 24-year-old Rick Peters became just the fourth Tiger rookie with three straight three-hit games June 24-27 (9-for-16, .563 BA, .588 OBP, .750 SLG, .600 BAbip) and six straight multi-hit games June 24-30 (17-for-29, .586 BA, .625 OBP, .690 SLG, .654 BAbip). Motown won nine consecutive wins through Saturday, June 28. Detroit was 14-13 in July when Alan Trammell 3-for-5, Kemp (HR, 3 RBI), Al Cowens 4-for-5 and Low Whitaker (4 RBI) led a 15-6 home win over California on Thursday, July 31. The squad went 15-17 in August with an 8-0 win in Arlington on Friday, August 8, behind Summers (HR, 4 RBI), Petry (9 IP, 0 ER, 5 H, 7 SO) and six Tiger steals. Tom Brookens was 5-for-5 (HR, 2 RBI), Rick Peters 4-for-6 and Wockenfuss (HR, 3 RBI) fueled an 8-6 win at Milwaukee on Wednesday, August 20. Reliever Aurelio Lopez (W 10-4, 6 IP, 0 ER, 2 H) led a 5-4 win at Chicago on Tuesday, August 26. Players were 15-14 in September and 2-3 in October. Kemp (HR, 6 RBI) led a 13-3 defeat of visiting Cleveland on Saturday, September 20. Lance Parrish went 3-for-4 (2 3B) during a 5-1 win over visiting New York on Saturday, September 27. Roger Weaver (7 IP, 2 ER) and Lopez (SV 21, 2 IP, 0 ER, 5 SO) paced an 8-2 triumph in Toronto on Monday, September 29, with Trammell 5-for-6 (2 2B, 2 SB) and Cowens 4-for-5. Lynn Jones (3B, 4 RBI) led a 7-6 win on Saturday, October 4, with 55,410 fans at Yankee Stadium. Detroit went 10-2 (.833) against Chicago and Seattle, with a mark of 10-3 (.769) over Cleveland. Motown finished 43-38 (.519) at home, 41-40 (.457) on the road and led league in runs (830), as their pitchers allowed 757.

Offense. Detroit had a .273 BA, .348 OBP, .409 SLG, .757 OPS, 2,310 TB, and 106 OPS+. Catcher Lance Parrish (.286 BA, 24 HR, 82 RBI) led in doubles (34), homers, isolated power (.213), extra base hits (64), total bases (276) and strikeouts (109). Richie Hebner (.290 BA, 12 HR, 82 RBI) and John Wockenfuss (.274 BA, 16 HR, 65 RBI) split time at first base. Lou Whitaker (.233 BA, HR, 45 RBI) at second led in walks (73). Tom Brookens (.275 BA, 10 HR, 66 RBI) at third led in games (151), triples (9) and power/speed number (11.3). Tiger of the Year Alan Trammell (.300 BA, 9 HR, 65 RBI) at short led in plate appearances (652), at bats (560), runs (107), hits (168), singles (133), WAR (4.8), oWAR (4.6), hitting, BAbip (.321), times on base (240) and outs (434). Player of the Year and most effective hitter leftfielder Steve Kemp (.293 BA, 21 HR, 101 RBI) led in runs batted in, base runs (88), runs produced (168), runs created (91), bases produced (315) and stolen base runs (0.9). Tiger Rookie of the Year Rick Peters (.291 BA, 2 HR, 42 RBI) was in center. Al Cowens (.280 BA, 5 HR, 42 RBI) in right led for in-play percentage (80%). Designated hitter Champ Summers (.297 BA, 17 HR, 60 RBI) led in on-base percentage (.393), slugging (.504), OPS (.897), OPS+ (143), total average (.907), base-out percentage (.920), gross production average (.303), batters run average (.198), secondary average (.360) and had a 17-game hitting streak. The leading Tiger pinch-hitters were Hebner at .545 (6-11, 2 HR, 6 RBI), Wockenfuss (HR, 6 RBI) and Summers (HR, 5 RBI).

1980s Team Hitting				
YEAR	OBP	SLG	OPS	OPS+
1980	.348	.409	.757	106
1981	.331	.368	.699	99
1982	.324	.418	.742	103
1983	.335	.427	.762	112
1984	.342	.432	.774	**114**
1985	.318	.424	.742	103
1986	.338	.424	.762	107
1987	**.349**	**.451**	**.800**	**114**
1988	.324	.378	.703	100
1989	.318	.351	.669	91

Pitching. Detroit had a 4.25 ERA, 40 CG, 9 SHO, 558 walks, 741 SO, 97 ERA+, 4.28 FIP, 1.406 WHIP, 9.2 H/9, 3.4 BB/9, and 4.5 SO/9. The staff led league in starts (163). Pitcher of the Year and most effective pitcher Aurelio Lopez (13-6, 3.77 ERA, 3.92 FIP, 4.17 DICE) led league in games (67), with staff lead for win percentage (.684), games finished (59), saves (21), LOB% (77.0), ERA, ERA+ (110), SO/9 (7.0) and strikeouts to walks (2.16). Dan Petry (10-9, 3.94 ERA, 3.92 FIP, 4.17 DICE) led in SHO (3) and HR/9 (0.5). Dan Schatzeder (11-13, 4.02 ERA) led in WHIP (1.225), pWAR (3.5), H/9 (8.3) and walks per nine (2.7). Jack Morris (16-15, 4.18 ERA) led in wins, losses, starts (36), innings (250), hits (252), walks (87), strikeouts (112), earned runs (116), runs (125) and quality starts (16). Milt Wilcox (13-11, 4.49 ERA) led in complete games (13), homers (24) and HBP (6). Dave Rozema (6-9, 3.92 ERA) led in wild pitches (9). Mark Fidrych (2-3, 5.68 ERA), Bruce Robbins (4-2, 6.62 ERA), Pat Underwood (3-6, 3.59 ERA), Dave Tobik (1-0, 3.98 ERA), Roger Weaver (3-4, 4.10 ERA) and John Hiller (1-0, 4.40 ERA). Schatzeder had home shutouts versus Oakland on Saturday, July 26 (9 IP, 0 ER, 5 H) and Minnesota on Friday, September 5 (9 IP, 0 ER, 5 H).

Defense. Detroit committed 133 errors for a .979 fielding percentage and led the division in putouts (4,402). League leaders were Morris in pitcher putouts (31), Brookens in errors (29) at third base, leftfielder Kemp in double plays (3) and Cowens in rightfield fielding (.988). Second baseman Whitaker and shortstop Trammell tied for the Tiger team lead in dWAR (1.3).

Richie Hebner was 2-for-5, scored two runs, and hit two homers with six RBIs versus New York at home on Tuesday, May 20. He then logged a 2-for-4 effort, scoring two runs, hit a double and finished with six RBIs at Cleveland on Tuesday, June 24.

Stan Younger (.318 BA) was assigned to the class "A" Lakeland Tigers. The class "AA" Montgomery Rebels featured pitcher Larry Pashnick (13-4 .765, 2.96 ERA). Jerry Ujdur (9-4 .692, 3.37 ERA) pitched for the class "AAA" Evansville Triplets.

1980s Hitting Games		
1.	Lou Whitaker	1,418
2.	Alan Trammell	1,389
3.	Tom Brookens	1,146
4.	Chet Lemon	1,099
5.	Lance Parish	906
6.	Kirk Gibson	881
7.	Larry Herndon	843
8.	Darrell Evans	727
9.	Dave Bergman	598
10.	Pat Sheridan	416

Team. A 50-day baseball strike began on June 12, as Detroit finished 31-26 (.544) in the first half, 29-23 (.558) in the second half and 60-49 (.550) overall for Sparky Anderson, with an attendance of 1,149,144. Players were 8-11 in April with a 2-0 shutout in Toronto on Thursday, April 16, with Milt Wilcox (7.1 IP, 0 ER, 3 H, 6 SO) and Kirk Gibson 4-for-4. Motown lost 10 straight games thru April 19-29. Michigander Rick Leach of Flint Southwestern High School excelled at class "AAA" Toledo (13 GM, 2 HR, 16 RBI, .409 BA). He made his MLB debut on Thursday, April 30 when Dave Rozema (9 IP, 0 ER, 2 H) of Grand Rapids Community College shutout Seattle 2-0. The club was 15-13 in May when closer Kevin Saucier was flawless May 19-August 20 (11 GM, 1-0, 7 SV, 20 IP, 0.00 ERA, .150 BA, .150 SLG, .161 BAbip). The Tigers won 12-3 in Milwaukee on Monday, May 25, with John Wockenfuss (3 RBI), Lance Parrish 3-for-5, Richie Hebner 3-for-5 (HR, 3 RBI), Lynn Jones 4-for-5 (2 RBI) and Jack Morris (W 6-3, 9 IP, 3 ER, 6 SO). Detroit went 8-2 in June including a 4-3 12-inning victory over visiting Milwaukee on Monday, June 1, as Jones was 4-for-6. Wilcox was spectacular June 2-August 31 (6 GM, 6-0, 46.2 IP, 0.96 ERA, .194 BA, .256 OBP, .255 SLG, .211 BAbip). Aurelio Lopez (W 3-1, 6 IP, 0 ER, 4 H, 6 SO) and Saucier (SV 7, 3 IP, 0 ER, 1 H) threw a 5-0 shutout in Texas on Tuesday, June 9. Motown had a mark of 13-8 in August with nine straight wins. Wilcox (W 9-5, 9 IP, 1 ER, 5 H) won 3-1 in Chicago on Monday, August 31. The Tigers were 15-12 in September and 1-3 in October. Catchers Bill Fahey (HR, 2 RBI) and Parrish (HR, 2 RBI) led a 12-inning 11-9 win over Cleveland at home on Saturday, September 12. Wockenfuss (2 HR, 3 RBI) aided a 6-3 win in Baltimore on Tuesday, September 22, with rookie reliever George Cappuzzello (W 1-0, 7.1 IP, 0 ER, 3 H). Morris (W 14-6, 6 IP, 0 ER, 1 H, 5 SO) pitched a 14-0 home shutout of Baltimore on Tuesday, September 29, as Rick Leach had a pinch-hit three-run triple during the five-run fifth inning. Motown and reliever Lopez (4 IP, 0 ER, 1 H) fell 5-4 to visiting Baltimore in 10-innings on Thursday, October 1, as Steve Kemp went 4-for-5. Detroit went 9-3 (.750) with Minnesota and Texas. The players were 32-23 (.582) at home and 28-26 (.519) on the road. The Bengals scored 427 runs and allowed opponents 404. Class "AA" Birmingham featured stars Mike Laga (31 HR, 86 RBI), Howard Johnson (.266 BA, 22 HR, 83 RBI), Glenn Wilson (.306 BA, 18 HR, 82 RBI), Stan Younger (47 SB), and Mark Dacko (13-7 .650).

P * KEVIN SAUCIER

Offense. Detroit had a .256 BA, .331 OBP, .368 SLG, .699 OPS, 1,323 TB and 99 OPS+. Catcher Lance Parrish (.244 BA, 10 HR, 46 RBI) led in doubles (18) and homers. Richie Hebner (.226 BA, 5 HR, 28 RBI) was at first. Lou Whitaker (.263 BA, 5 HR, 36 RBI) at second led the league in games (109). Tom Brookens (.243 BA, 4 HR, 25 RBI) manned third base. Shortstop Alan Trammell (.258 BA, 2 HR, 31 RBI) led league in sacrifice hits (16), with team lead for plate appearances (463), at bats (392), runs (52), singles (81) and outs (323). Steve Kemp (.277 BA, 9 HR, 49 RBI) at left led in runs (52), hits (103), doubles (18), runs batted in, on-base percentage (.389), oWAR (3.2), secondary average (.347), times on base (174), base runs (63), runs produced (92), runs created (61), extra base hits (31), total bases (156), bases produced (235) and walks (70). Al Cowens (.261 BA, HR, 18 RBI) was the centerfielder. Right field was split between Lynn Jones (.259 BA, 2 HR, 19 RBI) the leader for in-play percentage (83%) and Player of the Year, Tiger of the Year and most effective hitter Kirk Gibson (.328 BA, 9 HR, 40 RBI) that led in slugging (.479), OPS (.848), OPS+ (141), gross production average (.286), batters run average (.176), hitting, BAbip (.393), power/speed number (11.8), steals (17), stolen base runs (2.1), strikeouts (64) and hit streak (10). Key reserves were John Wockenfuss (.215 BA, 9 HR, 25 RBI) that led in isolated power (.180), Champ Summers (.255 BA, 3 HR, 21 RBI) and Rick Peters (.256 BA, 15 RBI). The leading Tiger pinch-hitter was Jones at .308 (4-13, HR, 3 RBI).

1980s Hitting Runs		
1.	Alan Trammell	815
2.	Lou Whitaker	814
3.	Chet Lemon	531
4.	Kirk Gibson	525
5.	Lance Parrish	465
6.	Tom Brookens	422
7.	Larry Herndon	358
8.	Darrell Evans	357
9.	Dave Bergman	164
10.	Steve Kemp	140

Pitching. The Tigers recorded a 3.53 ERA, 33 CG, 373 walks, 476 SO, 107 ERA+ of 107, 3.97 FIP, 1.251 WHIP, 3.5 BB/9, and 4.4 SO/9. Pitchers led league in shutouts (3) and H/9 (7.8). Pitcher of the Year Jack Morris (14-7, 3.05 ERA) led MLB in wins and walks (78), as he led staff in win percentage (.667), starts (25), complete games (15), innings (198), hits (153), homers (14), strikeouts (97), earned runs (67), runs (69) and pWAR (3.4). The most effective pitcher Kevin Saucier (4-2, 1.65 ERA) led staff in games (38), games finished (23), saves (13), LOB% (81.0), earned run average, ERA+ (230), WHIP (0.959), H/9 (4.8), HR/9 (0.2) and R/9 (2.0). Dan Petry (10-9, 3.00 ERA) led in shutouts (2) and SO/9 (5.0). Milt Wilcox (12-9, 3.03 ERA) led in HBP (6), WP (4), FIP (3.48), DICE (3.88), BB/9 (2.8) and SO/BB (1.52). Dan Schatzeder (6-8, 6.06 ERA), Dave Rozema (5-5, 3.63 ERA), Howard Bailey (1-4, 7.36 ERA), Dave Tobik (2-2, 2.69 ERA), George Cappuzzello (1-1, 3.48 ERA) and Aurelio Lopez (5-2, 3.64 ERA). Tobik was exemplary the period of May 10-August 22 (12 GM, 2-0, 31.1 IP, 1 ER, 0.29 ERA, .159 BA, .178 SLG, .185 BAbip, 0 HR).

Defense. The Bengals led the American League in fewest errors (67), fielding average (.978) and defensive efficiency (.740). Tiger league leaders were pitchers Morris in fielding average (1.000) and Schatzeder in errors (3). Whitaker at second base led in assists (354), as shortstop Trammell led team in defensive WAR (2.4). Jones led all right fielders in double plays (2).

Kirk Gibson went 4-for-4 on April 16, with a stellar second half (.375 BA, .547 SLG, .429 BAbip), that included August 22-31 (19-for-38, .500 BA, .525 OBP, .763 SLG, .548 BAbip). He dominated lefthanders (45-123, .366 BA, .512 SLG, .456 BAbip).

Kevin Saucier acquired in an off-season trade with the Texas Rangers shined April 15-August 20 (20 GM, 10 SV, 31.2 IP, 0.28 ERA, .133 BA, .220 OBP, .143 SLG, .155 BAbip). Mark Williams (11-4 .733, 2.15 ERA, 5 SHO) pitched for class "A" Lakeland.

1980s Hitting Hits	
1. Alan Trammell	1,504
2. Lou Whitaker	1,452
3. Chet Lemon	988
4. Lance Parrish	915
5. Kirk Gibson	876
6. Tom Brookens	821
7. Larry Herndon	765
8. Darrell Evans	559
9. Dave Bergman	364
10. Matt Nokes	304

Team. Detroit was fourth for Sparky Anderson at 83-79 (.512), with 1,636,058 fans. The team went 13-8 in April as relievers Kevin Saucier (3.2 IP, 0 ER, 4 SO) and Elias Sosa (2 IP, 0 ER) aided a 4-2 home win versus Toronto on Thursday, April 15. Motown was 16-9 in May when Larry Herndon went 3-for-4 (3 HR, 7 RBI) for a 11-9 win over visiting Oakland on Tuesday, May 18. Herndon was 5-for-5 (2 3B) in a 11-3 win against the Athletics on Thursday, May 20. The Bengals were 9-16 in June including a Pat Underwood (8 IP, 2 ER) 8-3 win on Tuesday, June 8, a doubleheader win the next day 2-1 behind Jack Morris (9 IP, 1 ER) and an 18-inning 4-3 victory suspended in the 15th inning and completed on Friday, September 24, behind Kirk Gibson 4-for-6 and reliever Dave Tobik (8.2 IP, 0 ER, 4 H). The Tigers went 1-14 June 13-29. Detroit was 13-16 during July including a 18-2 win at Minnesota on Thursday, July 15, with Herndon (5 RBI) and Tom Brookens (HR, 4 RBI). The squad had a 15-15 mark in August with a Dan Petry (W 12-6, 9 IP, 1 ER, 4 H, 6 SO) 7-1 triumph in Kansas City on Wednesday, August 4 behind Chet lemon (HR, 3 RBI) and Enos Cabell 4-for-5. Lou Whitaker was 4-for-4 versus Toronto at home on Thursday and Jack Morris (9 IP, 0 ER, 4 H) shutout Toronto 6-0 on Friday behind Lance Parrish (2 HR, 4 RBI). Whitaker had six straight multi-hit games August 8-13 (4 HR, 10 RBI, 9 R, .517 BA). 23-year-old rookie Glenn Wilson (HR, 2 RBI), Whitaker 3-for-5 (2 HR, 5 RBI), Richie Hebner (HR, 2 RBI) and Jerry Ujdur (9 IP, 1 ER, 4 H, 7 SO) led a 10-1 home win of New York on Tuesday, August 10. Detroit closed 14-13 in September and 3-2 in October, with a 10-5 win at Baltimore on Thursday, September 23, with reliver Dave Rucker (6.2 IP, 0 ER, 4 H), Herndon 3-for-5 (2 HR, 4 RBI) and 21-year-old rookie Howard Johnson (HR, 2 RBI). Morris (9 IP, 0 ER, 6 H) shutout Cleveland 4-0 at home on Saturday, September 25. Rucker (9 IP, 1 ER, 5 H) and Parrish (HR, 4 RBI) led a 4-1 victory in Cleveland on Saturday, October 2. Players were 9-3 (.750) against Minnesota and Oakland, 47-34 (.580) at home, 36-45 (.444) in the road, scored 729 runs and allowed 685. Class "AAA" Evansville had Mike Laga (34 HR, 90 RBI), with Tim Welke of Coldwater High School an American Association umpire. Kenny Baker (.342 BA) and Barbaro Garbey (99 RBI) played at class "AA" Birmingham, as Scott Tabor (8-2 .800) pitched for class "A" Lakeland.

P * DAN PETRY

Offense. Detroit hit .266, .324 OBP, .418 SLG, .742 OPS, 2,337 TB and 103 OPS+. Player of the Year, Tiger of the Year, and most effective hitter Lance Parrish (.284 BA, 32 HR, 87 RBI) set an American League record for home runs by a catcher (32). The *"Big Wheel"* led Motown in slugging (.529), OPS (.867), OPS+ (135), total average (.832), base-out percentage (.844), gross production average (.284), oWAR (4.6), batters run average (.179), secondary average (.325), isolated power (.245) and strikeouts (99). First base had the trio of Enos Cabell (.261 BA, 2 HR, 37 RBI) that led for in-play percentage (86%), Rick Leach (.239 BA, 3 HR, 12 RBI) and Richie Hebner (.274, 8 HR, 18 RBI). Lou Whitaker (.286 BA, 15 HR, 65 RBI) at second led in WAR (5.4) and stolen base runs (1.5), with Tom Brookens (.231 BA, 9 HR, 58 RBI) at third. Shortstop Alan Trammell (.258 BA, 9 HR, 57 RBI, 157 GM) led in doubles (34) and steals (19). Larry Herndon (.292 BA, 23 HR, 88 RBI, 157 GM) in left led in plate appearances (659), at bats (614), runs (92), hits (179), singles (122), triples (13), runs batted in, times on base (218), base runs (90), runs produced (157), runs created (98), power/speed number (15.8), extra base hits (57), total bases (295), bases produced (345) and outs (470). Centerfielder Kirk Gibson (.278 BA, 8 HR, 35 RBI). Tiger Rookie of the Year Glenn Wilson (.292 BA, 12 HR, 34 RBI) in right led for BAbip (.311) and had a 19-game hitting streak. Right-fielder Chet Lemon (.266 BA, 19 HR, 52 RBI) led MLB in HBP (15). He led team in on-base percentage (.368) and walks (56). The designated hitters were Mike Ivie (.232 BA, 14 HR, 38 RBI) and Jerry Turner (.248 BA, 8 HR, 27 RBI). John Wockenfuss (.301 BA, 8 HR, 32 RBI). Wockenfuss at .364 (4-11, 2 HR, 5 RBI) led pinch-hitters. Wilson had five straight multi-RBI games August 7-10 (12-for-20, 3 HR, 10 RBI, .600 BA, .600 OBP, 1.200 SLG, .600 BAbip). Bruce Fields (28 SB) hit .337 at class "A" Macon.

1980s Hitting Doubles	
1. Alan Trammell	267
2. Lance Parrish	262
3. Lou Whitaker	252
4. Chet Lemon	202
5. Tom Brookens	157
6. Kirk Gibson	137
7. Larry Herndon	110
8. Darrell Evans	72
9. Dave Bergman	50
10. Matt Nokes	43

Pitching. Detroit had five SHO, 554 walks, 740 SO, 106 ERA+, 4.43 FIP, 1.327 WHIP, 3.4 BB/9, and 4.6 SO/9, as staff led league in CG (45), ERA (3.80) and H/9 (8.5). Pitcher of the Year and most effective pitcher Dan Petry (15-9, 3.22 ERA) led in starts (38), win percentage (.625), walks (100), ERA, ERA+ (126), pWAR (4.2), HR/9 (0.5), R/9 (3.6) and quality starts (22). Milt Wilcox (12-10, 3.62 ERA) led in HBP (7). Jerry Ujdur (10-10, 3.69 ERA) led league in LOB% (80.5) and team in WHIP (1.230) and H/9 (7.6). Jack Morris (17-16, 4.06 ERA) led in wins, losses, complete games (17), SHO (3), innings (266.1), hits (247), homers (37), strikeouts (135), WP (10), earned runs (120), runs (131), and BB/9 (3.2). Dave Rozema (3-0, 1.63 ERA). Dave Tobik (4-9, 3.56 ERA) led in games (51), games finished (31), saves (9), FIP (3.68), DICE (3.96), SO/9 (5.7) and SO/BB (1.66). Larry Pashnick (4-4, 4.01 ERA), Pat Underwood (4-8, 4.73 ERA), Kevin Saucier (3-1, 3.12 ERA), Dave Rucker (5-6, 3.38 ERA), Elias Sosa (3-3, 4.43), Bob James (0-2, 5.03 ERA) and Aurelio Lopez (3-1, 5.27 ERA). Saucier excelled April 11-May 28 (17 GM, 3-1, 19 IP, 1.42 ERA, .215 BA). Class "AA" Birmingham had Bryan Kelly (8-3 .727), Dave Gumpert (2.17 ERA, 14 SV) and Paul Gibson (2.68 ERA, 12 SV).

Defense. The team had 117 errors (.981). Motown led league in defensive efficiency (.725) and led division in assists (1,844). League leaders were pitcher Petry in fielding (1.000) and putouts (28), catcher Parrish in wild pitches (41), Whitaker in fielding (.988), chances (811), assists (470) and double plays (120) at second. Trammell led team dWAR (2.1) at shortstop.

Outfielder Larry Herndon tied a major-league record with four home runs in consecutive plate appearances during home wins of 7-6 over Minnesota on Sunday, May 16 (1 HR, 1 RBI) and then 11-9 facing Oakland on Tuesday, May 18 (3 HR, 7 RBI).

1980s Hitting Triples		
1.	Lou Whitaker	43
2.	Alan Trammell	39
3.	Larry Herndon	37
4.	Tom Brookens	36
5.	Kirk Gibson	35
6.	Chet Lemon	28
7.	Lance Parrish	17
8.	Dave Bergman	10
	Rick Peters	10
10.	Richie Hebner	9
	Pat Sheridan	9

Team. Detroit (92-70 .568) finished second for Sparky Anderson, with 1,829,636 fans. The squad went 8-9 in April when Dan Petry (W 2-0, 8 IP, 2 ER) led a 13-2 win at New York on Tuesday, April 12, with 55,579 fans, behind Tom Brookens 4-for-5 (HR, 3 RBI) and Glenn Wilson 3-for-5 (3 RBI). Milt Wilcox (9 IP, 0 ER, 1 H, 8 SO) had a 6-0 shutout in Chicago on Friday, April 15, as Chet Lemon was 3-for-4 (3 RBI). The Tigers had a 14-14 record in May including a 12-5 home win over Texas on Sunday, May 22, with Brookens 4-for-4 (HR), Wilson (2 HR, 4 RBI) and Lance Parrish (3 RBI). The team went 18-10 in June with Lou Whitaker the Player of the Month (28 GM, .388 BA, .433 OBP, .612 SLG, .413 BAbip). Detroit won 12-1 in Arlington on Friday, June 3, behind Jack Morris (7 IP, 1 ER, 7 SO) and Enos Cabell 4-for-6 (3 RBI). Motown won 11-4 at Cleveland on Friday, June 17, led by Parrish 4-for-4 (2 RBI) and Brookens (4 RBI). Petry (9 IP, 0 ER, 5 H) had a 9-0 shutout in Baltimore on Friday, June 24, paced by Lemon (HR, 3 RBI) and Larry Herndon 4-for-5. Lemon (2 HR, 5 RBI) and Herndon (HR, 2 RBI) led another 9-3 victory over the Orioles on Saturday. The Bengals were 19-9 in July with a home sweep of California July 11-13. Lemon (3 RBI), Herndon 5-for-6 (HR, 3 RBI) and Dave Rozema (W 6-0) led a 12-6 victory on Monday. Aurelio Lopez (7 IP, 0 ER, 3 H, 5 SO) led a 14-inning 5-4 triumph on Tuesday and a Petry (9 IP, 1 ER) 7-1 win on Wednesday. Detroit won 4-3 in Anaheim on Sunday, July 24, with Trammell 5-for-5 and Morris (10 IP, 3 ER, 9 SO). Morris (8 IP, 1 ER, 3 H, 10 SO), Parrish (HR, 4 RBI), Lemon (HR, 3 RBI) and John Wockenfuss (HR, 2 RBI) led a 10-1 win over visiting Kansas City on Thursday, July 29. The Tigers were 15-15 in August, as Cabell (HR, 4 RBI) and Juan Berenguer (7 IP, 1 ER) logged a 9-1 victory at Minnesota on Saturday, August 20. Motown closed 18-11 in September and 0-2 in October, as Glenn Abbott (W 7-4, 9 IP, 0 ER, 4 H) shutout Cleveland 5-0 at home on September 14. The Bengals were, 9-3 (.750) versus Minnesota, 12-6 (.667) in extra-inning games, (48-33 (.593) at home and 44-37 (.543) on the road. Players scored 789 runs and allowed 679. Bill Nahorodny (.335 BA, 21 HR, 94 RBI) and Barbaro Garbey (.321 BA) played for class "AAA" Evansville.

1B * ENOS CABELL

Offense. Detroit had a .274 BA, .335 OBP, .427 SLG, .762 OPS, 2,387 TB and 112 OPS+. Player of the Year catcher Lance Parrish (.269 BA, 27 HR, 114 RBI) led in doubles (42), homers, runs batted in, slugging (.483), runs produced (167), isolated power (.213), extra base hits (72), strikeouts (106) and outs (479). Enos Cabell (.311 BA, 5 HR, 46 RBI) at first led for in-play percentage (84%). The most effective hitter Lou Whitaker (.320 BA, 12 HR, 72 RBI) at second led in games (161), plate appearances (720), at bats (643), runs (94), hits (206), singles (148), WAR (6.7), oWAR (6.3), hitting, times on base (273), base runs (107), runs created (112), total bases (294), bases produced (378) and walks (67). Tom Brookens (.214 BA, 6 HR, 32 RBI) was at third. Comeback Player of the Year Alan Trammell (.319 BA, 14 HR, 66 RBI) at short led in on-base percentage (.385), OPS (.856), OPS+ (138), total average (.873), base-out percentage (.905), gross production average (.291), batters run average (.177), power/speed number (19.1), stolen bases (30) and stolen base runs (3.0). Left-fielder Larry Herndon (.302 BA, 20 HR, 92 RBI, 9 3B), Chet Lemon (.255 BA, 24 HR, 69 RBI) in center led MLB in HBP (20), with Glenn Wilson (.268 BA, 11 HR, 65 RBI) in right. Designated hitter Kirk Gibson (.227 BA, 15 HR, 51 RBI, 9 3B) led in secondary average (.347). Reserves Johnny Grubb (.254 BA, 4 HR, 22 RBI), John Wockenfuss (.269 BA, 9 HR, 44 RBI) and Rick Leach (.248 BA, 3 HR, 26 RBI). The leading Tiger pinch-hitters were Whitaker at .429 (3-7), Grubb .400 (4-10, HR, 4 RBI), Wockenfuss (HR, 10 RBI) and Cabell at .333 (2-6).

1980s Hitting Home Runs		
1.	Lance Parrish	176
2.	Kirk Gibson	149
3.	Lou Whitaker	143
4.	Darrell Evans	141
5.	Chet Lemon	137
6.	Alan Trammell	130
7.	Larry Herndon	83
8.	Tom Brookens	62
9.	Matt Nokes	58
10.	John Wockenfuss	42

Pitching. Motown recorded a 3.80 ERA, 42 CG, seven SHO, 522 walks, 875 SO, 103 ERA+, 4.21 FIP, 1.268 WHIP, 3.2 BB/9, and 5.4 SO/9. Pitchers led league in homers (170), WP (59) and H/9 (8.2). Pitcher of the Year and most effective pitcher Jack Morris (20-13, 3.34 ERA) led MLB in innings (293.2), wild pitches (18) and batters faced (1,204). He led league in strikeouts (232), with staff lead for wins, losses, complete games (20), hits (257), FIP (3.38), DICE (3.63), pWAR (4.0), SO/BB (2.80) and quality starts (26). Dan Petry (19-11, 3.92 ERA, 2 SHO, 2.5 BB/9) led MLB in starts (38) and homers (37), as *"Peaches"* led staff in walks (99), earned runs (116) and runs (126). Juan *"El Gasolino"* Berenguer (9-5, 3.14 ERA) led in WHIP (1.148), H/9 (6.3) and SO/9 (7.4). Dave Rozema (8-3, 3.43 ERA, 0.9 HR/9, 2.5 BB/9) led in win percentage (.727). Milt Wilcox (11-10, 3.97 ERA, 2 SHO) and Glenn Abbott (2-1, 1.93 ERA). Aurelio Lopez (9-8, 2.81 ERA) led in games (57), games finished (46), saves (18), LOB% (84.0), ERA, ERA+ (140) and R/9 (2.8). Tiger Rookie of the Year Dave Gumpert (0-2, 2.64 ERA), Doug Bair (7-3, 3.88 ERA) and Howard Bailey (5-5, .488 ERA). Rozema went undefeated for the period of May 23-July 20 (9 GM, 5-0, 2.80 ERA, .214 BA, .237 BAbip). Glenn Abbott acquired on Tuesday, August 23 for $100,000, excelled during September (5 GM, 2-0, 1.14 ERA).

Defense. Detroit had 125 errors for a .980 fielding average and led league in defensive efficiency (.726). League leaders were Petry in pitcher double plays (10), Trammell in fielding (.979) at short and Herndon for errors (15) in left field. Lemon at center led team in dWAR (2.4), as Parrish led in catcher chances (772), chances per game (5.9) and caught stealing (54).

Jack Morris was dominate July 14-September 1 (10-0, 1.83 ERA, .185 BA). Tiger of the Year Whitaker had an 18-game hit streak June 5-22 (.456 BA, .722 SLG). His 206 hits were the most by a left-handed hitter since Charlie Gehringer's 209 in 1937.

Keith Comstock (12-3 .800), Colin Ward (10-3 .769), Don Heinkel (19-6 .760), Don Gordon (9-5 .643, 10 SV), George Foussianes (106 R, 22 HR, 81 RBI, 98 BB), Stan Younger (.309 BA, 43 SB) and Scott Earl (36 SB) were at class "AA" Birmingham.

1980s Hitting Runs Batted In	
1. Alan Trammell	637
2. Lou Whitaker	619
3. Lance Parrish	582
4. Chet Lemon	504
5. Kirk Gibson	495
6. Darrell Evans	405
7. Tom Brookens	376
8. Larry Herndon	364
9. Matt Nokes	181
10. John Wockenfuss	166

Team. Detroit won the Eastern Division for Manger of the Year Sparky Anderson at 104-58 (.642), with 2,704,794 fans. The Tigers swept Kansas City the ALCS and won the World Series over San Diego in five games, with Alan Trammell the MVP. The team went 18-2 in April as Trammell was named Player of the Month (20 GM, .403 BA, .495 OBP, .584 SLG, .426 BAbip). with a record 9-0 start. Jack Morris (W 2-0, 9 IP, 0 ER, 0 H, 8 SO) threw a 4-0 no-hitter in Chicago on Saturday, April 7, as the first base umpire was Michigander Tim McClelland from Jackson. Dan Petry (9 IP, 1 ER, 4 H, 7 SO) and Darrell Evans (HR, 3 RBI) led a 5-1 win of visiting Texas on Tuesday, April 10. Motown was 19-7 in May as Morris (W 9-1, 9 IP, 0 ER, 4 H, 10 SO) led a 5-1 victory in Anaheim on Thursday, May 24 for their ninth win in a row. The victory set MLB best 40-game start at 35-5 and tied the MLB record of 17 straight road wins. Milt Wilcox was undefeated thru May 24 (6-0, 3.08 ERA) with nine straight wins dating back to September 1983. The squad was 18-12 in June with a 14-2 home win against Baltimore on Friday, June 1, behind Trammell (HR, 3 RBI), Chet Lemon (HR, 3 RBI) and Petry (W 8-2, 6 IP, 0 ER, 3 H). Motown went 16-12 in July as Willie Hernandez (2-0, 7 SV, 1.31 ERA, .118 BA, .200 OBP, .109 BAbip) was named Player of the Month. Hernandez (SV 16, 3 IP, 0 ER, 1 H, 5 SO) saved a 5-2 Dave Rozema (W 5-1, 6 IP, 1 ER) win at Texas on Saturday, July 7. Wilcox (W 11-6, 8 IP 0 ER, 3 H) had a 3-0 home shutout of Boston on Sunday, July 29. Detroit was 16-15 in August including a 14-1 home win versus Oakland on Monday, August 20, with Darrell Evans 3-for-3 (HR), Lemon (HR, 3 RBI) and Morris (W 16-8, 7 IP, 1 ER, 6 SO). Players closed 17-10 in September with a 11-3 win at New York on Saturday, September 29, led by Juan Berenguer (6 IP, 1 ER), with a ninth inning Howard Johnson pinch-hit three-run double. Detroit went 11-2 (.846) versus Milwaukee, 10-2 (.833) with Texas and 11-2 (.846) in extra-innings. Motown was 30-12 (.714) in blowout games, 53-29 (.646) at home and 51-29 (.638) on the road. Players scored 829 runs and allowed 643. Class "AAA" Evansville had Scott Earl (41 SB) of Glen Oaks Community College in Centreville, Michigan. Jim Walewander (47 SB) played for class "A" Lakeland.

OF* CHET LEMON

Offense. Motown hit .271, .342 OBP, .432 SLG, .774 OPS, 2,436 TB, 114 OPS+, and league best 187 homers. Catcher Lance Parrish (.237 BA, 33 HR, 98 RBI) led in at bats (578), homers, runs batted in, strikeouts (120) and outs (464). Dave Bergman (.273 BA, 7 HR, 44 RBI) was at first. Lou Whitaker (.289 BA, 13 HR, 56 RBI) at second led in singles (122). Howard Johnson (.248 BA, 12 HR, 50 RBI) played third base. Alan Trammell (.314 BA, 14 HR, 69 RBI, 5.2 oWAR) at short led in hits (174), on-base percentage (.382), WAR (6.7), hitting, BAbip (.333), times on base (237), base runs (94) and hit streak (20). Larry Herndon (.280 BA, 7 HR, 43 RBI) was in left and Chet Lemon (.287 BA, 20 HR, 76 RBI) in center. Player of the Year and most effective hitter Kirk Gibson (.282 BA, 27 HR, 91 RBI, 5.2 oWAR) at right led MLB in power/speed number (28.0). He led club in games (149), runs (92), triples (10), slugging (.516), OPS (.879), OPS+ (142), total average (.926), base-out percentage (.950), gross production average (.293), batters run average (.187), secondary average (.390), runs produced (156), runs created (100), isolated power (.234), extra base hits (60), total bases (274), bases produced (366), stolen bases (29) and stolen base runs (3.3). Designated hitter Darrell Evans (.232 BA, 16 HR, 63 RBI) led in walks (77). The Tiger Rookie of the Year was reserve first baseman Barbaro Garbey (.287 BA, 5 HR, 52 RBI) that led for in-play percentage (83%). Tom Brookens (.246 BA, 5 HR, 26 RBI). The leading Tiger pinch-hitters were Rusty Kuntz at .417 (5-12), Ruppert Jones .400 (6-15, HR, 4 RBI), John Grubb .348 (8-23, 3 HR, 6 RBI), Garbey .320 (8-25, 9 RBI), Bergman .303 (7-23, HR, 7 RBI) and Herndon at .292 (7-24, HR, 6 RBI).

1980s Hitting On-Base Percentage	
1. Alan Trammell	.357
Darrell Evans	.357
3. Kirk Gibson	.356
4. Lou Whitaker	.353
5. Chet Lemon	.348
6. Dave Bergman	.346
7. Larry Herndon	.331
8. Pat Sheridan	.326
9. Lance Parrish	.318
10. Tom Brookens	.296

Pitching. Detroit had 19 CG, four SHO, 489 walks, 914 SO, 3.74 FIP, 3.0 BB/9, and 5.6 SO/9. The staff led league in win percentage (.642), saves (51), ERA (3.49), ERA+ (113), WHIP (1.262) and H/9 (8.3). The Most Valuable Player, Cy Young Award winner, Pitcher of the Year, Tiger of the Year, and most effective pitcher Willie Hernandez (9-3, 1.92 ERA) led MLB in games (80) and games finished (68). He led his staff in saves (32), LOB% (83.1), earned run average, ERA+ (204), FIP (2.58), DICE (2.81), WHIP (0.941), pWAR (4.8), H/9 (6.2), HR/9 (0.4), SO/9 (7.2), SO/BB (3.11) and R/9 (1.9). Dan Petry (18-8, 3.24 ERA) led in shutouts (2), hits (231) and home runs (21). Jack Morris (19-11, 3.60 ERA) led the league in wild pitches (14), as he led the club in wins, losses, complete games (9), innings (240.1), walks (87), strikeouts (148), earned runs (96), runs (108) and quality starts (26). Milt Wilcox (17-8, 4.00 ERA) led in HBP (8). Dave Rozema (7-6, 3.74 ERA) led in BB/9 (1.6). Juan Berenguer (11-10, 3.48 ERA), Glenn Abbott (3-4, 5.93 ERA) and Randy O'Neal (2-1, 3.38 ERA). The bullpen had Aurelio Lopez (10-1, 2.94 ERA) that led in win percentage (.909). Bill Scherrer (1-0, 1.89 ERA), Doug Bair (5-3, 3.75 ERA) and Sid Monge (1-0, 4.25 ERA). Scott Tabor (10-4 .714) was at class "AA" Birmingham and Ramon Pena (6-1 .857, 1.67 ERA) at class "A" Lakeland.

Defense. Motown had 127 errors (.979). League leaders were Parrish in catcher double plays (11), Lemon in fielding (.995) at center and team in dWAR (2.3). Gibson led in outfield errors (12). Detroit had a record tying six double plays on April 13.

Jack Morris (W 2-0, 9 IP, 0 ER, 0 H, 6 BB, 8 SO) pitched a 4-0 no-hitter at Chicago on Saturday, April 7, during a televised NBC "Game of the Week". He walked the bases loaded in the fourth inning, then pitched out of it with a double-play and strikeout.

Dave Bergman came to bat in a 3-3 tie versus Toronto, with two out and two on in the 10th-inning at home on June 4. He fouled off seven Roy Lee Jackson pitches and on pitch number 13 hit an upper deck three-run walk-off homer to right field.

Detroit Tigers 1985 American League

1980s Hitting Slugging Percentage	
1. Lance Parrish	.505
2. Kirk Gibson	.482
3. Darrell Evans	.450
4. Chet Lemon	.442
5. Larry Herndon	.436
6. Alan Trammell	.431
7. Lou Whitaker	.420
8. Dave Bergman	.376
9. Tom Brookens	.369
10. Pat Sheridan	.356

Team. Detroit finished third with Sparky Anderson at 84-77 (.522) and 2,286,609 fans. The Tigers won their first six games for a 11-7 record in April. Lou Whitaker (2 HR, 4 RBI), Kirk Gibson (HR, 3 RBI) and Dan Petry (6 IP, 0 ER, 4 H) led an 8-1 home win over Cleveland on Wednesday, April 10. Walt Terrell (9 IP, 0 ER, 4 H) pitched a 5-0 shutout in Milwaukee on Sunday, April 28, with Alan Trammell (HR, 2 RBI) and Lance Parrish (HR, 2 RBI). The club went 14-12 in May when Darrell Evans homered in four straight games May 15-18 (4 HR, 10 RBI, .647 BA, .667 OBP, .1412 SLG, .538 BAbip). Motown won 10-2 win at Oakland on Friday, May 17, behind Parrish 4-for-4, Evans (HR, 4 RBI), Tom Brookens 4-for-5 and Jack Morris (6 IP, 0 ER, 6 SO). Players were 16-11 in June when Randy O'Neal (7 IP, 1 ER, 4 H), Whitaker 4-for 5, Gibson (HR, 5 RBI) and Chet Lemon (HR, 3 RBI) paced a 10-1 triumph in Toronto on Saturday, June 8. Frank Tanana was 2-7 (5.91 ERA) with Texas when acquired on Thursday, June 20. The Detroit native was rejuvenated after returning home with three quality starts (2-0, 2.57 ERA). Motown had a 12-16 mark in July including an 8-0 shutout on Sunday, July 14, with Terrell (W 10-4, 7.1 IP, 0 ER, 1 H, 5 SO). The Bengals won 6-5 in 15-innings over Texas at home on Saturday, July 20, as Morris (8.2 IP, 3 ER) and Aurelio Lopez (3 IP, 1 ER, 1 H, 6 SO) pitched. The squad was 16-13 in August, when they lost to Milwaukee 14-4 at home on Sunday, August 4. The franchise fell to 11-16 in September and 4-2 in October. Players managed a 14-8 home win against California on Tuesday, September 3, behind Lemon (HR, 3 RBI) and Gibson 4-for-4 (2 HR, 5 RBI). Terrell (9 IP, 0 ER, 6 H, 6 SO) shutout Toronto 2-0 at home on Thursday, October 3. Evans was the first player in MLB to hit 40 homers in both leagues. He became the oldest American League home run leader at the age of 38. Detroit was 44-37 (.543) at home, 40-40 (.500) on the road, scored 729 runs and allowed 688. Scotti Madison hit .341 at class "AAA" Nashville. Class "AA" Birmingham had Bruce Fields of Lansing Everett High School (.323 BA) and Fred Breining (8-4, 2.88 ERA), with Charles McHugh (9-5) at class "A" Lakeland.

1B * DARRELL EVANS

Offense. The team registered a .253 BA, .318 OBP, .424 SLG, .742 OPS, 2,363 TB, and 103 OPS+. All-Star catcher Lance Parrish (.273 BA, 28 HR, 98 RBI) led in runs batted in. Darrell Evans (.248 BA, 40 HR, 94 RBI) at first base led MLB in homers and AB/HR (12.6). Evans led league in isolated power (.271). He led club in slugging (.519), secondary average (.432) and walks (85). Gold Glove, Silver Slugger and All-Star Lou Whitaker (.279 BA, 21 HR, 73 RBI) at second led in plate appearances (701), at bats (609), runs (102), hits (170), triples (8), times on base (252) and hit streak (14), with Tom Brookens (.237 BA, 7 HR, 47 RBI) at third. All-Star Alan Trammell (.258 BA, 13 HR, 57 RBI) at short led in singles (115), in-play percentage (78%) and outs (480). Larry Herndon (.244 BA, 12 HR, 37 RBI) was in left and Chet Lemon (.265 BA, 18 HR, 68 RBI) at center. Player of the Year and most effective hitter right fielder Kirk Gibson (.287 BA, 29 HR, 97 RBI) led in games (154), doubles (37), on-base percentage (.364), OPS (.882), OPS+ (140), total average (.953), base-out percentage (.963), gross production average (.293), WAR (5.4), oWAR (5.2), batters run average (.188), hitting, BAbip (.325), base runs (104), runs produced (164), runs created (110), power/speed number (29.5), extra base hits (71), total bases (301), bases produced (402), stolen bases (30), stolen base runs (6.6) and strikeouts (137). Designated hitters were John Grubb (.245 BA, 5 HR, 25 RBI) and Tiger Rookie of the Year Nelson Simmons (.239 BA, 10 HR, 33 RBI). The best pinch-hitters were Herndon at .600 (3-5, 4 RBI), Alejandro Sanchez .333 (6-18, 2 HR, 4 RBI) and Grubb (HR, 8 RBI). Parrish hit a homer in three straight games during August 22-24 (4 HR, 6 RBI, 1.375 SLG).

1980s Hitting On-Base plus Slugging	
1. Kirk Gibson	838
2. Lance Parrish	.823
3. Darrell Evans	.806
4. Chet Lemon	.790
5. Alan Trammell	.788
6. Lou Whitaker	.773
7. Larry Herndon	.767
8. Dave Bergman	.722
9. Pat Sheridan	.682
10. Tom Brookens	.664

Pitching. Detroit had a 3.78 ERA, 31 CG, 556 walks, 943 SO, 108 ERA+, 3.84 FIP, 1.284 WHIP, 3.4 BB/9, and 5.8 SO/9. Motown led league in shutouts (11), intentional walks (67), wild pitches (62), hits per nine (8.1) and tough losses (20). Pitcher of the Year and All-Star Jack Morris (16-11, 3.33 ERA) led league in wild pitches (15), as he led staff in wins, starts (35), complete games (13), shutouts (4), innings (257), walks (110), strikeouts (191), hit by pitch (5), LOB% (75.6), pWAR (4.9) and quality starts (26). Frank Tanana (10-7, 3.34 ERA) led in FIP (3.14), DICE (3.46) and SO/9 (7.0). All-Star Dan Petry (15-13, 3.36 ERA) led in losses and homers (24). Walt Terrell (15-10, 3.85 ERA) led in win percentage (.600), hits (221), earned runs (98), runs (107) and HR/9 (0.4). Randy O'Neal (5-5, 3.24 ERA), Milt Wilcox (1-3, 4.85 ERA) and Juan Berenguer (5-6, 5.59 ERA). Bill Scherrer (3-2, 4.36 ERA) led league in intentional walks (13). All-Star and the most effective pitcher Willie Hernandez (8-10, 2.70 ERA) led in games (74), games finished (64), saves (31), earned run average, ERA+ (151), WHIP (0.900), H/9 (6.9), BB/9 (1.2), SO/BB (5.43) and R/9 (3.2). Chuck Cary (0-1, 3-42 ERA), Aurelio Lopez (3-7, 4.80 ERA) and Doug Bair (2-0, 6.24). Hernandez was spectacular during the three-week period of April 26-May 15 (9 GM, 10.1 IP, 0 ER 0.00 ERA, 6 SV, .059 BA, .086 OBP, .174 OPS, .071 BAbip).

Defense. Detroit made 143 errors for a .977 fielding average. League leaders were pitchers Petry in fielding (1.000) and Terrell in double plays (8). Gold Glove catcher Parrish led in fielding (.993) and wild pitches (40). Brookens led in errors (23) at third, Herndon in double plays (4) at left, and Gibson in outfield errors (11). Trammell at short led the club in dWAR (1.9).

First year Tiger righthander Walt Terrell was splendid during home games (17 GM, 9-2, 2.86 ERA, .215 BA, .293 OBP, .293 SLG, .244 BABIP). He was equally as impressive during the first half (19 GM, 10-4, .235 BA, .311 OBP, .328 SLG, .263 BABIP).

Darrell Evans was 5-for-5 (HR, 3 RBI) on Saturday, June 15, with his 300th homer off 46-year-old Phil Niekro and 55,623 Yankee Stadium fans. Evans crushed Yankee pitching at home September 17-19 (5 HR, 7 RBI, .636 BA, .692 OBP, 2.000 SLG).

1980s Pitching Wins	
1. Jack Morris	162
2. Frank Tanana	61
Milt Wilcox	61
4. Walt Terrell	54
5. Aurelio Lopez	43
6. Willie Hernandez	36
7. Mike Henneman	31
8. Doyle Alexander	29
Dave Rozema	29
10. Jeff Robinson	26

Team. Detroit finished third for Sparky Anderson at 87-75 (.537), with an attendance of 1,899,437. The squad went 10-9 in April, as Kirk Gibson went 4-for-4 (2 HR, 5 RBI) in a 6-5 win over Boston at home on Monday, April 7, with 51,437 fans. Frank Tanana (9 IP, 1 ER), Lance Parrish (HR, 4 RBI) and Chet Lemon 3-for-4 led a 6-1 win over visiting Cleveland on Friday, April 18. Tanana won four straight starts April 18-May 4 (4-0, 34.2 IP, 1.04 ERA, .175 BA, .233 OBP, .242 SLG, .206 BABIP). The Bengals were 13-13 in May, with a 4-1 home win versus Oakland on Saturday, May 24, with Parrish (2 HR, 3 RBI) and Jack Morris (9 IP, 1 ER, 3 H, 8 SO). The club was 14-15 in June including a 11-2 win over Baltimore at home on Wednesday, June 25, behind Morris (W 7-4, 9 IP, 1 ER, 9 SO) and Gibson (2 HR, 5 RBI). Tanana went undefeated June 2-August 8 (10 GM, 5-0, 65.2 IP, 3.29 ERA, .255 BA). Detroit was 17-11 in July with Morris the Pitcher of the Month (6 GM, 5-1, 0.54 ERA, .188 BA, .222 OBP). John Grubb went on a four-game tear July 22-25 at home (6-for-10, 4 HR, 11 RBI, .600 BA, .583 OBP, 1.800 SLG). Morris (W 11-6, 8 IP, 0 ER, 4 H, 6 SO) defeated the visiting Minnesota Twins 12-2 on Wednesday, July 23, aided Gibson (HR, 3 RBI) and Grubb with a sixth inning pinch-hit grand slam home run. The Tigers were 14-16 in August when the team swept back-to-back home double-headers with Cleveland on Tuesday, August 5, as Darrell Evans (HR, 3 RBI) led a 6-5 win followed by a 11-9 Tanana (W 9-4, 7 IP, 2 ER) win with Lou Whitaker (2 HR, 3 RBI) and Tom Brookens (HR, 3 RBI). Players completed the sweep on Thursday with a Morris (W 13-7, 7 IP, 0 ER, 4 H, 5 SO) 15-1 win paced by Whitaker (3 RBI) and Gibson (HR, 3 RBI), followed by a Mark Thurmond (6 IP, 0 ER) 6-2 gem in game two behind Whitaker (3 RBI). Walt Terrell (W 11-9, 9 IP, 0 ER, 1 H) threw a one-hit 3-0 shutout of the Angels at home on Wednesday, August 20. Tanana (W10-6, 9 IP, 0 ER, 10 SO), Darnell Coles (5 RBI), Grubb 3-for-4 (3 RBI) and Gibson (HR, 3 RBI) led a 14-0 shutout of Seattle a home on Saturday, August 23. The team closed 14-11 in September and 5-0 in October. Pitchers Bryan Kelly (6.1 IP, 2 ER, 2 H, 6 SO) and Willie Hernandez (W 8-6, 2.2 IP, 0 ER, 0 H, 5 SO) led a 7-2 win versus visiting Baltimore on Saturday, September 13. Motown logged a 11-4 victory in Baltimore on Saturday, October 4, with Gibson (HR, 4 RBI), Larry Herndon (HR, 3 RBI) and Mike Heath (HR, 3 RBI). Players went 12-1 (.923) against the Orioles, including 7-0 at Memorial Stadium. Detroit was 49-32 (.605) at home, and 38-43 (.469) on the road. The Bengals scored 798 runs and allowed 714. Michigan native Bruce Fields of Lansing Everett High School hit .368 for the class "AAA" Nashville Sounds to win the American Association batting title.

C * LANCE PARRISH

Offense. Detroit had a .263 BA, .338 OBP, .424 SLG, .762 OPS, 2,335 TB and 107 OPS+. All-Star and Silver Slugger Lance Parrish (.257 BA, 22 HR, 62 RBI) at catcher led in isolated power (.226). Darrell Evans (.241 BA, 29 HR, 85 RBI) at first led in homers and walks (91). All-Star Lou Whitaker (.269 BA, 20 HR, 73 RBI) at second led in at bats (584), singles (105), outs (459) and hit streak (16). Darnell Coles (.273 BA, 20 HR, 86 RBI) was at third. Alan Trammell (.277 BA, 21 HR, 75 RBI) at short led in plate appearances (653), runs (107), hits (159), doubles (33), triples (7), WAR (6.4), oWAR (5.5), hitting, times on base (223), base runs (88), runs produced(161), runs created (93), extra base hits (61), total bases (269) and bases produced (353). Larry Herndon (.247 BA, 8 HR, 37 RBI) and Dave Collins (.270 BA, HR, 27 RBI) that led for in-play percentage (78%) were the leftfielders. Chet Lemon (.251 BA, 12 HR, 53 RBI) in center. Player of the Year and most effective hitter Kirk Gibson (.268 BA, 28 HR, 86 RBI) in right led in on-base percentage (.371), slugging (.492), OPS (.863), OPS+ (133), total average (.950), base-out percentage (.968), gross production average (.290), batter run average (.182), secondary average (.442), power/speed number (30.7), steals (34), stolen base runs (6.6) and strikeouts (107). The designated hitter was Johnny Grubb (.333 BA, 13 HR, 51 RBI). Infielder Tom Brookens (.270 BA, 3 HR, 25 RBI) led in BAbip (.307). Pat Sheridan (.237 BA, 6 HR, 19 RBI). The top pinch-hitters were Whitaker at .667 (4-6), Evans .375 (3-8, 2 HR, 5 RBI), Harry Spilman .300 (3-10), Grubb (HR, 7 RBI) and Herndon (3 HR, 12 RBI). Coles and Gibson led for runs batted in (86). Al Liebert (.327 BA) and Blane Fox (55 SB) were stars for class "A" Gastonia.

1980s Pitching Winning Percentage	
1. Aurelio Lopez	.632
2. Jeff Robinson	.605
3. Jack Morris	.577
4. Dave Rozema	.558
5. Frank Tanana	.545
6. Milt Wilcox	.545
7. Juan Berenguer	.543
8. Willie Hernandez	.537
9. Walt Terrell	.529
10. Doyle Alexander	.500

Pitching. Detroit had a 4.02 ERA, 33 CG, 10 SHO, 571 walks, 880 SO, 103 ERA+, 4.45 FIP, 1.347 WHIP, 8.6 H/9, 3.6 BB/9, and 5.5 SO/9. Staff led league in IBB (61) and cheap wins (17). Pitcher of the Year, Tiger of the Year, and most effective pitcher Jack Morris (21-8, 3.27 ERA) led the majors with six shutouts. He led staff in wins, starts (35), complete games (15), innings (267), hits (229), homers (40), strikeouts (223), wild pitches (12), earned run average, ERA+ (127), WHIP (1.165), pWAR (5.1) and quality starts (20). Walt Terrell (15-12, 4.56 ERA) led in losses, walks (98), earned runs (110) and runs (116). Tiger Rookie of the Year Eric King (11-4, 3.51 ERA) led in win percentage (.733). Frank Tanana (12-9, 4.16 ERA), Randy O'Neal (3-7, 4.33 ERA), Dan Petry (5-10, 4.66 ERA) and Dave LaPoint (3-6, 5.72 ERA). Willie Hernandez (8-7, 3.55 ERA) led in games (64), games finished (54), saves (24), LOB% (82.3), FIP (3.82), DICE (4.05), BB/9 (2.1), SO/9 (7.8) and SO/BB (3.67). Mark Thurmond (4-1, 1.92 ERA), Bill Campbell (3-6, 3.88 ERA) and Jim Slaton (0-0, 4.05 ERA). Steve Searcy (11-6 .647, 3.30 ERA) was with class "AA" Glens Falls.

Defense. The Detroit defense committed 108 errors during the 1986 season for a .982 fielding average and led the Eastern Division in assists (1,707). Tiger league leaders were pitchers Terrell and Petry with a perfect fielding percentage of 1.000.

Jack Morris was superb in July (6 GM, 5-1, 0.54 ERA, 50 IP, 47 SO, 4 CG, 3 SHO, .188 BA, .222 OBP, .261 SLG, .248 BABIP) recording three straight shutouts compiling a streak of 44.2 consecutive innings without allowing an earned run. He had a September to remember as well (7 GM, 6-0, 2.26 ERA, 63.2 IP, 48 SO, 5 CG, 2 SHO, .187 BA, .245 OBP, .326 SLG, .195 BABIP).

1980s Pitching Games Started	
1. Jack Morris	332
2. Milt Wilcox	151
3. Frank Tanana	150
4. Walt Terrell	131
5. Doyle Alexander	78
6. Juan Berenguer	60
Jeff Robinson	60
8. Dave Rozema	56
9. Dan Schatzeder	40
10. Jerry Ujdur	37

Team. Sparky Anderson Detroit (98-62 .605) to first place, with 2,061,830 fans. Players lost the ALCS in five games to Minnesota, when Mike Reilly from Battle Creek St. Philip Catholic Central High School was an umpire. The Tigers were 9-12 in April when Billy Bean 4-for-6, Dave Bergman 4-for-5 and Tom Brookens (HR, 3 RBI) led a 13-2 win over visiting Kansas City on Saturday, April 15. The Bengals won 12-4 in Anaheim on Thursday, April 30, with Jack Morris (9 IP, 8 SO), as 23-year-old rookie Matt Nokes hit a grand slam. Detroit finished 15-11 in May including a 15-2 home win facing California on Tuesday, May 12. The win was led by Mike Heath 4-for-6 (HR, 2 RBI) and Darnell Coles (HR, 4 RBI). The squad was 17-9 in June including a 15-3 win at Cleveland on Wednesday, June 3, aided by Morris (W 7-2, 7 IP, 2 ER), Chet Lemon 3-for-5 (HR, 4 RBI) and Brookens (HR, 4 RBI). Detroit won 18-8 in Boston on Sunday, June 7, with Nokes 3-for-5 (2 HR, 4 RBI), Lemon 3-for-3 (HR, 4 RBI) and Brookens (HR, 3 RBI). Morris (W 8-2), Bill Madlock 4-for-5 (2 RBI) and Kirk Gibson 3-for-5 (2 RBI) led an 8-5 win against visiting Milwaukee on Tuesday, June 9. Reliever Eric King (4.2 IP, 2 H, 0 ER) and Madlock went 3-for-5 (3 HR, 4 RBI) to lead an 11-inning 8-7 home win over Baltimore on June 28. The Bengals had three straight ninth-inning homers from pinch-hitter John Grubb, Nokes and Madlock to tie the game at seven, as Alan Trammell had a walk-off single for the win. Motown went 17-9 in July with a 12-5 Tiger win in Anaheim on Saturday, July 11, behind Mike Henneman (W 4-0, 4.2 IP, 0 ER, 2 H), Heath (4 RBI), Trammell 5-for-6 (3 RBI) and Lou Whitaker's pinch-hit two-run double. Detroit swept the Twins at home August 18-20. Morris (W 14-6, 7 IP, 2 ER, 3 H, 7 SO) and Larry Herndon (2 HR, 5 RBI) paced a 11-2 win on Tuesday. Walt Terrell (9 IP, 1 ER) led a 7-1 victory on Wednesday. Doyle Alexander (8 IP, 0 ER, 5 H) made his home debut with an 8-0 shutout on Thursday with 45,804 fans at Tiger Stadium. The club closed 17-12 in September and 4-0 in October. Trammell was the Player of the Month (7 HR, 20 RBI, .417 BA, .677 SLG) and Alexander the Pitcher of the Month (6-0, 1.09 ERA, 2 SHO, .200 BA, .225 BAbip). Herndon homered as Tanana (W 15-10, 9 IP, 0 ER, 6 H, 9 SO) shutout Toronto 1-0 at home on Sunday, October 4, to clinch the division title. Detroit went 11-2 (.846) against Boston, 54-27 (.667) at home, 44-37 (.543) on the road, scored 896 runs and allowed 735. Pedro Chavez (.339 BA) was at class "AA" Glens Falls and Pat Austin (45 SB) played for class "A" Lakeland.

P * WALT TERRELL

Offense. Detroit had a .272 BA, .349 OBP, .451 SLG, .800 OPS, 2,548 TB and 114 OPS+. Tiger Rookie of the Year and All-Star catcher Matt Nokes (.289 BA, 32 HR, 87 RBI) led in isolated power (.247). Darrell Evans (.257 BA, 34 HR, 99 RBI) at first led in homers, secondary average (.447) and walks (100). Lou Whitaker (.265 BA, 16 HR, 59 RBI) at second led in plate appearances (684), at bats (604), runs (110), doubles (38), triples (6) and outs (462). Tom Brookens (.241 BA, 13 HR, 59 RBI) was at third. Player of the Year, Tiger of the Year, and most effective hitter Alan Trammell (.343 BA, 28 HR, 105 RBI) at short led MLB in oWAR (8.3). He led club in games (151), hits (205), singles (140), runs batted in, on-base percentage (.402), slugging (.551), OPS (.953), OPS+ (155), total average (1.015), base-out percentage (1.019), gross production average (.319), WAR (8.2), batters run average (.221), hitting, BAbip (.335), in-play percentage (79%), times on base (268), base runs (120), runs produced (186), runs created (132), extra base hits (65), total bases (329), bases produced (410) stolen base runs (5.1) and hit streak (21). Kirk Gibson (.277 BA, 24 HR, 79 RBI) in left led in power/speed number (25.0), steals (26) and strikeouts (117). Chet Lemon (.277 BA, 20 HR, 75 RBI) was in center, Pat Sheridan (.259 BA, 6 HR, 49 RBI) in right and Bill Madlock (.279 BA, 14 HR, 50 RBI) the designated hitter. Larry Herndon (.324 BA, 9 HR, 47 RBI) and Mike Heath (.281 BA, 8 HR, 33 RBI). The top pinch-hitters were Evans at .600 (6-10, 4 RBI), Lemon .455 (5-11, 3 RBI) and Herndon at .381 (8-21, 5 RBI). Evans reached base in eight consecutive games as a pinch-hitter June 20-September 10.

1980s Pitching Complete Games	
1. Jack Morris	133
2. Dan Petry	45
3. Milt Wilcox	39
4. Walt Terrell	35
5. Frank Tanana	20
6. Doyle Alexander	13
7. Dan Schatzeder	10
8. Jeff Robinson	9
9. Jerry Ujdur	7
10. Dave Rozema	5

Pitching. The Tigers had a 4.02 ERA, 33 CG, eight SHO, 563 walks, 976 SO, 106 ERA+, 4.37 FIP, 1.369 WHIP, 8.8 H/9, 3.5 BB/9 and 6.0 SO/9. The Pitcher of the Year, Sporting News Rookie Pitcher of the Year, and most effective pitcher Mike Henneman (11-3, 2.98 ERA) led in win percentage (.786), earned run average, ERA+ (143), FIP (3.42), DICE (3.55), WHIP (1.200), HR/9 (0.7) and R/9 (3.4). Walt Terrell (17-10, 4.05 ERA, 21 QS) led in starts (35), hits (254), walks (94), earned runs (110) and runs (123). Jack Morris (18-11, 3.38 ERA, 21 QS) led MLB in wild pitches (24). He led the staff in wins, losses, complete games (11), innings (266), homers (39), strikeouts (208), LOB% (78.8), pWAR (5.1) and H/9 (7.7). Frank Tanana (15-10, 3.91 ERA) led in shutouts (3), BB/9 (2.3) and SO/BB (2.61). Dan Petry (9-7, 5.61 ERA) led in HBP (10). Doyle Alexander (9-0, 1.53 ERA) and rookie Jeff Robinson (9-6, 5.37 ERA). Willie Hernandez (3-4, 3.67 ERA) led in games finished (31). Nate Snell (1-2, 3.96 ERA), Mark Thurmond (0-1, 4.23 ERA) and Eric King (6-9, 4.89 ERA). Class "AAA" Toledo had Paul Gibson (14-7 .667), Bill Laskey (12-6 .667) and Nate Snell (6-1 .857, 2.34 ERA). Terrell closed year undefeated August 15-October 4 (8-0, 3.12 ERA).

Defense. The Detroit defense committed 122 errors in 1987 for a .980 fielding average, as they led all the Eastern Division teams in chances (6,193). Tiger league leaders were pitchers Jack Morris and Frank Tanana in fielding percentage (1.000).

Detroit traded John Smoltz ("AA" Glens Falls, 4-10, 5.68 ERA) for Doyle Alexander (Atlanta, 5-10, 4.13 ERA) on August 12. Doyle (9-0, 1.53 ERA) was a reminder of the 1972 acquisition of Woodie Fryman (10-3, 2.06 ERA) that led to a division title.

Class "A" Fayetteville had 218 stolen bases, led by Basilio Cabrera 38, Milt Cuyler 27, Phil Clark 25, Manny Mantrana 25, Darryl Martin 25, Arnie Beyeler 20, Ramon Solano 14, Zack Doster 13, Paul Foster 13, Torey Lovullo 6, and Dean Decillis 5.

1980s Pitching Earned Run Average	
1. Dave Rozema	2.34
2. Willie Hernandez	2.98
3. Aurelio Lopez	3.62
4. Jack Morris	3.66
5. Juan Berenguer	3.87
Frank Tanana	3.87
7. Milt Wilcox	3.89
8. Doyle Alexander	3.91
9. Walt Terrell	4.10
10. Jeff Robinson	4.15

Team. Detroit finished second for manager Sparky Anderson at 88-74 (.543), with 2,081,162 fans. The club was 13-8 in April, as Frank Tanana of Detroit Catholic Central High School went undefeated during the month (5-0, 3.62 ERA). The club won 11-4 in Kansas City on Saturday, April 9, behind Alan Trammell 4-for-5 and Lou Whitaker 4-for-6 (2 RBI). Tanana (7.1 IP, 1 ER, 5 H) won 4-1 versus Texas at home on Tuesday, April 12. Players were 15-12 in May, that included Jack Morris (9 IP, 0 ER, 2 H) outdueling Dan Petry (9 IP, 1 ER). Trammell homered for a 1-0 victory in California on Wednesday, May 4. Detroit had a 18-9 record in June when Jeff Robinson (W 8-2, 9 IP, 0 ER, 5 H) shutout Baltimore 1-0 at home on Wednesday, June 15. Motown had a 15-12 mark in July including a Doyle Alexander (W 8-4, 7 IP, 0 ER, 5 SO) 11-0 home win against the Angels on Friday, July 1. Dave Bergman led off a seven run second inning with a homer and had a two-run single later in the inning. Bergman reached base 12 out of 13 plate appearances July 22-26 (4 GM, 6-for-7 .857 BA, 4 BB, .909 OBP, 1.000 SLG, 1.000 BAbip). Walt Terrell (9 IP, 0 ER, 5 H) shutout visiting Texas 3-0 on Saturday, July 30. The squad went 14-16 in August, with an 18-6 in Boston on Sunday, August 14. The Tigers hammered Roger Clemens (1.1 IP, 8 ER, 5 H, 3 BB) and Mike Smithson (1.1 IP, 5 ER, 6 H, 2 BB). Bergman (2 RBI), Chet Lemon (HR, 5 RBI) and Darrell Evans (5 RBI) had three hits apiece. Detroit closed 11-17 in September and 2-0 in October. Evans slugged his 400th career home run in a 3-1 home win over Cleveland on Tuesday, September 20. 22-year-old rookie Torey Lovullo was impressive the week of September 23-30 (.429 BA, .429 OBP, .857 SLG, .417 BAbip). Motown was 9-3 (.750) against Chicago and Seattle. The Bengals were 50-31 (.617) at home, including 6-0 (1.000) versus both Kansas City and New York, and finished 38-43 (.469) on the road. Motown scored 703 runs and allowed 658. The Eastern League Champion Glens Falls Tigers (90-57 .584) were led by Shawn Holman (52 GM, 8-3 .727, 1.87 ERA, 10 SV) and Eastern League Pitcher of the Year Cesar Mejia (14-5 .737, 2.43 ERA, 4 SHO) that threw a no-hitter on April 17.

P * JEFF ROBINSON

Offense. Detroit finished with a .250 BA, .324 OBP, .378 SLG, .703 OPS, 2,056 TB and 100 OPS+. Catcher Matt Nokes (.251 BA, 16 HR, 53 RBI) led in isolated power (.173). First was manned by Ray Knight (.217 BA, 3 HR, 33 RBI) that led for in-play percentage (82%) and Dave Bergman (.294 BA, 5 HR, 35 RBI). Lou Whitaker (.275 BA, 12 HR, 55 RBI) at second led in on-base percentage (.376). Tom Brookens (.243 BA, 5 HR, 38 RBI) was the third baseman. Player of the Year, Tiger of the Year and most effective hitter Alan Trammell (.311 BA, 15 HR, 69 RBI) at short led in runs (73), hits (145), singles (105), runs batted in, slugging (.464), OPS (.836), OPS+ (138), total average (.794), base-out percentage (.809), gross production average (.284), WAR (6.0), oWAR (5.4), batters run average (.173), hitting, BAbip (.316), base runs (76), runs produced (127), runs created (81), power/speed number (9.5) and hit streak (12). Pat Sheridan (.254 BA, 11 HR, 47 RBI) and Luis Salazar (.270 BA) played in left. Gold Glove centerfielder Gary Pettis (.210 BA, 3 HR, 36 RBI) led in steals (44) and stolen base runs (7.2). Chet Lemon (.264 BA, 17 HR, 64 RBI, 144 GM) in right led in plate appearances (582), at bats (512), doubles (29), times on base (201), extra base hits (50), total bases (223), bases produced (283) and outs (401). Designated hitter Darrell Evans (.208 BA, 22 HR, 64 RBI) led in homers, secondary average (.357), walks (84) and strikeouts (84). Larry Herndon (.224 BA, 4 HR, 20 RBI). The leading pinch-hitters were Salazar at .556 (5-9, 4 RBI), Fred Lynn .500 (2-4, HR, 5 RBI) and Whitaker .333 (3-9). Class "AA" Glens Falls had the Eastern League MVP Rob Richie (.309 BA, 14 HR, 82 RBI).

1980s Pitching Innings Pitched	
1. Jack Morris	2,443.2
2. Milt Wilcox	977.1
3. Frank Tanana	971.0
4. Walt Terrell	897.0
5. Dave Rozema	737.2
6. Aurelio Lopez	586.0
7. Doyle Alexander	540.1
8. Willie Hernandez	483.2
9. Juan Berenguer	427.2
10. Jeff Robinson	377.1

Pitching. The Tigers had a 3.71 ERA, 34 CG, six SHO, 497 walks, 890 SO, 103 ERA+, 3.98 FIP, 1.285 WHIP, 8.5 H/9, 3.1 BB/9, and 5.5 SO/9, as staff led league in intentional walks (68) and quality starts (94). Pitcher of the Year Jeff Robinson (13-6, 2.98 ERA) led league in H/9 (6.3). He led staff in win percentage (.684) and pWAR (3.7). The most effective pitcher Mike Henneman (9-6, 1.87 ERA) led league in intentional walks (10), with club lead in games (65), games finished (51), saves (22), LOB% (85.0), ERA, ERA+ (205), FIP (3.35), DICE (3.58), WHIP (1.051), HR/9 (0.7) and R/9 (6.3). Jack Morris (15-13, 3.94 ERA) led in wins, innings (235), walks (83), strikeouts (168), wild pitches (11) and quality starts (20). Walt Terrell (7-16, 3.97 ERA) led in losses and complete games (11). Doyle Alexander (14-11, 4.32 ERA) led in hits (260), homers (30), earned runs (110), runs (122), walks per nine (1.8) and SO/BB (2.74). Frank Tanana (14-11, 4.21 ERA). Willie Hernandez (6-5, 3.06 ERA) led in SO/9 (7.8). Tiger Rookie of the Year Paul Gibson (4-2, 2.93 ERA). Robinson and Morris led in shutouts (2). Henneman excelled July 18-August 22 (13 GM, 2-0, 5 SV, 17.2 IP, 0 ER, 0.00 ERA, .177 BA, .215 OBP, .194 SLG, .224 BAbip). Robinson was undefeated during April 26-June 25 (10 GM, 7-0, 2.34 ERA, .202 BA, .227 BAbip). Eric King (4-1, 3.41) and Don Heinkel (0-0, 3.96 ERA). Steve Searcy (13-7 .650, 2.59 ERA) was at class "AAA" Toledo.

Defense. The Detroit committed 109 errors for a .982 fielding percentage and led the league in defensive efficiency (.718). The lone Tiger league leader was Morris with 31 pitcher putouts, as shortstop Trammell led his team in defensive War 1.5).

Frank Tanana went 11-4 in first half, 5-0 in April, 4-0 versus Texas and 2-0 when Tim Welke from Coldwater High School was the home plate umpire. Alan Trammell had four-hit games of 4-for-5 on April 9, 4-for-5 on May 20 and 4-for-6 on August 27.

The class "A" Lakeland Tigers had 226 steals, with leaders Milt Cuyler 50, Basilio Cabrera 30, Blane Fox 28, Lance Hudson 26, Wayne Housie 24, Phil Clark 16, Arnie Beyeler 14, Doyle Bathazar 10, Dean Decillis 9, Ron Marigny 5 and Luis Galindo 4.

1980s Pitching Walks		
1.	Jack Morris	858
2.	Walt Terrell	365
3.	Milt Wilcox	359
4.	Frank Tanana	293
5.	Aurelio Lopez	237
6.	Juan Berenguer	207
7.	Jeff Robinson	172
8.	Jeff King	157
9.	Doyle Alexander	148
10.	Willie Hernandez	138

Team. Detroit finished last with Sparky Anderson at 59-103 (.364), with an attendance of 1,543,656. The club was 8-14 in April including a Jeff Robinson (9 IP, 0 ER, 4 H, 7 SO) 3-0 home shutout of the Twins on Thursday, April 13. Players were 14-14 in May when Keith Moreland excelled May 10-17 (.519 BA, .567 OBP, .741 SLG, .542 BAbip) raising his average from .259 to .346. Moreland had multiple hits in four straight games May 10-14 and was 4-for-4 on May 17. Motown and Doyle Alexander (7 IP, 0 ER, 3 H, 5 SO) won 4-2 at Chicago on Monday, May 29, as Matt Nokes (HR, 4 RBI) hit a fourth-inning grand slam homer. The Bengals won 10-3 the next day behind Lou Whitaker (HR, 3 RBI), Moreland (HR, 4 RBI) and Frank Tanana (6.1 IP, 3 ER, 6 SO). The squad went 8-18 in June when reliever Mike Schwabe (6.1 IP, 2 ER, 4 H) won 16-5 in Baltimore on Friday, June 30. Fred Lynn went 3-for-4, Chet Lemon (HR, 5 RBI) and Mike Heath 4-for-5 (2 HR, 3 RBI) scoring four runs, as Detroit had an eight run eighth inning. The club was 6-21 in July that included a 16-inning 5-4 loss at California on Saturday, July 22, when Tiger starter Paul Gibson (10 IP, 4 ER, 6 SO) faced 40 batters and threw 154 pitches. The Bengals logged a 11-22 mark in August with 12 straight losses to end the month. Native Detroiter Frank Tanana (9 IP, 0 ER, 2 H, 10 SO) threw a 136 pitch 4-0 home shutout of Baltimore on Wednesday, August 16. The team closed 11-14 in September and 1-0 in October, as Lynn (2 HR, 4 RBI) scored four runs in a 12-3 Jack Morris (9 IP, 3 ER) win over visiting Cleveland on Sunday, September 3. Doyle Alexander (6.2 IP, 1 ER, 4 H) had a 5-1 home win over Kansas City the next day, with Doug Strange 3-for-4 (HR, 2 RBI) and Lynn (HR, 2 RBI) hit his 300th home run. Lynn went 4-for-5 during a Steve Searcy (7 IP, 2 ER) 9-2 triumph at Minnesota on Sunday, September 17. Lynn was superb September 3-17 (10 GM, 15-for-37, 3 HR, 12 RBI, .405 BA, .432 OBP, .730 SLG)). Detroit finished 38-43 (.469) at home, including 6-0 (1.000) versus Kansas City and 6-1 (.857) against Cleveland. The Bengals were 21-60 (.259) on the road, scored 617 runs and allowed their opponents 816.

P * MIKE HENNEMAN

Offense. Detroit finished with a .242 BA, .318 OBP, .351 SLG, .669 OPS, 1,909 TB and 91 OPS+. Mike Heath (.263 BA, 10 HR, 43 RBI) was the catcher, with Dave Bergman (.268 BA, 7 HR, 37 RBI) at first base. Player of the Year, Tiger of the Year and most effective hitter Lou Whitaker (.251 BA, 28 HR, 85 RBI) at second led in games (148), plate appearances (611), at bats (509), hits (128), doubles (21), homers, runs batted in, slugging (.462), OPS (.822), OPS+ (133), total average (.844), base-out percentage (.855), gross production average (.278), WAR (5.3), oWAR (5.1), batters run average (.166), secondary average (.391), times on base (220), base runs (86), runs produced (134), runs created (85), isolated power (.210), power/speed number (9.9), extra base hits (50), total bases (235), bases produced (330), walks (89) and outs (401). Rick Schu (.214 BA, 7 HR, 21 RBI) was at third and Alan Trammell (.243 BA, 5 HR, 43 RBI) at short, with Fred Lynn (.241 BA, 11 HR, 46 RBI) in left. Gold Glove centerfielder Gary Pettis (.257 BA, HR, 18 RBI) led in singles (99), triples (6), on-base percentage (.375), BAbip (.335), steals (43), stolen base runs (3.9) and strikeouts (106). Chet Lemon (.237 BA, 7 HR, 47 RBI) played in right. Designated hitter Keith Moreland (.299 BA, 5 HR, 35 RBI) led in hitting, in-play percentage (81%) and hit streak (11). Reserves Gary Ward (.251 BA, 9 HR, 29 RBI), Matt Nokes (.250 BA, 9 HR, 39 RBI), Kenny Williams (.205 BA, 6 HR, 23 RBI) and Mike Brumley (.198 BA, HR, 11 RBI). The best pinch-hitter was Lemon at .308 (4-13, 5 RBI). Whitaker and Pettis led in runs (77).

1980s Pitching Strikeouts		
1.	Jack Morris	1,629
2.	Frank Tanana	646
3.	Milt Wilcox	528
4.	Walt Terrell	450
5.	Aurelio Lopez	413
6.	Willie Hernandez	384
7.	Juan Berenguer	337
	Doyle Alexander	265
9.	Jeff Robinson	252
10.	Dave Rozema	221

Pitching. The team had a 4.53 ERA, 24 CG, three SHO, 652 walks, 831 SO, 85 ERA+, 4.43 FIP, 1.518 WHIP, 9.5 H/9, 4.1 BB/9, and 5.2 SO/9. Staff led league in homers (150), intentional walks (91), earned runs (719), runs (816), left on base (1,236), batters faced (6,334) and tough losses (25). Pitcher of the Year and All-Star Mike Henneman (11-4, 3.70 ERA) led in games (60), wins, win percentage (.733), games finished (35), FIP (3.67), DICE (3.91), hits per nine (8.4), homers per nine (0.4) and strikeouts per nine (6.9). The most effective pitcher Frank Tanana (10-14, 3.58 ERA, 33 GS, 1 SHO) led staff in innings (223.2), strikeouts (147), hit by pitch (8), LOB% (73.0), earned run average, ERA+ (108), WHIP (1.346), pWAR (3.1), BB/9 (3.0), SO/BB (1.99), R/9 (4.2) and quality starts (21). Doyle Alexander (6-18, 4.44 ERA, 33 GS, 1 SHO) led MLB in losses, with staff lead for hits (245), homers (28), walks (76), earned runs (110) and runs (118). Jack Morris (6-14, 4.86 ERA) led in complete games (10) and wild pitches (12). Tiger Rookie of the Year Kevin Ritz (4-6, 4.38 ERA), Jeff Robinson (4-5, 4.73 ERA, 1 SHO) and Charles Hudson (1-5, 6.35 ERA). Willie Hernandez (2-2, 5.74 ERA) led in saves (15). Frank Williams (3-3, 3.64 ERA), Ed Nunez (3-4, 4.17 ERA), Paul Gibson (4-8, 4.64 ERA) and Mike Schwabe (2-4, 6.04 ERA). Alexander and Tanana led the league in tough Losses (7). Tanana dominated White Sox batters in 1989 (3 GM, 3-0, 2.70 ERA, 0.986 WHIP, .202 BA).

Defense. Motown had 130 errors for a .979 fielding average. League leaders were pitcher Tanana in fielding (1.000), catcher Heath in assists (66) and double plays (10), Whitaker in putouts (327) at second and Trammell in team dWAR (2.3) at short.

Keith Moreland excelled May 10-17 (14-for-27 .519 BA, .567 OBP, .741 SLG, .542 BAbip). He had an 11-game hit streak May 22-June 1 (.375 BA, .444 OBP, .650 SLG). Moreland reached base in 30 straight games June 10-July 16 (.325 BA, .408 OBP).

Billy Bean (.315 BA) and Shawn Holman (3-1 .750, 1.91 ERA, 11 SV) were at class "AAA" Toledo. Rusty Meacham (10-3 .769, 2.29 ERA) was at class "A" Fayetteville. The class "A" Lakeland Tigers had Shawn Hare (.324 BA), Basilio Cabrera (45 SB), Dave Richards (7-3 .700, 1.80 ERA), with closers Dan O'Neill (4-1 .800, 0.98 ERA, 10 SV) and Kurt Knudsen (2.15 ERA, 10 SV).

Player of the Decade. Travis Fryman (.274 BA, 149 HR, 679 RBI) was Player of the Decade. He was a four-time All-Star selection and averaged 20 home runs and 93 runs batted 1991-1997. Travis earned the 1992 shortstop Silver Slugger Award. Fryman led the team in defensive WAR in 1992 and 1995-1997, as he led third basemen in fielding for 1996 (.979) and 1997 (.978). Highlights by year included 2-for-5 (3B, 4 RBI) on Wednesday, September 19, 1990 in Anaheim; 4-for-6 (3 RBI) in Milwaukee on Monday, May 27, 1991; 2-for-4 (2B, 3B, 5 RBI) in Toronto on Thursday, June 18, 1992; 5-for-5 (2 2B, 3B, HR, 4 RBI, 12 TB) facing the Yankees at home on Wednesday, July 28, 1993; 5-for-5 (2 RBI) at Baltimore on Wednesday, June 1, 1994; 2-for-4 (2 HR, 4 RBI) against Boston at home on Wednesday, August 2, 1995. He had four straight multi-hit games September 22-25, 1996 (10-for-17, .588 BA, .632 OBP, .647 SLG, .588 BAbip); and six straight multi-hit games June 24-29, 1997 (14-for-28 .500 BA, .643 SLG, .560 BAbip).

1990s

Year	W – L	Pct.	Pl
1990	79-83	.488	3
1991	84-78	.519	2
1992	75-87	.463	6
1993	**85-77**	**.525**	3
1994	53-62	.461	5
1995	60-84	.417	4
1996	53-109	.327	5
1997	79-83	.488	3
1998	65-97	.401	5
1999	69-92	.429	3
	702-852	.452	

All-Decade Team. Manager Sparky Anderson (1990s: 436-471 .481) retired at the end of the 1995 season after 26 years. He was 2,194-1,834 (.545) overall, with Cincinnati nine years (863-586 .596) and 18 years in Detroit (1,331-1,248 .516). He was the 1984 and 1987 American League Manager of the Year. Catcher Mickey Tettleton (.249 BA, 112 HR, 333 RBI) led team in OPS (.867), OPS+ (135), total average (.923), gross production average (.294), secondary average (.453) and walk percentage (18.3). Tony Clark (.275 BA, 127 HR, 402 RBI) at first led in slugging (.503) and total base average (1.9). Second baseman Lou Whitaker (.277 BA, 95 HR, 363 RBI). Alan Trammell (.283 BA, 47 HR, 282 RBI) at short led in strikeout percentage (9.0). Third baseman Travis Fryman (.274 BA, 149 HR, 679 RBI) led in games (1,096), plate appearances (4,792), at-bats (4,297), hits (1,176), singles (769), doubles (229), triples (29), oWAR (24.8), dWAR (6.8), times on base (1,597), extra base hits (407), total bases (1,910), bases produced (2,358) and strikeouts (931). Left fielder Bobby Higginson (.277 BA, 104 HR, 356 RBI). Centerfielder Tony Phillips (.281 BA, 61 HR, 309 RBI) led in on-base percentage (.395) and BAbip (.319). Right-fielder Rob Deer (.212 BA, 71 HR, 167 RBI). Designated hitter Cecil Fielder (.258 BA, 245 HR, 758 RBI) led in home runs (245), runs batted in (758), extra bases on long hits (884) and for bases produced average (2.4).

Pitcher of the Decade. Bill Gullickson (51-36 .586, 4.68 ERA) led in losses, starts (116), complete games (11), high quality starts (46), innings (722.2), hits (826), homers (109), earned runs (376), runs (403), BB/9 (2.03), batters faced (3,093), pitches (10,368), no decisions (29) and cheap wins (12). His best year as a Tiger was 1991 (20-9 .690, 3.90 ERA), with an impressive May 23-June 26 (6 GM, 4-1, 2.17 ERA). His 1991 totals included 10-4 at home and 10-5 on the road; 11-4 in first half and 9-5 after the All-Star break; and 4-0 against Seattle. Gullickson was solid in 1992 (14-13 .519, 4.34 ERA) when he finished 3-0 versus the Seattle Mariners. His 1993 season (13-9 .591, 5.37 ERA) included a 6-2 record pitching in away games, 6-0 (2.68 ERA) during August and 2-0 against Seattle. Gullickson dominated the Mariners (11 GM, 9-0 1.000, 81.2 IP, 2.86 ERA) during the 1990s decade. There were 40,455 fans in attendance when he defeated Seattle in the Kingdome, with a 13-0 shutout on Saturday, May 9, 1992 (W 5-2, 9 IP, 0 ER, 5 H).

1990s
Attendance

Year	Attn.	Avg.	Rk
1990	1,495,785	18,466	13
1991	1,641,661	20,267	12
1992	1,423,963	17,800	13
1993	1,971,421	24,339	12
1994	1,184,783	20,427	13
1995	1,180,979	16,402	11
1996	1,168,610	14,427	13
1997	1,365,157	16,854	13
1998	1,409,391	17,400	11
1999	**2,026,441**	**25,018**	09

All-Decade Pitchers. All-Star David Wells (26-19 .578, 3.78 ERA) went 19-5 .792 at home during the 1990s. His 1995 season (10-3 .769, 3.04 ERA, 159 ERA+) included 13 of 18 games were high-quality starts. Wells pitched well at home in 1995 (8-0 1.000, 2.95 ERA, 73.1 IP, 18 BB, 48 SO). Justin Thompson (36-43 .456, 3.98 ERA) led in losses, quality starts (60), strikeouts (427), pWAR (13.1), pick offs (15) and tough losses (15), as the 1997 All-Star (15-11 .577, 3.02 ERA) dominated lefthanders (.182 BA, .222 BAbip). Brian Moehler (35-42 .455, 4.50 ERA) led in dominant starts (10) and shutouts (6), with 1998 (14-13 .519, 3.90 ERA) his best when he went 9-3 (.750, 2.83 ERA) at home. Frank Tanana (25-31 .530, 4.44 ERA) was his best in 1991 (13-12 .520, 3.77 ERA) when he was superb May 29-July 27 (9 GM, 5-2, 1,84 ERA, .222 BA). Doug Brocail (12-10 .545, 2.83 ERA) led for technical runs allowed (3.11), earned run average, ERA+ (168), WHIP (1.168), H/9 (7.32), RA/9 (3.11) and holds (50). Mike Henneman (26-21 .553, 3.19 ERA) led in games (311), games finished (255), saves (117), intentional walks (46), wild pitches (26), FIP (3.41), DICE (3.44), HR/9 (0.48) and starred in 1991 (10-2 .833, 2.88 ERA, 21 SV, 146 ERA+). Todd Jones (10-12 .455, 3.92 ERA) closed in 1997 (5-4 .556, 3.09 ERA, 31 SV, 149 ERA+) and was exemplary for June 18-August 13 (21 GM, 1-0, 22.1 IP, 2 ER, 0.81 ERA, 15 SV, .207 BA). Paul Gibson (10-11 .476, 3.82 ERA) was superb May 2-June 21 of 1990 (20 GM, 2-0, 32 IP, 2 ER, 0.56 ERA). Joe Boever (16-10 .615, 5.01 ERA) led the 1990s in win percentage, with his best year in 1994 (9-2 .818, 3.98 ERA), including success facing lefthanders (.214 BA, .241 BAbip) and going undefeated during games at home (23 GM, 7-0 1.000, 3.15 ERA).

Alan Trammell opened 1990 on a 10-game hitting streak, reached base in the first 22 games, 4-for-5 (3 RBI) on Tuesday, May 22, 4-for-5 (1 HR) on Monday, July 16, 4-for-5 (3 2B, 1 HR, 3 RBI) on Sunday, August 12, and won a Silver Slugger Award.

Cecil Fielder was the first player to hit a home run against a team in four different cities during a season. He homered facing the Oakland Athletics in Las Vegas on April 6, at Detroit on April 28, in Oakland on June 25 and at New York on August 23.

1990s Team Hitting				
YEAR	AVG	HR	RBI	SB
1990	.259	172	714	82
1991	.247	209	778	109
1992	.256	182	746	66
1993	**.275**	178	**853**	104
1994	.265	161	622	46
1995	.247	159	619	73
1996	.256	204	741	87
1997	.258	176	743	**161**
1998	.264	165	691	122
1999	.261	**212**	704	108

Team. Sparky Anderson led third place Detroit (79-83 .488), with 1,495,785 fans. The team went 8-12 in April, defeating Milwaukee 13-5 at home on Saturday, April 28, with Cecil Fielder (2 HR, 6 RBI) and Chet Lemon (HR, 2 RBI). Players were 12-17 in May including a 11-7 loss in Toronto, as 49,206 SkyDome fans witnessed 10 home runs. Fielder 4-for-5 (3 HR, 5 RBI) and Lemon (2 HR) had the five Detroit homers. Jeff Robinson (9 IP, 0 ER, 4 H, 7 SO) had a 12-0 shutout in Texas on Wednesday, May 16, with Tony Phillips (4 RBI) and Alan Trammell (HR, 3 RBI). The club was 16-12 in June including a sweep in Cleveland. Dan Petry (W 5-2, 5 IP, 0 ER, 4 SO) and Ed Nunez (SV 1, 4 IP, 0 ER, 4 SO) threw a 6-2 win on Tuesday, June 5. Fielder (3 HR, 5 RBI) led a 6-4 win on Wednesday, as Brian Dubois (8 IP, 0 ER, 4 H) paced an 8-0 shutout on Thursday. Detroit finished 13-15 in July that included a 13-7 win at Comiskey Park on Tuesday, July 3, behind Lou Whitaker (3B, HR, 5 RBI), Fielder (HR, 3 RBI) and Jerry Don Gleaton (SV 2, 4 IP, 0 ER). Players won 17-9 at home over Boston on Saturday, July 28, led by Larry Sheets (HR, 6 RBI), with a 10-run sixth inning. The Tigers were 14-13 in August with Player of the Month Fielder (.298 BA, 9 HR, 25 RBI, 21 BB, .432 OBP, .681 SLG). Petry (7.2 IP, 2 ER), Dave Bergman 4-for-5 (2 RBI) and John Shelby with a three-run ninth inning pinch-hit homer led a 7-2 win at Boston on Sunday, August 5. Motown beat visiting Oakland 14-4 on Saturday, August 25, with Shelby (HR, 3 RBI) and Fielder (2 HR, 5 RBI) that became the first Tiger to clear the left-field roof. Motown closed 14-13 in September and 2-1 in October, as Walt Terrell (7 IP 0 ER, 4 H, 5 SO) and Trammell (HR, 3 RBI) led a 5-0 home shutout of Toronto on Monday, September 3. Ward (HR, 4 RBI) and Fielder (2 HR, 5 RBI) powered a 10-3 win in New York on Wednesday, October 3, as Fielder became the first Tiger since 1938 to hit 50 homers. Future Hall-of-Famer Jack Morris (9 IP, 6 H, 3 ER) got the win in his last game as a Tiger. Motown finished 49-32 (.605) at home, and 35-46 (.432) on the road. Detroit scored 750 runs, as they allowed 754.

1B * CECIL FIELDER

Offense. Detroit had a .259 BA, .337 OBP, .409 SLG, .746 OPS, 2,239 TB and 107 OPS+. Mike Heath (.270 BA, 7 HR, 38 RBI) caught. Player of the Year, All-Star, Silver Slugger, Tiger of the Year, and most effective hitter Cecil Fielder (.277 BA, 51 HR, 132 RBI) at first led MLB in homers, runs batted in, slugging (.592), AB/HR (11.2) and strikeouts (182). He led league in extra base hits (77), isolated power (.314) and total bases (339). Cecil led club in games (159), runs (104), on-base percentage (.377), OPS (.969), OPS+ (167), total average (1.007), base-out percentage (1.009), GPA (.318), oWAR (6.6), batters run average (.223), SecA (.469), times on base (254), base runs (120), runs produced (185), runs created (128) and bases produced (429). Lou Whitaker (.237 BA, 18 HR, 60 RBI) at second led in hit streak (12). Tony Phillips (.251 BA, 8 HR, 55 RBI) at third led in plate appearances (687), at bats (573), triples (5), steals (19), walks (99) and outs (459). Shortstop Alan Trammell (.304 BA, 14 HR, 89 RBI) led in hits (170), singles (118), doubles (37), on-base percentage (.377), WAR (6.7) and hitting. Gary Ward (.256 BA, 9 HR, 46 RBI) was in left. Lloyd Moseby (.248 BA, 14 HR, 51 RBI) at center led in power/speed number (15.4) and stolen base runs (2.1), with Chet Lemon (.258 BA, 5 HR, 32 RBI) in right. Designated hitters Dave Bergman (.278 BA, 2 HR, 26 RBI) and Larry Sheets (.261 BA, 10 HR, 52 RBI) that led for in-play percentage (80%). Tiger Rookie of the Year Travis Fryman (.297 BA, 9 HR, 27 RBI). The leading pinch-hitters were Heath at .429 (3-7) and Ward .357 (5-14, 8 RBI).

1990s Team Hitting				
YEAR	OBP	SLG	OPS	OPS+
1990	.337	.409	.746	107
1991	.333	.416	.749	105
1992	.337	.407	.744	108
1993	.362	.434	.796	**115**
1994	**.352**	**.454**	**.806**	107
1995	.327	.404	.731	90
1996	.323	.420	.743	87
1997	.332	.415	.747	95
1998	.323	.415	.738	91
1999	.326	.443	.768	95

Pitching. The Tigers had a 4.39 ERA, 15 CG, four SHO, 856 SO, 92 ERA+, 4.49 FIP, 1.442 WHIP, 8.8 H/9, 4.2 BB/9, and 5.4 SO/9, as staff led league in BB (661), IBB (86) and earned runs (697). Pitcher of the Year Jack Morris (15-18, 4.51 ERA) led MLB in starts (36 and earned runs (125), with league lead in CG (11), IBB (13) and runs (144). He led Detroit in wins, losses, SHO (3), IP (249.2), hits (231), homers (26), walks (97), SO (162) and quality starts (18). The most effective pitcher Jerry Don Gleaton (1-3, 2.94 ERA) led in ERA, ERA+ (137), FIP (3.26), DICE (3.45), WHIP (1.052), H/9 (6.8), BB/9 (2.7), SO/9 (6.1), SO/BB (2.24) and R/9 (2.9). He excelled April 25-June 19 (17 GM, 1.40 ERA), July 14-August 12 (12 GM, 2.16 ERA) and August 15-October 1 (12 GM, 0.63 ERA). Frank Tanana (9-8, 5.31 ERA) led in HBP (9). Walt Terrell (6-4, 4.54 ERA) led MLB in HBP (12, eight as a Tiger). He led staff in winning percentage (.600). Dan Petry (10-9, 4.45 ERA), Steve Searcy (2-7, 4.66 ERA), Brian Dubois (3-5, 5.09 ERA) and Jeff Robinson (10-9, 5.96 ERA). Mike Henneman (8-6, 3.05 ERA) led in games (69), GF (53), saves (22) and HR/9 (0.4). Paul Gibson (5-4, 3.05 ERA) led in LOB% (83.1) and pWAR (2.2). Ed Nunez (3-1, 2.24 ERA) and Clay Parker (2-2, 3.18 ERA). Randy Marshall was a phenomenal 20-2 (.909, 2.12 ERA, 0.910 WHIP) at class "A" Fayetteville (13-0) and class "A+" Lakeland (7-2). Class "AA" London had stars John Kiely (3-0 1.000, 1.76 ERA, 12 SV), Mike Wilkins (13-5 .722, 2.42 ERA), Rusty Meacham (15-9 .625, 3.13 ERA) and Dave Haas (13-8 .619, 2.99 ERA).

Defense. Detroit made 131 errors for a .979 fielding average. Tiger league leaders were pitchers Tanana and Petry in fielding average (1.000), Morris led in putouts (38) and allowed 45 stolen bases. Fielder led in double plays (137) at first base. Trammell led shortstops in double plays (102) and the team in dWAR (2.0). Moseby led centerfielders in double plays (5).

Fielder became the fourth American League player with two three-homer games on May 6 at Toronto (3 HR, 5 RBI) and again at Cleveland on June 6 (3 HR, 5 RBI). Class "AAA" Toledo had stars Milt Cuyler (52 SB) and Steve Searcy (10-5 .667, 2.92 ERA).

Class "A+" Central Division champs Lakeland (83-49 .629) featured John DeSilva (8-1 .889, 1.48 ERA), John Doherty (5-1 .833, 1.10 ERA, 10 SV), Greg Gohr (13-5 .722, 2.62 ERA), Marty Willis (10-6 .625, 2.65 ERA) and Lino Rivera (1-0, 0.41 ERA, 14 SV).

1990s Hitting Games	
1. Lou Whitaker	1,418
2. Alan Trammell	1,389
3. Tom Brookens	1,146
4. Chet Lemon	1,099
5. Lance Parish	906
6. Kirk Gibson	881
7. Larry Herndon	843
8. Darrell Evans	727
9. Dave Bergman	598
10. Pat Sheridan	416

Team. Detroit finished third for Sparky Anderson at 84-78 (.519), with an attendance of 1,641,661. The team went 10-9 in April when Frank Tanana (9 IP, 0 ER) had a 16-0 shutout in Chicago on Thursday, April 18, led by Alan Trammell 4-for-5, Tony Phillips 4-for-6 (HR, 3 RBI), Cecil Fielder (HR, 4 RBI), Rob Deer (2 HR, 4 RBI) and Lou Whitaker 3-for-3. The club was 13-14 in May with Deer 4-for-4 (2 HR, 3 RBI) in an 8-7 win over visiting Texas on Sunday, May 5. Fielder (HR, 3 RBI) and Milt Cuyler (HR, 4 RBI) hit a three-run homer and grand slam for a seven run first inning during the Dan Petry (8 IP, 2 ER) 8-3 home win against Minnesota on Sunday, May 19. Pete Incaviglia 3-for-4 (HR, 5 RBI) hit a first inning grand slam in a 11-5 win facing Baltimore at home on Monday, May 20. The Tigers won 15-9 in 5:37 at Milwaukee on Monday, May 27, with a seven-run 14th inning, behind Mickey Tettleton (HR, 3 RBI), Travis Fryman 4-for-6 (3 RBI), Cuyler (3 RBI), Andy Allanson (HR, 4 RBI) and John Shelby (HR, 2 RBI). Fielder walked five times and scored four runs. Players finished 14-14 in June when Tanana was spectacular June 7-28 (5 GM, 3-1, 37.2 IP, 0.96 ERA), .163 BA, .232 OBP, .264 SLG, .176 BABIP). He pitched a 5-0 shutout (9 IP, 4 H, 3 SO) in California on Friday, June 7. The Tigers shutout the Athletics 2-0 in Oakland on Tuesday, June 18, when Tanana (8.2 IP, 4 H, 5 SO) was pulled after 149 pitches. Bill Gullickson (W 9-3, 9 IP, 2 ER) and Tettleton (2 HR, 6 RBI) powered a 9-2 victory over California at home on Friday, June 21. Players were 14-12 in July when 25-year-old rookie Scott Livingstone had an impressive two-weeks MLB debut July 19-August 4 (11 GM, .390 BA, .479 OBP, .512 SLG, .484 BAbip). as Walt Terrell (9 IP, 1 ER), Fielder (2 HR) and Deer (HR) led a 3-1 home win of California on Wednesday, July 31. Detroit went 18-12 in August winning 4-0 in 5:12 at Toronto with 50,307 fans in the SkyDome. Detroit scored four runs in the 14th inning, as Mark Salas hit a three-run pinch-hit home run and Tettleton Homered. The club closed 11-15 in September and 4-2 in October, with a 6-4 win over the Brewers on Saturday, September 14, as Fielder became the first to hit a home run out of Milwaukee's County Stadium. Gullickson (W 20-9, 7 IP, 3 ER), Fielder (HR, 4 RBI) and Deer (HR, 3 RBI) led the way for a 10-5 win in Boston on Thursday, October 3. Lou Whitaker reached base in an incredible 50 consecutive games May 31-August 6 (.326 BA, .421 OBP, .558 SLG). The Bengals finished 12-4 (.750) in extra-inning games and were 25-16 (.610) during blowout games. Players had a superb 49-32 (.605) record at home and 35-46 (.432) on the road. Detroit scored 817 runs as pitchers allowed 794.

P * BILL GULLICKSON

Offense. Detroit had a .247 BA, .333 OBP, .416 SLG, .749 OPS, 2,310 TB and 105 OPS+. Catcher Mickey Tettleton (.263 BA, 31 HR, 89 RBI) led in secondary average (.429) and walks (101). Player of the Year, All-Star, Tiger of the Year, and most effective hitter Cecil Fielder (.261 BA, 44 HR, 133 RBI) at first base led MLB in games (162), home runs and runs batted. He led Motown in plate appearances (712), at bats (612), runs (102), hits (163), slugging (.513), times on base (247), base runs (107), runs produced (191), runs created (111), isolated power (.252), extra base hits (69), total bases (320), bases produced (398) and outs (482). Lou Whitaker (.279 BA, 23 HR, 78 RBI) at second led in on-base percentage (.391), OPS (.881), OPS+ (141), total average (.942), base-out percentage (.949), gross production average (.298), WAR (6.8), oWAR (5.7) and batters run average (.191). Travis Fryman (.259 BA, 21 HR, 91 RBI) at third led in doubles (36), BAbip (.313) and power/speed number (15.3). Shortstop Alan Trammell (.248 BA, 9 HR, 55 RBI) led for in-play percentage (78%), with Lloyd Moseby (.262 BA, 6 HR, 35 RBI) in left. Tiger Rookie of the Year Milt Cuyler (.257 BA, 3 HR, 33 RBI) at center led in triples (7), steals (41), stolen base runs (6.3) and hit streak (15). Right-fielder Rob Deer (.179 BA, 25 HR, 64 RBI) led MLB in strikeouts (175). Designated hitter Pete Incaviglia (.214 BA, 11 HR, 38 RBI). Tony Phillips (.284 BA, 17 HR, 72 RBI) led in singles (111) and hitting. Dave Bergman (7 HR, 29 RBI, .237 BA). The leading pinch-hitters were Phillips at .333. (2-6), Tettleton .308 (4-13, HR, 5 RBI) and Whitaker at .308 (4-13, HR, 5 RBI). Skeeter Barnes (.330 BA) played at class "AAA" Toledo, with Lou Frazier (42 SB) at class "AA" London.

1990s Hitting Runs	
1. Alan Trammell	815
2. Lou Whitaker	814
3. Chet Lemon	531
4. Kirk Gibson	525
5. Lance Parrish	465
6. Tom Brookens	422
7. Larry Herndon	358
8. Darrell Evans	357
9. Dave Bergman	164
10. Steve Kemp	140

Pitching. Motown had a 4.51 ERA, 18 CG, four SHO, 593 BB, 739 SO, 93 ERA+, 4.44 FIP, 1.491 WHIP, 9.7 H/9, 3.7 BB/9, and 4.6 SO/9. Staff led league in hits (1,570) and IBB (88). Pitcher of the Year Bill Gullickson (20-9, 3.90 ERA) led MLB in wins. He led league in starts (35) and IBB (13). He led staff in quality starts (20), innings (226.1), BB/9 (1.7) and SO/BB (2.07). The most effective pitcher Mike Henneman (10-2, 2.88 ERA) led in winning (.833), GF (50), saves (21), LOB% (76.6), ERA, ERA+ (146), FIP (2.93), DICE (3.07), HR/9 (0.2) and R/9 (3.1). Frank Tanana (13-12, 3.77 ERA, 2 SHO) led in homers (26), strikeouts (107) and pWAR (2.7). Walt Terrell (12-14, 4.24 ERA, 2 SHO) led league in hits (257). He led team in losses, CG (8), BB (79), WP (8), earned runs (103) and runs (115). Mark Leiter (9-7, 4.21 ERA) led in HBP (6), WHIP (1.300), H/9 (8.4) and SO/9 (6.9), Dan Petry (2-3, 4.94 ERA) and Scott Aldred (2-4, 5.18 ERA). Paul Gibson (5-7, 4.59 ERA) led in GM (68). Jerry Don Gleaton (3-2, 4.06 ERA), John Cerutti (3-6, 4.57 ERA), and Dan Gakeler (1-4, 5.74 ERA). Class "AA" London had Buddy Groom (7-1 .875). John Doherty (2.22 ERA, 15 SV), Brian Warren (8-2 .800) and Frank Gonzales (11-5 .688) was at class "A" Lakeland.

Defense. Detroit committed 104 errors for a .983 fielding percentage. League leading Tigers were pitchers Terrell and Gullickson in fielding percentage(1.000). Terrell also led in double plays (5). Whitaker at second led in fielding percentage (.994). Deer led in chances (322) and putouts (307) in right-field. Outfielder Cuyler led the Bengals in defensive WAR (1.9).

Cecil Fielder had five multi-homer games on May 22 (2 HR, 3 RBI), July 12 (2 HR, 2 RBI), on July 23 (2 HR, 5 RBI), July 31 (2 HR, 2 RBI) and on August 13 (2 HR, 5 HR). Mickey Tettleton cleared the Tiger Stadium right-field roof on June 22 and June 2.

1990s Hitting Hits	
1. Travis Fryman	1,176
2. Cecil Fielder	947
3. Tony Phillips	771
4. Bobby Higginson	660
5. Lou Whitaker	650
6. Alan Trammell	606
7. Tony Clark	603
8. Damion Easley	469
Mickey Tettleton	469
10. Deivi Cruz	370

Team. Detroit finished sixth under Sparky Anderson at 75-87 (.463), with an attendance of 1,423,963. The team went 7-14 in April that included Cecil Fielder (2 HR, 6 RBI) starring in a 10-9 home loss to Toronto on Wednesday, April 8. The franchise was 14-14 in May, as the Bengals won 8-4 over visiting Oakland on Sunday, May 3, led by Tony Phillips (HR, 4 RBI). Detroit won 8-1 over Kansas City at home on Tuesday, May 26, behind Mark Carreon (HR, 3 RBI) and Bill Gullickson (W 6-2, 9 IP, 1 ER, 6 H). The club managed a 14-14 record during June, including a Fielder (2 HR, 5 RBI) powered 10-4 home win with Milwaukee on Wednesday, June 3. Lou Whitaker destroyed pitching June 4-8 (11-for-16, .688 BA, .750 OBP, 1.438 SLG, 2.188 OPS, .667 BAbip). Players beat Baltimore 15-1 at home on Saturday, June 13, aided by Rob Deer (2 HR, 5 RBI) and Mark Leiter (9 IP, 1 ER, 6 SO). Motown won 14-10 in Toronto on Thursday, June 18, with 50,392 fans in the SkyDome, led by Travis Fryman (5 RBI) and Mickey Tettleton with four walks. Deer (2 HR, 4 RBI) led an 8-3 13-inning triumph at Chicago the next day, as reliever Walt Terrell (4 IP, 0 ER) got the win. Detroit had a 13-14 July record that included a 14-inning 5-4 home win over Seattle on Monday, July 6, as Fryman had three sacrifice hits. Fielder (2 HR, 6 RBI) and reliver John Doherty (5 IP, 0 ER) paced a 9-6 win in Cleveland on Friday, July 31, with 53,419 fans. The squad was 15-13 during August when Frank Tanana (7.2 IP, 1 ER) led a 5-1 win of visiting New York on Tuesday, August 11. Fryman went 4-for-5 (3 RBI) in a 10-3 win at Arlington on Saturday, August 15. The Tigers closed 12-15 in September and 0-3 in October. Motown defeated the visiting Indians 13-3 on Sunday, September 27, behind Deer (HR, 4 RBI), Tettleton (HR, 3 RBI) and Fielder (HR, 2 RBI), as Anderson became the winningest Tiger manager with 1,132 wins. The squad went 38-42 (.475) at home, including a 6-1 against Boston and 37-45 (.451) on the road, with a 6-0 mark facing Texas. Players scored 791 runs and allowed opponents 794. The class "AA" London Tigers featured stars Ivan Cruz (14 HR, 104 RBI) and Lou Frazier (58 SB).

DH * TONY PHILLIPS

Offense. Detroit had a .256 BA, .337 OBP, .407 SLG, .744 OPS, 2,245 TB and 108 OPS+. Most effective hitter Mickey Tettleton (.238 BA, 32 HR, 83 RBI) was the Silver Slugger at catcher and led the league in walks (122). He led Motown in secondary average (.451) and bases produced (368). Player of the Year and Tiger of the Year first baseman Cecil Fielder (.244 BA, 35 HR, 124 RBI) became the first player since Babe Ruth in 1921 to lead MLB in runs batted in for three consecutive seasons. He led the Bengals in homers. Lou Whitaker (278 BA, 19 HR, 71 RBI) at second led in gross production average (.289). Tiger Rookie of the Year Scott Livingstone (.282 BA, 4 HR, 46 RBI) at third led for hitting. All-Star and Silver Slugger Travis Fryman (.266 BA, 20 HR, 96 RBI) at short led MLB in at bats (659) and outs (512). He led his club in games (161), hits (175), triples (4), power/speed number (11.4) and total bases (274). Dan Gladden (.254 BA, 7 HR, 42 RBI) in left led with a 12-game hitting streak. Milt Cuyler (.241 BA, 3 HR, 28 RBI) roamed center. Rob Deer (.247 BA, 32 HR, 64 RBI) in right led in slugging (.547), OPS (.884), OPS+ (145), total average (.886) and isolated power (.300). Designated hitter Tony Phillips (.276 BA, 10 HR, 64 RBI) led MLB in runs (114). He led club in plate appearances (733), doubles (32), on-base percentage (.387) and WAR (5.0). Gary Pettis (.202 BA, HR, 12 RBI) led in steals (13). Mark Carreon (.232 BA, 10 HR, 41 RBI). The leading Tiger pinch-hitters were Shawn Hare at .750 (3-4, 4 RBI) and Phil Clark at .500 (3-6). Fielder failed to make the All-Star team despite having terrific numbers (18 HR, 75 RBI) at the break. Hare hit .330 in his 57 games assigned to class "AAA" Toledo.

1990s Hitting Doubles	
1. Travis Fryman	229
2. Cecil Fielder	141
Lou Whitaker	141
4. Bobby Higginson	137
5. Tony Phillips	129
6. Alan Trammell	120
7. Tony Clark	113
8. Damion Easley	106
9. Mickey Tettleton	85
10. Deivi Cruz	83

Pitching. The Tigers had a 4.60 ERA, 10 CG, two SHO, 564 walks, 693 SO, 86 ERA+, 4.46 FIP, 1.461 WHIP, 9.6 H/9, 3.5 BB/9, and 4.3 SO/9. The staff led league in hits (1,534), intentional walks (88) and earned runs (733). Pitcher of the Year and most effective pitcher Bill Gullickson (14-13, 4.34 ERA, 1 SHO) led in wins, losses, starts (34), complete games (4), innings (221.2), hits (228), homers (35), earned runs (107), runs (109), pWAR (1.7) and BB/9 (2.0). Frank Tanana (13-11, 4.39 ERA) led in walks (90), strikeouts (91), hit by pitch (7), wild pitches (11) and quality starts (18). Dave Haas (5-3, 3.94 ERA, 1 SHO), Mark Leiter (8-5, 4.18 ERA), Walt Terrell (7-10, 5.20 ERA), Eric King (4-6, 5.22 ERA), Kevin Ritz (2-5, 5.60 ERA) and Scott Aldred (3-8, 6.78 ERA). Mike Munoz (1-2, 3.00 ERA) led in games (65), LOB% (81.8), earned run average, ERA+ (133), H/9 (8.3), HR/9 (0.6) and R/9 (3.0). Mike Henneman (2-6, 3.96 ERA) led in games finished (53), saves (24), FIP (3.07), DICE (3.28), WHIP (1.228), SO/9 (6.8) and SO/BB (2.90). John Kiely (4-2, 2.13 ERA), John Doherty (7-4, 3.88 ERA), Kurt Knudsen (2-3, 4.58 ERA), Les Lancaster (3-4, 6.33 ERA, 12 IBB) and Buddy Groom (0-5, 5.82 ERA). Class "AA" London had Mike Lumley (8-3 .727, 2.52 ERA) and closer Jeff Braley (64 GM, 2.53 ERA, 15 SV). Sean Whiteside (8-4, 2.45 ERA) was at class "A-" Niagara Falls.

Defense. Detroit committed 116 errors during the 1992 season for a .981 fielding percentage. The Tiger league leaders were catcher Tettleton in fielding percentage (.996), as Bengal shortstop Fryman led the franchise in defensive WAR (1.6).

Mickey Tettleton led the league in walks (122) and excelled June 10-16 (.435 BA, .500 OBP, .870 SLG, 1.370 OPS, .500 BAbip). He had four walks at Toronto on June 18 and again versus the Angels at home on July 12. Mickey walked in 11 straight games July 29-August 9 (.553 OBP). Tettleton homered in each game of a home series with the Milwaukee Brewers September 4-6.

Class "A" Fayetteville had pitchers Rich Kelley (13-5 .722, 2.82 ERA), Ben Blomdahl (10-4 .714, 2.70 ERA) and Tom Schwarber (1.53 ERA, 24 SV), with Greg Coppeta (7-3 .700, 2.36) and Felipe Lira (11-5 .688, 2.39 ERA) assigned to class "A+" Lakeland.

1990s Hitting Triples		
1.	Travis Fryman	29
2.	Tony Phillips	15
3.	Bobby Higginson	14
4.	Juan Encarnacion	11
	Brian Hunter	11
6.	Kirk Gibson	10
7.	Curtis Pride	9
8.	Milt Cuyler	8
	Mickey Tettleton	8
10.	Lou Whitaker	7

Team. Detroit was third under Sparky Anderson at 85-77 (.525) with 1,971,421 fans. The Tigers were 15-7 in April including a 20-4 home win versus Oakland on Tuesday, April 13, behind Cecil Fielder 4-for-4, Mickey Tettleton (HR, 4 RBI), Rob Deer (HR, 3 RBI), Tony Phillips (4 BB) and Travis Fryman (4 R, HR, 5 RBI). The Bengals defeated Seattle 20-3 at home on Saturday, April 17, with a seven run sixth inning. Tettleton (HR, 4 RBI), Gary Thurman (4 RBI), Chad Kreuter 4-for-5 (3 RBI), and Fielder (2 RBI), as Fryman (4-for-5) scored five runs. Detroit was 15-11 in May that included a 12-inning 7-6 victory at home versus New York on Friday, May 7, behind Tettleton (2 HR, 6 RBI). Alan Trammell went 4-for-6 (HR, 3 RBI) in a home loss to New York on Saturday, May 8. The Tigers won 13-8 in Toronto on Wednesday, May 12, with 50,488 in the SkyDome, with Phillips (HR, 5 RBI), Fielder (2 HR, 4 RBI) and Kirk Gibson (2 HR). Motown went 13-16 in June, with a 10-2 mark for the period June 5-15. John Doherty (W 7-2, 7 IP, 0 ER) and Tettleton (HR, 4 RBI) led a 7-3 win at home over Milwaukee on Sunday, June 20. Players were 10-18 in July as Fryman (5-for-5, 4 RBI) hit for the cycle during a 12-7 loss to New York at home on Wednesday, July 28. The squad was 18-11 in August, as Bill Gullickson was Pitcher of the Month (7 GM, 6-0, 2.68 ERA, .221 BA, .217 BAbip). Gullickson (W 7-6, 9 IP, 1 ER, 3 H) pitched a 5-1 victory over Boston at home on Friday, August 6, with homers by Dan Gladden, Gibson and Scott Livingstone. Motown beat the Red Sox at home on Sunday, behind Fielder (2 HR, 5 RBI) and Tom Bolton (8 IP, 1 ER). Detroit went 10-1 for the period August 16-28. Trammell excelled August 13-27 (12 GM, .510 BA, .547 OBP, .776 SLG). The Bengals beat visiting Seattle 7-4 on Wednesday, August 25, as Fryman was 4-for-5 (HR, 4 RBI). The club closed 13-12 in September and 1-2 in October. Mike Moore (9 IP, 0 ER, 2 H, 6 SO) threw a 4-0 shutout in Chicago on Friday, September 10, led by Eric Davis (2 HR, 3 RBI). Eight Tigers pitched in a 14-8 loss to Toronto at home on Wednesday, September 15. Fryman went 7-for-10 in a doubleheader at Baltimore on Sunday, September 26. Detroit was 44-37 (.543) at home, 41-40 (.506) on the road, scored 899 runs and allowed 837. Shannon Penn (53 SB) starred at class "AA" London.

SS * TRAVIS FRYMAN

Offense. Detroit had a .275 BA, .362 OBP, .434 SLG, .796 OPS, 2,438 TB and 115 OPS+. Chad Kreuter (.286 BA, 15 HR, 51 RBI) caught. Player of the Year and All-Star Cecil Fielder (.267 BA, 30 HR, 117 RBI) at first led in games (154), runs batted in and outs (448). Second baseman Lou Whitaker (.290 BA, 9 HR, 67 RBI) led in total average (.907) and base-out percentage (.921). Scott Livingstone (.293 BA, 2 HR, 39 RBI) played third. Short was split between All-Star Travis Fryman (.300 BA, 22 HR, 97 RBI) and Alan Trammell (.329 BA, 12 HR, 60 RBI, .299 GPA). Fryman led squad in at bats (607), hits (182), doubles (37), oWAR (6.3), runs produced (173), runs created (112), extra base hits (64), total bases (295), bases produced (381). Trammell led in slugging (.496), OPS (.885), OPS+ (138), batters run average (.191) hitting, in-play percentage (79%) and hit streak (16). Dan Gladden (.267 BA, 13 HR, 56 RBI) was in left. Tiger of the Year and most effective hitter Tony Phillips (.313 BA, 7 HR, 57 RBI, .299 GPA) led MLB in walks (132). *"Tony the Tiger"* led team for plate appearances (707), runs (113), on-base percentage (.443), WAR (5.6), BAbip (.369), times on base (313), base runs (108), steals (16) and walks (132). Centerfielder Milt Cuyler (.213 BA, 19 RBI). Rob Deer (.217 BA, 14 HR, 39 RBI) in right led MLB in strikeouts (169), with 120 as a Tiger. Mickey Tettleton (.245 BA, 32 HR, 110 RBI) led in homers, secondary average (.448), isolated power (.247) and strikeouts (139). Anderson used the versatile Tettleton at first base (59), catcher (56) and in the outfield (55). Designated hitter Kirk Gibson (.261 BA, 13 HR, 62 RBI) led in triples (6), power/speed number (13.9) and stolen base runs (0.9). The Tiger Rookie of the Year was Chris Gomez (.250 BA, 11 RBI). The top pinch-hitters were Kreuter at .500 (4-8, 1 HR, 7 RBI), Skeeter Barnes .352 (6-17, 6 RBI), Scott Livingstone .333 (3-9) and Whitaker at .313 (5-16, 5 RBI).

1990s Hitting Home Runs		
1.	Cecil Fielder	235
2.	Travis Fryman	149
3.	Tony Clark	127
4.	Mickey Tettleton	112
5.	Bobby Higginson	104
6.	Lou Whitaker	95
7.	Rob Deer	71
	Damion Easley	71
9.	Tony Phillips	61
10.	Alan Trammell	47

Pitching. Detroit logged a 4.65 ERA, 11 CG, five SHO, 542 walks, 828 SO, 92 ERA+, 4.77 FIP, 1.454 WHIP, 9.7 H/9, 3.4 BB/9, and 5.2 SO/9. The Staff led league in homers (188), and IBB (92). Pitcher of the Year and most effective pitcher Mike Henneman (5-3, 2.64 ERA) led in win percentage (.625), games finished (50), saves (24), LOB% (77.0), ERA, ERA+ (164), FIP (3.52), DICE (3.53), hits per nine (8.7), HR/9 (0.5), SO/9 (7.3) and R/9 (3.5). David Wells (11-9, 4.19 ERA) led in strikeouts (139), HBP (7), wild pitches (13), WHIP (1.203), pWAR (2.9), BB/9 (2.0), SO/BB (3.31) and quality starts (17). John Doherty (14-11, 4.44 ERA) led in wins and losses. Mike Moore (13-9, 5.22 ERA) led MLB in starts (36) and homers (35). He led staff for CG (4), shutouts (3), innings (213.2), hits (227), walks (89), earned runs (124) and runs (135). Bill Gullickson (13-9, 5.37 ERA), Mark Leiter (6-6, 4.73 ERA), Bill Krueger (6-4, 3.40 ERA), Tom Bolton (6-6, 4.47 ERA) and Kurt Knudsen (3-2, 4.78 ERA). Bob MacDonald (3-3, 5.35 ERA) led in games (68). Class "AAA" Toledo had Buddy Groom (9-3 .750, 2.74 ERA), with Felipe Lira (10-4 .714, 3.38 ERA) at class "AA" London. Brian Maxcy (12-4 .750, 2.93 ERA, 9 SV) and John Grimm (1.45 ERA, 10 SV) pitched at class "A" Fayetteville. Shannon Withem (10-2 .833) and Phil Stidham (25 GM, 1.52 ERA, 9 SV) were with class "A+" Lakeland.

Defense. Detroit committed 132 errors during the 1993 season for a .979 fielding percentage. The lone Tiger league leader was Bill Gullickson for pitcher fielding percentage (1.000), as catcher Chad Kreuter led the Bengals for defensive WAR (0.9).

Bill Gullickson went 6-0 in August (2.68 ERA), including a 5-1 home win over the Boston Red Sox on August 6 (9 IP, 1 ER, 3 H). 30-year-old journeyman outfielder John Cangelosi logged a 20-game hitting streak and 39 steals for class "AAA" Toledo.

Cecil Fielder had five multiple homer games during the season, including 3-for-5 (2 HR, 4 RBI) on May 12, 3-for-3 (2 HR, 7 RBI) on June 6, 2-for-3 (2 HR, 3 RBI) on June 15, 2-for-4 (2 HR, 2 RBI) on June 18 and then 3-for-4 (2 HR, 5 RBI) on August 8.

1990s Hitting Runs Batted In	
1. Cecil Fielder	758
2. Travis Fryman	679
3. Tony Clark	402
4. Lou Whitaker	363
5. Bobby Higginson	356
6. Mickey Tettleton	333
7. Tony Phillips	309
8. Alan Trammell	282
9. Damion Easley	247
10. Kirk Gibson	169

Team. Detroit finished last under Sparky Anderson at 53-62 (.461), with an attendance of 1,184,783. The first season with three-divisions closed on August 11, 1994, when owners locked the players out. The squad went 7-14 in April, with an 8-3 win in New York on Sunday, April 10, led by Cecil Fielder (2 HR, 3 RBI). The Bengals won 9-5 at home against Kansas City on Tuesday, April 19, when Kirk Gibson went 3-for-4 (2 HR, 6 RBI). The squad was 16-11 in May including a 14-7 home win versus Texas on Wednesday, May 4, as the Tigers scored six runs in the third and eighth innings, with Lou Whitaker (2 HR, 7 RBI) and Alan Trammell 3-for-5 (3 RBI). Rookie Chris Gomez (HR, 6 RBI) and Mickey Tettleton (3 RBI) led a 13-6 win in Toronto on Tuesday, May 17. Detroit had a record of 13-14 in June, including a 9-8 win over the Twins on Friday, June 3, aided by Junior Feliz 4-for-6 (HR, 2 RBI), and Fielder (HR, 2 RBI) with a 13th-inning walk-off homer. Minnesota won 21-7 the next day with 31 Twins reaching base, as Juan Samuel went 3-for-3 (HR, 3 RBI). Gibson (2 HR, 7 RBI) led a 11-5 victory at California on Saturday, June 11. The Tigers won a 13-inning 10-8 game in 4:58 at Milwaukee on Tuesday, June 14. Travis Fryman went 4-for-6 (4 RBI) as Detroit scored four runs in the 13th inning, as the Brewers scored two runs in their last at-bat. Whitaker hit a ninth inning walk-off grand slam to cap a six-run rally for a Joe Boever (W 6-0) 7-5 win of Cleveland on Tuesday, June 21. The Tigers were 12-17 in July with a 14-2 win over the Royals at Kauffman Stadium on Friday, July 15, behind David Wells (7 IP, 1 ER), and Fielder 3-for-5 (HR, 5 RBI), as Fryman 2-for-2 (4 BB, HR, 2 RBI) reached base six times. Wells (9 IP, 1 ER) led a 9-1 home win against Seattle on Tuesday, July 26, as Fryman 4-for-5 (2 2B, 2 3B, 4 RBI) broke an 0-26 slump. Detroit finished 5-6 in August with a 10-4 home win against Milwaukee on Tuesday, August 9, led by Fielder (HR, 6 RBI) and Whitaker 4-for-5. David Wells (9 IP, 0 ER, 3 H, 8 SO) shutout the Brewers 4-0 on Wednesday. Motown went 7-2 in extra innings, 34-24 (.586) at home, 19-38 (.333) on the road, scored 652 runs and allowed 671. Class "A" Fayetteville had shortstop Matt Brunson (50 SB), outfielder Glen Barker (41 SB) and pitcher Scott Norman (14-7 .667, 2.78 ERA, 2 SHO).

P * MIKE MOORE

Offense. Detroit had a .265 BA, .352 OBP, .454 SLG, .806 OPS, 1,797 TB and 107 OPS+. Catcher Mickey Tettleton (.248 BA, 17 HR, 51 RBI) led in on-base percentage (.419), total average (.992), base-out percentage (.996), gross production average (.304), secondary average (.499) and walks (97). Player of the Year Cecil Fielder (.259 BA, 28 HR, 90 RBI) at first led in homers and runs batted in. Lou Whitaker (.301 BA, 12 HR, 43 RBI) was at second. All-Star third baseman Travis Fryman (.263 BA, 18 HR, 85 RBI) led MLB in strikeouts (128) and sacrifice flies (13), with league high 464 at bats. He led Motown in doubles (34), triples (5), extra base hits, total bases (220) and outs (364). The tandem of Alan Trammell (.267 BA, 8 HR, 28 RBI) leader for in-play percentage (80%) and Tiger Rookie of the Year Chris Gomez (.257 BA, 8 HR, 53 RBI) split time at shortstop. The most effective hitter Tony Phillips (.281 BA, 19 HR, 61 RBI) in left led MLB in plate appearances (538). He led Detroit in runs (91), hits (123), singles (82), WAR (4.7), oWAR (3.7), times on base (220), base runs (86), runs created (84), power/speed number (15.4), bases produced (313) and steals (13). The trio of Eric Davis (.183 BA, 3 HR, 13 RBI), Milt Cuyler (.241 BA, 1 HR, 11 RBI) and Juan Samuel (.309 BA, 5 HR, 21 RBI) played centerfield. Junior Felix (.306 BA, 13 HR, 49 RBI) in right led for hitting, BAbip (.366) and hit streak (17). Tiger of the Year designated hitter Kirk Gibson (.276 BA, 23 HR, 72 RBI) led in slugging (.548), OPS (.906), OPS+ (130) and isolated power (.273). The leading pinch-hitters were Samuel at .400 (2-5) and Gibson (2 HR, 8 RBI). Felix closed his MLB career in style July 30-August 11 (.414 BA, .500 OBP, .517 SLG, .545 BAbip).

1990s Hitting On-Base Percentage	
1. Tony Phillips	.395
2. Mickey Tettleton	.387
3. Lou Whitaker	.379
4. Bobby Higginson	.364
5. Tony Clark	.351
Cecil Fielder	.351
7. Damion Easley	.348
8. Alan Trammell	.347
9. Travis Fryman	.334
10. Deivi Cruz	.284

Pitching. Detroit had a 5.38 ERA, 15 CG, one SHO, 449 walks, 560 SO, 91 ERA+, 5.32 FIP, 1.560 WHIP, 10.1 H/9, 4.0 BB/9, and 5.0 SO/9. Pitchers led league for intentional walks (74). Pitcher of the Year Joe Boever (9-2, 3.98 ERA) led league in IBB (12), with team lead for games (46), win percentage (.818) and games finished (27). The most effective pitcher David Wells (5-7, 3.96 ERA) led in complete games (5), shutouts (1), FIP (4.07), DICE (3.94), WHIP (1.231), pWAR (2.7), BB/9 (1.9) and SO/BB (2.96). Storm Davis (2-4, 3.56 ERA) led in ERA, ERA+ (137), H/9 (6.8) and HR/9 (0.6). Moore (11-10, 5.42 ERA) led MLB in walks (89). He led staff in wins, homers (27) and quality starts (10). Belcher (7-15, 5.89 ERA) led the majors in losses and league for runs (124). He led Motown in innings (162), hits (192), strikeouts (76) and earned runs (106). Bill Gullickson (4-5, 5.93 ERA), Greg Gohr (2-2, 4.50 ERA), John Doherty (6-7, 6.48 ERA) and Sean Bergman (2-1, 5.60 ERA). Buddy Groom (0-1, 3.94 ERA) led in LOB% (79.2), SO/9 (7.6) and R/9 (3.9). Mike Henneman (1-3, 5.19 ERA) led in saves (8). Mike Gardiner (2-2, 4.14 ERA). Class "A" Jamestown had Eric Dinyar (5-1, 3.38 ERA, 5 SV) and Kenny Marrero (4-1, 2.11 ERA, 8 SV). Belcher and Moore led league in starts (25). Davis and Moore led in WP (10). Belcher and Gullickson led in HBP (4).

Defense. Detroit made 82 errors for a .981 fielding percentage. Tiger league leaders were pitchers Belcher in double plays (5), Moore in fielding percentage (1.000) and putouts (22). Fielder in assists (108) at first base and Fryman led third basemen in chances (313) and assists (221). Phillips led leftfielders in chances (247) and putouts (236), as well his team in dWAR (0.6).

Tim Belcher had a poor month of April (0-4, 9.56 ERA) and then pitched much better in June (4-0, 3.40 ERA). David Wells finished 0-3 in June (5.40 ERA, 11 BB, 18 SO), as he returned to form during the month of July (3-1, 2.96 ERA, 5 BB, 26 SO).

Class "AAA" Toledo had 205 stolen bases, led by Shannon Penn (45) and Rudy Pemberton (30). Eddie Gaillard (6-1 .857, 2.84 ERA) was at class "A+" Lakeland in the Florida State League, as Michigander Bill Welke from Coldwater was an FSL umpire.

1990s Hitting Slugging Percentage	
1. Tony Clark	.503
2. Cecil Fielder	.487
3. Mickey Tettleton	.480
4. Bobby Higginson	.477
5. Lou Whitaker	.464
6. Damion Easley	.461
7. Travis Fryman	.444
8. Alan Trammell	.410
9. Tony Phillips	.405
10. Deivi Cruz	.369

Team. Detroit (60-84 .417) finished fourth for Sparky Anderson with 1,180,979 fans. The club went 2-3 in April including a Juan Samuel (HR, 3 RBI) and Cecil Fielder (HR, 2 RBI) led 5-4 win in Anaheim with 51,145 fans on Wednesday, April 26. The Bengals were 13-15 in May with a 10-8 home win against Seattle on Monday, May 22, behind Fielder (2 HR, 4 RBI). Detroit won 14-3 over Minnesota on Wednesday, aided by Mike Moore (7 IP, 0 ER) and Travis Fryman 4-for-5 (HR). Players lost 14-12 in Chicago on Sunday, May 28, with their seven home runs the MLB record for a losing team. Chad Curtis (2 HR), Lou Whitaker (HR, 2 RBI), Fielder (2 HR, 5 RBI) and Kirk Gibson 4-for-6 (2 HR, 2 RBI) homered. The squad was 15-13 in June including a 15-inning 5-4 loss in 4:58 at Chicago on Friday, June 2, with Danny Bautista (3 RBI). John Flaherty (2 HR, 4 RBI) and Samuel (HR, 2 RBI) paced an 8-2 triumph in Minnesota on Sunday, June 11. Samuel (4 RBI) and Curtis (HR, 2 RBI) led a Motown 10-8 home win over Baltimore on Sunday, June 18. Detroit was 10-16 in July including a 12-5 home win facing Kansas City 12-5 on Thursday, July 6, behind Fryman 4-for-5 (HR) and Fielder (HR, 3 RBI). David Wells (W 8-3, 9 IP, 1 ER) had a 3-1 win the next day over the Royals. The club was 7-21 in August as Sean Bergman (9 IP, 0 ER, 4 H, 7 SO) shutout Boston 5-0 at home on Wednesday, August 2, with Fryman (2 HR, 4 RBI) and Whitaker (3 BB, HR). The Bengals lost to visiting Chicago 15-7 on Tuesday, August 22, aided by Chris Gomez, 4-for-5 (HR, 2 RBI) and Fielder (HR, 2 RBI). Fielder had a homer in four straight games August 20-23 (4 HR, 6 RBI, 1.133 SLG). Motown closed 13-15 in September and 0-1 in October. Whitaker hit a three-run walk-off homer in a 5-3 victory over Milwaukee on Wednesday, September 13. Players were 35-37 (.486) at home, 25-47 (.347) on the road, scored 654 runs and allowed opponents 844. Rudy Pemberton (.344 BA), Joe Hall (.320 BA), Randy Marshall (7-3 .700, 2.30 ERA) and Mike Christopher (2.23 ERA, 21 SV) were at class "AAA" Toledo. Ivan Cruz (31 HR, 93 RBI) and Glen Barker (39 SB) played at class "AA" Jacksonville. Class "A" Fayetteville had Brandon Reed (3-0, 1.000, 0.97 ERA, 41 SV), Jason Jordan (10-4 .714, 2.28 ERA) and Matt Skrmetta (9-4 .692, 2.71 ERA).

P * DAVID WELLS

Offense. Detroit finished with a .247 BA, .327 OBP, .404 SLG, .731 OPS, 1,967 TB and 90 OPS+. Catcher John Flaherty (.243 BA, 11 HR, 40 RBI) led for in-play percentage (77%). Player of the Year Cecil Fielder (.243 BA, 31 HR, 82 RBI) at first led in homers, runs batted in, slugging (.472), OPS (.818), OPS+ (111), total average (.796), base-out percentage (.801), gross production average (.274), batters run average (.163), secondary average (.379), isolated power (.229), walks (75) and strikeouts (116). Second baseman Lou Whitaker (.293 BA, 14 HR, 44 RBI). Tiger of the Year Travis Fryman (.275 BA, 15 HR, 81 RBI) at third led in singles (115), WAR (3.9), hitting, BAbip (.307) and runs produced (145). Chris Gomez (.223 BA, 11 HR, 50 RBI) at short led in stolen base runs (0.6). Tiger Rookie of the Year Bobby Higginson (.224 BA, 14 HR, 43 RBI) was in left. The most effective hitter Chad Curtis (.268 BA, 21 HR, 67 RBI) at center led MLB in outs (463). He led the league in plate appearances (670) and power/speed number (23.6). Curtis led Detroit in at bats (586), runs (96), hits (157), doubles (29), on-base percentage (.349), times on base (234), base runs (86), runs created (89), extra base hits (53), total bases (255), bases produced (352), stolen bases (27) and 18-game hit streak. Danny Bautista (.203 BA, 7 HR, 27 RBI) was in right, with Kirk Gibson (.260 BA, 9 HR, 35 RBI) the designated hitter. The leading pinch-hitters were Bautista at .500 (3-6), Gibson .500 (3-6, HR, 7 RBI), Franklin Stubbs (7 RBI), Whitaker (HR, 7 RBI) and Alan Trammell at .364 (4-11).

1990s Hitting On-Base plus Slugging	
1. Mickey Tettleton	.867
2. Tony Clark	.855
3. Lou Whitaker	.843
4. Bobby Higginson	.841
5. Cecil Fielder	.839
6. Damion Easley	.808
7. Tony Phillips	.800
8. Travis Fryman	.779
9. Alan Trammell	.757
10. Deivi Cruz	.653

Pitching. Motown had a 5.49 ERA, five CG, one SHO, 536 walks, 729 SO, 88 ERA+, 5.06 FIP, 1.604 WHIP, 10.7 H/9, 3.8 BB/9, and 5.1 SO/9, as staff led league in games finished (139), hits (1,509), IBB (79), and batters faced (5,774). Pitcher of the Year and most effective pitcher David Wells (10-3, 3.04 ERA) led in wins, win percentage (.769), complete games (3), LOB% (77.7), ERA, ERA+ (159), WHIP (1.205), pWAR (4.6), H/9 (8.3), SO/BB (2.24), runs per nine (3.7) and quality starts (14). Felipe Lira (9-13, 4.31 ERA) led in innings (146.1), strikeouts (89) and HBP (8). Sean Bergman (7-10, 5.12 ERA, 1 SHO) led in starts (28) and wild pitches (13). Mike Moore (5-15, 7.53 ERA) led league in losses, with staff lead in hits (179), homers (24), walks (68), earned runs (111) and runs (118). Jose Lima (3-9, 6.11 ERA) led in walks per nine (2.2). C.J. Nitkowski (1-4, 7.09 ERA). Mike Henneman (0-1, 1.53 ERA) led in saves (18). John Doherty (5-9, 5.10 ERA) led in HR/9 (0.8). Brian Bohannon (1-1, 5.54 ERA). Joe Boever (5-7, 6.39 ERA) led in games (60), games finished (27) and SO/9 (6.5). Mike Christopher (4-0, 3.82 ERA), Brian Maxcy (4-5, 6.88 ERA) and Buddy Groom (1-3, 7.52 ERA). Class "AA" Jacksonville had Trever Miller (8-2, 2.72 ERA) and John Kelly (2.09 ERA, 29 SV), as Eddie Gaillard (1.31 ERA, 25 SV) and Mike Salazar (7-3, 3.19 ERA) were with class "A+" Lakeland.

Defense. Detroit committed 106 errors for a .981 fielding average and led the Central Division in assists (1,594). League leaders were Lira in pitcher fielding (1.000), Flaherty led in catcher errors (11) and stolen bases (78). Fryman at third led in chances (458), assists (337), and double plays (38), with club lead in dWAR (1.8), as Higginson led outfielders in assists (13).

Closer Mike Henneman was in top form when not allowing an earned run during the periods of April 29-June 1 (10 GM, 0.00 ERA, 11 IP, 9 SO, .135 BA, .220 OBP, 5 SV) and June 19-August 6 (12 GM, 0.00 ERA, 12 IP, 10 SO, .171 BA, .227 OBP, 8 SV).

All-Star David Wells stood 1-3 thru May 22, and then won his last nine decisions as a Tiger. Wells finished 4-0 in June (2.91 ERA, .234 BA, .314 OBP, .252 BABIP) and 4-0 in July (2.52 ERA, .219 BA, .265 OBP, .252 BABIP) his last month with Detroit.

1990s Pitching Wins		
1.	Bill Gullickson	51
2.	Brian Moehler	35
	Frank Tanana	35
4.	Justin Thompson	35
5.	John Doherty	32
6.	Mike Moore	29
7.	Mike Henneman	26
	David Wells	26
9.	Mark Leiter	23
10.	Felipe Lira	20

Team. Detroit finished fifth for Buddy Bell at 53-109 (.327), with 1,168,610 fans. The club was 9-18 in April, as Travis Fryman opened with four straight multi-hit games (2 HR, 8 RBI, .400 BA, .850 SLG). Bobby Higginson 4-for-6 (HR, 3 RBI) and Fryman (2 HR, 3 RBI) led a 15-inning 10-9 win at Oakland in 4:47 on Thursday, April 4. Players won 13-8 in Toronto on Tuesday, April 16, behind Cecil Fielder 3-for-4 (3 HR, 5 RBI) and John Flaherty 3-for-5 (2 HR). The Motor City dropped a 24-11 slugfest loss at home to Minnesota on Wednesday, April 24, with Eddie Williams (HR, 3 RBI), Higginson 4-for-5 (3 RBI), and Mark Lewis (2 HR, 3 RBI). Detroit went 4-23 in May including 1-11 at home and lost 12 in a row thru Monday, May 27. Players went 1-19 for May 14-June 6, as Greg Gohr (7 IP, 2 ER) won 5-4 at Kansas City on Wednesday, May 29. The Squad had a 10-17 June record with a Higginson (5 RBI) led 10-8 win in Oakland on Tuesday, June 25. The Bengals were 12-14 in July when Melvin Nieves erupted with an MLB leading power surge July 15-August 22 (19 GM, 12 HR, 24 RBI, .316 BA, .855 SLG). Higginson had an RBI in five straight games July 27-August 1 (12-for-20 .600 BA, 2 HR, 9 RBI, .625 OBP, 1.050 SLG, .556 BAbip). Fielder (2 HR, 5 RBI) paced a 14-6 win in Seattle on Sunday, July 28. Fielder's last week as a Tiger July 25-31 (6 GM, .417 BA, 4 HR, 10 RBI, 1.000 SLG) was remarkable. The Tigers were 14-15 in August including a 13-7 win at Yankee Stadium on Saturday, August 10, led by Damion Easley (HR, 4 RBI), Tony Clark (3 RBI) and Andujar Cedeno (HR, 4 RBI). The Tiger five run first inning was the difference in a 16-11 victory over visiting Chicago on Tuesday, August 20, aided by Nieves 2-for-3 (HR, 5 RBI) and Kimera Bartee 3-for-5. Players closed 4-22 in September including 0-16 at home. Omar Olivares (4 IP, 0 ER), Nieves (HR, 3 RBI), and Fryman (3 RBI) led a 10-1 win at Milwaukee on Friday, September 20. Detroit was 27-54 (.333) at home, 26-55 (.321) on the road, scored 784 runs and allowed a league record 1,103 runs. The Tigers set the MLB record of 0-58 (10.01 ERA) in games decided by four or more runs. Phil Nevin was at class "AA" Jacksonville (98 GM, .294 BA, 24 HR, 69 RBI) and Detroit (38 GM, .292 BA, 8 HR, 19 RBI), with four straight multi-RBI games September 2-6. Class "A" Fayetteville had Clay Bruner (14-5 .737, 2.59 ERA), Dave Melendez (11-4 .733, 2.62 ERA), Bryan Corey (1.21 ERA, 34 SV) and Gabe Kapler (.300 BA, 26 HR, 99 RBI).

3B * PHIL NEVIN

Offense. Detroit had a .256 BA, .323 OBP, .420 SLG, .743 OPS, 2,324 TB and 87 OPS+. Brad Ausmus (.248 BA, 4 HR, 22 RBI) caught. Tiger Rookie of the Year Tony Clark (.250, 27 HR, 72 RBI) at first led in homers. Second baseman Mark Lewis (.270 BA, 11 HR, 55 RBI, 71% IP%) led in stolen base runs (1.2). Player of the Year, All-Star, and Tiger of the Year Travis Fryman (.268 BA, 22 HR, 100 RBI) at third led in games (157), plate appearances (688), at bats (616), runs (90), hits (165), singles (108), runs batted in, times on base (226), runs produced (168), total bases (269), bases produced (330) and outs (483). Andujar Cedeno (.196 BA, 7 HR, 20 RBI), Chris Gomez (.242 BA, HR, 16 RBI) and Alan Trammell (.233 BA, HR, 16 RBI) split time at shortstop. The most effective hitter Bobby Higginson (.320 BA, 26 HR, 81 RBI) in leftfield led for doubles (35), on-base percentage (.404), slugging (.577), OPS (.982), OPS+ (145), total average (1.045), base-out percentage (1.053), gross production average (.326), WAR (3.6), oWAR (3.9), batters run average (.232), hitting, secondary average (.411), base runs (96), runs created (103), isolated power (.257), extra base hits (61), walks (65) and hit streak (12). Kimera Bartee (.253 BA, HR, 14 RBI) led in BAbip (.388), stolen bases (20) and shared center with Chad Curtis (.263 BA, 10 HR, 37 RBI) the team leader in power/speed number (12.3). Right-fielder Melvin Nieves (.246 BA, 24 HR, 60 RBI) led in strikeouts (158). The designated hitters were Cecil Fielder (.248 BA, 26 HR, 80 RBI) and Eddie Williams (6 HR, 26 RBI, .200 BA). Curtis Pride (.300 BA, 10 HR, 31 RBI) led in triples (5). The top pinch-hitters were Higginson at .333 (3-9, 2 HR) and Ruben Sierra at .333 (2-6).

1990s Pitching Winning Percentage		
1.	Bill Gullickson	.586
2.	David Wells	.578
3.	Mark Leiter	.561
4.	Mike Henneman	.553
5.	Frank Tanana	.530
6.	John Doherty	.508
7.	Justin Thompson	.486
8.	Mike Moore	.460
9.	Brian Moehler	.455
10.	Felipe Lira	.370

Pitching. Pitchers logged a 6.38 ERA, 10 CG, four SHO, 957 SO, 80 ERA+, 5.83 FIP, 1.733 WHIP, 10.7 H/9, 4.9 BB/9, and 6.0 SO/9. Pitchers led league in hits (1,699), homers (241), walks (784), intentional walks (63), WP (82), earned runs (1,015), runs (1,103), batters faced (6,713) and runs per game (6.81). Pitcher of the Year and most effective pitcher Omar Olivares (7-11, 4.89 ERA) led in wins, CG (4) and pWAR (3.6). Felipe Lira (6-14, 5.22 ERA) led in losses, starts (32), shutouts (2), innings (194.62), hits (204), homers (30), strikeouts (113), HBP (10), earned runs (113), runs (123), WHIP (1.387), BB/9 (3.1) and quality starts (15). Greg Gohr (4-8, 7.17 ERA), Justin Thompson (1-6, 4.58 ERA), C.J. Nitkowski (2-3, 8.08 ERA) and Scott Aldred (0-4, 9.35 ERA). Richie Lewis (4-6, 4.18 ERA) led league in IBB (9). He led club in WP (14), LOB% (75.9), ERA, ERA+ (122), H/9 (7.8) and R/9 (4.5). Mike Myers (1-5, 5.01 ERA) led MLB in games (83), with team lead for FIP (4.01), DICE (3.84), HR/9 (0.8), SO/9 (9.6) and SO/BB (2.03). Gregg Olson (3-0, 5.01 ERA) led in GF (28) and saves (8). Brian Williams (3-10, 6.77 ERA) led in walks (85). Joey Eishen (1-1, 3.24 ERA), A.J. Sager (4-5, 5.01 ERA), Jose Lima (5-6, 5.70 ERA) and Greg Keagle (3-6, 7.39 ERA). Eishen was impressive to start his Bengal career August 3-24 (10.1 IP, 0.00 ERA, .206 BA, .226 BAbip).

Defense. Detroit made 137 errors for a .978 fielding average. League leaders were Lira in pitcher fielding (1.000), Fryman in fielding (.979), assists (271) at third, and led club in dWar (0.9). Nieves led in errors for outfielders (13) and in rightfield (9).

Phil Hiatt (42 HR, 119 RBI) was at class "AAA" Toledo, with Bubba Trammell (.328 BA) and Brian Moehler (15-6 .714) at class "AA" Jacksonville. Dave Roberts (112 R, 65 SB) played at Visalia, with Rich Almanzar (.306 BA, 53 BS) at class "A+" Lakeland.

Detroit bashed 204 homers led by Tony Clark 27, Cecil Fielder 26, Bobby Higginson 26, Melvin Nieves 24, Travis Fryman 22, Mark Lewis 11, Chad Curtis 10, Curtis Pride 10, and Phil Nevin 8. Felipe Lira excelled June 17-July 13 (3-0, 1.64 ERA, .210 BA).

1990s Pitching Games Started	
1. Bill Gullickson	116
2. Brian Moehler	98
3. Frank Tanana	93
4. Justin Thompson	90
5. Mike Moore	86
6. Felipe Lira	69
7. David Wells	64
8. John Doherty	61
9. Mark Leiter	42
10. Sean Bergman	37

Team. Detroit finished third for Buddy Bell at 79-83 (.488), with 1,365,157 fans. The team was 11-16 in April including a 15-12 win at Chicago on Saturday, April 5, behind Tony Clark 4-for-6 (2 HR), Damion Easley (HR, 3 RBI) and Brian Hunter 4-for-5 (3 RBI, 3 SB). Brian Johnson (HR, 4 RBI) led a 10-4 win over Minnesota at home on Monday, April 7. Bobby Higginson (HR, 4 RBI) hit a grand slam home run during a 10-5 victory the next day versus the Twins. Players were 14-11 in May, as Omar Olivares (9 IP, 0 ER, 3 H, 7 SO) shutout Cleveland 6-0 at home on Saturday, May 10, aided by Clark (HR, 3 RBI) and Higginson (HR, 2 RBI). Detroit best visiting Texas 13-5 at home on Sunday, May 25, with Higginson 4-for-5 (HR, 5 RBI). Olivares (9 IP, 0 ER, 4 H) shutout Anaheim 6-0 at home the next day paced by Travis Fryman (3 RBI). The Tigers took a 4-2 win in Seattle on Saturday, May 31, with a crowd of 57,118. Olivares (6.2 IP, 2 ER, 6 SO) and Bob Hamelin 2-for-4 (2 RBI) led the way. The squad went 11-15 in June as Hamelin was superb the week of June 2-8 (10-for-16, .625 BA, .647 OBP, 1.188 SLG, .727 BAbip). Hunter had four steals on June 26. Motown hit six homers to defeat the visiting Mets 14-0 on Monday, June 30, behind Justin Thompson (8 IP, 0 ER, 4 H), Higginson (4 R, 3 HR, 7 RBI), and Hunter 4-for-4 that scored four runs. Detroit had a 13-14 mark in July as Melvin Nieves homered in four straight games July 14-17 (4 HR, 8 RBI, 1.000 SLG). Willie Blair was undefeated in July (6-0 1.000). Blair (W 10-4, 9 IP, 1 ER, 3 H) and Easley (HR, 3 RBI) led a 3-1 win in Chicago on Tuesday, July 29. Closer Todd Jones shined June 18-August 13 (21 GM, 1-0, 15 SV, 0.81 ERA, .207 BA). The Tigers were 14-16 in August that included a 16-1 victory in Milwaukee on Friday, August 22. The offense was led by Higginson 5-for-6, Fryman (4 RBI), Clark (4 RBI), Nieves (HR, 3 RBI) and Hamelin (HR, 2 RBI). The club closed 16-11 in September with a 12-4 victory at Atlanta on Wednesday, September 3, with Clark (HR, 5 RBI). Motown was 42-39 (.519) at home, 37-44 (.457) on the road, scored 784 runs and allowed 790. Class "A+" Lakeland had Alejandro Freire (.323 BA, 24 HR, 92 RBI), Gabe Kapler (.295 BA, 19 HR, 87 RBI, 40 SB), Dave Darwin (10-1 .909, 2.50 ERA), Keilan Smith (9-2 .818, 2.57 ERA), and Victor Santos (10-5 .667, 3.23 ERA).

SS * DEIVE CRUZ

Offense. Detroit had a .258 BA, .332 OBP, .415 SLG, .747 OPS, 2,275 TB and 95 OPS+. Raul Casanova (.243 BA, 5 HR, 24 RBI) was the catcher. Player of the Year Tony Clark (.276 BA, 32 HR, 117 RBI) at first led in homers, runs batted in, secondary average (.381), times on base (256), base runs (106), runs produced (190), runs created (109), isolated power (.224), extra base hits (63), total bases (290), bases produced (384) and walks (93). Damion Easley (.264 BA, 22 HR, 72 RBI) at second led in doubles (37) and power/speed number (24.6) Third baseman Travis Fryman (.274 BA, 22 HR, 102 RBI). Tiger Rookie of the Year Deivi Cruz (.241 BA, 2 HR, 40 RBI) at shortstop led for in-play percentage (82%). The most effective hitter was leftfielder Bobby Higginson (.299 BA, 27 HR, 101 RBI). He led in on-base percentage (.379), slugging (.520), OPS (.899), OPS+ (133), total average (.905), base-out percentage (.923), gross production average (.301), oWAR (4.5), batters run average (.197), hitting, and hitting streak (14). Centerfielder Brian Hunter (.269 BA, 4 HR, 45 RBI) led MLB in games (162), steals (74) and outs (525). Brian led league in caught stealing (18). Hunter led club for plate appearances (738), at bats (658), runs (112), hits (177), singles (137), triples (7) and stolen base runs (11.4). Melvin Nieves (.228 BA, 20 HR, 64 RBI) in right led in BAbip (.337) and strikeouts (157). Designated hitter Bob Hamelin (.270 BA, 18 HR, 52 RBI). The top pinch-hitter was Phil Nevin at .471 (8-17, 2 HR, 6 RBI). Higginson had four straight multi-hit games September 19-22 (.471 BA, .588 SLG, .533 BAbip). Class "AA" Jacksonville had Juan Encarnacion (.323 BA, 26 HR, 90 RBI) and Jesse Ibarra (25 HR, 91 RBI).

1990s Pitching Complete Games	
1. Bill Gullickson	11
Jack Morris	11
3. Mike Moore	9
Justin Thompson	9
5. Brian Moehler	8
David Wells	8
7. Frank Tanana	7
8. John Doherty	5
9. Felipe Lira	4
10. Three Players	3

Pitching. Motown logged a 4.56 ERA, 13 CG, five SHO, 552 walks, 982 SO, 101 ERA+, 4.59 FIP, 1.403 WHIP, 9.2 H/9, 3.4 BB/9, and 6.1 SO/9. Detroit led the league in tough losses (19) and youngest staff (27.5). Pitcher of the Year and the most effective pitcher Justin Thompson (15-11, 3.02 ERA, 4 CG) led in starts (32), innings (223.1), walks (66), strikeouts (151), earned run average, ERA+ (152), WHIP (1.137), pWAR (7.7), H/9 (7.6), SO/BB (2.29), R/9 (3.3) and quality starts (25). Willie Blair (16-8, 4.17 ERA) led in wins, win percentage (.667) and BB/9 (2.4). Brian Moehler (11-12, 4.67 ERA) led in losses, hits (198), homers (22), earned runs (91) and runs (97). Omar Olivares (5-6, 4.70 ERA) led in shutouts (2) and HBP (9). Scott Sanders (3-8, 5.33 ERA), Felipe Lira (5-7, 5.77 ERA, 7 WP) and Greg Keagle (3-5, 6.55 ERA). Todd Jones (5-4, 3.09 ERA, 7 WP) led in games finished (51), saves (31), FIP (3.21), DICE (3.10), HR/9 (0.4) and SO/9 (9.0). Doug Brocail (3-4, 3.23 ERA) led in LOB% (82.8). Mike Myers (0-4, 5.70 ERA) led league in games (88). A.J. Sager (3-4, 4.18 ERA) and Dan Miceli (3-2, 5.01 ERA, 4 IBB). Closer Jones dominated hitters during the period of June 18-September 25 (37 GM, 4-0, 23 SV, 39.2 IP, 43 SO, 1.82 ERA, .218 BA). Justin Thompson had nine strikeouts on May 21 at Baltimore, June 1 in Seattle, and June 7 versus Seattle at home.

Defense. Detroit had 92 errors to lead the league in fielding (.985) and led Central Division in defensive efficiency (.698), chances (6,149) and putouts (4,337). League leaders were Thompson in pitcher fielding (1.000), Clark in chances (1,533) and putouts (1,423) at first. Leftfielder Higginson led in assists (17) and double plays (5). Hunter in center led outfielders in chances (419) and putouts (407). Third baseman Fryman led in fielding (.978) and putouts (126), with team best dWAR (1.3).

Brian Hunter went 4-for-5 on April 5 and 4-for-4 on June 30. Class "A" West Michigan (92-39 .702) featured star players Robert Fick (.341 BA), Scott Sollmann (40 SB), Frankie Cordero (50 GM, 6-1 .857, 0.99 ERA, 35 SV, 11.1 SO/9), Dave Borkowski (15-3 .833), Clay Bruner (15-3 .833), Greg Romo (12-6 .667), Craig Quintel (11-6 .647, 1.96 ERA), and Russ Spear (11-6 .647).

1990s Pitching Earned Run Average		
1.	Mike Henneman	3.19
2.	David Wells	3.78
3.	Justin Thompson	3.92
4.	Mark Leiter	4.36
5.	Frank Tanana	4.44
6.	Brian Moehler	4.50
7.	Bill Gullickson	4.68
8.	John Doherty	4.86
9.	Felipe Lira	5.07
10.	Mike Moore	5.90

Team. Motown (65-97 .401) finished fifth in the Central Division under Buddy Bell (52-85) and Larry Parrish (13-12), with 1,409,391 fans. The Tigers won their opener 11-6 in Tampa on Tuesday, March 31, led by Joe Randa 3-for-5 (3 RBI), Joe Oliver (3 RBI), Luis Gonzalez 3-for-5 (HR, 2 RBI) and Damion Easley 3-for-5. Detroit went 5-18 in April with a 7-2 defeat of visiting Texas on Thursday, April 30, led by Brian Moehler (9 IP, 2 ER, 6 SO) and Easley 3-for-4 (HR, 4 RBI). The team went 15-12 in May that included a 17-3 win in Seattle on Friday, May 1, behind Bobby Higginson 4-for-6 (2 HR, 3 RBI), Andy Tomberlin 4-for-4 (3 RBI) and Paul Bako (3 RBI). Easley drove in runners at an astounding rate during May 13-25 (13 GM, 8 HR, 24 RBI, .412 BA, .980 SLG). Damion (2 HR, 6 RBI) led Motown to a 12-11 win at Minnesota on Wednesday, May 20. Easley (2 HR, 5 RBI) then led an 8-7 home win against Chicago on Friday, May 29. Detroit had a 10-18 record in June with Justin Thompson (9 IP, 0 ER, 3 H, 6 SO) winning 4-1 at Minnesota on Sunday, June 7, as Higginson (2 RBI) and Tony Clark had back-to-back eighth-inning homers. Thompson (9 IP, 1 ER, 5 H) pitched a dominate game for a 7-1 win in Kansas City at Kauffman Stadium on Saturday, June 13, as Gonzalez was 2-for-3 (3 RBI). Bako starred during a three-game inter-league series with the Cincinnati Reds June 26-28 (6-for-9 .667 BA, .700 OBP, 1.000 SLG, 1.700 OPS, .857 BAbip). Motown was 13-15 in July with a Thompson (9 IP, 1 ER, 10 SO) gem during a 3-1 home win against Boston on Sunday, July 19. The last place Tigers (42-55 .433) beat the first place Yankees (69-25 .734) in 5:50 during a 17-inning contest at Yankee Stadium on Monday, July 20. The squad went 8-22 during August when 22-year-old rookie Juan Encarnacion caught fire for the week of August 2-26 (8 GM, .406 BA, .412 OBP, .625 SLG, .444 BAbip). The club endured a nine-game losing streak thru Wednesday, August 12. Bryce Florie (8.1 IP, 3 ER, 5 H, 10 SO) led a 6-4 win over Oakland at home on Sunday, August 16. Players went 13-12 in September, losing a 12-inning game to Chicago 17-16 in 5:12 at home on Monday, September 14. Encarnacion was 5-for-6 (5 R, HR, 4 RBI), Higginson (HR, 4 RBI) and Randa (HR, 4 RBI), as 10 Tiger pitchers allowed 31 runners to reach base. Players were 32-49 (.395) at home and 33-48 (.407) on the road. Detroit scored 722 runs and allowed 863. Pedro Santana (64 SB), Ryan Grimmett (48 SB) and Craig Johnson (14-6 .700, 2.79 ERA) played for class "A" West Michigan.

1B * TONY CLARK

Offense. Detroit had a .264 BA, .323 OBP, .415 SLG, .738 OPS, 2,353 TB and 91 OPS+. Catcher Paul Bako (.272 BA, 3 HR, 30 RBI) led in BAbip (.357). Player of the Year and most effective hitter Tony Clark (.291 BA, 34 HR, 103 RBI) at first led in hits (175), homers, runs batted in, on-base percentage (.358), slugging (.522), OPS (.880), OPS+ (126), total average (.852), base-out percentage (.860), gross production average (.292), batters run average (.187), hitting, secondary average (.336), base runs (105), runs created (112), isolated power (.231), extra base hits (71), total bases (314), bases produced (380), walks (63) and strikeouts (128). Tiger of the Year Damion Easley (.271 BA, 27 HR, 100 RBI) led in doubles (38), WAR (5.6), oWAR (4.0), runs produced (157), power/speed number (19.3) and hitting streak (19), with a Gold Glove at second. Joe Randa (.254 BA, 9 HR, 50 RBI) was at third. Deivi Cruz (.260 BA, 5 HR, 45 RBI) at shortstop led for in-play percentage (83%). Leftfielder Luis Gonzalez (267 BA, 23 HR, 71 RBI) led in triples (5). Centerfielder Brian Hunter (.254 BA, 4 HR, 36 RBI) led in singles (115), stolen bases (42), stolen base runs (5.4) and outs (467). Bobby Higginson (.284 BA, 25 HR, 85 RBI) at right led in plate appearances (686), at bats (612), runs (92), times on base (243) and walks (63), with designated hitter Frank Catalanotto (.282 BA, 6 HR, 25 RBI). The leading pinch-hitter was Kimera Bartee at .571 (4-7, HR, 3 RBI). Scott Sollmann (59 SB) was at class "A+" Lakeland.

1990s Pitching Innings Pitched		
1.	Bill Gullickson	722.2
2.	Brian Moehler	603.1
3.	Justin Thompson	588.0
4.	Frank Tanana	580.1
5.	John Doherty	514.1
6.	Mike Moore	500.2
7.	Felipe Lira	436.1
8.	David Wells	428.2
9.	Mike Henneman	391.2
10.	Mark Leiter	353.1

Pitching. The Tigers had a 4.93 ERA, nine CG, three SHO, 595 walks, 947 SO, 96 ERA+, 4.81 FIP, 1.484 WHIP, 9.7 H/9, 3.7 BB/9, and 5.9 SO/9, as staff led league for IBB (53). Pitcher of the Year and most effective pitcher Doug Brocail (5-2, 2.73 ERA) led in ERA, ERA+ (173), FIP (2.71), DICE (2.57), WHIP (1.037), H/9 (6.8), HR/9 (0.3), SO/BB (3.06), and runs per nine (3.3). Brian Moehler (14-13, 3.90 ERA) led in wins, win percentage (.519), shutouts (3), homers (30), pWAR (4.2), BB/9 (2.3) and quality starts (20). Justin Thompson (11-15, 4.05 ERA) led in losses, starts (34), complete games (5), innings (222), hits (227), walks (79), strikeouts (149), earned runs (100) and runs (114). Brian Powell (3-8, 6.35 ERA) and Frank Castillo (3-9, 6.83 ERA). Bryce Florie (8-9, 4.80 ERA), Seth Greisinger (6-9, 5.12 ERA) and Tim Worrell (2-6, 5.98 ERA). Sean Runyan (1-4, 3.58 ERA) led MLB in games (88) and team in LOB% (80.4). Todd Jones (1-4, 4.97 ERA) led in GF (53), saves (28) and SO/9 (8.1). Tiger Rookie of the Year Matt Anderson (5-1, 3.27 ERA), Dean Crow (2-2, 3.94 ERA), Doug Bochtler (0-2, 6.15 ERA) and A.J. Sager (4-2, 6.52 ERA). Class "AA" Jacksonville had Brian Powell (10-2 .833). Brocail excelled during May (0.90 ERA, .176 BA), July (1.59 ERA, .205 BA) and September (1.35 ERA, .149 BA).

Defense. Detroit had 115 errors (.982), led division in chances (6,266) and led league in assists (1,812). League leaders were Thompson in pitcher fielding (1.000), caught stealing (16), and pickoffs (8). Florie led in double plays (5), Easley led in fielding (.985) and putouts (285) at second. Easley and shortstop Cruz led team in dWAR (2.2). Higginson in right led in assists (15).

The first-place class "AA" Jacksonville Suns (86-54 .614) featured Southern League MVP and USA Minor League Player of the Year Gabe Kapler (.322 BA, 113 R, 47 2B, 28 HR, 146 RBI, 319 TB) and Robert Fick (.318 BA, 101 R, 47 2B, 18 HR, 114 RBI). Others included Carlos Villalobos (.320 BA, 96 R, 18 HR, 80 RBI) and Javier Cardona (.331 BA), with Dave Roberts (.326 BA).

Anderson was the first pick in the 1997 draft. He started 1998 with class "A+" Lakeland and class "AA" Jacksonville (30 GM, 13 SV, 0.66 ERA, 0.927 WHIP), with a stellar MLB debut period of June 25-July 29 (15 GM, 2-0, 15.1 IP, 0.59 ERA, .220 BA).

1990s Pitching Walks	
1. Mike Moore	246
2. Frank Tanana	234
3. Justin Thompson	204
4. Brian Moehler	184
5. Felipe Lira	169
6. Bill Gullickson	163
7. Mike Henneman	145
8. Mark Leiter	137
9. John Doherty	136
10. Greg Keagle	106

Team. Detroit finished third for manager Larry Parrish at 69-92 (.429) with 2,026,441 fans. The Tigers were 11-12 in April that included a 9-2 win at home over Boston on Wednesday, April 21, behind Brian Moehler (6.2 IP, 2 ER), Dean Palmer 3-for-4 (2 HR, 5 RBI), Brian Hunter 3-for-4 (2 2B) and Deivi Cruz 3-for-4, as Tony Clark (HR, 2 RBI) and Frank Catalanotto clubbed home runs. Motown suffered a dreadful 22-6 loss in Seattle on Thursday, April 29, as 29 Mariners reached base, with an 11-run fifth inning and six-run sixth. Tiger Mel Rojas (1.2 IP, 11 ER, 8 H, 1 BB, 2 HBP, 3 HR) had a short stay in Motown April 18-May 3 (5 GM, 6.1 IP, 16 ER, 12 H, 22.74 ERA, .387 BA, .487 OBP, .839 SLG). Players finished 10-18 in May with a Bobby Higginson (2 HR, 5 RBI) and Jeff Weaver (6 IP, 2 ER, 5 SO) led 9-3 win over visiting Cleveland on Sunday, May 16. Detroit won 10-5 facing Chicago at home on Thursday, May 27, aided by Weaver (W 6-3, 8 IP, 2 ER), Brad Ausmus 3-for-4 (HR, 3 RBI), and Higginson (3 RBI), as Luis Polonia was 5-for-5 and scored four runs. The Bengals were 12-15 in June losing an 8-7 14-inning game in St. Louis on Saturday, June 12, when Tony Clark (HR, 3 RBI), Dean Palmer and Deivi Cruz hit homered. Motown was 9-17 in July as Ausmus had two triples in a 9-8 home loss to the Yankees on Tuesday, July 6. The Tigers were 11-16 in August with a nine-game losing streak. Francisco Cordero (H 1, 1.1. IP, 4 SO) and Todd Jones (SV 18, 1 IP, 3 SO) struck out the seven batters they faced during a 3-1 win in Arlington on Thursday, August 12. The Bengals won 12-3 in Anaheim on Sunday, August 22, led by Palmer 3-for-5 (3 RBI) and Juan Encarnacion 3-for-5 (HR, 5 RBI). The club closed 15-13 in September and 1-1 in October, including 8-2 in their last 10 games. Motown won 9-7 in Oakland on Monday, September 6, aided by Polonia 4-for-5 (3B, 2 RBI, 2 SB), and Clark 3-for-3 (3 R, 2 2B, HR, 4 RBI). C.J. Nitkowski (7 IP, 0 ER, 2 H) and Karim Garcia 4-for-4 (2 HR, 3 RBI) paced the 7-0 shutout in Chicago on September 14. Closer Todd Jones was awesome during July 28-September 9 (10 GM, 1-0, 6 SV, 0.96 ERA, .152 BA, .200 BABIP). Detroit logged a 11-3 home win over Kansas City on Saturday, September 25, led by Nitkowski (6.1 IP, 2 ER, 10 SO), Polonia (3 RBI), Ausmus 3-for-4 (HR, 3 RBI) and Encarnacion (HR, 3 RBI). Motown was 38-43 (.469) at home, 31-49 (.388) on the road, scored 747 runs and allowed 882. Rich Gomez (.303 BA, 66 SB) was assigned to class "A" West Michigan, with Rod Lindsey (61 SB) at class "A+" Lakeland.

3B * DEAN PALMER

Offense. Detroit finished with a .261 BA, .326 OBP, .443 SLG, .768 OPS, 2,426 TB and 95 OPS+. Catcher Brad Ausmus (.275 BA, 9 HR, 54 RBI) led in on-base percentage (.365) and WAR (3.4). The most effective hitter Tony Clark (.280 BA, 31 HR, 99 RBI) at first led Motown in hits (150), total average (.855), times on base (220), base runs (92), runs created (98), walks (64) and hit streak (19). Second baseman Damion Easley (.266 BA, 20 HR, 65 RBI). Player of the Year, Tiger of the Year and Silver Slugger Dean Palmer (.263 BA, 38 HR, 100 RBI) at third led in plate appearances (631), at bats (560), runs (92), homers, runs batted in, oWAR (3.1), secondary average (.357), base runs (92), runs produced (154), runs created (98), isolated power (.255),extra base hits (65), total bases (290), bases produced (350), strikeouts (153) and outs (432). Shortstop Deivi Cruz (.284 BA, 13 HR, 58 RBI) led in games (155), singles (99) and doubles (35). Juan Encarnacion (.255 BA, 19 HR, 74 RBI) at left led in power/speed number (24.1), steals (33) and stolen base runs (2.7), with Tiger Rookie of the Year Gabe Kapler (.245 BA, 18 HR, 49 RBI) in center and Bobby Higginson (.239 BA, 12 HR, 46 RBI) in right. Designated hitter Luis Polonia (.324 BA, 10 HR, 32 RBI) led in triples (8), slugging (.526), OPS (.882), OPS+ (123), base-out percentage (.892), gross production average (.292), batters run average (.187), hitting, BAbip (.334) and in-play percentage (83%). Frank Catalanotto (.276 BA, 11 HR, 35 RBI) and Karim Garcia (.240 BA, 14 HR, 32 RBI). The best pinch-hitters were Polonia at .333 (2-6) and Catalanotto .292 (7-24, HR, 6 RBI). Clark reached base in 26 consecutive games during the month of July 10-August 10, that included a 19-game hitting streak (10 HR, 30 RBI, .370 BA, .427 OBP, .822 SLG). Dave McCarty (31 HR) played with class "AAA" Toledo.

1990s Pitching Strikeouts	
1. Justin Thompson	383
2. Brian Moehler	328
3. Frank Tanana	312
4. David Wells	293
5. Bill Gullickson	290
6. Mike Henneman	278
7. Felipe Lira	269
8. Mark Leiter	248
9. Mike Moore	215
10. John Doherty	174

Pitching. The team had a 5.17 ERA, four CG, two SHO, 583 walks, 976 SO, 94 ERA+, 5.05 FIP, 1.486 WHIP, 9.7 H/9, 3.7 BB/9, and 6.2 SO/9. Motown shined April 16-22 (5-1, 54 IP, 0.83 ERA, .172 BA). Pitcher of the Year and most effective pitcher Doug Brocail (4-4, 2.52 ERA, 2.7 BB/9) led in games (70), LOB% (83.3), ERA, ERA+ (194), WAR (3.1), FIP (3.40), DICE (3.27), WHIP (1.037), pWAR (3.1), H/9 (6.6), SO/BB (3.12) and R/9 (2.5). Dave Mlicki (14-12, 4.60 ERA) led in wins, win percentage (.538), walks (70) and strikeouts (119). Mlicki went 10-4 in the second half. Brian Moehler (10-16, 5.04 ERA) led league in losses, as he led staff in starts (32), shutouts (2), innings (196.1), hits (229), earned runs (110) and runs (116). Jeff Weaver (9-12, 5.55 ERA) led MLB in hit by pitch (17) and staff for homers (27). Thompson (9-11, 5.11 ERA), Dave Borkowski (2-6, 6.10 ERA) and Willie Blair (3-11, 6.85 ERA). Todd Jones (4-4, 3.80 ERA) led in games finished (62), saves (30) and SO/9 (8.7). C.J. Nitkowski (4-5, 4.30 ERA) led league in balks (3). Masao Kida (1-0, 6.26 ERA) led in wild pitches (7). Bryce Florie (2-1, 4.56 ERA), Matt Anderson (2-1, 5.68 ERA), Nelson Cruz (2-5, 5.67 ERA) and Francisco Cordero (2-2, 3.32 ERA). Cruz began at class "AAA" Toledo (7-1 .875, 2.73 ERA). Class "AA" Jacksonville had Southern League Pitcher of the Year Cordero (4-1, 27 SV, 1.38 ERA) and Victor Santos (12-6 .667). Bill Snyder (4-1, 1.92 ERA, 16 SV) was at class "A+" Lakeland.

Defense. Motown had 106 errors for a .982 fielding average and led division in defensive efficiency (.688). League leaders were Moehler and Weaver in pitcher fielding (1.000). Ausmus led in catcher fielding (.998) and led the Tigers in dWAR (1.6).

Tony Clark labored in first half (70 GM, 8 HR, 38 RBI, .240 BA, .384 SLG). He went on a tear in second half (73 GM, 23 HR, 61 RBI, .317 BA, .622 SLG). Class "AA" Jacksonville had Chris Wakeland (.321 BA) and Javier Cardona (.309 BA, 26 HR, 92 RBI).

Player of the Decade. Miguel Cabrera (.308 BA, 71 HR, 230 RBI) was Player of the Decade after two superb years in 2008 (.292 BA, 37 HR, 127 RBI, 130 OPS+, 331 TB) and 2009 (.324 BA, 34 HR, 103 RBI, 144 OPS+, 334 TB). The decade leader in slugging (.542), on-base plus slugging (.915), OPS+ (137), total average (.904), gross production average (.303), total base average (2.1) and bases produced average (2.5). Cabrera went 5-for-6 (2 2B, 6 RBI) during a 19-4 win at Kaufman Stadium in Kansas City on Monday, July 21, 2008, and 3-for-5 (2B, HR, 6 RBI) in a 15-2 win over visiting Texas on Friday, April 10, 2009. Miguel hit a cool .500 during the two weeks of April 14-20 (3 HR, 6 RBI, .586 OBP, .960 SLG, 1.546 OPS, .500 BAbip) and August 15-21 (HR, 5 RBI, .556 OBP, .720 SLG, 1.276 OPS, .571 BAbip). He dominated pitching of the Milwaukee Brewers (.538 BA) and Los Angeles Dodgers (.417) as a Tiger during the decade.

MGR * JIM LEYLAND

2000s			
Year	W – L	Pct.	Pl
2000	79-83	.488	3
2001	66-96	.407	4
2002	55-106	.342	5
2003	43-119	.265	5
2004	72-90	.444	4
2005	71-91	.438	4
2006	**95-67**	**.586**	2
2007	88-74	.543	2
2008	74-88	.457	5
2009	86-77	.528	2
	729-891	.450	

All-Decade Team. Manager Jim Leyland (343-306 .529) led the Tigers to a wild card playoff berth in 2006, as they would lose the World Series to St. Louis. Justin Verlander (65-43 .602, 3.92 ERA) was the staff leader. All-Star catcher Ivan Rodriguez (.298 BA, 62 HR, 300 RBI) reached the 2004 All-Star game (.369 BA, 12 HR, 59 RBI, 176 TB, .409 BAbip) and finished (.334 BA, 19 HR, 86 RBI) with a Silver Slugger and Gold Glove awards. First baseman Miguel Cabrera (.308, 71 HR, 230 RBI) was a road warrior in Toronto (.429 BA) and Seattle (.405 BA). Second baseman Placido Polanco (.311 BA, 37 HR, 285 RBI) led in singles (617), in-play percentage (85.5) and strikeout percentage (5.7). Polanco hit exactly.341 at home and on the road in 2007 (.341 BA, 9 HR, 67 RBI). Shortstop Carlos Guillen (.301 BA, 86 HR, 402 RBI) led in offensive WAR (22.2) was superb in 2004 (.318 BA, 20 HR, 97 RBI), 2006 (.320 BA, 19 HR, 85 RBI) and 2007 (.296 BA, 21 HR, 102 RBI). Third baseman Brandon Inge (.236 BA, 123 HR, 494 RBI) led in games (1,153), plate appearances (4,293), at bats (3,823), doubles (173), runs batted in (494), defensive WAR (12.1), times on base (1,299), extra base hits (327), extra bases on long hits (604), total bases (1,505), bases produced (1,884), sacrifice hits (38) and strikeouts (975), and an All-Star for 2009 (27 HR, 84 RBI). Left fielder Bobby Higginson (.268 BA, 83 HR, 353 RBI) starred in 2000 (.300 BA, 30 HR, 102 RBI, 104 R, 44 2B, 321 TB). Centerfielder Curtis Granderson (.272 BA, 102 HR, 299 RBI) led in triples (57) and steals (67). Right-fielder Magglio Ordonez (.320 BA, 90 HR, 442 RBI) led in on-base percentage (.392), hitting, BAbip (.340) and 20-game hit streak in 2005. Ordonez was an All-Star in 2006 (.298 BA, 24 HR, 104 RBI), Silver Slugger and MVP runner-up in 2007 (.363 BA, 28 HR, 139 RBI, 54 2B, 166 OPS+). Designated hitter Dmitri Young (.279 BA, 82 HR, 267 RBI) became an All-Star selection for the first time in 2003 (.297 BA, 29 HR, 85 RBI).

Pitcher of the Decade. Justin Verlander (65-43 .602, 3.92 ERA) led his team during the decade in wins, shutouts (3), balks (10), hit by pitch (46), pitcher WAR (15.2) and starter win percentage. He was the 2006 American League Rookie of the Year (17-9 .654, 3.63 ERA). *"JV"* went 8-3 (.727) at home, 10-4 (.714) in the first half, 4-1 (1.73 ERA) in May and 3-0 (1.01 ERA) in July. He finished 2007 (at 18-6 .750, 3.66 ERA) leading the league in win percentage, 10-3 (.769) at home, 10-3 (.769) in the first half, with 3-0 records against Kansas City and Seattle. His best year was in 2009 (19-9 .679, 3.45 ERA) when he was 10-2 (.833) at home, 10-4 (.714) in the first half, 5-0 (1.52 ERA) in May, 4-0 against Cleveland (0.90 ERA) and 3-0 versus Chicago (1.40 ERA). Justin went 8-1 (1.75 ERA) for April 28-June 21, 2009. He went 35-16 (.686) at Comerica Park during the 2000s.

P * JUSTIN VERLANDER

2000s Attendance			
Year	Attn.	Avg.	Rk
2000	2,438,617	30,106	7
2001	1,921,305	23,720	9
2002	1,503,623	18,795	12
2003	1,368,245	16,892	13
2004	1,917,004	23,667	9
2005	2,024,431	24,993	10
2006	2,595,937	32,049	5
2007	3,047,133	37,619	3
2008	**3,202,645**	**39,539**	3
2009	2,567,165	31,693	4

All-Decade Pitchers. Verlander pitched the first Comerica Park no-hitter on June 12, 2007, during a 4-0 victory over visiting Milwaukee (9 IP, 0 H, 0 ER, 4 BB, 12 SO). Jeff Weaver (30-39 .435, 3.97 ERA) led the decade in shutouts (3) and quality start percentage (.600), with a combined 7-0 record in inter-league play 2000-2001. Jeremy Bonderman (59-67 .468, 4.78 ERA) was decade leader in quality starts (83), dominant starts (15), intentional walks (22) and wild pitches (40). Steve Sparks (29-36 .446, 4.45 ERA) led for complete games (12), dominant start percentage (.115) and complete game percentage (.154). Nate Robertson (51-68 .429, 4.87 ERA) had decade highs in losses, starts (168), innings (1,042.2), hits (1,149), homers (145), walks (374), earned runs (564), runs (609), batters faced (4,558), pitches (16,305), no decisions (50), cheap wins (17) and plate appearances (4,567). Bobby Seay (10-5 .667, 4.00 ERA) was the Tigers leader in win percentage, FIP (3.48), DICE (3.33), HR/9 (0.49) and relief win percentage. Jamie Walker (12-12 .500, 3.33 ERA) led the staff in games (327), WHIP (1.174), BB/9 (1.9), SO/BB (3.5) and in holds (59). Joel Zumaya (11-11 .500, 3.15 ERA) led the 2000s in technical runs allowed (3.52), left on-base percentage (80.4), earned run average, ERA+ (144), H/9 (7.20), SO/9 (9.25) and RA/9 (3.52). Fernando Rodney (15-30 .333, 4.28 ERA) led during the 2000s for wins and losses in relief, with a team high 37 saves in 2009. Todd Jones (13-20 .394, 4.18 ERA) led in games finished (234) and saves (146). He dominated hitters for the period May 1-July 29, 2000 (32 GM, 0.61 ERA, .180 BA, 24 SV).

Several impressive scoreless streaks for Todd Jones were May 25-July 29, 2000 (22 GM, 15 SV, 21.2 IP, 6 BB, 26 SO, 0.00 ERA, .157 BA, .157 SLG) and June 24-July 28, 2006 (12 GM, 1-0, 9 SV, 11.2 IP, 3 BB, 7 SO, 0.00 ERA, .150 BA, .175 SLG, 182 BAbip).

2000s Team Hitting				
YEAR	AVG	HR	RBI	SB
2000	.275	177	785	83
2001	.260	139	691	**133**
2002	.248	124	546	65
2003	.240	153	553	98
2004	.272	201	800	86
2005	.272	168	678	66
2006	.274	**203**	785	60
2007	**.287**	177	**857**	103
2008	.271	200	780	63
2009	.260	183	718	72

Team. Phil Garner led third place Detroit (79-83 .488), with 2,438,617 fans. Players were 6-17 in April with a 10-5 win facing visiting Tampa on Friday, April 14, led by Juan Gonzalez (HR, 3 RBI). Bobby Higginson 4-for-4 (2 HR), Gonzalez and Dean Palmer homered in a 9-4 loss in Chicago on Sunday, April 23. Detroit went 12-14 in May including a 10-4 win over visiting Cleveland on Tuesday, May 23, with Higginson (HR, 4 RBI). The team was 15-12 in June with a 16-3 win versus Toronto at home on Tuesday, June 13, behind Higginson 4-for-4 (2 HR, 7 RBI), Damion Easley (3 RBI), Shane Halter 4-for-5 and Brad Ausmus 4-for-5 (4 R, HR, 2 RBI). The Bengals won 18-6 at Toronto on Tuesday, June 20, with eight Tiger home runs, led by Tony Clark (2 HR, 4 RBI), Higginson (HR, 3 RBI), Gonzalez (HR, 3 RBI), and Robert Fick (HR, 3 RBI). Reliever C.J. Nitkowski (4 IP, 1 ER, 5 SO), Wendell Magee (HR, 4 RBI) and Higginson (3 HR, 6 RBI) led a 14-8 win at Cleveland on Saturday, June 24. Detroit went 15-13 July with a 15-inning 4-2 victory in 5:20 at Milwaukee on Saturday, July 8, paced by pitchers Hideo Nomo (6 IP, 2 ER, 7 SO) and Nelson Cruz (W 2-0, 4 IP, 0 ER, 7 SO). The Tigers were 18-10 in August when Steve Sparks was selected Pitcher of the Month (6 GM, 5-0, 1.69 ERA, .188 BA, .234 OBP, .215 BAbip). Motown ponded visiting Baltimore 14-3 on Thursday, August 10, aided by Higginson 3-for-4 (4 RBI), Easley 3-for-3 (2 BB, 2 RBI), Gonzalez 3-for-5 and Rich Becker 2-for-3 (3 BB, RBI). Detroit won 11-4 the next day in Oakland, behind Becker (HR, 3 RBI) and Palmer (3 RBI). Sparks (9 IP, 0 ER, 5 H, 6 SO) had a 9-0 shutout in Seattle on Tuesday, August 15, with Palmer (HR, 4 RBI) and Gonzalez 4-for-5 (HR, 2 RBI). Easley excelled August 6-12 (.520 BA, .613 OBP, .840 SLG). The squad closed 12-17 in September and 1-0 in October. Nomo (8 IP, 0 ER, 5 H, 7 SO) shutout the Angels 5-0 at home on Monday, September 4, with Easley (3 RBI). Halter was 4-for-5 in a 12-11 home win against Minnesota on Sunday, October 1, as he became the fourth MLB player to play all nine positions in a game. Detroit finished 43-38 (.531) at home, 36-45 (.444) on the road, scored 823 runs and allowed 827. Billy McMillon hit a robust .345 at class "AAA" Toledo.

P * TODD JONES

Offense. Detroit had a .275 BA, .343 OBP, .438 SLG, .781 OPS, 2,473 TB and 102 OPS+. Brad Ausmus (.266 BA, 7 HR, 51 RBI) caught, with Tony Clark (.274 BA, 13 HR, 37 RBI) and Shane Halter (.261 BA, 3 HR, 27 RBI) at first. Second baseman Damion Easley (.259 BA, 14 HR, 58 RBI). Dean Palmer (.256 BA, 29 HR, 102 RBI) at third led in strikeouts (146). Shortstop Deivi Cruz (.302 BA, 10 HR, 82 RBI) led in games (156), singles (115), doubles (46), hitting, in-play percentage (87%) and outs (451). Player of the Year, Tiger of the Year and most effective hitter Bobby Higginson (.300 BA, 30 HR, 102 RBI) in left led for plate appearances (678), at bats (597), runs (104), hits (179), homers, runs batted in, on-base percentage (.377), slugging (.538), OPS (.915), OPS+ (135), total average (.960), base-out percentage (.968), gross production average (.304), WAR (5.3), oWAR (5.4), batters run average (.202), secondary average (.382), base runs (113), runs produced (176), runs created (121), isolated power (.238), power/speed number (20.0), extra base hits (78), total bases (321), bases produced (410), stolen base runs (2.7) and walks (74). Centerfielder Juan Encarnacion (.289 BA, 14 HR, 72 RBI) led in triples (6), BAbip (.322), and steals (16), with a 19-game hitting streak. Juan Gonzalez (.289 BA, 22 HR, 67 RBI) and Wendell Magee Jr. (.274 BA, 7 HR, 31 RBI) were in right. Designated hitter Luis Polonia (.273 BA, 6 HR, 25 RBI). Reserves Rich Becker (.244 BA, 7 HR, 34 RBI) and Tiger Rookie of the Year Jose Macias (.254 BA, 2 HR, 24 RBI). The best pinch-hitters were Billy McMillon at .714 (5-7) and Magee .385 (10-26, HR, 5 RBI). Encarnacion excelled during April 25-May 2 (.406 BA, .500 SLG, .462 BAbip).

2000s Team Hitting				
YEAR	OBP	SLG	OPS	OPS+
2000	.343	.438	.781	102
2001	.320	.409	.730	97
2002	.300	.379	.679	86
2003	.300	.375	.675	83
2004	.337	.449	.786	**108**
2005	.321	.428	.750	100
2006	.329	.449	.777	99
2007	**.345**	**.458**	**.802**	**108**
2008	.340	.444	.784	105
2009	.331	.416	.747	95

Pitching. Motown had a 4.71 ERA, six CG, one SHO, 496 walks, 978 SO, 99 ERA+, 4.50 FIP, 1.440 WHIP, 9.9 H/9, and 6.1 SO/9. The staff led league in tough losses (19) and walks per nine (3.1). Pitcher of the Year, All-Star, Rolaids Relief Man, and most effective pitcher Todd Jones (2-4, 3.52 ERA) led league in saves (42), with staff lead for games finished (60), LOB% (76.8), ERA, ERA+ (134), FIP (3.48), DICE (3.34), SO/9 (9.4), SO/BB (2.68) and runs per nine (3.9). Jeff Weaver (11-15, 4.32 ERA) led league in hit by pitch (15), club in losses, innings (200), WHIP (1.285) and pWAR (3.2). Brian Moehler (12-9, 4.50 ERA) led in wins and hits (222). Hideo Nomo (8-12, 4.74 ERA) led in starts (31), homers (31), walks (89), strikeouts (181), wild pitches (16), earned runs (100) and quality starts (17). Willie Blair (10-6, 4.88 ERA) led in win percentage (.625). Steve Sparks (7-5, 4.07 ERA) and Dave Mlicki (6-11, 5.58 ERA). Matt Anderson (3-2, 4.72 ERA) led in games (69) and hits per nine (7.4). Nelson Cruz (5-2, 3.07 ERA), Danny Patterson (5-1, 3.97 ERA), Doug Brocail (5-4, 4.09 ERA) and C.J. Nitkowski (4-9, 5.25 ERA). Class "AA" Jacksonville had Kris Keller (2.91 ERA, 26 SV) and Kevin Mobley (6-0, 2.70 ERA). Class "A" West Michigan featured Michigander Andy Van Hekken (16-6 .727, 2.45 ERA) out of Holland High School, Calvin Chipperfield (12-3 .800, 2.13 ERA) and Greg Watson (2.16 ERA, 30 SV). Sean Buller (5-2 .714, 1.99 ERA) pitched for the class "A+" Lakeland Tigers.

Defense. Detroit had 105 errors for a .983 fielding average, leading the division in chances (6,189) and assists (1,754). League leaders were pitchers Nomo in caught stealing (14), Moehler and Mlicki in fielding (1.000). Catcher Ausmus led in chances (974), putouts (898), assists (68), caught stealing (48%), team dWAR (2.3). Higginson led in outfielder assists (19), leftfielders in chances (331), putouts (305), assists (19), errors (7) and double plays (3). Easley led second basemen in fielding (.990).

Todd Jones was exemplary for May 2-July 29 (32 GM, 24 SV, 0.61 ERA, .180 BA), May 2-21 (9 GM, 0.00 ERA, .167 BA) and May 25-July 29 (22 GM, 0.00 ERA, .157 BA). Andres Torres (65 SB) and Rich Gomez (48 SB) were stars for class "A+" Lakeland.

2000s Hitting Games	
1. Brandon Inge	1,153
2. Carlos Guillen	721
3. Bobby Higginson	691
4. Curtis Granderson	674
5. Craig Monroe	672
6. Magglio Ordonez	671
7. Placido Polanco	632
8. Ivan Rodriguez	529
9. Omar Infante	494
10. Dmitri Young	487

Team. Phil Garner led fourth place Detroit (66-96 .407), with an 1,921,305 fans. The club was 8-15 in April including a 10-9 victory in Chicago on Friday, April 6, with a Deivi Cruz two-run homer and Tony Clark grand slam during an eight-run sixth inning. Steve Sparks (9 IP, 0 ER, 4 H) shutout Cleveland 1-0 at home on Saturday, April 14. The Bengals were 14-13 in May with a 18-2 win at Tampa Bay on Friday, May 18, with a nine-run fifth inning and scored six runs in the eighth. Rookie Victor Santos (6 IP, 2 ER, 3 H, 8 SO) got the win aided by Juan Encarnacion (HR, 4 RBI) and Jose Macias (4 RBI). The squad went 10-17 in June that included a 4-3 18-inning loss in 5:52 at Boston on Tuesday, June 5. Detroit defeated Milwaukee at home 9-4 on Friday, June 8, as Damion Easley 4-for-5 (4 RBI) hit for the cycle. Sparks (9 IP, 1 ER, 3 H) threw just 84 pitches during a 7-1 win over the visiting Yankees on Tuesday, June 19, behind Dean Palmer (HR, 3 RBI), Easley 4-for-4 and Roger Cedeno (3 SB). Players were 14-13 in July that included a 12-4 home win over New York on Wednesday, July 18, as Cedeno went 4-for-5 (4 R, 2 HR, 6 RBI). Jose Lima (9 IP, 1 ER) with a dominate start and Easley (4 RBI) beat the Yankees 11-2 on Thursday. The Tigers had an August mark of 9-20. Motown won 19-6 victory in Texas on Wednesday, August 8. The Bengals had a record tying 13-run ninth inning, as 18 Tigers went to bat, with a Randall Simon three-run triple, a Cruz two-run homer and a Shane Halter grand slam. Detroit hammered pitchers Mike Venafro (0 IP, 6 ER) and Brandon Villafuerte (0.1 IP, 7 ER). The 21-hit attack was led by Easley 6-for-6 (HR, 3 RBI), Simon (HR, 5 RBI) and Halter (HR, 5 RBI). Players closed 9-14 in September and 2-4 in October. Steve Sparks (14-9) excelled September 19-October 6 (4-0, 1.54 ERA). Players beat visiting Minnesota 9-5 on Wednesday, October 3. Detroit was 8-1 (.889) against Texas, 37-44 (.457) at home and 29-52 (.358) on the road, scored 724 runs and allowed 876. Chris Wakeland (23 HR, 84 RBI) was at class "AAA" Toledo, as Michigander Mike VanVleet of Battle Creek was an International League umpire. 21-year-old Andy Van Hekken from Holland High School was a combined 15-4 (.789) in the minors. Nate Cornejo (12-3 .800, 2.68 ERA) was assigned to class "AA" Erie.

P * STEVE SPARKS

Offense. The team had a .260 BA, .320 OBP, .409 SLG, .730 OPS, 2,267 TB and 97 OPS+. Catcher Robert Fick (.272 BA, 19 HR, 61 RBI) led in homers and isolated power (.204). Player of the Year, All-Star, and most effective hitter first baseman Tony Clark (.287 BA, 16 HR, 75 RBI) led in runs batted in, on-base percentage (.374), slugging (.481), OPS (.856), OPS+ (131), total average (.838), base-out percentage (.844), gross production average (.289), batters run average (.180), BAbip (.345), secondary average (.336) and strikeouts (108). Damion Easley (.250 BA, 11 HR, 65 RBI) at second led in games (154), plate appearances (658), at bats (585) and outs (462). Third had Jose Macias (.268 BA, 8 HR, 51 RBI) and Shane Halter (.284 BA, 12 HR, 65 RBI) that led for doubles (32) and oWAR (3.2). Deivi Cruz (.256 BA, 7 HR, 52 RBI) at short led for in-play percentage (83%), Bobby Higginson (.277 BA, 17 HR, 71 RBI) at left led in runs (84), WAR (3.4), times on base (232), base runs (88), runs produced (138), runs created (88), power/speed number (18.4), total bases (241), bases produced (341), walks (80) and hit streak (14). Centerfielder Roger Cedeno (.293 BA, 6 HR, 48 RBI) led league in caught stealing (18). He led Detroit in hits (153), singles (122), triples (11), hitting, stolen bases (55) and stolen base runs (7.5). Juan Encarnacion (.242 BA, 12 HR, 52 RBI) was in right, with designated hitter Dean Palmer (.222 BA, 11 HR, 40 RBI). Randall Simon enjoyed a consistent year beginning with class "AAA" Toledo (.338 BA, 10 HR, 31 RBI) and then joined the Tigers (.305 BA, 6 HR, 37 RBI). The leading Bengal pinch-hitter was Macias at .625 (5-8, HR).

2000s Hitting Runs	
1. Brandon Inge	449
2. Curtis Granderson	435
Carlos Guillen	435
4. Placido Polanco	393
5. Bobby Higginson	363
Magglio Ordonez	363
7. Craig Monroe	324
8. Ivan Rodriguez	267
9. Dmitri Young	255
10. Marcus Thames	216

Pitching. Detroit had a 5.01 ERA, one SHO, 553 walks, 859 SO, 86 ERA+, 4.80 FIP, 1.523 WHIP, 10.2 H/9, 3.5 BB/9, and 5.4 SO/9, as staff led league in CG (16) and left on base (1,197). Pitcher of the Year Steve Sparks (14-9, 3.65 ERA) led MLB in complete games (8), with staff lead for wins, win percentage (.609), shutouts (1), innings (232), hits (244) and pWAR (4.5). Jeff Weaver (13-16, 4.08 ERA) led league in batters faced (985). He led staff in losses, walks (68), strikeouts (152), HBP (14), earned runs (104), runs (116) and quality starts (21). Jose Lima (5-10, 4.71 ERA) led in homers (23). Chris Holt (7-9, 5.77 ERA), Adam Pettyjohn (1-6, 5.82 ERA) and Dave Mlicki (4-8, 7.33 ERA). Tiger of the Year and most effective pitcher Danny Patterson (5-4, 3.06 ERA) led in LOB% (75.3), ERA, ERA+ (140), WHIP (1.175), H/9 (8.9), BB/9 (1.7) and R/9 (3.3). Matt Anderson (3-1) led in games (62), games finished (41), saves (22), WP (9), FIP (2.62), DICE (2.57), HR/9 (0.3), SO/9 (8.4) and SO/BB (2.89). Tiger Rookie of the Year Victor Santos (2-2, 3.30 ERA), Todd Jones (4-5, 4.62 ERA), C.J. Nitkowski (0-3, 5.56 ERA) and Heath Murray (1-7, 6.54 ERA). Mike Steele (1.16 ERA, 19 SV) was at class "A" West Michigan. Sparks went 6-1 May 14-July 17 (3.45 ERA) and then was 4-0 August 26-October 6 (1.52 ERA). Weaver and Sparks led in starts (33).

Defense. Detroit led the Central Division in errors (131) for lowest fielding average (.979). League leaders were pitcher Weaver in fielding (1.000), Easley led second basemen in assists (496) and double plays (113). Centerfielder Cedeno led outfielders in errors (12), as Higginson led leftfielders in chances (339), putouts (321), assists (10) and errors (8). Macias at third led the club in defensive WAR (0.9). Players executed a triple-play against Seattle at home on Wednesday, August 1.

Victor Santos started his MLB career with a 0.00 earned run average thru 27.1 innings. The longest streak to start a career since Fernando Valenzuela in 1981. Class "AA" Erie featured Mike Rivera (33 HR, 101 RBI) and Eric Munson (26 HR, 102 RBI).

West Michigan had 205 steals. The leaders were Nook Logan 67, Ryan Neill 35, Miles Durham 33, Ron Merrill 15, Mikel Woods 13, Matt Walker 11, Hugh Quattlebaum 8, Miguel Pequero 5, Miles Luuloa 5, Jerry Amador 4, and Jack Hannahan 4.

2000s Hitting Hits	
1. Brandon Inge	901
2. Magglio Ordonez	807
3. Placido Polanco	806
4. Carlos Guillen	801
5. Curtis Granderson	702
6. Bobby Higginson	676
7. Ivan Rodriguez	620
8. Craig Monroe	607
9. Dmitri Young	500
10. Omar Infante	403

Team. Detroit (55-106 .342) finished last under Phil Garner (0-6) and Luis Pujols, with 1,423,963 fans. The squad was 8-17 in April when they started 0-11. Steve Sparks (8 IP, 2 ER) led an 8-2 win over visiting White Sox on Friday, April 19, with Randall Simon 4-for-4, Mike Rivera (2 RBI) and Oscar Salazar (HR, 2 RBI). The Bengals were 12-15 in May with a Mark Redman (9 IP, 1 ER, 4 H) 4-1 win at Cleveland on Monday, May 27. Players were 7-20 in June with a 7-6 home loss to Toronto on Sunday, June 2, when Simon Went 4-for-4 (HR, 4 RBI). Players were 13-14 in July with a 17-9 loss in Chicago on Tuesday, July 2. The Tigers hit six homers by Dmitri Young 3-for-5 (2 HR, 3 RBI), Damion Easley (HR, 2 RBI), Robert Fick (HR, 2 RBI), Wendell Magee (HR) and George Lombard 3-for-4 (HR). Detroit swept Kansas City at home July 23-25, with a 10-1 win on Tuesday led by Redman (8 IP, 1 ER, 4 H, 6 SO) and Magee (4 RBI), 3-0 triumph behind Jose Lima (7 IP, 0 ER, 2 H, 5 SO) and Simon (HR) on Wednesday, as Mike Maroth (6 IP, 2 ER, 6 SO), Juan Acevedo (SV 18, 1 IP, 0 ER) and Fick (HR, 3 RBI) paced the 5-2 victory on Thursday. Detroit won 8-5 at Cleveland on Friday, July 26. The 3-4-5 hitters Bobby Higginson 4-for-5 (4 R, HR, 2 RBI), Simon 4-for-5 (2 RBI) and Fick 4-for-5 (2 RBI) were a combined 12-for-15 (.800). The Tigers were 10-19 in August with a 10-7 home loss to Oakland on Sunday, August 25, as Simon went 3-for-5 (HR, 5 RBI). The franchise closed 5-21 during September that included a gem from Andy Van Hekken (9 IP, 0 ER). The lefthander from Holland, Michigan, shutout Cleveland 4-0 at home during his major-league debut on September 3. The team won a 12-inning 7-6 game in Kansas City on Wednesday, September 25, with Simon 4-for-6 (HR, 3 RBI) and Shane Halter (HR, 2 RBI). Players finished 7-37 in blowout games, was 33-47 (.413) at home, and 22-59 (.272) on the road. Detroit scored 575 runs as pitchers allowed opponents 864. Class "AAA" Toledo had Franklyn German (1.59 ERA, 13 SV), Eric Munson (24 HR, 84 RBI) and Andres Torres (42 SB). Jeremy Johnson (7-1 .875) and Nook Logan (55 SB) were assigned to class "A+" Lakeland.

P * MARK REDMAN

Offense. Detroit had a .248 BA, .300 OBP, .379 SLG, .679 OPS, 2,051 TB and 86 OPS+. Catcher Brandon Inge (.202 BA, 7 HR, 24 RBI) led in strikeouts (101). Tiger Rookie of the Year and most effective hitter Carlos Pena (.253 BA, 12 HR, 36 RBI) at first led in slugging (.462), OPS (.783), OPS+ (113), total average (.730), batters run average (.148), secondary average (.304), and isolated power (.209). He led rookies in hit streak (12). Damion Easley (.224 BA, 8 HR, 30 RBI) and Damian Jackson (.257 BA, HR, 25 RBI) were at second. Chris Truby (.199 BA, 2 HR, 15 RBI) and Craig Paquette (.194 BA, 4 HR, 20 RBI) were at third. Shane Halter (.239 BA, 10 HR, 39 RBI) at short led in triples (6). Bobby Higginson (.282 BA, 10 HR, 63 RBI) at left led in on-base percentage (.345) and power/speed number (10.9) and stolen base runs (0.6). Wendell Magee (.271 BA, 6 HR, 35 RBI) at center led in BAbip (.312). All-Star Robert Fick (.270 BA, 17 HR, 63 RBI) in right led in games (148), plate appearances (614), at bats (556), runs (66), hits (150), doubles (36), WAR (1.7), oWAR (2.0), times on base (203), base runs (75), runs created (80), extra base hits (55), total bases (241), bases produced (287), walks (46), outs (429) and hit streak (18). Player of the Year and Tiger of the Year designated hitter Randall Simon (.301 BA, 19 HR, 82 RBI) led league in at bats per strikeout (16.1). He led club in singles (108), homers, runs batted in, hitting, in-play percentage (87%) and runs produced (114). George Lombard (.241 BA, 5 HR, 13 RBI) led in stolen bases (13). The top pinch-hitters were Ryan Jackson at 1.000 (2-2), Hiram Bocachica .333 (2-6) and Simon .333 (2-6). Pena and Higginson led for gross production average (.260).

2000s Hitting Doubles	
1. Brandon Inge	173
2. Carlos Guillen	167
3. Magglio Ordonez	159
4. Placido Polanco	139
5. Bobby Higginson	133
6. Craig Monroe	130
7. Curtis Granderson	125
8. Ivan Rodriguez	124
9. Dmitri Young	100
10. Omar Infante	81

Pitching. The Tigers had a 4.92 ERA, 11 CG, four SHO, 463 walks, 794 SO, 87 ERA+, 4.44 FIP, 1.454 WHIP, 10.1 H/9, 2.9 BB/9 and 5.1 SO/9, as the staff led league in hits (1,593). Pitcher of the Year and most effective pitcher Jeff Weaver (6-8, 3.18 ERA) led in win percentage (.429), SHO (3), FIP (3.17), DICE (3.21), HR/9 (0.3) and R/9 (3.7). Mark Redman (8-15, 4.21 ERA) led in innings (203), strikeouts (109) and wild pitches (11). Steve Sparks (8-16, 5.52 ERA) led in losses, starts (31), hits (238), homers (23), walks (67), HBP (12), earned runs (116), runs (134) and quality starts (16). Nate Cornejo (1-5, 5.04 ERA) and Jose Lima (4-6, 7.77 ERA). Juan Acevedo (1-5, 2.65 ERA) led in games (65), games finished (48), saves (28), ERA and ERA+ (161). Jamie Walker (1-1, 3.71 ERA) led in LOB% (80.2), WHIP (.939), H/9 (6.6), BB/9 (1.9), SO/9 (8.2) and SO/BB (4.44). Jeff Farnsworth (2-3, 5.79 ERA) led for IBB (8). Julio Santana (3-5, 2.84 ERA), Oscar Henriquez (1-1, 4.50 ERA), Jose Paniagua (0-1, 5.83 ERA) and Adam Bernero (4-7, 6.20 ERA). Fernando Rodney started at class "AA" Erie (1-0, 1.33 ERA, 11 SV) then joined Detroit (1-3, 6.00 ERA). Mike Maroth was at class "AAA" Toledo (8-1 .889, 2.82 ERA and Motown (6-10, 4.48 ERA). Brian Powell started at Toledo (10-3 .769) and then became a Tiger (1-5, 4.84 ERA). Acevedo had extraordinary periods of excellence for April 29-June 9 (12 GM, 1-0, 7 SV, 17.1 IP, 0.00 ERA, .123 BA, .138 OBP, .158 SLG, .156 BAbip), then June 23-July 27 (13 GM, 8 SV, 13.1 IP, 0.00 ERA) and August 20-September 29 (12 GM, 3 SV, 11.2 IP, 0 ER, 0.00 ERA, .214 BA, .267 OBP, .243 BAbip).

Defense. Players led the league in errors (142) for a .977 fielding average and led division in assists (1,719). League leaders were Maroth in pitcher fielding (1.000), leftfielder Higginson in assists (15), errors (7) and double plays (3). Right-fielder Fick led all outfielders in assists (21), errors (12) and double plays (5). Third baseman Halter at third base led club in dWAR (0.7),

The third base experiment with Chris Truby (89 GM, .199 BA, 2 HR, 15 RBI, 78 TB, .496 OPS, 36 OPS+) and Craig Paquette (72 GM, .194 BA, 4 HR, 20 RBI, 77 TB, .528 OPS, 44 OPS+) failed miserably (161 GM, .197 BA, .218 OBP, .293 SLG, .241 BAbip).

Class "A" West Michigan had John Birtwell (7-2 .778, 1.59 ERA), Matt Coenen (14-8 .636, 3.38 ERA), Juan Francia (53 SB), Mike Kobow (1.99 ERA, 31 SV), Kevin McDowell (11-6 .647), Jason Moates (11-5 .688), and Juan Tejeda (.300 BA, 106 RBI).

2000s Hitting Triples	
1. Curtis Granderson	57
2. Carlos Guillen	33
3. Brandon Inge	31
4. Bobby Higginson	19
5. Shane Halter	17
Omar Infante	17
7. Carlos Pena	14
Ivan Rodriguez	14
9. Juan Encarnacion	13
Placido Polanco	13
Dmitri Young	13

Team. Detroit finished last under Alan Trammell at 43-119 (.265), with 1,368,245 fans. The club started 1-17 (.056) with records of 0-1 in March and 3-20 in April. Players won 4-1 in Oakland on Wednesday, April 23, with 20-year-old rookie Jeremy Bonderman (8 IP, 1 ER, 3 H) notching his first MLB win. The squad was 11-18 in May, as Motown won in Baltimore 7-6 on May 6, as Dmitri Young went 5-for-5 (2 HR, 5 RBI) with 15 total bases. The Bengals defeated the Orioles 9-4 the next day, as Craig Monroe (HR, 4 RBI) and Brandon Inge (2 HR, 3 RBI) led the way. Detroit lost 10-9 in Cleveland on Monday, May 19 when Carlos Pena (3 HR, 7 RBI) hit three home runs. The team had 5-22 record for June that included a 17-inning 10-9 home loss to New York on Sunday, June 1, in 5:10, with Steve Sparks (7.2 IP, 2 ER) the seventh Tiger pitcher. Detroit edged Colorado 9-7 at home on Saturday, June 14, behind Warren Morris 4-for-5 (HR), Eric Munson (HR, 3 RBI) and Kevin Witt 3-for-4 (2 RBI). The Bengals were 9-17 in July as Matt Roney (7 IP, 0 ER, 1 H) shutout visiting Toronto 5-0 on Tuesday, July 1, aided by Monroe (HR, 3 RBI) and Ramon 2-for-4 (HR). Will Ledezma (7 IP, 0 ER) defeated Boston at home 3-0 on Sunday, July 13. The Tigers won 5-1 facing Kansas City at home on Saturday, July 26. Bonderman (8 IP, 1 ER, 3 H) and Santiago (2 RBI) led the way. Motown finished 6-23 during August that included a 14-8 loss to the visiting Angels on Saturday, August 23, with Monroe (2 HR, 6 RBI). Detroit defeated Anaheim 10-9 the next day paced by Pena (HR, 2 RBI) and Inge (HR, 3 RBI). Pena homered in four of five games August 23-28. Bobby Higginson (HR, 4 RBI) and Ben Petrick (2 RBI) led an 8-4 home victory against Chicago on Friday, August 29. The Bengals were 9-18 in September with a Mike Maroth (6 IP, 0 ER) and Morris (HR, 2 RBI) led 3-0 shutout of the Royals at home on Friday, September 12. Detroit closed 5-1 in their final six games, including a 12-6 loss at Kauffman Stadium on Monday, September 22, as A.J. Hinch hit a two-run homer in his lone pinch-hit appearance. Motown beat the Royals 15-6 the next day, with Infante 4-for-6 (3 R, 2 2B, RBI), Monroe 3-for-5 (3 R, HR, 3 RBI), Morris (HR, 3 RBI) and Santiago 3-for-4. The Tigers defeated Minnesota 9-8 at home on Saturday, September 27 after trailing 8-0, with Pena (4 RBI), Monroe 4-for-5 (3 RBI), and Alex Sanchez had four steals. Motown closed 23-58 (.284) at home, and 20-61 (.247) on the road. Detroit scored 591 times and allowed opponents to score 928 runs, as that was the largest run differential in franchise history. Fernando Rodney (1-1, 1.33 ERA, 23 SV) was at class "AAA" Toledo.

DH * DMITRI YOUNG

Offense. Detroit had a .240 BA, .300 OBP, .375 SLG, .675 OPS, 2,050 TB and 83 OPS+. Brandon Inge (.203 BA, 8 HR, 30 RBI) caught, with Carlos Pena (.248 BA, 18 HR, 50 RBI) at first. Warren Morris (.272 BA, 6 HR, 37 RBI) was at second and Eric Munson (.240 BA, 18 HR, 50 RBI) manned third. Shortstop Ramon Santiago (.225 BA, 2 HR, 29 RBI) led MLB in sacrifice hits (18). Tiger Rookie of the Year Craig Monroe (.240 BA, 23 HR, 70 RBI) played leftfield. Centerfielder Alex Sanchez (.289 BA, HR, 22 RBI) led MLB in caught stealing (18), with team highs for in-play percentage (83%), stolen bases (44) and stolen base runs (2.4). Bobby Higginson (.235 BA, 14 HR, 52 RBI) in right led for power/speed number (10.2) and walks (59). Player of the Year, Tiger of the Year, and most effective hitter Dmitri Young (.297 BA, 29 HR, 85 RBI) was the designated hitter. He led in games (155), plate appearances (635), at bats (562), runs (78), hits (167), singles (97), doubles (34), triples (7), homers, runs batted in, on-base percentage (.372), slugging (.537), OPS (.909), OPS+ (144), total average (.903), base-out percentage (.906), gross production average (.302), WAR (3.4), oWAR (4.7), batters run average (.200), hitting, BAbip (.339), secondary average (.345), times on base (236), base runs (101), runs produced (134), runs created (112), isolated power (.240), extra base hits (70), total bases (302), bases produced (362), strikeouts (130), outs (416) and hitting streak (16). The top pinch-hitters were Munson at .600 (3-5, HR, 4 RBI), Sanchez .600 (3-5) and Higginson .500 (2-4).

2000s Hitting Home Runs	
1. Brandon Inge	123
2. Curtis Granderson	102
3. Craig Monroe	101
4. Marcus Thames	99
5. Magglio Ordonez	90
6. Carlos Guillen	86
7. Bobby Higginson	83
Dmitri Young	82
9. Carlos Pena	75
10. Miguel Cabrera	71

Pitching. Motown had a 5.30 ERA, three CG, 557 walks, 764 SO, 81 ERA+, 5.01 FIP, 1.510 WHIP, 10.1 H/9, 3.5 BB/9, and 4.8 SO/9. Pitchers led league in tough losses (27). Pitcher of the Year and most effective pitcher Jamie Walker (4-3, 3.32 ERA) led in games (78), LOB% (74.2), ERA, ERA+ (130), FIP (4.32), DICE (4.29), WHIP (1.200), H/9 (8.4), SO/9 (6.2), SO/BB (2.65) and R/9 (4.2). Nate Cornejo (6-17, 4.67 ERA) led in complete games (2), innings (194.2), hits (236), walks (58), pWAR (1.5), HR/9 (0.8) and quality starts (17). Mike Maroth (9-21, 5.73 ERA) led MLB in losses and earned runs (123). He led league for homers (34), with staff lead in wins, starts (33), hit by pitch (8), runs (131), and BB/9 (2.3). Jeremy Bonderman (6-19, 5.56 ERA) led in strikeouts (108) and wild pitches (12). Adam Bernero (1-12, 6.08 ERA) and Gary Knotts (3-8, 6.04 ERA). Steve Sparks (0-6, 4.72 ERA) led in games finished (24). Chris Spurling (1-3, 4.68 ERA), Chris Mears (1-3, 5.44 ERA, 5 SV), Nate Robertson (1-2, 5.44 ERA), Matt Roney (1-9, 5.45 ERA), Will Ledezma (3-7, 5.79 ERA), Fernando Rodney (1-3, 6.07 ERA) and Franklyn German (2-4, 6.04 ERA, 5 SV). Lefty Jon Connolly (16-3 .842, 1.41 ERA, 2 SHO) was an exemplary pitcher with class "A" West Michigan.

Defense. Detroit led the league in errors (138) and assists (1,813), with a .978 fielding average. League leaders were pitchers Maroth in caught stealing (11), pickoffs (7) and Sparks in double plays (6). Inge led catchers in double plays (11) and caught stealing (40). He led team in defensive WAR (1.5). Pena had 13 errors at first, as Sanchez committed six errors in centerfield.

Homero Rivera (13-4, 2.97 ERA), Brian Schmack (2.05 ERA, 29 SV) and Rob Henkel (9-3) were at class "AA" Erie. Mike Kobow (5-1, 1.05 ERA, 15 SV) was at class "A+" Lakeland, where D.J. Reyburn of Hope College was a Florida State League umpire.

<u>Team</u>. Alan Trammell led Detroit (72-90 .444) to fourth place, with 1,917,004 fans. The club went 12-11 in April including a 17-3 win over Cleveland at home on Friday, April 23, led by Brandon Inge (HR, 4 RBI), Eric Munson (4 R, HR, 4 RBI), and Ivan Rodriguez (3 RBI). Highlights included an 11-run sixth inning, as 14 Tigers went to bat. The club was 11-16 during May with a 10-inning 16-15 loss at Arlington in 3:59 on Saturday, May 8, with Alex Sanchez (3 RBI) and Rodriguez (3 RBI). The exciting fifth inning had Detroit scoring eight runs and Texas 10. Gary Knotts (W 1-0, 5 IP, 1 ER, 2 H, 5 SO) and Esteban Yan (SV 2, 4 IP, 0 ER, 0 H, 4 SO) two-hit the Rangers for a 7-1 triumph at home on Friday, May 14. The Bengals had 27 hits in a 17-7 victory over the Royals at Kauffman Stadium on Thursday, May 27. Carlos Pena went 6-for-6 (4 R, 2 HR, 5 RBI, 13 TB), Omar Infante 4-for-4 and Sanchez 4-for-6. The team had a 14-12 mark in June when Rodriguez was Player of the Month (17 RBI, .500 BA, .542 OBP, .733 SLG, .541 BAbip). Pena hit a walk-off grand slam in a 9-5 win over Arizona on Sunday, June 27. Motown was 13-15 in July when Mike Maroth was undefeated July 9-August 21 (5-0, 2.94 ERA), Maroth (9 IP, 0 ER,1 H, 7 SO) threw 127 pitches for a one-hit 8-0 shutout of visiting on Friday, July 16. Munson (HR, 2 RBI), Carlos Guillen (2 RBI) and Rodriguez (2 RBI) paced the win. Marcus Thames (HR, 5 RBI) led a 9-2 win in Chicago on Sunday, July 25. He hit a homer in four straight games July 22-26. The Bengals were 11-17 in August as Jeremy Bonderman (9 IP 0 ER, 7 H, 14 SO) shutout visiting Chicago 7-0 on Monday, August 23. Nate Robertson (W 12-7, 9 IP, 1 ER, 7 SO) and Craig Monroe (2 HR, 5 RBI) powered a 9-1 win in Kansas City on Monday, August 30. Detroit closed 10-17 in September and 1-2 for October. Motown split doubleheader on Thursday, September 9, with a 26-5 loss in the opener. The Tiger staff allowed 34 Royals to reach on 26 hits and eight walks, with an 11 run third inning. Bonderman (8 IP, 6 H, 0 ER, 9 SO) and Monroe (HR, 4 RBI) aided an 8-0 game two win. Bonderman (9 IP, 4 H, 0 ER, 9 SO) had an 8-0 shutout in Tampa on Thursday, September 30. Detroit went 38-43 (.469) at home, 34-47 (.420) on the road, scored 827 runs and allowed 844. Class "AA" Erie featured Kurt Airosa (34 HR, 94 RBI), Juan Tejeda (23 HR, 92 RBI), Curtis Granderson (.303 BA, 21 HR, 93 RBI), Wil Ledezma (10-3 .769) and Roberto Novoa (7-0 1.000, 2.96 ERA), as Michigander D.J. Reyburn of Grand Rapids was an Eastern League umpire. Tony Giarratano hit .376 at class "A+" Lakeland. Class "A" West Michigan had stars Kelly Hunt (21 HR, 102 RBI), Juan Francia (.320 BA, 37 SB) and Virgil Vasquez (14-6 .700).

2000s Hitting Runs Batted In	
1. Brandon Inge	494
2. Magglio Ordonez	442
3. Carlos Guillen	402
4. Craig Monroe	379
5. Bobby Higginson	353
6. Curtis Granderson	299
7. Placido Polanco	285
8. Ivan Rodriguez	268
9. Dmitri Young	267
10. Marcus Thames	255

C * IVAN RODRIGUEZ

<u>Offense</u>. Detroit had a .272 BA, .337 OBP, .449 SLG, .786 OPS, 2,526 TB and 108 OPS+. All-Star, King Tiger, Tiger of the Year and Silver Slugger catcher Ivan Rodriguez (.334 BA, 19 HR, 86 RBI) led in at bats (527), hits (176), singles (123), on-base percentage (.383), hitting and hit streak (14). Carlos Pena (.241 BA, 27 HR, 82 RBI) at first led in homers, secondary average (.389), stolen base runs (1.5) and strikeouts (146). Omar Infante (.264 BA, 16 HR, 55 RBI) at second led in outs (393). Third had Eric Munson (.212 BA, 19 HR, 49 RBI) that led in isolated power (.234) and Brandon Inge (.287 BA, 13 HR, 64 RBI). Player of the Year, King Tiger, All-Star and most effective hitter Carlos Guillen (.318 BA, 20 HR, 97 RBI) at short led in plate appearances (583), runs (97), doubles (37), triples (10), runs batted in, slugging (.542), OPS (.921), OPS+ (143), total average (.922), base-out percentage (.937), gross production average (.306), WAR (4.6), oWAR (5.9), batters run average (.205), base runs (98), runs produced (174), runs created (107), power/speed number (15.0), extra base hits (67), total bases (283) and bases produced (347). Rondell White (.270 BA, 19 HR, 67 RBI) and Monroe (.293 BA, 18 HR, 72 RBI) played leftfield. Sanchez (.322 BA, 2 HR, 26 RBI) led in BAbip (.374), in-play percentage (80%) and steals (19) sharing center with Tiger Rookie of the Year Nook Logan (.278 BA, 10 RBI). Bobby Higginson (.246 BA, 12 HR, 64 RBI) was in right, with designated hitter Dmitri Young (.272 BA, 18 HR, 60 RBI). The top pinch-hitters were Inge at .667 (2-3) and Monroe .500 (2-4, HR). Pena and Higginson led in walks (70).

<u>Pitching</u>. The Tigers had a 4.93 ERA, seven CG, four SHO, 530 walks, 995 SO, 91 ERA+, 4.60 FIP, 1.439 WHIP, 9.6 H/9, 3.3 BB/9, and 6.2 SO/9. Staff led league in wild pitches (71). Pitcher of the Year and most effective pitcher Jamie Walker (3-4, 3.20 ERA) led in games (70), LOB% (76.3), ERA, ERA+ (140), FIP (3.62), DICE (3.57), WHIP (1.253), walks per nine (1.7), strikeouts to walks (4.42) and runs per nine (3.9). Mike Maroth (11-13, 4.31 ERA, 33 GS, 17 QS) led in innings (217), hits (244) and pWAR (3.3). Jeremy Bonderman (11-13, 4.89 ERA) led league in shutouts (2) and team in walks (73), strikeouts (168) and hit by pitch (10). Nate Robertson (12-10, 4.90 ERA, 17 QS) led in wins, win percentage (.545) and homers (30). Jason Johnson (8-15, 5.13 ERA, 33 GS) led in losses, earned runs (112), and runs (121). Gary Knotts (7-6, 5.25 ERA) led in wild pitches (11). Wil Ledezma (4-3, 4.39 ERA). Ugueth Urbina (4-6, 4.50 ERA) led in games finished (46), saves (21), H/9 (6.3) and SO/9 (9.3). Esteban Yan (3-6, 3.83 ERA) led in homers per nine (0.8). Al Levine (3-4, 4.58 ERA), Danny Patterson (0-4, 4.75 ERA) and Steve Colyer (1-0, 6.47 ERA). Walker was superb April 13-May 14 (12 GM, 0.69 ERA, 13 IP, 12 SO).

2000s Hitting On-Base Percentage	
1. Magglio Ordonez	.382
2. Miguel Cabrera	.373
Carlos Guillen	.373
4. Placido Polanco	.355
5. Bobby Higginson	.352
6. Curtis Granderson	.344
7. Dmitri Young	.340
8. Robert Fick	.335
9. Carlos Pena	.331
10. Ivan Rodriguez	.326

<u>Defense</u>. Players made a league high 144 errors for a .977 fielding average. League leaders were Maroth in pitcher fielding (1.000), catcher Rodriguez in errors (11), Monroe in outfield errors (11) and errors in left (8). Sanchez led in errors (9) in center and right-fielder Higginson led all outfielders in assists with 13. Third baseman Inge led team in defensive WAR (0.6).

Pudge Rodriguez entered the All-Star game on July 13 at Houston with an MLB leading .369 average (45 R, 23 2B, 12 HR, 59 RBI). He went 2-for-4 with a first-inning triple in a 9-4 American League victory when Astro Roger Clemens allowed six runs.

Ugueth Urbina excelled the period of July 25-August 24 (11 GM, 0.75 ERA, 12 IP, .053 BA, .122 OBP, .158 SLG, .034 BAbip). Marcus Thames was exceptional in his 64 games at class "AAA" Toledo (.329 BA, 24 HR, 59 RBI, .410 OBP, .735 SLG, 172 TB).

2000s Hitting Slugging Percentage	
1. Miguel Cabrera	.542
2. Marcus Thames	.501
3. Magglio Ordonez	.495
4. Carlos Guillen	.486
Dmitri Young	.486
6. Curtis Granderson	.484
7. Carlos Pena	.461
8. Ivan Rodriguez	.453
9. Craig Monroe	.451
10. Robert Fick	.440

Team. Detroit finished fourth for Alan Trammell at 71-91 (.438), with 2,024,431 fans. The team went 11-11 in April including an opening day 11-2 win over Kansas City at home on Monday, April 4, with 44,105 fans, led by Jeremy Bonderman (7 IP, 1 ER, 7 SO), Brandon Inge (HR, 3 RBI) and Dmitri Young 4-for-4 (3 HR, 5 RBI) that scored four runs. Bonderman (8 IP, 1 ER) threw a 7-1 win in Kansas City on Saturday, April 16. Ugueth Urbina excelled April 17-June 7 (19 GM, 1-1, 9 SV, 21.1 IP, 26 SO, 0.84 ERA, .149 BA, .250 OBP, .213 BAbip) and was promptly traded to Philadelphia for Placido Polanco. The Bengals were 12-15 in May with a Bonderman (8 IP, 1 ER, 4 H, 8 SO) 2-1 triumph at Anaheim on Saturday, May 7, followed by a 10-1 win over the Angels the next day with a crowd of 43,587, behind Inge (HR, 2 RBI), Ivan Rodriguez (3 RBI) and Mike Maroth (8 IP, 1 ER, 3 H). Nate Robertson (8 IP, 0 ER) logged a 2-0 victory in Texas on Monday. Players were 13-13 in June with Jason Johnson logging home wins of 5-3 against Baltimore on Friday, June 3 (8 IP, 1 ER, 6 SO) and 8-2 against San Francisco on Saturday, June 18 (8 IP, 1 ER), when Inge 3-for-4 (3 RBI), Rodriguez 3-for-4 and Omar Infante 3-for-4 led the way. Bonderman (7 IP, 1 ER, 4 H) and Chris Shelton (HR, 2 RBI) led a defeat of San Diego 3-1 at home on Thursday, June 16. Comerica Park hosted the 76th All-Star game on Tuesday, July 12, with Michiganders Tim Welke of Glen Oaks Community College in Centreville, Michigan, the first base umpire and former Tiger Dave Campbell of Manistee the ESPN radio analyst. Detroit was 14-15 in July defeating the visiting Twins 12-6 on Friday, July 22, as Craig Monroe went 5-for-5 (3 2B, 6 RBI). Infante recorded a run batted in during six straight games July 19-23. The Bengals were 13-13 in August, as Carlos Pena dominated August 19-29 (8 GM, 7 HR, 15 RBI, .481 BA, .563 OBP, 1.333 SLG). Motown had a 17-6 home win over Toronto on Sunday, August 21, behind Inge (3 RBI), Pena (HR, 3 RBI), Curtis Granderson (HR, 3 RBI) and Monroe (HR, 2 RBI). Polanco had five straight multi-hit games August 15-20 (.440 BA, .440 OBP, .440 SLG, .440 BAbip). Motown closed 8-22 in September and 0-2 in October. Detroit was 39-42 (.486) at home, 32-49 (.347) on the road, scored 723 runs and allowed 787. Class "AA" Erie featured Don Kelly (.340 BA) and Joel Zumaya (8-3, 2.77 ERA).

1B * CHRIS SHELTON

Offense. Hitters had a .272 BA, .321 OBP, .428 SLG, .750 OPS, 2,398 TB and 100 OPS+. All-Star catcher Pudge Rodriguez (.276 BA, 14 HR, 50 RBI) led in doubles (33). The most effective hitter was rookie Chris Shelton (.299 BA, 18 HR, 59 RBI) at first base. He led in slugging (.510), OPS (.870), OPS+ (132), total average (.837), base-out percentage (.840), secondary average, (.299) and isolated power (.211). Tiger of the Year and King Tiger Placido Polanco (.338 BA, 6 HR, 36 RBI) at second led in on-base percentage (.386), WAR (4.3), oWAR (3.1), batters run average (.177), hitting and in-play percentage (86%). Brandon Inge (.261 BA, 16 HR, 72 RBI) at third led in games (160), plate appearances (694), at bats (616), runs (75), hits (161), singles (105), triples (9), times on base (227), base runs (83), runs created (85), extra base hits (56), total bases (258), bases produced (328), walks (63), strikeouts (140) and outs (487). Omar Infante (.222 BA, 9 HR, 43 RBI) shared short with Carlos Guillen (.320 BA, 5 HR, 23 RBI) who led in BAbip (.358). Leftfielder Rondell White (.313 BA, 12 HR, 53 RBI) led with a 20-game hitting streak. Player of the Year Craig Monroe (.277 BA, 20 HR, 89 RBI) led MLB in sacrifice flies (12). He led club in runs batted in, runs produced (138), power/speed number (11.4) and hit .467 (21 RBI, .800 SLG) with the bases loaded. Nook Logan (.258 BA, HR, 17 RBI) at center led in steals (23) and stolen base runs (3.3). Magglio Ordonez (.302 BA, 8 HR, 46 RBI) was in right. Designated hitter Dmitri Young (.271 BA, 21 HR, 72 RBI) led in homers (21). Carlos Pena (.235 BA, 18 HR, 44 RBI) and Tiger Rookie of the Year Curtis Granderson (.272 BA, 8 HR, 20 RBI). The best pinch-hitters were Logan at 1.000 (3-3, 3 RBI), and Young at .667 (4-6). Shelton and Polanco led in gross production average (.289).

2000s Hitting On-Base plus Slugging	
1. Miguel Cabrera	.915
2. Magglio Ordonez	.876
3. Carlos Guillen	.858
4. Curtis Granderson	.828
5. Dmitri Young	.826
6. Marcus Thames	.808
7. Carlos Pena	.792
8. Bobby Higginson	.786
9. Ivan Rodriguez	.780
10. Robert Fick	.775

Pitching. Detroit had a 4.51 ERA, seven CG, no SHO, 461 walks, 907 SO, 94 ERA+, 4.57 FIP, 1.369 WHIP, 9.4 H/9, 2.9 BB/9 and 5.7 SO/9. Pitcher of the Year and most effective pitcher Jeremy Bonderman (14-13, 4.57 ERA) led in win percentage (.519), complete games (4), strikeouts (145), FIP (3.90), DICE (3.88), pWAR (1.4), SO/9 (6.9) and SO/BB (2.54). Jason Johnson (8-13, 4.54 ERA) led in innings (210), wild pitches (17), BB/9 (2.1) and quality starts (19). Mike Maroth (14-14, 4.74 ERA) led in starts (34), hits (235), homers (30), HBP (9), earned runs (110) and runs (123). Nate Robertson (7-16, 4.48 ERA) led in losses and walks (65). Sean Douglass (5-5, 5.56 ERA) and Will Ledezma (2-4, 7.07 ERA). Fernando Rodney (2-3, 2.86 ERA) led in games finished (26). Jamie Walker (4-3, 3.70 ERA) led in games (66). Ugueth Urbina (1-3, 2.63 ERA, 163 ERA+). Chris Spurling (3-4, 3.44 ERA) led in ERA (3.44) and ERA+ (124). Franklyn German (4-0, 3.66 ERA) led in LOB% (82.8). Kyle Farnsworth (1-1, 2.32 ERA, 184 ERA+), Craig Dingman (2-3, 3.66 ERA) and Troy Percival (1-3, 5.76 ERA, 8 SV). Kevin Whelan (0.73 ERA, 11 SV) was at class "A" West Michigan. Justin Verlander was 11-2 (.846, 1.29 ERA) in the minors. Kyle Farnsworth excelled April 26-July 19 (32 GM, 0.62 ERA, .176 BA). Fernando Rodney shined for the month of July 5-August 6 (10 GM, 0.00 ERA, .152 BA). Rodney and Urbina led the Tigers in saves (9).

Defense. Motown committed 110 errors for a .982 fielding average, as they led the league in assists (1,791) and double plays (171). Tiger league leaders were pitchers Maroth in fielding (1.000) and pickoffs (11), Bonderman in errors (5). Catcher Rodriguez in runners caught stealing (51%). Inge led third basemen in chances (530), assists (378), errors (23) and double plays (42). Monroe led leftfielder in double plays (4). Logan led for errors (6) in centerfield, as he led his club in dWAR (1.8).

Class "AAA" Toledo had Sean Douglas (9-1 .900, 2.87 ERA), Jason Karnuth (7-2 .778, 2.13 ERA, 23 SV), Marcus Thames (.340 BA) and Ramon Martinez (3 GM, 11-for-15, .733 BA). Class "A+" Lakeland featured stars Jordan Tata (13-2 .867, 2.79 ERA), Nate Bumstead (12-4 .750, 2.58 ERA), Chris Homer (7-4 .636, 3.09 ERA, 29 SV) and Brent Clevlen (.302 BA, 18 HR, 102 RBI).

2000s Pitching Wins	
1. Justin Verlander	65
2. J. Bonderman	59
3. Nate Robertson	51
4. Mike Maroth	50
5. Jeff Weaver	30
6. Kenny Rogers	29
Steve Sparks	29
8. Zach Miner	25
9. A. Galarraga	19
10. Jason Johnson	16

Team. Detroit (95-67 .586) was second for Jim Leyland, with 2,595,937 fans. Michiganders Paul Emmel of Midland and Tim McClelland from Jackson were umpires as the Wildcard Tigers beat New York 3-1 in the ALDS. They swept Oakland 4-0 in the ALCS, with umpire Mike Reilly of Battle Creek. They lost the World Series to St. Louis in five games, with McClelland working the series. Motown was 16-9 in April with a 14-3 win in Kansas City on Wednesday, April 5, behind Ivan Rodriguez 5-for-5 (HR, 5 RBI) and Jeremy Bonderman (6.2 IP, 1 ER, 3 H, 8 SO). On Sunday, April 16, in his 12th game, Chris Shelton became the fastest to reach eight homers in league history. Detroit beat Minnesota 18-1 at home on Saturday, April 29. The 23-hit attack was led by Rodriguez 4-for-6, Carlos Guillen 3-for-4 (2 HR, 5 RBI), Magglio Ordonez 3-for-4 (HR, 2 RBI) and Curtis Granderson (HR, 3 RBI). Players were 19-9 in May including a 13-8 win at Kansas City on Thursday, May 25, with Rodriguez (HR, 5 RBI), Marcus Thames (2 HR, 3 RBI), Craig Monroe 4-for-4 (HR) and Granderson 4-for-6. The Bengals were 20-7 in June when Rodriguez (HR, 5 RBI) and Joel Zumaya (SV, 3 IP, 0 ER, 0 H, 4 SO) led a 10-5 win in Toronto on Sunday, June 11. Kenny Rogers (W 10-3, 8 IP, 2 ER) won 12-3 in Wrigley Field on Sunday, June 18, with eight Tiger homers, Guillen (HR, 3 RBI), Shelton (2 HR, 3 RBI) and Brandon Inge (2 HR). Motown went 15-10 in July, as Justin Verlander (W 11-4, 7 IP, 2 H, 0 ER, 6 SO) and Placido Polanco (3 RBI) led a 6-0 home win versus Kansas City on Saturday, July 15. The next day Thames (2 HR, 5 RBI) starred in a 9-6 loss to the Royals. The squad was 13-16 in August including a 10-4 win in Tampa on Tuesday, August 1, with Guillen 4-for-5 (HR, 2 RBI) hitting for the cycle, and Brent Clevlen (2 HR). Players closed 12-15 in September and 0-1 in October, with a Bonderman (6 IP, 2 ER, 7 SO) 17-2 win of visiting Baltimore on Friday, September 15, led by Inge (HR, 4 RBI) and Ordonez (HR, 3 RBI). Rogers (W 17-6, 8 IP, 1 ER, 5 H), Granderson (HR, 4 RBI) and Guillen (3 RBI) paced a 15-4 win at Kansas City on Saturday, September 23. Detroit was 15-3 (.833) for inter-league, 14-4 (.778) against Kansas City, 46-35 (.568) at home, 49-32 (.605) on the road, scored 822 runs and allowed 675. Josh Phelps (24 HR, 90 RBI) and Ryan Ludwick (28 HR, 80 RBI) were at class "AAA" Toledo.

P * KENNY ROGERS

Offense. Detroit had a .274 BA, .329 OBP, .449 SLG, .777 OPS, 2,531 TB, 99 OPS+ and 203 homers. Ivan Rodriguez (.300 BA, 13 HR, 69 RBI) was an All-Star and Gold Glove catcher. First baseman Chris Shelton (.273 BA, 16 HR, 47 RBI). ALCS MVP Placido Polanco (.295 BA, 4 HR, 52 RBI) at second led league in at bats per strikeout (17.1) and his team for in-play percentage (87%). Brandon Inge (.253 BA, 27 HR, 83 RBI) was at third. Tiger of the Year and most effective hitter Carlos Guillen (.320 BA, 19 HR, 85 RBI) at short led in runs (100), doubles (41), on-base percentage (.400), OPS (.920), OPS+ (136), total average (.934), base-out percentage (.957), gross production average (.310), WAR (6.0), oWAR (6.2), batters run average (.208), hitting, BAbip (.351), times on base (249), base runs (106), runs produced (166), runs created (113), power/speed number (19.5), bases produced (373), steals (20) and walks (71). Craig Monroe (.255 BA, 28 HR, 92 RBI) in left led for homers. Curtis Granderson (.260 BA, 19 HR, 68 RBI) at center led league in strikeouts (174), with club lead for plate appearances (679), at bats (596), triples (9) and outs (463). Player of the Year and All-Star right-fielder Magglio Ordonez (.298 BA, 24 HR, 104 RBI) led in hits (177), singles (120), runs batted in and total bases (283). Designated hitter Marcus Thames (.256 BA, 26 HR, 60 RBI) led for slugging (.549), secondary average (.399) and isolated power (.293). Leading the pinch-hitters were Vance Wilson at .400 (2-5), Alexis Gomez .364 (4-11) and Shelton .333 (2-6). Monroe and Guillen led in extra base hits (65). Rodriguez and Monroe led in hit streak (14). Guillen torched Minnesota at home May 16-18 (7-for-8, .875 BA, .909 OBP, 1.125 SLG, 1.000 BAbip).

2000s Pitching Winning Percentage	
1. Justin Verlander	602
2. Kenny Rogers	.537
3. Jamie Walker	.500
4. Mike Maroth	.446
Steve Sparks	.446
6. Jeff Weaver	.435
7. Nate Robertson	.429
8. Todd Jones	.394
9. Jason Johnson	.364
10. Fernando Rodney	.333

Pitching. Players had three CG, one SHO, 489 walks, 1,003 SO, 4.32 FIP, 1.318 WHIP, 8.8 H/9, 3.0 BB/9 and 6.2 SO/9, as staff led league in ERA (3.84), ERA+ (118), HR/9 (1.0) and cheap wins (21). Pitcher of the Year and Tiger Rookie of the Year Justin Verlander (17-9, 3.63 ERA, 1 SHO) was 4-1 (1.73 ERA) in May, 3-0 (1.01 ERA) in July and led in pWAR (4.0). King Tiger, Gold Glove, and All-Star Kenny Rogers (17-8, 3.84 ERA) led in win percentage (.680) and HBP (9). Nate Robertson (13-13, 3.84 ERA) led in losses, homers (29), walks (67) and quality starts (20). Jeremy Bonderman (14-8, 4.08 ERA) led league in starts (34), with team lead in innings (214), hits (214), strikeouts (202), earned runs (97), runs (104) , FIP (3.29) and DICE (3.14). Mike Maroth (5-2, 4.19 ERA) and Zach Miner (7-6, 4.84 ERA). Most effective pitcher Joel Zumaya (6-3, 1.94 ERA) led in ERA, ERA+ (233), H/9 (6.0), SO/9 (10.5) and R/9 (2.2). Jamie Walker (0-1, 2.81 ERA) led in LOB% (91.3), WHIP (1.146) and SO/BB (4.63). Fernando Rodney (7-4, 3.52 ERA) led in games (63). Todd Jones (2-6, 3.94 ERA) led in GF (56) and saves (37). Wil Ledezma (3-3, 3.58 ERA), Jason Grilli (2-3, 4.21 ERA) and Ramon Colon (2-0, 4.89 ERA). Class "AAA" Toledo had Lee Gardner (2.92 ERA, 30 SV), with P.J. Finigan (9-2 .818) and Kevin Whelan (4-1 .800, 2.67 ERA, 27 SV) at class "A+" Lakeland. Zumaya dominated May 21-July 13 (21 GM, 25.1 IP, 0.71 ERA, .161 BA) and July 15-September 5 (16 GM, 24.1 IP, 0.74 ERA, .138 BA, .175 SLG, .182 BAbip). Bonderman had six straight strikeouts at Milwaukee on Monday, June 19.

Defense. Detroit had 106 errors (.983), led in defensive efficiency (.701), chances (6,230) and assists (1,780). League leaders were Rogers in pitcher errors (5), and caught stealing (86%), catcher Rodriguez in fielding (.998) and runners caught stealing (51%). Inge at third led in chances (555), putouts (143), assists (398) and team dWAR (2.8). Guillen led in errors (28) at short, Monroe led for assists (12) in left, with a club record of three on September 12. Granderson at center led in fielding (.997).

Class "A" West Michigan (89-48, 2.96 ERA) had Burke Badenhop (14-3 .824, 2.84 ERA), Anthony Claggett (7-2 .778, 0.91 ERA, 14 SV), Ramon Garcia (7-2 .778, 1.92 ERA), Matt Rusch (9-3 .750, 1.79 ERA) and Sendy Vasquez (13-6 .684, 2.97 ERA).

2000s Pitching Games Started		
1.	Nate Robertson	168
2.	J. Bonderman	164
3.	Mike Maroth	143
4.	Justin Verlander	132
5.	Jeff Weaver	80
6.	Steve Sparks	79
7.	Kenny Rogers	74
8.	Jason Johnson	66
9.	Nate Cornejo	56
10.	A. Galarraga	53

Team. Jim Leyland led second-place Detroit (88-74 .543), with a record 3,047,133 fans. The club went 14-11 in April as Carlos Guillen (HR, 4 RBI) and Ivan Rodriguez (HR, 6 RBI) led a 12-5 home win versus Kansas City on Monday, April 16. Magglio Ordonez drove in a run during eight straight games April 16-25. Jeremy Bonderman won eight straight starts April 30-June 20 (8-0 1.000). The team was 16-12 in May including 11-1 for the period April 29-May 12. Bonderman (6.1 IP, 1 ER, 8 SO) won 14-2 in Tampa on Tuesday, May 29, as Gary Sheffield (2 HR, 5 RBI) and Rodriguez (HR, 3 RBI) led the 22-hit barrage. Players were 16-10 in June as Justin Verlander (9 IP, 0 ER, 0 H, 12 SO) no-hit Milwaukee at home 4-0 on Tuesday, June 12, with umpire Paul Emmel from Central Michigan University. Chad Durbin (W 6-3, 6 IP, 1 ER, 5 SO) won 15-1 at Washington on Tuesday, June 19, with Sean Casey (HR, 4 RBI), Inge (3 RBI) and a Marcus Thames two-run pinch-hit homer. Motown was 15-12 in July with a Bonderman (W 9-1, 8 IP, 0 ER, 7 SO) 1-0 win at home against Minnesota on Sunday, July 1. Andrew Miller (7 IP, 1 ER, 3 H, 6 SO) and Thames (HR, 5 RBI) led a 9-2 home win over Boston on Friday, July 6. Detroit beat the White Sox 13-9 on the road Wednesday, July 25, as Ryan Raburn went 4-for-5 (2 HR, 7 RBI). Players were 11-18 in August with Player of the Month Ordonez (10 HR, 31 RBI, .393 BA, .692 SLG). Motown beat visiting Oakland 11-6 on Sunday, August 12, when Ordonez (2 HR, 4 RBI) hit two homers in the eight-run second inning. Guillen (HR, 4 RBI) led an 8-5 win with at New York, with 53,914 fans on Thursday, August 16. Verlander (W 14-5, 7 IP, 0 ER, 3 H, 6 SO) beat the Yankees 16-0 at home on Monday, August 27, behind Inge (4 RBI) and Raburn (3 RBI). The team closed 16-11 in September, as reliever Tim Byrdak (W 2-0, 4 IP, 0 ER, 0 H, 5 SO) led a 5-4 win over the Royals at home on Friday, September 21. Motown was 14-4 (.778) for inter-league, 45-36 (.556) at home and 43-38 (.531) on the road, scored 887 runs and allowed 797. Curtis Granderson (38 2B, 23 3B, 23 HR, 26 SB) joined Willie Mays in the 20-20-20-20 club. Manager Tom Brookens led class "A" West Michigan (83-57) to the Midwest League title with pitchers Ed Clelland (24 GM, 2-0 1.000, 0.79 ERA, 6 SV), Casey fine (6-1 .857, 3.10 ERA, 6 SV, 11 SO/9), Brett Jensen (5-1 .833, 1.79 ERA, 23 SV, 9.8 SO/9), Matt O'Brien 7-2 .778, 2.19 ERA), and Josh Rainwater (7-2 .778, 2.32 ERA), with Duane Below (13-5 .722, 2.97 ERA, 9.9 SO/9) of Britton-Macon High School.

1B * SEAN CASEY

Offense. Detroit had a .287 BA, .345 OBP, .458 SLG, .802 OPS, 2,635 TB and 108 OPS+. All-Star, Gold Glove catcher Ivan Rodriguez (.281 BA, 11 HR, 63 RBI), with Sean Casey (.296 BA, 4 HR, 54 RBI) at first. All-Star, Silver Slugger, Defensive Player of the Year, and Gold Glove second baseman Placido Polanco (.341 BA, 9 HR, 67 RBI) led MLB in at bats per strikeout (19.6). *"Polly"* led Motown in singles (152) and in-play percentage (86%). Brandon Inge (.236 BA, 14 HR, 71 RBI) at third led in strikeouts (150). All-Star shortstop Carlos Guillen (.296 BA, 21 HR, 102 RBI). Craig Monroe (.222 BA, 11 HR, 55 RBI) was in left. Centerfielder Curtis Granderson (.302 BA, 23 HR, 74 RBI) led MLB in stolen base percentage (96.30) and triples (23). He led his team in games (158), runs (122), WAR (7.6), isolated power (.250), power/speed number (24.4), extra base hits (84), stolen bases (26), stolen base runs (7.2) and outs (438). Player of the Year, All-Star, Tiger of the Year, King Tiger, Silver Slugger, and most effective hitter right-fielder Magglio Ordonez (.363 BA, 28 HR, 139 RBI) led MLB in hitting and doubles (54). Magglio led the Tigers in plate appearances (679), hits (216), homers, runs batted in, on-base percentage (.434), slugging (.595), OPS (1.029), OPS+ (166), total average (1.088), base-out percentage (1.089), gross production average (.344), oWAR (7.2), batters run average (.258), BAbip (.381), times on base (294), base runs (140), runs produced (228), runs created (154), total bases (354), bases produced (434) and hit streak (15). Designated hitter Gary Sheffield (.265 BA, 25 HR, 75 RBI) led in secondary average (.401) and walks (84). Marcus Thames (.242 BA, 18 HR, 54 RBI) and the Tiger Rookie of the Year Ryan Raburn (.304 BA, 4 HR, 27 RBI). The leading pinch-hitters were Casey at .500 (6-12, 3 RBI), Timo Perez .400 (2-5) and Thames at .333 (3-9, 2 HR, 5 RBI).

2000s Pitching Complete Games		
1.	Steve Sparks	12
2.	Jeff Weaver	10
3.	J.Bonderman	6
	Justin Verlander	6
5.	Nate Robertson	4
6.	Nate Cornejo	3
	Jason Johnson	3
	Mike Maroth	3
	Mark Redman	3
10.	Jose Lima	2

Pitching. Motown had a 4.57 ERA, 566 walks, 1,047 SO, 100 ERA+, 4.67 FIP, 1.426 WHIP, 9.3 H/9, 3.5 BB/9, and 6.5 SO/9. The staff led league in WP (75). Pitcher of the Year and All-Star Justin Verlander (18-6, 3.66 ERA,1 CG, 1 SHO) led the MLB in wild pitches (17) and HBP (19). He led league in win percentage (.750). *"JV"* led staff in wins, starts (32), innings (201.2), walks (67), strikeouts (183), SO/9 (8.2) and quality starts (21). Nate Robertson (9-13, 4.76) led in losses and hits (199). Jeremy Bonderman (11-9, 5.01 ERA) led league in cheap wins (5), as he led team for HR (23), ER (97), runs (105), BB/9 (2.5) and SO/BB (3.02). Kenny Rogers (3-4, 4.43), Chad Durbin (8-7, 4.72 ERA), Mike Maroth (5-2, 5.06 ERA) and Andrew Miller (5-5, 5.63 ERA). The most effective pitcher Bobby Seay (3-0, 2.33 ERA) led in LOB% (80.2), ERA, ERA+ (197), FIP (2.98), DICE (2.74), WHIP (1.144), H/9 (7.4), HR/9 (0.2) and R/9 (2.3). Todd Jones (1-4, 4.26 ERA) led in GM (63), GF (54) and SV (38). Zack Miner (3-4, 3.02 ERA), Tim Byrdak (3-0, 3.20 ERA), Fernando Rodney (2-6, 4.26 ERA) and Jason Grilli (5-3, 4.75). Seay pitched 21 straight scoreless games May 27-July 28 (13 IP, 0.00 ERA). Jones earned his 300th save at Minnesota on Sunday, September 16.

Defense. Detroit had 99 errors (.984). League leaders were pitchers Maroth in caught stealing percentage (75%), Verlander in fielding (1.000) and Polanco in fielding (1.000) at second, Inge in chances (434), assists (325) and errors (18) at third, with team best dWAR (1.9). Granderson led in outfield chances (439), putouts (424), centerfield errors (5) and double plays (4).

Class "A+" Lakeland recorded 200 stolen bases led by Ovandy Suero 75, Wilkin Ramirez 28, Cameron Maybin 25, and Will Rhymes 24. The class "AA" Erie SeaWolves had Eddie Bonine (14-5 .737) and Jeff Larish (28 HR, 101 RBI). The class "AAA" Toledo Mudhens featured Mike Hessman (31 HR, 101 RBI), Virgil Vasquez (12-5 .706) *and Aquilino Lopez (2.35 ERA, 26 SV).*

Detroit Tigers 2008 American League

2000s Pitching Earned Run Average	
1. Jamie Walker	3.33
2. Justin Verlander	3.92
3. Jeff Weaver	3.97
4. Todd Jones	4.18
5. Zach Miner	4.24
6. Fernando Rodney	4.28
7. Steve Sparks	4.45
8. Kenny Rogers	4.66
9. Jeremy Bonderman	4.78
10. Mike Maroth	4.80

Team. The team finished fifth for Jim Leyland at 74-88 (.457), with a record ,202,645 fans. The team began 0-1 in March and 13-14 in April. Miguel Cabrera 4-for-6 (HR, 5 RBI), Edgar Renteria (HR, 5 RBI) and 26-year-old rookie Armando Galarraga (6.2 IP, 1 H, 2 ER, 6 SO) led a 13-2 win at Cleveland on Wednesday, April 16. Motown swept Texas at home April 22-24, including 10-2 on Tuesday, April 22, with Renteria 4-for-4. Carlos Guillen (5 RBI) and Cabrera (HR, 3 RBI) led a 19-6 victory the next day that included a 11-run sixth inning. The Bengals won 8-2 on Thursday with five home runs and Magglio Ordonez (2 HR, 4 RBI). The squad was 10-17 in May with the 2-3-4 hitters of Placido Polanco (4 R, 4-for-5), Gary Sheffield (3 RBI) and Ordonez (4 R, 2 HR, 6 RBI) guiding a 19-3 win over visiting Minnesota on Saturday, May 24. The Tigers mauled Boof Bonser (3 IP, 9 R) and Brian Bass (1.1 IP, 7 R). Detroit went 19-8 in June when Marcus Thames hit a home run in five straight games June 13-17 (6 HR, 8 RBI, .375 BA, .444 OBP, 1.500 SLG). Galarraga (W 7-2, 6 IP, 0 ER, 5 SO) and Polanco 4-for-4 (2 RBI) paced a 7-2 win in San Francisco on Wednesday, June 18. Players were 13-13 in July as Cabrera was selected Player of the Month (8 HR, 31 RBI, .330 BA, .613 SLG). The 2007 home run champion Cabrera homered in four of five games July 4-9 (5 HR, 8 RBI). Nate Robertson (9 IP, 1 ER, 4 H) started a 15-inning 2-1 win at Seattle on Sunday, July 6. Ordonez sizzled during July 20-26 (.609 BA, .609 OBP, .957 SLG). The Tigers had a 10-run eighth inning during a 19-4 slaughter at Kansas City on Monday, July 21, behind Cabrera 5-for-6 (6 RBI), Matt Joyce 4-for-6 (HR, 5 RBI) and Sheffield (HR, 3 RBI), with Guillen scoring five runs. Players recorded a 14-12 win at Cleveland on Wednesday, July 30, as Curtis Granderson went 5-for-7, Polanco (3 RBI), Cabrera (HR, 4 RBI) and Sheffield 4-for-7. Detroit finished 11-17 during August, as Galarraga (W 12-4, 6 IP, 3 ER, 5 SO) and Joyce (2 HR, 4 RBI) ran a 11-3 win in Texas on Tuesday, August 19, that included a nine run Tiger seventh inning. Galarraga was undefeated for July 23-August 19 (5-0, 2.54 ERA, .219 BA). Motown closed 8-18 in September, as Freddy Garcia (5 IP, 0 ER, 2 H) started a 17-4 stampede in Texas on Wednesday, September 17, with Ordonez (4 RBI), Cabrera 4-for-5 (HR, 3 RBI), Renteria (3 RBI) and Dusty Ryan 4-for-5. Players went 13-5 (.722) for inter-league play, 7-3 (.700) over Seattle, 40-41 (.494) at home, 34-47 (.420) on the road, scored 821 runs and allowed 857.

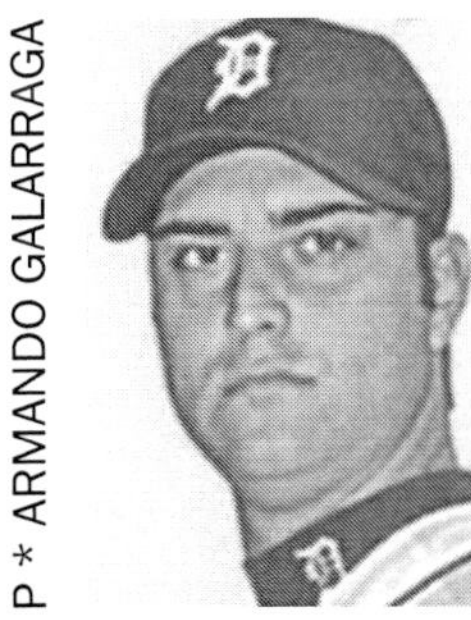
P * ARMANDO GALARRAGA

Offense. Detroit logged a .271 BA, .340 OBP, .444 SLG, .784 OPS, 2,504 TB, 105 OPS+ and 200 home runs. Ivan Rodriguez (.295 BA, 5 HR, 32 RBI) that led in BAbip (.340) and Brandon Inge (.205 BA, 11 HR, 51 RBI) split catching. Tiger of the Year, King Tiger and Player of the Year Miguel Cabrera (.292 BA, 37 HR, 127 RBI) at first led league in homers and total bases (331). He led team in games (160), plate appearances (684), at bats (616), hits (180), doubles (36), runs batted in, slugging (.537), OPS (.887), OPS+ (130), batters run average (.188), times on base (239), base runs (107), runs produced (175), runs created (116), extra base hits (75), bases produced (388), strikeouts (126) and outs (461). Placido Polanco (.307 BA, 8 HR, 58 RBI) at second led league for AB/SO (13.5), with club lead in singles (133), WAR (4.4) and in-play percentage (85%). Carlos Guillen (.286 BA, 10 HR, 54 RBI) was at third and Edgar Renteria (.270 BA, 10 HR, 55 RBI) at short. Left had Matt Joyce (.252 BA, 12 HR, 33 RBI) and Marcus Thames (.241 BA, 25 HR, 56 RBI) that led in isolated power (.275). Curtis Granderson (.280 BA, 22 HR, 66 RBI) at center led league in triples (13). He led club in runs (112), total average (.868), base-out percentage (.878), oWAR (4.8), secondary average (.356), power/speed number (15.5), steals (12), walks (71) and hit streak (15). Magglio Ordonez (.317 BA, 21 HR, 103 RBI) in right led in hitting. Designated hitter Gary Sheffield (.225 BA, 19 HR, 57 RBI). The leading pinch-hitters were Jeff Larish at .455 (5-11, 2 RBI), Thames .400 (4-10, HR, 5 RBI) and Ryan Raburn at .333 (3-9, HR).

2000s Pitching Innings Pitched	
1. Nate Robertson	1,042.2
2. J. Bonderman	1,005.0
3. Mike Maroth	880.0
4. Justin Verlander	840.0
5. Steve Sparks	614.2
6. Jeff Weaver	551.0
7. Kenny Rogers	440.2
8. Jason Johnson	406.2
9. Zach Miner	357.0
10. Fernando Rodney	330.0

Pitching. Detroit had a 4.90 ERA, one CG, 644 walks, 991 SO, 91 ERA+, 4.79 FIP, 1.512 WHIP, 9.6 H/9, 4.0 BB/9, and 6.2 SO/9, as staff led the league in IBB (63). Pitcher of the Year, Tiger Rookie of the Year, and most effective pitcher Armando Galarraga (13-7, 3.73 ERA) led in wins, win percentage (.650), homers (28), LOB% (75.6), earned run average, ERA+ (119), WHIP (1.192), pWAR (4.0), H/9 (7.7), BB/9 (3.1), R/9 (4.2) and quality starts (16). Justin Verlander (11-17, 4.84 ERA) led MLB in losses and league in balks (3). He led his staff in starts (33), complete games (1), innings (201), walks (87), strikeouts (163) and hit by pitch (14). Nate Robertson (7-11, 6.35 ERA) led league in earned runs (119). He led team in hits (218) and runs (124). Kenny Rogers (9-13, 5.70 ERA) and Jeremy Bonderman (3-4, 4.29 ERA). Bobby Seay (1-2, 4.47 ERA) led in games (60), FIP (3.43), DICE (3.30), HR/9 (0.6), SO/9 (9.3) and SO/BB (2.32). Todd Jones (4-1, 4.97 ERA) led in games finished (37) and saves (18). Aquilino Lopez (4-1, 3.55 ERA, 6 WP), Freddy Dolsi (1-5, 3.97 ERA), Zach Miner (8-5, 4.27 ERA), Fernando Rodney (0-6, 4.91 ERA), Casey Fossum (3-1, 5.66 ERA) and Clay Rapada (3-0, 4.22 ERA). New Tiger Lopez was impressive March 31-May 1 (11 GM, 2-0, 18.1 IP, 14 SO, 0.49 ERA, .224 BA, .232 OBP).

Defense. Detroit had 113 errors for a .981 fielding percentage. The Tiger league leaders were pitcher Rogers in chances (77), assists (50) and double plays (11), as he won the Fielding Bible Award as the best fielding pitcher in MLB. Polanco led in putouts (323) at second base and was the club leader in defensive WAR (1.8). Ordonez led all right fielders in errors (5).

The class "AAA" Toledo Mud Hens had stars Freddy Guzman (56 SB), Eddie Bonine (12-4 .750) and Blaine Neal (1.21 ERA, 26 SV). Class "A" West Michigan featured Alfredo Figaro (12-2 .857, 2.05 ERA), Jon Kibler (14-5 .737, 1.75 ERA), Wilton Garcia (9-4 .692) and Kyle Peter (42 SB). Tonah Nickerson (12-4 .750) and Ryan Strieby (29 HR, 94 RBI) were at class "A+" Lakeland.

2000s Pitching Walks	
1. Nate Robertson	374
2. J. Bonderman	344
3. Justin Verlander	282
4. Mike Maroth	245
5. Steve Sparks	194
6. Fernando Rodney	170
7. Kenny Rogers	158
8. Jeff Weaver	153
9. Zach Miner	145
10. A. Galarraga	128

Team. Jim Leyland led second place Detroit (86-77 .528), with 2,567,165 fans. The club went 11-10 in April including an 15-2 home win over Texas on Friday, April 10, led by Armando Galarraga (7 IP, 1 ER, 8 SO) and Miguel Cabrera (HR, 6 RBI). Motown was 17-11 in May with Pitcher of the Month Justin Verlander (5-0, 41.1 IP, 56 SO, 1.52 ERA, .178 BA). Players beat the visiting Athletics 14-1 on Friday, May 15, behind Edwin Jackson (7 IP, 1 ER, 6 SO), Ryan Raburn (HR, 5 RBI) and Brandon Inge (HR, 5 RBI). Raburn (HR, 3 RBI) and Cabrera (4 RBI) aided Rick Porcello (6 IP, 1 ER, 3 H, 5 SO) for a 9-1 win over Oakland on Saturday. Dontrelle Willis (6.1 IP, 1 H, 0 ER, 5 SO) led a 4-0 home shutout of Texas on Tuesday, May 19. Jackson (8 IP, 0 ER, 2 H, 7 SO) paced a 3-0 shutout in Baltimore on Sunday, May 31. The Bengals were 15-13 in June, as Verlander (W 7-2, 9 IP, 1 ER, 9 SO) had a 2-1 win at Chicago on Wednesday, June 10. Motown beat visiting Milwaukee 10-4 on Friday, June 19, behind Marcus Thames (2 HR, 4 RBI). The Bengals recorded a 10-14 record in July. Placido Polanco (3 RBI) paced a 11-9 16-inning win at Minnesota in 5:07 on Friday, July 3. Clete Thomas went 3-for-4 (HR, 5 RBI), Inge (2 HR, 3 RBI), Thames 4-for-4 and Verlander (W 10-4, 7 IP, 0 ER, 5 H, 8 SO) to lead a 10-1 win at home over Cleveland on Sunday, July 12. The Tigers were 16-13 in August, with a Verlander (W 13-6, 8 IP, 0 ER, 4 H, 8 SO) 2-0 triumph in Boston on Thursday, August 13, and a 1-0 home win over Kansas City the next day by Jarrod Washburn (8 IP, 0 ER, 3 H). Cabrera hit his 200th homer at Oakland on Sunday, August 23. The club closed 16-12 in September and 1-4 in October. Carlos Guillen (HR, 4 RBI) guided a 6-5 win at Cleveland on Thursday, September 24. Detroit was the first to lose a three-game lead with four games to play. They lost tie-breaker game 163 to Minnesota 6-5 on Tuesday, October 6. Players were 14-4 (.778) against Cleveland and 7-2 (.778) facing Texas. Motown finished 51-30 (.630) at home, 35-47 (.427) away, scored 743 runs and allowed 745. Gustavo Nunez (.315 BA, 45 SB) was at class "A" West Michigan, with Don Kelly (.331 BA) at class "AAA" Toledo.

C * GERALD LAIRD

Offense. Motown had a .260 BA, .331 OBP, .416 SLG, .747 OPS, 2,307 TB and 95 OPS+. Gerald Laird (.225 BA, 4 HR, 33 RBI) caught. Player of the Year and most effective hitter Miguel Cabrera (.324 BA, 34 HR, 103 RBI) at first led in runs (96), hits (198), doubles (34), homers, runs batted in, on-base percentage (.396), slugging (.547), OPS (.942), OPS+ (144), total average (.941), base-out percentage (.945), gross production average (.315), WAR (5.1), oWAR (5.2), batters run average (.216), hitting, BAbip (.348), times on base (271), base runs (120), runs produced (165), runs created (132), extra base hits (68), total bases (334), bases produced (408) and hit streak (17). Placido Polanco (.285 BA, 10 HR, 72 RBI) at second led in singles (131) and in-play percentage (84%). All-Star Brandon Inge (.230 BA, 27 HR, 84 RBI) at third led league in games and team in strikeouts (170). Short had Ramon Santiago (.267 BA, 7 HR, 35 RBI) and Adam Everett (.238 BA, 3 HR, 44 RBI) that led league in sacrifice hits (15). Ryan Raburn (.291, 16 HR, 45 RBI) at left led in secondary average (.345) and isolated power (.241). All-Star and Marvin Miller Man of the Year Curtis Granderson (.249 BA, 30 HR, 71 RBI) at center led in plate appearances (710), at bats (631), triples (8), power/speed number (24.0), steals (20), stolen base runs (2.4), walks (72) and outs (486). Magglio Ordonez (.310 BA, 9 HR, 50 RBI) and Clete Thomas (.240 BA, 7 HR, 39 RBI) manned right. Marcus Thames (.252 BA, 13 HR, 36 RBI) and Carlos Guillen (.242 BA, 11 HR, 41 RBI) were designated hitters. Pinch-hitting had Avila at .500 (2-4, 3 RBI) and Thames .429 (6-14, HR, 3 RBI). Ordonez had hits in his last 13 games of 2009 and in the first six games of 2010 for a 19-game hit streak (4 HR, 16 RBI, .480 BA, .524 OBP, .747 SLG, .464 BAbip).

2000s Pitching Strikeouts	
1. J. Bonderman	817
2. Justin Verlander	746
3. Nate Robertson	709
4. Mike Maroth	420
5. Jeff Weaver	363
6. Steve Sparks	316
7. Fernando Rodney	314
8. A. Galarraga	221
9. Jason Johnson	218
10. Kenny Rogers	217

Pitching. Detroit had a 4.29 ERA, four CG, one SHO, 594 walks, 1,102 SO, 104 ERA+, 4.53 FIP, 1.412 WHIP, 9.0 H/9, 3.7 BB/9 and 6.9 SO/9. Pitcher of the Year, All-Star, Tiger of the Year, King Tiger, and most effective pitcher Justin Verlander (19-9, 3.45 ERA, 3 CG, 1 SHO) led MLB in wins, innings (240), strikeouts (269), starts (35) and batters faced (982). He led league for balks (4) and SO/9 (10.1), Verlander led staff in win percentage (.679), hits (219), wild pitches (8), earned runs (92), runs (99), WAR (5.5), FIP (2.80), DICE (2.70), pWAR (5.5), BB/9 (2.4), SO/BB (4.27) and quality starts (22). All-Star Edwin Jackson (13-9, 3.62 ERA) led in homers (27) and walks (70). Tiger Rookie of the Year Rick Porcello (14-9, 3.96 ERA). Armando Galarraga (6-10, 5.64 ERA) led in losses. Brandon Lyon (6-5, 2.86 ERA) led league in IBB (9), with club lead in LOB% (80.8), earned run average, ERA+ (158), WHIP (1.106), H/9 (6.4) and runs per nine (2.9). He excelled in June (11 GM, 0.56 ERA) and July 7-August 21 (15 GM, 0.00 ERA). Fernando Rodney led the league in games finished (65), club in games (73) and saves (37). Bobby Seay (6-3, 4.25 ERA) led in HR/9 (0.6). Fu-Te Ni (0-0, 2.61 ERA), Ryan Perry (0-1, 3.79 ERA), Zach Miner (7-5, 4.29 ERA), Joel Zumaya (3-3, 4.94 ERA) and Nate Robertson (2-3, 5.44 ERA). The class "A" West Michigan Whitecaps had Mark Sorensen (8-2 .800, 2.44 ERA) and Casey Crosby (10-4 .714, 2.41). Jackson was undefeated for May 10-July 10 (5-0, 38 IP, 1.89 ERA).

Defense. Players had 88 errors (.985) and led division in defensive efficiency (.694). League leaders were Verlander in pitcher caught stealing (16) and caught stealing ratio (64%). Catcher Laird in fielding (.997), assists (78), caught stealing (42) and caught stealing ratio (42%). Cabrera in assists (105) at first, Gold Glover Polanco in fielding (.997) at second. Inge in chances (444), putouts (143), and errors (20) at third. Raburn led for errors (5) in left field. Granderson and Inge led in dWAR (1.6).

32-year-old Journeyman righthander Nate Bump found his form with Camden (8-2 .800, 2.49 ERA) in the Atlantic League. He then joined the Detroit class "AAA" affiliate in Toledo (7-1 .875, 2.38 ERA) at midseason for a combined 15-3 (.833) record.

Player of the Decade. Miguel Cabrera (.317 BA, 268 HR, 941 RBI) thoroughly dominated the American league, as an All-Star during the first seven years of the decade. He won four batting titles in a five-year period of 2011 (.344), 2012 (.330), 2013 (.348) and 2015 (.338). The former third baseman in the National League switched back there for his best seasons as a Tiger, with back-to-back MVP selections in 2012 (.330 BA, 44 HR, 139 RBI, 164 OPS+, 377 TB) and 2013 (.348 BA, 44 HR, 137 RBI, 190 OPS+, 353 TB). Cabrera became the first major-leaguer in 45 years to win a Triple Crown in 2012, as he led the American League in hitting (.330), home runs (44) and runs batted in (139). Several of his many decade highlights included finishing fifth or better in MVP voting five times and an All-Star game selectee for seven straight years from 2010 to 2016.

2010s

Year	W - L	Pct.	Pl
2010	81-81	.500	3
2011	**95-67**	**.586**	1
2012	88-74	.543	1
2013	93-69	.574	1
2014	90-72	.556	1
2015	74-87	.460	4
2016	86-75	.534	2
2017	64-98	.395	5
2018	64-98	.395	3
2019	47-114	.292	5
	782-835	.484	

All-Decade Team. Manager Brad Ausmus (314-332 .486) led Detroit to the Central Division title in 2014 (90-72 .556), with a second-place finish in 2016 (86-75 .534). Pitcher Justin Verlander (118-71 .624, 3.28 ERA) won the Cy Young in 2011 (24-5 .828, 2.40 ERA, 172 ERA+) and runner-up for the award in 2012 (17-8 .680, 2.64 ERA, 161 ERA+) and 2016 (16-9 .640, 3.04 ERA, 140 ERA+). Catcher Alex Avila (.244 BA, 72 HR, 300 RBI) earned a Silver Slugger Award in 2011 (.295 BA, 19 HR, 82 RBI, 142 OPS+) as an All-Star. Avila led the league for runners caught stealing in 2011, 2012 and 2014. First baseman Miguel Cabrera was a four-time batting champion during the decade. Second baseman Ian Kinsler (.275 BA, 78 HR, 300 RBI) earned an All-Star selection in 2014 (.275 BA, 17 HR, 92 RBI), with MVP votes for 2015 (.296 BA, 11 HR, 73 RBI) and a Gold Glove in 2016 (.288 BA, 28 HR, 83 RBI). Shortstop Jhonny Peralta (.275 BA, 53 HR, 242 RBI) was at his best in 2011 (.299 BA, 21 HR, 86 RBI) as an All-Star. Third baseman Nicholas Castellanos (.274, 104 HR, 424 RBI) had solid years in 2017 (.272 BA, 26 HR, 101 RBI) and 2018 (.298 BA, 23 HR, 89 RBI). Left-fielder Justin Upton (.260 BA, 59 HR, 181 RBI) made the All-Star team and a Silver Slugger Award in 2017 (.279 BA, 28 HR, 94 RBI). Center-fielder Austin Jackson (.277 BA, 46 HR, 234 RBI) was the Tiger Rookie of the Year in 2010 (.293 BA, 4 HR, 41 RBI) and the second Detroit player to lead all rookies for hits (181), runs (103), doubles (34), triples (10) and stolen bases (27), as would hit .300 in 2012. Right-fielder J.D. Martinez (.300 BA, 99 HR, 285 RBI) was average with Houston (252 GM, .251 BA, 24 HR, 126 RBI, .387 SLG, 88 OPS+) then became an All-Star for the Tigers in 2015 (.282 BA, 38 HR, 102 RBI, 319 TB). Designated hitter Victor Martinez (.290 BA, 115 HR, 540 RBI) shined in 2011 (.330 BA, 12 HR, 103 RBI). He was an All-Star and MVP runner-up in 2014 (.335 BA, 32 HR, 103 RBI, .409 OBP, 28 IBB, 172 OPS+).

Pitcher of the Decade. Justin Verlander (118-71 .624, 3.28 ERA) was the decade leader in wins, losses, starts (248), complete games (17), shutouts (4), quality starts (174), high quality starts (131), dominant starts (27), innings (1,671), hits (1,428), homers (160), walks (484), strikeouts (1,627), hit by pitch (37), wild pitches (41), earned runs (609), runs (664), pWAR (40.8), batters faced (6,835), pickoffs (14), pitches (27,381), no decisions (59), cheap wins (14), tough losses (27), quality start percentage (.702), high quality starts percentage (.528) and complete game percentage (.069). He followed his Cy Young year of 2011 (24-5 .828, 2.40 ERA, 172 ERA+), with an impressive 2012 (17-8 .680, 2.64 ERA, 161 ERA+) for a spectacular two-year period (41-13 .759, 2.52 ERA, 166 ERA+, 2.97 FIP, 0.987 WHIP, 9.0 SO/9). He threw a 9-0 no-hitter versus the Blue Jays in the Rogers Centre on May 7, 2011 (9 IP, 0 H, 0 ER). Verlander's decade totals included 21-4 during inter-league games, 12-3 versus Minnesota and 15-4 facing the White Sox.

2010s Attendance

Year	Attn.	Avg.	Rk
2010	2,461,237	30,386	6
2011	2,642,045	32,618	6
2012	3,028,033	37,383	5
2013	**3,083,397**	**38,067**	3
2014	2,917,209	36,015	4
2015	2,726,048	33,655	5
2016	2,493,859	31,173	7
2017	2,321,599	28,662	7
2018	1,856,970	22,926	10
2019	1,501,430	18,536	12

All-Decade Pitchers. Max Scherzer (82-35 .701) had terrific years in his Cy Young year of 2013 (21-3 .875, 2.90 ERA, 240 SO, 144 ERA+, 10.1 SO/9, 0.970 WHIP) and 2014 (18-5 .783, 3.15 ERA, 252 SO, 10.3 SO/9). Doug Fister (32-20 .615, 3.29 ERA) went 8-1 (1.79 ERA, 273 ERA+, 2.48 FIP, 0.839 WHIP) after his trade to Detroit on July 30, 2011, and led the decade in FIP (3.20), BB/9 (1.8), SO/BB (4.10) and dominant start percentage (.132). Reliever Drew Smyly (16-12 .571, 3.53 ERA) excelled in 2013 (6-0, 2.37 ERA, 176 ERA+, 2.31 FIP, 1.039 WHIP, 9.6 SO/9). Michael Fulmer (24-31 .436, 3.81 ERA) earned the 2016 Rookie of the Year Award (11-7 .611, 3.06 ERA), with a one-month scoreless innings streak May 21-June 17 (6 GM, 33.2 IP, 0.00 ERA, .141 BA). He continued for an equally impressive two-month period May 21-July 21 (10 GM, 9-1 .900, 65.1 IP, 0.83 ERA, .153 BA, .192 BAbip). Joaquin Benoit (13-7 .650, 2.89 ERA) was decade leader in technical runs allowed (3.08), left on-base percentage (81.3), earned run average, ERA+ (145), WHIP (1.075), RA/9 (3.08) and holds (68). Al Alburquerque 17-6 .739, 3.20 ERA) was decade leader in relief wins and relief win percentage, as Justin Wilson 7-9 .438, 3.55 ERA) had decade high totals for FIP (3.20) and DICE (3.05), with a flawless April 4-28, 2017 (11 GM, 1-0, 9.2 IP, 0.00 ERA, .000 BA, .000 BAbip, .000 SLG, .091 OBP, .091 OPS). Alex Wilson (11-12 .478, 3.20 ERA) was superb in 2016 (4-0 1.000, 2.96 ERA, 144 ERA+). Jose Valverde (7-13 .350, 3.22 ERA) was an All-Star in 2010-2011 led decade in games finished (210), saves (119) and H/9 (6.84).

Detroit had a formable duo in 2013 with Cy Young award winner Max Scherzer (21-3 .875, 2.90, 144 ERA+, 0.970 WHIP) and Anibal Sanchez (14-8 .636, 2.57 ERA, 162 ERA+, 2.39 FIP, 0.4 HR/9) for a combined 35-11 .761, 2.75 ERA. Max led the American League in wins, winning percentage, and WHIP, as Anibal led league in earned run average, ERA+, FIP and HR/9.

Detroit Tigers 2010 American League

Team. Detroit finished third with Jim Leyland at 81-81 (.500), with an attendance of 2,461,237. The club went 14-10 in April as 23-year-old Austin Jackson was the Rookie of the Month (.364 BA, .422 OBP, .495 SLG, .530 BAbip). Dontrelle Willis (6 IP, 0 ER, 4 H, 6 SO) led a 3-0 home shutout of Minnesota on Thursday, April 29. The squad had a 12-14 mark in May when Miguel Cabrera 3-for-4 (3 HR, 4 RBI) hit three homers in a 5-4 loss at home to Oakland on Friday, May 28. Max Scherzer (5.2 IP, 0 ER, 2 H, 14 SO) won 10-2 over the Athletics on Sunday, as Cabrera went 4-for-5 (HR, 4 RBI) and Brandon Inge 3-for-3 (HR). The team logged a 15-12 June record when Armando Galarraga (9 IP, 0 ER, 1 H) shutout Cleveland 1-0 at home on Wednesday, June 2. Umpire Tim Joyce's safe call allowed Jason Donald the lone hit that prevented a perfect game. Video replay indicated Donald was out at first base. Motown won seven in a row thru Friday, June 18. Detroit went 11-15 in July, as Scherzer (8 IP, 1 ER, 3 H, 7 SO) and Brennan Boesch 3-for-4 paced a 7-1 win over visiting Seattle on Friday, July 2. Justin Verlander (W 10-5, 7 IP, 1 ER, 10 SO) defeated the Mariners 6-1 on Saturday, behind Inge (3 RBI). The club had a 3-13 stretch for July 11-29. The players were 13-16 in August that included a 13-8 victory in Chicago on Sunday, August 15, aided by Jhonny Peralta (2 HR, 3 RBI), and Cabrera 2-for-3 (HR). Scherzer (6 IP, 0 ER, 2 H, 6 SO) logged a 3-1 win in New York the next day led by Ryan Raburn (HR, 2 RBI). The squad finished 15-11 in September with a 5-1 home win against the White Sox on Wednesday, September 8. Jeremy Bonderman (8 IP, 1 ER, 3 H, 8 SO), Inge (2 RBI) and Alex Avila (2 RBI) led the win. Players were 8-1 during September 17-26. Scherzer started the year 1-4 (7.29 ERA, .323 BA, .563 SLG) and then went 11-7 (2.46 ERA, .220 BA, .293 OBP) after his return from class "AAA" Toledo. The Tigers finished 52-29 (.642) at home, 29-52 (.358) on the road, scored 751 runs as pitchers allowed 743.

2010s
Team Hitting

YEAR	AVG	HR	RBI	SB
2010	.268	152	717	69
2011	.277	169	750	49
2012	.268	163	698	59
2013	**.283**	176	**767**	35
2014	.277	155	731	**106**
2015	.270	151	660	83
2016	.267	**211**	719	58
2017	.258	187	699	65
2018	.241	135	597	70
2019	.240	149	556	57

OF * AUSTIN JACKSON

Offense. Detroit had a .268 BA, .335 OBP, .415 SLG, .750 OPS, 2,343 TB and 102 OPS+. Rookie Alex Avila (.228 BA, 7 HR, 31 RBI) and Gerald Laird (.207 BA, 5 HR, 25 RBI) were the catchers. Player of the Year and most effective hitter Miguel Cabrera (.328 BA, 38 HR, 126 RBI) at first base led MLB in runs batted in, and OPS+ (178). He led the league in on-base percentage (.420), adjusted batting runs (64), total average (1.116), times on base (272), runs created (141), and intentional walks (32). Cabrera led Motown in runs (111), doubles (45), homers, slugging (.622), OPS (1.042), base-out percentage (1.121), gross production average (.344), WAR (6.4), oWAR (7.0), batters run average (.261), hitting, secondary average (.456), base runs (132), runs produced (199), isolated power (.294), extra base hits (84), total bases (341), bases produced (433), and walks (89), with a 20-game hitting streak. 27-year-old Rookie Will Rhymes (.304 BA, HR, 19 RBI) and Carlos Guillen (.273 BA, 6 HR, 34 RBI) were at second base. The Marvin Miller Man of the Year Brandon Inge (.247 BA, 13 HR, 70 RBI) manned third base. Ramon Santiago (.263 BA, 3 HR, 22 RBI) and Jhonny Peralta (.253 BA, 8 HR, 38 RBI) were at shortstop. Ryan Raburn (.280 BA, 15 HR, 62 RBI) and Don Kelly (.244 BA, 9 HR, 27 RBI) were leftfielders. 23-year-old Tiger Rookie of the Year Austin Jackson (.293 BA, 4 HR, 41 RBI) played centerfield and led the league in BAbip (.396) and strikeouts (170). He led club in games (151), plate appearances (675), at bats (618), hits (181), singles (133), triples (10), steals (27), stolen base runs (4.5), strikeouts (170) and outs (454). Magglio Ordonez (.303 BA, 12 HR, 59 RBI) and Brennan Boesch (.256 BA, 14 HR, 67 RBI) were in right field. DH Johnny Damon (.271 BA, 8 HR, 51 RBI) led in power/speed number (9.3). The leading Tiger pinch-hitters were Jackson at .500 (2-4), Scott Sizemore (HR, 3 RBI) and Damon at .455 (5-11). Jackson was selected an outfielder for the 2010 Topps Major League Rookie All-Star Team.

Pitching. The Tigers had a 4.30 ERA, six CG, one SHO, 537 walks, 1,056 SO, 98 ERA+, 4.15 FIP, 1.372 WHIP, 9.0 H/9, 3.3 BB/9 and 6.6 SO/9. Pitcher of the Year, All-Star and most effective pitcher Justin Verlander (18-9, 3.37 ERA, 11 WP) led in wins, winning (.667), starts (33), CG (4), innings (224.1), hits (190), walks (71), strikeouts (219), FIP (2.97), DICE (2.89), pWAR (4.4) and SO/BB (3.08). Rick Porcello (10-12, 4.92 ERA, 11 WP) led in losses and BB/9 (2.1). Jeremy Bonderman (8-10, 5.53 ERA) led in homers (25), HBP (10), earned runs (105), and runs (113). Armando Galarraga (4-9, 4.49 ERA) led in SHO (1). Max Scherzer (12-11, 3.50 ERA). Dontrelle Willis (1-2, 4.98 ERA). Joel Zumaya (2-1, 2.58 ERA). All-Star Jose Valverde (2-4, 3.00 ERA) led in games finished (55), saves (26), ERA, ERA+ (140), WHIP (1.159), H/9 (5.9), SO/9 (9.0) and R/9 (3.4). Ryan Perry (3-5, 3.59 ERA) led in LOB% (76.4). Phil Coke (.7-5, 3.76 ERA) led in games (74) and HR/9 (0.3). Daniel Schlereth (2-0, 2.89 ERA), Brad Thomas (6-2, 3.89 ERA), Eddie Bonine (4-1, 4.63) and Robbie Weinhardt 2-2, 6.14 ERA). Schlereth dominated August 20-October 3 (2-0, 13.2 IP, 0.66 ERA, 14 SO, .208 BA).

2010s
Team Hitting

YEAR	OBP	SLG	OPS	OPS+
2010	.335	.415	.750	102
2011	.340	.434	.773	109
2012	.335	.422	.757	103
2013	**.346**	.434	**.780**	111
2014	.331	.426	.757	**113**
2015	.328	.420	.748	105
2016	.331	**.438**	.769	106
2017	.324	.424	.748	98
2018	.300	.380	.680	83
2019	.294	.388	.682	78

Defense. Detroit committed 109 errors for a .982 fielding percentage. Tiger league leaders were first baseman Cabrera in errors (13), third baseman Brandon Inge in fielding percentage (.977) and Brennan Boesch led all outfielders with 10 errors.

Miguel Cabrera's honors included All-Star, Silver Slugger, Tiger of the Year, King Tiger and Player of the Year. He had hitting streaks during *April 30-May 13 (12 GM, .476 BA), June 19-July 16 (20 GM, .397 BA) and for August 18-31 (13 GM, .367 BA).*

Class "A" West Michigan had Corey Jones (.360 BA), Kenny Faulk (2.16 ERA, 12 SV) and Jared Wesson (7-2 .778), with Alden Carrithers (.359 BA), Kody Kaiser (.325 BA), Adam Wilk (9-5 .643) and Lester Oliveros (1.89 ERA, 9 SV) at class "A+" Lakeland.

2010s Hitting Games	
1. Miguel Cabrera	1,360
2. Victor Martinez	969
3. Nick Castellanos	837
4. Alex Avila	731
5. Austin Jackson	670
6. Ian Kinsler	607
7. Jose Iglesias	558
8. Don Kelly	544
9. Jhonny Peralta	460
10. J.D. Martinez	458

Team. Jim Leyland led Detroit (95-67 .586) to the Central Division title, with 2,642,045 fans. Motown beat New York in the ALDS 3-2, with umpire Michigander Bill Welke from Coldwater. The Bengals lost the ALCS in six games to Texas, as they were the first team to have a single, double, triple and homer in order during a postseason game. The squad was 0-1 in March and 12-14 in April including a 10-7 win in New York on Sunday, April 3, with Brennan Boesch 4-for-4 (4 R, 4 RBI) and Miguel Cabrera (4 RBI). Alex Avila (HR, 5 RBI) led a 7-3 victory at Baltimore on Wednesday, April 6. Detroit won 8-4 at Oakland on Friday, April 15, with a seven-run 10th-inning. The Tigers were 16-11 in May when Justin Verlander (9 IP, 9 ER, 0 H) pitched his second no-hitter 9-0 at Toronto in the Rogers Centre on Saturday, May 7. The team went 16-12 in June with a 4-1 home win over Seattle on Thursday, June 9, as Avila tripled twice. Verlander (W 10-3, 8 IP, 0 ER, 4 H, 14 SO) led a 6-0 home win over Arizona on Saturday, June 25, with Sparky Anderson's number 11 retired on Sunday. Cabrera (2 HR, 4 RBI) and the Tigers lost 16-9 to the visiting Mets on Wednesday, June 29. Verlander was stellar in June (6-0, 0.92 ERA, 9.9 SO/9), as he improved to 11-3. Players were 13-13 in July as Victor Martinez (4 RBI) and Carlos Guillen (4 RBI) led a Rick Porcello (W 11-6, 8 IP, 2 ER, 6 SO) 12-2 win over the Angels at home on Friday, July 29. Detroit closed 18-10 in August with a 4:43 14-inning 3-2 loss in Cleveland on Tuesday, August 9, with reliever Duane Below (4 IP, 0 ER, 0 H, 3 SO) of Britton, Michigan. Players were 20-6 in September with a 12-game win streak the longest since 1934. Doug Fister was the Pitcher of the Month (5-0, 34 IP, 34 SO, 0.53 ERA, .127 BA, .156 OBP, .195 SLG, .159 BAbip). Max Scherzer (W 14-8, 7 IP, 0 ER, 6 SO), Avila 4-for-6, Andy Dirks (HR, 4 RBI) and Cabrera (HR, 4 RBI) thumped Chicago 18-2 at home on Sunday, September 4. Fister (8 IP, 1 ER, 4 H, 13 SO) paced a 4-2 win at Cleveland on Monday. Detroit was 14-4 (.778) against Minnesota, 50-31 (.617) at home, 45-36 (.556) on the road, scored 787 runs and allowed 711. Drew Smyly went 11-6 (2.07 ERA) overall in the minors.

1B * MIGUEL CABREA

Offense. Detroit had a .277 BA, .340 OBP, .434 SLG, .773 OPS, 2,412 TB and 109 OPS+. All-Star and Silver Slugger catcher Alex Avila (.295 BA, 19 HR, 82 RBI) led in BAbip (.366). USA Today MVP, Player of the Year, All-Star, King Tiger, Luis Aparicio Award, and most effective hitter Miguel Cabrera (.344 BA, 30 HR, 105 RBI) at first led MLB in hitting, on-base percentage (.448), doubles (48), runs created (149), and times on base (308). *"Miggy"* led the league in games (161), as he led Motown in plate appearances (688), runs (111), hits (197), homers, runs batted in, slugging (.586), OPS (1.033), OPS+ (179), total average (1.118), base-out percentage (1.119), gross production average (.348), WAR (7.6), oWAR (7.9), batters run average (.262), secondary average (.432), base runs (143), runs produced (186), isolated power (.241), extra base hits (78), total bases (335), bases produced (445) and walks (108). Ramon Santiago (.260 BA, 5 HR, 30 RBI) and Ryan Raburn (.256 BA, 14 HR, 49 RBI) were at second, with Brandon Inge (.197 BA, 3 HR, 23 RBI) at third. All-Star Jhonny Peralta (.299 BA, 21 HR, 86 RBI) was at short and Brennan Boesch (.283 BA, 16 HR, 54 RBI) in leftfield. Centerfielder Austin Jackson (.249 BA, 10 HR, 45 RBI) led league in triples (11). *"Ajax"* led club in at bats (591), power/speed number (13.8), stolen bases (22), stolen base runs (3.6), strikeouts (181) and outs (477). Right-fielder Magglio Ordonez (.255 BA, 5 HR, 32 RBI) led in hit streak (18). Designated hitter Victor Martinez (.330 BA, 12 HR, 103 RBI) led for singles (126) and in-play percentage (81%). Wilson Betemit (.292 BA, 5 HR, 19 RBI, 133 OPS+) at third was acquired at the trade deadline. The leading Tiger pinch-hitters were Danny Worth at .667 (2-3), Don Kelly .444 (4-9, HR, 3 RBI) and Andy Dirks at .300 (3-10, HR, 4 RBI).

2010s Hitting Runs	
1. Miguel Cabrera	799
2. Austin Jackson	447
3. Victor Martinez	405
4. Ian Kinsler	401
5. Nick Castellanos	365
6. Alex Avila	267
7. J.D. Martinez	257
8. Jose Iglesias	212
9. Jhonny Peralta	199
10. Brennan Boesch	176

Pitching. Motown had a 4.04 ERA, four CG, two SHO, 492 BB, 1,115 SO, 103 ERA+, 3.95 FIP, 1.318 WHIP, 8.8 H/9, 3.1 BB/9, and 7.0 SO/9. Pitchers led league in saves (52). The MVP, Cy Young, USA Today Top Pitcher, Pitcher of the Year, Tiger of the Year, All-Star and most effective pitcher Justin Verlander (24-5, 2.40 ERA) led MLB in ERA+ (172), WHIP (0.920), starts (34), wins, innings (251), H/9 (6.2), strikeouts (250) and quality starts (28), "JV" led league in pWAR (8.6), win percentage (.828), ERA and team win percentage in his starts (.735). He led staff in BB/9 (2.0) and SO/BB (4.39). Max Scherzer (15-9, 4.43 ERA, 12 WP) led in homers (29). Brad Penny (11-11, 5.30 ERA) led in losses, hits (222), walks (62), earned runs (107) and runs (117). Rick Porcello (14-9, 4.75 ERA) led in HBP (8). Doug Fister (8-1, 1.79 ERA, 231 ERA+) led league in HR/9 (0.5). Joaquin Benoit (4-3, 2.95 ERA) led in FIP (2.96), DICE (2.93) and SO/9 (9.3). All-Star, Reliever of the Year, Delivery Man of the Year and Rolaids Relief Man Jose Valverde (2-4, 2.24 ERA 185 ERA+) led MLB in games finished (70) and saves (49) a new team record. *"Papa Grande"* led staff in LOB% (82.9) and HR/9 (0.6). Tiger Rookie of the Year Al Alburquerque (6-1, 1.87 ERA, 223 ERA+), Dan Schlereth (2-2, 3.49 ERA), Phil Coke (3-9, 4.47 ERA) and Ryan Perry (2-0, 5.35 ERA). Class "A" West Michigan had pitching stars Bruce Rondon (2.03 ERA, 19 SV, 13.7 SO/9) and Kevin Eichhorn (11-5 .688).

Defense. Detroit committed 103 errors for a .983 fielding average. Tiger league leaders were pitchers Max Scherzer in fielding average (1.000), Doug Fister in chances (58) and Justin Verlander with five errors. Alex Avila led all catchers in fielding average (.995), chances (1,018), putouts (940) and in runners caught stealing (40). Miguel Cabrera at first led in errors (13) and double plays (117). Centerfielder Austin Jackson won the Fielding Bible Award and led MLB in dWAR (3.1).

Justin Verlander was stellar in June (6-0 1.000, 0.92 ERA), first half (12-4 .750, 2.15 ERA), second half (12-1 .923, 2.79 ERA), at home (10-3 .769, 2.37 ERA), away (14-2 .875, 2.43 ERA), night (16-4 .800, 2.67 ERA) and during days (8-1 .889, 1.78 ERA).

Duane Below (9-4 .692, 3.13 ERA) of Britton, Michigan, and Brendan Wise (50 GM, 1.90 ERA) were at class "AAA" Toledo. Class "A+" Lakeland had Kenny Faulk (2.56 ERA, 20 SV), with Chance Ruffin (2.03 ERA, 19 SV) at Toledo and class "AA" Erie.

2010s Hitting Hits	
1. Miguel Cabrera	1,595
2. Victor Martinez	1,033
3. Nick Castellanos	862
4. Austin Jackson	743
5. Ian Kinsler	681
6. Alex Avila	547
7. Jose Iglesias	513
8. J.D. Martinez	509
9. Jhonny Peralta	463
10. James McCann	368

Team. Motown (88-74 .543) won the Central Division for Jim Leyland, with 3,028,033 fans. Detroit defeated Oakland in the ALDS (3-2), with Michigan umpires Scott Barry of Quincy and Jeff Kellogg of Coldwater. Motown swept New York (4-0) in ALCS, with Delmon Young MVP. San Francisco won the World Series in sweep. The squad was 11-11 in April including a 10-0 home shutout of Boston on Saturday, April 7, behind Miguel Cabrera (2 HR, 3 RBI), Prince Fielder 2-for-3 (2 HR, 2 RBI) and Alex Avila (HR, 2 RBI). The Bengals won 13-12 in 11-innings over the Red Sox on Sunday in 4:45, with Cabrera (HR, 5 RBI), Jhonny Peralta (3 RBI) and Austin Jackson 4-for-6. Players were 13-16 in May as Andy dirks had five straight multi-hit games May 5-10 (.571 BA, .609 OBP, 1.000 SLG). Justin Verlander (9 IP, 0 ER, 1 H, 12 SO) shutout Pittsburgh 6-0 at home on Friday, May 18, aided by Young (HR, 3 RBI). Max Scherzer (7 IP, 2 ER, 4 H, 15 SO) beat the Pirates 4-3 on Sunday. Fielder mashed in Minnesota May 25-27 (9-for-12, .750 BA, .786 OBP, .917 SLG). Players were 14-13 in June when Scherzer (8 IP, 0 ER, 12 SO) shutout visiting Colorado 5-0 on Sunday, June 17, as Quintin Berry went 5-for-5. Rick Porcello (7 IP, 0 ER, 4 H) and Jackson (HR, 3 RBI) paced a 6-2 win at Texas on Saturday, June 30. Players were 16-10 in July with a 5-1 win over Minnesota at home on July 4, led by Verlander (W 9-5, 9 IP, 1 ER, 4 H, 7 SO) and Cabrera (2 HR, 3 RBI). Detroit beat visiting Chicago 6-4 on Sunday, July 22, as Cabrera hit his 300th homer. The club went 16-11 in August when Cabrera was Player of the Month (8 HR, 24 RBI, .357 BA, .663 SLG). Anibal Sanchez (6 IP, 1 ER, 5 SO), and Fielder (HR, 4 RBI) led a 10-2 win over Cleveland at home on Friday, August 3. The club went 16-12 in September and 2-1 in October. The Tigers won 8-0 facing Minnesota at home on Saturday, September 22, behind Young (HR, 3 RBI) and Doug Fister (9 IP, 0 ER, 7 SO). Fister (7.2 IP, 2 ER, 10 SO) paced led a 5-4 home win on Thursday, as he struck out nine straight Royals for a league record. Motown was 13-5 (.722) with Kansas City, 50-31 (.617) at home, 38-43 (.469) away, scored 726 runs and allowed 670. Berry was the first Tiger since 1918 with a hit in his first six games. He set a league record of 21 steals without being caught. Fister struggled April 7-July 2 (1-6 .167, 4.61 ERA) then was better July 3-September 26 (9-3 .750, 2.75 ERA). Marcus Lemon, son of Chet Lemon, hit .324 for his hometown Lakeland Tigers. Bruce Rondon (52 GM, 1.53 ERA, 29 SV, 11.2 SO/9) was in the minors.

1B * PRINCE FIELDER

Offense. Detroit had a .268 BA, .335 OBP, .422 SLG, .757 OPS, 2,313 TB and 103 OPS+. Alex Avila (.243 BA, 9 HR, 48 RBI) caught. All-Star and Silver Slugger Prince Fielder (.313 BA, 30 HR, 108 RBI) at first led MLB in games (162), times on base (284), hit by pitch (17), and IBB (18). *"Uncle Phil"* led club in on-base percentage (.412) and walks (85). Omar Infante (.257 BA, 4 HR, 20 RBI) and Ramon Santiago (.206 BA, 2 HR, 17 RBI) were at second. Third baseman Miguel Cabrera (.330 BA, 44 HR, 139 RBI) was recognized with MVP, Triple Crown, Player of the Year, Hank Aaron Award, Silver Slugger, Luis Aparicio Award, Tiger of the Year, King Tiger, and most effective hitter. Cabrera led MLB in OPS (.999), total bases (377), homers, runs batted in, double plays grounded into (28), and extra base hits (84). He led the league in hitting, slugging (.606) and runs created (139). *"Miggy"* led the club in plate appearances (697), runs (109), hits (205), doubles (40), OPS+ (164), total average (1.007), gross production average (.328), WAR (7.2), secondary average (.387), isolated power (.277) and bases produced (447). Shortstop Jhonny Peralta (.239 BA, 13 HR, 63 RBI). The leftfielders were Andy Dirks (.322 BA, 8 HR, 35 RBI) and Tiger Rookie of the Year Quintin Berry (.258 BA, 2 HR, 29 RBI) that led MLB in SB% (21-for-21 100%) and team in stolen bases (21). Austin Jackson (.300 BA, 16 HR, 66 RBI) at center led league in triples (10) and club in power/speed number (13.7). Brennan Boesch (.240 BA, 12 HR, 54 RBI) was in right, with Delmon Young (.267 BA, 18 HR, 74 RBI) the designated hitter. Dirks led all pinch-hitters .429 (3-7).

2010s Hitting Doubles	
1. Miguel Cabrera	324
2. Nick Castellanos	208
3. Victor Martinez	188
4. Austin Jackson	140
5. Ian Kinsler	129
6. Alex Avila	118
7. Jose Iglesias	113
8. J.D. Martinez	111
9. Jhonny Peralta	94
10. Brennan Boesch	73

Pitching. Motown had a 3.75 ERA, three SHO, 438 walks , 1,318 SO, 113 ERA+, 3.63 FIP, 1.291 WHIP, 8.9 H/9, 2.8 BB/9 and 8.3 SO/9. Staff led league in CG (9), pWAR (26.2), HR/9 (0.9). Pitcher of the Year Justin Verlander (17-8, 2.64 ERA, 1 SHO) led MLB in pWAR (8.1), CG (6), ERA+ (161), IP (238.1), SO (239) and BF (956). *"JV"* led league in quality starts (25), with club lead for wins, starts (33), WHIP (1.057), and R/9 (3.1). Max Scherzer (16-7, 3.74 ERA) led MLB in SO/9 (11.1). *"Mad Max"* led club in win percentage (.696) and HR (23). Rick Porcello (10-12, 4.59 ERA) led league in hits (226). He led club in losses, earned runs (90), and runs (101). Drew Smyly (4-3, 3.99 ERA) led league in ND (11). Doug Fister (10-10, 3.45 ERA, 1 SHO) and Anibal Sanchez (4-6, 3.74 ERA, 1 SHO). Brayan Villarreal (3-5, 2.63 ERA) led in WP (9), ERA, ERA+ (162) and H/9 (6.3). Octavio Dotel (5-3, 3.57 ERA) led in FIP (2.30), DICE (2.21), BB/9 (1.9) and SO/BB (5.17). Joaquin Benoit (5-3, 3.68 ERA) led in GM (73) and LOB% (81.7). Jose Valverde (3-4, 3.78 ERA) led league in GF (67) and club in SV (35). Michigander Duane Below (2-1, 3.88 ERA) from Lenawee County and Phil Coke (2-3, 4.00 ERA). Class "A" West Michigan had Jade Todd (6-2 .750, 1.65 ERA). Tyler Clark (6-1 .857, 0.63 ERA) and Luis Sanz (11-3 .786) were at class "A+" Lakeland.

Defense. Detroit committed 99 errors (.983 FA). Tiger league leaders were Porcello in pitcher errors (5), Avila in catcher fielding (.994), passed balls (10) and caught stealing (34). Fielder led in chances (1,372), putouts (1,256) and errors (11) at first base. Cabrera led in putouts (127) at third base, as centerfielder Jackson was the Wilson Defensive Player of the Year.

Nick Castellanos was dominate at class "A+" Lakeland (55 GM, 87-for-215, .405 BA). Brad Eldred was a star at class "AAA" Toledo (63 GM, 24 HR, 65 RBI, .305 BA, .695 SLG, 164 TB), with a blazing start in his first 13 games (.388 BA, 13 HR, 35 RBI).

Justin Verlander's streak of consecutive 100-pitch games from Friday, June 18, 2010, through Sunday, September 2, 2012, came to an end at 80. His record in those games was a phenomenal 47-16 (.746), as he averaged 116 pitches per contest.

2010s Hitting Triples	
1. Austin Jackson	43
2. Nick Castellanos	32
3. Ian Kinsler	18
4. Rajai Davis	13
5. Anthony Gose	10
JaCoby Jones	10
7. J.D. Martinez	9
8. Niko Goodrum	8
Omar Infante	8
Mikie Mahtook	8
James McCann	8
Victor Reyes	8

Team. Jim Leyland led Central Division champs Detroit (93-69 .574), with 3,083,397 fans. The Tigers defeated Oakland in the ALDS (3-2) and lost the ALCS to Boston (4-2). The club was 15-10 in April with a 10-0 home shutout of Atlanta on Friday, April 26, led by Matt Tuiasosopo (HR, 5 RBI) and Anibal Sanchez (8 IP, 0 ER, 5 H, 17 SO), with a franchise strikeout record. The team went 14-14 in May with Cabrera the Player of the Month (.379 BA, 12 HR, 33 RBI). The Bengals won 17-2 in Houston on Saturday, May 4, aided by Max Scherzer (8 IP, 1 ER, 3 H, 8 SO), Cabrera 4-for-4 (2 HR, 6 RBI), Victor Martinez (HR, 4 RBI) and Torii Hunter 4-for-5 (2 RBI). Players lost 11-8 at Texas on Sunday, May 19, as Cabrera was 4-for-4 (3 HR, 5 RBI) and scored four runs. Cabrera had five consecutive multi-RBI games May 19-May 24 (10-for-19, 6 HR, 15 RBI, .526 BA, .625 OBP, 1.526 SLG). The squad had a 14-13 June record including a 10-1 defeat of visiting Tampa Bay on Tuesday, June 4, behind Prince Fielder (HR, 4 RBI), Omar Infante (HR, 3 RBI) and Sanchez (7 IP, 1 ER, 4 H, 9 SO). Detroit went 18-8 in July with a 11-1 victory over Washington at home on Wednesday, July 31, led by Hunter 4-for-5 (HR, 3 RBI), Alex Avila (HR, 2 RBI) and Justin Verlander (6 IP, 1 ER, 6 SO). Players were 19-11 in August that included a 16-1 17-game stretch. Cabrera had a run batted in during seven straight games August 6-12. Doug Fister (6 IP, 2 ER, 8 SO) led a 14-inning 6-5 win at Cleveland in 4:47 on Wednesday, August 7. The 10-3 win the next day was their twelfth straight win, as Scherzer (7 IP, 2 ER) became the third MLB pitcher to start a season 17-1. Scherzer (W 19-1, 6 IP, 0 ER, 3 H, 11 SO) shutout the Mets 3-0 in New York on Saturday, August 24. Motown closed 13-13 in September including a Sanchez (W 13-7, 7 IP, 1 ER) 16-2 win at Kauffman Stadium on Friday, September 6. The 26-hit attack had Austin Jackson (4 RBI), Andy Dirks 5-for-5 and Infante 5-for-5 (6 RBI), as first two Tigers with five hits in a game since 1917. Detroit highlights included 33-15 (.800) in blowout games, 15-4 (.789) with Cleveland, 51-30 (.630) at home, 42-39 (.519) on the road, scored 796 runs and allowed 624. Devon Travis hit .351 with consistent play for class "A+" Lakeland (55 GM .351 BA) and class "A" West Michigan (77 GM .352 BA).

P * MAX SCHERZER

Offense. Detroit finished with a .283 BA, .346 OBP, .434 SLG, .780 OPS, 2,491 TB and 111 OPS+. Alex Avila (.227 BA, 11 HR, 47 RBI) caught. All-Star Prince Fielder (.279 BA, 25 HR, 106 RBI) at first base led MLB in games (162), with team highs for plate appearances (712), at bats (624) and outs (475). Omar Infante (.318 BA) at second led for in-play percentage (84%). MVP, Player of the Year, All-Star, Tiger of the Year, Hank Aaron Award, Silver Slugger, and most effective hitter Miguel Cabrera (.348 BA, 44 HR, 137 RBI) at third led MLB in hitting, on-base percentage (.442), slugging (.636), OPS (1.078), OPS+ (190), total average (1.184), runs created (155). He led Motown in runs (103), hits (193), homers, runs batted in, base-out percentage (1.183), gross production average (.358), WAR (7.3), oWAR (9.1), batters run average (.281), secondary average (.456), times on base (288), base runs (140), runs produced (196), isolated power (.288), extra base hits (71), total bases (353), bases produced (446), walks (90) and hitting streak (15). All-Star shortstop Jhonny Peralta (.303 BA, 11 HR, 55 RBI) led in BAbip (.374). Leftfielder Andy Dirks (.256 BA, 9 HR, 37 RBI) led in stolen base runs (1.5). Wilson Defensive Team member Austin Jackson (.272 BA, 12 HR, 49 RBI) in centerfield led in triples (7), power/speed number (9.6), stolen bases (8) and strikeouts (129). All-Star and Silver Slugger right-fielder Torii Hunter (.304 BA, 17 HR, 84 RBI) led in doubles (37). Designated hitter Victor Martinez (.301 BA, 14 HR, 83 RBI) led the league in at bats per strikeout (9.8). "*V-Mart*" led the Bengals for singles (132). Others were utilityman Don Kelly (.222 BA, 6 HR, 23 RBI) and the Tiger Rookie of the Year Jose Iglesias (.259 BA, 2 HR, 10 RBI) at shortstop. The best pinch-hitter was Matt Tuiasosopo at .286 (4-14, HR, 7 RBI).

2010s Hitting Home Runs	
1. Miguel Cabrera	268
2. Victor Martinez	115
3. Nick Castellanos	104
4. J.D. Martinez	99
5. Ian Kinsler	78
6. Alex Avila	72
7. Justin Upton	59
8. Prince Fielder	55
9. Jhonny Peralta	53
10. Austin Jackson	46

Pitching. Detroit had a 3.61 ERA, three CG, one SHO, 462 walks, 116 ERA+, 1.252 WHIP, 8.4 H/9 and 2.8 BB/9, as staff led league for strikeouts (1,428), balks (7), FIP (3.27), pWAR (27.1), HR/9 (0.8), SO/9 (8.8), SO/BB (3.9) and quality starts (108). All-Star, Cy Young Award, Pitcher of the Year, All-Star, King Tiger, and most effective pitcher Max Scherzer (21-3, 2.90 ERA) led MLB in wins and win percentage (.875). He led league in WHIP (.970), with staff lead for pWAR (6.4), strikeouts (240), and quality starts (25). Anibal Sanchez (14-8, 2.57 ERA) led league in earned run average, ERA+ (162), FIP (2.39) and HR/9 (0-4). Doug Fister (14-9, 3.67 ERA) led in hits (229), HBP (16) earned runs (85) and BB/9 (1.9). All-Star Justin Verlander (13-12, 3.46 ERA) led MLB in starts (34), with club lead in losses, innings (218.1), homers (19), walks (75) and runs (94). Rick Porcello (13-8, 4.32 ERA) and Jose Alvarez (1-5, 5.82 ERA). Joaquin Benoit (4-1, 2.01 ERA) led in games (66), games finished (43), saves (24), LOB% (87.3), ERA+ (207), H/9 (6.3) and R/9 (2.0). Drew Smyly (6-0, 2.37 ERA) led in FIP (2.31), DICE (2.26) and strikeouts to walks (4.76). Luke Putkonen (1-3, 3.03 ERA), rookie Bruce Rondon (1-2, 3.45 ERA), Al Alburquerque (4-3, 4.59 ERA), Darin Downs (0-2, 4.84 ERA) and Phil Coke (0-5, 5.40 ERA). Melvin Mercedes (5-2 .714, 1.19 ERA, 23 SV) was at class "A+" Lakeland and "AA" Erie, with Blaine Hardy (8-3 .727, 1.67 ERA) at Erie and class "AAA" Toledo.

Defense. Players led the division in fewest errors (76), fielding average (.987) and putouts (4,388). Tiger league leaders were Fister in pitcher fielding average (1.000), chances (53) and putouts (23), as he and Verlander would lead for double plays (5). Peralta led all shortstops in fielding average (.991) and centerfielder Jackson led the Bengals for defensive WAR (0.9).

Max Scherzer was extraordinary at home (12-1 .923, .220 BA), on the road (9-2 .818, .177 BA), in first half (13-1 .928, .206 BA), in second half (8-2 .800, .187 BA), facing righthanders (.165 BA, .219 OBP, .223 BAbip) and facing lefthanders (.222 BA).

Will Startup (7-1) and Justin Souza (5-2, 2.63 ERA, 19 SV) were at class "AA" Erie. Class "A" West Michigan had stars Jordan John (9-4, 2.92 ERA), Corey Knebel (2-1, 0.87 ERA, 15 SV), Joshua Turley (8-4, 2.09 ERA) and Guido Knudson (1-2, 1.79 ERA).

2010s Hitting Runs Batted In		
1.	Miguel Cabrera	941
2.	Victor Martinez	540
3.	Nick Castellanos	424
4.	Alex Avila	300
	Ian Kinsler	300
6.	J.D. Martinez	285
7.	Jhonny Peralta	242
8.	Austin Jackson	234
9.	Prince Fielder	214
10.	Justin Upton	181

Team. Detroit (90-72 .556) won the Central for Brad Ausmus, with 2,917,209 fans. Motown lost the ALDS to Baltimore (3-0), with Michigan umpires Scott Barry from Quincy and Jeff Kellogg from Coldwater. The team was 1-0 in March and 13-9 in April with a 10-4 home win over Baltimore on Friday, April 4, with Miguel Cabrera 4-for-5 (HR, 3 RBI) and Rajai Davis (HR, 3 RBI). Players were 17-12 in May as Max Scherzer (4-1, 1.72 ERA, 47 IP, 60 SO, 11.5 SO/9) became the first Tiger with seven strikeouts per game in his first seven starts. Cabrera 4-for-5 (HR, 4 RBI) and Danny Worth (3 RBI) led a 11-4 home win over Houston on Tuesday, May 6. Cabrera had three straight three-hit games May 17-19 (9-for-14, .643 BA). The club was 14-13 in June when Nicholas Castellanos became the fifth Tiger rookie with three straight three-hit games June 5-7 (9-for-12, .750 BA). Scherzer (W 8-2, 9 IP, 0 ER, 3 H, 8 SO) had a 4-0 shutout in Chicago on Thursday, June 12. Ian Kinsler had seven straight multiple hit games June 21-28 (3 HR, 9 RBI, .500 BA). Detroit went 13-13 in July as J.D. Martinez (HR, 2 RBI) and Porcello (W 11-4, 9 IP, 0 ER, 4 H) shutout Oakland at home 3-0 on Tuesday, July 1. Porcello was the first Tiger since 1986 with back-to-back shutouts and the first Tiger since 1944 without a walk or strikeout in a shutout. The club fell 2-1 in Anaheim on Friday, July 25, when Drew Smyly (5.2 IP, 2 ER, 11 SO) was the first Tiger left-hander with 11 strikeouts in 21 years. Motown had a 16-15 mark in August when Victor Martinez was selected Player of the Month (6 HR, 30 RBI, .350 BA). Eight Bengal pitchers threw 325 pitches during a 6:37 19-inning 6-5 loss to Toronto at the Rogers Centre on Sunday, August 10. Scherzer (W 14-4, 8 IP, 0 ER, 3 H, 14 SO) won 5-2 at home over Pittsburgh on Thursday, August 14. Davis had three steals in an 8-1 home loss to Seattle on Sunday, August 17. V-Mart (HR, 5 RBI) aided a Porcello (9 IP, 0 ER, 3 H) 6-0 shutout in Tampa on Wednesday, August 20. David Price (8 IP, 0 ER, 1 H, 9 SO) lost 1-0 to the Rays on Thursday, as the first pitcher in 100 years to lose a complete game one-hitter with no walks or earned runs. Detroit closed 16-10 in September with Cabrera Player of the Month (8 HR, 18 RBI, .379 BA). Price (7 IP, 1 ER, 8 SO) paced a 12-1 win at Cleveland on Monday, September 1, behind Cabrera 4-for-5 (4 R, 2 HR, 3 RBI), and V-Mart (HR, 2 RBI), with a ninth-inning Tyler Collins (HR, 3 RBI) pinch-hit three-run homer. Motown was 45-36 (.556) both at home and away. The Tigers scored 757 runs and allowed 705.

OF * RAJAI DAVIS

Offense. Detroit had a .277 BA, .331 OBP, .426 SLG, .757 OPS, 2,399 TB, and 113 OPS+. Alex Avila (.218 BA, 11 HR, 47 RBI) caught. All-Star Miguel Cabrera (.313 BA, 25 HR, 109 RBI) at first led MLB in sacrifice flies (11). *"Miggy"* led the league in doubles (52), with team lead for runs (101), hits (191), runs batted in, runs produced (185), extra base hits (78) and total bases (320). All-Star Ian Kinsler (.275 BA, 17 HR, 92 RBI) at second led MLB in at bats (684), plate appearances (726) and outs (528). *"Kins"* led Motown in games (161), singles (127), WAR (5.8), in-play percentage (82%) and power/speed number (15.9). Tiger Rookie of the Year Nicholas Castellanos (.259 BA, 11 HR, 66 RBI) was at third base. Andrew Romine (.227 BA, 2 HR, 12 RBI) and Eugenio Saurez (.242 BA, 4 HR, 23 RBI) were at short. The leftfielders were Rajai Davis (.282 BA, 8 HR, 51 RBI) that led squad in steals (36) and J.D. Martinez (.315 BA, 23 HR, 76 RBI). *"J.D."* led in BAbip (.389), isolated power (.238) and 14-game hitting streak. Centerfielder Austin Jackson (.273 BA, 4 HR, 33 RBI) was leader for triples (5), with Torii Hunter (.286 BA, 17 HR, 83 RBI) in right. Player of the Year, All-Star, Silver Slugger, Tiger of the Year, King Tiger, Silver Slugger, and most effective hitter designated hitter Victor Martinez (.335 BA, 32 HR, 103 RBI) led MLB in OPS (.974), IBB (28) and at bats per strikeout (13.4). "V-Mart" led league on on-base percentage (.409). Victor led his squad in homers, OPS+ (172), total average (1.000), base-out percentage (1.005), gross production average (.325), oWAR (5.9), batters run average (.231), hitting, secondary average (.357), times on base (262), base runs (119), runs created (130), bases produced (390) and walks (70). The best pinch-hitters were Castellanos at .400 (2-5), Steven Moya .400 (2-5) and Tyler Collins .373 (3-8, HR, 4 RBI). Moya (.276 BA, 35 HR, 105 RBI) starred with the class "AA" Erie Seawolves, as Steven was selected the Eastern League MVP.

2010s Hitting On-Base Percentage		
1.	Miguel Cabrera	.399
2.	Prince Fielder	.387
3	J.D. Martinez	.361
4.	Alex Avila	.349
	Victor Martinez	.349
6.	Austin Jackson	.342
7.	Justin Upton	.333
8.	Andy Dirks	.332
	Jhonny Peralta	.332
10.	Ian Kinsler	.328

Pitching. The Tigers had a 4.01 ERA, five CG, four SHO, 462 BB, 1,244 SO, 97 ERA+, 3.60 FIP, 1.332 WHIP, 9.1 H/9, 2.9 BB/9 and 7.7 SO/9, as staff led league for balks (9) and HR/9 (0.8). Pitcher of the Year and All-Star Max Scherzer (18-5, 3.15 ERA) led league in wins. He led staff in win percentage (.783), starts (33), IP (220.1), SO (252), pWAR (5.7), SO/9 (10.3) and SO/BB (4.00). The most effective pitcher Anibal Sanchez (8-5, 3.43 ERA) led in FIP (2.71), DICE (2.58), WHIP (1.095), H/9 (7.7) and HR/9 (0.3). Rick Porcello (15-13, 3.43 ERA) led MLB in SHO (3). He led club in losses, CG (3) and BB/9 (1.8). Justin Verlander (15-12, 4.54 ERA) led league in ER (104) and runs (114). He led staff in hits (223) and BB (65). David Price (4-4, 3.59 ERA) led MLB in IP (248.1, 77.2 w/Det), SO (271, 82 w/Det), starts (34, 11 w/Det), hits (230, 74 Det) and BF (1,009, 320 w/Det). Drew Smyly (6-9, 3.93 ERA) and Kyle Lobstein (1-2, 4.35 ERA). Al Aburquerque (3-1, 2.51 ERA) led in games (72), LOB% (89.7), ERA, ERA+ (152) and R/9 (2.5). Joe Nathan (5-4, 4.81 ERA) led in GF (54) and saves (35). Blaine Hardy (2-1, 2.54 ERA), Joba Chamberlain (2-5, 3.57 ERA), Phil Coke (5-2, 3.88 ERA), Evan Reed (0-1, 4.18 ERA) and Ian Krol (0-0, 4.96 ERA). Wilsen Palacios (10-4 .714) was at Erie, with Joshua Turley (7-1 .875, 1.85 ERA) and Angel Nesbitt (2-0, 0.79 ERA, 14 SV) at Lakeland.

Defense. The Bengals committed 101 errors for a .983 fielding average. Tiger league leaders at pitcher were Verlander in errors (6) and Smyly in pickoffs (7). Avila led all catchers in caught stealing (36) and doubles plays (9), as first baseman Cabrera led in assists (98). Kinsler at second led league in chances (766), and putouts (290), with team lead for dWAR (2.9).

Class "A" West Michigan had Wynton Bernard (.323 BA, 45 SB), Austin Kubitza (10-2 .833, 2.34 ERA), Jonathon Crawford (8-3 .727, 2.85 ERA) and Kevin Ziomek (10-6 .625, 2.27 ERA), with Johan Belisario (5-0 1.000, 0.79 ERA) at class "A" Connecticut.

Team. Brad Ausmus led fifth place Detroit (74-87 .460), with 2,726,048 fans. The club was 15-8 in April starting 6-0 with a record 10 hits per game. Motown swept Minnesota at home with a David Price (8.2 IP, 0 ER, 5 H) led 4-0 win on Monday, April 6, won 11-0 the next day with Anibal Sanchez (6.2 IP, 0 ER, 3 H, 6 SO), Ian Kinsler (4 RBI) and Anthony Gose (3 RBI), as Shane Greene (8 IP, 0 ER, 4 H) and J.D. Martinez (HR, 3 RBI) led a 7-1 victory on Thursday. Miguel Cabrera went 8-for-9 at Cleveland April 11-12 with games of 4-for-5 and 4-for-4 (2 HR, 4 RBI), as he reached base seven straight at-bats and nine times in 10 plate appearances. The Bengals were 13-16 in May with a 4-3 10-inning win at St. Louis on Saturday, May 16, as Cabrera hit his 400th homer. Players were 11-13 in June when Price shined June 1-July 17 (5-0, 50⅔ IP, 1.60 ERA, 52 SO). Sanchez was superb June 9-July 22 (7-0, 3.16 ERA). The "*Martinez Road Show*" was at Yankee Stadium, with Victor (HR, 4 RBI) and J.D. (3 HR, 6 RBI) pacing a 12-4 win on Sunday, June 21. Detroit went 11-16 in July as Price (W 9-2, 8 IP, 0 ER, 8 SO) won 4-2 in Minnesota on Thursday, July 9. J.D. Martinez hit a 467-foot homer for the longest in Comerica Park history during a 11-9 loss to Seattle on Tuesday, July 21. The Tigers were 10-17 in August including a 15-8 win in Chicago on Wednesday, August 19, with Nicholas Castellanos 4-for-5 (2 HR, 5 RBI), as Daniel Norris was the first Tiger pitcher to homer in his first plate appearance and first American League pitcher with a regular season homer at Wrigley Field. Alfredo Simon (9 IP, 0 ER, 1 H) shutout Texas 4-0 at home on Thursday. Blaine Hardy's year-long homerless streak closed on Sunday, August 23, after 84⅔ innings, as he set the Tiger lefthander record of 87 consecutive homerless appearances. Justin Verlander (9 IP, 1 H, 0 ER, 9 SO) shutout the Angels 5-0 at home Wednesday, August 26. Motown closed 13-15 in September and 1-2 in October with an 8-7 13-inning home win in 5:03 over Tampa Bay on Tuesday, September 8, as 10 Tigers pitched. The class "AA" Eastern League Pitcher of the Year Michael Fulmer (10-3, 2.24 ERA) was with Binghamton (6-2 1.88) and Erie (4-1, 2.84 ERA). Players were 38-43 (.469) at home, and 36-44 (.450) on the road. Detroit scored 689 runs and allowed 803.

2010s Hitting Slugging Percentage	
1. J.D. Martinez	.551
2. Miguel Cabrera	.544
3. Justin Upton	.500
4. Prince Fielder	.491
5. Nick Castellanos	.459
6. Torii Hunter	.456
7. Victor Martinez	.440
8. Ian Kinsler	.436
9. Jhonny Peralta	.433
10. Brennan Boesch	.414

P * ALFREDO SIMON

Offense. Detroit logged a .270 BA, .328 OBP, .420 SLG, .748 OPS, 2,355 TB and 105 OPS+. Tiger Rookie of the Year James McCann (.264 BA) caught. All-Star, Silver Slugger, and most effective hitter Miguel Cabrera (.338 BA, 18 HR, 76 RBI) at first led MLB in hitting. He led the league in on-base percentage (.440) and BAbip (.384), with Tiger lead for OPS (.974), OPS+ (169), total average (1.016), base-out percentage (1.020), gross production average (.332), oWAR (4.8), batters run average (.235), secondary average (.375), walks (77) and hitting streak (13). Ian Kinsler (.296 BA, 11 HR, 73 RBI) at second base led club in plate appearances (675), at bats (624), runs (94), hits (185), singles (132), doubles (35), WAR (5.9), times on base (231) and outs (463). Nicholas Castellanos (.255 BA, 15 HR, 73 RBI) played third base. All-Star shortstop Jose Iglesias (.300 BA) led Motown for in-play percentage (82%), with Yoenis Cespedes (.293 BA, 18 HR, 61 RBI) in left. Centerfielder Anthony Gose (.254 BA) led in stolen bases (23). Player of the Year, Silver Slugger, Tiger of the Year and King Tiger right-fielder J.D. Martinez (.282 BA, 38 HR, 102 RBI) led team in games (158), homers, runs batted in, slugging (.535), base runs (101), runs produced (157), runs created (110), isolated power (.253), extra base hits (73), total bases (319), bases produced (375) and strikeouts (178). The Designated hitter was Victor Martinez (.245 BA, 11 HR, 64 RBI). Tyler Collins (.266 BA, 4 HR, 25 RBI). Rajai Davis (.258 BA, 8 HR, 30 RBI) led in triples (11), power/speed number (11.1) and stolen base runs (0.6). The leading Tiger pinch-hitters were McCann at .500 (3-6, 2 RBI) and Collins .333 (2-6, HR).

Pitching. Motown had a 4.64 ERA, seven CG, four SHO, 489 BB, 1,100 SO, 86 ERA+, 4.46 FIP, 1.368 WHIP, 9.3 H/9, 3.0 BB/9 and 6.8 SO/9. Staff led league in HR (193), ER (746), runs (803) and tied MLB record without an earned run in the first 32 innings, with shutouts in first two games for the first time, 30⅔ straight innings without a walk thru Friday, April 17, the best streak in 100 years. Pitcher of the Year, All-Star, most effective pitcher, and Cy Young runner-up David Price (9-4, 2.53 ERA) led league in ERA (2.45, 2.53 w/Det) and ERA+ (164, 158 w/Det). He led club in win percentage (.692), DICE (2.92), SO/9 (8.5), SO/BB (4.76) and quality starts (15). Justin Verlander (5-8, 3.38 ERA) led in pWAR (2.3) and H/9 (7.6). Anibal Sanchez (10-10, 4.99 ERA) led league in HR (29). Alfredo Simon (13-12, 5.05 ERA) led in wins, losses, starts (31), innings (187), hits (201), BB (68), HBP (8), WP (14), ER (105) and runs (112). Matt Boyd (1-4, 6.57 ERA), Kyle Lobstein (3-8, 5.94 ERA) and Shane Greene (4-8, 6.88 ERA). Alex Wilson (3-3, 2.19 ERA) led in LOB% (82.1), ERA, ERA+ (183), WHIP (1.029), BB/9 (1.4) and R/9 (2.4). Al Alburquerque (4-1, 4.21 ERA) led MLB in balks (4). Joakim Soria (3-1, 2.85 ERA) led in GF (35) and SV (23). Blaine Hardy (5-3, 3.08 ERA) led in GM (70), FIP (2.89) and HR/9 (0.3). Bruce Rondon (1-0, 5.81 ERA) and Tom Gorzelanny (2-2, 5.95 ERA).

2010s Hitting On-Base plus Slugging	
1. Miguel Cabrera	.943
2. J.D. Martinez	.912
3. Prince Fielder	.878
4. Justin Upton	.833
5. Victor Martinez	.789
6. Nick Castellanos	.783
Torii Hunter	.783
8. Ian Kinsler	.764
Jhonny Peralta	.764
10. Austin Jackson	.755

Defense. Detroit committed 86 errors (.986). The Tiger league leaders were pitchers Sanchez and Simon in fielding (1.000), McCann led all MLB catchers in fielding (1.000), Gold Glove leftfielder Cespedes led in errors (5), J.D. Martinez led right fielders in fielding (.993), as second baseman Kinsler won a Fielding Bible Award and led the Bengals in defensive WAR (2.6).

David Price had 22⅔ straight innings with no earned runs September 28, 2014-April 17, 2015 (2-0, 0.00 ERA, 5 BB, 19 SO). He was traded to the Toronto Blue Jays on Thursday July 30, 2015, for pitchers Matt Boyd, Jairo Labourt and Daniel Norris.

Class "AA" Erie had Wynton Bernard (.301 BA, 43 SB) and Jeff Ferrell (1.67 ERA, 12 SV), with Joe Jimenez (5-1 .833, 1.47 ERA, 17 SV, 0.791 WHIP), Johan Belisario (1.79 ERA, 12 SV) and Spencer Turnbull (11-3 .786, 3.01 ERA) at class "A" West Michigan.

Team. Detroit finished second for Brad Ausmus at 86-75 (.534), with an attendance of 2,595,937. Players went 13-10 in April with Jordan Zimmermann named Pitcher of the Month (5-0, 0.55 ERA, .224 BA). Zimmermann started his Tiger career with $24\frac{1}{3}$ consecutive scoreless innings April 8-25. Victor Martinez was the first player since 1914 with a pinch-hit homer in his team's first two games. Comerica Park at 31 degrees on Saturday, April 9 was the coldest game in team history. Motown had an 8-2 home win over Pittsburgh 8-2 on Tuesday, April 12, led by Justin Upton 4-for-5 (HR, 2 RBI) and J.D. Martinez 4-for-5 (2 RBI). Zimmermann (W 3-0, 6.1 IP, 0 ER, 8 SO) led a 3-2 win at Kansas City on Wednesday, April 20. The team finished 11-17 in May as 23-year-old rookie Michael Fulmer (7.2 IP, 0 ER, 3 H) pitched a 4-1 win at Oakland on Friday, May 27. The Bengals were 17-11 in June when J.D. Martinez had six straight multi-hit games June 8-14 (.609 BA, .679 OBP, .870 SLG, .700 BAbip). V-Mart hit the 3-3-3-3 jackpot (3 R, 3 H, 3 HR, 3 RBI) with homers from both sides in a 10-4 six-homer win at Kauffman Stadium on Thursday, June 16. The Tigers won 10-7 at Tampa Bay on Thursday, June 30, aided by Cameron Maybin (4 RBI) and an eight-run ninth inning. Detroit was 16-10 in July with Justin Verlander the Pitcher of the Month (4-0, 1.69 ERA, .171 BA, .238 BAbip). Upton (HR, 3 RBI) and Tyler Collins (HR, 3 RBI) aided a 14-6 home victory over Houston on Friday, July 29. Motown beat the Astros 11-0 on Sunday, with Mike Pelfrey (5 IP, 0 ER, 4 SO), Cabrera (HR, 4 RBI), Upton (HR, 2 RBI) and James McCann (HR, 4 RBI). Motown went 10-1 for July 25-August 6. Detroit was 15-13 in August as Upton (2 HR, 6 RBI) and Verlander (W 13-7, 6 IP, 1 ER, 3 H) paced a 10-5 win over visiting Boston on Sunday, August 21. The team closed 14-12 in September and 0-2 in October, with Cabrera the Player of the Month (10 HR, 27 RBI, .349 BA, .670 SLG). Verlander (W 15-8, 6 IP, 2 ER,11 SO) won 4-2 at Minnesota on Thursday, September 22. Cabrera (HR, 5 RBI), Upton 2-for-3 (HR, 3 RBI) and Verlander (W 16-8, 7.2 IP, 12 SO) shutout Cleveland 12-0 at home on Tuesday, September 27. Daniel Norris (6.2 IP, 1 ER, 8 SO) and Cabrera (2 HR, 3 RBI) led a 6-2 win in Atlanta on Friday, September 30, as Ian Kinsler's 28th homer tied Lou Whitaker's 1989 team mark for a second baseman, with a new record of eight homers to lead-off an inning in a season. The squad went 15-4 (.789) with Minnesota including 9-0 (1.000) at Target Field. Players were 45-35 (.563) at home, 41-40 (.506) on the road, scored 750 runs and allowed 721.

2010s Pitching Wins	
1. Justin Verlander	118
2. Max Scherzer	82
3. Rick Porcello	62
4. Anibal Sanchez	46
5. Doug Fister	32
6. Matt Boyd	31
7. Jordan Zimmermann	25
8. Michael Fulmer	24
9. Al Alburquerque	17
Phil Coke	17
Shane Greene	17

OF * CAMERON MAYBIN

Offense. Detroit had a .267 BA, .331 OBP, .438 SLG, .769 OPS, 2,421 TB and 108 OPS+. James McCann (.221 BA, 12 HR, 48 RBI) and Jarrod Saltalamacchia (.171 BA, 12 HR, 38 RBI) caught. Player of the Year, All-Star, Silver Slugger, and most effective hitter Miguel Cabrera (.316 BA, 38 HR, 108 RBI, 679 PA) at first grounded into an MLB high 26 double plays. He led league in IBB (15), with team lead for games (158), hits (188), singles (118), homers, runs batted in, on-base percentage (.393), slugging (.563), OPS (.956), OPS+ (155), total average (.956), base-out percentage (.957), gross production average (.318), oWAR (5.4), batters run average (.221), hitting (.316), secondary average (.373), times on base (267), base runs (121), runs created (132), isolated power (.247), extra base hits (70), total bases (335), bases produced (410) and walks (75). Ian Kinsler (.288 BA, 28 HR, 83 RBI, 679 PA) at second led in at bats (618), runs (117), WAR (6.0), runs produced (172), power/speed number (18.7) and outs (454). Nicholas Castellanos (.285 BA, 18 HR, 58 RBI) manned third base. Jose Iglesias (.255 BA, 4 HR, 32 RBI, 14 HS) at short led league in at bats per strikeout (9.3) and led the Tigers for in-play percentage (81%). Left-fielder Justin Upton (.246 BA, 31 HR, 87 RBI) led in strikeouts (179). Centerfielder Cameron Maybin (.315 BA, 4 HR, 43 RBI) led in triples (5), BAbip (.383) and steals (15). J.D. Martinez (.307 BA, 22 HR, 68 RBI, 14 HS) at right led in doubles (35). Designated hitter Victor Martinez (.289 BA, 27 HR, 86 RBI). Andrew Romine (.236 BA, 2 HR, 16 RBI) led in stolen base runs (2.4). The top pinch-hitters were Kinsler at .667 (2-3), Victor Martinez .500 (4-8, 3 HR, 6 RBI), McCann .333 (2-6, HR) and Tyler Collins at .300 (3-10, HR).

Pitching. Motown had a 4.24 ERA, three complete games, one SHO, 462 walks, 1,232 strikeouts, 98 ERA+, 4.16 FIP, 1.316 WHIP, 8.9 H/9, 2.9 BB/9 and 7.8 SO/9, with league best HR/9 (1.1). Pitcher of the Year, Tiger of the Year, and most effective pitcher Justin Verlander (16-9, 3.04 ERA) led MLB in pWAR (7.4). He led the league in strikeouts (254) and WHIP (1.001). Verlander led his staff in wins, win percentage (.640), starts (34), complete games (2), innings (227.2), walks (57), LOB% (79.9) and SO/BB (4.46). Rookie of the Year and Tiger Rookie of the Year Michael Fulmer (11-7, 3.06 ERA) led in hit by pitch (9). Fulmer set team rookie record of $33\frac{1}{3}$ straight scoreless innings streak and became second in MLB history with four straight scoreless outings of six or more innings with three or less hits. Jordan Zimmermann (9-7, 4.87 ERA) led in BB/9 (2.2) and the first Tiger to start a season with three scoreless starts (19.1 IP, 0.00 ERA, 15 SO) of six innings or more. Anibal Sanchez (7-13, 5.87 ERA) led in losses, wild pitches (7), earned runs (100) and runs (108). Daniel Norris (4-2, 3.38 ERA), Matt Boyd (6-5, 4.53 ERA) and Mike Pelfrey (4-10, 5.07 ERA). Alex Wilson (4-0, 2.96 ERA) led in ERA, ERA+ (144). Kyle Ryan (4-2, 3.07 ERA) led in HR/9 (0.3). Francisco Rodriguez (3-4, 3.24 ERA) led in GF (55) and saves (44). Justin Wilson (4-5, 4.14 ERA) led in games (66). Bruce Rondon (5-2, 2.97 ERA) and Mark Lowe (1-3, 7.12 ERA). Joe Jimenez (1.51 ERA, 30 SV, 13.1 SO/9, 0.801 WHIP) split time at Lakeland (17 GM, 0.00 ERA, 10 SV), Erie (21 GM, 2.18 ERA, 12 SV) and Toledo (17 GM, 2.30 ERA, 8 SV).

2010s Pitching Winning Percentage	
1. Al Alburquerque	.739
2. Max Scherzer	.701
3. Warrick Saupold	.667
4. Joaquin Benoit	.650
5. Justin Verlander	.624
6. David Price	.619
7. Doug Fister	.615
8. Blaine Hardy	.583
9. Kyle Ryan	.571
Drew Smyly	.571

Defense. Club had 75 errors for league lead in fielding (.987). League leaders were catcher McCann in DP (9) and MLB record 139 games to start career without an error, Cabrera in assists (95) at first, Kinsler in chances (744) at second and led team in dWAR (1.8) with a Gold Glove. Iglesias led in fielding (.991) at short and Upton in chances (261) and putouts (253) in left.

The class "A" West Michigan Whitecaps had stars Will Maddox (.339 BA), Matt Hall (8-0 1.000, 1.09 ERA), Kyle Dowdy (10-3 .769, 2.84 ERA), Toller Boardman (8-3 .727, 2.10 ERA), Gerson Moreno (1.08 ERA, 11 SV) and Jake Shull (1.23 ERA, 7 SV).

2010s Pitching Games Started	
1. Justin Verlander	248
2. Max Scherzer	161
3. Rick Porcello	149
4. Anibal Sanchez	130
5. Matt Boyd	116
6. J. Zimmermann	95
7. Daniel Norris	76
8. Michael Fulmer	75
9. Doug Fister	68
10. Drew Smyly	36

Team. Motown (64-98 .395) closed fifth for Brad Ausmus, with 2,321,599 fans. The club went 12-12 during April, as JaCoby Jones became the first Tiger with his first home run on opening day since 1965, as they had a homer in their first 13 games for a team record. John Hicks (HR, 5 RBI) led a 13-4 win in Minnesota on Sunday, April 23. Players defeated visiting Seattle 19-9 on Tuesday, with a 24-hit attack and a nine-run fifth inning. The combined 40 hits were a Comerica Park record, with Ian Kinsler 4-for-5, Tyler Collins (3 RBI), Justin Upton (3 RBI) and James McCann (HR, 4 RBI). The Tigers were 13-16 in May including a 13-11 13-inning loss in 5:19 at home to Baltimore on Tuesday, May 16, as Victor Martinez (HR, 3 RBI) and J.D. Martinez (4 BB, 2 HR, 5 RBI) paced Motown. Detroit had a 9-3 home win over Texas on Saturday, May 20 aided by Nicholas Castellanos (HR, 3 RBI), with consecutive first inning homers from Alex Avila (HR, 3 RBI), Miguel Cabrera and J.D. Martinez. Detroit split a doubleheader at Chicago on Saturday, May 27, as umpire John Libka from Mayville, Michigan, made his MLB debut. Buck Farmer (6.1 IP, 0 ER, 3 H, 11 SO) and Dixon Machado 3-for-4 led a 4-3 game two win. The Bengals were 10-15 in June including a 15-5 win over the visiting White Sox 15-5 on Friday, June 2, behind Cabrera (4 RBI), and Machado (3 RBI), as J.D. Martinez, Hicks and Mikie Mahtook homered. Players went 12-14 in July with a 9-3 triumph in Kansas City on Tuesday, July 18, led by Castellanos 4-for-5 (2 HR, 5 RBI). The Bengals hammered first-place Houston 13-1 at home on Sunday, July 30, with Upton 4-for-5 (HR, 6 RBI), McCann 3-for-4 (HR, 3 RBI) and Verlander (6 IP, 0 ER, 6 SO). Motown was 11-17 in August with a Jordan Zimmermann (7 IP, 0 ER, 6 SO) 2-0 win in New York on Wednesday, August 2. The team closed 6-23 in September and 0-1 in October, as Castellanos excelled September 5-19 (.446 BA, .466 OBP, .821 SLG). Detroit won 5-4 in Toronto on Friday, September 8, with a triple play and Castellanos (HR, 4 RBI). Matt Boyd (9 IP, 0 ER, 1 H, 5 SO) came within one out of a no-hitter in a 12-0 home shutout of the White Sox on Sunday, September 17, led by rookie Jeimer Candelario (HR, 4 RBI) and Castellanos (HR, 4 RBI). Alex Presley excelled September 15-27 (.405 BA, .450 OBP, .541 SLG, .452 BAbip). Andrew Romine was the fifth player to play all nine positions in an MLB game at Minnesota on Saturday, September 30. Detroit was 34-47 (.420) at home, 30-51 (.432) on the road, scored 735 runs and allowed 894 runs.

OF * MIKIE MAHTOOK

Offense. Detroit had a .258 BA, .324 OBP, .424 SLG, .748 OPS, 2,355 TB and 98 OPS+. James McCann (.253 BA, 13 HR, 49 RBI) caught, with Miguel Cabrera (.249 BA, 16 HR, 60 RBI) at first. Second baseman Ian Kinsler (.236 BA, 22 HR, 52 RBI) led in runs (90), power/speed number (17.1) and steals (14). Nicholas Castellanos (.272 BA, 26 HR, 101 RBI) at third base led league in triples (10). He led team for games (157), plate appearances (665), at bats (614), hits (167), singles (95), runs batted in, runs produced (148), runs created (96), extra base hits (72), total bases (301), bases produced (346), outs (469) and hit streak (17). Jose Iglesias (.255 BA, 6 HR, 54 RBI) at short led for in-play percentage (80%). Player of the Year, All-Star, Tiger of the Year, and most effective hitter leftfielder Justin Upton (.279 BA, 28 HR, 94 RBI) led in doubles (37), homers, on-base percentage (.362), slugging (.542), OPS (.904), OPS+ (135), total average (.918), gross production average (.298), hitting, secondary average (.399), isolated power (.264), walks (57) and strikeouts (147). Centerfielder Mikie Mahtook (.276 BA, 12 HR, 38 RBI) led in stolen base runs (1.8). J.D. Martinez (.305 BA, 16 HR, 39 RBI) in right led MLB for slugging (.690, .630 w/Det) and AB/HR (9.6, 12.5 w/Det). Designated hitter Victor Martinez (.255 BA, 10 HR, 47 RBI). Andrew Romine (.233 BA, 4 HR, 25 RBI) and Tiger Rookie of the Year Dixon Machado (.259 BA, HR, 11 RBI). The leading pinch-hitters were Romine at .500 (4-8), Alex Avila .429 (6-14), McCann .400 (2-5) and Machado at .364 (4-11). Upton recorded a run batted in during six consecutive games May 31-June 7 (10-for-21, .476 BA, 3 HR, 11 RBI, .522 OBP, 1.048 SLG, .467 BAbip).

2010s Pitching Complete Games	
1. Justin Verlander	17
2. Rick Porcello	4
3. Doug Fister	3
Anibal Sanchez	3
5. Michael Fulmer	2
Armando Galarraga	2
Alfredo Simon	2
8. Matt Boyd	1
Max Scherzer	1

Pitching. The Tigers logged a 5.36 ERA, two complete games, one SHO, 538 walks, 1,202 SO, 84 ERA+, 4.73 FIP, 1.496 WHIP, 10.1 H/9, 3.4 BB/9, and 7.6 SO/9. Pitchers led league in hits (1,587), IBB (42), earned runs (846), runs (894), left on base (1,143) and tough losses (17). Pitcher of the Year Justin Verlander 10-8, 3.82 ERA) led staff in win Percentage (.556), innings (172), walks (67), strikeouts (176), pWAR (4.5) and R/9 (4.0). The most effective pitcher Michael Fulmer (10-12, 3.83 ERA) led the league in HR/9 (0.7). He led staff in HBP (8), FIP (3.67), DICE (3.52), WHIP (1.154) and BB/9 (2.2). Matt Boyd (6-11, 5.27 ERA) led in SHO (1). Jordan Zimmermann (8-13, 6.08 ERA) led MLB in earned runs (108), as he led club in losses, starts (29), hits (204), homers (29) and runs (111). Anibal Sanchez (3-7, 6.41 ERA) led in SO/BB (3.59). Daniel Norris (5-8, 5.31 ERA) and Buck Farmer (5-5, 6.75 ERA). Shane Greene (4-3, 2.66 ERA) led in games (71), LOB% (84.2), ERA, ERA+ (169), H/9 (6.7) and R/9 (2.8). Justin Wilson (3-4, 2.68 ERA) led in saves (13), with a record SO/9 (12.3). Daniel Stumpf (0-1, 3.82 ERA), Alex Wilson (2-5, 4.50 ERA) and Warwick Saupold (3-2, 4.88 ERA). Blaine Hardy (1-0, 5.94 ERA), Chad Bell (0-3, 6.93 ERA) and Francisco Rodriguez (2-5, 7.82 ERA). Minors league stars were Artie Lewicki (14-4 .778) and Bryan Garcia (2.13 ERA, 17 SV). Class "AAA" Toledo had Blaine Hardy (7-3 .700, 0.910 WHIP). Greene excelled June 25-August 15 (2-0, 0.00 ERA, 3 SV, 16.1 IP, 18 SO, .164 BA, .182 SLG).

Defense. Detroit made 84 errors for a .985 fielding average. League leaders were catcher McCann in stolen bases (57), Cabrera in fielding (.999) at first, Castellanos in errors (18) at third, Iglesias in fielding (.987) at short, as he led team in dWAR (1.1). Upton led in chances (335), putouts (318) and errors (8) in left. Detroit had a triple-play at Toronto on September 8.

Justin Upton had notable games on June 11 (HR, 5 RBI), July 30 (4-for-5, HR, 6 RBI) and on August 4 (HR, 4 RBI). Class "A" West Michigan had Gregory Soto (10-1 .909, 2.25 ERA), Spenser Watkins (9-3 .750), Jacob Robson (.329 BA) and Michigan native Blaise Salter (.330 BA) of Orchard Lake St. Mary's High School. Spencer Trumbull (7-3 .700) was at class "A+" Lakeland.

2010s Pitching Earned Run Average		
1.	David Price	2.90
2.	Al Alburquerque	3.20
	Alex Wilson	3.20
4.	Jose Valverde	3.22
5.	J. Verlander	3.28
6.	Doug Fister	3.29
7.	Max Scherzer	3.52
8.	Drew Smyly	3.53
9.	Justin Wilson	3.55
10.	Blaine Hardy	3.73

Team. Detroit finished third for Ron Gardenhire at 64-98 (.395), with 1,856,970 fans. The club was 0-1 in March and 11-15 during April including a 13-8 win against visiting Baltimore on Thursday, April 19, behind Leonys Martin (HR, 4 RBI), Jeimer Candelario 4-for-4 (HR, 3 RBI) and Jose Iglesias (3 RBI). Mike Fiers (5.1 IP, 2 ER, 10 H) became the first Tiger since 1908 to surrender 10 hits in less than six innings with no strikeouts and get a win over Kansas City 12-4 at home on Saturday, April 21, with Miguel Cabrera (3 RBI) and Nicholas Castellanos (HR, 3 RBI). The team went 15-14 in May as Francisco Liriano (8 IP, 0 ER, 1 H, 5 SO) entered the seventh with a no-hitter during a 11-inning 3-2 loss in Seattle on Sunday, May 20. James McCann (HR, 4 RBI) hit a grand slam in a Matt Boyd (5 IP, 0 ER, 2 H, 4 SO) 9-3 home win over the Angels on Monday, May 28. The squad was 10-18 in June when Castellanos doubled at Boston on Tuesday, June 5, to extend the franchise record for consecutive games with a two-base hit to 53. Castellanos (3 HR, 7 RBI, .417 BA, 1.167 SLG) led a three-game sweep of the White Sox at Chicago June 15-17, including (2 HR, 5 RBI) in game two. The Tigers were 10-14 in July with a Jordan Zimmermann (7 IP, 1 ER, 6 SO) 9-1 win in Toronto on Sunday, July 1, aided by JaCoby Jones (HR, 2 RBI) and a Castellanos (HR, 4 RBI) grand slam. Players went 8-19 in August that included a 1-0 13-inning loss at Oakland on Friday, August 3, as Blaine Hardy (7 IP, 0 ER, 1 H, 6 SO) entered the seventh inning with a no-hitter. Castellanos went 5-for-5 (HR, 5 RBI) in a 9-5 home win over the White Sox on Monday, August 13. The Tigers lost 7-5 in Yankee Stadium in the Bronx on Friday, on August 31, as Zimmermann (6 IP, 1 ER, 3 H, 6 SO) had a quality start. Detroit closed 10-17 in September with an 11-8 home win over Kansas City on Thursday, September 20, behind rookies Ronny Rodriguez 3-for-5 and Christin Stewart (2 HR, 6 RBI). Players were 38-43 (.563) at home, and 26-55 (.506) on the road, including 6-0 (1.000) at Comiskey Park. Motown scored 630 times and allowed 796 runs. Matt Hall (27 GM, 5-2, 1.58 ERA) and Caleb Thielbar (27 GM, 3-0, 1.42 ERA) was with class "AA" Erie.

P * MIKE FIERS

Offense. Motown logged a .241 BA, .300 OBP, .380 SLG, .680 OPS, 2,085 TB and 85 OPS+. Catcher James McCann (.220 BA, 8 HR, 39 RBI) had a 10-game hit streak. John Hicks (.260 BA, 9 HR, 32 RBI) and Jim Adduci (.267 BA, 3 HR, 21 RBI) were at first. Tiger Rookie of the Year Niko Goodrum (.245 BA, 16 HR, 53 RBI) at second led in secondary average (.300) and power/speed number (13.7). Rookie Jeimer Candelario (.224 BA, 19 HR, 54 RBI) at third led in walks (66) and strikeouts (160). Shortstop Jose Iglesias (.269 BA, 5 HR, 48 RBI) led in steals (15). JaCoby Jones (.207 BA, 11 HR, 34 RBI) at left led in triples (6). Mikie Mahtook (.202 BA, 9 HR, 29 RBI) and Leonys Martin (.251 BA, 9 HR, 29 RBI) played in centerfield. Player of the Year, Tiger of the Year, and most effective hitter right-fielder Nicholas Castellanos (.298 BA, 23 HR, 89 RBI) led in games (157), plate appearances (678), at bats (620), runs (88), hits (185), singles (111), doubles (46), homers, runs batted in, on-base percentage (.354), slugging (.500), OPS (.854), OPS+ (130), total average (.824), base-out percentage (.828), gross production average (.284), WAR (2.9), oWAR (4.7), batters run average (.177), hitting, BAbip (.361), times on base (240), base runs (100), runs produced (154), runs created (110), isolated power (.202), extra-base hits (74), total bases (310), bases produced (361) and outs (447). Designated hitter Victor Martinez (.251 BA, 9 HR, 54 RBI). Miguel Cabrera (.299 BA, 3 HR, 22 RBI). Victor Reyes (.222 BA, HR, 12 RBI) led in stolen base runs (2.1). The top pinch-hitter was Martinez at .375 (3-8). Castellanos scorched pitching during period of April 21-25 (10-for-14 .714 BA, 2 HR, 9 RBI, .733 OBP, 1.214 SLG, .667 BAbip).

2010s Pitching Innings		
1.	J. Verlander	1,671.0
2.	Max Scherzer	1,013.0
3.	Rick Porcello	902.2
4.	Anibal Sanchez	798.1
5.	Matt Boyd	638.2
6.	J. Zimmermann	508.2
7.	Michael Fulmer	456.0
8.	Doug Fister	440.2
9.	Daniel Norris	396.1
10.	Phil Coke	323.2

Pitching. The Tigers recorded a 4.58 ERA, 491 walks, 1,215 SO, 95 ERA+, 4.59 FIP, 1.343 WHIP, 9.0 H/9, 3.1 BB/9 and 7.7 SO/9. Pitcher of the Year Mike Fiers (7-6, 3.48 ERA) led in win percentage (.538), LOB% (83.1) and pWAR (2.8). The most effective pitcher Alex Wilson (2-4, 3.36 ERA) led in earned run average, ERA+ (133), WHIP (1.054), H/9 (7.3) and R/9 (3.5). Matt Boyd (9-13, 4.39 ERA) led in wins, losses, starts (31), innings (170.1), hits (146), strikeouts (159), HBP (11), earned runs (83), runs (87) and quality starts (14). Michael Fulmer (3-12, 4.69 ERA). Francisco Liriano (5-12, 4.58 ERA) led in walks (73) and wild pitches (9). Jordan Zimmermann (7-8, 4.52 ERA) led in homers (28), BB/9 (1.8) and SO/BB (4.27). Daniel Norris (0-5, 5.68 ERA). All-Star Joe Jimenez (5-4, 4.31 ERA) led in games (68), FIP (2.91), DICE (2.74), HR/9 (0.7) and SO/9 (11.2). Shane Greene (4-6, 5.12 ERA) led in games finished (58) and saves (32), Louis Coleman (4-1, 3.51 ERA), Blaine Hardy (4-5, 3.56 ERA), Buck Farmer (3-4, 4.15 ERA), Daniel Stumpf (1-5, 4.93 ERA) and Warwick Saupold (4-1, 4.46 ERA). Drew VerHagen (3-3, 4.63 ERA) was stellar during the period of August 14-September 22 (14 GM, 1-0, 15 IP, 0.60 ERA, .185 BA, .204 SLG, .238 BAbip). Class "AAA" Toledo featured closers Johnny Barbato (33 GM, 1.45 ERA, 12 SV) and Zac Houston (33 GM, 1.18 ERA, 10 SV). Caleb Thielbar (7-1 .875, 2.05 ERA) and Matt Hall (9-2 .818, 2.13 ERA) split the year at class "AA" Erie and Toledo. The class "A" West Michigan Whitecaps had Clate Schmidt (9-2 .818, 2.59 ERA) and Billy Lescher (1.23 ERA, 8 SV), as class (A+) Lakeland had Anthony Castro (9-4 .692, 2.93 ERA) and Spenser Watkins (8-4 .667, 2.24 ERA).

Defense. Detroit made 95 errors for a .984 fielding average and led Central Division in defensive efficiency (.694). Outfielder JaCoby Jones led MLB for defensive runs saved rating (24) and team leader in dWAR (2.3). League leaders were Candelario in third base fielding (.973), as Mahtook led for double plays (2) in left. Castellanos led all right fielders in putouts with 287.

August 13-19 Player of the Week Castellanos (.393 BA, .485 OBP, .714 SLG, .450 BABIP) was 5-for-5 (HR, 5 RBI) at home with the White Sox on August 13. Dawel Lugo hit a two-run homer at Milwaukee on September 28 in his only pinch-hit appearance.

Rookie Joe Jimenez had a 1.56 ERA in minors 2013-17 (153 GM, 15-7, 56 SV, 13.0 SO/9). He then became a 2018 All-Star selection March 30-July 15 (46 GM, 4-1, 2.72 ERA, .216 BA), including May 9-June 23 (20 GM, 1-0, .147 BA) with a 0.47 ERA.

2010s Pitching Walks	
1. J. Verlander	484
2. Max Scherzer	305
3. Anibal Sanchez	230
4. Rick Porcello	211
5. Matt Boyd	202
6. Daniel Norris	130
7. Michael Fulmer	128
8. Buck Farmer	127
9. Al Alburquerque	125
Phil Coke	125

Team. Detroit was last under Ron Gardenhire at 47-114 (.292), with an attendance of 1,501,430. The club went 2-2 in March as Jordan Zimmermann (7IP, 0 ER, 1 H) and a Christian Stewart (HR, 2 RBI) 10th-inning two-run homer led the 2-0 win in the Rogers Centre on Thursday, March 28, with 45,048 fans. Matt Moore (7 IP, 0 ER, 2 H, 6 SO) made his Tiger debut during a 4-3 win over the Blue Jays on Sunday, with Jeimer Candelario 5-for-6 (2 RBI). Motown finished 11-12 in April with a Daniel Norris (5 IP, 0 ER, 2 H, 6 SO) and Shane Greene (SV 10, 1 IP, 0 ER, 0 H, 2 SO) 4-3 win over the visiting White Sox on Sunday, April 21. Greene had a franchise record 12 saves in April. John Hicks went 3-for-3 (2 BB) during a 12-11 loss in 4:02 at Chicago on Friday, April 26, despite five Tiger homers from Nicholas Castellanos, Miguel Cabrera 4-for-6 (HR, 3 RBI), Grayson Greiner, JaCoby Jones and Ronny Rodriguez. The Bengals were 9-19 in May as Brandon Dixon hit .400 May 23-June 1 (9 GM, .419 OBP, .733 SLG) and Jones hit .421 May 24-June 11 (16 GM, .468 OBP, .772 SLG). Matt Boyd (6 IP, 0 ER, 8 SO) pitched a 3-0 win in Baltimore on Tuesday, May 28. Spencer Turnbull (6 IP, 1 ER) led an 8-2 triumph at Atlanta on Friday, May 31, as Niko Goodrum went 5-for-5 (2 HR, 3 RBI, 4 R) as the first MLB player since 1934 to record five hits in a players first game in his home state. Detroit was 5-20 in June as Jones 3-for-4 (2 HR, 5 RBI) and Stewart homered in a 9-3 win over Minnesota at home on Saturday, June 8. The squad went 5-20 during July including a 11-5 victory at Comiskey Park in Chicago on the Fourth of July, as Boyd (W 6-6, 5.1 IP, 0 BB, 13 SO) became the first pitcher in the live-ball era since 1920 with no walks and 13 strikeouts in six or less innings. Detroit won 12-8 at Kansas City on Sunday, July 14, with Harold Castro 4-for-6 (2 RBI), Dixon (2 RBI), Candelario (3 RBI), Gordon Beckham (HR, 2 RBI) and Goodrum 4-for-5 (2 RBI, 2 SB). Norris (5 IP, 0 ER, 3 H, 5 SO), Dixon (HR, 4 RBI) and Beckham (HR, 3 RBI) led a 9-1 win in Anaheim on Wednesday, July 31. Players were 8-21 in August including a 5-2 win over Kansas City at home on Friday, August 9, with Edwin Jackson (6.1 IP, 1 ER, 4 H) and Dawel Lugo 3-for-4 (2 RBI). Pitchers Norris (3 IP, 0 ER) and Drew VerHagen (5 IP, 0 ER) led a 3-0 win in Tampa on Tuesday, August 16, with Boyd (7 IP, 1 ER, 2 H, 2 BB, 9 SO) on the hill in a 5-4 loss on Thursday. Players were 7-20 in September, as Tyler Alexander (6 IP, 1 ER, 4 H) and Jordy Mercer (HR, 2 RBI) led 5-2 home win over Baltimore on Monday, September 16. Motown set a league record for futility against an opponent when 1-18 (.053) against Cleveland. Detroit had an MLB record tying 59 losses at home (22-59 .272), was 25-55 (.313) on the road, scored 582 runs and allowed 915. Pitcher Tim Adleman was a combined 13-4 (.765) at Long Island, Erie, and Toledo.

P * SHANE GREENE

Offense. Detroit had a .240 BA, .294 OBP, .388 SLG, .682 OPS, 2,154 TB and 78 OPS+. The Tigers led the league in triples (41) and strikeouts (1,595). John Hicks (.210 BA, 13 HR, 35 RBI) and Grayson Greiner (.202 BA, 5 HR, 19 RBI) caught. Brandon Dixon (.248 BA, 15 HR, 52 RBI) at first led in homers (15). Second base had Harold Castro (.291 BA, 5 HR, 38 RBI) that led in hitting, BAbip (.367) and IP% (72), with Gordon Beckham (.215 BA, 6 HR, 15 RBI), Josh Harrison (.175 BA, HR, 8 RBI), and Ronny Rodriguez (.221 BA, 14 HR, 43 RBI). Dawel Lugo (.245 BA, 6 HR, 26 RBI) and Jeimer Candelario (.203 BA, 8 HR, 32 RBI) shared third. The shortstops were Jordy Mercer (.270 BA, 9 HR, 22 RBI) and Niko Goodrum (12 HR, 45 RBI, .248 BA) that led in runs (61), triples (5), WAR (1.6), oWAR (1.8), secondary average (.303), runs produced (94), power/speed number (12.0), steals (12), stolen base runs (1.8) and strikeouts (138). Christin Stewart (.233 BA, 10 HR, 40 RBI) was in left. JaCoby Jones (.235 BA, 11 HR, 26 RBI) at center led in isolated power (.195). Nicholas Castellanos (11 HR, 37 RBI, .273 BA) at right led MLB in doubles (58, 37 w/Det). He led club in slugging (.462), OPS (.790), OPS+ (105), total average (.738), gross production average (.263), batters run average (.151) and extra base hits (51). Player of the Year designated hitter Miguel Cabrera (12 HR, 59 RBI, .282 BA) led in games (136), plate appearances (549), at bats (493), hits (139), singles (106), runs batted in, on-base percentage (.346), times on base (190), base runs (65), runs created (68), total bases (196), bases produced (244), walks (48) and outs (377). The leading Tiger pinch-hitters were Dixon at .571 (4-7, HR, 4 RBI), Harold Castro .400 (2-5) and Hicks (2 HR, 5 RBI).

2010s Pitching Strikeouts	
1. Justin Verlander	1,627
2. Max Scherzer	1,081
3. Anibal Sanchez	738
4. Matt Boyd	625
5. Rick Porcello	566
6. J. Zimmermann	362
7. Daniel Norris	360
8. Michael Fulmer	356
9. Doug Fister	353
10. Shane Greene	290

Pitching. Motown logged a 5.24 ERA, 536 BB, 1,368 SO, 92 ERA+, 4.84 FIP, 1.459 WHIP, 9.8 H/9, 3.4 BB/9 and 8.6 SO/9. Staff led league in hits (1,555). Pitcher of the Year Matt Boyd (9-12, 4.56 ERA) led MLB in homers (39) and balks (4), with league best in lefthander strikeouts (238). He led staff in wins, starts (32), innings (185.1), hits (178), earned runs (94), runs (101), pWAR (3.5), WHIP (1.230), SO/BB (4.76) and quality starts (14). The most effective pitcher Buck Farmer (6-6, 3.72 ERA) led in games (73), FIP (3.88), DICE (3.67), H/9 (8.2) and R/9 (4.3). Joe Jimenez (4-7, 4.37 ERA) led in LOB% (77.2) and team record SO/9 (12.4). Spencer Turnbull (3-17, 4.61) led MLB in losses and league in HBP (16). *"Red Bull"* led team in walks (59), WP (9) and HR/9 (0.8). Jordan Zimmermann (1-13, 6.91 ERA) led in BB/9 (2.0). Daniel Norris (3-13, 4.49 ERA), Tyler Alexander (1-4, 4.86 ERA), Tyson Ross (1-5, 6.11 ERA), Edwin Jackson (2-5, 8.47 ERA) and Ryan Carpenter (1-6, 9.30 ERA). All-Star Shane Greene (0-2, 1.18 ERA) led in GF (32) and SV (22). Nick Ramirez (5-4, 4.07 ERA), Jose Cisnero (0-4, 4.33 ERA), Dan Stumpf (1-1, 4.34 ERA), Blaine Hardy (1-1, 4.47 ERA), Victor Alcantara (3-2, 4.85), Greg Soto (0-5, 5.77 ERA) and Drew VerHagen (4-3, 5.90 ERA). Greene was exceptional for May 4-July 2 (16 GM, 9 SV, 16 IP, 0.00 ERA, .153 BA, .231 OBP, .220 SLG, .178 BAbip).

Defense. Detroit made 74 errors for a .981 fielding average. Tiger league leaders were pitchers Soto in errors (3), Hardy and VerHagen in fielding average (1.000), as Hicks led in catcher fielding average (1.000). Candelario led Motown in dWAR (0.8).

Shane Greene set league records with seven saves during the club's first 10 games thru Sunday, April 7 and for recording his eighth save in the team's first 12 games on Wednesday, April 10. He became the first Tiger to save his team's first 10 wins.

Team. Detroit (23-35 .397) finished fifth for managers Ron Gardenhire (21-28 .429) and Lloyd McClendon (2-6 .250) during the COVID-19 pandemic. The Bengals were 5-3 in July including JaCoby Jones with a memorable week July 25-31 (3 HR, 7 RBI, .435 BA, .480 OBP, .957 SLG, .500 BAbip). The Bengals won 3-2 in Cincinnati on Sunday, July 26, with Spencer Turnbull (5 IP, 1 ER, 3 H, 8 SO) and C.J. Cron (HR, 2 RBI). Motown won 5-4 win over Kansas City at home on Wednesday, July 29, behind Jonathan Schoop (HR, 3 RBI) and Jones 3-for-3 (2 2B, HR, RBI). Turnbull (W 1-0, 6 IP, 2 ER, 3 H, 6 SO) led a 7-2 victory against visiting Cincinnati on Friday, July 31, aided by Austin Romine 2-for-3 (2 RBI) and Travis Demeritte with a two-run pinch-hit double. Players were 11-13 in August when Tyler Alexander (3.2 IP, 0 ER, 0 H, 10 SO) struck out the first nine batters faced during a 4-3 loss to the Reds on Sunday. The feat set a new MLB record for the most consecutive strikeouts by a relief pitcher. The Bengals won an 11-inning 17-13 decision in 4:33 at Pittsburgh on Friday, August 7, with Niko Goodrum (5 RBI), Jeimer Candelario (3 RBI), Cron (HR, 2 RBI), Romine (2 RBI) and Jones (2 RBI). Detroit defeated the Pirates 11-5 the next day with five homers, aided by Miguel Cabrera 3-for-4 (HR, 3 RBI), Cron 2-for-4 (HR, 2 RBI) and Candelario 3-for-5 (HR). Motown beat the visiting White Sox 5-1 on Monday, August 10, behind Goodrum 4-for-4 (HR) and Jones (HR, 2 RBI). Willie Castro shined August 10-September 26 (16-for-33, .485 BA, .514 OBP, .606 SLG, .615 BAbip). Schoop starred August 17-September 1 (21-for-48, 4 HR, 11 RBI, .438 BA, .500 OBP, .708 SLG). The club lost nine straight games thru Thursday, August 20. Motown defeated the Cubs 7-1 at home on Tuesday, August 25, aided by Turnbull (W 3-2, 5.2 IP, 0 ER, 3 H, 5 SO) and Schoop (HR, 4 RBI). Cabrera excelled August 25-September 4 (15-for-35, .429 BA, .571 SLG, .483 BAbip). Reyes excelled during September 1-6 (12-for-26, 2 HR, 6 RBI, .462 BA, .481 OBP, .769 SLG, .500 BAbip).The Tigers closed 7-19 in September, as pitchers Michael Fulmer (3 IP, 0 ER, 3 H, 6 SO) and Daniel Norris (W 3-1, 2.1 IP, 1 ER, 5 SO) led a 12-1 victory at Milwaukee on Tuesday, September 1. Victor Reyes went 4-for-6 (HR, 5 RBI), Grayson Greiner (HR, 2 RBI), Candelario (2 RBI) and Christin Stewart 2-for-3 (HR). Players prevailed 10-8 in Minnesota on Sunday, September 6, with Willi Castro (HR, 3 RBI), Greiner (HR, 2 RBI) and Candelario 3-for-5 (RBI), as rookie Sergio Alcantara homered in his first MLB at-bat. Candelario hit his stride for September 6-10 (12-for-21, 3 HR, 10 RBI, .571 BA, .609 OBP, 1.190 SLG, .643 BAbip). Pitchers Turnbull (W 4-2, 6 IP, 0 ER, 3 H) and Gregory Soto (1 IP, 0 ER, 0 H, 3 SO) led an 8-3 win over visiting Milwaukee on Tuesday, September 8, with Jorge Bonifacio (2 RBI) and Candelario (HR, 4 RBI). The Tigers rallied with a five-run seventh inning to win 6-3 in St. Louis on Thursday, September 10, with Candelario 3-for-3 (HR, 3 RBI), Bonifacio 3-for-4 (HR, 2 RBI), Reyes 3-for-4, and Jordan Zimmermann (3 IP, 0 ER). Motown shutout visiting Kansas City 6-0 on Tuesday, September 15, behind Matt Boyd (5.2 IP, 0 ER, 2 H, 5 SO), Candelario 3-for-5, Bonafacio 2-for-3 (2 RBI), Willi Castro 3-for-5 (HR) and Cabrera 2-for-2 (3 BB, HR). The Bengals were 12-15 (.444) at home, and 11-20 (.355) on the road. Detroit scored 249 runs and allowed 318 runs.

P * DANIEL NORRIS

Offense. Detroit had a .245 BA, .303 OBP, .397 SLG, .700 OPS, 751 TB and 91 OPS+, with league high in triples (12). Austin Romine (.238 BA, 2 HR, 17 RBI) caught. King Tiger and Tiger of the Year Jeimer Candelario (.297 BA, 7 HR, 29 RBI) at first base led in doubles (11), triples (3), WAR (2.0), oWAR (1.5), secondary average (.314), times on base (76), base runs (32), runs created (34), batter runs (18), isolated power (.205), extra base hits (21), total bases (93) and bases produced (114). Jonathan Schoop (.278 BA, 8 HR, 23 RBI) was at second base, with 21-year-old rookie Isaac Paredes (.220 BA, 1 HR, 6 RBI) at third. Niko Goodrum (.184 BA, 5 HR, 20 RBI) led in power/speed number (5.8), stolen base percentage (87.5), stolen base runs (1.5) and strikeouts (69), as he shared short with Player of the Year, Tiger Rookie of the Year, and most effective hitter Willi Castro (.349 BA, 6 HR, 24 RBI). He led in on-base percentage (.381), slugging (.550), OPS (.932), OPS+ (150), total average (.929), base-out percentage (.932), gross production average (.309), batters run average (.210), hitting, total base average (2.0), and record BAbip (.448). Christin Stewart (.167 BA, 3 HR, 9 RBI) played in left. Centerfield had JaCoby Jones (.268 BA, 5 HR, 14 RBI) and Victor Reyes (.277 BA, 4 HR, 14 RBI, 57 GM, 30 R) that led in hits (56), singles (43), in-play percentage (71.83), run scoring percentage (41.27) and steals (8). Jorge Bonafacio (.221 BA, 2 HR, 17 RBI) and Daz Cameron (.193 BA, 3 RBI played in right. Designated hitter Miguel Cabrera (.250 BA, 10 HR, 35 RBI) led in plate appearances (231), at bats (204), homers, runs batted in, runs produced (53), walks (24), outs (158) and hitting streak (13). The leading pinch-hitter was Harold Castro at .600 (3-5, 2 RBI).

Pitching. The Tigers logged a 5.63 ERA, 192 walks, 444 SO, 82 ERA+, 5.17 FIP, 1.428 WHIP, 9.3 H/9, 3.5 BB/9 and 8.1 SO/9, with league's youngest staff (26.6). Pitcher of the Year Bryan Garcia (2-1, 1.66 ERA) led staff in games finished (12), LOB% (79.3), earned run average, record ERA+ (279), HR/9 (0.0) and RA/9 (2.5). The most effective pitcher Jose Cisnero (3-3, 3.03 ERA) led in games (29), FIP (2.65), DICE (2.46) and WHIP (1.112). Spencer Turnbull (4-4, 3.97 ERA) led in wins, walks (29), IBB (1) and pWAR (1.0). Tarik Skubal (1-4, 5.63 ERA). Matt Boyd (3-7, 6.71 ERA, 5 HBP) led MLB in homers (15) and earned runs (45), with league lead in losses. He led staff in starts (12), complete games (1), innings (60.1), hits (67), strikeouts (60), wild pitches (5), and runs (46). Casey Mize (0-1, 6.75 ERA, 5 HBP), Ivan Nova (1-1, 8.53 ERA) and Michael Fulmer (0-2, 8.79 ERA). Daniel Norris (3-1, 3.25 ERA). Gregory Soto (0-1, 4.30 ERA) led in H/9 (6.3) and SO/9 (11.3). Tyler Alexander (2-3, 3.96 ERA). Buck Farmer (1-0, 3.80 ERA) led in BB/9 (2.1). Joe Jimenez (1-3, 7.15 ERA, 5 HBP) led in saves (5) and SO/BB (3.67). Kyle Funkhouser (1-1, 7.27 ERA), Rony Garcia (1-0, 8.14 ERA) and Michigander John Schreiber (0-1, 6.32 ERA) from Wyandotte. Soto was extraordinary July 24-August 17 (10 GM, 10.1 IP, 0.00 ERA, .114 BA, .184 OBP, .143 SLG, .190 BAbip, 12.2 SO/9). Jose Cisnero excelled July 31-September 4 (15 GM, 15.2 IP, 0.57 ERA, .132 BA, .207 OBP, .189 SLG, .194 BAbip).

Defense. Motown had 27 errors for a .987 fielding average. Tiger league leaders were Boyd, Fulmer, Norris, and Turnbull in pitcher fielding (1.000), as Turnbull led in double plays (3); catchers Romine and Greiner in fielding (1.000), outfielders Stewart in left, Jones in center and Reyes in right for fielding (1.000). Shortstop Goodrum led Detroit in defensive WAR (0.4).

Rookie Bryan Garcia was exemplary August 3-September 21 (20 GM, 1-0, 3 SV, 16.2 IP, 0.54 ERA, .197 BA, .213 SLG, .226 BAbip). Daniel Norris dominated hitters August 3-September 8 (7 GM, 3-0, 19.1 IP, 1.86 ERA, .219 BA, .230 OBP, .283 BAbip).

Team. Former Tiger A.J. Hinch led Detroit (77-85 .475) to third place, with 1,102,621 fans. The club went 8-19 in April, as 22-year-old Rule V draft pick Akil Baddoo excelled in spring training (5 HR, .325 BA, .750 SLG). He hit his first MLB pitch for a homer on Sunday, April 4, with a grand slam on Monday and walk-off single on Tuesday. The club had a mark of 14-13 in May when Robbie Grossman (5 RBI) and Matt Boyd (6 IP, 0 ER) paced an 8-7 home win over Kansas City on Tuesday, May 11. Jose Cisnero shined May 12-July 9 (25 GM, 4 SV, 24.1 IP, 0.37 ERA, .143 BA, .209 OBP, .156 SLG, .204 BAbip). Harold Castro had five straight multi-hit games May 16-25 (12-for-21, .571 BA, .591 OBP, .619 SLG, .571 BAbip). Gregory Soto dominated May 14-July 3 (17 GM, 1-0, 2 SV, 17 IP, 0.53 ERA, .080 BA, .175 OBP, .140 SLG, .100 BAbip). Spencer Turnbull (9 IP, 0 ER, 0 H, 9 SO) threw a 5-0 no-hitter in Seattle on Tuesday, May 18. Motown won 7-5 in Kansas City on Friday, May 21, led by Miguel Cabrera 3-for-5 (2 HR, 5 RBI). Players were 14-13 in June when they lost 9-8 on the road to the White Sox on Friday, June 4, with Jonathan Schoop 4-for-4 (2 HR, 5 RBI) and Eric Haase (HR, 2 RBI). Detroit was 14-12 in July, as Haase from Dearborn Divine Child High School was Rookie of the Month (9 HR, 29 RBI, .627 SLG). Motown won 11-5 at home over the White Sox on Saturday, July 3, led by Haase 3-for-4 (2 HR, 6 RBI) and Schoop (HR, 3 RBI). The Tigers won 14-0 at home facing Texas on Monday, July 19, aided by Casey Mize (4 IP, 0 ER, 1 H), Cabrera (5 RBI), Baddoo (HR, 4 RBI), and Victor Reyes 4-for-5. Haase drove in a run during five straight games July 25-29 (2 HR, 11 RBI,.722 SLG). Detroit won 6-5 at Minnesota on Tuesday, July 27, as opposing catchers (Haase and Mitch Garver) hit grand slams for the first time in league history. The eight run fourth inning led to a 17-14 Tiger win the next day, as nine position players drove in a run. The club was 12-14 in August, as Tarik Skubal (5 IP, 0 ER) and Reyes (2 3B, 3 RBI) paced an 8-1 home win facing Boston on Thursday, August 5. Cabrera hit his 500th homer in a 5-3 win at Toronto on Sunday, August 22. Detroit closed 14-12 in September and 1-2 in October, with a 15-5 win in Cincinnati on Friday, September 3, behind Jeimer Candelario 4-for-5 (HR, 2 RBI), Schoop 4-for-6 (HR), Grossman (HR, 3 RBI), and Dustin Garneau (2 HR, 3 RBI). Cabrera had nine straight hits September 7-10. Motown won 5-1 in Pittsburgh on Wednesday, September 8, with Cabrera 4-for-4 (3 RBI) and Grossman 4-for-5 (HR). Tyler Alexander (6 IP, 1 ER) and Joe Jimenez (W 6-1) led a 5-2 road win over the White Sox on Sunday, October 3. Players were 42-39 (.519) at home, 35-46 (.432) away, scored 697 runs and allowed 756. Class "AAA" Toledo had Aderlin Rodriguez (29 HR, 94 RBI) and Ricardo Pinto (11-3 .786). Riley Greene (24 HR, 84 RBI) and Spencer Torkelson (30 HR, 91 RBI) were minor league stars.

C * ERIC HAASE

Offense. Detroit had a .242 BA, .308 OBP, .399 SLG, .707 OPS, 2,146 TB and 97 OPS+, with league high in triples (37) and SO% (25.3). The catchers were Eric Haase (.231 BA, 22 HR, 61 RBI) that led in slugging (.459), AB/HR (16.0), AB/RBI (5.8), and isolated power (.228), with Jake Rogers (.239 BA, 6 HR, 17 RBI). Player of the Year Jonathan Schoop (.278 BA, 22 HR, 84 RBI, 156 GM, 86 RC) at first led in plate appearances (674), at bats (623), hits (173), singles (120), runs batted in, runs produced (147), total bases (271), and outs (473), with a 16-game hit streak. Willi Castro (.220 BA, 9 HR, 38 RBI) at second led in RS% (41.59) and GIDP% (6.1). The most effective hitter was Tiger of the Year Jeimer Candelario (.271 BA, 16 HR, 67 RBI, 86 RC) at third led MLB in doubles (42). He led squad in OPS (.795), OPS+ (122), gross production average (.269), WAR (3.7), oWAR (4.1), batters run average (.156), and extra base hits (61). Shortstop Niko Goodrum (.214 BA, 9 HR, 33 RBI). Robbie Grossman (.239 BA, 23 HR, 67 RBI, 156 GM, 3.0 SBR) in left led in runs (88), home runs (23), on-base percentage (.357), total average (.817), base-out percentage (.820), secondary average (.379), times on base (239), base runs (84), batter runs (46), power/speed number (21.4), bases produced (349), steals (20), walks (98) and strikeouts (155). 22-year-old rookie Akil Baddoo (.259 BA, 13 HR, 55 RBI, 3.0 SBR) in center led in triples (7) and SB% (81.8), Victor Reyes (.258 BA, 5 HR, 22 RBI) in right. Designated hitter Miguel Cabrera (.256 BA, 15 HR, 75 RBI) led in sacrifice flies (9) and grounded into a double play (21). The top pinch-hitters were Cabrera at 1.000 (2-2) and Haase .667 (4-6, HR, 3 RBI) with four straight pinch-hits. Schoop ruled the month of June (10 HR, 27 RBI, .340 BA, .698 SLG). Jacob Robson (28-for-66, .424 BA, .712 SLG) mastered his brief stay with class "AA" Erie.

Pitching. Motown logged a 4.32, 571 walks, 1,259 SO, 99 ERA+, 4.60 FIP, 1.367 WHIP, 8.7 H/9, 3.6 BB/9, 8.0 SO/9, and 2.20 SO/BB. Staff led league in hit by pitch (82), runners left on base (1,149), passed balls (18), tough losses (13), triples (28) and runners caught stealing (32). Pitcher of the Year and most effective pitcher Michael Fulmer (5-6, 2.97 ERA, 2 IBB) led in TRA (3.49), ERA, ERA+ (143), FIP (3.46), and DICE (3.29). Spencer Turnbull (4-2, 2.88 ERA) and Matt Boyd (3-8, 3.89 ERA). Casey Mize (7-9, 3.71 ERA) led in games started (30), complete games (1), innings (150.1), hit by pitch (11), WHIP (1.137), quality starts (12), no decisions (14) and triples allowed (5). Tyler Alexander (2-4, 3.81 ERA) led in BB/9 (2.4). Wily Peralta (4-5, 3.07). Tarik Skubal (8-12, 4.34 ERA) led league in homers allowed on the road (22) and to righthanders (34). He led staff in wins, losses, hits (141), homers (35), walks (47), SO (164), earned runs (72), runs (76), LOB% (81.4), and cheap wins (4). Matt Manning (4-7, 5.80 ERA) and Jose Urena (4-8, 5.81 ERA). Gregory Soto (6-3, 3.39 ERA, 2 IBB) led in games finished (38), saves (18), wild pitches (11) and H/9 (6.5). Jose Cisnero (4-4, 3.65 ERA) led in games (67). Kyle Funkhouser (7-4, 3.42 ERA) led in winning percentage (.636) and HR/9 (0.8). Joe Jimenez (6-1, 5.96 ERA) led in SO/9 (11.3). Alex Lange (1-3, 4.04 ERA), Derek Holland (3-2, 5.07 ERA), Daniel Norris (1-3, 5.89 ERA), Buck Farmer (0-0, 6.37 ERA) and Bryan Garcia (3-2, 7.55 ERA).

Defense. The Bengals committed 83 errors during the 2021 season for a .986 fielding percentage. Tiger MLB leaders were Alexander, Boyd, Farmer, Lange, Manning, and Turnbull in pitcher fielding (1.000). Catcher Rogers and shortstop Short led team in defensive WAR (0.5). Grossman split time in left field and right field as he led all MLB outfielders in fielding (1.000).

Kyle Funkhouser was exemplary for the periods of June 20-July 20 (10 GM, 3-0, 15.1 IP, 15 SO, 0.00 ERA, .173 BA, .212 SLG), and September 10-29 (9 GM, 1-0, 8 IP, 0.00 ERA, .207 BA). He excelled at home (30 GM, 4-1, 1.00 ERA, .154 BA, .191 BAbip).

Matt Boyd started strong April 1-May 15 (2-3, 41.2 IP, 1.94 ERA, .203 BA). Casey Mise found his niche during May (4-1, 31 IP, 27 SO, 1.74 ERA, .162 BA, .195 BAbip). Wily Peralta excelled for August 15-September 25 (1-1, 27 IP, 1.67 ERA, .223 BA).

TIGER PLAYOFF HISTORY

Division Series: 4-1 (12-10 .545), League Championship Series: 3-4 (16-15 .516), World Series: 4-7 (27-37 .422)

1907 WORLD SERIES

The Chicago Cubs (107-45) left nothing to chance, sweeping the Tigers (92-58) in four straight. Game one resulted in a 3-3 tie, called on account of darkness after 12 innings. To get that tie, however, the Cubs had to score twice in the bottom of the ninth against Tiger right-hander Wild Bill Donovan, who was 25-4 in the regular season. Game two finally resulted in a decision, as Jack Pfiester scattered nine hits to beat the Tigers, 3-1. The third game was much the same, but this time Ed Reulbach held Detroit to a single run, while the Cubbies scored five. Second baseman Johnny Evers was the hitting star with three hits including a pair of doubles. The Series shifted to Detroit for Game four, but the change of scenery did the Tigers little good. Once again, they could manage just one run, this time against Orval Overall, while the Cubs scored six times against Donovan. The first two of those six runs came courtesy of Overall himself, who drove home Evers and Wildfire Schulte with a single to right field in the fifth. Overall permitted five hits to top the Tigers, 6-1. Mordecai "Three Finger" Brown, the Cubs' ace most seasons, finally pitched in game five, and responded with a 2-0 shutout, thus clinching the World Championship for Chicago. Ty Cobb, playing in his first of three straight World Series, batted just .200 and scored a run.

1908 WORLD SERIES

A year later the 1908 Series was a rematch, with the Chicago Cubs (99-55) facing the Detroit Tigers (90-63). The big news came before the series, as the Cubs and Tigers both captured their pennants on the very last day of the regular season. In Detroit for Game one, the Cubs trailed 6-5 as they came to bat in the ninth. Tiger knuckleballer "Kickapoo" Eddie Summers had been pitching well in relief to that point, but the Cubs strung together six straight hits and five runs against Summers for a 10-6 triumph. The clubs traveled to Chicago for Game two, which remained scoreless after seven innings. But just as they had done in the ninth inning of Game one, the Cubs exploded again, this time for six runs in the eighth. Shortstop Joe Tinker got things started with a two-run homer, and Orval Overall cruised to a 6-1 victory. The Tigers finally got on the board in Game three, George Mullin winning an 8-3 decision, as Ty Cobb went 4-for-5 with a double and two RBIs. Back in Detroit, Cub ace Mordecai "Three Finger" Brown, 29-9 during the regular season, baffled the Tigers, allowing four hits and no runs. Summers was no match for Brown, as the Cubs won 3-0. The Cubs scored one in the first inning and one in the fifth in game five, with Overall pitching a 2-0 shutout for the title, as Chicago clinched their second straight World Series Championship.

1909 WORLD SERIES

The highlight going in was the anticipated matchup between the two greatest ballplayers in the world, Pittsburgh's Honus Wagner and Detroit's Ty Cobb. The star of the Series would be neither of them, however, but a reserve pitcher named Babe Adams (12-3 during the regular season). Adams got the start for Pittsburgh (110-42) in Game one and bested the Tigers (98-54) 4-1. Detroit evened the Series the next day, as Wild Bill Donovan beat Pirate ace Howie Camnitz, 7-2. Following a travel day, the Series resumed in Detroit, but the Pirates knocked out Tigers starter Ed Summers in the first inning on the way to scoring five runs. The Bucs led 6-0 after six innings, with all six runs unearned. Motown scored four times in the seventh on a pair of two-run singles from Donie Bush and Ty Cobb. The Pirates came up with two runs of insurance in the ninth, which proved handy when the Tigers scored a pair of their own in the bottom of the inning for an 8-6 game three victory. The next day, George Mullin tossed a five-hit 5-0 shutout win in game four, as Cobb knocked in a pair of runs and the Tigers evened the Series at two games apiece. In a strange scheduling twist, the Series moved back to Pittsburgh for game five, and Adams topped the Tigers again. He was not nearly as sharp in the opener, but he was sharp enough to beat Summers 8-4. Back in Detroit, Mullin won game six 5-4, thus forcing a seventh game. Babe Adams, with just one day of rest since his Game five victory, returned with his best effort, tossing a six-hit shutout. Meanwhile, the Pirate hitters pounded Donovan and Mullin for eight runs, with the Pirates rolling to the title. They made this one close, but for the third straight year, the Tigers lost the World Series. Cobb would play another 19 seasons, although never again reached the fall classic.

1934 WORLD SERIES

Detroit (101-53) and St. Louis (95-58) reached the World Series, as the Cardinals clinched on the last day, with the Tigers winning their first pennant since 1909 by seven games over New York. Cardinals ace Dizzy Dean, who won an incredible 30 games in 1934 started the opener in Detroit. St. Louis scored three times in the first three innings aided by five Tiger errors and scored another four runs in the sixth. Dean went the distance to earn the 8-3 decision. Game two was a thriller, as pinch-hitter Gee Walker's RBI single in the bottom of the ninth tied the score 2-2 headed for extra innings. In the bottom of the 12th, Goose Goslin's single to center scored Charlie Gehringer with the winning run for Detroit. The next afternoon in St. Louis, Dizzy Dean's brother Paul started and held the Tigers to a single run. Right fielder Jack Rothrock's two-run triple led the Redbirds to a 4-1 triumph. The Bengals bounced back in Game four behind Eldon Auker, who clung to a 5-4 lead until the eighth, when Motown erupted for five runs for a 10-4 victory. Detroit's Tommy Bridges, who was roughed up in Game three, outpitched Dizzy Dean in Game five, beating the Cardinals ace 3-1. Back in Detroit for Game six, Paul Dean who had pitched eight innings two days earlier returned for a complete game 4-3 victory to even the series at three games apiece. Dean also drove in the decisive run with an RBI single to right field in the seventh inning. Dizzy Dean started the decisive game seven, with the series on the line facing Auker for the Tigers. St. Louis scored seven runs in the third inning and two more in the sixth on a Joe Medwick triple. Fans threw soda bottles and fruit at Medwick when he took his defensive position in the field, prompting Commissioner Kenesaw Mountain Landis to order him to leave the game. Dean scattered six hits during an 11-0 shutout. The Cardinals were World Series champions, as the Dizzy and Paul Dean won all four games.

1935 WORLD SERIES

Detroit (93-58) had never won a World Series championship, while the Chicago Cubs (100-54) lost their last four World Series appearances since their Fall Classic triumph in 1908 against the Bengals. The Cubs took game one in Motown against Schoolboy Rowe (9 IP, 2 ER, 8 SO) on a Lon Warneke (9 IP, 0 ER, 4 H) 3-0 shutout and Frank Demaree home run. The Tigers evened things up, emphatically, with four first inning runs followed with three more in the fourth for a 7-0 lead. Tommy Bridges (9 IP, 2 ER) Charlie Gehringer 2-for-3 (3 RBI) and AL MVP Hank Greenberg (HR, 2 RBI) led an 8-3 Game two win. Cubs starter Charlie Root (0 IP, 4 ER, 4 H) failed to retire a hitter. Demaree homered again for the cubs in the second inning. Detroit scored four runs eighth inning runs for an 5-3 edge in game three at Wrigley Field, as Chicago tied it in the ninth for extra innings. Motown scored an unearned run off Larry French in the top of the 11th inning, as reliever Schoolboy Rowe (4 IP, 2 ER, 3 SO) retired three straight Chicago hitters to complete the victory. Goose Goslin (2 RBI) and Billy Rogell each were 3-for-5 at the plate for the Bengals. Game four was a 2-1 squeaker, with Detroit's Alvin "General" Crowder (9 IP, 1 ER, 5 H) topping Chicago's Tex Carleton (7 IP, 1 ER). Crowder singled and scored the first Detroit run, with their second run an unearned tally in the sixth on two Cub errors. Chuck Klein (HR, 2 RBI) hit a third inning two-run homer for a 2-0 lead in game five. Warneke 6 IP, 0 ER, 3 H) tossed six scoreless innings before retiring with a sore shoulder. The Cubs avoided elimination with a 3-1 victory at home. Cub Billy Herman was 3-for-4 (HR, 3 RBI) with the score tied at 3-3 after eight innings. Stan Hack led off the top of the ninth with a triple but was stranded when Tiger starter Tommy Bridges (9 IP, 3 ER, 7 SO) worked out of the jam. Goose Goslin's two-out single to right field in the ninth scored Mickey Cochrane with the game-winning, walk-off, championship-clinching run. On their fifth try, the Tigers had finally won a World Series. Detroit series leaders were hitters Pete Fox (.385 BA), Gehringer (.375 BA), pitchers Crowder (1-0, 1.00 ERA), Bridges (2-0, 2.50 ERA) and Rowe (1-2, 2.57 ERA). Herman (HR, 6 RBI, .333 BA), Klein (.333 BA), Warneke (2-0, 0.54 ERA) and Carleton (0-1, 1.29 ERA) led the Cubs.

1940 WORLD SERIES

The Detroit Tigers (90-64) faced the Cincinnati Reds (100-53), who had lost the Fall Classic to the Bronx Bombers the previous year. The Series opened in Cincinnati, but the Tigers cruised to a 7-2 victory behind Bobo Newsom (9 IP, 2 ER), Dick Bartell (2 RBI), Bruce Campbell (2 RBI) and Pinky Higgins (2 RBI). Tragedy struck the next day, however, when Newsom's father, in town for the Series, suffered a fatal heart attack. The Reds turned the tables in Game two as their ace, Bucky Walters (9 IP, 3 ER, 3 H) and Jimmy Ripple (HR, 2 RBI) led a 5-3 victory at home. Play shifted to Motown for Game three, and the Bengals took advantage playing at home with a 7-4 Tommy Bridges (9 IP, 3 ER) win led by Higgins (HR, 3 RBI), Rudy York (HR, 2 RBI) and Campbell 3-for-4. The Tigers scored four runs seventh inning runs on the strength of two-run home runs by York and Higgins. Red right-hander Paul Derringer (9 IP, 2 ER, 5 H), who did not make it out of the first inning of game one, registered a 5-2 game four victory at Detroit to even the series. Bobo Newsom (9 IP, 0 ER, 3 H, 7 SO) was brilliant in Game five with an 8-0 three-hit shutout for the 55,189 fans at Tiger Stadium, despite the emotional loss of his father. The Tigers were led by Hank Greenberg 3-for-5 (HR, 4 RBI) with a monumental three-run homer in the third inning, and Campbell 3-for-4 (2 RBI). Back in Ohio for game six, Cincinnati and Bucky Walters (9 IP, 0 ER, 5 H) shutout the Bengals 4-0 and hit an eighth inning two-run home run to force a deciding game seven. Newsom (8 IP, 2 ER, 6 SO) pitched well in game seven at home on just one day's rest, and after six innings, he owned a 1-0 lead. Derringer (9 IP, 0 ER) allowed just an unearned run in the third. The Reds scored twice in the seventh and Derringer closed out the Series with a perfect ninth inning for the title. Billy Werber (.370 BA), Jimmy Wilson (.353 BA) and Ripple (HR, 6 RBI, .333 BA) led the Reds, as Campbell (HR, 5 RBI, .360 BA), AL MVP Greenberg (HR, 6 RBI, .357 BA) and Higgins (HR, 6 RBI, .333 BA) paced Detroit during the World Series.

1945 WORLD SERIES

The 1945 World Series is remembered as the last wartime Fall Classic, and thus as one devoid of stars, but both the Tigers (88-65) and Cubs (98-56) featured some fine players. Future Hall of Famers Hank Greenberg (.311 BA, 166 OPS+) and Hal Newhouser (25-9, 1.81 ERA, 8 SHO, 195 ERA+) led Detroit, while the Cubs enjoyed the services of Phil Cavaretta (.355 BA, 166 OPS+), Stan Hack (.323 BA) and Andy Pafko (110 RBI). The Series opened in Detroit, with the Cubs starting Hank Borowy a combined 21-7, 2.65 ERA in 1945 between the Yankees (10-5) and Cubs (11-2, NL best 2.13 ERA). Borowy (9 IP, 0 ER) led a 9-0 shutout, with Cavaretta and Pafko each 3-for-4 scoring three runs apiece. Bill Nicholson 2-for-4 (3 RBI) had a two-run triple in the first inning. Virgil Trucks (9 IP, 1 ER), Doc Cramer 3-for-4 and Greenberg (HR, 3 RBI) led a 4-1 win in game two. Trucks had been discharged from the United States Navy less than a week earlier. Though the war was over, wartime travel restrictions were still in effect, so the teams stayed in Motown for Game three. Chicago's Claude Passeau (9 IP, 0 ER, 1 H) was brilliant, logging a one hit 3-0 win. Dizzy Trout (9 IP, 0 ER, 5 H, 6 SO) allowed an unearned run in a 4-1 game four triumph at Wrigley Field to even the series 2-2. Game five featured a rematch of the opener, but this time Tigers ace Newhouser (9 IP, 9 SO) bested Borowy 8-4, as Greenberg was 3-for-5, with three doubles and three runs scored. Chicago led 7-3 late in game six, but the Tigers tied the game the eighth inning, as the fourth run scored came on a Greenberg Home run to left. Stan Hack finished the game 4-for-5 (3 RBI), as he dropped a game-winning two-out double to left field in the 12th inning. Pinch-runner Bill Schuster scored the winning run from first base in the dramatic walk-off win to force a seventh and deciding game seven, as Borowy (4 IP, 0 ER) earned the victory in relief. Cub manager Charlie Grimm elected to start his ace Borowy in Game seven on one day of rest with the title on the line. Borowy allowed singles to the first three batters he faced, was lifted, and Detroit wound up scoring five first inning runs. That was all Hal Newhouser (9 IP, 3 ER, 10 SO) needed, as the Tigers mauled the Cubs 9-3, with Doc Cramer 3-for-5 and Paul Richards 2-for-4 (4 RBI) had two doubles for the World Championship. Series totals had Cramer at .379 (11-29), Greenberg (2 HR, 7 RBI) and Richards (6 RBI) to lead Detroit. The Cubs were led by Cavaretta .423 (11-26, 5 RBI), Hack .367 (11-30), Livingston .354 (8-22) and Peanuts Lowry at .310 (9-29).

1968 WORLD SERIES

1968 was the Year of the Pitcher, as two shining examples pitched for World Series teams from St. Louis (97-65) and Detroit (103-59). The Cardinal ace was Bob Gibson, who went 22-9 with a microscopic 1.12 ERA in the regular season. The Tiger staff was led by Denny McLain, who at 31-6, became the first 30-game winner in Major League Baseball since Dizzy Dean won 30 games for St. Louis back in 1934. Game one in St. Louis matched Cy Young Award winners Gibson (9 IP, 0 ER. 5 H, 17 SO) and McLain. Gibson set a World Series record with 17 strikeouts and shutout the Bengals 4-0. The Tigers took Game two 8-1 at Busch Stadium, behind Mickey Lolich (9 IP, 1 ER, 9 SO). The Tigers were led offensively by homers from Willie Horton, Lolich (2 RBI) and Norm Cash. The World Series moved to Detroit for Game three won by the Cardinals 7-3. Tim McCarver (HR, 3 RBI) had a three-run homer in the fifth inning, followed by an Orlando Cepeda (HR, 3 RBI) three-run blast in the seventh. Lou Brock went 3-for-4 with three stolen bases, as Al Kaline (HR, 2 RBI) and Dick McAuliffe homered for Detroit. Gibson (9 IP, 1 ER, 5 H, 10 SO) led St. Louis to a convincing 10-1 game four victory in Motown in a rematch of Cy Young Award winners. Brock 3-for-5 (HR, 4 RBI) logged a double, triple, home run, stolen base and drove home four runners, as Gibson (HR, 2 RBI) helped his cause with a fourth-inning homer. The lone bright spot for the 53,634 Tiger Stadium faithful was a Jim Northrup dinger in the fourth inning, as St. Louis took a commanding 3-1 series advantage. Brock went 3-for-5 with two steals as Cepeda (HR, 2 RBI) hit a two-run homer in the three-run first inning. Lolich (9 IP, 3 ER, 8 SO) shut St. Louis down for the next eight innings. In the meantime, the Bengals scored two runs in the fourth, and then three more in the seventh for a 5-2 victory. The clubs traveled back to St. Louis for Game six, with McLain (9 IP, 1 ER, 7 SO) leading a 13-1 win facing seven Cardinal pitchers. Kaline 3-for-4 (HR, 4 RBI), Northrup (HR, 4 RBI), Cash (2 RBI) and Horton (2 RBI) powered the Tigers lineup. Northrup's grand slam keyed a 10-run third inning, as Detroit evened the series 3-3. Game seven in St. Louis featured Bob Gibson (9 IP, 4 ER, 8 SO) against Mickey Lolich (9 IP, 1 ER) on two days of rest. They matched shutout innings until the top of the seventh. Centerfielder Curt Flood misjudged a flyball for a Northrup triple, with two runs scored. Bill Freehan then doubled in Northrup. Both clubs scored a run in the ninth for a Detroit 4-1 victory, with the Bengals winning their first World Series since 1945. Tiger All-Stars Cash (.385 BA, 5 RBI), Kaline (.379 BA, 2 HR, 8 RBI) and Horton (.304 BA) led the way, as series MVP Lolich (3-0, 1.67 ERA, 3 CG, 27 IP, 21 SO) tied a World Series record by winning three games.

1972 AMERICAN LEAGUE CHAMPIONSHIP SERIES

Eastern Division champions Detroit (86-70) faced the Western Division winners Oakland (93-62). Game one starters were Catfish Hunter (8 IP, 1 ER, 4 H) for the Athletics and 25-game winner Mickey Lolich (10 IP, 2 ER) for the Tigers at Oakland. Norm Cash hit a second-inning home run for Detroit, as the game headed to extra innings tied 1-1. Al Kaline hit a homer in the top of the eleventh, as Oakland pinch-hitter Gonzalo Marquez hit a two-run single in the bottom of the inning for a 3-2 walk-off win. Blue Moon Odom (9 IP, 0 ER, 3 H) pitched Oakland to a 3-0 three-hit shutout at home. Bert Campaneris (2 SB) was already 3-for-3 in the game when he headed to his at-bat in the seventh inning against Tiger Lerrin LaGrow. The first pitch hit him in the ankle and after staggering for a moment, threw his bat at LaGrow who ducked away. The bench-clearing incident resulted in Campaneris and LaGrow being suspended for the remainder of the ALCS. Joe Coleman (9 IP, 0 ER, 14 SO) took the mound for the game three 3-0 win in Motown, as he finished with an ALCS record 14 strikeouts. Ike Brown (2 RBI) and Bill Freehan hit a home run and Ike Brown (2 RBI) led the win. Hunter (7.1 IP, 1 ER) and Lolich (9 IP, 1 ER) started game four in Detroit. Dick McAuliffe had a Tiger third inning home run and Mike Epstein went yard for Oakland to tie game 1-1 in the seventh. The Athletics scored two runs in the tenth inning for a temporary 3-1 lead. Jim Northrup had a run scoring hit to cap a three-run tenth and 4-3 walk-off Tiger win. Woodie Fryman (8 IP, 1 ER, 4 H) faced Odom (5 IP, 1 R, 2 H) in the deciding game five, with 50,276 in Tiger Stadium. Oakland manager Dick Williams called on 1971 Cy Young winner Vida Blue (4 IP, 0 ER, 3 SO) to save the 2-1 win for a trip to the World Series. Campaneris (.429 BA), Matty Alou (.381 BA) Odom (2-0, 0.00 ERA, 14 IP) and Hunter (1.17 ERA, 15.1 IP) led Oakland, with Lolich (1.42 ERA, 19 IP), Coleman (1-0, 0.00 ERA, 9 IP) and Northrup (.357 BA) leading the Motown effort. The Bengals hit a meager .198 in a pitching dominated series.

1984 AMERICAN LEAGUE CHAMPIONSHIP SERIES

Manager Sparky Anderson guided the Detroit Tigers (104-58) to the Eastern Division crown during the teams 84th season in 1984. Motown led the standings wire-to-wire, with the teams most wins and best 162-game winning percentage (.642). The Bengals opened the season 9-0, with another nine-game win streak in May. Players set the 40-game all-time best mark of 35-5 and were a perfect 17-0 in their first 17 games played on the road. Detroit opened their season 11-2 in their first 13 home games and were 19-5 at home after having played 24 games in Motown. Their ALCS opponent Kansas City (84-78) meanwhile squeaked to a Western Division title for the right to face baseballs best team. The Royals reached the ALCS despite the disadvantage of scoring 673 runs, while their pitching staff allowed opponents to score 686. Game one in Kansas City had the Royals Bud Black (17-12) starting against Tiger ace Jack Morris (19-11). Detroit and Morris (7 IP, 1 ER) won with a convincing 8-1 score in Royals Stadium. Three Tigers slammed home runs with Alan Trammell 3-for-3 (HR, 3 RBI), Lance Parrish (HR, 2 RBI) and Larry Herndon. Game two in Kansas City featured starters Dan Petry (7 IP, 2 ER, 4 H) for Detroit facing off with Bret Saberhagen (8 IP, 2 ER) for the Royals. The game went into extra innings tied 3-3, as Motown scored two runs on an eleventh inning double by Johnny Grubb. Reliever Aurelio Lopez (3 IP, 0 ER) got the 5-3 extra inning win. Kirk Gibson (HR, 2 RBI) was a factor as well with a double and home run off Saberhagen. Milt Wilcox (8 IP, 0 ER, 2 H, 8 SO) and Willie Hernandez (1 IP, 0 ER, 0 H) outdueled Charlie Leibrandt (8 IP, 1 ER, 3 H, 6 SO) in a game three series pennant clinching 1-0 Tiger shutout win. The Detroit pitching duo allowed two hits, with a crowd of 52,168 fans in attendance at Tiger Stadium. Gibson hit .417 to be named the ALCS MVP, followed by teammates Trammell (.364 BA) and Barbaro Garbey (.333 BA). Detroit pitching (3-0, 1.24 ERA) shut down the Royals who managed to hit a deficient .170 (18-for-106, .214 OBP, .198 SLG) as a team. The Bengals advanced to square off with the National League Champion San Diego Padres in the World Series.

1984 WORLD SERIES

The 1984 World Series will be remembered as a mismatch, with Detroit (104-58) trouncing National League Champion San Diego (92-70) in five games. In the very first inning of the Series, Detroit collected four base hits, but scored just once. Then in the bottom of the frame, San Diego grabbed a 2-1 lead on Terry Kennedy's two-run double. It was still 2-1 in the fifth when Larry Herndon (HR, 2 RBI) homered with two out and a man on for the final score of 3-2, with 57,908 at Jack Murphy Stadium. Jack Morris (9 IP, 2 ER, 9 SO) held the Padres scoreless after the first inning. San Diego showed life in Game two, bouncing back from a 3-0 deficit in the first inning for a 5-3 triumph at home to even the Series with 57,911 in attendance. Relievers Andy Hawkins (5.1 IP, 0 ER, 1 H) and Craig Lefferts (3 IP, 0 ER, 1 H, 5 SO) held the Tigers to just two hits after the first frame. DH Kurt Bevacqua was 3-for-4 (HR, 3 RBI), Garry Templeton 3-for-4 and Alan Wiggins 3-for-5 led the Padre offense. Milt Wilcox (6 IP, 1 ER) and regular season MVY and Cy Young winner Willie Hernandez (2.1 IP, 0 ER, 1 H) led Detroit to a 5-2 game three win at home. The Tigers scored four second inning runs aided by a two-run shot by Marty Castillo (HR, 2 RBI). Tiger Alan Trammell (2 HR, 4 RBI), a San Diego native, went 3-for-4 with a pair of two-run home runs in the first and third innings, accounting for all of Detroit's runs in their 4-2 game four win and a commanding 3-1 series lead. Jack Morris (9 IP, 2 ER, 5 H) went the distance in the win. Kirk Gibson got the Tigers started in the first inning of Game five in Tiger Stadium with a two-run round-tripper. The Padres fought back to tie the contest at three-all in the fourth, and after scoring a run in the eighth they trailed 5-4. Then Gibson struck again, this time in the eighth inning with a three-run right field upper deck home run. Reliever Aurelio Lopez (2.1 IP, 0 ER, 0 H, 4 SO), Gibson (2 HR, 5 RBI) and Parrish with a homer led the 8-4 win to take the series. Series MVP Trammell (.450 BA, 2 HR, 6 RBI), Gibson (.333 BA, 2 HR, 7 RBI), Herndon (.333 BA), Castillo (.333 BA) and Morris (2-0, 2.00 ERA, 2 CG) led the way. The Padres series leader was Kurt Bevacqua (.412 BA, 2 HR, 4 RBI).

1987 AMERICAN LEAGUE CHAMPIONSHIP SERIES

Detroit (98-64) lost three of four games in Toronto to trail the Blue Jays by 3.5 games with a week to go. The Bengals finished 6-2 from that point on to win the division by two games. Motown won their last four games, including sweeping a three-game series at home over Toronto to end the season. Minnesota (85-77) scored 786 runs in 1987 and allowed 806, as they limped into the ALCS with a 2-7 record in their last nine games. The Twins watched their seven-game lead with a week to go dwindle down to a two after losing the last five games of the season. Tiger Doyle Alexander (9-0, 1.53 ERA, 279 ERA+) was phenomenal down the stretch and started game one against Frank Viola at the Metrodome. The Twins had a three-run fifth inning and scored four more in the eighth for an 8-5 victory. Gary Gaetti (2 HR, 2 RBI) hit two solo homers and Tom Brunansky (3 RBI) doubled twice. Mike Heath (HR, 2 RBI) and Kirk Gibson hit home runs for Detroit. Bert Blyleven (7.1 IP, 3 ER, 6 SO) and 55,245 fans enjoyed a 6-3 Twins victory over Jack Morris in game two at Minneapolis. The Minnesota attack was led by Dan Gladden (2 RBI), Tim Laudner (2 RBI) and Kent Hrbek who hit a home for the Twins, as Chet Lemon (HR, 2 RBI) and Lou Whitaker homered for Detroit. The Bengals scored five in third inning of game three, with a two-run pinch-hit double by Larry Herndon. Detroit held on the 7-6 win at home, as Mike Henneman (3 IP, 0 ER, 1 H) got the win in relief. Herndon (2 RBI) and Pat Sheridan (HR, 2 RBI) led the Tigers. Kirby Puckett and Greg Gagne connected for home runs for a Twins 5-3 game four win in Motown, with Frank Viola (5 IP, 2 ER) the winner. Blyleven (6 IP, 3 ER) recorded a game five 9-5 win in Detroit, as Tom Brunansky 3-for-5 (HR, 3 RBI) and Gladden 3-for-6 (2 RBI) had two doubles for Minnesota. Gibson 3-for-4 led Detroit, along with home runs from Rookie catcher Matt Nokes (HR, 2 RBI) and Lemon. The pennant winners were World Series bound on the strength of ALCS MVP Gaetti (.300 BA), Brunansky (.412 BA, 2 HR, 9 RBI) and Gladden (.350 BA).

Crafty Tiger Lefthander Kenny Rogers set two Records in 2006 with 23 Consecutive Post Season Scoreless Innings.

The Post Season Scoreless Streak for a Lefthanded Pitcher and the American League Post Season Scoreless Streak

7.2 Innings, 0 Earned Runs, 5 Hits, 2 Walks and 8 Strikeouts versus New York in ALDS on October 6, 2006, at home.
7.1 Innings, 0 Earned Runs, 2 Hits, 2 Walks and 6 Strikeouts versus Oakland in ALCS on October 13, 2006, at home.
8.0 Innings, 0 Earned Runs, 2 Hits, 3 Walks and 5 Strikeouts versus St. Louis in WS on October 22, 2006, at home.

2006 AMERICAN LEAGUE DIVISION SERIES

The Wild Card Detroit Tigers (95–67) finished second in the Central Division. The Eastern Division champion Yankees (97-65) scored five third inning runs in game one off Nate Robertson. Chien-Ming Wang (6.2 IP, 3 ER) led the 8-4 Yankees win. Craig Monroe and Curtis Granderson homered for Motown, as Bobby Abreu (4 RBI), Derek Jeter 5-for-5 (HR) and Jason Giambi (HR, 2 RBI) led New York. Johnny Damon launched a three-run home run off Justin Verlander for a 3-1 lead in game two at Yankee Stadium. Carlos Guillen homered to tie the game 3-3 in the sixth. Granderson tripled in the seventh for the winning run of a 4-3 win. Tiger Kenny Rogers (7.2 IP, 0 ER, 5 H, 8 SO) led a 6-0 game three shutout. At 41 years and 330 days he became the oldest starting pitcher to record his first postseason win. Motown got to Randy Johnson (5.2 IP, 5 ER, 8 H, 2 BB) early and often to build a 5-0 lead, as Granderson capped the scoring with a leadoff seventh-inning home run off Brian Bruney. Detroit defeated New York 8–3 in game four behind Jeremy Bonderman (8.1 IP, 2 ER) to complete the series sweep. In the second inning, Magglio Ordonez hit a leadoff home run and later Craig Monroe crushed a two-run home run off Jaret Wright to give the Tigers a 3–0 lead. Ivan Rodriguez singled in a another run in the next Tiger at-bat. Detroit scored another three runs in the fifth for a commanding 9-0 lead, as Bonderman had a no-hitter through five innings. Yankee hitters ended their twenty-inning scoreless streak on Hideki Matsui's groundout in the seventh. Bonderman left in the ninth, with Jamie Walker allowing a Jorge Posada two-run homer before getting Robinson Cano to ground out to end the game. The Tigers advanced to the 2006 ALCS to face the Oakland Athletics. The game is notable as it was Cory Lidle's final appearance before dying in an airplane crash four days later, and was the final ALDS game televised by FOX due to the new television contracts.

2006 AMERICAN LEAGUE CHAMPIONSHIP SERIES

Detroit (95-67) faced Western Division Champion Oakland (93-69) in the ALCS. The series was a rematch of the in 1972 ALCS series won by the Athletics. The Bengals took game one in Oakland 5-1 behind Nate Robertson (5 IP, 0 ER, 4 SO), scoring twice in the third and three times in the fourth. Brandon Inge 3-for-3 (HR, 2 RBI) and Ivan Rodriguez homered for Detroit. Oakland 0-for-13 with runners in scoring position and four double plays by Detroit were LCS records. Justin Verlander and Detroit won game two 8-5 in Oakland, after trailing 3-1. Alexis Gomez (HR, 4 RBI) hit a two-run home run in the sixth, Curtis Granderson hit a homer in the ninth and Craig Monroe was 2-for-3 (2 RBI) for Motown. Milton Bradley went 4-for-5 (2 HR, 4 RBI) for Oakland. The Bengals took a 3-0 lead in game three on a Monroe fifth inning home run off Rich Harden. Kenny Rogers (7.1 IP, 0 ER, 2 H, 6 SO) continued his post season dominance, with Todd Jones picking up the save. Tiger Jeremy Bonderman (6.2 IP, 3 ER) faced Dan Haren in Game four. Jay Payton homered in the fourth to make it 3–0 Athletics. Magglio Ordonez hit a solo homer in the sixth to tie the game 3-3. Huston Street got two outs, then allowed back-to-back singles to Polanco and Monroe before Ordonez launched a three-run walk-off home run for the win, as Detroit advanced to the World Series. Ordonez (2 HR, 4 RBI) and Placido Polanco 3-for-5 led the Tiger attack. Ordonez's blast was the first pennant-winning home run since Aaron Boone's in the 2003 ALCS game seven and came on the 30th Anniversary of New York Yankee Chris Chambliss hitting a pennant-winning walk-off home run in Game five of the 1976 ALCS. Detroit manager Jim Leyland, who led the Florida Marlins to the 1997 World Series title, became the seventh manager in history to win pennants in both leagues. Series leaders were ALCS MVP Polanco (.529 BA), Gomez (4 RBI, .444 BA), Monroe (4 RBI, .429 BA), Granderson (.333 BA), Inge (.333 BA) and Ordonez (2 HR, 6 RBI) for the Bengals, as Bradley led Oakland (2 HR, 5 RBI, .500 BA). The Detroit pitching staff recorded a 2.25 earned run average in the series led by Rogers (1-0, 0.00 ERA) and Robertson (1-0, 0.00 ERA).

2006 WORLD SERIES

Detroit (95-67) faced St. Louis (83-78) in the World Series for the third time, as the Cardinals won in 1934 and Tigers in 1968. Two rookies started Game one for the first time: Anthony Reyes (5-8) for St. Louis, with the fewest wins for a game one starter, and Justin Verlander (17-9) for the Bengals. Scott Rolen put a halt to his record 0-15 skid with a homer in the second. Albert Pujols hit a two-run homer in the third. Reyes (8 IP, 2 ER, 4 H) retired a World Series rookie record seventeen in a row for a 7-2 win in Motown. The Cardinals scored three runs in the third and sixth innings. Bengal Craig Monroe homered in the ninth. 42,533 fans endured the 44 °F temperature at Comerica Park for game two. Kenny Rogers (8 IP, 0 ER, 2 H, 5 SO) ran his postseason scoreless streak to 23 straight innings with a 3-1 Tiger victory. The scoreless streak is a league mark and MLB record for a left-hander. Monroe hit a fifth inning homer for a 3-0 lead. Todd Jones closed the game after allowing a run. Carlos Guillen 3-for-3 fell a home run shy of a cycle, as Monroe became the fifth player to hit a home run in each of his first two World Series games. Chris Carpenter (8 IP, 0 ER, 3 H, 6 SO) led a 5–0 St. Louis game three win at home. The redbirds scored on a Jim Edmonds two-run double in the fourth, two in the seventh and a run in the eighth. David Eckstein went 4-for-5 (3 2B, 2 RBI) during a 5-4 Cardinal win. Sean Casey 3-for-4 (HR, 2 RBI), Ivan Rodriguez 3-for-4 and Jeremy Bonderman (5.1 IP, 2 ER, 4 SO) gave Motown a chance. Former Tiger Jeff Weaver (8 IP, 1 ER, 4 H, 9 SO) led St. Louis to a 4-2 win in game five. Both teams scored two fourth inning runs, with Sean Casey a two-run homer for Detroit. Cardinal Adam Wainwright struck out Bandon Inge for the save, and the first World Series to end on a strikeout since 1988. Detroit pitchers committed one error per game for a World Series record of five. St. Louis had the worst record for a World Series champion. Series leaders were Rolen (.421 BA), Yadier Molina (.412 BA), series MVP Eckstein (.364), Carpenter (1-0, 0.00 ERA) and Reyes (1-0, 2.25 ERA) for St. Louis, as Casey (2 HR, 5 RBI, .529 BA), Guillen (.353 BA) and Inge (.353 BA) led Detroit.

2011 American League Division Series

Detroit (95-67) won their first Central title and faced New York (97-65). Cy Young winner Tiger Justin Verlander (24-5, 2.40 ERA) started game one versus CC Sabathia. Bengal Delmon Young had a home run in the first. The game was suspended due to rain in the second inning and resumed the next day with Doug Fister and Iván Nova pitching. Fister (8-1, 1.79 ERA) dominated after his trade to Motown. Yankee Robinson Cano was 3-for-5 (2 2B, HR, 6 RBI) with a grand slam in the six-run sixth inning, with his six RBI game a Yankee postseason record. Iván Nova (6.1 IP, 2 ER, 5 SO) and Mariano Rivera led the 9-3 win at home. Tiger Max Scherzer (6 IP, 0 ER, 2 H, 5 SO) outpitched Freddie Garcia in a game two 5-3 win in New York, as Miguel Cabrera was 3-for-4 (HR, 3 RBI) and Magglio Ordonez 3-for-3. Curtis Granderson and Nick Swisher homered for New York. Verlander (8 IP, 4 ER, 11 SO) and Sabathia (5.1 IP, 4 ER, 7 H, 6 BB) started game three in Detroit. Bengal José Valverde recorded his 50th consecutive save in a 5-4 win. Ramon Santiago (2 RBI) and Delmon Young with a homer in the seventh led the Bengals, as Brett Gardner (2 RBI) led New York. A.J. Burnett (5.2 IP, 1 ER) escaped a bases loaded first inning in a 10-1 game four win in Detroit. Derek Jeter's two-run double for New York started the scoring, with a fourth inning Victor Martinez homer for the Bengals. New York tacked on two more in the fifth inning and erupted for six runs in the eighth. Relievers Rafael Soriano, Phil Hughes and Boone Logan struck out six Tigers in the last 3 ⅓ hitless innings. The Bengals behind Fister (5 IP, 1 ER, 4 SO) closed the series with an 3-2 win before a Yankee Stadium III record crowd of 50,960. Back-to-back first inning homers by Don Kelly and Young gave Detroit the lead. Young's third homer was a new Tiger playoff series record. Cano with a fifth inning homer and a bases loaded Mark Teixeira walk scored the New York runs. Sabathia entered in the fifth for his first game in relief. Rivera had a scoreless ninth in his final postseason appearance, as Valverde logged his 51st straight save. Series leaders were Ordonez (.455 BA), Brandon Inge (.429 BA), Don Kelly (.364 BA) and Scherzer (1-0, 1.23 ERA) for Detroit, as Jorge Posada (.429 BA), Gardner (.412 BA, 5 RBI) and Cano (318 BA, 2 HR, 9 RBI) led New York.

2011 American League Championship Series

This was the first postseason meeting between the Rangers (96-66) and Tigers (95-67). C.J. Wilson (16-7, 2.94 ERA) faced Justin Verlander (24-5, 2.40 ERA) in game one. Texas scored two runs in the second, with a Nelson Cruz fourth inning homer for a 3-0 lead against Verlander and a 3-2 win at home. Detroit had loaded the bases in the first and fifth innings, with Ramon Santiago 3-for-4, as Bengal relievers (4 IP, 0 ER, 1 H) shut the Rangers down. Closer Neftali Feliz allowed a hit then struck out three hitters for the save. Josh Hamilton and Adrián Beltre each had an RBI in the first to give the Rangers an early 2-0 lead in game two in Texas. Ryan Raburn hit a three-run third inning homer, followed by a Nelson Cruz seventh inning Ranger home run. The Bengals escaped a ninth inning bases load jam, although paid the price in the eleventh when Cruz hit the first ever walk-off grand slam in post season history. Raburn (HR, 3 RBI) powered Detroit, as Cruz 3-for-4 (2 HR, 5 RBI) and reliever Scott Feldman (4.1 IP, 0 ER, 1 H, 4 SO) led Texas to a 7-4 home win for a 2-0 series lead. The Rangers scored a game three first inning in Motown on three straight singles. Víctor Martínez hit a solo home run in the fourth, scored another in the fifth, and led 4-1 after a sixth inning Jhonny Peralta homer and Austin Jackson single. Miguel Cabrera (HR, 2 RBI) connected for a home run in the seventh, as Detroit won 5-2 at home behind Doug Fister (7.1 IP, 2 ER). Matt Harrison (5 IP, 2 ER, 3 H) and Cruz (HR, 3 RBI) outlasted Tiger starter Rick Porcello (6.2 IP, 2 ER, 6 SO) in Detroit for a 7-3 win. Cabrera doubled home two third inning runners, with the Rangers scoring three runs in the sixth. The game entered extra innings 3-3, as Texas scored four eleventh inning runs capped by a Cruz hit a three-run homer. Cabrera (2 RBI) walked three times for the Bengals. Verlander (7.1 IP, 4 ER, 8 SO) faced Wilson (6 IP, 6 ER, 8 H, 2 BB) for game five at Detroit in a repeat of game one starters. Tiger Alex Avila homered in the Third to tie the game and took a 2-1 lead with a Delmon Young home run the next inning. The Bengals scored four sixth inning runs on the first combined natural cycle on four consecutive at-bats in playoff history, with a Raburn single, Cabrera double, Martínez triple, and another homer by Young to make it 6–2. Cruz hit a two-run home run in the eight to chase Verlander. Young (2 HR, 3 RBI) was 2-for-3 in the Tiger 7-5 win, as Cruz (HR, 2 RBI) and Josh Hamilton (2 RBI) led the Rangers. Texas won the series with a convincing 15-5 victory in Arlington. Cabrera and Peralta homered for Detroit in the first and second innings for a 2-0 lead. Texas scored nine third inning runs on six hits and four walks, as 14 batters went to the plate. Michael Young had two two-run doubles during the Ranger sixth inning. Cabrera hit a solo home run in the eighth. The Ranger attack was led by Young (2 2B, HR, 5 RBI), Ian Kinsler (3 RBI), Cruz (HR, 2 RBI) and David Murphy (2 RBI) 2-for-2 with three walks, as Martinez 3-for-4, Cabrera (2 HR, 2 RBI), Jackson (2 RBI) led Detroit. Series leaders for Texas were Yorvit Torrealba (.444 BA), Murphy (.4512 BA), ALCS MVP Cruz (.364 BA, 7 R, 6 HR, 13 RBI), Hamilton (.308 BA) and Kinsler (6 RBI), as Cabrera (.400 BA, 3 HR, 7 RBI) and Ramon Santiago (.375 BA) led Motown. The Rangers won despite a 6.59 ERA by starters Holland (8.59), Wilson (6.75), Lewis (6.35) and Harrison (3.60).

Justin Verlander Set the Record of 30 Consecutive Post Season Scoreless Innings Against the Same Team 2012-2013

6.0 Innings, 0 Earned Runs, 2 Hits, 4 Walks and 11 Strikeouts versus the A's in ALCS on October 6, 2012, in Detroit.
9.0 Innings, 0 Earned Runs, 4 Hits, 1 Walks and 11 Strikeouts versus the A's in ALCS on October 11, 2012, in Oakland.
7.0 Innings, 0 Earned Runs, 4 Hits, 1 Walks and 11 Strikeouts versus the A's in ALDS on October 5, 2013, in Oakland.
8.0 Innings, 0 Earned Runs, 2 Hits, 1 Walks and 10 Strikeouts versus the A's in ALDS on October 10, 2013, at Oakland.

2012 American League Division Series

Western Division champion Oakland (94-68) advanced to face Detroit (88-74) winners of the Central Division. Game one in Motown had Jarrod Parker (13-8) against Justin Verlander (17-8). Verlander (7 IP, 1 ER, 3 H, 11 SO) pitched a high-quality start leading a 3-1 game one win, as he allowed a Coco Crisp home run to start the game. Parker (6.1 IP, 2 ER, 5 SO) recorded a quality start, although the Tigers scored single runs in the first, third and in the fifth on an Alex Avila homer. Pat Neshek, pitching for the first time since the death of his one-day-old son, got out of a seventh inning jam with two Tigers on, with Infante grounding into a force out and striking out Austin Jackson. Quintin Berry and Avila both went 2-for-3 at the plate. Game two at Detroit had Tommy Milone (13-10) facing Doug Fister (10-10). Once again, the Detroit starter Fister (7 IP, 2 ER, 8 SO) logged a high-quality start against a quality start for the Athletics in Milone (6 IP, 1 ER, 6 SO). The Bengals took a 3-2 lead in the seventh when centerfielder Crisp bobbled a short fly by Cabrera for an error allowing two Tigers to score. After back-to-back one-out ninth inning singles by Infante and Cabrera, Prince Fielder was intentionally walked, bringing Don Kelly to the plate. Kelly, a .186 hitter during the regular season, delighted the home crowd by hitting a walk-off sacrifice fly to right for a 5-4 Tiger win. Miguel Cabrera went 3-for-5 with two doubles, as Josh Reddick homered for Oakland. Athletics starter Brett Anderson (6 IP, 0 ER, 2 H, 6 SO) led a game three 2-0 victory at home, as Sean Smith hit a fifth inning homer off Detroit starter Anibal Sanchez (6.1 IP, 2 ER). Fielder was victimized twice by the Oakland defense with a Crisp over-the-wall catch on a potential home run, and then Yoenis Cespedes robbing him of an extra base hit with a diving catch in left-center. Josh Donaldson was 2-for-3 for Oakland and Jhonny Peralta 2-for-2 for the Bengals. Max Scherzer (5.1 IP, 0 ER, 3 H, 8 SO) clearly outpitched Athletics Starter A.J. Griffin (5 IP, 2 ER, 7 H) in game four, although Oakland won 4-3 at the Oakland County Coliseum to even the series 2-2. Oakland entered their last at-bat trailing 3-1, as the sixth Tiger pitcher closer José Valverde (0.2 IP, 3 ER, 4 H) allowed three runs. Crisp singled in the third run of the comeback for a dramatic walk-off win. The Athletics led the league with 14 regular season walk-off wins. Smith (2 RBI) led Oakland, as Fielder had a fourth inning homer for Detroit. Verlander (9 IP, 0 ER, 4 H, 11 SO) faced Parker (6.1 IP, 4 ER) in a rematch of game one starters and shutout the Athletics 6-0 in game five at Oakland to win the series. Infante 2-for-3 and Austin Jackson (2 RBI) led the Bengal attack. Series leaders for Detroit were Verlander (2-0, 0.56 ERA, 16 IP) with an American League Division Series record 22 strikeouts, Infante (.353 BA) and Berry (.300 BA). Cespedes (.316 BA), Anderson (1-0, 0.00 ERA) and Milone (1.50 ERA) paced Oakland.

2012 American League Championship Series

Detroit (88-74) advanced to face New York (95-67) for the pennant. The game one starters at Yankee Stadium were Andy Pettitte (6.2 IP, 2 ER) and Doug Fister (6.1 IP, 0 ER, 5 SO). The Yankees failed to score after loading the bases in the first, second and sixth innings, with New York 1-for-10 with runners in scoring position. Fister threw six shutout innings, as Detroit broke through for RBI singles by Prince Fielder and Delmon Young in the sixth. A home run by Delmon Young and an RBI single by Avisail García after a Peralta double in the eighth gave the Bengals a 4–0 lead. In the bottom of the ninth, Detroit brought in closer José Valverde (0.2 IP, 4 ER, 3 H, BB) who allowed an Ichiro Suzuki two-run homer and a game-tying two run shot from Raúl Ibanez. Valverde would lose his closer role after getting trampled in his last two appearances (1.1 IP, 7 ER, 7 H, 47.37 ERA, 42 pitches). Detroit scored two 12th inning runs on a Delmon Young double and a single by Andy Dirks for the 6-4 win. Derek Jeter broke his left ankle during the inning and missed the rest of the post season. Young 3-for-6 (HR, 3 RBI) and Peralta 3-for-5 led the Tigers, as Suzuki was 4-for-6 (HR, 2 RBI) and Ibanez (HR, 2 RBI) led the Bronx Bombers. Ibanez's clutch homers in both the ALDS and ALCS brought him distinction as the only player in history with three homers in the ninth inning or later in one postseason. The game was Jeter's 158th and final playoff game, with his second inning single setting the record for post season hits at 200. Tiger Anibal Sanchez (7 IP, 0 ER, 3 H, 7 SO) led a game two 3-0 shutout of the Yankees in New York. Yankee starter Hiroki Kuroda (7.2 IP, 3 ER, 5 H, 11 SO) retired the first 15 hitters, including striking out seven of the first nine. Detroit scored in the seventh and two more in the eighth, as new closer Phil Coke (2 IP, 0 ER, 3 SO) got the save. All-Stars Alex Rodriguez (2-for-21) and Curtis Granderson (3-for-28) were post season disappointments. Justin Verlander (8.1 IP, 1 ER, 3 H, 132 pitches) led a 2-1 victory at Comerica Park over New York. Young hit his seventh post-season home run with the Tigers in the fourth off Phil Hughes, who was removed with a stiff back. Verlander was working on a shutout when he allowed a ninth inning home run by Eduardo Nunez. The home run by Nunez ended a streak of 30 ⅓ scoreless innings by Tigers starters in the postseason, breaking the 1974 record of 29 innings set by the Oakland Athletics. Coke (.2 IP, 1 SO) earned his second consecutive save. Robinson Cano singled in the ninth to end his MLB record single post-season hitless streak at 0-for-29. Detroit starters went 37 innings without allowing an earned run. Max Scherzer (5.2 IP, 1 ER, 2 H, 10 SO) took a no-hitter into the sixth inning, as Detroit won 8-1 at home to complete the series sweep. The Tigers jumped on CC Sabathia (3.2 IP, 6 R, 11 H, 2 BB) with a run in first and third innings, followed by a pair of two-run homers by Cabrera and Peralta in the fourth. Austin Jackson homered off Derek Lowe in the seventh inning, and Peralta closed the scoring with his second homer in the eighth. Coke (2 IP, 0 ER, 0 H) closed the game and dealt the Bronx Bombers their first postseason series sweep since the 1980 ALCS against Kansas City, and the first time they were swept in a seven game series since the 1976 World Series versus Cincinnati. The Tiger series leaders were Avisail Garcia (.455 BA), Peralta (.389 BA), ALCS MVP Young (2 HR, 6 RBI, .353 BA) and Cabrera (.313 BA). Suzuki (.353 BA) led New York that hit .157 against Tiger pitching. Tiger starters allowed only two earned runs in the ALCS, posting a 0.66 ERA, led by Sanchez (1-0, 0.00 ERA), Fister (0.00 ERA), Verlander (1-0, 1.08 ERA) and Scherzer (1-0, 1.59 ERA). Cabrera set a major league record by having at least one hit in all 17 of his League Championship Series games thus far in his career. Cabrera set a new franchise record by reaching base safely in all 20 of his postseason games since joining the team prior to the 2007 season.

2012 World Series

The National League champion San Francisco Giants (94-68) advanced after defeating the St. Louis Cardinals 4-3 in the NLCS. Their opponent the Detroit Tigers (88-74) swept the New York Yankees. The 2012 World Series was the first since 1954 (Giants Willie Mays and Indians Bobby Avila) to feature the batting champions from each league, Buster Posey (.336 BA) of the Giants and Miguel Cabrera (.330 BA) of the Tigers. This was the first World Series since 1988 (Dodgers Kirk Gibson and Jose Canseco of Oakland) to feature both of that year's League MVPs, with the Giants' Buster Posey and Detroit's Miguel Cabrera. Game one featured Barry Zito (5.2 IP, 1 ER) and Justin Verlander. San Francisco opened a 6-0 lead on the strength of Sandoval's record tying three homer game, with home runs in the first, two-run dinger in the third and solo shot in the fifth. Other World Series records set by Sandoval included being the first to hit three homers in a game one and homer in his first three plate appearances. The Giants scored their final two runs in the seventh inning off José Valverde, with his third straight disastrous post season appearance in a row (3 GM, 1.2 IP, 9 ER, 11 H, 48.80 ERA). Jhonny Peralta slammed a two-run ninth inning homer, as the Giants won game one 8-3 at home. Tim Lincecum (2.1 IP, 0 ER, 0 H, 5 SO) relived Zito, with this the third time three CY Young winners pitched in a World Series since game three in 1983. Sandoval went 4-for-4 (3 HR, 3 R, 4 RBI). Madison Bumgarner (7 IP, 0 ER, 2 H, 8 SO) outdueled Tiger Doug Fister (6 IP, 1 ER) during a 2-0 game two shutout at home. San Francisco scored a run in the seventh and eighth innings. The Giants became the first team with back-to-back shutouts since the 1966 Baltimore Orioles, with a 2-0 game three blanking of the Bengals in Motown. The Bengals started Anibal Sanchez (7 IP, 2 ER, 8 SO) against Ryan Vogelsong (5.2 IP, 0 ER) who pitched out of a fifth inning bases loaded jam. Lincecum (2.1 IP, 0 ER, 0 H, 3 SO) returned for another perfect outing for the Giants. Matt Cain (7 IP, 3 ER, 5 SO) faced Max Scherzer (6.1 IP, 3 ER, 8 SO) in Detroit for game four. Cabrera hit a two-run home run in the third to take a 2-1 lead and snap a 20-inning Tiger scoreless streak. The Giants regained the lead on a Posey two-run blast in the sixth, as Delmon Young homered to tie it in the bottom of the inning. Bengal Phil Coke struck out three consecutive Giants in the ninth to set a World Series record of seven consecutive strikeouts, dating back to games two and three. NLCS MVP Marco Scutaro had a single in the tenth for the 4-3 victory to complete the series sweep over the Tigers. Sandoval (3 HR, 4 RBI, .500 BA) won the series MVP award to lead San Francisco, as Young (.357 BA) and Omar Infante (.333 BA) led Detroit. San Francisco logged a 1.46 ERA, with Bumgarner (1-0, 00.0 ERA), Vogelsong (1-0, 0.00 ERA) and Zito (1-0, 1.59 ERA), as the Tigers hit .159. Detroit became only the third team (1990 Oakland and 2007 Colorado) to be swept in the World Series after sweeping the LCS.

2013 American League Division Series

Detroit (93-69) started Max Scherzer (21-3) in game one versus Oakland's (96-66) 40-year-old Bartolo Colón (18-6). Scherzer (7 IP, 2 ER, 3 H, 11 SO) allowed one hit in the first six innings against Colón (6 IP, 3 ER). Yoenis Cespedes hit a two-run homer in the seventh, but the A's lost 3-2 at home. Joaquín Benoit (1.1 IP, 0 ER, 0 H, 3 SO) got the save. Game two had Tiger Justin Verlander (7 IP, 0 ER, 4 H, 11 SO) and Sonny Gray (8 IP, 0 ER, 4 H, 9 SO) at Oakland, with Bengal Don Kelly 2-for-3 and Stephen Vogt had the walk-off hit in a 1-0 victory. The A's scored one, two and three runs in innings three thru five of game three in Motown, as homers were hit by Josh Reddick in the fourth, Brandon Moss and Seth Smith in the fifth. Detroit scored three runs in the fourth to end a 20-inning scoreless streak by Oakland pitchers. Coco Crisp went 3-for-4 to lead the 6-3 A's win. Tiger rookie lefthander Jose Alvarez (3 IP, 0 ER, 0 H, 3 SO) excelled. Jed Lowrie had an RBI single off Fister (6 IP, 3 ER) in the first and then hit a two-run fifth inning homer. Oakland starter Dan Straily (6 IP, 3 ER, 8 SO) had a no-hitter for four innings, when Jhonny Peralta hit a fifth inning three-run homer to tie the game 3-3. Reliever Scherzer allowed the A's a run in the seventh, as Victor Martinez had a two-run homer for Detroit in the seventh. Motown scored three more runs in the eighth for an 8-4 lead. Cespedes drove in two in the ninth for a Tigers 8-6 win. Martinez 3-for-4 (HR), Peralta 2-for-3 (HR, 3 RBI) and Omar Infante (2 RBI) led Motown, as Crisp 4-for-5 and Lowrie (HR, 3 RBI) led the A's. Game five starters on Oakland were Verlander (8 IP, 0 ER, 2 H, 10 SO) and Gray (5 IP, 3 ER, 6 H). Cabrera had a two-run homer in the fourth, with another Tiger run in the sixth. Verlander retired the first 16 hitters during the 3-0 shutout, as Martinez was 3-for-4. Series leaders were Martinez (.450 BA), Peralta (HR, 5 RBI, .417 BA) and Verlander (1-0, 0.00 ERA) for Detroit, as Crisp (.389 BA), Cespedes (HR, 4 RBI, .381 BA) and Smith (.313 BA) led the A's. Oakland made 57 strikeouts for a best-of-five playoff record, as Jackson and Moss each fanned an ALDS record 13 times. Verlander had 30 consecutive scoreless innings against the A's, a record against one team in the playoffs. The A's lost their last six Game fives and was 1–12 in playoff-clinching games since 2000.

2013 American League Championship Series

Eastern Division champion Boston (97-65) faced Detroit (93-69) in the playoffs for the first time. Tiger pitchers Anibal Sánchez (6 IP, 0 E 0 H, 12 SO) led a 1-0 shutout at Fenway Park, with 17 strikeouts and held Boston hitless for 8⅓ innings. Jhonny Peralta was 3-for-4, with a sixth inning RBI single. Scherzer (7 IP, 1 ER, 2 H, 13 SO) dominated game two in Boston, with a no-hitter for 5 ⅔ innings. Clay Buchholz (5.2 IP, 5 ER, 8 H) allowed an Alex Avila RBI single in the second and four sixth inning runs for Detroit. The sixth included a Miguel Cabrera homer and a two-run shot by Avila. Dustin Pedroia doubled in a sixth inning run to end 23 straight scoreless innings by Tiger pitchers, going back to Game five of the ALDS against Oakland. Avid Ortiz hit a grand slam in the eighth to tie the game, as Boston scored 6-5 walk-off win on a Jarrod Saltalamacchia single. Justin Verlander (8 IP, 1 ER, 4 H, 10 SO) lost game three 1-0 to Boston at home. John Lackey (6.2 IP, 0 ER, 4 H, 8 SO) and Mike Napoli with a seventh inning homer led the way. Cabrera failed to reach base for the first time in 33 career playoff games. Tiger Doug Fister (6 IP, 1 ER, 7 SO) started game four versus Jake Peavy (3 IP, 7 ER, 5 H, 3 BB) in Detroit. The Bengals scored five in the second and two runs in the fourth. The Red Sox scored three runs during the 7-3 loss. The Tigers tied the series 2-2 behind Torii Hunter (2 RBI), Cabrera (2 RBI) and Austin Jackson (2 RBI), as Jacoby Ellsbury went 4-for-5 with a double and triple for Boston. Jon Lester (5.1 IP, 2 ER) for Boston and Sánchez (6 IP, 3 ER, 5 SO) started game five in Detroit. Napoli homered to center during a three run Boston second inning, as he scored again the next inning. Motown scored a run in the fifth, sixth and seventh innings. Napoli went 3-for-4 and Koji Uehara (1.2 IP, 0 ER, 0 H, 2 SO) saved the 4-3 win. Buchholz (5 IP, 2 ER, 4 H, 4 SO) and Scherzer (6.1 IP, 3 ER, 4 H, 8 SO) faced off in Boston for game six. The Red Sox scored in the fifth, as Victor Martinez had a two-run single for Detroit in the sixth. Shane Victorino (HR, 4 RBI) in a 2-23 series slump, hit a seventh inning grand slam for the 5-2 score and series win. Series leaders were ALCS MVP Uehara (5 GM, 1-0, 6 IP, 0.00 ERA), Lackey (1-0, 0.00 ERA), Ellsbury (.318 BA) and Napoli (.300 BA) for the Red Sox. Martinez (.364 BA), Jose Iglesias (.357 BA), Jackson (.318 BA), Verlander (0-1, 1.13 ERA) and Fister (1-0, 1.50 ERA) led the Bengals.

2014 American League Division Series

Central champs Detroit (90-72) faced Eastern Division winners Baltimore (96-66) for the first time in the playoffs. Chris Tillman (13-6) and Cy Young winner Max Scherzer (18-5) started game one at Baltimore, when Oriole Nelson Cruz had a two-run homer in the first. Detroit tied it the next inning on home runs by Victor Martinez and J.D. Martinez. J.J. Hardy homered for Baltimore in the seventh and Miguel Cabrera for Motown in the eighth. Baltimore had a team playoff and LDS record eight run eighth for the 12-3 win, as Alejandro doubled twice in the inning when 12 Orioles went to bat. Tillman (5 IP, 2 ER, 6 SO), Cruz (HR, 3 RBI), De Aza (2 RBI) and Jonathan Schoop (2 RBI) led Baltimore. Wei-Yin Chen and Tiger Justin Verlander started game two. Nick Markakis had a two-run homer in the third, as the Bengals scored five times in the fourth highlighted by back-to-back homers, with a three-run shot from J.D. Martinez and a solo bomb by Nicholas Castellanos. Detroit led 6-3 when former Tiger Delmon Young doubled home three runs in the eighth. The Orioles took game two 7-6 at home for a 2-0 series advantage. Bud Norris (6.1 IP, 0 ER, 2 H, 6 SO) and David Price (8 IP, 2 ER, 5 H, 6 SO) staged a duel in Motown for game three. Cruz (HR, 2 RBI) hammered a two-run home run in the sixth as Detroit scratched out a run in the ninth. Baltimore swept the series behind Cruz (2 HR, 5 RBI, .500 BA), De Aza (.375 BA), Hardy (.300 BA), Steve Pearce (.300 BA), Schoop (.300 BA) and Norris (1-0, 0.00 ERA), as Cabrera (.354 BA) and Victor Martinez (.333 BA) led Detroit. The Bengals had won each of their previous four ALDS they had played, as the Orioles advanced to the ALCS for the first time in 17 years.

TIGER OWNERS
(BOLD INDICATES MEMBER OF MICHIGAN SPORTS HALL OF FAME)

James D. Burns
1901

James Dennis "Jimmy" Burns was born in the Southwest Detroit neighborhood of Springwells, Michigan on July 28, 1865. He was an American baseball team owner, businessman, hotel operator and politician. Jimmy bought the Detroit Tigers in 1900 and transitioned the team into the majors, as one of the eight charter franchises for the inaugural American League season in 1901. Home games were played in Bennett Park located at the corner of Michigan Avenue and Trumble Avenue. Sunday home games were played in Burns Park at the corner of Toledo Avenue and Waterman Avenue in Springwells. Bennett Park had a capacity of 14,000 while Burns Park could accommodate a mere 3,500 fans. Burns was elected sheriff of Wayne County, Michigan, and served a four-year term. He also served three times as a delegate from the State of Michigan to the Democratic National Convention, in 1908, 1912, and 1916. Jimmy owned the Burns Hotel and Ste. Claire Hotel in addition to the Burns and Campbell Bar and Metropole Restaurant and Grill. Burns was a member of the Benevolent and Protective Order of Elks and Loyal Order of Moose. He died in Detroit, Michigan on January 2, 1928, at the age of 62.

Samuel F. Angus
1901-1903

Samuel Floyd Angus was born in April of 1855 at Prairie Depot, Ohio. He worked as a book agent and was a life insurance agent. Sam was regional manager for the National Life Insurance Company and for the Home Life Insurance Company. Angus built the 79-mile Detroit, Ypsilanti, Ann Arbor and Jackson Railway in 1898 and then the 61-mile Toledo, Fremont, and Norwalk Railway the next year. He led a group acquiring the Detroit Tigers from James D. Burns in November of 1901. Sam became the majority owner in 1902 and sold the franchise in October of 1903. Angus began the annual tradition of conducting a Tiger spring training during the spring of 1903 in Shreveport, Louisiana. He acquired outfielder Sam Crawford and pitcher Bill Donovan prior to the 1903 season. The two led Detroit to the American League pennant in 1907. Sam was a 32nd degree Mason, member of the Turtle Lake club, the New York Athletic Club, the Detroit Boat Club, the Lake St. Clair Shooting and Fishing Club, and Ohio Society of New York. Angus died in Detroit, Michigan in February 1908 at the age of 52.

William H. Yawkey
1903-1908

William Hoover "Bill" Yawkey was born in Bay City, Michigan on August 22, 1875. He was a lumber and mining executive. Bill was the son of lumber tycoon William C. Yawkey, the richest man in Michigan. His father was in the process of purchasing the team from Sam Angus when he died. Frank Navin, then the Tigers bookkeeper and vice president, persuaded Bill to complete the deal. Yawkey was the sole owner of the Detroit Tigers 1903-1908, and then part-owner with Navin from 1908 to 1919. In 1908, he sold almost half of the club's stock to Navin, making him a full partner. Bill was an avid outdoorsman owning a moose lodge in Cook County, Minnesota, and a hunting preserve at South Island in South Carolina. Yawkey was a 32nd Degree Mason. He died in Augusta, Georgia on March 5, 1919, at the age of 43 from pneumonia. Augusta resident Ty Cobb was with Yawkey during his illness. Upon his death, Bill left his $40 million estate to his 14-year old adopted son Tom Yawkey, the owner and president of the Boston Red Sox 1933-1976, and Vice President of the American League 1956-1973.

Francis J. Navin
1908-1935

Francis Joseph "Frank" Navin was a Michigan native born in Adrian on April 18, 1871. He was one of nine children of Irish immigrants. Frank attended the Detroit College of Law and worked as an accountant in the insurance company of Sam Angus. Angus bought the Tigers in 1901, and transferred Navin to the Tigers as bookkeeper, secretary, treasurer, business manager, farm director, chief ticket agent and advertising manager. Frank purchased $5000 worth of franchise stock in 1903 and then bought almost half of the club in 1908. Navin was principal owner of the Tigers for 27 years, from 1908 to 1935. His signing of outfielder Ty Cobb and manager Hughie Jennings was vital to the team becoming title contenders, with three straight trips to the World Series 1907-1909. Frank was one of the few that understood the game and business aspects of baseball. Navin acquired Mickey Cochrane who led Detroit to back-to-back pennants in 1934 and 1935. He served as vice president and then acting president of the American League. Frank died in Detroit on November 13, 1935, at the age of 64.

Walter O. Briggs Sr.
1935-1952

Walter Owen Briggs Sr. was born in Ypsilanti, Michigan on February 27, 1877. Briggs was an American entrepreneur and professional sports owner. He worked at the Michigan Central Railroad and later opened Briggs Manufacturing Company in 1908, which specialized in the manufacturing of automobile bodies for the auto industry and later plumbing fixtures. Walter was part owners 1919-1935, after he and John Kelsey purchased 25 percent of the Yawkey interest in 1919. Briggs bought out Kelsey in 1927 to become a full partner of Navin. He became sole owner when Navin died in 1935. Walter renovated and expanded Navin Field, including double-decking the grandstand resulting in a bowl configuration and reopened as Briggs Stadium in 1938, with a new seating capacity of 58,000. Briggs enjoyed pennants in 1940 and 1945, with a World Championship in 1945. He helped found the Detroit Zoo in 1928 providing many exhibits. Frank supported Eastern Michigan University and the Detroit Symphony Orchestra. Briggs died in Miami Beach, Florida on January 17, 1952, at the age of 74.

Walter O. Briggs Jr.
1952-1956

Walter Owen "Spike" Briggs Jr. was born in Detroit, Michigan on January 20, 1912. Briggs was an American Major League Baseball executive. He graduated from Georgetown University. Spike became owner of the Tigers when he inherited the team upon the death of his father, Walter O. Briggs Sr., Briggs would own the franchise for five seasons from 1952 to 1956. Though Briggs wanted to retain ownership of the team and Briggs Stadium in his family, the estate administrators and courts ordered both to be sold. A group led by radio executives John Fetzer and Fred Knorr bought the club in 1956 with Briggs to be retained as the executive vice president. The following season Spike was also named Tiger general manager, but resigned from both posts in April 1957. He was succeeded as general manager by former Tiger player John McHale who had been the director of minor league operations for the previous four years. Spike died in Detroit on July 31, 1970, at the age of 58.

Frederick A. Knorr II
1956-1960

Frederick August Knorr II was born on July 9, 1913. A Michigan native from Detroit, Knorr graduated from Hillsdale College in Hillsdale, Michigan. He was a radio executive and part-owner of the Detroit Tigers in Major League Baseball from 1956 until his death in 1960. Fred worked at WHLS in Port Huron, Michigan, and later bought four Michigan radio stations, including WKMH. Knorr and John Fetzer led a group including Bing Crosby that purchased the Tigers and Briggs Stadium from the Briggs estate for $5,500,000 in 1956. The new owners agreed to retain Walter O. "Spike" Briggs, Jr., as executive vice president. Fred served as Tiger president until he was replaced on April 19, 1957. The Tigers under Knorr supported the integration of baseball, a position contrary to the former owners. On June 6, 1958, Ozzie Virgil, Sr. became the first black player for the Tigers. Fred died while vacationing in Fort Lauderdale, Florida, on December 26, 1960, at the age of 47.

John E. Fetzer
1956-1983

John Earl Fetzer was born in Decatur, Indiana on March 25, 1901. He was a radio and television executive building a transmitter-receiver in 1917. Fetzer built a radio station for Emmanuel Missionary College (now known as Andrews University) at Berrien Springs, Michigan in 1923. Fetzer bought that station in 1930, renamed it WKZO and relocated it to Kalamazoo, the last major city in Michigan without a station. He created a directional antenna for night broadcasting. John was sued by a station in Omaha, Nebraska, resulting in the Supreme Court deciding the case in his favor. His broadcasting empire grew during WWII and expanded into television, with Fetzer Cablevision (now known as Charter Communications). John became Tiger part-owner in 1956 and then the sole owner 1961-1983. Fetzer sold the Tigers to Domino's Pizza founder and owner Tom Monaghan following the 1983 season. He died in Honolulu, Hawaii on February 20, 1991, at the age of 89.

Thomas S. Monaghan
1983-1992

Thomas Stephen Monaghan is an Irish American entrepreneur born on March 25, 1937 (age 83) and raised in the St. Joseph Home for Children in Jackson, Michigan 1943-1949. Monaghan enlisted in the U.S. Marine Corps in 1956 and was honorably discharged in 1959. While a University of Michigan student, he borrowed $900 with brother James to buy DomiNick's Pizza at Ypsilanti in 1960 and opened three more stores that year. Tom became sole owner and invented an insulated box for pizza deliveries, with nearly three Domino's Pizza franchises opening daily in the 1980s. Monaghan owned the Tigers 1983-1992, as the team won the World Series in his first year as owner in 1984. Monaghan owns Domino's Farms Office Park, located in the Ann Arbor Charter Township, Michigan. He retired after 38 years of day-to-day operations and sold 93 percent of the Domino's Pizza company to Bain Capital for about $1 billion. Tom dedicates his time and fortune to Catholic causes.

Michael Ilitch Sr.
1992-2017

Michael Ilitch Sr. was born in Detroit, Michigan on July 20, 1929. A graduate of Cooley High School in Detroit, Ilitch served four years in the U.S. Marine Corps. He then played pro baseball in the minors for his hometown Detroit Tigers, New York Yankees, and Washington Senators 1952-1955. Mike and his wife, Marian, opened Little Caesars Pizza Treat at Garden City in 1959. Ilitch owned the Detroit Red Wings 1982-2017, with four Stanley Cup Championships. He owned the Tigers 1992-2017, as Comerica Park opened in 2000, with team in the 2006 and 2012 World Series. Mike owned the Fox Theatre, Olympia Entertainment and the Arena Football League Detroit Drive 1988-1992. Ilitch was inducted into the Hockey Hall of Fame in 2003, U.S. Hockey Hall of Fame in 2004 and the Michigan Military and Veterans Hall of Honor in 2019. He ranked #86 on the *Forbes* list of "400 Richest Americans" worth over $6.1 billion. Ilitch died on February 10, 2017, at the age of 87.

Christopher P. Ilitch
2017-Present

Christopher Paul Ilitch was born at Detroit, Michigan in June of 1965 (age 55). He graduated from Cranbrook High School in Bloomfield Hills and was a member of the 1983 MHSAA B-C-D state hockey championship team. Christopher earned a bachelor's degree in business from the University of Michigan in 1987 and worked for IBM. Ilitch is chairman of Ilitch Charities, the president and CEO of Ilitch Holdings, with estimated revenues over $2 billion. The Little Caesars Love Kitchen was established in 1985 to help those in need, with more than three million people served. He is the owner of the NHL Detroit Red Wings and MLB Detroit Tigers, becoming owner of both teams and all related properties upon the death of his father Mike in 2017. Christopher serves as chairman of the Detroit Metro Convention and Visitors Bureau Board of Directors.

Bing Crosby and Tom Selleck had similarities of having a star on the Hollywood Walk of Fame and were part owners of the Tigers. Crosby was a singer, comedian, and actor. Known for the movies *"Going My Way"* and *"The Bells of St. Mary's"*. Commissioner Ford Frick ruled in 1957 that Crosby could retain his small interest in the Tigers when he became a stockholder with the Pittsburgh Pirates.

Selleck is an actor and film producer born in Detroit on January 29, 1945. Known for his TV roles as Thomas Magnum in *"Magnum P.I."* where he wore a Tiger baseball cap, and as New York City Police Commissioner Frank Reagan on *"Blue Bloods"*. The Michigan native spent three weeks of the 1992 spring training schedule with the Tigers to prepare for his upcoming movie role in *"Mr. Baseball"*.

TIGER EXECUTIVES
(BOLD INDICATES MEMBER OF MICHIGAN SPORTS HALL OF FAME)

Presidents

- James D. Burns 1901
- Samuel F. Angus 1902-1903
- William H. Yawkey 1904-1907
- **Frank J. Navin 1908-1935**
- **Walter O. Briggs Sr. 1936-1952**
- Walter O. Briggs Jr. 1952-1956
- Frederick A. Knorr 1957
- Harvey R. Hansen 1957-1959
- Bill DeWitt 1959-1960
- **John E. Fetzer 1961-1978**
- **Jim Campbell 1978-1990**
- **Bo Schembechler 1990-1992**
- **Michael Illitch Sr. 1992-1995, 2001**
- John McHale Jr. 1995-2001
- Dave Dombrowski 2002-2015
- Christopher Illitch 2015-present

General Managers

- **Mickey Cochrane 1936-1938**
- Jack Zeller 1938-1945
- George Trautman 1946
- Billy Evans 1946-1951
- **Charlie Gehringer 1952-1953**
- Muddy Ruel 1954-1956
- Walter O. Briggs Jr. 1957
- John McHale 1957-1959
- Rick Ferrell 1959-1962
- **Jim Campbell 1963-1983**
- Bill Lajoie 1984-1990
- Joe McDonald 1991-1992
- Jerry Walker 1993
- Joe Klein 1994-1995
- Randy Smith 1996-2002
- Dave Dombrowski 2002-2015
- Al Avila 2015-present

Bengal owner and president Walter O. Briggs Sr. is pictured at Briggs Stadium in Detroit prior to a day game on Friday, June 24, 1938. There were 15,300 fans watch the Tigers defeat the New York Yankees 12-8. Hank Greenberg led Motown with two home runs and five runs batted in, with Don Ross 4-for-5. The Bronx Bombers were led by Lou Gehrig with two doubles and a homer, as Joe DiMaggio and Joe Gordon also hit home runs. Tiger righthander Jake Wade (W 1-2, 4 IP, 1 ER, 3 SO) got the win in relief. Briggs and his son Spike owned the Tigers 1936-1956. Walter O. Briggs Sr. established the general manager leadership position for the club in 1936.

TIGER MANAGERS
(BOLD INDICATES MEMBER OF NATIONAL BASEBALL HALL OF FAME)

George Stallings

YEARS	W-L	PCT	PL
1901	74-61	.548	3
	74-61	.548	

George Stallings

Frank Dwyer

YEARS	W-L	PCT	PL
1902	52-83	.385	7
	52-83	.385	

Ed Barrow

YEARS	W-L	PCT	PL
1903	65-71	.478	5
1904	32-46	.410	7
	97-117	.453	

Bobby Lowe

YEARS	W-L	PCT	PL
1904	30-44	.405	7
	30-44	.405	

Bill Armour

YEARS	W-L	PCT	PL
1905	79-75	.516	3
1906	71-78	.477	6
	150-152	.497	

Hughie Jennings

YEARS	W-L	PCT	PL
1907	92-58	.613	1
1908	90-63	.588	1
1909	98-54	.645	1
1910	86-68	.558	3
1911	89-65	.578	2
1912	69-84	.451	6
1913	66-87	.431	6
1914	80-73	.523	4
1915	100-54	.649	2
1916	87-67	.565	3
1917	78-75	.510	4
1918	55-71	.437	7
1919	80-60	.571	4
1920	61-93	.396	7
	1131-972	.538	

Ty Cobb

YEARS	W-L	PCT	PL
1921	71-82	.464	6
1922	79-75	.513	3
1923	83-71	.539	2
1924	86-68	.558	3
1925	81-73	.526	4
1926	79-75	.513	6
	479-444	.519	

George Moriarty

YEARS	W-L	PCT	PL
1927	82-71	.536	4
1928	68-86	.442	6
	150-157	.489	

Bucky Harris

YEARS	W-L	PCT	PL
1929	70-84	.455	6
1930	75-79	.487	5
1931	61-93	.396	7
1932	76-75	.503	5
1933	75-79	.487	5
1955	79-75	.513	5
1956	82-72	.532	5
	516-557	.481	

Del Baker

Del Baker

YEARS	W-L	PCT	PL
1933	75-79	.487	5
1938	37-19	.661	4
1939	81-73	.526	5
1940	90-64	.584	1
1941	75-79	.487	4
1942	73-81	.474	5
	358-317	.530	

Mickey Cochrane

1934	101-53	.656	1
1935	93-58	.616	1
1936	83-71	.539	2
1937	89-65	.578	2
1938	47-51	.480	4
	413-297	.582	

Steve O'Neill

YEARS	W-L	PCT	PL
1943	78-76	.506	5
1944	88-66	.571	2
1945	88-65	.575	1
1946	92-62	.597	2
1947	85-69	.552	2
1948	78-76	.506	5
	509-414	.551	

Red Rolfe

YEARS	W-L	PCT	PL
1949	87-67	.565	4
1950	95-59	.617	2
1951	73-81	.474	5
1952	23-49	.319	8
	278-256	.521	

Fred Hutchinson

YEARS	W-L	PCT	PL
1952	27-55	.329	8
1953	60-94	.390	6
1954	68-86	.442	5
	155-235	.397	

Jack Tighe

YEARS	W-L	PCT	PL
1957	78-76	.506	4
1958	21-28	.429	5
	99-104	.488	

Bill Norman

YEARS	W-L	PCT	PL
1958	56-49	.533	5
1959	2-15	.118	4
	58-64	.475	

Jimmy Dykes

YEARS	W-L	PCT	PL
1959	74-63	.540	4
1960	44-52	.458	6
	118-115	.506	

Billy Hitchcock

YEARS	W-L	PCT	PL
1960	1-0	1.000	6
	1-0	1.000	

Fred Hutchinson

Joe Gordon

YEARS	W-L	PCT	PL
1960	26-31	.456	6
	26-31	.456	

Bob Scheffing

Bob Scheffing

YEARS	W-L	PCT	PL
1961	101-61	.623	2
1962	85-76	.528	4
1963	24-36	.400	5
	210-173	.548	

Chuck Dressen

YEARS	W-L	PCT	PL
1963	55-47	.539	5
1964	85-77	.525	4
1965	65-55	.542	4
1966	16-10	.615	3
	221-189	.539	

Bob Swift

YEARS	W-L	PCT	PL
1965	24-18	.571	4
1966	32-25	.561	3
	56-43	.566	

Frank Skaff

YEARS	W-L	PCT	PL
1966	40-39	.506	3
	40-39	.506	

Mayo Smith

YEARS	W-L	PCT	PL
1967	91-71	.562	2
1968	103-59	.636	1
1969	90-72	.556	2
1970	79-83	.488	4
	363-285	.560	

Billy Martin

YEARS	W-L	PCT	PL
1971	91-71	.562	2
1972	86-70	.551	1
1973	71-63	.530	3
	253-208	.549	

Joe Schultz

YEARS	W-L	PCT	PL
1973	14-14	.500	3
	14-14	.500	

Ralph Houk

YEARS	W-L	PCT	PL
1974	72-90	.444	6
1975	57-102	.358	6
1976	74-87	.460	5
1977	74-88	.457	4
1978	86-76	.531	5
	363-443	.450	

Les Moss

YEARS	W-L	PCT	PL
1979	27-26	.509	5
	27-26	.509	

Dick Tracewski

YEARS	W-L	PCT	PL
1979	2-0	1.000	5
	2-0	1.000	

Sparky Anderson

YEARS	W-L	PCT	PL
1979	56-50	.528	5
1980	84-78	.519	5
1981	60-49	.550	2
1982	83-79	.512	4
1983	92-70	.568	2
1984	104-58	.642	1
1985	84-77	.522	3
1986	87-75	.537	3
1987	98-64	.605	1
1988	88-74	.543	2
1989	59-103	.364	7
1990	79-83	.488	3
1991	84-78	.519	2
1992	75-87	.463	6
1993	85-77	.525	3
1994	53-62	.461	5
1995	60-84	.417	4
	1331-1248	.516	

Buddy Bell

YEARS	W-L	PCT	PL
1996	53-109	.327	5
1997	79-83	.488	3
1998	53-85	.384	5
	184-277	.399	

Larry Parrish

YEARS	W-L	PCT	PL
1998	12-14	.462	5
1999	69-92	.429	3
	82-104	.441	

Phil Garner

YEARS	W-L	PCT	PL
2000	79-83	.488	3
2001	66-96	.407	5
2002	0-6	.000	5
	145-185	.439	

Luis Pujols

YEARS	W-L	PCT	PL
2002	55-100	.355	5
	55-100	.355	

Alan Trammell

YEARS	W-L	PCT	PL
2003	43-119	.265	5
2004	72-90	.444	4
2005	71-91	.438	4
	186-300	.383	

Jim Leyland

YEARS	W-L	PCT	PL
2006	95-67	.586	2
2007	88-74	.543	2
2008	74-88	.457	5
2009	86-77	.528	2
2010	81-81	.500	3
2011	95-67	.586	1
2012	88-74	.543	1
2013	93-69	.574	1
	700-597	.540	

Brad Ausmus

YEARS	W-L	PCT	PL
2014	90-72	.556	1
2015	74-87	.460	5
2016	86-75	.534	2
2017	64-98	.395	5
	314-332	.486	

Brad Ausmus

Ron Gardenhire

YEARS	W-L	PCT	PL
2018	64-98	.395	3
2019	47-114	.292	5
2020	21-29	.420	5
	132-241	.354	

Lloyd McClendon

YEARS	W-L	PCT	PL
2020	2-6	.250	5
	2-6	.250	

A.J. Hinch

YEARS	W-L	PCT	PL
2021	77-85	.475	3
	77-85	.475	

Detroit Tigers
American League
1901-2021
9,446-9,311 .504

TIGER COACHES
(BOLD INDICATES MEMBER OF NATIONAL BASEBALL HALL OF FAME)

Rick Adair, 1996-1999
Felipe Alou, 2002
Rick Anderson, 2018-2020
Brad Andress. 1990-1999
Luke Appling, 1960
Del Baker, 1933-1938
Kimera Bartee, 2021
Dick Bartell, 1949-1952
Rafael Belliard, 2006-08, 2010, 2013
Mick Billmeyer, 2014-2017
Wayne Blackburn, 1963-1964, 1975
Roger Bresnahan, 1930-1931
Eddie Brinkman, 1979
Tom Brookens, 2010-2013
Gates Brown, 1978-1984
Jimmy Burke, 1914-1917
Fred Carisch, 1923-1924
Jeremy Carroll, 2020
Phil Cavarretta, 1961-1963
Dave Clark, 2014-2020
Phil Clark, 2018-2019
Bob Cluck, 2003-2005
Bob Coleman, 1932
Darnell Coles, 2014
Billy Consolo, 1979-1992
Scott Coolbaugh, 2021
Jack Coombs, 1920
Roger Craig, 1980-1984
Doc Cramer, 1948
Tony Cuccinello, 1967-1968
José Cruz Jr., 2021
Jim Davenport, 1991
Cot Deal, 1973-1974
Bill Donovan, 1918
Rich Dubee, 2017
Jean Dubuc, 1930-1931
Leon Durham, 2017
Jewel Ens, 1932
Glenn Ezell, 1996
Bill Fahey, 1983
Rick Ferrell, 1950-1953
Tom Ferrick, 1960-1962
Chris Fetter, 2021
Bruce Fields, 2003-2005
Art Fowler, 1971-1973
Terry Francona, 1996
Charlie Gehringer, 1942
Kirk Gibson, 2003-2005
Fred Gladding, 1976-1978

Joe Gordon, 1956
Alex Grammas, 1980-1991
Johnny Grodzicki, 1979
Chip Hale, 2021
Steve Hamilton, 1975
Toby Harrah, 1998, 2013
Fred Hatfield, 1977-1978
Don Heffner, 1961
Jim Hegan, 1974-1978
Tommy Henrich, 1958-1959
Chuck Hernandez, 2006-2008
Larry Herndon, 1992-1998
Mike Hessman, 2021
Perry Hill, 1997-1999
Gordie Hinkle, 1939
Billy Hitchcock, 1955-1960
Johnny Hopp, 1954
Dan Howley, 1919, 1921-1922
Willis Hudlin, 1957-1959
Jeff Jones, 1995, 1998-2000,
2002, 2007-2015
Wally Joyner, 2014-2016
Ted Kazanski, 1969
Mick Kelleher, 2003-2005
Fred Kendall, 1996-1998
Rick Knapp, 2009-2011
Red Kress, 1940
Gene Lamont, 2006-2017
Rafael Landestoy, 2002
Lefty Leifield, 1927-1928
Steve Liddle, 2018-2019
George Lombard, 2021
Don Lund, 1957-1958
Ted Lyons, 1949-1953
Bill Madlock, 2000-2001
Doug Mansolino, 2000-2002
Jon Matlack, 1996
George McBride, 1925-1926, 1929
Steve McCatty, 2002
Lloyd McClendon, 2006-13, 2017-20
Deacon McGuire, 1912-1916
Bob Melvin, 2000
Benny Meyer, 1928-1930
Bing Miller, 1938-1941
Art Mills, 1944-1948
Wally Moses, 1967-1970
Billy Muffett, 1985-1994
Pat Mullin, 1963-1966
George Myatt, 1962-1963

Hal Naragon, 1967-1969
Dave Newhan, 2015-2016
Juan Nieves, 2021
Ron Oester, 1996
Len Okrie, 1970
Steve O'Neill, 1941
Ed Ott, 2001-2002
Stubby Overmire, 1963-1966
Lance Parrish, 1999-2001, 2003-2005
Larry Parrish, 1997-1998
Josh Paul, 2020-2021
Cy Perkins, 1934-1937
Jeff Pico, 2019-2020
Vada Pinson, 1985-1991
Luis Pujols, 2002
Tim Remes, 2019-2020
Grover Resinger, 1969-1970
Merv Rettenmund, 2002
Mike Roarke, 1965-1966, 1970
Mike Rojas, 2011-2013
Gene Roof, 1992-1995
Schoolboy Rowe, 1954-1955
A.J. Sager, 2018
Johnny Sain, 1967-1969
Juan Samuel, 1999-2005
Ramon Santiago, 2018-2021
Boss Schmidt, 1929
Joe Schultz, 1971-1976
Shaq Shaughnessy, 1928
Merv Shea, 1939-1942
Frank Shellenback, 1946-1947
Charlie Silvera, 1971-1973
Frank Skaff, 1965-1966, 1971
Don Slaught, 2006
Bill Sweeney, 1947-1948
Bob Swift, 1953-1954, 1963-1966
Jack Tighe, 1955-1956
● Dick Tracewski, 1972-1995
Alan Trammell, 1999
Ralph Treuel, 1995
Andy Van Slyke, 2006-2009
Joe Vavra, 2019-2020
Al Vincent, 1943-1944
Omar Vizquel, 2014-2017
Dan Warthen, 1999-2002
Jerry White, 1997-1998
Jo-Jo White, 1960
Dan Whitmer, 1992-1994
Otto Williams, 1925

● The longest serving coach in Detroit Tiger franchise history

TIGER COACHES WHO MANAGED IN THE MAJOR LEAGUES
(BOLD INDICATES MEMBER OF NATIONAL BASEBALL HALL OF FAME)

Felipe Alou	Montreal (NL) 1992-2001 San Francisco (NL) 2003-2006
Luke Appling	Oakland (AL) 1967
Del Baker	Detroit (AL) 1933, 1936-1940 Boston (AL) 1960
Roger Bresnahan	St. Louis (NL) 1909-1912 Chicago (NL) 1915
Jimmy Burke	St. Louis (NL) 1905 St. Louis (AL) 1918-1920
Phil Cavarretta	Chicago (NL) 1951-1953
Dave Clark	Houston (NL) 2009
Jack Coombs	Philadelphia (NL) 1919
Roger Craig	San Diego (NL) 1978-1979 San Francisco (NL) 1985-1992
Jim Davenport	San Francisco (NL) 1985
Bill Donovan	New York (AL) 1915-1917 Philadelphia (NL) 1921
Jewel Ens	Pittsburgh (NL) 1929-1931
Terry Francona	Philadelphia (NL) 1997-2000 Boston (AL) 2004-2011 Cleveland (AL) 2013-2021
Kirk Gibson	Arizona (NL) 2010-2014
Joe Gordon	Cleveland (AL) 1958-1960 Detroit (AL) 1960 Oakland (AL) 1961 Kansas City (AL) 1969
Alex Grammas	Pittsburgh (NL) 1969 Milwaukee (AL) 1976-1977
Chip Hale	Arizona (NL) 2015-2016
Toby Harrah	Texas (AL) 1992
Don Heffner	Cincinnati (NL) 1966
Billy Hitchcock	Detroit (AL) 1960 Baltimore (AL) 1962-1963 Atlanta (NL) 1966-1967
Dan Howley	St. Louis (AL) 1927-1929 Cincinnati (NL) 1930-1932
Gene Lamont	Chicago (AL) 1992-1995 Pittsburgh (NL) 1997-2000
Ted Lyons	Chicago (AL) 1946-1948
George McBride	Washington (AL) 1921
Lloyd McClendon	Pittsburgh (NL) 2001-2005 Seattle (AL) 2014-2015 Detroit (AL) 2020
Deacon McGuire	Washington (NL) 1898 Boston (AL) 1907-1908 Cleveland (AL) 1909-1911
Bob Melvin	Seattle (AL) 2003-2004 Arizona (NL) 2005-2009 Oakland (AL) 2011-2021
George Myatt	Philadelphia (NL) 1969
Steve O'Neill	Cleveland (AL) 1935-1937 Detroit (AL) 1943-1948 Boston (AL) 1950-1951 Philadelphia (NL) 1952-1954
Larry Parrish	Detroit (AL) 1998-1999
Cy Perkins	Detroit (AL) 1937
Luis Pujols	Detroit (AL) 2002
Juan Samuel	Baltimore (AL) 2010
Joe Schultz	Seattle (AL) 1969 Detroit (AL) 1973
Frank Skaff	Detroit (AL) 1966
Bob Swift	Detroit (AL) 1965-1966
Jack Tighe	Detroit (AL) 1957-1958
Dick Tracewski	Detroit (AL) 1979
Alan Trammell	Detroit (AL) 2003-2005 Arizona (NL) 2014
Jo-Jo White	Cleveland (AL) 1960

TIGER SCOUTS
(BOLD INDICATES MEMBER OF NATIONAL BASEBALL HALL OF FAME)

Matty Alou
Ruben Amaro Sr.
Eddie Bane
Larry Bearnarth
Reno Bertoia
Arnie Beyeler
Max Bishop
Wayne Blackburn
Gary Blaylock
Tommy Bridges
Gates Brown
Billy Bruton
Buster Chatham
Harlong Clift
Mickey Cochrane
Jim Command

Tony Giuliani
Jerry Don Gleaton
Joe Gordon
Mike Guerra
Alan Hargesheimer
Ray Hayward
Joe Holden
Willis Hudlin
Lefty Jamerson
George Kell
Hal Keller
Don Kelly
Joe Klein
Johnny Klippstein
Marty Krug
Bill Lajoie

Dave Owen
Marv Owen
Larry Parrish
Ted Pawelek
Orlando Pena
Ned Pettigrew
Dee Phillips
Scott Reid
Dave Roberts
Schoolboy Rowe
Tom Runnells
Bob Scheffing
LeGrant Scott
Frank Shellenback
Frank Skaff
Vic Sorrell

Max Bishop

Billy Bruton

George Moriarty

Bruce Connatser
Murray Cook
Jim Davenport
Boots Day
Mike de la Hoz
Bernie DeViveiros
Mel Didier
High East
Dick Egan
Wish Egan
Hoot Evers
Al Federoff
Rick Ferrell
Jack Fournier
Pete Fox
Denny Galehouse

Eddie Lake
Jesse Landrum
Nemo Leibold
Dave Littlefield
Max Macon
Runt Marr
Joe Mathes
Bob Mavis
Charlie Metro
George Moriarty
Pat Mullin
Hal Newhouser
Bill Norman
Jim Olander
Stephen G. O'Rourke
Stubby Overmire

Steve Souchock
George Spencer
Bob Swift
Bruce Tanner
Jack Tighe
Al Vincent
Jerry Walker
Dan Warthen
Vic Wertz
Jeff Wetherby
Harrison Wickel
Del Wilber
Rob Wilfong
John Williams
John Young
Jack Zeller

(BOLD INDICATES MEMBER OF NATIONAL BASEBALL HALL OF FAME)

Glenn Abbott, RHP, 1983–1984
Al Aber, LHP, 1953–1957
Juan Acevedo, RHP, 2002
Bob Adams, C, 1977
Jim Adduci, OF-DH-1B, 2017–2018
Hank Aguirre, LHP, 1958–1967
Pat Ahearne, RHP, 1995
Eddie Ainsmith, C, 1919–1921
Bill Akers, IF, 1929–1931
Al Alburquerque, RHP, 2011–2015
Sergio Alcantara, 2B-3B, 2020
Victor Alcantara, RHP, 2017–2019
Scott Aldred, LHP, 1990–1992, 1996
Dale Alexander, 1B-OF, 1929–1932
Doyle Alexander, RHP, 1987–1989
Tyler Alexander, LHP, 2019-2021
Andy Allanson, C, 1991
Dusty Allen, IF-OF, 2000
Rod Allen, DH-OF, 1984
Ernie Alten, LHP, 1920
George Alusik, OF, 1958–1962
Luis Alvarado, IF, 1977
Gabe Alvarez, INF-DH-OF, 1998–2000
José Álvarez, LHP, 2013
Ossie Álvarez, IF, 1959
Sandy Amoros, OF, 1960
Bob Anderson, RHP, 1963
Josh Anderson, OF, 2009
Matt Anderson, RHP, 1998–2003
Jimmy Archer, C-INF, 1907
George Archie, IF, 1938
Harry Arndt, IF-OF, 1902
Fernando Arroyo, RHP, 1975–1979
Elden Auker, RHP, 1933–1938
Brad Ausmus, C, 1996, 1999–2000
Earl Averill, OF, 1939–1940
Steve Avery, LHP, 2003
Alex Avila, C-DH-1B, 2009–2015, 2017
Mike Aviles, IF-OF-DH, 2016
Erick Aybar, IF, 2016
Doc Ayers, RHP, 1919–1921
Sandy Baez, RHP, 2018–2019
Bill Bailey, LHP, 1918
Howard Bailey, LHP, 1981–1983
Doug Bair, RHP, 1983–1985
Del Baker, C, 1914–1916
Doug Baker, IF, 1984–1987
Jeff Baker, IF, 2012
Steve Baker, RHP, 1978–1979
Paul Bako, C, 1998
Billy Baldwin, OF, 1975
Collin Balester, RHP, 2012
Chris Bando, C, 1988
Johnny Barbato, RHP, 2018
Ray Bare, RHP, 1975–1977
Clyde Barfoot, RHP, 1926
Frank Barnes, LHP, 1929
Sam Barnes, IF, 1921
Skeeter Barnes, IF-OF, 1991–1994
Jimmy Barrett, OF, 1901–1905
Kimera Bartee, OF, 1996–1999
Dick Bartell, IF, 1940–1941
Al Baschang, OF, 1912
Johnny Bassler, C, 1921–1927
Matt Batts, C, 1952–1954
Paddy Baumann, IF-OF, 1911–1914
Harry Baumgartner, RHP, 1920
John Baumgartner, IF, 1953
Danny Bautista, OF, 1993–1996
Denny Bautista, RHP, 2008
José Bautista, RHP, 1997
Yorman Bazardo, RHP, 2007–2008
Trey Beamon, OF, 1998
Billy Bean, OF, 1987–1989
Billy Beane, OF, 1988
Dave Beard, RHP, 1989
Gene Bearden, LHP, 1951
Boom-Boom Beck, RHP, 1944
Erve Beck, IF, 1902
Heinie Beckendorf, C, 1909–1910
Rich Becker, OF, 2000–2001
Gordon Beckham, INF-DH, 2019
Wayne Belardi, IF, 1954–1956
Tim Belcher, RHP, 1994
Francis Beltran, RHP, 2008
Beau Bell, OF, 1939
Chad Bell, LHP, 2017–2018
Duane Below, LHP, 2011–2013
Joaquín Benoit, RHP, 2011–2013
Al Benton, RHP, 1938–1948
Lou Berberet, C, 1959–1960
Juan Berenguer, RHP, 1982–1985
Dave Bergman, IF, 1984–1992
Sean Bergman, RHP, 1993–1996
Tony Bernazard, IF, 1991
Adam Bernero, RHP, 2000–2003
Johnny Bero, IF, 1948
Geronimo Berroa, DH, 1998
Neil Berry, IF, 1948–1952
Quintin Berry, OF, 2012
Reno Bertoia, IF, 1953–58, 1961–1962
Wilson Betemit, IF, 2011
Jason Beverlin, RHP, 2002
Monte Beville, C, 1904
Steve Bilko, IF, 1960
Jack Billingham, RHP, 1978–1980
Josh Billings, RHP, 1927–1929
Babe Birrer, RHP, 1955
Bud Black, RHP, 1952–1956
Willie Blair, RHP, 1996–2001
Ike Blessitt, OF, 1972
Ben Blomdahl, RHP, 1995
Jimmy Bloodworth, IF, 1942–1946
Lu Blue, IF, 1921–1927
Hiram Bocachica, OF, 2002–2003
Doug Bochtler, RHP, 1998
Randy Bockus, RHP, 1989
Brennan Boesch, OF, 2010–2012
George Boehler, RHP, 1912–1916
Joe Boever, RHP, 1993–1995
John Bogart, RHP, 1920
Brian Bohanon, LHP, 1995
Bernie Boland, RHP, 1915–1920
Frank Bolling, IF, 1954–1960
Milt Bolling, IF, 1958
Cliff Bolton, C, 1937
Tom Bolton, LHP, 1993
Jeremy Bonderman, RHP, 2003–10, 2013
Jorge Bonifacio, OF, 2020
Eddie Bonine, RHP, 2008–2010
Dan Boone, RHP, 1921
Ray Boone, IF, 1953–1958
Dave Borkowski, RHP, 1999–2001
Red Borom, IF, 1944–1945
Steve Boros, IF, 1957–1962
Hank Borowy, RHP, 1950–1957
Dave Boswell, RHP, 1971
Matt Boyd, LHP, 2015–2021
Jim Brady, LHP, 1956
Ralph Branca, RHP, 1953–1954
Jim Brideweser, IF, 1956
Rocky Bridges, IF, 1959–1960
Tommy Bridges, RHP, 1930–1946
Ed Brinkman, IF, 1971–1974
Doug Brocail, RHP, 1997–2000
Rico Brogna, IF, 1992–1994
Ike Brookens, RHP, 1975
Tom Brookens, IF, 1979–1988
Louis Brower, IF, 1931
Chris Brown, IF, 1989
Darrell Brown, OF, 1981
Dick Brown, C, 1961–1962
Gates Brown, OF, 1963–1975
Ike Brown, IF, 1969–1974
Frank Browning, RHP, 1910
Bob Bruce, RHP, 1959–1961
Andy Bruckmiller, RHP, 1905
Mike Brumley, IF, 1989
Arlo Brunsberg, C, 1966
Will Brunson, LHP, 1998–1999
Bill Bruton, OF, 1961–1964
Johnny Bucha, C, 1953
Don Buddin, IF, 1962
Fritz Buelow, C, 1901–1904
George Bullard, IF, 1954
Jim Bunning, RHP, 1955–1963
Les Burke, IF, 1923–1926
Bill Burns, LHP, 1912
George Burns, IF, 1914–1917
Jack Burns, IF, 1903-1904
Jack Burns, IF, 1936
Joe Burns, OF, 1913
Pete Burnside, LHP, 1959–1960
Sheldon Burnside, LHP, 1978–1979
Beau Burrows, RHP, 2020-2021
Donie Bush, IF, 1908–1921
Sal Butera, C, 1983
Harry Byrd, RHP, 1957
Tim Byrdak, LHP, 2007
Enos Cabell, IF, 1982–1983
Miguel Cabrera, 1B-3B-DH, 2008–21
Greg Cadaret, LHP, 1994
Bob Cain, LHP, 1951
Les Cain, P, 1968–1972
Paul Calvert, RHP, 1950–1951
Daz Cameron, RF, 2020-2021

Bill Campbell, RHP, 1986
Bruce Campbell, OF, 1940–1941
Dave Campbell, IF, 1967–1969
Paul Campbell, IF, 1948–1950
Jeimer Candelario, 3B-1B, 2017–21
Guy Cantrell, RHP, 1930
Jose Capellan, RHP, 2007
George Cappuzzello, LHP, 1981
Javier Cardona, C, 2000–2002
Fred Carisch, C, 1923
Drew Carlton, RHP, 2021
Ryan Carpenter, LHP, 2018–2019
Charlie Carr, IF, 1903–1904
Mark Carreon, OF, 1992
Ezequiel Carrera, OF, 2014
Ownie Carroll, RHP, 1925–1930
Frank Carswell, OF, 1953
Chuck Cary, LHP, 1985–1986
Jerry Casale, RHP, 1961–1962
Raul Casanova, C, 1996–1999
Doc Casey, IF, 1901–1902
Joe Casey, C, 1909–1911
Sean Casey, IF, 2006–2007
Norm Cash, IF, 1960–1974
Ron Cash, IF, 1973–1974
Nick Castellanos, OF-3B, 2013–2019
George Caster, RHP, 1945–1946
Frank Castillo, RHP, 1998
Marty Castillo, IF, 1981–1985
Harold Castro, IF-OF-DH, 2018–2021
Anthony Castro, RHP, 2020
Willi Castro, SS-3B, 2019-2021
Frank Catalanotto, OF, 1997–1999
Pug Cavet, LHP, 1911–1915
Andujar Cedeño, IF, 1996
Roger Cedeño, OF, 2000–2001
John Cerutti, LHP, 1991
Yoenis Cespedes, OF, 2015
Joba Chamberlain, RHP, 2014–2015
Dean Chance, RHP, 1971
Harry Chiti, C, 1960–1961
Mike Chris, LHP, 1979
Neil Chrisley, OF, 1959–1960
Bob Christian, OF, 1968
Mark Christman, IF, 1938–1939
Mike Christopher, RHP, 1995–1996
Eddie Cicotte, RHP, 1905
Al Cicotte, RHP, 1958
Jose Cisnero, RHP, 2019-2021
Davey Claire, IF, 1920
Danny Clark, IF, 1922
Jermaine Clark, OF, 2001
Mel Clark, OF, 1957
Phil Clark, OF, 1992
Tony Clark, IF, 1995–2001
Nig Clarke, C, 1905
Rufe Clarke, RHP, 1923–1924
Al Clauss, LHP, 1913
Brent Clevlen, OF, 2006–2007
Flea Clifton, IF, 1934–1937
Joe Cobb, DH, 1918
Ty Cobb, OF, 1905–1926
Mickey Cochrane, C, 1934–1937
Jack Coffey, IF, 1918
Slick Coffman, RHP, 1937–1939
Phil Coke, LHP, 2010–2014
Rocky Colavito, OF, 1960–1963
Nate Colbert, IF, 1975
Bert Cole, LHP, 1921–1925
Joe Coleman Sr., RHP, 1955
Joe Coleman Jr., RHP, 1971–1976
Louis Coleman, RHP, 2018
Vince Coleman, OF, 1997
Darnell Coles, IF, 1986–1987, 1990
Orlin Collier, RHP, 1931
Dave Collins, OF, 1986
Kevin Collins, IF, 1970–1971
Rip Collins, RHP, 1923–1927
Tyler Collins, OF, 2014–2017
Roman Colon, RHP, 2005–2007
Steve Colyer, LHP, 2004
Wayne Comer, OF, 1967–1968, 1972
Ralph Comstock, RHP, 1913
Dick Conger, RHP, 1940
Allen Conkwright, RHP, 1920
Bill Connelly, RHP, 1950
Earl Cook, RHP, 1941
Duff Cooley, OF, 1905
Jack Coombs, RHP, 1920
Wilbur Cooper, LHP, 1926
Tim Corcoran, IF, 1977–1980
Francisco Cordero, RHP, 1999
Nate Cornejo, RHP, 2001–2004
Red Corriden, IF, 1912
Chuck Cottier, IF, 1961
Johnny Couch, RHP, 1917
Bill Coughlin, IF, 1904–1908
Ernie Courtney, IF, 1903
Harry Coveleski, LHP, 1914–1918
Tex Covington, RHP, 1911–1912
Al Cowens, OF, 1980–1981
Red Cox, RHP, 1920
Doc Cramer, OF, 1942–1948
Jim Crawford, LHP, 1976–1978
Sam Crawford, OF, 1903–1917
Doug Creek, LHP, 2005
Jack Crimian, RHP, 1957
Leo Cristante, RHP, 1955
Davey Crockett, IF, 1901
C.J. Cron, 1B, 2020
Jack Cronin, RHP, 1901–1902
Casey Crosby, LHP, 2012
Frank Croucher, IF, 1939–1941
Dean Crow, RHP, 1998
Alvin Crowder, RHP, 1934–1936
Francisco Cruceta, RHP, 2008
Roy Crumpler, LHP, 1920
Deivi Cruz, IF, 1997–2001
Fausto Cruz, IF, 1996
Jacob Cruz, OF, 2002
Nelson Cruz, RHP, 1999–2000
William Cuevas, RHP, 2017
Roy Cullenbine, OF, 1938–39, 45–47
John Cummings, LHP, 1996–1997
George Cunningham, RHP-OF, 1916–19
Jim Curry, IF, 1918
Chad Curtis, OF, 1995–1996
George Cutshaw, IF, 1922–1923
Milt Cuyler, OF, 1990–1995
Jack Dalton, OF, 1916
Mike Dalton, LHP, 1991
Johnny Damon, OF, 2010
Chuck Daniel, RHP, 1957
Vic Darensbourg, LHP, 2005
Jeff Datz, C, 1989
Doc Daugherty, PH, 1951
Hooks Dauss, RHP, 1912–1926
Jerry Davie, RHP, 1959
Eric Davis, OF, 1993–1994
Harry Davis, IF, 1932–1933
Rajai Davis, OF, 2014–2015
Storm Davis, RHP, 1993–1994
Woody Davis, RHP, 1938
Frankie De La Cruz, RHP, 2007
Ivan DeJesus, IF, 1988
Charlie Deal, IF, 1912–1913
Rob Deer, OF, 1991–1993
John Deering, RHP, 1903
Tony DeFate, IF, 1917
Mark DeJohn, IF, 1982
Miguel Del Pozo, LHP, 2021
Jim Delahanty, IF, 1909–1912
Jim Delsing, OF, 1952–1956
Travis Demeritte, RF-RHP, 2019-2020
Don Demeter, OF, 1964–1966
Steve Demeter, IF, 1959
Ray Demmitt, OF, 1914
Matt den Dekker, OF, 2017
Bill Denehy, RHP, 1971
Gene Desautels, C, 1930-1933
John DeSilva, RHP, 1993
Bernie DeViveiros, IF, 1927
Mike DiFelice, C, 2004
Bob Didier, C, 1973
Steve Dillard, IF, 1978
Pop Dillon, IF, 1901–1902
Craig Dingman, RHP, 2004–2005
Andy Dirks, OF, 2011–2013
George Disch, RHP, 1905
Glenn Dishman, LHP, 1997
Jack Dittmer, IF, 1957
Brandon Dixon, INF-OF-DH, 2019
Brent Dlugach, IF, 2009
Pat Dobson, RHP, 1967–1969
Larry Doby, OF, 1959
John Doherty, RHP, 1992–1995
Frank Doljack, OF, 1930–1934
Freddy Dolsi, RHP, 2008–2009
Red Donahue, RHP, 1906
Jim Donohue, RHP, 1961
Bill Donovan, RHP-IB-OF, 1903–12, 1918
Dick Donovan, RHP, 1954
Tom Doran, C, 1905
Octavio Dotel, RHP, 2012–2013
Sean Douglass, RHP, 2005
Snooks Dowd, IF, 1919
Darin Downs, LHP, 2012–2013
Red Downs, IF, 1907–1908
Jess Doyle, RHP, 1925–1927
Delos Drake, OF, 1911
Lee Dressen, IF, 1918
Lew Drill, C, 1904–1905
Walt Dropo, IF, 1952–1954
Brian Dubois, LHP, 1989–1990
Jean Dubuc, RHP, 1912–1916

Joe Dugan, IF, 1931
Roberto Durán, LHP, 1997–1998
Chad Durbin, RHP, 2006–2007
Bob Dustal, RHP, 1963
Ben Dyer, IF, 1916-1919
Duffy Dyer, C, 1980–1981
Scott Earl, IF, 1984
Damion Easley, IF, 1996–2002
Mal Eason, RHP, 1903
Paul Easterling, OF, 1928–1930
Zeb Eaton, RHP, 1944–1945
Eric Eckenstahler, LHP, 2002–2003
Wish Egan, RHP, 1902
Dick Egan, LHP, 1963–1964
Howard Ehmke, RHP, 1916–17, 1919-22
Joey Eischen, LHP, 1996
Harry Eisenstat, LHP, 1938–1939
Kid Elberfeld, IF, 1901–1903
Heinie Elder, LHP, 1913
Brad Eldred, IF, 2012
Babe Ellison, IF, 1916–1920
Juan Encarnacion, OF, 1997–2001
Dave Engle, C, 1986
Gil English, IF, 1936–1937
John Ennis, RHP, 2004
Eric Erickson, RHP, 1916–1919
Hal Erickson, RHP, 1953
Tex Erwin, C, 1907
John Eubank, RHP, 1905–1907
Darrell Evans, IF-DH, 1984–1988
Adam Everett, IF, 2009–2010
Hoot Evers, OF, 1941–1952, 1954
Roy Face, RHP, 1968
Bill Fahey, C, 1981–1983
Ferris Fain, IF, 1955
Bob Farley, IF, 1962
Buck Farmer, RHP, 2014–2021
Ed Farmer, RHP, 1973
Jeff Farnsworth, RHP, 2002
Kyle Farnsworth, RHP, 2005, 2008
John Farrell, RHP, 1996
Bill Faul, RHP, 1962–1964
Al Federoff, IF, 1951–1952
Junior Felix, OF, 1994
Neftalí Feliz, RHP, 2015
Jack Feller, C, 1958
Chico Fernández, IF, 1960–1963
Jose Fernandez, LHP, 2019
Jeff Ferrell, RHP, 2015, 2017
Cy Ferry, RHP, 1904
Robert Fick, IF, 1998–2002
Mark Fidrych, RHP, 1976–1980
Cecil Fielder, IF, 1990–1996
Prince Fielder, IF, 2012–2013
Bruce Fields, OF, 1986
Daniel Fields, OF, 2015
Casey Fien, RHP, 2009–2010
Mike Fiers, RHP, 2018
Alfredo Figaro, RHP, 2009–2010
Jim Finigan, IF, 1957
Happy Finneran, RHP, 1918
Bill Fischer, RHP, 1958, 1960–1961
Carl Fischer, LHP, 1933–1935
Ed Fisher, RHP, 1902
Fritz Fisher, LHP, 1964
Doug Fister, RHP, 2011–2013
Ira Flagstead, OF, 1917–1923
John Flaherty, C, 1994–1996
Les Fleming, IF, 1939
Scott Fletcher, IF, 1995
Tom Fletcher, LHP, 1962
Van Fletcher, RHP, 1955
Bryce Florie, RHP, 1997–1999
Ben Flowers, RHP, 1955
Bubba Floyd, IF, 1944
Doug Flynn, IF, 1985
Hank Foiles, C, 1960
Jason Foley, RHP, 2021
Jim Foor, LHP, 1971–1972
Gene Ford, RHP, 1905
Casey Fossum, LHP, 2008
Larry Foster, RHP, 1963
Bob Fothergill, OF, 1922–1930
Steve Foucault, RHP, 1977–1978
Pete Fox, OF, 1933–1940
Terry Fox, RHP, 1961–1966
Paul Foytack, RHP, 1953–1963
Ray Francis, LHP, 1923
Tito Francona, OF-PH, 1958
Moe Franklin, IF, 1941–1942
Jeff Frazier, OF, 2010
Vic Frazier, RHP, 1933–1934
Bill Freehan, C, 1961–1976
George Freese, IF, 1953
Luke French, LHP, 2009
Cy Fried, LHP, 1920
Owen Friend, IF, 1953
Emil Frisk, OF, 1901
Bill Froats, LHP, 1955
Travis Fryman, IF, 1990–1997
Woodie Fryman, LHP, 1972–1974
Charlie Fuchs, RHP, 1942
Tito Fuentes, IF, 1977
Frank Fuller, IF, 1915–1916
Carson Fulmer, RHP, 2020
Michael Fulmer, RHP, 2016–18, 2020-21
Liz Funk, OF, 1930
Kyle Funkhouser, RHP, 2020-2021
Charlie Furbush, LHP, 2011
Chick Gagnon, IF, 1922
Eddie Gaillard, RHP, 1997
Del Gainer, IF, 1909–1914
Dan Gakeler, RHP, 1991
Armando Galarraga, RHP, 2008–2010
Doug Gallagher, LHP, 1962
Chick Galloway, IF, 1928
John Gamble, IF, 1972–1973
Barbaro Garbey, IF, 1984–1985
Alex Garbowski, PH, 1952
Avisail García, OF, 2012–2013
Bryan García, RHP, 2019-2021
Freddy García, RHP, 2008
Luis García, IF, 1999
Karim García, OF, 1999–2000
Pedro García, IF, 1976
Rony García, RHP, 2020-2021
Mike Gardiner, RHP, 1993–1995
Dustin Garneau, C, 2021
Reed Garrett, RHP, 2019
Ned Garver, RHP, 1952–1956
Charlie Gehringer, IF, 1924–1942
Charlie Gelbert, IF, 1937
Rufe Gentry, RHP, 1943–1948
Mike Gerber, OF, 2018
Franklyn Germán, RHP, 2002–2006
Dick Gernert, IF, 1960–1961
Doc Gessler, OF, 1903
Tony Giarratano, IF, 2005
Frank Gibson, C, 1913
Kirk Gibson, OF, 1979–87, 1993–1995
Paul Gibson, LHP, 1988–1991
Sam Gibson, RHP, 1926–1928
Floyd Giebell, RHP, 1939–1941
Bill Gilbreth, LHP, 1971–1972
George Gill, RHP, 1937–1939
Bob Gillespie, RHP, 1944
Joe Ginsberg, C, 1948–1953
Matt Ginter, RHP, 2005
Dan Gladden, OF, 1992–1993
Fred Gladding, RHP, 1961–1967
John Glaiser, RHP, 1920
Norm Glaser, RHP, 1920
Kid Gleason, IF, 1901–1902
Jerry Don Gleaton, LHP, 1990–1991
Gary Glover, RHP, 2008
Ed Glynn, LHP, 1975–1978
Greg Gohr, RHP, 1993–1996
Izzy Goldstein, RHP, 1932
Purnal Goldy, OF, 1962–1963
Alexis Gómez, OF, 2005–2006
Chris Gomez, IF, 1993–1996
Álex González, IF, 2014
Dan Gonzales, OF, 1979–1980
Enrique Gonzalez, RHP,2010–2011
Juan Gonzalez, OF, 2000
Julio Gonzalez, IF, 1983
Luis Gonzalez, OF, 1998
Andrew Good, RHP, 2005
Niko Goodrum, IF-OF-DH, 2018–2021
Johnny Gorsica, RHP, 1940–1947
Tom Gorzelanny, LHP, 2015
Anthony Gose, OF, 2015–2016
Goose Goslin, OF, 1934–1937
Johnny Grabowski, C, 1931
Skinny Graham, RHP, 1929
Bill Graham, RHP, 1966
Curtis Granderson, OF, 2004–2009
Mark Grater, RHP, 1993
Beiker Graterol, RHP, 1999
Ted Gray, LHP, 1946–1954
Lenny Green, OF, 1967–1968
Hank Greenberg, 1B-OF, 1930,
1933-1941, 1945-1946-1946
Al Greene, DH, 1979
Paddy Greene, IF, 1903
Shane Greene, RHP, 2015–2019
Grayson Greiner, C, 2018–2021
Seth Greisinger, RHP, 1998, 2002
Ed Gremminger, IF, 1904
Art Griggs, IF, 1918
Jason Grilli, RHP, 2005–2008
Steve Grilli, RHP, 1975–1977
Marv Grissom, RHP, 1949
Steve Gromek, RHP, 1953–1957
Buddy Groom, LHP, 1992–1995

Robbie Grossman, OF, 2021
Johnny Groth, OF, 1946–52, 1957–60
Charlie Grover, RHP, 1913
Johnny Grubb, OF, 1983–1987
Joe Grzenda, LHP, 1961
Carlos Guillen, IF, 2004–2011
Bill Gullickson, RHP, 1991–1994
Dave Gumpert, RHP, 1982–1983
César Gutierrez, IF, 1969–1971
Dave Haas, RHP, 1991–1993
Eric Haase, C-LF-DH, 2020-2021
Sammy Hale, IF, 1920–1921
Charley Hall, RHP, 1918
Herb Hall, RHP, 1918
Joe Hall, OF, 1995–1997
Marc Hall, RHP, 1913–1914
Matt Hall, LHP, 2018–2019
Tom Haller, C, 1972
Shane Halter, IF, 2000–2003
Bob Hamelin, DH, 1997
Earl Hamilton, LHP, 1916
Jack Hamilton, RHP, 1964–1965
Luke Hamlin, RHP, 1933–1934
Fred Haney, IF, 1922–1925
Don Hankins, RHP, 1927
Jack Hannahan, IF, 2006
Jim Hannan, RHP, 1971
Charlie Harding, RHP, 1913
Blaine Hardy, LHP, 2014–2019
Shawn Hare, OF, 1991–1992
Pinky Hargrave, C, 1928–1930
Dick Harley, OF, 1902
Brian Harper, C, 1986
George Harper, OF, 1916–1918
Terry Harper, OF, 1987
Denny Harriger, RHP, 1998
Andy Harrington, PH, 1925
Bob Harris, RHP, 1938–1939
Bucky Harris, IF, 1929–1931
Gail Harris, IF, 1958–1960
Gene Harris, RHP, 1994
Ned Harris, OF, 1941–1946
Josh Harrison, 2B-DH, 2019
Earl Harrist, RHP, 1953
Bill Haselman, C, 1998–1999
Fred Hatfield, IF, 1952–1956
Clyde Hatter, LHP, 1935–1937
Brad Havens, LHP, 1989
Ray Hayworth, C, 1926–1938
Bob Hazle, OF, 1958
Bill Heath, C, 1967
Mike Heath, C, 1986–1990
Richie Hebner, IF, 1980–1982
Don Heffner, IF, 1944
Jim Hegan, C, 1958
Harry Heilmann, OF, 1914–1929
Don Heinkel, RHP, 1988
Mike Henneman, RHP, 1987–1995
Les Hennessey, IF, 1913
Oscar Henriquez, RHP, 2002
Dwayne Henry, RHP, 1995
Roy Henshaw, LHP, 1942–1944
Ray Herbert, RHP, 1950–51, 1953-54
Babe Herman, OF, 1937
Willie Hernández, LHP, 1984–1989
Fernando Hernández, RHP, 1997
Larry Herndon, OF, 1982–1988
Art Herring, RHP, 1929–1933
Whitey Herzog, OF, 1963
Mike Hessman, IF, 2007
Gus Hetling, IF, 1906
Phil Hiatt, IF, 1996
Charlie Hickman, IF, 1904–1905
Buddy Hicks, IF, 1956
John Hicks, 1B-C-DH, 2016–2019
Pinky Higgins, IF, 1939–1944, 1946
Bobby Higginson, OF, 1995–2005
Ed High, LHP, 1901
Hugh High, OF, 1913–1914
Erik Hiljus, RHP, 1999–2000
Derek Hill, CF, 2020-2021
John Hiller, LHP, 1965–1980
A. J. Hinch, C, 2003
Billy Hitchcock, IF, 1942–1946, 1953
Billy Hoeft, LHP, 1952–1959
Chief Hogsett, LHP, 1929–1936, 1944
Bryan Holaday, C, 2012–2015, 2017
Fred Holdsworth, RHP, 1972–1974
Derek Holland, LHP, 2021
Michael Hollimon, IF, 2008–2009
Carl Holling, RHP, 1921–1922
Ken Holloway, RHP, 1922–1928
Shawn Holman, RHP, 1989
Ducky Holmes, OF, 1901–1902
Chris Holt, RHP, 2000–2001
Vern Holtgrave, RHP, 1965
Kevin Hooper, IF, 2005–2006
Joe Hoover, IF, 1943–1945
Johnny Hopp, OF, 1952
Willie Horton, OF, 1963–1977
Tim Hosley, C, 1970–1971
Gene Host, LHP, 1956
Chuck Hostetler, OF, 1944–1945
Frank House, C, 1950–1957, 1961
Fred House, RHP, 1913
Art Houtteman, RHP, 1945–50, 1952-53
Frank Howard, OF, 1972–1973
Waite Hoyt, RHP, 1930–1931
Clarence Huber, IF, 1920–1921
Charles Hudson, RHP, 1989
Frank Huelsman, OF, 1904
Aubrey Huff, 1B, 2009
Tom Hughes, OF, 1930
Mark Huismann, RHP, 1988
Terry Humphrey, C, 1975
Bob Humphreys, RHP, 1962
Brian L. Hunter, OF, 1996–1999
Torii Hunter, OF, 2013–2014
Jimmy Hurst, OF, 1997
Drew Hutchinson, LHP, 2021
Fred Hutchinson, RHP, 1939–41, 1946-53
Tim Hyers, IF, 1996
José Iglesias, SS-3B-DH, 2013, 2015–18
Gary Ignasiak, LHP, 1973
Pete Incaviglia, OF, 1991, 1998
Omar Infante, IF, 2002–07, 2012–13
Brandon Inge, IF, 2001–2012
Riccardo Ingram, OF, 1994
Ed Irvin, IF, 1912
Mike Ivie, IF, 1982–1983
Austin Jackson, OF, 2010–2014
Damian Jackson, IF, 2002
Edwin Jackson, RHP, 2009, 2019
Herb Jackson, RHP, 1905
Ron Jackson, IF, 1981
Ryan Jackson, IF, 2000–2002
Baby Doll Jacobson, OF, 1915
Charlie Jaeger, RHP, 1904
Art James, OF, 1975
Bill James, RHP, 1915–1919
Bob James, RHP, 1982–1983
Kevin Jarvis, RHP, 1997
Paul Jata, IF, 1972
Myles Jaye, RHP, 2017
Gregg Jefferies, IF, 1999–2000
Hughie Jennings, IF, 1907–1918
Marcus Jensen, C, 1997–1998
Willie Jensen, RHP, 1912
Eduardo Jimenez, RHP, 2019
Jason Jiménez, LHP, 2002
Joe Jiménez, RHP, 2017–2021
Augie Johns, LHP, 1926–1927
Alex Johnson, OF, 1976
Brian Johnson, C, 1996–1997
Dave Johnson, RHP, 1993
Earl Johnson, LHP, 1951
Howard Johnson, IF, 1982–1984
Jason Johnson, RHP, 2004–2005
Jim Johnson, RHP, 2014
Ken Johnson, LHP, 1952
Mark Johnson, RHP, 2000
Roy Johnson, OF, 1929–1932
Syl Johnson, RHP, 1922–1925
Alex Jones, LHP, 1903
Bob Jones, IF, 1917–1925
Dalton Jones, IF, 1970–1972
Davy Jones, OF, 1906–1912
Deacon Jones, RHP, 1916–1918
Elijah Jones, RHP, 1907–1909
JaCoby Jones, 3B-OF-DH, 2016–2021
Jacque Jones, OF, 2008
Ken Jones, RHP, 1924
Lynn Jones, OF, 1979–1983
Ruppert Jones, OF, 1984
Sam Jones, RHP, 1962
Todd Jones, RHP, 1997–01, 2006–2008
Tom Jones, IF, 1909–1910
Tracy Jones, OF, 1989–1990
Milt Jordan, RHP, 1953
Matt Joyce, OF, 2008
Jair Jurrjens, RHP, 2007
Walt Justis, RHP, 1905
Jeff Kaiser, LHP, 1991
Al Kaline, OF, 1953–1974
Rudy Kallio, RHP, 1918–1919
Harry Kane, LHP, 1903
Gabe Kapler, OF, 1998–1999
Jason Karnuth, RHP, 2005
Marty Kavanagh, IF, 1914–1916, 1918
Greg Keagle, RHP, 1996–1998
George Kell, IF, 1946–1952
Mick Kelleher, IF, 1981–1982
Kris Keller, RHP, 2002
Charlie Keller, OF, 1950–1951
Bryan Kelly, P, 1986–1987

Don Kelly, OF 2009–2014
Steve Kemp, OF, 1977–1981
Bob Kennedy, OF, 1956
Vern Kennedy, RHP, 1938–1939
Logan Kensing, RHP, 2016
Russ Kerns, PH, 1945
John Kerr, IF, 1923–1924
Masao Kida, RHP, 1999–2000
John Kiely, RHP, 1991–1993
Mike Kilkenny, LHP, 1969–1972
Red Killefer, OF, 1907–1909
Ed Killian, LHP, 1904–1910
Bruce Kimm, C, 1976–1977
Chad Kimsey, RHP, 1936
Chick King, OF, 1954–1956
Eric King, RHP, 1986–1988, 1992
Gene Kingsale, OF, 2003
Dennis Kinney, LHP, 1981
Ian Kinsler, IF, 2014–2017
Matt Kinzer, RHP, 1990
Jay Kirke, OF, 1910
Rube Kisinger, RHP, 1902–1903
Frank Kitson, RHP, 1903–1905
Danny Klassen, IF, 2003
Al Klawitter, RHP, 1913
Ron Kline, RHP, 1961–1962
Johnny Klippstein, P, 1967
Corey Knebel, RHP, 2014
Rudy Kneisch, LHP, 1926
Ray Knight, IF, 1988
Gary Knotts, RHP, 2003–2004
John Knox, IF, 1972–1975
Kurt Knudsen, RHP, 1992–1994
Guido Knudson, RHP, 2015
Alan Koch, RHP, 1963–1964
Brad Kocher, C, 1912
Mark Koenig, IF, 1930–1931
Don Kolloway, IF, 1949–1952
Howie Koplitz, RHP, 1961–1962
George Korince, RHP, 1966–1967
Frank Kostro, IF, 1962–1963
Pete Kozma, IF-DH, 2018
Marc Krauss, IF, 2015
Wayne Krenchicki, IF, 1983
Chuck Kress, IF, 1954
Red Kress, IF, 1939–1940
Lou Kretlow, RHP, 1946–1949
Chad Kreuter, C, 1992–1994
Ian Krol, LHP, 2014–2015, 2021
Bill Krueger, LHP, 1993–1994
Dick Kryhoski, IF, 1950–1951
Harvey Kuenn, OF, 1952–1959
Rusty Kuntz, OF, 1984–1985
Chet Laabs, OF, 1937–1939
Clem Labine, RHP, 1960
Jairo Labourt, LHP, 2017
Ed Lafitte, RHP, 1909–1912
Mike Laga, IF, 1982–1986
Lerrin LaGrow, RHP, 1970–1975
Gerald Laird, C, 2009–2010, 2012
Joe Lake, RHP, 1912–1913
Eddie Lake, IF, 1946–1950
Al Lakeman, C, 1954
Chris Lambert, RHP,2008–2009
Gene Lamont, C, 1970–1975

Les Lancaster, RHP, 1992
Jim Landis, OF, 1967
Marvin Lane, OF, 1971–1976
Alex Lange, RHP, 2021
Dave LaPoint, LHP, 1986
Jeff Larish, IF, 2008–2010
Steve Larkin, RHP, 1934
Frank Lary, RHP, 1954–1964
Fred Lasher, RHP, 1967–1970
Chick Lathers, IF, 1910–1911
Charley Lau, C, 1956–1959
Bill Lawrence, OF, 1932
Roxie Lawson, RHP, 1933–1939
Bill Laxton, LHP, 1976
Jack Lazorko, RHP, 1986
Rick Leach, OF, 1981–1983
Razor Ledbetter, RHP, 1915
Wilfredo Ledezma, LHP, 2003–2007
Don Lee, RHP, 1957–1958
Ron LeFlore, OF, 1974–1979
Bill Leinhauser, OF, 1912
Mark Leiter, RHP, 1991–1994
Bill Lelivelt, RHP, 1909–1910
Dave Lemanczyk, RHP, 1973–1976
Chet Lemon, OF, 1982–1990
Don Lenhardt, OF, 1952
Jim Lentine, OF, 1980
Arcenio Leon, RHP, 2017
Dutch Leonard, LHP, 1919–21, 1924-25
Ted Lepcio, IF, 1959
Pete LePine, OF, 1902
George Lerchen, OF, 1952
Don Leshnock, LHP, 1972
Al Levine, RHP, 2004
Artie Lewicki, RHP, 2017–2018
Colby Lewis, RHP, 2006
Mark Lewis, IF, 1995–1996
Richie Lewis, RHP, 1996
José Lima, RHP, 1993–96, 2001–02
Em Lindbeck, PH, 1960
Jim Lindeman, OF, 1990
Chris Lindsay, IF, 1905–1906
Rod Lindsey, OF, 1998–2002
Carl Linhart, PH, 1952
Johnny Lipon, IF, 1942–1952
Felipe Lira, RHP, 1995–1997, 1999
Francisco Liriano, LHP, 2018
Dick Littlefield, LHP, 1952
Jack Lively, RHP, 1911
Scott Livingstone, IF, 1991–1994
Kyle Lobstein, LHP, 2014–2015
Harry Lochhead, IF, 1901
Bob Logan, LHP, 1937
Nook Logan, OF, 2004–2006
Mickey Lolich, LHP, 1963–1975
George Lombard, OF, 2002
Herman Long, IF, 1903
Aurelio López, RHP, 1979–1985
Aquilino López, RHP, 2007–2008
Lefty Lorenzen, LHP, 1913
Art Loudell, RHP, 1910
Baldy Louden, IF, 1912–1913
Shane Loux, RHP, 2002–2003
Slim Love, LHP, 1919–1920
Torey Lovullo, IF, 1988–1989

Grover Lowdermilk, RHP, 1915–1916
Bobby Lowe, IF, 1904–1907
Mark Lowe, RHP, 2016
Dwight Lowry, C, 1984–1987
Willie Ludolph, RHP, 1924
Dawel Lugo, 2B-3B-DH, 2018–2020
Urbano Lugo, RHP, 1990
Jerry Lumpe, IF, 1964–1967
Don Lund, OF, 1949–1954
Scott Lusader, OF, 1987–1990
Billy Lush, OF, 1903
Red Lynn, RHP, 1939
Fred Lynn, OF, 1988–1989
Brandon Lyon, RHP, 2009
Duke Maas, RHP, 1955–1957
Frank MacCormack, RHP, 1976
Bob MacDonald, LHP, 1993
Dixon Machado, IF-DH, 2015–2018
Dave Machemer, IF, 1979
Jose Macias, IF, 1999–2002
Morris Madden, LHP, 1987
Elliott Maddox, OF, 1970
Dave Madison, RHP, 1952–1953
Scotti Madison, IF, 1985–1986
Bill Madlock, IF, 1987
Wendell Magee, OF, 2000–2002
Billy Maharg, IF, 1912
Mickey Mahler, LHP, 1985
Mikie Mahtook, OF-DH, 2017–2019
Bob Maier, IF, 1945
Alex Main, RHP, 1914
George Maisel, OF, 1916
Tom Makowski, LHP, 1975
Herm Malloy, RHP, 1907–1908
Harry Malmberg, IF, 1955
Hal Manders, RHP, 1941–1942, 1946
Vincent Maney, IF, 1912
Clyde Manion, C, 1920–1927
Phil Mankowski, IF, 1976–1979
Matt Manning, RHP, 2021
Joe Mantiply, LHP, 2016
Jeff Manto, IF, 1998
Jerry Manuel, IF, 1975–1976
Heinie Manush, OF, 1923–1927
Cliff Mapes, OF, 1952
Firpo Marberry, RHP, 1933–1935
Leo Marentette, RHP, 1965
Dick Marlowe, RHP, 1951–1956
Mike Maroth, LHP, 2002–2007
Buck Marrow, RHP, 1932
Mike Marshall, RHP, 1967
Jefry Marté, IF, 2015
Luis Marte, RHP, 2011–2012
Billy Martin, IF, 1958
John Martin, LHP, 1983
Leonys Martín, CF-DH, 2018
J.D. Martinez, OF, 2014–2017
Ramón Martínez, IF, 2005
Víctor Martínez, DH-C-1B, 2011, 2013-18
Roger Mason, RHP, 1984
Walt Masterson, RHP, 1956
Tom Matchick, IF, 1967–1969
Eddie Mathews, IF, 1967–1968
Bob Mavis, PR, 1949
Brian Maxcy, RHP, 1995–1996

Charlie Maxwell, OF, 1955–1962
Milt May, C, 1976–1979
Cameron Maybin, OF, 2007, 2016, 2020
Eddie Mayo, IF, 1944–1948
Nomar Mazara, RF, 2021
Sport McAllister, OF, 1901–1903
Zach McAllister, RHP, 2018
Dick McAuliffe, IF, 1960–1973
Macay McBride, LHP, 2007
James McCann, C-DH, 2014–2018
Arch McCarthy, RHP, 1902
Barney McCosky, OF, 1939–1946
Benny McCoy, IF, 1938–1939
Pat McCoy, LHP, 2014
Ed McCreery, RHP, 1914
Lance McCullers, RHP, 1990
Jeff McCurry, RHP, 1996
Mickey McDermott, LHP, 1958
Red McDermott, OF, 1912
Allen McDill, LHP, 2000
John McDonald, IF, 2005
Orlando McFarlane, C, 1966
Jim McGarr, IF, 1912
Dan McGarvey, OF, 1912
Casey McGehee, IF, 2016
Pat McGehee, RHP, 1912
Deacon McGuire, C, 1902–1903, 1912
John McHale, IF, 1943–1948
Matty McIntyre, OF, 1904–1910
Archie McKain, LHP, 1939–1941
David McKay, RHP, 2019-2020
Red McKee, C, 1913–1916
Denny McLain, RHP, 1963–1970
Pat McLaughlin, RHP, 1937, 1945
Wayne McLeland, RHP, 1951–1952
Sam McMackin, LHP, 1902
Don McMahon, RHP, 1968–1969
Frank McManus, C, 1904
Marty McManus, IF, 1927–1931
Billy McMillon, OF, 2000–2001
Fred McMullin, IF, 1914
Carl McNabb, PH, 1945
Eric McNair, IF, 1941–1942
Norm McRae, RHP, 1969–1970
Bill McTigue, LHP, 1916
Rusty Meacham, RHP, 1991
Chris Mears, RHP, 2003
Phil Meeler, RHP, 1972
Mitch Meluskey, C, 2002
Bob Melvin, C, 1985
Orlando Mercado, C, 1987
Melvin Mercedes, RHP, 2014
Jordy Mercer, INF-DH, 2019-2020
Win Mercer, RHP, 1902
Herm Merritt, IF, 1921
José Mesa, RHP, 2007
Scat Metha, IF, 1940
Charlie Metro, OF, 1943–1944
Dan Meyer, IF, 1974–1976
Dutch Meyer, IF, 1940–1942
Dan Miceli, RHP, 1997
Gene Michael, IF, 1975
Jim Middleton, RHP, 1921
Ed Mierkowicz, OF, 1945–1948
Andrew Miller, LHP, 2006–2007
Bob Miller, LHP, 1953–1956
Bob Miller, RHP, 1973
Eddie Miller, OF, 1982
Hack Miller, C, 1944–1945
Justin Miller, RHP, 2014
Matt Miller, LHP, 2001–2002
Orlando Miller, IF, 1997
Roscoe Miller, RHP, 1901–1902
Trever Miller, LHP, 1996
Zach Miner, RHP, 2006–2009
Clarence Mitchell, LHP, 1911
Willie Mitchell, LHP, 1916–1919
Casey Mize, RHP, 2020-2021
Dave Mlicki, RHP, 1999–2001
Brian Moehler, RHP, 1996–2002
Herb Moford, RHP, 1958
John Mohardt, OF, 1922
Bob Molinaro, OF, 1975, 1977, 1983
Dustin Molleken, RHP, 2016
Bill Monbouquette, RHP, 1966–1967
Sid Monge, LHP, 1984
Craig Monroe, OF, 2002–2007
Manny Montejo, RHP, 1961
Anse Moore, OF, 1946
Bill Moore, RHP, 1925
Jackie Moore, C, 1965
Matt Moore, LHP, 2019
Mike Moore, RHP, 1993–1995
Roy Moore, LHP, 1922–1923
Jake Mooty, RHP, 1944
Jerry Morales, OF, 1979
Harry Moran, LHP, 1912
Keith Moreland, OF, 1989
Chet Morgan, OF, 1935–1938
Tom Morgan, RHP, 1958–1960
George Moriarty, IF, 1909–1915
Hal Morris, IF, 2000
Jack Morris, RHP, 1977–1990
Warren Morris, IF, 2003
Bill Morrisette, RHP, 1920
Jim Morrison, IF, 1987–1988
Bubba Morton, OF, 1961–1963
Lloyd Moseby, OF, 1990–1991
Jerry Moses, C, 1974
John Moses, OF, 1991
Don Mossi, LHP, 1959–1963
Steven Moya, OF, 2014–2016
Les Mueller, RHP, 1941–1945
Edward Mujica, RHP, 2017
Billy Mullen, IF, 1926
George Mullin, RHP-OF, 1902–1913
Pat Mullin, OF, 1940–1953
Mike Munoz, LHP, 1991–1993
Eric Munson, IF, 2000–2004
John Murphy, IF, 1903
Dwayne Murphy, OF, 1988
Heath Murray, LHP, 2001
Glenn Myatt, C, 1936
Mike Myers, LHP, 1995–1997
Russ Nagelson, OF, 1970
Bill Nahorodny, C, 1983
Kid Nance, OF, 1901
Ray Narleski, RHP, 1959
Joe Nathan, RHP, 2014–2015
Efren Navarro, 1B-DH, 2017
Julio Navarro, RHP, 1964–1966
Bots Nekola, LHP, 1933
Lynn Nelson, RHP, 1940
Ángel Nesbitt, RHP, 2015
Jack Ness, IF, 1911
Jim Nettles, OF, 1974
Johnny Neun, IF, 1925–1928
Phil Nevin, IF, 1995–1997
Hal Newhouser, LHP, 1939–1953
Bobo Newsom, RHP, 1939–1941
Fu-Te Ni, LHP, 2009–2010
Simon Nicholls, IF, 1903
Fred Nicholson, OF, 1917
Joe Niekro, RHP, 1970–1972
Bob Nieman, OF, 1953–1954
Melvin Nieves, OF, 1996–1997
Ron Nischwitz, LHP, 1961–1962, 1965
C. J. Nitkowski, LHP, 1995–96, 1999–01
Matt Nokes, C, 1986–1990
Dickie Noles, RHP, 1987
Hideo Nomo, RHP, 2000
Daniel Norris, LHP, 2015–2021
Lou North, RHP, 1913
Jim Northrup, OF, 1964–1974
Greg Norton, IF, 2004
Randy Nosek, RHP, 1989–1990
Ivan Nova, RHP, 2020
Roberto Novoa, RHP, 2004
Edwin Nunez, RHP, 1989–1990
Renato Nunez, 1B, 2021
John O'Connell, IF, 1902
Charley O'Leary, IF, 1904–1912
Ollie O'Mara, IF, 1912
Randy O'Neal, RHP, 1984–1986
Frank O'Rourke, IF, 1924–1926
Prince Oana, RHP, 1943–1945
Ben Oglivie, OF, 1974–1977
Frank Okrie, LHP, 1920
Red Oldham, LHP, 1914–15, 1920-22
Omar Olivares, RHP, 1996–1997
Lester Oliveros, RHP, 2011
Andrew Oliver, LHP, 2010–2011
Joe Oliver, C, 1997–1998
Ole Olsen, RHP, 1922–1923
Gregg Olson, RHP, 1996
Karl Olson, OF, 1957
Eddie Onslow, IF, 1912–1913
Jack Onslow, C, 1912
Magglio Ordonez, OF, 2005–2011
Joe Orengo, IF, 1944
Joe Orrell, RHP, 1943–1945
Jose Ortega, RHP, 2012–2014
Bobo Osborne, IF, 1957–1962
Jimmy Outlaw, OF, 1943–1949
Stubby Overmire, LHP, 1943–1949
Frank Owen, RHP, 1901
Marv Owen, IF, 1931–1937
Ray Oyler, IF, 1965–1968
John Pacella, RHP, 1986
Phil Page, LHP, 1928–1930
David Palmer, RHP, 1989
Dean Palmer, IF, 1999–2003
Jose Paniagua, RHP, 2002
Stan Papi, IF, 1980–1981
Craig Paquette, IF, 2002–2003

Isaac Paredes, 3B, 2020-2021
Johnny Paredes, IF, 1990–1991
Mark Parent, C, 1996
Clay Parker, RHP, 1990
Salty Parker, IF, 1936
Slicker Parks, RHP, 1921
Bobby Parnell, RHP, 2016
Lance Parrish, C, 1977–1986
Dixie Parsons, C, 1939–1943
Steve Partenheimer, IF, 1913
Johnny Pasek, C, 1933
Larry Pashnick, RHP, 1982–1983
Bob Patrick, OF, 1941–1942
Daryl Patterson, RHP, 1968–1971
Danny Patterson, RHP, 2000–2004
Jarrod Patterson, IF, 2001
David Pauley, RHP, 2011
Fred Payne, C, 1906–1908
Terry Pearson, RHP, 2002
Marv Peasley, LHP, 1910
Al Pedrique, IF, 1989
Mike Pelfrey, RHP, 2016
Rudy Pemberton, OF, 1995
Brayan Pena, C, 2013
Carlos Pena, IF, 2002–2006
Orlando Pena, RHP, 1965–1967
Ramon Pena, RHP, 1989
Shannon Penn, DH, 1995–1996
Brad Penny, RHP, 2011
Gene Pentz, RHP, 1975
Pepper Peploski, IF, 1913
Don Pepper, IF, 1966
Jhonny Peralta, IF, 2010–2013
Wily Peralta, RHP, 2021
Troy Percival, RHP, 2005
Hernan Perez, 2B, 2012–2015
Neifi Perez, IF, 2006–2007
Timo Perez, OF, 2007
Matt Perisho, LHP, 2001–2002
Cy Perkins, C, 1934
Hub Pernoll, LHP, 1910–1912
Ron Perranoski, LHP, 1971–1972
Pol Perritt, RHP, 1921
Boyd Perry, IF, 1941
Clay Perry, IF, 1908
Hank Perry, OF, 1912
Jim Perry, RHP, 1973
Ryan Perry, RHP, 2009–2011
Johnny Pesky, IF, 1952–1954
John Peters, C, 1915
Rick Peters, OF, 1979–1981
Dustin Peterson, OF-DH-1B, 2019
Ben Petrick, C, 2003
Dan Petry, RP, 1979–1987, 1990–1991
Gary Pettis, OF, 1988–1989, 1992
Adam Pettyjohn, LHP, 2001
Dave Philley, OF, 1957
Bubba Phillips, IF, 1955, 1963–1964
Eddie Phillips, C, 1929
Jack Phillips, IF, 1955–1957
Red Phillips, RHP, 1934–1936
Tony Phillips, OF, 1990–1994
Billy Pierce, LHP, 1945–1948
Jack Pierce, IF, 1975
Tony Piet, IF, 1938
Herman Pillette, RHP, 1922–1924
Luis Pineda, RHP, 2001
Babe Pinelli, IF, 1920
Wally Pipp, IF, 1913
Cotton Pippen, RHP, 1939–1940
Chris Pittaro, IF, 1985
Al Platte, OF, 1913
Johnny Podres, LHP, 1966–1967
Boots Poffenberger, RHP, 1937–1938
Placido Polanco, IF, 2005–2009
Luis Polonia, OF, 1998–2000
Jim Poole, LHP, 1999–2000
Rick Porcello, RHP, 2009–2014
Jay Porter, C, 1955–1957
Lew Post, OF, 1902
Brian Powell, RHP, 1998–1999, 2002
Ray Powell, OF, 1913
Ted Power, RHP, 1988
Del Pratt, IF, 1923–1924
Joe Presko, RHP, 1957–1958
Alex Presley, OF, 2016–2017
David Price, LHP, 2014–2015
Jim Price, C, 1967–1971
Jerry Priddy, IF, 1950–1953
Curtis Pride, OF, 1996–1997
Jim Proctor, RHP, 1959
Augie Prudhomme, RHP, 1929
Tim Pugh, RHP, 1997
David Purcey, LHP, 2011
Billy Purtell, IF, 1914
Luke Putkonen, RHP, 2012–2014
Ed Putman, C, 1979
George Quellich, OF, 1931
Mike Rabelo, C, 2006–2007
Ryan Raburn, OF, 2004, 2007–2012
Dick Radatz, RHP, 1969
Rip Radcliff, OF, 1941–1943
Ed Rakow, RHP, 1964–1965
Erasmo Ramirez, RHP, 2021
Nick Ramirez, LHP, 2019-2020
Wilkin Ramírez, OF, 2009
Wilson Ramos, C, 2021
Joe Randa, IF, 1998
Clay Rapada, LHP, 2007–2009
Earl Rapp, OF, 1949
Jim Ray, RHP, 1974
Robbie Ray, LHP, 2014
Bugs Raymond, RHP, 1904
Mark Redman, LHP, 2001–2002
Wayne Redmond, OF, 1965–1969
Bob Reed, RHP, 1969–1970
Evan Reed, RHP, 2013–2014
Jody Reed, IF, 1997
Rich Reese, IF, 1973
Phil Regan, RHP, 1960–1965
Frank Reiber, C, 1933–1936
Zac Reininger, RHP, 2017–2019
Alex Remneas, RHP, 1912
Erwin Renfer, RHP, 1913
Tony Rensa, C, 1930
Edgar Renteria, IF, 2008
Víctor Reyes, OF-DH, 2018–2021
Bob Reynolds, RHP, 1975
Ross Reynolds, RHP, 1914–1915
Billy Rhiel, IF, 1932–1933
Will Rhymes, IF, 2010–2011
Dennis Ribant, RHP, 1968
Harry Rice, OF, 1928–1930
Paul Richards, C, 1943–1946
Nolen Richardson, IF, 1929–1932
Rob Richie, OF, 1989
Hank Riebe, C, 1942–1949
Topper Rigney, IF, 1922–1925
Juan Rincon, RHP, 2009
Billy Ripken, IF, 1998
Kevin Ritz, RHP, 1989–1992
Mike Rivera, C, 2001–2002
Mike Roarke, C, 1961–1964
Bruce Robbins, LHP, 1979–1980
Bip Roberts, IF, 1998
Dave Roberts, LHP, 1976–1977
Leon Roberts, OF, 1974–1975
Willis Roberts, RHP, 1999
Jerry Robertson, RHP, 1970
Nate Robertson, LHP, 2003–2009
Aaron Robinson, C, 1949–1951
Eddie Robinson, IF, 1957
Jeff Robinson, RHP, 1987–1990
Rabbit Robinson, IF, 1904
Jacob Robson, OF, 2021
Fernando Rodney, RHP, 2002–03, 2005–09
Aurelio Rodríguez, IF, 1971–1979
Francisco Rodríguez, RHP, 2016–2017
Ivan Rodriguez, C, 2004–2008
Ronny Rodríguez, IF-DH-OF, 2018–2019
Steve Rodriguez, IF, 1995
Joe Rogalski, RHP, 1938
Billy Rogell, IF, 1930–1939
Jake Rogers, C-DH, 2019, 2021
Kenny Rogers, LHP, 2006–2008
Saul Rogovin, RHP, 1949–1951
Mel Rojas, RHP, 1999
Bill Roman, IF, 1964–1965
Ed Romero, IF, 1990
Andrew Romine, IF, 2014–2017
Austin Romine, C, 2020
Henri Rondeau, OF, 1913
Bruce Rondon, RHP, 2013, 2015–2017
Matt Roney, RHP, 2003
Jim Rooker, LHP, 1968
Trevor Rosenthal, RHP, 2019
Cody Ross, OF, 2003
Don Ross, IF, 1938, 1942–1945
Tyson Ross, RHP, 2019
Claude Rossman, IF, 1907–1909
Larry Rothschild, RHP, 1981–1982
Jack Rowan, RHP, 1906
Schoolboy Rowe, LHP, 1933–1942
Rich Rowland, C, 1990–1993
Dave Rozema, RHP, 1977–1984
Art Ruble, OF, 1927
Dave Rucker, LHP, 1981–1983
Muddy Ruel, C, 1931–1932
Chance Ruffin, RHP, 2011
Vern Ruhle, RHP, 1974–1977
Sean Runyan, LHP, 1998–2000
Jack Russell, RHP, 1937

Dusty Ryan, C, 2008–2009
Kyle Ryan, LHP, 2014–2017
Erik Sabel, RHP, 2002
A. J. Sager, RHP, 1996–1998
Mark Salas, C, 1990–1991
Luis Salazar, IF, 1988
Oscar Salazar, IF, 2002
Jarrod Saltalamacchia, C-1B, 2016, 2018
Ron Samford, IF, 1955–1957
Juan Samuel, IF, 1994–1995
Joe Samuels, RHP, 1930
Alejandro Sánchez, OF, 1985
Alex Sanchez, OF, 2003–2004
Anibal Sanchez, RHP, 2012–2017
Reggie Sanders, IF, 1974
Scott Sanders, RHP, 1997–1998
Julio Santana, RHP, 2002
Marino Santana, RHP, 1998
Pedro Santana, IF, 2001
Ramon Santiago, IF, 2002–03, 06–13
Omir Santos, C, 2011–2012
Víctor Santos, RHP, 2001
Dane Sardinha, C, 2008–2009
Joe Sargent, IF, 1921
Kevin Saucier, LHP, 1981–1982
Warwick Saupold, RHP, 2016–2018
Dennis Saunders, RHP, 1970
Jay Sborz, RHP, 2010
Bob Scanlan, RHP, 1996
Ray Scarborough, RHP 1953
Germany Schaefer, IF, 1905–1909
Biff Schaller, OF, 1911
Wally Schang, C, 1931
Dan Schatzeder, LHP, 1980–1981
Frank Scheibeck, IF, 1906
Fred Scherman, LHP, 1969–1973
Bill Scherrer, LHP, 1984–1986
Max Scherzer, RHP, 2010–2014
Lou Schiappacasse, OF, 1902
Daniel Schlereth, LHP, 2010–2012
Brian Schmack, RHP, 2003–2004
Boss Schmidt, C, 1906–1911
Jonathan Schoop, 2B-1B, 2020-2021
John Schreiber, RHP, 2019-2020
Rick Schu, IF, 1989
Heinie Schuble, IF, 1929–1935
Barney Schultz, RHP, 1959
Bob Schultz, LHP, 1955
Mike Schwabe, RHP, 1989–1990
Chuck Scrivener, IF, 1975–1977
Johnnie Seale, LHP, 1964–1965
Steve Searcy, LHP, 1988–1991
Tom Seats, LHP, 1940
Bobby Seay, LHP, 2006–2010
Frank Secory, OF, 1940
Chuck Seelbach, RHP, 1971–1974
Ray Semproch, RHP, 1960
Rip Sewell, RHP, 1932
Dick Sharon, OF, 1973–1974
Al Shaw, C, 1901
Bob Shaw, RHP, 1957–1958
Merv Shea, C, 1927–1929, 1939
Larry Sheets, DH, 1990
Gary Sheffield, OF, 2007–2008
John Shelby, OF, 1990–1991
Hugh Shelley, OF, 1935
Chris Shelton, IF, 2004–2006
Pat Sheridan, OF, 1986–1989
Larry Sherry, RHP, 1964–1967
Jimmy Shevlin, IF, 1930
Ivey Shiver, OF, 1931
Ron Shoop, C, 1959
Zack Short, SS, 2021
Chick Shorten, OF, 1919–1921
Joe Siddall, C, 1998–1999
Ruben Sierra, OF, 1996
Ed Siever, LHP, 1901–1902, 1906–1908
Frank Sigafoos, IF, 1929
Al Simmons, OF, 1936
Hack Simmons, IF, 1910
Nelson Simmons, OF, 1984–1985
Alfredo Simón, RHP, 2015
Randall Simon, IF, 2001–2002
Duke Sims, C, 1972–1973
Matt Sinatro, C, 1989
Duane Singleton, OF, 1996
Dave Sisler, RHP, 1959–1960
Scott Sizemore, IF, 2010–2011
Dave Skeels, RHP, 1910
Lou Skizas, OF, 1958
John Skopec, LHP, 1903
Tarik Skubal, LHP, 2020-2021
Jim Slaton, RHP, 1978, 1986
Bill Slayback, RHP, 1972–1974
Lou Sleater, LHP, 1957–1958
Jim Small, OF, 1955–1957
Bob Smith, LHP, 1959
Chad Smith, RHP, 2014
Clay Smith, RHP, 1940
George C. Smith, IF, 1963–1965
George S. Smith, RHP, 1926–1929
Heinie Smith, IF, 1903
Jack Smith, IF, 1912
Jason Smith, IF, 2004–2005
Rufus Smith, LHP, 1927
Willie Smith, OF, 1963
Josh Smoker, LHP, 2018
Drew Smyly, LHP, 2012–2014
Nate Snell, RHP, 1987
Clint Sodowsky, RHP, 1995–1996
Joakim Soria, RHP, 2014–2015
Vic Sorrell, RHP, 1928–1937
Elías Sosa, RHP, 1982
Gregory Soto, LHP, 2019-2021
Steve Souchock, OF, 1951–1955
Steve Sparks, RHP, 2000–2003
Joe Sparma, RHP, 1964–1969
Kid Speer, LHP, 1909
George Spencer, RHP, 1958–1960
Tubby Spencer, C, 1916–1918
Charlie Spikes, OF, 1978
Harry Spilman, IF, 1986
Chris Spurling, RHP, 2003, 2005–206
Max St. Pierre, C, 2010
Tuck Stainback, OF, 1940–1941
Matt Stairs, OF, 2006
Gerry Staley, RHP, 1961
Oscar Stanage, C, 1909–1925
Mickey Stanley, OF, 1964–1978
Joe Staton, IF, 1972–1973
Rusty Staub, OF-DH, 1976–1979
Bill Steen, RHP, 1915
Dave Stegman, OF, 1978–1980
Ben Steiner, IF, 1947
Todd Steverson, OF, 1995
Christin Stewart, LF-DH, 2018–2020
Lefty Stewart, LHP, 1921
Phil Stidham, RHP, 1994
Bob Stoddard, RHP, 1985
John Stone, OF, 1928–1933
Lil Stoner, RHP, 1922–1929
Jesse Stovall, RHP, 1904
Mike Strahler, RHP, 1973
Bob Strampe, RHP, 1972
Doug Strange, IF, 1989
Walt Streuli, C, 1954–1956
Sailor Stroud, RHP, 1910
Marlin Stuart, RHP, 1949–1952
Franklin Stubbs, IF, 1995
Jim Stump, RHP, 1957–1959
Daniel Stumpf, LHP, 2017–2019
Tom Sturdivant, RHP, 1963
Eugenio Suárez, IF, 2014
Joe Sugden, C, 1912
George Suggs, RHP, 1908–1909
Billy Sullivan, C, 1916
Billy Sullivan, Jr., C, 1940–1941
Charlie Sullivan, RHP, 1928, 1930-1931
Jackie Sullivan, IF, 1944
Joe Sullivan, LHP, 1935–1936
John Sullivan, C, 1905
John Sullivan, C, 1963–1965
Russ Sullivan, OF, 1951–1953
Champ Summers, OF, 1979–1981
Ed Summers, RHP, 1908–1912
George C. Susce, C, 1932
George D. Susce, RHP, 1958–1959
Gary Sutherland, IF, 1974–1976
Suds Sutherland, RHP, 1921
Bill Sweeney, IF, 1928
Bob Swift, C, 1944–1953
Bob Sykes, LHP, 1977–1978
Ken Szotkiewicz, IF, 1970
Frank Tanana, LHP, 1985–1992
Jordan Tata, RHP, 2006–2007
Jackie Tavener, IF, 1921–1928
Ben Taylor, IF, 1952
Bill Taylor, OF, 1957–1958
Bruce Taylor, RHP, 1977–1979
Gary Taylor, RHP, 1969
Tony Taylor, IF, 1971–1973
Wiley Taylor, RHP, 1911
Birdie Tebbetts, C, 1936–1947
Teheran, Julio, RHP, 2021
Walt Terrell, RHP, 1985–88, 1990–92
John Terry, P, 1902
Mickey Tettleton, C-DH-OF-1B, 1991–94
Marcus Thames, OF, 2004–2009
Brad Thomas, LHP, 2010–2011
Clete Thomas, OF, 2008–2012
Frosty Thomas, RHP, 1905
Bud Thomas, RHP, 1939–1941

George Thomas, OF, 1957–61, 63–65
Ira Thomas, C, 1908
Jason Thompson, IF, 1976–1980
Justin Thompson, LHP, 1996–1999
Sam Thompson, OF, 1906
Tim Thompson, C, 1958
Gary Thurman, OF, 1993
Mark Thurmond, LHP, 1986–1987
Tom Timmermann, RHP, 1969–1973
Ron Tingley, C, 1995
Dave Tobik, RHP, 1978–1982
Jim Tobin, RHP, 1945
Kevin Tolar, LHP, 2000–2001
Tim Tolman, OF, 1986–1987
Andy Tomberlin, OF, 1998
Earl Torgeson, IF, 1955–1957
Andrés Torres, OF, 2002–2004
Carlos Torres, RHP, 2019
Dick Tracewski, IF, 1966–1969
Alan Trammell, IF, 1977–1996
Bubba Trammell, OF, 1997
Allan Travers, RHP, 1912
Tom Tresh, OF, 1969
Matt Treanor, C, 2009
Gus Triandos, C, 1963
Dizzy Trout, RHP, 1939–1952
Bun Troy, RHP, 1912
Chris Truby, IF, 2002
Virgil Trucks, RHP, 1941–1943, 1945-1952, 1956
Mike Trujillo, RHP, 1988–1989
John Tsitouris, RHP, 1957
Matt Tuiasosopo, OF-INF-DH, 2013
Spencer Turnbull, RHP, 2018–2021
Jacob Turner, RHP, 2011–2012, 2018
Jerry Turner, OF, 1982
Bill Tuttle, OF, 1952–1957
Guy Tutwiler, IF, 1911–1913
Bob Uhl, RHP, 1940
George Uhle, RHP, 1929–1933
Jerry Ujdur, RHP, 1980–1983
Pat Underwood, LHP, 1979–1983
Al Unser, C, 1942–1944
Justin Upton, OF, 2016–2017
Tom Urbani, LHP, 1996
Ugueth Urbina, RHP, 2004–2005
Urena, Jose, RHP, 2021
Lino Urdaneta, RHP, 2004
José Valdez, RHP, 2015–2016
Vito Valentinetti, RHP, 1958
José Valverde, RHP, 2010–2013
Andy Van Hekken, LHP, 2002–2004
Todd Van Poppel, RHP, 1996
Elam Vangilder, RHP, 1928–1929
Virgil Vasquez, RHP, 2007
Bobby Veach, OF, 1912–1923
Coot Veal, IF, 1958–1960, 1963
Lou Vedder, RHP, 1920
José Veras, RHP, 2013
Randy Veres, RHP, 1996
Drew VerHagen, RHP, 2014–2019
Justin Verlander, RHP, 2005–2017
Tom Veryzer, IF, 1973–1977
George Vico, IF, 1948–1949
Brandon Villafuerte, RHP, 2000
Brayan Villarreal, RHP, 2011–2013
Fernando Vina, IF, 2004
Ozzie Virgil, IF, 1958–1961
Joe Vitiello, DH, 2004
Ossie Vitt, IF, 1912–1918
Jake Wade, LHP, 1936–1938
Hal Wagner, C, 1947–1948
Mark Wagner, IF, 1976–1980
Dick Wakefield, OF, 1941–1949
Chris Wakeland, OF, 2001
Matt Walbeck, C, 1996–97, 2002–03
Jim Walewander, IF, 1987–1988
Dixie Walker, OF, 1938–1939
Frank Walker, OF, 1917–1918
Gee Walker, OF, 1931–1937
Hub Walker, OF, 1931, 1935, 1945
Jamie Walker, LHP, 2002–2006
Luke Walker, LHP, 1974
Mike Walker, RHP, 1996
Tom Walker, RHP, 1975
Jim H. Walkup, LHP, 1927
Jim E. Walkup, RHP, 1939
Jim Walsh, LHP, 1921
Steve Wapnick, RHP, 1990
Gary Ward, OF, 1989–1990
Hap Ward, OF, 1912
Jon Warden, LHP, 1968
Jack Warner, IF, 1925–1928
John Warner, C, 1905–1906
Jarrod Washburn, LHP, 2009
Johnny Watson, IF, 1930
Jeff Weaver, RHP, 1999–2002
Jim Weaver, OF, 1985
Roger Weaver, RHP, 1980
Earl Webb, OF, 1932–1933
Skeeter Webb, IF, 1945–1947
Thad Weber, RHP, 2012
Herm Wehmeier, RHP, 1958
Dick Weik, RHP, 1953–1954
Robbie Weinhardt, RHP, 2010–2011
Milt Welch, C, 1945
Casper Wells, OF, 2010–2011
David Wells, LHP, 1993–1995
Ed Wells, LHP, 1923–1927
Don Wert, IF, 1963–1970
Vic Wertz, OF, 1947–52, 1961–63
Charlie Wheatley, RHP, 1912
Kevin Whelan, RHP, 2014
Jack Whillock, RHP, 1971
Lou Whitaker, IF, 1977–1995
Derrick White, IF, 1995
Hal White, RHP, 1941–43, 1946-52
Jo-Jo White, OF, 1932–1938
Rondell White, OF, 2004–2005
Earl Whitehill, LHP, 1923–1932
Sean Whiteside, LHP, 1995
Kevin Wickander, LHP, 1995
Dave Wickersham, RHP, 1964–1967
Jimmy Wiggs, RHP, 1905–1906
Bill Wight, LHP, 1952–1953
Milt Wilcox, RHP, 1977–1985
Adam Wilk, LHP, 2011–2012
Ed Willett, RHP, 1906–1913
Brian Williams, RHP, 1996
Eddie Williams, IF, 1996
Frank Williams, RHP, 1989
Johnnie Williams, RHP, 1914
Kenny Williams, OF, 1989–1990
Lefty Williams, LHP, 1913–1914
Carl Willis, RHP, 1984
Dontrelle Willis, LHP, 2008–2010
Alex Wilson, RHP, 2015–2018
Bobby Wilson, C, 2016, 2019
Earl Wilson, RHP, 1966–1970
Glenn Wilson, OF, 1982–1983
Josh Wilson, IF, 2015
Icehouse Wilson, PH, 1934
Jack Wilson, RHP, 1942
Justin Wilson, LHP, 2016–2017
Mutt Wilson, RHP, 1920
Red Wilson, C, 1954–1960
Squanto Wilson, C, 1911
Vance Wilson, C, 2005–2006
Walter Wilson, RHP, 1945
Al Wingo, OF, 1924–1928
George Winter, RHP, 1908
Casey Wise, IF, 1960
Hughie Wise, C, 1930
Kevin Witt, DH, 2003
John Wockenfuss, C-IB-OF, 1974–1983
Pete Wojey, RHP, 1956–1957
Randy Wolf, LHP, 2015
Bob Wood, C, 1904–1905
Jake Wood, IF, 1961–1967
Jason Wood, IF, 1998–1999
Joe Wood, IF, 1943
Larry Woodall, C, 1920–1929
Hal Woodeshick, LHP, 1956, 1961
Ron Woods, OF, 1969
Mark Woodyard, RHP, 2005–2006
Danny Worth, OF, 2010–2014
Ralph Works, RHP, 1909–1912
Tim Worrell, RHP, 1998
Yats Wuestling, IF, 1929–1930
John Wyatt, RHP, 1968
Whit Wyatt, RHP, 1929–1933
Esteban Yan, RHP, 2004
Emil Yde, LHP, 1929
Joe Yeager, IF, 1901–1903
Archie Yelle, C, 1917–1919
Tom Yewcic, C, 1957
Rudy York, IF, 1934–1945
Eddie Yost, IF, 1959–1960
Delmon Young, OF, 2011–2012
Dmitri Young, OF, 2002–2006
Ernie Young, OF, 2003
John Young, IF, 1971
Matt Young, OF, 2012
Kip Young, RHP, 1978–1979
Ralph Young, IF, 1915–1921
Chris Zachary, RHP, 1972
Carl Zamloch, RHP, 1913
Bill Zepp, RHP, 1971
Gus Zernial, OF, 1958–1959
Jordan Zimmermann, RHP, 2016–2020
Joel Zumaya, RHP, 2006–2010
George Zuverink, RHP, 1954–1955

TIGER PLAYERS WHO MANAGED IN THE MAJOR LEAGUES
(BOLD INDICATES MEMBER OF NATIONAL BASEBALL HALL OF FAME)

Brad Ausmus	Detroit (AL) 2014-2017 Los Angeles (AL) 2019
Del Baker	Detroit (AL) 1933, 1936-1942 Boston (AL) 1960
Steve Boros	Oakland (AL) 1983-1984 San Diego (NL) 1986
Donie Bush	Washington (AL) 1923 Pittsburgh (NL) 1927-1929 Chicago (AL) 1930-1931 Cincinnati (NL) 1933
Ty Cobb	Detroit (AL) 1921-1926

Ty Cobb resting on baseball field, holding a baseball bat.

Mickey Cochrane	Detroit (AL) 1934-1938
Jack Coombs	Philadelphia (NL) 1919
Red Corriden	Chicago (AL) 1950
Chuck Cottier	Seattle (AL) 1984-1986
Lary Doby	Chicago (AL) 1978
Bill Donovan	New York (AL) 1915-1917 Philadelphia (NL) 1921
Kid Elberfeld	New York (AL) 1908
John Farrell	Toronto (AL) 2011-2012 Boston (AL) 2013-2017
Doc Gessler	Pittsburgh (FL) 1914
Kirk Gibson	Arizona (NL) 2010-2014
Kid Gleason	Chicago (AL) 1919-1923
Fred Haney	St. Louis (AL) 1939-1941 Pittsburgh (NL) 1953-1955 Milwaukee (NL) 1956-1959
Bucky Harris	Washington (AL) 1924-1928, 1935-1942, 1950-1954 Detroit (AL) 1929-1933, 1955-56 Boston (AL) 1934 Philadelphia (NL) 1943 New York (AL) 1947-1948
Don Heffner	Cincinnati (NL) 1966
Whitey Herzog	Texas (AL) 1973 California (AL) 1974 Kansas City (AL) 1975-1979 St. Louis (NL) 1980-1990
Pinky Higgins	Boston (AL) 1955-1962
A.J. Hinch	Arizona (NL) 2009-2010 Houston (AL) 2015-2019 Detroit (AL) 2021
Billy Hitchcock	Detroit (AL) 1960 Baltimore (AL) 1962-1963 Atlanta (NL) 1966-1967
Frank Howard	San Diego (NL) 1981 New York (NL) 1983
Fred Hutchinson	Detroit (AL) 1952-1954 St. Louis (NL) 1956-1958 Cincinnati (NL) 1959-1964
Hughie Jennings	Detroit (AL) 1907-1920 New York (NL) 1924-1925
Gabe Kapler	Philadelphia (NL) 2018-2019 San Francisco (NL) 2020-2021
Bob Kennedy	Chicago (NL) 1963-1965 Oakland (AL) 1968
Bruce Kimm	Chicago (NL) 2002
Ray Knight	Cincinnati (NL) 1996-1997, 2003

Harvey Kuenn	Milwaukee (AL) 1975, 1982-1983
Gene Lamont	Chicago (AL) 1992-1995 Pittsburgh (NL) 1997-2000
Johnny Lipon	Cleveland (AL) 1971
Torey Lovullo	Arizona (NL) 2017-2021
Bobby Lowe	Detroit (AL) 1904
Jerry Manuel	Chicago (AL) 1998-2003 New York (NL) 2008-2010
Billy Martin	Minnesota (AL) 1969 Detroit (AL) 1971-1973 Texas (AL) 1973-1975 New York (AL) 1975-1979, 1983, 1985, 1988 Oakland (AL) 1980-1982
Eddie Mathews	Atlanta (NL) 1972-1974
Deacon McGuire	Washington (NL) 1898 Boston (AL) 1907-1908 Cleveland (AL) 1909-1911

Boston Red Sox manager Deacon McGuire standing on field.

Marty McManus	Boston (AL) 1932-1933
Bob Melvin	Seattle (AL) 2003-2004 Arizona (NL) 2005-2009 Oakland (AL) 2011-2021
Charlie Metro	Chicago (NL) 1962 Kansas City (AL) 1970
Gene Michael	New York (AL) 1981-1982 Chicago (NL) 1986-1987
Jackie Moore	Oakland (AL) 1984-1986
George Moriarty	Detroit (AL) 1927-1928
Johnny Neun	New York (AL) 1946 Cincinnati (NL) 1947-1948
Jack Onslow	Chicago (AL) 1949-1950
Salty Parker	New York (NL) 1967 Houston (NL) 1972
Al Pedrique	Arizona (NL) 2004
Cy Perkins	Detroit (AL) 1937
Johnny Pesky	Boston (AL) 1963-1964, 1980
Phil Regan	Baltimore (AL) 1995
Paul Richards	Chicago (AL) 1951-1954, 1976 Baltimore (AL) 1955-1961
Larry Rothschild	Tampa Bay (AL) 1998-2001
Muddy Ruel	St. Louis (AL) 1947
Juan Samuel	Baltimore (AL) 2010
Heinie Smith	New York (NL) 1902
Billy Sullivan	Chicago (AL) 1909
Bob Swift	Detroit (AL) 1965-1966
Birdie Tebbetts	Cincinnati (NL) 1954-1958 Milwaukee (NL) 1961-1962 Cleveland (AL) 1963-1966
Dick Tracewski	Detroit (AL) 1979
Alan Trammell	Detroit (AL) 2003-2005 Arizona (NL) 2014
Ossie Vitt	Cleveland (AL) 1938-1940
Jo-Jo White	Cleveland (AL) 1960
Rudy York	Boston (AL) 1959
Eddie Yost	Washington (AL) 1963

TIGER BROADCASTERS
(BOLD INDICATES MEMBER OF MICHIGAN SPORTS HALL OF FAME)

Radio

- **Ty Tyson** (1927–1942, 1951)
- **Harry Heilmann** (1934–1950)
- Paul Williams (1951)
- **Van Patrick** (1952–1959)
- Dizzy Trout (1953–1955)
- Mel Ott (1956–1958)
- **George Kell** (1959–1963)
- **Ernie Harwell** (1960–1991, 1993, 1999–2002)
- Bob Scheffing (1964)
- Gene Osborn (1965–1966)
- **Ray Lane** (1967–1972)
- **Paul Carey** (1973–1991)
- Bob Rathbun (1992–1994)
- Rick Rizzs (1992–1994)
- **Frank Beckmann** (1995–1998)
- Lary Sorensen (1995–1998)
- Jim Price (1998-2021)
- Dan Dickerson (2000-2021)
- **Al Kaline** (2009)
- John Keating (2009)
- Dan Petry (2012)

The legendary tandem of Ernie Harwell, play by play, and Paul Carey, color commentator, were inducted into the Michigan Sports Hall of Fame. The duo covered the team on the Detroit Tigers Radio Network for 19 major league seasons 1973-1991.

Television

- **Ty Tyson** (1947–1952)
- Paul Williams (1947-1952
- **Harry Heilmann** (1947–1950)
- **Van Patrick** (1953–1959)
- Dizzy Trout (1953–1955)
- Mel Ott (1956–1958)
- **George Kell** (1959–1963, 1965–1996)
- **Ernie Harwell** (1960–1964, 1994–1998)
- Bob Scheffing (1964)
- **Ray Lane** (1965–1966, 1999–2003)
- Larry Osterman (1967–1977, 1984–1992)
- Don Kremer (1975–1976)
- **Al Kaline** (1976–2001)
- Joe Pellegrino (1977–1978)
- Mike Barry (1978–1979)
- Larry Adderley (1981–1983)
- Hank Aguirre (1981–1983)
- **Norm Cash** (1981–1983)
- **Bill Freehan** (1984–1985)
- **Jim Northrup** (1985–1994)
- Jim Price (1993–1997)
- Fred McLeod (1995–1997)
- Josh Lewin (1998–2001)
- **Frank Beckmann** (1999–2003)
- **Kirk Gibson** (1998-2002, 2015-2021)
- Tom Paciorek (2000)
- **Lance Parrish** (2002)
- Mario Impemba (2002-2018)
- Rod Allen (2003-2018)
- **Jack Morris** (2003, 2014-2016, 2018-2021)
- Matt Shepard (2018-2021)

STADIUMS

Bennett Park
Northwest corner of Michigan Avenue and Trumbull Avenue, Detroit, Michigan
Tuesday, 28 April 1896 – Sunday, 10 September 1911
Capacity: 14,000
Dimensions: Left field - 285', Left-center field – 420', Center field – 390', Right-center field – 326', Right field – 315'

Burns Park (Sunday home games)
Southwest corner of Toledo Avenue and Waterman Avenue, Springwells Township, Michigan
Sunday, 6 May 1900 – Sunday, 7 September 1902
Capacity: 3,500

Navin Field 1912-1937 Briggs Stadium 1938-1960, Tiger Stadium 1961-1999
2121 Trumbull Avenue, Detroit, Michigan 48216
Saturday, 20 April 1912 – Monday, 27 September 1999
Capacity: 46,945 at closing (Highest 58,000 1938-1960)
Dimensions: Left field - 230', Left-center field – 365', Center field – 440', Right-center field – 370', Right field – 325'

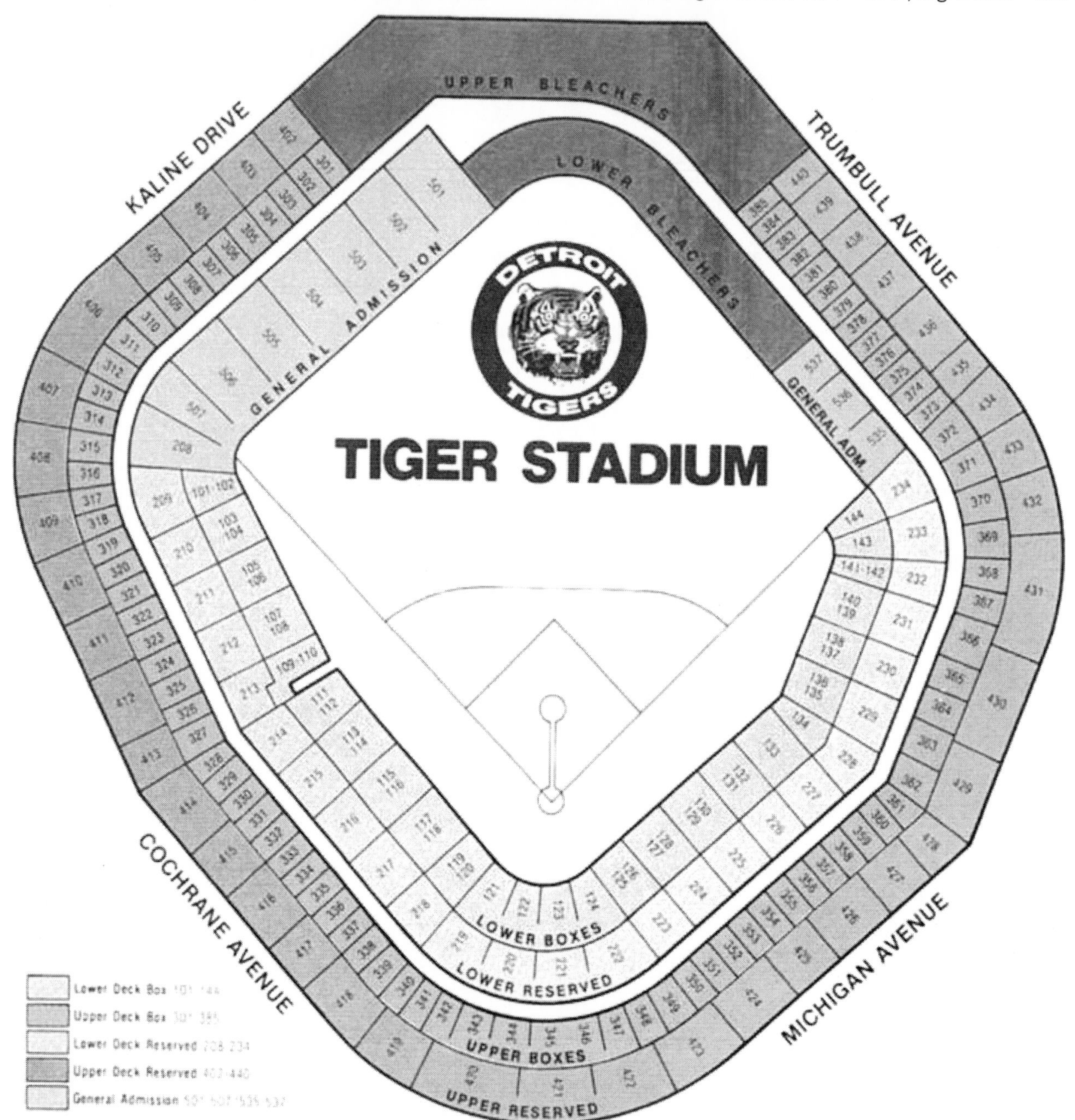

Comerica Park 1999-Present
2100 Woodward Avenue, Detroit, Michigan 48216
Thursday, 20 April 2000 - Present
Capacity: 41,083 (Highest 41,681 2014)
Dimensions: Left field - 345', Left-center field – 370', Center field – 420', Right-center field – 365', Right field – 330'

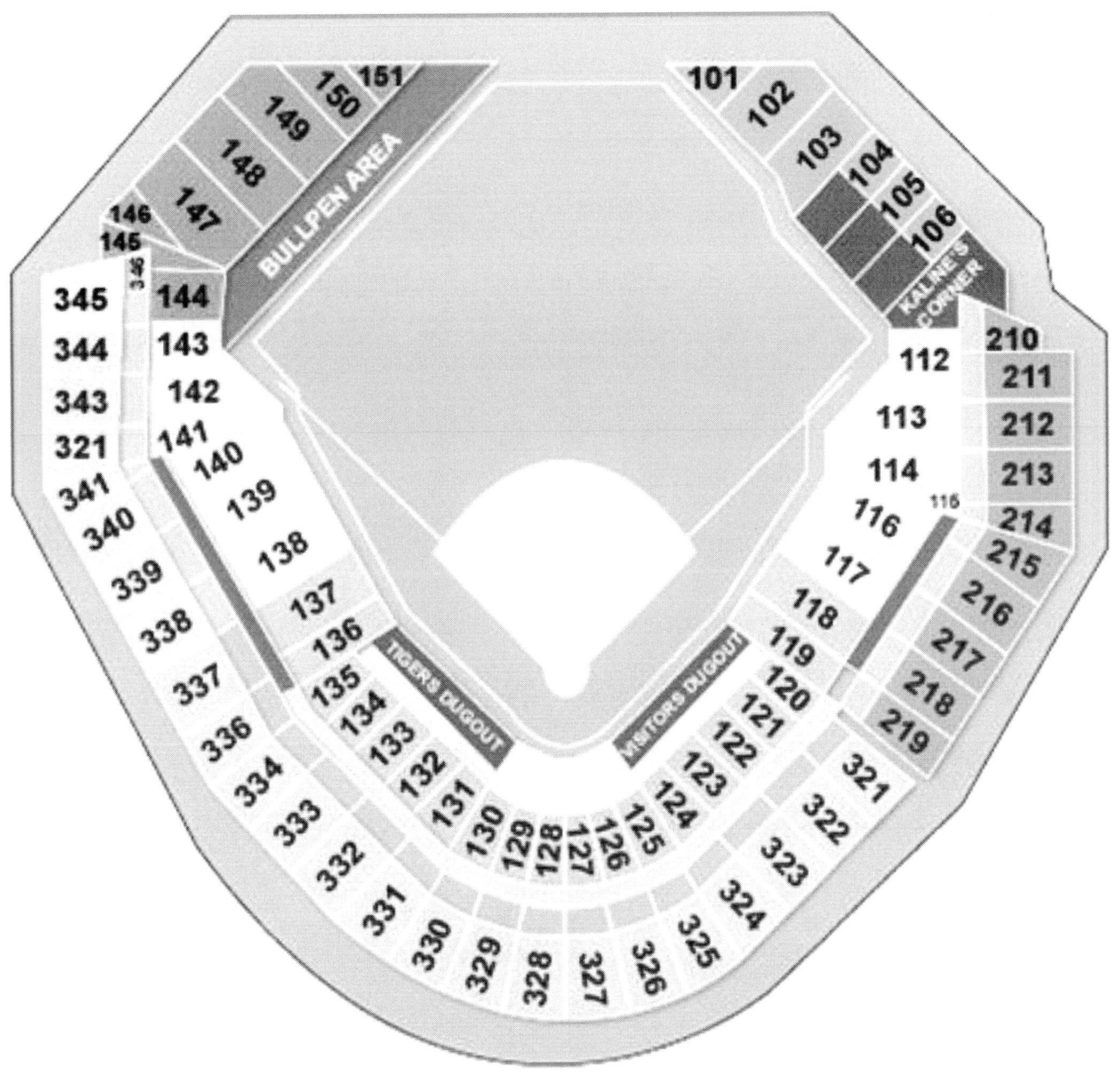

Did You Know?

Brian Moehler won the last game at Tiger Stadium and first in Comerica Park. Moehler (6 IP, 2 ER, 5 SO) led an 8-2 win against Kansas City on Monday, September 27, 1999, with 43,356 fans. Luis Polonia, Karim Garcia, and Robert Fick (5 RBI) hit home runs. Damion Easley went 3-for-3, with Fick's bomb the 30th to reach the right field roof and 11,111 homer in stadium history, as Michigander Rocky Roe from Southfield and Eastern Michigan University was the Homeplate umpire. Moehler (6 IP, 1 ER) took the mound for a 5-2 victory over Seattle on Tuesday, April 11, 2000, with 39,168 fans. Free-agent signee Greg Jefferies went 2-for-4 (2 RBI) in his home debut, with triples by Bobby Higginson (2 RBI) and Polonia. Michigan native Rick Reed of Detroit and Eastern Michigan University was home plate umpire in the Comerica Park opener.

Joker Marchant Stadium 1966-Present
2301 Lakeland Hills Boulevard, Lakeland, Florida 33805
Saturday, 12 March 1966 - Present
Capacity: 8,500 (Highest 41,681 2014)
Dimensions: Left field - 340', Center field – 420', Right field – 340'

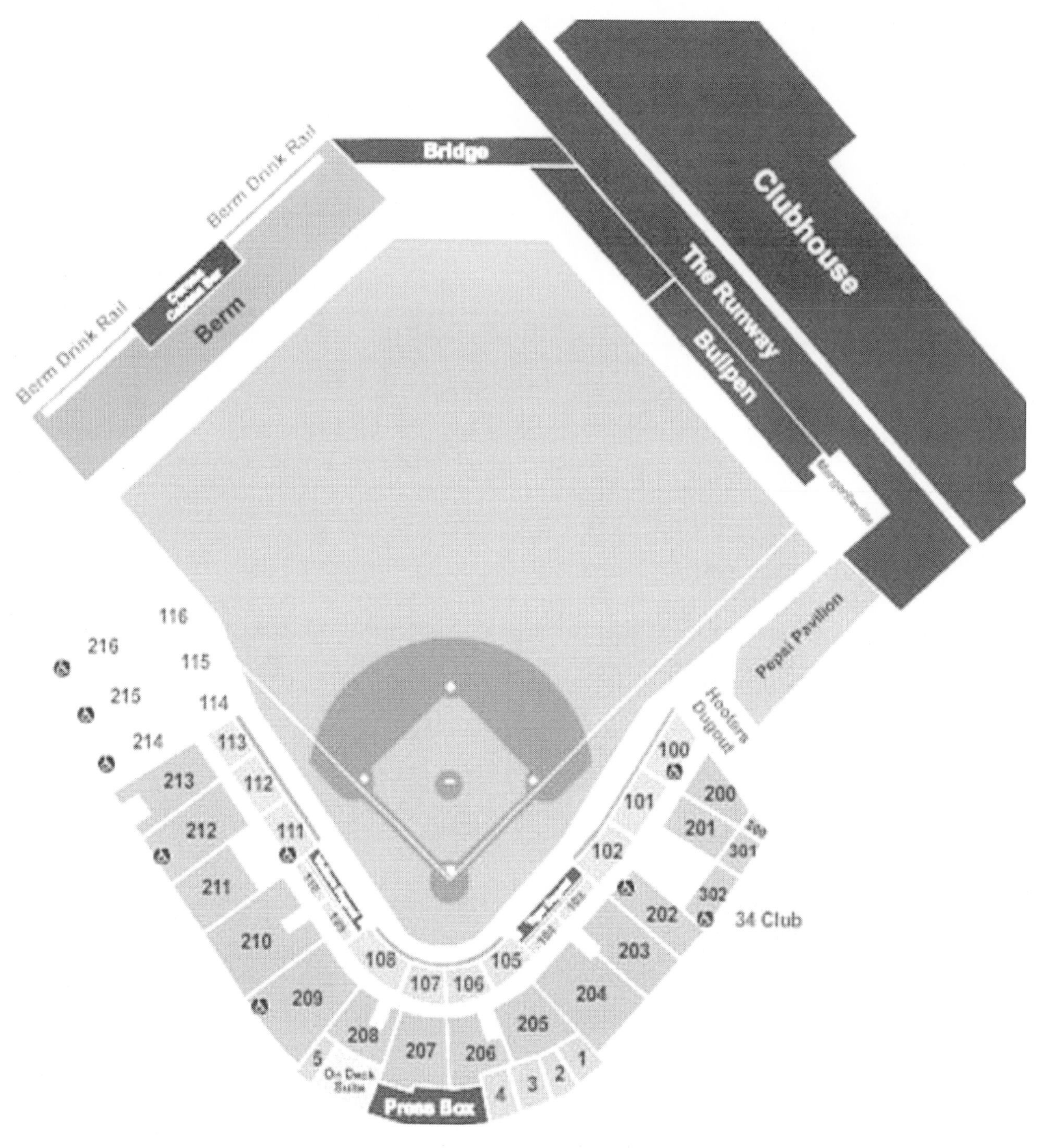

SPRING TRAINING SITES

1901	Detroit, Michigan	1913-1915	Gulfport, Mississippi	1931	Sacramento, California
1902	Ypsilanti, Michigan	1916-1918	Waxahachie, Texas	1932	Palo Alto, California
1903-1904	Shreveport, Louisiana	1919-1920	Macon, Georgia	1933	San Antonio, Texas
1905-1907	Augusta, Georgia	1921	San Antonio, Texas	1934-1943	Lakeland, Florida
1908	Hot Springs, Arkansas	1922-1926	Augusta, Georgia	1943-1945	Evansville, Florida
1909-1910	San Antonio, Texas	1927-1928	San Antonio, Texas	1946-2019	Lakeland, Florida
1911-1912	Monroe, Louisiana	1929	Phoenix, Arizona	2020	Detroit, Michigan
		1930	Tampa, Florida	2021	Lakeland, Florida

ALL-TIME TIGER FIRST TEAM
MANAGER: MICKEY COCHRANE 1934-1938 (348-250 .582) WORLD CHAMPIONS IN 1935, LOST WORLD SERIES IN 1934
BOLD INDICATES CATEGORY LEADER BY POSITION

POS	PITCHERS	W%	TRA	ERA	ERA+	FIP	DICE	WHIP	H/9	HR/9	BB/9	SO/9	SO/BB	RA/9	LOB%
SP	DOUG FISTER	.615	3.74	3.29	128	3.20	**3.13**	1.191	8.97	0.67	1.76	7.21	**4.10**	3.74	72.9
	MAX SCHERZER	**.701**	3.73	3.52	117	3.32	3.24	1.197	8.07	0.96	2.71	**9.60**	3.54	3.73	75.4
	JUSTIN VERLANDER	.616	3.79	3.49	123	3.48	3.37	1.191	7.97	0.86	2.75	8.51	3.10	3.79	73.7
	DENNY MCLAIN	.654	3.42	3.13	110	3.55	4.04	**1.112**	**7.46**	1.10	2.54	6.50	2.56	3.42	**78.2**
	HARRY COVELESKI	.616	3.39	**2.34**	123	2.67	3.29	1.131	7.80	0.11	2.37	3.52	1.48	3.39	68.9
	EARL WILSON	.587	3.51	3.18	107	3.46	3.95	1.170	7.76	1.01	2.77	6.63	2.40	3.51	77.3
	BILL DONOVAN	.593	3.38	2.49	109	**2.62**	3.21	1.192	7.84	0.11	2.88	4.54	1.58	3.38	70.3
RP	JOAQUIN BENOIT	.650	3.08	2.89	145	3.39	3.34	**1.075**	6.92	1.09	2.76	9.95	3.61	3.08	81.3
	FRED GLADDING	.703	2.96	2.70	132	3.32	3.77	1.231	7.58	0.72	3.50	7.00	2.00	2.96	81.2
	WILLIE HERNANDEZ	.537	3.26	2.98	135	3.52	3.76	1.121	7.52	0.97	2.57	7.15	2.78	3.26	78.9
	DOUG BROCAIL	.548	3.36	3.06	155	3.68	3.55	1.211	7.84	0.79	3.06	7.70	2.52	3.36	77.7
	AL ALBURQUERQUE	**.739**	3.20	3.20	127	3.34	3.24	1.33	7.00	0.64	5.00	**11.04**	2.21	3.20	79.8
	JUSTIN WILSON	.438	3.73	3.55	123	3.20	**3.05**	1.172	7.55	1.00	3.00	10.91	**3.64**	3.73	74.8
	JOHN HILLER	.534	3.17	2.83	134	3.39	3.80	1.268	7.54	0.80	3.88	7.51	1.94	3.17	80.2

POS	POSITION PLAYERS	OBP	SLG	OPS	OPS+	TA	BOP	GPA	BA	BABIP	SECA	IP%	RS%	TBA	BPA
C	MICKEY COCHRANE	**.444**	.430	**.874**	126	**.975**	**.975**	**.307**	**.313**	.324	.349	74.31	**35.81**	1.46	2.29
	MICKEY TETTLETON	.387	**.480**	.867	**135**	.923	.924	.294	.249	.277	**.453**	55.01	24.06	1.59	**2.35**
	LANCE PARRISH	.317	.469	.786	114	.722	.726	.260	.263	.280	.283	69.51	28.88	**1.75**	2.06
1B	HANK GREENBERG	**.412**	**.616**	**1.028**	**161**	**1.128**	**1.127**	**.339**	.319	.329	**.460**	66.46	33.75	**2.33**	**2.96**
	MIGUEL CABRERA	.387	.529	.916	145	.912	.913	.306	.309	.336	.348	66.89	25.61	1.96	2.45
	DALE ALEXANDER	.391	.512	.903	129	.908	.911	.304	**.331**	**.344**	.273	79.20	31.54	1.93	2.33
2B	CHARLIE GEHRINGER	**.404**	**.480**	**.884**	124	**.924**	**.926**	**.302**	**.320**	.320	**.304**	81.06	**40.89**	**1.83**	**2.42**
	JIM DELAHANTY	.394	.399	.793	**129**	.829	.837	.277	.306	**.332**	.242	76.69	34.73	1.42	1.97
	LOU WHITAKER	.363	.426	.789	117	.781	.787	.270	.276	.290	.297	73.42	34.17	1.53	2.09
SS	CARLOS GUILLEN	.366	**.476**	**.842**	**121**	**.822**	**.825**	**.284**	.297	**.326**	**.297**	72.34	32.78	1.75	**2.23**
	HARVEY KUENN	.360	.426	.786	112	.717	.721	.268	**.314**	.319	.187	**87.20**	34.32	**1.77**	2.13
	ALAN TRAMMELL	.352	.415	.767	110	.738	.746	.262	.285	.298	.248	77.91	34.10	1.50	1.97
3B	RAY BOONE	.372	**.482**	**.854**	**130**	.835	.839	.288	.291	.288	.319	75.23	25.79	**1.75**	2.23
	GEORGE KELL	.391	.433	.824	119	.775	.782	.284	**.325**	.331	.212	**84.90**	34.00	1.73	2.18
	EDDIE YOST	**.425**	.417	.842	127	**.937**	**.938**	**.296**	.269	.284	**.412**	64.30	30.44	1.46	**2.40**
LF	GOOSE GOSLIN	.376	.456	.832	111	.838	.839	.283	.297	.301	.287	79.87	**37.87**	1.70	2.21
	ROCKY COLAVITO	.364	**.501**	**.865**	130	**.862**	**.864**	.289	.271	.257	**.378**	70.58	28.03	**1.86**	**2.42**
	BOB FOTHERGILL	.379	.482	.861	122	.828	.836	**.291**	**.337**	**.350**	.203	**84.66**	36.72	1.47	1.70
CF	TY COBB	**.434**	**.516**	**.950**	**171**	**1.099**	**1.096**	**.324**	**.368**	**.385**	.320	81.04	39.31	**1.95**	**2.67**
	HEINIE MANUSH	.379	.475	.853	120	.853	.861	.289	.321	.329	.235	81.24	**41.93**	1.62	1.94
	BARNEY MCCOSKY	.386	.434	.820	110	.811	.815	.282	.312	.329	.254	**81.31**	38.46	1.74	2.30
RF	HARRY HEILMANN	.410	.518	**.927**	**149**	**.971**	**.972**	**.314**	**.342**	.352	.290	79.04	33.01	1.90	2.35
	J.D. MARTINEZ	.361	**.551**	.912	147	.905	.906	.300	.300	**.363**	.349	59.86	27.15	**2.04**	**2.42**
	AL KALINE	.376	.480	.855	134	.849	.852	.289	.297	.296	.316	75.90	31.04	1.71	2.21
DH	CHAMP SUMMERS	**.388**	**.508**	**.896**	**143**	**.927**	**.928**	**.302**	.293	.301	.364	68.09	27.63	1.41	1.85
	DMITRI YOUNG	.340	.486	.826	120	.776	.778	.274	.279	**.311**	.289	67.97	29.37	**1.79**	2.10
UT	TONY PHILLIPS	**.395**	.405	**.800**	**120**	**.831**	**.834**	**.279**	.281	**.319**	**.324**	67.11	35.48	1.54	**2.36**
	MARTY MCMANUS	.359	.434	.793	103	.785	.793	.270	**.287**	.295	.266	79.48	34.55	**1.57**	2.07

ALL-TIME TIGER SECOND TEAM

MANAGER: MAYO SMITH 1967-1970 (363-285 .560) WORLD CHAMPIONS IN 1968

BOLD INDICATES CATEGORY LEADER BY POSITION

POS	PITCHERS	W%	TRA	ERA	ERA+	FIP	DICE	WHIP	H/9	HR/9	BB/9	SO/9	SO/BB	RA/9	LOB%
	MARK FIDRYCH	.604	3.56	3.10	126	3.33	3.66	1.203	8.67	0.50	2.16	3.71	1.72	3.56	72.2
	MICKEY LOLICH	.542	3.79	3.45	105	3.19	3.66	1.222	8.28	0.88	2.71	7.17	2.64	3.79	74.5
	ED SUMMERS	.602	3.64	2.42	111	2.64	3.32	1.152	8.38	0.17	1.99	3.26	1.64	3.64	67.8
SP	JIM BUNNING	.576	3.84	3.45	116	3.59	4.07	1.208	8.15	1.07	2.72	6.78	2.49	3.84	76.0
	HAL NEWHOUSER	.575	3.61	3.07	130	3.18	3.65	1.313	8.07	0.41	3.75	5.41	1.44	3.61	73.1
	ED KILLIAN	.575	**3.29**	2.38	109	2.78	3.46	1.218	8.21	**0.05**	2.75	2.92	1.06	**3.29**	71.5
	DON MOSSI	.573	3.94	3.49	116	3.59	4.03	1.174	8.81	1.06	**1.75**	5.03	2.87	3.94	73.3
	BRANDON LYON	.545	2.86	2.86	158	4.06	3.97	1.106	6.41	0.80	3.55	6.52	1.84	2.86	80.8
	DREW SMYLY	.571	3.75	3.53	116	3.51	3.42	1.236	8.53	0.96	2.60	8.47	3.26	3.75	75.7
	MIKE HENNEMAN	.626	3.58	3.05	136	3.40	3.54	1.305	8.39	0.54	0.36	6.45	1.92	3.58	74.9
RP	ALEX WILSON	.478	3.50	3.20	135	3.87	3.72	1.164	8.37	0.85	2.11	5.85	2.77	3.50	75.8
	KEVIN SAUCIER	.700	**2.62**	**2.32**	**170**	3.68	4.03	1.243	**6.15**	0.10	5.04	4.63	0.92	**2.62**	78.9
	TERRY FOX	.605	3.19	2.77	137	3.77	4.22	1.211	8.26	0.81	2.64	4.13	1.56	3.19	79.5
	JOEL ZUMAYA	.520	3.43	3.05	147	3.94	3.80	1.350	7.26	0.77	4.89	9.01	1.84	3.43	79.1

POS	POSITION PLAYERS	OBP	SLG	OPS	OPS+	TA	BOP	GPA	BA	BABIP	SECA	IP%	RS%	TBA	BPA
	IVAN RODRIGUEZ	.328	.449	.777	103	.689	.694	.260	.298	**.337**	.203	76.06	31.23	**1.75**	1.97
C	MATT NOKES	.322	.458	.780	115	.711	.716	.259	.268	.269	.264	74.16	24.00	1.45	1.68
	ALEX AVILA	.350	.404	.754	106	.730	.734	.258	.245	.323	.319	55.74	22.95	1.23	1.72
	RUDY YORK	.369	.503	.873	128	.869	.870	.292	.282	.286	.361	70.37	28.84	1.86	2.39
1B	PRINCE FIELDER	.387	.491	.878	136	.877	.879	.297	.295	.314	.329	68.47	22.59	1.83	2.33
	TONY CLARK	.355	.502	.857	121	.837	.839	.285	.277	.317	.345	61.61	27.67	1.84	2.29
	IAN KINSLER	.328	.436	.764	108	.715	.718	.256	.275	.294	.243	76.20	40.22	1.78	2.15
2B	PLACIDO POLANCO	.355	.418	.773	103	.697	.703	.264	.311	.319	.169	**85.46**	37.24	1.71	1.98
	DAMION EASLEY	.339	.428	.767	101	.748	.752	.260	.260	.286	.279	69.62	32.53	1.57	2.02
	TOPPER RIGNEY	**.389**	.393	.782	105	.788	.805	.273	.296	.318	.253	75.22	30.82	1.32	1.89
SS	BILLY ROGELL	.362	.381	.742	89	.725	.731	.258	.274	.288	.246	79.78	35.49	1.39	1.95
	JHONNY PERALTA	.332	.433	.764	106	.691	.696	.257	.275	.312	.242	70.99	26.07	1.58	1.91
	TRAVIS FRYMAN	.334	.444	.779	106	.737	.743	.262	.274	.313	.269	68.36	31.63	1.74	2.15
3B	NICK CASTELLANOS	.324	.459	.783	110	.722	.725	.260	.274	**.333**	.256	66.62	26.02	1.73	2.01
	JEIMER CANDELARIO	.336	.415	.751	104	.773	.771	.255	.249	.311	.329	61.91	29.95	1.52	2.12
	DICK WAKEFIELD	.396	.447	.843	**131**	.842	.843	.290	.293	.315	.319	72.16	29.92	1.51	2.09
LF	BOBBY VEACH	.370	.444	.814	130	.811	.822	.278	.311	.323	.237	81.99	34.00	1.65	2.09
	JOHN STONE	.362	.460	.822	110	.792	.795	.278	.303	.319	.244	80.96	36.69	1.73	2.11
	CURTIS GRANDERSON	.344	.484	.828	114	.838	.840	.276	.272	.321	**.337**	64.57	37.50	1.85	2.36
CF	HOOT EVERS	.368	.436	.803	112	.760	.765	.274	.290	.302	.264	77.32	32.64	1.54	2.00
	RON LEFLORE	.348	.406	.754	108	.769	.772	.258	.297	.353	.246	73.14	40.59	1.68	2.38
	KIRK GIBSON	.354	.480	.834	125	.872	.875	.279	.273	.306	.358	64.70	33.83	1.70	2.29
RF	MAGLIO ORDONEZ	.373	.476	.849	123	.802	.805	.287	.312	.330	.264	75.70	28.49	1.78	2.17
	GEE WALKER	.351	.469	.820	108	.808	.811	.275	.317	.331	.225	**84.32**	38.97	1.80	2.14
DH	LUIS POLONIA	.343	.477	.819	109	.805	.811	.273	**.302**	.309	.257	81.78	32.52	1.71	2.09
	JOHNNY GRUBB	.373	.446	.819	125	.827	.830	.279	.269	.279	.342	68.80	22.96	0.98	1.34
UT	JOHN WOCKENFUSS	.346	**.439**	.785	116	.747	.750	.266	.261	.263	.303	72.74	25.50	1.20	1.56
	RYAN RABURN	.311	.430	.740	96	.676	.681	.247	.256	.314	.250	64.69	35.43	1.19	1.42

ALL-TIME TIGER THIRD TEAM
MANAGER: STEVE O'NEILL 1943-1948 (509-414 .551) WORLD CHAMPIONS IN 1945
BOLD INDICATES CATEGORY LEADER BY POSITION

POS	PITCHERS	W%	TRA	ERA	ERA+	FIP	DICE	WHIP	H/9	HR/9	BB/9	SO/9	SO/BB	RA/9	LOB%
SP	WILLIE MITCHELL	.556	3.57	2.83	98	2.77	3.47	1.255	8.33	0.14	2.97	3.97	1.34	3.57	71.0
	DAVE WICKERSHAM	.541	3.90	3.40	104	3.67	4.11	1.248	8.18	0.80	3.05	5.46	1.79	3.90	73.7
	DAVID WELLS	.578	4.22	3.78	122	4.19	4.13	1.211	8.73	1.18	2.16	6.15	2.84	4.22	72.9
	DAVE ROZEMA	.553	3.90	3.38	120	3.99	4.29	1.230	8.99	0.91	2.08	3.60	1.73	3.90	73.9
	FRANK LARY	.528	3.96	3.46	116	3.62	4.14	1.271	8.85	0.81	2.59	4.62	1.78	3.96	73.6
	ED SIEVER	.531	4.00	2.61	121	2.80	3.29	1.233	9.30	0.13	1.80	2.63	1.46	4.00	65.9
	GEORGE MULLIN	.539	3.92	2.76	102	2.86	3.41	1.270	8.50	0.10	2.93	3.66	1.25	3.92	67.4
RP	ORLANDO PENA	.471	3.66	3.01	116	3.66	4.12	1.309	8.82	1.13	2.96	7.31	2.47	3.66	80.4
	HANK AGUIRRE	.500	3.65	3.29	115	3.59	4.04	1.208	7.87	0.85	3.00	5.76	1.92	3.65	75.3
	JOSE VALVERDE	.350	3.66	3.22	131	3.88	3.81	1.203	6.84	0.76	3.98	8.01	2.01	3.66	74.7
	BOBBY SEAY	.667	4.00	4.00	114	3.48	3.33	1.338	8.48	0.49	3.56	7.83	2.20	4.00	72.1
	JAMIE WALKER	.500	3.80	3.33	131	4.16	4.11	1.174	8.60	1.30	1.97	6.83	3.47	3.80	78.1
	STEVE FOUCAULT	.450	3.79	3.14	132	3.31	3.62	1.343	9.03	0.64	3.06	6.13	2.00	3.79	74.4
	JUAN ACEVEDO	.167	3.98	2.65	161	3.63	3.67	1.219	8.20	0.48	2.77	5.18	1.87	3.98	69.7

POS	POSITION PLAYERS	OBP	SLG	OPS	OPS+	TA	BOP	GPA	BA	BABIP	SECA	IP%	RS%	TBA	BPA
C	JOHNNY BASSLER	.420	.367	.786	106	.811	.822	.280	.308	.318	.249	**78.22**	21.79	1.07	1.63
	BILL FREEHAN	.340	.412	.752	112	.704	.709	.256	.262	.269	.254	74.90	23.74	1.41	1.78
	RED WILSON	.343	.366	.709	91	.656	.669	.246	.262	.275	.236	77.85	27.98	1.12	1.54
1B	NORM CASH	.374	.490	.865	139	.883	.884	.291	.272	.273	.376	66.77	25.85	1.60	2.13
	LU BLUE	.403	.403	.806	110	.845	.852	.282	.295	.313	.290	75.95	**40.71**	1.48	2.21
	CECIL FIELDER	.351	.498	.849	126	.837	.839	.283	.258	.277	.382	59.62	25.08	1.87	2.40
2B	DICK MCAULIFFE	.345	.408	.753	111	.733	.737	.257	.249	.266	.301	70.34	30.84	1.45	2.00
	JERRY PRIDDY	.355	.380	.735	95	.673	.679	.255	.267	.294	.239	74.24	31.08	1.41	1.93
	FRANK BOLLING	.326	.388	.714	91	.651	.659	.244	.261	.272	.222	78.59	32.19	1.44	1.83
SS	DONIE BUSH	.357	.301	.658	92	.688	.706	.236	.250	.274	.257	74.92	**42.70**	1.12	1.94
	JOHNNY LIPON	.355	.337	.692	83	.631	.642	.244	.268	.279	.202	81.51	32.75	1.25	1.79
	EDDIE LAKE	.364	.317	.681	85	.679	.687	.243	.229	.246	**.297**	71.10	39.06	1.05	1.81
3B	DEAN PALMER	.327	.460	.787	103	.764	.767	.262	.244	.279	.334	59.30	28.05	1.68	2.13
	PINKY HIGGINS	.364	.400	.764	102	.709	.716	.264	.280	.286	.247	79.38	28.81	1.46	1.96
	MARV OWEN	.342	.374	.717	84	.657	.667	.248	.278	.295	.188	81.45	31.24	1.40	1.76
LF	STEVE KEMP	.376	.450	.826	125	.820	.823	.282	.284	.298	.319	71.13	28.61	1.65	2.23
	AL WINGO	**.406**	.423	.829	114	.854	.860	.289	.309	.332	.279	75.92	35.08	1.12	1.60
	CHARLIE MAXWELL	.363	.465	.828	120	.837	.840	.280	.268	.274	.346	68.41	28.03	1.47	1.95
CF	AUSTIN JACKSON	.342	.413	.755	105	.726	.731	.257	.277	.357	.251	65.23	41.34	1.65	2.15
	JIMMY BARRETT	.382	.358	.741	117	.770	.775	.262	.292	.332	.243	74.53	38.06	1.37	2.05
	CHET LEMON	.349	.437	.786	117	.747	.751	.266	.263	.280	.285	70.85	28.84	1.48	1.88
RF	ROY CULLENBINE	**.412**	.454	.865	134	.935	.936	.299	.270	.268	**.427**	68.34	27.89	1.41	2.18
	VIC WERTZ	.376	.476	.852	125	.841	.842	.288	.286	.298	.331	71.81	30.53	1.59	2.07
	SAM CRAWFORD	.362	.448	.810	145	.819	.826	.275	.309	.321	.254	84.01	34.17	1.69	2.15
DH	DARRELL EVANS	.357	.450	.806	121	.820	.822	.273	.238	.234	**.395**	63.69	25.12	1.45	2.07
	GARY SHEFFIELD	.354	.433	.788	106	.805	.807	.268	.247	.251	.368	67.07	**34.12**	1.60	**2.30**
UT	NIKO GOODRUM	.306	.401	.707	90	.683	.685	.238	.232	.315	.296	56.95	31.45	1.40	1.88
	SHANE HALTER	.309	.399	.708	91	.629	.640	.239	.251	.294	.227	68.88	26.42	1.22	1.49

ALL-TIME TIGER FOURTH TEAM

MANAGER: HUGHIE JENNINGS 1907-1920 (1,131-972 .538) LOST THE WORLD SERIES IN 1907, 1908 AND 1909

BOLD INDICATES CATEGORY LEADER BY POSITION

POS	PITCHERS	W%	TRA	ERA	ERA+	FIP	DICE	WHIP	H/9	HR/9	BB/9	SO/9	SO/BB	RA/9	LOB%
SP	VIRGIL TRUCKS	.543	3.93	3.50	113	3.47	4.00	1.305	8.09	0.61	3.66	5.23	1.43	3.93	72.2
	JACK MORRIS	.569	4.09	3.73	108	3.92	4.18	1.266	8.18	0.95	3.21	5.86	1.82	4.09	72.9
	BERNIE BOLAND	.578	3.69	3.09	94	3.05	3.70	1.251	7.75	0.10	3.51	3.11	0.89	3.69	72.9
	DIZZY TROUT	.513	3.82	3.20	125	3.34	3.79	1.344	8.70	0.38	3.40	4.16	1.23	3.82	71.8
	BOBO NEWSOM	.588	4.14	3.59	**131**	3.62	3.80	1.373	8.55	0.57	3.81	5.95	1.56	4.14	71.3
	MICHAEL FULMER	.426	4.33	3.95	111	4.03	3.88	1.243	8.59	1.02	2.60	7.30	2.81	4.33	71.7
	ED WILLETT	.545	4.10	2.89	99	3.09	3.62	1.256	8.44	0.10	2.86	2.96	1.03	4.10	66.1
RP	AURELIO LOPEZ	.639	3.67	3.41	119	4.10	4.38	1.258	7.69	1.09	3.64	6.55	1.80	3.67	78.4
	PAT DOBSON	.355	3.45	3.06	109	3.72	4.26	1.221	7.31	0.93	3.67	6.15	1.68	3.45	78.3
	JERRY DON GLEATON	.444	3.65	3.47	118	3.79	3.96	1.266	7.75	0.68	3.65	5.87	1.61	3.65	74.7
	TOM TIMMERMANN	.491	3.83	3.39	105	3.26	3.77	1.284	8.31	0.57	3.24	5.46	1.68	3.83	72.4
	BLAINE HARDY	.583	4.07	3.73	117	4.11	3.95	1.329	8.79	0.99	3.17	7.12	2.25	4.07	75.0
	EDWIN NUNEZ	.545	3.95	3.01	131	3.84	4.05	1.392	7.64	0.67	4.89	7.17	1.47	3.95	74.3
	FRED LASHER	.625	3.76	3.49	98	3.75	4.28	1.314	7.25	0.75	4.58	6.43	1.40	3.76	75.5

POS	POSITION PLAYERS	OBP	SLG	OPS	OPS+	TA	BOP	GPA	BA	BABIP	SECA	IP%	RS%	TBA	BPA
C	MIKE HEATH	.314	.395	.708	97	.622	.628	.240	.266	.298	.197	74.59	28.07	1.18	1.41
	LARRY WOODALL	.347	.333	.680	77	.634	.650	.239	.268	.282	.194	81.96	31.25	0.80	1.12
	FRANK HOUSE	.310	.377	.686	85	.602	.611	.234	.251	.245	.210	81.71	25.17	1.17	1.44
1B	CARLOS PENA	.331	.461	.792	112	.774	.777	.264	.244	.294	.342	57.55	27.82	1.58	2.04
	JASON THOMPSON	.343	.436	.779	113	.746	.750	.263	.256	.266	.314	69.30	23.54	1.56	2.05
	CLAUDE ROSSMAN	.318	.364	.682	115	.620	.641	.234	.280	.308	.164	82.16	25.81	1.35	1.65
2B	OMAR INFANTE	.305	.399	.704	87	.633	.642	.237	.266	.299	.201	76.32	32.71	1.34	1.60
	JAKE WOOD	.314	.364	.678	84	.642	.646	.232	.251	.293	.228	71.80	40.23	1.14	1.54
	EDDIE MAYO	.326	.352	.678	86	.586	.604	.235	.265	.271	.171	83.44	32.51	1.33	1.71
SS	JACKIE TAVENER	.321	.372	.694	79	.645	.666	.238	.260	.287	.206	77.86	33.64	1.30	1.68
	JOSE IGLESIAS	.312	.364	.676	83	.590	.598	.231	.268	.296	.157	80.61	31.18	1.25	1.50
	DEIVI CRUZ	.293	.390	.683	77	.562	.576	.230	.271	.289	.145	83.57	31.62	1.33	1.45
3B	BRANDON INGE	.304	.387	.691	83	.631	.640	.234	.234	.282	.244	64.30	27.14	1.27	1.60
	TOM BROOKENS	.297	.369	.665	83	.596	.608	.226	.246	.272	.203	75.81	35.26	1.08	1.37
	OSSIE VITT	.324	.302	.626	86	.596	.626	.221	.243	.252	.200	80.95	41.46	1.09	1.64
LF	WILLIE HORTON	.337	.472	.808	127	.754	.757	.269	.276	.289	.280	70.96	23.42	1.68	2.00
	BOBBY HIGGINSON	.358	.455	.813	113	.811	.815	.275	.272	.289	.323	70.25	29.92	1.64	2.18
	MARCUS THAMES	.307	.501	.808	108	.770	.772	.263	.245	.268	.340	59.86	29.55	1.51	1.78
CF	JOHNNY GROTH	.370	.410	.780	107	.717	.721	.269	.293	.305	.230	80.14	30.00	1.26	1.64
	JUAN ENCARNACION	.310	.444	.753	95	.710	.715	.250	.269	.308	.246	71.80	33.80	1.67	2.00
	BILLY BRUTON	.336	.396	.732	97	.704	.710	.250	.266	.285	.255	75.49	38.76	1.40	1.89
RF	ROY JOHNSON	.355	.438	.793	102	.790	.792	.269	.287	.308	.270	80.22	44.99	1.78	2.36
	TORII HUNTER	.327	.456	.783	115	.704	.711	.261	.295	.328	.205	75.61	34.32	1.84	2.04
	PAT MULLIN	.358	.453	.811	115	.789	.792	.274	.271	.281	.311	73.53	32.00	1.31	1.71
DH	RUSTY STAUB	.353	.434	.787	117	.739	.746	.267	.277	.267	.279	79.64	24.94	1.66	2.13
	VICTOR MARTINEZ	.349	.440	.789	115	.720	.724	.267	.290	.299	.239	77.98	22.98	1.62	1.95
UT	JIMMY OUTLAW	.339	.337	.676	87	.594	.601	.237	.268	.288	.174	**82.08**	34.89	1.06	1.43
	FRED HATFIELD	.335	.325	.660	82	.594	.606	.232	.248	.271	.196	75.77	29.71	1.05	1.46

ALL-TIME TIGER FIFTH TEAM

MANAGER: SPARKY ANDERSON 1979-1995 (1,331-1,248 .516) WORLD CHAMPIONS IN 1984

BOLD INDICATES CATEGORY LEADER BY POSITION

POS	PITCHERS	W%	TRA	ERA	ERA+	FIP	DICE	WHIP	H/9	HR/9	BB/9	SO/9	SO/BB	RA/9	LOB%
SP	FRED HUTCHINSON	.572	4.19	3.73	113	3.71	4.14	1.281	9.14	0.78	2.39	3.63	1.52	4.19	70.6
	TOMMY BRIDGES	.584	4.21	3.57	126	3.88	3.95	1.368	8.52	0.58	3.80	5.33	1.40	4.21	70.7
	JOE COLEMAN	.547	4.29	3.82	97	3.64	4.12	1.351	8.48	0.83	3.68	6.39	1.74	4.29	72.4
	FRANK KITSON	.456	4.37	3.02	91	2.88	3.30	1.246	9.46	0.24	1.75	3.28	1.87	4.37	63.9
	JUAN BERENGUER	.543	4.31	3.87	102	4.07	4.33	1.319	7.51	0.95	4.36	7.09	1.63	4.31	72.3
	HOOKS DAUSS	.551	4.23	3.30	102	3.33	3.68	1.320	9.04	0.23	2.83	3.19	1.13	4.23	67.1
	JEAN DUBUC	.545	4.13	3.06	98	3.31	3.79	1.287	8.06	0.09	3.52	2.78	0.79	4.13	65.9
RP	FRED LASHER	.625	3.76	3.49	98	3.75	4.28	1.314	7.25	0.75	4.58	6.43	1.40	3.76	75.5
	DAVE SISLER	.500	3.49	3.08	131	3.98	4.45	1.390	6.97	0.48	5.54	5.20	0.94	3.49	76.6
	JOBA CHAMBERLAIN	.222	4.34	3.71	106	3.78	3.65	1.388	9.42	0.85	3.07	7.84	2.55	4.34	73.1
	FRED SCHERMAN	.625	3.73	3.39	107	4.02	4.53	1.367	8.10	0.76	4.21	4.94	1.18	3.73	77.0
	KYLE RYAN	.571	4.08	3.87	107	4.29	4.15	1.336	8.93	0.77	3.09	4.92	1.59	4.08	73.3
	DAVE TOBIK	.385	3.89	3.65	112	4.17	4.47	1.280	7.93	1.05	3.59	5.63	1.57	3.89	76.0
	UGUETH URBINA	.357	4.09	3.87	114	4.50	4.46	1.291	6.53	1.22	5.09	9.63	1.89	4.09	76.9

POS	POSITION PLAYERS	OBP	SLG	OPS	OPS+	TA	BOP	GPA	BA	BABIP	SECA	IP%	RS%	TBA	BPA
C	RAY HAYWORTH	.333	.336	.670	72	.592	.601	.234	.268	.292	.161	81.42	29.22	1.03	1.32
	BIRDIE TEBBETTS	.326	.350	.676	73	.590	.597	.234	.260	.272	.184	83.38	24.72	1.11	1.44
	JAMES MCCANN	.288	.366	.653	76	.550	.556	.221	.240	.298	.184	66.28	21.84	1.24	1.45
1B	WALT DROPO	.308	.408	.716	96	.612	.617	.241	.266	.279	.200	79.03	25.06	1.51	1.73
	DON KOLLOWAY	.332	.356	.688	81	.578	.585	.238	.279	.292	.148	84.93	34.69	1.21	1.49
	GEORGE BURNS	.313	.362	.675	101	.616	.636	.232	.266	.288	.166	80.32	33.33	1.28	1.56
2B	RALPH YOUNG	.344	.300	.644	84	.611	.637	.230	.251	.268	.196	77.76	33.28	1.06	1.65
	GERMANY SCHAEFER	.300	.316	.616	94	.591	.618	.214	.250	.286	.192	76.31	37.97	1.13	1.58
	JERRY LUMPE	.308	.321	.629	78	.539	.551	.219	.248	.265	.162	81.43	32.61	1.09	1.40
SS	CHICO FERNANDEZ	.302	.345	.647	72	.568	.584	.222	.243	.259	.201	77.22	28.28	1.16	1.53
	RAMON SANTIAGO	.312	.333	.645	74	.574	.595	.224	.244	.281	.174	72.16	32.24	0.90	1.15
	JOE HOOVER	.300	.316	.616	74	.525	.547	.214	.243	.287	.149	74.49	43.43	1.16	1.49
3B	BOB JONES	.314	.337	.651	75	.571	.600	.226	.265	.277	.148	83.91	39.30	1.18	1.48
	DON WERT	.316	.346	.662	88	.584	.595	.229	.244	.263	.203	75.21	26.72	1.21	1.58
	GEORGE MORIARTY	.307	.313	.620	82	.614	.636	.216	.251	.276	.192	80.11	30.41	1.08	1.56
LF	LARRY HERNDON	.331	.436	.767	110	.702	.707	.258	.278	.303	.244	74.74	30.12	1.42	1.72
	CRAIG MONROE	.303	.451	.754	97	.682	.688	.249	.259	.283	.258	70.29	33.28	1.57	1.83
	JIM DELSING	.349	.394	.744	103	.710	.713	.256	.260	.268	.268	77.06	29.68	1.26	1.70
CF	JO-JO WHITE	.363	.344	.707	82	.714	.719	.249	.264	.293	.252	76.26	45.60	0.98	1.54
	BRIAN HUNTER	.317	.342	.659	73	.660	.666	.228	.261	.308	.226	75.21	40.32	1.39	2.08
	DOC CRAMER	.330	.352	.682	90	.577	.587	.237	.282	.288	.136	88.49	33.37	1.33	1.61
RF	PETE FOX	.351	.430	.781	97	.744	.749	.265	.302	.317	.212	82.70	43.00	1.69	2.08
	ROB DEER	.318	.439	.757	107	.749	.750	.253	.212	.262	.381	49.70	29.72	1.53	2.09
	BEN OGLIVIE	.326	.444	.770	113	.721	.726	.258	.275	.295	.257	73.57	28.74	1.35	1.68
DH	RANDALL SIMON	.327	.454	.781	112	.681	.687	.261	.302	.298	.187	85.13	23.48	1.59	1.72
	DELMON YOUNG	.296	.422	.718	91	.607	.613	.239	.268	.296	.185	74.30	27.05	1.64	1.77
UT	DON KELLY	.297	.340	.637	74	.568	.577	.219	.234	.256	.203	74.68	38.17	0.65	0.84
	AUSTIN ROMINE	.293	.313	.605	66	.542	.552	.210	.236	.295	.173	69.65	39.08	0.67	0.90

ALL-TIME TIGERS DEPTH CHART – TOP 150 PLAYERS
PLAYERS RANKED BY AVERAGE FOR EACH OF THE CATEGORIES LISTED
BOLD INDICATES MEMBER OF NATIONAL BASEBALL HALL OF FAME AND CATEGORY LEADER

PLAYERS 1-50	RK	AVG	OBP	SLG	OPS	OPS+	TA	BOP	GPA	BA	BABIP	SECA	IP%	RS%	ISO	TBA	BPA
TY COBB	**1**	**9.20**	**.434**	.516	.950	**171**	1.099	1.096	.324	**.368**	**.385**	.320	81.04	39.31	.148	1.95	2.67
CHARLIE GEHRINGER	2	13.67	.404	.480	.884	124	.924	.926	.302	.320	.320	.304	81.06	40.89	.160	1.83	2.42
HARRY HEILMANN	3	13.93	.410	.518	.927	149	.971	.972	.314	.342	.352	.290	79.04	33.01	.175	1.90	2.35
HANK GREENBERG	4	14.40	.412	**.616**	**1.028**	161	**1.128**	**1.127**	**.339**	.319	.329	**.460**	66.46	33.75	**.297**	**2.33**	**2.96**
DALE ALEXANDER	5	17.87	.391	.512	.903	129	.908	.911	.304	.331	.344	.273	79.20	31.54	.181	1.93	2.33
HEINIE MANUSH	6	22.80	.379	.475	.853	120	.853	.861	.289	.321	.329	.235	81.24	41.93	.153	1.62	1.94
MIGUEL CABRERA	7	22.93	.392	.539	.931	149	.936	.937	.311	.313	.338	.357	66.94	25.83	.226	2.01	2.50
J.D. MARTINEZ	8	24.27	.361	.551	.912	147	.905	.906	.300	.300	.363	.349	59.86	27.15	.251	2.04	2.42
GOOSE GOSLIN	9	25.40	.376	.456	.832	111	.838	.839	.283	.297	.301	.287	79.87	37.87	.158	1.70	2.21
BOB FOTHERGILL	10	25.93	.379	.482	.861	122	.828	.836	.291	.337	.350	.203	84.66	36.72	.145	1.47	1.70
AL KALINE	11	26.53	.376	.480	.855	134	.849	.852	.289	.297	.296	.316	75.90	31.04	.182	1.71	2.21
GEE WALKER	12	26.60	.351	.469	.820	108	.808	.811	.275	.317	.331	.225	84.32	38.97	.152	1.80	2.14
RUDY YORK	13	26.87	.369	.503	.873	128	.869	.870	.292	.282	.286	.361	70.37	28.84	.222	1.86	2.39
SAM CRAWFORD	14	26.93	.362	.448	.810	145	.819	.826	.275	.309	.321	.254	84.01	34.17	.139	1.69	2.15
BARNEY MCCOSKY	15	27.20	.386	.434	.820	110	.811	.815	.282	.312	.329	.254	81.31	38.46	.122	1.74	2.30
CARLOS GUILLEN	16	28.60	.366	.476	.842	121	.822	.825	.284	.297	.326	.297	72.34	32.78	.180	1.75	2.23
JOHN STONE	17	28.60	.362	.460	.822	110	.792	.795	.278	.303	.319	.244	80.96	36.69	.157	1.73	2.11
PRINCE FIELDER	18	29.00	.387	.491	.878	136	.877	.879	.297	.295	.314	.329	68.47	22.59	.196	1.83	2.33
BOBBY VEACH	19	29.20	.370	.444	.814	130	.811	.822	.278	.311	.323	.237	81.99	34.00	.133	1.65	2.09
KIRK GIBSON	20	29.20	.354	.480	.834	125	.872	.875	.279	.273	.306	.358	64.70	33.83	.207	1.70	2.29
CURTIS GRANDERSON	21	29.33	.344	.484	.828	114	.838	.840	.276	.272	.321	.337	64.57	37.50	.211	1.85	2.36
ROY JOHNSON	22	29.47	.355	.438	.793	102	.790	.792	.269	.287	.308	.270	80.22	44.99	.152	1.78	2.36
GEORGE KELL	23	29.87	.391	.433	.824	119	.775	.782	.284	.325	.331	.212	84.90	34.00	.107	1.73	2.18
ROCKY COLAVITO	24	30.07	.364	.501	.865	130	.862	.864	.289	.271	.257	.378	70.58	28.03	.230	1.86	2.42
VIC WERTZ	25	30.67	.376	.476	.852	125	.841	.842	.288	.286	.298	.331	71.81	30.53	.190	1.59	2.07
RAY BOONE	26	31.07	.372	.482	.854	130	.835	.839	.288	.291	.288	.319	75.23	25.79	.191	1.75	2.23
MAGGLIO ORDONEZ	27	31.13	.373	.476	.849	123	.802	.805	.287	.312	.330	.264	75.70	28.49	.164	1.78	2.17
LU BLUE	28	31.40	.403	.403	.806	110	.845	.852	.282	.295	.313	.290	75.95	40.71	.108	1.48	2.21
DICK WAKEFIELD	29	31.93	.396	.447	.843	131	.842	.843	.290	.293	.315	.319	72.16	29.92	.154	1.51	2.09
ROY CULLENBINE	30	32.67	.412	.454	.865	134	.935	.936	.299	.270	.268	.427	68.34	27.89	.184	1.41	2.18
TONY CLARK	31	32.67	.355	.502	.857	121	.837	.839	.285	.277	.317	.345	61.61	27.67	.225	1.84	2.30
NORM CASH	32	32.80	.374	.490	.865	139	.883	.884	.291	.272	.273	.376	66.77	22.85	.218	1.60	2.13
MICKEY TETTLETON	33	34.00	.387	.480	.867	135	.923	.924	.294	.249	.277	.453	55.01	24.06	.232	1.59	2.35
AL WINGO	34	34.27	.406	.423	.829	114	.854	.860	.289	.309	.332	.279	75.92	35.08	.114	1.12	1.60
STEVE KEMP	35	35.20	.376	.450	.826	125	.820	.823	.282	.284	.298	.319	71.13	28.61	.167	1.65	2.23
PETE FOX	36	35.60	.351	.430	.781	97	.744	.749	.265	.302	.317	.212	82.70	43.00	.128	1.69	2.08
TONY PHILLIPS	37	35.93	.395	.405	.800	120	.831	.834	.279	.281	.319	.324	67.11	35.48	.124	1.54	2.36
JIM DELAHANTY	38	36.07	.394	.399	.793	129	.829	.837	.277	.306	.332	.242	76.69	34.73	.093	1.42	1.97
MARTY MCMANUS	39	36.13	.359	.434	.793	103	.785	.793	.270	.287	.295	.266	79.48	34.55	.147	1.57	2.07
CECIL FIELDER	40	36.40	.351	.498	.849	126	.837	.839	.283	.258	.277	.382	59.62	25.08	.241	1.87	2.40
HARVEY KUENN	41	37.60	.360	.426	.786	112	.717	.721	.268	.314	.319	.187	87.20	34.32	.112	1.77	2.13
BOBBY HIGGINSON	42	38.13	.358	.455	.813	113	.811	.815	.275	.272	.289	.323	70.25	29.92	.183	1.64	2.18
DMITRI YOUNG	43	38.20	.340	.486	.826	120	.776	.778	.274	.279	.311	.289	67.97	29.37	.207	1.79	2.10
HOOT EVERS	44	38.67	.368	.436	.803	112	.760	.765	.274	.290	.302	.264	77.32	32.64	.146	1.54	2.00
LOU WHITAKER	45	39.07	.363	.426	.789	117	.781	.787	.270	.276	.290	.297	73.42	34.17	.150	1.53	2.09
CHARLIE MAXWELL	46	39.33	.363	.465	.828	120	.837	.840	.280	.268	.274	.346	68.41	28.03	.197	1.47	1.95
RON LEFLORE	47	39.60	.348	.406	.754	108	.769	.772	.258	.297	.353	.246	73.14	40.59	.109	1.68	2.38
PAT MULLIN	48	41.33	.358	.453	.811	115	.789	.792	.274	.271	.281	.311	73.53	32.00	.182	1.31	1.71
PLACIDO POLANCO	49	41.60	.355	.418	.773	103	.697	.703	.264	.311	.319	.169	85.46	37.24	.107	1.71	1.98
IAN KINSLER	50	42.13	.328	.436	.764	108	.715	.718	.256	.275	.294	.243	76.20	40.22	.161	1.78	2.15

AVERAGE COLUMN TIEBREAKER: PLAYER WITH THE HIGHER OPS+ NUMBER IS RANKED FIRST

ALL-TIME TIGERS DEPTH CHART – TOP 150 PLAYERS
PLAYERS RANKED BY AVERAGE FOR EACH OF THE CATEGORIES LISTED
BOLD INDICATES MEMBER OF NATIONAL BASEBALL HALL OF FAME AND CATEGORY LEADER

PLAYERS 51-100	RK	AVG	OBP	SLG	OPS	OPS+	TA	BOP	GPA	BA	BABIP	SECA	IP%	RS%	ISO	TBA	BPA
ALAN TRAMMELL	51	43.73	.352	.415	.767	110	.738	.746	.262	.285	.298	.248	77.91	34.10	.130	1.50	1.97
AUSTIN JACKSON	52	44.13	.342	.413	.755	105	.726	.731	.257	.277	.357	.251	65.23	41.34	.136	1.65	2.15
RUSTY STAUB	53	44.47	.353	.434	.787	117	.739	.746	.267	.277	.267	.279	79.64	24.94	.157	1.66	2.13
WILLIE HORTON	54	44.53	.337	.472	.808	127	.754	.757	.269	.276	.289	.280	70.96	23.42	.196	1.68	2.00
TRAVIS FRYMAN	55	44.80	.334	.444	.779	106	.737	.743	.262	.274	.313	.269	68.36	31.63	.171	1.74	2.15
TOPPER RIGNEY	56	45.13	.389	.393	.782	105	.788	.805	.273	.296	.318	.253	75.22	30.82	.097	1.32	1.89
JIMMY BARRETT	57	45.33	.382	.358	.741	117	.770	.775	.262	.292	.332	.243	74.54	38.06	.066	1.37	2.05
DARRELL EVANS	58	46.47	.357	.450	.806	121	.820	.822	.273	.238	.234	.395	63.96	25.12	.212	1.45	2.07
CARLOS PENA	59	46.80	.331	.461	.792	112	.774	.777	.264	.244	.294	.342	57.55	27.82	.217	1.58	2.04
IVAN RODRIGUEZ	60	46.93	.328	.449	.777	103	.689	.694	.260	.298	.337	.203	76.06	31.23	.151	1.75	1.97
LANCE PARRISH	61	47.40	.317	.469	.786	114	.722	.726	.260	.263	.280	.283	69.51	28.88	.207	1.75	2.06
VICTOR MARTINEZ	62	47.60	.349	.440	.789	115	.720	.724	.267	.290	.299	.239	77.98	22.98	.150	1.62	1.95
CHET LEMON	63	47.87	.349	.437	.786	117	.747	.751	.266	.263	.280	.285	70.85	28.84	.174	1.48	1.88
DAMION EASLEY	64	47.93	.339	.428	.767	101	.748	.752	.260	.260	.286	.279	69.62	32.53	.168	1.57	2.02
DEAN PALMER	65	48.00	.327	.460	.787	103	.764	.767	.262	.244	.279	.334	59.30	28.05	.216	1.68	2.13
BILLY ROGELL	66	48.33	.362	.381	.742	89	.725	.731	.258	.274	.288	.246	79.78	35.49	.107	1.39	1.95
NICHOLAS CASTELLANOS	67	48.40	.324	.459	.783	110	.722	.725	.260	.274	.333	.256	66.62	26.02	.186	1.73	2.01
MARCUS THAMES	68	48.40	.307	.501	.808	108	.770	.772	.263	.245	.268	.340	59.86	29.55	.256	1.51	1.78
JOHNNY GROTH	69	48.40	.370	.410	.780	107	.717	.721	.269	.293	.305	.230	80.14	30.00	.117	1.26	1.64
FRED HANEY	70	49.00	.383	.359	.742	94	.730	.747	.262	.297	.313	.207	78.56	43.58	.062	1.16	1.67
JUAN ENCARNACION	71	49.13	.310	.444	.753	95	.710	.715	.250	.269	.308	.246	71.80	33.80	.174	1.67	2.00
JOHNNY BASSLER	72	50.27	.420	.367	.786	106	.811	.822	.280	.308	.318	.249	78.22	21.79	.058	1.07	1.63
PINKY HIGGINS	73	50.53	.364	.400	.764	102	.709	.716	.264	.280	.286	.247	79.38	28.81	.120	1.46	1.96
BEN OGLIVIE	74	51.53	.326	.444	.770	113	.721	.726	.258	.275	.295	.257	73.57	28.74	.169	1.35	1.68
JASON THOMPSON	75	51.60	.343	.436	.779	113	.746	.750	.263	.256	.266	.314	69.30	23.54	.180	1.56	2.05
BILLY BRUTON	76	51.87	.336	.396	.732	97	.704	.710	.250	.266	.285	.255	75.49	38.76	.131	1.40	1.89
DICK MCAULIFFE	77	52.27	.345	.408	.753	111	.733	.737	.257	.249	.266	.301	70.34	30.84	.158	1.45	2.00
LARRY HERNDON	78	52.27	.331	.436	.767	110	.702	.707	.258	.278	.303	.244	74.74	30.12	.158	1.42	1.72
JOHN WOCKENFUSS	79	52.67	.346	.439	.785	116	.747	.750	.266	.261	.263	.303	72.74	25.50	.178	1.20	1.56
JIM NORTHRUP	80	52.67	.332	.430	.762	115	.703	.706	.257	.267	.280	.258	75.42	28.65	.163	1.49	1.85
CRAIG MONROE	81	53.40	.303	.451	.754	97	.682	.688	.249	.259	.283	.258	70.29	33.28	.192	1.57	1.83
JEIMER CANDALARIO	82	53.67	.336	.415	.751	104	.720	.721	.255	.249	.311	.288	61.91	29.95	.165	1.52	1.98
JHONNY PERALTA	83	54.67	.332	.433	.764	106	.691	.696	.257	.275	.312	.242	70.99	26.07	.158	1.58	1.91
JIM DELSING	84	55.20	.349	.394	.744	103	.710	.713	.256	.260	.268	.268	77.06	29.68	.134	1.26	1.70
JO-JO WHITE	85	56.53	.363	.344	.707	82	.714	.719	.249	.264	.293	.252	76.26	45.60	.080	0.98	1.54
ALEX AVILA	86	57.73	.350	.404	.754	106	.730	.734	.258	.245	.323	.319	55.74	22.95	.159	1.23	1.72
GATES BROWN	87	57.87	.330	.420	.750	110	.710	.714	.254	.257	.259	.279	75.63	32.58	.163	0.90	1.16
BILL FREEHAN	88	58.47	.340	.412	.752	112	.704	.709	.256	.262	.269	.254	74.90	23.74	.150	1.41	1.78
JERRY PRIDDY	89	58.47	.355	.380	.735	95	.673	.679	.255	.267	.294	.239	74.24	31.08	.113	1.41	1.93
MARV OWEN	90	58.60	.342	.374	.717	84	.657	.667	.248	.278	.295	.188	81.45	31.24	.097	1.40	1.76
RYAN RABURN	91	58.80	.311	.430	.740	96	.676	.681	.247	.256	.314	.250	64.69	35.43	.174	1.19	1.42
JOHNNY LIPON	92	59.13	.355	.337	.692	83	.631	.642	.244	.268	.279	.202	85.51	32.75	.069	1.25	1.79
BRENNAN BOESCH	93	59.67	.315	.414	.729	96	.672	.675	.245	.259	.298	.237	70.14	31.38	.155	1.48	1.80
DAVY JONES	94	60.00	.355	.309	.663	100	.688	.698	.237	.269	.294	.225	78.85	47.19	.039	1.04	1.68
EDDIE LAKE	95	60.53	.364	.317	.681	85	.679	.687	.243	.229	.246	.297	71.10	39.06	.088	1.05	1.81
FRANK BOLLING	96	60.60	.326	.388	.714	91	.651	.659	.244	.261	.272	.222	78.59	32.19	.127	1.44	1.83
MATTY MCINTYRE	97	61.20	.338	.337	.675	112	.654	.664	.236	.261	.291	.216	78.24	36.23	.075	1.27	1.80
NIKO GOODRUM	98	61.33	.306	.401	.707	90	.683	.685	.238	.232	.315	.296	56.95	31.45	.169	1.40	1.88
DONIE BUSH	99	62.27	.357	.301	.658	92	.688	.706	.236	.250	.274	.257	74.92	42.70	.051	1.12	1.94
BRIAN HUNTER	100	62.53	.317	.342	.659	73	.660	.666	.228	.261	.308	.226	75.21	40.32	.081	1.39	2.08

AVERAGE COLUMN TIEBREAKER: PLAYER WITH THE HIGHER OPS+ NUMBER IS RANKED FIRST

ALL-TIME TIGERS DEPTH CHART – TOP 150 PLAYERS
PLAYERS RANKED BY AVERAGE FOR EACH OF THE CATEGORIES LISTED
BOLD INDICATES MEMBER OF NATIONAL BASEBALL HALL OF FAME AND CATEGORY LEADER

PLAYERS 101-150	RK	AVG	OBP	SLG	OPS	OPS+	TA	BOP	GPA	BA	BABIP	SECA	IP%	RS%	ISO	TBA	BPA
OMAR INFANTE	101	63.00	.305	.399	.704	87	.633	.642	.237	.266	.299	.201	76.32	32.71	.132	1.34	1.60
BILL TUTTLE	102	63.67	.330	.368	.699	89	.616	.625	.241	.263	.275	.206	79.79	32.14	.106	1.37	1.78
JACKIE TAVENER	103	63.67	.321	.372	.694	79	.645	.666	.238	.260	.287	.206	77.86	33.64	.112	1.30	1.68
WALT DROPO	104	65.00	.308	.408	.716	96	.612	.617	.241	.266	.279	.200	79.03	25.06	.142	1.51	1.73
CLAUDE ROSSMAN	105	65.07	.318	.364	.682	115	.620	.641	.234	.280	.308	.164	82.16	25.81	.084	1.35	1.65
DOC CRAMER	106	65.60	.330	.352	.682	90	.577	.587	.237	.282	.288	.136	**88.49**	33.37	.070	1.33	1.61
GEORGE BURNS	107	65.87	.313	.362	.675	101	.616	.636	.232	.266	.288	.166	80.32	33.33	.096	1.28	1.56
DON KOLLOWAY	108	65.93	.332	.356	.688	81	.578	.585	.238	.279	.292	.148	84.93	34.69	.076	1.21	1.48
PAT SHERIDAN	109	66.13	.326	.372	.698	93	.666	.674	.240	.251	.292	.249	68.65	34.97	.121	1.00	1.40
JAKE WOOD	110	66.33	.314	.364	.678	84	.642	.646	.232	.251	.293	.228	71.80	40.23	.113	1.14	1.54
RED WILSON	111	66.53	.343	.366	.709	91	.656	.669	.246	.262	.275	.236	77.85	27.98	.104	1.12	1.54
EDDIE MAYO	112	67.27	.326	.352	.678	86	.586	.604	.235	.265	.271	.171	83.44	32.51	.088	1.33	1.71
JIMMY OUTLAW	113	67.33	.339	.337	.676	87	.594	.601	.237	.268	.288	.174	82.08	34.89	.069	1.06	1.43
MICKEY STANLEY	114	68.27	.298	.377	.675	90	.588	.596	.228	.248	.257	.207	79.88	34.82	.129	1.25	1.52
MIKE HEATH	115	69.07	.314	.395	.708	97	.622	.628	.240	.266	.298	.197	74.59	28.07	.129	1.18	1.41
DEIVI CRUZ	116	69.47	.293	.390	.683	77	.562	.576	.230	.271	.289	.145	83.57	31.62	.119	1.33	1.45
LARRY WOODALL	117	70.00	.347	.333	.680	77	.634	.650	.239	.268	.282	.194	81.96	31.25	.065	0.80	1.12
BOB JONES	118	70.20	.314	.337	.651	75	.571	.600	.226	.265	.277	.148	83.91	39.30	.073	1.18	1.48
JOSE IGLESIAS	119	70.27	.312	.364	.676	83	.590	.598	.231	.268	.296	.157	80.61	31.18	.096	1.25	1.50
BRANDON INGE	120	70.33	.304	.387	.691	83	.631	.640	.234	.234	.282	.244	64.30	27.14	.153	1.27	1.60
DAVE BERGMAN	121	70.47	.346	.368	.714	100	.666	.674	.248	.259	.276	.243	74.78	25.00	.109	0.83	1.15
SHANE HALTER	122	70.67	.309	.399	.708	91	.629	.640	.239	.251	.294	.227	68.88	26.42	.148	1.22	1.49
OSSIE VITT	123	71.13	.324	.302	.626	86	.596	.626	.221	.243	.252	.200	80.95	41.46	.059	1.09	1.64
FRANK HOUSE	124	72.27	.310	.377	.686	85	.602	.611	.234	.251	.245	.210	81.71	25.71	.126	1.17	1.44
TOM BROOKENS	125	72.27	.297	.369	.665	83	.596	.608	.226	.246	.272	.203	75.81	35.26	.123	1.08	1.37
RALPH YOUNG	126	73.67	.344	.300	.644	84	.611	.637	.230	.251	.268	.196	77.76	33.28	.049	1.06	1.65
GERMANY SCHAEFER	127	73.73	.300	.316	.616	94	.591	.618	.214	.250	.286	.192	76.31	37.97	.067	1.13	1.58
RAY HAYWORTH	128	74.60	.333	.336	.670	72	.592	.601	.234	.268	.292	.161	81.42	29.22	.068	1.03	1.32
BIRDIE TEBBETTS	129	75.53	.326	.350	.676	73	.590	.597	.234	.260	.272	.184	83.38	24.72	.090	1.11	1.44
MILT CUYLER	130	75.53	.304	.324	.627	72	.599	.613	.218	.239	.293	.206	71.18	**47.48**	.084	0.95	1.36
GEORGE MORIARTY	131	76.40	.307	.313	.620	82	.614	.636	.216	.251	.276	.192	80.11	30.41	.062	1.08	1.56
GEORGE MULLIN	132	76.87	.315	.342	.657	99	.585	.593	.227	.261	.304	.167	77.77	30.15	.080	0.88	1.10
FRED HATFIELD	133	77.13	.335	.325	.660	82	.594	.606	.232	.248	.271	.196	75.77	29.71	.077	1.05	1.46
DON WERT	134	78.47	.316	.346	.662	88	.584	.595	.229	.244	.263	.203	75.21	26.72	.102	1.21	1.58
JERRY LUMPE	135	78.87	.308	.321	.629	78	.539	.551	.219	.248	.265	.162	81.43	32.61	.073	1.09	1.40
BILL COUGHLIN	136	80.27	.291	.279	.569	80	.511	.723	.201	.236	.266	.140	78.85	35.40	.043	0.99	1.34
CHICO FERNANDEZ	137	80.67	.302	.345	.647	72	.568	.584	.222	.243	.259	.201	77.22	28.28	.102	1.16	1.53
DON KELLY	138	80.93	.297	.340	.637	74	.568	.577	.219	.234	.256	.203	74.68	38.17	.106	0.65	0.84
AURELIO RODRIGUEZ	139	81.73	.274	.356	.631	76	.519	.529	.213	.239	.258	.163	79.57	28.23	.117	1.25	1.43
RAMON SANTIAGO	140	82.00	.312	.333	.645	74	.574	.595	.224	.244	.281	.174	72.16	32.24	.089	0.90	1.15
ANDREW ROMINE	141	83.87	.293	.313	.605	66	.542	.552	.210	.236	.295	.173	69.65	39.08	.077	0.67	0.90
BOSS SCHMIDT	142	84.27	.270	.307	.577	80	.474	.500	.198	.243	.261	.103	85.66	32.60	.064	0.95	1.08
JAMES MCCANN	143	84.80	.288	.366	.653	76	.550	.556	.221	.240	.298	.184	66.28	21.84	.126	1.24	1.45
CHARLEY O'LEARY	144	86.47	.272	.271	.543	68	.462	.494	.190	.227	.245	.120	83.20	34.65	.044	0.92	1.18
EDDIE BRINKMAN	145	90.00	.276	.306	.582	65	.475	.491	.201	.222	.240	.153	78.96	27.84	.083	1.00	1.23
DIZZY TROUT	146	90.73	.264	.325	.589	58	.494	.511	.200	.217	.261	.177	68.86	32.22	.108	0.59	0.72
BOB SWIFT	147	90.93	.322	.282	.604	64	.524	.539	.216	.232	.248	.185	78.25	20.17	.050	0.74	1.10
OSCAR STANAGE	148	92.40	.284	.295	.579	69	.486	.504	.202	.234	.268	.131	78.76	22.75	.061	0.94	1.17
HOOKS DAUSS	149	96.40	.284	.266	.550	54	.494	.518	.194	.189	.248	.205	62.66	28.45	.077	0.55	0.81
TOMMY BRIDGES	150	99.33	.237	.223	.460	19	.360	.406	.162	.180	.247	.117	64.04	32.94	.043	0.53	0.70

AVERAGE COLUMN TIEBREAKER: PLAYER WITH THE HIGHER OPS+ NUMBER IS RANKED FIRST

ALL-TIME TIGERS DEPTH CHART – TOP 10 BY POSITION

PLAYERS RANKED BY AVERAGE FOR EACH OF THE CATEGORIES LISTED

BOLD INDICATES MEMBER OF NATIONAL BASEBALL HALL OF FAME AND CATEGORY LEADER

CATCHER	RK	AVG	OBP	SLG	OPS	OPS+	TA	BOP	GPA	BA	BABIP	SECA	IP%	RS%	ISO	TBA	BPA
MICKEY COCHRANE	**1**	**3.00**	**.444**	.430	**.874**	126	**.975**	**.975**	**.307**	**.313**	.324	.349	74.31	**35.81**	.118	1.46	2.29
MICKEY TETTLETON	2	4.40	.387	**.480**	.867	**135**	.923	.924	.294	.249	.277	**.453**	55.01	24.06	**.232**	1.59	**2.35**
LANCE PARRISH	3	5.33	.317	.469	.786	114	.722	.726	.260	.263	.280	.283	69.51	28.88	.207	**1.75**	2.06
IVAN RODRIGUEZ	4	5.87	.328	.449	.777	103	.689	.694	.260	.298	**.337**	.203	76.06	31.23	.151	**1.75**	1.97
MATT NOKES	5	6.60	.322	.458	.780	115	.711	.716	.259	.268	.269	.264	74.16	24.00	.190	1.45	1.68
ALEX AVILA	6	6.80	.350	.404	.754	106	.730	.734	.258	.245	.323	.319	55.74	22.95	.159	1.23	1.72
JOHNNY BASSLER	7	6.93	.420	.367	.786	106	.811	.822	.280	.308	.318	.249	78.22	21.79	.058	1.07	1.63
BILL FREEHAN	8	7.40	.340	.412	.752	112	.704	.709	.256	.262	.269	.254	74.90	23.74	.150	1.41	1.78
RED WILSON	9	8.73	.343	.366	.709	91	.656	.669	.246	.262	.275	.236	77.85	27.98	.104	1.12	1.54
MIKE HEATH	10	9.07	.314	.395	.708	97	.622	.628	.240	.266	.298	.197	74.59	28.07	.129	1.18	1.41

FIRST BASE	RK	AVG	OBP	SLG	OPS	OPS+	TA	BOP	GPA	BA	BABIP	SECA	IP%	RS%	ISO	TBA	BPA
HANK GREENBERG	**1**	**2.13**	**.412**	**.616**	**1.028**	**161**	**1.128**	**1.127**	**.339**	.319	.329	**.460**	66.46	33.75	**.297**	**2.33**	**2.96**
MIGUEL CABRERA	2	3.87	.387	.529	.916	145	.912	.913	.306	.309	.336	.348	66.89	25.61	.219	1.96	2.45
DALE ALEXANDER	3	4.27	.391	.512	.903	129	.908	.911	.304	**.331**	**.344**	.273	79.20	31.54	.181	1.93	2.33
RUDY YORK	4	5.73	.369	.503	.873	128	.869	.870	.292	.282	.286	.361	70.37	28.84	.222	1.86	2.39
PRINCE FIELDER	5	6.47	.387	.491	.878	136	.877	.879	.297	.295	.314	.329	68.47	22.59	.196	1.83	2.33
TONY CLARK	6	7.13	.355	.502	.857	121	.837	.839	.285	.277	.317	.345	61.61	27.67	.225	1.84	2.30
NORM CASH	7	7.20	.374	.490	.865	139	.883	.884	.291	.272	.273	.376	66.77	22.85	.218	1.60	2.13
LU BLUE	8	7.20	.403	.403	.806	110	.845	.852	.282	.295	.313	.290	75.95	**40.71**	.108	1.48	2.21
CECIL FIELDER	9	7.80	.351	.498	.849	126	.837	.839	.283	.258	.277	.382	59.62	25.08	.241	1.87	2.40
CARLOS PENA	10	9.93	.331	.461	.792	112	.774	.777	.264	.244	.294	.342	57.55	27.82	.217	1.58	2.04

SECOND BASE	RK	AVG	OBP	SLG	OPS	OPS+	TA	BOP	GPA	BA	BABIP	SECA	IP%	RS%	ISO	TBA	BPA
CHARLIE GEHRINGER	**1**	**1.47**	**.404**	**.480**	**.884**	124	**.924**	**.926**	**.302**	**.320**	.320	**.304**	81.06	**40.89**	.160	**1.83**	**2.42**
JIM DELAHANTY	2	4.53	.394	.399	.793	**129**	.829	.837	.277	.306	**.332**	.242	76.69	34.73	.093	1.42	1.97
LOU WHITAKER	3	4.60	.363	.426	.789	117	.781	.787	.270	.276	.290	.297	73.42	34.17	.150	1.53	2.09
IAN KINSLER	4	4.93	.328	.436	.764	108	.715	.718	.256	.275	.294	.243	76.20	40.22	.161	1.78	2.15
PLACIDO POLANCO	5	5.40	.355	.418	.773	103	.697	.703	.264	.311	.319	.169	**85.46**	37.24	.107	1.71	1.98
DAMION EASLEY	6	6.13	.339	.428	.767	101	.748	.752	.260	.260	.286	.279	69.62	32.53	**.168**	1.57	2.02
DICK MCAULIFFE	7	7.33	.345	.408	.753	111	.733	.737	.257	.249	.266	.301	70.34	30.84	.158	1.45	2.00
JERRY PRIDDY	8	8.13	.355	.380	.735	95	.673	.679	.255	.267	.294	.239	74.24	31.08	.113	1.41	1.93
FRANK BOLLING	9	8.73	.326	.388	.714	91	.651	.659	.244	.261	.272	.222	78.59	32.19	.127	1.44	1.83
OMAR INFANTE	10	9.20	.305	.399	.704	87	.633	.642	.237	.266	.299	.201	76.32	32.71	.132	1.34	1.60

SHORTSTOP	RK	AVG	OBP	SLG	OPS	OPS+	TA	BOP	GPA	BA	BABIP	SECA	IP%	RS%	ISO	TBA	BPA
CARLOS GUILLEN	**1**	**2.60**	.366	**.476**	**.842**	**121**	**.822**	**.825**	**.284**	.297	**.326**	**.297**	72.34	32.78	**.180**	1.75	**2.23**
HARVEY KUENN	2	3.47	.360	.426	.786	112	.717	.721	.268	**.314**	.319	.187	**87.20**	34.32	.112	**1.77**	2.13
ALAN TRAMMELL	3	4.47	.352	.415	.767	110	.738	.746	.262	.285	.298	.248	77.91	34.10	.130	1.50	1.97
TOPPER RIGNEY	4	5.07	**.389**	.393	.782	105	.788	.805	.273	.296	.318	.253	75.22	30.82	.097	1.32	1.89
BILLY ROGELL	5	5.40	.362	.381	.742	89	.725	.731	.258	.274	.288	.246	79.78	35.49	.107	1.39	1.95
JHONNY PERALTA	6	6.67	.332	.433	.764	106	.691	.696	.257	.275	.312	.242	70.99	26.07	.158	1.58	1.91
DONIE BUSH	7	9.00	.357	.301	.658	92	.688	.706	.236	.250	.274	.257	74.92	42.70	.051	1.12	1.94
JOHNNY LIPON	8	9.07	.355	.337	.692	83	.631	.642	.244	.268	.279	.202	85.51	32.75	.069	1.25	1.79
EDDIE LAKE	9	9.13	.364	.317	.681	85	.679	.687	.243	.229	.246	**.297**	71.10	39.06	.088	1.05	1.81
JACKIE TAVENER	10	9.13	.321	.372	.694	79	.645	.666	.238	.260	.287	.206	77.86	33.64	.112	1.30	1.68

THIRD BASE	RK	AVG	OBP	SLG	OPS	OPS+	TA	BOP	GPA	BA	BABIP	SECA	IP%	RS%	ISO	TBA	BPA
RAY BOONE	**1**	**3.73**	.372	**.482**	**.854**	**130**	.835	.839	.288	.291	.288	.319	75.23	25.79	.191	**1.75**	2.23
GEORGE KELL	2	3.80	.391	.433	.824	119	.775	.782	.284	**.325**	.331	.212	**84.90**	34.00	.107	1.73	2.18
EDDIE YOST	3	4.53	**.425**	.417	.842	127	**.937**	**.938**	**.296**	.269	.284	**.412**	64.30	30.44	.148	1.46	**2.40**
TRAVIS FRYMAN	4	5.33	.334	.444	.779	106	.737	.743	.262	.274	.313	.269	68.36	31.63	.171	1.74	2.15
NICHOLAS CASTELLANOS	5	6.40	.324	.459	.783	110	.722	.725	.260	.274	**.333**	.256	66.62	26.02	.186	1.73	2.01
JEIMER CANDELARIO	6	6.60	.336	.415	.751	104	.773	.771	.255	.249	.311	.329	61.91	29.95	.165	1.52	2.12
DEAN PALMER	7	6.80	.327	.460	.787	103	.764	.767	.262	.244	.279	.334	59.30	28.05	**.216**	1.68	2.13
PINKY HIGGINS	8	7.00	.364	.400	.764	102	.709	.716	.264	.280	.286	.247	79.38	28.81	.120	1.46	1.96
MARV OWEN	9	8.27	.342	.374	.717	84	.657	.667	.248	.278	.295	.188	81.45	31.24	.097	1.40	1.76
BRANDON INGE	10	10.73	.304	.387	.691	83	.631	.640	.234	.234	.282	.244	64.30	27.14	.153	1.27	1.60

AVERAGE COLUMN TIEBREAKER: PLAYER WITH THE HIGHER OPS+ NUMBER IS RANKED FIRST

LEFT FIELD	RK	AVG	OBP	SLG	OPS	OPS+	TA	BOP	GPA	BA	BABIP	SECA	IP%	RS%	ISO	TBA	BPA
GOOSE GOSLIN	**1**	**5.00**	.376	.456	.832	111	.838	.839	.283	.297	.301	.287	79.87	37.87	.158	1.70	2.21
ROCKY COLAVITO	2	5.07	.364	**.501**	**.865**	130	**.862**	**.864**	.289	.271	.257	**.378**	70.58	28.03	.230	**1.86**	**2.42**
BOB FOTHERGILL	3	5.67	.379	.482	.861	122	.828	.836	**.291**	**.337**	**.350**	.203	**84.66**	36.72	.145	1.47	1.70
DICK WAKEFIELD	4	6.00	.396	.447	.843	**131**	.842	.843	.290	.293	.315	.319	72.16	29.92	.154	1.51	2.09
BOBBY VEACH	5	6.73	.370	.444	.814	130	.811	.822	.278	.311	.323	.237	81.99	34.00	.133	1.65	2.09
JOHN STONE	6	6.73	.362	.460	.822	110	.792	.795	.278	.303	.319	.244	80.96	36.69	.157	1.73	2.11
STEVE KEMP	7	6.93	.376	.450	.826	125	.820	.823	.282	.284	.298	.319	71.13	28.61	.167	1.65	2.23
AL WINGO	8	7.20	**.406**	.423	.829	114	.854	.860	.289	.309	.332	.279	75.92	35.08	.114	1.12	1.60
CHARLIE MAXWELL	9	8.07	.363	.465	.828	120	.837	.840	.280	.268	.274	.346	68.41	28.03	.197	1.47	1.95
WILLIE HORTON	10	8.93	.337	.472	.808	127	.754	.757	.269	.276	.289	.280	70.96	23.42	.196	1.68	2.00

CENTER FIELD	RK	AVG	OBP	SLG	OPS	OPS+	TA	BOP	GPA	BA	BABIP	SECA	IP%	RS%	ISO	TBA	BPA
TY COBB	**1**	**1.87**	**.434**	**.516**	**.950**	**171**	**1.099**	**1.096**	**.324**	**.368**	**.385**	.320	81.04	39.31	.148	**1.95**	**2.67**
HEINIE MANUSH	2	4.07	.379	.475	.853	120	.853	.861	.289	.321	.329	.235	81.24	41.93	.153	1.62	1.94
BARNEY MCCOSKY	3	4.73	.386	.434	.820	110	.811	.815	.282	.312	.329	.254	81.31	38.46	.122	1.74	2.30
CURTIS GRANDERSON	4	5.40	.344	.484	.828	114	.838	.840	.276	.272	.321	**.337**	64.57	37.50	**.211**	1.85	2.36
HOOT EVERS	5	7.07	.368	.436	.803	112	.760	.765	.274	.290	.302	.264	77.32	32.64	.146	1.54	2.00
RON LEFLORE	6	7.13	.348	.406	.754	108	.769	.772	.258	.297	.353	.246	73.14	40.59	.109	1.68	2.38
AUSTIN JACKSON	7	8.07	.342	.413	.755	105	.726	.731	.257	.277	.357	.251	65.23	41.34	.136	1.65	2.15
JIMMY BARRETT	8	8.47	.382	.358	.741	117	.770	.775	.262	.292	.332	.243	74.53	38.06	.066	1.37	2.05
CHET LEMON	9	8.80	.349	.437	.786	117	.747	.751	.266	.263	.280	.285	70.85	28.84	.174	1.48	1.88
JOHNNY GROTH	10	9.40	.370	.410	.780	107	.717	.721	.269	.293	.305	.230	80.14	30.00	.117	1.26	1.64

RIGHT FIELD	RK	AVG	OBP	SLG	OPS	OPS+	TA	BOP	GPA	BA	BABIP	SECA	IP%	RS%	ISO	TBA	BPA
HARRY HEILMANN	**1**	**3.00**	.410	.518	**.927**	**149**	**.971**	**.972**	**.314**	**.342**	.352	.290	79.04	33.01	.175	1.90	2.35
J.D. MARTINEZ	2	4.47	.361	**.551**	.912	147	.905	.906	.300	.300	**.363**	.349	59.86	27.15	**.251**	**2.04**	**2.42**
AL KALINE	3	5.73	.376	.480	.855	134	.849	.852	.289	.297	.296	.316	75.90	31.04	.182	1.71	2.21
KIRK GIBSON	4	6.67	.354	.480	.834	125	.872	.875	.279	.273	.306	.358	64.70	33.83	.207	1.70	2.29
MAGGLIO ORDONEZ	5	7.00	.373	.476	.849	123	.802	.805	.287	.312	.330	.264	75.70	28.49	.164	1.78	2.17
GEE WALKER	6	7.07	.351	.469	.820	108	.808	.811	.275	.317	.331	.225	**84.32**	38.97	.152	1.80	2.14
ROY CULLENBINE	7	7.33	**.412**	.454	.865	134	.935	.936	.299	.270	.268	**.427**	68.34	27.89	.184	1.41	2.18
VIC WERTZ	8	7.33	.376	.476	.852	125	.841	.842	.288	.286	.298	.331	71.81	30.53	.190	1.59	2.07
SAM CRAWFORD	9	7.40	.362	.448	.810	145	.819	.826	.275	.309	.321	.254	84.01	34.17	.139	1.69	2.15
ROY JOHNSON	10	8.27	.355	.438	.793	102	.790	.792	.269	.287	.308	.270	80.22	**44.99**	.152	1.78	2.36

DESIGNATED HITTER	RK	AVG	OBP	SLG	OPS	OPS+	TA	BOP	GPA	BA	BABIP	SECA	IP%	RS%	ISO	TBA	BPA
CHAMP SUMMERS	**1**	**2.40**	**.388**	**.508**	**.896**	**143**	**.927**	**.928**	**.302**	.293	.301	.364	68.09	27.63	**.215**	1.41	1.85
DMITRI YOUNG	2	3.80	.340	.486	.826	120	.776	.778	.274	.279	**.311**	.289	67.97	29.37	.207	**1.79**	2.10
LUIS POLONIA	3	3.80	.343	.477	.819	109	.805	.811	.273	**.302**	.309	.257	81.78	32.52	.175	1.71	2.09
JOHNNY GRUBB	4	4.67	.373	.446	.819	125	.827	.830	.279	.269	.279	.342	68.80	22.96	.177	.98	1.34
DARRELL EVANS	5	4.67	.357	.450	.806	121	.820	.822	.273	.238	.234	**.395**	63.96	25.12	.212	1.45	2.07
GARY SHEFFIELD	6	5.33	.354	.433	.788	106	.805	.807	.268	.247	.251	.368	67.07	**34.12**	.186	1.60	**2.30**
RUSTY STAUB	7	5.67	.353	.434	.787	117	.739	.746	.267	.277	.267	.279	79.64	24.94	.157	1.66	2.13
VICTOR MARTINEZ	8	6.00	.349	.440	.789	115	.720	.724	.267	.290	.299	.239	77.98	22.98	.150	1.62	1.95
RANDALL SIMON	9	6.27	.327	.454	.781	112	.681	.687	.261	**.302**	.298	.187	**85.13**	23.48	.152	1.59	1.72
DELMON YOUNG	10	7.67	.296	.422	.718	91	.607	.613	.239	.268	.296	.185	74.30	27.05	.154	1.64	1.77

UTILITY	RK	AVG	OBP	SLG	OPS	OPS+	TA	BOP	GPA	BA	BABIP	SECA	IP%	RS%	ISO	TBA	BPA
TONY PHILLIPS	**1**	**2.40**	**.395**	.405	**.800**	**120**	**.831**	**.834**	**.279**	.281	**.319**	**.324**	67.11	35.48	.124	1.54	**2.36**
MARTY MCMANUS	2	2.80	.359	.434	.793	103	.785	.793	.270	**.287**	.295	.266	79.48	34.55	.147	**1.57**	2.07
JOHN WOCKENFUSS	3	4.00	.346	**.439**	.785	116	.747	.750	.266	.261	.263	.303	72.74	25.50	**.178**	1.20	1.56
RYAN RABURN	4	5.07	.311	.430	.740	96	.676	.681	.247	.256	.314	.250	64.69	35.43	.174	1.19	1.42
NIKO GOODRUM	5	5.60	.306	.401	.707	90	.683	.685	.238	.232	.315	.296	56.95	31.45	.169	1.40	1.88
SHANE HALTER	6	5.93	.309	.399	.708	91	.629	.640	.239	.251	.294	.227	68.88	26.42	.148	1.22	1.49
JIMMY OUTLAW	7	6.40	.339	.337	.676	87	.594	.601	.237	.268	.288	.174	**82.08**	34.89	.069	1.06	1.43
FRED HATFIELD	8	7.27	.335	.325	.660	82	.594	.606	.232	.248	.271	.196	75.77	29.71	.077	1.05	1.46
DON KELLY	9	8.33	.297	.340	.637	74	.568	.577	.219	.234	.256	.203	74.68	38.17	.106	0.65	0.84
AUSTIN ROMINE	10	8.67	.293	.313	.605	66	.542	.552	.210	.236	.295	.173	69.65	**39.08**	.077	0.67	0.90

AVERAGE COLUMN TIEBREAKER: PLAYER WITH THE HIGHER OPS+ NUMBER IS RANKED FIRST

ALL-TIME TIGERS DEPTH CHART – TOP 50 STARTING PITCHERS
PITCHERS RANKED BY AVERAGE PER EACH OF THE CATEGORIES LISTED
BOLD INDICATES MEMBER OF NATIONAL BASEBALL HALL OF FAME AND CATEGORY LEADER

STARTERS 1-50	RK	AVG	W%	TRA	ERA	ERA+	FIP	DICE	WHIP	H/9	HR/9	BB/9	SO/9	SO/BB	RA/9	LOB%
DOUG FISTER	**1**	**11.71**	.615	3.74	3.29	128	3.20	**3.13**	1.191	8.97	0.67	1.76	7.21	**4.10**	3.74	72.90
MAX SCHERZER	2	12.79	**.701**	3.73	3.52	117	3.32	3.24	1.197	8.07	0.96	2.71	**9.60**	3.54	3.73	75.36
JUSTIN VERLANDER	3	13.50	.616	3.79	3.49	123	3.48	3.37	1.191	7.97	0.86	2.75	8.51	3.10	3.79	73.67
DENNY MCLAIN	4	14.50	.654	3.42	3.13	110	3.55	4.04	**1.112**	**7.46**	1.10	2.54	6.50	2.56	3.42	**78.16**
HARRY COVELESKI	5	15.79	.616	3.39	**2.34**	123	2.67	3.29	1.131	7.80	0.11	2.37	3.52	1.48	3.39	68.93
EARL WILSON	6	15.93	.587	3.51	3.18	107	3.46	3.95	1.170	7.76	1.01	2.77	6.63	2.40	3.51	77.34
BILL DONOVAN	7	16.29	.593	3.38	2.49	109	**2.62**	3.21	1.192	7.84	0.11	2.88	4.54	1.58	3.38	70.30
MARK FIDRYCH	8	18.07	.604	3.56	3.10	126	3.33	3.66	1.203	8.67	0.50	2.16	3.71	1.72	3.56	72.16
MICKEY LOLICH	9	18.07	.542	3.79	3.45	105	3.19	3.66	1.222	8.28	0.88	2.71	7.17	2.64	3.79	74.46
ED SUMMERS	10	18.50	.602	3.64	2.42	111	2.64	3.32	1.152	8.38	0.17	1.99	3.26	1.64	3.64	67.75
JIM BUNNING	11	19.50	.576	3.84	3.45	116	3.59	4.07	1.208	8.15	1.07	2.72	6.78	2.49	3.84	76.01
HAL NEWHOUSER	12	20.71	.575	3.61	3.07	130	3.18	3.65	1.313	8.07	0.41	3.75	5.41	1.44	3.61	73.10
ED KILLIAN	13	21.07	.575	**3.29**	2.38	109	2.78	3.46	1.218	8.21	**0.05**	2.75	2.92	1.06	**3.29**	71.45
DON MOSSI	14	21.57	.573	3.94	3.49	116	3.59	4.03	1.174	8.81	1.06	**1.75**	5.03	2.87	3.94	73.26
WILLIE MITCHELL	15	22.86	.556	3.57	2.83	98	2.77	3.47	1.255	8.33	0.14	2.97	3.97	1.34	3.57	70.96
DAVE WICKERSHAM	16	24.50	.541	3.90	3.40	104	3.67	4.11	1.248	8.18	0.80	3.05	5.46	1.79	3.90	73.68
DAVID WELLS	17	25.71	.578	4.22	3.78	122	4.19	4.13	1.211	8.73	1.18	2.16	6.15	2.84	4.22	72.85
DAVE ROZEMA	18	26.86	.553	3.90	3.38	120	3.99	4.29	1.230	8.99	0.91	2.08	3.60	1.73	3.90	73.90
FRANK LARY	19	26.93	.528	3.96	3.46	116	3.62	4.14	1.271	8.85	0.81	2.59	4.62	1.78	3.96	73.58
ED SIEVER	20	27.57	.531	4.00	2.61	121	2.80	3.29	1.233	9.30	0.13	1.80	2.63	1.46	4.00	65.89
GEORGE MULLIN	21	27.79	.539	3.92	2.76	102	2.86	3.41	1.270	8.50	0.10	2.93	3.66	1.25	3.92	67.36
VIRGIL TRUCKS	22	28.00	.543	3.93	3.50	113	3.47	4.00	1.305	8.09	0.61	3.66	5.23	1.43	3.93	72.24
JACK MORRIS	23	28.14	.569	4.09	3.73	108	3.92	4.18	1.266	8.18	0.95	3.21	5.86	1.82	4.09	72.89
BERNIE BOLAND	24	28.64	.578	3.69	3.09	94	3.05	3.70	1.251	7.75	0.10	3.51	3.11	0.89	3.69	68.73
DIZZY TROUT	25	29.57	.513	3.82	3.20	125	3.34	3.79	1.344	8.70	0.38	3.40	4.16	1.23	3.82	71.78
BOBO NEWSOM	26	29.79	.588	4.14	3.59	**131**	3.62	3.80	1.373	8.55	0.57	3.81	5.95	1.56	4.14	71.28
MICHAEL FULMER	27	31.00	.421	4.33	3.95	111	4.03	3.88	1.243	8.59	1.02	2.60	7.30	2.81	4.33	71.68
ED WILLETT	28	31.21	.545	4.10	2.89	99	3.09	3.62	1.256	8.44	0.10	2.86	2.96	1.03	4.10	66.15
FRED HUTCHINSON	29	32.57	.572	4.19	3.73	113	3.71	4.14	1.281	9.14	0.78	2.39	3.63	1.52	4.19	70.59
TOMMY BRIDGES	30	32.79	.584	4.21	3.57	126	3.88	3.95	1.368	8.52	0.58	3.80	5.33	1.40	4.21	70.74
JOE COLEMAN	31	32.79	.547	4.29	3.82	97	3.64	4.12	1.351	8.48	0.83	3.68	6.39	1.74	4.29	72.40
FRANK KITSON	32	33.50	.456	4.37	3.02	91	2.88	3.30	1.246	9.46	0.24	1.75	3.28	1.87	4.37	63.85
JUAN BERENGUER	33	34.36	.543	4.31	3.87	102	4.07	4.33	1.319	7.51	0.95	4.36	7.09	1.63	4.31	72.32
HOOKS DAUSS	34	35.00	.551	4.23	3.30	102	3.33	3.68	1.320	9.04	0.23	2.83	3.19	1.13	4.23	67.09
JEAN DUBUC	35	35.29	.545	4.13	3.06	98	3.31	3.79	1.287	8.06	0.09	3.52	2.78	0.79	4.13	65.90
SCHOOLBOY ROWE	36	35.50	.629	4.49	4.01	113	3.75	3.75	1.331	9.47	0.56	2.51	4.12	1.64	4.49	67.09
SPENCER TURNBULL	37	35.86	.306	4.64	4.25	109	3.63	3.43	1.323	8.46	0.63	3.45	8.49	2.46	4.64	68.09
MILT WILCOX	38	36.43	.564	4.34	3.91	103	3.99	4.28	1.324	8.69	0.86	3.23	5.12	1.58	4.34	71.55
STEVE GROMEK	39	36.50	.523	4.15	3.77	104	4.26	4.84	1.272	9.09	1.21	2.36	3.84	1.63	4.15	75.95
DOYLE ALEXANDER	40	37.50	.500	4.26	3.91	100	4.15	4.36	1.325	9.46	1.02	2.47	4.41	1.79	4.26	73.37
ANIBAL SANCHEZ	41	37.86	.484	4.79	4.43	94	3.93	3.81	1.299	9.10	1.19	2.59	8.32	3.21	4.79	69.49
JOE SPARMA	42	37.86	.520	4.29	3.84	88	3.81	4.31	1.378	7.97	0.75	4.43	6.07	1.37	4.29	72.17
BILLY HOEFT	43	38.57	.487	4.31	4.02	98	3.68	4.24	1.368	9.04	0.88	3.27	5.32	1.63	4.31	72.73
JUSTIN THOMPSON	44	39.07	.456	4.40	3.98	119	4.37	4.24	1.335	8.75	0.99	3.27	5.94	1.82	4.40	72.04
RICK PORCELLO	45	39.07	.547	4.67	4.30	97	4.03	3.95	1.359	10.03	0.93	2.21	5.49	2.49	4.67	69.91
NED GARVER	46	39.29	.487	4.19	3.68	106	3.78	4.34	1.325	9.22	0.77	2.71	3.26	1.20	4.19	71.68
FRANK TANANA	47	39.64	.539	4.49	4.08	99	4.18	4.39	1.357	9.15	1.06	3.06	5.56	1.82	4.49	72.53
WOODIE FRYMAN	48	40.00	.468	4.45	4.13	90	3.81	4.29	1.353	8.75	0.95	3.43	5.99	1.75	4.45	72.05
BILL JAMES	49	40.29	.493	4.06	3.01	92	3.46	4.17	1.429	8.21	0.11	4.65	3.15	0.68	4.06	70.39
DUTCH LEONARD	50	40.43	.495	4.62	3.79	102	3.52	3.67	1.372	9.62	0.41	2.73	4.21	1.54	4.62	66.53

AVERAGE COLUMN TIEBREAKERS
FIRST TIEBREAKER IS THE PITCHER WITH THE HIGHER ERA+ NUMBER IS RANKED FIRST
THE SECOND TIEBREAKER IS THE PITCHER WITH THE LOWER WHIP NUMBER IS RANKED FIRST

ALL-TIME TIGERS DEPTH CHART – TOP 50 RELIEF PITCHERS
PITCHERS RANKED BY AVERAGE PER EACH OF THE CATEGORIES LISTED
BOLD INDICATES MEMBER OF NATIONAL BASEBALL HALL OF FAME AND CATEGORY LEADER

RELIEVERS 1-50	RK	AVG	W%	TRA	ERA	ERA+	FIP	DICE	WHIP	H/9	HR/9	BB/9	SO/9	SO/BB	RA/9	LOB%
JOAQUIN BENOIT	**1**	**7.71**	.650	3.08	2.89	145	3.39	3.34	**1.075**	6.92	1.09	2.76	9.95	3.61	3.08	**81.34**
FRED GLADDING	2	13.07	.703	2.96	2.70	132	3.32	3.77	1.231	7.58	0.72	3.50	7.00	2.00	2.96	81.24
WILLIE HERNANDEZ	3	13.29	.537	3.26	2.98	135	3.52	3.76	1.121	7.52	0.97	2.57	7.15	2.78	3.26	78.89
DOUG BROCAIL	4	14.21	.548	3.36	3.06	155	3.68	3.55	1.211	7.84	0.79	3.06	7.70	2.52	3.36	77.68
AL ALBURQUERQUE	5	14.36	**.739**	3.20	3.20	127	3.34	3.24	1.333	7.00	0.64	5.00	**11.04**	2.21	3.20	79.83
JUSTIN WILSON	6	16.36	.438	3.73	3.55	123	3.20	**3.05**	1.172	7.55	1.00	3.00	10.91	**3.64**	3.73	74.80
JOHN HILLER	7	16.57	.534	3.17	2.83	134	3.39	3.80	1.268	7.54	0.80	3.88	7.51	1.94	3.17	80.18
BRANDON LYON	8	16.79	.545	2.86	2.86	158	4.06	3.97	1.106	6.41	0.80	3.55	6.52	1.84	2.86	80.81
DREW SMYLY	9	18.07	.571	3.75	3.53	116	3.51	3.42	1.236	8.53	0.96	2.60	8.47	3.26	3.75	75.73
MIKE HENNEMAN	10	18.79	.626	3.57	3.05	136	3.40	3.54	1.305	8.39	0.54	3.36	6.45	1.92	3.57	74.85
ALEX WILSON	11	19.50	.478	3.50	3.20	135	3.87	3.72	1.164	8.37	0.85	2.11	5.85	2.77	3.50	75.80
KEVIN SAUCIER	12	20.64	.700	**2.62**	**2.32**	**170**	3.68	4.03	1.243	**6.15**	0.10	5.04	4.63	0.92	**2.62**	78.90
TERRY FOX	13	20.79	.605	3.19	2.77	137	3.77	4.22	1.211	8.26	0.81	2.64	4.13	1.56	3.19	79.51
JOEL ZUMAYA	14	21.21	.520	3.43	3.05	147	3.94	3.80	1.350	7.25	0.77	4.89	9.01	1.84	3.43	79.07
ORLANDO PENA	15	22.64	.471	3.66	3.01	116	3.66	4.12	1.309	8.82	1.13	2.96	7.31	2.47	3.66	80.37
HANK AGUIRRE	16	22.93	.500	3.65	3.29	115	3.59	4.04	1.208	7.87	0.85	3.00	5.76	1.92	3.65	75.35
JOSE VALVERDE	17	23.00	.350	3.66	3.22	131	3.88	3.81	1.203	6.84	0.76	3.98	8.01	2.01	3.66	74.69
BOBBY SEAY	18	23.57	.667	4.00	4.00	114	3.48	3.33	1.338	8.48	0.49	3.56	7.83	2.20	4.00	72.14
JAMIE WALKER	19	23.93	.500	3.80	3.33	131	4.16	4.11	1.174	8.60	1.30	1.97	6.83	3.47	3.80	78.11
STEVE FOUCAULT	20	24.29	.450	3.79	3.14	132	3.31	3.62	1.343	9.03	0.64	3.06	6.13	2.00	3.79	74.39
JUAN ACEVEDO	21	25.14	.167	3.98	2.65	161	3.63	3.67	1.219	8.20	0.48	2.77	5.18	1.87	3.98	69.69
AURELIO LOPEZ	22	26.21	.639	3.67	3.41	119	4.10	4.38	1.258	7.69	1.09	3.64	6.55	1.80	3.67	78.39
PAT DOBSON	23	26.21	.355	3.45	3.06	109	3.72	4.26	1.221	7.31	0.93	3.67	6.15	1.68	3.45	78.26
JERRY DON GLEATON	24	26.50	.444	3.65	3.47	118	3.79	3.96	1.266	7.75	0.68	3.65	5.87	1.61	3.65	74.70
TOM TIMMERMANN	25	26.57	.491	3.83	3.39	105	3.26	3.77	1.284	8.31	0.57	3.24	5.46	1.68	3.83	72.44
BLAINE HARDY	26	27.93	.583	4.07	3.73	117	4.11	3.95	1.329	8.79	0.99	3.17	7.12	2.25	4.07	74.96
ED NUNEZ	27	28.57	.545	3.95	3.01	131	3.84	4.05	1.392	7.64	0.67	4.89	7.17	1.47	3.95	74.29
FRED LASHER	28	29.50	.625	3.76	3.49	98	3.75	4.28	1.314	7.25	0.75	4.58	6.43	1.40	3.76	75.50
JOSE CISNERO	29	32.50	.389	4.62	3.69	121	3.93	3.74	1.334	7.75	0.85	4.26	9.66	2.27	4.62	70.28
DAVE SISLER	30	31.86	.500	3.49	3.08	131	3.98	4.45	1.390	6.97	0.48	5.54	5.20	0.94	3.49	76.62
JOBA CHAMBERLAIN	31	32.21	.222	4.34	3.71	106	3.78	3.65	1.388	9.42	0.85	3.07	7.84	2.55	4.34	73.10
FRED SCHERMAN	32	33.36	.625	3.73	3.39	107	4.02	4.53	1.367	8.10	0.76	4.21	4.94	1.18	3.73	77.03
KYLE RYAN	33	34.57	.571	4.08	3.87	107	4.29	4.15	1.336	8.93	0.77	3.09	4.92	1.59	4.08	73.31
UGUETH URBINA	34	34.71	.357	4.09	3.87	114	4.50	4.46	1.291	6.53	1.22	5.09	9.63	1.89	4.09	76.92
DAVE TOBIK	35	34.79	.385	3.89	3.65	112	4.17	4.47	1.280	7.93	1.05	3.59	5.63	1.57	3.89	75.96
DANNY PATTERSON	36	34.79	.476	4.26	4.02	111	4.11	4.04	1.334	9.65	0.78	2.35	4.90	2.08	4.26	72.58
ESTEBAN YAN	37	35.50	.333	4.45	3.83	117	3.90	3.85	1.425	9.52	0.83	3.31	7.14	2.16	4.45	72.77
LARRY SHERRY	38	35.93	.514	4.28	3.85	92	3.79	4.23	1.374	8.05	0.83	4.31	6.72	1.56	4.28	72.86
DARRYL PATTERSON	39	37.43	.563	4.10	3.55	99	3.96	4.44	1.430	8.26	0.76	4.61	6.13	1.33	4.10	75.31
GEORGE CUNNINGHAM	40	37.71	.390	4.66	3.13	88	**2.87**	3.58	1.304	8.38	**0.04**	3.36	3.15	0.94	4.66	61.62
BRUCE RONDON	41	37.71	.533	5.16	5.00	85	3.58	3.46	1.388	8.30	0.89	4.19	10.72	2.56	5.16	66.62
AL BENTON	42	38.07	.526	4.25	3.46	121	3.86	4.24	1.401	8.91	0.57	3.69	3.77	1.02	4.25	70.90
MARK THURMOND	43	38.64	.667	3.57	3.18	133	4.62	4.79	1.482	10.09	0.95	3.26	3.02	0.93	3.57	**81.35**
TOM MORGAN	44	39.07	.353	4.54	3.81	107	3.97	4.33	1.242	9.62	1.17	**1.56**	4.05	2.59	4.54	69.76
TODD JONES	45	39.64	.418	4.62	4.07	113	4.06	3.97	1.456	9.26	0.77	3.85	6.98	1.81	4.62	71.10
RYAN PERRY	46	40.57	.455	4.52	4.07	106	4.28	4.20	1.438	8.37	0.78	4.57	7.20	1.57	4.52	72.14
PHIL COKE	47	40.64	.415	4.81	4.25	97	3.63	3.56	1.523	10.23	0.56	3.48	6.78	1.95	4.81	69.54
FERNANDO RODNEY	48	40.86	.333	4.69	4.28	104	4.15	4.04	1.424	8.18	0.85	4.64	8.56	1.85	4.69	71.14
SYL JOHNSON	49	40.93	.600	4.70	4.15	95	4.07	4.08	1.376	9.41	0.65	2.97	4.20	1.41	4.70	67.67
SHANE GREENE	50	41.14	.425	5.09	4.72	92	4.19	4.03	1.323	8.63	1.12	3.28	8.34	2.54	5.09	67.57

AVERAGE COLUMN TIEBREAKERS
FIRST TIEBREAKER IS THE PITCHER WITH THE HIGHER ERA+ NUMBER IS RANKED FIRST
THE SECOND TIEBREAKER IS THE PITCHER WITH THE LOWER WHIP NUMBER IS RANKED FIRST

MEMBERS OF THE TIGER ORGANIZATION IN THE NATIONAL BASEBALL HALL OF FAME (INDIVIDUALS WITH A CONNECTION TO THE DETROIT TIGER FRANCHISE)

Name	Year
Ty Cobb	1936
Roger Bresnahan	1945
Hughie Jennings	1945
Mickey Cochrane	1947
Carl Hubbell	1947
Charlie Gehringer	1949
Mel Ott	1951
Harry Heilmann	1952
Ed Barrow	1953
Al Simmons	1953
Gabby Harnett	1955
Ted Lyons	1955
Hank Greenberg	1956
Sam Crawford	1957
Luke Appling	1964
Heinie Manush	1964
Goose Goslin	1968
Waite Hoyt	1969
Billy Evans	1973
Sam Thompson	1974
Earl Averill	1975
Bucky Harris	1975
Eddie Mathews	1978
Al Kaline	1980
George Kell	1983
Rick Ferrell	1984
Hal Newhouser	1992
Jim Bunning	1996
Larry Doby	1998
Sparky Anderson	2000
Joe Gordon	2009
Whitey Herzog	2010
John Smoltz	2015
Ivan Rodriguez	2017
Jack Morris	2018
Alan Trammell	2018

Hall of Famers Mickey Cochrane, Charlie Gehringer, Goose Goslin and Hank Greenberg.

Ty Cobb – Inducted 1936
Tiger Player 1905-1926
Tiger Manager 1921-1926

Roger Bresnahan – Inducted 1945
Tiger Coach
1930-1931

Hughie Jennings – Inducted 1945
Tiger Manager 1907-1920
Tiger Player 1907-1918

Mickey Cochrane – Inducted 1947
Tiger Player 1934-1937, Tiger Manager 1934-1938
General Manager 1936-1938

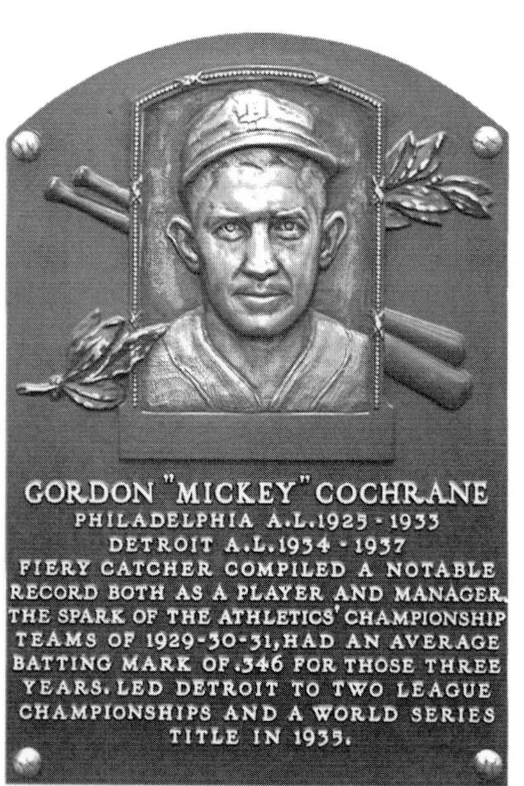

Carl Hubbell – Inducted 1947
Tiger Minor League Player
Fort Worth 1927

CARL HUBBELL
NEW YORK N.L.1928-1943
HAILED FOR IMPRESSIVE PERFORMANCE IN
1934 ALL-STAR GAME WHEN HE STRUCK OUT
RUTH,GEHRIG,FOXX,SIMMONS AND CRONIN
IN SUCCESSION.NICKNAMED GIANTS'
MEAL-TICKET.WON 253 GAMES IN MAJORS,
SCORING 16 STRAIGHT IN 1936.COMPILED
STREAK OF 46 1/3 SCORELESS INNINGS IN
1933.HOLDER OF MANY RECORDS.

Charlie Gehringer – Inducted 1949
Tiger Player 1924-1942, Tiger Coach 1942
Tiger General Manager 1951-53, VP 1950s

CHARLES L. GEHRINGER
SECOND BASEMAN WITH DETROIT A.L.FROM
1925 THROUGH 1941 AND COACH IN 1942.
COMPILED LIFETIME BATTING AVERAGE
OF.321.IN 2323 GAMES,COLLECTED 2839
HITS.NAMED MOST VALUABLE PLAYER IN
A.L.IN 1937.BATTED.321 IN WORLD SERIES
COMPETITION AND HAD A.500 AVERAGE
FOR SIX ALL-STAR GAMES.

Mel Ott – Inducted 1951
Tiger Radio and Television
1956-1958

MELVIN T.(MEL)OTT
NEW YORK (N.L.) 1926-48
ONE OF FEW PLAYERS TO JUMP FROM A HIGH
SCHOOL TEAM INTO MAJORS.PLAYED OUTFIELD
AND THIRD BASE AND MANAGED CLUB FROM
DEC.1941 THROUGH JULY 1948.HIT 511 HOME
RUNS,N.L.RECORD WHEN HE RETIRED.ALSO
LED IN MOST RUNS SCORED,MOST RUNS BATTED
IN,TOTAL BASES,BASES ON BALLS AND EXTRA
BASES ON LONG HITS.HAD A.304 LIFETIME
BATTING AVERAGE.PLAYED IN ELEVEN ALL STAR
GAMES AND IN THREE WORLD SERIES.

Harry Heilmann – Inducted 1952
Tiger Player 1914, 1916-1929
Tiger Radio 1934-1950

HARRY EDWIN HEILMANN
DETROIT,A.L.-CINCINNATI,N.L.
1916-1932
RIGHT HANDED HITTING OUTFIELDER AND
FIRST BASEMAN,WON AMERICAN LEAGUE
BATTING CHAMPIONSHIP FOUR TIMES
1921,'23,'25 AND'27.IN 1923,BATTED.403.
COLLECTED 2660 HITS AND 183 HOME RUNS
IN 2,146 MAJOR LEAGUE GAMES.HAD
LIFETIME BATTING AVERAGE OF.342 AND
FIELDING MARK OF.975.

Ed Barrow – Inducted 1953
Tiger Manager
1903-1904

EDWARD GRANT BARROW
CLUB EXECUTIVE, MANAGER, LEAGUE PRESIDENT IN MINORS AND MAJORS FROM 1894 TO 1945. CONVERTED BABE RUTH FROM PITCHER TO OUTFIELDER AS MANAGER BOSTON A.L. IN 1918. DISCOVERED HONUS WAGNER AND MANY OTHER GREAT STARS. WON WORLD SERIES IN 1918. BUILT NEW YORK YANKEES INTO OUTSTANDING ORGANIZATION IN BASEBALL AS BUSINESS MANAGER FROM 1920 TO 1945, WINNING 14 PENNANTS, 10 WORLD SERIES.

Al Simmons – Inducted 1953
Tiger Player
1936

ALOYSIUS HARRY SIMMONS
PLAYED WITH 7 MAJOR LEAGUE CLUBS 1924-1944. STAR WITH PHILA.(A.L.). BATTED .308 TO .392 FROM 1924 TO 1934. LEADING BATTER .381 IN 1930, .390 IN 1931. MOST HITS BY A.L. RIGHT-HANDED BATTER WITH 2831. LED LEAGUE RUNS BATTED IN, RUNS SCORED, HITS AND TOTAL BASES SEVERAL SEASONS. HIT 3 HOME RUNS, JULY 15, 1932. LIFETIME BATTING AVERAGE .334.

Gabby Hartnett – Inducted 1955
Tiger Minor League Manager
Buffalo - 1946

CHARLES LEO (GABBY) HARTNETT
CHICAGO N.L. 1922 TO 1940
NEW YORK N.L. 1941
CAUGHT 100 OR MORE GAMES PER SEASON FOR 12 YEARS, EIGHT IN SUCCESSION, 1930 TO 1937 FOR LEAGUE RECORD. SET MARK FOR CONSECUTIVE CHANCES FOR CATCHER WITHOUT ERROR, 452 IN 1933-34. HIGHEST FIELDING AVERAGE FOR CATCHER IN 100 OR MORE GAMES IN 7 SEASONS; MOST PUTOUTS N.L. 7292; MOST CHANCES ACCEPTED N.L. 8546. LIFETIME BATTING AVERAGE .297.

Ted Lyons – Inducted 1955
Tiger Coach
1949-1953

THEODORE AMAR LYONS
CHICAGO A.L. 1923 TO 1946
ENTIRE ACTIVE PITCHING CAREER OF 21 SEASONS WITH CHICAGO A.L. WON 260 GAMES, LOST 230. TIED FOR LEAGUE'S MOST VICTORIES 1925 AND 1927. BEST EARNED RUN AVERAGE, 2.10 IN 1942 WHEN HE STARTED AND FINISHED ALL 20 GAMES. PITCHED NO-HIT GAME, AUG. 21, 1926 AGAINST BOSTON. PITCHED 21-INNING GAME MAY 24, 1929.

Hank Greenberg – Inducted 1956
Tiger Player
1930, 1933-1941, 1945-1946

Luke Appling – Inducted 1964
Tiger First Base Coach
1960

Sam Crawford – Inducted 1957
Tiger Player
1903-1917

Heinie Manush – Inducted 1964
Tiger Player
1923-1927

Goose Goslin – Inducted 1968
Tiger Player
1934-1937

LEON ALLEN GOSLIN
"GOOSE"
WASHINGTON A.L. 1921 TO 1930, 1933, 1938
ST. LOUIS A.L. 1930 TO 1932
DETROIT A.L. 1934 TO 1937
BATTED .344 IN 1924, .334 IN 1925, .354 IN 1926, .334 IN 1927. LED A.L. IN BATTING IN 1928 WITH .379 AVERAGE. RUNS BATTED IN FOR 1924-129. HIT .300 OR BETTER 11 YEARS. LIFETIME TOTAL OF 2735 HITS, BATTING AVERAGE .316. MADE 37 HITS IN 5 WORLD SERIES.

Billy Evans – Inducted 1973
Tiger General Manager
1947-1951

WILLIAM GEORGE EVANS
UMPIRE AND EXECUTIVE
EMPLOYED BY AMERICAN LEAGUE IN 1906 AT AGE 22, MAKING HIM YOUNGEST UMPIRE EVER IN MAJORS. SERVED ON A.L. STAFF THROUGH 1927. OFFICIATED IN SIX WORLD SERIES. GENERAL MANAGER OF CLEVELAND INDIANS, 1927-1935. FARM DIRECTOR OF BOSTON RED SOX 1936-1940 PRESIDENT OF SOUTHERN ASSOCIATION, 1942-1946. GENERAL MANAGER OF DETROIT TIGERS. 1947-1951.

Waite Hoyt – Inducted 1969
Tiger Player
1930-1931

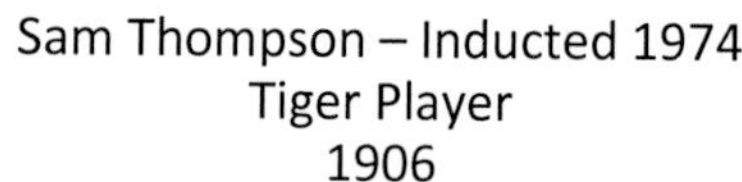

Sam Thompson – Inducted 1974
Tiger Player
1906

WAITE CHARLES HOYT
"SCHOOLBOY"
NEW YORK YANKEE PITCHER 1921-1930. LIFETIME RECORD: 237 GAMES WON, 182 GAMES LOST, .566 AVERAGE, EARNED RUN AVERAGE 3.59. PITCHED 3 GAMES IN 1921 WORLD SERIES AND GAVE NO EARNED RUNS. ALSO PITCHED FOR BOSTON, DETROIT AND PHILADELPHIA A.L. AND BROOKLYN, NEW YORK AND PITTSBURGH N.L.

SAMUEL LUTHER THOMPSON
DETROIT N.L., PHILADELPHIA N.L. 1885-1898; DETROIT A.L. 1906
ONE OF THE FOREMOST SLUGGERS OF HIS DAY. LIFETIME BATTING AVERAGE .336, BATTED BETTER THAN .400 TWICE. GREAT CLUTCH HITTER. COLLECTED 200 OR MORE HITS IN A SEASON THREE TIMES. TOPPED N.L. IN HOME RUNS AND RUNS BATTED IN TWICE.

Earl Averill – Inducted 1975
Tiger Player
1939-1940

HOWARD EARL AVERILL
"ROCK"
CLEVELAND A.L. DETROIT A.L.
BOSTON N.L. 1929-1941
COMPILED .318 CAREER BATTING AVERAGE AND HIT 238 HOME RUNS. TWICE MADE MORE THAN 200 HITS IN SEASON, PACING LEAGUE WITH 232 IN 1936. DROVE IN 100 OR MORE RUNS FIVE TIMES. RAPPED FOUR HOMERS, THREE CONSECUTIVELY IN FIRST GAME AND BATTED IN 11 RUNS IN 1930 TWIN-BILL.

Eddie Mathews – Inducted 1978
Tiger Player
1967-1968

EDWIN LEE MATHEWS
BOSTON N.L., MILWAUKEE N.L., ATLANTA N.L., HOUSTON N.L., DETROIT A.L., 1952-1968
BECAME SEVENTH PLAYER IN MAJOR LEAGUE HISTORY TO HIT 500 HOME RUNS. FINISHED CAREER WITH 512. HIT 30 OR MORE HOMERS NINE YEARS IN ROW, 1953-1961, REACHING 40 MARK FOUR TIMES. ESTABLISHED RECORD FOR HOMERS IN SEASON BY THIRD BASEMAN WITH 47 IN 1953. LED N.L. IN HOME RUNS TWICE AND IN WALKS FOUR TIMES. HAD FIVE SEASONS OF 100 OR MORE RUNS BATTED IN.

Bucky Harris – Inducted 1975
Tiger Player 1929, 1932
Tiger Manager 1929-1933, 1955-1956

STANLEY RAYMOND HARRIS
"BUCKY"
SERVED 40 YEARS IN MAJORS AS PLAYER, MANAGER AND EXECUTIVE, INCLUDING 29 AS PILOT. SLICK SECOND SACKER EARNED TAG OF "BOY WONDER" BY GUIDING WASHINGTON TO 1924 WORLD TITLE AS 27-YEAR-OLD IN DEBUT AS PLAYER-PILOT. WON A.L. FLAG AGAIN IN 1925. LED 1947 YANKEES TO WORLD TITLE. MANAGED DETROIT, BOSTON RED SOX AND PHILADELPHIA PHILLIES.

Al Kaline – Inducted 1980
Tiger Player 1953-1974, Television 1975-2002
Assistant to General Manager 2003-2020

ALBERT WILLIAM KALINE
DETROIT A.L., 1953-1974
TWELFTH PLAYER TO REACH ELITE 3,000-HIT PLATEAU. SOCKED 399 HOMERS AND ATTAINED .297 CAREER AVERAGE, WITH NINE YEARS IN .300 CLASS. FINISHED IN ALL-TIME TOP 15 WITH 2,834 GAMES, 3,007 HITS, 1,583 RUNS BATTED IN AND 4,852 TOTAL BASES. PLAYED 100 OR MORE GAMES 20 YEARS AND HAD 242 CONSECUTIVE ERRORLESS GAMES IN OUTFIELD, 1970-1972, FOR A.L. RECORDS. LED IN HITS AND WON BATTING TITLE IN 1955 AT AGE 20.

George Kell – Inducted 1983
Tiger Player 1946-1952, Radio 1960-1963
Television 1959-1963, 1965-1975, 1980-1995

GEORGE CLYDE KELL
PHILADELPHIA A. L. 1943-1946
DETROIT A. L. 1946-1952
BOSTON A. L. 1952-1954
CHICAGO A. L. 1954-1956
BALTIMORE A. L. 1956-1957
PREMIER A. L. THIRD BASEMAN OF 1940'S AND 1950'S. SOLID HITTER AND SURE-HANDED FIELDER WITH STRONG, ACCURATE ARM. BATTED OVER .300 9 TIMES, LEADING LEAGUE WITH .343 IN 1949. LED A. L. THIRD BASEMEN IN FIELDING PCT. 7 TIMES, ASSISTS 4 TIMES AND PUTOUTS AND DOUBLE PLAYS TWICE.

Hal Newhouser – Inducted 1992
Tiger Player 1939-1953
Tiger Scout

HAROLD NEWHOUSER
(PRINCE HAL)
DETROIT, A.L., 1939-1953
CLEVELAND, A.L., 1954-1955
ONLY PITCHER IN MAJOR LEAGUE HISTORY TO WIN BACK-TO-BACK MVP AWARDS (1944-1945). STRIKEOUT KING WITH BLAZING FAST BALL. 207-150 OVER 17 CAMPAIGNS. CONSECUTIVE SEASONS OF 29-9, 25-9 and 26-9 WITH CORRESPONDING ERA'S OF 2.22, 1.81 and 1.94 FROM 1944-1946. HURLED PENNANT-CLINCHER IN 1945 FOLLOWED BY 2 WORLD SERIES VICTORIES OVER CUBS.

Rick Ferrell – Inducted 1984
Tiger Coach 1950-1954, Scouting Director 1950s
Vice President and General Manager 1959-1962

RICHARD BENJAMIN FERRELL
ST. LOUIS A.L. 1929-1933, 1941-1943
BOSTON A.L. 1933-1937
WASHINGTON A.L. 1937-1941, 1944-1947
CAUGHT MORE GAMES (1,806) THAN ANY OTHER AMERICAN LEAGUER. DURABLE DEFENSIVE STAND-OUT WITH FINE ARM. EXPERT AT HANDLING PITCHERS. MET CHALLENGE OF 4 KNUCKLE-BALLERS IN SENATORS' STARTING ROTATION. OFTEN FORMED BATTERY WITH BROTHER, WES. HIT OVER .300 4 TIMES. SECOND ONLY TO DICKEY IN A.L. CAREER PUTOUTS AT RETIREMENT.

Jim Bunning – Inducted 1996
Tiger Player
1955-1963

JAMES PAUL DAVID BUNNING
DETROIT, A.L. 1955-1963
PHILADELPHIA, N.L. 1964-1967, 1970-1971
PITTSBURGH, N.L. 1968-1969
LOS ANGELES, N.L. 1969
MAINTAINED DEDICATION AND CONSISTENCY THROUGHOUT 17 SEASONS WHILE POSTING CAREER RECORD OF 224-184 WITH 3.27 ERA. INTIMIDATING RIGHT-HANDED SIDEARMER WON 100 GAMES, PITCHED NO-HITTER AND STRUCK OUT 1,000 IN BOTH LEAGUES. 1964 PERFECT GAME WAS FIRST IN N.L. IN 20TH CENTURY. SECOND ALL-TIME IN STRIKEOUTS (2,855) UPON RETIREMENT IN 1971. ENJOYED SECOND CAREER AS MULTI-TERM U.S. CONGRESSMAN

Larry Doby – Inducted 1998
Tiger Player
1959

LAWRENCE EUGENE DOBY
CLEVELAND, A.L. 1947-55, 1958
CHICAGO, A.L. 1956-57, 1959
DETROIT, A.L., 1959
EXCEPTIONAL ATHLETIC PROWESS AND A STAUNCH CONSTITUTION LED TO A SUCCESSFUL PLAYING CAREER AFTER INTEGRATING THE AMERICAN LEAGUE IN 1947. A SEVEN-TIME ALL-STAR WHO BATTED .283 WITH 253 HOME RUNS AND 970 RBI IN 13 MAJOR LEAGUE SEASONS. THE POWER-HITTING CENTER FIELDER PACED THE A.L. IN HOME RUNS TWICE AND COLLECTED 100 RBI FIVE TIMES, WHILE LEADING THE INDIANS TO PENNANTS IN 1948 AND 1954. APPOINTED MANAGER OF THE WHITE SOX IN 1978, THE SECOND AFRICAN-AMERICAN TO LEAD A MAJOR LEAGUE CLUB. PLAYED FOUR SEASONS WITH NEWARK IN THE NEGRO NATIONAL LEAGUE. FOLLOWING PLAYER CAREER WORKED AS A SCOUT AND MAJOR LEAGUE BASEBALL EXECUTIVE.

Joe Gordon – Inducted 2009
Tiger Scout 1953-1955, Tiger Coach 1956
Tiger Manager 1960

JOSEPH LOWELL GORDON
"JOE" "FLASH"
NEW YORK, A.L., 1938-1943, 1946
CLEVELAND, A.L., 1947-1950
AN ACROBATIC SECOND BASEMAN WITH TREMENDOUS POWER WHO HELPED LEAD HIS TEAMS TO SIX PENNANTS IN 11 SEASONS, WINNING FIVE WORLD SERIES TITLES. RENOWNED FOR SUPERB DEFENSIVE RANGE, THE NINE-TIME ALL-STAR AND 1942 A.L. MVP LED THE LEAGUE IN ASSISTS FOUR TIMES AND DOUBLE PLAYS THREE TIMES. SET CAREER A.L. HOME RUN RECORD FOR SECOND BASEMEN. DROVE IN MORE THAN 100 RUNS FOUR TIMES AND HIT 20 OR MORE HOME RUNS SEVEN TIMES. ALSO MANAGED PARTS OF FIVE SEASONS WITH CLEVELAND, DETROIT AND KANSAS CITY ATHLETICS AND ROYALS.

Sparky Anderson – Inducted 2000
Tiger Manager
1979-1995

GEORGE LEE ANDERSON
"SPARKY"
CINCINNATI, N.L., 1970-1978
DETROIT, A.L., 1979-1995
ONE OF THE GAME'S MOST SUCCESSFUL AND COLORFUL MANAGERS, HIS 2,194 WINS RANK THIRD IN HISTORY BEHIND CONNIE MACK AND JOHN MCGRAW. THE CRANK THAT TURNED THE BIG RED MACHINE, HIS SKILLFUL LEADERSHIP HELPED THOSE CINCINNATI TEAMS DOMINATE IN THE 1970s. REVERED AND TREASURED BY HIS PLAYERS FOR HIS HUMILITY, HUMANITY, ETERNAL OPTIMISM AND KNOWLEDGE OF THE GAME. BASEBALL'S ONLY MANAGER TO WIN A WORLD SERIES IN BOTH LEAGUES AND LEAD TWO FRANCHISES IN VICTORIES. HIS TEAMS WON THREE WORLD SERIES, SEVEN DIVISION TITLES AND FIVE PENNANTS, COMPILING A .619 POST-SEASON WINNING PERCENTAGE.

Whitey Herzog – Inducted 2010
Tiger Player
1963

DORREL NORMAN ELVERT HERZOG
"WHITEY", "THE WHITE RAT"
TEXAS, A.L., 1973
CALIFORNIA, A.L., 1974
KANSAS CITY, A.L., 1975-1979
ST. LOUIS, N.L., 1980-1990
AN ARCHITECT AND RESPECTED LEADER WHO BUILT AND MANAGED TEAMS TO SIX DIVISION TITLES, THREE PENNANTS AND THE 1982 WORLD SERIES TITLE. RENOWNED FOR BEING TWO STEPS AHEAD OF OPPOSING MANAGERS, MAXIMIZED PLAYER CONTRIBUTIONS WITH A STERN YET GOOD-NATURED STYLE, EMPHASIZING SPEED, PITCHING AND DEFENSE. TWICE POSTED 100-WIN SEASONS, AND WAS NAMED 1985 MANAGER OF THE YEAR. A TWO-TIME EXECUTIVE OF THE YEAR AS GENERAL MANAGER, ALSO WITH PLAYER DEVELOPMENT CONTRIBUTIONS WITH METS AND ANGELS. TOTALED EIGHT SEASONS AS A MAJOR LEAGUE PLAYER.

John Smoltz – Inducted 2015
Tiger Minor League Player
Lakeland 1986, Glens Falls 1987

JOHN ANDREW SMOLTZ
ATLANTA, N.L. 1988-99, 2001-08; BOSTON, A.L. 2009;
ST. LOUIS, N.L. 2009
A WORKHORSE POWER PITCHER, TRADED HIS STARTING DOMINANCE TO DEVELOP INTO PREMIER CLOSER BEFORE RETURNING TO ROTATION. BECAME THE FIRST PLAYER IN HISTORY WITH 200 WINS AND 150 SAVES. WITH A DYNAMIC FASTBALL, A DECEPTIVE SLIDER AND A DARTING SPLITTER, FANNED 3,084 BATTERS AND WAS NAMED TO EIGHT ALL-STAR TEAMS. THE 1996 N.L. CY YOUNG AWARD WINNER AND 1992 NLCS MVP. SET N.L. RECORD WITH 55 SAVES IN 2002. PITCHED BEST WHEN GAME WAS BIGGEST, RECORDING A 15-4 POST-SEASON RECORD, HELPING BRAVES TO 1995 WORLD SERIES TITLE.

Ivan Rodriguez – Inducted 2017
Tiger Player
2004-2008

IVÁN RODRÍGUEZ TORRES
"PUDGE"
TEXAS, A.L. 1991-2002, 2009; FLORIDA, N.L. 2003;
DETROIT, A.L. 2004-08; NEW YORK, A.L. 2008;
HOUSTON, N.L. 2009; WASHINGTON, N.L. 2010-11
A RUGGED DO-IT-ALL CATCHER WHOSE POWERFUL ARM AND CONSISTENT BAT PRODUCED RECORDS AT THE PLATE AND BEHIND IT. HIT .296 OVER 21 SEASONS, AMASSING MORE HITS, DOUBLES, AND TOTAL BASES THAN ANY OTHER BACKSTOP. CAUGHT 2,427 MAJOR LEAGUE GAMES, MOST IN HISTORY, AND EARNED AN UNMATCHED 13 GOLD GLOVE AWARDS AT THE POSITION. RENOWNED FOR HIS ABILITY TO NAB WOULD-BE BASE STEALERS, LEADING THE LEAGUE A RECORD NINE TIMES. SELECTED TO 14 ALL-STAR GAMES AND NAMED 1999 A.L. MOST VALUABLE PLAYER WITH THE RANGERS. LED MARLINS TO 2003 WORLD SERIES TITLE, AFTER WINNING NLCS MVP.

Jack Morris – Inducted 2018
Tiger Player 1977-1990
Television 2003, 2015-2016, 2019

JOHN SCOTT MORRIS
"JACK"
DETROIT, A.L. 1977-90; MINNESOTA, A.L. 1991;
TORONTO, A.L. 1992-93; CLEVELAND, A.L. 1994
INTENSE COMPETITOR WITH A SPIRITED DRIVE AND DETERMINATION WHO PROPELLED HIS TEAMS AS STAFF ACE. THREE-TIME 20-GAME WINNER AND FIVE-TIME ALL-STAR HARNESSED SPLIT-FINGERED FASTBALL TO BECOME WINNINGEST PITCHER OF THE 1980S. WON 19 REGULAR SEASON GAMES – AND EACH OF HIS THREE POSTSEASON APPEARANCES – FOR DETROIT'S 1984 JUGGERNAUT. DURABLE WORKHORSE TOTALED 175 COMPLETE GAMES, MOST OF ANY PITCHER SINCE 1975, AND MADE RECORD 14 STRAIGHT OPENING DAY STARTS. WINNER OF FOUR WORLD CHAMPIONSHIP RINGS WITH THREE CLUBS. EARNED 1991 WORLD SERIES M.V.P. HONORS, CARRYING MINNESOTA TO TITLE WITH 10-INNING SHUTOUT IN GAME 7.

Alan Trammell – Inducted 2018
Tiger Player 1977-1996, Tiger Manager 2003-2005
Assistant to General Manager 2014-Present

ALAN STUART TRAMMELL
DETROIT, A.L. 1977-96
CATALYST FOR DOMINANT TIGERS TEAMS OF THE 1980S WHO SHOWCASED ALL-AROUND EXCELLENCE FOR TWO DECADES AT SHORTSTOP. SIX-TIME ALL-STAR AND WINNER OF FOUR GOLD GLOVE AWARDS, HIT .300-OR-BETTER IN SEVEN SEASONS. DEVELOPED POWER LATER IN CAREER TO STEP INTO CLEAN-UP SLOT, A RARITY FOR MIDDLE INFIELDERS OF HIS ERA. UPON RETIREMENT, RANKED AMONG TOP 10 SHORTSTOPS ALL-TIME IN HITS, DOUBLES AND HOME RUNS, AS WELL AS DEFENSIVE GAMES AND FIELDING PERCENTAGE. NAMED MOST VALUABLE PLAYER OF 1984 WORLD SERIES AFTER BATTING .450 WITH TWO HOMERS AND SIX RBI IN DETROIT'S FIVE-GAME VICTORY OVER SAN DIEGO.

MEMBERS OF TIGER ORGANIZATION IN STATE HALL OF FAMES
(BOLD INDICATES MEMBER OF NATIONAL BASEBALL HALL OF FAME)

Alabama Sports Hall of Fame

Name	Year
Heinie Manush	1972
Del Pratt	1972
Dixie Walker	1973
Virgil Trucks	1974
Billy Hitchcock	1975
Frank House	1975
Rip Sewell	1976
Frank Lary	1978
Rudy York	1979
Frank Bolling	1982
Jimmy Outlaw	1990
Alex Grammas	1993
Chase Riddle	2000
Jim Davenport	2006
Todd Jones	2017
Luis Gonzalez	2019

Arizona Fall League Hall of Fame

Name	Year
Jerry Manuel	2002
Terry Francona	2005
Troy Percival	2005
Torii Hunter	2007
Eric Wedge	2008
Bob Melvin	2013
Max Scherzer	2017

Arizona Sports Hall of Fame

Name	Year
Luis Gonzalez	2015

Arkansas Sports Hall of Fame

Name	Year
Schoolboy Rowe	1962
Ray Winder	1962
George Kell	1964
Johnny Sain	1966
George Harper	1970
Willis Hudlin	1977
Torii Hunter	2008

Delaware Sports Hall of Fame

Name	Year
Jack Crimian	1985
Billy Bruton	1991
John Wockenfuss	1993

Florida Sports Hall of Fame

Name	Year
Fred Hutchinson	1968
Rip Sewell	1982
Johnny Damon	2016
Gary Sheffield	2018

Georgia Sports Hall of Fame

Name	Year
Luke Appling	1964
Ty Cobb	1964
Whitt Wyatt	1976
Rudy York	1977
George Stallings	1979
Wally Moses	1989
Ray Knight	1995
Paul Richards	1996
Jo-Jo White	1997
Ernie Harwell	2008
John Smoltz	2012

Iowa Sports Hall of Fame

Name	Year
Jack Coombs	1956
Bing Miller	1961
Earl Whitehill	1963
Jack Dittmer	1988
Ed Barrow	**2007**

Kansas Sports Hall of Fame

Name	Year
Elden Auker	1969
Ralph Houk	1977
Don Heinkel	2011
Mike Pelfrey	2019
Nate Robertson	2019

Kentucky Sports Hall of Fame

Name	Year
Jim Bunning	**1986**
Woodie Fryman	2005
Doug Flynn	2006

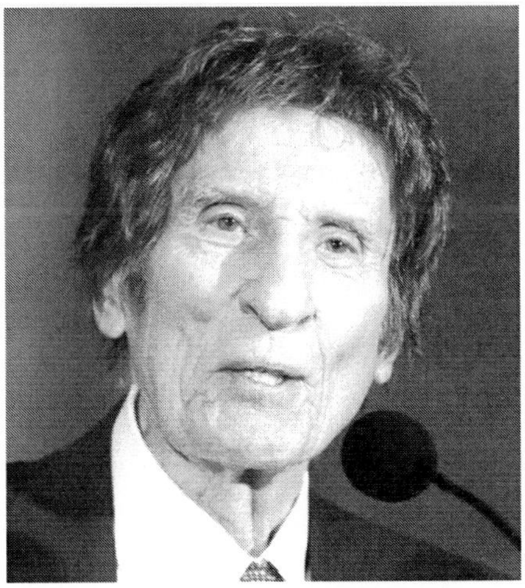

Michael Ilitch Sr.

Louisiana Sports Hall of Fame

Name	Year
Ted Lyons	1960
Mel Ott	**1963**
Rusty Staub	1989
Earl Wilson	1996
Mel Didier	2003

Maryland State Athletic Hall of Fame

Name	Year
Charlie Keller	1958
Johnny Neun	1961
Al Kaline	**1972**
Billy Ripken	2002

Michigan Jewish Sports Hall of Fame

Name	Year
Hank Greenberg	**1985**
Harry Eisenstat	1993
Joe Ginsberg	1995
Jerry Green	2004
Eli Zaret	2013
Larry Sherry	2019

Michigan Military and Veterans Hall of Honor

Name	Year
Michael Ilitch Sr.	2019

Michigan Sports Hall of Fame

Name	Year
Ty Cobb	**1955**
Mickey Cochrane	**1956**
Charlie Gehringer	**1956**
Harry Heilmann	**1956**
Sam Crawford	**1958**
Hank Greenberg	**1958**
Hughie Jennings	**1958**
Wish Egan	1960
Schoolboy Rowe	1961
George Mullin	1962
Hal Newhouser	**1962**
Ralph Young	1962
Tommy Bridges	1963
Heinie Manush	**1964**
Goose Goslin	**1965**
Walter Briggs Sr.	1969
George Kell	**1969**
Billy Rogell	1970
Rudy York	1972
Frank Navin	1976
Al Kaline	**1978**
Jim Bunning	**1981**
Bill Freehan	1982
Mickey Lolich	1982
Vic Wertz	1983
Norm Cash	1984
John Fetzer	1984
Jim Campbell	1985
Virgil Trucks	1985
Dick McAuliffe	1986
Willie Horton	1987
Don Lund	1987
Ernie Harwell	**1989**
John Hiller	1989
Bo Schembechler	1989
Denny McLain	1991
Van Patrick	1991
Sparky Anderson	1992
Paul Carey	1992
Harvey Kuenn	1993
Mickey Stanley	1994
Barney McCosky	1995
Ty Tyson	1996
Ray Lane	1997
Charlie Maxwell	1997
Kirk Gibson	1999
Jim Northrup	2000
Alan Trammell	**2000**
Lou Whitaker	2000
Jack Morris	**2001**
Gates Brown	2002
Lance Parrish	2002
Billy Pierce	2003
Michael Ilitch Sr.	2004
Frank Tanana	2006
Frank Beckmann	2007
Rick Leach	2010
Willie Hernandez	2012
Jim Leyland	2017
Dan Fife	2019

Mississippi Sports Hall of Fame

Eric McNair	1963
Claude Passeau	1964
Willie Mitchell	1966
Gee Walker	1969
Skeeter Webb	1978
Jim Davenport	1983

Missouri Sports Hall of Fame

Vern Kennedy	1955
Whitey Herzog	**1994**
Jerry Lumpe	1994
Vince Coleman	2016
Al Nipper	2018

Larry Doby

New Jersey Hall of Fame

Lary Doby	2010

Sports Hall of Fame of New Jersey

Larry Doby	1993
Goose Goslin	**1999**
Doc Cramer	2004

New Mexico Sports Hall of Fame

Cody Ross	

New York Baseball Hall of Fame

Brendan Harris	2011
Brendan Ryan	2012
Ralph Branca	2013
Ed Kranepool	2013
Dave Lemanczyk	2013
Dale Long	2013
Lou Whitaker	2013
Rocky Colavito	2014
John Doherty	2014
Roy Face	2014
John Flaherty	2015
John Antonelli	2016
John Cerutti	2016
David Palmer	2016
Andy Van Slyke	2017
Billy Martin	2018
Joe Nathan	2018

North Carolina Sports Hall of Fame

Rick Ferrell	1964
General Crowder	1967
Jim Perry	1973
Roger Craig	1985
Jack Coombs	1987
Mike Caldwell	1998
Vic Sorrell	1999

Oklahoma Sports Hall of Fame

Carl Hubbell	**1986**
Gary Ward	2000
Don Demeter	2010
Pete Incaviglia	2010
Mike Moore	2019
Mickey Tettleton	2019

Oregon Sports Hall of Fame

Earl Averill	1980
Joe Gordon	1980
Larry Jansen	1980
Johnny Pesky	1980
Syl Johnson	1981
Mickey Lolich	1984
Walter McCredie	1990
Jack Wilson	1994
George Freese	2008

Pennsylvania Sports Hall of Fame

Jimmy Dykes	1965
Charlie Gelbert	1966
Wilbur Cooper	1967
Roy Face	1970
Nellie Fox	1971
Rip Sewell	1973
Danny Litwhiler	1974
Vic Wertz	1977
Dick Gernert	1980
Don Wert	1980
Tom Ferrick	1984
Steve O'Neill	1993
Dick Tracewski	1997
Harry Coveleski	1998
Tom Brookens	1999
Hughie Jennings	**2000**
Tom O'Malley	2002
Steve Bilko	2003
Joe Page	2003
Bucky Harris	2005
Jim Leyland	2012
Jeff Manto	2012

Rhode Island Heritage Hall of Fame

Gabby Harnett	1972
Clem Labine	1989
Birdie Tebbetts	2015

South Carolina Athletic Hall of Fame

Bobo Newsom	1969
Larry Doby	1973
Chick Galloway	1976
Don Buddin	1996
Art Fowler	1996
Jerry Martin	2007

South Dakota Sports Hall of Fame

Dave Collins	
Sparky Anderson	

Tennessee Sports Hall of Fame

Dale Alexander	1968
Tommy Bridges	1971
Phil Garner	2002

Texas Sports Hall of Fame

Paul Richards	1959
Jake Atz	1963
Pinky Higgins	1965
Clarence Kraft	1969
Al Vincent	1979
Firpo Marberry	1982
Ted Lyons	1985
Norm Cash	2001
Wayne Graham	2005
Eddie Mathews	**2012**
Ivan Rodriguez	**2014**

Virginia Sports Hall of Fame

George McQuinn	1978
Clyde McCullough	1983
Hank Foiles	1987
Sean Casey	2014
Johnny Grubb	2015

Washington Sports Hall of Fame

Fred Hutchinson	1962
Earl Averill	1964
Bob Johnson	1964
Earl Torgeson	1969
George Burns	1974
Gerry Staley	1977
Roy Johnson	1978
Jack Fournier	1979
Jo-Jo White	1980
Earl Johnson	1983
Harlond Clift	1997
Ira Flagstead	2003
Hub Kittle	2003
Edo Vanni	2005

Earl Averill

Wisconsin Athletic Hall of Fame

Al Simmons	**1951**
George McBride	1952
Billy Sullivan	1953
Ed Konetchy	1961
Davy Jones	1964
Pants Rowland	1964
Eddie Mathews	**1976**
Harvey Kuenn	1988
Red Wilson	1990

MEMBERS OF TIGER ORGANIZATION IN FOREIGN AND OTHER HALL OF FAMES
(BOLD INDICATES MEMBER OF NATIONAL BASEBALL HALL OF FAME)

Baseball Australia Hall of Fame

Mark Ettles	2018

Canada's Sports Hall of Fame

John Hiller	1999

Canadian Baseball Hall of Fame

John Hiller	1985
Reno Bertoia	1988
Nig Clarke	1996
Frank O'Rourke	1996
John McHale	1997
Sparky Anderson	**2007**
Doug Melvin	2012
Rusty Staub	2012
Felipe Alou	2015
Matt Stairs	2015
Lloyd Moseby	2018

Caribbean Baseball Hall of Fame

Sandy Amoros	1999
Orlando Pena	2000
Jerry White	2006
Neifi Perez	2012
Juan Gonzalez	2015
Felipe Alou	2016
Geronimo Berroa	2016
Luis Polonia	2016

Federacion de Peloteros Profesionales Cubanos en el Exilio

Mike Guerra	1969
Sandy Amoros	1978
Tony Taylor	1981
Mike Cuellar	1984
Preston Gomez	1984
Luis Aloma	1986
Max Lanier	1986
Orlando Pena	1986
Tito Fuentes	1997
Chico Fernandez	1997
Manuel Hidalgo	1997
Chico Fernandez	1997
Rocky Nelson	1997
Don Lenhardt	2007
Sal Maglie	2007

Hispanic Heritage Baseball Museum HOF

Tito Fuentes	2002
Felipe Alou	2003
Tony Taylor	2004
Omar Vizquel	2007
Juan Samuel	2010
Luis Gonzalez	2011
Luis Salazar	2011
Ruben Sierra	2011
Carlos Guillen	2012
Ivan Rodriguez	**2017**

International Jewish Sports Hall of Fame

Hank Greenberg	**1979**
Brad Ausmus	2020

Japanese Baseball Hall of Fame

Hideo Nomo	2014

Latino Baseball Hall of Fame

Felipe Alou	2010
Ben Oglivie	2012
Aurelio Rodriguez	2012
Mike Cuellar	2013
Juan Gonzalez	2013
Aurelio Lopez	2014
Murray Cook	2014
Luis Salazar	2014
Ozzie Virgil Sr.	2014
Luis Gonzalez	2015
Edgar Renteria	2016
Ivan Rodriguez	**2016**
Omar Vizquel	2016
Tony Taylor	2018

Sandy Amoros

Mexican Pro Baseball Hall of Fame

Ruben Amaro Sr.	1986
Aurelio Lopez	1993
Aurelio Rodriguez	1995
George Brunet	1999
Jack Pierce	2001
Sid Monge	2004

Ontario Sports Hall of Fame

John Hiller	2017

Salón de la Fama del Beisbol Cubano

Jacinto Calvo	1948
Emilio Palmero	1954
Tony Taylor	1980
Orlando Pena	1986
Tito Fuentes	1997

Venezuelan Baseball Hall of Fame

Urbano Lugo	2009
Luis Salazar	2011
Omar Vizquel	2018

American Sportscasters Assoc. HOF

Ernie Harwell	**1991**

Arizona Fall League Hall of Fame

Jerry Manuel	2002
Terry Francona	2005
Troy Percival	2005
Torii Hunter	2007
Eric Wedge	2008
Bob Melvin	2013
Max Scherzer	2016

Italian American Sports Hall of Fame

Phil Cavarretta	1979
Rocky Colavito	1981
Sal Maglie	1982
Billy Martin	1990
Tony Cuccinello	1995
Babe Pinelli	2000
Ralph Branca	2003

Jewish Sports Hall of Fame

Hank Greenberg	**1995**
Sean Rogovin	1998
Brad Ausmus	2004
Elliott Maddox	2004

National Sports Media Hall of Fame

Ernie Harwell	**1989**

Philadelphia Sports Hall of Fame

1981	**Al Simmons**	**OF**
1982	**Mickey Cochrane**	**C**
1984	**Jim Bunning**	**P**
1984	Jimmy Dykes	3B
1988	Wally Moses	OF
1996	**Sam Thompson**	**OF**
1997	Ferris Fain	1B
2001	Gus Zernial	OF
2002	Tony Taylor	2B
2008	Juan Samuel	2B

Philadelphia Sports Hall of Fame

2006	**Al Simmons**	**OF**
2007	**Mickey Cochrane**	**C**
2011	Jimmy Dykes	3B
2015	**Sam Thompson**	**OF**
2016	**Goose Goslin**	**OF**
2017	Bob Johnson	1B

Polish American Sports Hall of Fame

Al Simmons	**1975**
Steve Gromek	1981
Ron Perranoski	1983
Joe Niekro	1992
Barney McCosky	1995
Frank Tanana	1996
Alan Trammell	**1998**
Johnny Podres	2002
Mark Fidrych	2009

(BOLD INDICATES MEMBER OF NATIONAL BASEBALL HALL OF FAME)

Year	Player	Pos.
1933	**Charlie Gehringer**	**2B**
1934	Tommy Bridges	P
1934	**Mickey Cochrane**	**C**
1934	**Charlie Gehringer**	**2B**
1935	Tommy Bridges	P
1935	**Mickey Cochrane**	**C**
1935	**Charlie Gehringer**	**2B**
1935	Schoolboy Rowe	P
1936	Tommy Bridges	P
1936	**Charlie Gehringer**	**2B**
1936	**Goose Goslin**	**LF**
1936	Schoolboy Rowe	P

Vern Kennedy

Year	Player	Pos.
1937	Tommy Bridges	P
1937	**Charlie Gehringer**	**2B**
1937	**Hank Greenberg**	**1B**
1937	Gee Walker	LF
1938	**Charlie Gehringer**	**2B**
1938	**Hank Greenberg**	**1B**
1938	Vern Kennedy	P
1938	Rudy York	C
1939	Tommy Bridges	P
1939	**Hank Greenberg**	**1B**
1939	Bobo Newsom	P
1940	Tommy Bridges	P
1940	**Hank Greenberg**	**LF**
1940	Bobo Newsom	P
1941	Al Benton	P
1941	Birdie Tebbetts	C
1941	Rudy York	1B
1942	Al Benton	P
1942	**Hal Newhouser**	**P**
1942	Birdie Tebbetts	C
1942	Rudy York	1B
1943	**Hal Newhouser**	**P**
1943	Dick Wakefield	LF
1943	Rudy York	1B
1944	Pinky Higgins	3B

Year	Player	Pos.
1944	**Hal Newhouser**	**P**
1944	Dizzy Trout	P
1944	Rudy York	1B
1945	**Hank Greenberg**	**LF**
1945	Eddie Mayo	2B
1945	**Hal Newhouser**	**P**
1946	**Hal Newhouser**	**P**
1947	**George Kell**	**3B**
1947	Pat Mullin	RF
1947	**Hal Newhouser**	**P**
1947	Dizzy Trout	P
1948	Hoot Evers	CF
1948	**George Kell**	**3B**
1948	Pat Mullin	RF
1948	**Hal Newhouser**	**P**
1949	**George Kell**	**3B**
1949	Virgil Trucks	P
1949	Vic Wertz	RF
1950	Hoot Evers	LF
1950	Ted Gray	P
1950	Art Houtteman	P
1950	**George Kell**	**3B**
1951	Fred Hutchinson	P
1951	**George Kell**	**3B**
1951	Vic Wertz	RF
1952	Vic Wertz	RF
1953	Harvey Kuenn	SS

Birdie Tebbetts

Year	Player	Pos.
1954	Ray Boone	3B
1954	Harvey Kuenn	SS
1955	Billy Hoeft	P
1955	**Al Kaline**	**RF**
1955	Harvey Kuenn	SS
1956	Ray Boone	3B
1956	**Al Kaline**	**RF**
1956	Harvey Kuenn	SS
1956	Charlie Maxwell	LF
1957	**Jim Bunning**	**P**
1957	**Al Kaline**	**RF**
1957	Harvey Kuenn	SS

Year	Player	Pos.
1957	Charlie Maxwell	LF
1958	**Al Kaline**	**RF**
1958	Harvey Kuenn	CF
1959	**Jim Bunning**	**P**
1959	**Al Kaline**	**CF**
1959	Harvey Kuenn	RF
1960	**Al Kaline**	**CF**
1960	Frank Lary	P
1961	**Jim Bunning**	**P**
1961	Norm Cash	1B
1961	Rocky Colavito	LF
1961	**Al Kaline**	**RF**

Bill Freehan

Year	Player	Pos.
1961	Frank Lary	P
1962	Hank Aguirre	P
1962	**Jim Bunning**	**P**
1962	Rocky Colavito	LF
1962	**Al Kaline**	**RF**
1963	**Jim Bunning**	**P**
1963	**Al Kaline**	**RF**
1964	Bill Freehan	C
1964	**Al Kaline**	**RF**
1964	Jerry Lumpe	2B
1965	Bill Freehan	C
1965	Willie Horton	LF
1965	**Al Kaline**	**CF**
1965	Dick McAuliffe	SS
1966	Norm Cash	1B
1966	Bill Freehan	C
1966	**Al Kaline**	**CF**
1966	Dick McAuliffe	SS
1966	Denny McLain	P
1967	Bill Freehan	C
1967	**Al Kaline**	**RF**
1967	Dick McAuliffe	2B
1968	Bill Freehan	C
1968	Willie Horton	LF
1968	Denny McLain	P
1968	Don Wert	3B

1969	Bill Freehan	C
1969	Mickey Lolich	P
1969	Denny McLain	P
1970	Bill Freehan	C
1970	Willie Horton	LF
1971	Norm Cash	1B
1971	Bill Freehan	C
1971	**Al Kaline**	**RF**
1971	Mickey Lolich	P
1972	Norm Cash	1B
1972	Joe Coleman	P
1972	Bill Freehan	C
1972	Mickey Lolich	P
1973	Eddie Brinkman	SS
1973	Bill Freehan	C
1973	Willie Horton	LF
1974	John Hiller	P
1974	**Al Kaline**	**DH**
1975	Bill Freehan	C
1976	Mark Fidrych	P
1976	Ron LeFlore	CF
1976	Rusty Staub	RF
1977	Mark Fidrych	P
1977	Jason Thompson	1B
1978	Jason Thompson	1B
1979	Steve Kemp	LF
1980	Lance Parrish	C

Eddie Brinkman

1980	**Alan Trammell**	**SS**
1981	**Jack Morris**	**P**
1982	Lance Parrish	C
1983	Aurelio Lopez	P
1983	Lance Parrish	C
1983	Lou Whitaker	2B
1984	Willie Hernandez	P
1984	Chet Lemon	CF
1984	**Jack Morris**	**P**
1984	Lance Parrish	C
1984	**Alan Trammell**	**SS**
1985	Willie Hernandez	P

Carlos Guillen

1985	**Jack Morris**	**P**
1984	Lou Whitaker	2B
1985	Lance Parrish	C
1985	Dan Petry	P
1985	**Alan Trammell**	**SS**
1985	Lou Whitaker	2B
1986	Willie Hernandez	P
1986	Lance Parrish	C
1986	Lou Whitaker	2B
1987	**Jack Morris**	**P**
1987	Matt Nokes	C
1987	**Alan Trammell**	**SS**
1987	Lou Whitaker	2B
1988	Doyle Alexander	P
1988	**Alan Trammell**	**SS**
1989	Mike Henneman	P
1990	Cecil Fielder	1B
1990	**Alan Trammell**	**SS**
1991	Cecil Fielder	1B
1992	Travis Fryman	SS
1993	Cecil Fielder	1B
1993	Travis Fryman	SS
1994	Travis Fryman	3B
1994	Mickey Tettleton	C
1995	David Wells	P
1996	Travis Fryman	3B
1997	Justin Thompson	P
1998	Damion Easley	2B
1999	Brad Ausmus	C
2000	Todd Jones	P
2001	Tony Clark	1B
2002	Robert Fick	RF
2003	Dmitri Young	DH
2004	Carlos Guillen	SS
2004	**Ivan Rodriguez**	**C**
2005	**Ivan Rodriguez**	**C**
2006	Magglio Ordonez	RF
2006	**Ivan Rodriguez**	**C**
2006	Kenny Rogers	P
2007	Carlos Guillen	SS
2007	Magglio Ordonez	RF
2007	Placido Polanco	2B
2007	**Ivan Rodriguez**	**C**
2007	Justin Verlander	P
2008	Carlos Guillen	SS
2009	Curtis Granderson	CF
2009	Brandon Inge	3B
2009	Edwin Jackson	P
2009	Justin Verlander	P
2010	Miguel Cabrera	1B
2010	Jose Valverde	P
2010	Justin Verlander	P
2011	Alex Avila	C
2011	Miguel Cabrera	1B
2011	Jhonny Peralta	SS
2011	Jose Valverde	P
2011	Justin Verlander	P
2012	Miguel Cabrera	3B
2012	Prince Fielder	1B
2012	Justin Verlander	P
2013	Miguel Cabrera	3B
2013	Prince Fielder	1B
2013	Torii Hunter	RF
2013	Jhonny Peralta	SS
2013	Max Scherzer	P
2013	Justin Verlander	P
2014	Miguel Cabrera	1B
2014	Ian Kinsler	2B

Joe Jimenez

2014	Victor Martinez	DH
2014	Max Scherzer	P
2015	Miguel Cabrera	1B
2015	Jose Iglesias	SS
2015	J.D. Martinez	RF
2015	David Price	P
2016	Miguel Cabrera	1B
2017	Michael Fulmer	P
2017	Justin Upton	LF
2018	Joe Jimenez	P
2019	Shane Greene	P
2021	Gregory Soto	P

All-Century Team (1999 Fan Vote)
OF Ty Cobb 777,056

All-Star Award (Associated Press)
1983	Lou Whitaker	2B
	Lance Parrish	C
1984	Willie Hernandez	RP
1985	Darrell Evans	DH
1987	Alan Trammell	SS
1988	Alan Trammell	SS
1990	Cecil Fielder	1B
1991	Cecil Fielder	1B
	Mickey Tettleton	C

All-Time Team (1997 BWAA)
CF Runner-up Ty Cobb

Andrew "Rube" Foster Legacy Award
2011 Dave Dombrowski GM

Babe Ruth Award (NY area BBWAA chapter)
1968	Mickey Lolich	LHP
1984	Jack Morris	RHP

Best Major League Baseball Player (ESPY Award)
2013	Miguel Cabrera	3B
2014	Miguel Cabrera	1B

Best Regular Season Game (Sports Illustrated)
Twins-Tigers, October 6, 2009

Blooper of the Year Award (This Year in Baseball Awards)
2006 Sean Casey is thrown out on a sure-fire single.

Closer of the Year Award (GIBBY Awards)
2011 Jose Valverde Detroit

Bullpen of the Week
2016 6/20-6/26 Detroit Tigers

Chalmers Award (MVP)
1911 Ty Cobb CF

Club Retailer of the Year Award
2011 Detroit Tigers

Comeback Player of the Year Award (The Sporting News)
1965	Norm Cash	1B
1971	Norm Cash	1B
1973	John Hiller	LHP
1983	Alan Trammell	SS

Commissioner's Trophy
1968	Detroit Tigers
1984	Detroit Tigers

Defensive Player of the Year (GIBBY)
2007 Placido Polanco 2B

DHL Delivery Man of the Year Award
2011 Jose Valverde RHP

DHL Hometown Heroes (Best player of Franchise)
Ty Cobb OF Detroit

Edgar Martinez Outstanding Designated Hitter Award (BWAA 2000-2020)
2014 Victor Martinez DH

Executive of the Year (Sporting News)
1940	Walter Briggs Sr.	Detroit
1968	Jim Campbell	Detroit
2011	Dave Dombrowski	Detroit

Fielding Bible Awards (Baseball Info Solutions)
2006	Ivan Rodriguez	C
2008	Kenny Rogers	P
2011	Austin Jackson	CF
2015	Ian Kinsler	2B

Fireman of the Year (Sporting News)
1973	John Hiller	Detroit
2000	Todd Jones	Detroit

Ford C. Frick Award
1981 Ernie Harwell

Frank Slocum Big B.A.T. Award (Baseball Assistance Team)
2007 Sean Casey

Heart and Hustle Award (MLB Players Alumni Association)
2017	Ian Kinsler	Detroit
2018	JaCoby Jones	Detroit
2019	Niko Goodrum	Detroit

Hitter of the Year Award (GIBBY)
2012	Miguel Cabrera	Detroit
2013	Miguel Cabrera	Detroit

Honor Rolls of Baseball (National Baseball Hall of Fame)
1953 Ed Barrow Executive

Hutch Award
1969	Al Kaline	OF
1973	John Hiller	LHP

J.G. Taylor Spink Award (BWAA)
1968	Harry G. Salsinger
1972	Fred Lieb
2001	Joe Falls
2015	Tom Gage

Jack Graney Award (Canadian Baseball Hall of Fame)
2002 Ernie Harwell WXYT Detroit

Joe Black MVP Award (Arizona Fall League)
2004 Chris Shelton DH

Lou Aparicio Award
2007	Magglio Ordonez	OF
2011	Miguel Cabrera	1B
2012	Miguel Cabrera	3B
2013	Miguel Cabrera	3B
2015	Miguel Cabrera	1B

Lou Gehrig Memorial Award (Phi Delta Theta Fraternity)
1968 Al Kaline OF

Major league Executive of the Year (Baseball America)
2006 Dave Dombrowski Detroit

Major League Quadruple Triple Crown
	H	HR	RBI	AVG	
1909	216	9	107	.377	Ty Cobb

Major League Triple Crown
	HR	RBI	AVG	
1909	9	107	.377	Ty Cobb

MLB MVP (GIBBY Awards)
2012	Miguel Cabrera	Detroit
2013	Miguel Cabrera	Detroit

Manager of the Year (AP)
1961	Bob Scheffing	101-61
1968	Mayo Smith	103-59

Manager of the Year (Baseball America)
2006 Jim Leyland 95-67

Manager of the Year (This Year in Baseball Awards)
2006 Jim Leyland 95-67

Manager of the Year (Sporting News)
1950	Red Rolfe	95-59
1968	Mayo Smith	103-59

Manager of the Year Award (Major League Baseball)
1984	Sparky Anderson	104-58
1987	Sparky Anderson	98-64
2006	Jim Leyland	95-67

Marvin Miller Man of the Year Award
(Players Choice Awards)

2009	Curtis Granderson	OF
2010	Brandon Inge	3B

Most Valuable Player (BWAA)

1934	Mickey Cochrane	C
1935	Hank Greenberg	1B
1937	Charlie Gehringer	2B
1940	Hank Greenberg	LF
1944	Hal Newhouser	LHP
1945	Hal Newhouser	LHP
1968	Denny McLain	RHP
1984	Willie Hernandez	LHP
2011	Justin Verlander	RHP
2012	Miguel Cabrera	3B
2013	Miguel Cabrera	3B

Most Valuable Player (Sporting News)

1935	Hank Greenberg	1B
1937	Charlie Gehringer	2B
1940	Hank Greenberg	LF
1945	Eddi Mayo	2B

Organization of the Year
(Baseball America)

1997	Detroit Tigers	AL

Outstanding Designated Hitter Award
(Associated Press 1973-1999)

1975	Willie Horton	DH
1978	Rusty Staub	DH

Outstanding Pitcher of the Year
(Players Choice Awards)

2011	Justin Verlander	RHP
2013	Max Scherzer	RHP

Outstanding Player of the Year
(Players Choice Awards)

2012	Miguel Cabrera	3B
2013	Miguel Cabrera	3B

Outstanding Rookie of the Year
(Players Choice Awards)

2006	Justin Verlander	RHP
2010	Austin Jackson	CF
2016	Michael Fulmer	RHP

Pitcher of the Year (Baseball Digest)

2011	Justin Verlander	RHP
2013	Max Scherzer	RHP

Pitcher of the Year (Sporting News)

1944	Hal Newhouser	LHP
1945	Hal Newhouser	LHP
1968	Denny McLain	RHP
1969	Denny McLain	RHP
1981	Jack Morris	RHP
1984	Willie Hernandez	LHP
2011	Justin Verlander	RHP
2012	Justin Verlander	RHP

Pitching Triple Crown

1945	Hal Newhouser	LHP
2011	Justin Verlander	RHP

Player of the Year (Associated Press)

1990	Cecil Fielder	1B

Player of the Year (Baseball Digest)

2012	Miguel Cabrera	3B
2013	Miguel Cabrera	3B

Player of the Year (Players Choice)

2011	Justin Verlander	RHP
2012	Miguel Cabrera	3B
2013	Miguel Cabrera	3B

Player of the Year (Sporting News)

1945	Hal Newhouser	LHP
1968	Denny McLain	RHP
2011	Justin Verlander	RHP
2012	Miguel Cabrera	3B
2013	Miguel Cabrera	3B

Quadruple Triple Crown

	H	HR	RBI	AVG	
1909	216	9	107	.377	Ty Cobb

Rawlings Award
(Woman Executive of the Year)

1989	Pat Hamilton	Toledo
1996	Audrey Zielinski	Detroit

Red Smith Award
(Associated Press Sports Editors)

2010	Mitch Albom	Det. Free Press

Reliever of the Month

2019	Shane Greene	APR

Roberto Clemente Award

1973	Al Kaline	OF

Rookie of the Month Award
(Major League Baseball)

2006	Justin Verlander	MAY	RHP
2009	Rick Porcello	MAY	RHP
2010	Austin Jackson	APR	OF
2010	Brennan Boesch	MAY	OF
2010	Brennan Boesch	JUN	OF

Rookie of the Year (Baseball America)

2006	Justin Verlander	RHP

Rookie of the Year (BWAA)

1953	Harvey Kuenn	SS
1976	Mark Fidrych	RHP
1978	Lou Whitaker	2B
2006	Justin Verlander	RHP
2016	Michael Fulmer	RHP

Rookie of the Year (Sporting News)

1953	Harvey Kuenn	SS
1976	Mark Fidrych	RHP
1977	Dave Rozema	RHP
1987	Mike Henneman	RHP
2006	Justin Verlander	RHP
2010	Austin Jackson	OF
2016	Michael Fulmer	RHP

Sabermetric Triple Crown

	TB	RC	OBP	
1909	296	126	.431	Ty Cobb
1915	274	138	.486	Ty Cobb
1917	335	148	.444	Ty Cobb

Scout of the Year Award (East)

1994	Steve Souchock	Detroit
2010	Murray Cook	Detroit

Scout of the Year Award (Midwest)

1990	Dee Phillips	Detroit

Setup Man of the Year Award
(This Year in Baseball Awards)

2006	Joel Zumaya	Detroit

Slocum Award

1940	Edward G. Barrow
1942	Mel Ott
1947	Shag Shaughnessy
1948	Bucky Harris
1973	Al Kaline
1979	Ralph Houk
1992	Ernie Harwell
1996	Sparky Anderson
2003	Gene Michael

Starting Pitcher of the Year (MLB)

2011	Justin Verlander	RHP

Starting Pitcher of the Year
(Sporting News)

2013	Max Scherzer	RHP

Starting Pitcher of the Year Award
(GIBBY Awards)

2011	Justin Verlander	Detroit

Triple Crown

	HR	RBI	AVG	
1909	9	107	.377	Ty Cobb
2012	44	139	.330	Miguel Cabrera

Willie, Mickey, and the Duke Award
(NY BWAA)

2008	The Summer of 1968: Pitchers Bob Gibson, Denny McLain, and Luis Tiant

Championship Series MVP

1984	Kirk Gibson	OF
2006	Placido Polanco	2B

Charles Isham Taylor Legacy Award

2006	Jim Leyland	Detroit

Comeback Player of the Year (Sporting News)

1965	Norm Cash	1B
1971	Norm Cash	1B
1973	John Hiller	LHP
1983	Alan Trammell	SS

Cy Young Award (BWAA)

1968	Denny McLain	31-6	1.96
1969	Denny McLain	24-9	2.80
1984	Willie Hernandez	9-3	1.92
2011	Justin Verlander	24-5	2.40
2013	Max Scherzer	21-3	2.90

Edgar Martinez Award

1975	Willie Horton	DH
1978	Rusty Staub	DH
2014	Victor Martinez	DH

Hank Aaron Award (Major League Baseball)

2012	Miguel Cabrera	3B
2013	Miguel Cabrera	3B

Hilton Smith Legacy Award (Negro Leagues Baseball Museum)

2011	Jose Valverde	Detroit

Josh Gibson Legacy Award

2008	Miguel Cabrera	Detroit
2012	Miguel Cabrera	Detroit

Larry Doby Legacy Award (Negro Leagues Baseball Museum)

2006	Justin Verlander	Detroit
2016	Michael Fulmer	Detroit

Rookie of the Month Award

2006	May	Justin Verlander
2009	May	Rick Porcello
2010	April	Austin Jackson
2010	May	Brennan Boesch
2010	June	Brennan Boesch
2021	July	Eric Haase

Pitcher of the Month

1984	April	Jack Morris
1984	July	Willie Hernandez
1986	July	Jack Morris
1987	Sep	Doyle Alexander
1993	Aug	Bill Gullickson
2000	Aug	Steve Sparks
2009	May	Justin Verlander
2011	June	Justin Verlander
2011	Sept	Doug Fister
2016	April	Jordan Zimmermann
2016	July	Justin Verlander

Player of the Month

1974	Sep	Al Kaline
1976	April	Willie Horton
1976	May	Ron LeFlore
1976	June	Mark Fidrych
1983	June	Lou Whitaker
1984	April	Alan Trammell
1987	Sep	Alan Trammell
1990	Aug	Cecil Fielder
2004	June	Ivan Rodriguez
2007	Aug	Magglio Ordonez
2008	July	Miguel Cabrera
2012	Aug	Miguel Cabrera
2013	May	Miguel Cabrera
2013	Aug	Miguel Cabrera
2014	Aug	Victor Martinez
2014	Sep	Miguel Cabrera
2016	Sep	Miguel Cabrera

Player of the Week

1975	Aug 3	Willie Horton
1976	Apr 25	Willie Horton
1976	May 9	Ron LeFlore
1976	Jun 6	Ben Oglivie
1978	Jun 25	Jason Thompson
1979	Jun 3	Lance Parrish
1980	May 18	Alan Trammell
1980	Aug 24	Tom Brookens
1980	Sep 21	Steve Kemp
1981	Aug 30	Kirk Gibson
1981	Oct 4	Kirk Gibson
1982	May 23	Larry Herndon
1983	Apr 17	Milt Wilcox
1983	Jun 12	Lou Whitaker
1984	Apr 8	Jack Morris
1984	Jun 24	Lance Parrish
1985	May 19	Darrell Evans
1985	Jun 9	Kirk Gibson
1985	Sep 22	Darrell Evans
1986	Apr 13	Kirk Gibson
1986	Jun 29	Kirk Gibson
1986	Jul 13	Jack Morris
1986	Jul 20	Kirk Gibson
1986	Jul 27	Johnny Grubb
1986	Sep 28	Jack Morris
1987	Sep 20	Alan Trammell
1988	Jul 3	Pat Sheridan
1988	Oct 2	Chet Lemon
1990	May 13	Cecil Fielder
1990	Aug 19	Cecil Fielder
1991	May 26	Tony Phillips
1991	Aug 25	Walt Terrell
1992	Sep 27	Rob Deer
1993	Apr 18	Travis Fryman
1993	Jun 20	Cecil Fielder
1993	Aug 15	Dan Gladden
1993	Aug 29	Mickey Tettleton
1995	May 28	Kirk Gibson
1996	Sep 29	Tony Clark
1997	Apr 20	Tony Clark
1997	Jul 6	Brian Hunter
1998	May 24	Damion Easley
1998	Sep 13	Joe Randa
2000	Jun 18	Bobby Higginson
2000	Jun 25	Tony Clark
2000	Oct 1	Bobby Higginson
2001	Jul 15	Bobby Higginson
2002	Jun 16	Robert Fick
2004	Jul 11	Jason Johnson
2004	Aug 22	Bobby Higginson
2002	Jul 28	Randall Simon
2003	Jun 1	Dmitri Young
2005	Apr 10	Dmitri Young
2006	Apr 9	Chris Shelton
2006	May 28	Justin Verlander
2007	Apr 29	Magglio Ordonez
2007	Jun 10	Gary Sheffield
2007	Jun 17	Justin Verlander
2007	Jun 24	Carlos Guillen
2007	Jul 15	Curtis Granderson
2008	Apr 20	Miguel Cabrera
2008	May 25	Magglio Ordonez
2008	Jul 13	Matthew Joyce
2008	Jul 27	Miguel Cabrera
2010	Apr 11	Miguel Cabrera
2010	Jun 6	Armando Galarraga
2010	Jul 11	Miguel Cabrera
2011	May 8	Justin Verlander
2011	May 15	Victor Martinez
2011	Jun 19	Justin Verlander
2011	Sep 4	Austin Jackson
2011	Sep 18	Justin Verlander
2012	Apr 8	Miguel Cabrera
2012	Sep 16	Miguel Cabrera
2012	Sep 30	Justin Verlander
2013	Apr 14	Prince Fielder
2013	May 5	Ryan Raburn
2013	June 23	Max Scherzer
2013	Aug 11	Cabrera/Jackson
2014	Jun 22	J.D. Martinez
2014	Sep 7	Miguel Cabrera
2015	Apr 12	Miguel Cabrera
2015	July 5	J.D. Martinez
2016	May 1	Victor Martinez
2016	May 22	Cabrera/Maybin
2016	Sep 25	Justin Upton
2016	Oct 2	Miguel Cabrera
2017	May 21	J.D. Martinez
2017	July 16	J.D. Martinez
2018	Aug 19	Nicholas Castellanos
2020	Sep 13	Jeimer Candelario
2021	May 23	Spencer Turnbull

Rookie of the Year Award (BWAA)
Renamed Jackie Robinson Award 1987

1953	Harvey Kuenn	SS
1976	Mark Fidrych	RHP
1978	Lou Whitaker	2B
2006	Justin Verlander	RHP
2016	Michael Fulmer	RHP

Rawlings Gold Glove - Catcher

1965	Bill Freehan	C
1966	Bill Freehan	C
1967	Bill Freehan	C
1968	Bill Freehan	C
1969	Bill Freehan	C
1983	Lance Parrish	C
1984	Lance Parrish	C
1985	Lance Parrish	C
2004	Ivan Rodriguez	C
2006	Ivan Rodriguez	C
2007	Ivan Rodriguez	C

Rawlings Gold Glove - Outfield

1957	Al Kaline	OF
1958	Al Kaline	OF
1959	Al Kaline	OF
1961	Al Kaline	OF
1962	Al Kaline	OF
1963	Al Kaline	OF
1964	Al Kaline	OF
1965	Al Kaline	OF
1966	Al Kaline	OF
1967	Al Kaline	OF
1968	Mickey Stanley	OF
1969	Mickey Stanley	OF
1970	Mickey Stanley	OF
1973	Mickey Stanley	OF
1988	Gary Pettis	OF
1989	Gary Pettis	OF
2015	Yoenis Cespedes	OF

Rawlings Gold Glove - Pitcher

1961	Frank Lary	P
2006	Kenny Rogers	P

Rawlings Gold Glove - Second Base

1958	Frank Bolling	2B
1983	Lou Whitaker	2B
1984	Lou Whitaker	2B
1985	Lou Whitaker	2B
2007	Placido Polanco	2B
2009	Placido Polanco	2B
2016	Ian Kinsler	2B
2018	Ian Kinsler	2B

Rawlings Gold Glove - Shortstop

1980	Alan Trammell	SS
1981	Alan Trammell	SS
1983	Alan Trammell	SS
1984	Alan Trammell	SS

Rawlings Gold Glove - Third Base

1976	Aurelio Rodriguez	3B

Silver Bat Award (Batting Champion)

1949	George Kell	.343
1955	Al Kaline	.340
1961	Norm Cash	.361
2007	Magglio Ordonez	.363
2011	Miguel Cabrera	.344
2012	Miguel Cabrera	.330
2013	Miguel Cabrera	.348
2015	Miguel Cabrera	.338

Dean Palmer

Silver Slugger Award - Catcher

1980	Lance Parrish	C
1982	Lance Parrish	C
1983	Lance Parrish	C
1984	Lance Parrish	C
1986	Lance Parrish	C
1987	Matt Nokes	C
1991	Mickey Tettleton	C
1992	Mickey Tettleton	C
2004	Ivan Rodriguez	C
2011	Alex Avila	C

Silver Slugger Award - DH

2014	Victor Martinez	DH

Silver Slugger Award - First Base

1990	Cecil Fielder	1B
1991	Cecil Fielder	1B
2010	Miguel Cabrera	1B
2012	Prince Fielder	1B
2015	Miguel Cabrera	1B
2016	Miguel Cabrera	1B

Silver Slugger Award - Outfield

2007	Magglio Ordonez	OF
2013	Torii Hunter	OF
2015	J.D. Martinez	OF

Silver Slugger Award - Second Base

1983	Lou Whitaker	2B
1984	Lou Whitaker	2B
1985	Lou Whitaker	2B
1987	Lou Whitaker	2B
1998	Damion Easley	2B
2007	Placido Polanco	2B

Silver Slugger Award - Shortstop

1987	Alan Trammell	SS
1988	Alan Trammell	SS
1990	Alan Trammell	SS
1992	Travis Fryman	SS

Silver Slugger Award - Third Base

1999	Dean Palmer	3B
2012	Miguel Cabrera	3B
2013	Miguel Cabrera	3B

Sophomore of the Year Award

1954	Harvey Kuenn	SS
1955	Al Kaline	CF

TSN Manager of the Year Award

1987	Sparky Anderson	98-64
2006	Jim Leyland	95-67

TSN Player of the Year Award

1945	Eddie Mayo	2B
1955	Al Kaline	RF
1963	Al Kaline	RF
1990	Cecil Fielder	1B

Walter "Buck" Leonard Legacy Award
(Negro Leagues Baseball Museum)

2007	Magglio Ordonez	Detroit
2011	Miguel Cabrera	Detroit
2012	Miguel Cabrera	Detroit
2013	Miguel Cabrera	Detroit
2015	Miguel Cabrera	Detroit

Wilbur "Bullet" Rogan Legacy Award
(Negro Leagues Baseball Museum)

2011	Justin Verlander	Detroit
2013	Max Scherzer	Detroit

William Harridge Trophy
American League Champion

1907	Detroit Tigers
1908	Detroit Tigers
1909	Detroit Tigers
1934	Detroit Tigers
1935	Detroit Tigers
1940	Detroit Tigers
1945	Detroit Tigers
1968	Detroit Tigers
1984	Detroit Tigers
2006	Detroit Tigers
2012	Detroit Tigers

Wilson Defensive Player of the Year

2012	Austin Jackson	OF
2013	Austin Jackson	OF
2014	Ian Kinsler	2B

Tiger of the Year Award
(BWAA - Detroit Chapter)

Year	Player	Position
1965	Don Wert	3B
1966	Al Kaline	CF-RF
1967	Bill Freehan	C
1968	Denny McLain	RHP
1969	Denny McLain	RHP
1970	Tom Timmerman	RHP
1971	Mickey Lolich	LHP
1972	Ed Brinkman	SS
1973	John Hiller	LHP
1974	Al Kaline	DH
1975	Willie Horton	DH
1976	Mark Fidrych	RHP
1977	Ron LeFlore	CF
1978	Ron LeFlore	CF
1979	Steve Kemp	LF
1980	Alan Trammell	SS
1981	Kirk Gibson	RF-CF
1982	Lance Parrish	C
1983	Lou Whitaker	2B
1984	Willie Hernandez	LHP
1985	Darrell Evans	1B
1986	Jack Morris	RHP
1987	Alan Trammell	SS
1988	Alan Trammell	SS
1989	Lou Whitaker	2B
1990	Cecil Fielder	1B
1991	Cecil Fielder	1B
1992	Cecil Fielder	1B
1993	Tony Philips	2B-LF
1994	Kirk Gibson	DH-OF
1995	Travis Fryman	3B
1996	Travis Fryman	3B
1997	Tony Clark	1B
	Bobby Higginson	LF
1998	Damion Easley	2B
1999	Dean Palmer	3B
2000	Bobby Higginson	LF
2001	Steve Sparks	RHP
2002	Randall Simon	DH-1B
2003	Dmitri Young	DH-LF
2004	Ivan Rodriguez	C
2005	Placido Polanco	2B
2006	Carlos Guillen	SS
2007	Magglio Ordonez	RF
2008	Miguel Cabrera	1B
2009	Justin Verlander	RHP
2010	Miguel Cabrera	1B
2011	Justin Verlander	RHP
2012	Miguel Cabrera	3B
2013	Miguel Cabrera	3B
2014	Victor Martinez	DH
2015	J.D. Martinez	RF
2016	Justin Verlander	RHP
2017	Justin Upton	LF
2018	Nicholas Castellanos	RF
2019	Matt Boyd	LHP
2020	Jeimer Candelario	1B
2021	Jeimer Candelario	3B

Tiger Rookie of the Year Award
(BWAA – Detroit Chapter)

Year	Player	Position
1969	Mike Kilkenny	LHP
1970	Elliott Maddox	3B-LF
1971	No Selection	
1972	Chuck Seelbach	RHP
1973	Dick Sharon	RF
1974	Ron LeFlore	CF
1975	Vern Ruhle	RHP
1976	Mark Fidrych	RHP
1977	Dave Rozema	RHP
1978	Lou Whitaker	2B
1979	Lynn Jones	CF
1980	Rick Peters	CF
1981	No Selection	
1982	Glenn Wilson	CF
1983	Dave Gumpert	RHP
1984	Barbaro Garbey	1B
1985	Nelson Simmons	DH-LF
1986	Eric King	RHP
1987	Matt Nokes	C
1988	Paul Gibson	LHP
1989	Kevin Ritz	RHP
1990	Travis Fryman	SS
1991	Milt Cuyler	CF
1992	Scott Livingstone	3B
1993	Chris Gomez	SS
1994	Chris Gomez	SS
1995	Bobby Higginson	RF-LF
1996	Tony Clark	1B
1997	Deivi Cruz	SS
1998	Matt Anderson	RHP
1999	Gabe Kapler	CF
2000	Jose Macias	2B-3B
2001	Victor Santos	RHP
2002	Carlos Pena	1B
2003	Craig Monroe	LF
2004	Nook Logan	CF
2005	Curtis Granderson	CF
2006	Justin Verlander	RHP
2007	Ryan Raburn	OF
2008	Armando Galarraga	RHP
2009	Rick Porcello	RHP
2010	Austin Jackson	CF
2011	Al Alburquerque	RHP
2012	Quintin Berry	LF
2013	Jose Iglesias	SS
2014	Nicholas Castellanos	3B
2015	James McCann	C
2016	Michael Fulmer	RHP
2017	Dixon Machado	SS-2B
2018	Niko Goodrum	2B
2019	Harold Castro	2B-CF
2020	Willi Castro	SS
2021	Akil Baddoo	OF

King Tiger Award
(Mayo Smith Society)

Year	Player	Position
2004	Carlos Guillen	SS
	Ivan Rodriguez	C
2005	Placido Polanco	2B
2006	Kenny Rogers	LHP
2007	Magglio Ordonez	RF
2008	Miguel Cabrera	1B
2009	Justin Verlander	RHP
2010	Miguel Cabrera	1B
2011	Justin Verlander	RHP
2012	Miguel Cabrera	3B
2013	Max Scherzer	RHP
2014	Victor Martinez	DH
2015	J.D. Martinez	RF
2016	Ian Kinsler	2B
	Justin Verlander	RHP
2017	Nicholas Castellanos	RF
2018	Niko Goodrum	2B
2019	Matt Boyd	LHP
2020	Jeimer Candelario	1B

Placido Polanco

Bill MacAdam Tenth Man Award
(Detroit Baseball Society)

Year	Player
2011	Don Kelly
2012	Quintin Berry
2013	Don Kelly
2014	No Selection
2015	Rajai Davis
2016	Andrew Romine
2017	John Hicks
2018	Niko Goodrum
2019	No Selection
2020	No Selection

Tigers Legend Award
(Detroit Baseball Society)

Year	Player
2015	Mickey Stanley
2020	Lance Parrish

Minor League Player of the Year

1938	Fred Hutchinson	P
1986	Gregg Jefferies	SS
1987	Gregg Jefferies	SS
2005	Delmon Young	RF

Minor League Player of the Year (Baseball America)

1986	Gregg Jefferies	SS
1987	Gregg Jefferies	SS
2005	Delmon Young	RF

Minor League Player of the Year (USA Today)

1998	Gabe Kapler	OF
2003	Prince Fielder	1B
2005	Francisco Liriano	LHP
2007	Justin Upton	OF
2008	David Price	LHP

Appalachian League Hall of Fame

Boyce Cox	2019
Alan Trammell	2019
Lou Whitaker	2020

California League Hall of Fame

Vada Pinson	2016
Gary Sheffield	2016
Omar Vizquel	2016

California League Manager of the Year

1957	Roy Partee
1960	Billy DeMars
1965	Harry Malmberg
1971	Roy Majtyka
1972	Tom Burgess
1977	Stan Wasiak
1978	Stan Wasiak
1986	Tom Kotchman
1987	Dave Machemer
1988	Dave Huppert
1996	Carlos Lezcano
2000	Mark Parent
2002	Bill Plummer
2006	Gary Thurman
2010	Carlos Lezcano
2016	Howard Johnson
2018	Rick Magnante
2019	Shawn Roof

California League MVP

1942	Salvador Taormina	OF
1955	Pumpsie Green	SS
1957	Vada Pinson	OF
1963	Jose Vidal	OF
1988	Paul Faries	INF
1998	Brad Penny	RHP

California League Pitcher of the Year

1998	Brad Penny	RHP

California League Rookie of the Year

1971	Johnny Grubb	OF-3B
1987	Gary Sheffield	SS
1988	Paul Faries	2B
2004	Erick Aybar	SS
2012	C.J. Cron	1B

Carolina League Manager of the Year

1945	Herb Brett
1948	Buddy Bates
1949	Ace Parker
1851	Ace Parker
1952	Herb Brett
1953	Herb Brett
1956	Johnny Pesky
1957	Bobby Mavis
1967	Clyde Mccullough
1969	Al Federoff
1974	Johnny Lipon
1976	Tony Torchia
1982	Bill Dancy
1991	Brian Graham
1998	Chris Cron
1999	Eric Wedge
2001	Brad Komminsk
2003	Dave Clark
2004	Torey Lovullo
2005	Ivan DeJesus
2013	Jason Wood
2018	Omar Vizquel

Carolina League MVP

1960	Ed Olivares	OF
1962	Rusty Staub	1B
1963	Jim Price	C
1981	Brad Komminsk	OF
1982	Juan Samuel	2B
1986	Gregg Jefferies	SS
2001	Victor Martinez	C
2003	Chris Shelton	1B
2004	Brad Eldred	1B
2005	Leo Daigle	1B

Carolina League Pitcher of the Year

1982	Charles Hudson	RHP
1992	John Cummings	LHP
1994	Bart Evans	RHP
2005	Jim Johnson	RHP

Eastern League Most Valuable Pitcher

1988	Cesar Mejia	RHP
1990	Mike Gardiner	RHP
1993	Joey Eischen	LHP
1994	Juan Acevedo	RHP
1998	Brent Stentz	RHP
2015	Michael Fulmer	RHP
2019	Matt Manning	RHP

Eastern League Manager of the Year

1963	Johnny Lipon
1970	John Davis
1976	Roy Majtyka
1983	Bill Dancy
1986	Bob Schaefer
1990	Chris Chambliss
1995	Bill Dancy
2002	Brad Komminsk
2003	Marty Pevey
2005	Torey Lovullo
2007	Matt Walbeck
2008	Brad Komminsk
2010	Mat Walbeck
2014	Billy McMillon
2017	Bobby Mitchell

Eastern League MVP

1975	Dave Bergman
1977	Harry Spilman
1988	Rob Richie
1991	Matt Stairs
2002	Victor Martinez
2014	Steven Moya

Eastern League Rookie of the Year

1994	Juan Acevedo	RHP
2006	Kory Castro	3B/RF

Florida State League Hall of Fame

Johnny Lipon	2009
Stan Wasiak	2009
Felipe Alou	2010
Jim Leyland	2010
Ivan Rodriguez	2011
Dave Huppert	2012
Lloyd Moseby	2012
Lou Whitaker	2012
Al Nipper	2013
Kirk Gibson	2015
Justin Verlander	2015
Gene Lamont	2016
Joe McDonald	2017

FSL Manager of the Year

Mark Meleski	1997
Mike Rojas	2005

FSL Most Valuable Pitcher

2005	Jordan Tata	RHP

Florida State League MVP

2005	Brent Clevlen	OF

International League Rookie of Year

1961	Tom Tresh	SS
1964	Jim Northrup	OF
1996	Billy McMillon	OF
2000	Aubrey Huff	3B
2005	Francisco Liriano	LHP
2009	Austin Jackson	OF

International League Hall of Fame

Charlie Keller	1947
Steve O'Neill	1947
Frank Shaughnessy	1947
Dixie Walker	1947
Jewel Ens	1950
Dan Howley	1950
Eddie Onslow	1951
Fred Hutchinson	1954
Luke Hamlin	1955
George Stallings	1959
Ike Boone	2003
Dale Alexander	2008
Gene Cook	2008
George Quellich	2008
Steve Demeter	2009
Rube Kisinger	2009
Frank Carswell	2010
Bob Seeds	2010
Mack Jones	2013
Larry Parrish	2013
Jim Weber	2014
Lee Gardner	2017
Mike Hessman	2018

International League MVP

1932	Marv Owen	3B
1933	Red Rolfe	SS
1934	Ike Boone	OF/MGR
1938	Ollie Carnegie	OF
1941	Fred Hutchinson	RHP
1946	Eddie Robinson	1B
1948	Jimmy Bloodworth	2B
1951	Archie Wilson	OF
1953	Rocky Nelson	1B
1958	Rocky Nelson	1B
1959	Pancho Herrera	1B
1968	Merv Rettenmund	OF
1969	Luis Alvarado	SS
1976	Joe Lis	1B
1989	Tom O'Malley	3B
1994	Jeff Manto	3B-1B
1996	Phil Hiatt	3B
2002	Raul Gonzalez	OF
2003	Fernando Seguignol	DH
2004	Jhonny Peralta	SS
2006	Kevin Witt	1B
2007	Mike Hessman	3B

IL Manager of the Year

1967	Jack Tighe
1968	Jack Tighe
1969	Clyde McCullough
1984	Tony Torchia
2001	Eric Wedge
2008	Rick Sweet
2009	Rick Sweet
2005	Larry Parrish
2015	Ron Johnson
2016	Al Pedrique
2017	Al Pedrique

IL Most Valuable Pitcher

1955	Jack Crimian	RHP
1956	Lynn Lovenguth	RHP
1960	Al Cicotte	RHP
1965	Sam Jones	RHP
1868	Dave Roberts	LHP
1970	Rob Gardner	LHP
1971	Roric Harrison	RHP
1973	Dick Pole	RHP
1978	Juan Berenguer	RHP
1983	Walt Terrell	RHP
1984	Brad Havens	LHP
1988	Steve Searcy	LHP
1998	Shannon Withem	RHP
2016	Jake Thompson	RHP

Kinston Pro Baseball Hall of Fame

Charlie Keller	1983
George Suggs	1983
Cecil Fielder	1994
Jim Price	1995
Gordie Mackenzie	2005
Sean Casey	2009
Gene Michael	2010

Midwest League Manager of the Year

1956	Len Okrie
1959	Stubby Overmire
1967	Alex Cosmidis
1970	Frank Calo
1971	Joe Sparks
1975	John Sullivan
1976	Salty Parker
1984	Tom Gamboa
1985	Duffy Dyer
1997	Bruce Fields
2000	Bruce Fields
2006	Matt Walbeck
2007	Tom Brookens
2009	Marty Pevey
2017	Mike Rabelo

Midwest League Prospect of the Year

1960	Bob Sprout	LHP
1961	Dennis Ribant	RHP
1993	Johnny Damon	OF
1997	Francisco Cordero	RHP
2003	Prince Fielder	1B
2006	Cameron Maybin	CF

Midwest League MVP

1962	Tony Torchia	1B
1983	Curt Ford	OF
1985	Eddie Williams	3B
1995	Jesus Ibarra	1B
1997	Robert Fick	1B
2003	Prince Fielder	1B
2006	Jeff Baisley	3B
2007	Gorkys Hernandez	CF
2014	Wynton Bernard	RF/CF

New York-Penn League Hall of Fame

Jim Leyland	2015

Northwest League MVP

1991	Joe Randa	3B

Pacific Coast League Hall of Fame

Pop Dillon	
Red Killefer	
Walt McCredie	
Herman Pillette	
Frenchy Uhalt	
Ossie Vitt	
Johnny Bassler	1943
Steve Bilko	2003
Ike Boone	2003
Oscar Eckhardt Jr.	2003
Sam Gibson	2003
Fred Haney	2003
Earl Rapp	2004
Bill Sweeney	2004
Pants Rowland	2005
Babe Ellison	2006
Earl Averill	2009
Dave Barbee	2014

Pacific Coast League Most Valuable Player

1933	Bobo Newsom	RHP
1936	Willie Ludolph	RHP
1938	Fred Hutchinson	RHP
1940	George Archie	1B
1944	Les Scarsella	OF
1945	Bob Joyce	RHP
1946	Les Scarsella	OF
1947	Tony Lupien	1B
1950	Catfish Metkovich	OF
1953	Dale Long	1B
1954	Jack Phillips	1B
1955	Steve Bilko	1B
1956	Steve Bilko	1B
1957	Steve Bilko	1B
1958	Earl Averill	C
1967	Rick Joseph	3B
1972	Tom Paciorek	1B
1984	Alejandro Sanchez	OF
1994	Billy Ashley	OF
2001	Phil Hiatt	3B
2003	Graham Koonce	1B-DH

Pacific Coast League Manager of the Year

1967	Johnny Lipon
1972	Andy Seminick
1974	Rocky Bridges
1977	Rocky Bridges
1994	Rick Sweet

PCL Pitcher of the Year

2008	Shane Loux	RHP

South Atlantic League MVP

1981	Jeff Reynolds	3B
2010	J.D. Martinez	OF

South Atlantic League Hall of Fame

Sparky Anderson	1994
Ty Cobb	1994
John Moss	1994
Bob Bonifay	1995
Goose Goslin	1995
Roy Majtyka	1996
Dwight Lowry	1998
Murray Cook	2001
Doug Flynn	2003
Jack Farnsworth	2005
Buddy Bell	2008
Vince Coleman	2008
Lena Blackburne	2013

Southern League Hall of Fame

Peter Bragan	2014
Billy Hitchcock	2014
Alan Trammell	2014
Lou Whitaker	2015

Southern League Manager of the Year

1972	Joe Sparks
1977	Ed Brinkman
1982	Gene Lamont
1983	Roy Majtyka
1990	Ron Gardenhire/Jerry Manuel
1991	Chris Chambliss
1993	Terry Francona
1995	Bruce Kimm
2010	Bill Dancy

Southern League MVP

1977	Alan Trammell	SS
1998	Gabe Kapler	OF
2005	Delmon Young	RF

Southern League Most Outstanding Pitcher

1972	Bill Campbell	RHP
1983	Don Heinkel	RHP
1990	Brian Barnes	LHP
1999	Francisco Cordero	RHP
2003	Joel Hanrahan	RHP
2011	Matt Moore	LHP

Texas League Pitcher of the Year

1946	Prince Oana	RHP
1950	Wayne McLeland	RHP
1952	Hal Erickson	RHP
1964	Chris Zachary	RHP
1973	Frank Tanana	LHP
1985	Juan Nieves	LHP
2013	David Martinez	RHP

Texas League Player of the Year

1932	Hank Greenberg	1B
1935	Rudy York	1B
1938	Dizzy Trout	RHP
1942	Dick Wakefield	OF
1967	Nate Colbert	1B
1971	Enos Cabell	1B
1987	Greg Jefferies	SS
1995	Johnny Damon	CF

Texas League Hall of Fame

Jake Atz	2004
Paul Easterling	2004
Hank Greenberg	2004
Clarence Kraft	2004
Joe Pate	2004
Al Simmons	2004
Paul Wachtel	2004
Ziggy Sears	2005
Al Vincent	2005
Augie Johns	2006
Del Pratt	2006
Ed Konetchy	2008
Randy Ready	2009
Eddie Palmer	2010
Gregg Jefferies	2011
Nig Clarke	2015
Frank Tanana	2015
Tom Walker	2015

Joe Bauman Home Run Award

2002	Ivan Cruz	DH
2003	Graham Koonce	
2006	Kevin Witt	

Lary Doby Award MVP Futures Game

2012	Nicholas Castellanos	DH

King of Baseball Award

1953	Frank "Shag" Shaughnessy
1963	Donie Bush
1974	Fred Haney
1980	Billy Hitchcock
1992	Johnny Lipon

Larry MacPhail Award (Top promotional effort)

2007	West Michigan Whitecaps

College Baseball Awards

Golden Spikes Award (USA Baseball)

1980	Terry Francona	1B
1992	Phil Nevin	3B
2007	David Price	LHP

College Baseball Hall of Fame

Pete Incaviglia	Oklahoma St.	2007
Fred Lynn	USC	2007
Keith Moreland	Texas	2009
Don Heinkel	Wichita St.	2010
Terry Francona	Arizona	2011

College Player of the Year (Baseball America)

1985	Pete Incaviglia	OF
1992	Phil Nevin	3B
2006	Andrew Miller	LHP
2007	David Price	LHP

Johnny Bench Award

2010	Bryan Holaday	TCU

Roger Clemens Award

2006	Andrew Miller	UNC
2007	David Price	Vanderbilt

Clint Hartung Award

1950s	Billy Consolo	SS
1980s	Brad Komminsk	OF

Dick Howser Trophy

2007	David Price	LHP	Vanderbilt

Brooks Wallace Award (Most Outstanding Collegiate Player)

2007	David Price	LHP	Vanderbilt

Most Outstanding Player Award (College World Series)

1980	Terry Francona	1B
1992	Phil Nevin	3B
2017	Alex Faedo	RHP

High School Baseball Awards

Gatorade Player of the Year

1987-88	Michigan	Steve Avery	P/CF

High School Player of the Year (Baseball America)

2005	Justin Upton	IF

National Baseball Gatorade Player of the Year

1986	Gary Sheffield	INF
1988	Mark Lewis	INF
1990	Todd Van Poppel	RHP
1992	A.J. Hinch	C
2005	Justin Upton	OF
2007	Rick Porcello	RHP

Player of the Year (USA Today)

1990	Todd Van Poppel	RHP
1998	Gerald Laird	C
1999	Cody Ross	OF
2003	Delmon Young	OF
2004	Justin Upton	IF
2005	Justin Upton	IF
2005	Cameron Maybin	OF
2007	Rick Porcello	RHP
2009	Jacob Turner	RHP
2015	Daz Cameron	OF
2019	Riley Greene	OF

TIGERS LEADING MAJOR LEAGUE BASEBALL IN HITTING

Games

1904 Jimmy Barrett 162
1909 Donie Bush 157
1933 Charlie Gehringer 155
Billy Rogell 155
1934 Charlie Gehringer 154
Marv Owen 154
Billy Rogell 154
1945 Rudy York 155
1947 Eddie Lake 158
1950 Johnny Groth 157
George Kell 157
Jerry Priddy 157
1954 Harvey Kuenn 155
1955 Bill Tuttle 154
1961 Rocky Colavito 163
1973 Eddie Brinkman 162
1991 Cecil Fielder 162
1997 Brian Hunter 162
2012 Prince Fielder 162
2013 Prince Fielder 162

Plate Appearances

1904 Jimmy Barrett 719
1913 Donie Bush 694
1914 Donie Bush 721
1918 Donie Bush 594
1946 Eddie Lake 705
1947 Eddie Lake 732
1953 Harvey Kuenn 731
1994 Tony Phillips 538
2014 Ian Kinsler 726

At-Bats

1941 Doc Cramer 630
1943 Dick Wakefield 633
1953 Harvey Kuenn 679
1954 Harvey Kuenn 656
1992 Travis Fryman 659
2014 Ian Kinsler 684

Hit by the Pitch

1923 Heinie Manush 17
1924 Heinie Manush 16
1962 Norm Cash 13
1967 Bill Freehan 20
1982 Chet Lemon 15
1983 Chet Lemon 20
2012 Prince Fielder 17

Bases on Balls

1909 Donie Bush 88
1914 Donie Bush 112
1938 Hank Greenberg 119
1959 Eddie Yost 135
1960 Eddie Yost 125
1993 Tony Phillips 132

On-Base Percentage

1909 Ty Cobb .431
1910 Ty Cobb .455
1913 Ty Cobb .466
1915 Ty Cobb .486
1917 Ty Cobb .444
1918 Ty Cobb .440
1961 Norm Cash .487
2011 Miguel Cabrera .448
2013 Miguel Cabrera .442

Runs

1908 Matty McIntyre 105
1911 Ty Cobb 148
1915 Ty Cobb 144
1916 Ty Cobb 113
1917 Donie Bush 112
1934 Charlie Gehringer 135
1938 Hank Greenberg 143
1978 Ron LeFlore 126
1992 Tony Phillips 114

Billy Rogell

Triples

1903 Sam Crawford 25
1908 Ty Cobb 20
1910 Sam Crawford 19
1913 Sam Crawford 23
1914 Sam Crawford 26
1917 Ty Cobb 24
1919 Bobby Veach 17
1940 Barney McCosky 19
1961 Jake Wood 14
2007 Curtis Granderson 23

Home Runs

1909 Ty Cobb 9
1935 Hank Greenberg 36
1938 Hank Greenberg 58
1943 Rudy York 34
1946 Hank Greenberg 44
1985 Darrell Evans 40
1990 Cecil Fielder 51
1991 Cecil Fielder 44
2012 Miguel Cabrera 44

Runs Batted In

1907 Ty Cobb 119
1909 Ty Cobb 107
1911 Ty Cobb 127
1917 Bobby Veach 110
1918 Bobby Veach 84
1935 Hank Greenberg 168
1937 Hank Greenberg 184
1940 Hank Greenberg 150
1990 Cecil Fielder 132
1991 Cecil Fielder 133
1992 Cecil Fielder 124
2010 Miguel Cabrera 126
2012 Miguel Cabrera 139

Doubles

1911 Ty Cobb 47
1915 Bobby Veach 40
1917 Ty Cobb 44
1919 Bobby Veach 45
1924 Harry Heilmann 45
1934 Hank Greenberg 63
1940 Hank Greenberg 50
1950 George Kell 56
1955 Harvey Kuenn 38
1958 Harvey Kuenn 39
1961 Al Kaline 41
2007 Magglio Ordonez 54
2011 Miguel Cabrera 48
2019 Castellanos (37 Det.) 58
2021 Jeimer Candelario 42

On-Base Plus Slugging

1909 Ty Cobb .947
1910 Ty Cobb 1.004
1911 Ty Cobb 1.086
1912 Ty Cobb 1.040
1915 Ty Cobb .973
1917 Ty Cobb 1.014
1918 Ty Cobb .955
1940 Hank Greenberg 1.103
1961 Norm Cash 1.148
2012 Miguel Cabrera .999
2013 Miguel Cabrera 1.078
2014 Victor Martinez .974

OPS+

1909 Ty Cobb 192
1910 Ty Cobb 205
1911 Ty Cobb 196
1912 Ty Cobb 200
1913 Ty Cobb 194
1915 Ty Cobb 185
1917 Ty Cobb 209
1918 Ty Cobb 194
2010 Miguel Cabrera 178
2013 Miguel Cabrera 190

Total Average

1909	Ty Cobb	1.193
1910	Ty Cobb	1.312
1911	Ty Cobb	1.459
1913	Ty Cobb	1.305
1915	Ty Cobb	1.267
1916	Ty Cobb	1.134
1917	Ty Cobb	1.253
1918	Ty Cobb	1.131
1940	Hank Greenberg	1.222
2013	Miguel Cabrera	1.184

Intentional Bases on Balls

2012	Prince Fielder	18
2014	Victor Martinez	28

Stolen Bases

1909	Ty Cobb	76
1911	Ty Cobb	83
1915	Ty Cobb	96
1916	Ty Cobb	68
1917	Ty Cobb	55
1997	Brian Hunter	74

Caught Stealing

1912	Ty Cobb	34
1915	Ty Cobb	38
1930	Charlie Gehringer	15
2003	Al. Sanchez (18 Det.)	24

Isolated Power

1935	Hank Greenberg	.300
1937	Hank Greenberg	.332
1938	Hank Greenberg	.369
1940	Hank Greenberg	.330
1943	Rudy York	.256
1946	Hank Greenberg	.327
1985	Darrell Evans	.271
1990	Cecil Fielder	.314

Power/Speed Number

1937	Gee Walker	20.2
1938	Charlie Gehringer	16.5
1984	Kirk Gibson	28.0

Secondary Average

1909	Ty Cobb	.356
1913	Ty Cobb	.399
1916	Ty Cobb	.346
1917	Ty Cobb	.384
1938	Hank Greenberg	.586
1940	Hank Greenberg	.497
1945	R. Cullenbine (.373 Det.)	.386

Strikeouts

1961	Jake Wood	141
1990	Cecil Fielder	182
1991	Rob Deer	175
1993	Rob Deer (120 Det.)	169
1994	Travis Fryman	128

Sacrifice Flies

1958	Frank Bolling	9
1994	Travis Fryman	13
2005	Craig Monroe	12
2014	Miguel Cabrera	11

Sacrifice Hits

1903	Billy Lush	34
1909	Donie Bush	52
1915	Ossie Vitt	42
1920	Donie Bush	48
1944	Eddie Mayo	28
2003	Ramon Santiago	18

Grounded into Double Plays

1943	Jimmy Bloodworth	29
1945	Rudy York	23
1955	Bill Tuttle	25
1968	Mickey Stanley	22
1977	Rusty Staub	27
2012	Miguel Cabrera	28
2016	Miguel Cabrera	26

Alex Sanchez

Batting Average on Balls in Play

1907	Ty Cobb	.380
1909	Ty Cobb	.399
1910	Ty Cobb	.410
1911	Ty Cobb	.443
1912	Ty Cobb	.424
1913	Ty Cobb	.414
1915	Ty Cobb	.397
1917	Ty Cobb	.400
1918	Ty Cobb	.398
1919	Ty Cobb	.400
1925	Harry Heilmann	.398
1926	Heinie Manush	.382
1927	Harry Heilmann	.394
1949	George Kell	.348
1961	Norm Cash	.370
1976	Ron LeFlore	.391
2010	Austin Jackson	.396

Total Bases

1907	Ty Cobb	283
1909	Ty Cobb	296
1911	Ty Cobb	367
1913	Sam Crawford	298
1917	Ty Cobb	335
1935	Hank Greenberg	389
1940	Hank Greenberg	384
2012	Miguel Cabrera	377

Batting Average

1907	Ty Cobb	.350
1909	Ty Cobb	.377
1911	Ty Cobb	.420
1912	Ty Cobb	.410
1913	Ty Cobb	.390
1915	Ty Cobb	.369
1917	Ty Cobb	.383
1918	Ty Cobb	.382
1919	Ty Cobb	.384
1923	Harry Heilmann	.403
1926	Heinie Manush	.378
1927	Harry Heilmann	.398
1949	George Kell	.343
1955	Al Kaline	.340
1961	Norm Cash	.361
2007	Magglio Ordonez	.363
2011	Miguel Cabrera	.344
2013	Miguel Cabrera	.348
2015	Miguel Cabrera	.338

Slugging

1909	Ty Cobb	.517
1910	Ty Cobb	.549
1911	Ty Cobb	.620
1912	Ty Cobb	.584
1917	Ty Cobb	.570
1918	Ty Cobb	.515
1940	Hank Greenberg	.670
1990	Cecil Fielder	.592
2013	Miguel Cabrera	.636
2017	J.D. Martinez (.630 Det.)	.690

Runs Created

1935	Hank Greenberg	159
1937	Hank Greenberg	172
1940	Hank Greenberg	166
1961	Norm Cash	178
2011	Miguel Cabrera	149
2013	Miguel Cabrera	155

Outs

1946	Eddie Lake	464
1953	Harvey Kuenn	486
1954	Harvey Kuenn	493
1992	Travis Fryman	512
1995	Chad Curtis	463
1997	Brian Hunter	525

At-Bats

1944	Dizzy Trout	1321
1945	Hal Newhouser	1132
1971	Mickey Lolich	1415
1983	Jack Morris	1101
2012	Justin Verlander	884
2014	David Price (304 Det.)	959

Balks

1914	Red Oldham	3
1925	Ed Wells	3
1926	Rip Collins	3
1927	Earl Whitehill	2
1928	Ken Holloway	1
1938	Vern Kennedy	2
1940	Bobo Newsom	2
1944	Hal Newhouser	2
1952	Bill Wight	4
1956	Paul Foytack	3
1957	Frank Lary	2
1958	Jim Bunning	3
2015	Al Alburquerque	4
2019	Matt Boyd	4

Bases on Balls per Nine Innings

1951	Fred Hutchinson	1.3

Bases on Balls

1919	Howard Ehmke	107
1956	Paul Foytack	142
1981	Jack Morris	78
1994	Mike Moore	89

Batters Faced

1944	Dizzy Trout	1421
1945	Hal Newhouser	1261
1971	Mickey Lolich	1538
1983	Jack Morris	1204
2009	Justin Verlander	982
2012	Justin Verlander	956
2014	David Price (320 Det.)	1009

George Mullin

Batting Average

1918	H. Finneran (.393 Det.)	.315
1934	General Crowder	.315
1944	Johnny Gorsica	.296
1991	Walt Terrell	.301
1994	Bill Gullickson	.322
2003	Nate Cornejo	.307
2011	Brad Penny	.306
2012	Rick Porcello	.310

Batting Average on Balls in Play

1918	H. Finneran (.400 Det.)	.327
1934	General Crowder	.337
1945	Stubby Overmire	.306
1956	Billy Hoeft	.324
1973	Woodie Fryman	.327
2012	Rick Porcello	.310

Bunt Hits

1993	Bill Gullickson	10
1995	Sean Bergman	8
1998	Brian Moehler	7
2008	Nate Robertson	9
2010	Jeremy Bonderman	9
2013	Doug Fister	8

Caught Stealing

1953	Ted Gray	13
1955	Frank Lary	12
1961	Jim Bunning	11
1970	Mickey Lolich	16
1973	Mickey Lolich	19
1974	Mickey Lolich	32
2009	Justin Verlander	16
2010	Max Scherzer	13
2014	Max Scherzer	10

Cheap Wins

1924	Earl Whitehill	7
1926	Earl Whitehill	5
1943	Virgil Trucks	5
1956	Billy Hoeft	5
1959	Jim Bunning	6
1966	Mickey Lolich	5
1974	Joe Coleman	6
1983	Dan Petry	7
1986	Jack Morris	7

Complete Games

1944	Dizzy Trout	33
1945	Hal Newhouser	29
1947	Hal Newhouser	24
1961	Frank Lary	22
2001	Steve Sparks	8
2012	Justin Verlander	6

Infield Hits

2013	Doug Fister	37

Sean Bergman

Double Plays Grounded into

1935	General Crowder	30
1957	Frank Lary	35
1983	Dan Petry	36
1991	Walt Terrell	35

Doubles Allowed

1971	Mickey Lolich	49
1973	Mickey Lolich	56
1988	Doyle Alexander	52
1991	Bill Gullickson	51
2012	Rick Porcello	53

Earned Runs

1908	George Mullin	100
1926	Earl Whitehill	112
1974	Mickey Lolich	142
1990	Jack Morris	125
2003	Mike Maroth	123
2017	Jordan Zimmermann	108
2020	Matt Boyd	45

Earned Run Average

1944	Dizzy Trout	2.12
1945	Hal Newhouser	1.81
1946	Hal Newhouser	1.94
1951	Saul Rogovin (5.25 Det.)	2.78
1962	Hank Aguirre	2.21
1976	Mark Fidrych	2.34

Earned Run Average Plus

1940	Bobo Newsom	168
1944	Dizzy Trout	167
1945	Hal Newhouser	195
1946	Hal Newhouser	190
1951	Saul Rogovin (81 Det.)	146
1962	Hank Aguirre	185
1976	Mark Fidrych	159
2011	Justin Verlander	172
2012	Justin Verlander	161

Jerry Casale

Fielding Independent Pitching

1945	Hal Newhouser	2.45
1946	Hal Newhouser	1.97

Games

1984	Willie Hernandez	80
1996	Mike Myers	83
1998	Sean Runyan	88

Games in Relief

1916	Bernie Boland	37
1928	George Smith	37
1940	Al Benton	42
1984	Willie Hernandez	80
1996	Mike Myers	83
1998	Sean Runyan	88

Games Finished

1933	Chief Hogsett	34
1935	Chief Hogsett	30
1984	Willie Hernandez	68
2011	Jose Valverde	70
2012	Jose Valverde	67

Games Started

1936	Tommy Bridges	38
1939	Bobo Newsom (31 Det.)	37
1944	Dizzy Trout	40
1945	Hal Newhouser	36
1968	Denny McLain	41
1971	Mickey Lolich	45
1983	Dan Petry	38
1990	Jack Morris	36
1993	Mike Moore	36
2009	Justin Verlander	35
2011	Justin Verlander	34
2013	Justin Verlander	34
2014	David Price (11 Det.)	34

Hits Per Nine Innings

1945	Hal Newhouser	6.9
1946	Hal Newhouser	6.6

Home Runs

1931	Earl Whitehill	22
1946	Virgil Trucks	23
1963	Jim Bunning	38
1966	Denny McLain	42
1967	Denny McLain	35
1968	Denny McLain	31
1974	Mickey Lolich	38
1983	Dan Petry	37
1993	Mike Moore	35
2020	Matt Boyd	15

Home Runs – Grand Slams

1923	Syl Johnson	1
1926	Ed Wells	1
1931	Tommy Bridges	1
1932	Earl Whitehill	2
1941	Johnny Gorsica	2
1951	Bob Cain	3
1953	Bill Wight	2
1955	Al Aber	2
	Ned Garver	2
1958	Jim Bunning	3
1959	Ray Narleski	4
1962	Jerry Casale	2
1967	Denny McLain	2
1972	Joe Coleman	2
1980	Dan Schatzeder	2
	Roger Weaver	2
1986	Willie Hernandez	2
	Dave LaPoint	2
1989	Willie Hernandez	2
	Charles Hudson	2
1995	Joe Boever	3
1996	Gregg Olson	3
2017	Francisco Rodriguez	2

Home Runs - Home

1931	Earl Whitehill	11
1946	Virgil Trucks	15
1948	Fred Hutchinson	20
1950	Art Houtteman	21
1953	Ned Garver	15
1954	Steve Gromek	18
1957	Jim Bunning	23
1958	Jim Bunning	22
1963	Jim Bunning	24
1967	Earl Wilson	21
1968	Denny McLain	22
1971	Mickey Lolich	25
1972	Mickey Lolich	21
1973	Mickey Lolich	21
1974	Joe Coleman	19
	Mickey Lolich	19
1978	Jim Slaton	19
1987	Jack Morris	29
1992	Bill Gullickson	24
2019	Matt Boyd	26

Hits

1907	George Mullin	346
1944	Dizzy Trout	314
1947	Hal Newhouser	268
1971	Mickey Lolich	336
2014	David Price (74 Det.)	230

Home Runs - Road

1931	Earl Whitehill	11
1959	Jim Bunning	18
1966	Denny McLain	21
	Earl Wilson	21
1967	Denny McLain	17
1974	Mickey Lolich	19
1983	Dan Petry	21
1986	Jack Morris	24
1993	Mike Moore	21
2020	Matt Boyd	9

Holds

1919	Hooks Dauss	1
1920	Red Oldham	1
1921	Carl Holling	1
	Pol Perritt	1
	Suds Sutherland	1
1945	George Caster (1 Det.)	3
1956	Al Aber	4
1959	Pete Burnside	4
	Dave Sisler	4

Hit by the Pitch

1908	Ed Summers	20
1914	Hooks Dauss	18
1915	Harry Coveleski	20
1922	Howard Ehmke	23
1924	Earl Whitehill	13
1954	Steve Gromek	12
1956	Frank Lary	12
1957	Frank Lary	12
1960	Frank Lary	19
1965	Mickey Lolich	12
1990	Walt Terrell (8 Det.)	12
1999	Jeff Weaver	17
2000	Jeff Weaver	15
2007	Justin Verlander	19

Matt Boyd

Home Runs - Right-handers

1931	Earl Whitehill	17
1936	Tommy Bridges	16
1948	Fred Hutchinson	15
1953	Billy Hoeft	22
1954	Billy Hoeft	21
1971	Mickey Lolich	33
1972	Mickey Lolich	26
1973	Mickey Lolich	29
1974	Mickey Lolich	32
1993	David Wells	24
2003	Mike Maroth	30
2019	Matt Boyd	32
2020	Matt Boyd	14

Innings Pitched

1944	Dizzy Trout	352.1
1945	Hal Newhouser	313.1
1968	Denny McLain	336.0
1971	Mickey Lolich	376.0
1983	Jack Morris	293.2
2009	Justin Verlander	240.0
2011	Justin Verlander	251.0
2012	Justin Verlander	238.1
2014	David Price (77.2 Det.)	248.1

Bobo Newsom

Home Runs - Lefthanders

1946	Virgil Trucks	14
1954	Steve Gromek	14
1958	Jim Bunning	18
1963	Jim Bunning	24
1966	Denny McLain	22
1967	Denny McLain	19
1968	Denny McLain	19
1974	Joe Coleman	20
1982	Jack Morris	22
1983	Dan Petry	21
1991	Bill Gullickson	15
1992	Bill Gullickson	18
1999	Jeff Weaver	20
2008	Armando Galarraga	21

No Decisions in Games Started

1921	Dutch Leonard	10
1922	Red Oldham	9
1924	Rip Collins	9
1925	Earl Whitehill	11
1937	Jake Wade	9
1940	Hal Newhouser	10
1942	Al Benton	11
1968	Joe Sparma	12
1974	Joe Coleman	15
1997	Omar Olivares	15
2020	Michael Fulmer	8

Home Runs - Per Nine Innings

1902	Ed Siever	0.0
1904	Ed Killian	0.0
	George Mullin	0.0
1905	Ed Killian	0.0
1906	Red Donahue	0.0
1907	George Mullin	0.0
	Ed Siever	0.0
1908	George Mullin	0.0
1909	George Mullin	0.0
1913	Jean Dubuc	0.0
	Ed Willett	0.0
1915	Hooks Dauss	0.0
1917	Bernie Boland	0.0
1918	Bernie Boland	0.0
	George Cunningham	0.0
	Rudy Kallio	0.0
1942	Virgil Trucks	0.161
1955	Frank Lary	0.383

On-Base Plus Slugging

1918	H. Finneran (.854 Det.)	.782
1973	Woodie Fryman	.808
1974	Lerrin LaGrow	.770
1975	Joe Coleman	.828
1990	Frank Tanana	.801
1991	Walt Terrell	.791
2020	Matt Boyd	.900

Runs

1919	Hooks Dauss	125
1920	Hooks Dauss	158
1926	Earl Whitehill	136
1974	Joe Coleman	160
1990	Jack Morris	144
1994	Tim Belcher	124

Pitches

2009	Justin Verlander	3937
2011	Justin Verlander	3941
2012	Justin Verlander	3768
2013	Justin Verlander	3692
2014	David Price (1166 Det.)	3730
2016	Justin Verlander	3668
2017	Justin Verlander	3531

Quality Starts

1944	Dizzy Trout	31
1945	Hal Newhouser	31
1961	Frank Lary	25
1968	Denny McLain	35
2011	Justin Verlander	28
2016	Justin Verlander	27
2017	Justin Verlander	23

Losses

1923	Herman Pillette	19
1939	Vern Kennedy (3 Det.)	20
1941	Bobo Newsom	20
1970	Mickey Lolich	19
1989	Doyle Alexander	18
1994	Tim Belcher	15
1995	Mike Moore	15
2003	Mike Maroth	21
2008	Justin Verlander	17
2019	Spencer Turnbull	17

Passed Balls

1929	George Uhle	5
1930	George Uhle	4
1937	Boots Poffenberger	5

Spencer Turnbull

Quality Start Percentage

1943	Tommy Bridges	82%
1944	Hal Newhouser	79%
1945	Hal Newhouser	86%
1954	Steve Gromek	75%
1962	Hank Aguirre	82%

Pickoffs

1940	Bobo Newsom	4
1946	Hal Newhouser	3
1950	Art Houtteman	4
1970	Mickey Lolich	13
2003	Mike Maroth	7
2014	Drew Smyly (5 Det.)	7

Pitches per Plate Appearance

2012	Max Scherzer	4.15

Plate Appearances

1944	Dizzy Trout	1421
1945	Hal Newhouser	1261
1971	Mickey Lolich	1538
1983	Jack Morris	1204
2009	Justin Verlander	982
2012	Justin Verlander	956
2014	David Price (320 Det.)	1009

Reached on Error

1970	Mickey Lolich	23
1990	Jack Morris	21

Sacrifice Hits

1931	Earl Whitehill	29
1932	Whit Wyatt	22
1947	Hal Newhouser	27
1960	Jim Bunning	23
1972	Mickey Lolich	23
2020	Spencer Turnbull	2

Shutouts

1932	Tommy Bridges	4
1935	Schoolboy Rowe	6
1944	Dizzy Trout	7
1945	Hal Newhouser	8
1949	Virgil Trucks	6
1955	Billy Hoeft	7
1967	Mickey Lolich	6
1969	Denny McLain	9
1986	Jack Morris	6
2014	Rick Porcello	3

Sacrifice Flies

1956	Billy Hoeft	12
1981	Jack Morris	9
2005	Mike Maroth	11
	Nate Robertson	11
2009	Armando Galarraga	11

Steve Gromek

Slugging Percentage

1918	Happy Finneran	.412
1934	General Crowder	.468
1974	Mickey Lolich	.426
1975	Joe Coleman	.465
2002	Steve Sparks	.486
2020	Matt Boyd	.552

Strikeouts

1944	Hal Newhouser	187
1945	Hal Newhouser	212
1949	Virgil Trucks	153
1971	Mickey Lolich	308
2009	Justin Verlander	269
2011	Justin Verlander	250
2012	Justin Verlander	239
2014	David Price (82 Det.)	271

Stolen Bases

1931	Tommy Bridges	22
1933	Tommy Bridges	22
1969	Mickey Lolich	24
	Denny McLain	24
1974	Joe Coleman	46

Strikeouts per Nine Innings

1945	Hal Newhouser	6.1
1946	Hal Newhouser	8.5
2012	Max Scherzer	11.1

Strikeouts to Walks

1961	Don Mossi	2.91

Tough Losses

1921	Dutch Leonard	7
1943	Hal Newhouser	9
1947	Hal Newhouser	9
1954	Steve Gromek	8
1955	Frank Lary	10
1997	Justin Thompson	8
2003	Jeremy Bonderman	8
	Mike Maroth	8
2006	Nate Robertson	7

Total Bases

1971	Mickey Lolich	509
1974	Mickey Lolich	492
1988	Doyle Alexander	420
1991	Bill Gullickson	387
2014	David price (112 Det.)	360

Triples Allowed

2006	Jeremy Bonderman	10

Win-Loss Percentage

1907	Bill Donovan	.862
1968	Denny McLain	.838
2013	Max Scherzer	.875

Intentional Walks

1989	Mike Henneman	15
1994	Joe Boever	12

Mike Henneman

Saves

1940	Al Benton	17
1973	John Hiller	38
2011	Jose Valverde	49

Wild Pitches

1920	Dutch Leonard	13
1945	Hal Newhouser	10
1947	Hal Newhouser	11
1983	Jack Morris	18
1987	Jack Morris	24
2007	Justin Verlander	17

Wins Above Replacement - Pitcher

1944	Dizzy Trout	9.3
1945	Hal Newhouser	11.3
1958	Frank Lary	6.7
1962	Hank Aguirre	7.4
1976	Mark Fidrych	9.6
2012	Justin Verlander	8.1
2016	Justin Verlander	7.4

Wins

1909	George Mullin	29
1944	Hal Newhouser	29
1945	Hal Newhouser	25
1946	Hal Newhouser	26
1967	Earl Wilson	22
1968	Denny McLain	31
1971	Mickey Lolich	25
1981	Jack Morris	14
1991	Bill Gullickson	20
2009	Justin Verlander	19
2011	Justin Verlander	24
2013	Max Scherzer	21

Walks Plus Hits per Innings Pitched

1946	Hal Newhouser	1.069
2011	Justin Verlander	0.920
2013	Max Scherzer	0.970
2016	Justin Verlander	1.001

At-Bats

1908	Sam Crawford	591
1913	Sam Crawford	609
1917	Ty Cobb	588
1929	Roy Johnson	640
1941	Doc Cramer	630
1943	Dick Wakefield	633
1950	George Kell	641
1953	Harvey Kuenn	679
1954	Harvey Kuenn	656
1992	Travis Fryman	659
1994	Travis Fryman	464
2014	Ian Kinsler	684

Bases on Balls

1903	Jimmy Barrett	74
1904	Jimmy Barrett	79
1909	Donie Bush	88
1910	Donie Bush	78
1911	Donie Bush	98
1912	Donie Bush	117
1914	Donie Bush	112
1938	Hank Greenberg	119
1959	Eddie Yost	135
1960	Eddie Yost	125
1992	Mickey Tettleton	122
1993	Tony Phillips	132

Batting Average

1907	Ty Cobb	.350
1908	Ty Cobb	.324
1909	Ty Cobb	.377
1910	Ty Cobb	.383
1911	Ty Cobb	.420
1912	Ty Cobb	.410
1913	Ty Cobb	.390
1914	Ty Cobb	.368
1915	Ty Cobb	.369
1917	Ty Cobb	.383
1918	Ty Cobb	.382
1919	Ty Cobb	.384
1921	Harry Heilmann	.394
1923	Harry Heilmann	.403
1925	Harry Heilmann	.393
1926	Heinie Manush	.378
1927	Harry Heilmann	.398
1937	Charlie Gehringer	.371
1949	George Kell	.343
1955	Al Kaline	.340
1959	Harvey Kuenn	.353
1961	Norm Cash	.361
2007	Magglio Ordonez	.363
2011	Miguel Cabrera	.344
2012	Miguel Cabrera	.330
2013	Miguel Cabrera	.348
2015	Miguel Cabrera	.338

Batting Average on Balls in Play

1907	Ty Cobb	.380
1908	Ty Cobb	.345
1909	Ty Cobb	.399
1910	Ty Cobb	.410
1911	Ty Cobb	.443
1912	Ty Cobb	.424
1913	Ty Cobb	.414
1915	Ty Cobb	.397
1917	Ty Cobb	.400
1918	Ty Cobb	.398
1919	Ty Cobb	.400
1921	Harry Heilmann	.399
1925	Harry Heilmann	.398
1926	Heinie Manush	.382
1927	Harry Heilmann	.394
1934	Hank Greenberg	.369
1937	Charlie Gehringer	.371
1949	George Kell	.348
1955	Al Kaline	.339
1959	Harvey Kuenn	.364
1961	Norm Cash	.370
1976	Ron LeFlore	.391
2010	Austin Jackson	.396
2015	Miguel Cabrera	.384
2016	J.D. Martinez	.378

Caught Stealing

1912	Ty Cobb	34
1915	Ty Cobb	38
1930	Charlie Gehringer	15
1950	Hoot Evers	9
1997	Brian Hunter	18
2001	Roger Cedeno	15
2003	Alex Sanchez	18

Doubles

1908	Ty Cobb	36
1909	Sam Crawford	35
1911	Ty Cobb	47
1915	Bobby Veach	40
1917	Ty Cobb	44
1919	Bobby Veach	45
1924	Harry Heilmann	45
1929	Charlie Gehringer	45
	Roy Johnson	45
1934	Hank Greenberg	63
1936	Charlie Gehringer	60
1940	Hank Greenberg	50
1943	Dick Wakefield	38
1950	George Kell	56
1951	George Kell	36
1955	Harvey Kuenn	38
1958	Harvey Kuenn	39
1959	Harvey Kuenn	42
1961	Al Kaline	41
2007	Magglio Ordonez	54
2011	Miguel Cabrera	48
2014	Miguel Cabrera	52

Games

Year	Player	Games
1904	Jimmy Barrett	162
1909	Donie Bush	157
1920	Bobby Veach	154
1922	Topper Rigney	155
	Bobby Veach	155
1926	Jackie Tavener	156
1929	Dale Alexander	155
	Charlie Gehringer	155
1930	Dale Alexander	154
	Charlie Gehringer	154
1933	Charlie Gehringer	155
	Billy Rogell	155
1934	Charlie Gehringer	154
	Marv Owen	154
	Billy Rogell	154
1940	Rudy York	155
1943	Dick Wakefield	155
	Rudy York	155
1945	Rudy York	155
1946	Eddie Lake	155
1947	Eddie Lake	158
1949	Vic Wertz	155
1950	Johnny Groth	157
	George Kell	157
	Jerry Priddy	157
1951	Jerry Priddy	154
1954	Harvey Kuenn	155
1955	Bill Tuttle	154
1961	Rocky Colavito	163
1965	Don Wert	162
1972	Eddie Brinkman	156
1973	Eddie Brinkman	162
1976	Rusty Staub	161
1981	Lou Whitaker	109
1991	Cecil Fielder	162
1997	Brian Hunter	162
2009	Brandon Inge	161
2011	Miguel Cabrera	161
2012	Prince Fielder	162
2013	Prince Fielder	162

Eddie Lake

Grounded into Double Plays

1943	Jimmy Bloodworth	29
1945	Rudy York	23
1955	Bill Tuttle	25
1968	Mickey Stanley	22
1976	Rusty Staub	23
1977	Rusty Staub	27
2008	Magglio Ordonez	27
2012	Miguel Cabrera	28
2016	Miguel Cabrera	26

Hit by the Pitch

1902	Dick Harley	12
1914	George Burns	12
1917	Tubby Spencer	9
	Bobby Veach	9
1923	Heinie Manush	17
1924	Heinie Manush	16
1962	Norm Cash	13
1964	Bill Freehan	8
1967	Bill Freehan	20
1968	Bill Freehan	24
1982	Chet Lemon	15
1983	Chet Lemon	20
2012	Prince Fielder	17

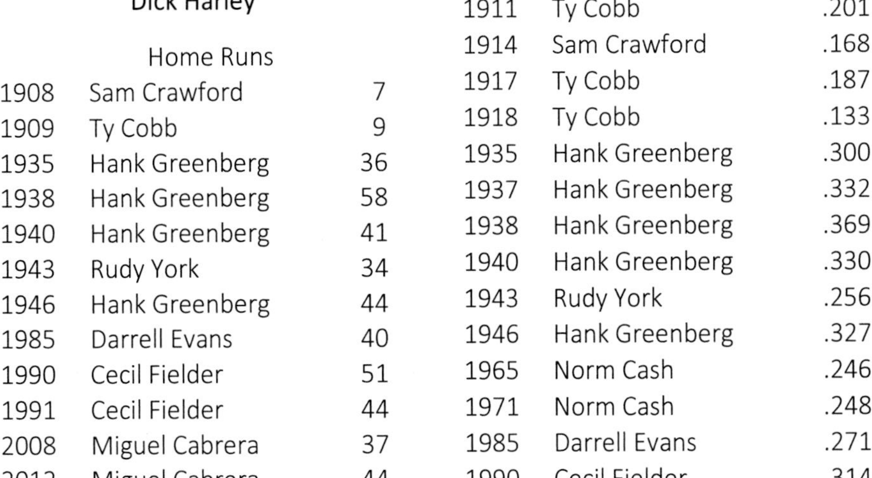

Dick Harley

Home Runs

1908	Sam Crawford	7
1909	Ty Cobb	9
1935	Hank Greenberg	36
1938	Hank Greenberg	58
1940	Hank Greenberg	41
1943	Rudy York	34
1946	Hank Greenberg	44
1985	Darrell Evans	40
1990	Cecil Fielder	51
1991	Cecil Fielder	44
2008	Miguel Cabrera	37
2012	Miguel Cabrera	44

Hits

1907	Ty Cobb	212
1908	Ty Cobb	188
1909	Ty Cobb	216
1911	Ty Cobb	248
1912	Ty Cobb	226
1915	Ty Cobb	208
1917	Ty Cobb	225
1919	Ty Cobb	191
	Bobby Veach	191
1921	Harry Heilmann	237
1929	Dale Alexander	215
	Charlie Gehringer	215
1934	Charlie Gehringer	214
1940	Barney McCosky	200
1943	Dick Wakefield	200
1950	George Kell	218
1951	George Kell	191
1953	Harvey Kuenn	209
1954	Harvey Kuenn	201
1955	Al Kaline	200
1956	Harvey Kuenn	196
1959	Harvey Kuenn	198
1961	Norm Cash	193

Intentional Bases on Balls

1950	Vic Wertz	8
1959	Al Kaline	12
1961	Norm Cash	19
1963	Al Kaline	12
1967	Bill Freehan	15
2010	Miguel Cabrera	32
2012	Prince Fielder	18
2014	Victor Martinez	28
2016	Miguel Cabrera	15

Isolated Power

1907	Sam Crawford	.137
1908	Ty Cobb	.152
1910	Ty Cobb	.167
1911	Ty Cobb	.201
1914	Sam Crawford	.168
1917	Ty Cobb	.187
1918	Ty Cobb	.133
1935	Hank Greenberg	.300
1937	Hank Greenberg	.332
1938	Hank Greenberg	.369
1940	Hank Greenberg	.330
1943	Rudy York	.256
1946	Hank Greenberg	.327
1965	Norm Cash	.246
1971	Norm Cash	.248
1985	Darrell Evans	.271
1990	Cecil Fielder	.314

On-Base Percentage

1903	Jimmy Barrett	.407
1909	Ty Cobb	.431
1910	Ty Cobb	.455
1913	Ty Cobb	.466
1915	Ty Cobb	.486
1917	Ty Cobb	.444
1918	Ty Cobb	.440
1959	Eddie Yost	.435
1960	Eddie Yost	.414
1961	Norm Cash	.487
2010	Miguel Cabrera	.420
2011	Miguel Cabrera	.448
2013	Miguel Cabrera	.442
2014	Victor Martinez	.409
2015	Miguel Cabrera	.440

On-Base Plus Slugging

1907	Ty Cobb	.848
1908	Ty Cobb	.844
1909	Ty Cobb	.947
1910	Ty Cobb	1.004
1911	Ty Cobb	1.086
1912	Ty Cobb	1.040
1915	Ty Cobb	.973
1917	Ty Cobb	1.014
1918	Ty Cobb	.955
1925	Ty Cobb	1.066
1940	Hank Greenberg	1.103
1959	Al Kaline	.940
1961	Norm Cash	1.148
2012	Miguel Cabrera	.999
2013	Miguel Cabrera	1.078
2014	Victor Martinez	.974

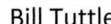

Bill Tuttle

OPS+

Year	Player	OPS+
1907	Ty Cobb	167
1908	Ty Cobb	170
1909	Ty Cobb	192
1910	Ty Cobb	205
1911	Ty Cobb	196
1912	Ty Cobb	200
1913	Ty Cobb	194
1915	Ty Cobb	185
1917	Ty Cobb	209
1918	Ty Cobb	194
1925	Ty Cobb	171
1959	Al Kaline	151
2010	Miguel Cabrera	178
2013	Miguel Cabrera	190

Outs

Year	Player	Outs
1908	Germany Schaefer	476
1911	Donie Bush	461
1914	Donie Bush	482
1931	Roy Johnson	471
1943	Joe Hoover	478
1944	Eddie Mayo	509
1946	Eddie Lake	464
1953	Harvey Kuenn	486
1954	Harvey Kuenn	493
1955	Bill Tuttle	481
1974	Gary Sutherland	489
1992	Travis Fryman	512
1995	Chad Curtis	463
1997	Brian Hunter	525
2014	Ian Kinsler	528

Plate Appearances

Year	Player	PA
1904	Jimmy Barrett	719
1908	Matty McIntyre	678
1909	Donie Bush	678
1913	Donie Bush	694
1914	Donie Bush	721
1915	Donie Bush	703
1918	Donie Bush	594
1922	Bobby Veach	705
1929	Charlie Gehringer	717
1943	Dick Wakefield	697
1946	Eddie Lake	705
1947	Eddie Lake	732
1953	Harvey Kuenn	731
1963	Rocky Colavito	692
1994	Tony Phillips	538
1995	Chad Curtis	670
2014	Ian Kinsler	726

Power/Speed Number

Year	Player	Power/Speed
1908	Sam Crawford	9.5
1909	Ty Cobb	16.1
1910	Ty Cobb	14.2
1917	Bobby Veach	11.6
1929	Charlie Gehringer	17.6
1932	Roy Johnson	16.5
1937	Gee Walker	20.2
1938	Charlie Gehringer	16.5
1946	Eddie Lake	10.4
1947	Eddie Lake	11.5
1984	Kirk Gibson	28.0
1995	Chad Curtis	23.6

Donie Bush

Runs Batted In

Year	Player	RBI
1907	Ty Cobb	119
1908	Ty Cobb	108
1909	Ty Cobb	107
1910	Sam Crawford	120
1911	Ty Cobb	127
1914	Sam Crawford	104
1915	Sam Crawford	112
	Bobby Veach	112
1917	Bobby Veach	110
1918	Bobby Veach	84
1925	Harry Heilmann	134
1935	Hank Greenberg	168
1937	Hank Greenberg	184
1940	Hank Greenberg	150
1943	Rudy York	118
1946	Hank Greenberg	127
1955	Ray Boone	116
1990	Cecil Fielder	132
1991	Cecil Fielder	133
1992	Cecil Fielder	124
2010	Miguel Cabrera	126
2012	Miguel Cabrera	139

Runs Created

Year	Player	Runs Created
1903	Sam Crawford	98
1907	Ty Cobb	106
1908	Ty Cobb	100
1909	Ty Cobb	126
1911	Ty Cobb	168
1915	Ty Cobb	138
1916	Ty Cobb	125
1917	Ty Cobb	148
1918	Ty Cobb	95
1935	Hank Greenberg	159
1937	Hank Greenberg	172
1940	Hank Greenberg	166
1943	Rudy York	109
1950	George Kell	124
1959	Harvey Kuenn	117
1961	Norm Cash	178
2010	Miguel Cabrera	141
2011	Miguel Cabrera	149
2012	Miguel Cabrera	139
2013	Miguel Cabrera	155

Runs

Year	Player	Runs
1907	Sam Crawford	102
1908	Matty McIntyre	105
1909	Donie Bush	115
	Ty Cobb	115
1910	Ty Cobb	106
1911	Ty Cobb	148
1915	Ty Cobb	144
1916	Ty Cobb	113
1917	Donie Bush	112
1929	Charlie Gehringer	131
1934	Charlie Gehringer	135
1938	Hank Greenberg	143
1959	Eddie Yost	115
1968	Dick McAuliffe	95
1978	Ron LeFlore	126
1992	Tony Phillips	114

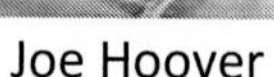

Joe Hoover

Sacrifice Flies

1958	Frank Bolling	9
1963	Bubba Phillips	10
1983	Lance Parrish	13
1994	Travis Fryman	13
2005	Craig Monroe	12
2014	Miguel Cabrera	11

Sacrifice Hits

1901	Kid Nance	24
1903	Billy Lush	34
1909	Donie Bush	52
1915	Ossie Vitt	42
1920	Donie Bush	48
1943	Joe Hoover	28
1944	Eddie Mayo	28
1946	George Kell	15
1958	Billy Martin	13
1968	Denny McLain	16
1969	Denny McLain	13
1981	Alan Trammell	16
1983	Alan Trammell	15
2003	Ramon Santiago	18
2009	Adam Everett	15

Bubba Phillips

Secondary Average

1909	Ty Cobb	.356
1910	Ty Cobb	.421
1911	Ty Cobb	.416
1913	Ty Cobb	.399
1915	Ty Cobb	.430
1916	Ty Cobb	.346
1917	Ty Cobb	.384
1925	Ty Cobb	.386
1938	Hank Greenberg	.586
1940	Hank Greenberg	.497
1945	Roy Cullenbine	.386
1965	Norm Cash	.411

Slugging

1907	Ty Cobb	.468
1908	Ty Cobb	.476
1909	Ty Cobb	.517
1910	Ty Cobb	.549
1911	Ty Cobb	.620
1912	Ty Cobb	.584
1917	Ty Cobb	.570
1918	Ty Cobb	.515
1940	Hank Greenberg	.670
1943	Rudy York	.527
1959	Al Kaline	.530
1990	Cecil Fielder	.592
2012	Miguel Cabrera	.606
2013	Miguel Cabrera	.636

Stolen Bases

1907	Ty Cobb	53
1909	Ty Cobb	76
1911	Ty Cobb	83
1915	Ty Cobb	96
1916	Ty Cobb	68
1917	Ty Cobb	55
1929	Charlie Gehringer	27
1930	Marty McManus	23
1978	Ron LeFlore	68
1997	Brian Hunter	74

Strikeouts

1901	Jimmy Barrett	64
1938	Hank Greenberg	95
1961	Jake Wood	141
1990	Cecil Fielder	182
1991	Rob Deer	175
1993	Rob Deer	169
1994	Travis Fryman	128
2006	Curtis Granderson	174
2010	Austin Jackson	170

Total Average

1907	Ty Cobb	.929
1908	Ty Cobb	.906
1909	Ty Cobb	1.193
1910	Ty Cobb	1.312
1911	Ty Cobb	1.459
1913	Ty Cobb	1.305
1915	Ty Cobb	1.267
1916	Ty Cobb	1.134
1917	Ty Cobb	1.253
1918	Ty Cobb	1.131
1925	Ty Cobb	1.240
1940	Hank Greenberg	1.222
1959	Eddie Yost	.997
2010	Miguel Cabrera	1.124
2013	Miguel Cabrera	1.184

Total Bases

1907	Ty Cobb	283
1908	Ty Cobb	276
1909	Ty Cobb	296
1911	Ty Cobb	367
1913	Sam Crawford	298
1915	Ty Cobb	274
1917	Ty Cobb	335
1935	Hank Greenberg	389
1940	Hank Greenberg	384
1943	Rudy York	301
1955	Al Kaline	321
1962	Rocky Colavito	309
1990	Cecil Fielder	339
2008	Miguel Cabrera	331
2012	Miguel Cabrera	377

Cecil Fielder

Triples

1903	Sam Crawford	25
1908	Ty Cobb	20
1910	Sam Crawford	19
1911	Ty Cobb	24
1913	Sam Crawford	23
1914	Sam Crawford	26
1915	Sam Crawford	19
1917	Ty Cobb	24
1918	Ty Cobb	14
1919	Bobby Veach	17
1929	Charlie Gehringer	19
1931	Roy Johnson	19
1940	Barney McCosky	19
1950	Hoot Evers	11
1961	Jake Wood	14
2007	Curtis Granderson	23
2008	Curtis Granderson	13
2011	Austin Jackson	11
2012	Austin Jackson	10
2017	Nicholas Castellanos	10

At-Bats

Year	Player	At-Bats
1939	Bobo Newsom	1120
1944	Dizzy Trout	1321
1945	Hal Newhouser	1132
1947	Hal Newhouser	1074
1949	Hal Newhouser	1105
1956	Frank Lary	1126
1959	Jim Bunning	942
1960	Frank Lary	1052
1968	Denny McLain	1206
1969	Denny McLain	1215
1971	Mickey Lolich	1415
1983	Jack Morris	1101
2001	Steve Sparks	899
2011	Justin Verlander	904
2012	Justin Verlander	884
2014	David Price	959

Balks

Year	Player	Balks
1904	Ed Killian	1
1914	Red Oldham	3
1925	Ed Wells	3
1926	Rip Collins	3
1927	Earl Whitehill	2
1928	Ken Holloway	1
1937	Slick Coffman	2
1938	Vern Kennedy	2
1940	Bobo Newsom	2
1944	Hal Newhouser	2
1952	Bill Wight	4
1953	Ned Garver	1
	Billy Hoeft	1
1955	Ned Garver	1
	Steve Gromek	1
1956	Paul Foytack	3
1957	Frank Lary	2
1958	Jim Bunning	3
1960	Pete Burnside	2
1962	Paul Foytack	2
1963	Bill Faul	3
1999	C.J. Nitkowski	3
2008	Justin Verlander	3
2009	Justin Verlander	4
2011	Justin Verlander	2
2015	Al Alburquerque	4
2019	Matt Boyd	4

Bases on Balls per Nine Innings

Year	Player	BB/9
1947	Fred Hutchinson	2.5
1948	Fred Hutchinson	2.0
1949	Fred Hutchinson	2.5
1950	Fred Hutchinson	1.9
1951	Fred Hutchinson	1.3
1955	Steve Gromek	1.8
1961	Don Mossi	1.8
1977	Dave Rozema	1.4

Bases on Balls Allowed

Year	Player	BB
1903	George Mullin	106
1904	George Mullin	131
1905	George Mullin	138
1906	George Mullin	108
1919	Howard Ehmke	107
1927	Earl Whitehill	105
1943	Hal Newhouser	111
1944	Rufe Gentry	108
1956	Paul Foytack	142
1981	Jack Morris	78
1994	Mike Moore	89

Batters Faced

Year	Player	Batters Faced
1905	George Mullin	1428
1906	George Mullin	1361
1939	Bobo Newsom	1261
1944	Dizzy Trout	1421
1945	Hal Newhouser	1261
1956	Frank Lary	1269
1968	Denny McLain	1288
1969	Denny McLain	1304
1971	Mickey Lolich	1538
1983	Jack Morris	1204
2001	Jeff Weaver	985
2009	Justin Verlander	982
2012	Justin Verlander	956
2014	David Price	1009

Willie Blair

Batting Average Allowed

Year	Player	Avg.
1918	Happy Finneran	.315
1934	General Crowder	.315
1944	Johnny Gorsica	.296
1945	Stubby Overmire	.295
1976	Vern Ruhle	.288
1991	Walt Terrell	.301
1994	Bill Gullickson	.322
2002	Steve Sparks	.306
2003	Nate Cornejo	.307
2008	Nate Robertson	.315
2011	Brad Penny	.306
2012	Rick Porcello	.310

Batting Average on Balls in Play

Year	Player	Avg.
1918	Happy Finneran	.327
1922	Red Oldham	.321
1924	Lil Stoner	.330
1934	General Crowder	.337
1945	Stubby Overmire	.306
1951	Ted Gray	.290
1956	Billy Hoeft	.324
1962	Jim Bunning	.294
1966	Mickey Lolich	.298
1973	Woodie Fryman	.327
1975	Joe Coleman	.315
2000	Brian Moehler	.332
2012	Rick Porcello	.345

Bunt Hits Allowed

Year	Player	Bunt Hits
1988	Doyle Alexander	8
1993	Bill Gullickson	10
1995	Sean Bergman	8
1998	Brian Moehler	7
2008	Nate Robertson	9
2010	Jeremy Bonderman	9
2013	Doug Fister	8
2016	Michael Fulmer	5
	Mike Pelfrey	5
2020	Spencer Turnbull	2

Caught Stealing

Year	Player	Caught Stealing
1921	Dutch Leonard	17
1931	Vic Sorrell	15
1953	Ted Gray	13
1955	Frank Lary	12
1961	Jim Bunning	11
1970	Mickey Lolich	16
1973	Mickey Lolich	19
1974	Mickey Lolich	32
1998	Justin Thompson	16
2000	Hideo Nomo	14
2003	Mike Maroth	11
2009	Justin Verlander	16
2010	Max Scherzer	13
2014	Max Scherzer	10

Cheap Wins

Year	Player	Cheap Wins
1918	Bernie Boland	3
1923	Hooks Dauss	7
1924	Earl Whitehill	7
1925	Lil Stoner	5
	Earl Whitehill	5
1926	Earl Whitehill	5
1929	Vic Sorrell	5
1943	Virgil Trucks	5
1956	Billy Hoeft	5
1959	Jim Bunning	6
1966	Mickey Lolich	5
1974	Joe Coleman	6
1983	Dan Petry	7
1986	Jack Morris	7
1997	Willie Blair	5
2007	Jeremy Bonderman	5

Complete Games

1905	George Mullin	35
1939	Bobo Newsom	24
1944	Dizzy Trout	33
1945	Hal Newhouser	29
1947	Hal Newhouser	24
1958	Frank Lary	19
1960	Frank Lary	15
1961	Frank Lary	22
1968	Denny McLain	28
1971	Mickey Lolich	29
1976	Mark Fidrych	24
1990	Jack Morris	11
2001	Steve Sparks	8
2012	Justin Verlander	6

George Mullin

Double Plays Grounded into

1933	Firpo Marberry	32
1935	General Crowder	30
1944	Dizzy Trout	24
1957	Frank Lary	35
1958	Frank Lary	29
1981	Jack Morris	25
1983	Dan Petry	36
1991	Walt Terrell	35
2013	Doug Fister	26

Doubles Allowed

1939	Bobo Newsom	54
1944	Dizzy Trout	46
1950	Art Houtteman	41
1955	Ned Garver	41
1956	Billy Hoeft	46
1971	Mickey Lolich	49
1973	Mickey Lolich	56
1988	Doyle Alexander	52
1991	Bill Gullickson	51
2008	Kenny Rogers	55
2012	Rick Porcello	53

Earned Runs

1907	George Mullin	103
1908	George Mullin	100
1910	George Mullin	92
1914	Hooks Dauss	96
1918	Hooks Dauss	83
1922	Howard Ehmke	131
1926	Earl Whitehill	112
1949	Hal Newhouser	109
1955	Ned Garver	102
1959	Paul Foytack	124
1966	Denny McLain	115
1970	Mickey Lolich	115
1974	Mickey Lolich	142
1990	Jack Morris	125
2003	Mike Maroth	123
2008	Nate Robertson	119
2014	Justin Verlander	104
2017	Jordan Zimmermann	108
2020	Matt Boyd	45

Earned Run Average

1902	Ed Siever	1.91
1944	Dizzy Trout	2.12
1945	Hal Newhouser	1.81
1946	Hal Newhouser	1.94
1951	Saul Rogovin	2.78
1962	Hank Aguirre	2.21
1976	Mark Fidrych	2.34
2011	Justin Verlander	2.40
2013	Anibal Sanchez	2.57
2015	David Price (2.53 Det.)	2.45

Earned Run Average Plus

1902	Ed Siever	195
1940	Bobo Newsom	168
1944	Dizzy Trout	167
1945	Hal Newhouser	195
1946	Hal Newhouser	190
1951	Saul Rogovin	146
1962	Hank Aguirre	185
1976	Mark Fidrych	159
2011	Justin Verlander	172
2012	Justin Verlander	161
2013	Anibal Sanchez	162
2015	David Price (158 Det.)	164

Fielding Independent Pitching

1945	Hal Newhouser	2.45
1946	Hal Newhouser	1.97
1947	Hal Newhouser	2.85
1948	Hal Newhouser	3.19
1950	Fred Hutchinson	3.67
	Dizzy Trout	3.67
1960	Jim Bunning	2.86
1962	Hank Aguirre	2.99
2013	Anibal Sanchez	2.39

Games

1915	Harry Coveleski	50
1973	John Hiller	65
1984	Willie Hernandez	80
1996	Mike Myers	83
1997	Mike Myers	88
1998	Sean Runyan	88
2011	Jose Valverde	75

Games in Relief

1916	Bernie Boland	37
1919	Doc Ayers	25
1928	George Smith	37
1940	Al Benton	42
1973	John Hiller	65
1984	Willie Hernandez	80
1996	Mike Myers	83
1997	Mike Myers	88
1998	Sean Runyan	88
2011	Jose Valverde	75

Games Finished

1933	Chief Hogsett	34
1935	Chief Hogsett	30
1973	John Hiller	60
1984	Willie Hernandez	68
2009	Fernando Rodney	65
2011	Jose Valverde	70
2012	Jose Valverde	67

Games Started

1905	George Mullin	41
1925	Earl Whitehill	33
1934	Tommy Bridges	35
1936	Bobo Newsom	38
1939	Bobo Newsom	37
1944	Dizzy Trout	40
1945	Hal Newhouser	36
1956	Frank Lary	38
1959	Paul Foytack	37
1960	Frank Lary	36
1968	Denny McLain	41
1969	Denny McLain	41
1971	Mickey Lolich	45
1983	Dan Petry	38
1990	Jack Morris	36
1991	Bill Gullickson	35
1993	Mike Moore	36
1994	Tim Belcher	25
	Mike Moore	25
2006	Jeremy Bonderman	34
2009	Justin Verlander	35
2011	Justin Verlander	34
2013	Justin Verlander	34

Hits

1905	George Mullin	303
1907	George Mullin	346
1915	Harry Coveleski	271
1944	Dizzy Trout	314
1947	Hal Newhouser	268
1949	Hal Newhouser	277
1955	Ned Garver	251
1956	Frank Lary	289
1960	Frank Lary	262
1962	Jim Bunning	262
1969	Denny McLain	288
1971	Mickey Lolich	336
1991	Walt Terrell	257
2012	Rick Porcello	226
2014	David Price (74 Det.)	230

Hit by the Pitch

1908	Ed Summers	20
1912	Ed Willett	17
1914	Hooks Dauss	18
1915	Harry Coveleski	20
1916	Hooks Dauss	16
1921	Hooks Dauss	13
	Howard Ehmke	13
1922	Howard Ehmke	23
1924	Earl Whitehill	13
1930	Chief Hogsett	9
1931	Art Herring	8
1933	Tommy Bridges	6
1954	Steve Gromek	12
1956	Frank Lary	12
1957	Frank Lary	12
1958	Frank Lary	12
1960	Frank Lary	19
1965	Mickey Lolich	12
1973	Joe Coleman	10
1974	Joe Coleman	12
1999	Jeff Weaver	17
2000	Jeff Weaver	15
2007	Justin Verlander	19
2019	Spencer Turnbull	16

Hits - Infield

1999	Brian Moehler	27
2001	Jeff Weaver	28
2005	Jason Johnson	29
2013	Doug Fister	37

Hits Per Nine Innings

1933	Tommy Bridges	7.4
1941	Al Benton	7.4
1942	Hal Newhouser	6.7
1945	Hal Newhouser	6.9
1946	Hal Newhouser	6.6
1962	Hank Aguirre	6.8
1988	Jeff Robinson	6.3
2011	Justin Verlander	6.2
2016	Justin Verlander	6.8

Holds

1919	Hooks Dauss	1
1920	Red Oldham	1
1921	Carl Holling	1
	Pol Perritt	1
	Suds Sutherland	1
1923	Bert Cole	1
	Herman Pillette	1
1935	Elden Auker	2
	Chief Hogsett	2
1937	Jack Russell	1
1945	George Caster	3
1956	Al Aber	4
1959	Pete Burnside	4
	Dave Sisler	4

Ray Narleski

Home Runs

1910	Sailor Stroud	9
1931	Earl Whitehill	22
1935	Tommy Bridges	22
1946	Virgil Trucks	23
1948	Fred Hutchinson	32
1950	Art Houtteman	29
1953	Ted Gray	25
1954	Steve Gromek	26
1955	Steve Gromek	26
1959	Jim Bunning	37
1963	Jim Bunning	38
1966	Denny McLain	42
1967	Denny McLain	35
1968	Denny McLain	31
1972	Mickey Lolich	29
1974	Mickey Lolich	38
1983	Dan Petry	37
1989	Doyle Alexander	28
1992	Bill Gullickson	35
1993	Mike Moore	35
2003	Mike Maroth	34
2015	Anibal Sanchez	29
2019	Matt Boyd	39
2020	Matt Boyd	15

Home Runs – Grand Slams

1921	Dutch Leonard	1
1922	Bert Cole	1
	Hooks Dauss	1
	Red Oldham	1
1923	Syl Johnson	1
1926	Ed Wells	1
1929	Phil Page	1
1931	Tommy Bridges	1
1932	Earl Whitehill	2
1941	Johnny Gorsica	2
1947	Al Benton	1
	Dizzy Trout	1
1950	Art Houtteman	2
1951	Bob Cain	3
1952	Ted Gray	2
1953	Bill Wight	2
1955	Al Aber	2
	Ned Garver	2
1958	Jim Bunning	3
1959	Ray Narleski	4
1962	Jerry Casale	2
1967	Denny McLain	2
1968	Pat Dobson	1
	Denny McLain	1
	Dennis Ribant	1
	Joe Sparma	1
	John Wyatt	1
1970	Mickey Lolich	2
1972	Joe Coleman	2
1980	Dan Schatzeder	2
	Roger Weaver	2
1986	Willie Hernandez	2
	Dave LaPoint	2
1989	Willie Hernandez	2
	Charles Hudson	2
1993	Bob MacDonald	2
	Mike Moore	2
1995	Joe Boever	3
1996	Gregg Olson	3
2002	Jose Paniagua	2
2004	Gary Knotts	2
2011	Daniel Schlereth	2
2017	Francisco Rodriguez	2

Home Runs - Road

1923	Hooks Dauss	6
1929	Earl Whitehill	9
1931	Earl Whitehill	11
1948	Fred Hutchinson	12
1955	Steve Gromek	14
1959	Jim Bunning	18
1966	Denny McLain	21
	Earl Wilson	21
1967	Denny McLain	17
1974	Mickey Lolich	19
1983	Dan Petry	21
1986	Jack Morris	24
1993	Mike Moore	21
2003	Mike Maroth	20
2011	Max Scherzer	18
2020	Matt Boyd	9

Home Runs - Home

1931	Earl Whitehill	11
1946	Virgil Trucks	15
1948	Fred Hutchinson	20
1950	Art Houtteman	21
1953	Ned Garver	15
1954	Steve Gromek	18
1957	Jim Bunning	23
1958	Jim Bunning	22
1959	Paul Foytack	20
1962	Jim Bunning	17
1963	Jim Bunning	24
1966	Denny McLain	21
1967	Earl Wilson	21
1968	Denny McLain	22
1971	Mickey Lolich	25
1972	Mickey Lolich	21
1973	Mickey Lolich	21
1974	Joe Coleman	19
	Mickey Lolich	19
1978	Jim Slaton	19
1987	Jack Morris	29
1990	Frank Tanana	16
1992	Bill Gullickson	24
2019	Matt Boyd	26

Home Runs by Right-handers

1918	Happy Finneran	5
1921	Howard Ehmke	8
1925	Earl Whitehill	9
1930	George Uhle	13
1931	Earl Whitehill	17
1936	Tommy Bridges	16
1948	Fred Hutchinson	16
1949	Hal Newhouser	18
1953	Billy Hoeft	22
1954	Billy Hoeft	21
1959	Jim Bunning	24
	Paul Foytack	24
1961	Don Mossi	20
1968	Mickey Lolich	21
1971	Mickey Lolich	33
1972	Mickey Lolich	26
1973	Mickey Lolich	29
1974	Mickey Lolich	32
1989	Frank Tanana	19
1993	David Wells	24
2003	Mike Maroth	30
2019	Matt Boyd	32
2020	Matt Boyd	14

Home Runs - Per Nine Innings

1904	Ed Killian	0.0
	George Mullin	0.0
1905	Ed Killian	0.0
1902	Ed Siever	0.0
1906	Red Donahue	0.0
1907	George Mullin	0.0
	Ed Siever	0.0
1908	George Mullin	0.0
1909	George Mullin	0.0
1913	Jean Dubuc	0.0
	Ed Willett	0.0
1915	Hooks Dauss	0.0
1917	Bernie Boland	0.0
1918	Bernie Boland	0.0
	George Cunningham	0.0
	Rudy Kallio	0.0
1922	Herman Pillette	0.2
1933	Carl Fischer	0.2
1939	Dizzy Trout	0.3
1942	Hal Newhouser	0.2
	Virgil Trucks	0.2
	Hal White	0.2
1943	Hal Newhouser	0.1
1944	Stubby Overmire	0.1
1945	Hal Newhouser	0.1
1948	Hal Newhouser	0.3
	Dizzy Trout	0.3
1955	Frank Lary	0.4
1971	Joe Coleman	0.5
2011	Doug Fister	0.5
2013	Anibal Sanchez	0.4
2017	Michael Fulmer	0.7

Home Runs by Lefthanders

1918	Hooks Dauss	2
1946	Virgil Trucks	14
1948	Fred Hutchinson	16
1954	Steve Gromek	14
1955	Steve Gromek	16
1956	Steve Gromek	15
1958	Jim Bunning	18
1959	Jim Bunning	13
1963	Jim Bunning	24
1966	Denny McLain	22
1967	Denny McLain	19
1968	Denny McLain	19
1974	Joe Coleman	20
1982	Jack Morris	22
1983	Dan Petry	21
1989	Doyle Alexander	14
1991	Bill Gullickson	15
1992	Bill Gullickson	18
1999	Jeff Weaver	20
2008	Armando Galarraga	21

Innings Pitched

1905	George Mullin	347.2
1944	Dizzy Trout	352.1
1945	Hal Newhouser	313.1
1956	Frank Lary	294.0
1957	Jim Bunning	267.1
1958	Frank Lary	260.1
1960	Frank Lary	274.1
1968	Denny McLain	336.0
1969	Denny McLain	325.0
1971	Mickey Lolich	376.0
1983	Jack Morris	293.2
2009	Justin Verlander	240.0
2011	Justin Verlander	251.0
2012	Justin Verlander	238.1
2014	David Price (77.2 Det)	248.1

Jean Dubuc

Losses

1923	Herman Pillette	19
1939	Vern Kennedy	20
1941	Bobo Newsom	20
1947	Hal Newhouser	17
1951	Ted Gray	14
	Dizzy Trout	14
1952	Art Houtteman	20
1970	Mickey Lolich	19
1974	Mickey Lolich	21
1989	Doyle Alexander	18
1994	Tim Belcher	15
1995	Mike Moore	15
1999	Brian Moehler	16
2003	Mike Maroth	21
2008	Justin Verlander	17
2019	Spencer Turnbull	17
2020	Matt Boyd	7

No Decisions in Games Started

1921	Dutch Leonard	10
1922	Red Oldham	9
1924	Rip Collins	9
1925	Earl Whitehill	11
1937	Jake Wade	9
1940	Hal Newhouser	10
1941	Hal Newhouser	8
1942	Al Benton	11
1946	Virgil Trucks	8
1951	Ted Gray	8
1968	Joe Sparma	12
1973	Mickey Lolich	11
1974	Joe Coleman	15
1997	Omar Olivares	15
2012	Drew Smyly	11
2020	Michael Fulmer	8

Jake Wade

On-Base Percentage Allowed

1929	Ownie Carroll	.376
1944	Rufe Gentry	.365
1952	Dizzy Trout	.361
1966	Mickey Lolich	.329
1968	Joe Sparma	.326
2008	Kenny Rogers	.377
2011	Brad Penny	.361

On-Base Plus Slugging Allowed

1918	Happy Finneran	.782
1929	Vic Sorrell	.816
1967	Denny McLain	.706
1973	Woodie Fryman	.808
1974	Lerrin LaGrow	.770
1975	Joe Coleman	.828
1990	Frank Tanana	.801
1991	Walt Terrell	.791
2002	Steve Sparks	.852
2003	Mike Maroth	.846
2008	Nate Robertson	.891
2011	Brad Penny	.844
2015	Alfredo Simon	.808
2020	Matt Boyd	.900

Passed Balls

1920	Dutch Leonard	3
1929	George Uhle	5
1930	George Uhle	4
1937	Boots Poffenberger	5
1949	Virgil Trucks	3
1952	Virgil Trucks	3
1979	Jack Morris	5
	Dan Petry	5
2020	Daniel Norris	2

Pickoffs

1920	Hooks Dauss	3
1928	Ownie Carroll	4
1940	Bobo Newsom	4
1943	Hal Newhouser	3
1946	Hal Newhouser	3
1950	Art Houtteman	4
1952	Bill Wight	4
1967	Earl Wilson	6
1969	Mickey Lolich	7
1970	Mickey Lolich	13
1998	Justin Thompson	8
2003	Mike Maroth	7
2005	Mike Maroth	11
2014	Drew Smyly	7
2020	Tyler Alexander	2

Pitches

2009	Justin Verlander	3937
2010	Justin Verlander	3745
2011	Justin Verlander	3941
2012	Justin Verlander	3768
2013	Justin Verlander	3692
2014	David Price (1166 Det.)	3730
2016	Justin Verlander	3668
2017	Justin Verlander	3531

Pitches per Plate Appearance

2012	Max Scherzer	4.15

Plate Appearances

1939	Bobo Newsom	1261
1944	Dizzy Trout	1421
1945	Hal Newhouser	1261
1956	Frank Lary	1268
1968	Denny McLain	1288
1969	Denny McLain	1304
1971	Mickey Lolich	1538
1983	Jack Morris	1204
2001	Jeff Weaver	985
2009	Justin Verlander	982
2012	Justin Verlander	956
2014	David Price	1009

Reached on Error

1970	Mickey Lolich	23
1990	Jack Morris	21

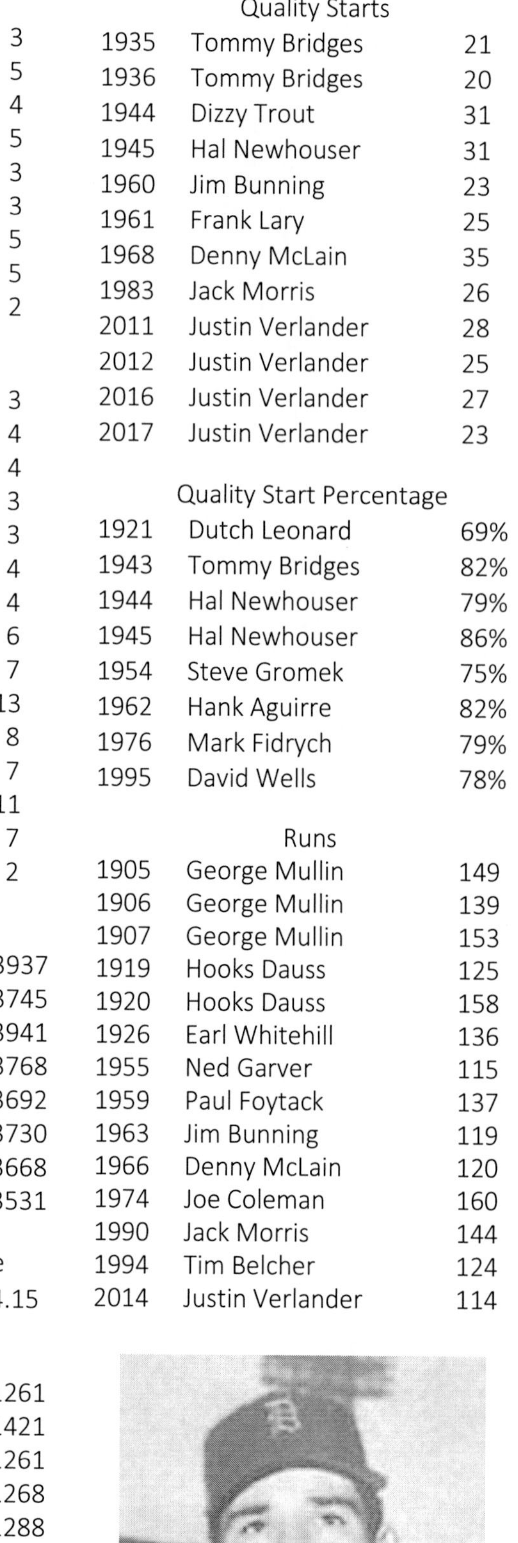

Quality Starts

1935	Tommy Bridges	21
1936	Tommy Bridges	20
1944	Dizzy Trout	31
1945	Hal Newhouser	31
1960	Jim Bunning	23
1961	Frank Lary	25
1968	Denny McLain	35
1983	Jack Morris	26
2011	Justin Verlander	28
2012	Justin Verlander	25
2016	Justin Verlander	27
2017	Justin Verlander	23

Quality Start Percentage

1921	Dutch Leonard	69%
1943	Tommy Bridges	82%
1944	Hal Newhouser	79%
1945	Hal Newhouser	86%
1954	Steve Gromek	75%
1962	Hank Aguirre	82%
1976	Mark Fidrych	79%
1995	David Wells	78%

Runs

1905	George Mullin	149
1906	George Mullin	139
1907	George Mullin	153
1919	Hooks Dauss	125
1920	Hooks Dauss	158
1926	Earl Whitehill	136
1955	Ned Garver	115
1959	Paul Foytack	137
1963	Jim Bunning	119
1966	Denny McLain	120
1974	Joe Coleman	160
1990	Jack Morris	144
1994	Tim Belcher	124
2014	Justin Verlander	114

Bill Wight

Sacrifice Hits

1931	Earl Whitehill	29
1932	Whit Wyatt	22
1936	Tommy Bridges	17
1947	Hal Newhouser	27
1953	Dick Marlowe	16
1954	Ned Garver	19
1960	Jim Bunning	23
1972	Mickey Lolich	23
1973	Joe Coleman	16
1998	Justin Thompson	10
2001	Jeff Weaver	12
2004	Nate Robertson	12
2005	Jason Johnson	9
2019	Daniel Norris	5
2020	Spencer Turnbull	2

Al Benton

Shutouts

1905	Ed Killian	8
1926	Ed Wells	4
1932	Tommy Bridges	4
1935	Schoolboy Rowe	6
1943	Dizzy Trout	5
1944	Dizzy Trout	7
1945	Hal Newhouser	8
1949	Virgil Trucks	6
1950	Art Houtteman	4
1955	Billy Hoeft	7
1967	Mickey Lolich	6
1968	Denny McLain	9
1986	Jack Morris	6
2002	Jeff Weaver	3
2004	Jeremy Bonderman	2
2014	Rick Porcello	3

Sacrifice Flies

1956	Billy Hoeft	12
1971	Mickey Lolich	12
1980	Jack Morris	13
1981	Jack Morris	9
2000	Jeff Weaver	9
2005	Mike Maroth	11
	Nate Robertson	11
2009	Armando Galarraga	11

Saves

1903	George Mullin	2
1940	Al Benton	17
1973	John Hiller	38
2000	Todd Jones	42
2011	Jose Valverde	49

Slugging Percentage Allowed

1918	Happy Finneran	.412
1934	General Crowder	.468
1945	Stubby Overmire	.373
1953	Billy Hoeft	.443
1962	Don Mossi	.429
1967	Denny McLain	.410
1973	Woodie Fryman	.453
1974	Mickey Lolich	.426
1975	Joe Coleman	.465
2002	Steve Sparks	.486
2003	Mike Maroth	.502
2008	Nate Robertson	.518
2011	Brad Penny	.483
2015	Alfredo Simon	.466
2020	Matt Boyd	.552

Strikeouts

1935	Tommy Bridges	163
1936	Tommy Bridges	175
1944	Hal Newhouser	187
1945	Hal Newhouser	212
1949	Virgil Trucks	153
1959	Jim Bunning	201
1960	Jim Bunning	201
1971	Mickey Lolich	308
1983	Jack Morris	232
2009	Justin Verlander	269
2011	Justin Verlander	250
2012	Justin Verlander	239
2014	David Price (82 Det.)	271
2016	Justin Verlander	254

Stolen Bases Allowed

1931	Tommy Bridges	22
1933	Tommy Bridges	22
1951	Saul Rogovin	11
1969	Mickey Lolich	24
	Denny McLain	24
1974	Joe Coleman	46
1990	Jack Morris	45

Strikeouts per Nine Innings

1920	Doc Ayers	4.4
1923	Syl Johnson	4.7
1942	Tommy Bridges	5.0
	Hal Newhouser	5.0
1944	Hal Newhouser	5.4
1945	Hal Newhouser	6.1
1946	Hal Newhouser	8.5
1960	Jim Bunning	7.2
2009	Justin Verlander	10.1
2012	Max Scherzer	11.1

Jeff Weaver

Strikeouts to Walks

1921	Dutch Leonard	1.90
1934	Schoolboy Rowe	1.84
1935	Schoolboy Rowe	2.06
1947	Fred Hutchinson	1.85
1948	Fred Hutchinson	1.92
1950	Fred Hutchinson	1.48
1951	Fred Hutchinson	1.96
1954	Billy Hoeft	1.93
1959	Frank Lary	2.98
1960	Jim Bunning	3.14
1961	Don Mossi	2.91
1968	Denny McLain	4.44

Tough Losses

1921	Dutch Leonard	7
1923	Hooks Dauss	7
1936	Elden Auker	5
1943	Hal Newhouser	9
1944	Dizzy Trout	7
1947	Hal Newhouser	9
1951	Ted Gray	6
1953	Ted Gray	6
1954	Steve Gromek	8
1955	Frank Lary	10
1985	Jack Morris	8
1989	Doyle Alexander	7
	Frank Tanana	7
1996	Felipe Lira	6
1997	Justin Thompson	8
2000	Jeff Weaver	7
2001	Jeff Weaver	6
2002	Steve Sparks	6
2003	Jeremy Bonderman	8
	Mike Maroth	8
2006	Nate Robertson	7

Total Bases Allowed

1944	Dizzy Trout	405
1948	Fred Hutchinson	375
1949	Hal Newhouser	372
1955	Ned Garver	361
1959	Paul Foytack	383
1968	Denny McLain	382
1969	Denny McLain	423
1971	Mickey Lolich	509
1974	Mickey Lolich	492
1988	Doyle Alexander	420
1991	Bill Gullickson	387
2014	David price	360

Triples Allowed

1929	George Uhle	20
1952	Art Houtteman	12
1960	Frank Lary	12
1969	Denny McLain	9
1994	Tim Belcher	7
2002	Mark Redman	8
	Steve Sparks	8
2006	Jeremy Bonderman	10
2013	Anibal Sanchez	8
2014	Rick Porcello	10
2015	Alfredo Simon	10
2016	Jordan Zimmermann	7
2021	Casey Mize	5

Walks Plus Hits per Innings Pitched

1933	Firpo Marberry	1.229
1946	Hal Newhouser	1.069
1948	Fred Hutchinson	1.226
1949	Fred Hutchinson	1.161
2011	Justin Verlander	0.920
2013	Max Scherzer	0.970
2016	Justin Verlander	1.001

Intentional Walks

1956	Billy Hoeft	12
1974	John Hiller	19
1985	Bill Scherrer	13
1988	Mike Henneman	10
1989	Mike Henneman	15
1990	Jack Morris	13
1991	Bill Gullickson	13
1992	Les Lancaster	12
1994	Joe Boever	12
1995	Joe Boever	12
1996	Richie Lewis	9
2009	Brandon Lyon	9

Wild Pitches

1902	George Mullin	13
1912	Jean Dubuc	16
1913	Jean Dubuc	13
1920	Dutch Leonard	13
1931	Tommy Bridges	9
1945	Hal Newhouser	10
1947	Hal Newhouser	11
1975	Joe Coleman	15
1983	Jack Morris	18
1984	Jack Morris	14
1985	Jack Morris	15
1987	Jack Morris	24
2007	Justin Verlander	17

Wins Above Replacement - Pitcher

1944	Dizzy Trout	9.3
1945	Hal Newhouser	11.3
1947	Hal Newhouser	5.8
1948	Hal Newhouser	6.5
1954	Steve Gromek	5.6
1958	Frank Lary	6.7
1960	Jim Bunning	6.6
1962	Hank Aguirre	7.4
1966	Earl Wilson	5.9
1969	Denny McLain	8.1
1976	Mark Fidrych	9.6
2011	Justin Verlander	8.6
2012	Justin Verlander	8.1
2016	Justin Verlander	7.4

Firpo Marberry

Wins

1909	George Mullin	29
1936	Tommy Bridges	23
1943	Dizzy Trout	20
1944	Hal Newhouser	29
1945	Hal Newhouser	25
1946	Hal Newhouser	26
1948	Hal Newhouser	21
1956	Frank Lary	21
1957	Jim Bunning	20
1967	Earl Wilson	22
1968	Denny McLain	31
1969	Denny McLain	24
1971	Mickey Lolich	25
1981	Jack Morris	14
1991	Bill Gullickson	20
2009	Justin Verlander	19
2011	Justin Verlander	24
2013	Max Scherzer	21
2014	Max Scherzer	18

Win-Loss Percentage

1907	Bill Donovan	.862
1909	George Mullin	.784
1935	Elden Auker	.720
1940	Schoolboy Rowe	.842
1945	Hal Newhouser	.735
1968	Denny McLain	.838
2007	Justin Verlander	.750
2011	Justin Verlander	.828
2013	Max Scherzer	.875
2014	Max Scherzer	.783
2015	David Price (.692 Det.)	.783

1901 Kid Elberfeld
1902 Jimmy Barrett
1903 Sam Crawford
1904 Sam Crawford
1905 Sam Crawford
1906 Ty Cobb
1907 Ty Cobb
1908 Ty Cobb
1909 Ty Cobb
1910 Ty Cobb
1911 Ty Cobb
1912 Ty Cobb
1913 Ty Cobb
1914 Ty Cobb
1915 Ty Cobb
1916 Ty Cobb
1917 Ty Cobb
1918 Ty Cobb
1919 Bobby Veach
1920 Bobby Veach
1921 Harry Heilmann
1922 Ty Cobb
1923 Harry Heilmann
1924 Harry Heilmann
1925 Harry Heilmann
1926 Harry Heilmann
1927 Harry Heilmann
1928 Harry Heilmann
1929 Dale Alexander
1930 Charlie Gehringer
1931 Dale Alexander
1932 Charlie Gehringer
1933 Charlie Gehringer
1934 Hank Greenberg
1935 Hank Greenberg
1936 Charlie Gehringer
1937 Hank Greenberg
1938 Hank Greenberg
1939 Hank Greenberg
1940 Hank Greenberg
1941 Rudy York
1942 Rudy York
1943 Rudy York
1944 Rudy York
1945 Roy Cullenbine
1946 Hank Greenberg
1947 George Kell
1948 Hoot Evers
1949 Vic Wertz
1950 Vic Wertz
1951 Vic Wertz
1952 Walt Dropo
1953 Ray Boone
1954 Ray Boone
1955 Al Kaline
1956 Al Kaline
1957 Al Kaline
1958 Al Kaline
1959 Al Kaline
1960 Rocky Colavito

Kid Elberfeld

1961 Norm Cash
1962 Rocky Colavito
1963 Al Kaline
1964 Bill Freehan
1965 Willie Horton
1966 Norm Cash
1967 Al Kaline
1968 Willie Horton
1969 Willie Horton
1970 Willie Horton
1971 Norm Cash
1972 Norm Cash
1973 Willie Horton
1974 Bill Freehan
1975 Willie Horton
1976 Rusty Staub
1977 Jason Thompson
1978 Rusty Staub
1979 Steve Kemp
1980 Steve Kemp
1981 Kirk Gibson
1982 Lance Parrish
1983 Lance Parrish
1984 Kirk Gibson
1985 Kirk Gibson
1986 Kirk Gibson
1987 Alan Trammell
1988 Alan Trammell
1989 Lou Whitaker
1990 Cecil Fielder
1991 Cecil Fielder
1992 Cecil Fielder
1993 Cecil Fielder
1994 Cecil Fielder
1995 Cecil Fielder
1996 Travis Fryman
1997 Tony Clark
1998 Tony Clark
1999 Dean Palmer
2000 Bobby Higginson
2001 Tony Clark
2002 Randall Simon
2003 Dmitri Young
2004 Carlos Guillen
2005 Craig Monroe
2006 Magglio Ordonez
2007 Magglio Ordonez
2008 Miguel Cabrera
2009 Miguel Cabrera
2010 Miguel Cabrera
2011 Miguel Cabrera
2012 Miguel Cabrera
2013 Miguel Cabrera
2014 Victor Martinez
2015 J.D. Martinez
2016 Miguel Cabrera
2017 Justin Upton
2018 Nicholas Castellanos
2019 Miguel Cabrera
2020 Willi Castro
2021 Jonathan Schoop

Year	Player	Games
1901	**Jimmy Barrett**	**135**
	Kid Gleason	**135**
1902	**Jimmy Barrett**	**136**
1903	**Sam Crawford**	**137**
1904	**Jimmy Barrett**	**162**
1905	Sam Crawford	154
1906	Bill Coughlin	147
1907	Claude Rossman	153
1908	Germany Schaefer	153
1909	Donie Bush	157
1910	Sam Crawford	154
1911	Donie Bush	150
1912	Sam Crawford	149
1913	Donie Bush	153
	Sam Crawford	153
1914	Donie Bush	157
	Sam Crawford	157
1915	Ty Cobb	156
	Sam Crawford	156
1916	Ossie Vitt	153
	Ralph Young	153
1917	Bobby Veach	154
1918	Donie Bush	128
1919	Harry Heilmann	140
1920	Bobby Veach	154
1921	Lu Blue	153
1922	Topper Rigney	155
	Bobby Veach	155
1923	Ty Cobb	145
1924	Ty Cobb	155
1925	Lu Blue	150
	Harry Heilmann	150
1926	Jackie Tavener	156
1927	Heinie Manush	151
1928	Charlie Gehringer	154
1929	Dale Alexander	155
	Charlie Gehringer	155
1930	Dale Alexander	154
	Charlie Gehringer	154
1931	Roy Johnson	151
1932	Charlie Gehringer	152
1933	Charlie Gehringer	155
	Billy Rogell	155
1934	Three Batters	154
1935	Hank Greenberg	152
1936	Charlie Gehringer	154
	Marv Owen	154
1937	Hank Greenberg	154
1938	Pete Fox	155
	Hank Greenberg	155
1939	Barney McCosky	147
1940	Rudy York	155
1941	Rudy York	155
1942	Barney McCosky	154
1943	Dick Wakefield	155
	Rudy York	155
1944	Eddie Mayo	154
1945	Rudy York	155
1946	Eddie Lake	155
1947	Eddie Lake	158
1948	George Vico	144
1949	Vic Wertz	155
1950	Three Batters	157
1951	Jerry Priddy	154
1952	Johnny Groth	141
1953	Harvey Kuenn	155
1954	Harvey Kuenn	155
1955	Bill Tuttle	154
1956	Al Kaline	153
1957	Harvey Kuenn	151
1958	Frank Bolling	154
1959	Eddie Yost	148

George Vico

Year	Player	Games
1960	Al Kaline	147
1961	**Rocky Colavito**	**163**
1962	Rocky Colavito	161
1963	Rocky Colavito	160
1964	Dick McAuliffe	162
1965	Don Wert	162
1966	Norm Cash	160
1967	Bill Freehan	155
1968	Bill Freehan	155
1969	Mickey Stanley	149
1970	Dick McAuliffe	146
1971	Eddie Brinkman	159
1972	Eddie Brinkman	156
1973	Eddie Brinkman	162
1974	Aurelio Rodriguez	159
1975	Willie Horton	159
1976	Rusty Staub	161
1977	Rusty Staub	158
	Jason Thompson	158
1978	Rusty Staub	162
1979	Ron LeFlore	148
1980	Tom Brookens	151
1981	Lou Whitaker	109
1982	Larry Herndon	157
	Alan Trammell	157
1983	Lou Whitaker	161
1984	Kirk Gibson	149
1985	Tom Brookens	156
1986	Darrell Evans	151
	Alan Trammell	151
1987	Alan Trammell	151
1988	Darrell Evans	144
	Chet Lemon	144
1989	Lou Whitaker	148
1990	Cecil Fielder	159
1991	Cecil Fielder	162
1992	Travis Fryman	161
1993	Cecil Fielder	154
1994	Travis Fryman	114
	Tony Phillips	114
1995	Chad Curtis	144
	Travis Fryman	144
1996	Travis Fryman	157
1997	Brian Hunter	162
1998	Tony Clark	157
	Bobby Higginson	157
1999	Deivi Cruz	155
2000	Deivi Cruz	156
2001	Damion Easley	154
2002	Robert Fick	148
2003	Dmitri Young	155
2004	Omar Infante	142
	Carlos Pena	142
2005	Brandon Inge	160
2006	Brandon Inge	159
	Curtis Granderson	159
2007	Curtis Granderson	158
2008	Miguel Cabrera	160
2009	Brandon Inge	161
2010	Austin Jackson	151
2011	Miguel Cabrera	161
2012	Prince Fielder	162
2013	Prince Fielder	162
2014	Ian Kinsler	161
2015	J.D. Martinez	158
2016	Miguel Cabrera	158
2017	Nicholas Castellanos	157
2018	Nicholas Castellanos	157
2019	Miguel Cabrera	136
2020	Miguel Cabrera	57
	Victor Reyes	57
2021	Robbie Grossman	156
	Jonathan Schoop	156

Year	Player	PA
1901	**Jimmy Barrett**	**630**
1902	Jimmy Barrett	594
1903	Jimmy Barrett	615
1904	**Jimmy Barrett**	**714**
1905	Sam Crawford	631
1906	Sam Crawford	610
1907	Ty Cobb	646
1908	Matty McIntyre	672
1909	Donie Bush	676
1910	Sam Crawford	650
1911	Donie Bush	692
1912	Sam Crawford	644
1913	Donie Bush	694
1914	**Donie Bush**	**721**
1915	Donie Bush	703
1916	Ossie Vitt	705
1917	Donie Bush	673
1918	Donie Bush	593
1919	Donie Bush	602
1920	Ralph Young	703
1921	Lu Blue	709
1922	Bobby Veach	704
1923	Ty Cobb	647
1924	**Ty Cobb**	**726**
1925	Harry Heilmann	664
1926	Jackie Tavener	613
1927	Heinie Manush	659
1928	Charlie Gehringer	691
1929	Charlie Gehringer	715
1930	Charlie Gehringer	699
1931	Roy Johnson	697
1932	Charlie Gehringer	692
1933	Charlie Gehringer	705
1934	Charlie Gehringer	708
1935	Hank Greenberg	710
1936	**Charlie Gehringer**	**731**
1937	Hank Greenberg	701
1938	Charlie Gehringer	688
1939	Barney McCosky	692
1940	Rudy York	685
1941	Rudy York	687
1942	Doc Cramer	682
1943	Dick Wakefield	697
1944	Eddie Mayo	696
1945	Rudy York	655
1946	Eddie Lake	703
1947	**Eddie Lake**	**732**
1948	Hoot Evers	606
1949	Vic Wertz	695
1950	Jerry Priddy	729
1951	George Kell	674
1952	Jerry Groth	580
1953	Harvey Kuenn	731
1954	Harvey Kuenn	696
1955	Bill Tuttle	698
1956	Al Kaline	693
1957	Harvey Kuenn	679
1958	Frank Bolling	681
1959	Eddie Yost	675
1960	Eddie Yost	636
1961	Jake Wood	731

Doc Cramer

Year	Player	PA
1962	Rocky Colavito	707
1963	Rocky Colavito	692
1964	Jerry Lumpe	688
1965	Don Wert	697
1966	Norm Cash	679
1967	Dick McAuliffe	675
1968	Dick McAuliffe	658
1969	Mickey Stanley	651
1970	Dick McAuliffe	639
1971	Aurelio Rodriguez	639
1972	Aurelio Rodriguez	639
1973	Mickey Stanley	661
1974	Gary Sutherland	652
1975	Willie Horton	667
1976	Rusty Staub	690
1977	Ron LeFlore	698
1978	**Ron LeFlore**	**741**
1979	Ron LeFlore	654
1980	Alan Trammell	652
1981	Alan Trammell	463
1982	Larry Herndon	659
1983	Lou Whitaker	720
1984	Lance Parrish	629
	Lou Whitaker	629
1985	Lou Whitaker	701
1986	Alan Trammell	653
1987	Lou Whitaker	684
1988	Chet Lemon	582
1989	Lou Whitaker	611
1990	Tony Phillips	687
1991	Cecil Fielder	712
1992	Tony Phillips	733
1993	Tony Phillips	707
1994	Tony Phillips	538
1995	Chad Curtis	670
1996	Travis Fryman	688
1997	Brian Hunter	738
1998	Bobby Higginson	685
1999	Dean Palmer	631
2000	Bobby Higginson	679
2001	Damion Easley	658
2002	Robert Fick	614
2003	Dmitri Young	635
2004	Carlos Guillen	583
2005	Brandon Inge	694
2006	Curtis Granderson	679
2007	Maggio Ordonez	679
2008	Miguel Cabrera	684
2009	Curtis Granderson	710
2010	Austin Jackson	675
2011	Miguel Cabrera	688
2012	Miguel Cabrera	697
2013	Prince Fielder	712
2014	Ian Kinsler	726
2015	Ian Kinsler	675
2016	Miguel Cabrera	679
	Ian Kinsler	679
2017	Nicholas Castellanos	665
2018	Nicholas Castellanos	678
2019	Miguel Cabrera	549
2020	Miguel Cabrera	231
2021	Jonathan Schoop	674

Year	Player	At Bats
1901	**Kid Gleason**	**547**
1902	Doc Casey	520
1903	**Sam Crawford**	**550**
1904	**Jimmy Barrett**	**624**
1905	Sam Crawford	575
1906	Sam Crawford	563
1907	Ty Cobb	605
1908	Sam Crawford	591
1909	Sam Crawford	589
1910	Sam Crawford	588
1911	Ty Cobb	591
1912	Sam Crawford	581
1913	Sam Crawford	609
1914	Donie Bush	596
1915	Sam Crawford	612
1916	Ossie Vitt	597
1917	Ty Cobb	588
1918	Donie Bush	500
1919	Bobby Veach	538
1920	Bobby Veach	612
1921	Bobby Veach	612
1922	Bobby Veach	618
1923	Ty Cobb	556
1924	**Ty Cobb**	**625**
1925	Harry Heilmann	573
1926	Jackie Tavener	532
1927	Heinie Manush	593
1928	Charlie Gehringer	603
1929	**Roy Johnson**	**640**
1930	Charlie Gehringer	610
1931	Roy Johnson	621
1932	Charlie Gehringer	618
1933	Charlie Gehringer	628
1934	Goose Goslin	614
1935	Hank Greenberg	619
1936	**Charlie Gehringer**	**641**
1937	Gee Walker	635
1938	Pete Fox	634
1939	Barney McCosky	611
1940	Barney McCosky	589
1941	Rudy York	590
1942	Doc Cramer	630
1943	Dick Wakefield	633
1944	Eddie Mayo	607
1945	Rudy York	595
1946	Eddie Lake	587
1947	Eddie Lake	602
1948	Hoot Evers	538
1949	Vic Wertz	608
1950	**George Kell**	**641**
1951	George Kell	598
1952	Johnny Groth	524
1953	**Harvey Kuenn**	**679**
1954	Harvey Kuenn	656
1955	Harvey Kuenn	620
1956	Al Kaline	617
1957	Harvey Kuenn	624
1958	Frank Bolling	610
1959	Harvey Kuenn	561
1960	Rocky Colavito	555
1961	Jake Wood	663

Gary Sutherland

Year	Player	At Bats
1962	Rocky Colavito	601
1963	Rocky Colavito	597
1964	Jerry Lumpe	624
1965	Don Wert	609
1966	Norm Cash	603
1967	Dick McAuliffe	557
1968	Mickey Stanley	583
1969	Mickey Stanley	592
1970	Mickey Stanley	568
1971	Aurelio Rodriguez	604
1972	Aurelio Rodriguez	601
1973	Mickey Stanley	602
1974	Gary Sutherland	619
1975	Willie Horton	615
1976	Rusty Staub	589
1977	Ron LeFlore	652
1978	Ron LeFlore	666
1979	Ron LeFlore	600
1980	Alan Trammell	560
1981	Alan Trammell	392
1982	Larry Herndon	614
1983	Lou Whitaker	643
1984	Lance Parrish	578
1985	Lou Whitaker	609
1986	Lou Whitaker	584
1987	Lou Whitaker	604
1988	Chet Lemon	512
1989	Lou Whitaker	509
1990	Cecil Fielder	573
	Tony Phillips	573
1991	Cecil Fielder	624
1992	Travis Fryman	659
1993	Travis Fryman	607
1994	Travis Fryman	464
1995	Chad Curtis	586
1996	Travis Fryman	616
1997	Brian Hunter	658
1998	Bobby Higginson	612
1999	Dean Palmer	560
2000	Bobby Higginson	597
2001	Damion Easley	585
2002	Robert Fick	556
2003	Dmitri Young	562
2004	Ivan Rodriguez	527
2005	Brandon Inge	616
2006	Curtis Granderson	596
2007	Curtis Granderson	612
2008	Miguel Cabrera	616
2009	Curtis Granderson	631
2010	Austin Jackson	618
2011	Austin Jackson	591
2012	Miguel Cabrera	622
2013	Prince Fielder	624
2014	**Ian Kinsler**	**684**
2015	Ian Kinsler	624
2016	Ian Kinsler	618
2017	Nicholas Castellanos	614
2018	Nicholas Castellanos	620
2019	Miguel Cabrera	493
2020	Miguel Cabrera	204
2021	Jonathan Schoop	623

Year	Player	Runs
1901	**Jimmy Barrett**	**110**
1902	Jimmy Barrett	93
1903	Jimmy Barrett	95
1904	Jimmy Barrett	83
1905	Sam Crawford	73
1906	Sam Crawford	65
1907	Sam Crawford	102
1908	Matty McIntyre	105
1909	**Ty Cobb**	**116**
1910	Ty Cobb	106
1911	**Ty Cobb**	**147**
1912	Ty Cobb	119
1913	Donie Bush	98
1914	Donie Bush	97
1915	Ty Cobb	144
1916	Ty Cobb	113
1917	Donie Bush	112
1918	Ty Cobb	83
1919	Ty Cobb	92
1920	Bobby Veach	92
1921	Ty Cobb	124
1922	Lu Blue	131
1923	Harry Heilmann	121
1924	Ty Cobb	115
1925	Al Wingo	104
1926	Heinie Manush	95
1927	Charlie Gehringer	110
1928	Charlie Gehringer	108
1929	Charlie Gehringer	131
1930	Charlie Gehringer	144
1931	Roy Johnson	107
1932	Charlie Gehringer	112
1933	Charlie Gehringer	103
1934	Charlie Gehringer	135
1935	Charlie Gehringer	123
1936	Charlie Gehringer	144
1937	Hank Greenberg	137
1938	Hank Greenberg	144
1939	Barney McCosky	120
1940	Hank Greenberg	129
1941	Rudy York	91
1942	Rudy York	81
1943	Dick Wakefield	91
1944	Pinky Higgins	79
1945	Roy Cullenbine	80
1946	Eddie Lake	105
1947	Eddie Lake	96
1948	Pat Mullin	91
1949	George Kell	97
1950	George Kell	114
1951	George Kell	92
1952	Walt Dropo	56
	Johnny Groth	56
1953	Harvey Kuenn	94
1954	Harvey Kuenn	81
1955	Al Kaline	121
1956	Al Kaline	96
	Harvey Kuenn	96
	Charlie Maxwell	96
1957	Al Kaline	83
1958	Frank Bolling	91
1959	Eddie Yost	115
1960	Eddie Yost	78
1961	Rocky Colavito	129
1962	Norm Cash	94
1963	Rocky Colavito	91
1964	Dick McAuliffe	85
1965	Don Wert	81
1966	Norm Cash	98
1967	Al Kaline	94
1968	Dick McAuliffe	95
1969	Norm Cash	81
1970	Mickey Stanley	83
1971	Norm Cash	72
	Jim Northrup	72
1972	Aurelio Rodriguez	65
1973	Mickey Stanley	81
1974	Al Kaline	71
1975	Ron LeFlore	66
1976	Ron LeFlore	93
1977	Ron LeFlore	100
1978	Ron LeFlore	126
1979	Ron LeFlore	110
1980	Alan Trammell	107
1981	Steve Kemp	52
	Alan Trammell	52
1982	Larry Herndon	92
1983	Lou Whitaker	94
1984	Kirk Gibson	92
1985	Lou Whitaker	102
1986	Alan Trammell	107
1987	Lou Whitaker	110
1988	Alan Trammell	73
1989	Gary Pettis	77
	Lou Whitaker	77
1990	Cecil Fielder	104
1991	Cecil Fielder	102
1992	Tony Phillips	114
1993	Tony Phillips	113
1994	Tony Phillips	91
1995	Chad Curtis	96
1996	Travis Fryman	90
1997	Brian Hunter	112
1998	Bobby Higginson	92
1999	Dean Palmer	92
2000	Bobby Higginson	104
2001	Bobby Higginson	84
2002	Robert Fick	66
2003	Dmitri Young	78
2004	Carlos Guillen	97
2005	Brandon Inge	75
2006	Carlos Guillen	100
2007	Curtis Granderson	122
2008	Curtis Granderson	112
2009	Miguel Cabrera	96
2010	Miguel Cabrera	111
2011	Miguel Cabrera	111
2012	Miguel Cabrera	109
2013	Miguel Cabrera	103
2014	Miguel Cabrera	101
2015	Ian Kinsler	94
2016	Ian Kinsler	117
2017	Ian Kinsler	90
2018	Nicholas Castellanos	88
2019	Niko Goodrum	61
2020	Jeimer Candelario	30
	Victor Reyes	30
2021	Robbie Grossman	88

Victor Reyes

Year	Player	Hits
1901	**Jimmy Barrett**	**159**
1902	Jimmy Barrett	154
1903	**Sam Crawford**	**184**
1904	Jimmy Barrett	167
1905	Sam Crawford	171
1906	Sam Crawford	166
1907	**Ty Cobb**	**212**
1908	Ty Cobb	188
1909	**Ty Cobb**	**216**
1910	Ty Cobb	196
1911	**Ty Cobb**	**248**
1912	Ty Cobb	227
1913	Sam Crawford	193
1914	Sam Crawford	183
1915	Ty Cobb	208
1916	Ty Cobb	201
1917	Ty Cobb	225
1918	Ty Cobb	161
1919	Ty Cobb	191
	Bobby Veach	191
1920	Bobby Veach	188
1921	Harry Heilmann	237
1922	Ty Cobb	211
1923	Harry Heilmann	211
1924	Ty Cobb	211
1925	Harry Heilmann	225
1926	Heinie Manush	188
1927	Harry Heilmann	201
1928	Charlie Gehringer	193
1929	Dale Alexander	215
	Charlie Gehringer	215
1930	Charlie Gehringer	201
1931	John Stone	191
1932	Charlie Gehringer	184
1933	Charlie Gehringer	204
1934	Charlie Gehringer	214
1935	Hank Greenberg	203
1936	Charlie Gehringer	227
1937	Gee Walker	213
1938	Pete Fox	186
1939	Barney McCosky	190
1940	Barney McCosky	200
1941	Pinky Higgins	161
1942	Barney McCosky	176
1943	Dick Wakefield	200
1944	Doc Cramer	169
1945	Rudy York	157
1946	Eddie Lake	149
1947	George Kell	188
1948	Hoot Evers	169
1949	Vic Wertz	185
1950	George Kell	218
1951	George Kell	191
1952	Johnny Groth	149
1953	Harvey Kuenn	209
1954	Harvey Kuenn	201
1955	Al Kaline	200
1956	Harvey Kuenn	196
1957	Harvey Kuenn	173
1958	Harvey Kuenn	179
1959	Harvey Kuenn	198

Jerry Lumpe

Year	Player	Hits
1960	Al Kaline	153
1961	Norm Cash	193
1962	Rocky Colavito	164
1963	Al Kaline	172
1964	Jerry Lumpe	160
1965	Don Wert	159
1966	Norm Cash	168
1967	Bill Freehan	146
1968	Jim Northrup	153
1969	Jim Northrup	160
1970	Mickey Stanley	143
1971	Aurelio Rodriguez	153
1972	Aurelio Rodriguez	142
1973	Mickey Stanley	147
1974	Gary Sutherland	157
1975	Willie Horton	169
1976	Rusty Staub	176
1977	Ron LeFlore	212
1978	Ron LeFlore	198
1979	Ron LeFlore	180
1980	Alan Trammell	168
1981	Steve Kemp	103
1982	Larry Herndon	179
1983	Lou Whitaker	206
1984	Alan Trammell	174
1985	Lou Whitaker	170
1986	Alan Trammell	159
1987	Alan Trammell	205
1988	Alan Trammell	145
1989	Lou Whitaker	128
1990	Alan Trammell	170
1991	Cecil Fielder	163
1992	Travis Fryman	175
1993	Travis Fryman	182
1994	Tony Phillips	123
1995	Chad Curtis	157
1996	Travis Fryman	165
1997	Brian Hunter	177
1998	Tony Clark	175
1999	Tony Clark	150
2000	Bobby Higginson	179
2001	Roger Cedeno	153
2002	Robert Fick	150
2003	Dmitri Young	167
2004	Ivan Rodriguez	176
2005	Brandon Inge	161
2006	Magglio Ordonez	177
2007	Magglio Ordonez	216
2008	Miguel Cabrera	180
2009	Miguel Cabrera	198
2010	Austin Jackson	181
2011	Miguel Cabrera	197
2012	Miguel Cabrera	205
2013	Miguel Cabrera	193
2014	Miguel Cabrera	191
2015	Ian Kinsler	185
2016	Miguel Cabrera	188
2017	Nicholas Castellanos	167
2018	Nicholas Castellanos	185
2019	Miguel Cabrera	139
2020	Victor Reyes	56
2021	Jonathan Schoop	173

Year	Player	Singles
1901	**Jimmy Barrett**	**130**
1902	Jimmy Barrett	125
1903	**Jimmy Barrett**	**138**
1904	**Jimmy Barrett**	**152**
1905	Sam Crawford	117
1906	Sam Crawford	123
1907	**Ty Cobb**	**165**
1908	Matty McIntyre	131
1909	Ty Cobb	164
1910	Ty Cobb	139
1911	**Ty Cobb**	**169**
1912	Ty Cobb	166
1913	Ty Cobb	129
	Sam Crawford	129
1914	Donie Bush	128
1915	Ty Cobb	161
1916	Ty Cobb	155
1917	Ty Cobb	151
1918	Ty Cobb	125
1919	Ty Cobb	141
1920	Ralph Young	146
1921	Harry Heilmann	161
1922	Ty Cobb	149
1923	Harry Heilmann	138
1924	Ty Cobb	159
1925	Harry Heilmann	161
1926	Heinie Manush	131
1927	Bob Fothergill	133
1928	Charlie Gehringer	142
1929	Charlie Gehringer	138
1930	Dale Alexander	135
1931	John Stone	142
1932	Harry Davis	110
	Charlie Gehringer	110
1933	Charlie Gehringer	144
1934	Charlie Gehringer	146
1935	Charlie Gehringer	142
1936	Charlie Gehringer	140
1937	Charlie Gehringer	154
1938	Pete Fox	134
1939	Barney McCosky	139
1940	Barney McCosky	138
1941	Barney McCosky	124
1942	Doc Cramer	136
1943	Doc Cramer	159
1944	Doc Cramer	138
1945	Doc Cramer	113
1946	Eddie Lake	116
1947	George Kell	149
1948	Hoot Evers	120
1949	Vic Wertz	133
1950	George Kell	148
1951	George Kell	150
1952	Johnny Groth	121
1953	Harvey Kuenn	167
1954	Harvey Kuenn	162
1955	Al Kaline	141
1956	Harvey Kuenn	145
1957	Harvey Kuenn	128
1958	Harvey Kuenn	129
1959	Harvey Kuenn	140

Harry Davis

Year	Player	Singles
1960	Al Kaline	105
1961	Jake Wood	129
1962	Billy Bruton	108
1963	Al Kaline	118
1964	Jerry Lumpe	127
1965	Don Wert	123
1966	Don Wert	117
1967	Don Wert	106
1968	Mickey Stanley	118
1969	Jim Northrup	99
1970	Mickey Stanley	98
1971	Aurelio Rodriguez	101
1972	Aurelio Rodriguez	101
1973	Mickey Stanley	102
1974	Gary Sutherland	131
1975	Willie Horton	130
1976	Ron LeFlore	137
1977	Tito Fuentes	156
	Ron LeFlore	156
1978	Ron LeFlore	153
1979	Ron LeFlore	139
1980	Alan Trammell	133
1981	Alan Trammell	81
1982	Larry Herndon	122
1983	Lou Whitaker	148
1984	Lou Whitaker	122
1985	Alan Trammell	115
1986	Lou Whitaker	105
1987	Alan Trammell	140
1988	Alan Trammell	105
1989	Gary Pettis	99
1990	Alan Trammell	118
1991	Tony Phillips	111
1992	Tony Philips	122
1993	Tony Phillips	143
1994	Tony Phillips	82
1995	Travis Fryman	115
1996	Travis Fryman	108
1997	Brian Hunter	137
1998	Brian Hunter	115
1999	Deivi Cruz	99
2000	Deivi Cruz	115
2001	Roger Cedeno	122
2002	Randall Simon	108
2003	Dmitri Young	97
2004	Ivan Rodriguez	123
2005	Brandon Inge	105
2006	Magglio Ordonez	120
2007	Placido Polanco	152
2008	Placido Polanco	133
2009	Placido Polanco	131
2010	Austin Jackson	133
2011	Victor Martinez	126
2012	Miguel Cabrera	121
2013	Victor Martinez	132
2014	Ian Kinsler	127
2015	Ian Kinsler	132
2016	Miguel Cabrera	118
2017	Nicholas Castellanos	95
2018	Nicholas Castellanos	111
2019	Miguel Cabrera	106
2020	Victor Reyes	43
2021	Jonathan Schoop	120

Year	Player	Doubles
1901	**Ducky Holmes**	**28**
1902	Jimmy Barrett	19
1903	Charlie Carr	23
	Sam Crawford	23
1904	Sam Crawford	22
1905	**Sam Crawford**	**38**
1906	Sam Crawford	25
1907	Sam Crawford	34
1908	Ty Cobb	36
1909	Sam Crawford	35
1910	Ty Cobb	36
1911	**Ty Cobb**	**47**
1912	Ty Cobb	30
	Sam Crawford	30
1913	Sam Crawford	32
1914	George Burns	22
	Ty Cobb	22
	Sam Crawford	22
1915	Bobby Veach	40
1916	Bobby Veach	33
1917	Ty Cobb	44
1918	Bobby Veach	21
1919	Bobby Veach	45
1920	Bobby Veach	39
1921	Harry Heilmann	43
	Bobby Veach	43
1922	Ty Cobb	42
1923	Harry Heilmann	44
1924	Harry Heilmann	45
1925	Harry Heilmann	40
	Frank O'Rourke	40
1926	Harry Heilmann	41
1927	**Harry Heilmann**	**50**
1928	Harry Heilmann	38
1929	Charlie Gehringer	45
	Roy Johnson	45
1930	Charlie Gehringer	47
1931	Dale Alexander	47
1932	Charlie Gehringer	44
1933	Charlie Gehringer	42
	Billy Rogell	42
1934	**Hank Greenberg**	**63**
1935	Hank Greenberg	46
1936	Charlie Gehringer	60
1937	Hank Greenberg	49
1938	Pete Fox	35
1939	Hank Greenberg	42
1940	Hank Greenberg	50
1941	Rudy York	29
1942	Pinky Higgins	34
1943	Dick Wakefield	38
1944	Pinky Higgins	32
1945	Roy Cullenbine	27
1946	Hank Greenberg	29
1947	George Kell	29
1948	Hoot Evers	33
1949	George Kell	38
1950	George Kell	56
1951	George Kell	36
1952	Jerry Priddy	23
1953	Harvey Kuenn	33
1954	Harvey Kuenn	28
1955	Harvey Kuenn	38
1956	Al Kaline	32
	Harvey Kuenn	32
1957	Harvey Kuenn	30

Harry Heilmann

Year	Player	Doubles
1958	Harvey Kuenn	39
1959	Harvey Kuenn	42
1960	Al Kaline	29
1961	Al Kaline	41
1962	Rocky Colavito	30
1963	Rocky Colavito	29
1964	Al Kaline	31
1965	Norm Cash	23
1966	Al Kaline	29
1967	Al Kaline	28
1968	Jim Northrup	29
1969	Jim Northrup	31
1970	Al Kaline	24
1971	Aurelio Rodriguez	30
1972	Aurelio Rodriguez	23
1973	Aurelio Rodriguez	27
1974	Al Kaline	28
1975	Aurelio Rodriguez	20
1976	Rusty Staub	28
1977	Rusty Staub	34
1978	Ron LeFlore	30
	Rusty Staub	30
1979	Steve Kemp	26
	Lance Parrish	26
1980	Lance Parrish	34
1981	Steve Kemp	18
	Lance Parrish	18
1982	Alan Trammell	34
1983	Lance Parrish	42
1984	Chet Lemon	34
	Alan Trammell	34
1985	Kirk Gibson	37
1986	Alan Trammell	33
1987	Lou Whitaker	38
1988	Chet Lemon	29
1989	Lou Whitaker	21
1990	Alan Trammell	37
1991	Travis Fryman	36
1992	Tony Phillips	32
1993	Travis Fryman	37
1994	Travis Fryman	34
1995	Chad Curtis	29
1996	Bobby Higginson	35
1997	Damion Easley	37
1998	Damion Easley	38
1999	Deivi Cruz	35
2000	Deivi Cruz	46
2001	Shane Halter	32
2002	Robert Fick	36
2003	Dmitri Young	34
2004	Carlos Guillen	37
2005	Ivan Rodriguez	33
2006	Carlos Guillen	41
2007	Magglio Ordonez	54
2008	Miguel Cabrera	36
2009	Miguel Cabrera	34
2010	Miguel Cabrera	45
2011	Miguel Cabrera	48
2012	Miguel Cabrera	40
2013	Torii Hunter	37
2014	Miguel Cabrera	52
2015	Ian Kinsler	35
2016	J.D. Martinez	35
2017	Justin Upton	37
2018	Nicholas Castellanos	46
2019	Nicholas Castellanos	37
2020	Jeimer Candelario	11
2021	Jeimer Candelario	42

Year	Player	Triples
1901	**Kid Gleason**	**12**
1902	Dick Harley	8
1903	**Sam Crawford**	**25**
1904	Sam Crawford	16
1905	Sam Crawford	10
1906	Sam Crawford	16
1907	Sam Crawford	17
1908	Ty Cobb	20
1909	Sam Crawford	14
1910	Sam Crawford	19
1911	Ty Cobb	24
1912	Ty Cobb	23
1913	Sam Crawford	23
1914	**Sam Crawford**	**26**
1915	Sam Crawford	19
1916	Bobby Veach	15
1917	Ty Cobb	24
1918	Ty Cobb	14
1919	Bobby Veach	17
1920	Bobby Veach	15
1921	Ty Cobb	16
1922	Ty Cobb	16
1923	Harry Heilmann	11
	Topper Rigney	11
1924	Harry Heilmann	16
1925	Ty Cobb	12
1926	Charlie Gehringer	17
1927	Heinie Manush	18
1928	Charlie Gehringer	16
1929	Charlie Gehringer	19
1930	Charlie Gehringer	15
1931	Roy Johnson	19
1932	Harry Davis	13
1933	Pete Fox	13
1934	Marv Owen	9
1935	Hank Greenberg	16
1936	Charlie Gehringer	12
1937	Hank Greenberg	14
1938	Pete Fox	10
1939	Barney McCosky	14
1940	Barney McCosky	19
1941	Bruce Campbell	10
1942	Barney McCosky	11
1943	Rudy York	11
1944	Doc Cramer	9
1945	Doc Cramer	8
1946	George Kell	9
1947	Eddie Lake	6
	Pat Mullin	6
1948	Pat Mullin	11
1949	George Kell	9
1950	Hoot Evers	11
1951	Pat Mullin	6
	Jerry Priddy	6
1952	Pat Mullin	5
1953	Harvey Kuenn	7
1954	Bill Tuttle	11
1955	Al Kaline	8
1956	Al Kaline	10
1957	Frank Bolling	6
	Harvey Kuenn	6
1958	Gail Harris	8
1959	Harvey Kuenn	7
1960	Charlie Maxwell	5
1961	Jake Wood	14
1962	Al Kaline	6
1963	Billy Bruton	8
1964	Bill Freehan	8

Juan Samuel

Year	Player	Triples
1965	Dick McAuliffe	6
1966	Dick McAuliffe	8
1967	Dick McAuliffe	7
1968	Dick McAuliffe	10
1969	Dick McAuliffe	5
	Jim Northrup	5
1970	Mickey Stanley	11
1971	Aurelio Rodriguez	7
1972	Mickey Stanley	6
1973	Jim Northrup	7
1974	Bill Freehan	5
	Aurelio Rodriguez	5
1975	Ron LeFlore	6
	Aurelio Rodriguez	6
1976	Ron LeFlore	8
1977	Tito Fuentes	10
	Ron LeFlore	10
1978	Lou Whitaker	7
1979	Ron LeFlore	10
1980	Tom Brookens	9
1981	Al Cowens	4
	Steve Kemp	4
	Lou Whitaker	4
1982	Larry Herndon	13
1983	Kirk Gibson	9
	Larry Herndon	9
1984	Kirk Gibson	10
1985	Lou Whitaker	8
1986	Alan Trammell	7
1987	Lou Whitaker	6
1988	Tom Brookens	5
	Pat Sheridan	5
1989	Gary Pettis	6
1990	Lloyd Moseby	5
	Tony Phillips	5
1991	Milt Cuyler	7
1992	Travis Fryman	4
1993	Milt Cuyler	7
1994	Travis Fryman	5
	Juan Samuel	5
1995	Travis Fryman	5
	Bobby Higginson	5
1996	Curtis Pride	5
1997	Brian Hunter	7
1998	Luis Gonzalez	5
1999	Luis Polonia	8
2000	Juan Encarnacion	6
2001	Roger Cedeno	11
2002	Shane Halter	6
2003	Dmitri Young	7
2004	Carlos Guillen	10
2005	Brandon Inge	9
2006	Curtis Granderson	9
2007	Curtis Granderson	23
2008	Curtis Granderson	13
2009	Curtis Granderson	8
2010	Austin Jackson	10
2011	Austin Jackson	11
2012	Austin Jackson	10
2013	Austin Jackson	7
2014	Austin Jackson	5
2015	Rajai Davis	11
2016	Cameron Maybin	5
2017	Nicholas Castellanos	10
2018	Jacoby Jones	6
2019	Niko Goodrum	5
	Victor Reyes	5
2020	Jeimer Candelario	3
2021	Akil Baddoo	7

Year	Player	HR
1901	**Jimmy Barrett**	**4**
	Ducky Holmes	**4**
1902	**Jimmy Barrett**	**4**
1903	**Sam Crawford**	**4**
1904	Sam Crawford	2
	Charlie Hickman	2
	Matty McIntyre	2
1905	**Sam Crawford**	**6**
1906	Bill Coughlin	2
	Sam Crawford	2
	Charley O'Leary	2
	Germany Schaefer	2
1907	Ty Cobb	5
1908	**Sam Crawford**	**7**
1909	**Ty Cobb**	**9**
1910	Ty Cobb	8
1911	Ty Cobb	8
1912	Ty Cobb	7
1913	**Sam Crawford**	**9**
1914	Sam Crawford	8
1915	George Burns	5
1916	Ty Cobb	5
1917	Bobby Veach	8
1918	Harry Heilmann	5
1919	Harry Heilmann	8
1920	**Bobby Veach**	**11**
1921	**Harry Heilmann**	**19**
1922	**Harry Heilmann**	**21**
1923	Harry Heilmann	18
1924	Harry Heilmann	10
1925	Harry Heilmann	13
1926	Heinie Manush	14
1927	Harry Heilmann	14
1928	Harry Heilmann	14
1929	**Dale Alexander**	**25**
1930	Dale Alexander	20
1931	John Stone	10
1932	Charlie Gehringer	19
1933	Charlie Gehringer	12
	Hank Greenberg	12
1934	**Hank Greenberg**	**26**
1935	**Hank Greenberg**	**36**
1936	Goose Goslin	24
1937	**Hank Greenberg**	**40**
1938	**Hank Greenberg**	**58**
1939	Hank Greenberg	33
1940	Hank Greenberg	41
1941	Rudy York	27
1942	Rudy York	21
1943	Rudy York	34
1944	Rudy York	18
1945	Roy Cullenbine	18
	Rudy York	18
1946	Hank Greenberg	44
1947	Roy Cullenbine	24
1948	Pat Mullin	23
1949	Vic Wertz	20
1950	Vic Wertz	27
1951	Vic Wertz	27
1952	Walt Dropo	23
1953	Ray Boone	22
1954	Ray Boone	20
1955	Al Kaline	27
1956	Charlie Maxwell	28

Brandon Dixon

Year	Player	HR
1957	Charlie Maxwell	24
1958	Gail Harris	20
1959	Charlie Maxwell	31
1960	Rocky Colavito	35
1961	Rocky Colavito	45
1962	Norm Cash	39
1963	Al Kaline	27
1964	Dick McAuliffe	24
1965	Norm Cash	30
1966	Norm Cash	32
1967	Al Kaline	25
1968	Willie Horton	36
1969	Willie Horton	28
1970	Jim Northrup	24
1971	Norm Cash	32
1972	Norm Cash	22
1973	Norm Cash	19
1974	Bill Freehan	18
1975	Willie Horton	25
1976	Jason Thompson	17
1977	Jason Thompson	31
1978	Jason Thompson	26
1979	Steve Kemp	26
1980	Lance Parrish	24
1981	Lance Parrish	10
1982	Lance Parrish	32
1983	Lance Parrish	27
1984	Lance Parrish	33
1985	Darrell Evans	40
1986	Darrell Evans	29
1987	Darrell Evans	34
1988	Darrell Evans	22
1989	Lou Whitaker	28
1990	Cecil Fielder	51
1991	Cecil Fielder	44
1992	Cecil Fielder	35
1993	Mickey Tettleton	32
1994	Cecil Fielder	28
1995	Cecil Fielder	31
1996	Tony Clark	27
1997	Tony Clark	32
1998	Tony Clark	34
1999	Dean Palmer	38
2000	Bobby Higginson	30
2001	Robert Fick	19
2002	Randall Simon	19
2003	Dmitri Young	29
2004	Carlos Pena	27
2005	Dmitri Young	21
2006	Craig Monroe	28
2007	Magglio Ordonez	28
2008	Miguel Cabrera	37
2009	Miguel Cabrera	34
2010	Miguel Cabrera	38
2011	Miguel Cabrera	30
2012	Miguel Cabrera	44
2013	Miguel Cabrera	44
2014	Victor Martinez	32
2015	J.D. Martinez	38
2016	Miguel Cabrera	38
2017	Justin Upton	28
2018	Nicholas Castellanos	23
2019	Brandon Dixon	15
2020	Miguel Cabrera	10
2021	Robbie Grossman	23

YEARLY TIGER HITTING LEADERS – RUNS BATTED IN

1901	**Kid Elberfeld**	**76**
1902	Kid Elberfeld	64
1903	**Sam Crawford**	**89**
1904	Sam Crawford	73
1905	Sam Crawford	75
1906	Sam Crawford	72
1907	**Ty Cobb**	**119**
1908	Ty Cobb	108
1909	Ty Cobb	107
1910	**Sam Crawford**	**120**
1911	**Ty Cobb**	**127**
1912	Sam Crawford	109
1913	Sam Crawford	83
1914	Sam Crawford	104
1915	Sam Crawford	112
	Bobby Veach	112
1916	Bobby Veach	91
1917	Bobby Veach	103
1918	Bobby Veach	78
1919	Bobby Veach	101
1920	Bobby Veach	113
1921	**Harry Heilmann**	**139**
1922	Bobby Veach	126
1923	Harry Heilmann	115
1924	Harry Heilmann	114
1925	Harry Heilmann	134
1926	Harry Heilmann	103
1927	Harry Heilmann	120
1928	Harry Heilmann	107
1929	Dale Alexander	137
1930	Dale Alexander	135
1931	Dale Alexander	87
1932	John Stone	108
1933	Charlie Gehringer	105
1934	**Hank Greenberg**	**139**
1935	**Hank Greenberg**	**170**
1936	Goose Goslin	125
1937	**Hank Greenberg**	**183**
1938	Hank Greenberg	146
1939	Hank Greenberg	112
1940	Hank Greenberg	150
1941	Rudy York	111
1942	Rudy York	90
1943	Rudy York	118
1944	Rudy York	98
1945	Roy Cullenbine	93
1946	Hank Greenberg	127
1947	George Kell	93
1948	Hoot Evers	103
1949	Vic Wertz	133
1950	Vic Wertz	123
1951	Vic Wertz	94
1952	Walt Dropo	70
1953	Walt Dropo	96
1954	Ray Boone	85
1955	Ray Boone	116
1956	Al Kaline	128
1957	Al Kaline	90
1958	Al Kaline	85
1959	Charlie Maxwell	95
1960	Rocky Colavito	87
1961	Rocky Colavito	140

Darnell Coles

1962	Rocky Colavito	112
1963	Al Kaline	101
1964	Norm Cash	83
1965	Willie Horton	104
1966	Willie Horton	100
1967	Al Kaline	78
1968	Jim Northrup	90
1969	Willie Horton	91
1970	Jim Northrup	80
1971	Norm Cash	91
1972	Norm Cash	61
1973	Aurelio Rodriguez	58
1974	Al Kaline	64
1975	Willie Horton	92
1976	Rusty Staub	96
1977	Jason Thompson	105
1978	Rusty Staub	121
1979	Steve Kemp	105
1980	Steve Kemp	101
1981	Steve Kemp	49
1982	Larry Herndon	88
1983	Lance Parrish	114
1984	Lance Parrish	98
1985	Lance Parrish	98
1986	Darnell Coles	86
	Kirk Gibson	86
1987	Alan Trammell	105
1988	Alan Trammell	69
1989	Lou Whitaker	85
1990	Cecil Fielder	132
1991	Cecil Fielder	133
1992	Cecil Fielder	124
1993	Cecil Fielder	117
1994	Cecil Fielder	90
1995	Cecil Fielder	82
1996	Travis Fryman	100
1997	Tony Clark	117
1998	Tony Clark	103
1999	Dean Palmer	100
2000	Bobby Higginson	102
	Dean Palmer	102
2001	Tony Clark	75
2002	Randall Simon	82
2003	Dmitri Young	85
2004	Carlos Guillen	97
2005	Craig Monroe	89
2006	Magglio Ordonez	104
2007	Magglio Ordonez	139
2008	Miguel Cabrera	127
2009	Miguel Cabrera	103
2010	Miguel Cabrera	126
2011	Miguel Cabrera	105
2012	Miguel Cabrera	139
2013	Miguel Cabrera	137
2014	Miguel Cabrera	109
2015	J.D. Martinez	102
2016	Miguel Cabrera	108
2017	Nicholas Castellanos	101
2018	Nicholas Castellanos	89
2019	Miguel Cabrera	59
2020	Miguel Cabrera	35
2021	Jonathan Schoop	84

Year	Player	HBP
1901	**Doc Casey**	**10**
1902	**Dick Harley**	**12**
1903	Joe Yeager	9
1904	Rabbit Robinson	5
1905	Bill Coughlin	7
1906	John Warner	7
1907	Bill Coughlin	8
1908	Bill Coughlin	7
	Matty McIntyre	7
1909	Jim Delahanty	9
1910	Tom Jones	10
1911	Jim Delahanty	10
1912	Baldy Louden	11
	George Moriarty	11
1913	George Moriarty	7
1914	**George Burns**	**12**
1915	Ty Cobb	10
1916	George Burns	7
1917	Tubby Spencer	9
	Bobby Veach	9
1918	Bobby Veach	4
1919	Ira Flagstead	7
1920	Bobby Veach	7
1921	Ira Flagstead	6
1922	Bobby Veach	8
1923	**Heinie Manush**	**17**
1924	Heinie Manush	16
1925	Frank O'Rourke	11
1926	Frank O'Rourke	7
1927	Jack Warner	6
1928	Charlie Gehringer	6
1929	Charlie Gehringer	6
1930	Charlie Gehringer	7
1931	Hub Walker	4
1932	Charlie Gehringer	3
	Gee Walker	3
1933	Marv Owen	4
1934	Mickey Cochrane	4
	Pete Fox	4
	Marv Owen	4
1935	Pete Fox	6
1936	Gee Walker	8
1937	Gee Walker	5
1938	Billy Rogell	5
1939	Six Players	2
1940	Dick Bartell	5
1941	Four Players	3
1942	Jimmy Bloodworth	5
1943	Jimmy Bloodworth	3
1944	Joe Hoover	6
1945	Doc Cramer	3
	Roy Cullenbine	3
1946	Eddie Lake	4
1947	Hoot Evers	6
1948	George Vico	7
1949	George Vico	4
1950	Hoot Evers	4
	Vic Wertz	4
1951	George Kell	4
1952	Fred Hatfield	6
1953	Walt Dropo	6
1954	Wayne Belardi	5
	Fred Hatfield	5
1955	Fred Hatfield	5
	Al Kaline	5
1956	Wayne Belardi	8
1957	Charlie Maxwell	5
1958	Frank Bolling	4
	Gail Harris	4

JaCoby Jones

Year	Player	HBP
1959	Eddie Yost	12
1960	Eddie Yost	8
1961	Norm Cash	9
1962	Norm Cash	13
1963	Jake Wood	7
1964	Bill Freehan	8
1965	Bill Freehan	7
1966	Al Kaline	5
1967	**Bill Freehan**	**20**
1968	**Bill Freehan**	**24**
1969	Bill Freehan	8
1970	Jim Northrup	7
1971	Bill Freehan	9
1972	Bill Freehan	6
1973	Bill Freehan	11
1974	Bill Freehan	5
1975	Bill Freehan	6
1976	Rusty Staub	7
1977	Steve Kemp	5
1978	Tim Corcoran	5
1979	Rusty Staub	5
1980	Rick Peters	6
1981	Alan Trammell	3
	Champ Summers	3
1982	Chet Lemon	15
1983	Chet Lemon	20
1984	Kirk Gibson	8
1985	Chet Lemon	10
1986	Chet Lemon	8
1987	Bill Madlock	10
1988	Chet Lemon	7
1989	Chet Lemon	8
1990	Cecil Fielder	5
	Lloyd Moseby	5
1991	Cecil Fielder	6
1992	Travis Fryman	6
1993	Five Players	4
1994	Junior Felix	8
1995	Chad Curtis	7
1996	Melvin Nieves	6
1997	Damion Easley	16
1998	Damion Easley	16
1999	Damion Easley	19
2000	Damion Easley	11
2001	Damion Easley	13
2002	Damion Easley	11
2003	Dmitri Young	11
2004	Rondell White	8
2005	Dmitri Young	9
2006	Brandon Inge	7
	Placido Polanco	7
2007	Brandon Inge	11
	Placido Polanco	11
2008	Brandon Inge	8
2009	Brandon Inge	17
2010	Ryan Raburn	8
2011	Brennan Boesch	5
2012	Prince Fielder	17
2013	Prince Fielder	9
2014	Torii Hunter	7
2015	Victor Martinez	7
2016	Ian Kinsler	13
2017	James McCann	9
2018	JaCoby Jones	11
2019	Jeimer Candelario	7
	Christian Stewart	7
2020	Jonathan Schoop	4
2021	Willie Castro	8
	Robbie Grossman	8

YEARLY TIGER HITTING LEADERS – REACHED ON ERROR

Year	Player	RoE
1930	**Charlie Gehringer**	**9**
1931	**Dale Alexander**	**11**
1932	Charlie Gehringer	8
1933	**Marv Owen**	**11**
1934	Marv Owen	8
1935	**Pete Fox**	**12**
1936	Gee Walker	9
1937	**Gee Walker**	**12**
1938	Billy Rogell	7
1939	Barney McCosky	10
1940	Birdie Tebbetts	5
1941	Rudy York	5
1942	Barney McCosky	6
1943	Doc Cramer	3
	Joe Hoover	3
1944	Joe Hoover	3
1945	Skeeter Webb	4
1946	Jimmy Bloodworth	4
	Jimmy Outlaw	4
1947	**Eddie Lake**	**14**
1948	George Kell	7
1949	George Kell	9
1950	Jerry Priddy	11
1951	Hoot Evers	8
	Johnny Lipon	8
1952	Jerry Priddy	7
1953	Ray Boone	13
1954	Harvey Kuenn	11
1955	Al Kaline	13
1956	Al Kaline	13
1957	**Harvey Kuenn**	**16**
1958	Frank Bolling	11
1959	Frank Bolling	12
1960	Frank Bolling	10
	Al Kaline	10
1961	**Al Kaline**	**18**
1962	Rocky Colavito	10
1963	Al Kaline	14
1964	Jerry Lumpe	11
1965	Willie Horton	14
1966	Willie Horton	10
1967	Bill Freehan	12
1968	Mickey Stanley	12
1969	Mickey Stanley	15
1970	Mickey Stanley	17
1971	Aurelio Rodriguez	9
	Mickey Stanley	9
1972	Mickey Stanley	11
1973	Mickey Stanley	17
1974	Gary Sutherland	10
1975	Ron LeFlore	11
1976	Ron LeFlore	14
1977	Ron LeFlore	12
1978	Steve Kemp	12
	Ron LeFlore	12
1979	Ron LeFlore	10
1980	Tom Brookens	11

Jerry Priddy

Year	Player	RoE
1981	Steve Kemp	5
	Rick Peters	5
	Lou Whitaker	5
1982	Enos Cabell	8
	Lou Whitaker	8
1983	Glenn Wilson	12
1984	Lou Whitaker	13
1985	Darrell Evans	8
	Kirk Gibson	8
1986	Alan Trammell	12
1987	Alan Trammell	11
1988	Gary Pettis	11
1989	Alan Trammell	11
1990	Tony Phillips	10
1991	Cecil Fielder	11
1992	Travis Fryman	12
1993	Travis Fryman	9
1994	Cecil Fielder	7
1995	Chad Curtis	8
	Travis Fryman	8
1996	Travis Fryman	9
1997	Deivi Cruz	10
1998	Deivi Cruz	14
1999	Juan Encarnacion	10
2000	Juan Encarnacion	10
2001	Damion Easley	13
2002	Damian Jackson	8
2003	Dmitri Young	7
2004	Rondell White	9
2005	Craig Monroe	9
2006	Brandon Inge	11
2007	Placido Polanco	10
2008	Edgar Renteria	10
2009	Placido Polanco	9
2010	Austin Jackson	9
2011	Austin Jackson	8
2012	Quintin Berry	6
	Austin Jackson	6
	Delmon Young	6
2013	Austin Jackson	8
2014	Victor Martinez	9
2015	Yoenis Cespedes	7
	Anthony Gose	7
2016	Jose Iglesias	8
2017	Mikie Mahtook	7
2018	Nicholas Castellanos	10
2019	Nicholas Castellanos	9
2020	Jonathan Schoop	4
2021	Robbie Grossman	6

TOP FIVE SEASONS FOR ATTENDANCE

1.	3,202,645	2008	COMERICA PARK	74-88 .457	FIFTH PLACE	AL CENTRAL
2.	3,083,397	2013	COMERICA PARK	93-69 .574	FIRST PLACE	AL CENTRAL
3.	3,047,133	2007	COMERICA PARK	88-74 .543	SECOND PLACE	AL CENTRAL
4.	3,028,033	2012	COMERICA PARK	88-74 .543	FIRST PLACE	AL CENTRAL
5.	2,917,209	2014	COMERICA PARK	90-72 .556	FIRST PLACE	AL CENTRAL

Year	Player	OBP
1901	**Kid Elberfeld**	**.397**
1902	**Jimmy Barrett**	**.397**
1903	**Jimmy Barrett**	**.407**
1904	Jimmy Barrett	.353
1905	Sam Crawford	.357
1906	Ty Cobb	.360
1907	Ty Cobb	.380
1908	Matty McIntyre	.392
1909	**Ty Cobb**	**.431**
1910	**Ty Cobb**	**.458**
1911	**Ty Cobb**	**.467**
1912	Ty Cobb	.458
1913	**Ty Cobb**	**.467**
1914	Ty Cobb	.466
1915	**Ty Cobb**	**.486**
1916	Ty Cobb	.452
1917	Ty Cobb	.444
1918	Ty Cobb	.440
1919	Ty Cobb	.429
1920	Ty Cobb	.416
1921	Ty Cobb	.452
1922	Ty Cobb	.462
1923	Harry Heilmann	.481
1924	Johnny Bassler	.441
1925	Ty Cobb	.468
1926	Harry Heilmann	.445
1927	Harry Heilmann	.475
1928	Charlie Gehringer	.395
1929	Harry Heilmann	.412
1930	Charlie Gehringer	.404
1931	Dale Alexander	.401
1932	Charlie Gehringer	.370
1933	Charlie Gehringer	.393
1934	Charlie Gehringer	.450
1935	Mickey Cochrane	.452
1936	Charlie Gehringer	.431
1937	Charlie Gehringer	.458
1938	Hank Greenberg	.438
1939	Charlie Gehringer	.423
1940	Hank Greenberg	.433
1941	Barney McCosky	.401
1942	Barney McCosky	.365
1943	Dick Wakefield	.377
1944	Dick Wakefield	.464
1945	Roy Cullenbine	.398
1946	Roy Cullenbine	.477
1947	Dick Wakefield	.412
1948	Dick Wakefield	.406
1949	George Kell	.424
1950	Hoot Evers	.408
	Vic Wertz	.408
1951	George Kell	.386
1952	Johnny Groth	.348
1953	Ray Boone	.395
1954	Ray Boone	.376
1955	Al Kaline	.421
1956	Charlie Maxwell	.414
1957	Charlie Maxwell	.377
1958	Al Kaline	.374
1959	Eddie Yost	.435
1960	Eddie Yost	.414
1961	**Norm Cash**	**.487**

Champ Summers

Year	Player	OBP
1962	Norm Cash	.382
1963	Norm Cash	.386
1964	Al Kaline	.383
1965	Al Kaline	.388
1966	Al Kaline	.392
1967	Al Kaline	.411
1968	Al Kaline	.392
1969	Norm Cash	.368
1970	Norm Cash	.383
1971	Al Kaline	.416
1972	Al Kaline	.374
1973	Dick McAuliffe	.366
	Jim Northrup	.366
1974	Bill Freehan	.361
1975	Gary Sutherland	.321
1976	Rusty Staub	.386
1977	Ron LeFlore	.363
1978	Steve Kemp	.379
1979	Steve Kemp	.398
1980	Champ Summers	.393
1981	Steve Kemp	.389
1982	Chet Lemon	.368
1983	Alan Trammell	.385
1984	Alan Trammell	.382
1985	Kirk Gibson	.364
1986	Kirk Gibson	.371
1987	Alan Trammell	.402
1988	Lou Whitaker	.376
1989	Gary Pettis	.375
1990	Cecil Fielder	.377
	Alan Trammell	.377
1991	Lou Whitaker	.391
1992	Tony Phillips	.387
1993	Tony Phillips	.443
1994	Mickey Tettleton	.419
1995	Chad Curtis	.349
1996	Bobby Higginson	.404
1997	Bobby Higginson	.379
1998	Tony Clark	.358
1999	Brad Ausmus	.365
2000	Bobby Higginson	.377
2001	Tony Clark	.374
2002	Bobby Higginson	.345
2003	Dmitri Young	.372
2004	Ivan Rodriguez	.383
2005	Placido Polanco	.386
2006	Carlos Guillen	.400
2007	Magglio Ordonez	.434
2008	Carlos Guillen	.376
	Magglio Ordonez	.376
2009	Miguel Cabrera	.396
2010	Miguel Cabrera	.420
2011	Miguel Cabrera	.448
2012	Prince Fielder	.412
2013	Miguel Cabrera	.442
2014	Victor Martinez	.409
2015	Miguel Cabrera	.440
2016	Miguel Cabrera	.393
2017	Justin Upton	.362
2018	Nicholas Castellanos	.354
2019	Miguel Cabrera	.346
2020	Willi Castro	.381
2021	Robbie Grossman	.357

Year	Player	SLG
1901	**Kid Elberfeld**	**.428**
1902	Jimmy Barrett	.387
1903	**Sam Crawford**	**.489**
1904	Sam Crawford	.361
1905	Sam Crawford	.430
1906	Sam Crawford	.407
1907	Ty Cobb	.468
1908	Ty Cobb	.475
1909	**Ty Cobb**	**.517**
1910	**Ty Cobb**	**.554**
1911	**Ty Cobb**	**.621**
1912	Ty Cobb	.586
1913	Ty Cobb	.535
1914	Ty Cobb	.513
1915	Ty Cobb	.487
1916	Ty Cobb	.493
1917	Ty Cobb	.570
1918	Ty Cobb	.515
1919	Bobby Veach	.519
1920	Bobby Veach	.474
1921	Harry Heilmann	.606
1922	Harry Heilmann	.598
1923	**Harry Heilmann**	**.632**
1924	Harry Heilmann	.533
1925	Ty Cobb	.598
1926	Heinie Manush	.564
1927	Harry Heilmann	.616
1928	Harry Heilmann	.507
1929	Dale Alexander	.580
1930	Charlie Gehringer	.534
1931	John Stone	.464
1932	Charlie Gehringer	.497
1933	Charlie Gehringer	.468
	Hank Greenberg	.468
1934	Hank Greenberg	.600
1935	Hank Greenberg	.628
1936	Charlie Gehringer	.555
1937	**Hank Greenberg**	**.668**
1938	**Hank Greenberg**	**.683**
1939	Hank Greenberg	.622
1940	Hank Greenberg	.670
1941	Bruce Campbell	.457
1942	Ned Harris	.430
1943	Rudy York	.527
1944	Rudy York	.439
1945	Roy Cullenbine	.451
1946	Hank Greenberg	.604
1947	Pat Mullin	.470
1948	Pat Mullin	.504
1949	Johnny Groth	.471
1950	Hoot Evers	.551
1951	Vic Wertz	.511
1952	Walt Dropo	.479
1953	Ray Boone	.556
1954	Ray Boone	.466
1955	Al Kaline	.546
1956	Charlie Maxwell	.534
1957	Charlie Maxwell	.482
1958	Al Kaline	.490
1959	Al Kaline	.530
1960	Norm Cash	.501

Bruce Campbell

Year	Player	SLG
1961	Norm Cash	.662
1962	Al Kaline	.593
1963	Al Kaline	.514
1964	Al Kaline	.469
1965	Norm Cash	.512
1966	Al Kaline	.534
1967	Al Kaline	.541
1968	Willie Horton	.543
1969	Jim Northrup	.508
1970	Willie Horton	.501
1971	Norm Cash	.531
1972	Al Kaline	.475
1973	Willie Horton	.501
1974	Bill Freehan	.479
1975	Willie Horton	.421
1976	Ben Oglivie	.492
1977	Jason Thompson	.487
1978	Jason Thompson	.472
1979	Steve Kemp	.543
1980	Champ Summers	.504
1981	Kirk Gibson	.479
1982	Lance Parrish	.529
1983	Lance Parrish	.483
1984	Kirk Gibson	.516
1985	Darrell Evans	.519
1986	Kirk Gibson	.492
1987	Alan Trammell	.551
1988	Alan Trammell	.464
1989	Lou Whitaker	.462
1990	Cecil Fielder	.592
1991	Cecil Fielder	.513
1992	Rob Deer	.547
1993	Alan Trammell	.496
1994	Kirk Gibson	.548
1995	Cecil Fielder	.472
1996	Bobby Higginson	.577
1997	Bobby Higginson	.520
1998	Tony Clark	.522
1999	Luis Polonia	.526
2000	Bobby Higginson	.538
2001	Tony Clark	.481
2002	Randall Simon	.459
2003	Dmitri Young	.537
2004	Carlos Guillen	.542
2005	Chris Shelton	.510
2006	Marcus Thames	.549
2007	Magglio Ordonez	.595
2008	Miguel Cabrera	.537
2009	Miguel Cabrera	.547
2010	Miguel Cabrera	.622
2011	Miguel Cabrera	.586
2012	Miguel Cabrera	.606
2013	Miguel Cabrera	.636
2014	Victor Martinez	.565
2015	J.D. Martinez	.535
2016	Miguel Cabrera	.563
2017	Justin Upton	.542
2018	Nicholas Castellanos	.500
2019	Nicholas Castellanos	.462
2020	Willi Castro	.550
2021	Eric Haase	.459

Year	Player	OPS
1901	**Kid Elberfeld**	**.825**
1902	Jimmy Barrett	.784
1903	**Sam Crawford**	**.855**
1904	Sam Crawford	.670
1905	Sam Crawford	.786
1906	Ty Cobb	.766
1907	Ty Cobb	.848
1908	Ty Cobb	.842
1909	**Ty Cobb**	**.947**
1910	**Ty Cobb**	**1.012**
1911	**Ty Cobb**	**1.088**
1912	Ty Cobb	1.043
1913	Ty Cobb	1.002
1914	Ty Cobb	.979
1915	Ty Cobb	.973
1916	Ty Cobb	.944
1917	Ty Cobb	1.014
1918	Ty Cobb	.955
1919	Ty Cobb	.944
1920	Ty Cobb	.867
1921	Harry Heilmann	1.051
1922	Harry Heilmann	1.030
1923	**Harry Heilmann**	**1.113**
1924	Harry Heilmann	.961
1925	Ty Cobb	1.066
1926	Heinie Manush	.985
1927	Harry Heilmann	1.091
1928	Harry Heilmann	.897
1929	Dale Alexander	.977
	Harry Heilmann	.977
1930	Charlie Gehringer	.938
1931	John Stone	.852
1932	Charlie Gehringer	.867
1933	Charlie Gehringer	.862
1934	Hank Greenberg	1.005
1935	Hank Greenberg	1.039
1936	Charlie Gehringer	.987
1937	Hank Greenberg	1.105
1938	**Hank Greenberg**	**1.122**
1939	Hank Greenberg	1.042
1940	Hank Greenberg	1.103
1941	Barney McCosky	.827
1942	Ned Harris	.781
1943	Rudy York	.893
1944	Dick Wakefield	1.040
1945	Roy Cullenbine	.849
1946	Roy Cullenbine	1.014
1947	Pat Mullin	.829
1948	Pat Mullin	.889
1949	George Kell	.892
1950	Hoot Evers	.959
1951	Vic Wertz	.894
1952	Vic Wertz	.851
1953	Ray Boone	.951
1954	Ray Boone	.842
1955	Al Kaline	.967
1956	Charlie Maxwell	.948
1957	Charlie Maxwell	.858
1958	Al Kaline	.864
1959	Al Kaline	.940
1960	Norm Cash	.903

Chris Shelton

Year	Player	OPS
1961	**Norm Cash**	**1.148**
1962	Al Kaline	.969
1963	Al Kaline	.889
1964	Al Kaline	.851
1965	Norm Cash	.883
1966	Al Kaline	.927
1967	Al Kaline	.952
1968	Willie Horton	.895
1969	Jim Northrup	.866
1970	Willie Horton	.855
1971	Norm Cash	.903
1972	Al Kaline	.849
1973	Willie Horton	.863
1974	Bill Freehan	.840
1975	Willie Horton	.740
1976	Rusty Staub	.818
1977	Ron LeFlore	.838
1978	Jason Thompson	.836
1979	Steve Kemp	.941
1980	Champ Summers	.897
1981	Kirk Gibson	.848
1982	Lance Parrish	.867
1983	Alan Trammell	.856
1984	Kirk Gibson	.879
1985	Kirk Gibson	.882
1986	Kirk Gibson	.863
1987	Alan Trammell	.953
1988	Alan Trammell	.836
1989	Lou Whitaker	.822
1990	Cecil Fielder	.969
1991	Lou Whitaker	.881
1992	Rob Deer	.884
1993	Alan Trammell	.885
1994	Kirk Gibson	.906
1995	Cecil Fielder	.818
1996	Bobby Higginson	.982
1997	Bobby Higginson	.899
1998	Tony Clark	.880
1999	Luis Polonia	.882
2000	Bobby Higginson	.915
2001	Tony Clark	.856
2002	Randall Simon	.779
2003	Dmitri Young	.909
2004	Carlos Guillen	.921
2005	Chris Shelton	.870
2006	Carlos Guillen	.920
2007	Magglio Ordonez	1.029
2008	Miguel Cabrera	.887
2009	Miguel Cabrera	.942
2010	Miguel Cabrera	1.042
2011	Miguel Cabrera	1.033
2012	Miguel Cabrera	.999
2013	Miguel Cabrera	1.078
2014	Victor Martinez	.974
2015	Miguel Cabrera	.974
2016	Miguel Cabrera	.956
2017	Justin Upton	.904
2018	Nicholas Castellanos	.854
2019	Nicholas Castellanos	.790
2020	Willi Castro	.932
2021	Jeimer Candelario	.795

1901	**Kid Elberfeld**	**124**
1902	Jimmy Barrett	114
1903	**Sam Crawford**	**159**
1904	Sam Crawford	114
1905	Sam Crawford	149
1906	Ty Cobb	132
1907	**Ty Cobb**	**167**
1908	**Ty Cobb**	**169**
1909	**Ty Cobb**	**193**
1910	**Ty Cobb**	**206**
1911	Ty Cobb	196
1912	Ty Cobb	200
1913	Ty Cobb	194
1914	Ty Cobb	190
1915	Ty Cobb	185
1916	Ty Cobb	179
1917	**Ty Cobb**	**209**
1918	Ty Cobb	194
1919	Ty Cobb	166
1920	Ty Cobb	132
1921	Harry Heilmann	167
1922	Ty Cobb	169
	Harry Heilmann	169
1923	Harry Heilmann	194
1924	Harry Heilmann	149
1925	Ty Cobb	171
926	Heinie Manush	154
1927	Harry Heilmann	180
1928	Harry Heilmann	132
1929	Harry Heilmann	149
1930	Charlie Gehringer	134
1931	John Stone	120
1932	Charlie Gehringer	119
1933	Charlie Gehringer	126
1934	Hank Greenberg	156
1935	Hank Greenberg	170
1936	Charlie Gehringer	142
1937	Hank Greenberg	172
1938	Hank Greenberg	169
1939	Hank Greenberg	156
1940	Hank Greenberg	171
1941	Barney McCosky	110
1942	Ned Harris	112
1943	Rudy York	152
1944	Dick Wakefield	190
1945	Roy Cullenbine	139
1946	Roy Cullenbine	175
1947	Dick Wakefield	127
1948	Pat Mullin	132
1949	George Kell	136
1950	Hoot Evers	141
1951	Vic Wertz	140
1952	Vic Wertz	135
1953	Ray Boone	156
1954	Ray Boone	131
1955	Al Kaline	162
1956	Charlie Maxwell	148
1957	Charlie Maxwell	131
1958	Al Kaline	130
1959	Al Kaline	151
1960	Norm Cash	140

Hoot Evers

1961	Norm Cash	201
1962	Al Kaline	152
1963	Al Kaline	144
1964	Al Kaline	134
1965	Norm Cash	148
1966	Al Kaline	161
1967	Al Kaline	176
1968	Willie Horton	165
1969	Jim Northrup	136
1970	Willie Horton	133
1971	Norm Cash	149
1972	Al Kaline	149
1973	Willie Horton	136
1974	Bill Freehan	139
1975	Willie Horton	106
1976	Rusty Staub	137
1977	Ron LeFlore	123
1978	Jason Thompson	131
1979	Steve Kemp	149
1980	Champ Summers	143
1981	Kirk Gibson	141
1982	Lance Parrish	135
1983	Alan Trammell	138
1984	Kirk Gibson	142
1985	Kirk Gibson	140
1986	Kirk Gibson	133
1987	Alan Trammell	155
1988	Alan Trammell	138
1989	Lou Whitaker	133
1990	Cecil Fielder	167
1991	Lou Whitaker	141
1992	Rob Deer	145
1993	Alan Trammell	138
1994	Kirk Gibson	130
1995	Cecil Fielder	111
1996	Bobby Higginson	145
1997	Bobby Higginson	133
1998	Tony Clark	126
1999	Luis Polonia	123
2000	Bobby Higginson	135
2001	Tony Clark	131
2002	Randall Simon	112
2003	Dmitri Young	144
2004	Carlos Guillen	143
2005	Chris Shelton	132
2006	Carlos Guillen	136
2007	Magglio Ordonez	166
2008	Miguel Cabrera	130
2009	Miguel Cabrera	144
2010	Miguel Cabrera	178
2011	Miguel Cabrera	179
2012	Miguel Cabrera	164
2013	Miguel Cabrera	190
2014	Victor Martinez	172
2015	Miguel Cabrera	169
2016	Miguel Cabrera	155
2017	Justin Upton	135
2018	Nicholas Castellanos	130
2019	Nicholas Castellanos	105
2020	Willi Castro	153
2021	Jeimer Candelario	122

Year	Player	Rating
1901	**Jimmy Barrett**	**1.6**
1902	**Jimmy Barrett**	**1.0**
1903	Sam Crawford	1.2
1904	Sam Crawford	1.4
1905	**Sam Crawford**	**1.0**
1906	Sam Crawford	1.4
1907	**Ty Cobb**	**1.0**
1908	**Ty Cobb**	**1.0**
1909	**Ty Cobb**	**1.0**
1910	**Ty Cobb**	**1.0**
1911	**Ty Cobb**	**1.0**
1912	**Ty Cobb**	**1.0**
1913	Ty Cobb	1.2
1914	Ty Cobb	1.2
1915	**Ty Cobb**	**1.0**
1916	**Ty Cobb**	**1.0**
1917	**Ty Cobb**	**1.0**
1918	**Ty Cobb**	**1.0**
1919	Ty Cobb	1.2
1920	Ty Cobb	1.6
1921	Ty Cobb	1.2
1922	Harry Heilmann	1.4
1923	**Harry Heilmann**	**1.0**
1924	**Harry Heilmann**	**1.0**
1925	Ty Cobb	1.4
1926	Harry Heilmann	1.2
1927	**Harry Heilmann**	**1.0**
1928	**Harry Heilmann**	**1.0**
1929	Dale Alexander	1.8
1930	**Charlie Gehringer**	**1.0**
1931	John Stone	1.4
1932	**Charlie Gehringer**	**1.0**
1933	**Charlie Gehringer**	**1.0**
1934	**Hank Greenberg**	**1.0**
1935	**Hank Greenberg**	**1.0**
1936	**Charlie Gehringer**	**1.0**
1937	**Hank Greenberg**	**1.0**
1938	**Hank Greenberg**	**1.0**
1939	**Hank Greenberg**	**1.0**
1940	**Hank Greenberg**	**1.0**
1941	Barney McCosky	1.8
1942	Barney McCosky	1.2
1943	**Rudy York**	**1.0**
1944	Dick Wakefield	1.4
1945	Hank Greenberg	1.8
1946	Hank Greenberg	1.4
1947	Roy Cullenbine	1.6
1948	Pat Mullin	1.4
1949	George Kell	1.2
1950	Vic Wertz	1.4
1951	**Vic Wertz**	**1.0**
1952	Vic Wertz	1.6
1953	Ray Boone	1.2
1954	**Ray Boone**	**1.0**
1955	**Al Kaline**	**1.0**
1956	Charlie Maxwell	1.6
1957	Charlie Maxwell	1.4
1958	**Al Kaline**	**1.0**
1959	Al Kaline	1.4
1960	Al Kaline	2.4

Jason Thompson

Year	Player	Rating
1961	**Norm Cash**	**1.0**
1962	Al Kaline	1.4
1963	Al Kaline	1.2
1964	**Al Kaline**	**1.0**
1965	Norm Cash	1.2
1966	Al Kaline	1.2
1967	**Al Kaline**	**1.0**
1968	**Willie Horton**	**1.0**
1969	Jim Northrup	1.2
1970	Willie Horton	1.8
1971	Norm Cash	1.4
1972	Norm Cash	1.4
1973	Willie Horton	1.2
1974	**Bill Freehan**	**1.0**
1975	Willie Horton	1.2
1976	Ron LeFlore	1.4
1977	**Ron LeFlore**	**1.0**
1978	Jason Thompson	1.4
1979	Steve Kemp	1.2
1980	Steve Kemp	1.8
1981	Kirk Gibson	1.4
1982	Lance Parrish	1.2
1983	Lou Whitaker	1.6
1984	Kirk Gibson	1.2
1985	**Kirk Gibson**	**1.0**
1986	Kirk Gibson	1.4
1987	**Alan Trammell**	**1.0**
1988	**Alan Trammell**	**1.0**
1989	**Lou Whitaker**	**1.0**
1990	**Cecil Fielder**	**1.0**
1991	Cecil Fielder	1.8
1992	Mickey Tettleton	2.0
1993	Tony Phillips	2.0
1994	Tony Phillips	2.0
1995	Chad Curtis	1.4
1996	**Bobby Higginson**	**1.0**
1997	Bobby Higginson	1.2
1998	**Tony Clark**	**1.0**
1999	Tony Clark	1.6
2000	**Bobby Higginson**	**1.0**
2001	Tony Clark	1.4
2002	Carlos Pena	1.8
2003	**Dmitri Young**	**1.0**
2004	**Carlos Guillen**	**1.0**
2005	Chris Shelton	1.6
2006	**Carlos Guillen**	**1.0**
2007	**Magglio Ordonez**	**1.0**
2008	Miguel Cabrera	1.4
2009	**Miguel Cabrera**	**1.0**
2010	**Miguel Cabrera**	**1.0**
2011	**Miguel Cabrera**	**1.0**
2012	**Miguel Cabrera**	**1.0**
2013	**Miguel Cabrera**	**1.0**
2014	**Victor Martinez**	**1.0**
2015	Miguel Cabrera	1.4
2016	**Miguel Cabrera**	**1.0**
2017	Justin Upton	1.2
2018	**Nicholas Castellanos**	**1.0**
2019	Nicholas Castellanos	1.2
2020	Willi Castro	1.2
2021	Jeimer Candelario	2.0

YEARLY TIGER HITTING LEADERS – TOTAL AVERAGE

Year	Player	Average
1901	**Kid Elberfeld**	**.910**
1902	Jimmy Barrett	.848
1903	Jimmy Barrett	.873
1904	Sam Crawford	.637
1905	Sam Crawford	.797
1906	Ty Cobb	.759
1907	**Ty Cobb**	**.919**
1908	Ty Cobb	.903
1909	**Ty Cobb**	**1.193**
1910	**Ty Cobb**	**1.321**
1911	**Ty Cobb**	**1.464**
1912	Ty Cobb	1.106
1913	Ty Cobb	1.310
1914	Ty Cobb	1.098
1915	Ty Cobb	1.170
1916	Ty Cobb	1.071
1917	Ty Cobb	1.253
1918	Ty Cobb	1.131
1919	Ty Cobb	1.056
1920	Ty Cobb	.875
1921	Ty Cobb	1.132
1922	Harry Heilmann	1.135
1923	Harry Heilmann	1.288
1924	Harry Heilmann	1.042
1925	Ty Cobb	1.206
1926	Harry Heilmann	1.040
1927	Harry Heilmann	1.265
1928	Harry Heilmann	.910
1929	Harry Heilmann	1.013
1930	Charlie Gehringer	.958
1931	Dale Alexander	.821
1932	Charlie Gehringer	.857
1933	Charlie Gehringer	.855
1934	Hank Greenberg	1.071
1935	Hank Greenberg	1.138
1936	Charlie Gehringer	1.075
1937	Hank Greenberg	1.277
1938	Hank Greenberg	1.306
1939	Hank Greenberg	1.152
1940	Hank Greenberg	1.215
1941	Barney McCosky	.816
1942	Bob Harris	.737
1943	Rudy York	.871
1944	Dick Wakefield	1.162
1945	Roy Cullenbine	.882

Year	Player	Average
1946	Roy Cullenbine	1.202
1947	Roy Cullenbine	.898
1948	Dick Wakefield	.921
1949	George Kell	.877
1950	Vic Wertz	.978
1951	Vic Wertz	.888
1952	Walt Dropo	.709
1953	Ray Boone	.985
1954	Ray Boone	.814
1955	Al Kaline	.993
1956	Charlie Maxwell	1.015
1957	Charlie Maxwell	.876
1958	Al Kaline	.823
1959	Eddie Yost	.992
1960	Norm Cash	.984
1961	Norm Cash	1.358

Bob Harris

Year	Player	Average
1962	Al Kaline	.980
1963	Norm Cash	.876
1964	Al Kaline	.852
1965	Al Kaline	.899
1966	Al Kaline	.969
1967	Al Kaline	1.009
1968	Willie Horton	.867
1969	Jim Northrup	.847
1970	Norm Cash	.821
1971	Norm Cash	.933
1972	Al Kaline	.807
1973	Norm Cash	.828
1974	Bill Freehan	.806
1975	Willie Horton	.648
1976	Rusty Staub	.794
1977	Jason Thompson	.808

Year	Player	Average
1978	Jason Thompson	.817
1979	Steve Kemp	.949
1980	Champ Summers	.907
1981	Kirk Gibson	.818
	Steve Kemp	.818
1982	Lance Parrish	.832
1983	Alan Trammell	.873
1984	Kirk Gibson	.926
1985	Kirk Gibson	.953
1986	Kirk Gibson	.950
1987	Alan Trammell	1.015
1988	Alan Trammell	.794
1989	Lou Whitaker	.844
1990	Cecil Fielder	1.007
1991	Lou Whitaker	.942
1992	Rob Deer	.886
1993	Lou Whitaker	.907
1994	Mickey Tettleton	.992
1995	Cecil Fielder	.796
1996	Bobby Higginson	1.045
1997	Bobby Higginson	.905
1998	Tony Clark	.852
1999	Tony Clark	.855
2000	Bobby Higginson	.960
2001	Tony Clark	.838
2002	Bobby Higginson	.720
2003	Dmitri Young	.903
2004	Carlos Guillen	.922
2005	Chris Shelton	.837
2006	Carlos Guillen	.934
2007	Magglio Ordonez	1.088
2008	Curtis Granderson	.868
2009	Miguel Cabrera	.941
2010	Miguel Cabrera	1.116
2011	Miguel Cabrera	1.118
2012	Miguel Cabrera	1.007
2013	Miguel Cabrera	1.184
2014	Victor Martinez	1.000
2015	Miguel Cabrera	1.016
2016	Miguel Cabrera	.956
2017	Justin Upton	.918
2018	Nicholas Castellanos	.824
2019	Nicholas Castellanos	.738
2020	Willie Castro	.929
2021	Robbie Grossman	.817

Year	Player	BOP
1901	**Kid Elberfeld**	**.913**
1902	Jimmy Barrett	.850
1903	Jimmy Barrett	.879
1904	Sam Crawford	.647
1905	Sam Crawford	.799
1906	Ty Cobb	.772
1907	**Ty Cobb**	**.921**
1908	Ty Cobb	.907
1909	**Ty Cobb**	**1.181**
1910	**Ty Cobb**	**1.305**
1911	**Ty Cobb**	**1.449**
1912	Ty Cobb	1.196
1913	Ty Cobb	1.298
1914	Ty Cobb	1.166
1915	Ty Cobb	1.261
1916	Ty Cobb	1.132
1917	Ty Cobb	1.243
1918	Ty Cobb	1.126
1919	Ty Cobb	1.054
1920	Ty Cobb	.911
1921	Ty Cobb	1.171
1922	Harry Heilmann	1.143
1923	Harry Heilmann	1.289
1924	Harry Heilmann	1.052
1925	Ty Cobb	1.235
1926	Harry Heilmann	1.057
1927	Harry Heilmann	1.267
1928	Harry Heilmann	.922
1929	Harry Heilmann	1.032
1930	Charlie Gehringer	.993
1931	John Stone	.844
1932	Charlie Gehringer	.876
1933	Charlie Gehringer	.866
1934	Hank Greenberg	1.081
1935	Hank Greenberg	1.144
1936	Charlie Gehringer	1.077
1937	Hank Greenberg	1.283
1938	Hank Greenberg	1.316
1939	Hank Greenberg	1.156
1940	Hank Greenberg	1.221
1941	Barney McCosky	.828
1942	Bob Harris	.752
1943	Rudy York	.884
1944	Dick Wakefield	1.173
1945	Roy Cullenbine	.883
1946	Roy Cullenbine	1.200
1947	Roy Cullenbine	.905
1948	Dick Wakefield	.925
1949	George Kell	.895
1950	Vic Wertz	.980
1951	Vic Wertz	.896
1952	Walt Dropo	.715
1953	Ray Boone	.989
1954	Ray Boone	.822
1955	Al Kaline	1.012
1956	Charlie Maxwell	1.017
1957	Charlie Maxwell	.884
1958	Al Kaline	.836
1959	Eddie Yost	.997
1960	Norm Cash	.992

Robbie Grossman

Year	Player	BOP
1961	Norm Cash	1.368
1962	Al Kaline	.980
1963	Norm Cash	.886
1964	Al Kaline	.856
1965	Norm Cash	.912
1966	Al Kaline	.983
1967	Al Kaline	1.015
1968	Willie Horton	.878
1969	Jim Northrup	.854
1970	Norm Cash	.828
1971	Norm Cash	.934
1972	Al Kaline	.813
1973	Norm Cash	.830
1974	Bill Freehan	.812
1975	Ben Oglivie	.664
1976	Ron LeFlore	.829
1977	Ron LeFlore	.832
1978	Ron LeFlore	.824
1979	Steve Kemp	.967
1980	Champ Summers	.920
1981	Kirk Gibson	.844
1982	Lance Parrish	.844
1983	Alan Trammell	.905
1984	Kirk Gibson	.950
1985	Kirk Gibson	.963
1986	Kirk Gibson	.968
1987	Alan Trammell	1.019
1988	Alan Trammell	.809
1989	Lou Whitaker	.855
1990	Cecil Fielder	1.009
1991	Lou Whitaker	.949
1992	Mickey Tettleton	.899
1993	Lou Whitaker	.921
1994	Mickey Tettleton	.996
1995	Cecil Fielder	.801
1996	Bobby Higginson	1.053
1997	Bobby Higginson	.923
1998	Tony Clark	.860
1999	Luis Polonia	.892
2000	Bobby Higginson	.968
2001	Tony Clark	.844
2002	Bobby Higginson	.741
2003	Dmitri Young	.906
2004	Carlos Guillen	.937
2005	Chris Shelton	.840
2006	Carlos Guillen	.957
2007	Magglio Ordonez	1.089
2008	Curtis Granderson	.878
2009	Miguel Cabrera	.945
2010	Miguel Cabrera	1.121
2011	Miguel Cabrera	1.119
2012	Miguel Cabrera	1.009
2013	Miguel Cabrera	1.183
2014	Victor Martinez	1.005
2015	Miguel Cabrera	1.020
2016	Miguel Cabrera	.957
2017	Justin Upton	.933
2018	Nicholas Castellanos	.828
2019	Nicholas Castellanos	.739
2020	Willi Castro	.932
2021	Robbie Grossman	.820

Year	Player	GPA
1901	**Kid Elberfeld**	**.286**
1902	Jimmy Barrett	.276
1903	**Sam Crawford**	**.287**
1904	Jimmy Barrett	.234
1905	Sam Crawford	.268
1906	Ty Cobb	.258
1907	**Ty Cobb**	**.288**
1908	Ty Cobb	.284
1909	**Ty Cobb**	**.323**
1910	**Ty Cobb**	**.343**
1911	**Ty Cobb**	**.365**
1912	Ty Cobb	.352
1913	Ty Cobb	.344
1914	Ty Cobb	.338
1915	Ty Cobb	.340
1916	Ty Cobb	.326
1917	Ty Cobb	.342
1918	Ty Cobb	.327
1919	Ty Cobb	.322
1920	Ty Cobb	.300
1921	Ty Cobb	.352
	Harry Heilmann	.352
1922	Ty Cobb	.349
1923	**Harry Heilmann**	**.374**
1924	Harry Heilmann	.326
1925	Ty Cobb	.360
1926	Harry Heilmann	.334
1927	Harry Heilmann	.368
1928	Harry Heilmann	.302
1929	Harry Heilmann	.327
1930	Charlie Gehringer	.315
1931	Dale Alexander	.292
1932	Charlie Gehringer	.291
1933	Charlie Gehringer	.294
1934	Charlie Gehringer	.332
	Hank Greenberg	.332
1935	Hank Greenberg	.342
1936	Charlie Gehringer	.333
1937	Hank Greenberg	.363
1938	Hank Greenberg	.368
1939	Hank Greenberg	.344
1940	Hank Greenberg	.363
1941	Barney McCosky	.287
1942	Barney McCosky	.267
1943	Rudy York	.296
1944	Dick Wakefield	.353
1945	Roy Cullenbine	.292
1946	Roy Cullenbine	.349
1947	Dick Wakefield	.289
1948	Dick Wakefield	.301
1949	George Kell	.308
1950	Hoot Evers	.321
1951	Vic Wertz	.300
1952	Walt Dropo	.264
1953	Ray Boone	.317
1954	Ray Boone	.286
1955	Al Kaline	.326
1956	Charlie Maxwell	.320
1957	Charlie Maxwell	.290
1958	Al Kaline	.291
1959	Al Kaline	.317
1960	Norm Cash	.306

Roy Cullenbine

Year	Player	GPA
1961	**Norm Cash**	**.384**
1962	Al Kaline	.317
1963	Al Kaline	.297
1964	Al Kaline	.289
1965	Norm Cash	.295
1966	Al Kaline	.310
1967	Al Kaline	.320
1968	Willie Horton	.294
1969	Jim Northrup	.288
1970	Willie Horton	.285
1971	Al Kaline	.303
1972	Al Kaline	.287
1973	Willie Horton	.288
1974	Bill Freehan	.282
1975	Willie Horton	.249
1976	Rusty Staub	.282
1977	Ron LeFlore	.282
1978	Jason Thompson	.282
1979	Steve Kemp	.315
1980	Champ Summers	.303
1981	Kirk Gibson	.286
1982	Lance Parrish	.284
1983	Alan Trammell	.291
1984	Kirk Gibson	.293
1985	Kirk Gibson	.293
1986	Kirk Gibson	.290
1987	Alan Trammell	.319
1988	Alan Trammell	.284
1989	Lou Whitaker	.278
1990	Cecil Fielder	.318
1991	Lou Whitaker	.298
1992	Lou Whitaker	.289
1993	Tony Phillips	.299
	Lou Whitaker	.299
1994	Mickey Tettleton	.304
1995	Cecil Fielder	.274
1996	Bobby Higginson	.326
1997	Bobby Higginson	.301
1998	Tony Clark	.292
1999	Luis Polonia	.292
2000	Bobby Higginson	.304
2001	Tony Clark	.289
2002	Bobby Higginson	.260
2003	Dmitri Young	.302
2004	Carlos Guillen	.306
2005	Placido Polanco	.289
	Chris Shelton	.289
2006	Carlos Guillen	.310
2007	Maggilo Ordonez	.344
2008	Miguel Cabrera	.292
	Maggilo Ordonez	.292
2009	Miguel Cabrera	.315
2010	Miguel Cabrera	.344
2011	Miguel Cabrera	.348
2012	Miguel Cabrera	.328
2013	Miguel Cabrera	.358
2014	Victor Martinez	.325
2015	Miguel Cabrera	.332
2016	Miguel Cabrera	.318
2017	Justin Upton	.298
2018	Nicholas Castellanos	.284
2019	Nicholas Castellanos	.263
2020	Willi Castro	.309
2021	Jeimer Candelario	.269

Year	Player	WAR
1901	**Kid Elberfeld**	**3.8**
1902	Jimmy Barrett	3.1
1903	**Sam Crawford**	**5.6**
1904	Jimmy Barrett	3.1
1905	Sam Crawford	5.3
1906	Sam Crawford	3.2
1907	**Ty Cobb**	**6.8**
1908	Ty Cobb	6.1
1909	**Ty Cobb**	**9.8**
1910	**Ty Cobb**	**10.5**
1911	**Ty Cobb**	**10.7**
1912	Ty Cobb	9.2
1913	Ty Cobb	7.4
1914	Sam Crawford	6.2
1915	Ty Cobb	9.5
1916	Ty Cobb	8.0
1917	**Ty Cobb**	**11.3**
1918	Ty Cobb	6.6
1919	Bobby Veach	6.6
1920	Bobby Veach	4.2
1921	Harry Heilmann	6.8
1922	Ty Cobb	6.7
1923	Harry Heilmann	9.3
1924	Harry Heilmann	6.4
1925	Harry Heilmann	6.9
1926	Harry Heilmann	5.2
1927	Harry Heilmann	7.2
1928	Charlie Gehringer	4.5
1929	Charlie Gehringer	5.8
1930	Charlie Gehringer	6.5
1931	John Stone	3.4
1932	Charlie Gehringer	4.7
1933	Charlie Gehringer	7.2
1934	Charlie Gehringer	8.4
1935	Charlie Gehringer	7.8
1936	Charlie Gehringer	7.4
1937	Hank Greenberg	7.7
1938	Hank Greenberg	7.0
1939	Hank Greenberg	5.5
1940	Hank Greenberg	7.1
1941	Barney McCosky	3.2
1942	Rudy York	3.0
1943	Rudy York	6.3
1944	Pinky Higgins	4.0
1945	Roy Cullenbine	5.4
1946	Hank Greenberg	6.5
1947	Roy Cullenbine	4.3
1948	Pat Mullin	3.5
1949	George Kell	4.8
1950	George Kell	4.9
1951	Vic Wertz	4.4
1952	Vic Wertz	2.2
1953	Ray Boone	4.6
1954	Ray Boone	4.4
1955	Al Kaline	8.2
1956	Al Kaline	6.5
1957	Al Kaline	5.5
1958	Al Kaline	6.5
1959	Al Kaline	6.0
1960	Norm Cash	2.8
1961	Norm Cash	9.2

Barney McCosky

Year	Player	WAR
1962	Rocky Colavito	5.7
1963	Al Kaline	5.4
1964	Al Kaline	5.6
1965	Norm Cash	5.4
1966	Dick McAuliffe	6.0
1967	Al Kaline	7.5
1968	Bill Freehan	7.0
1969	Jim Northrup	5.0
1970	Al Kaline	3.2
1971	Bill Freehan	4.3
1972	Bill Freehan	4.2
1973	Dick McAuliffe	2.6
1974	Bill Freehan	4.0
1975	Aurelio Rodriguez	1.9
1976	Ron LeFlore	5.3
1977	Jason Thompson	3.8
1978	Jason Thompson	5.5
1979	Lou Whitaker	4.5
1980	Alan Trammell	4.8
1981	Steve Kemp	3.8
	Alan Trammell	3.8
	Lou Whitaker	3.8
1982	Lou Whitaker	5.4
1983	Lou Whitaker	6.7
1984	Alan Trammell	6.7
1985	Kirk Gibson	5.4
1986	Alan Trammell	6.3
1987	Alan Trammell	8.2
1988	Alan Trammell	6.0
1989	Lou Whitaker	5.3
1990	Alan Trammell	6.7
1991	Lou Whitaker	6.7
1992	Tony Phillips	5.0
1993	Tony Phillips	5.6
1994	Tony Phillips	4.7
1995	Travis Fryman	3.9
1996	Bobby Higginson	3.6
1997	Tony Clark	3.5
	Travis Fryman	3.5
1998	Damion Easley	5.6
1999	Brad Ausmus	3.4
2000	Bobby Higginson	5.3
2001	Bobby Higginson	3.4
2002	Robert Fick	1.7
2003	Dmitri Young	3.4
2004	Carlos Guillen	4.6
2005	Placido Polanco	4.3
2006	Carlos Guillen	6.0
2007	Curtis Granderson	7.6
2008	Placido Polanco	4.4
2009	Miguel Cabrera	5.1
2010	Miguel Cabrera	6.4
2011	Miguel Cabrera	7.5
2012	Miguel Cabrera	7.2
2013	Miguel Cabrera	7.3
2014	Ian Kinsler	5.7
2015	Ian Kinsler	6.0
2016	Ian Kinsler	6.1
2017	Justin Upton	5.2
2018	Nicholas Castellanos	2.9
2019	Niko Goodrum	1.6
2020	Jeimer Candelario	2.0
2021	Jeimer Candelario	3.7

1901	**Kid Elberfeld**	**4.0**
1902	Jimmy Barrett	2.7
1903	**Sam Crawford**	**5.3**
1904	Jimmy Barrett	3.0
1905	Sam Crawford	5.1
1906	Sam Crawford	3.6
1907	**Ty Cobb**	**6.5**
1908	Ty Cobb	6.4
1909	**Ty Cobb**	**9.5**
1910	**Ty Cobb**	**9.6**
1911	**Ty Cobb**	**10.2**
1912	Ty Cobb	8.9
1913	Ty Cobb	7.6
1914	Sam Crawford	6.7
1915	Ty Cobb	9.9
1916	Ty Cobb	8.7
1917	**Ty Cobb**	**10.6**
1918	Ty Cobb	6.8
1919	Ty Cobb	6.1
1920	Ty Cobb	3.8
1921	Harry Heilmann	7.3
1922	Ty Cobb	7.2
1923	Harry Heilmann	8.9
1924	Harry Heilmann	6.2
1925	Harry Heilmann	7.1
1926	Harry Heilmann	5.8
	Heinie Manush	5.8
1927	Harry Heilmann	7.7
1928	Charlie Gehringer	5.0
1929	Charlie Gehringer	5.8
1930	Charlie Gehringer	6.5
1931	John Stone	3.2
1932	Charlie Gehringer	4.4
1933	Charlie Gehringer	5.4
1934	Charlie Gehringer	7.5
1935	Hank Greenberg	7.3
1936	Charlie Gehringer	6.9
1937	Hank Greenberg	7.5
1938	Hank Greenberg	6.8
1939	Hank Greenberg	5.3
1940	Hank Greenberg	7.2
1941	Barney McCosky	2.7
1942	Pinky Higgins	2.4
1943	Rudy York	5.2
1944	Dick Wakefield	4.1
1945	Roy Cullenbine	4.4
1946	Hank Greenberg	5.8

1947	George Kell	3.5
1948	Pat Mullin	3.5
1949	George Kell	4.6
1950	George Kell	4.6
1951	George Kell	3.8
1952	Jerry Priddy	2.2
1953	Ray Boone	5.1
1954	Ray Boone	4.1
1955	Al Kaline	7.1
1956	Al Kaline	5.3
1957	Charlie Maxwell	3.7
1958	Al Kaline	3.6
1959	Al Kaline	5.4
	Harvey Kuenn	5.4
	Eddie Yost	5.4
1960	Eddie Yost	3.8

Shane Halter

1961	Norm Cash	8.5
1962	Rocky Colavito	4.1
1963	Al Kaline	5.2
1964	Bill Freehan	4.6
1965	Norm Cash	4.2
1966	Al Kaline	5.9
	Dick McAuliffe	5.9
1967	Al Kaline	6.6
1968	Bill Freehan	6.6
1969	Jim Northrup	4.4
1970	Al Kaline	3.2
	Dick McAuliffe	3.2
1971	Bill Freehan	4.1
1972	Bill Freehan	4.1
1973	Willie Horton	2.8
1974	Bill Freehan	4.1

1975	Bill Freehan	1.8
1976	Ron LeFlore	5.5
1977	Ron LeFlore	4.7
1978	Ron LeFlore	5.2
1979	Steve Kemp	4.5
1980	Alan Trammell	4.6
1981	Steve Kemp	3.2
1982	Lance Parrish	4.6
1983	Lou Whitaker	6.3
1984	Kirk Gibson	5.2
1985	Kirk Gibson	5.2
1986	Alan Trammell	5.5
1987	Alan Trammell	8.2
1988	Alan Trammell	5.3
1989	Lou Whitaker	5.1
1990	Cecil Fielder	6.5
1991	Lou Whitaker	5.6
1992	Mickey Tettleton	4.9
1993	Travis Fryman	6.3
1994	Tony Phillips	3.7
1995	Chad Curtis	2.4
	Travis Fryman	2.4
1996	Bobby Higginson	3.9
1997	Bobby Higginson	4.5
1998	Damion Easley	4.0
1999	Dean Palmer	3.1
2000	Bobby Higginson	5.3
2001	Shane Halter	3.2
2002	Robert Fick	1.9
2003	Dmitri Young	4.7
2004	Carlos Guillen	5.8
2005	Placido Polanco	3.1
2006	Carlos Guillen	6.1
2007	Magglio Ordonez	7.2
2008	Curtis Granderson	4.8
2009	Miguel Cabrera	5.2
2010	Miguel Cabrera	6.9
2011	Miguel Cabrera	7.9
2012	Miguel Cabrera	7.7
2013	Miguel Cabrera	9.1
2014	Victor Martinez	5.8
2015	Miguel Cabrera	4.8
2016	Miguel Cabrera	5.5
2017	Justin Upton	3.9
2018	Nicholas Castellanos	4.7
2019	Niko Goodrum	1.8
2020	Jeimer Candelario	1.5
2021	Jeimer Candelario	4.1

Year	Player	dWAR
1901	**Doc Casey**	**1.0**
1902	**Kid Elberfeld**	**1.1**
1903	Charlie Carr	0.4
1904	Charley O'Leary	0.8
1905	Bill Coughlin	0.3
	Matty McIntyre	0.3
1906	Ty Cobb	-0.4
1907	Charley O'Leary	0.6
1908	Boss Schmidt	0.9
1909	**Donie Bush**	**2.2**
1910	Donie Bush	2.0
1911	Donie Bush	0.9
	Oscar Stanage	0.9
1912	Donie Bush	1.8
1913	Donie Bush	0.9
1914	**Donie Bush**	**2.4**
	George Moriarty	**2.4**
1915	Ossie Vitt	1.7
1916	**Ossie Vitt**	**2.5**
1917	Oscar Stanage	0.7
1918	Bob Jones	0.0
1919	Eddie Ainsmith	0.3
1920	Babe Pinelli	0.5
1921	Bob Jones	0.9
1922	Bob Jones	0.9
1923	Bob Jones	1.0
1924	Topper Rigney	1.0
1925	Jackie Tavener	0.7
1926	Jackie Tavener	0.5
1927	Charlie Gehringer	0.9
1928	Jackie Tavener	0.4
1929	Marty McManus	0.4
1930	Charlie Gehringer	1.1
1931	Marty McManus	0.6
1932	Billy Rogell	1.4
1933	Charlie Gehringer	2.3
	Billy Rogell	2.3
1934	Billy Rogell	2.2
1935	**Billy Rogell**	**2.7**
1936	Billy Rogell	1.5
1937	Charlie Gehringer	1.1
1938	Billy Rogell	1.3
1939	Charlie Gehringer	0.8
1940	Birdie Tebbetts	0.3
1941	Birdie Tebbetts	0.4
1942	Jimmy Bloodworth	1.1
1943	Jimmy Bloodworth	0.9
1944	Eddie Mayo	2.4
1945	Eddie Mayo	2.1
1946	George Kell	0.6
	Eddie Lake	0.6
1947	George Kell	0.7
1948	Johnny Lipon	0.7
1949	Johnny Lipon	1.1
1950	**Jerry Priddy**	**2.7**
1951	Jerry Priddy	0.5
1952	Fred Hatfield	0.5
1953	Fred Hatfield	0.1
1954	Harvey Kuenn	1.7
1955	Frank House	0.7
1956	Harvey Kuenn	0.7
1957	Al Kaline	1.4
1958	Al Kaline	2.2
1959	Frank Bolling	1.6
1960	Chico Fernandez	1.3
1961	Al Kaline	2.2

Ray Oyler

Year	Player	dWAR
1962	Rocky Colavito	0.8
1963	Bill Freehan	0.6
1964	Bill Freehan	1.7
1965	Don Wert	1.4
1966	Jerry Lumpe	1.1
1967	**Ray Oyler**	**2.7**
1968	Jim Northrup	1.4
1969	Don Wert	0.8
1970	Bill Freehan	1.2
1971	Eddie Brinkman	1.8
1972	Eddie Brinkman	1.9
1973	Bill Freehan	1.8
1974	Eddie Brinkman	1.9
1975	Aurelio Rodriguez	1.2
1976	Bruce Kimm	0.9
1977	Milt May	1.3
1978	Alan Trammell	1.7
1979	Lance Parrish	1.7
1980	Alan Trammell	1.3
1981	Alan Trammell	2.4
1982	Alan Trammell	2.1
1983	Chet Lemon	2.3
1984	Chet Lemon	2.2
	Alan Trammell	2.2
1985	Alan Trammell	1.8
1986	Alan Trammell	1.8
1987	Alan Trammell	0.9
1988	Alan Trammell	1.5
1989	Alan Trammell	2.2
1990	Alan Trammell	2.0
1991	Milt Cuyler	1.8
1992	Travis Fryman	1.6
1993	Chad Kreuter	0.8
1994	Tony Phillips	0.5
1995	Travis Fryman	1.8
1996	Travis Fryman	0.8
1997	Travis Fryman	1.2
1998	Deivi Cruz	2.2
1999	Brad Ausmus	1.5
2000	Brad Ausmus	2.2
	Damion Easley	2.2
2001	Jose Macias	0.9
2002	Shane Halter	0.6
2003	Brandon Inge	1.4
2004	Brandon Inge	0.6
2005	Nook Logan	1.8
2006	**Brandon Inge**	**2.7**
2007	Brandon Inge	1.9
2008	Placido Polanco	1.8
2009	Adam Everett	1.5
	Curtis Granderson	1.5
	Brandon Inge	1.5
2010	Don Kelly	2.0
2011	**Austin Jackson**	**3.4**
2012	Alex Avila	1.3
2013	Austin Jackson	0.7
	Jhonny Peralta	0.7
2014	Ian Kinsler	2.9
2015	Ian Kinsler	2.6
2016	Ian Kinsler	1.7
2017	Jose Iglesias	1.1
2018	JaCoby Jones	2.5
2019	Jeimer Candelario	0.8
2020	Niko Goodrum	0.4
2021	Jake Rogers	0.5
	Zack Short	0.5

Year	Player	BRA
1901	**Kid Elberfeld**	**.166**
1902	Jimmy Barrett	.152
1903	**Sam Crawford**	**.171**
1904	Sam Crawford	.109
1905	Sam Crawford	.152
1906	Sam Crawford	.137
1907	**Ty Cobb**	**.175**
1908	Ty Cobb	.171
1909	**Ty Cobb**	**.214**
1910	**Ty Cobb**	**.248**
1911	**Ty Cobb**	**.285**
1912	Ty Cobb	.265
1913	Ty Cobb	.243
1914	Ty Cobb	.235
1915	Ty Cobb	.233
1916	Ty Cobb	.218
1917	Ty Cobb	.247
1918	Ty Cobb	.222
1919	Ty Cobb	.217
1920	Ty Cobb	.185
1921	Harry Heilmann	.263
1922	Harry Heilmann	.253
1923	**Harry Heilmann**	**.293**
1924	Harry Heilmann	.219
1925	Ty Cobb	.277
1926	Harry Heilmann	.228
1927	Harry Heilmann	.284
1928	Harry Heilmann	.192
1929	Harry Heilmann	.226
1930	Charlie Gehringer	.212
1931	Dale Alexander	.179
	John Stone	.179
1932	Charlie Gehringer	.183
1933	Charlie Gehringer	.183
1934	Hank Greenberg	.239
1935	Hank Greenberg	.257
1936	Charlie Gehringer	.239
1937	Hank Greenberg	.291
1938	**Hank Greenberg**	**.298**
1939	Hank Greenberg	.256
1940	Hank Greenberg	.289
1941	Barney McCosky	.169
1942	Ned Harris	.150
1943	Rudy York	.191
1944	Dick Wakefield	.267
1945	Roy Cullenbine	.178
1946	Roy Cullenbine	.255
1947	Dick Wakefield	.170
1948	Pat Mullin	.194
1949	George Kell	.193
1950	Hoot Evers	.221
1951	Vic Wertz	.195
1952	Vic Wertz	.176
1953	Ray Boone	.217
1954	Ray Boone	.175
1955	Al Kaline	.230
1956	Charlie Maxwell	.220
1957	Charlie Maxwell	.180
1958	Al Kaline	.182
1959	Al Kaline	.217
1960	Norm Cash	.202
1961	**Norm Cash**	**.321**
1962	Al Kaline	.222
1963	Al Kaline	.192
1964	Al Kaline	.179
1965	Norm Cash	.190
1966	Al Kaline	.209
1967	Al Kaline	.222
1968	Willie Horton	.191
1969	Jim Northrup	.182
1970	Willie Horton	.177
1971	Norm Cash	.197
1972	Al Kaline	.177
1973	Willie Horton	.181
1974	Bill Freehan	.171
1975	Willie Horton	.134
1976	Rusty Staub	.167
1977	Ron LeFlore	.172
1978	Jason Thompson	.171
1979	Steve Kemp	.215
1980	Champ Summers	.198
1981	Kirk Gibson	.176
1982	Lance Parrish	.179
1983	Alan Trammell	.177
1984	Kirk Gibson	.187
1985	Kirk Gibson	.188
1986	Kirk Gibson	.182
1987	Alan Trammell	.221
1988	Alan Trammell	.173
1989	Lou Whitaker	.166
1990	Cecil Fielder	.223
1991	Lou Whitaker	.191
1992	Rob Deer	.184
1993	Alan Trammell	.191
1994	Junior Felix	.195
	Kirk Gibson	.195
1995	Cecil Fielder	.163
1996	Bobby Higginson	.232
1997	Bobby Higginson	.197
1998	Tony Clark	.187
1999	Luis Polonia	.187
2000	Bobby Higginson	.202
2001	Tony Clark	.180
2002	Randall Simon	.147
2003	Dmitri Young	.200
2004	Carlos Guillen	.205
2005	Chris Shelton	.184
2006	Carlos Guillen	.208
2007	Magglio Ordonez	.258
2008	Miguel Cabrera	.188
2009	Miguel Cabrera	.216
2010	Miguel Cabrera	.261
2011	Miguel Cabrera	.262
2012	Miguel Cabrera	.238
2013	Miguel Cabrera	.281
2014	Victor Martinez	.231
2015	Miguel Cabrera	.235
2016	Miguel Cabrera	.221
2017	Justin Upton	.196
2018	Nicholas Castellanos	.177
2019	Nicholas Castellanos	.151
2020	Willi Castro	.210
2021	Jeimer Candelario	.156

Junior Felix

YEARLY TIGER HITTING LEADERS – BATTING AVERAGE

1901	**Kid Elberfeld**	**.308**
1902	Jimmy Barrett	.303
1903	**Sam Crawford**	**.335**
1904	Jimmy Barrett	.268
1905	Sam Crawford	.297
1906	Ty Cobb	.320
1907	**Ty Cobb**	**.350**
1908	Ty Cobb	.324
1909	**Ty Cobb**	**.377**
1910	**Ty Cobb**	**.385**
1911	**Ty Cobb**	**.420**
1912	Ty Cobb	.410
1913	Ty Cobb	.390
1914	Ty Cobb	.368
1915	Ty Cobb	.369
1916	Ty Cobb	.371
1917	Ty Cobb	.383
1918	Ty Cobb	.382
1919	Ty Cobb	.384
1920	Ty Cobb	.334
1921	Harry Heilmann	.394
1922	Ty Cobb	.401
1923	Harry Heilmann	.403
1924	Johnny Bassler	.346
	Harry Heilmann	.346
1925	Harry Heilmann	.393
1926	Heinie Manush	.378
1927	Harry Heilmann	.398
1928	Harry Heilmann	.328
1929	Bob Fothergill	.354
1930	Charlie Gehringer	.330
1931	John Stone	.327
1932	Gee Walker	.323
1933	Charlie Gehringer	.325
1934	Charlie Gehringer	.356
1935	Charlie Gehringer	.330
1936	Charlie Gehringer	.354
1937	Charlie Gehringer	.371
1938	Hank Greenberg	.315
1939	Charlie Gehringer	.325
1940	Hank Greenberg	.340
	Barney McCosky	.340
1941	Barney McCosky	.324
1942	Barney McCosky	.293
1943	Dick Wakefield	.316
1944	Dick Wakefield	.355
1945	Eddie Mayo	.285
1946	Roy Cullenbine	.335
1947	George Kell	.320
1948	Hoot Evers	.314
1949	George Kell	.343
1950	George Kell	.340
1951	George Kell	.319
1952	Johnny Groth	.284
1953	Ray Boone	.312
1954	Harvey Kuenn	.306
1955	Al Kaline	.340
1956	Harvey Kuenn	.332
1957	Al Kaline	.295
1958	Harvey Kuenn	.319
1959	Harvey Kuenn	.353

Johnny Groth

1960	Norm Cash	.286
1961	Norm Cash	.361
1962	Al Kaline	.304
1963	Al Kaline	.312
1964	Bill Freehan	.300
1965	Al Kaline	.281
1966	Al Kaline	.288
1967	Al Kaline	.308
1968	Al Kaline	.287
1969	Jim Northrup	.295
1970	Willie Horton	.305
1971	Al Kaline	.294
1972	Al Kaline	.313
1973	Willie Horton	.316
1974	Bill Freehan	.297
1975	Ben Oglivie	.286
1976	Ron LeFlore	.316
1977	Ron LeFlore	.325
1978	Ron LeFlore	.297
1979	Steve Kemp	.318
1980	Alan Trammell	.300
1981	Kirk Gibson	.328
1982	Larry Herndon	.292
1983	Lou Whitaker	.320
1984	Alan Trammell	.314
1985	Kirk Gibson	.287
1986	Alan Trammell	.277
1987	Alan Trammell	.343
1988	Alan Trammell	.311
1989	Dave Bergman	.268
1990	Alan Trammell	.304
1991	Tony Phillips	.284
1992	Scott Livingstone	.282
1993	Alan Trammell	.329
1994	Junior Felix	.306
1995	Travis Fryman	.275
1996	Bobby Higginson	.320
1997	Bobby Higginson	.299
1998	Tony Clark	.291
1999	Luis Polonia	.324
2000	Deivi Cruz	.302
2001	Roger Cedeno	.293
2002	Randall Simon	.301
2003	Dmitri Young	.297
2004	Ivan Rodriguez	.334
2005	Placido Polanco	.338
2006	Carlos Guillen	.320
2007	Magglio Ordonez	.363
2008	Magglio Ordonez	.317
2009	Miguel Cabrera	.324
2010	Miguel Cabrera	.328
2011	Miguel Cabrera	.344
2012	Miguel Cabrera	.330
2013	Miguel Cabrera	.348
2014	Victor Martinez	.335
2015	Miguel Cabrera	.338
2016	Miguel Cabrera	.316
2017	Justin Upton	.279
2018	Nicholas Castellanos	.298
2019	Harold Castro	.291
2020	Willi Castro	.349
2021	Harold Castro	.283

Year	Player	Avg
1901	**Jimmy Barrett**	**.327**
1902	**Jimmy Barrett**	**.338**
1903	**Sam Crawford**	**.360**
1904	Jimmy Barrett	.313
1905	Sam Crawford	.307
1906	Ty Cobb	.359
1907	**Ty Cobb**	**.380**
1908	Ty Cobb	.344
1909	**Ty Cobb**	**.399**
1910	**Ty Cobb**	**.413**
1911	**Ty Cobb**	**.444**
1912	Ty Cobb	.426
1913	Ty Cobb	.415
1914	Ty Cobb	.389
1915	Ty Cobb	.397
1916	Ty Cobb	.394
1917	Ty Cobb	.400
1918	Ty Cobb	.398
1919	Ty Cobb	.401
1920	Ty Cobb	.354
1921	Harry Heilmann	.399
1922	Ty Cobb	.416
1923	Harry Heilmann	.414
1924	Harry Heilmann	.360
1925	Harry Heilmann	.398
1926	Bob Fothergill	.385
1927	Harry Heilmann	.394
1928	Harry Heilmann	.339
1929	Bob Fothergill	.354
1930	John Stone	.346
1931	Dale Alexander	.344
	John Stone	.344
1932	Gee Walker	.339
1933	Hank Greenberg	.343
1934	Hank Greenberg	.369
1935	Hank Greenberg	.339
1936	Gee Walker	.358
1937	Charlie Gehringer	.371
1938	Dixie Walker	.322
1939	Hank Greenberg	.331
	Barney McCosky	.331
1940	Barney McCosky	.360
1941	Barney McCosky	.343
1942	Barney McCosky	.304
1943	Dick Wakefield	.341
1944	Dick Wakefield	.366
1945	Jimmy Outlaw	.293
1946	Roy Cullenbine	.347
1947	Vic Wertz	.345
1948	Hoot Evers	.320
1949	George Kell	.348
1950	George Kell	.341
1951	George Kell	.327
1952	Johnny Groth	.301
1953	Johnny Pesky	.324
1954	Walt Dropo	.308
1955	Al Kaline	.339
1956	Harvey Kuenn	.333
	Charlie Maxwell	.333
1957	Reno Bertoia	.309
1958	Harvey Kuenn	.327
1959	Harvey Kuenn	.364
1960	Norm Cash	.295
1961	Norm Cash	.370
1962	Billy Bruton	.291
1963	Al Kaline	.302
1964	Billy Bruton	.324
1965	Don Demeter	.296
1966	Dick McAuliffe	.288
1967	Jim Northrup	.308
1968	Al Kaline	.299
1969	Jim Northrup	.308
1970	Willie Horton	.306
1971	Al Kaline	.311
	Mickey Stanley	.311
1972	Al Kaline	.321
1973	Willie Horton	.334
1974	Bill Freehan	.295
1975	Ron LeFlore	.331
1976	Ron LeFlore	.391
1977	Ron LeFlore	.378
1978	Ron LeFlore	.335
1979	Ron LeFlore	.343
1980	Alan Trammell	.321
1981	Kirk Gibson	.393
1982	Larry Herndon	.310
1983	Alan Trammell	.341
	Lou Whitaker	.341
1984	Alan Trammell	.333
1985	Kirk Gibson	.325
1986	Dave Collins	.302
1987	Alan Trammell	.335
1988	Alan Trammell	.316
1989	Gary Pettis	.335
1990	Mike Heath	.315
	Alan Trammell	.315
1991	Travis Fryman	.313
1992	Travis Fryman	.309
1993	Tony Phillips	.369
1994	Junior Felix	.366
1995	Travis Fryman	.307
1996	Kimera Bartee	.388
1997	Melvin Nieves	.337
1998	Tony Clark	.317
1999	Luis Polonia	.334
2000	Juan Encarnacion	.322
2001	Tony Clark	.345
2002	Wendall MaGee	.312
2003	Dmitri Young	.339
2004	Alex Sanchez	.374
2005	Carlos Guillen	.358
2006	Carlos Guillen	.351
2007	Magglio Ordonez	.381
2008	Magglio Ordonez	.334
2009	Miguel Cabrera	.348
2010	Austin Jackson	.396
2011	Alex Avila	.366
2012	Austin Jackson	.371
2013	Jhonny Peralta	.374
2014	J.D. Martinez	.389
2015	Miguel Cabrera	.384
2016	Cameron Maybin	.383
2017	Justin Upton	.351
2018	Nicholas Castellanos	.361
2019	Harold Castro	.367
2020	**Willi Castro**	**.448**
2021	Harold Castro	.351

Willi Castro

Year	Player	Average
1901	**Kid Elberfeld**	**.306**
1902	Jimmy Barrett	.277
1903	**Billy Lush**	**.314**
1904	Sam Crawford	.221
1905	Sam Crawford	.257
1906	Matty McIntyre	.256
1907	Ty Cobb	.238
1908	Ty Cobb	.277
1909	**Ty Cobb**	**.356**
1910	**Ty Cobb**	**.422**
1911	Ty Cobb	.416
1912	Donie Bush	.333
1913	Ty Cobb	.400
1914	Ty Cobb	.362
1915	**Ty Cobb**	**.430**
1916	Ty Cobb	.347
1917	Ty Cobb	.384
1918	Ty Cobb	.311
1919	Ira Flagstead	.293
1920	Ty Cobb	.264
1921	Ty Cobb	.331
1922	Harry Heilmann	.378
1923	Harry Heilmann	.374
1924	Harry Heilmann	.339
1925	Ty Cobb	.386
1926	Lu Blue	.352
1927	Harry Heilmann	.372
1928	Harry Heilmann	.289
1929	Harry Heilmann	.329
1930	Charlie Gehringer	.325
1931	Roy Johnson	.295
1932	Charlie Gehringer	.311
1933	Hank Greenberg	.278
1934	Hank Greenberg	.374
1935	**Hank Greenberg**	**.443**
1936	Goose Goslin	.378
1937	**Hank Greenberg**	**.512**
1938	**Hank Greenberg**	**.586**
1939	Hank Greenberg	.502
1940	Hank Greenberg	.497
1941	Rudy York	.356
1942	Rudy York	.295
1943	Rudy York	.403
1944	Dick Wakefield	.420
1945	Roy Cullenbine	.373
1946	Hank Greenberg	.488
1947	Roy Cullenbine	.496
1948	Dick Wakefield	.410
1949	Aaron Robinson	.369
1950	Vic Wertz	.386
1951	Vic Wertz	.375
1952	Vic Wertz	.418
1953	Ray Boone	.371
1954	Ray Boone	.306
1955	Earl Torgeson	.363
1956	Earl Torgeson	.412
1957	Charlie Maxwell	.362
1958	Charlie Maxwell	.327
1959	Eddie Yost	.430
1960	Norm Cash	.405

Ira Flagstead

Year	Player	Average
1961	Norm Cash	.544
1962	Norm Cash	.481
1963	Norm Cash	.379
1964	Norm Cash	.344
1965	Norm Cash	.411
1966	Al Kaline	.415
1967	Al Kaline	.428
1968	Willie Horton	.348
1969	Norm Cash	.317
1970	Norm Cash	.373
1971	Norm Cash	.381
1972	Norm Cash	.295
1973	Norm Cash	.342
1974	Bill Freehan	.281
1975	Bill Freehan	.232
1976	Jason Thompson	.318
1977	Jason Thompson	.340
1978	Jason Thompson	.311
1979	Steve Kemp	.361
1980	Champ Summers	.360
1981	Steve Kemp	.347
1982	Lance Parrish	.325
1983	Kirk Gibson	.347
1984	Kirk Gibson	.390
1985	Darrell Evans	.432
1986	Kirk Gibson	.442
1987	Darrell Evans	.447
1988	Darrell Evans	.357
1989	Lou Whitaker	.391
1990	Cecil Fielder	.469
1991	Mickey Tettleton	.429
1992	Mickey Tettleton	.451
1993	Mickey Tettleton	.448
1994	Mickey Tettleton	.499
1995	Cecil Fielder	.379
1996	Bobby Higginson	.411
1997	Tony Clark	.381
1998	Tony Clark	.336
1999	Dean Palmer	.357
2000	Bobby Higginson	.382
2001	Tony Clark	.336
2002	Robert Fick	.245
2003	Dmitri Young	.345
2004	Carlos Pena	.389
2005	Chris Shelton	.299
2006	Marcus Thames	.399
2007	Gary Sheffield	.401
2008	Curtis Granderson	.356
2009	Ryan Raburn	.345
2010	Miguel Cabrera	.456
2011	Miguel Cabrera	.432
2012	Miguel Cabrera	.387
2013	Miguel Cabrera	.456
2014	Victor Martinez	.357
2015	Miguel Cabrera	.375
2016	Miguel Cabrera	.373
2017	Justin Upton	.399
2018	Niko Goodrum	.300
2019	Niko Goodrum	.303
2020	JaCoby Jones	.320
2021	Robbie Grossman	.379

Year	Player	Pct
1901	**Sport McAllister**	**88%**
1902	**Kid Gleason**	**89%**
1903	Charlie Carr	88%
1904	Bobby Lowe	86%
1905	Sam Crawford	85%
1906	**Sam Crawford**	**89%**
1907	Sam Crawford	87%
1908	Boss Schmidt	87%
1909	Sam Crawford	83%
1910	Sam Crawford	84%
1911	Ty Cobb	83%
1912	Ty Cobb	85%
	Sam Crawford	85%
1913	Sam Crawford	85%
1914	Bobby Veach	83%
1915	Sam Crawford	84%
1916	Sam Crawford	85%
1917	George Burns	84%
1918	Bob Jones	85%
	Bobby Veach	85%
1919	Ty Cobb	87%
1920	Bobby Veach	86%
1921	Bob Jones	86%
1922	George Cutshaw	87%
1923	Del Pratt	84%
1924	Bob Jones	86%
	Del Pratt	86%
1925	Heinie Manush	81%
1926	Bob Fothergill	83%
1927	Heinie Manush	85%
1928	Bob Fothergill	85%
1929	**Bob Fothergill**	**89%**
1930	Liz Funk	83%
	Charlie Gehringer	83%
1931	**Mark Koenig**	**92%**
1932	Gee Walker	87%
1933	Pete Fox	87%
1934	Goose Goslin	82%
	Marv Owen	82%
1935	Gee Walker	87%
1936	Gee Walker	86%
1937	Pete Fox	84%
	Marv Owen	84%
1938	Chet Morgan	88%
1939	Pete Fox	84%
	Birdie Tebbetts	84%
1940	Birdie Tebbetts	87%
1941	Rip Radcliff	90%
1942	Doc Cramer	90%
1943	Doc Cramer	91%
1944	Doc Cramer	89%

Year	Player	Pct
1945	Doc Cramer	86%
	Bob Maier	86%
1946	George Kell	87%
1947	George Kell	86%
1948	George Kell	85%
1949	Don Kolloway	85%
1950	Don Kolloway	86%
1951	George Kell	86%
1952	Johnny Groth	83%
1953	Harvey Kuenn	88%
1954	**Harvey Kuenn**	**92%**
1955	Harvey Kuenn	89%
1956	Harvey Kuenn	84%
1957	Harvey Kuenn	87%
1958	Harvey Kuenn	84%
1959	Harvey Kuenn	84%
1960	Frank Bolling	82%

Boss Schmidt

Year	Player	Pct
1961	Chico Fernandez	82%
1962	Dick Brown	77%
1963	Bubba Phillips	85%
1964	Jerry Lumpe	82%
1965	Jerry Lumpe	81%
1966	Jerry Lumpe	82%
1967	Don Wert	79%
1968	Mickey Stanley	81%
1969	Mickey Stanley	80%
1970	Cesar Gutierrez	84%
1971	Mickey Stanley	82%
1972	Eddie Brinkman	82%
1973	Bill Freehan	80%
	Mickey Stanley	80%
1974	Gary Sutherland	89%
1975	Dan Meyer	87%
1976	Dan Meyer	86%
1977	Tito Fuentes	82%
	Milt May	82%
	Tom Veryzer	82%
1978	Tim Corcoran	83%
	Aurelio Rodriguez	83%
1979	Aurelio Rodriguez	83%
1980	Al Cowens	80%
1981	Lynn Jones	83%
1982	Enos Cabell	86%
1983	Enos Cabell	84%
1984	Barbaro Garbey	83%
1985	Alan Trammell	78%
1986	Dave Collins	78%
1987	Alan Trammell	79%
1988	Ray Knight	82%
1989	Alan Trammell	80%
1990	Larry Sheets	80%
1991	Alan Trammell	78%
1992	Scott Livingstone	83%
1993	Alan Trammell	79%
1994	Alan Trammell	80%
1995	John Flaherty	77%
1996	Travis Fryman	71%
	Mark Lewis	71%
1997	Deivi Cruz	82%
1998	Deivi Cruz	83%
1999	Luis Polonia	83%
2000	Deivi Cruz	87%
2001	Deivi Cruz	83%
2002	Randall Simon	87%
2003	Alex Sanchez	83%
2004	Alex Sanchez	80%
2005	Placido Polanco	86%
2006	Placido Polanco	87%
2007	Placido Polanco	86%
2008	Placido Polanco	85%
2009	Placido Polanco	84%
2010	Don Kelly	75%
	Magglio Ordonez	75%
2011	Victor Martinez	81%
2012	Delmon Young	74%
2013	Omar Infante	84%
2014	Ian Kinsler	82%
2015	Jose Iglesias	82%
2016	Jose Iglesias	81%
2017	Jose Iglesias	80%
2018	Jose Iglesias	82%
	Victor Martinez	82%
2019	Harold Castro	72%
2020	Victor Reyes	49%
2021	Harold Castro	72%

Year	Player	Times on Base
1901	**Jimmy Barrett**	**240**
1902	Jimmy Barrett	234
1903	**Jimmy Barrett**	**243**
1904	**Jimmy Barrett**	**249**
1905	Sam Crawford	224
1906	Sam Crawford	205
1907	Ty Cobb	241
1908	**Matty McIntyre**	**258**
1909	**Ty Cobb**	**270**
1910	Ty Cobb	264
1911	**Ty Cobb**	**300**
1912	Ty Cobb	275
1913	Sam Crawford	245
1914	Donie Bush	265
1915	**Ty Cobb**	**336**
1916	Ty Cobb	281
1917	Ty Cobb	290
1918	Ty Cobb	204
1919	Ty Cobb	230
1920	Ralph Young	260
1921	Harry Heilmann	292
1922	Ty Cobb	270
1923	Harry Heilmann	290
1924	Ty Cobb	297
1925	Harry Heilmann	293
1926	Harry Heilmann	255
1927	Harry Heilmann	275
1928	Charlie Gehringer	268
1929	Charlie Gehringer	285
1930	Charlie Gehringer	277
1931	John Stone	249
1932	Charlie Gehringer	255
1933	Charlie Gehringer	275
1934	Charlie Gehringer	316
1935	Hank Greenberg	290
1936	Charlie Gehringer	314
1937	Hank Greenberg	305
1938	Hank Greenberg	297
1939	Barney McCosky	262
1940	Hank Greenberg	289
1941	Rudy York	246
1942	Barney McCosky	244
1943	Dick Wakefield	262
1944	Pinky Higgins	246
1945	Roy Cullenbine	250
1946	Eddie Lake	256
1947	George Kell	252
1948	Hoot Evers	224
1949	Vic Wertz	265
1950	George Kell	285
1951	George Kell	256
1952	Johnny Groth	200
1953	Harvey Kuenn	260
1954	Ray Boone	233
1955	Al Kaline	287
1956	Al Kaline	265
1957	Harvey Kuenn	220
1958	Harvey Kuenn	230
1959	Eddie Yost	292
1960	Eddie Yost	262
1961	Norm Cash	326

Pinky Higgins

Year	Player	Times on Base
1962	Rocky Colavito	262
1963	Rocky Colavito	247
1964	Al Kaline	232
1965	Don Wert	235
1966	Norm Cash	238
1967	Dick McAuliffe	245
1968	Bill Freehan	231
1969	Jim Northrup	215
1970	Dick McAuliffe	228
1971	Al Kaline	208
1972	Aurelio Rodriguez	172
1973	Mickey Stanley	195
1974	Al Kaline	212
1975	Willie Horton	213
1976	Rusty Staub	266
1977	Ron LeFlore	253
1978	Ron LeFlore	267
1979	Ron LeFlore	232
1980	Alan Trammell	240
1981	Steve Kemp	174
1982	Larry Herndon	218
1983	Lou Whitaker	273
1984	Alan Trammell	237
1985	Lou Whitaker	252
1986	Alan Trammell	223
1987	Alan Trammell	268
1988	Chet Lemon	201
1989	Lou Whitaker	220
1990	Cecil Fielder	254
1991	Cecil Fielder	247
1992	Tony Phillips	282
1993	Tony Phillips	313
1994	Tony Phillips	220
1995	Chad Curtis	234
1996	Travis Fryman	226
1997	Tony Clark	256
1998	Bobby Higginson	243
1999	Tony Clark	220
2000	Bobby Higginson	255
2001	Bobby Higginson	232
2002	Robert Fick	203
2003	Dmitri Young	236
2004	Carlos Guillen	220
	Ivan Rodriguez	220
2005	Brandon Inge	227
2006	Carlos Guillen	249
2007	Magglio Ordonez	294
2008	Miguel Cabrera	239
2009	Miguel Cabrera	271
2010	Miguel Cabrera	272
2011	Miguel Cabrera	308
2012	Prince Fielder	284
2013	Miguel Cabrera	288
2014	Victor Martinez	262
2015	Ian Kinsler	231
2016	Miguel Cabrera	267
2017	Nicholas Castellanos	213
2018	Nicholas Castellanos	240
2019	Miguel Cabrera	190
2020	Miguel Cabrera	76
	Jeimer Candelario	76
2021	Robbie Grossman	239

Year	Player	AB/HR
1901	**Sport McAllister**	**102.0**
1902	Jimmy Barrett	127.3
1903	Sam Crawford	137.5
1904	Sam Crawford	281.0
1905	**Sam Crawford**	**95.8**
1906	Charley O'Leary	221.5
1907	Ty Cobb	121.0
1908	**Sam Crawford**	**84.4**
1909	**Ty Cobb**	**63.7**
1910	**Ty Cobb**	**63.6**
1911	Ty Cobb	73.9
1912	Ty Cobb	79.0
1913	Sam Crawford	67.7
1914	Sam Crawford	72.8
1915	George Burns	78.4
1916	Ty Cobb	108.4
1917	Bobby Veach	71.4
1918	**Harry Heilmann**	**57.2**
1919	Ira Flagstead	57.4
1920	**Bobby Veach**	**55.6**
1921	**Harry Heilmann**	**31.7**
1922	**Harry Heilmann**	**21.7**
1923	Harry Heilmann	29.1
1924	Heinie Manush	46.9
1925	Ty Cobb	34.6
1926	Heinie Manush	35.6
1927	Harry Heilmann	36.1
1928	Pinky Hargrave	32.0
1929	Dale Alexander	25.0
1930	Dale Alexander	30.1
1931	John Stone	58.4
1932	Charlie Gehringer	32.5
1933	Hank Greenberg	37.4
1934	Hank Greenberg	22.8
1935	**Hank Greenberg**	**17.2**
1936	Goose Goslin	23.8
1937	**Rudy York**	**10.7**
1938	**Hank Greenberg**	**9.6**
1939	Hank Greenberg	15.2
1940	Hank Greenberg	14.0
1941	Rudy York	21.9
1942	Rudy York	27.5
1943	Rudy York	16.8
1944	Dick Wakefield	23.0
1945	Roy Cullenbine	29.1
1946	Hank Greenberg	11.9
1947	Roy Cullenbine	19.3
1948	Pat Mullin	21.6
1949	Aaron Robinson	25.5
1950	Vic Wertz	20.7
1951	Vic Wertz	18.6
1952	Vic Wertz	16.8
1953	Ray Boone	17.5
1954	Ray Boone	27.2
1955	Al Kaline	21.8
1956	Charlie Maxwell	17.9
1957	Charlie Maxwell	20.5
1958	Gail Harris	22.6
1959	Charlie Maxwell	16.7
1960	Rocky Colavito	15.9
1961	Norm Cash	13.0
	Rocky Colavito	13.0

Eric Munson

Year	Player	AB/HR
1962	Norm Cash	13.0
1963	Norm Cash	19.0
1964	Don Demeter	20.0
1965	Norm Cash	15.6
1966	Al Kaline	16.5
1967	Al Kaline	18.3
1968	Willie Horton	14.2
1969	Willie Horton	18.1
1970	Jim Northrup	21.0
1971	Norm Cash	14.1
1972	Norm Cash	20.0
1973	Norm Cash	19.1
1974	Bill Freehan	24.7
1975	Willie Horton	24.6
1976	Ben Oglivie	20.3
1977	Jason Thompson	18.9
1978	Jason Thompson	22.7
1979	Steve Kemp	18.8
1980	Champ Summers	20.4
1981	John Wockenfuss	19.1
1982	Lance Parish	15.2
1983	Chet Lemon	20.5
1984	Lance Parrish	17.5
1985	Darrell Evans	12.6
1986	Lance Parrish	14.9
1987	Matt Nokes	14.4
1988	Darrell Evans	19.9
1989	Lou Whitaker	18.2
1990	Cecil Fielder	11.2
1991	Cecil Fielder	14.2
1992	Rob Deer	12.3
1993	Mickey Tettleton	16.3
1994	Kirk Gibson	14.3
1995	Cecil Fielder	15.9
1996	Tony Clark	13.9
1997	Bob Hamelin	17.7
1998	Tony Clark	17.7
1999	Dean Palmer	14.7
2000	Dean Palmer	18.1
2001	Robert Fick	21.1
2002	Randall Simon	25.4
2003	Eric Munson	17.4
2004	Eric Munson	16.9
2005	Chris Shelton	21.6
2006	Marcus Thames	13.4
2007	Gary Sheffield	19.8
2008	Marcus Thames	12.6
2009	Ryan Raburn	16.3
2010	Miguel Cabrera	14.4
2011	Miguel Cabrera	19.1
2012	Miguel Cabrera	14.1
2013	Miguel Cabrera	12.6
2014	Victor Martinez	17.5
2015	J.D. Martinez	15.7
2016	Miguel Cabrera	15.7
2017	Justin Upton	16.4
2018	Nicholas Castellanos	27.0
2019	John Hicks	24.5
2020	JaCoby Jones	19.4
2021	Eric Haase	16.0

Year	Player	AB/RBI
1901	**Sport McAllister**	**5.4**
1902	Kid Elberfeld	7.6
1903	Sam Crawford	6.2
1904	Sam Crawford	7.7
1905	Sam Crawford	7.7
1906	Sam Crawford	7.8
1907	**Ty Cobb**	**5.1**
1908	Ty Cobb	5.4
1909	Ty Cobb	5.4
1910	**Sam Crawford**	**4.9**
1911	**Ty Cobb**	**4.7**
1912	Sam Crawford	5.3
1913	Ty Cobb	6.4
1914	Sam Crawford	5.6
1915	Bobby Veach	5.1
1916	Harry Heilmann	6.2
	Bobby Veach	6.2
1917	Bobby Veach	5.5
1918	Bobby Veach	6.4
1919	Bobby Veach	5.3
1920	Bobby Veach	5.4
1921	**Harry Heilmann**	**4.3**
1922	Harry Heilmann	4.9
	Bobby Veach	4.9
1923	Harry Heilmann	4.6
1924	Harry Heilmann	5.0
1925	**Ty Cobb**	**4.1**
1926	Harry Heilmann	4.9
1927	Harry Heilmann	4.2
1928	Pinky Hargrave	5.1
1929	**Harry Heilmann**	**3.8**
1930	Dale Alexander	4.5
1931	Dale Alexander	5.9
1932	John Stone	5.4
1933	Hank Greenberg	5.3
1934	Hank Greenberg	4.3
1935	**Hank Greenberg**	**3.7**
1936	Goose Goslin	4.6
1937	**Hank Greenberg**	**3.2**
1938	Rudy York	3.6
1939	Hank Greenberg	4.4
1940	Hank Greenberg	3.8
1941	Rudy York	5.3
1942	Pinky Higgins	6.3
1943	Rudy York	4.8
1944	Dick Wakefield	5.2
1945	Roy Cullenbine	5.6
1946	Hank Greenberg	4.1
1947	Roy Cullenbine	5.9
1948	Hoot Evers	5.2
1949	Vic Wertz	4.6
1950	Vic Wertz	4.5
1951	Vic Wertz	5.3
1952	Vic Wertz	5.6
1953	Ray Boone	4.1
1954	Ray Boone	6.4
1955	Ray Boone	4.3
1956	Al Kaline	4.8
1957	Charlie Maxwell	6.0
1958	Gail Harris	5.4
1959	Al Kaline	5.4
1960	Norm Cash	5.6

Victor Martinez

Year	Player	AB/RBI
1961	Norm Cash	4.1
1962	Al Kaline	4.2
1963	Al Kaline	5.5
1964	Don Demeter	5.5
1965	Willie Horton	4.9
1966	Willie Horton	5.3
1967	Al Kaline	5.9
1968	Willie Horton	6.0
1969	Willie Horton	5.6
1970	Willie Horton	5.4
1971	Norm Cash	5.0
1972	Bill Freehan	6.7
1973	Dick McAuliffe	7.3
1974	Bill Freehan	7.4
1975	Willie Horton	6.7
1976	Rusty Staub	6.1
1977	Jason Thompson	5.6
1978	Rusty Staub	5.3
1979	Steve Kemp	4.7
1980	Richie Hebner	4.2
1981	John Wockenfuss	6.9
1982	Lance Parrish	5.6
1983	Lance Parrish	5.3
1984	Kirk Gibson	5.8
1985	Darrell Evans	5.4
1986	Kirk Gibson	5.1
1987	Darrell Evans	5.0
1988	Darrell Evans	6.8
	Alan Trammell	6.8
1989	Lou Whitaker	6.0
1990	Cecil Fielder	4.3
1991	Cecil Fielder	4.7
1992	Cecil Fielder	4.8
1993	Mickey Tettleton	4.7
1994	Kirk Gibson	4.6
1995	Cecil Fielder	6.0
1996	Cecil Fielder	4.9
1997	Tony Clark	5.0
1998	Tony Clark	5.8
1999	Tony Clark	5.4
2000	Dean Palmer	5.1
2001	Tony Clark	5.7
2002	Randall Simon	5.9
2003	Craig Monroe	6.1
2004	Carlos Guillen	5.4
2005	Craig Monroe	6.4
2006	Magglio Ordonez	5.7
2007	Magglio Ordonez	4.3
2008	Miguel Cabrera	4.9
2009	Ryan Raburn	5.8
2010	Miguel Cabrera	4.3
2011	Victor Martinez	5.2
2012	Miguel Cabrera	4.5
2013	Miguel Cabrera	4.1
2014	Victor Martinez	5.4
2015	Miguel Cabrera	5.6
2016	Miguel Cabrera	5.5
2017	Justin Upton	4.9
2018	Nicholas Castellano	7.0
2019	Brandon Dixon	7.5
2020	Willi Castro	5.4
2021	Eric Haase	5.8

Year	Player	AB/SO
1901	**Sport McAllister**	**43.7**
1902	**Kid Elberfeld**	**48.8**
1903	Joe Yeager	16.1
1904	Rabbit Robinson	16.0
1905	Sam Crawford	18.5
1906	Sam Crawford	28.2
1907	Sam Crawford	20.1
1908	Sam Crawford	21.1
1909	Sam Crawford	18.4
1910	Sam Crawford	17.3
1911	Sam Crawford	15.9
1912	Ty Cobb	18.4
1913	Sam Crawford	21.8
1914	Sam Crawford	18.8
1915	Ossie Vitt	25.5
1916	Sam Crawford	32.2
1917	Ossie Vitt	34.1
1918	Ossie Vitt	44.5
1919	Ty Cobb	22.6
1920	Bobby Veach	27.8
1921	Ty Cobb	26.7
1922	George Cutshaw	38.4
1923	Ty Cobb	39.7
1924	Del Pratt	42.9
1925	**Johnny Bassler**	**57.3**
1926	Harry Heilmann	26.4
1927	Harry Heilmann	31.6
1928	Charlie Gehringer	27.4
1929	Charlie Gehringer	33.4
1930	Charlie Gehringer	35.9
1931	Mark Koenig	30.3
1932	Earl Webb	18.8
1933	Charlie Gehringer	23.3
1934	Charlie Gehringer	24.0
1935	Charlie Gehringer	38.1
1936	Charlie Gehringer	49.3
1937	Charlie Gehringer	22.6
1938	Charlie Gehringer	27.0
1939	Charlie Gehringer	25.4
1940	Charlie Gehringer	30.3
1941	Rip Radcliff	29.2
1942	Doc Cramer	35.0
1943	Doc Cramer	46.6
1944	Doc Cramer	27.5
1945	Doc Cramer	25.8
1946	George Kell	31.0
1947	George Kell	36.8
1948	George Kell	24.5
1949	George Kell	40.2
1950	George Kell	35.6
1951	George Kell	33.2
1952	Joe Ginsberg	14.6
1953	Harvey Kuenn	21.9
1954	Harvey Kuenn	50.5
1955	Harvey Kuenn	23.0
1956	Harvey Kuenn	17.4
1957	Harvey Kuenn	22.3
1958	Harvey Kuenn	16.5
1959	Harvey Kuenn	15.2
1960	Al Kaline	11.7
1961	Al Kaline	14.0

Mark Koenig

Year	Player	AB/SO
1962	Al Kaline	10.2
1963	Al Kaline	11.5
1964	Al Kaline	10.3
1965	Jerry Lumpe	14.8
1966	Jerry Lumpe	8.8
1967	Al Kaline	9.7
1968	Mickey Stanley	10.2
1969	Mickey Stanley	10.6
1970	Cesar Gutierrez	10.6
1971	Bill Freehan	10.8
1972	Eddie Brinkman	10.1
1973	Bill Freehan	12.7
1974	Gary Sutherland	16.7
1975	Dan Meyer	18.8
1976	Dan Meyer	13.4
1977	Rusty Staub	13.3
1978	Rusty Staub	18.3
1979	Aurelio Rodriguez	8.6
1980	Al Cowens	10.1
1981	Lynn Jones	17.4
1982	Alan Trammell	10.4
1983	Enos Cabell	9.6
1984	Barbaro Garbey	9.3
1985	Lou Whitaker	10.9
1986	Alan Trammell	10.1
1987	Alan Trammell	12.7
1988	Alan Trammell	10.1
1989	Alan Trammell	10.0
1990	Dave Bergman	12.1
1991	Lou Whitaker	10.4
1992	Scott Livingstone	9.8
	Lou Whitaker	9.8
1993	Alan Trammell	10.6
1994	Alan Trammell	8.3
1995	John Flaherty	7.5
1996	Bobby Higginson	6.7
1997	Deivi Cruz	7.9
1998	Luis Gonzalez	8.8
1999	Luis Polonia	10.4
2000	Deivi Cruz	13.6
2001	Deivi Cruz	9.0
	Jose Macias	9.0
2002	Randall Simon	16.1
2003	Alex Sanchez	8.6
2004	Alex Sanchez	6.6
2005	Placido Polanco	21.4
2006	Placido Polanco	17.1
2007	Placido Polanco	19.6
2008	Placido Polanco	13.5
2009	Placido Polanco	13.4
2010	Magglio Ordonez	8.5
2011	Victor Martinez	10.6
2012	Prince Fielder	6.9
2013	Omar Infante	10.3
2014	Victor Martinez	13.4
2015	Jose Iglesias	9.5
2016	Jose Iglesias	9.3
2017	Jose Iglesias	7.1
2018	Victor Martinez	9.5
2019	Miguel Cabrera	4.6
2020	Victor Reyes	2.1
2021	Jonathan Schoop	4.7

YEARLY TIGER HITTING LEADERS – NUMBER OF PITCHES

Year	Player	Pitches
1988	**Chet Lemon**	**2,195**
1989	**Lou Whitaker**	**2,231**
1990	**Cecil Fielder**	**2,632**
1991	**Cecil Fielder**	**2,708**
1992	**Tony Phillips**	**2,904**
1993	**Tony Phillips**	**2,948**
1994	Tony Phillips	2,337
1995	Chad Curtis	2,615
1996	Travis Fryman	2,576
1997	Brian Hunter	2,726
1998	Bobby Higginson	2,606
1999	Dean Palmer	2,451
2000	Bobby Higginson	2,712
2001	Bobby Higginson	2,487
2002	Robert Fick	2,420
2003	Dmitri Young	2,357
2004	Carlos Pena	2,277
2005	Brandon Inge	2,781
2006	Curtis Granderson	2,778
2007	Curtis Granderson	2,690
2008	Curtis Granderson	2,678
2009	Curtis Granderson	2,818
2010	Austin Jackson	2,704
2011	Austin Jackson	2,646
2012	Miguel Cabrera	2,620
2013	Prince Fielder	2,618
2014	Victor Martinez	2,586
2015	J.D. Martinez	2,605
2016	Justin Upton	2,606
2017	Nicholas Castellanos	2,605
2018	Jeimer Candelario	2,674
2019	Miguel Cabrera	2,046
2020	Miguel Cabrera	913
2021	Robbie Grossman	2,827

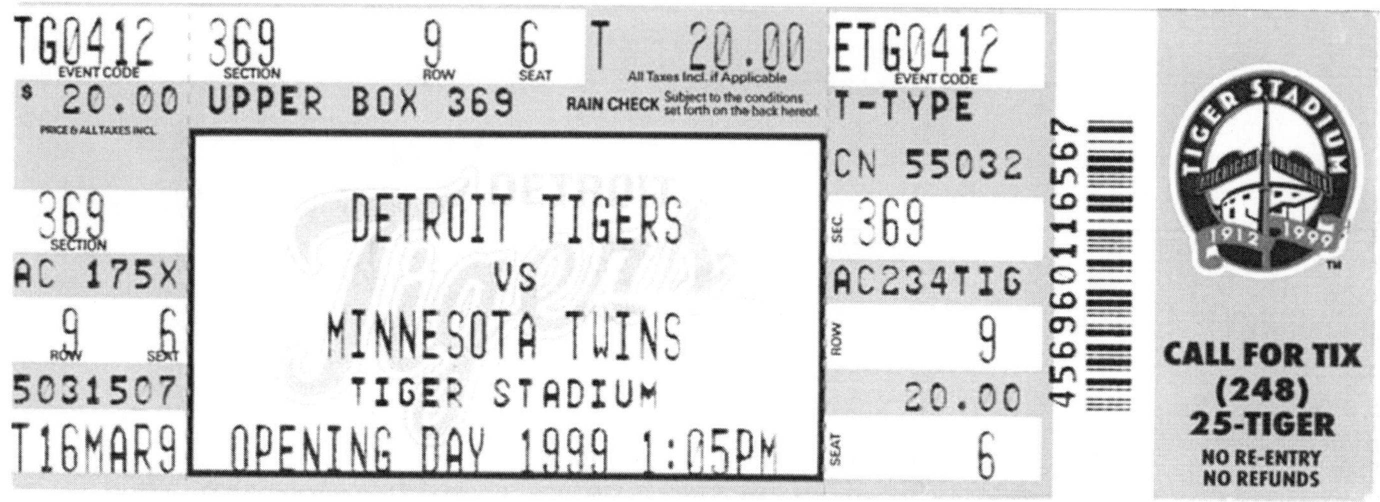

Ticket for the final opening day at Tiger Stadium on Saturday, April 10, 1999. Major league baseball had been played at the corner of Michigan and Trumbull for over a century. Some of the best MLB players including Ty Cobb, Charlie Gehringer, Hank Greenberg, George Kell, Al Kaline and Alan Trammell played there. General contractor Hunkin and Conkey broke ground in October of 1911, with plans from the Osborne Engineering Company. The park opened on April 20, 1912, with last MLB game played on September 27, 1999. Ruth hit a 575-foot home run on July 18, 1921, that is believed to be the longest. The Bambino would later hit his 700th career home run there on July 13, 1934.

YEARLY TIGER HITTING LEADERS – PITCHES PER PLATE APPEARANCES

Year	Player	Pitches per PA
1988	**Darrell Evans**	**4.03**
1989	**Gary Pettis**	**4.13**
1990	Cecil Fielder	4.11
1991	**Rob Deer**	**4.26**
1992	**Mickey Tettleton**	**4.34**
1993	Mickey Tettleton	4.33
1994	**Mickey Tettleton**	**4.46**
1995	Bobby Higginson	4.14
1996	Cecil Fielder	4.09
1997	Bobby Higginson	3.99
1998	Bobby Higginson	3.81
1999	Tony Clark	3.92
2000	Bobby Higginson	3.99
2001	Tony Clark	4.05
2002	Brandon Inge	4.21
2003	Brandon Inge	4.06
2004	Carlos Pena	4.04
2005	Chris Shelton	4.24
2006	Chris Shelton	4.17
2007	Brandon Inge	4.23
2008	Curtis Granderson	4.24
2009	Brandon Inge	4.09
2010	Johnny Damon	4.10
	Brandon Inge	4.10
2011	Alex Avila	4.03
2012	Alex Avila	4.15
2013	Alex Avila	4.08
2014	Austin Jackson	4.19
2015	Anthony Gose	3.96
2016	Justin Upton	4.16
2017	Justin Upton	4.19
2018	Jeimer Candelario	4.30
2019	Jeimer Candelario	4.20
2020	Niko Goodrum	4.33
2021	Robbie Grossman	4.21

Year	Player	Base Runs
1901	**Jimmy Barrett**	**79**
1902	Jimmy Barrett	78
1903	**Sam Crawford**	**87**
1904	Jimmy Barrett	66
1905	Sam Crawford	83
1906	Sam Crawford	72
1907	**Ty Cobb**	**95**
1908	Ty Cobb	90
1909	**Ty Cobb**	**115**
1910	**Ty Cobb**	**120**
1911	**Ty Cobb**	**148**
1912	Ty Cobb	131
1913	Ty Cobb	102
	Sam Crawford	102
1914	Sam Crawford	104
1915	Ty Cobb	138
1916	Ty Cobb	118
1917	Ty Cobb	135
1918	Ty Cobb	89
1919	Ty Cobb	101
1920	Bobby Veach	91
1921	Harry Heilmann	143
1922	Ty Cobb	126
1923	Harry Heilmann	144
1924	Harry Heilmann	123
1925	Harry Heilmann	137
1926	Harry Heilmann	112
1927	Harry Heilmann	136
1928	Harry Heilmann	103
1929	Dale Alexander	128
1930	Charlie Gehringer	120
1931	John Stone	98
1932	Charlie Gehringer	106
1933	Charlie Gehringer	109
1934	Hank Greenberg	137
1935	Hank Greenberg	144
1936	Charlie Gehringer	142
1937	**Hank Greenberg**	**155**
1938	Hank Greenberg	152
1939	Hank Greenberg	121
1940	Hank Greenberg	149
1941	Rudy York	96
1942	Barney McCosky	88
1943	Rudy York	106
1944	Pinky Higgins	87
	Rudy York	87
1945	Roy Cullenbine	95
1946	Hank Greenberg	110
1947	George Kell	90
1948	Pat Mullin	93
1949	Vic Wertz	105
1950	George Kell	117
1951	Vic Wertz	94
1952	Walt Dropo	65
1953	Harvey Kuenn	88
1954	Ray Boone	92
1955	Al Kaline	126
1956	Al Kaline	117
1957	Al Kaline	88
1958	Al Kaline	93
1959	Harvey Kuenn	105
1960	Eddie Yost	88

Pat Mullin

Year	Player	Base Runs
1961	**Norm Cash**	**159**
1962	Rocky Colavito	112
1963	Al Kaline	98
1964	Al Kaline	91
1965	Norm Cash	87
1966	Norm Cash	97
1967	Al Kaline	99
1968	Willie Horton	90
1969	Jim Northrup	92
1970	Al Kaline	80
1971	Norm Cash	83
1972	Norm Cash	64
1973	Mickey Stanley	68
1974	Al Kaline	73
1975	Willie Horton	80
1976	Rusty Staub	97
1977	Ron LeFlore	101
1978	Jason Thompson	98
1979	Steve Kemp	100
1980	Steve Kemp	88
1981	Steve Kemp	63
1982	Larry Herndon	90
1983	Lou Whitaker	107
1984	Alan Trammell	94
1985	Kirk Gibson	104
1986	Alan Trammell	88
1987	Alan Trammell	120
1988	Alan Trammell	76
1989	Lou Whitaker	86
1990	Cecil Fielder	120
1991	Cecil Fielder	107
1992	Mickey Tettleton	98
1993	Tony Phillips	108
1994	Tony Phillips	86
1995	Chad Curtis	86
1996	Bobby Higginson	96
1997	Tony Clark	106
1998	Tony Clark	105
1999	Tony Clark	92
	Dean Palmer	92
2000	Bobby Higginson	113
2001	Bobby Higginson	88
2002	Robert Fick	75
2003	Dmitri Young	101
2004	Carlos Guillen	98
2005	Brandon Inge	83
2006	Carlos Guillen	106
2007	Magglio Ordonez	140
2008	Miguel Cabrera	107
2009	Miguel Cabrera	120
2010	Miguel Cabrera	132
2011	Miguel Cabrera	143
2012	Miguel Cabrera	133
2013	Miguel Cabrera	140
2014	Victor Martinez	119
2015	J.D. Martinez	101
2016	Miguel Cabrera	121
2017	Nicholas Castellanos	89
2018	Nicholas Castellanos	100
2019	Miguel Cabrera	65
2020	Jeimer Candelario	32
2021	Robbie Grossman	84

Year	Player	Runs Produced
1901	**Jimmy Barrett**	**171**
1902	Jimmy Barrett	133
	Kid Elberfeld	133
1903	**Sam Crawford**	**173**
1904	Sam Crawford	120
1905	Sam Crawford	142
1906	Sam Crawford	135
1907	**Ty Cobb**	**211**
1908	Ty Cobb	192
1909	**Ty Cobb**	**214**
1910	Sam Crawford	198
1911	**Ty Cobb**	**266**
1912	Ty Cobb	195
1913	Sam Crawford	152
1914	Sam Crawford	170
1915	Ty Cobb	240
1916	Bobby Veach	180
1917	Ty Cobb	203
1918	Ty Cobb	144
1919	Bobby Veach	185
1920	Bobby Veach	194
1921	Harry Heilmann	234
1922	Bobby Veach	213
1923	Harry Heilmann	218
1924	Harry Heilmann	211
1925	Harry Heilmann	218
1926	Harry Heilmann	184
1927	Harry Heilmann	212
1928	Charlie Gehringer	176
	Harry Heilmann	176
1929	Charlie Gehringer	224
1930	Charlie Gehringer	226
1931	Dale Alexander	159
1932	Charlie Gehringer	200
1933	Charlie Gehringer	196
1934	Charlie Gehringer	250
1935	Hank Greenberg	253
1936	Charlie Gehringer	245
1937	**Hank Greenberg**	**281**
1938	Hank Greenberg	232
1939	Hank Greenberg	192
1940	Hank Greenberg	238
1941	Rudy York	175
1942	Rudy York	150
1943	Rudy York	174
1944	Rudy York	157

Year	Player	Runs Produced
1945	Roy Cullenbine	155
1946	Hank Greenberg	173
1947	George Kell	163
1948	Hoot Evers	174
1949	Vic Wertz	209
1950	George Kell	207
1951	Vic Wertz	153
1952	Walt Dropo	103
	Johnny Groth	103
1953	Ray Boone	144
	Walt Dropo	144
1954	Ray Boone	141
1955	Al Kaline	196
1956	Al Kaline	197
1957	Al Kaline	150
1958	Al Kaline	153

Craig Monroe

Year	Player	Runs Produced
1959	Harvey Kuenn	161
1960	Al Kaline	130
1961	Rocky Colavito	224
1962	Rocky Colavito	165
1963	Al Kaline	163
1964	Bill Freehan	131
1965	Willie Horton	144
1966	Norm Cash	159
1967	Al Kaline	147
1968	Jim Northrup	145
1969	Norm Cash	133
1970	Jim Northrup	127
1971	Norm Cash	131
1972	Aurelio Rodriguez	108
1973	Mickey Stanley	121
1974	Al Kaline	122

Year	Player	Runs Produced
1975	Willie Horton	129
1976	Rusty Staub	154
1977	Rusty Staub	163
1978	Ron LeFlore	176
1979	Steve Kemp	167
1980	Steve Kemp	168
1981	Steve Kemp	92
1982	Larry Herndon	157
1983	Lance Parrish	167
1984	Kirk Gibson	156
1985	Kirk Gibson	164
1986	Alan Trammell	161
1987	Alan Trammell	186
1988	Alan Trammell	127
1989	Lou Whitaker	134
1990	Cecil Fielder	185
1991	Cecil Fielder	191
1992	Cecil Fielder	169
1993	Travis Fryman	173
1994	Travis Fryman	133
	Tony Phillips	133
1995	Travis Fryman	145
1996	Travis Fryman	168
1997	Tony Clark	190
1998	Damion Easley	157
1999	Dean Palmer	154
2000	Bobby Higginson	176
2001	Bobby Higginson	138
2002	Randall Simon	114
2003	Dmitri Young	134
2004	Carlos Guillen	174
2005	Craig Monroe	138
2006	Carlos Guillen	166
2007	Magglio Ordonez	228
2008	Miguel Cabrera	175
2009	Miguel Cabrera	165
2010	Miguel Cabrera	199
2011	Miguel Cabrera	186
2012	Miguel Cabrera	204
2013	Miguel Cabrera	196
2014	Miguel Cabrera	185
2015	J.D. Martinez	157
2016	Ian Kinsler	172
2017	Nicholas Castellanos	148
2018	Nicholas Castellanos	154
2019	Niko Goodrum	94
2020	Miguel Cabrera	53
2021	Jonathan Schoop	147

Year	Player	Pct
1901	**Doc Casey**	**53%**
1902	Jimmy Barrett	39%
	Ducky Holmes	39%
1903	Sam Crawford	41%
1904	Bobby Lowe	38%
	Matty McIntyre	38%
1905	Germany Schaefer	35%
1906	Chris Lindsay	37%
1907	Davy Jones	51%
1908	Germany Schaefer	50%
1909	Donie Bush	48%
1910	Davy Jones	49%
1911	**Davy Jones**	**57%**
1912	Donie Bush	44%
1913	Donie Bush	42%
1914	Donie Bush	37%
	Marty Kavanagh	37%
1915	Ossie Vitt	52%
1916	Ossie Vitt	42%
1917	Donie Bush	46%
1918	Bob Jones	44%
1919	Ralph Young	42%
1920	Ty Cobb	42%
1921	Ty Cobb	46%
1922	Lu Blue	48%
1923	Fred Haney	43%
1924	Heinie Manush	47%
1925	Fred Haney	47%
1926	Johnny Neun	47%
1927	Charlie Gehringer	50%
1928	Harry Rice	42%
1929	Roy Johnson	46%
1930	Roy Johnson	50%
1931	Charlie Gehringer	44%
1932	Heinie Schuble	48%
1933	Pete Fox	44%
1934	Jo-Jo White	51%
1935	Pete Fox	50%
1936	Gee Walker	44%
1937	Pete Fox	44%
1938	Chet Morgan	46%
1939	Barney McCosky	45%
1940	Barney McCosky	45%
1941	Barney McCosky	35%
1942	Doc Cramer	33%
1943	Joe Hoover	43%
1944	Joe Hoover	46%
1945	Skeeter Webb	39%
1946	Eddie Lake	39%
1947	Vic Wertz	39%
1948	Pat Mullin	34%
1949	George Kell	38%
	Pat Mullin	38%
1950	Johnny Lipon	40%
1951	George Kell	35%
1952	Fred Hatfield	28%
1953	Harvey Kuenn	36%
1954	Frank Bolling	34%
	Harvey Kuenn	34%
1955	Harvey Kuenn	42%
1956	Harvey Kuenn	35%
1957	Al Kaline	31%
	Harvey Kuenn	31%
1958	Frank Bolling	37%
1959	Harvey Kuenn	38%
1960	Frank Bolling	33%

Nook Logan

Year	Player	Pct
1961	Billy Bruton	41%
1962	Jake Wood	55%
1963	Billy Bruton	41%
1964	Gates Brown	37%
1965	Jerry Lumpe	37%
1966	Dick McAuliffe	37%
1967	Al Kaline	35%
1968	Mickey Stanley	41%
1969	Al Kaline	34%
1970	Mickey Stanley	40%
1971	Dick McAuliffe	35%
1972	Willie Horton	34%
	Al Kaline	34%
1973	Mickey Stanley	36%
1974	Aurelio Rodriguez	33%
1975	Dan Meyer	37%
1976	Ron LeFlore	40%
1977	Tito Fuentes	35%
	Ron LeFlore	35%
	Tom Veryzer	35%
1978	Ron LeFlore	45%
1979	Ron LeFlore	45%
1980	Alan Trammell	42%
1981	Lou Whitaker	35%
1982	Larry Herndon	35%
1983	Tom Brookens	46%
1984	Tom Brookens	39%
1985	Tom Brookens	35%
	Lou Whitaker	35%
1986	Alan Trammell	43%
1987	Lou Whitaker	44%
1988	Gary Pettis	44%
1989	Gary Pettis	39%
1990	Tony Phillips	37%
1991	Milt Cuyler	42%
1992	Dan Gladden	38%
	Tony Phillips	38%
1993	Alan Trammell	38%
1994	Lou Whitaker	43%
1995	Chad Curtis	35%
1996	Kimera Bartee	44%
1997	Brian Hunter	45%
1998	Deivi Cruz	36%
1999	Deivi Cruz	34%
2000	Damion Easley	36%
2001	Roger Cedeno	39%
2002	Wendell Magee	28%
2003	Alex Sanchez	32%
2004	Dmitri Young	43%
2005	Nook Logan	44%
2006	Craig Monroe	41%
2007	Curtis Granderson	45%
2008	Curtis Granderson	43%
2009	Clete Thomas	42%
2010	Austin Jackson	43%
2011	Brennan Boesch	41%
	Austin Jackson	41%
2012	Austin Jackson	40%
2013	Austin Jackson	45%
2014	Ian Kinsler	40%
2015	Rajai Davis	45%
2016	Ian Kinsler	43%
2017	Andrew Romine	43%
2018	JaCoby Jones	38%
2019	Niko Goodrum	35%
2020	JaCoby Jones	45%
2021	Willie Castro	42%

Year	Player	Runs
1901	**Jimmy Barrett**	**84**
1902	Jimmy Barrett	83
1903	**Sam Crawford**	**92**
1904	Jimmy Barrett	71
1905	Sam Crawford	88
1906	Sam Crawford	78
1907	**Ty Cobb**	**104**
1908	Ty Cobb	99
1909	**Ty Cobb**	**124**
1910	Ty Cobb	123
1911	**Ty Cobb**	**154**
1912	Ty Cobb	130
1913	Sam Crawford	105
1914	Sam Crawford	105
1915	Ty Cobb	139
1916	Ty Cobb	119
1917	Ty Cobb	138
1918	Ty Cobb	89
1919	Bobby Veach	101
1920	Bobby Veach	97
1921	Harry Heilmann	137
1922	Ty Cobb	117
1923	Harry Heilmann	135
1924	Harry Heilmann	121
1925	Harry Heilmann	129
1926	Harry Heilmann	107
1927	Harry Heilmann	127
1928	Charlie Gehringer	104
1929	Dale Alexander	129
1930	Charlie Gehringer	123
1931	John Stone	99
1932	Charlie Gehringer	109
1933	Charlie Gehringer	109
1934	Charlie Gehringer	130
	Hank Greenberg	130
1935	Hank Greenberg	145
1936	Charlie Gehringer	139
1937	**Hank Greenberg**	**155**
1938	Hank Greenberg	152
1939	Hank Greenberg	121
1940	Hank Greenberg	147
1941	Rudy York	97
1942	Barney McCosky	88
1943	Rudy York	106
1944	Rudy York	88
1945	Roy Cullenbine	95
1946	Hank Greenberg	112

Year	Player	Runs
1947	Roy Cullenbine	88
	George Kell	88
1948	Pat Mullin	93
1949	Vic Wertz	103
1950	Vic Wertz	114
1951	Vic Wertz	94
1952	Walt Dropo	66
1953	Harvey Kuenn	88
1954	Ray Boone	92
1955	Al Kaline	124
1956	Al Kaline	118
1957	Al Kaline	91
1958	Al Kaline	93
1959	Eddie Yost	107
1960	Eddie Yost	90
1961	Norm Cash	153

Bobby Higginson

Year	Player	Runs
1962	Rocky Colavito	113
1963	Al Kaline	99
1964	Al Kaline	92
1965	Norm Cash	89
1966	Norm Cash	98
	Al Kaline	98
1967	Al Kaline	98
1968	Willie Horton	93
1969	Jim Northrup	94
1970	Al Kaline	79
	Jim Northrup	79
1971	Norm Cash	87
1972	Norm Cash	66
1973	Willie Horton	68
1974	Bill Freehan	73
	Al Kaline	73
1975	Willie Horton	79
1976	Rusty Staub	97
1977	Ron LeFlore	107
1978	Ron LeFlore	103
1979	Steve Kemp	99
1980	Steve Kemp	88
1981	Steve Kemp	63
1982	Larry Herndon	93
1983	Lou Whitaker	107
1984	Kirk Gibson	101
1985	Kirk Gibson	111
1986	Alan Trammell	94
1987	Alan Trammell	122
1988	Alan Trammell	77
1989	Lou Whitaker	88
1990	Cecil Fielder	123
1991	Cecil Fielder	109
1992	Mickey Tettleton	98
1993	Travis Fryman	109
1994	Tony Phillips	87
1995	Chad Curtis	92
1996	Bobby Higginson	96
1997	Tony Clark	107
1998	Tony Clark	107
1999	Dean Palmer	97
2000	Bobby Higginson	117
2001	Bobby Higginson	91
2002	Robert Fick	77
2003	Dmitri Young	106
2004	Carlos Guillen	100
2005	Brandon Inge	85
2006	Carlos Guillen	107
2007	Magglio Ordonez	135
2008	Miguel Cabrera	110
2009	Miguel Cabrera	121
2010	Miguel Cabrera	130
2011	Miguel Cabrera	136
2012	Miguel Cabrera	133
2013	Miguel Cabrera	138
2014	Victor Martinez	118
2015	J.D. Martinez	105
2016	Miguel Cabrera	121
2017	Nicholas Castellanos	93
2018	Nicholas Castellanos	104
2019	Miguel Cabrera	65
2020	Jeimer Candelario	32
2021	Robbie Grossman	90

Year	Player	Runs Created
1901	**Jimmy Barrett**	**79**
1902	Jimmy Barrett	78
1903	**Sam Crawford**	**98**
1904	Jimmy Barrett	66
1905	Sam Crawford	88
1906	Sam Crawford	78
1907	**Ty Cobb**	**108**
1908	Ty Cobb	101
1909	**Ty Cobb**	**127**
1910	Ty Cobb	129
1911	**Ty Cobb**	**171**
1912	Ty Cobb	148
1913	Sam Crawford	110
1914	Sam Crawford	109
1915	Ty Cobb	133
1916	Ty Cobb	121
1917	Ty Cobb	149
1918	Ty Cobb	95
1919	Bobby Veach	111
1920	Bobby Veach	102
1921	Harry Heilmann	162
1922	Ty Cobb	137
1923	Harry Heilmann	159
1924	Harry Heilmann	130
1925	Harry Heilmann	149
1926	Harry Heilmann	119
1927	Harry Heilmann	148
1928	Harry Heilmann	110
1929	Dale Alexander	144
1930	Charlie Gehringer	132
1931	John Stone	105
1932	Charlie Gehringer	114
1933	Charlie Gehringer	116
1934	Hank Greenberg	144
1935	Hank Greenberg	160
1936	Charlie Gehringer	154
1937	**Hank Greenberg**	**173**
1938	Hank Greenberg	166
1939	Hank Greenberg	131
1940	Hank Greenberg	166
1941	Rudy York	97
1942	Barney McCosky	90
1943	Rudy York	110
1944	Rudy York	90
1945	Roy Cullenbine	94
1946	Hank Greenberg	118
1947	George Kell	94
1948	Pat Mullin	96
1949	Vic Wertz	109
1950	George Kell	125
1951	Vic Wertz	98
1952	Walt Dropo	70
1953	Harvey Kuenn	93
1954	Ray Boone	95
1955	Al Kaline	135
1956	Al Kaline	125
1957	Al Kaline	95
1958	Al Kaline	100
1959	Harvey Kuenn	113
1960	Rocky Colavito	83
	Al Kaline	83
1961	Norm Cash	172
1962	Rocky Colavito	115
1963	Al Kaline	106
1964	Al Kaline	94
1965	Norm Cash	89
1966	Norm Cash	101
1967	Al Kaline	102
1968	Willie Horton	98
1969	Jim Northrup	99
1970	Al Kaline	79
	Jim Northrup	79
1971	Norm Cash	89
1972	Norm Cash	66
1973	Willie Horton	75
1974	Bill Freehan	77
1975	Willie Horton	83
1976	Rusty Staub	98
1977	Ron LeFlore	113
1978	Jason Thompson	101
1979	Steve Kemp	106
1980	Steve Kemp	91
1981	Steve Kemp	61
1982	Larry Herndon	98
1983	Lou Whitaker	112
1984	Kirk Gibson	100
1985	Kirk Gibson	110
1986	Alan Trammell	93
1987	Alan Trammell	132
1988	Alan Trammell	81
1989	Lou Whitaker	85
1990	Cecil Fielder	128
1991	Cecil Fielder	111
1992	Mickey Tettleton	93
1993	Travis Fryman	112
1994	Tony Phillips	84
1995	Chad Curtis	89
1996	Bobby Higginson	103
1997	Tony Clark	109
1998	Tony Clark	112
1999	Tony Clark	98
	Dean Palmer	98
2000	Bobby Higginson	121
2001	Bobby Higginson	88
2002	Robert Fick	80
2003	Dmitri Young	112
2004	Carlos Guillen	107
2005	Brandon Inge	85
2006	Carlos Guillen	113
2007	Magglio Ordonez	154
2008	Miguel Cabrera	116
2009	Miguel Cabrera	132
2010	Miguel Cabrera	143
2011	Miguel Cabrera	150
2012	Miguel Cabrera	148
2013	Miguel Cabrera	156
2014	Victor Martinez	130
2015	J.D. Martinez	110
2016	Miguel Cabrera	132
2017	Nicholas Castellanos	96
2018	Nicholas Castellanos	110
2019	Miguel Cabrera	68
2020	Jeimer Candelario	34
2021	Jeimer Candelario	86
	Jonathan Schoop	86

Walt Dropo

Year	Player	RC/27
1901	**Jimmy Barrett**	**2.92**
1902	Jimmy Barrett	2.90
1903	**Sam Crawford**	**3.64**
1904	Jimmy Barrett	2.44
1905	Sam Crawford	3.26
1906	Sam Crawford	2.89
1907	**Ty Cobb**	**3.98**
1908	Ty Cobb	3.75
1909	**Ty Cobb**	**4.72**
1910	**Ty Cobb**	**4.78**
1911	**Ty Cobb**	**6.34**
1912	Ty Cobb	5.47
1913	Sam Crawford	4.09
1914	Sam Crawford	4.04
1915	Ty Cobb	4.93
1916	Ty Cobb	4.47
1917	Ty Cobb	5.51
1918	Ty Cobb	3.53
1919	Bobby Veach	4.11
1920	Bobby Veach	3.79
1921	Harry Heilmann	6.01
1922	Ty Cobb	5.08
1923	Harry Heilmann	5.90
1924	Harry Heilmann	4.82
1925	Harry Heilmann	5.52
1926	Harry Heilmann	4.42
1927	Harry Heilmann	5.47
1928	Harry Heilmann	4.09
1929	Dale Alexander	5.34
1930	Charlie Gehringer	4.88
1931	John Stone	3.89
1932	Charlie Gehringer	4.21
1933	Charlie Gehringer	4.28
1934	Hank Greenberg	5.33
1935	Hank Greenberg	5.92
1936	Charlie Gehringer	5.69
1937	**Hank Greenberg**	**6.42**
1938	Hank Greenberg	6.17
1939	Hank Greenberg	4.84
1940	Hank Greenberg	6.16
1941	Rudy York	3.59
1942	Barney McCosky	3.34
1943	Rudy York	4.08
1944	Rudy York	3.34
1945	Roy Cullenbine	3.48
1946	Hank Greenberg	4.37
1947	George Kell	3.46
1948	Pat Mullin	3.56
1949	Vic Wertz	4.04
1950	George Kell	4.62
1951	Vic Wertz	3.63
1952	Walt Dropo	2.61
1953	Harvey Kuenn	3.46
1954	Ray Boone	3.52
1955	Al Kaline	5.01
1956	Al Kaline	4.64
1957	Al Kaline	3.50
1958	Al Kaline	3.69
1959	Harvey Kuenn	4.19
1960	Rocky Colavito	3.09

Jeimer Candelario

Year	Player	RC/27
1961	Norm Cash	6.38
1962	Rocky Colavito	4.25
1963	Al Kaline	3.93
1964	Al Kaline	3.49
1965	Norm Cash	3.29
1966	Norm Cash	3.74
1967	Al Kaline	3.77
1968	Willie Horton	3.63
1969	Jim Northrup	3.66
1970	Jim Northrup	2.94
1971	Norm Cash	3.30
1972	Norm Cash	2.45
1973	Willie Horton	2.76
1974	Bill Freehan	2.85
1975	Willie Horton	3.06
1976	Rusty Staub	3.64
1977	Ron LeFlore	4.17
1978	Jason Thompson	3.75
1979	Steve Kemp	3.92
1980	Steve Kemp	3.36
1981	Steve Kemp	2.25
1982	Larry Herndon	3.63
1983	Lou Whitaker	4.14
1984	Kirk Gibson	3.69
1985	Kirk Gibson	4.06
1986	Alan Trammell	3.46
1987	Alan Trammell	4.90
1988	Alan Trammell	2.98
1989	Lou Whitaker	3.14
1990	Cecil Fielder	4.74
1991	Cecil Fielder	4.11
1992	Mickey Tettleton	3.45
1993	Travis Fryman	4.14
1994	Tony Phillips	3.10
1995	Chad Curtis	3.30
1996	Bobby Higginson	3.80
1997	Tony Clark	4.04
1998	Tony Clark	4.16
1999	Tony Clark	3.64
	Dean Palmer	3.64
2000	Bobby Higginson	4.48
2001	Bobby Higginson	3.28
2002	Robert Fick	2.95
2003	Dmitri Young	4.16
2004	Carlos Guillen	3.98
2005	Brandon Inge	3.15
2006	Carlos Guillen	4.18
2007	Magglio Ordonez	5.69
2008	Miguel Cabrera	4.28
2009	Miguel Cabrera	4.89
2010	Miguel Cabrera	5.30
2011	Miguel Cabrera	5.55
2012	Miguel Cabrera	5.49
2013	Miguel Cabrera	5.78
2014	Victor Martinez	4.80
2015	J.D. Martinez	4.06
2016	Miguel Cabrera	4.88
2017	Nicholas Castellanos	3.57
2018	Nicholas Castellanos	4.06
2019	Miguel Cabrera	2.51
2020	Jeimer Candelario	1.26
2021	Jonathan Schoop	3.19

1901 Jimmy Barrett 86.1
1902 Jimmy Barrett 85.8
1903 Sam Crawford 96.8
1904 Jimmy Barrett 72.7
1905 Sam Crawford 92.6
1906 Sam Crawford 80.4
1907 Ty Cobb 108.4
1908 Ty Cobb 102.9
1909 Ty Cobb 128.7
1910 Ty Cobb 133.5
1911 Ty Cobb 174.6
1912 Ty Cobb 132.8
1913 Sam Crawford 113.8
1914 Sam Crawford 105.2
1915 Ty Cobb 130.9
1916 Ty Cobb 116.4
1917 Ty Cobb 152.6
1918 Ty Cobb 98.5
1919 Ty Cobb 112.4
1920 Bobby Veach 100.7
1921 Harry Heilmann 161.4
1922 Ty Cobb 131.2
1923 Harry Heilmann 158.9
1924 Harry Heilmann 131.5
1925 Harry Heilmann 148.6
1926 Harry Heilmann 118.8
1927 Harry Heilmann 149.6
1928 Harry Heilmann 111.5
1929 Dale Alexander 141.3
1930 Charlie Gehringer 129.6
1931 John Stone 104.4
1932 Charlie Gehringer 116.2
1933 Charlie Gehringer 120.1
1934 Charlie Gehringer 146.8
1935 Hank Greenberg 166.4
1936 Charlie Gehringer 162.1
1937 Hank Greenberg 182.8
1938 Hank Greenberg 176.5
1939 Hank Greenberg 132.1
1940 Hank Greenberg 165.2
1941 Rudy York 97.7
1942 Barney McCosky 88.4
1943 Rudy York 104.1
1944 Rudy York 87.8

1945 Roy Cullenbine 99.4
1946 Hank Greenberg 115.4
1947 George Kell 89.1
1948 Pat Mullin 100.6
1949 Vic Wertz 106.2
1950 Vic Wertz 124.3
1951 Vic Wertz 98.1
1952 Walt Dropo 63.8
1953 Harvey Kuenn 92.3
1954 Ray Boone 93.1
1955 Al Kaline 133.0
1956 Al Kaline 126.2
1957 Charlie Maxwell 92.3
1958 Al Kaline 93.8
1959 Harvey Kuenn 113.7
1960 Eddie Yost 95.7

Harvey Kuenn

1961 Norm Cash 188.6
1962 Rocky Colavito 131.0
1963 Al Kaline 112.4
1964 Al Kaline 104.7
1965 Norm Cash 95.8
1966 Al Kaline 107.3
1967 Al Kaline 115.8
1968 Willie Horton 104.3
1969 Jim Northrup 105.3
1970 Al Kaline 76.8
1971 Norm Cash 92.3
1972 Norm Cash 64.8
1973 Willie Horton 68.1
1974 Bill Freehan 74.8
1975 Willie Horton 77.4
1976 Rusty Staub 96.6

1977 Ron LeFlore 102.4
1978 Jason Thompson 102.8
1979 Steve Kemp 103.0
1980 Steve Kemp 86.4
1981 Steve Kemp 61.2
1982 Larry Herndon 87.3
1983 Lou Whitaker 109.1
1984 Kirk Gibson 99.1
1985 Kirk Gibson 110.6
1986 Alan Trammell 88.9
1987 Alan Trammell 131.1
1988 Alan Trammell 76.8
1989 Lou Whitaker 88.5
1990 Cecil Fielder 127.6
1991 Cecil Fielder 109.4
1992 Mickey Tettleton 99.0
1993 Travis Fryman 114.1
1994 Tony Phillips 88.3
1995 Chad Curtis 84.8
1996 Bobby Higginson 103.0
1997 Tony Clark 110.7
1998 Tony Clark 108.8
1999 Tony Clark 97.1
2000 Bobby Higginson 123.6
2001 Bobby Higginson 87.6
2002 Robert Fick 76.5
2003 Dmitri Young 108.9
2004 Carlos Guillen 103.2
2005 Brandon Inge 82.0
2006 Carlos Guillen 107.7
2007 Magglio Ordonez 149.9
2008 Miguel Cabrera 112.4
2009 Miguel Cabrera 126.0
2010 Miguel Cabrera 138.7
2011 Miguel Cabrera 147.3
2012 Miguel Cabrera 137.3
2013 Miguel Cabrera 153.8
2014 Victor Martinez 124.7
2015 J.D. Martinez 107.7
2016 Miguel Cabrera 124.8
2017 Nicholas Castellanos 92.2
2018 Nicholas Castellanos 110.1
2019 Miguel Cabrera 65.2
2020 Jeimer Candelario 34.4
2021 Jeimer Candelario 88.8

1920	**Bobby Veach**	**48**
1921	**Harry Heilmann**	**93**
1922	Ty Cobb	77
1923	**Harry Heilmann**	**98**
1924	Harry Heilmann	79
1925	Harry Heilmann	88
1926	Harry Heilmann	70
1927	Harry Heilmann	92
1928	Harry Heilmann	61
1929	Charlie Gehringer	81
1930	Charlie Gehringer	73
1931	John Stone	51
1932	Charlie Gehringer	59
1933	Charlie Gehringer	62
1934	Charlie Gehringer	85
	Hank Greenberg	85
1935	**Hank Greenberg**	**98**
1936	Charlie Gehringer	93
1937	**Hank Greenberg**	**112**
1938	Hank Greenberg	109
1939	Hank Greenberg	84
1940	Hank Greenberg	106
1941	Rudy York	51
1942	Barney McCosky	43
1943	Rudy York	61
1944	Dick Wakefield	47
1945	Roy Cullenbine	56
1946	Hank Greenberg	73
1947	Roy Cullenbine	50
1948	Pat Mullin	55
1949	George Kell	59
1950	Vic Wertz	73
1951	Vic Wertz	55
1952	Walt Dropo	31
1953	Ray Boone	50
1954	Ray Boone	52
1955	Al Kaline	80
1956	Al Kaline	73
1957	Charlie Maxwell	50

1958	Al Kaline	53
1959	Al Kaline	68
	Eddie Yost	68
1960	Eddie Yost	51
1961	**Norm Cash**	**116**
1962	Rocky Colavito	68
1963	Al Kaline	58
1964	Al Kaline	53
1965	Norm Cash	50
1966	Al Kaline	60
1967	Al Kaline	65
1968	Willie Horton	53
1969	Jim Northrup	53
1970	Al Kaline	44

Lou Whitaker

1971	Norm Cash	52
1972	Norm Cash	30
1973	Willie Horton	36
1974	Bill Freehan	41
1975	Willie Horton	32
1976	Rusty Staub	55
1977	Ron LeFlore	56
1978	Ron LeFlore	55
1979	Steve Kemp	62
1980	Steve Kemp	52
1981	Steve Kemp	35
1982	Larry Herndon	44
	Lance Parrish	44
1983	Lou Whitaker	58

1984	Kirk Gibson	59
1985	Kirk Gibson	69
1986	Kirk Gibson	53
1987	Alan Trammell	82
1988	Alan Trammell	42
1989	Lou Whitaker	47
1990	Cecil Fielder	78
1991	Cecil Fielder	61
1992	Mickey Tettleton	53
1993	Travis Fryman	63
	Tony Phillips	63
1994	Tony Phillips	53
1995	Chad Curtis	43
1996	Bobby Higginson	63
1997	Tony Clark	62
1998	Tony Clark	61
1999	Tony Clark	54
2000	Bobby Higginson	72
2001	Bobby Higginson	46
2002	Robert Fick	34
2003	Dmitri Young	64
2004	Carlos Guillen	62
2005	Chris Shelton	38
2006	Carlos Guillen	67
2007	Magglio Ordonez	95
2008	Miguel Cabrera	64
2009	Miguel Cabrera	77
2010	Miguel Cabrera	90
2011	Miguel Cabrera	97
2012	Miguel Cabrera	90
2013	Miguel Cabrera	100
2014	Victor Martinez	78
2015	Miguel Cabrera	63
2016	Miguel Cabrera	79
2017	Justin Upton	51
2018	Nicholas Castellanos	57
2019	Miguel Cabrera	29
2020	Jeimer Candelario	18
2021	Robbie Grossman	46

Year	Player	Runs
1901	**Jimmy Barrett**	**85**
1902	Jimmy Barrett	84
1903	**Sam Crawford**	**91**
1904	Jimmy Barrett	74
1905	Sam Crawford	87
1906	Sam Crawford	78
1907	**Ty Cobb**	**104**
1908	Ty Cobb	97
1909	**Ty Cobb**	**125**
1910	Ty Cobb	124
1911	**Ty Cobb**	**152**
1912	Ty Cobb	122
1913	Sam Crawford	105
1914	Sam Crawford	102
1915	Ty Cobb	132
1916	Ty Cobb	116
1917	Ty Cobb	137
1918	Ty Cobb	90
1919	Ty Cobb	100
1920	Bobby Veach	92
1921	Harry Heilmann	135
1922	Ty Cobb	113
1923	Harry Heilmann	133
1924	Harry Heilmann	118
1925	Harry Heilmann	128
1926	Harry Heilmann	105
1927	Harry Heilmann	125
1928	Harry Heilmann	102
1929	Dale Alexander	126
1930	Charlie Gehringer	117
1931	John Stone	96
1932	Charlie Gehringer	106
1933	Charlie Gehringer	108
1934	Charlie Gehringer	128
1935	Hank Greenberg	144
1936	Charlie Gehringer	136
1937	**Hank Greenberg**	**153**
1938	**Hank Greenberg**	**153**
1939	Hank Greenberg	120
1940	Hank Greenberg	147
1941	Rudy York	99
1942	Barney McCosky	89
1943	Rudy York	108
1944	Rudy York	90
1945	Roy Cullenbine	97
1946	Hank Greenberg	114
1947	Roy Cullenbine	91
1948	Pat Mullin	94
1949	Vic Wertz	106
1950	Vic Wertz	115
1951	Vic Wertz	96
1952	Walt Dropo	68
1953	Harvey Kuenn	89
1954	Ray Boone	94
1955	Al Kaline	124
1956	Al Kaline	119
1957	Al Kaline	90
1958	Al Kaline	94
1959	Eddie Yost	107
1960	Eddie Yost	91
1961	**Norm Cash**	**154**

Robert Fick

Year	Player	Runs
1962	Rocky Colavito	116
1963	Al Kaline	100
1964	Al Kaline	93
1965	Norm Cash	88
1966	Norm Cash	100
1967	Al Kaline	100
1968	Willie Horton	93
1969	Jim Northrup	94
1970	Al Kaline	81
1971	Norm Cash	87
1972	Norm Cash	66
1973	Mickey Stanley	69
1974	Al Kaline	75
1975	Willie Horton	83
1976	Rusty Staub	99
1977	Ron LeFlore	104
1978	Ron LeFlore	103
1979	Steve Kemp	100
1980	Steve Kemp	90
1981	Steve Kemp	65
1982	Larry Herndon	93
1983	Lou Whitaker	107
1984	Kirk Gibson	98
1985	Kirk Gibson	110
1986	Alan Trammell	91
1987	Alan Trammell	124
1988	Alan Trammell	77
1989	Lou Whitaker	89
1990	Cecil Fielder	124
1991	Cecil Fielder	111
1992	Mickey Tettleton	99
1993	Travis Fryman	108
	Tony Phillips	108
1994	Tony Phillips	88
1995	Chad Curtis	89
1996	Bobby Higginson	96
1997	Tony Clark	108
1998	Tony Clark	108
1999	Tony Clark	95
	Dean Palmer	95
2000	Bobby Higginson	116
2001	Bobby Higginson	90
2002	Robert Fick	76
2003	Dmitri Young	104
2004	Carlos Guillen	99
2005	Brandon Inge	84
2006	Carlos Guillen	106
2007	Magglio Ordonez	136
2008	Miguel Cabrera	111
2009	Miguel Cabrera	122
2010	Miguel Cabrera	131
2011	Miguel Cabrera	138
2012	Miguel Cabrera	135
2013	Miguel Cabrera	141
2014	Victor Martinez	119
2015	J.D. Martinez	105
2016	Miguel Cabrera	124
2017	Nicholas Castellanos	91
2018	Nicholas Castellanos	102
2019	Miguel Cabrera	69
2020	Jeimer Candelario	32
2021	Robbie Grossman	90

YEARLY TIGER HITTING LEADERS – HOME RUN AVERAGE

Year	Player	HR Avg
1901	**Sport McAllister**	**5.88**
1902	Jimmy Barrett	4.72
1903	Sam Crawford	4.36
1904	Sam Crawford	2.14
1905	**Sam Crawford**	**6.26**
1906	Charley O'Leary	2.71
1907	Ty Cobb	4.96
1908	**Sam Crawford**	**7.11**
1909	**Ty Cobb**	**9.42**
1910	**Ty Cobb**	**9.49**
1911	Ty Cobb	8.12
1912	Ty Cobb	7.59
1913	Sam Crawford	8.87
1914	Sam Crawford	8.25
1915	George Burns	7.65
1916	Ty Cobb	5.54
1917	Bobby Veach	8.41
1918	**Harry Heilmann**	**10.49**
1919	Ira Flagstead	10.45
1920	**Bobby Veach**	**10.78**
1921	**Harry Heilmann**	**18.94**
1922	**Harry Heilmann**	**27.69**
1923	Harry Heilmann	20.61
1924	Heinie Manush	12.80
1925	Ty Cobb	17.35
1926	Heinie Manush	16.87
1927	Harry Heilmann	16.63
1928	Pinky Hargrave	18.75
1929	Dale Alexander	23.96
1930	Dale Alexander	19.93
1931	John Stone	10.27
1932	Charlie Gehringer	18.45
1933	Hank Greenberg	16.04
1934	Hank Greenberg	26.31
1935	**Hank Greenberg**	**34.89**
1936	Goose Goslin	25.17
1937	**Rudy York**	**56.00**
1938	**Hank Greenberg**	**62.59**
1939	Hank Greenberg	39.60
1940	Hank Greenberg	42.93
1941	Rudy York	27.46
1942	Rudy York	21.84
1943	Rudy York	35.73
1944	Dick Wakefield	26.09
1945	Roy Cullenbine	20.65
1946	Hank Greenberg	50.48
1947	Roy Cullenbine	31.03
1948	Pat Mullin	27.82
1949	Aaron Robinson	23.56
1950	Vic Wertz	28.98
1951	Vic Wertz	32.34
1952	Walt Dropo	30.07
1953	Ray Boone	34.29
1954	Ray Boone	22.10
1955	Al Kaline	27.55
1956	Charlie Maxwell	33.60
1957	Charlie Maxwell	29.27
1958	Gail Harris	26.61
1959	Charlie Maxwell	35.91
1960	Rocky Colavito	37.84

Charley O'Leary

Year	Player	HR Avg
1961	Rocky Colavito	46.31
1962	Norm Cash	46.15
1963	Norm Cash	31.64
1964	Don Demeter	29.93
1965	Norm Cash	38.54
1966	Al Kaline	36.33
1967	Al Kaline	32.75
1968	Willie Horton	42.19
1969	Willie Horton	33.07
1970	Jim Northrup	28.57
1971	Norm Cash	42.48
1972	Norm Cash	30.00
1973	Norm Cash	31.40
1974	Bill Freehan	24.27
1975	Willie Horton	24.39
1976	Ben Oglivie	29.51
1977	Jason Thompson	31.79
1978	Jason Thompson	26.49
1979	Steve Kemp	31.84
1980	Champ Summers	29.39
1981	John Wockenfuss	31.40
1982	Lance Parrish	39.51
1983	Chet Lemon	29.33
1984	Lance Parrish	34.26
1985	Darrell Evans	47.52
1986	Lance Parrish	40.37
1987	Matt Nokes	41.65
1988	Darrell Evans	30.21
1989	Lou Whitaker	33.01
1990	Cecil Fielder	53.40
1991	Cecil Fielder	42.31
1992	Rob Deer	48.85
1993	Mickey Tettleton	36.78
1994	Kirk Gibson	41.82
1995	Cecil Fielder	37.65
1996	Tony Clark	43.09
1997	Bob Hamelin	33.96
1998	Tony Clark	33.89
1999	Dean Palmer	40.71
2000	Dean Palmer	33.21
2001	Robert Fick	28.43
2002	Randall Simon	23.65
2003	Eric Munson	34.50
2004	Eric Munson	35.51
2005	Chris Shelton	27.84
2006	Marcus Thames	44.83
2007	Gary Sheffield	30.36
2008	Marcus Thames	47.47
2009	Ryan Raburn	36.78
2010	Miguel Cabrera	41.61
2011	Miguel Cabrera	31.47
2012	Miguel Cabrera	42.44
2013	Miguel Cabrera	47.57
2014	Victor Martinez	34.22
2015	J.D. Martinez	38.26
2016	Miguel Cabrera	38.32
2017	Justin Upton	36.60
2018	Nicholas Castellanos	22.26
2019	John Hicks	24.45
2020	JaCoby Jones	30.93
2021	Eric Haase	37.61

Year	Player	Ratio
1901	Six Batters	0.01
1902	Three Batters	0.01
1903	**Sam Crawford**	**0.01**
1904	Seven Batters	0.00
1905	**Sam Crawford**	**0.01**
1906	Eight Batters	0.00
1907	**Ty Cobb, Sam Crawford**	**0.01**
1908	**Three Batters**	**0.01**
1909	**Ty Cobb**	**0.02**
1910	**Ty Cobb**	**0.02**
1911	Four Batters	0.01
1912	Ty Cobb, Sam Crawford	0.01
1913	Four Batters	0.01
1914	Four Batters	0.01
1915	Five Batters	0.01
1916	Three Batters	0.01
1917	Three Batters	0.01
1918	**Harry Heilmann**	**0.02**
1919	**Ira Flagstead**	**0.02**
1920	**H. Heilmann, B. Veach**	**0.02**
1921	**H. Heilmann, B. Veach**	**0.03**
1922	**Harry Heilmann**	**0.05**
1923	Harry Heilmann	0.03
1924	Harry Heilmann	0.02
	Heinie Manush	0.02
1925	Ty Cobb	0.03
1926	Heinie Manush	0.03
1927	Harry Heilmann	0.03
1928	Pinky Hargrave	0.03
	Harry Heilmann	0.03
1929	Dale Alexander	0.04
1930	Dale Alexander	0.03
	Charlie Gehringer	0.03
1931	John Stone	0.02
1932	C. Gehringer, J. Stone	0.03
1933	Hank Greenberg	0.03
1934	Hank Greenberg	0.04
1935	**Hank Greenberg**	**0.06**
1936	Goose Goslin	0.04
1937	**Rudy York**	**0.09**
1938	**Hank Greenberg**	**0.10**
1939	Hank Greenberg	0.07
1940	Hank Greenberg	0.07
1941	Rudy York	0.05
1942	Rudy York	0.04
1943	Rudy York	0.06
1944	Dick Wakefield	0.04
1945	Roy Cullenbine, R. York	0.03
1946	Hank Greenberg	0.08
1947	Roy Cullenbine	0.05
1948	Pat Mullin	0.05
1949	P. Mullin, A. Robinson	0.04
1950	Vic Wertz	0.05
1951	Vic Wertz	0.05
1952	Walt Dropo	0.05
1953	Ray Boone	0.06
1954	Ray Boone	0.04
1955	Frank House, Al Kaline	0.05
1956	Charlie Maxwell	0.06
1957	Charlie Maxwell	0.05
1958	Gail Harris	0.04
1959	Charlie Maxwell	0.06
1960	Rocky Colavito	0.06
1961	N. Cash, Rocky Colavito	0.08
1962	Norm Cash	0.08

John Wockenfuss

Year	Player	Ratio
1963	Norm Cash, Al Kaline	0.05
1964	N. Cash, Don Demeter	0.05
1965	N. Cash, Willie Horton	0.06
1966	Al Kaline	0.06
1967	Three Batters	0.05
1968	Willie Horton	0.07
1969	Willie Horton	0.06
1970	W. Horton, J. Northrup	0.05
1971	Norm Cash	0.07
1972	Norm Cash	0.05
1973	Norm Cash	0.05
1974	Bill Freehan	0.04
1975	Willie Horton	0.04
1976	Ben Oglivie	0.05
1977	B. Oglivie, J. Thompson	0.05
1978	J. Thompson, R. Staub	0.04
1979	Steve Kemp	0.05

Year	Player	Ratio
1980	Champ Summers	0.05
1981	John Wockenfuss	0.05
1982	Lance Parrish	0.07
1983	Chet Lemon	0.05
1984	Lance Parrish	0.06
1985	Darrell Evans	0.08
1986	Lance Parrish	0.07
1987	D. Evans, Matt Nokes	0.07
1988	Darrell Evans	0.05
1989	Lou Whitaker	0.06
1990	Cecil Fielder	0.09
1991	Cecil Fielder	0.07
1992	Rob Deer	0.08
1993	Mickey Tettleton	0.06
1994	Cecil Fielder, K. Gibson	0.07
1995	Cecil Fielder	0.06
1996	Tony Clark, Cecil Fielder	0.07
1997	Tony Clark	0.06
	Bob Hamelin	0.06
	Melvin Nieves	0.06
1998	Tony Clark	0.06
1999	Dean Palmer	0.07
2000	Dean Palmer	0.06
2001	Robert Fick	0.05
2002	Randall Simon	0.04
2003	Eric Munson	0.06
2004	Eric Munson, C. Pena	0.06
2005	Chris Shelton	0.05
2006	Marcus Thames	0.07
2007	Magglio Ordonez	0.05
	Gary Sheffield	0.05
2008	Marcus Thames	0.08
2009	M. Cabrera, R. Raburn	0.06
2010	Miguel Cabrera	0.07
2011	Miguel Cabrera	0.05
2012	Miguel Cabrera	0.07
2013	Miguel Cabrera	0.08
2014	Victor Martinez	0.06
2015	J.D. Martinez	0.06
2016	Miguel Cabrera	0.06
2017	Justin Upton	0.06
2018	Candelario, Goodrum,	0.04
	Nicholas Castellanos	0.04
2019	Brandon Dixon	0.04
	John Hicks	0.04
	JaCoby Jones	0.04
2020	M. Cabrera, W. Castro	0.05
	J. Candelario, J. Schoop	0.05
2021	Eric Haase	0.06

YEARLY TIGER HITTING LEADERS – HOME RUN PERCENTAGE

Year	Player	HR %
1901	**Sport McAllister**	**0.9**
1902	Jimmy Barrett	0.7
1903	Sam Crawford	0.7
1904	Sam Crawford	0.3
	Ed Gremminger	0.3
	Matty McIntyre	0.3
1905	**Sam Crawford**	**1.0**
1906	Charley O'Leary	0.4
	Germany Schaefer	0.4
1907	Ty Cobb	0.8
1908	**Sam Crawford**	**1.1**
1909	**Ty Cobb**	**1.4**
1910	**Ty Cobb**	**1.4**
1911	Ty Cobb	1.2
1912	Ty Cobb	1.1
1913	Sam Crawford	1.3
1914	Sam Crawford	1.2
1915	George Burns	1.1
1916	George Burns	0.8
	Ty Cobb	0.8
1917	Bobby Veach	1.2
1918	**Harry Heilmann**	**1.5**
1919	**Ira Flagstead**	**1.5**
1920	**Bobby Veach**	**1.6**
1921	**Harry Heilmann**	**2.8**
1922	**Harry Heilmann**	**4.0**
1923	Harry Heilmann	2.9
1924	Heinie Manush	1.9
1925	Ty Cobb	2.4
1926	Heinie Manush	2.5
1927	Harry Heilmann	2.3
1928	Pinky Hargrave	2.8
1929	Dale Alexander	3.6
1930	Dale Alexander	3.0
1931	John Stone	1.5
1932	Charlie Gehringer	2.7
1933	Hank Greenberg	2.4
1934	Hank Greenberg	3.9
1935	**Hank Greenberg**	**5.1**
1936	Goose Goslin	3.6
1937	**Rudy York**	**8.4**
1938	**Hank Greenberg**	**8.5**
1939	Earl Averill	5.5
	Hank Greenberg	5.5
1940	Hank Greenberg	6.1
1941	Rudy York	3.9
1942	Rudy York	3.2
1943	Rudy York	5.1
1944	Dick Wakefield	3.6
1945	Roy Cullenbine	2.8
1946	Hank Greenberg	7.3
1947	Roy Cullenbine	4.0
1948	Pat Mullin	4.0
1949	Pat Mullin	3.4
1950	Vic Wertz	4.1
1951	Vic Wertz	4.6
1952	Walt Dropo	4.7
1953	Ray Boone	5.0
1954	Ray Boone	3.2
1955	Frank House	4.2
1956	Charlie Maxwell	4.7
1957	Charlie Maxwell	4.1
1958	Gail Harris	4.0
1959	Charlie Maxwell	5.1

Don Demeter

Year	Player	HR %
1960	Rocky Colavito	5.7
1961	Rocky Colavito	6.4
1962	Al Kaline	6.4
1963	Norm Cash	4.4
	Al Kaline	4.4
1964	Don Demeter	4.7
1965	Norm Cash	5.4
1966	Al Kaline	5.1
1967	Al Kaline	4.5
1968	Willie Horton	6.2
1969	Willie Horton	4.9
1970	Willie Horton	4.2
	Jim Northrup	4.2
1971	Norm Cash	6.1
1972	Norm Cash	4.4
1973	Norm Cash	4.5
1974	Bill Freehan	3.6
1975	Willie Horton	3.7
1976	Ben Oglivie	4.6
1977	Jason Thompson	4.6
1978	Jason Thompson	3.9
1979	Steve Kemp	4.6
1980	Champ Summers	4.2
1981	John Wockenfuss	4.5
1982	Lance Parrish	6.0
1983	Chet Lemon	4.2
1984	Lance Parrish	5.2
1985	Darrell Evans	6.7
1986	Lance Parrish	5.9
1987	Matt Nokes	6.3
1988	Darrell Evans	4.2
1989	Lou Whitaker	4.7
1990	Cecil Fielder	8.0
1991	Cecil Fielder	6.2
1992	Rob Deer	7.1
1993	Mickey Tettleton	5.1
1994	Kirk Gibson	6.1
1995	Cecil Fielder	5.4
1996	Tony Clark	6.7
1997	Melvin Nieves	5.0
1998	Tony Clark	5.1
1999	Dean Palmer	6.0
2000	Dean Palmer	4.8
2001	Robert Fick	4.2
2002	Randall Simon	3.8
2003	Craig Monroe	5.0
	Eric Munson	5.0
2004	Eric Munson	5.3
2005	Chris Shelton	4.2
2006	Marcus Thames	6.7
2007	Gary Sheffield	4.2
2008	Marcus Thames	7.3
2009	Ryan Raburn	5.5
2010	Miguel Cabrera	5.9
2011	Miguel Cabrera	4.4
2012	Miguel Cabrera	6.3
2013	Miguel Cabrera	6.7
2014	Victor Martinez	5.0
2015	J.D. Martinez	5.8
2016	Miguel Cabrera	5.6
2017	Justin Upton	5.4
2018	Nicholas Castellanos	3.4
2019	John Hicks	3.9
2020	JaCoby Jones	4.6
2021	Eric Haase	5.8

Year	Player	HR
1901	**D. Holmes, S. McAllister**	**3**
1902	**Jimmy Barrett**	**3**
1903	Jimmy Barrett	2
1904	Bill Donovan	1
	Ed Gremminger	1
	Charley O'Leary	1
1905	S. Crawford, C. Hickman	2
1906	S. Crawford, B. Lowe	1
	Charley O'Leary	1
1907	Ty Cobb, Red Downs,	1
	Germany Schaefer	1
1908	Sam Crawford	2
1909	**Ty Cobb**	**6**
1910	Ty Cobb, Sam Crawford	4
1911	Ty Cobb	5
1912	Sam Crawford	2
1913	Sam Crawford	3
1914	Sam Crawford	3
1915	G. Burns. M. Kavanagh	3
1916	Ty Cobb, Bobby Veach	2
1917	George Burns, Ty Cobb,	1
	George Cunningham,	1
	H. Heilmann, B. Veach	1
1918	Harry Heilmann	2
1919	I. Flagstead, H. Heilmann	3
1920	H. Heilmann, B. Veach	5
1921	**Harry Heilmann**	**7**
1922	**Harry Heilmann**	**8**
1923	**Harry Heilmann**	**11**
1924	Harry Heilmann	5
1925	Harry Heilmann	6
1926	Heinie Manush	8
1927	Harry Heilmann	10
1928	Harry Heilmann	10
1929	**Marty McManus**	**12**
1930	Dale Alexander	10
1931	Roy Johnson	5
1932	Charlie Gehringer	6
1933	Hank Greenberg	9
1934	**Hank Greenberg**	**15**
1935	**Hank Greenberg**	**18**
1936	Goose Goslin	12
1937	**Hank Greenberg**	**25**
1938	**Hank Greenberg**	**39**
1939	Hank Greenberg	16
1940	Hank Greenberg	27
1941	Rudy York	18
1942	Rudy York	14

Year	Player	HR
1943	Rudy York	19
1944	Rudy York	13
1945	Roy Cullenbine	11
1946	Hank Greenberg	29
1947	Roy Cullenbine	15
1948	Pat Mullin	11
1949	Vic Wertz	12
1950	Vic Wertz	16
1951	Vic Wertz	13
1952	Walt Dropo	11
1953	Bob Nieman	12
1954	Ray Boone	10
1955	Al Kaline	16
1956	Ray Boone	16
1957	Charlie Maxwell	15
1958	Gail Harris	13
1959	Charlie Maxwell	21

Bobby Lowe

Year	Player	HR
1960	Rocky Colavito	17
1961	Norm Cash	21
1962	Norm Cash	25
1963	Al Kaline	22
1964	Norm Cash	14
1965	Norm Cash	17
1966	Norm Cash, Al Kaline	18
1967	Al Kaline	15
1968	Willie Horton	20
1969	Willie Horton, Al Kaline	13
	Jim Northrup	13
1970	W. Horton, J. Northrup	13
1971	Norm Cash	14
1972	Norm Cash	11
1973	G. Brown, Jim Northrup,	9
	Mickey Stanley	9
1974	Bill Freehan	10

Year	Player	HR
1975	Dan Meyer	8
1976	Rusty Staub	9
1977	Jason Thompson	15
1978	Rusty Staub	16
1979	S. Kemp, C. Summers	17
1980	Steve Kemp	15
1981	Lance Parrish	8
1982	Lance Parrish	22
1983	Chet Lemon	14
1984	Lance Parrish	13
1985	Darrell Evans	21
1986	D. Evans, Kirk Gibson	15
1987	Darrell Evans	19
1988	Darrell Evans	14
1989	Lou Whitaker	17
1990	Cecil Fielder	25
1991	Cecil Fielder	27
1992	Cecil Fielder	18
	Mickey Tettleton	18
1993	Cecil Fielder	20
1994	C. Fielder, Tony Phillips	12
1995	Cecil Fielder	16
1996	Tony Clark	17
1997	Tony Clark	18
1998	Damion Easley	19
1999	Dean Palmer	24
2000	Dean Palmer	15
2001	Robert Fick	8
2002	Randall Simon	13
2003	C. Monroe, D. Young	10
2004	Eric Munson	13
2005	Carlos Pena	14
2006	B. Inge, Craig Monroe	12
2007	Magglio Ordonez	17
2008	Miguel Cabrera	19
2009	Miguel Cabrera	19
2010	Miguel Cabrera	17
2011	Miguel Cabrera	15
2012	Miguel Cabrera	28
2013	Miguel Cabrera	17
2014	Victor Martinez	15
2015	J.D. Martinez	20
2016	Miguel Cabrera	20
2017	Nicholas Castellanos	14
2018	Jeimer Candelario	10
	Nicholas Castellanos	10
2019	JaCoby Jones	7
2020	Jonathan Schoop	6
2021	Robbie Grossman	12

Year	Player	HR
1901	**Jimmy Barrett**	**3**
1902	Doc Casey, Ducky Holmes	2
1903	**Sam Crawford**	**3**
1904	S. Crawford, C. Hickman,	2
	Matty McIntyre	2
1905	**Sam Crawford**	**4**
1906	Germany Schaefer	2
1907	**Ty Cobb, Sam Crawford**	**4**
1908	**Sam Crawford**	**5**
1909	Ty Cobb, Sam Crawford	3
1910	Ty Cobb	4
1911	Ty Cobb, Sam Crawford	3
1912	**Ty Cobb**	**6**
1913	Ty Cobb, Sam Crawford	4
1914	Sam Crawford	5
1915	George Burns, Ty Cobb,	2
	Sam Crawford, B. Veach	2
1916	George Burns	4
1917	**Bobby Veach**	**7**
1918	Cobb, Heilmann, Veach	3
1919	Harry Heilmann	5
1920	Bobby Veach	6
1921	**Harry Heilmann**	**12**
1922	**Harry Heilmann**	**13**
1923	Harry Heilmann	7
1924	Heinie Manush	6
1925	Ty Cobb	10
1926	Heinie Manush	6
1927	H. Manush, Oscar Stanage	5
1928	Pinky Hargrave	8
1929	**Dale Alexander**	**15**
1930	Dale Alexander	10
1931	John Stone	8
1932	Charlie Gehringer	13
1933	John Stone, Gee Walker	7
1934	Hank Greenberg	11
1935	**Hank Greenberg**	**18**
1936	Goose Goslin	12
1937	**Rudy York**	**18**
1938	**Hank Greenberg**	**19**
1939	Hank Greenberg	17
1940	H. Greenberg, Rudy York	14
1941	Rudy York	9
1942	Rudy York	7
1943	Rudy York	15

Year	Player	HR
1944	Rudy York	5
1945	Rudy York	9
1946	Hank Greenberg	15
1947	Roy Cullenbine	9
1948	Pat Mullin	12
1949	Vic Wertz	8
1950	Hoot Evers, Vic Wertz	11
1951	Vic Wertz	14
1952	Walt Dropo	12
1953	Ray Boone	14
1954	Ray Boone	10
1955	Al Kaline	11
1956	Al Kaline, C. Maxwell	14
1957	Al Kaline	13
1958	Frank Bolling	11
1959	Al Kaline	11

Germany Schaefer

Year	Player	HR
1960	Rocky Colavito	18
1961	**Rocky Colavito**	**27**
1962	Rocky Colavito	18
1963	Rocky Colavito	9
1964	Don Demeter	12
1965	Willie Horton	14
1966	Willie Horton	15
1967	Norm Cash, Bill Freehan	12
1968	Willie Horton	16
1969	Willie Horton	15
1970	Jim Northrup	11
1971	Norm Cash	18
1972	Norm Cash	11
1973	Norm Cash, Willie Horton	11
1974	Willie Horton	9
1975	Willie Horton	19

Year	Player	HR
1976	Jason Thompson	10
1977	Jason Thompson	16
1978	Jason Thompson	13
1979	Lance Parrish	11
1980	Lance Parrish	17
1981	K. Gibson, J. Wockenfuss	5
1982	Larry Herndon	14
1983	Lance Parrish	15
1984	Lance Parrish	20
1985	Darrell Evans	19
1986	D. Evans, Lance Parrish	14
1987	Matt Nokes	18
1988	D. Evans, Alan Trammell	8
1989	Lou Whitaker	11
1990	Cecil Fielder	26
1991	Cecil Fielder	17
1992	Rob Deer	19
1993	Mickey Tettleton	16
1994	Cecil Fielder	16
1995	Cecil Fielder	15
1996	Cecil Fielder	17
1997	Tony Clark	14
1998	Tony Clark	16
1999	Tony Clark	19
2000	Bobby Higginson	18
2001	Robert Fick	11
2002	Carlos Pena	7
2003	Dmitri Young	19
2004	Carlos Pena	17
2005	Craig Monroe, D. Young	11
2006	C. Monroe, M. Ordonez	16
2007	Curtis Granderson	13
2008	Miguel Cabrera	18
2009	Curtis Granderson	20
2010	Miguel Cabrera	21
2011	Miguel Cabrera	15
2012	Miguel Cabrera	16
2013	**Miguel Cabrera**	**27**
2014	Victor Martinez	17
2015	J.D. Martinez	18
2016	Miguel Cabrera	18
2017	Justin Upton	15
2018	Nicholas Castellanos	13
2019	Brandon Dixon	10
2020	Miguel Cabrera	5
2021	Eric Haase	14

Year	Player	HR
1901	Three Batters	1
1902	**Jimmy Barrett**	**2**
1903	Billy Lush	1
1904	25 Batters	0
1905	**Sam Crawford**	**3**
1906	Germany Schaefer	2
1907	Ty Cobb	2
1908	Sam Crawford	2
1909	**Ty Cobb**	**4**
1910	Three Batters	2
1911	**Ty Cobb**	**4**
1912	Donie Bush, Ty Cobb	2
1913	**Sam Crawford**	**4**
1914	Sam Crawford	3
1915	George Burns	2
1916	Four Batters	1
1917	Harry Heilmann	2
1918	Bobby Veach	2
1919	H. Heilmann, Ira Flagstead	2
1920	**Bobby Veach**	**5**
1921	**H. Heilmann, Bobby Veach**	**5**
1922	Harry Heilmann	3
1923	**Harry Heilmann**	**5**
1924	Harry Heilmann	3
1925	**Harry Heilmann**	**10**
1926	Heinie Manush	4
1927	Harry Heilmann	5
1928	H. Heilmann, Harry Rice	3
1929	H. Heilmann, M. McManus	5
1930	D. Alexander, C. Gehringer	3
1931	Roy Johnson	4
1932	Three Batters	5
1933	John Stone	4
1934	Hank Greenberg	7
1935	**Hank Greenberg**	**12**
1936	Al Simmons	5
1937	Hank Greenberg	10
1938	H. Greenberg, Rudy York	9
1939	Rudy York	6
1940	**Hank Greenberg**	**13**
1941	Rudy York	9
1942	Rudy York	6
1943	Rudy York	7
1944	Three Players	1
1945	Roy Cullenbine	3
1946	Hank Greenberg	10
1947	Hoot Evers	6
1948	Hoot Evers	6
1949	Vic Wertz	8
1950	Vic Wertz	8
1951	Hoot Evers, Jerry Priddy	5
1952	Walt Dropo	9
1953	Ray Boone	5
1954	Ray Boone	4
1955	Ray Boone	9
1956	R. Boone, Harvey Kuenn	5
1957	Ray Boone	5
1958	Gail Harris	3
1959	Al Kaline	9
1960	Rocky Colavito	8
1961	Rocky Colavito	10
1962	Steve Boros	8
1963	Al Kaline	10
1964	Don Demeter	11
1965	Willie Horton	10
1966	**Norm Cash, W. Horton**	**13**
1967	**Al Kaline**	**14**
1968	**Willie Horton**	**16**
1969	Al Kaline	15
1970	Three Players	7
1971	Willie Horton	10
1972	Mickey Stanley	7
1973	Frank Howard	12
1974	Ed Brinkman, W. Horton	9
1975	Willie Horton	11
1976	Rusty Staub	7
1977	Ron LeFlore	11
1978	Lance Parrish	13
1979	John Wockenfuss	14
1980	**L. Parrish, J. Wockenfuss**	**16**
1981	L. Parrish, J. Wockenfuss	6
1982	Lance Parrish	12
1983	Larry Herndon	11
1984	Lance Parrish	14
1985	Darrell Evans, L. Parrish	9
1986	Darrell Evans	9
1987	Alan Trammell	11
1988	Chet Lemon	9
1989	Gary Ward	9
1990	**Cecil Fielder**	**25**
1991	Cecil Fielder	13
1992	Rob Deer	14
1993	Travis Fryman	9
1994	Travis Fryman	7
1995	Cecil Fielder, Juan Samuel	6
1996	Cecil Fielder	7
1997	Tony Clark	10
1998	Tony Clark	10
1999	Dean Palmer	10
2000	Juan Encarnacion	7
2001	Bobby Higginson	8
2002	Robert Fick, Carlos Pena	5
2003	Craig Monroe	14
2004	Carlos Pena, Dmitri Young	8
2005	Craig Monroe	7
2006	Magglio Ordonez	9
2007	Magglio Ordonez	8
2008	Marcus Thames	13
2009	Ryan Raburn	12
2010	Brandon Inge, Ryan Raburn	7
2011	Jhonny Peralta, R. Raburn	7
2012	Delmon Young	7
2013	Miguel Cabrera	13
2014	Victor Martinez	12
2015	J.D. Martinez	10
2016	M. Cabrera, J. McCann	9
2017	Nicholas Castellanos	11
2018	Jeimer Candelario	6
	Nicholas Castellanos	6
2019	M. Cabrera, N. Castellanos	4
2020	M. Cabrera, J. Candelario	2
	N. Goodrum, J. Jones	2
2021	Eric Haase	11

Al Simmons

Year	Player	HR
1901	**Jimmy Barrett**	**4**
1902	Three Players	2
1903	**Sam Crawford**	**4**
1904	S. Crawford, M. McIntyre	2
1905	Sam Crawford	3
1906	Bill Coughlin, S. Crawford	2
1907	**Sam Crawford**	**4**
1908	**Sam Crawford**	**5**
1909	**Ty Cobb**	**5**
1910	**Ty Cobb**	**5**
1911	Ty Cobb, Sam Crawford	4
1912	Ty Cobb	4
1913	**Sam Crawford**	**5**
1914	**Sam Crawford**	**5**
1915	Sam Crawford	4
1916	**Ty Cobb**	**5**
1917	**Bobby Veach**	**7**
1918	Harry Heilmann	5
1919	Harry Heilmann	6
1920	**Harry Heilmann**	**7**
1921	**Harry Heilmann**	**14**
1922	**Harry Heilmann**	**18**
1923	Harry Heilmann	13
1924	Heinie Manush	9
1925	Ty Cobb	8
1926	Heinie Manush	10
1927	Harry Heilmann	9
1928	Harry Heilmann	11
1929	**Dale Alexander**	**21**
1930	Dale Alexander	17
1931	John Stone	7
1932	Charlie Gehringer	14
1933	Charlie Gehringer	10
1934	Hank Greenberg	19
1935	**Hank Greenberg**	**24**
1936	Goose Goslin	22
1937	**Hank Greenberg**	**30**
1938	**Hank Greenberg**	**49**
1939	Hank Greenberg	29
1940	Hank Greenberg	28
1941	Rudy York	18
1942	Rudy York	15
1943	Rudy York	27
1944	Rudy York	17
1945	Rudy York	16
1946	Hank Greenberg	34
1947	Roy Cullenbine	21
1948	Pat Mullin	20
1949	Aaron Robinson	13
1950	Vic Wertz	19
1951	Vic Wertz	24
1952	Walt Dropo	14
1953	Ray Boone	17
1954	Ray Boone	16
1955	Al Kaline	21
1956	Charlie Maxwell	25
1957	Al Kaline, Charlie Maxwell	22
1958	Gail Harris	17
1959	Charlie Maxwell	26
1960	Rocky Colavito	27

Bill Coughlin

Year	Player	HR
1961	Norm Cash	36
1962	Norm Cash	33
1963	Norm Cash	22
1964	Norm Cash	21
1965	Norm Cash	22
1966	Al Kaline	22
1967	Norm Cash	19
1968	Norm Cash	21
1969	Willie Horton	20
1970	Jim Northrup	17
1971	Norm Cash	24
1972	Norm Cash	21
1973	Norm Cash	19
1974	Bill Freehan	11
1975	Willie Horton	14
1976	Jason Thompson	16
1977	Jason Thompson	22
1978	Jason Thompson	16
1979	Champ Summers	19
1980	Steve Kemp, C. Summers	15
1981	Kirk Gibson, Steve Kemp	5
1982	Lance Parrish	20
1983	Chet Lemon, L. Parrish	18
1984	Lance Parrish	19
1985	Darrell Evans	31
1986	Kirk Gibson	21
1987	Darrell Evans	29
1988	Darrell Evans	22
1989	Lou Whitaker	23
1990	Cecil Fielder	26
1991	Cecil Fielder	31
1992	Cecil Fielder	26
1993	Mickey Tettleton	25
1994	Cecil Fielder	22
1995	Cecil Fielder	25
1996	Bobby Higginson	25
1997	Tony Clark	22
1998	Tony Clark	24
1999	Dean Palmer	28
2000	Bobby Higginson	26
2001	Robert Fick	17
2002	Randall Simon	16
2003	Dmitri Young	20
2004	Carlos Pena	19
2005	Dmitri Young	17
2006	Craig Monroe	26
2007	Granderson, Ordonez	20
2008	Miguel Cabrera	28
2009	Curtis Granderson	28
2010	Miguel Cabrera	32
2011	Miguel Cabrera	24
2012	Miguel Cabrera	40
2013	Miguel Cabrera	31
2014	Victor Martinez	20
2015	J.D. Martinez	28
2016	Miguel Cabrera	29
2017	Justin Upton	18
2018	Nicholas Castellanos	17
2019	Brandon Dixon	12
2020	Miguel Cabrera	8
2021	Robbie Grossman	15

Year	Player	HR
1901	**J. Barrett, Ducky Holmes**	**4**
1902	**Jimmy Barrett**	**4**
1903	**Sam Crawford**	**4**
1904	S. Crawford, M. McIntyre	2
1905	**Sam Crawford**	**6**
1906	Sam Crawford	2
1907	Ty Cobb	5
1908	**Sam Crawford**	**7**
1909	**Ty Cobb**	**9**
1910	Ty Cobb	8
1911	Ty Cobb	8
1912	Ty Cobb	7
1913	**Sam Crawford**	**9**
1914	Sam Crawford	8
1915	Sam Crawford	4
1916	Ty Cobb	5
1917	Bobby Veach	8
1918	Ty Cobb, Bobby Veach	3
1919	Bobby Veach	3
1920	**Bobby Veach**	**11**
1921	**Bobby Veach**	**16**
1922	Bobby Veach	9
1923	Ty Cobb	6
1924	Heinie Manush	9
1925	Ty Cobb	12
1926	Heinie Manush	14
1927	Heinie Manush	6
1928	C. Gehringer, Harry Rice	6
1929	Charlie Gehringer	13
1930	**Charlie Gehringer**	**16**
1931	John Stone	10
1932	**Charlie Gehringer**	**19**
1933	Charlie Gehringer	12
1934	Goose Goslin	13
1935	Charlie Gehringer	19
1936	**Goose Goslin**	**24**
1937	Charlie Gehringer	14
1938	Charlie Gehringer	20
1939	Charlie Gehringer	16
1940	Charlie Gehringer	10
1941	Bruce Campbell	15
1942	Bob Harris	9
1943	Dick Wakefield	7
1944	Dick Wakefield	12
1945	Eddie Mayo	10

Year	Player	HR
1946	Dick Wakefield	12
1947	Pat Mullin	15
1948	Pat Mullin	23
1949	Vic Wertz	20
1950	**Vic Wertz**	**27**
1951	**Vic Wertz**	**27**
1952	Pat Mullin	7
1953	Jim Delsing	11
1954	Frank House	9
1955	Frank House	15
1956	**Charlie Maxwell**	**28**
1957	Charlie Maxwell	24
1958	Gail Harris	20
1959	**Charlie Maxwell**	**31**
1960	Charlie Maxwell	24
1961	**Norm Cash**	**41**

Jim Delsing

Year	Player	HR
1962	Norm Cash	39
1963	Norm Cash	26
1964	Dick McAuliffe	24
1965	Norm Cash	30
1966	Norm Cash	32
1967	N. Cash, Dick McAuliffe	22
1968	Norm Cash	25
1969	Jim Northrup	25
1970	Jim Northrup	24
1971	Norm Cash	32
1972	Norm Cash	22
1973	Norm Cash	19
1974	Jim Northrup	11
1975	Ben Oglivie	9
1976	Jason Thompson	17
1977	Jason Thompson	31

Year	Player	HR
1978	Jason Thompson	26
1979	Steve Kemp	26
1980	Steve Kemp	21
1981	Kirk Gibson, Steve Kemp	9
1982	Lou Whitaker	15
1983	Kirk Gibson	15
1984	Kirk Gibson	27
1985	Darrell Evans	40
1986	Darrell Evans	29
1987	Darrell Evans	34
1988	Darrell Evans	22
1989	Lou Whitaker	28
1990	Lou Whitaker	18
1991	Lou Whitaker	23
1992	Lou Whitaker	19
1993	Kirk Gibson	13
1994	Kirk Gibson	23
1995	Bobby Higginson	14
1996	Bobby Higginson	26
1997	Bobby Higginson	27
1998	Luis Gonzalez	23
1999	Bobby Higginson	12
2000	Bobby Higginson	30
2001	Robert Fick	19
2002	Randall Simon	19
2003	Eric Munson, Carlos Pena	18
2004	Carlos Pena	27
2005	Carlos Pena	18
2006	Curtis Granderson	19
2007	Curtis Granderson	23
2008	Curtis Granderson	22
2009	Curtis Granderson	30
2010	Brennan Boesch	14
2011	Alex Avila	19
2012	Prince Fielder	30
2013	Prince Fielder	25
2014	Alex Avila	11
2015	Anthony Gose	5
2016	Steven Moya	5
2017	Alex Avila	11
2018	Leonys Martin	9
2019	Christin Stewart	10
2020	Christin Stewart	3
2021	Akil Baddoo	13

Year	Player	HR
1901	**K. Elberfeld, Doc Nance**	**3**
1902	Kid Elberfeld	1
1903	Charlie Carr	2
1904	E. Grimminger, C. O'Leary	1
1905	Germany Schaeffer	2
1906	Coughlin, O'Leary, Schaefer	2
1907	R. Downs, G. Schaefer	1
1908	**Germany Schaefer**	**3**
1909	George Moriarty	1
1910	**Jim Delahanty**	**3**
1911	**J. Delahanty, O. Stanage**	**3**
1912	Baldy Louden	1
1913	Del Gainer, Ossie Vitt	2
1914	**George Burns**	**5**
1915	**George Burns**	**5**
1916	George Burns	4
1917	**Harry Heilmann**	**5**
1918	**Harry Heilmann**	**5**
1919	**Harry Heilmann**	**8**
1920	**Harry Heilmann**	**9**
1921	**Harry Heilmann**	**19**
1922	**Harry Heilmann**	**21**
1923	Harry Heilmann	18
1924	Harry Heilmann	10
1925	Harry Heilmann	13
1926	Harry Heilmann	9
1927	Harry Heilmann	14
1928	Harry Heilmann	14
1929	**Dale Alexander**	**25**
1930	Dale Alexander	20
1931	Alexander, McManus	3
	Marv Owen	3
1932	Gee Walker	8
1933	Hank Greenberg	12
1934	**Hank Greenberg**	**26**
1935	**Hank Greenberg**	**36**
1936	Al Simmons	13
1937	**Hank Greenberg**	**40**
1938	**Hank Greenberg**	**58**
1939	Hank Greenberg	33
1940	Hank Greenberg	41
1941	Rudy York	27
1942	Rudy York	21
1943	Rudy York	34
1944	Rudy York	18

Year	Player	HR
1945	Rudy York	18
1946	Hank Greenberg	44
1947	Eddie Lake	12
1948	Hoot Evers	10
1949	Johnny Groth	11
1950	Hoot Evers	21
1951	Hoot Evers	11
1952	Walt Dropo	23
1953	Ray Boone	22
1954	Ray Boone	20
1955	Al Kaline	27
1956	Al Kaline	27
1957	Al Kaline	23
1958	Al Kaline	16
1959	Al Kaline	27
1960	Rocky Colavito	35

Baldy Louden

Year	Player	HR
1961	Rocky Colavito	45
1962	Rocky Colavito	37
1963	Al Kaline	27
1964	Don Demeter	22
1965	Willie Horton	29
1966	Al Kaline	29
1967	Al Kaline	25
1968	Willie Horton	36
1969	Willie Horton	28
1970	Willie Horton	17
1971	Willie Horton	22
1972	Mickey Stanley	14
1973	W. Horton, M. Stanley	17
1974	Bill Freehan	18
1975	Willie Horton	25
1976	Willie Horton	14

Year	Player	HR
1977	Ron LeFlore	16
1978	Ron LeFlore	12
1979	Lance Parrish	19
1980	Lance Parrish	24
1981	Lance Parrish	10
1982	Lance Parrish	32
1983	Lance Parrish	27
1984	Lance Parrish	33
1985	Lance Parrish	28
1986	Lance Parrish	22
1987	Alan Trammell	28
1988	Chet Lemon	17
1989	Mike Heath	10
1990	Cecil Fielder	51
1991	Cecil Fielder	44
1992	Cecil Fielder	35
1993	Cecil Fielder	30
1994	Cecil Fielder	28
1995	Cecil Fielder	31
1996	Cecil Fielder	26
1997	D. Easley, Travis Fryman	22
1998	Damion Easley	27
1999	Dean Palmer	38
2000	Dean Palmer	29
2001	J. Encarnacion, S. Halter	12
2002	Shane Halter	10
2003	Craig Monroe	23
2004	I. Rodriguez, R. White	19
2005	Craig Monroe	20
2006	Craig Monroe	28
2007	Magglio Ordonez	28
2008	Miguel Cabrera	37
2009	Miguel Cabrera	34
2010	Miguel Cabrera	38
2011	Miguel Cabrera	30
2012	Miguel Cabrera	44
2013	Miguel Cabrera	44
2014	Miguel Cabrera	25
2015	J.D. Martinez	38
2016	Miguel Cabrera	38
2017	Justin Upton	28
2018	Nicholas Castellanos	23
2019	Brandon Dixon	15
2020	Miguel Cabrera	10
2021	E. Haase, R. Grossman	22

Year	Player	HR
1901	**Kid Gleason**	**3**
	Sport McAllister	**3**
1902	**Doc Casey**	**3**
1903	Billy Lush	1
1904	Bill Donovan	1
1905	Three Switch Hitters	0
1906	Three Switch Hitters	0
1907	Two Switch Hitters	0
1908	Boss Schmidt	1
1909	Boss Schmidt	1
1910	**Donie Bush**	**3**
1911	Donie Bush, Bill Donovan	1
1912	Donie Bush	2
1913	Donie Bush	1
1914	Three Switch Hitters	0
1915	Donie Bush	1
1916	Ralph Young	1
1917	Ralph Young	1
1918	Six Switch Hitters	0
1919	Ralph Young	1
1920	Donie Bush	1
1921	**Lu Blue**	**5**
1922	**Lu Blue**	**6**
1923	Lu Blue	1
1924	Lu Blue	2
1925	Lu Blue	3
1926	Lu Blue	1
1927	Lu Blue	1
1928	**Pinky Hargrave**	**10**
1929	Pinky Hargrave	3
1930	Pinky Hargrave	5
1931	Billy Rogell	2
1932	Billy Rogell	9
1933	Billy Rogell	0
1934	Billy Rogell	3
1935	Billy Rogell	6
1936	Billy Rogell	6
1937	Billy Rogell	8
1938	Billy Rogell	3
1939	Roy Cullenbine	6
1940	Two Switch Hitters	0
1941	Archie McKain	0
1942	Charlie Fuchs	0
1943	No Switch Hitters	0
1944	No Switch Hitters	0

Year	Player	HR
1945	**Roy Cullenbine**	**18**
1946	Roy Cullenbine	15
1947	**Roy Cullenbine**	**24**
1948	Ted Gray	0
1949	Ted Gray	0
1950	Ted Gray	0
1951	Ted Gray	0
1952	George Lerchen	1
1953	Two Switch Hitters	0
1954	Two Switch Hitters	0
1955	Steve Gromek	0
1956	Three Switch Hitters	0
1957	Dave Philley	2
1958	No Switch Hitters	0
1959	No Switch Hitters	0
1960	Casey Wise	2

Dave Philley

Year	Player	HR
1961	Ron Nischwitz	0
1962	Two Switch Hitters	0
1963	Mickey Lolich	0
1964	Two Switch Hitters	0
1965	Three Switch Hitters	0
1966	Mickey Lolich	0
1967	Mickey Lolich	0
1968	Two Switch Hitters	0
1969	Tom Tresh	13
1970	Three Switch Hitters	0
1971	Two Switch Hitters	0
1972	Two Switch Hitters	0
1973	Three Switch Hitters	0
1974	Mickey Lolich	0
1975	Gene Michael	3
1976	Jerry Manuel	0

Year	Player	HR
1977	Tito Fuentes	5
1978	Bob Sykes	0
1979	Rick Peters	0
1980	Rick Peters	2
1981	Two Switch Hitters	0
1982	Howard Johnson	4
1983	Howard Johnson	3
1984	Howard Johnson	12
1985	Nelson Simmons	10
1986	Dave Collins	1
1987	Jim Walewander	1
1988	Gary Pettis	3
1989	M. Brumley, T. Lovullo,	1
	Gary Pettis, Doug Strange	1
1990	Tony Phillips	8
1991	**Mickey Tettleton**	**31**
1992	**Mickey Tettleton**	**32**
1993	**Mickey Tettleton**	**32**
1994	Tony Phillips	19
1995	Tony Clark	3
1996	Tony Clark	27
1997	**Tony Clark**	**32**
1998	**Tony Clark**	**34**
1999	Tony Clark	31
2000	Tony Clark	13
2001	Tony Clark	16
2002	Dmitri Young	7
2003	Dmitri Young	29
2004	Carlos Guillen	20
2005	Dmitri Young	21
2006	Carlos Guillen	19
2007	Carlos Guillen	21
2008	Carlos Guillen	10
2009	Carlos Guillen	11
2010	Carlos Guillen	6
2011	Victor Martinez	12
2012	Ramon Santiago	2
2013	Victor Martinez	14
2014	Victor Martinez	32
2015	Victor Martinez	11
2016	Victor Martinez	27
2017	Victor Martinez	10
2018	Jeimer Candelario	19
2019	Niko Goodrum	12
2020	Jeimer Candelario	7
2021	Robbie Grossman	23

Year	Player	HR
1901	**Kid Gleason, D. Holmes**	**2**
1902	Buelow, Casey, Gleason	1
1903	**Sam Crawford**	**2**
1904	**Sam Crawford**	**2**
1905	**Sam Crawford**	**4**
1906	S. Crawford, G. Schaefer	1
1907	Ty Cobb	2
1908	**Ty Cobb**	**4**
1909	**Ty Cobb**	**9**
1910	Ty Cobb	6
1911	Ty Cobb	4
1912	Sam Crawford	2
1913	Sam Crawford	6
1914	Ty Cobb	2
1915	George Burns, D. Bush,	1
	Ty Cobb, Marty Kavanagh	1
1916	Ty Cobb	3
1917	Ty Cobb	3
1918	Ty Cobb, Harry Heilmann	2
1919	Harry Heilmann	1
1920	H. Heilmann, Bob Jones	1
1921	Ty Cobb	4
1922	Bob Jones	3
1923	Fred Haney	2
1924	Heinie Manush	1
1925	Lu Blue	2
1926	Heinie Manush	2
1927	B. Fothergill, C. Gehringer,	1
	Jackie Tavener	1
1928	Chick Galloway	1
	C. Gehringer, John Stone	1
1929	Roy Johnson	2
1930	Akers, Gehringer, Rice	1
1931	John Stone	1
1932	John Stone	1
1933	29 Batters	0
1934	Hank Greenberg	1
1935	C. Gehringer, Billy Rogell	1
1936	M. Cochrane, G. Goslin	1
1937	30 Batters	0
1938	Christman, Greenberg	1
1939	Pete Fox, C. Gehringer	1
1940	B. Campbell, B. McCosky	1
1941	Bob Harris, Pat Mullin	1
1942	Barney McCosky	1
1943	27 Batters	0
1944	Doc Cramer, D. Wakefield	2
1945	36 Batters	0
1946	36 Batters	0
1947	27 Batters	0
1948	32 Batters	0
1949	Johnny Groth	1
1950	Hoot Evers	2
1951	32 Batters	0
1952	44 Batters	0
1953	Don Lund	1
1954	35 Batters	0
1955	Bill Tuttle	1
1956	37 Batters	0
1957	40 Batters	0
1958	39 Batters	0

Juan Gonzalez

Year	Player	HR
1959	Al Kaline	1
1960	37 Batters	0
1961	Norm Cash	1
1962	Jake Wood	1
1963	Jake Wood	1
1964	Al Kaline, Jerry Lumpe	1
1965	Norm Cash, D. McAuliffe	1
1966	Willie Horton	1
1967	Dick McAuliffe	1
1968	32 Batters	0
1969	32 Batters	0
1970	34 Batters	0
1971	Willie Horton, Tony Taylor	1
1972	38 Batters	0
1973	22 Batters	0
1974	25 Batters	0
1975	Ron LeFlore	1
1976	Ben Oglivie	1
1977	Ron LeFlore, Steve Kemp	1
1978	Lou Whitaker	1
1979	24 Batters	0
1980	20 Batters	0
1981	19 Batters	0
1982	21 Batters	0
1983	Kirk Gibson, Lou Whitaker	1
1984	21 Batters	0
1985	23 Batters	0
1986	Mike Heath	1
1987	25 Batters	0
1988	22 Batters	0
1989	24 Batters	0
1990	23 Batters	0
1991	Lou Whitaker	1
1992	19 Batters	0
1993	18 Batters	0
1994	18 Batters	0
1995	23 Batters	0
1996	27 Batters	0
1997	Bobby Higginson	1
1998	32 Batters	0
1999	28 Batters	0
2000	Juan Gonzalez	1
2001	D. Easley, Shane Halter	1
2002	Wendell Magee	1
2003	Shane Halter	1
2004	Carlos Guillen	1
2005	Curtis Granderson	1
2006	27 Batters	0
2007	Curtis Granderson	1
2008	28 Batters	0
2009	29 Batters	0
2010	28 Batters	0
2011	26 Batters	0
2012	Austin Jackson	1
2013	25 Batters	0
2014	28 Batters	0
2015	James McCann	1
2016	28 Batters	0
2017	Nicholas Castellanos	1
2018	30 Batters	0
2019	29 Batters	0
2020	JaCoby Jones	1
2021	E. Haase, V. Reyes	1

1901	**D. Holmes, Joe Yeager**	**1**
1902	**Erve Beck, D. McGuire**	**1**
1903	26 Batters	0
1904	25 Batters	0
1905	**Sam Crawford**	**1**
1906	24 Batters	0
1907	24 Batters	0
1908	**Germany Schaefer**	**1**
1909	29 Batters	0
1910	**Donie Bush**	**1**
1911	**Ty Cobb**	**1**
1912	**Eddie Onslow**	**1**
1913	**Ty Cobb, Sam Crawford**	**1**
1914	30 Batters	0
1915	27 Batters	0
1916	**George Burns**	**1**
1917	**Ty Cobb**	**1**
1918	36 Batters	0
1919	**Harry Heilmann**	**1**
1920	38 Batters	0
1921	34 Batters	0
1922	**Bobby Veach**	**2**
1923	Fred Haney	1
1924	Heinie Manush	2
1925	Ty Cobb	1
1926	Al Wingo	1
1927	Gehringer, McManus	1
1928	Heilmann, Rice, Tavener	1
1929	**Marty McManus**	**2**
1930	B. Fothergill, C. Gehringer	1
1931	33 Batters	0
1932	John Stone	1
1933	31 Batters	0
1934	29 Batters	0
1935	27 Batters	0
1936	M. Cochrane, G. Goslin	1
1937	**H. Greenberg, Rudy York**	**2**
1938	**Hank Greenberg**	**2**
1939	Five Batters	1
1940	Hank Greenberg	1
1941	Rudy York	1
1942	Pinky Higgins	1
1943	27 Batters	0
1944	Al Unser	1
	Dick Wakefield	1
1945	Zeb Eaton	1

1946	Pat Mullin	1
1947	29 Batters	0
1948	33 Batters	0
1949	Four Batters	1
1950	Three Batters	1
1951	35 Batters	0
1952	Four Batters	1
1953	**Ray Boone**	**2**
1954	Five Batters	1
1955	Frank House	1
1956	Four Batters	1
1957	43 Batters	0
1958	Three Batters	1
1959	**Eddie Yost**	**2**
1960	Three Batters	1
1961	**Norm Cash**	**2**

Erve Beck

1962	Three Batters	1
1963	Three Batters	1
1964	Dick McAuliffe	1
1965	Four Batters	1
1966	Six Batters	1
1967	**Jim Northrup**	**2**
1968	**Jim Northrup**	**4**
1969	Willie Horton	3
1970	Four Batters	1
1971	Norm Cash	2
1972	Bill Freehan	2
1973	Dick McAuliffe	2
1974	Bill Freehan	1
1975	N. Colbert, A. Rodriguez	1
1976	Rusty Staub	1
1977	Milt May, J. Thompson	1

1978	Five Batters	1
1979	Three Batters	1
1980	Four Batters	1
1981	34 Batters	0
1982	Alan Trammell	2
1983	Lance Parrish	2
1984	Five Batters	1
1985	Darrell Evans	2
1986	Darrell Evans	2
1987	Matt Nokes	2
1988	Pat Sheridan	2
1989	Matt Nokes	1
1990	Cecil Fielder	2
1991	Five Batters	1
1992	Cecil Fielder	2
1993	Dan Gladden	3
1994	Lou Whitaker	2
1995	Travis Fryman	2
1996	Cecil Fielder	2
1997	Bobby Higginson	3
1998	Four Batters	1
1999	Three Batters	1
2000	Three Batters	1
2001	Three Batters	1
2002	Randall Simon	1
2003	Carlos Pena, Cody Ross	1
2004	B. Inge, Carlos Pena	2
2005	Dmitri Young	2
2006	B. Inge, Craig Monroe	1
2007	C. Guillen, M. Thames	2
2008	E. Renteria, M. Thames	2
2009	Brandon Inge	2
2010	Brennan Boesch	1
2011	Three Batters	1
2012	Miguel Cabrera	1
2013	Five Batters	1
2014	Three Batters	1
2015	Nicholas Castellanos	2
2016	Four Batters	1
2017	Justin Upton	3
2018	Nicholas Castellanos,	1
	L. Martin, James McCann	1
2019	M. Cabrera, John Hicks,	1
	R. Rodriguez. C. Stewart	1
2020	I. Paredes, J. Schoop	1
2021	Akil Baddoo, M. Cabrera	1
	E. Haase, Rogers, Schoop	1

Year	Player	ISO
1901	**Kid Elberfeld**	**.120**
1902	Jimmy Barrett	.084
1903	**Sam Crawford**	**.155**
1904	Sam Crawford	.107
1905	Sam Crawford	.132
1906	Sam Crawford	.112
1907	Sam Crawford	.137
1908	Ty Cobb	.151
1909	Ty Cobb	.140
1910	**Ty Cobb**	**.169**
1911	**Ty Cobb**	**.201**
1912	Ty Cobb	.174
1913	Sam Crawford	.172
1914	Sam Crawford	.168
1915	Marty Kavanagh	.157
1916	Harry Heilmann	.129
1917	Ty Cobb	.187
1918	Ty Cobb	.133
1919	Bobby Veach	.164
1920	Bobby Veach	.167
1921	**Harry Heilmann**	**.213**
1922	**Harry Heilmann**	**.242**
1923	Harry Heilmann	.229
1924	Harry Heilmann	.188
1925	Ty Cobb	.219
1926	Heinie Manush	.187
1927	Harry Heilmann	.218
1928	Harry Heilmann	.179
1929	Dale Alexander	.236
1930	Charlie Gehringer	.205
1931	Roy Johnson	.159
1932	Charlie Gehringer	.199
1933	Hank Greenberg	.167
1934	**Hank Greenberg**	**.261**
1935	**Hank Greenberg**	**.300**
1936	Goose Goslin	.212
1937	**Rudy York**	**.344**
1938	**Hank Greenberg**	**.369**
1939	Hank Greenberg	.310
1940	Hank Greenberg	.330
1941	Rudy York	.197
1942	Rudy York	.168
1943	Rudy York	.256
1944	Dick Wakefield	.221
1945	Roy Cullenbine	.174
1946	Hank Greenberg	.327
1947	Pat Mullin	.214
1948	Pat Mullin	.216
1949	Pat Mullin	.181
1950	Hoot Evers	.228
1951	Vic Wertz	.226
1952	Walt Dropo	.200
1953	Ray Boone	.244
1954	Ray Boone	.171
1955	Al Kaline	.206
1956	Al Kaline	.216
1957	Charlie Maxwell	.205
1958	Gail Harris	.208
1959	Charlie Maxwell	.210
1960	Rocky Colavito	.225
1961	Norm Cash	.301
1962	Al Kaline	.289
1963	Norm Cash, Al Kaline	.201
1964	Don Demeter	.204
1965	Norm Cash	.246
1966	Al Kaline	.246
1967	Al Kaline	.234
1968	Willie Horton	.258
1969	Jim Northrup	.214
1970	Willie Horton	.197
1971	Norm Cash	.248
1972	Norm Cash	.186
1973	Norm Cash	.209
1974	Bill Freehan	.182
1975	Bill Freehan	.152
1976	Ben Oglivie	.207
1977	Jason Thompson	.217
1978	Jason Thompson	.185
1979	Steve Kemp	.224
1980	Lance Parrish	.213
1981	John Wockenfuss	.180
1982	Lance Parrish	.245
1983	Lance Parrish	.213
1984	Kirk Gibson	.234
1985	Darrell Evans	.271
1986	Lance Parrish	.226
1987	Matt Nokes	.247
1988	Matt Nokes	.173
1989	Lou Whitaker	.210
1990	Cecil Fielder	.314
1991	Cecil Fielder	.252
1992	Rob Deer	.300
1993	Mickey Tettleton	.247
1994	Kirk Gibson	.273
1995	Cecil Fielder	.229
1996	Bobby Higginson	.257
1997	Tony Clark	.224
1998	Tony Clark	.231
1999	Dean Palmer	.255
2000	Bobby Higginson	.238
2001	Robert Fick	.204
2002	Robert Fick	.164
2003	Dmitri Young	.240
2004	Eric Munson	.234
2005	Chris Shelton	.211
2006	Marcus Thames	.293
2007	Curtis Granderson	.250
2008	Marcus Thames	.275
2009	Ryan Raburn	.241
2010	Miguel Cabrera	.294
2011	Miguel Cabrera	.241
2012	Miguel Cabrera	.277
2013	Miguel Cabrera	.288
2014	J.D. Martinez	.238
2015	J.D. Martinez	.253
2016	Miguel Cabrera	.247
2017	Justin Upton	.264
2018	Nicholas Castellanos	.202
2019	JaCoby Jones	.195
2020	JaCoby Jones	.247
2021	Eric Haase	.228

Matt Nokes

Year	Player	PSN
1901	**Ducky Holmes**	**7.2**
1902	Jimmy Barrett	6.9
1903	Sam Crawford	6.5
1904	Sam Crawford	3.6
1905	**Sam Crawford**	**9.4**
1906	Bill Coughlin	3.8
	Germany Schaefer	3.8
1907	Ty Cobb	9.1
1908	**Sam Crawford**	**9.5**
1909	**Ty Cobb**	**16.1**
1910	Ty Cobb	14.2
1911	Ty Cobb	14.6
1912	Ty Cobb	12.6
1913	Sam Crawford	10.6
1914	Sam Crawford	12.1
1915	Sam Crawford	6.9
1916	Ty Cobb	9.3
1917	Bobby Veach	11.6
1918	Harry Heilmann	7.2
1919	Harry Heilmann	7.5
1920	Bobby Veach	11.0
1921	Ty Cobb	15.5
1922	Harry Heilmann	11.6
1923	Harry Heilmann	12.0
1924	Harry Heilmann	11.3
1925	Ty Cobb	12.5
1926	Heinie Manush	12.3
1927	Harry Heilmann	12.3
1928	Harry Heilmann	9.3
	Marty McManus	9.3
1929	**Charlie Gehringer**	**17.6**
1930	Charlie Gehringer	17.4
1931	Roy Johnson	12.9
1932	Gee Walker	12.6
1933	Gee Walker	13.4
1934	Hank Greenberg	13.4
1935	Pete Fox	14.5
1936	**Goose Goslin**	**17.7**
1937	**Gee Walker**	**20.2**
1938	Charlie Gehringer	16.5
1939	Hank Greenberg	12.9
1940	Hank Greenberg	10.5
1941	Pinky Higgins	6.9
1942	Barney McCosky	8.6
1943	Rudy York	8.7
1944	Rudy York	7.8

Year	Player	PSN
1945	Rudy York	9.0
1946	Eddie Lake	10.4
1947	Eddie Lake	11.5
1948	Hoot Evers	4.6
1949	Hoot Evers	6.5
1950	Hoot Evers	8.1
1951	Hoot Evers	6.9
1952	Walt Dropo	3.7
1953	Don Lund	4.5
1954	Ray Boone	6.7
1955	Al Kaline	9.8
1956	Al Kaline	11.1
1957	Al Kaline	14.9
1958	Al Kaline	9.7
1959	Al Kaline	14.6
1960	Al Kaline	16.8

Don Lund

Year	Player	PSN
1961	Billy Bruton	19.2
1962	Billy Bruton	14.9
1963	Jake Wood	13.7
1964	Gates Brown	12.7
1965	Norm Cash	10.0
1966	Al Kaline	8.5
1967	Al Kaline	12.1
1968	Dick McAuliffe	10.7
1969	Mickey Stanley	10.7
1970	Mickey Stanley	11.3
1971	Jim Northrup	9.7
1972	Jim Northrup	5.3
1973	Jim Northrup	6.0
1974	Mickey Stanley	6.2
1975	Ron LeFlore	12.4
1976	Ben Oglivie	11.3

Year	Player	PSN
1977	**Ron LeFlore**	**22.7**
1978	Ron LeFlore	20.4
1979	Ron LeFlore	16.1
1980	Tom Brookens	11.3
1981	Kirk Gibson	11.8
1982	Larry Herndon	15.8
1983	Alan Trammell	19.1
1984	**Kirk Gibson**	**28.0**
1985	**Kirk Gibson**	**29.5**
1986	**Kirk Gibson**	**30.7**
1987	Kirk Gibson	25.0
1988	Alan Trammell	9.5
1989	Lou Whitaker	9.9
1990	Lloyd Moseby	15.4
1991	Travis Fryman	15.3
1992	Travis Fryman	11.4
1993	Kirk Gibson	13.9
1994	Tony Phillips	15.4
1995	Chad Curtis	23.6
1996	Chad Curtis	12.3
1997	Damion Easley	24.6
1998	Damion Easley	19.3
1999	Juan Encarnacion	24.1
2000	Bobby Higginson	20.0
2001	Bobby Higginson	18.4
2002	Bobby Higginson	10.9
2003	Bobby Higginson	10.2
2004	Carlos Guillen	15.0
2005	Craig Monroe	11.4
2006	Carlos Guillen	19.5
2007	Curtis Granderson	24.4
2008	Curtis Granderson	15.5
2009	Curtis Granderson	24.0
2010	B. Boesch, J. Damon	9.3
2011	Austin Jackson	13.8
2012	Austin Jackson	13.7
2013	Austin Jackson	9.6
2014	Ian Kinsler	15.9
2015	Rajai Davis	11.1
2016	Ian Kinsler	18.7
2017	Ian Kinsler	17.1
2018	Niko Goodrum	13.7
2019	Niko Goodrum	12.0
2020	Niko Goodrum	5.8
2021	Robbie Grossman	21.4

Year	Player	XBH
1901	**Ducky Holmes**	**42**
1902	Jimmy Barrett	29
1903	**Sam Crawford**	**52**
1904	Sam Crawford	40
1905	**Sam Crawford**	**54**
1906	Sam Crawford	43
1907	**Sam Crawford**	**55**
1908	**Ty Cobb**	**60**
1909	Sam Crawford	55
1910	Ty Cobb	57
1911	**Ty Cobb**	**79**
1912	Ty Cobb	60
1913	Sam Crawford	64
1914	Sam Crawford	56
1915	Sam Crawford	54
1916	Bobby Veach	51
1917	Ty Cobb	74
1918	Bobby Veach	37
1919	Bobby Veach	65
1920	Bobby Veach	65
1921	Harry Heilmann	76
1922	Ty Cobb	62
1923	Harry Heilmann	73
1924	Harry Heilmann	71
1925	Harry Heilmann	64
1926	Harry Heilmann	58
1927	Harry Heilmann	73
1928	Harry Heilmann	62
1929	**Dale Alexander**	**83**
1930	Charlie Gehringer	78
1931	Roy Johnson	64
1932	Charlie Gehringer	74
1933	Charlie Gehringer	60
1934	**Hank Greenberg**	**96**
1935	**Hank Greenberg**	**98**
1936	Charlie Gehringer	87
1937	**Hank Greenberg**	**103**
1938	Hank Greenberg	85
1939	Hank Greenberg	82
1940	Hank Greenberg	99
1941	Rudy York	59
1942	Rudy York	51
1943	Rudy York	67
1944	Rudy York	52
1945	Roy Cullenbine	50
1946	Hank Greenberg	78
1947	Pat Mullin	49
1948	Pat Mullin	50
1949	Vic Wertz	52
1950	George Kell	70
1951	Vic Wertz	55
1952	Walt Dropo	43
1953	Bob Nieman	52
1954	Ray Boone	46
1955	Al Kaline	59
1956	Al Kaline	69
1957	Al Kaline	56
1958	Al Kaline	57
1959	Harvey Kuenn	58
1960	Rocky Colavito	54
1961	Rocky Colavito	77
1962	Rocky Colavito	69

Bob Nieman

Year	Player	XBH
1963	Al Kaline	54
1964	Al Kaline	53
1965	Norm Cash	54
1966	Al Kaline	59
1967	Al Kaline	55
1968	Willie Horton	58
1969	Jim Northrup	61
1970	Jim Northrup	48
1971	Aurelio Rodriguez	52
1972	Aurelio Rodriguez	41
1973	Mickey Stanley	45
1974	Al Kaline	43
1975	Willie Horton	39
	Aurelio Rodriguez	39
1976	Rusty Staub	46
1977	Jason Thompson	60
1978	Rusty Staub	55
1979	Steve Kemp	55
1980	Lance Parrish	64
1981	Steve Kemp	31
1982	Larry Herndon	57
1983	Lance Parrish	72
1984	K. Gibson, Chet Lemon	60
1985	Kirk Gibson	71
1986	Alan Trammell	61
1987	Alan Trammell	65
1988	Chet Lemon	50
1989	Lou Whitaker	50
1990	Cecil Fielder	77
1991	Cecil Fielder	69
1992	Cecil Fielder	57
	Mickey Tettleton	57
1993	Travis Fryman	64
1994	Travis Fryman	57
1995	Chad Curtis	53
1996	Bobby Higginson	61
1997	Tony Clark	63
1998	Tony Clark	71
1999	Dean Palmer	65
2000	Bobby Higginson	78
2001	Shane Halter	51
	Bobby Higginson	51
2002	Robert Fick	55
2003	Dmitri Young	70
2004	Carlos Guillen	67
2005	Brandon Inge	56
2006	Carlos Guillen	65
	Craig Monroe	65
2007	Curtis Granderson	84
2008	Miguel Cabrera	75
2009	Miguel Cabrera	68
2010	Miguel Cabrera	84
2011	Miguel Cabrera	78
2012	Miguel Cabrera	84
2013	Miguel Cabrera	71
2014	Miguel Cabrera	78
2015	J.D. Martinez	73
2016	Miguel Cabrera	70
2017	Nicholas Castellanos	72
2018	Nicholas Castellanos	74
2019	Nicholas Castellanos	51
2020	Jeimer Candelario	21
2021	Jeimer Candelario	61

Year	Player	Extra Bases
1901	**Ducky Holmes**	**60**
1902	Jimmy Barrett	43
1903	**Sam Crawford**	**85**
1904	Sam Crawford	60
1905	Sam Crawford	76
1906	Sam Crawford	63
1907	Sam Crawford	80
1908	**Ty Cobb**	**88**
1909	Sam Crawford	81
1910	Ty Cobb	86
1911	**Ty Cobb**	**119**
1912	Ty Cobb	97
1913	Sam Crawford	105
1914	Sam Crawford	98
1915	Sam Crawford	81
1916	Bobby Veach	72
1917	Ty Cobb	110
1918	Ty Cobb	56
	Bobby Veach	56
1919	Bobby Veach	88
1920	Bobby Veach	102
1921	**Harry Heilmann**	**128**
1922	Harry Heilmann	110
1923	Harry Heilmann	120
1924	Harry Heilmann	107
1925	Harry Heilmann	101
1926	Heinie Manush	93
1927	Harry Heilmann	110
1928	Harry Heilmann	100
1929	**Dale Alexander**	**148**
1930	Charlie Gehringer	125
1931	Roy Johnson	99
1932	Charlie Gehringer	123
1933	Charlie Gehringer	90
1934	**Hank Greenberg**	**155**
1935	**Hank Greenberg**	**186**
1936	Charlie Gehringer	129
1937	**Hank Greenberg**	**197**
1938	**Hank Greenberg**	**205**
1939	Hank Greenberg	155
1940	Hank Greenberg	189
1941	Rudy York	116
1942	Rudy York	97
1943	Rudy York	146
1944	Rudy York	95
1945	Roy Cullenbine	91
1946	Hank Greenberg	171
1947	Roy Cullenbine	92
1948	Pat Mullin	107
1949	Vic Wertz	98
1950	Vic Wertz	126
1951	Vic Wertz	113
1952	Walt Dropo	92
1953	Ray Boone	94
1954	Ray Boone	93
1955	Al Kaline	121
1956	Al Kaline	133
1957	Al Kaline	106
1958	Al Kaline	96
1959	Charlie Maxwell	109
1960	Rocky Colavito	125
1961	Rocky Colavito	169

Roy Johnson

Year	Player	Extra Bases
1962	Rocky Colavito	145
1963	Al Kaline	111
1964	Dick McAuliffe	104
1965	Norm Cash	115
1966	Norm Cash	120
1967	Al Kaline	107
1968	Willie Horton	132
1969	Jim Northrup	116
1970	Jim Northrup	99
1971	Norm Cash	112
1972	Norm Cash	82
1973	Mickey Stanley	84
1974	Bill Freehan	81
1975	Willie Horton	90
1976	Rusty Staub	79
1977	Jason Thompson	127
1978	Jason Thompson	109
1979	Steve Kemp	110
1980	Lance Parrish	118
1981	Steve Kemp	53
1982	Lance Parrish	119
1983	Lance Parrish	129
1984	Kirk Gibson	124
1985	Darrell Evans	137
1986	Alan Trammell	110
1987	Alan Trammell	124
1988	Chet Lemon	88
1989	Lou Whitaker	107
1990	Cecil Fielder	180
1991	Cecil Fielder	157
1992	Cecil Fielder	127
1993	Mickey Tettleton	129
1994	Cecil Fielder	104
1995	Cecil Fielder	113
1996	Bobby Higginson	113
1997	Tony Clark	130
1998	Tony Clark	139
1999	Dean Palmer	143
2000	Bobby Higginson	142
2001	Bobby Higginson	91
2002	Robert Fick	91
2003	Dmitri Young	135
2004	Carlos Guillen	117
2005	Brandon Inge	97
2006	Craig Monroe	123
2007	Curtis Granderson	153
2008	Miguel Cabrera	151
2009	Miguel Cabrera	136
2010	Miguel Cabrera	161
2011	Miguel Cabrera	138
2012	Miguel Cabrera	172
2013	Miguel Cabrera	160
2014	Miguel Cabrera	129
	Victor Martinez	129
2015	J.D. Martinez	151
2016	Miguel Cabrera	147
2017	Nicholas Castellanos	134
2018	Nicholas Castellanos	125
2019	Nicholas Castellanos	76
2020	Jeimer Candelario	38
2021	Robbie Grossman	98
	Jonathan Schoop	98

Year	Player	XBH%
1901	**Ducky Holmes**	**7.1**
1902	Ducky Holmes	5.2
1903	**Sam Crawford**	**8.6**
1904	Sam Crawford	6.5
1905	**Sam Crawford**	**8.6**
1906	Sam Crawford	7.0
1907	**Sam Crawford**	**8.7**
1908	**Ty Cobb**	**9.4**
1909	Sam Crawford	8.3
1910	Ty Cobb	9.5
1911	**Ty Cobb**	**12.1**
1912	Ty Cobb	9.9
1913	Sam Crawford	9.5
1914	Ty Cobb	8.5
1915	Marty Kavanagh	8.0
	Bobby Veach	8.0
1916	Harry Heilmann	8.4
1917	Ty Cobb	11.1
1918	Ty Cobb	7.6
1919	Bobby Veach	10.9
1920	Bobby Veach	9.7
1921	Harry Heilmann	11.3
1922	Harry Heilmann	11.0
1923	Harry Heilmann	11.7
1924	Harry Heilmann	10.5
1925	Ty Cobb	11.2
1926	Heinie Manush	10.1
1927	**Harry Heilmann**	**12.2**
1928	Bob Fothergill	10.7
1929	**Bob Fothergill**	**13.3**
1930	Charlie Gehringer	11.2
1931	Roy Johnson	9.2
1932	Charlie Gehringer	10.7
1933	Hank Greenberg	9.6
1934	**Hank Greenberg**	**14.4**
1935	Hank Greenberg	13.8
1936	Gee Walker	12.2
1937	**Hank Greenberg**	**14.7**
1938	Hank Greenberg	12.5
1939	Hank Greenberg	13.6
1940	**Hank Greenberg**	**14.8**
1941	Bruce Campbell	9.1
1942	Pinky Higgins	8.1
1943	Rudy York	10.1
1944	Dick Wakefield	9.6
1945	Roy Cullenbine	7.9
1946	Hank Greenberg	12.9
1947	Pat Mullin	10.5
1948	Dick Wakefield	9.2
1949	Johnny Groth	8.4
1950	Hoot Evers	11.0
1951	Vic Wertz	9.5
1952	Walt Dropo	8.8
1953	Ray Boone	9.9
1954	Jim Delsing	7.5
1955	Ray Boone	8.8
1956	Al Kaline	10.0
1957	Al Kaline	8.8
1958	Al Kaline	9.4
1959	Harvey Kuenn	9.4
1960	Rocky Colavito	8.8

Aurelio Rodriguez

Year	Player	XBH%
1961	Rocky Colavito	10.9
1962	Al Kaline	11.3
1963	Al Kaline	8.8
1964	Don Demeter	9.6
1965	Norm Cash	9.8
1966	Al Kaline	10.3
1967	Al Kaline	10.0
1968	Willie Horton	10.0
1969	Jim Northrup	10.1
1970	Willie Horton	9.2
1971	Willie Horton	9.6
1972	Norm Cash	7.6
	Mickey Stanley	7.6
1973	Norm Cash	9.0
1974	Bill Freehan	8.0
1975	Bill Freehan	7.3
1976	Ben Oglivie	9.2
1977	Ben Oglivie	9.5
1978	Aurelio Rodriguez	8.2
1979	Steve Kemp	9.6
1980	Lance Parrish	10.8
1981	Lance Parrish	7.8
1982	Lance Parrish	10.0
1983	Lance Parrish	10.9
1984	Chet Lemon	10.5
1985	Kirk Gibson	10.6
1986	Alan Trammell	9.3
1987	Alan Trammell	9.7
1988	Chet Lemon	8.6
1989	Lou Whitaker	8.3
1990	Cecil Fielder	12.0
1991	Travis Fryman	9.7
1992	Rob Deer	11.8
1993	Mickey Tettleton	9.7
1994	Junior Felix	11.5
1995	John Flaherty	8.9
1996	Bobby Higginson	12.2
1997	Damion Easley	10.3
	Bobby Higginson	10.3
1998	Tony Clark	10.6
1999	Luis Polonia	11.0
2000	Bobby Higginson	11.5
2001	Shane Halter	10.0
2002	Robert Fick	8.9
2003	Dmitri Young	10.9
2004	Carlos Guillen	11.4
2005	Craig Shelton	9.9
2006	Marcus Thames	12.3
2007	Curtis Granderson	12.4
2008	Miguel Cabrera	10.9
2009	Ryan Raburn	10.0
2010	Miguel Cabrera	13.0
2011	Miguel Cabrera	11.3
2012	Miguel Cabrera	12.1
2013	Miguel Cabrera	10.9
2014	J.D. Martinez	11.7
2015	Yoenis Cespedes	11.2
2016	J.D. Martinez	11.4
2017	Justin Upton	12.5
2018	Nicholas Castellanos	10.9
2019	Nicholas Castellanos	11.6
2020	JaCoby Jones	13.0
2021	Jeimer Candelario	9.7

Year	Player	Pct.
1901	**Ducky Holmes**	**26.6**
1902	Ducky Holmes	22.6
1903	**Billy Lush**	**28.4**
1904	Sam Crawford	28.0
1905	**Sam Crawford**	**31.6**
1906	Sam Crawford	25.9
1907	Sam Crawford	29.3
1908	**Ty Cobb**	**31.9**
1909	Sam Crawford	29.7
1910	Sam Crawford	29.4
1911	**Ty Cobb**	**31.9**
1912	Sam Crawford	29.1
1913	**Sam Crawford**	**33.2**
1914	Sam Crawford	30.6
1915	Marty Kavanagh	31.6
1916	**Harry Heilmann**	**33.9**
1917	Ty Cobb	32.9
1918	Harry Heilmann	26.6
	Bobby Veach	26.6
1919	**Bobby Veach**	**34.0**
1920	**Bobby Veach**	**34.6**
1921	**Bobby Veach**	**34.8**
1922	**Harry Heilmann**	**35.8**
1923	Harry Heilmann	34.6
1924	**Harry Heilmann**	**36.0**
1925	**Frank O'Rourke**	**36.9**
1926	Lu Blue	31.7
1927	Harry Heilmann	36.3
1928	Bob Fothergill	37.3
1929	**Harry Heilmann**	**40.4**
1930	Charlie Gehringer	38.8
1931	Roy Johnson	37.0
1932	Charlie Gehringer	40.2
1933	Hank Greenberg	35.6
1934	**Hank Greenberg**	**47.8**
1935	**Hank Greenberg**	**48.3**
1936	Charlie Gehringer	38.3
1937	**Hank Greenberg**	**51.5**
1938	Hank Greenberg	48.6
1939	**Hank Greenberg**	**52.6**
1940	Hank Greenberg	50.8
1941	Rudy York	38.6
1942	Pinky Higgins	35.3
1943	Rudy York	43.2
1944	Dick Wakefield	32.7
1945	Roy Cullenbine	34.5
1946	**Hank Greenberg**	**53.8**
1947	Pat Mullin	48.0
1948	Dick Wakefield	40.4
1949	Johnny Groth	34.3
1950	Vic Wertz	39.5
1951	Vic Wertz	38.5
1952	Pat Mullin	39.1
1953	Ray Boone	36.7
1954	Jim Delsing	34.8
1955	Ray Boone	34.5
1956	Al Kaline	35.6
1957	Charlie Maxwell	36.8
1958	Gail Harris	37.4
1959	Charlie Maxwell	34.6
1960	Charlie Maxwell	39.5

Billy Lush

Year	Player	Pct.
1961	Rocky Colavito	45.6
1962	Norm Cash	46.3
1963	Norm Cash	34.6
	Gus Triandos	34.6
1964	Don Demeter	39.8
1965	Norm Cash	43.5
1966	Al Kaline	42.8
1967	Al Kaline	39.0
1968	Willie Horton	39.7
1969	Jim Northrup	38.1
1970	Bill Freehan	37.9
1971	Dick McAuliffe	40.4
1972	Mickey Stanley	35.3
1973	Norm Cash	40.0
1974	Bill Freehan	30.3
1975	Bill Freehan	32.4
1976	Ben Oglivie	34.5
1977	Ben Oglivie	39.8
1978	Aurelio Rodriguez	33.3
1979	Jerry Morales	40.9
1980	Lance Parrish	40.5
1981	Lance Parrish	35.3
1982	Lance Parrish	38.4
1983	Lance Parrish	44.2
1984	Chet Lemon	41.1
1985	Darrell Evans	45.6
1986	Alan Trammell	38.4
1987	Darrell Evans	42.2
1988	Chet Lemon	37.0
1989	Lou Whitaker	39.1
1990	Cecil Fielder	48.4
1991	Rob Deer	51.3
1992	**Rob Deer**	**54.6**
1993	Mickey Tettleton	47.7
1994	Travis Fryman	46.7
1995	Cecil Fielder	41.7
1996	Melvin Nieves	48.1
1997	Melvin Nieves	47.6
1998	Juan Gonzalez	43.2
1999	Dean Palmer	44.2
2000	Bobby Higginson	43.6
2001	Shane Halter	39.8
2002	Shane Halter	38.8
2003	Dmitri Young	41.9
2004	Eric Munson	51.5
2005	Omar Infante	43.3
2006	Marcus Thames	53.9
2007	Curtis Granderson	45.4
2008	Brandon Inge	43.7
2009	Curtis Granderson	38.9
2010	Miguel Cabrera	46.7
2011	Alex Avila	40.9
2012	Miguel Cabrera	41.0
2013	Miguel Cabrera	36.8
2014	Miguel Cabrera	40.8
2015	J.D. Martinez	43.5
2016	Justin Upton	43.6
2017	Justin Upton	50.8
2018	Niko Goodrum	44.0
2019	JaCoby Jones	47.1
2020	JaCoby Jones	53.8
2021	Eric Haase	43.2

Year	Player	Total Bases
1901	**Ducky Holmes**	**218**
1902	Jimmy Barrett	197
1903	**Sam Crawford**	**269**
1904	Sam Crawford	203
1905	Sam Crawford	247
1906	Sam Crawford	229
1907	**Ty Cobb**	**283**
1908	Ty Cobb	276
1909	**Ty Cobb**	**296**
1910	Ty Cobb	279
1911	**Ty Cobb**	**367**
1912	Ty Cobb	323
1913	Sam Crawford	298
1914	Sam Crawford	281
1915	Ty Cobb	274
1916	Ty Cobb	267
1917	Ty Cobb	335
1918	Ty Cobb	217
1919	Bobby Veach	279
1920	Bobby Veach	290
1921	Harry Heilmann	365
1922	Ty Cobb	297
1923	Harry Heilmann	331
1924	Harry Heilmann	304
1925	Harry Heilmann	326
1926	Heinie Manush	281
1927	Harry Heilmann	311
1928	Harry Heilmann	283
1929	Dale Alexander	363
1930	Charlie Gehringer	326
1931	Roy Johnson	272
1932	Charlie Gehringer	307
1933	Charlie Gehringer	294
1934	Hank Greenberg	356
1935	**Hank Greenberg**	**389**
1936	Charlie Gehringer	356
1937	**Hank Greenberg**	**397**
1938	Hank Greenberg	380
1939	Hank Greenberg	311
1940	Hank Greenberg	384
1941	Rudy York	269
1942	Barney McCosky	247
	Rudy York	247
1943	Rudy York	301
1944	Rudy York	256
1945	Rudy York	246
1946	Hank Greenberg	316
1947	George Kell	242
1948	Pat Mullin	250
1949	Vic Wertz	283
1950	George Kell	310
1951	Vic Wertz	256
1952	Walt Dropo	220
1953	Harvey Kuenn	262
1954	Harvey Kuenn	256
1955	Al Kaline	321
1956	Al Kaline	327
1957	Al Kaline	276
1958	Al Kaline	266
1959	Harvey Kuenn	281
1960	Rocky Colavito	263

Magglio Ordonez

Year	Player	Total Bases
1961	Norm Cash	354
1962	Rocky Colavito	309
1963	Al Kaline	283
1964	Al Kaline	246
1965	Willie Horton	251
1966	Norm Cash	288
1967	Al Kaline	248
1968	Willie Horton	278
1969	Jim Northrup	276
1970	Jim Northrup	231
1971	Aurelio Rodriguez	242
1972	Aurelio Rodriguez	214
1973	Mickey Stanley	231
1974	Al Kaline	217
1975	Willie Horton	259
1976	Rusty Staub	255
1977	Ron LeFlore	310
1978	Rusty Staub	279
1979	Steve Kemp	266
1980	Lance Parrish	276
1981	Steve Kemp	156
1982	Larry Herndon	295
1983	Lou Whitaker	294
1984	Kirk Gibson	274
1985	Kirk Gibson	301
1986	Alan Trammell	269
1987	Alan Trammell	329
1988	Chet Lemon	223
1989	Lou Whitaker	235
1990	Cecil Fielder	339
1991	Cecil Fielder	320
1992	Travis Fryman	274
1993	Travis Fryman	295
1994	Travis Fryman	220
1995	Chad Curtis	255
1996	Travis Fryman	269
1997	Tony Clark	290
1998	Tony Clark	314
1999	Dean Palmer	290
2000	Bobby Higginson	321
2001	Bobby Higginson	241
2002	Robert Fick	241
2003	Dmitri Young	302
2004	Carlos Guillen	283
2005	Brandon Inge	258
2006	Magglio Ordonez	283
2007	Magglio Ordonez	354
2008	Miguel Cabrera	331
2009	Miguel Cabrera	334
2010	Miguel Cabrera	341
2011	Miguel Cabrera	335
2012	Miguel Cabrera	377
2013	Miguel Cabrera	353
2014	Miguel Cabrera	320
2015	J.D. Martinez	319
2016	Miguel Cabrera	335
2017	Nicholas Castellanos	301
2018	Nicholas Castellanos	310
2019	Miguel Cabrera	196
2020	Jeimer Candelario	93
2021	Jonathan Schoop	271

YEARLY TIGER HITTING LEADERS – TOTAL BASE AVERAGE

Year	Player(s)	TBA
1901	**Ducky Holmes**	**1.7**
1902	Three Batters	1.4
1903	**Sam Crawford**	**2.0**
1904	Sam Crawford	1.4
1905	Sam Crawford	1.6
1906	Sam Crawford	1.6
1907	Ty Cobb, Sam Crawford	1.9
1908	Ty Cobb, Sam Crawford	1.8
1909	Ty Cobb	1.9
1910	**Ty Cobb**	**2.0**
1911	**Ty Cobb**	**2.5**
1912	Ty Cobb	2.3
1913	Ty Cobb, Sam Crawford	1.9
1914	Ty Cobb, Sam Crawford	1.8
1915	Ty Cobb	1.8
1916	Ty Cobb	1.8
1917	Ty Cobb	2.2
1918	Ty Cobb	2.0
1919	Ty Cobb	2.1
1920	Bobby Veach	1.9
1921	T. Cobb, Harry Heilmann	2.4
1922	Harry Heilmann	2.3
1923	Harry Heilmann	2.3
1924	Harry Heilmann	2.0
1925	Harry Heilmann	2.2
1926	Heinie Manush	2.1
1927	Harry Heilmann	2.2
1928	Harry Heilmann	1.9
1929	Dale Alexander	2.3
1930	Charlie Gehringer	2.1
1931	Roy Johnson, J. Stone	1.8
1932	C. Gehringer, John Stone	2.0
1933	Charlie Gehringer	1.9
1934	Hank Greenberg	2.3
1935	**Hank Greenberg**	**2.6**
1936	Charlie Gehringer	2.3
1937	**Hank Greenberg**	**2.6**
1938	Hank Greenberg	2.5
1939	Hank Greenberg	2.3
1940	**Hank Greenberg**	**2.6**
1941	Three Batters	1.7
1942	B. McCosky, Rudy York	1.6
1943	Rudy York	1.9
1944	Dick Wakefield	2.0
1945	R. Cullenbine, Rudy York	1.6
1946	Hank Greenberg	2.2
1947	Three Batters	1.6
1948	Hoot Evers, Pat Mullin	1.8
1949	George Kell, Vic Wertz	1.8
1950	Three Batters	2.0
1951	Vic Wertz	1.9
1952	Walt Dropo	1.9
1953	Ray Boone	2.1
1954	R. Boone, Harvey Kuenn	1.7
1955	Al Kaline	2.1
1956	Al Kaline	2.1
1957	Al Kaline	1.9
1958	Al Kaline, Harvey Kuenn	1.8
1959	Al Kaline, Harvey Kuenn	2.0
1960	Rocky Colavito	1.8
1961	Norm Cash	2.2

Rondell White

Year	Player(s)	TBA
1962	Al Kaline	2.4
1963	Al Kaline	2.0
1964	Bill Freehan, Al Kaline	1.7
1965	Willie Horton	1.8
1966	Three Batters	1.8
1967	Al Kaline	1.9
1968	Willie Horton	1.9
1969	Jim Northrup	1.9
1970	Willie Horton	1.9
1971	Willie Horton	1.9
1972	Three Batters	1.4
1973	Willie Horton	1.9
1974	Bill Freehan	1.6
1975	Willie Horton	1.6
1976	Ron LeFlore	1.7
1977	Ron LeFlore	2.0
1978	Jason Thompson	1.8
1979	Steve Kemp	2.0
1980	Lance Parrish	1.9
1981	Kirk Gibson	1.7
1982	Larry Herndon, L. Parrish	1.9
1983	Larry Herndon, L. Parrish	1.9
1984	Alan Trammell	1.9
1985	Kirk Gibson	2.0
1986	Three Batters	1.8
1987	Alan Trammell	2.2
1988	Alan Trammell	1.7
1989	Lou Whitaker	1.6
1990	Cecil Fielder	2.1
1991	Cecil Fielder	2.0
1992	Rob Deer	2.0
1993	Travis Fryman	2.0
1994	Cecil Fielder	2.0
1995	Chad Curtis	1.8
1996	Bobby Higginson	2.0
1997	Bobby Higginson	1.9
1998	Tony Clark	2.0
1999	Luis Polonia	2.0
2000	Bobby Higginson	2.1
2001	Three Batters	1.6
2002	Randall Simon	1.7
2003	Dmitri Young	1.9
2004	Carlos Guillen	2.1
2005	Chris Shelton, R. White	1.9
2006	Four Batters	1.8
2007	Magglio Ordonez	2.3
2008	Miguel Cabrera	2.1
2009	Miguel Cabrera	2.1
2010	Miguel Cabrera	2.3
2011	Miguel Cabrera	2.1
2012	Miguel Cabrera	2.3
2013	Miguel Cabrera	2.4
2014	Victor Martinez	2.1
2015	Yoenis Cespedes	2.0
	J.D. Martinez	2.0
2016	Miguel Cabrera	2.1
	J.D. Martinez	2.1
2017	Justin Upton	2.0
2018	Nicholas Castellanos	2.0
2019	Nicholas Castellanos	1.9
2020	Willi Castro	2.0
2021	Jonathan Schoop	1.7

Year	Player	TBP
1901	**Kid Elberfeld**	**0.40**
1902	**Jimmy Barrett**	**0.40**
1903	**Jimmy Barrett**	**0.41**
1904	Jimmy Barrett	0.35
1905	Sam Crawford	0.36
1906	Ty Cobb	0.36
1907	Ty Cobb	0.38
1908	Matty McIntyre	0.39
1909	**Ty Cobb**	**0.43**
1910	**Ty Cobb**	**0.46**
1911	**Ty Cobb**	**0.47**
1912	Ty Cobb	0.46
1913	**Ty Cobb**	**0.47**
1914	**Ty Cobb**	**0.47**
1915	**Ty Cobb**	**0.49**
1916	Ty Cobb	0.45
1917	Ty Cobb	0.44
1918	Ty Cobb	0.44
1919	Ty Cobb	0.43
1920	Ty Cobb	0.42
1921	Ty Cobb	0.45
1922	Ty Cobb	0.46
1923	Harry Heilmann	0.48
1924	Johnny Bassler	0.44
1925	Ty Cobb	0.47
1926	Harry Heilmann	0.45
1927	Harry Heilmann	0.47
1928	Charlie Gehringer	0.40
1929	Harry Heilmann	0.41
1930	Gehringer, McManus	0.40
1931	Dale Alexander	0.40
1932	Charlie Gehringer	0.37
1933	Charlie Gehringer	0.39
1934	Charlie Gehringer	0.45
1935	Mickey Cochrane	0.45
1936	Charlie Gehringer	0.43
1937	Charlie Gehringer	0.46
1938	Hank Greenberg	0.44
1939	Gehringer, Greenberg	0.42
1940	Gehringer, Greenberg	0.43
1941	Barney McCosky	0.40
1942	Barney McCosky	0.37
1943	Dick Wakefield	0.38
1944	Dick Wakefield	0.46
1945	Roy Cullenbine	0.40
1946	Roy Cullenbine	0.48
1947	Dick Wakefield	0.41
1948	Dick Wakefield	0.41
1949	George Kell	0.42
1950	Three Batters	0.41
1951	George Kell	0.39
1952	Johnny Groth	0.35
1953	Ray Boone	0.39
1954	Ray Boone	0.38
1955	Al Kaline	0.43
1956	Charlie Maxwell	0.42
1957	Charlie Maxwell	0.38
1958	Al Kaline, Harvey Kuenn	0.38
1959	Eddie Yost	0.44
1960	Eddie Yost	0.42

Marty McManus

Year	Player	TBP
1961	**Norm Cash**	**0.49**
1962	Norm Cash, Al Kaline	0.38
1963	Norm Cash	0.39
1964	Al Kaline	0.38
1965	Al Kaline	0.39
1966	Al Kaline	0.40
1967	Al Kaline	0.42
1968	Al Kaline	0.39
1969	Norm Cash	0.37
1970	Norm Cash	0.39
1971	Al Kaline	0.42
1972	Al Kaline	0.38
1973	McAuliffe, Northrup	0.37
1974	Bill Freehan	0.36
1975	Four Batters	0.32
1976	Rusty Staub	0.39
1977	Ron LeFlore	0.37
1978	Steve Kemp	0.38
1979	S. Kemp, Lou Whitaker	0.40
1980	Champ Summers	0.40
1981	Steve Kemp	0.39
1982	Chet Lemon	0.37
1983	Alan Trammell	0.39
1984	Alan Trammell	0.38
1985	Kirk Gibson	0.37
1986	Kirk Gibson	0.37
1987	Alan Trammell	0.41
1988	Three Batters	0.38
1989	Gary Pettis	0.38
1990	Three Batters	0.38
1991	Lou Whitaker	0.40
1992	T. Phillips, L. Whitaker	0.39
1993	Tony Phillips	0.45
1994	Mickey Tettleton	0.42
1995	Three Batters	0.35
1996	Bobby Higginson	0.41
1997	T. Clark, B. Higginson	0.38
1998	T. Clark, B. Higginson	0.36
1999	Brad Ausmus	0.37
2000	Bobby Higginson	0.38
2001	Tony Clark	0.38
2002	Bobby Higginson	0.35
2003	Dmitri Young	0.37
2004	Ivan Rodriguez	0.39
2005	Placido Polanco	0.39
2006	Carlos Guillen	0.40
2007	Magglio Ordonez	0.44
2008	C. Guillen, M. Ordonez	0.38
2009	Miguel Cabrera	0.40
2010	Miguel Cabrera	0.43
2011	Miguel Cabrera	0.45
2012	Prince Fielder	0.42
2013	Miguel Cabrera	0.44
2014	Victor Martinez	0.41
2015	Miguel Cabrera	0.44
2016	Miguel Cabrera	0.40
2017	Justin Upton	0.36
2018	Nicholas Castellanos	0.36
2019	Miguel Cabrera	0.35
2020	Willie Castro	0.39
2021	Robbie Grossman	0.36

YEARLY TIGER HITTING LEADERS – BASES PRODUCED

Year	Player	Bases
1901	**Jimmy Barrett**	**307**
1902	Jimmy Barrett	295
1903	**Sam Crawford**	**312**
1904	Jimmy Barrett	281
1905	**Sam Crawford**	**319**
1906	Sam Crawford	291
1907	**Ty Cobb**	**356**
1908	Ty Cobb	349
1909	**Ty Cobb**	**420**
1910	Ty Cobb	408
1911	**Ty Cobb**	**494**
1912	Ty Cobb	427
1913	Sam Crawford	363
1914	Sam Crawford	375
1915	Ty Cobb	488
1916	Ty Cobb	413
1917	Ty Cobb	451
1918	Ty Cobb	292
1919	Bobby Veach	331
1920	Bobby Veach	337
1921	Harry Heilmann	420
1922	Ty Cobb	361
1923	Harry Heilmann	414
1924	Harry Heilmann	395
1925	Harry Heilmann	399
1926	Harry Heilmann	341
1927	Harry Heilmann	394
1928	Charlie Gehringer	356
1929	Charlie Gehringer	428
1930	Charlie Gehringer	414
1931	Roy Johnson	377
1932	Charlie Gehringer	384
1933	Charlie Gehringer	367
1934	Hank Greenberg	428
1935	Hank Greenberg	480
1936	Charlie Gehringer	443
1937	**Hank Greenberg**	**507**
1938	Hank Greenberg	506
1939	Hank Greenberg	410
1940	Hank Greenberg	483
1941	Rudy York	364
1942	Barney McCosky	326
1943	Rudy York	390
1944	Rudy York	329
1945	Roy Cullenbine	340
1946	Hank Greenberg	401
1947	Roy Cullenbine	336
1948	Pat Mullin	328
1949	Vic Wertz	365
1950	Vic Wertz	389
1951	Vic Wertz	334
1952	Walt Dropo	248
1953	Harvey Kuenn	318
1954	Ray Boone	328
1955	Al Kaline	409
1956	Al Kaline	404
1957	Al Kaline	330
1958	Al Kaline	327
1959	Eddie Yost	371
1960	Eddie Yost	328

Ron LeFlore

Year	Player	Bases
1961	Norm Cash	489
1962	Rocky Colavito	407
1963	Rocky Colavito	345
1964	Al Kaline	325
1965	Norm Cash	322
1966	Norm Cash	356
1967	Dick McAuliffe	340
1968	Willie Horton	327
1969	Jim Northrup	332
1970	Jim Northrup	292
1971	Norm Cash	300
1972	Norm Cash	246
1973	Mickey Stanley	279
1974	Al Kaline	284
1975	Willie Horton	304
1976	Rusty Staub	341

Year	Player	Bases
1977	Ron LeFlore	386
1978	Ron LeFlore	403
1979	Ron LeFlore	379
1980	Steve Kemp	315
1981	Steve Kemp	235
1982	Larry Herndon	345
1983	Lou Whitaker	378
1984	Kirk Gibson	366
1985	Kirk Gibson	402
1986	Alan Trammell	353
1987	Alan Trammell	410
1988	Chet Lemon	283
1989	Lou Whitaker	330
1990	Cecil Fielder	429
1991	Cecil Fielder	398
1992	Mickey Tettleton	368
1993	Travis Fryman	381
1994	Tony Phillips	313
1995	Chad Curtis	352
1996	Travis Fryman	330
1997	Tony Clark	384
1998	Tony Clark	380
1999	Dean Palmer	350
2000	Bobby Higginson	410
2001	Bobby Higginson	341
2002	Robert Fick	287
2003	Dmitri Young	362
2004	Carlos Guillen	347
2005	Brandon Inge	328
2006	Carlos Guillen	373
2007	Magglio Ordonez	434
2008	Miguel Cabrera	388
2009	Miguel Cabrera	408
2010	Miguel Cabrera	433
2011	Miguel Cabrera	445
2012	Miguel Cabrera	447
2013	Miguel Cabrera	446
2014	Victor Martinez	390
2015	J.D. Martinez	375
2016	Miguel Cabrera	410
2017	Nicholas Castellanos	346
2018	Nicholas Castellanos	361
2019	Miguel Cabrera	244
2020	Jeimer Candelario	114
2021	Robbie Grossman	349

Year	Player	BPA
1901	**Jimmy Barrett**	**2.3**
1902	Jimmy Barrett	2.2
1903	**Sam Crawford**	**2.3**
1904	Sam Crawford	1.8
1905	Sam Crawford	2.1
1906	Sam Crawford	2.0
1907	**Ty Cobb**	**2.4**
1908	Ty Cobb	2.3
1909	**Ty Cobb**	**2.7**
1910	**Ty Cobb**	**2.9**
1911	**Ty Cobb**	**3.4**
1912	Ty Cobb	3.1
1913	Ty Cobb	2.8
1914	Ty Cobb	2.7
1915	Ty Cobb	3.1
1916	Ty Cobb	2.8
1917	Ty Cobb	3.0
1918	Ty Cobb	2.6
1919	Ty Cobb	2.6
1920	Ty Cobb	2.4
1921	Ty Cobb	3.0
1922	Harry Heilmann	2.9
1923	Harry Heilmann	2.9
1924	Harry Heilmann	2.6
1925	Ty Cobb, H. Heilmann	2.7
1926	H. Heilmann, H. Manush	2.4
1927	Harry Heilmann	2.8
1928	Gehringer, Heilmann	2.3
1929	Charlie Gehringer	2.8
1930	Charlie Gehringer	2.7
1931	Roy Johnson	2.5
1932	Charlie Gehringer	2.5
1933	Charlie Gehringer	2.4
1934	Hank Greenberg	2.8
1935	Hank Greenberg	3.2
1936	Charlie Gehringer	2.9
1937	Hank Greenberg	3.3
1938	Hank Greenberg	3.3
1939	Hank Greenberg	3.0
1940	Hank Greenberg	3.3
1941	Rudy York	2.3
1942	B. McCosky, Rudy York	2.1
1943	Rudy York	2.5
1944	Dick Wakefield	2.8
1945	Roy Cullenbine	2.3
1946	Hank Greenberg	2.8
1947	Roy Cullenbine	2.4
1948	Pat Mullin	2.4
1949	George Kell, Vic Wertz	2.4
1950	Hoot Evers, Vic Wertz	2.6
1951	Vic Wertz	2.4
1952	Walt Dropo	2.2
1953	Ray Boone	2.6
1954	Ray Boone	2.2
1955	Al Kaline	2.7
1956	Al Kaline	2.6
1957	Charlie Maxwell	2.3
1958	Al Kaline, H. Kuenn	2.2
1959	Al Kaline	2.6
1960	Eddie Yost	2.3
1961	Norm Cash	3.1

Justin Upton

Year	Player	BPA
1962	Al Kaline	2.9
1963	Al Kaline	2.4
1964	Al Kaline	2.2
1965	Norm Cash	2.3
1966	Al Kaline	2.4
1967	Al Kaline	2.6
1968	Willie Horton	2.3
1969	Jim Northrup	2.2
1970	W. Horton, Al Kaline	2.2
1971	Norm Cash, W. Horton	2.2
1972	Norm Cash, Bill Freehan	1.8
1973	Willie Horton	2.1
1974	Bill Freehan	2.0
1975	W. Horton, Ron LeFlore	1.9
1976	Ron LeFlore	2.5
1977	Ron LeFlore	2.5
1978	Ron LeFlore	2.6
1979	Ron LeFlore	2.6
1980	Steve Kemp	2.3
1981	Steve Kemp	2.2
1982	Lance Parrish	2.3
1983	A. Trammell, L. Whitaker	2.3
1984	Kirk Gibson	2.5
1985	Kirk Gibson	2.6
1986	Kirk Gibson	2.7
1987	Alan Trammell	2.7
1988	A. Trammell, L. Whitaker	2.1
1989	Gary Pettis, L. Whitaker	2.2
1990	Cecil Fielder	2.7
1991	Cecil Fielder	2.5
1992	Rob Deer	2.5
1993	T. Fryman, Tony Phillips	2.5
1994	Tony Phillips	2.7
1995	Chad Curtis	2.4
1996	Bobby Higginson	2.5
1997	Bobby Higginson	2.5
1998	Tony Clark	2.4
1999	Tony Clark, Luis Polonia	2.4
2000	Bobby Higginson	2.7
2001	R. Cedeno, B. Higginson	2.3
2002	Bobby Higginson	2.0
2003	Dmitri Young	2.3
2004	Carlos Guillen	2.6
2005	Chris Shelton	2.2
2006	Carlos Guillen	2.4
2007	Magglio Ordonez	2.8
2008	Curtis Granderson	2.5
2009	Miguel Cabrera	2.6
2010	Miguel Cabrera	2.9
2011	Miguel Cabrera	2.8
2012	Miguel Cabrera	2.8
2013	Miguel Cabrera	3.0
2014	Victor Martinez	2.6
2015	Miguel Cabrera	2.6
2016	Miguel Cabrera	2.6
2017	Justin Upton	2.5
2018	Nicholas Castellanos	2.3
2019	Nicholas Castellanos	2.2
2020	Jeimer Candelario	2.2
2021	Robbie Grossman	2.2

Year	Player	SB
1901	**Ducky Holmes**	**35**
1902	Jimmy Barrett	24
1903	Jimmy Barrett	27
1904	Sam Crawford	20
1905	Sam Crawford	22
1906	B. Coughlin, G. Schaefer	31
1907	**Ty Cobb**	**49**
1908	Germany Schaefer	40
1909	**Ty Cobb**	**76**
1910	Ty Cobb	65
1911	**Ty Cobb**	**83**
1912	Ty Cobb	61
1913	Ty Cobb	51
1914	Donie Bush, Ty Cobb	35
1915	**Ty Cobb**	**96**
1916	Ty Cobb	68
1917	Ty Cobb	55
1918	Ty Cobb	34
1919	Ty Cobb	28
1920	Donie Bush, Ty Cobb	15
1921	Ty Cobb	22
1922	Topper Rigney	17
1923	Fred Haney	13
1924	Ty Cobb	23
1925	Lu Blue	19
1926	Lu Blue	13
1927	Jackie Tavener	19
1928	Harry Rice	20
1929	Charlie Gehringer	27
1930	Marty McManus	23
1931	Roy Johnson	33
1932	Gee Walker	30
1933	Gee Walker	26
1934	Jo-Jo White	28
1935	Jo-Jo White	19
1936	Gee Walker	17
1937	Gee Walker	23
1938	Pete Fox	16
1939	Pete Fox	23
1940	Barney McCosky	13
1941	Barney McCosky	8
1942	Barney McCosky	11
1943	Ned Harris, Joe Hoover	6
1944	Eddie Mayo	9
1945	Skeeter Webb	8
1946	Eddie Lake	15
1947	Eddie Lake	11
1948	Johnny Lipon	4
1949	G. Kell, Don Holloway	7
1950	Johnny Lipon	9
1951	George Kell	10
1952	Pat Mullin	4
1953	Harvey Kuenn	6
1954	Al Kaline, Harvey Kuenn	9
1955	Earl Torgeson	9
1956	Harvey Kuenn	9
1957	Al Kaline	11
1958	Red Wilson	10
1959	Al Kaline	10
1960	Al Kaline	19
1961	Jake Wood	30

Jo-Jo White

Year	Player	SB
1962	Jake Wood	24
1963	Jake Wood	18
1964	Billy Bruton	14
1965	Jerry Lumpe	7
1966	Don Wert	6
1967	Mickey Stanley	9
1968	Dick McAuliffe	8
1969	Mickey Stanley	8
1970	Mickey Stanley	10
1971	Jim Northrup	7
1972	Tony Taylor	5
1973	Tony Taylor	9
1974	Ron LeFlore	23
1975	Ron LeFlore	28
1976	Ron LeFlore	58
1977	Ron LeFlore	39
1978	Ron LeFlore	68
1979	Ron LeFlore	78
1980	T. Brookens, Rick Peters	13
1981	Kirk Gibson	17
1982	Alan Trammell	19
1983	Alan Trammell	30
1984	Kirk Gibson	29
1985	Kirk Gibson	30
1986	Kirk Gibson	34
1987	Kirk Gibson	26
1988	Gary Pettis	44
1989	Gary Pettis	43
1990	Tony Phillips	19
1991	Milt Cuyler	41
1992	Gary Pettis	13
1993	Tony Phillips	16
1994	Tony Phillips	13
1995	Chad Curtis	27
1996	Kimera Bartee	20
1997	Brian Hunter	74
1998	Brian Hunter	42
1999	Juan Encarnacion	33
2000	Juan Encarnacion	16
2001	Roger Cedeno	55
2002	George Lombard	13
2003	Alex Sanchez	44
2004	Alex Sanchez	19
2005	Nook Logan	23
2006	Carlos Guillen	20
2007	Curtis Granderson	26
2008	Curtis Granderson	12
2009	Curtis Granderson	20
2010	Austin Jackson	27
2011	Austin Jackson	22
2012	Quintin Berry	21
2013	Austin Jackson	8
2014	Rajai Davis	36
2015	Anthony Gose	23
2016	Cameron Maybin	15
2017	Ian Kinsler	14
2018	Jose Iglesias	15
2019	Niko Goodrum	12
2020	Victor Reyes	8
2021	Robbie Grossman	20

YEARLY TIGER HITTING LEADERS – CAUGHT STEALING

Year	Player	CS
1920	**Ralph Young**	**13**
1921	**Lu Blue**	**17**
1922	Ty Cobb	13
1923	Lu Blue	11
1924	Ty Cobb	14
1925	Al Wingo	13
1926	Frank O'Rourke	13
1927	Bob Fothergill	15
1928	Marty McManus	13
	Harry Rice	13
1929	Roy Johnson	15
1930	Charlie Gehringer	15
1931	**Roy Johnson**	**21**
1932	Charlie Gehringer	8
	Jo-Jo White	8
1933	Billy Rogell, Gee Walker	9
1934	Pete Fox	10
1935	Jo-Jo White	10
1936	Billy Rogell	10
1937	Pete Fox	8
1938	Pete Fox	7
1939	Pete Fox	12
1940	Barney McCosky	9
1941	Pinky Higgins	4
	Rip Radcliff	4
1942	Jimmy Bloodworth	8
1943	Ned Harris	8
1944	Eddie Mayo	13
1945	Bob Maier	11
1946	Eddie Lake	9
1947	George Kell	11
1948	Eddie Mayo	9
1949	Eddie Lake	8
1950	Hoot Evers	9
1951	Johnny Lipon	6
1952	Johnny Groth	10
1953	Johnny Pesky	7
1954	Harvey Kuenn	9
1955	Al Kaline	8
1956	Harvey Kuenn	5
1957	Frank Bolling, Al Kaline	9
1958	Harvey Kuenn	10
1959	Al Kaline	4
1960	Rocky Colavito	6
1961	Jake Wood	9
1962	Billy Bruton	7
1963	Billy Bruton	7
1964	Billy Bruton	5
	Dick McAuliffe	5
1965	Willie Horton	9
	Dick McAuliffe	9
1966	Dick McAuliffe	7
	Jim Northrup	7
1967	Dick McAuliffe	5
1968	Dick McAuliffe	7
1969	Dick McAuliffe	5
1970	Dick McAuliffe	6
	Jim Northrup	6
1971	Bill Freehan	7
1972	Jim Northrup	7
1973	Tony Taylor	5

Pat Sheridan

Year	Player	CS
1974	Ron LeFlore	9
1975	Ron LeFlore	20
1976	Ron LeFlore	20
1977	Ron LeFlore	19
1978	Ron LeFlore	16
1979	R. LeFlore, A. Trammell	14
1980	Alan Trammell	12
1981	Rick Peters	6
1982	Tom Brookens	9
	Larry Herndon	9
1983	Alan Trammell	10
	Lou Whitaker	10
1984	Alan Trammell	13
1985	Lance Parrish	6
1986	Dave Collins	12
	Alan Trammell	12
1987	Pat Sheridan	13
1988	Gary Pettis	10
1989	Gary Pettis	15
1990	Alan Trammell	10
1991	Milt Cuyler	10
1992	Tony Phillips	10
1993	Tony Phillips	11
1994	Junior Felix	6
1995	Chad Curtis	15
1996	Kimera Bartee	10
	Chad Curtis	10
1997	Brian Hunter	18
1998	Brian Hunter	12
1999	Juan Encarnacion	12
2000	Brad Ausmus	5
	Luis Polonia	5
2001	Roger Cedeno	15
2002	Bobby Higginson	5
	Ramon Santiago	5
2003	Alex Sanchez	18
2004	Alex Sanchez	13
2005	Brandon Inge	6
	Nook Logan	6
2006	Carlos Guillen	9
2007	Carlos Guillen	8
2008	Magglio Ordonez	5
2009	Curtis Granderson	6
2010	Austin Jackson	6
2011	Austin Jackson	5
2012	Austin Jackson	9
2013	Austin Jackson	4
2014	Rajai Davis	11
2015	Anthony Gose	11
2016	Ian Kinsler	6
	Cameron Maybin	6
2017	Nicholas Castellanos	5
	Ian Kinsler	5
	Justin Upton	5
2018	Jose Iglesias	6
2019	Niko Goodrum	3
	Victor Reyes	3
2020	Victor Reyes	2
2021	Niko Goodrum	5
	Robbie Grossman	5

1901 No Qualified Players
1902 No Qualified Players
1903 No Qualified Players
1904 No Qualified Players
1905 No Qualified Players
1906 No Qualified Players
1907 No Qualified Players
1908 No Qualified Players
1909 No Qualified Players
1910 No Qualified Players
1911 No Qualified Players
1912 George Moriarty .769 30-9
1913 No Qualified Players
1914 George Moriarty .694 34-15
1915 George Burns .750 9-3
1916 No Qualified Players
1917 No Qualified Players
1918 No Qualified Players
1919 No Qualified Players
1920 Donie Bush .682 15-7
1921 Ralph Young .917 11-1
1922 Bobby Veach .900 9-1
1923 Bobby Veach .769 10-3
1924 Heinie Manush .737 14-5
1925 Lu Blue .792 19-5
1926 Ty Cobb .692 9-4
1927 Larry Woodall .900 9-1
1928 Bob Fothergill .727 8-3
1929 Charlie Gehringer .730 27-10
1930 Marty McManus .742 23-8
1931 Hub Walker .909 10-1
1932 Gee Walker .833 30-6
1933 Gee Walker .743 26-9
1934 Jo-Jo White .824 28-6
1935 Pete Fox .778 14-4
1936 Goose Goslin .778 14-4
1937 Gee Walker .767 23-7
1938 Charlie Gehringer .933 14-1
1939 Barney McCosky .833 20-4
1940 Charlie Gehringer 1.000 10-0
1941 Barney McCosky .727 8-3
1942 Barney McCosky .688 11-5
1943 Joe Hoover .545 6-5
1944 Paul Richards .727 8-3
1945 Skeeter Webb .533 8-7

1946 Eddie Lake .625 15-9
1947 Hoot Evers .533 8-7
1948 Eddie Mayo .100 1-9
1949 George Kell .583 7-5
1950 Johnny Lipon .600 9-6
1951 George Kell .769 10-3
1952 Johnny Groth .167 2-10
1953 Harvey Kuenn .545 6-5
1954 Al Kaline .643 9-5
1955 Harvey Kuenn .727 8-3
1956 Harvey Kuenn .643 9-5
1957 Al Kaline .550 11-9
1958 Red Wilson 1.000 10-0
1959 Eddie Yost .818 9-2
1960 Al Kaline .826 19-4
1961 Al Kaline .933 14-1

Red Wilson

1962 Jake Wood .889 24-3
1963 Jake Wood .783 18-5
1964 Billy Bruton .737 14-5
1965 Norm Cash .500 6-6
1966 Al Kaline .500 5-5
1967 Mickey Stanley .818 9-2
1968 Al Kaline .600 6-4
1969 Mickey Stanley .667 8-4
1970 Mickey Stanley .909 10-1
1971 Jim Northrup .636 7-4
1972 Jim Northrup .364 4-7
1973 Tony Taylor .643 9-5
1974 Ben Oglivie .800 12-3
1975 Dan Meyer .727 8-3
1976 Dan Meyer 1.000 10-0
1977 Ron LeFlore .672 39-19

1978 Ron LeFlore .810 68-16
1979 Ron LeFlore .848 78-14
1980 Lou Whitaker .667 8-4
1981 Kirk Gibson .773 17-5
1982 Lou Whitaker .786 11-3
1983 Kirk Gibson .824 14-3
1984 Kirk Gibson .763 29-9
1985 Kirk Gibson .882 30-4
1986 Kirk Gibson .850 34-6
1987 Alan Trammell .913 21-2
1988 Gary Pettis .815 44-10
1989 Alan Trammell .833 10-2
1990 Lou Whitaker .800 8-2
1991 Alan Trammell .846 11-2
1992 Gary Pettis .765 13-4
1993 Milt Cuyler .867 13-2
1994 Tony Phillips .722 13-5
1995 Kirk Gibson .818 9-2
1996 Kimera Bartee .667 20-10
1997 Travis Fryman .842 16-3
1998 Brian Hunter .778 42-12
1999 Damion Easley .786 11-3
2000 Bobby Higginson .833 15-3
2001 Roger Cedeno .786 55-15
2002 George Lombard .867 13-2
2003 Ramon Santiago .714 10-4
2004 Nook Logan .800 8-2
2005 Nook Logan .793 23-6
2006 Ivan Rodriguez .727 8-3
2007 Curtis Granderson .963 26-1
2008 Gary Sheffield .818 9-2
2009 Josh Anderson .867 13-2
2010 Johnny Damon .917 11-1
2011 Austin Jackson .815 22-5
2012 Quintin Berry 1.000 21-0
2013 Austin Jackson .667 8-4
2014 Ian Kinsler .789 15-4
2015 Rajai Davis .692 18-8
2016 Cameron Maybin .714 15-6
2017 Ian Kinsler .737 14-5
2018 Victor Reyes .900 9-1
2019 Niko Goodrum .800 12-3
2020 Victor Reyes .800 8-2
2021 Akil Baddoo .818 18-4

Year	Player	Runs
1901	**Ducky Holmes**	**10.5**
1902	Jimmy Barrett	7.2
1903	Jimmy Barrett	8.1
1904	Sam Crawford	6.0
1905	Sam Crawford	6.6
1906	Bill Coughlin	9.3
	Germany Schaefer	9.3
1907	**Ty Cobb**	**14.7**
1908	Ty Cobb	12.0
1909	**Ty Cobb**	**22.8**
1910	Ty Cobb	19.5
1911	**Ty Cobb**	**24.9**
1912	Sam Crawford	4.5
1913	Ty Cobb	15.3
1914	George Moriarty	1.2
1915	Ty Cobb	6.0
1916	Ty Cobb	6.0
1917	Ty Cobb	16.5
1918	Ty Cobb	10.2
1919	Ty Cobb	8.4
1920	Donie Bush	0.3
1921	Ralph Young	2.7
1922	Bobby Veach	2.1
1923	Bobby Jones	1.5
1924	Heinie Manush	1.2
1925	Lu Blue	2.7
1926	Heinie Manush	0.3
1927	Jack Warner	1.8
1928	Bob Fothergill	0.6
1929	Charlie Gehringer	2.1
1930	Marty McManus	2.1
1931	Charlie Gehringer	1.5
1932	Gee Walker	5.4
1933	Gee Walker	2.4
1934	Jo-Jo White	4.8
1935	Pete Fox	1.8
1936	Goose Goslin	1.8
1937	Gee Walker	2.7
1938	Charlie Gehringer	3.6
1939	Barney McCosky	3.6
1940	Charlie Gehringer	3.0
1941	Frank Croucher	0.6
	Barney McCosky	0.6
1942	Barney McCosky	0.3
1943	Paul Richards	0.3
1944	Paul Richards	0.6
1945	Roy Cullenbine	0.6
1946	Hoot Evers	1.5
1947	Vic Wertz	0.6
1948	Bob Swift	0.3

Year	Player	Runs
1949	Neil Berry	0.0
1950	Aaron Robinson	-0.6
	Vic Wertz	-0.6
1951	George Kell	1.2
1952	Pat Mullin	0.0
1953	Walt Dropo	0.6
1954	Ray Boone, Frank House	0.0
1955	Earl Torgeson	2.7
1956	Al Kaline	1.5
1957	Ray Boone, Frank House	-0.3
	Charlie Maxwell	-0.3
1958	Red Wilson	3.0
1959	Eddie Yost	1.5
1960	Al Kaline	3.3
1961	Al Kaline, Jake Wood	3.6
1962	Jake Wood	5.4
1963	Jake Wood	2.4

Andrew Romine

Year	Player	Runs
1964	Billy Bruton	1.2
1965	Jerry Lumpe	2.1
1966	Bill Freehan	0.3
1967	Jim Northrup	1.5
	Mickey Stanley	1.5
1968	Norm Cash	-0.3
1969	Don Wert	0.3
1970	Mickey Stanley	2.4
1971	Dick McAuliffe	0.6
1972	Gates Brown	0.9
1973	Norm Cash	0.3
	Aurelio Rodriguez	0.3
1974	Eddie Brinkman	0.6
	Bill Freehan	0.6
	Aurelio Rodriguez	0.6
1975	Bill Freehan, Dan Meyer	0.6
1976	Ron LeFlore	5.4

Year	Player	Runs
1977	Ron LeFlore	0.3
1978	Ron LeFlore	10.8
1979	Ron LeFlore	15.0
1980	Steve Kemp	0.9
1981	Kirk Gibson	2.1
1982	Lou Whitaker	1.5
1983	Alan Trammell	3.0
1984	Kirk Gibson	3.3
1985	Kirk Gibson	6.6
1986	Kirk Gibson	6.6
1987	Alan Trammell	5.1
1988	Gary Pettis	7.2
1989	Gary Pettis	3.9
1990	Lloyd Moseby	2.1
1991	Milt Cuyler	6.3
1992	Mark Carreon	0.3
1993	Kirk Gibson	0.9
1994	Tony Phillips	0.9
	Alan Trammell	0.9
1995	Chris Gomez	0.6
1996	Mark Lewis	1.2
1997	Brian Hunter	11.4
1998	Brian Hunter	5.4
1999	Juan Encarnacion	2.7
2000	Bobby Higginson	2.7
2001	Roger Cedeno	7.5
2002	Bobby Higginson	0.6
2003	Alex Sanchez	2.4
2004	Carlos Pena	1.5
2005	Nook Logan	3.3
2006	Carlos Guillen	0.6
	Ivan Rodriguez	0.6
2007	Curtis Granderson	7.2
2008	Placido Polanco	1.5
	Gary Sheffield	1.5
2009	Curtis Granderson	2.4
2010	Austin Jackson	4.5
2011	Austin Jackson	3.6
2012	Alex Avila, M. Cabrera	0.6
2013	Andy Dirks	1.5
2014	Rajai Davis	4.2
2015	Rajai Davis	0.6
2016	Andrew Romine	2.4
2017	Mikie Mahtook	1.8
2018	Niko Goodrum	1.2
2019	Niko Goodrum	1.8
2020	Niko Goodrum	1.5
2021	Akil Baddoo	3.0
	Robbie Grossman	3.0

Year	Player	Runs
1901	**Jimmy Barrett**	**171**
1902	Jimmy Barrett	168
1903	**Jimmy Barrett**	**173**
1904	Jimmy Barrett	156
1905	Sam Crawford	150
1906	Sam Crawford	126
1907	Ty Cobb	145
1908	**Matty McIntyre**	**184**
1909	**Ty Cobb**	**204**
1910	**Ty Cobb**	**224**
1911	**Ty Cobb**	**248**
1912	Ty Cobb	195
1913	Ty Cobb	193
1914	Donie Bush, S. Crawford	189
1915	**Ty Cobb**	**285**
1916	Ty Cobb	221
1917	Ty Cobb	239
1918	Ty Cobb	154
1919	Ty Cobb	163
1920	Ralph Young	172
1921	Harry Heilmann	226
1922	Ty Cobb	200
1923	Harry Heilmann	252
1924	Harry Heilmann	225
1925	Harry Heilmann	231
1926	Harry Heilmann	199
1927	Harry Heilmann	240
1928	Charlie Gehringer	187
1929	Charlie Gehringer	213
1930	Charlie Gehringer	210
1931	Roy Johnson	177
1932	Charlie Gehringer	191
1933	Charlie Gehringer	195
1934	Charlie Gehringer	260
1935	Hank Greenberg	268
1936	Charlie Gehringer	256
1937	**Hank Greenberg**	**304**
1938	**Hank Greenberg**	**319**
1939	Hank Greenberg	245
1940	Hank Greenberg	286
1941	Rudy York	204
1942	Barney McCosky	169
1943	Rudy York	208
1944	Pinky Higgins	179
1945	Roy Cullenbine	214
1946	Hank Greenberg	217
1947	Roy Cullenbine	239
1948	Pat Mullin	187
1949	Vic Wertz	202
1950	Vic Wertz	231
1951	Vic Wertz	189
1952	Johnny Groth	119
1953	Jim Delsing	154
1954	Ray Boone	179
1955	Al Kaline	233
1956	Al Kaline	211
1957	Charlie Maxwell	178
1958	Al Kaline	163
1959	Eddie Yost	259
1960	Eddie Yost	**226**

Matty McIntyre

Year	Player	Runs
1961	**Norm Cash**	**334**
1962	Rocky Colavito	230
1963	Norm Cash	193
1964	Al Kaline	183
1965	Norm Cash	178
1966	Al Kaline	197
1967	Al Kaline	205
1968	Dick McAuliffe	173
1969	Jim Northrup	160
1970	Dick McAuliffe	178
1971	Al Kaline	173
1972	Norm Cash	122
1973	Mickey Stanley	121
1974	Al Kaline	147
1975	Willie Horton	133
1976	Rusty Staub	195
1977	Jason Thompson	185
1978	Steve Kemp	199
1979	Steve Kemp	188
1980	Steve Kemp	173
1981	Steve Kemp	144
1982	Larry Herndon	140
1983	Lou Whitaker	191
1984	Kirk Gibson	174
1985	Kirk Gibson	199
1986	Darrell Evans	185
1987	Darrell Evans	213
1988	Darrell Evans	149
1989	Lou Whitaker	189
1990	Cecil Fielder	237
1991	Mickey Tettleton	215
1992	Mickey Tettleton	235
1993	Tony Phillips	255
1994	Tony Phillips	198
1995	Chad Curtis	168
1996	Bobby Higginson	184
1997	Tony Clark	218
1998	Tony Clark	186
1999	Tony Clark	173
2000	Bobby Higginson	212
2001	Bobby Higginson	182
2002	Robert Fick	131
2003	Dmitri Young	179
2004	Carlos Guillen	170
2005	Brandon Inge	156
2006	Carlos Guillen	198
2007	Magglio Ordonez	250
2008	Miguel Cabrera	183
	Curtis Granderson	183
2009	Miguel Cabrera	214
2010	Miguel Cabrera	255
2011	Miguel Cabrera	287
2012	Miguel Cabrera	231
2013	Miguel Cabrera	271
2014	Victor Martinez	215
2015	Miguel Cabrera	195
2016	Miguel Cabrera	223
2017	Justin Upton	157
2018	Nicholas Castellanos	166
2019	Miguel Cabrera	122
2020	Jeimer Candelario	57
2021	Robbie Grossman	196

Year	Player	Walks
1901	**Jimmy Barrett**	**76**
1902	Jimmy Barrett	74
1903	Jimmy Barrett	74
1904	**Jimmy Barrett**	**79**
1905	Sam Crawford	50
1906	Matty McIntyre	56
1907	Davy Jones	60
1908	**Matty McIntyre**	**83**
1909	**Donie Bush**	**88**
1910	Donie Bush	78
1911	**Donie Bush**	**98**
1912	**Donie Bush**	**117**
1913	Donie Bush	80
1914	Donie Bush	112
1915	**Donie Bush, Ty Cobb**	**118**
1916	Ty Cobb	78
1917	Donie Bush	80
1918	Donie Bush	79
1919	Donie Bush	75
1920	Ralph Young	85
1921	Lu Blue	103
1922	Lu Blue	82
1923	Lu Blue	96
1924	Topper Rigney	102
1925	Lu Blue	83
1926	Lu Blue	90
1927	Harry Heilmann	72
1928	Charlie Gehringer	69
1929	Roy Johnson	67
1930	Charlie Gehringer	69
1931	Roy Johnson	72
1932	Charlie Gehringer	68
1933	Billy Rogell	79
1934	Charlie Gehringer	99
1935	Mickey Cochrane	96
1936	Goose Goslin	85
1937	Hank Greenberg	102
1938	**Hank Greenberg**	**119**
1939	Hank Greenberg	91
1940	Charlie Gehringer	101
1941	Charlie Gehringer	95
1942	Rudy York	73
1943	Rudy York	84
1944	Pinky Higgins	81
1945	Roy Cullenbine	102
1946	Eddie Lake	103
1947	**Roy Cullenbine**	**137**
1948	Pat Mullin	77
1949	Vic Wertz	80
1950	J. Growth, Jerry Priddy	95
1951	Vic Wertz	78
1952	Joe Ginsberg	51
	Johnny Groth	51
1953	Jim Delsing	66
1954	Ray Boone	71
1955	Al Kaline	82
1956	Charlie Maxwell	79
1957	Charlie Maxwell	76
1958	Charlie Maxwell	64
1959	Eddie Yost	135
1960	Eddie Yost	125
1961	Norm Cash	124
1962	Norm Cash	104
1963	Norm Cash	89
1964	Dick McAuliffe	77
1965	Norm Cash	77
1966	Al Kaline	81
1967	Dick McAuliffe	105
1968	Dick McAuliffe	82
1969	Norm Cash	63
1970	Dick McAuliffe	101
1971	Al Kaline	82
1972	Dick McAuliffe	59
1973	Gates Brown	52
1974	Al Kaline	65
1975	Gary Sutherland	45
1976	Rusty Staub	83
1977	Jason Thompson	73
1978	Steve Kemp	97
1979	Lou Whitaker	78
1980	Lou Whitaker	73
1981	Steve Kemp	70
1982	Chet Lemon	56
1983	Lou Whitaker	67
1984	Darrell Evans	77
1985	Darrell Evans	85
1986	Darrell Evans	91
1987	Darrell Evans	100
1988	Darrell Evans	84
1989	Lou Whitaker	89
1990	Tony Phillips	99
1991	Mickey Tettleton	101
1992	Mickey Tettleton	122
1993	Tony Phillips	132
1994	Mickey Tettleton	97
1995	Cecil Fielder	75
1996	Bobby Higginson	65
1997	Tony Clark	93
1998	T. Clark, B. Higginson	63
1999	T. Clark, B. Higginson	64
2000	Bobby Higginson	74
2001	Bobby Higginson	80
2002	Robert Fick	46
2003	Bobby Higginson	59
2004	B. Higginson, C. Pena	70
2005	Brandon Inge	63
2006	Carlos Guillen	71
2007	Gary Sheffield	84
2008	Curtis Granderson	71
2009	Curtis Granderson	72
2010	Miguel Cabrera	89
2011	Miguel Cabrera	108
2012	Prince Fielder	85
2013	Miguel Cabrera	90
2014	Victor Martinez	70
2015	Miguel Cabrera	77
2016	Miguel Cabrera	75
2017	Justin Upton	57
2018	Jeimer Candelario	66
2019	Miguel Cabrera	48
2020	Miguel Cabrera	20
2021	Robbie Grossman	98

Joe Ginsberg

Year	Player	IBB	Year	Player	IBB	Year	Player	IBB
1955	**Al Kaline**	**12**	1976	Rusty Staub	11	1997	Tony Clark	13
1956	Ray Boone	8	1977	Phil Mankowski	4	1998	Luis Gonzalez	7
1957	**Frank House**	**13**		Rusty Staub	4	1999	Tony Clark	7
1958	Harvey Kuenn	8	1978	Ron LeFlore	7	2000	Bobby Higginson	6
1959	Al Kaline	12	1979	Jason Thompson	8	2001	Tony Clark	10
1960	Charlie Maxwell	6	1980	Champ Summers	6	2002	R. Simon, D. Young	5
1961	**Norm Cash**	**19**	1981	Lance Parrish	6	2003	Dmitri Young	16
1962	Norm Cash	12	1982	Lance Parrish	5	2004	Ivan Rodriguez	6
1963	Al Kaline	12	1983	Lou Whitaker	8	2005	Dmitri Young	7
1964	Dick McAuliffe	8	1984	Darrell Evans	10	2006	Carlos Guillen	10
1965	Al Kaline	11	1985	Kirk Gibson	16	2007	Sean Casey	11
1966	Bill Freehan	9	1986	Darrell Evans	5	2008	Miguel Cabrera	6
1967	Bill Freehan	15		Lou Whitaker	5	2009	Miguel Cabrera	14
1968	Willie Horton	8	1987	Darrell Evans	8	**2010**	**Miguel Cabrera**	**32**
	Dick McAuliffe	8		Kirk Gibson	8	2011	Miguel Cabrera	22
1969	Willie Horton	10		Alan Trammell	8	2012	Prince Fielder	18
1970	Dick McAuliffe	7	1988	Alan Trammell	8	2013	Miguel Cabrera	19
	Don Wert	7	1989	Lou Whitaker	6	2014	Victor Martinez	28
1971	Bill Freehan	9	1990	Cecil Fielder	11	2015	Miguel Cabrera	15
	Al Kaline	9	1991	Cecil Fielder	12	2016	Miguel Cabrera	15
	Jim Northrup	9	1992	Mickey Tettleton	18	2017	Miguel Cabrera	6
1972	Norm Cash	13	1993	Cecil Fielder	15	2018	Nichola Castellanos	5
1973	Norm Cash	7	1994	Mickey Tettleton	10	2019	Miguel Cabrera	4
1974	Ben Oglivie	6	1995	Cecil Fielder	8	2020	Miguel Cabrera	1
1975	Willie Horton	11	1996	Cecil Fielder	8	2021	Robbie Grossman	3

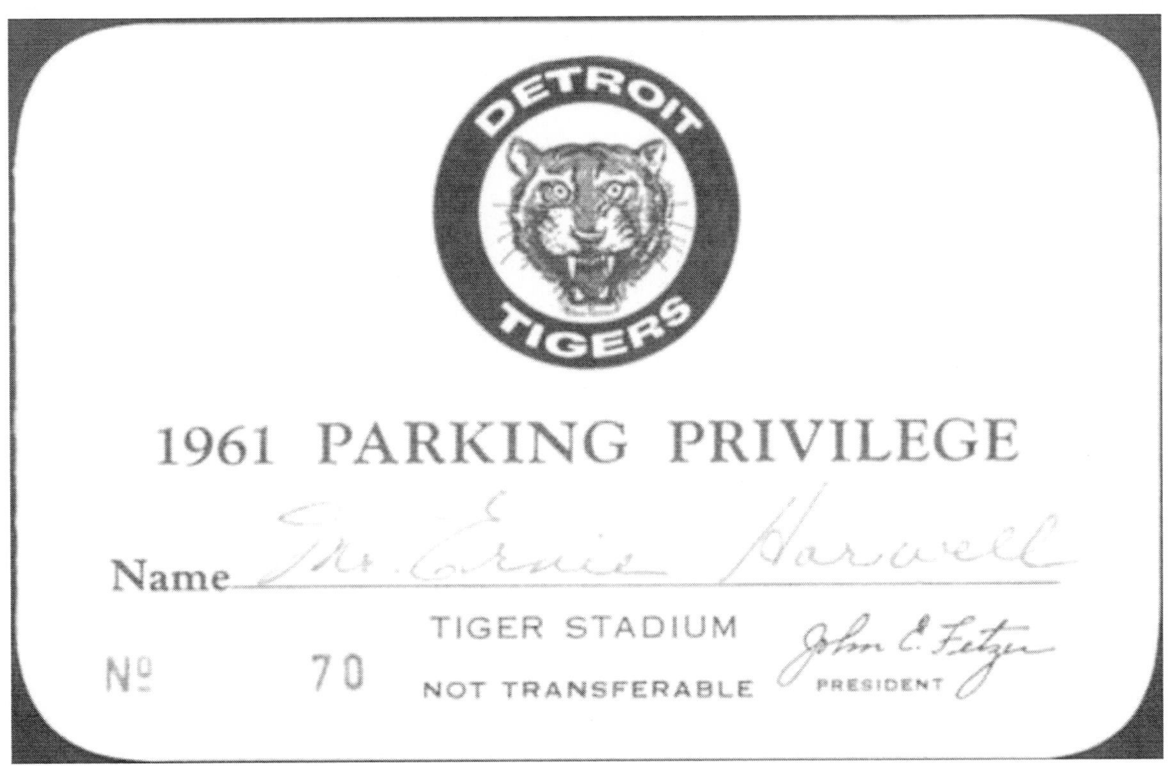
DETROIT TIGERS

1961 PARKING PRIVILEGE

Name Mr. Ernie Harwell

TIGER STADIUM

No 70

NOT TRANSFERABLE

John E. Fetzer PRESIDENT

1961 Detroit Tigers parking privilege credentials issued to radio and television broadcaster Ernie Harwell.

Year	Player	BB%
1901	**Jimmy Barrett**	**12.1**
1902	**Jimmy Barrett**	**12.5**
1903	**Billy Lush**	**13.3**
1904	Jimmy Barrett	11.1
1905	Matty McIntyre	8.7
1906	Davy Jones	11.1
1907	Davy Jones	10.6
1908	Matty McIntyre	12.4
1909	Donie Bush	13.0
1910	Donie Bush	12.9
1911	**Donie Bush**	**14.2**
1912	**Donie Bush**	**18.2**
1913	Ty Cobb	11.6
1914	Donie Bush	15.5
1915	Donie Bush, Ty Cobb	16.8
1916	Ty Cobb	12.3
1917	Donie Bush	11.9
1918	Ralph Young	14.7
1919	Donie Bush	12.5
1920	Ralph Young	12.1
1921	Lu Blue	14.5
1922	Johnny Bassler	13.7
1923	Johnny Bassler	15.9
1924	Topper Rigney	16.1
1925	Johnny Bassler	17.1
1926	Lu Blue	16.7
1927	Lu Blue	15.6
1928	Charlie Gehringer	10.0
1929	Harry Rice	10.0
1930	Marty McManus	10.5
1931	Marty McManus	11.8
1932	Earl Webb	10.3
1933	Billy Rogell	11.7
1934	Mickey Cochrane	14.9
1935	**Mickey Cochrane**	**18.4**
1936	Goose Goslin	12.9
1937	Hank Greenberg	14.6
1938	Hank Greenberg	17.5
1939	Hank Greenberg	15.1
1940	Charlie Gehringer	16.1
1941	Charlie Gehringer	17.7
1942	Birdie Tebbetts	13.9
1943	Rudy York	12.7
1944	Dick Wakefield	16.6

Year	Player	BB%
1945	Roy Cullenbine	16.1
1946	**Roy Cullenbine**	**21.0**
1947	**Roy Cullenbine**	**22.6**
1948	Dick Wakefield	17.8
1949	Aaron Robinson	17.8
1950	Aaron Robinson	20.9
1951	Vic Wertz	13.4
1952	Joe Ginsberg	14.0
1953	Jim Delsing	12.0
1954	Jim Delsing	11.5
1955	Earl Torgeson	16.5
1956	Frank House	22.4
1957	Charlie Maxwell	13.1
1958	Charlie Maxwell	13.7
1959	Eddie Yost	20.0
1960	Eddie Yost	19.7

Earl Torgeson

Year	Player	BB%
1961	Norm Cash	18.5
1962	Norm Cash	16.5
1963	Norm Cash	15.0
1964	Norm Cash	12.5
1965	Al Kaline	15.2
1966	Al Kaline	14.2
1967	Dick McAuliffe	15.6
1968	Al Kaline	14.1
1969	Norm Cash	11.3
1970	Norm Cash	15.9
1971	Al Kaline	16.4
1972	Dick McAuliffe	12.6
1973	Dick McAuliffe	12.4
1974	Al Kaline	10.3
1975	Gary Sutherland	8.1
1976	Jason Thompson	14.0

Year	Player	BB%
1977	Steve Kemp	11.2
1978	Steve Kemp	14.1
1979	Lou Whitaker	15.0
1980	John Wockenfuss	15.3
1981	Steve Kemp	15.7
1982	Chet Lemon	10.9
1983	Kirk Gibson	11.3
1984	Darrell Evans	15.9
1985	Darrell Evans	14.3
1986	Darrell Evans	15.1
1987	Darrell Evans	16.4
1988	Darrell Evans	16.2
1989	Gary Pettis	15.8
1990	Tony Phillips	15.2
1991	Mickey Tettleton	16.6
1992	Mickey Tettleton	18.5
1993	Tony Phillips	18.7
1994	Mickey Tettleton	22.0
1995	Cecil Fielder	13.2
1996	Cecil Fielder	14.4
1997	Tony Clark	14.1
1998	Tony Clark	9.4
1999	Bobby Higginson	14.4
2000	Brad Ausmus	11.4
2001	Bobby Higginson	12.6
2002	Shane Halter	8.5
2003	Bobby Higginson	10.9
2004	Bobby Higginson	13.2
2005	Brandon Inge	9.1
2006	Carlos Guillen	11.4
2007	Gary Sheffield	14.2
2008	Carlos Guillen	12.3
2009	Clete Thomas	10.6
2010	Miguel Cabrera	13.7
2011	Miguel Cabrera	15.7
2012	Alex Avila	14.1
2013	Miguel Cabrera	13.8
2014	Alex Avila	13.3
2015	Miguel Cabrera	15.1
2016	Miguel Cabrera	11.0
2017	Justin Upton	11.0
2018	Jeimer Candelario	10.7
2019	Jeimer Candelario	11.1
2020	Miguel Cabrera	10.4
2021	Robbie Grossman	14.6

1901	**Kid Elberfeld**	**3.2**
1902	**Kid Elberfeld**	**5.5**
1903	Billy Lush	1.3
1904	Rabbit Robinson	1.5
1905	Sam Crawford	1.6
1906	Sam Crawford	1.9
1907	Davy Jones	1.5
1908	S. Crawford, M. McIntyre	1.3
1909	Sam Crawford	1.5
1910	Ty Cobb	1.4
1911	Sam Crawford	1.7
1912	Donie Bush	2.2
1913	Donie Bush	2.5
1914	Ty Cobb	2.6
1915	Ossie Vitt	3.6
1916	Sam Crawford	3.7
1917	Ossie Vitt	3.7
1918	Ossie Vitt	5.3
1919	Donie Bush	2.1
1920	Ralph Young	2.8
1921	Johnny Bassler	3.6
1922	Johnny Bassler	5.2
1923	**Johnny Bassler**	**5.8**
1924	Johnny Bassler	5.6
1925	**Johnny Bassler**	**12.3**
1926	Lu Blue	5.0
1927	Harry Heilmann	4.5
1928	Charlie Gehringer	3.1
1929	Charlie Gehringer	3.4
1930	Charlie Gehringer	4.1
1931	Marty McManus	2.2
1932	Earl Webb	2.2
1933	Charlie Gehringer	2.5
1934	Charlie Gehringer	4.0
1935	Mickey Cochrane	6.4
1936	Charlie Gehringer	6.4
1937	Charlie Gehringer	3.6
1938	Charlie Gehringer	5.4
1939	Charlie Gehringer	4.3
1940	Charlie Gehringer	5.9
1941	Charlie Gehringer	3.7
1942	Pinky Higgins	3.4
1943	Doc Cramer	2.4
1944	Eddie Mayo	2.5
1945	Roy Cullenbine	2.8
1946	Roy Cullenbine	2.3
1947	George Kell	3.8
1948	Johnny Lipon	3.1
1949	George Kell	5.5
1950	George Kell	3.7
1951	George Kell	3.4
1952	Joe Ginsberg	2.4
1953	Jim Delsing	1.7
1954	Harvey Kuenn	2.2
1955	Earl Torgeson	2.1
1956	Boone, House, Torgeson	1.7
1957	Harvey Kuenn	1.7
1958	Harvey Kuenn	1.5
1959	Eddie Yost	1.8
1960	Eddie Yost	1.8
1961	Steve Boros, al Kaline	1.6

Steve Boros

1962	Rocky Colavito	1.4
1963	Norm Cash	1.2
1964	Al Kaline	1.5
1965	Jerry Lumpe	1.6
1966	Al Kaline	1.2
1967	Al Kaline	1.8
1968	Al Kaline	1.4
1969	Bill Freehan	1.0
1970	Al Kaline, Dick McAuliffe	1.6
1971	Jim Northrup	1.4
1972	Dick McAuliffe	1.0
1973	G. Brown, Bill Freehan	1.3
1974	Bill Freehan	1.0
1975	Gary Sutherland	1.1
1976	Rusty Staub	1.7
1977	Rusty Staub	1.3
1978	Rusty Staub	2.2
1979	Lou Whitaker	1.2
1980	Steve Kemp, Rick Peters,	1.1
	Trammell, Wockenfuss	1.1
1981	Lynn Jones	1.8
1982	Alan Trammell	1.1
1983	Lou Whitaker	1.0
1984	Darrell Evans	1.1
1985	Lou Whitaker	1.4
1986	Alan Trammell	1.0
1987	Alan Trammell	1.3
1988	D. Bergman, L. Whitaker	1.1
1989	Lou Whitaker	1.5
1990	Dave Bergman	1.9
1991	Lou Whitaker	2.0
1992	Lou Whitaker	1.8
1993	Lou Whitaker	1.7
1994	Mickey Tettleton	1.0
1995	Chad Curtis	0.8
1996	Bobby Higginson	1.0
1997	Bobby Higginson	0.8
1998	Luis Gonzalez	0.9
1999	Bobby Higginson	1.0
2000	Brad Ausmus	0.9
2001	Bobby Higginson	1.2
2002	Bobby Higginson	0.9
2003	Bobby Higginson	0.8
2004	Bobby Higginson	0.8
2005	Placido Polanco	1.3
2006	Carlos Guillen	0.8
2007	P. Polanco, G. Sheffield	1.2
2008	Carlos Guillen	0.9
2009	M. Ordonez, P. Polanco	0.8
2010	Magglio Ordonez	1.1
2011	Miguel Cabrera	1.2
2012	Prince Fielder	1.0
2013	Miguel Cabrera	1.0
2014	Victor Martinez	1.7
2015	Miguel Cabrera	0.9
2016	M. Cabrera, Jose Iglesias,	0.6
	Victor Martinez	0.6
2017	Ian Kinsler, V. Martinez	0.6
2018	Victor Martinez	0.7
2019	M. Cabrera, J. Candelario	0.4
2020	Miguel Cabrera	0.5
2021	Robbie Grossman	0.6

Year	Player	SF
1954	**Frank House**	**7**
1955	**Ray Boone**	**7**
	Earl Torgeson	**7**
1956	**Harvey Kuenn**	**8**
	Charlie Maxwell	**8**
1957	Al Kaline	7
1958	**Frank Bolling**	**9**
1959	Lou Berberet	7
1960	Al Kaline	5
1961	Rocky Colavito	8
1962	Rocky Colavito	7
1963	**Bubba Phillips**	**10**
1964	Norm Cash	7
	Bill Freehan	7
	Don Wert	7
1965	Norm Cash	4
	Willie Horton	4
	Jerry Lumpe	4
	Don Wert	4
1966	Al Kaline	6
	Don Wert	6
1967	Al Kaline	6
1968	Willie Horton	7
1969	Al Kaline	7
1970	Al Kaline	7
1971	Al Kaline	6
1972	Mickey Stanley	8
1973	Mickey Stanley	6
1974	Al Kaline	5
	Aurelio Rodriguez	5
1975	Willie Horton	8
1976	**Rusty Staub**	**11**
1977	Rusty Staub	10
1978	**Rusty Staub**	**11**
1979	Steve Kemp	8
	Jerry Morales	8
1980	Steve Kemp	9
1981	Tom Brookens	6
1982	Alan Trammell	6
1983	**Lance Parrish**	**13**
1984	Dave Bergman	6
	Kirk Gibson	6
	Lance Parrish	6
1985	Kirk Gibson	10
1986	Darnell Coles	8
1987	Darrell Evans	6
	Larry Herndon	6
	Alan Trammell	6
1988	Alan Trammell	7
1989	Lou Whitaker	9
1990	Alan Trammell	6
1991	Lou Whitaker	8
1992	Cecil Fielder	7
	Tony Phillips	7
1993	Travis Fryman	6
	Scott Livingstone	6
	Mickey Tettleton	6
1994	**Travis Fryman**	**13**
1995	Chad Curtis	7
	Travis Fryman	7
	Bobby Higginson	7
1996	Travis Fryman	10
1997	Travis Fryman	11
1998	Luis Gonzalez	8
1999	Damion Easley	6
2000	Dean Palmer	10
2001	Bobby Higginson	9
2002	Bobby Higginson	7
	Randall Simon	7
2003	Eric Munson	7
2004	Brandon Inge	6
2005	Craig Monroe	12
2006	Curtis Granderson	6
	Craig Monroe	6
2007	Carlos Guillen	8
2008	Miguel Cabrera	9
2009	Marcus Thames	6
2010	Miguel Cabrera	8
2011	Jhonny Peralta	9
2012	Prince Fielder	7
	Delmon Young	7
2013	Torri Hunter	10
2014	Miguel Cabrera	11
2015	Victor Martinez	7
2016	Miguel Cabrera	5
	Nicholas Castellanos	5
	J.D. Martinez	5
2017	Nicholas Castellanos	5
2018	Victor Martinez	7
2019	Christin Stewart	6
2020	Niko Goodrum	3
2021	Miguel Cabrera	9

View of Briggs Stadium, with a streetcar and vehicles in the foreground, as fans stand in line at the advance ticket office.

Year	Player	SH
1901	**Doc Nance**	**24**
1902	Kid Gleason	11
1903	**Billy Lush**	**34**
1904	Matty McIntyre	28
1905	C. O'Leary, G. Schaefer	29
1906	**Bill Coughlin**	**36**
1907	Claude Rossman	28
1908	**Germany Schaefer**	**43**
1909	**Donie Bush**	**52**
1910	Tom Jones	33
1911	Donie Bush	30
1912	George Moriarty	20
1913	Ossie Vitt	23
1914	George Moriarty	25
1915	Ossie Vitt	42
1916	Ossie Vitt	32
1917	Ossie Vitt, Ralph Young	31
1918	Ossie Vitt	20
1919	Ralph Young	46
1920	Donie Bush	48
1921	Donie Bush	40
1922	Topper Rigney	37
1923	Topper Rigney	33
1924	Topper Rigney	31
1925	Lu Blue	34
1926	H. Manush, J. Tavener	28
1927	M. McManus, J. Tavener	18
1928	Jackie Tavener	19
1929	Dale Alexander	18
1930	Liz Funk	23
1931	Marv Owen	12
1932	Harry Davis	17
1933	Marv Owen	15
1934	Billy Rogell	13
1935	Charlie Gehringer	17
1936	Marv Owen	12
1937	Pete Fox, Billy Rogell	10
1938	Pete Fox	8
1939	Pinky Higgins	14
1940	Dick Bartell	11
1941	Frank Croucher	11
1942	Barney McCosky	12
1943	Joe Hoover	28
1944	Eddie Mayo	28
1945	Doc Cramer	15
1946	George Kell	13
1947	Hoot Evers	14
1948	Eddie Mayo	18
1949	George Kell	16
1950	Johnny Lipon	18
1951	Jerry Priddy	12
1952	Ted Gray	8
1953	Don Lund	8
1954	Steve Gromek	10
1955	Bill Tuttle	13
1956	Frank Bolling	7
1957	Paul Foytack	12
1958	Billy Martin	13
1959	Jim Bunning, Frank Lary	8
1960	Chico Fernandez	19
1961	Boros, Foytack, Mossi	6

John Flaherty

Year	Player	SH
1962	Chico Fernandez	12
1963	Billy Bruton	10
1964	Dave Wickersham	12
1965	Jerry Lumpe	10
1966	Don Wert	11
1967	Ray Oyler	15
1968	Denny McLain	16
1969	Denny McLain	13
1970	Joe Niekro	15
1971	Mickey Lolich	16
1972	Joe Coleman	15
1973	Eddie Brinkman	14
1974	Eddie Brinkman	9
1975	Aurelio Rodriguez	8
1976	Aurelio Rodriguez	9
1977	Tito Fuentes	13
1978	Lou Whitaker	13
1979	Lou Whitaker	14
1980	Alan Trammell	13
1981	Alan Trammell	16
1982	Alan Trammell	9
1983	Alan Trammell	15
1984	Tom Brookens	8
1985	Alan Trammell	11
1986	Alan Trammell	11
1987	Tom Brookens	9
1988	L. Salazar, J. Walewander	10
1989	Gary Pettis	8
1990	Tony Phillips	9
1991	Milt Cuyler	12
1992	Milt Cuyler	8
1993	Lou Whitaker	7
1994	Chris Gomez, L. Whitaker	3
1995	John Flaherty	8
1996	Kimera Bartee	13
1997	Deivi Cruz	14
1998	Deivi Cruz	5
1999	Deivi Cruz	14
2000	Shane Halter	10
2001	Jose Macias	8
2002	George Lombard	7
2003	Ramon Santiago	18
2004	Alex Sanchez	12
2005	Nook Logan	12
2006	Vance Wilson	10
2007	Brandon Inge	7
2008	B. Inge, Ramon Santiago	5
2009	Adam Everett	15
2010	Ramon Santiago	8
2011	Austin Jackson	14
2012	Quintin Berry	6
2013	Ramon Santiago	6
2014	Eugenio Suarez	5
2015	J. Iglesias, James McCann	4
	Andrew Romine	4
2016	Jose Iglesias	7
2017	Jose Iglesias, Alex Presley	3
2018	Jose Iglesias	3
2019	Harold Castro, Jake Rogers	2
2020	Willi Castro	1
2021	Harold Castro	4

Year	Player	Total
1901	**Doc Nance**	**24**
1902	Kid Gleason	11
1903	**Billy Lush**	**34**
1904	Matty McIntyre	28
1905	C. O'Leary, G. Schaefer	29
1906	**Bill Coughlin**	**36**
1907	Claude Rossman	28
1908	**Germany Schaefer**	**43**
1909	**Donie Bush**	**52**
1910	Tom Jones	33
1911	Donie Bush	30
1912	George Moriarty	20
1913	Ossie Vitt	23
1914	George Moriarty	25
1915	Ossie Vitt	42
1916	Ossie Vitt	32
1917	Ossie Vitt, Ralph Young	31
1918	Ossie Vitt	20
1919	Ralph Young	46
1920	Donie Bush	48
1921	Donie Bush	40
1922	Topper Rigney	37
1923	Topper Rigney	33
1924	Topper Rigney	31
1925	Lu Blue	34
1926	H. Manush, J. Tavener	28
1927	M. McManus, J. Tavener	18
1928	Jackie Tavener	19
1929	Dale Alexander	18
1930	Liz Funk	23
1931	Marv Owen	12
1932	Harry Davis	17
1933	Marv Owen	15
1934	Billy Rogell	13
1935	Charlie Gehringer	17
1936	Marv Owen	12
1937	Pete Fox, Billy Rogell	10
1938	Pete Fox	8
1939	Pinky Higgins	14
1940	Dick Bartell	11
1941	Frank Croucher	11
1942	Barney McCosky	12
1943	Joe Hoover	28
1944	Eddie Mayo	28
1945	Doc Cramer	15
1946	George Kell	13
1947	Hoot Evers	14
1948	Eddie Mayo	18
1949	George Kell	16
1950	Johnny Lipon	18
1951	Jerry Priddy	12
1952	Ted Gray	8
1953	Don Lund	8
1954	Dropo, Gromek, Kuenn	10
1955	Bill Tuttle	18
1956	Frank Bolling	12
1957	Al Kaline	13
1958	Billy Martin	19
1959	Frank Bolling	9
1960	Chico Fernandez	22
1961	Steve Boros	13

Leon Roberts

Year	Player	Total
1962	Chico Fernandez	15
1963	Bubba Phillips	15
1964	D. Wert, D. Wickersham	13
1965	Jerry Lumpe	14
1966	Don Wert	17
1967	Ray Oyler	18
1968	Denny McLain	16
1969	Denny McLain	15
1970	Cesar Gutierrez	17
1971	Mickey Lolich	16
1972	Joe Coleman	15
1973	Eddie Brinkman	16
1974	Eddie Brinkman	12
1975	L. Roberts, A. Rodriguez	9
1976	Aurelio Rodriguez	14
1977	Tito Fuentes	18
1978	Lou Whitaker	21
1979	Lou Whitaker	18
1980	Alan Trammell	20
1981	Alan Trammell	19
1982	Alan Trammell	15
1983	Alan Trammell	19
1984	D. Bergman, T. Brookens	9
	K. Gibson, L. Whitaker	9
1985	Alan Trammell	20
1986	D. Coles, Alan Trammell	15
1987	Bill Madlock	12
1988	Luis Salazar	13
1989	Lou Whitaker	10
1990	Tony Phillips	11
1991	Milt Cuyler	14
1992	Tony Phillips	12
1993	Lou Whitaker	11
1994	Travis Fryman	14
1995	John Flaherty	10
1996	Kimera Bartee	13
1997	Deivi Cruz	17
1998	Luis Gonzalez	8
1999	Deivi Cruz	19
2000	Deivi Cruz	15
2001	Shane Halter	13
2002	B. Higginson, G. Lombard	8
	Chris Truby	8
2003	Ramon Santiago	20
2004	Brandon Inge	14
2005	Craig Monroe	13
2006	Curtis Granderson	13
2007	Brandon Inge	11
2008	Miguel Cabrera, B. Inge	9
2009	Adam Everett	19
2010	Ramon Santiago	10
2011	Austin Jackson	17
2012	Berry, P. Fielder, D. Young	7
2013	Torii Hunter	13
2014	Miguel Cabrera	11
2015	J. Iglesias, Victor Martinez	7
2016	Jose Iglesias	10
2017	Nicholas Castellanos	5
2018	Victor Martinez	7
2019	H. Castro, C. Stewart	6
2020	W. Castro, Niko Goodrum	3
2021	M. Cabrera, H. Castro	9

Year	Player	SO
1901	**Jimmy Barrett**	**64**
1902	Jimmy Barrett	61
1903	**Jimmy Barrett**	**67**
1904	**Jimmy Barrett**	**91**
1905	**Germany Schaefer**	**91**
1906	Germany Schaefer	57
1907	Bill Coughlin	67
1908	Germany Schaefer	75
1909	Donie Bush	74
1910	Donie Bush	82
1911	Oscar Stanage	79
1912	Oscar Stanage	55
1913	Del Gainer	45
1914	Oscar Stanage	58
1915	George Burns	51
1916	Oscar Stanage	48
1917	Harry Heilmann	54
1918	George Cunningham	34
1919	Harry Heilmann	41
1920	D. Bush, Harry Heilmann	32
1921	Lu Blue	47
1922	Lu Blue	48
1923	Lu Blue, Harry Heilmann	40
1924	Harry Heilmann	41
1925	Jackie Tavener	60
1926	Jackie Tavener	53
1927	Jack Warner	45
1928	Jackie Tavener	51
1929	Dale Alexander	63
1930	Dale Alexander	56
1931	Roy Johnson	51
1932	John Stone	64
1933	Hank Greenberg	78
1934	**Hank Greenberg**	**93**
1935	Hank Greenberg	91
1936	Goose Goslin	50
1937	**Hank Greenberg**	**101**
1938	Hank Greenberg	92
1939	Hank Greenberg	95
1940	Rudy York	88
1941	Rudy York	88
1942	Rudy York	71
1943	**Joe Hoover**	**101**
1944	Rudy York	73
1945	Rudy York	85
1946	Hank Greenberg	88
1947	Pat Mullin, Vic Wertz	66
1948	Vic Wertz	70
1949	Vic Wertz	61
1950	Jerry Priddy	95
1951	Jerry Priddy	73
1952	Walt Dropo	63
1953	Walt Dropo	69
1954	Bill Tuttle	60
1955	Al Kaline	57
1956	Charlie Maxwell	74
1957	Charlie Maxwell	84
1958	Billy Martin	62
1959	Charlie Maxwell	91
1960	Rocky Colavito	80

Billy Martin

Year	Player	SO
1961	**Jake Wood**	**141**
1962	Norm Cash	82
1963	Rocky Colavito	78
1964	Dick McAuliffe	96
1965	Willie Horton	101
1966	Willie Horton	103
1967	Dick McAuliffe	118
1968	Willie Horton	110
1969	Willie Horton	93
1970	Jim Northrup	68
1971	Aurelio Rodriguez	93
1972	Aurelio Rodriguez	104
1973	Aurelio Rodriguez	85
1974	Al Kaline	75
1975	Ron LeFlore	139
1976	Ron LeFlore	111
1977	Ron LeFlore	121
1978	Ron LeFlore	104
1979	Lance Parrish	105
1980	Lance Parrish	109
1981	Kirk Gibson	64
1982	Lance Parrish	99
1983	Lance Parrish	106
1984	Lance Parrish	120
1985	Kirk Gibson	137
1986	Kirk Gibson	107
1987	Kirk Gibson	117
1988	Darrell Evans	89
1989	Gary Pettis	106
1990	**Cecil Fielder**	**182**
1991	Rob Deer	175
1992	Cecil Fielder	151
1993	Mickey Tettleton	139
1994	Travis Fryman	128
1995	Cecil Fielder	116
1996	Melvin Nieves	158
1997	Melvin Nieves	157
1998	Tony Clark	128
1999	Dean Palmer	153
2000	Dean Palmer	146
2001	Tony Clark	108
2002	Brandon Inge	101
2003	Dmitri Young	130
2004	Carlos Pena	146
2005	Brandon Inge	140
2006	Curtis Granderson	174
2007	Brandon Inge	150
2008	Miguel Cabrera	126
2009	Brandon Inge	170
2010	Austin Jackson	170
2011	Austin Jackson	181
2012	Austin Jackson	134
2013	Austin Jackson	129
2014	Alex Avila	151
2015	J.D. Martinez	178
2016	Justin Upton	179
2017	Justin Upton	147
2018	Jeimer Candelario	160
2019	Niko Goodrum	138
2020	Niko Goodrum	69
2021	Robbie Grossman	155

Year	Player	Ratio
1901	**Sport McAllister**	**.08**
1902	**Kid Elberfeld**	**.08**
1903	Joe Yeager	.24
1904	Rabbit Robinson	.26
1905	Sam Crawford	.18
1906	Germany Schaefer	.54
1907	Sam Crawford	.15
1908	Sam Crawford	.15
1909	Sam Crawford	.17
1910	Sam Crawford	.20
1911	Ty Cobb, Sam Crawford	.17
1912	Ty Cobb	.13
1913	**Bush, Crawford, Vitt**	**.05**
1914	**S. Crawford, B. Veach**	**.05**
1915	**Ossie Vitt**	**.04**
1916	**Sam Crawford**	**.03**
1917	**Ossie Vitt**	**.03**
1918	**Ossie Vitt**	**.02**
1919	Ty Cobb	.04
1920	C. Shorten, Bobby Veach	.04
1921	Three Batters	.04
1922	J. Bassler, G. Cutshaw	.03
1923	Four Batters	.03
1924	**Del Pratt**	**.02**
1925	**Johnny Bassler**	**.02**
1926	Lu Blue, Harry Heilmann	.04
1927	Harry Heilmann	.03
1928	Charlie Gehringer	.04
1929	Charlie Gehringer	.03
1930	Charlie Gehringer	.03
1931	Mark Koenig	.03
1932	Earl Webb	.05
1933	Charlie Gehringer	.04
1934	Charlie Gehringer	.04
1935	Charlie Gehringer	.03
1936	**Charlie Gehringer**	**.02**
1937	Charlie Gehringer	.04
1938	C. Gehringer, C. Morgan	.04
1939	Charlie Gehringer	.04
1940	Charlie Gehringer	.03
1941	Rip Radcliff	.03
1942	Doc Cramer	.03
1943	**Doc Cramer**	**.02**
1944	Doc Cramer, Eddie Mayo	.04
1945	Doc Cramer	.04
1946	George Kell	.03
1947	George Kell	.03
1948	George Kell	.04
1949	**George Kell**	**.02**
1950	George Kell	.03
1951	George Kell	.03
1952	J. Ginsberg, J. Groth	.07
1953	Harvey Kuenn	.05
1954	**Harvey Kuenn**	**.02**
1955	Harvey Kuenn	.04
1956	Harvey Kuenn	.06
1957	Harvey Kuenn	.04
1958	Harvey Kuenn	.06
1959	Harvey Kuenn	.07
1960	Frank Bolling, Al Kaline	.09

Enos Cabell

Year	Player	Ratio
1961	Al Kaline	.07
1962	Al Kaline	.10
1963	Al Kaline, Bubba Phillips	.09
1964	Al Kaline, Jerry Lumpe	.10
1965	Jerry Lumpe	.07
1966	Jerry Lumpe	.11
1967	Al Kaline	.10
1968	Mickey Stanley	.10
1969	Mickey Stanley	.09
1970	Cesar Gutierrez	.09
1971	B. Freehan, Jim Northrup	.09
1972	Eddie Brinkman	.10
1973	Bill Freehan	.08
1974	Gary Sutherland	.06
1975	Dan Meyer	.05
1976	Dan Meyer	.07
1977	Milt May, Rusty Staub	.08
1978	Rusty Staub	.05
1979	A. Rodriguez, Trammell	.12
1980	Al Cowens, Rick Peters	.10
1981	Lynn Jones	.06
1982	Three Batters	.10
1983	Enos Cabell	.10
1984	Three Batters	.11
1985	Lou Whitaker	.09
1986	Alan Trammell	.10
1987	Alan Trammell	.08
1988	Ray Knight, A. Trammell	.10
1989	Alan Trammell	.10
1990	Dave Bergman	.08
1991	A. Trammell, L. Whitaker	.10
1992	Livingstone, Whitaker	.10
1993	Alan Trammell	.09
1994	Alan Trammell	.12
1995	John Flaherty	.13
1996	Bobby Higginson	.15
1997	Deivi Cruz	.13
1998	Luis Gonzalez	.11
1999	Luis Polonia	.10
2000	Deivi Cruz	.07
2001	Deivi Cruz, Jose Macias	.11
2002	Randall Simon	.06
2003	Alex Sanchez, W. Morris	.12
2004	Alex Sanchez	.15
2005	Placido Polanco	.05
2006	Placido Polanco	.06
2007	Placido Polanco	.05
2008	Placido Polanco	.07
2009	Placido Polanco	.07
2010	Magglio Ordonez	.12
2011	Victor Martinez	.09
2012	Prince Fielder	.14
2013	O. Infante, V. Martinez	.10
2014	Victor Martinez	.07
2015	Jose Iglesias	.11
2016	Jose Iglesias	.11
2017	Jose Iglesias	.14
2018	Victor Martinez	.10
2019	M. Cabrera, H. Castro	.08
2020	Victor Reyes	.08
2021	Jonathan Schoop	.08

1901	**Sport McAllister**	**2.1**
1902	**Kid Elberfeld**	**1.8**
1903	Joe Yeager	5.7
1904	Rabbit Robinson	5.4
1905	Sam Crawford	4.9
1906	Sam Crawford	3.3
1907	Ty Cobb	4.6
1908	Sam Crawford	4.3
1909	Sam Crawford	4.8
1910	Sam Crawford	5.2
1911	Sam Crawford	5.6
1912	Ty Cobb	4.9
1913	Sam Crawford	4.2
1914	Sam Crawford	4.6
1915	Ossie Vitt	3.2
1916	Sam Crawford	2.7
1917	Ossie Vitt	2.5
1918	Ossie Vitt	1.9
1919	Ty Cobb	4.0
1920	Bobby Veach	3.3
1921	Ty Cobb	3.3
1922	George Cutshaw	2.3
1923	Ty Cobb	2.2
1924	Del Pratt	2.0
1925	**Johnny Bassler**	**1.4**
1926	Harry Heilmann	3.2
1927	Harry Heilmann	2.7
1928	Charlie Gehringer	3.2
1929	Charlie Gehringer	2.7
1930	Charlie Gehringer	2.4
1931	Mark Koenig	3.1
1932	Earl Webb	4.8
1933	Charlie Gehringer	3.8
1934	Charlie Gehringer	3.5
1935	Charlie Gehringer	2.3
1936	Charlie Gehringer	1.8
1937	Charlie Gehringer	3.8
1938	Charlie Gehringer	3.1
1939	Charlie Gehringer	3.3
1940	Charlie Gehringer	2.7
1941	Rip Radcliff	3.2
1942	Doc Cramer	2.6
1943	Doc Cramer	2.0
1944	Eddie Mayo	3.3
1945	Doc Cramer	3.5

1946	George Kell	2.9
1947	George Kell	2.4
1948	George Kell	3.6
1949	George Kell	2.1
1950	George Kell	2.5
1951	George Kell	2.7
1952	Joe Ginsberg	5.8
1953	Harvey Kuenn	4.2
1954	Harvey Kuenn	1.9
1955	Harvey Kuenn	4.1
1956	Harvey Kuenn	5.2
1957	Harvey Kuenn	4.1
1958	Harvey Kuenn	5.5
1959	Harvey Kuenn	6.0
1960	Al Kaline	7.5
1961	Al Kaline	6.3

Earl Webb

1962	Al Kaline	8.6
1963	Al Kaline	7.8
1964	Al Kaline	8.4
1965	Jerry Lumpe	5.9
1966	Jerry Lumpe	10.5
1967	Al Kaline	8.5
1968	Mickey Stanley	8.9
1969	Mickey Stanley	8.6
1970	Cesar Gutierrez	8.6
1971	Bill Freehan	8.2
	Jim Northrup	8.2
1972	Ed Brinkman	8.9
1973	Bill Freehan	6.9
1974	Gary Sutherland	5.7
1975	Danny Meyer	5.0
1976	Danny Meyer	7.0
1977	Rusty Staub	6.8
1978	Rusty Staub	4.8
1979	Alan Trammell	10.6
1980	Al Cowens, Rick Peters	8.8
1981	Lynn Jones	5.1
1982	Alan Trammell	8.5
1983	Lou Whitaker	9.7
1984	Lou Whitaker	10.0
1985	Lou Whitaker	8.0
1986	Alan Trammell	8.7
1987	Alan Trammell	7.0
1988	Alan Trammell	8.9
1989	Alan Trammell	9.0
1990	Dave Bergman	7.7
1991	Lou Whitaker	7.9
1992	Lou Whitaker	8.4
1993	Alan Trammell	8.5
1994	Alan Trammell	11.2
1995	John Flaherty	12.3
1996	Bobby Higginson	13.2
1997	Deivi Cruz	12.1
1998	Luis Gonzalez	10.1
1999	Luis Polonia	9.0
2000	Deivi Cruz	6.9
2001	Jose Macias	10.1
2002	Randall Simon	5.9
2003	Alex Sanchez	10.8
2004	Alex Sanchez	14.2
2005	Placido Polanco	4.2
2006	Placido Polanco	5.4
2007	Placido Polanco	4.7
2008	Placido Polanco	6.8
2009	Placido Polanco	6.8
2010	Magglio Ordonez	10.4
2011	Victor Martinez	8.6
2012	Prince Fielder	12.2
2013	Omar Infante	9.2
2014	Victor Martinez	6.6
2015	Jose Iglesias	9.7
2016	Jose Iglesias	9.7
2017	Jose Iglesias	13.3
2018	Victor Martinez	9.6
2019	Miguel Cabrera	19.7
2020	Victor Reyes	21.1
2021	Jonathan Schoop	19.7

Year	Player	GIDP
1939	**Pinky Higgins**	**14**
1940	**Hank Greenberg**	**15**
1941	**Pinky Higgins**	**20**
1942	**Pinky Higgins**	**21**
1943	**Jimmy Bloodworth**	**29**
1944	Rudy York	18
1945	Rudy York	23
1946	Hank Greenberg	17
1947	Eddie Mayo	16
1948	George Vico	23
1949	Vic Wertz	19
1950	George Kell	23
1951	Jerry Priddy	18
1952	Walt Dropo	17
	Steve Souchock	17

Rocky Bridges

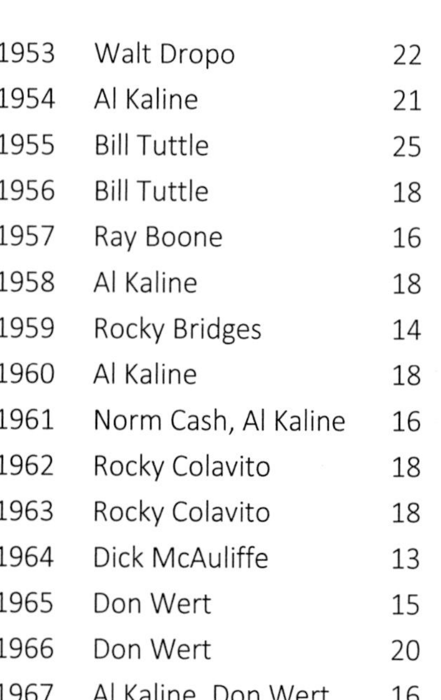

Year	Player	GIDP
1953	Walt Dropo	22
1954	Al Kaline	21
1955	Bill Tuttle	25
1956	Bill Tuttle	18
1957	Ray Boone	16
1958	Al Kaline	18
1959	Rocky Bridges	14
1960	Al Kaline	18
1961	Norm Cash, Al Kaline	16
1962	Rocky Colavito	18
1963	Rocky Colavito	18
1964	Dick McAuliffe	13
1965	Don Wert	15
1966	Don Wert	20
1967	Al Kaline, Don Wert	16

Year	Player	GIDP
1968	Mickey Stanley	22
1969	Mickey Stanley	14
	Don Wert	14
1970	Al Kaline	20
1971	Willie Horton	15
1972	Jim Northrup	16
1973	Eddie Brinkman	22
1974	Gary Sutherland	17
1975	Willie Horton	18
1976	Rusty Staub	23
1977	Rusty Staub	27
1978	Rusty Staub	24
1979	Ron LeFlore	16
1980	Steve Kemp	24
	Lance Parrish	24

Chet Lemon

Year	Player	GIDP
1981	Lance Parrish	16
1982	Larry Herndon	20
1983	Lance Parrish	21
1984	Chet Lemon	16
1985	Lance Parrish	10
1986	Lou Whitaker	20
1987	Chet Lemon	17
1988	Chet Lemon	18
1989	Mike Heath	18
1990	Cecil Fielder	15
1991	Cecil Fielder	17
1992	Cecil Fielder	14
1993	Cecil Fielder	22
1994	Cecil Fielder	17
1995	Travis Fryman	18

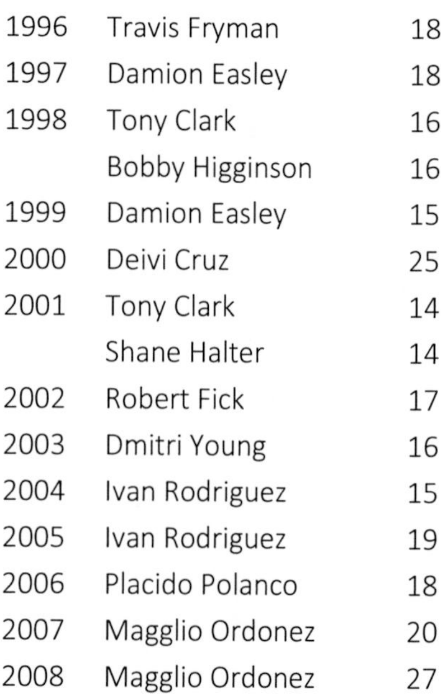

Year	Player	GIDP
1996	Travis Fryman	18
1997	Damion Easley	18
1998	Tony Clark	16
	Bobby Higginson	16
1999	Damion Easley	15
2000	Deivi Cruz	25
2001	Tony Clark	14
	Shane Halter	14
2002	Robert Fick	17
2003	Dmitri Young	16
2004	Ivan Rodriguez	15
2005	Ivan Rodriguez	19
2006	Placido Polanco	18
2007	Magglio Ordonez	20
2008	Magglio Ordonez	27

Mike Heath

Year	Player	GIDP
2009	Miguel Cabrera	22
2010	Miguel Cabrera	17
2011	Miguel Cabrera	24
2012	Miguel Cabrera	28
2013	Victor Martinez	23
2014	Miguel Cabrera	21
2015	Nicholas Castellanos	21
2016	Miguel Cabrera	26
2017	Miguel Cabrera	15
	Victor Martinez	15
2018	Victor Martinez	19
2019	Miguel Cabrera	18
2020	Jonathan Schoop	8
2021	Miguel Cabrera	21

Year	Player	DP%
1940	**Pete Fox**	**11.1**
1941	**Barney McCosky**	**5.6**
1942	Bob Harris	7.4
1943	Bob Harris	9.7
1944	Joe Hoover	8.3
1945	Jimmy Outlaw	6.7
1946	Pat Mullin	6.7
1947	Pat Mullin	6.3
1948	**Pat Mullin**	**4.8**
1949	Pat Mullin	7.3
1950	Aaron Robinson	5.9
1951	Pat Mullin	5.2
1952	Jerry Priddy	9.8
	Vic Wertz	9.8

1960

Norm Cash

121 Games, 428 Plate Appearances, Grounded into zero double plays, 81 double play opportunities, 0.0 double play percentage.

Year	Player	DP%
1953	Ray Boone	5.5
1954	Jim Delsing	6.4
1955	Jim Delsing	6.3
1956	**Charlie Maxwell**	**3.3**
1957	Charlie Maxwell	5.9
1958	Charlie Maxwell	6.3
1959	Harvey Kuenn	4.0
1960	**Norm Cash**	**0.0**
1961	Jake Wood	6.4
1962	Jake Wood	8.2
1963	Jake Wood	4.7
1964	Gates Brown	6.8
1965	Dick McAuliffe	4.6
1966	Jerry Lumpe	3.5

Year	Player	DP%
1967	Dick McAuliffe	1.8
1968	**Dick McAuliffe**	**0.0**
1969	Dick McAuliffe	4.6
1970	Dick McAuliffe	1.1
1971	Norm Cash	5.0
1972	Dick McAuliffe	3.3
1973	Dick McAuliffe	3.2
1974	Jim Northrup	8.1
1975	Ron LeFlore	3.2
1976	Jason Thompson	9.3
1977	Tom Veryzer	6.9
1978	Steve Kemp	6.3
1979	Alan Trammell	6.3
1980	Al Cowens	6.8

1968

Dick McAuliffe

151 Games, 658 Plate Appearances, Grounded into zero double plays, 78 double play opportunities, 0.0 double play percentage.

Year	Player	DP%
1981	Al Cowens	7.1
1982	Alan Trammell	5.5
1983	Kirk Gibson	2.4
1984	Kirk Gibson	3.0
1985	Lou Whitaker	3.5
1986	Lance Parrish	4.3
1987	Darrell Evans	1.5
1988	Gary Pettis	3.7
1989	Fred Lynn	5.5
1990	Alan Trammell	6.9
1991	Rob Deer	2.6
	Lou Whitaker	2.6
1992	Mickey Tettleton	4.1
1993	Kirk Gibson	2.1

Year	Player	DP%
1994	Kirk Gibson	2.3
1995	Bobby Higginson	5.1
1996	Kimera Bartee	2.0
1997	Melvin Nieves	3.9
1998	Paul Bako	5.5
1999	Bobby Higginson	2.1
2000	Bobby Higginson	3.3
2001	Roger Cedeno	6.3
2002	Damion Easley, C. Pena	7.6
2003	Carlos Pena	6.1
2004	Eric Munson	1.7
2005	Omar Infante	7.3
2006	**Marcus Thames**	**0.0**
2007	Curtis Granderson	3.7

2006

Marcus Thames

110 Games, 390 Plate Appearances, Grounded into zero double plays, 65 double play opportunities, 0.0 double play percentage.

Year	Player	DP%
2008	Brandon Inge	5.6
2009	Curtis Granderson	0.9
2010	Don Kelly	1.9
2011	Ryan Raburn	5.1
2012	Quintin Berry	5.8
2013	Andy Dirks	5.5
2014	Nicholas Castellanos	5.9
2015	J.D. Martinez	8.5
2016	Nicholas Castellanos	4.4
2017	Mikie Mahtook	5.5
2018	Leonys Martin	2.7
2019	Jeimer Candelario	4.0
2020	**Willi Castro**	**0.0**
2021	Willi Castro	6.1

Year	Player	Outs
1901	**Kid Gleason**	**412**
1902	Doc Casey	387
1903	Charlie Carr	407
1904	**Jimmy Barrett**	**465**
1905	Germany Schaefer	448
1906	Bill Coughlin	417
1907	Claude Rossman	441
1908	**Germany Schaefer**	**476**
1909	Donie Bush	439
1910	Sam Crawford	442
1911	Donie Bush	461
1912	Sam Crawford	424
1913	Donie Bush	460
1914	**Donie Bush**	**482**
1915	**Donie Bush**	**482**
1916	**Ossie Vitt**	**494**
1917	Donie Bush	428
1918	Donie Bush	396
1919	Ralph Young	406
1920	Ralph Young	456
1921	Bobby Veach	442
1922	Bobby Veach	453
1923	Ty Cobb	399
1924	Ty Cobb	443
1925	Lu Blue	408
1926	Jackie Tavener	426
1927	Heinie Manush	439
1928	Charlie Gehringer	432
1929	Roy Johnson	460
1930	Charlie Gehringer	437
1931	Roy Johnson	471
1932	Harry Davis	455
1933	Charlie Gehringer	434
1934	Goose Goslin	436
1935	Charlie Gehringer	430
1936	Billy Rogell	441
1937	Pete Fox	438
1938	Pete Fox	463
1939	Barney McCosky	441
1940	Dick Bartell	429
1941	Rudy York	458
1942	Doc Cramer	489
1943	Joe Hoover	478
1944	**Eddie Mayo**	**509**
1945	Rudy York	467
1946	Eddie Lake	464
1947	Eddie Lake	508
1948	George Vico	424
1949	Vic Wertz	452
1950	Jerry Priddy	489
1951	Jerry Priddy	465
1952	Jerry Groth	401
1953	Harvey Kuenn	486
1954	Harvey Kuenn	493
1955	Bill Tuttle	481
1956	Al Kaline	439
1957	Harvey Kuenn	482
1958	Frank Bolling	472
1959	Charlie Maxwell	405
1960	Rocky Colavito	444

Dick Bartell

Year	Player	Outs
1961	**Jake Wood**	**515**
1962	Rocky Colavito	463
1963	Rocky Colavito	463
1964	Jerry Lumpe	489
1965	Don Wert	483
1966	Norm Cash	457
1967	Dick McAuliffe	437
1968	Mickey Stanley	469
1969	Mickey Stanley	476
1970	Mickey Stanley	455
1971	Aurelio Rodriguez	476
1972	Aurelio Rodriguez	484
1973	Mickey Stanley	481
1974	Gary Sutherland	489
1975	Willie Horton	474
1976	Rusty Staub	448
1977	Rusty Staub	490
1978	Rusty Staub	505
1979	Ron LeFlore	452
1980	Alan Trammell	434
1981	Alan Trammell	323
1982	Larry Herndon	470
1983	Lance Parrish	479
1984	Lance Parrish	464
1985	Alan Trammell	480
1986	Lou Whitaker	459
1987	Lou Whitaker	462
1988	Chet Lemon	401
1989	Lou Whitaker	401
1990	Tony Phillips	459
1991	Cecil Fielder	482
1992	Travis Fryman	512
1993	Cecil Fielder	448
1994	Travis Fryman	364
1995	Chad Curtis	463
1996	Travis Fryman	483
1997	**Brian Hunter**	**525**
1998	Brian Hunter	467
1999	Dean Palmer	433
2000	Deivi Cruz	451
2001	Damion Easley	462
2002	Robert Fick	429
2003	Dmitri Young	416
2004	Omar Infante	393
2005	Brandon Inge	487
2006	Curtis Granderson	463
2007	Curtis Granderson	438
2008	Miguel Cabrera	461
2009	Curtis Granderson	486
2010	Austin Jackson	454
2011	Victor Martinez	462
2012	Miguel Cabrera	429
2013	Miguel Cabrera	416
2014	**Ian Kinsler**	**528**
2015	Ian Kinsler	463
2016	Ian Kinsler	454
2017	Nicholas Castellanos	469
2018	Nicholas Castellanos	447
2019	Miguel Cabrera	377
2020	Miguel Cabrera	158
2021	Jonathan Schoop	473

Year	Player	Streak
1901	**Kid Gleason**	**25**
1902	Jimmy Barrett	18
1903	Sam Crawford	20
1904	Matty McIntyre	17
1905	Sam Crawford	17
1906	**Ty Cobb**	**25**
1907	Ty Cobb	22
1908	Ty Cobb	15
1909	Sam Crawford	23
1910	Jim Delahanty	18
1911	**Ty Cobb**	**40**
1912	Ty Cobb	23
1913	Ty Cobb	12
1914	George Burns	13
1915	Sam Crawford	19
1916	George Burns	13
1917	Ty Cobb	35
1918	Ty Cobb	21
1919	Harry Heilmann	21
1920	Ty Cobb	20
1921	Harry Heilmann	23
1922	George Cutshaw	18
1923	Harry Heilmann	21
1924	Del Pratt	19
1925	Harry Heilmann	20
1926	Ty Cobb	21
1927	Charlie Gehringer	21
1928	Harry Heilmann	21
1929	Dale Alexander	16
1930	Dale Alexander	29
1931	John Stone	25
1932	John Stone	15
1933	Pete Fox	18
1934	Goose Goslin	30
1935	Pete Fox	29
1936	Al Simmons, G. Walker	16
1937	Gee Walker	27
1938	Gehringer, Greenberg	13
1939	Pinky Higgins	16
1940	Hank Greenberg	18
1941	Rip Radcliff	20
1942	Barney McCosky	15
1943	Dick Wakefield	21
1944	Doc Cramer	18
1945	Hank Greenberg	15
1946	R. Cullenbine, G. Kell	14
1947	Eddie Mayo	20
1948	George Kell, Eddie Mayo,	12
	Pat Mullin, George Vico	12
1949	George Kell	20
1950	George Kell	20
1951	Dick Kryhoski	13
1952	W. Dropo, Johnny Groth	11
1953	Harvey Kuenn	15
1954	Frank House, H. Kuenn	14
1955	Ray Boone, Al Kaline	15
1956	Ray Boone	16
1957	Frank Bolling	18
1958	Al Kaline	18
1959	Harvey Kuenn	22
1960	Rocky Colavito, Al Kaline	12

Harold Castro

Year	Player	Streak
1961	Al Kaline	22
1962	Billy Bruton	14
1963	Al Kaline	16
1964	Al Kaline	14
1965	Norm Cash	14
1966	Dick McAuliffe	11
1967	Dick McAuliffe	14
1968	Willie Horton	14
1969	Jim Northrup	13
1970	Willie Horton	16
1971	Willie Horton	15
1972	Bill Freehan	13
1973	Willie Horton	15
1974	Gary Sutherland	15
1975	Leon Roberts	17
1976	Ron LeFlore	30
1977	Ron LeFlore	17
1978	Ron LeFlore	27
1979	Ron LeFlore	15
1980	Champ Summers	17
1981	Kirk Gibson	10
1982	Glenn Wilson	19
1983	Lou Whitaker	18
1984	Alan Trammell	20
1985	Lou Whitaker	14
1986	Lou Whitaker	16
1987	Alan Trammell	21
1988	Alan Trammell	12
1989	Keith Moreland	11
1990	Lou Whitaker	12
1991	Milt Cuyler	15
1992	Dan Gladden	13
1993	Alan Trammell	16
1994	Junior Felix	17
1995	Chad Curtis	18
1996	B. Higginson, A. Trammell	12
1997	Bobby Higginson	14
1998	Damion Easley (May)	19
	Damion Easley (July)	19
1999	Tony Clark	19
2000	Juan Encarnacion	19
2001	Bobby Higginson	14
2002	Robert Fick, Dmitri Young	18
2003	Dmitri Young	16
2004	Ivan Rodriguez	14
2005	M. Ordonez, R. White	20
2006	C. Monroe, I. Rodriguez	14
2007	Magglio Ordonez	15
2008	Curtis Granderson	15
2009	Miguel Cabrera	17
2010	Miguel Cabrera	20
2011	Magglio Ordonez	18
2012	Austin Jackson	16
2013	Miguel Cabrera	15
2014	J.D. Martinez	14
2015	Miguel Cabrera	13
2016	J. Iglesias, J.D. Martinez	14
2017	Nicholas Castellanos	17
2018	James McCann	10
2019	Harold Castro	13
2020	Miguel Cabrera	13
2021	Jonathan Schoop	16

YEARLY TIGER HITTING LEADERS – INFIELD HITS

Year	Player	Infield Hits
1988	**Luis Salazar**	**23**
1989	Chet Lemon	19
1990	Alan Trammell	14
1991	**Tony Phillips**	**24**
1992	**Tony Phillips**	**36**

Delmon Young

Year	Player	Infield Hits
1993	Tony Phillips	27
1994	Junior Felix	13
1995	Chad Curtis	14
1996	Kimera Bartee	21
1997	**Brian Hunter**	**37**
1998	**Brian Hunter**	**48**
1999	Luis Polonia	20
2000	Luis Polonia	6
2001	Roger Cedeno	14
2002	Shane Halter	4
2003	Alex Sanchez	41
2004	Alex Sanchez	36
2005	Nook Logan	27
2006	Placido Polanco	19
2007	Placido Polanco	20
2008	Placido Polanco	24
2009	Placido Polanco	18
2010	Austin Jackson	32
2011	Austin Jackson	32
2012	Delmon Young	14
2013	Torii Hunter	20
2014	Rajai Davis	26
2015	Jose Iglesias	30
2016	Jose Iglesias	26
2017	Nicholas Castellanos	17
	Mike Mahtook	17
2018	Jose Iglesias	18
	JaCoby Jones	18

Jonathan Schoop

Year	Player	Infield Hits
2019	Harold Castro, V. Reyes	11
2020	Willi Castro	6
	Victor Reyes	6
	Jonathan Schoop	6
2021	Jonathan Schoop	23

YEARLY TIGER HITTING LEADERS – BUNT HITS

Year	Player	Bunt Hits
1988	**Luis Salazar**	**14**
1989	Gary Pettis	6
1990	Tony Phillips	8
1991	**Milt Cuyler**	**15**
1992	Tony Phillips	4
	Lou Whitaker	4

Omar Infante

Year	Player	Bunt Hits
1993	Chad Kreuter	4
1994	Junior Felix	4
1995	Danny Bautista	3
1996	Kimera Bartee	9
1997	D. Easley, B. Hunter	4
1998	Brian Hunter	5
1999	**Luis Polonia**	**15**
2000	Shane Halter	4
	Wendell Magee	4
	Luis Polonia	4
2001	Roger Cedeno	12
2002	Shane Halter	4
2003	**Alex Sanchez**	**30**
2004	Alex Sanchez	29
2005	Nook Logan	10
2006	A. Gomez, Brandon Inge	3
	Curtis Granderson	3
2007	Omar Infante	4
2008	P. Polanco, R. Raburn	3
2009	Gerald Laird	7
2010	Ramon Santiago	5
2011	Austin Jackson	8
2012	Quintin Berry	6
2013	Ramon Santiago	5
2014	Bryan Holaday	5
2015	Anthony Gose	7
2016	Jose Iglesias	3
	Cameron Maybin	3
2017	Jim Aducci, Tyler Collins	1
	Victor Martinez	1

Anthony Gose

Year	Player	Bunt Hits
2018	Leonys Martin	7
2019	V. Reyes, R. Rodriguez	3
2020	Victor Reyes	2
2021	Derek Hill	3

Year	Player	AB
1901	**Emil Frisk**	**6**
1902	Sport McAllister	5
1903	Sport McAllister	5
1904	**George Mullin**	**6**
1905	Jim Barrett, Tom Doran,	2
	Bobby Lowe, G. Mullin	2
1906	**George Mullin**	**8**
1907	**George Mullin**	**20**
1908	**Davy Jones**	**21**
1909	Davy Jones, G. Mullin	10
1910	Chick Lathers	14
1911	Biff Schaller, B. Schmidt	17
1912	Davy Jones	15
1913	**Jean Dubuc**	**28**
1914	**Jean Dubuc**	**32**
1915	Baby Doll Jacobson	20
	Marty Kavanagh	20
1916	Marty Kavanagh	18
1917	Sam Crawford	10
1918	George Cunningham	9
1919	Chick Shorten	10
1920	**Sammy Hale**	**34**
1921	Chick Shorten	29
1922	Danny Clark	21
1923	Heinie Manush	21
1924	Al Wingo	16
1925	Johnny Neun	21
1926	Johnny Neun	19
1927	Al Wingo	26
1928	Pinky Hargrave	31
1929	**Bob Fothergill**	**52**
1930	George Uhle	21
1931	George Uhle	18
1932	Billy Rhiel	25
1933	Jo-Jo White	23
1934	Frank Doljack	23
1935	Gee Walker, Jo-Jo White	13
1936	Jo-Jo White	28
1937	Goose Goslin	26
1938	Jo-Jo White	16
1939	Roy Cullenbine	23
1940	Earl Averill	32
1941	Billy Sullivan	20
1942	Charlie Gehringer	32
1943	Rip Radcliff	30
1944	Don Ross	15
1945	Chuck Hostetler	21
1946	Anse Moore	15
1947	Doc Cramer	22
1948	Fred Hutchinson	24
1949	Pat Mullin	17
1950	Charlie Keller	29
1951	Charlie Keller	32
1952	Johnny Hopp	29
1953	**Pat Mullin**	**57**
1954	Bob Nieman	26
1955	Charlie Maxwell	26
1956	Wayne Belardi	37
1957	Dave Philley	25
1958	Gus Zernial	38
1959	Neil Chrisley	43
1960	Sandy Amoros, N. Chrisley	44

Neil Chrisley

Year	Player	AB
1961	Charlie Maxwell	45
1962	Vic Wertz	53
1963	Whitey Herzog	35
1964	Jake Wood	29
1965	Gates Brown	34
1966	Gates Brown	40
1967	Jerry Lumpe	30
1968	Gates Brown	40
1969	Gates Brown	39
1970	Gates Brown	41
1971	Dalton Jones	45
1972	Gates Brown	28
1973	Frank Howard	26
1974	Gates Brown	53
1975	Gates Brown	35
1976	Ben Oglivie	38
1977	Tim Corcoran	32
1978	Aurelio Rodriguez	20
1979	John Wockenfuss	20
1980	Champ Summers	26
1981	Champ Summers	14
1982	Jerry Turner	24
1983	John Wockenfuss	24
1984	Barbaro Garbey	25
1985	Dave Bergman, J. Grubb	24
1986	Larry Herndon	26
1987	Dave Bergman, J. Grubb,	21
	Larry Herndon	21
1988	Dave Bergman, D. Evans	24
1989	Gary Ward	32
1990	Dave Bergman	33
1991	Dave Bergman	25
1992	Dave Bergman	22
1993	Skeeter Barnes	17
1994	Lou Whitaker	12
1995	Franklin Stubbs	25
1996	Curtis Pride	20
1997	Curtis Pride	22
1998	Frank Catalanotto	32
1999	Frank Catalanotto	24
2000	Wendell Magee	26
2001	Robert Fick	16
2002	H. Bocachica, R. Simon	6
2003	Kevin Witt	18
2004	Eric Munson	13
2005	Shelton, Wilson, D. Young	6
2006	Alexis Gomez	11
2007	Sean Casey	12
2008	Jeff Larish	11
2009	Ryan Raburn	18
2010	Ramon Santiago	18
2011	Ryan Raburn	11
2012	Ramon Santiago	8
2013	Andy Dirks	16
2014	Don Kelly	10
2015	Rajai Davis	20
2016	Jarrod Saltalamacchia	17
2017	Alex Avila	14
2018	V. Martinez, J. Adduci	8
2019	Ronny Rodriguez	12
2020	Harold Castro	5
2021	Harold Castro	14

Year	Player	PH
1901	**Emil Frisk, S. McAllister**	**2**
1902	Four Batters	0
1903	Long, McAllister, G. Mullin	1
1904	**George Mullin**	**2**
1905	Duff Cooley, Tom Doran	1
1906	**George Mullin, Fred Payne**	**3**
1907	**George Mullin**	**5**
1908	Ira Thomas	4
1909	Five Batters	1
1910	C. Lathers, Hack Simmons	3
1911	**Bill Schaller, Boss Schmidt**	**6**
1912	Davy Jones	4
1913	Hugh High	5
1914	**Jean Dubuc**	**6**
1915	**Marty Kavanagh**	**10**
1916	G. Burns, M. Kavanagh	2
1917	George Harper	3
1918	Tubby Spencer	3
1919	Chick Shorten	3
1920	**Sammy Hale**	**12**
1921	Chick Shorten	7
1922	Danny Clark, Clyde Manion	3
1923	Heinie Manush	9
1924	Al Wingo	7
1925	Heinie Manush, J. Neun	6
1926	Johnny Neun	6
1927	Al Wingo	5
1928	Pinky Hargrave	12
1929	**Bob Fothergill**	**19**
1930	John Stone, George Uhle	5
1931	Mark Koenig	4
1932	Billy Rhiel	12
1933	Jo-Jo White	10
1934	Jack Doljack	4
1935	Gee Walker	7
1936	Jo-Jo White	10
1937	Goose Goslin	6
1938	Tony Piet	3
1939	Roy Cullenbine	8
1940	Earl Averill	10
1941	McCosky, Rowe, Sullivan	3
1942	Charlie Gehringer	9
1943	Rip Radcliff	7
1944	Don Ross, Al Unser	2
1945	Six Batters	2
1946	Anse Moore	4
1947	Doc Cramer	6
1948	Dick Wakefield	8
1949	Paul Campbell	5
1950	Charlie Keller	10
1951	Charlie Keller	8
1952	Johnny Hopp	7
1953	Pat Mullin	13
1954	Bob Nieman	8
1955	Jack Phillips	8
1956	Earl Torgeson	10
1957	Dave Philley	10
1958	Gus Zernial	15
1959	Gus Zernial	6
1960	Neil Chrisley	10
1961	Charlie Maxwell	12

Jim Price

Year	Player	PH
1962	Vic Wertz	17
1963	Billy Bruton	6
1964	Jake Wood	7
1965	Gates Brown, Jake Wood	9
1966	Gates Brown	13
1967	Jim Price	5
1968	Gates Brown	18
1969	G. Brown, T. Matchick	8
1970	Dalton Jones	11
1971	Dalton Jones	13
1972	Al Kaline	10
1973	Frank Howard	5
1974	Gates Brown	16
1975	Gates Brown	6
1976	Ben Oglivie	9
1977	Tim Corcoran	10
1978	Aurelio Rodriguez	7
1979	John Wockenfuss	5
1980	Champ Summers	7
1981	Lynn Jones	4
1982	J. Turner, J. Wockenfuss	4
1983	John Wockenfuss	7
1984	B. Garbey, Johnny Grubb	8
1985	Dave Bergman	6
	Alejandro Sanchez	6
1986	Larry Herndon	6
1987	Larry Herndon	8
1988	Luis Salazar	5
1989	Gary Ward	6
1990	Dave Bergman	6
1991	M. Tettleton, L. Whitaker	4
1992	Dave Bergman	6
1993	Skeeter Barnes	6
1994	Gibson, Samuel, Whitaker	2
1995	Juan Samuel	6
1996	Bobby Higginson, C. Pride	3
1997	Phil Nevin	8
1998	Frank Catalanotto	8
1999	Frank Catalanotto	7
2000	Wendell Magee	10
2001	Jose Macias	5
2002	Hiram Bocachica,	2
	Ryan Jackson, R. Simon	2
2003	Four Batters	3
2004	Greg Norton	3
2005	Dmitri Young	4
2006	Alexis Gomez	4
2007	Sean Casey	6
2008	Jeff Larish	5
2009	Marcus Thames	6
2010	J. Damon, Ramon Santiago	5
2011	Don Kelly	4
2012	Andy Dirks	3
2013	Matt Tuiasosopo	4
2014	Tyler Collins	3
2015	Rajai Davis, J. McCann	3
2016	Victor Martinez	4
2017	Alex Avila	6
2018	Victor Martinez	3
2019	Brandon Dixon	4
2020	Harold Castro	3
2021	Eric Haase	4

YEARLY TIGER HITTING LEADERS – PINCH HIT AVERAGE (MINIMUM OF FIVE PINCH HIT AT-BATS)

Year	Player	Avg	H-AB
1901	**Emil Frisk**	**.333**	**2-6**
1902	Sport McAllister	.000	0-5
1903	Sport McAllister	.200	1-5
1904	**George Mullin**	**.333**	**2-6**
1905	No Qualified Hitters		
1906	**Fred Payne**	**.429**	**3-7**
1907	George Mullin	.250	5-20
1908	Ira Thomas	.364	4-11
1909	Davy Jones	.100	1-10
	George Mullin	.100	1-10
1910	Boss Schmidt	.400	2-5
1911	Biff Schaller	.353	6-17
	Boss Schmidt	.353	6-17
1912	**Hank Perry**	**.500**	**3-6**
1913	Hugh High	.263	5-19
1914	Harry Heilmann	.273	3-11
1915	**Marty Kavanagh**	**.500**	**10-20**
1916	**Sam Crawford**	**.500**	**3-6**
1917	George Harper	.333	3-9
1918	Tubby Spencer	.429	3-7
1919	Chick Shorten	.300	3-10
1920	Eddie Ainsmith	.400	2-5
1921	Larry Woodall	.444	4-9
1922	Fred Haney	.400	2-5
1923	**Del Pratt**	**.571**	**4-7**
1924	Al Wingo	.438	7-16
1925	Bob Fothergill	.500	4-8
1926	Heinie Manush	.444	4-9
1927	Charlie Gehringer	.375	3-8
1928	Marty McManus	.500	4-8
1929	Bob Fothergill	.365	19-52
1930	Roy Johnson	.286	2-7
1931	Bill Akers	.400	2-5
1932	Billy Rhiel	.480	12-25
1933	Heinie Schuble	.500	4-8
1934	Gee Walker	.294	5-17
1935	**Pete Fox**	**.600**	**3-5**
1936	Jo-Jo White	.357	10-28
1937	Jo-Jo White	.400	2-5
1938	Chet Laabs	.286	2-7
1939	**Red Kress**	**.800**	**4-5**
1940	Red Kress	.600	3-5
1941	Schoolboy Rowe	.500	3-6
1942	Ned Harris	.429	6-14
1943	Prince Oana	.333	3-9
1944	Don Ross	.133	2-15
1945	Hank Greenberg	.400	2-5
1946	Fred Hutchinson	.400	2-5
1947	Fred Hutchinson	.313	5-16
1948	Jimmy Outlaw	.417	5-12
1949	Paul Campbell	.625	5-8
1950	**Aaron Robinson**	**.800**	**4-5**
1951	Dick Kryhoski	.400	4-10
1952	Don Kolloway	.300	6-20
	Bud Souchock	.300	6-20
1953	Johnny Pesky	.387	12-31
1954	Matt Batts	.400	2-5
1955	Jack Phillips	.444	8-18
1956	Charlie Maxwell	.571	4-7
1957	Dave Philley	.400	10-25
1958	Bill Taylor	.500	3-6
1959	Charlie Maxwell	.375	3-8
1960	Johnny Groth	.500	4-8
1961	Al Kaline	.600	3-5
1962	Vic Wertz	.321	17-53
1963	Al Kaline	.600	3-5
1964	George Thomas	.353	6-17
1965	Don Demeter	.400	6-15
1966	Jim Northrup	.400	4-10
1967	Jim Northrup	.333	2-6
1968	Al Kaline	.500	5-10
1969	Tommy Matchick	.500	8-16
1970	Mickey Stanley	.400	2-5
1971	Mickey Stanley	.500	3-6
1972	Mickey Stanley	.600	3-5
1973	Dick McAuliffe	.286	2-7
1974	Willie Horton	.500	3-6
	Marv Lane	.500	3-6
1975	John Knox	.400	2-5
1976	Mickey Stanley	.316	6-19
1977	Milt May	.400	2-5
1978	Lou Whitaker	.500	3-6
1979	Champ Summers	.308	4-13
1980	Richie Hebner	.545	6-11
1981	Lynn Jones	.308	4-13
1982	John Wockenfuss	.364	4-11
1983	Lou Whitaker	.429	3-7
1984	Rusty Kuntz	.417	5-12
1985	Larry Herndon	.600	3-5
1986	Lou Whitaker	.667	4-6
1987	Darrell Evans	.600	6-10
1988	Luis Salazar	.556	5-9
1989	Chet Lemon	.308	4-13
1990	Mike Heath	.429	3-7
1991	Tony Phillips	.333	2-6
1992	Phil Clark	.500	3-6
1993	Chad Kreuter	.500	4-8
1994	Juan Samuel	.400	2-5
1995	Danny Bautista	.500	3-6
	Kirk Gibson	.500	3-6
1996	Bobby Higginson	.333	3-9
	Reuben Sierra	.333	2-6
1997	Phil Nevin	.471	8-17
1998	Kimera Bartee	.571	4-7
1999	Luis Polonia	.333	2-6
2000	Billy McMillon	.714	5-7
2001	Jose Macias	.625	5-8
2002	Hiram Bocachica	.333	2-6
	Randall Simon	.333	2-6
2003	Eric Munson	.600	3-5
	Alex Sanchez	.600	3-5
2004	Greg Norton	.250	3-12
2005	Dmitri Young	.667	4-6
2006	Vance Wilson	.400	2-5
2007	Sean Casey	.500	6-12
2008	Jeff Larish	.455	5-11
2009	Marcus Thames	.429	6-14
2010	Johnny Damon	.455	5-11
2011	Don Kelly	.444	4-9
2012	Andy Dirks	.429	3-7
2013	Matt Tuiasosopo	.286	4-14
2014	N. Castellanos	.400	2-5
	Stephen Moya	.400	2-5
2015	James McCann	.500	3-6
2016	Victor Martinez	.500	4-8
2017	Andrew Romine	.500	4-8
2018	Victor Martinez	.375	3-8
2019	Brandon Dixon	.571	4-7
2020	Harold Castro	.600	3-5
2021	Eric Haase	.667	4-6

Fred Payne

Year	Player	HR
1901	7 Batters	0
1902	4 Batters	0
1903	8 Batters	0
1904	7 Batters	0
1905	9 Batters	0
1906	**Germany Schaefer**	**1**
1907	9 Batters	0
1908	8 Batters	0
1909	8 Batters	0
1910	11 Batters	0
1911	10 Batters	0
1912	14 Batters	0
1913	16 Batters	0
1914	9 Batters	0
1915	8 Batters	0
1916	9 Batters	0
1917	**Sam Crawford**	**1**
1918	9 Batters	0
1919	7 Batters	0
1920	**Sammy Hale**	**1**
1921	11 Batters	0
1922	**Dan Clark, Ira Flagstead**	**1**
1923	**Heinie Manush**	**1**
1924	**Al Wingo**	**1**
1925	**Heinie Manush**	**1**
1926	16 Batters	0
1927	**Heinie Manush**	**1**
1928	**Pinky Hargrave**	**1**
1929	14 Batters	0
1930	16 Batters	0
1931	13 Batters	0
1932	**Gee Walker**	**1**
1933	14 Batters	0
1934	13 Batters	0
1935	15 Batters	0
1936	13 Batters	0
1937	**Goose Goslin**	**2**
1938	Chet Laabs	1
1939	Four Batters	1
1940	**Billy Sullivan**	**2**
1941	Dutch Meyer	1
1942	**Ned Harris**	**2**
1943	9 Batters	0
1944	Don Ross, Al Unser	1
1945	**Zeb Eaton**	**2**
1946	17 Batters	0
1947	F. Hutchinson, Pat Mullin	1
1948	**Dick Wakefield**	**3**
1949	Paul Campbell, Pat Mullin	2
1950	Aaron Robinson	1
1951	Charlie Keller, Pat Mullin	1
1952	Don Kolloway	2
1953	Matt Batts, Fred Hatfield	1
	Pat Mullin	1
1954	Five Batters	1
1955	C. Maxwell, Earl Torgeson	1
1956	Frank House	2
1957	22 Batters	0
1958	**Gus Zernial**	**3**
1959	Four Batters	1
1960	**Norm Cash**	**3**
1961	**Charlie Maxwell**	**3**
1962	**Vic Wertz**	**3**
1963	Gates Brown, Willie Horton	1
	Bubba Phillips	1
1964	Four Batters	1

Richie Hebner

Year	Player	HR
1965	Gates Brown, Jim Northrup	1
	George Thomas	1
1966	Gates Brown	2
1967	Jim Landis, Earl Wilson	1
1968	**Gates Brown**	**3**
1969	Four Batters	1
1970	Gates Brown, Norm Cash,	1
	Kevin Collins	1
1971	Gates Brown, Ike Brown	2
1972	Gates Brown	1
1973	**Frank Howard**	**3**
1974	**Gates Brown**	**3**
1975	Gates Brown, Dan Meyer	1
1976	**Ben Oglivie**	**3**
1977	Six Batters	1
1978	Aurelio Rodriguez	1
1979	C. Summers, J. Wockenfuss	2
1980	Richie Hebner	2
1981	Lynn Jones	1
1982	John Wockenfuss	2
1983	Johnny Grubb, Rick Leach,	1
	John Wockenfuss	1
1984	**Johnny Grubb**	**3**
1985	Alejandro Sanchez	2
1986	**Larry Herndon**	**3**
1987	Johnny Grubb	1
1988	Fred Lynn, Pat Sheridan	1
1989	21 Batters	0
1990	Larry Sheets, John Shelby	1
1991	Five Batters	1
1992	Dave Bergman	1
1993	Rob Deer, Chad Kreuter	1
1994	Kirk Gibson	2
1995	Kirk Gibson, Lou Whitaker	1
1996	Bobby Higginson	2
1997	Phil Nevin	2
1998	Four Batters	1
1999	F. Catalanotto, Jose Macias	1
2000	Rich Becker, Luis Polonia	1
	Wendell Magee	1
2001	Jose Macias	1
2002	15 Batters	0
2003	A.J. Hinch, Eric Munson	1
2004	Craig Monroe	1
2005	20 Batters	0
2006	Matt Stairs	1
	Marcus Thames	1
2007	Marcus Thames	2
2008	Ryan Raburn, M. Thames	1
2009	Aubrey Huff, Ryan Raburn,	1
	Marcus Thames	1
2010	R. Raburn, Scott Sizemore	1
2011	Five Batters	1
2012	17 Batters	0
2013	A. Dirks, Ramon Santiago	1
	Matt Tuiasosopo	1
2014	Tyler Collins, J.D. Martinez	1
2015	Tyler Collins	1
2016	**Victor Martinez**	**3**
2017	19 Batters	0
2018	Dawel Lugo	1
2019	John Hicks	2
2020	14 Batters	0
2021	Eric Haase, Victor Reyes	1
	Robbie Grossman	1

1916	**Sam Crawford**	**1**
	Harry Heilmann	**1**
1917	**Sam Crawford**	**1**
	George Harper	**1**
1918	**Tubby Spencer**	**1**
1919	**Ben Dyer, Ira Flagstead**	**1**
	Chick Shorten	**1**
1920	**Sammy Hale, C. Shorten**	**6**
1921	Chick Shorten	4
1922	Danny Clark	3
1923	Bob Fothergill, H. Manush	5
1924	**Al Wingo**	**9**
1925	Bob Fothergill	6
1926	Heinie Manush	6
1927	Al Wingo	6
1928	**Pinky Hargrave**	**11**
1929	**Bob Fothergill**	**13**
1930	George Uhle	5
1931	George Uhle	5
1932	Dale Alexander	4
1933	Jo-Jo White	8
1934	Mickey Cochrane	4
	Frank Doljack	4
1935	Goose Goslin	3
1936	Jo-Jo White	5
1937	Goose Goslin	6
1938	Chet Laabs, Birdie Tebbetts	2
1939	Rudy York	8
1940	Earl Averill	7
1941	Schoolboy Rowe	3
1942	Charlie Gehringer	5
1943	Prince Oana, Rip Radcliff	4
1944	Al Unser	5
1945	Zeb Eaton	6
1946	Pat Mullin	5
1947	Doc Cramer	6
1948	Dick Wakefield	10
1949	Pat Mullin	4
1950	Charlie Keller	11
1951	**Charlie Keller**	**13**
1952	Don Kolloway	8
	Bud Souchock	8
1953	Pat Mullin	9
1954	Jim Delsing	4

1955	Earl Torgeson	6
1956	Frank House	6
1957	Jay Porter	5
1958	Gus Zernial	12
1959	Gus Zernial	7
1960	Norm Cash	9
1961	C. Maxwell, Bubba Morton	9
1962	**Vic Wertz**	**14**
1963	Billy Bruton	5
1964	Billy Bruton, Don Demeter	5
1965	Gates Brown	7
1966	Gates Brown	9
1967	Jim Northrup	4
1968	Gates Brown	7
1969	Gates Brown	5
1970	Gates Brown	13

Frank Doljack

1971	Ike Brown	6
1972	Gates Brown	3
1973	Frank Howard	4
1974	Gates Brown	11
1975	Gates Brown, Dan Meyer	3
1976	Ben Oglivie	9
1977	Tim Corcoran	4
1978	Tim Corcoran, Milt May	3
1979	John Wockenfuss	5
1980	Richie Hebner	6
	John Wockenfuss	6
1981	Al Cowens, Lynn Jones	3
	Rick Leach	3
1982	John Wockenfuss	5
1983	John Wockenfuss	10
1984	Barbaro Garbey	9

1985	Johnny Grubb	8
1986	Larry Herndon	12
1987	Larry Herndon	5
1988	Fred Lynn	5
1989	Chet Lemon	5
1990	Gary Ward	8
1991	Mickey Tettleton	5
	Lou Whitaker	5
1992	Skeeter Barnes	5
1993	Chad Kreuter	7
1994	Kirk Gibson	8
1995	Kirk Gibson, Lou Whitaker	7
	Franklin Stubbs	7
1996	Curtis Pride	4
1997	Phil Nevin	6
1998	Frank Catalanotto	3
	Mike Tomberlin	3
1999	Frank Catalanotto	6
2000	Wendell Magee	5
2001	Robert Fick	3
2002	Hiram Bocachica	2
	Randall Simon	2
2003	Eric Munson	4
2004	Craig Monroe	2
2005	Nook Logan, Chris Shelton	3
2006	Omar Infante, Matt Stairs	2
2007	Marcus Thames	5
2008	Marcus Thames	5
2009	Aubrey Huff	5
2010	Scott Sizemore	3
2011	Andy Dirks	4
2012	Alex Avila, Quintin Berry	1
	B. Boesch, Ramon Santiago	1
	Andy Dirks, Jhonny Peralta	1
2013	Matt Tuiasosopo	7
2014	Tyler Collins	4
2015	Rajai Davis, James McCann	2
2016	Victor Martinez	6
2017	Alex Avila	2
2018	Dawel Lugo	2
2019	John Hicks	5
2020	Jorge Bonifacio	2
	Harold Castro	2
2021	Eric Haase	3

1901 Roscoe Miller
1902 Win Mercer
1903 George Mullin
1904 Bill Donovan
1905 Ed Killian
1906 Ed Siever
1907 Bill Donovan
1908 Ed Summers
1909 George Mullin
1910 George Mullin
1911 George Mullin
1912 Jean Dubuc
1913 Hooks Dauss
1914 Harry Coveleski
1915 Hooks Dauss
1916 Harry Coveleski
1917 Bernie Boland
1918 Bernie Boland
1919 Hooks Dauss
1920 Howard Ehmke

Frank Lary

1921 Dutch Leonard
1922 Herman Pillette
1923 Hooks Dauss
1924 Earl Whitehill
1925 Dutch Leonard
1926 Sam Gibson
1927 Earl Whitehill
1928 Ownie Carroll
1929 George Uhle
1930 Earl Whitehill
1931 George Uhle
1932 Earl Whitehill
1933 Firpo Marberry
1934 Schoolboy Rowe
1935 Tommy Bridges
1936 Tommy Bridges
1937 Eldon Auker
1938 Tommy Bridges
1939 Tommy Bridges
1940 Bobo Newsom

1941 Al Benton
1942 Virgil Trucks
1943 Dizzy Trout
1944 Hal Newhouser
1945 Hal Newhouser
1946 Hal Newhouser
1947 Fred Hutchinson
1948 Hal Newhouser
1949 Virgil Trucks
1950 Art Houtteman
1951 Virgil Trucks
1952 Hal Newhouser
1953 Ned Garver
1954 Steve Gromek
1955 Billy Hoeft
1956 Frank Lary
1957 Jim Bunning
1958 Frank Lary
1959 Don Mossi
1960 Frank Lary

Mickey Lolich

1961 Frank Lary
1962 Hank Aguirre
1963 Phil Regan
1964 Mickey Lolich
1965 Denny McLain
1966 Denny McLain
1967 Earl Wilson
1968 Denny McLain
1969 Denny McLain
1970 Les Cain
1971 Mickey Lolich
1972 Mickey Lolich
1973 John Hiller
1974 John Hiller
1975 Vern Ruhle
1976 Mark Fidrych
1977 Dave Rozema
1978 John Hiller
1979 Jack Morris
1980 Aurelio Lopez

1981 Jack Morris
1982 Dan Petry
1983 Jack Morris
1984 Willie Hernandez
1985 Jack Morris
1986 Jack Morris
1987 Mike Henneman
1988 Jeff Robinson
1989 Mike Henneman
1990 Jack Morris
1991 Bill Gullickson
1992 Bill Gullickson
1993 Mike Henneman
1994 Joe Boever
1995 David Wells
1996 Omar Olivares
1997 Justin Thompson
1998 Doug Brocail
1999 Doug Brocail
2000 Todd Jones

Justin Verlander

2001 Steve Sparks
2002 Jeff Weaver
2003 Jaimie Walker
2004 Jaimie Walker
2005 Jeremy Bonderman
2006 Justin Verlander
2007 Justin Verlander
2008 Armando Galarraga
2009 Justin Verlander
2010 Justin Verlander
2011 Justin Verlander
2012 Justin Verlander
2013 Max Scherzer
2014 Max Scherzer
2015 David Price
2016 Justin Verlander
2017 Shane Greene
2018 Mike Fiers
2019 Matt Boyd
2020 Bryan Garcia
2021 Michael Fulmer

1901 Ed High
1902 Jack Cronin
1903 No Selectee
1904 Bugs Raymond
1905 George Disch
1906 Jimmy Wiggs
1907 Elijah Jones
1908 George Suggs
1909 Ralph Works
1910 Hub Pernoll
1911 Tex Covington
1912 Hub Pernoll
1913 Carl Zamloch
1914 Ross Reynolds
1915 Red Oldham
1916 George Cunningham
1917 Deacon Jones
1918 Deacon Jones
1919 Doc Ayers
1920 Doc Ayers

Terry Fox

1921 Carl Holling
1922 Syl Johnson
1923 Bert Cole
1924 Ken Holloway
1925 Ken Holloway
1926 Hooks Dauss
1927 George Smith
1928 Elam Vangilder
1929 Lil Stoner
1930 Charlie Sullivan
1931 Charlie Sullivan
1932 Chief Hogsett
1933 Chief Hogsett
1934 Firpo Marberry
1935 Chief Hogsett
1936 Roxie Lawson
1937 George Gill
1938 Harry Eisenstat
1939 Bud Thomas
1940 Archie McKain

1941 Al Benton
1942 Roy Henshaw
1943 Johnny Gorsica
1944 Walter Beck
1945 George Caster
1946 George Caster
1947 Johnny Gorsica
1948 Stubby Overmire
1949 Dizzy Trout
1950 Hal White
1951 Gene Bearden
1952 Hal White
1953 Ray Herbert
1954 Bob Miller
1955 Al Aber
1956 Al Aber
1957 Harry Byrd
1958 Tom Morgan
1959 Tom Morgan
1960 Dave Sisler

George Caster

1961 Terry Fox
1962 Terry Fox
1963 Terry Fox
1964 Fred Gladding
1965 Terry Fox, Fred Gladding
1966 Orlando Pena
1967 Fred Gladding, Mike Marshall
1968 Daryl Patterson
1969 Tom Timmerman
1970 John Hiller
1971 Fred Scherman
1972 Chuck Seelbach
1973 John Hiller
1974 John Hiller
1975 John Hiller
1976 John Hiller
1977 Steve Foucault
1978 John Hiller
1979 Aurelio Lopez
1980 Aurelio Lopez

1981 Kevin Saucier
1982 Dave Tobik
1983 Aurelio Lopez
1984 Willie Hernandez
1985 Willie Hernandez
1986 Willie Hernandez
1987 Mike Henneman
1988 Mike Henneman
1989 Mike Henneman
1990 Ed Nunez
1991 Mike Henneman
1992 John Kiely
1993 Mike Henneman
1994 Storm Davis
1995 Mike Henneman
1996 Richie Lewis
1997 Todd Jones
1998 Doug Brocail
1999 Doug Brocail
2000 Todd Jones

John Hiller

2001 Danny Patterson
2002 Juan Acevedo
2003 Jamie Walker
2004 Jamie Walker
2005 Kyle Farnsworth
2006 Joel Zumaya
2007 Bobby Seay
2008 Aquilino Lopez
2009 Brandon Lyon
2010 Jose Valverde
2011 Al Alburquerque, J. Valverde
2012 Brayan Villarreal
2013 Joaquin Benoit, Drew Smyly
2014 Al Alburquerque
2015 Alex Wilson
2016 Alex Wilson
2017 Shane Greene, Justin Wilson
2018 Alex Wilson
2019 Shane Greene
2020 Bryan Garcia
2021 Michael Fulmer

Year	Pitcher	Games
1901	**Roscoe Miller, Ed Siever**	**38**
1902	Win Mercer, G. Mullin	35
1903	**George Mullin**	**41**
1904	**George Mullin**	**45**
1905	George Mullin	44
1906	George Mullin	40
1907	**George Mullin**	**46**
1908	Ed Summers	40
1909	Ed Willett	41
1910	George Mullin	38
1911	Ed Willett	38
1912	Jean Dubuc, Ed Willett	37
1913	Jean Dubuc	36
1914	Hooks Dauss	45
1915	**Harry Coveleski**	**50**
1916	Bernie Boland	46
1917	George Cunningham	44
1918	Hooks Dauss	33
1919	Bernie Boland	35
1920	Doc Ayers	46
1921	Red Oldham	40
1922	Howard Ehmke	45
1923	**Bert Cole**	**52**
1924	Ken Holloway	49
1925	Jess Doyle	45
1926	Ken Holloway, Ed Wells,	36
	Earl Whitehill	36
1927	Earl Whitehill	41
1928	George Smith	39
1929	Earl Whitehill	38
1930	Charlie Sullivan	40
1931	Tommy Bridges,	35
	Art Herring, Vic Sorrell	35
1932	Chief Hogsett	47
1933	Chief Hogsett	45
1934	Schoolboy Rowe	45
1935	Schoolboy Rowe	42
1936	Roxie Lawson, S. Rowe	41
1937	Elden Auker	39
1938	Slick Coffman	39
1939	Al Benton	37
1940	Al Benton	42
1941	Bobo Newsom	43
1942	Hal Newhouser	38
1943	Dizzy Trout	44
1944	Dizzy Trout	49
1945	Dizzy Trout	41
1946	Dizzy Trout	38
1947	Hal Newhouser	40
1948	Art Houtteman, V. Trucks	43
1949	Virgil Trucks	41
1950	Hal White	42
1951	Dizzy Trout	42
1952	Hal White	41
1953	Ray Herbert	43
1954	Ray Herbert	42
1955	Al Aber	39
1956	Paul Foytack	43
1957	Jim Bunning, Duke Maas	45
1958	Hank Aguirre	44
1959	Tom Morgan	46

Ed Siever

Year	Pitcher	Games
1960	Dave Sisler	41
1961	Hank Aguirre	45
1962	Ron Nischwitz	48
1963	Terry Fox	46
1964	Mickey Lolich	44
1965	Fred Gladding	46
1966	**Larry Sherry**	**55**
1967	Fred Gladding	42
1968	Pat Dobson	47
1969	Pat Dobson	49
1970	**Tom Timmermann**	**61**
1971	**Fred Scherman**	**69**
1972	Chuck Seelbach	61
1973	John Hiller	65
1974	John Hiller	59
1975	John Hiller, Tom Walker	36
1976	John Hiller	56
1977	John Hiller	45
1978	John Hiller	51
1979	Aurelio Lopez	61
1980	Aurelio Lopez	67
1981	Kevin Saucier	38
1982	Dave Tobik	51
1983	Aurelio Lopez	57
1984	**Willie Hernandez**	**80**
1985	Willie Hernandez	74
1986	Willie Hernandez	64
1987	M. Henneman, Eric King	55
1988	Mike Henneman	65
1989	Mike Henneman	60
1990	Mike Henneman	69
1991	Paul Gibson	68
1992	Mike Munoz	65
1993	Rob MacDonald	68
1994	Joe Boever	46
1995	Joe Boever	60
1996	**Mike Myers**	**83**
1997	**Mike Myers**	**88**
1998	**Sean Runyan**	**88**
1999	Doug Brocail	70
2000	Matt Anderson	69
2001	Matt Anderson	62
2002	Juan Acevedo	65
2003	Jaime Walker	78
2004	Jaime Walker	70
2005	Jaime Walker	66
2006	Fernando Rodney	63
2007	Todd Jones	63
2008	Bobby Seay	60
2009	Fernando Rodney	73
2010	Phil Coke	74
2011	Jose Valverde	75
2012	Joaquin Benoit	73
2013	Joaquin Benoit	66
2014	Al Alburquerque	72
2015	Blaine Hardy	70
2016	Justin Wilson	66
2017	Shane Greene	71
2018	Joe Jimenez	68
2019	Buck Farmer	73
2020	Jose Cisnero	29
2021	Jose Cisnero	67

Year	Pitcher	Wins
1901	**Roscoe Miller**	**23**
1902	Win Mercer	15
1903	George Mullin	19
1904	Bill Donovan, G. Mullin	17
1905	**Ed Killian**	**23**
1906	George Mullin	21
1907	**Bill Donovan, Ed Killian**	**25**
1908	Ed Summers	24
1909	**George Mullin**	**29**
1910	George Mullin	21
1911	George Mullin	18
1912	Jean Dubuc, Ed Willett	17
1913	Jean Dubuc	15
1914	Harry Coveleski	22
1915	Hooks Dauss	24
1916	Harry Coveleski	21
1917	Hooks Dauss	17
1918	Bernie Boland	14
1919	Hooks Dauss	21
1920	Howard Ehmke	15
1921	Howard Ehmke	13
1922	Herman Pillette	19
1923	Hooks Dauss	21
1924	Earl Whitehill	17
1925	Hooks Dauss	16
1926	Earl Whitehill	16
1927	Earl Whitehill	16
1928	Ownie Carroll	16
1929	George Uhle	15
1930	Earl Whitehill	17
1931	Vic Sorrell, Earl Whitehill	13
1932	Earl Whitehill	16
1933	Firpo Marberry	16
1934	Schoolboy Rowe	24
1935	Tommy Bridges	21
1936	Tommy Bridges	23
1937	Roxie Lawson	18
1938	Tommy Bridges	13
1939	Tommy Bridges	17
	Bobo Newsom	17
1940	Bobo Newsom	21
1941	Al Benton	15
1942	Virgil Trucks	14
1943	Dizzy Trout	20
1944	**Hal Newhouser**	**29**
1945	Hal Newhouser	25
1946	Hal Newhouser	26
1947	Fred Hutchinson	18
1948	Hal Newhouser	21
1949	Virgil Trucks	19
1950	Art Houtteman	19
1951	Virgil Trucks	13
1952	Ted Gray	12
1953	Ned Garver	11
1954	Steve Gromek	18
1955	Billy Hoeft	16
1956	Frank Lary	21
1957	Jim Bunning	20
1958	Frank Lary	16
1959	Bunning, Lary, Mossi	17
1960	Frank Lary	15

Dave Mlicki

Year	Pitcher	Wins
1961	Frank Lary	23
1962	Jim Bunning	19
1963	Phil Regan	15
1964	Dave Wickersham	19
1965	Denny McLain	16
1966	Denny McLain	20
1967	Earl Wilson	22
1968	**Denny McLain**	**31**
1969	Denny McLain	24
1970	Mickey Lolich	14
1971	Mickey Lolich	25
1972	Mickey Lolich	22
1973	Joe Coleman	23
1974	John Hiller	17
1975	Mickey Lolich	12
1976	Mark Fidrych	19
1977	Dave Rozema	15
1978	Jim Slaton	17
1979	Jack Morris	17
1980	Jack Morris	16
1981	Jack Morris	14
1982	Jack Morris	17
1983	Jack Morris	20
1984	Jack Morris	19
1985	Jack Morris	16
1986	Jack Morris	21
1987	Jack Morris	18
1988	Jack Morris	15
1989	Mike Henneman	11
1990	Jack Morris	15
1991	Bill Gullickson	20
1992	Bill Gullickson	14
1993	John Doherty	14
1994	Mike Moore	11
1995	David Wells	10
1996	Omar Olivares	7
1997	Willie Blair	16
1998	Brian Moehler	14
1999	Dave Mlicki	14
2000	Brian Moehler	12
2001	Steve Sparks	14
2002	Mark Redman, S. Sparks	8
2003	Mike Maroth	9
2004	Nate Robertson	12
2005	J. Bonderman, M. Maroth	14
2006	K. Rogers, J. Verlander	17
2007	Justin Verlander	18
2008	Armando Galarraga	13
2009	Justin Verlander	19
2010	Justin Verlander	18
2011	Justin Verlander	24
2012	Justin Verlander	17
2013	Max Scherzer	21
2014	Max Scherzer	18
2015	Alfredo Simon	13
2016	Justin Verlander	16
2017	M. Fulmer, J. Verlander	10
2018	Matt Boyd	9
2019	Matt Boyd	9
2020	Spencer Turnbull	4
2021	Tarik Skubal	8

Year	Pitcher	Losses
1901	**Jack Cronin, Ed Siever**	**15**
1902	**Win Mercer**	**18**
1903	Bill Donovan, Frank Kitson	16
1904	**George Mullin**	**23**
1905	George Mullin	21
1906	George Mullin	18
1907	George Mullin	20
1908	George Mullin	13
1909	Ed Willett	10
1910	G. Mullin, Ed Summers	12
1911	Ed Willett	14
1912	George Mullin	17
1913	Jean Dubuc, Ed Willett	14
1914	Hooks Dauss	15
1915	H. Coveleski, H. Dauss	13
1916	Hooks Dauss, Bill James	12
1917	Howard Ehmke	15
1918	Hooks Dauss	16
1919	Bernie Boland	16
1920	Hooks Dauss	21
1921	Hooks Dauss	15
1922	Howard Ehmke	17
1923	Herman Pillette	19
1924	Hooks Dauss, Lil Stoner	11
1925	Collins, Dauss, Whitehill	11
1926	Earl Whitehill	13
1927	Earl Whitehill	14
1928	Earl Whitehill	16
1929	Ownie Carroll	17
1930	Earl Whitehill	13
1931	T. Bridges, Earl Whitehill	16
1932	Vic Sorrell	14
1933	Carl Fischer, Vic Sorrell	15
1934	Tommy Bridges	11
1935	Schoolboy Rowe	13
1936	Elden Auker	16
1937	Tommy Bridges	12
1938	Elden Auker	10
1939	Schoolboy Rowe	12
1940	Al Benton	10
1941	Bobo Newsom	20
1942	Dizzy Trout	18
1943	Hal Newhouser	17
1944	Gentry, Gorsica, Trout	14
1945	Dizzy Trout	15
1946	Dizzy Trout	13
1947	Hal Newhouser	17
1948	Art Houtteman	16
1949	H. Newhouser, V. Trucks	11
1950	Hal Newhouser	13
1951	Ted Gray, Dizzy Trout	14
1952	Art Houtteman	20
1953	Ted Gray	15
1954	Steve Gromek	16
1955	Ned Garver	16
1956	Billy Hoeft	14
1957	Frank Lary	16
1958	Frank Lary	15
1959	Paul Foytack	14
1960	Frank Lary	15

Win Mercer

Year	Pitcher	Losses
1961	Jim Bunning	11
1962	Don Mossi	13
1963	Hank Aguirre	15
1964	Dave Wickersham	12
1965	Dave Wickersham	14
1966	Mickey Lolich, D. McLain	14
1967	Denny McLain	16
1968	Earl Wilson	12
1969	Mickey Lolich	11
1970	Mickey Lolich	19
1971	Mickey Lolich	14
1972	Joe Coleman, M. Lolich	14
1973	Joe Coleman, M. Lolich	15
1974	Mickey Lolich	21
1975	Joe Coleman, M. Lolich	18
1976	Dave Roberts	17
1977	Fernando Arroyo	18
1978	Dave Rozema, Milt Wilcox	12
1979	Milt Wilcox	10
1980	Jack Morris	15
1981	Dan Petry, Milt Wilcox	9
1982	Jack Morris	16
1983	Jack Morris	13
1984	Jack Morris	11
1985	Dan Petry	13
1986	Walt Terrell	12
1987	Jack Morris	11
1988	Walt Terrell	16
1989	Doyle Alexander	18
1990	Jack Morris	18
1991	Walt Terrell	14
1992	Bill Gullickson	13
1993	John Doherty	11
1994	Tim Belcher	15
1995	Mike Moore	15
1996	Felipe Lira	14
1997	Brian Moehler	12
1998	Justin Thompson	15
1999	Brian Moehler	16
2000	Jeff Weaver	15
2001	Jeff Weaver	16
2002	Steve Sparks	16
2003	Mike Maroth	21
2004	Jason Johnson	15
2005	Nate Robertson	16
2006	Nate Robertson	13
2007	Nate Robertson	13
2008	Justin Verlander	17
2009	Armando Galarraga	10
2010	Rick Porcello	12
2011	Brad Penny	11
2012	Rick Porcello	12
2013	Justin Verlander	12
2014	Rick Porcello	13
2015	Alfredo Simon	12
2016	Anibal Sanchez	13
2017	Jordan Zimmermann	13
2018	Matt Boyd	13
2019	Spencer Turnbull	17
2020	Matt Boyd	7
2021	Tarik Skubal	12

Year	Pitcher	Pct.	W-L
1901	**Roscoe Miller**	**.639**	**23-13**
1902	Win Mercer	.455	15-18
1903	George Mullin	.559	19-15
1904	Bill Donovan	.515	17-16
1905	Ed Killian	.622	23-14
1906	Ed Killian	.625	10-6
1907	**Bill Donovan**	**.862**	**25-4**
1908	Bill Donovan	.720	18-7
1909	George Mullin	.784	29-8
1910	Bill Donovan	.708	17-7
1911	Ralph Works	.688	11-5
1912	Jean Dubuc	.630	17-10
1913	Joe Lake	.533	8-7
1914	Harry Coveleski	.647	22-12
1915	Bill James	.700	7-3
1916	Bernie Boland	.769	10-3
1917	Willie Mitchell	.600	12-8
1918	Bernie Boland	.583	14-10
1919	Hooks Dauss	.700	21-9
1920	Howard Ehmke	.455	15-18
1921	Bert Cole	.636	7-4
1922	Syl Johnson	.700	7-3
1923	Bert Cole	.722	13-5
1924	Ken Holloway	.700	14-6
1925	Ken Holloway	.765	13-4
1926	Hooks Dauss	.667	12-6
1927	Rip Collins	.650	13-7
1928	Ownie Carroll	.571	16-12
1929	Emil Yde	.700	7-3
1930	Vic Sorrell	.593	16-11
1931	Vic Sorrell	.481	13-14
1932	Earl Whitehill	.571	16-12
1933	Schoolboy Rowe	.636	7-4
1934	Firpo Marberry	.750	15-5
	Schoolboy Rowe	.750	24-8
1935	Elden Auker	.720	18-7
1936	Tommy Bridges	.676	23-11
1937	George Gill	.733	11-4
1938	Harry Eisenstat	.600	9-6
1939	Tommy Bridges	.708	17-7
1940	Schoolboy Rowe	.842	16-3
1941	Al Benton	.714	15-6
1942	Virgil Trucks	.636	14-8
1943	Tommy Bridges	.632	12-7
1944	Hal Newhouser	.763	29-9
1945	Hal Newhouser	.735	25-9
1946	Hal Newhouser	.743	26-9
1947	Stubby Overmire	.688	11-5
1948	Hal Newhouser	.636	21-12
1949	Fred Hutchinson	.682	15-7
1950	Dizzy Trout	.722	13-5
1951	Virgil Trucks	.619	13-8
1952	Hal Newhouser	.500	9-9
1953	Ned Garver	.500	11-11
1954	Ned Garver	.560	14-11
1955	Billy Hoeft	.696	16-7
1956	Frank Lary	.618	21-13
1957	Jim Bunning	.714	20-8
1958	Jim Bunning	.538	14-12
1959	Don Mossi	.654	17-9
1960	Dave Sisler	.583	7-5

Eric King

Year	Pitcher	Pct.	W-L
1961	Frank Lary	.719	23-9
1962	Hank Aguirre	.667	16-8
1963	Phil Regan	.625	15-9
1964	Mickey Lolich	.667	18-9
1965	Denny McLain	.727	16-6
1966	Dave Wickersham	.727	8-3
1967	Earl Wilson	.667	22-11
1968	Denny McLain	.838	31-6
1969	Denny McLain	.727	24-9
1970	Les Cain	.630	12-7
1971	Joe Coleman	.690	20-9
1972	Woodie Fryman	.770	10-3
1973	John Hiller	.670	10-5
1974	John Hiller	.550	17-14
1975	Vern Ruhle	.480	11-12
1976	Mark Fidrych	.680	19-9
1977	Dave Rozema	.680	15-7
1978	John Hiller	.690	9-4
1979	Jack Morris	.710	17-7
1980	Aurelio Lopez	.680	13-6
1981	Jack Morris	.670	14-7
1982	Dan Petry	.630	15-9
1983	Dave Rozema	.730	8-3
1984	**Aurelio Lopez**	**.910**	**10-1**
1985	Walt Terrell	.600	15-10
1986	Eric King	.730	11-4
1987	Mike Henneman	.790	11-3
1988	Jeff Robinson	.680	13-6
1989	Mike Henneman	.730	11-4
1990	Mike Henneman	.570	8-6
1991	Mike Henneman	.830	10-2
1992	John Doherty	.636	7-4
1993	Gullickson, Moore	.590	13-9
1994	Joe Boever	.820	9-2
1995	David Wells	.770	10-3
1996	Jose Lima	.460	5-6
1997	Willie Blair	.670	16-8
1998	Brian Moehler	.519	14-13
1999	Dave Mlicki	.540	14-12
2000	Willie Blair	.625	10-6
2001	Steve Sparks	.610	14-9
2002	Jeff Weaver	.430	6-8
2003	Wil Ledezma	.300	3-7
	Mike Maroth	.300	9-21
2004	Nate Robertson	.545	12-10
2005	J. Bonderman	.520	14-13
2006	Kenny Rogers	.680	17-8
2007	Justin Verlander	.750	18-6
2008	A. Galarraga	.650	13-7
2009	Justin Verlander	.679	19-9
2010	Justin Verlander	.667	18-9
2011	Justin Verlander	.828	24-5
2012	Max Scherzer	.696	16-7
2013	Max Scherzer	.875	21-3
2014	Max Scherzer	.783	18-5
2015	David Price	.692	9-4
2016	Justin Verlander	.640	16-9
2017	Justin Verlander	.556	10-8
2018	Mike Fiers	.538	7-6
2019	Buck Farmer	.500	6-6
2020	Matt Boyd	.300	3-7
2021	Kyle Funkhouser	.636	7-4

Year	Pitcher	Innings
1901	**Roscoe Miller**	**332.0**
1902	Win Mercer	281.2
1903	George Mullin	320.2
1904	**George Mullin**	**382.1**
1905	George Mullin	347.2
1906	George Mullin	330.0
1907	George Mullin	357.1
1908	Ed Summers	301.0
1909	George Mullin	303.2
1910	George Mullin	289.0
1911	George Mullin	234.1
1912	Ed Willett	284.1
1913	Jean Dubuc	242.2
1914	Harry Coveleski	303.1
1915	Harry Coveleski	312.2
1916	Harry Coveleski	324.1
1917	Hooks Dauss	270.2
1918	Hooks Dauss	249.2
1919	Hooks Dauss	256.1
1920	Hooks Dauss	270.1
1921	Dutch Leonard	245.0
1922	Howard Ehmke	279.2
1923	Hooks Dauss	316.0
1924	Earl Whitehill	233.0
1925	Earl Whitehill	239.1
1926	Earl Whitehill	252.1
1927	Earl Whitehill	236.0
1928	Ownie Carroll	231.0
1929	George Uhle	249.0
1930	Vic Sorrell	233.1
1931	Earl Whitehill	271.1
1932	Vic Sorrell	234.1
1933	Firpo Marberry	238.1
1934	Tommy Bridges	275.0
1935	Schoolboy Rowe	275.2
1936	Tommy Bridges	294.2
1937	Elden Auker	252.2
1938	Vern Kennedy	190.1
1939	Bobo Newsom	246.0
1940	Bobo Newsom	264.0
1941	Bobo Newsom	250.1
1942	Al Benton	226.2
1943	Dizzy Trout	246.2
1944	Dizzy Trout	352.1
1945	Hal Newhouser	313.1
1946	Hal Newhouser	292.2
1947	Fred Hutchinson	219.2
1948	Hal Newhouser	272.1
1949	Hal Newhouser	292.0
1950	Art Houtteman	274.2
1951	Ted Gray	197.1
1952	Ted Gray	224.0
1953	Ned Garver	198.1
1954	Steve Gromek	252.2
1955	Frank Lary	235.0
1956	Frank Lary	294.0
1957	Jim Bunning	267.1
1958	Frank Lary	260.1
1959	Jim Bunning	249.2
1960	Frank Lary	274.1

Dutch Leonard

Year	Pitcher	Innings
1961	Frank Lary	275.1
1962	Jim Bunning	258.0
1963	Jim Bunning	248.1
1964	Dave Wickersham	254.0
1965	Mickey Lolich	243.2
1966	Denny McLain	264.1
1967	Earl Wilson	264.0
1968	Denny McLain	336.0
1969	Denny McLain	325.0
1970	Mickey Lolich	272.2
1971	Mickey Lolich	376.0
1972	Mickey Lolich	327.1
1973	Mickey Lolich	308.2
1974	Mickey Lolich	308.0
1975	Mickey Lolich	240.2
1976	Mark Fidrych	250.1
1977	Dave Rozema	218.1
1978	Jim Slaton	233.2
1979	Jack Morris	197.2
1980	Jack Morris	250.0
1981	Jack Morris	198.0
1982	Jack Morris	266.1
1983	Jack Morris	293.2
1984	Jack Morris	240.1
1985	Dan Petry	238.2
1986	Walt Terrell	217.1
1987	Jack Morris	266.0
1988	Doyle Alexander	229.0
1989	Frank Tanana	223.2
1990	Jack Morris	249.2
1991	Bill Gullickson	226.1
1992	Bill Gullickson	221.2
1993	Mike Moore	213.2
1994	Tim Belcher	162.0
1995	Felipe Lira	146.1
1996	Felipe Lira	194.2
1997	Justin Thompson	223.1
1998	Justin Thompson	222.0
1999	Brian Moehler	196.1
2000	Jeff Weaver	200.0
2001	Steve Sparks	232.0
2002	Mark Redman	203.0
2003	Nate Cornejo	194.2
2004	Mike Maroth	217.0
2005	Jason Johnson	210.0
2006	Jeremy Bonderman	214.0
2007	Justin Verlander	201.2
2008	Justin Verlander	201.0
2009	Justin Verlander	240.0
2010	Justin Verlander	224.1
2011	Justin Verlander	251.0
2012	Justin Verlander	238.0
2013	Justin Verlander	218.1
2014	Max Scherzer	220.1
2015	Alfredo Simon	187.0
2016	Justin Verlander	227.2
2017	Justin Verlander	172.0
2018	Matt Boyd	170.1
2019	Matt Boyd	185.1
2020	Matt Boyd	60.1
2021	Casey Mize	150.1

Year	Pitcher	Hits
1901	**Roscoe Miller**	**339**
1902	Win Mercer	282
	George Mullin	282
1903	George Mullin	284
1904	**George Mullin**	**345**
1905	George Mullin	303
1906	George Mullin	315
1907	**George Mullin**	**346**
1908	George Mullin	301
1909	George Mullin	258
1910	George Mullin	260
1911	Ed Willett	261
1912	Ed Willett	281
1913	Ed Willett	237
1914	Hooks Dauss	286
1915	Harry Coveleski	271
1916	Harry Coveleski	278
1917	Hooks Dauss	243
1918	Hooks Dauss	243
1919	Hooks Dauss	262
1920	Hooks Dauss	308
1921	Hooks Dauss	275
1922	Howard Ehmke	299
1923	Hooks Dauss	331
1924	Lil Stoner	271
1925	Earl Whitehill	267
1926	Earl Whitehill	271
1927	Lil Stoner	251
1928	Ownie Carroll	219
1929	George Uhle	283
1930	Earl Whitehill	248
1931	Earl Whitehill	287
1932	Earl Whitehill	255
1933	Vic Sorrell	233
1934	Schoolboy Rowe	259
1935	Tommy Bridges	277
1936	Tommy Bridges	289
1937	Tommy Bridges	267
1938	Vern Kennedy	215
1939	Bobo Newsom	222
1940	Bobo Newsom	235
1941	Bobo Newsom	265
1942	Dizzy Trout	214
1943	Dizzy Trout	204
1944	Dizzy Trout	314
1945	Dizzy Trout	252
1946	Dizzy Trout	244
1947	Hal Newhouser	268
1948	Hal Newhouser	249
1949	Hal Newhouser	277
1950	Fred Hutchinson	269
1951	Fred Hutchinson	204
1952	Art Houtteman	218
1953	Ned Garver	228
1954	Steve Gromek	236
1955	Ned Garver	251
1956	Frank Lary	289
1957	Frank Lary	250
1958	Frank Lary	249
1959	Paul Foytack	239
1960	Frank Lary	262

Nate Cornejo

Year	Pitcher	Hits
1961	Frank Lary	252
1962	Jim Bunning	262
1963	Jim Bunning	245
1964	Dave Wickersham	224
1965	Mickey Lolich	216
1966	Denny McLain	205
1967	Earl Wilson	216
1968	Denny McLain	241
1969	Denny McLain	288
1970	Mickey Lolich	272
1971	Mickey Lolich	336
1972	Mickey Lolich	282
1973	Mickey Lolich	315
1974	Mickey Lolich	310
1975	Mickey Lolich	260
1976	Dave Roberts	254

Year	Pitcher	Hits
1977	Fernando Arroyo	227
1978	Jim Slaton	235
1979	Milt Wilcox	201
1980	Jack Morris	252
1981	Jack Morris	153
1982	Jack Morris	247
1983	Jack Morris	257
1984	Dan Petry	231
1985	Walt Terrell	221
1986	Jack Morris	229
1987	Walt Terrell	254
1988	Doyle Alexander	260
1989	Doyle Alexander	245
1990	Jack Morris	231
1991	Walt Terrell	257
1992	Bill Gullickson	228
1993	Mike Moore	227
1994	Tim Belcher	192
1995	Mike Moore	179
1996	Felipe Lira	204
1997	Brian Moehler	198
1998	Justin Thompson	227
1999	Brian Moehler	229
2000	Brian Moehler	222
2001	Steve Sparks	244
2002	Steve Sparks	238
2003	Nate Cornejo	236
2004	Mike Maroth	244
2005	Mike Maroth	235
2006	Jeremy Bonderman	214
2007	Nate Robertson	199
2008	Nate Robertson	218
2009	Justin Verlander	219
2010	Justin Verlander	190
2011	Brad Penny	222
2012	Rick Porcello	226
2013	Doug Fister	229
2014	Justin Verlander	223
2015	Alfredo Simon	201
2016	Anibal Sanchez	171
	Justin Verlander	171
2017	Jordan Zimmermann	204
2018	Matt Boyd	146
2019	Matt Boyd	178
2020	Matt Boyd	67
2021	Tarik Skubal	141

Year	Pitcher	HR
1901	**Ed Siever**	**9**
1902	Win Mercer, Joe Yeager	5
1903	Frank Kitson	8
1904	Frank Kitson	7
1905	George Mullin	4
1906	Ed Siever	5
1907	Bill Donovan	3
1908	Ed Killian, Ed Summers	3
1909	Ed Willett	5
1910	**Sailor Stroud**	**9**
1911	George Mullin	7
1912	Joe Lake, Mullin, Ed Willett	3
1913	Hooks Dauss	4
1914	Harry Coveleski	4
1915	Jean Dubuc	6
1916	Harry Coveleski	6
1917	Howard Ehmke	3
1918	Hooks Dauss, Bill James	3
1919	B. Boland, Dutch Leonard	7
1920	**Hooks Dauss**	**11**
1921	**Howard Ehmke**	**15**
	Dutch Leonard	**15**
1922	Red Oldham	14
1923	K. Holloway, S. Johnson	12
1924	Lil Stoner	13
1925	Earl Whitehill	13
1926	Lil Stoner	11
1927	Ken Holloway	10
1928	**Lil Stoner**	**16**
1929	**Earl Whitehill**	**16**
1930	**George Uhle**	**18**
1931	**Earl Whitehill**	**22**
1932	Earl Whitehill	17
1933	Vic Sorrell	18
1934	Tommy Bridges	16
1935	**Tommy Bridges**	**22**
1936	Tommy Bridges	21
1937	Roxie Lawson	17
1938	George Gill	15
1939	Schoolboy Rowe	17
1940	Bobo Newsom	19
1941	Bobo Newsom	15
1942	Dizzy Trout	15
1943	Virgil Trucks	11
1944	Rufe Gentry, Dizzy Trout	9
1945	Les Mueller, Dizzy Trout	8
1946	**Virgil Trucks**	**23**
1947	F. Hutchinson, V. Trucks	14
1948	**Fred Hutchinson**	**32**
1949	Art Houtteman	19
	Hal Newhouser	19
1950	Art Houtteman	29
1951	Ted Gray	17
1952	Ted Gray	21
1953	Ted Gray	25
1954	Steve Gromek	26
1955	Steve Gromek	26
1956	Steve Gromek	25
1957	**Jim Bunning**	**33**
1958	Jim Bunning	28
1959	Jim Bunning	37
1960	Frank Lary	25

George Gill

Year	Pitcher	HR
1961	Don Mossi	29
1962	Jim Bunning	28
1963	**Jim Bunning**	**38**
1964	Dave Wickersham	28
1965	Denny McLain	25
1966	**Denny McLain**	**42**
1967	Denny McLain	35
1968	Denny McLain	31
1969	Denny McLain	25
1970	Joe Niekro	28
1971	Mickey Lolich	36
1972	Mickey Lolich	29
1973	Mickey Lolich	35
1974	Mickey Lolich	38
1975	Joe Coleman	27
1976	Vern Ruhle	19
1977	Dave Rozema	25
1978	Jim Slaton	27
1979	Jack Morris	19
1980	Milt Wilcox	24
1981	Jack Morris	14
1982	Jack Morris	37
1983	Dan Petry	37
1984	Dan Petry	21
1985	Dan Petry	24
1986	Jack Morris	40
1987	Jack Morris	39
1988	Doyle Alexander	30
1989	Doyle Alexander	28
1990	Jack Morris	26
1991	Frank Tanana	26
1992	Bill Gullickson	35
1993	Mike Moore	35
1994	Mike Moore	27
1995	Mike Moore	24
1996	Felipe Lira	30
1997	Brian Moehler	22
1998	Brian Moehler	30
1999	Willie Blair	29
2000	Hideo Nomo	31
2001	Jose Lima	23
2002	Steve Sparks	23
2003	Mike Maroth	34
2004	Nate Robertson	30
2005	Mike Maroth	30
2006	Nate Robertson	29
2007	Jeremy Bonderman	23
2008	Armando Galarraga	28
2009	Edwin Jackson	27
2010	Jeremy Bonderman	25
2011	Max Scherzer	29
2012	Max Scherzer	23
2013	Justin Verlander	19
2014	Rick Porcello, M. Scherzer	18
	Justin Verlander	18
2015	Anibal Sanchez	29
2016	A. Sanchez, J. Verlander	30
2017	Jordan Zimmermann	29
2018	Jordan Zimmermann	28
2019	Matt Boyd	39
2020	Matt Boyd	15
2021	Tarik Skubal	35

Year	Pitcher	Walks
1901	**Roscoe Miller**	**98**
1902	George Mullin	95
1903	**George Mullin**	**106**
1904	**George Mullin**	**131**
1905	**George Mullin**	**138**
1906	George Mullin	108
1907	George Mullin	106
1908	George Mullin	71
1909	George Mullin	78
1910	George Mullin	102
1911	Ed Willett	80
1912	Jean Dubuc	109
1913	Jean Dubuc	91
1914	Harry Coveleski	100
1915	Hooks Dauss	115
1916	Hooks Dauss	90
1917	Bill James	96
1918	Rudy Kallio	76
1919	Howard Ehmke	107
1920	Howard Ehmke	124
1921	Dauss, Ehmke, Oldham	81
1922	Howard Ehmke	101
1923	Herman Pillette	83
1924	Earl Whitehill	79
1925	Earl Whitehill	88
1926	Earl Whitehill	79
1927	Earl Whitehill	105
1928	Ownie Carroll	87
1929	Vic Sorrell	106
1930	Vic Sorrell	106
1931	Earl Whitehill	118
1932	Tommy Bridges	119
1933	Tommy Bridges	110
1934	Tommy Bridges	104
1935	Tommy Bridges	113
1936	Tommy Bridges	115
1937	Roxie Lawson	115
1938	Vern Kennedy	113
1939	Bobo Newsom	104
1940	Bobo Newsom	100
1941	Hal Newhouser	137
1942	Hal Newhouser	114
1943	Hal Newhouser	111
1944	Rufe Gentry	108
1945	Hal Newhouser	110
1946	Dizzy Trout	97
1947	Hal Newhouser	110
1948	Hal Newhouser	99
1949	Virgil Trucks	124
1950	Art Houtteman	99
1951	Ted Gray	95
1952	Ted Gray	101
1953	Ted Gray	76
1954	Ned Garver, G. Zuverink	62
1955	Frank Lary	89
1956	**Paul Foytack**	**142**
1957	Paul Foytack	104
1958	Jim Bunning	79
1959	Jim Bunning	75
1960	Jim Bunning	64
1961	Jim Bunning	71

Tarik Skubal

Year	Pitcher	Walks
1962	Paul Foytack	86
1963	Jim Bunning	69
1964	Dave Wickersham	81
1965	Joe Sparma	75
1966	Denny McLain	104
1967	Earl Wilson	92
1968	Joe Sparma	77
1969	Mickey Lolich	122
1970	Mickey Lolich	109
1971	Joe Coleman	96
1972	Joe Coleman	110
1973	Joe Coleman	93
1974	**Joe Coleman**	**158**
1975	Joe Coleman	85
1976	John Hiller	67
1977	John Hiller	61
1978	Jim Slaton	85
1979	Milt Wilcox	73
1980	Jack Morris	87
1981	Jack Morris	78
1982	Dan Petry	100
1983	Dan Petry	99
1984	Jack Morris	87
1985	Jack Morris	110
1986	Walt Terrell	98
1987	Walt Terrell	94
1988	Jack Morris	83
1989	Doyle Alexander	76
1990	Jack Morris	97
1991	Walt Terrell	79
1992	Frank Tanana	90
1993	Mike Moore	89
1994	Mike Moore	89
1995	Mike Moore	68
1996	Brian Williams	85
1997	Justin Thompson	66
1998	Justin Thompson	79
1999	Dave Mlicki	70
2000	Hideo Nomo	89
2001	Jeff Weaver	68
2002	Steve Sparks	67
2003	Jeremy Bonderman	58
	Nate Cornejo	58
2004	Jeremy Bonderman	73
2005	Nate Robertson	65
2006	Nate Robertson	67
2007	Justin Verlander	67
2008	Justin Verlander	87
2009	Edwin Jackson	70
2010	Justin Verlander	71
2011	Brad Penny	62
2012	M. Scherzer, J. Verlander	60
2013	Justin Verlander	75
2014	Justin Verlander	65
2015	Alfredo Simon	68
2016	Justin Verlander	57
2017	Justin Verlander	67
2018	Francisco Liriano	73
2019	Spencer Turnbull	59
2020	Spencer Turnbull	29
2021	Tarik Skubal	47

Year	Pitcher	Strikeouts
1901	**Ed Siever**	**85**
1902	George Mullin	78
1903	**Bill Donovan**	**187**
1904	George Mullin	161
1905	George Mullin	168
1906	George Mullin	123
1907	George Mullin	146
1908	Bill Donovan	141
1909	George Mullin	124
1910	Bill Donovan	107
1911	George Mullin	87
1912	Jean Dubuc	97
1913	Hooks Dauss	107
1914	Hooks Dauss	150
1915	Harry Coveleski	150
1916	Harry Coveleski	108
1917	Hooks Dauss	102
1918	Hooks Dauss	73
1919	Dutch Leonard	102
1920	Doc Ayers	103
1921	Dutch Leonard	120
1922	Howard Ehmke	108
1923	Hooks Dauss	105
1924	Rip Collins	75
1925	Earl Whitehill	83
1926	Earl Whitehill	109
1927	Earl Whitehill	95
1928	Earl Whitehill	93
1929	Earl Whitehill	103
1930	George Uhle	117
1931	Tommy Bridges	105
1932	Tommy Bridges	108
1933	Tommy Bridges	120
1934	Tommy Bridges	151
1935	Tommy Bridges	163
1936	Tommy Bridges	175
1937	Tommy Bridges	138
1938	Tommy Bridges	101
1939	Bobo Newsom	164
1940	Bobo Newsom	164
1941	Bobo Newsom	175
1942	Al Benton	102
1943	Hal Newhouser	144
1944	**Hal Newhouser**	**187**
1945	**Hal Newhouser**	**212**
1946	**Hal Newhouser**	**275**
1947	Hal Newhouser	176
1948	Hal Newhouser	143
1949	Virgil Trucks	153
1950	Ted Gray	102
1951	Ted Gray	131
1952	Ted Gray	138
1953	Ted Gray	115
1954	Billy Hoeft	114
1955	Billy Hoeft	133
1956	Paul Foytack	184
1957	Jim Bunning	182
1958	Jim Bunning	177
1959	Jim Bunning	201
1960	Jim Bunning	201

Hooks Dauss

Year	Pitcher	Strikeouts
1961	Jim Bunning	194
1962	Jim Bunning	184
1963	Jim Bunning	196
1964	Mickey Lolich	192
1965	Mickey Lolich	226
1966	Denny McLain	192
1967	Earl Wilson	184
1968	**Denny McLain**	**280**
1969	Mickey Lolich	271
1970	Mickey Lolich	230
1971	**Mickey Lolich**	**308**
1972	Mickey Lolich	250
1973	Mickey Lolich	214
1974	Mickey Lolich	202
1975	Mickey Lolich	139
1976	John Hiller	117
1977	John Hiller	115
1978	Milt Wilcox	132
1979	Jack Morris	113
1980	Jack Morris	112
1981	Jack Morris	97
1982	Jack Morris	135
1983	Jack Morris	232
1984	Jack Morris	148
1985	Jack Morris	191
1986	Jack Morris	223
1987	Jack Morris	208
1988	Jack Morris	168
1989	Frank Tanana	147
1990	Jack Morris	162
1991	Frank Tanana	107
1992	Frank Tanana	91
1993	David Wells	139
1994	Tim Belcher	76
1995	Felipe Lira	89
1996	Felipe Lira	113
1997	Justin Thompson	151
1998	Justin Thompson	149
1999	Dave Mlicki	119
2000	Hideo Nomo	181
2001	Jeff Weaver	152
2002	Mark Redman	109
2003	Jeremy Bonderman	108
2004	Jeremy Bonderman	168
2005	Jeremy Bonderman	145
2006	Jeremy Bonderman	202
2007	Justin Verlander	183
2008	Justin Verlander	163
2009	Justin Verlander	269
2010	Justin Verlander	219
2011	Justin Verlander	250
2012	Justin Verlander	239
2013	Max Scherzer	240
2014	Max Scherzer	252
2015	D. Price, Anibal Sanchez	138
2016	Justin Verlander	254
2017	Justin Verlander	176
2018	Matt Boyd	159
2019	Matt Boyd	238
2020	Matt Boyd	60
2021	Tarik Skubal	164

Year	Pitcher	Balks
1901	Seven Pitchers	0
1902	**Ed Siever**	**1**
1903	10 Pitchers	0
1904	**Ed Killian**	**1**
1905	**George Mullin**	**1**
1906	Nine Pitchers	0
1907	**George Mullin**	**1**
1908	**Ed Summers**	**1**
1909	**Ed Summers**	**1**
1910	13 Pitchers	0
1911	**Tex Covington**	**1**
1912	**Bill Burns**	**1**
1913	19 Pitchers	0
1914	**Red Oldham**	**3**
1915	Pug Cavet, Red Oldham	1
1916	Three Pitchers	1
1917	Hooks Dauss	1
1918	Eric Erickson	1
1919	Doc Ayers	1
1920	Howard Ehmke	2
1921	Seven Pitchers	1
1922	Bert Cole, Howard Ehmke	1
1923	Herman Pillette	1
	Earl Whitehill	1
1924	K. Holloway, H. Pillette	1
1925	**Ed Wells**	**3**
1926	**Rip Collins**	**3**
1927	Earl Whitehill	2
1928	Ken Holloway	1
1929	Three Pitchers	1
1930	14 Pitchers	0
1931	T. Bridges, George Uhle	1
1932	Tommy Bridges	1
1933	Vic Frazier	2
1934	Three Pitchers	1
1935	Four Pitchers	1
1936	Tommy Bridges, S. Rowe	1
1937	Slick Coffman	2
1938	Vern Kennedy	2
1939	Red Lynn, Dizzy Trout	1
1940	Bobo Newsom	2
1941	Four Pitchers	1
1942	Three Pitchers	1
1943	Three Pitchers	1
1944	Hal Newhouser	2
1945	Hal Newhouser	2
1946	F. Hutchinson, Dizzy Trout	1
1947	Dizzy Trout	1
1948	Dizzy Trout, Virgil Trucks	1
1949	12 Pitchers	0
1950	Four Pitchers	1
1951	Bob Cain	2
1952	**Bill Wight**	**3**
1953	Ned Garver, Billy Hoeft	1
1954	Ted Gray	1
1955	Ned Garver, Steve Gromek	1
1956	**Paul Foytack**	**3**
1957	Frank Lary	2
1958	**Jim Bunning**	**3**
1959	Five Pitchers	1
1960	Pete Burnside	2

Steve Baker

Year	Pitcher	Balks
1961	Don Mossi	2
1962	Paul Foytack	2
1963	**Bill Faul**	**3**
1964	Hank Aguirre	2
1965	Denny McLain	2
1966	Orlando Pena	2
1967	Joe Sparma	2
1968	Earl Wilson	2
1969	Denny McLain	2
1970	Five Pitchers	1
1971	Daryl Patterson	2
1972	20 Pitchers	0
1973	W. Fryman, F. Scherman	1
1974	Woodie Fryman	1
1975	Three Pitchers	1
1976	Steve Grilli, Bill Laxton	2
1977	**Jim Crawford**	**3**
1978	Steve Foucault, Jim Slaton	1
1979	Steve Baker	2
1980	Jack Morris, Dan Petry	2
1981	Jack Morris	2
1982	Four Pitchers	1
1983	**Dave Rozema**	**3**
1984	J. Berenguer, Milt Wilcox	2
1985	**Jack Morris**	**3**
1986	**Eric King**	**3**
1987	**Jeff Robinson**	**3**
1988	**Jack Morris**	**11**
1989	Seven Pitchers	1
1990	Jack Morris	2
1991	Five Pitchers	1
1992	Three Pitchers	1
1993	Five Pitchers	1
1994	Tim Belcher, Greg Gohr	1
1995	Brian Maxcy	2
1996	Richie Lewis	2
1997	Three Pitchers	1
1998	20 Pitchers	0
1999	C.J. Nitkowski	3
2000	Jeff Weaver, Greg Gohr	2
2001	Steve Sparks	2
2002	Steve Sparks	2
2003	J. Bonderman, Matt Roney	2
2004	Six Pitchers	1
2005	Wil Ledezma	2
2006	J. Bonderman, J. Verlander	1
2007	W. Ledezma, J. Verlander	2
2008	Justin Verlander	3
2009	Justin Verlander	4
2010	A. Galarraga, Rick Porcello	3
2011	Justin Verlander	2
2012	Brayan Villarreal	2
2013	Seven Pitchers	1
2014	Al Alburquerque	2
2015	Al Alburquerque	4
2016	Anibal Sanchez	2
2017	Four Pitchers	1
2018	Matt Boyd	2
2019	Matt Boyd	4
2020	23 Pitchers	0
2021	Three Pitchers	1

Year	Pitcher	HBP
1901	**Roscoe Miller**	**13**
1902	Win Mercer	10
1903	George Mullin	8
1904	**Ed Killian**	**17**
1905	Ed Killian	13
1906	George Mullin	15
1907	George Mullin	15
1908	**Ed Summers**	**20**
1909	Ed Willett	15
1910	Ed Willett	17
1911	Ed Willett	14
1912	Ed Willett	17
1913	Hooks Dauss	13
1914	Hooks Dauss	18
1915	**Harry Coveleski**	**20**
1916	Hooks Dauss	16
1917	Willie Mitchell	13
1918	Hooks Dauss	9
1919	Dutch Leonard	7
1920	Howard Ehmke	13
1921	Hooks Dauss, H. Ehmke	13
1922	**Howard Ehmke**	**23**
1923	Rip Collins, Ken Holloway	10
1924	Earl Whitehill	13
1925	Earl Whitehill	10
1926	Ken Holloway	8
	Earl Whitehill	8
1927	Earl Whitehill	9
1928	Ownie Carroll, Sam Gibson	7
1929	Ownie Carroll	8
1930	Chief Hogsett	9
1931	Art Herring	8
1932	Buck Marrow	6
1933	Tommy Bridges	6
1934	Auker, Bridges, Sorrell	3
1935	Elden Auker	9
1936	Tommy Bridges	5
1937	Elden Auker	6
1938	Elden Auker	5
1939	Tommy Bridges	6
1940	Johnny Gorsica	4
1941	Al Benton	3
1942	Hal White	5
1943	Roy Henshaw	3
1944	Gentry, Gorsica, Trout	4
1945	Jim Tobin	4
1946	Dizzy Trout, Virgil Trucks	3
1947	Dizzy Trout	3
1948	Ted Gray	3
1949	Ted Gray, Art Houtteman	5
1950	Art Houtteman	8
1951	Bob Cain	11
1952	Virgil Trucks	7
1953	Steve Gromek	8
1954	Steve Gromek	12
1955	Steve Gromek	9
1956	Frank Lary	12
1957	Frank Lary	12
1958	Frank Lary	12
1959	Jim Bunning, Frank Lary	11
1960	Frank Lary	19

Buck Marrow

Year	Pitcher	HBP
1961	Jim Bunning	9
1962	Jim Bunning	13
1963	Hank Aguirre	8
1964	Dave Wickersham	12
1965	Mickey Lolich	12
1966	Dave Wickersham	8
1967	Joe Sparma	8
1968	Mickey Lolich	11
1969	Mickey Lolich	14
1970	Les Cain	7
1971	J. Coleman, Mickey Lolich	7
1972	Mickey Lolich	11
1973	Joe Coleman	10
1974	Joe Coleman	12
1975	Joe Coleman	9
1976	Bill Laxton	6
1977	Dave Rozema	7
1978	Three Pitchers	8
1979	Milt Wilcox	11
1980	Milt Wilcox	6
1981	Milt Wilcox	6
1982	Milt Wilcox	7
1983	Juan Berenguer, Dan Petry	6
1984	Milt Wilcox	8
1985	Jack Morris	5
1986	Eric King	8
1987	Dan Petry	10
1988	Doyle Alexander, Eric King	5
1989	Frank Tanana	8
1990	Frank Tanana	9
1991	Mark Leiter	6
1992	Frank Tanana	7
1993	Tom Bolton, David Wells	7
1994	Tim Belcher, Bill Gullickson	4
1995	Felipe Lira	8
1996	Felipe Lira	10
1997	Omar Olivares	9
1998	Frank Castillo	5
1999	Jeff Weaver	17
2000	Jeff Weaver	15
2001	Jeff Weaver	14
2002	Steve Sparks	12
2003	Mike Maroth	8
2004	Jeremy Bonderman	10
2005	Mike Maroth	9
2006	Kenny Rogers	9
2007	Justin Verlander	19
2008	Justin Verlander	14
2009	A. Galarraga, J. Verlander	6
2010	Jeremy Bonderman	10
2011	Rick Porcello	8
2012	Doug Fister	7
2013	Doug Fister	16
2014	Max Scherzer	6
2015	Alfredo Simon	8
2016	Michael Fulmer	9
2017	Michael Fulmer	8
2018	Matt Boyd	11
2019	Spencer Turnbull	16
2020	Three Pitchers	5
2021	Casey Mize	11

Year	Pitcher	IBB
1955	**Ned Garver**	**10**
1956	**Billy Hoeft**	**12**
1957	**Paul Foytack**	**12**
1958	Herb Moford	6
1959	Frank Lary	4
1960	Jim Bunning	7
1961	Hank Aguirre	3
	Jim Bunning	3
	Don Mossi	3
1962	Hank Aguirre	7
1963	Terry Fox	5
	Phil Regan	5
1964	Hank Aguirre	4
	Fred Gladding	4
	Phil Regan	4
1965	Larry Sherry	10
1966	Mickey Lolich	8
1967	Earl Wilson	7
1968	Fred Lasher	7
1969	Mickey Lolich	10
1970	Tom Timmermann	11
1971	Fred Scherman	7
1972	Fred Scherman	9
1973	John Hiller	7
	Mickey Lolich	7
1974	**John Hiller**	**19**
1975	Joe Coleman	6
	Vern Ruhle	6
1976	John Hiller	9
1977	John Hiller	8
1978	Jack Morris	5
1979	Jack Billingham	11
1980	Dan Petry	14
	Dave Rozema	14
1981	Jack Morris	11
1982	Dave Tobik	8
1983	Aurelio Lopez	7
	Dan Petry	7
1984	Willie Hernandez	8
1985	Bill Scherrer	13
1986	Randy O'Neal	9
	Frank Tanana	9
1987	Eric King	10
1988	Mike Henneman	10
1989	Mike Henneman	15
1990	Jack Morris	13
1991	Bill Gullickson	13
1992	Les Lancaster	12
1993	Tom Bolton	10
	Mike Moore	10
1994	Joe Boever	12
1995	Joe Boever	12
1996	Richie Lewis	9
1997	A.J. Sager	6
1998	Bryce Florie	6
	Doug Botchtler	6
	Dean Crow	6
1999	Brian Moehler	5
2000	Matt Anderson	4
2001	C.J. Nitkowski	7
2002	Jeff Farnsworth	8
2003	Nate Cornejo	8
2004	Jeremy Bonderman	5
	Esteban Yan	5
2005	Chris Spurling	6
2006	Jeremy Bonderman	7
2007	Jeremy Bonderman	6
	Todd Jones	6
2008	Justin Verlander	8
2009	Brandon Lyon	9
2010	Phil Coke	4
	Fu-Te Ni	4
2011	Phil Coke	5
2012	Jose Valverde	5
2013	Phil Coke	7
2014	Ian Krol	4
	Rick Porcello	4
2015	Shane Greene	4
2016	Kyle Ryan	5
	Alex Wilson	5
2017	Warwick Saupold	5
	Alex Wilson	5
2018	Joe Jimenez	3
2019	Nick Ramirez	4
2020	John Schreiber	1
	Spencer Turnbull	1
2021	Michael Fulmer	2
	Gregory Soto	2

NED GARVER

Veteran righthander Ned Garver pitching in relief for the Detroit Tigers on Thursday, July 26, 1956. The Tigers lost to the visiting Baltimore Orioles 11-6, with a meager crowd of 5,468 fans in attendance at Briggs Stadium. The game had four future major league managers in outfielder Dick Williams and second baseman Billy Gardner for the Orioles, with shortstop Harvey Kuenn and outfielder Bob Kennedy for the Bengals.

Year	Pitcher	WP
1901	**Jack Cronin**	**5**
1902	**George Mullin**	**13**
1903	Bill Donovan	7
1904	Bill Donovan	11
1905	George Mullin	6
1906	George Mullin	11
1907	George Mullin	6
1908	George Mullin	12
1909	Ed Willett	11
1910	Ed Willett	10
1911	Ed Lafitte	8
1912	**Jean Dubuc**	**16**
1913	Jean Dubuc	11
1914	Hooks Dauss	8
1915	Jean Dubuc	11
1916	Hooks Dauss	8
1917	Three Pitchers	4
1918	Rudy Kallio	7
1919	Bernie Boland, D. Leonard	4
1920	Dutch Leonard	13
1921	Dutch Leonard	7
1922	Herman Pillette	6
1923	Rip Collins	5
1924	Rip Collins	4
1925	Four Pitchers	4
1926	Lil Stoner	6
1927	Sam Gibson, Lil Stoner	6
1928	Josh Billings	4
1929	O. Carroll, George Uhle	6
1930	Charlie Sullivan	6
1931	Tommy Bridges	9
1932	T. Bridges, Whit Wyatt	6
1933	Carl Fischer	4
1934	Vic Sorrell	4
1935	Tommy Bridges	5
1936	T. Bridges, Chad Kimsey	6
1937	Roxie Lawson	6
1938	Vern Kennedy	7
1939	Al Benton, Dizzy Trout	5
1940	Tommy Bridges	5
1941	Johnny Gorsica	5
1942	Dizzy Trout	8
1943	Dizzy Trout	6
1944	R. Gentry, H. Newhouser	4
1945	Hal Newhouser	10
1946	Hal Newhouser	8
1947	Hal Newhouser	11
1948	Virgil Trucks	7
1949	Ted Gray	7
1950	Three Pitchers	4
1951	Virgil Trucks	6
1952	Three Pitchers	5
1953	Ray Hebert	6
1954	Ray Herbert, Billy Hoeft	3
1955	Frank Lary	7
1956	Paul Foytack	8
1957	Paul Foytack, Frank Lary	5
1958	Jim Bunning	5
1959	Paul Foytack	6
1960	Dave Sisler	9
1961	Frank Lary	6

Alfredo Simon

Year	Pitcher	WP
1962	Jim Bunning	13
1963	Mickey Lolich	8
1964	Mickey Lolich	7
1965	Three Pitchers	7
1966	Mickey Lolich	11
1967	Earl Wilson	8
1968	Earl Wilson	7
1969	Mickey Lolich	14
1970	Mickey Lolich	14
1971	J. Coleman, Mickey Lolich	7
1972	Joe Coleman	9
1973	Mickey Lolich	12
1974	Joe Coleman	13
1975	Joe Coleman	15
1976	Jim Crawford	7
1977	Jim Crawford, John Hiller	6
1978	Jim Slaton	10
1979	Jack Morris	9
1980	Dave Rozema	9
1981	G. Cappuzzello, M. Wilcox	4
1982	Jack Morris	10
1983	**Jack Morris**	**18**
1984	Jack Morris	14
1985	Jack Morris	15
1986	Jack Morris	12
1987	**Jack Morris**	**24**
1988	Jack Morris	11
1989	Jack Morris	12
1990	Jack Morris, Jeff Robinson	16
1991	Walt Terrell	8
1992	Frank Tanana	11
1993	David Wells	13
1994	Storm Davis, Mike Moore	10
1995	Sean Bergman	13
1996	Richie Lewis	14
1997	Todd Jones, Felipe Lira	7
1998	Bryce Florie	9
1999	Masao Kida	7
2000	Hideo Nomo	16
2001	Matt Anderson	9
2002	Mark Redman	11
2003	Jeremy Bonderman	12
2004	Gary Knotts	11
2005	Jason Johnson	17
2006	R. Colon, Nate Robertson	6
2007	Justin Verlander	17
2008	Four Pitchers	6
2009	Justin Verlander	8
2010	Rick Porcello	11
	Justin Verlander	11
2011	R. Porcello, Max Scherzer	12
2012	Brayan Villarreal	9
2013	Al Aburquerque	9
2014	Max Scherzer	10
2015	Alfredo Simon	14
2016	Anibal Sanchez	7
2017	Three Players	5
2018	Francisco Liriano	9
2019	Spencer Turnbull	9
2020	Matt Boyd	5
2021	Gregory Soto	11

Year	Pitcher	ER
1901	**Roscoe Miller**	**109**
1902	George Mullin	106
1903	George Mullin	80
1904	George Mullin	102
1905	George Mullin	97
1906	George Mullin	102
1907	George Mullin	103
1908	George Mullin	100
1909	Ed Willett	76
1910	George Mullin	92
1911	Ed Willett	94
1912	Ed Willett	104
1913	Ed Willett	83
1914	Hooks Dauss	96
1915	Jean Dubuc	92
1916	Hooks Dauss	85
1917	Hooks Dauss	73
1918	Hooks Dauss	83
1919	Hooks Dauss	101
1920	Hooks Dauss	107
1921	**Hooks Dauss**	**112**
1922	**Howard Ehmke**	**131**
1923	Hooks Dauss	127
1924	Lil Stoner	113
1925	Earl Whitehill	124
1926	Earl Whitehill	112
1927	Lil Stoner	95
1928	Earl Whitehill	94
1929	Vic Sorrell	130
1930	Earl Whitehill	104
1931	Earl Whitehill	123
1932	Earl Whitehill	123
1933	Vic Sorrell	98
1934	Tommy Bridges	112
1935	General Crowder	114
1936	Schoolboy Rowe	123
1937	Roxie Lawson	127
1938	Vern Kennedy	107
1939	Bobo Newson	92
1940	Bobo Newsom	83
1941	Bobo Newsom	128
1942	Dizzy Trout	85
1943	Dizzy Trout	68
1944	Rufe Gentry	96
1945	Dizzy Trout	86
1946	Virgil Trucks	85
1947	Hal Newhouser	91
	Virgil Trucks	91
1948	Fred Hutchinson	106
1949	Hal Newhouser	109
1950	Art Houtteman	108
1951	Ted Gray	89
1952	Art Houtteman	107
1953	Billy Hoeft	106
1954	Billy Hoeft	89
1955	Ned Garver	102
1956	Billy Hoeft	112
1957	Frank Lary	105
1958	Paul Foytack	88
1959	Paul Foytack	124
1960	Frank Lary	107

Dave Roberts

Year	Pitcher	ER
1961	Frank Lary	99
1962	Jim Bunning	103
1963	Jim Bunning	107
1964	Dave Wickersham	97
1965	Mickey Lolich	93
1966	Denny McLain	115
1967	Denny McLain	99
1968	Mickey Lolich	78
1969	Denny McLain	101
1970	Mickey Lolich	115
1971	Mickey Lolich	122
1972	Mickey Lolich	91
1973	**Mickey Lolich**	**131**
1974	**Mickey Lolich**	**142**
1975	Joe Coleman	124
1976	Dave Roberts	112
1977	Fernando Arroyo	97
1978	Jim Slaton	107
1979	Milt Wilcox	95
1980	Jack Morris	116
1981	Jack Morris	67
1982	Jack Morris	120
1983	Dan Petry	116
1984	Jack Morris	96
1985	Walt Terrell	98
1986	Walt Terrell	110
1987	Walt Terrell	110
1988	Doyle Alexander	110
1989	Doyle Alexander	110
1990	Jack Morris	125
1991	Walt Terrell	103
1992	Bill Gullickson	107
1993	Mike Moore	124
1994	Tim Belcher	106
1995	Mike Moore	111
1996	Felipe Lira	113
1997	Brian Moehler	91
1998	Justin Thompson	100
1999	Brian Moehler	110
2000	Hideo Nomo	100
2001	Jeff Weaver	104
2002	Steve Sparks	116
2003	Mike Maroth	123
2004	Jason Johnson	112
2005	Mike Maroth	110
2006	Jeremy Bonderman	97
2007	Jeremy Bonderman	97
2008	Nate Robertson	119
2009	Justin Verlander	92
2010	Jeremy Bonderman	105
2011	Brad Penny	107
2012	Rick Porcello	90
2013	Doug Fister, R. Porcello	85
2014	Justin Verlander	104
2015	Alfredo Simon	105
2016	Anibal Sanchez	100
2017	Jordan Zimmermann	108
2018	Matt Boyd	83
2019	Matt Boyd	94
2020	Matt Boyd	45
2021	Tarik Skubal	72

Year	Pitcher	Runs
1901	**Roscoe Miller**	**168**
1902	George Mullin	155
1903	George Mullin	128
1904	George Mullin	154
1905	George Mullin	149
1906	George Mullin	139
1907	George Mullin	153
1908	George Mullin	142
1909	Ed Willett	112
1910	George Mullin	125
1911	Ed Willett	136
1912	Ed Willett	144
1913	Ed Willett	117
1914	Hooks Dauss	126
1915	Harry Coveleski	123
1916	Harry Coveleski	105
1917	Hooks Dauss	105
1918	Hooks Dauss	105
1919	Hooks Dauss	125
1920	Hooks Dauss	158
1921	Hooks Dauss	141
1922	Howard Ehmke	146
1923	Hooks Dauss	140
1924	Lil Stoner	130
1925	Earl Whitehill	135
1926	Earl Whitehill	136
1927	Lil Stoner	118
1928	Earl Whitehill	131
1929	Vic Sorrell	152
1930	Earl Whitehill	139
1931	Earl Whitehill	152
1932	E. Whitehill, W. Wyatt	136
1933	Vic Sorrell	112
1934	Tommy Bridges	117
1935	Tommy Bridges	129
1936	Tommy Bridges	141
1937	Roxie Lawson	141
1938	Vern Kennedy	123
1939	Schoolboy Rowe	113
1940	Bobo Newsom	110
1941	Bobo Newsom	140
1942	Dizzy Trout	98
1943	Hal Newhouser	88
1944	Rufe Gentry, D. Trout	104
1945	Dizzy Trout	108
1946	Virgil Trucks	94
1947	Hal Newhouser	105
	Virgil Trucks	105
1948	Fred Hutchinson	119
1949	Hal Newhouser	118
1950	Fred Hutchinson	119
1951	Ted Gray	103
1952	Ted Gray	118
1953	Billy Hoeft	113
1954	N. Garver, G. Zuverink	93
1955	Ned Garver	115
1956	Billy Hoeft	127
1957	Frank Lary	111
1958	Paul Foytack	98
1959	Paul Foytack	137
1960	Frank Lary	125
1961	Frank Lary	117
1962	Jim Bunning	112
1963	Jim Bunning	119
1964	Dave Wickersham	108
1965	Mickey Lolich	103
1966	Denny McLain	120
1967	Denny McLain	110
1968	Denny McLain	86
1969	Mickey Lolich	111
1970	Mickey Lolich	125
1971	Mickey Lolich	133
1972	Mickey Lolich	100
1973	Mickey Lolich	143
1974	Joe Coleman	160
1975	Joe Coleman	137
1976	Dave Roberts	122
1977	Fernando Arroyo	102
1978	Jim Slaton	117
1979	Milt Wilcox	105
1980	Jack Morris	125
1981	Jack Morris	69
1982	Jack Morris	131
1983	Dan Petry	126
1984	Jack Morris	108
1985	Walt Terrell	107
1986	Walt Terrell	116
1987	Walt Terrell	123
1988	Doyle Alexander	122
1989	Doyle Alexander	118
1990	Jack Morris	144
1991	Walt Terrell	115
1992	Bill Gullickson	109
1993	Mike Moore	135
1994	Tim Belcher	124
1995	Mike Moore	118
1996	Felipe Lira	123
1997	Brian Moehler	97
1998	Justin Thompson	114
1999	Brian Moehler	116
2000	H. Nomo, Jeff Weaver	102
2001	Jeff Weaver	116
2002	Steve Sparks	134
2003	Mike Maroth	131
2004	Jason Johnson	121
2005	Mike Maroth	123
2006	Jeremy Bonderman	104
2007	Jeremy Bonderman	105
2008	Nate Robertson	124
2009	Justin Verlander	99
2010	Jeremy Bonderman	113
2011	Brad Penny	117
2012	Rick Porcello	101
2013	Justin Verlander	94
2014	Justin Verlander	114
2015	Alfredo Simon	112
2016	Anibal Sanchez	108
2017	Jordan Zimmermann	111
2018	Matt Boyd	87
2019	Matt Boyd	101
2020	Matt Boyd	46
2021	Tarik Skubal	76

Brian Moehler

YEARLY TIGER PITCHING LEADERS – BATTERS FACED

Year	Pitcher	BF
1901	**Roscoe Miller**	**1408**
1902	Win Mercer	1170
1903	George Mullin	1312
1904	**George Mullin**	**1568**
1905	George Mullin	1428
1906	George Mullin	1361
1907	George Mullin	1470
1908	Ed Summers	1195
1909	George Mullin	1189
1910	George Mullin	1140
1911	Ed Willett	978
1912	Ed Willett	1172
1913	Ed Willett	1002
1914	Hooks Dauss	1218
1915	Harry Coveleski	1269
1916	Harry Coveleski	1248
1917	Hooks Dauss	1085
1918	Hooks Dauss	1027
1919	Hooks Dauss	1049
1920	Hooks Dauss	1159
1921	Dutch Leonard	1058
1922	Howard Ehmke	1232
1923	Hooks Dauss	1340
1924	Earl Whitehill	1026
1925	Earl Whitehill	1042
1926	Earl Whitehill	1099
1927	Earl Whitehill	1037
1928	Ownie Carroll	966
1929	George Uhle	1084
1930	Vic Sorrell	1021
1931	Earl Whitehill	1197
1932	Earl Whitehill	1064
1933	Vic Sorrell	999
1934	Tommy Bridges	1153
1935	Tommy Bridges	1195
1936	Tommy Bridges	1272
1937	Elden Auker	1081
1938	Vern Kennedy	877
1939	Bobo Newsom	1050
1940	Bobo Newsom	1101
1941	Bobo Newsom	1130
1942	Dizzy Trout	965
1943	Dizzy Trout	1019
1944	Dizzy Trout	1421
1945	Hal Newhouser	1261
1946	Hal Newhouser	1176
1947	Hal Newhouser	1216
1948	Hal Newhouser	1146
1949	Hal Newhouser	1228
1950	Art Houtteman	1147
1951	Ted Gray	876
1952	Ted Gray	967
1953	Ned Garver	868
1954	Steve Gromek	1049
1955	Frank Lary	997
1956	Frank Lary	1269
1957	Jim Bunning	1081
1958	Frank Lary	1085
1959	Jim Bunning	1037
1960	Frank Lary	1148
1961	Frank Lary	1127

Vern Kennedy

Year	Pitcher	BF
1962	Jim Bunning	1103
1963	Jim Bunning	1051
1964	Dave Wickersham	1064
1965	Mickey Lolich	1015
1966	Denny McLain	1080
1967	Earl Wilson	1083
1968	Denny McLain	1288
1969	Denny McLain	1304
1970	Mickey Lolich	1181
1971	Mickey Lolich	1538
1972	Mickey Lolich	1321
1973	Mickey Lolich	1286
1974	Mickey Lolich	1263
1975	Mickey Lolich	1016
1976	Dave Roberts	1048
1977	Dave Rozema	890
1978	Jim Slaton	1003
1979	Milt Wilcox	854
1980	Jack Morris	1074
1981	Jack Morris	798
1982	Jack Morris	1107
1983	Jack Morris	1204
1984	Jack Morris	1015
1985	Jack Morris	1077
1986	Jack Morris	1092
1987	Jack Morris	1101
1988	Jack Morris	997
1989	Doyle Alexander	977
1990	Jack Morris	1073
1991	B. Gullickson, W. Terrell	954
1992	Bill Gullickson	919
1993	Mike Moore	942
1994	Tim Belcher	750
1995	Felipe Lira	635
1996	Felipe Lira	850
1997	Justin Thompson	891
1998	Justin Thompson	946
1999	Brian Moehler	859
2000	Jeff Weaver	849
2001	Jeff Weaver	985
2002	Steve Sparks	868
2003	Mike Maroth	847
2004	Mike Maroth	928
2005	Mike Maroth	889
2006	Jeremy Bonderman	903
2007	Justin Verlander	866
2008	Justin Verlander	880
2009	Justin Verlander	982
2010	Justin Verlander	925
2011	Justin Verlander	969
2012	Justin Verlander	956
2013	Justin Verlander	925
2014	Max Scherzer	904
2015	Alfredo Simon	820
2016	Justin Verlander	903
2017	Justin Verlander	729
2018	Matt Boyd	709
2019	Matt Boyd	788
2020	Matt Boyd	271
2021	Tarik Skubal	634

1901 Roscoe Miller 4.55
1902 Ed Siever 3.49
1903 Bill Donovan 3.05
1904 Ed Killian 3.20
1905 Ed Killian 3.10
1906 Red Donahue 3.59
1907 Ed Siever 2.92
1908 Bill Donovan 2.89
1909 Ed Killian 2.34
1910 Bill Donovan 3.22
1911 George Mullin 3.80
1912 Jean Dubuc 3.82
1913 Hooks Dauss 4.04
1914 Harry Coveleski 3.23
1915 Hooks Dauss 3.34
1916 Harry Coveleski 2.91
1917 Willie Mitchell 3.21
1918 Bernie Boland 3.04
1919 Bernie Boland 3.45
1920 Howard Ehmke 4.46
1921 Dutch Leonard 4.59
1922 Herman Pillette 3.60
1923 Hooks Dauss 3.99
1924 Rip Collins 4.13
1925 Hooks Dauss 4.34
1926 Sam Gibson 4.31
1927 Earl Whitehill 4.19
1928 Ownie Carroll 3.90
1929 George Uhle 5.10
1930 George Uhle 4.14
1931 George Uhle 4.10
1932 Tommy Bridges 4.25
1933 Firpo Marberry 3.70
1934 Schoolboy Rowe 3.72
1935 Schoolboy Rowe 3.95
1936 Tommy Bridges 4.31
1937 Eldon Auker 4.52
1938 George Gill 4.50
1939 Bobo Newsom 3.66
1940 Schoolboy Rowe 3.62
1941 Al Benton 3.60
1942 Hal White 3.32
1943 Tommy Bridges 2.68
1944 Dizzy Trout 2.66
1945 Hal Newhouser 2.10

1946 Hal Newhouser 2.37
1947 Hal Newhouser 3.32
1948 Hal Newhouser 3.60
1949 Virgil Trucks 3.11
1950 Art Houtteman 3.67
1951 Fred Hutchinson 4.01
1952 Virgil Trucks 4.52
1953 Ned Garver 4.86
1954 Steve Gromek 3.03
1955 Billy Hoeft 3.07
1956 Frank Lary 3.55
1957 Jim Bunning 3.06
1958 Frank Lary 3.15
1959 Don Mossi 3.63
1960 Jim Bunning 3.29

Fred Scherman

1961 Don Mossi 3.63
1962 Hank Aguirre 2.79
1963 Hank Aguirre 3.83
1964 Mickey Lolich 3.41
1965 Denny McLain 2.98
1966 Earl Wilson 2.70
1967 Mickey Lolich 3.13
1968 Denny McLain 2.30
1969 Denny McLain 2.91
1970 Mickey Lolich 4.13
1971 Fred Scherman 3.03
1972 Mickey Lolich 2.75
1973 John Hiller 1.51
1974 John Hiller 3.06
1975 Mickey Lolich 4.45

1976 Mark Fidrych 2.73
1977 Dave Rozema 3.59
1978 Dave Rozema 3.57
1979 Aurelio Lopez 2.62
1980 Aurelio Lopez 4.06
1981 Kevin Saucier 2.02
1982 Dan Petry 3.59
1983 Aurelio Lopez 2.81
1984 Willie Hernandez 1.92
1985 Willie Hernandez 3.21
1986 Jack Morris 3.54
1987 Mike Henneman 3.35
1988 Mike Henneman 2.27
1989 Frank Tanana 4.23
1990 Jerry Don Gleaton 2.94
1991 Mike Henneman 3.09
1992 Mike Munoz 3.00
1993 Mike Henneman 3.52
1994 Buddy Groom 3.94
1995 Felipe Lira 4.55
1996 Richie Lewis 4.48
1997 Justin Thompson 3.30
1998 Doug Brocail 3.30
1999 Doug Brocail 2.52
2000 Todd Jones 3.94
2001 Danny Patterson 3.34
2002 Jamie Walker 3.92
2003 Jamie Walker 4.15
2004 Jamie Walker 3.90
2005 Craig Spurling 3.82
2006 Joel Zumaya 2.16
2007 Bobby Seay 2.33
2008 Armando Galarraga 4.18
2009 Brandon Lyon 2.86
2010 Jose Valverde 3.43
2011 Jose Valverde 2.61
2012 Justin Verlander 3.06
2013 Joaquin Benoit 2.01
2014 Al Alburquerque 2.51
2015 Alex Wilson 2.44
2016 Alex Wilson 3.21
2017 Justin Wilson 2.68
2018 Alex Wilson 3.50
2019 Buck Farmer 4.26
2020 Bryan Garcia 2.49
2021 Michael Fulmer 3.49

1901	**Roscoe Miller**	**62.86**
1902	**Win Mercer**	**66.58**
1903	**Bill Donovan**	**70.89**
1904	Ed Killian	70.72
1905	**Ed Killian**	**71.43**
1906	Bill Donovan	70.75
1907	**Ed Killian**	**74.12**
1908	**Ed Willett**	**75.04**
1909	**Ed Killian**	**78.59**
1910	Ed Summers	72.89
1911	George Mullin	71.06
1912	Jean Dubuc	68.75
1913	Marc Hall	66.78
1914	Harry Coveleski	71.07
1915	Hooks Dauss	70.54
1916	Harry Coveleski	71.89
1917	Bill James	74.57
1918	Bernie Boland	72.70
1919	Bernie Boland	71.82
1920	Howard Ehmke	67.59
1921	Dutch Leonard	68.00
1922	Herman Pillette	72.66
1923	Syl Johnson	69.56
1924	Earl Whitehill	66.61
1925	Hooks Dauss	69.64
1926	Sam Gibson	68.48
1927	Earl Whitehill	69.86
1928	Ownie Carroll	69.93
1929	Ownie Carroll	63.83
1930	George Uhle	71.14
1931	Earl Whitehill	68.04
1932	Tommy Bridges	72.52
1933	Firpo Marberry	71.07
1934	Tommy Bridges	71.64
1935	Eldon Auker	74.40
1936	Tommy Bridges	70.60
1937	Tommy Bridges	68.24
1938	George Gill	73.01
1939	Bobo Newsom	73.93
1940	Schoolboy Rowe	75.65
1941	Al Benton	73.93
1942	Hal White	75.36
1943	**Tommy Bridges**	**78.59**
1944	Dizzy Trout	76.47

1945	**Hal Newhouser**	**80.70**
1946	Hal Newhouser	79.00
1947	Hal Newhouser	74.85
1948	Hal Newhouser	71.64
1949	Fred Hutchinson	77.00
1950	Art Houtteman	77.92
1951	Ted Gray	70.80
1952	Ted Gray	69.09
1953	Ned Garver	69.08
1954	**Steve Gromek**	**81.91**
1955	Billy Hoeft	78.77
1956	Frank Lary	77.38
1957	**Jim Bunning**	**82.14**
1958	Frank Lary	79.07
1959	Jim Bunning	76.71
1960	Jim Bunning	75.76

Bernie Boland

1961	Don Mossi	76.83
1962	Hank Aguirre	77.68
1963	Hank Aguirre	76.81
1964	Mickey Lolich	77.43
1965	Denny McLain	81.28
1966	Earl Wilson	81.73
1967	Earl Wilson	78.97
1968	**Denny McLain**	**84.02**
1969	Denny McLain	78.40
1970	Mickey Lolich	74.96
1971	Fred Scherman	82.56
1972	Mickey Lolich	81.80
1973	**John Hiller**	**90.52**
1974	John Hiller	79.21
1975	Mickey Lolich	68.93
1976	John Hiller	82.13

1977	Dave Rozema	77.19
1978	Milt Wilcox	75.04
1979	Aurelio Lopez	84.72
1980	Aurelio Lopez	76.97
1981	Kevin Saucier	81.03
1982	Jerry Ujdur	80.49
1983	Aurelio Lopez	84.03
1984	Willie Hernandez	83.07
1985	Jack Morris	75.60
1986	Willie Hernandez	82.28
1987	Jack Morris	78.83
1988	Mike Henneman	85.03
1989	Frank Tanana	72.96
1990	Paul Gibson	83.08
1991	Mike Henneman	76.65
1992	Mike Munoz	81.79
1993	Mike Henneman	77.00
1994	Buddy Groom	79.21
1995	Felipe Lira	73.74
1996	Richie Lewis	75.89
1997	Doug Brocail	82.83
1998	Sean Runyan	80.36
1999	Doug Brocail	83.33
2000	Todd Jones	76.83
2001	Danny Patterson	75.27
2002	Jamie Walker	80.25
2003	Jamie Walker	74.18
2004	Jamie Walker	76.27
2005	Franklyn German	82.80
2006	**Jamie Walker**	**91.32**
2007	Bobby Seay	80.22
2008	Armando Galarraga	75.64
2009	Brandon Lyon	80.81
2010	Ryan Perry	76.41
2011	Jose Valverde	82.93
2012	Joaquin Benoit	81.73
2013	Joaquin Benoit	87.30
2014	Al Alburquerque	89.70
2015	Alex Wilson	82.09
2016	Justin Verlander	79.90
2017	Shane Greene	84.17
2018	Mike Fiers	83.06
2019	Joe Jimenez	77.16
2020	Bryan Garcia	79.31
2021	Tarik Skubal	81.38

1901 Joe Yeager 2.61
1902 Ed Siever 1.91
1903 George Mullin 2.25
1904 George Mullin 2.40
1905 Ed Killian 2.27
1906 Ed Siever 2.71
1907 Ed Killian 1.78
1908 Ed Summers 1.64
1909 Ed Killian 1.71
1910 Ed Willett 2.37
1911 George Mullin 3.07
1912 Jean Dubuc 2.77
1913 Hooks Dauss 2.48
1914 Harry Coveleski 2.49
1915 Harry Coveleski 2.45
1916 Harry Coveleski 1.97
1917 Bill James 2.09
1918 Bernie Boland 2.65
1919 Dutch Leonard 2.77
1920 Howard Ehmke 3.25
1921 Dutch Leonard 3.75
1922 Herman Pillette 2.85
1923 Hooks Dauss 3.62
1924 Rip Collins 3.21
1925 Hooks Dauss 3.16
1926 Sam Gibson 3.48
1927 Earl Whitehill 3.36
1928 Ownie Carroll 3.27
1929 George Uhle 4.08
1930 George Uhle 3.65
1931 George Uhle 3.50
1932 Tommy Bridges 3.36
1933 Tommy Bridges 3.09
1934 Elden Auker 3.42
1935 Tommy Bridges 3.51
1936 Tommy Bridges 3.60
1937 Elden Auker 3.88
1938 George Gill 4.12
1939 Bobo Newsom 3.37
1940 Bobo Newsom 2.83
1941 Al Benton 2.97
1942 T. Bridges, Virgil Trucks 2.74
1943 Tommy Bridges 2.39
1944 Dizzy Trout 2.12
1945 Hal Newhouser 1.81
1946 Hal Newhouser 1.94
1947 Hal Newhouser 2.87
1948 Hal Newhouser 3.01
1949 Virgil Trucks 2.81
1950 Art Houtteman 3.54
1951 Fred Hutchinson 3.68
1952 Virgil Trucks 3.97
1953 Ned Garver 4.45
1954 Steve Gromek 2.74
1955 Billy Hoeft 2.99
1956 Frank Lary 3.15
1957 Jim Bunning 2.69
1958 Frank Lary 2.90
1959 Don Mossi 3.36
1960 Jim Bunning 2.79

Alex Wilson

1961 Don Mossi 2.96
1962 Hank Aguirre 2.21
1963 Hank Aguirre 3.67
1964 Mickey Lolich 3.26
1965 Denny McLain 2.61
1966 Earl Wilson 2.59
1967 Mickey Lolich 3.04
1968 Denny McLain 1.96
1969 Denny McLain 2.80
1970 Mickey Lolich 3.80
1971 Fred Scherman 2.71
1972 Mickey Lolich 2.50
1973 John Hiller 1.44
1974 John Hiller 2.64
1975 Mickey Lolich 3.78
1976 Mark Fidrych 2.34
1977 Dave Rozema 3.09
1978 Dave Rozema 3.14
1979 Aurelio Lopez 2.41
1980 Aurelio Lopez 3.77
1981 Kevin Saucier 1.65
1982 Dan Petry 3.22
1983 Aurelio Lopez 2.81
1984 Willie Hernandez 1.92
1985 Willie Hernandez 2.70
1986 Jack Morris 3.27
1987 Mike Henneman 2.98
1988 Mike Henneman 1.87
1989 Frank Tanana 3.58
1990 Jerry Don Gleaton 2.94
1991 Mike Henneman 2.88
1992 Mike Munoz 3.00
1993 Mike Henneman 2.64
1994 Buddy Groom 3.94
1995 Felipe Lira 4.31
1996 Richie Lewis 4.18
1997 Justin Thompson 3.02
1998 Doug Brocail 2.73
1999 Doug Brocail 2.52
2000 Todd Jones 3.52
2001 Danny Patterson 3.06
2002 Juan Acevedo 2.65
2003 Jamie Walker 3.32
2004 Jamie Walker 3.20
2005 Craig Spurling 3.44
2006 Joel Zumaya 1.94
2007 Bobby Seay 2.33
2008 Armando Galarraga 3.73
2009 Brandon Lyon 2.86
2010 Jose Valverde 3.00
2011 Jose Valverde 2.24
2012 Justin Verlander 2.64
2013 Joaquin Benoit 2.01
2014 Al Alburquerque 2.51
2015 Alex Wilson 2.19
2016 Justin Verlander 3.04
2017 Shane Greene 2.66
2018 Alex Wilson 3.36
2019 Buck Farmer 3.72
2020 Bryan Garcia 1.66
2021 Michael Fulmer 2.97

Year	Pitcher	ERA+
1901	**Joe Yeager**	**140**
1902	**Ed Siever**	**187**
1903	George Mullin	132
1904	George Mullin	108
1905	Ed Killian	117
1906	Red Donahue	99
	Ed Siever	99
1907	Ed Killian	143
1908	Ed Summers	146
1909	Ed Killian	144
1910	Ed Willett	106
1911	George Mullin	109
1912	Jean Dubuc	121
1913	Hooks Dauss	118
1914	Harry Coveleski	110
1915	Harry Coveleski	120
1916	Harry Coveleski	143
1917	Bill James	127
1918	Bernie Boland	105
1919	Dutch Leonard	116
1920	Howard Ehmke	117
1921	Dutch Leonard	114
1922	Herman Pillette	141
1923	Hooks Dauss	110
1924	Rip Collins	132
1925	Hooks Dauss	139
1926	Sam Gibson	116
1927	Earl Whitehill	123
1928	Ownie Carroll	124
1929	George Uhle	104
1930	George Uhle	127
1931	George Uhle	125
1932	Tommy Bridges	133
1933	Tommy Bridges	139
1934	Eldon Auker	132
1935	Tommy Bridges	127
1936	Tommy Bridges	140
1937	Eldon Auker	119
1938	George Gill	116
1939	Bobo Newsom	137
1940	Bobo Newsom	155
1941	Al Benton	140
1942	Hal Newhouser	149
1943	Tommy Bridges	138
1944	Dizzy Trout	162
1945	Hal Newhouser	186
1946	Hal Newhouser	180
1947	Hal Newhouser	129
1948	Hal Newhouser	142
1949	Virgil Trucks	149
1950	Art Houtteman	129
1951	Fred Hutchinson	112
1952	Virgil Trucks	92
1953	Ned Garver	90
1954	Steve Gromek	136
1955	Billy Hoeft	132
1956	Frank Lary	132
1957	Jim Bunning	141
1958	Frank Lary	130
1959	Don Mossi	115
1960	Jim Bunning	139

Bryan Garcia

Year	Pitcher	ERA+
1961	Don Mossi	136
1962	Hank Aguirre	180
1963	Hank Aguirre	99
1964	Mickey Lolich	111
1965	Denny McLain	133
1966	Earl Wilson	133
1967	Mickey Lolich	106
1968	Denny McLain	152
1969	Denny McLain	130
1970	Mickey Lolich	98
1971	Fred Scherman	128
1972	Mickey Lolich	123
1973	**John Hiller**	**265**
1974	John Hiller	138
1975	Mickey Lolich	100
1976	Mark Fidrych	150
1977	Dave Rozema	132
1978	Dave Rozema	120
1979	Aurelio Lopez	176
1980	Aurelio Lopez	107
1981	Kevin Saucier	222
1982	Dan Petry	127
1983	Aurelio Lopez	145
1984	Willie Hernandez	208
1985	Willie Hernandez	154
1986	Jack Morris	128
1987	Mike Henneman	150
1988	Mike Henneman	213
1989	Frank Tanana	109
1990	Jerry Don Gleaton	133
1991	Mike Henneman	142
1992	Mike Munoz	132
1993	Mike Henneman	164
1994	Buddy Groom	122
1995	Felipe Lira	110
1996	Richie Lewis	120
1997	Justin Thompson	151
1998	Doug Brocail	171
1999	Doug Brocail	193
2000	Todd Jones	140
2001	Danny Patterson	146
2002	Juan Acevedo	169
2003	Jamie Walker	136
2004	Jamie Walker	145
2005	Craig Spurling	127
2006	Joel Zumaya	235
2007	Bobby Seay	194
2008	Armando Galarraga	117
2009	Brandon Lyon	156
2010	Jose Valverde	138
2011	Jose Valverde	182
2012	Justin Verlander	155
2013	Joaquin Benoit	199
2014	Al Alburquerque	152
2015	Alex Wilson	183
2016	Justin Verlander	136
2017	Shane Greene	172
2018	Alex Wilson	131
2019	Buck Farmer	130
2020	**Bryan Garcia**	**281**
2021	Michael Fulmer	143

1901 Roscoe Miller 1.80
1902 Ed Siever 1.20
1903 Bill Donovan 1.20
1904 Ed Killian 1.20
1905 Ed Killian 1.80
1906 Ed Siever 1.80
1907 Ed Siever 1.40
1908 Bill Donovan 1.40
1909 George Mullin 1.60
1910 Bill Donovan 1.40
1911 George Mullin 2.20
1912 Ed Willett 2.00
1913 Hooks Dauss 1.00
1914 Harry Coveleski 1.80
1915 Harry Coveleski 1.20
1916 Harry Coveleski 1.00
1917 Willie Mitchell 1.40
1918 Hooks Dauss 1.60
1919 Dutch Leonard 1.60
1920 Doc Ayers 2.40
1921 Dutch Leonard 1.00
1922 Herman Pillette 1.40
1923 Hooks Dauss 1.20
1924 Rip Collins 1.00
1925 Hooks Dauss 2.20
1926 Earl Whitehill 1.40
1927 Earl Whitehill 1.00
1928 Ownie Carroll 1.40
1929 George Uhle 1.00
1930 George Uhle 1.40
1931 George Uhle 1.00
1932 Vic Sorrell 1.80
1933 Firpo Marberry 2.00
1934 Schoolboy Rowe 1.20
1935 Schoolboy Rowe 1.20
1936 Schoolboy Rowe 1.40
1937 Eldon Auker 1.40
1938 Tommy Bridges 1.60
1939 Tommy Bridges 1.40
1940 Bobo Newsom 1.60
1941 Tommy Bridges 2.00
1942 Virgil Trucks 2.40
1943 Tommy Bridges 1.40
1944 Hal Newhouser 1.60
1945 Hal Newhouser 1.00
1946 Hal Newhouser 1.00
1947 Hal Newhouser 1.40
1948 Hal Newhouser 1.20
1949 Virgil Trucks 1.60
1950 Dizzy Trout 1.80
1951 Fred Hutchinson 1.00
1952 Virgil Trucks 1.80
1953 Ned Garver 1.60
1954 Ned Garver 1.80
1955 Billy Hoeft 1.00
1956 Frank Lary 1.00
1957 Jim Bunning 1.40
1958 Frank Lary 1.40
1959 Don Mossi 1.00
1960 Jim Bunning 1.00

Ned Garver

1961 Jim Bunning 1.60
1962 Hank Aguirre 1.00
1963 Mickey Lolich 2.20
1964 Mickey Lolich 1.00
1965 Denny McLain 1.40
1966 Earl Wilson 1.00
1967 Mickey Lolich 1.00
1968 Denny McLain 1.00
1969 Denny McLain 1.00
1970 Mickey Lolich 1.80
1971 Mickey Lolich 1.60
1972 Mickey Lolich 1.00
1973 John Hiller 1.00
1974 John Hiller 1.00
1975 Mickey Lolich 1.00
1976 Mark Fidrych 1.00
1977 Dave Rozema 1.00
1978 John Hiller 1.40
1979 Aurelio Lopez 1.20
1980 Aurelio Lopez 2.20
1981 Kevin Saucier 2.00
1982 Dan Petry 2.00
1983 Jack Morris 1.60
1984 Willie Hernandez 1.00
1985 Willie Hernandez 2.20
1986 Jack Morris 1.40
1987 Mike Henneman 1.60
1988 Mike Henneman 1.20
1989 Frank Tanana 1.40
1990 Jerry Don Gleaton 1.20
1991 Mike Henneman 2.00
1992 Bill Gullickson 1.60
1993 Mike Henneman 1.60
1994 David Wells 1.40
1995 David Wells 1.00
1996 Omar Olivares 1.80
1997 Justin Thompson 1.40
1998 Doug Brocail 1.40
1999 Doug Brocail 1.00
2000 Todd Jones 2.80
2001 Danny Patterson 1.80
2002 Jeff Weaver 1.40
2003 Jamie Walker 1.20
2004 Jamie Walker 1.40
2005 Jeremy Bonderman 2.40
2006 Joel Zumaya 2.00
2007 Bobby Seay 1.20
2008 Armando Galarraga 1.80
2009 Justin Verlander 1.40
2010 Justin Verlander 1.40
2011 Justin Verlander 1.60
2012 Justin Verlander 1.60
2013 Max Scherzer 2.40
2014 Anibal Sanchez 1.80
2015 David Price 2.00
2016 Justin Verlander 2.40
2017 Michael Fulmer 1.60
2018 Alex Wilson 2.20
2019 Buck Farmer 1.80
2020 Jose Cisnero 1.60
2021 Michael Fulmer 2.20

Year	Pitcher	Rating
1901	**Roscoe Miller**	**1.80**
1902	**Ed Siever**	**1.20**
1903	**Bill Donovan**	**1.20**
1904	**Ed Killian**	**1.20**
1905	Bill Donovan	1.80
	Ed Killian	1.80
1906	Red Donahue	1.80
	Ed Siever	1.80
1907	Ed Siever	1.40
1908	Bill Donovan	1.40
1909	George Mullin	1.60
1910	Bill Donovan	1.40
1911	George Mullin	2.20
1912	Ed Willett	2.00
1913	**Hooks Dauss**	**1.00**
1914	Harry Coveleski	1.40
1915	Harry Coveleski	1.20
1916	**Harry Coveleski**	**1.00**
1917	Willie Mitchell	1.40
1918	Hooks Dauss	1.60
1919	Dutch Leonard	1.60
1920	Doc Ayers	2.40
	Dutch Leonard	2.40
1921	**Dutch Leonard**	**1.00**
1922	Herman Pillette	1.40
1923	Hooks Dauss	1.20
1924	**Rip Collins**	**1.00**
1925	H. Dauss, Lil Stoner	2.20
1926	Earl Whitehill	1.40
1927	**Earl Whitehill**	**1.00**
1928	Ownie Carroll	1.40
1929	**George Uhle**	**1.00**
1930	George Uhle	1.40
1931	**George Uhle**	**1.00**
1932	Vic Sorrell	1.80
1933	Firpo Marberry	2.00
1934	Schoolboy Rowe	1.20
1935	Schoolboy Rowe	1.20
1936	Schoolboy Rowe	1.40
1937	Eldon Auker	1.40
1938	Tommy Bridges	1.60
1939	Tommy Bridges	1.40
1940	Bobo Newsom	1.60
1941	Tommy Bridges	2.00
1942	Tommy Bridges	2.40
	Virgil Trucks	2.40
1943	Tommy Bridges	1.40
1944	Hal Newhouser	1.60
1945	**Hal Newhouser**	**1.00**
1946	**Hal Newhouser**	**1.00**
1947	Hal Newhouser	1.40
1948	Hal Newhouser	1.20
1949	Virgil Trucks	1.60
1950	Dizzy Trout	1.80
1951	**Fred Hutchinson**	**1.00**
1952	Virgil Trucks	1.80
1953	Ned Garver	1.60
1954	Ned Garver	1.80
1955	**Billy Hoeft**	**1.00**
1956	**Frank Lary**	**1.00**
1957	Jim Bunning	1.40
1958	Frank Lary	1.40
1959	**Don Mossi**	**1.00**
1960	**Jim Bunning**	**1.00**

Willie Mitchell

Year	Pitcher	Rating
1961	Jim Bunning	1.60
1962	**Hank Aguirre**	**1.00**
1963	Hank Aguirre	2.20
	Mickey Lolich	2.20
1964	**Mickey Lolich**	**1.00**
1965	Denny McLain	1.40
1966	**Earl Wilson**	**1.00**
1967	**Mickey Lolich**	**1.00**
1968	**Denny McLain**	**1.00**
1969	**Denny McLain**	**1.00**
1970	Mickey Lolich	1.20
1971	Mickey Lolich	1.40
1972	Mickey Lolich	1.20
1973	Mickey Lolich	1.40
1974	**Mickey Lolich**	**1.00**
1975	**Mickey Lolich**	**1.00**
1976	**Mark Fidrych**	**1.00**
1977	**Dave Rozema**	**1.00**
1978	Dave Rozema	1.20
1979	**Jack Morris**	**1.00**
1980	Dan Petry	2.00
	Dan Schatzeder	2.00
1981	Dan Petry	1.80
1982	Dan Petry	1.40
1983	Jack Morris	1.40
1984	Dan Petry	1.40
1985	Frank Tanana	1.80
1986	**Jack Morris**	**1.00**
1987	Jack Morris	1.40
1988	Jack Morris	1.60
1989	**Frank Tanana**	**1.00**
1990	Jack Morris	1.40
1991	Bill Gullickson	1.60
1992	Bill Gullickson	1.40
1993	**David Wells**	**1.00**
1994	**David Wells**	**1.00**
1995	**David Wells**	**1.00**
1996	Omar Olivares	1.20
1997	**Justin Thompson**	**1.00**
1998	Brian Moehler	1.40
1999	Dave Mlicki	1.60
2000	Jeff Weaver	1.40
2001	Jeff Weaver	1.40
2002	**Jeff Weaver**	**1.00**
2003	Nate Cornejo	1.60
2004	Jeremy Bonderman	1.80
2005	Jeremy Bonderman	1.40
2006	Justin Verlander	2.00
2007	**Justin Verlander**	**1.00**
2008	Armando Galarraga	1.40
2009	**Justin Verlander**	**1.00**
2010	**Justin Verlander**	**1.00**
2011	**Justin Verlander**	**1.00**
2012	**Justin Verlander**	**1.00**
2013	Anibal Sanchez	1.40
2014	A. Sanchez, M. Scherzer	1.60
2015	David Price	1.20
2016	**Justin Verlander**	**1.00**
2017	Michael Fulmer	1.40
2018	Matt Boyd	1.40
2019	Matt Boyd	1.20
2020	Matt Boyd	1.20
2021	Casey Mize	2.40

1913 Carl Zamloch 1.40
1914 Ross Reynolds 2.00
1915 Red Oldham 1.40
1916 George Cunningham 1.40
1917 Deacon Jones 1.20
1918 Deacon Jones 1.00
1919 Doc Ayers 1.00
1920 Doc Ayers 1.00
1921 Carl Holling 1.00
1922 Syl Johnson 1.20
1923 Bert Cole 1.20
1924 Ken Holloway 1.40
1925 Ken Holloway 1.40
1926 Hooks Dauss 1.20
1927 George Smith 1.00
1928 Elam Vangilder 1.40

Chief Hogsett

1929 Lil Stoner 1.60
1930 Charlie Sullivan 1.00
1931 Charlie Sullivan 1.00
1932 Chief Hogsett 1.00
1933 Art Herring 1.00
1934 Chief Hogsett 1.40
1935 Chief Hogsett 1.20
1936 Chad Kimsey 1.60
1937 Slick Coffman 1.40
1938 Harry Eisenstat 1.00
1939 Archie McKain 1.20
1940 Archie McKain 1.40
1941 Al Benton 1.20
1942 Roy Henshaw 1.20
1943 Johnny Gorsica 1.20
1944 Walter Beck 1.00

1945 George Caster 1.00
1946 George Caster 1.00
1947 Art Houtteman 1.40
1948 Art Houtteman 1.40
1949 Dizzy Trout 1.40
1950 Hal White 1.20
1951 Dizzy Trout 1.40
1952 Hal White 1.60
1953 R. Herbert, D. Marlowe 1.40
1954 Bob Miller 1.00
1955 Al Aber 1.00
1956 Al Aber 1.60
1957 Harry Byrd 1.20
1958 Tom Morgan 1.40
1959 Pete Burnside 1.40
1960 Dave Sisler 1.20
1961 Terry Fox 1.00
1962 Terry Fox 1.00
1963 Bob Anderson 1.00
1964 Fred Gladding 1.40
1965 Orlando Pena 1.60
1966 Dave Wickersham 2.00
1967 F. Gladding 1.80
Mike Marshall 1.80
1968 Daryl Patterson 1.60
1969 Tom Timmerman 2.00
1970 John Hiller 1.40
1971 Fred Scherman 1.40
1972 John Hiller 1.40
1973 John Hiller 1.00
1974 John Hiller 1.00
1975 John Hiller 1.00
1976 John Hiller 1.20
1977 Steve Foucault 1.20
1978 John Hiller 1.20
1979 Aurelio Lopez 1.00
1980 Pat Underwood 1.60
1981 Kevin Saucier 1.20
1982 Kevin Saucier 1.60
1983 D. Gumpert, A. Lopez 1.60
1984 Willie Hernandez 1.00
1985 Willie Hernandez 1.20
1986 Mark Thurmond 1.80
1987 Mike Henneman 1.00
1988 Mike Henneman 1.00
1989 Henneman, Williams 2.00

1990 Ed Nunez 1.60
1991 Mike Henneman 1.00
1992 John Kiely 1.60
1993 Mike Henneman 1.20
1994 Buddy Groom 1.60
1995 Mike Henneman 1.00
1996 Richie Lewis 1.40
1997 Todd Jones 1.40
1998 Matt Anderson 1.80
1999 Doug Brocail 1.00
2000 Nelson Cruz, T. Jones 1.80
2001 Danny Patterson 1.40
2002 J. Acevedo, J. Santana 2.00
2003 Jamie Walker 1.20
2004 Jamie Walker 1.00
2005 Kyle Farnsworth 1.80

Michael Fulmer

2006 Joel Zumaya 1.20
2007 Bobby Seay 1.00
2008 Aquilino Lopez 1.60
2009 Fu-Te Ni 1.60
2010 Joel Zumaya 2.20
2011 Al Alburquerque 1.40
2012 Brayan Villarreal 1.40
2013 Joaquin Benoit 1.20
2014 Al Alburquerque 1.60
2015 Alex Wilson 1.40
2016 Alex Wilson 1.80
2017 Shane Greene 1.20
2018 Victor Alcantara 2.20
2019 Buck Farmer 1.20
2020 Jose Cisnero 1.40
2021 Michael Fulmer 1.00

Year	Pitcher	FIP
1901	**Jack Cronin**	**3.44**
1902	**Ed Siever**	**2.83**
1903	**Bill Donovan**	**2.64**
1904	Ed Killian	2.67
1905	Bill Donovan	2.84
1906	**Red Donahue**	**2.51**
1907	**Ed Siever**	**2.27**
1908	**Bill Donovan**	**1.78**
1909	George Mullin	2.29
1910	Bill Donovan	2.53
1911	Ed Lafitte	3.18
1912	Joe Lake	2.81
1913	Hooks Dauss	3.10
1914	Hooks Dauss	2.62
1915	Harry Coveleski	2.56
1916	Harry Coveleski	2.57
1917	Willie Mitchell	2.49
1918	George Cunningham	2.60
1919	Dutch Leonard	2.96
1920	Doc Ayers	3.14
1921	Dutch Leonard	3.81
1922	Hooks Dauss	3.60
1923	Hooks Dauss	3.49
1924	Rip Collins	3.64
1925	Earl Whitehill	4.35
1926	Earl Whitehill	3.45
1927	Earl Whitehill	3.89
1928	Earl Whitehill	3.70
1929	George Uhle	3.55
1930	Earl Whitehill	4.18
1931	George Uhle	3.96
1932	Vic Sorrell	3.94
1933	Carl Fischer	3.56
1934	Schoolboy Rowe	3.51
1935	Schoolboy Rowe	3.32
1936	Schoolboy Rowe	3.93
1937	Tommy Bridges	3.86
1938	Eldon Auker	4.62
1939	Tommy Bridges	3.41
1940	Tommy Bridges	3.55
1941	Bobo Newsom	3.49
1942	Tommy Bridges	2.87
1943	Tommy Bridges	2.68
1944	Hal Newhouser	2.58
1945	Hal Newhouser	2.45

Year	Pitcher	FIP
1946	Hal Newhouser	1.97
1947	Hal Newhouser	2.85
1948	Hal Newhouser	3.19
1949	Hal Newhouser	3.51
1950	Fred Hutchinson	3.67
	Dizzy Trout	3.67
1951	Fred Hutchinson	3.21
1952	Virgil Trucks	3.23
1953	Ned Garver	3.97
1954	Ned Garver	3.50
1955	Billy Hoeft	3.27
1956	Frank Lary	3.44
1957	Billy Hoeft	3.40
1958	Frank Lary	3.39
1959	Don Mossi	3.27
1960	Jim Bunning	2.86

Jose Cisnero

Year	Pitcher	FIP
1961	Jim Bunning	3.23
1962	Hank Aguirre	2.99
1963	Hank Aguirre	3.74
1964	Mickey Lolich	3.30
1965	Mickey Lolich	2.92
1966	Earl Wilson	2.97
1967	Mickey Lolich	2.65
1968	Denny McLain	2.53
1969	M. Lolich, D. McLain	3.05
1970	Tom Timmermann	3.21
1971	Joe Coleman	2.65
1972	Mickey Lolich	2.80
1973	John Hiller	2.25
1974	John Hiller	2.96
1975	Mickey Lolich	3.26
1976	Mark Fidrych	3.15

Year	Pitcher	FIP
1977	Dave Rozema	3.95
1978	Dave Rozema	3.71
1979	Aurelio Lopez	3.57
1980	A. Lopez, Dan Petry	3.92
1981	Milt Wilcox	3.48
1982	Dan Petry	3.70
1983	Jack Morris	3.38
1984	Willie Hernandez	2.58
1985	Willie Hernandez	3.27
1986	Willie Hernandez	3.82
1987	Mike Henneman	3.42
1988	Mike Henneman	3.35
1989	Mike Henneman	3.67
1990	Jerry Don Gleaton	3.26
1991	Mike Henneman	2.93
1992	Mike Henneman	3.07
1993	Mike Henneman	3.52
1994	Buddy Groom	4.47
1995	Brian Bohanon	4.42
1996	Mike Myers	4.01
1997	Todd Jones	3.21
1998	Doug Brocail	2.71
1999	Doug Brocail	3.40
2000	Todd Jones	3.48
2001	Matt Anderson	2.62
2002	Juan Acevedo	3.63
2003	Jamie Walker	4.32
2004	Jamie Walker	3.62
2005	Jeremy Bonderman	3.90
2006	Jeremy Bonderman	3.29
2007	Bobby Seay	2.98
2008	Bobby Seay	3.43
2009	Justin Verlander	2.80
2010	Justin Verlander	2.97
2011	Joaquin Benoit	2.96
2012	Octavio Dotel	2.30
2013	Anibal Sanchez	2.39
2014	Max Scherzer	2.85
2015	Blaine Hardy	2.89
2016	Shane Greene	3.13
2017	Justin Wilson	3.23
2018	Joe Jimenez	2.91
2019	Buck Farmer	3.88
2020	Jose Cisnero	2.65
2021	Michael Fulmer	3.46

Year	Pitcher	DICE
1901	**Jack Cronin**	**3.51**
1902	**Ed Siever**	**3.16**
1903	**Bill Donovan**	**2.89**
1904	Ed Killian	3.25
1905	Bill Donovan	3.32
1906	Red Donahue	3.15
1907	Ed Siever	3.09
1908	**Bill Donovan**	**2.67**
1909	George Mullin	3.08
1910	Bill Donovan	3.20
1911	Ed Lafitte	3.41
1912	Joe Lake	2.96
1913	Hooks Dauss	3.55
1914	Hooks Dauss	3.18
1915	Harry Coveleski	3.15
1916	Harry Coveleski	3.26
1917	Willie Mitchell	3.23
1918	George Cunningham	3.36
1919	Dutch Leonard	3.47
1920	Doc Ayers	3.39
1921	Dutch Leonard	3.71
1922	Hooks Dauss	3.59
1923	Hooks Dauss	3.55
1924	Rip Collins	3.60
1925	Earl Whitehill	4.24
1926	Earl Whitehill	3.53
1927	Earl Whitehill	3.86
1928	Earl Whitehill	3.79
1929	George Uhle	3.39
1930	Earl Whitehill	3.68
1931	George Uhle	3.84
1932	Vic Sorrell	3.92
1933	Carl Fischer	3.77
1934	Schoolboy Rowe	3.39
1935	Schoolboy Rowe	3.26
1936	Schoolboy Rowe	3.66
1937	Tommy Bridges	3.82
1938	Eldon Auker	4.70
1939	Tommy Bridges	3.43
1940	Tommy Bridges	3.71
1941	Bobo Newsom	3.83
1942	Tommy Bridges	3.45
1943	Tommy Bridges	3.27
1944	Hal Newhouser	3.04
1945	Hal Newhouser	2.91

Year	Pitcher	DICE
1946	**Hal Newhouser**	**2.58**
1947	Hal Newhouser	3.35
1948	Hal Newhouser	3.53
1949	Hal Newhouser	4.00
1950	F. Hutchinson, D. Trout	4.08
1951	Fred Hutchinson	3.66
1952	Virgil Trucks	3.84
1953	Ned Garver	4.38
1954	Ned Garver	4.10
1955	Billy Hoeft	3.86
1956	Frank Lary	4.07
1957	Billy Hoeft	3.94
1958	Frank Lary	3.91
1959	Don Mossi	3.73
1960	Jim Bunning	3.33

Billy Hoeft

Year	Pitcher	DICE
1961	Jim Bunning	3.66
1962	Hank Aguirre	3.37
1963	Hank Aguirre	4.26
1964	Mickey Lolich	3.69
1965	Mickey Lolich	3.41
1966	Earl Wilson	3.42
1967	Mickey Lolich	3.11
1968	Denny McLain	3.15
1969	M. Lolich, D. McLain	3.54
1970	Mickey Lolich	3.85
1971	Joe Coleman	3.20
1972	Mickey Lolich	3.40
1973	John Hiller	2.68
1974	John Hiller	3.38
1975	Mickey Lolich	3.67

Year	Pitcher	DICE
1976	Mark Fidrych	3.52
1977	Dave Rozema	4.21
1978	Dave Rozema	4.13
1979	Aurelio Lopez	3.83
1980	A. Lopez, Dan Petry	4.17
1981	Milt Wilcox	3.88
1982	Dan Petry	3.99
1983	Jack Morris	3.63
1984	Willie Hernandez	2.81
1985	Willie Hernandez	3.58
1986	Willie Hernandez	4.05
1987	Mike Henneman	3.55
1988	Mike Henneman	3.58
1989	Mike Henneman	3.91
1990	Jerry Don Gleaton	3.45
1991	Mike Henneman	3.07
1992	Mike Henneman	3.28
1993	Mike Henneman	3.53
1994	Buddy Groom	4.34
1995	Brian Bohanon	4.32
1996	Mike Myers	3.84
1997	Todd Jones	3.10
1998	**Doug Brocail**	**2.57**
1999	Doug Brocail	3.27
2000	Todd Jones	3.34
2001	**Matt Anderson**	**2.57**
2002	Juan Acevedo	3.67
2003	Jamie Walker	4.29
2004	Jamie Walker	3.57
2005	Jeremy Bonderman	3.88
2006	Jeremy Bonderman	3.14
2007	Bobby Seay	2.74
2008	Bobby Seay	3.30
2009	Justin Verlander	2.70
2010	Justin Verlander	2.89
2011	Joaquin Benoit	2.93
2012	**Octavio Dotel**	**2.21**
2013	Drew Smyly	2.26
2014	Max Scherzer	2.71
2015	Blaine Hardy	2.76
2016	Shane Greene	2.98
2017	Justin Wilson	3.07
2018	Joe Jimenez	2.74
2019	Buck Farmer	3.67
2020	Jose Cisnero	2.46
2021	Michael Fulmer	3.29

Year	Pitcher	WHIP
1901	**Joe Yeager**	**1.277**
1902	**Ed Siever**	**1.051**
1903	Bill Donovan	1.114
1904	Ed Killian	1.164
1905	Ed Killian	1.165
1906	Ed Siever	1.280
1907	Ed Siever	1.121
1908	Ed Summers	1.083
1909	**Ed Summers**	**1.047**
1910	Ed Willett	1.110
1911	George Mullin	1.306
1912	Ed Willett	1.284
1913	Hooks Dauss	1.200
1914	Harry Coveleski	1.157
1915	Harry Coveleski	1.145
1916	Harry Coveleski	1.051
1917	Willie Mitchell	1.176
1918	Bernie Boland	1.191
1919	Bernie Boland	1.245
1920	Doc Ayers	1.337
1921	Dutch Leonard	1.371
1922	Herman Pillette	1.329
1923	Syl Johnson	1.293
1924	Rip Collins	1.213
1925	Hooks Dauss	1.417
1926	Earl Whitehill	1.387
1927	Earl Whitehill	1.453
1928	Ownie Carroll	1.325
1929	George Uhle	1.369
1930	George Uhle	1.314
1931	George Uhle	1.238
1932	Vic Sorrell	1.327
1933	Firpo Marberry	1.229
1934	Schoolboy Rowe	1.278
1935	Schoolboy Rowe	1.233
1936	Schoolboy Rowe	1.345
1937	Elden Auker	1.373
1938	Elden Auker, G. Gill	1.494
1939	Tommy Bridges	1.247
1940	Schoolboy Rowe	1.260
1941	Al Benton	1.237
1942	Tommy Bridges	1.293
1943	Virgil Trucks	1.095
1944	Dizzy Trout	1.127
1945	Hal Newhouser	1.114
1946	Hal Newhouser	1.069
1947	Fred Hutchinson	1.238
1948	Fred Hutchinson	1.226
1949	Fred Hutchinson	1.161
1950	Art Houtteman	1.296
1951	Fred Hutchinson	1.227
1952	Art Houtteman	1.281
1953	Ted Gray	1.375
1954	Ned Garver	1.129
1955	Billy Hoeft	1.191
1956	Frank Lary	1.378
1957	Jim Bunning	1.070
1958	Paul Foytack	1.196
1959	Don Mossi	1.136
1960	Jim Bunning	1.115

Jerry Don Gleaton

Year	Pitcher	WHIP
1961	Jim Bunning	1.131
1962	Hank Aguirre	1.051
1963	Phil Regan	1.259
1964	Mickey Lolich	1.121
1965	Denny McLain	1.071
1966	**Earl Wilson**	**1.004**
1967	Mickey Lolich	1.083
1968	**Denny McLain**	**0.905**
1969	Denny McLain	1.092
1970	Joe Niekro	1.376
1971	Mickey Lolich	1.138
1972	Mickey Lolich	1.088
1973	John Hiller	1.021
1974	John Hiller, M. Lolich	1.260
1975	Mickey Lolich	1.346
1976	Mark Fidrych	1.079
1977	Dave Rozema	1.173
1978	Dave Rozema	1.175
1979	Aurelio Lopez	1.150
1980	Dan Schatzeder	1.225
1981	Kevin Saucier	0.959
1982	Jerry Ujdur	1.230
1983	Jack Morris	1.158
1984	Willie Hernandez	0.941
1985	**Willie Hernandez**	**0.900**
1986	Jack Morris	1.165
1987	Mike Henneman	1.200
1988	Mike Henneman	1.051
1989	Frank Tanana	1.346
1990	Jerry Don Gleaton	1.052
1991	Bill Gullickson	1.325
1992	Mike Henneman	1.228
1993	David Wells	1.203
1994	Mark Gardiner	1.295
1995	Felipe Lira	1.415
1996	Felipe Lira	1.387
1997	Justin Thompson	1.137
1998	Doug Brocail	1.037
1999	Doug Brocail	1.037
2000	Jeff Weaver	1.285
2001	Danny Patterson	1.175
2002	Jamie Walker	0.939
2003	Jamie Walker	1.200
2004	Jamie Walker	1.253
2005	Craig Spurling	1.132
2006	Jamie Walker	1.146
2007	Bobby Seay	1.144
2008	Armando Galarraga	1.192
2009	Brandon Lyon	1.106
2010	Jose Valverde	1.159
2011	Justin Verlander	0.920
2012	Justin Verlander	1.057
2013	Max Scherzer	0.970
2014	Al Alburquerque	1.169
2015	Alex Wilson	1.029
2016	Justin Verlander	1.001
2017	Justin Wilson	0.942
2018	Alex Wilson	1.054
2019	Matt Boyd	1.230
2020	Jose Cisnero	1.112
2021	Casey Mize	1.137

Year	Pitcher	WAR
1901	**Roscoe Miller**	**6.9**
1902	Win Mercer	6.1
1903	**Bill Donovan**	**7.0**
1904	Ed Killian	4.8
1905	**Ed Killian**	**7.2**
1906	George Mullin	4.7
1907	Ed Killian	6.5
1908	Bill Donovan	4.4
1909	George Mullin	4.6
1910	Bill Donovan	3.6
1911	George Mullin	5.5
1912	Jean Dubuc	4.4
1913	Hooks Dauss	3.4
1914	Harry Coveleski	5.4
1915	Hooks Dauss	5.5
1916	Harry Coveleski	6.9
1917	Bill James	2.9
1918	Bernie Boland	4.2
1919	Bernie Boland	4.9
1920	Howard Ehmke	4.2
1921	Dutch Leonard	4.2
1922	Herman Pillette	5.8
1923	Hooks Dauss	4.7
1924	Rip Collins	3.5
1925	Hooks Dauss	4.0
1926	Sam Gibson	3.4
1927	Earl Whitehill	4.9
1928	Ownie Carroll	5.1
1929	George Uhle	3.5
1930	George Uhle	6.2
1931	George Uhle	5.6
1932	Tommy Bridges	4.5
1933	Firpo Marberry	5.3
1934	Schoolboy Rowe	5.8
1935	Schoolboy Rowe	3.7
1936	Tommy Bridges	6.4
1937	Elden Auker	4.3
1938	George Gill	3.7
1939	**Bobo Newsom**	**7.2**
1940	**Bobo Newsom**	**7.4**
1941	Al Benton	5.5
1942	Al Benton	5.6
1943	Dizzy Trout	5.0
1944	**Dizzy Trout**	**9.3**
1945	**Hal Newhouser**	**11.3**
1946	Hal Newhouser	9.6
1947	Hal Newhouser	5.8
1948	Hal Newhouser	6.5
1949	Virgil Trucks	6.9
1950	Art Houtteman	6.0
1951	Fred Hutchinson	3.2
1952	Virgil Trucks	1.9
1953	Ned Garver	2.3
1954	Steve Gromek	5.6
1955	Billy Hoeft	5.0
1956	Frank Lary	6.3
1957	Jim Bunning	6.3
1958	Frank Lary	6.7
1959	Don Mossi	4.1
1960	Jim Bunning	6.6

Mike Fiers

Year	Pitcher	WAR
1961	Frank Lary	4.3
1962	Hank Aguirre	7.4
1963	Hank Aguirre	2.9
1964	Mickey Lolich	3.6
1965	Denny McLain	4.6
1966	Earl Wilson	4.5
1967	Mickey Lolich	2.7
1968	Denny McLain	7.4
1969	Denny McLain	8.1
1970	Mickey Lolich	4.5
1971	Mickey Lolich	8.5
1972	Mickey Lolich	7.4
1973	John Hiller	7.9
1974	John Hiller	4.1
1975	Mickey Lolich	4.0
1976	Mark Fidrych	9.6
1977	Dave Rozema	5.6
1978	Dave Rozema	4.0
1979	Jack Morris	5.8
1980	Dan Schatzeder	3.5
1981	Jack Morris	3.4
1982	Dan Petry	4.2
1983	Jack Morris	4.0
1984	Willie Hernandez	4.8
1985	Jack Morris	4.9
1986	Jack Morris	5.1
1987	Jack Morris	5.1
1988	Jeff Robinson	3.7
1989	Frank Tanana	3.1
1990	P. Gibson, Edwin Nunez	2.2
1991	Frank Tanana	2.7
1992	Bill Gullickson	1.6
1993	David Wells	2.9
1994	David Wells	2.7
1995	David Wells	4.6
1996	Omar Olivares	3.6
1997	Justin Thompson	7.7
1998	Brian Moehler	4.2
1999	Doug Brocail	3.1
2000	Jeff Weaver	3.2
2001	Steve Sparks	4.5
2002	M. Redman, Jeff Weaver	2.7
2003	Nate Cornejo	1.5
2004	Mike Maroth	3.3
2005	Jeremy Bonderman	1.4
2006	Justin Verlander	4.0
2007	Justin Verlander	4.2
2008	Armando Galarraga	4.0
2009	Justin Verlander	5.5
2010	Justin Verlander	4.4
2011	Justin Verlander	8.6
2012	Justin Verlander	8.1
2013	Max Scherzer	6.4
2014	Max Scherzer	5.7
2015	David Price	3.6
2016	Justin Verlander	7.2
2017	Justin Verlander	4.5
2018	Mike Fiers	2.8
2019	Matt Boyd	3.5
2020	Spencer Turnbull	1.0
2021	Casey Mize	3.2

1901	**Roscoe Miller**	**9.2**
1902	**Ed Siever**	**7.9**
1903	**Bill Donovan**	**7.2**
1904	Bill Donovan	7.7
1905	B. Donovan, Ed Killian	7.6
1906	George Mullin	8.6
1907	Bill Donovan	7.4
1908	Bill Donovan	7.8
1909	Ed Willett	7.3
1910	**Ed Willett**	**7.0**
1911	Bill Donovan	8.6
1912	Jean Dubuc	7.8
1913	Hooks Dauss	7.5
1914	Harry Coveleski	7.4
1915	Bernie Boland	7.4
1916	Jean Dubuc	7.1
1917	Bernie Boland	7.3
1918	Bernie Boland	7.8
1919	Bernie Boland	8.2
1920	Howard Ehmke	8.4
1921	Dutch Leonard	10.0
1922	Herman Pillette	8.8
1923	Syl Johnson	9.2
1924	Rip Collins	8.3
1925	Hooks Dauss	9.4
1926	Sam Gibson	9.1
1927	Earl Whitehill	9.1
1928	Ownie Carroll	8.5
1929	Earl Whitehill	9.8
1930	George Uhle	9.0
1931	George Uhle	8.9
1932	Tommy Bridges	7.8
1933	Tommy Bridges	7.4
1934	Tommy Bridges	8.1
1935	Schoolboy Rowe	8.9
1936	Tommy Bridges	8.8
1937	Jake Wade	8.7
1938	Vern Kennedy	10.2
1939	Bobo Newsom	8.1
1940	Tommy Bridges	7.8
1941	Al Benton	7.4
1942	**Hal Newhouser**	**6.7**
1943	Dizzy Trout	7.4
1944	Hal Newhouser	7.6
1945	Hal Newhouser	6.9
1946	**Hal Newhouser**	**6.6**
1947	Hal Newhouser	8.5
1948	Virgil Trucks	8.1
1949	Virgil Trucks	6.8
1950	Art Houtteman	8.4
1951	Dizzy Trout	8.1
1952	Ted Gray	8.5
1953	Ted Gray	8.5
1954	Ned Garver	7.9
1955	Billy Hoeft	7.7
1956	Paul Foytack	7.4
1957	Jim Bunning	7.2
1958	J. Bunning, Paul Foytack	7.7
1959	Jim Bunning	7.9
1960	Jim Bunning	7.8

Kevin Saucier

1961	Jim Bunning	7.8
1962	Hank Aguirre	6.8
1963	Phil Regan	8.5
1964	Hank Aguirre	7.5
1965	Denny McLain	7.1
1966	Earl Wilson	6.9
1967	Mickey Lolich	7.3
1968	**Denny McLain**	**6.5**
1969	Mickey Lolich	6.9
1970	Les Cain	8.3
1971	Fred Scherman	7.2
1972	Joe Coleman	6.9
1973	**John Hiller**	**6.4**
1974	John Hiller	7.6
1975	Vern Ruhle	9.4
1976	John Hiller	6.9
1977	Dave Rozema	9.2
1978	Milt Wilcox	8.7
1979	Aurelio Lopez	6.7
1980	Dan Schatzeder	8.3
1981	**Kevin Saucier**	**4.8**
1982	Jerry Udjur	7.6
1983	Aurelio Lopez	6.8
1984	Willie Hernandez	6.2
1985	Willie Hernandez	6.9
1986	Jack Morris	7.7
1987	Jack Morris	7.7
1988	Jeff Robinson	6.3
1989	Mike Henneman	8.4
1990	Jerry Don Gleaton	6.8
1991	Mike Henneman	8.6
1992	Mike Munoz	8.3
1993	Mike Henneman	8.7
1994	Mark Gardiner	8.1
1995	Felipe Lira	9.3
1996	Richie Lewis	7.8
1997	Justin Thompson	7.6
1998	Doug Brocail	6.8
1999	Doug Brocail	6.6
2000	Matt Anderson	7.4
2001	Danny Patterson	8.9
2002	Jamie Walker	6.6
2003	Jamie Walker	8.4
2004	Ugueth Urbina	6.3
2005	Chris Spurling	7.4
2006	Joel Zumaya	6.0
2007	Bobby Seay	7.4
2008	Armando Galarraga	7.7
2009	Brandon Lyon	6.4
2010	Jose Valverde	5.9
2011	Justin Verlander	6.2
2012	Justin Verlander	7.3
2013	Joaquin Benoit	6.3
2014	Al Alburquerque	7.2
2015	Alex Wilson	7.8
2016	Justin Verlander	6.8
2017	Justin Wilson	4.9
2018	D. Verhagen, A. Wilson	7.3
2019	Buck Farmer	8.2
2020	Gregory Soto	6.3
2021	Gregory Soto	6.5

Year	Pitcher	HR/9
1901	**Roscoe Miller**	**0.0**
1902	**Ed Siever**	**0.0**
1903	Bill Donovan, G. Mullin	0.1
1904	**Ed Killian, George Mullin**	**0.0**
1905	**Ed Killian**	**0.0**
1906	**Red Donahue**	**0.0**
1907	**George Mullin, Ed Siever**	**0.0**
1908	**George Mullin**	**0.0**
1909	**George Mullin**	**0.0**
1910	Ed Willett	0.1
1911	Ed LaFitte, Jack Lively	0.1
1912	Four Pitchers	0.1
1913	**Jean Dubuc, Ed Willett**	**0.0**
1914	Three Pitchers	0.1
1915	**Hooks Dauss**	**0.0**
1916	**Hooks Dauss, Jean Dubuc**	**0.0**
1917	**Bernie Boland**	**0.0**
1918	**Bernie Boland,**	**0.0**
	G. Cunningham, R. Kallio	**0.0**
1919	Howard Ehmke	0.2
1920	Red Oldham	0.2
1921	Hooks Dauss, R. Oldham	0.4
1922	Herman Pillette	0.2
1923	Three Pitchers	0.3
1924	Three Pitchers	0.3
1925	Hooks Dauss	0.4
1926	Earl Whitehill	0.2
1927	Earl Whitehill	0.2
1928	O. Carroll, E. VanGilder	0.2
1929	George Uhle	0.3
1930	Earl Whitehill	0.3
1931	Vic Sorrell	0.3
1932	Vic Sorrell, C. Hogsett	0.4
1933	Carl Fischer	0.2
1934	Elden Auker, S. Rowe	0.4
1935	Schoolboy Rowe	0.4
1936	Elden Auker	0.5
1937	Elden Auker	0.5
1938	Vern Kennedy	0.6
1939	Dizzy Trout	0.3
1940	Tommy Bridges	0.5
1941	Hal Newhouser	0.3
1942	Three Pitchers	0.2
1943	Hal Newhouser	0.1
1944	Stubby Overmire	0.1
1945	Hal Newhouser	0.1
1946	Hal Newhouser	0.3
1947	H. Newhouser, D. Trout	0.3
1948	H. Newhouser, D. Trout	0.3
1949	Ted Gray, Virgil Trucks	0.5
1950	Dizzy Trout	0.6
1951	F. Hutchinson, D. Trout	0.6
1952	Virgil Trucks	0.5
1953	Ned Garver	0.7
1954	Ned Garver	0.7
1955	Frank Lary	0.4
1956	Frank Lary	0.6
1957	Billy Hoeft	0.7
1958	Frank Lary	0.7
1959	Don Mossi	0.8

Rudy Kallio

Year	Pitcher	HR/9
1960	Jim Bunning	0.7
1961	Jim Bunning, Frank Lary	0.8
1962	Hank Aguirre	0.6
1963	Hank Aguirre	1.0
1964	Hank Aguirre	0.8
1965	Dave Wickersham	0.6
1966	Larry Sherry, Earl Wilson	0.9
1967	Mickey Lolich	0.6
1968	Joe Sparma	0.7
1969	M. Lolich, Denny McLain	0.7
1970	Tom Timmermann	0.3
1971	Joe Coleman	0.5
1972	F. Scherman, C. Seelbach	0.5
1973	John Hiller	0.5
1974	John Hiller	0.6
1975	Mickey Lolich	0.7
1976	Mark Fidrych	0.4
1977	F. Arroyo, Dave Rozema	1.0
1978	J. Billingham, D. Rozema	0.7
1979	Milt Wilcox	0.8
1980	Dan Petry	0.5
1981	Kevin Saucier	0.2
1982	Dan Petry	0.5
1983	Three Pitchers	0.9
1984	Willie Hernandez	0.4
1985	Walt Terrell	0.4
1986	Frank Tanana	1.1
1987	Mike Henneman	0.7
1988	Mike Henneman	0.7
1989	Mike Henneman	0.4
1990	Mike Henneman	0.4
1991	Mike Henneman	0.2
1992	Mike Munoz	0.6
1993	Mike Henneman	0.5
1994	Buddy Groom	1.1
1995	John Doherty	0.8
1996	Mike Myers	0.8
1997	Todd Jones	0.4
1998	Doug Brocail	0.3
1999	Doug Brocail	0.8
2000	Danny Patterson	0.6
2001	Matt Anderson	0.3
2002	Juan Acevedo	0.5
2003	Nate Cornejo	0.8
2004	Esteban Yan	0.8
2005	Jamie Walker	0.9
2006	Todd Jones, Joel Zumaya	0.6
2007	Bobby Seay	0.2
2008	Bobby Seay	0.6
2009	Bobby Seay	0.6
2010	Phil Coke	0.3
2011	Jose Valverde	0.6
2012	Jose Valverde	0.4
2013	Anibal Sanchez	0.4
2014	Joba Chamberlain	0.4
2015	Blaine Hardy	0.3
2016	Kyle Ryan	0.3
2017	Shane Greene	0.8
2018	Joe Jimenez	0.7
2019	Spencer Turnbull	0.8
2020	**Bryan Garcia**	**0.0**
2021	Kyle Funkhouser	0.8

YEARLY TIGER PITCHING LEADERS – WALKS PER NINE INNINGS

1901	**Jack Cronin**	**1.7**
1902	**Ed Siever**	**1.5**
1903	**Frank Kitson**	**1.3**
1904	Frank Kitson	1.7
1905	Frank Kitson	2.3
1906	Ed Siever	1.8
1907	Ed Siever	1.7
1908	Ed Summers	1.6
1909	Ed Summers	1.7
1910	Ed Summers	2.5
1911	George Mullin	2.3
1912	Joe Lake	2.2
1913	Hooks Dauss, Ed Willett	3.3
1914	Hooks Dauss	2.6
1915	Harry Coveleski	2.5
1916	Harry Coveleski	1.7
1917	Willie Mitchell	2.2
1918	Hooks Dauss	2.1
1919	Hooks Dauss	2.2
1920	Doc Ayers	2.7
1921	Dutch Leonard	2.3
1922	Hooks Dauss	2.4
1923	Hooks Dauss	2.2
1924	Rip Collins	2.6
1925	Earl Whitehill	3.3
1926	Earl Whitehill	2.8
1927	Ken Holloway	3.0
1928	Ownie Carroll	3.4
1929	George Uhle	2.1
1930	George Uhle	2.8
1931	George Uhle	2.3
1932	Vic Sorrell	3.0
1933	Firpo Marberry	2.3
1934	Elden Auker	2.5
1935	Schoolboy Rowe	2.2
1936	Schoolboy Rowe	2.3
1937	Tommy Bridges	3.3
1938	George Gill	2.7
1939	Tommy Bridges	2.8
1940	Schoolboy Rowe	2.3
1941	Johnny Gorsica	2.9
1942	Tommy Bridges	3.2
1943	Virgil Trucks	2.3
1944	J. Gorsica, S. Overmire	1.8
1945	Stubby Overmire	2.3
1946	F. Hutchinson, V. Trucks	2.9
1947	Fred Hutchinson	2.5
1948	Fred Hutchinson	2.0
1949	Fred Hutchinson	2.5
1950	Fred Hutchinson	1.9
1951	**Fred Hutchinson**	**1.3**
1952	Art Houtteman	2.6
1953	Billy Hoeft	2.6
1954	Steve Gromek	2.0
1955	Steve Gromek	1.8
1956	Frank Lary	3.6
1957	Jim Bunning	2.4
1958	Frank Lary	2.4
1959	Frank Lary, Don Mossi	1.9
1960	Don Mossi	1.8

Joe Niekro

1961	Don Mossi	1.8
1962	Don Mossi	1.8
1963	Jim Bunning	2.5
1964	Mickey Lolich	2.5
1965	Denny McLain	2.5
1966	Earl Wilson	2.1
1967	Mickey Lolich	2.5
1968	Denny McLain	1.7
1969	Denny McLain	1.9
1970	Joe Niekro	3.0
1971	Mickey Lolich	2.2
1972	Mickey Lolich	2.0
1973	Mickey Lolich	2.3
1974	Mickey Lolich	2.3
1975	Mickey Lolich	2.4
1976	Mark Fidrych	1.9
1977	Dave Rozema	1.4
1978	Dave Rozema	1.8
1979	Jack Morris	2.7
1980	Dan Schatzeder	2.7
1981	Milt Wilcox	2.8
1982	Jack Morris	3.2
1983	Jack Morris	2.5
1984	Willie Hernandez	2.3
1985	**Willie Hernandez**	**1.2**
1986	Willie Hernandez	2.1
1987	Frank Tanana	2.3
1988	Doyle Alexander	1.8
1989	Frank Tanana	3.0
1990	Jerry Don Gleaton	2.7
1991	Bill Gullickson	1.7
1992	Bill Gullickson	2.0
1993	David Wells	2.0
1994	Mark Gardiner	3.5
1995	John Doherty	2.9
1996	Felipe Lira	3.1
1997	Willie Blair	2.4
1998	Brian Moehler	2.3
1999	Doug Brocail, B. Moehler	2.7
2000	Brian Moehler	2.0
2001	Danny Patterson	1.7
2002	Jamie Walker	1.9
2003	Mike Maroth	2.3
2004	Jamie Walker	1.7
2005	Jason Johnson	2.1
2006	T. Jones, Jamie Walker	1.5
2007	Jeremy Bonderman	2.5
2008	Armando Galarraga	3.1
2009	Justin Verlander	2.4
2010	Rick Porcello	2.1
2011	Justin Verlander	2.0
2012	Octavio Dotel	1.9
2013	Doug Fister	1.9
2014	Rick Porcello	1.8
2015	Alex Wilson	1.4
2016	Justin Verlander	2.3
2017	Michael Fulmer	2.2
2018	Jordan Zimmermann	1.8
2019	Jordan Zimmermann	2.0
2020	Buck Farmer	2.1
2021	Tyler Alexander	2.4

1901 Ed Siever 2.7
1902 George Mullin 2.7
1903 Bill Donovan 5.5
1904 Bill Donovan 4.2
1905 Bill Donovan, G. Mullin 4.3
1906 Bill Donovan 3.6
1907 Bill Donovan 4.1
1908 Bill Donovan 5.2
1909 George Mullin 3.7
1910 Bill Donovan 4.7
1911 Bill Donovan 4.3
1912 Joe Lake 4.8
1913 Hooks Dauss 4.3
1914 Hooks Dauss 4.5
1915 Harry Coveleski 4.3
1916 Hooks Dauss 3.6
1917 H. Ehmke, Willie Mitchell 3.9
1918 Rudy Kallio 3.5
1919 Dutch Leonard 4.2
1920 Doc Ayers 4.4
1921 Dutch Leonard 4.4
1922 Howard Ehmke 3.5
1923 Hooks Dauss 3.0
1924 Rip Collins 3.1
1925 Earl Whitehill 3.1
1926 Earl Whitehill 3.9
1927 Sam Gibson 3.7
1928 Earl Whitehill 4.3
1929 Earl Whitehill 3.8
1930 G. Uhle, Earl Whitehill 4.4
1931 Tommy Bridges 5.5
1932 Tommy Bridges 4.8
1933 T. Bridges, Carl Fischer 4.6
1934 Schoolboy Rowe 5.0
1935 Tommy Bridges 5.3
1936 Tommy Bridges 5.3
1937 Tommy Bridges 5.1
1938 Elden Auker 2.6
1939 Bobo Newsom 6.0
1940 Tommy Bridges 6.1
1941 Bobo Newsom 6.3
1942 T. Bridges, B. Newsom 5.0
1943 Hal Newhouser 6.6
1944 Hal Newhouser 5.4
1945 Hal Newhouser 6.1
1946 Hal Newhouser 8.5
1947 Hal Newhouser 5.6
1948 Virgil Trucks 5.2
1949 Virgil Trucks 5.0
1950 Dizzy Trout 4.3
1951 Ted Gray 6.0
1952 Virgil Trucks 5.9
1953 Ted Gray 5.9
1954 Billy Hoeft 5.9
1955 Billy Hoeft 5.4
1956 Paul Foytack 6.5
1957 Jim Bunning 6.1
1958 Jim Bunning 7.3
1959 Jim Bunning 7.2
1960 Jim Bunning 7.2

Carl Fischer

1961 Jim Bunning 6.5
1962 Hank Aguirre 6.5
1963 Jim Bunning 7.1
1964 Mickey Lolich 7.4
1965 Mickey Lolich 8.3
1966 Mickey Lolich 7.6
1967 Mickey Lolich 7.7
1968 Mickey Lolich 8.1
1969 Mickey Lolich 8.7
1970 Les Cain 7.8
1971 J. Coleman, M. Lolich 7.4
1972 Joe Coleman 7.1
1973 John Hiller 8.9
1974 John Hiller 8.0
1975 Joe Coleman 5.6
1976 John Hiller 8.7
1977 Dave Rozema 3.8
1978 Milt Wilcox 5.5
1979 Aurelio Lopez 7.5
1980 Aurelio Lopez 7.0
1981 Dan Petry 5.0
1982 Milt Wilcox 5.2
1983 Jack Morris 7.1
1984 Willie Hernandez 7.2
1985 Jack Morris 6.7
1986 Willie Hernandez 7.8
1987 M. Henneman, J. Morris 7.0
1988 Willie Hernandez 7.8
1989 Mike Henneman 6.9
1990 Jerry Don Gleaton 6.1
1991 Mike Henneman 6.5
1992 Mike Henneman 6.8
1993 Mike Henneman 7.3
1994 Buddy Groom 7.6
1995 Joe Boever 6.5
1996 Mike Myers 9.6
1997 Todd Jones 9.0
1998 Todd Jones 8.1
1999 Todd Jones 8.7
2000 Todd Jones 9.4
2001 Matt Anderson 8.4
2002 Jamie Walker 8.2
2003 Jamie Walker 6.2
2004 Ugueth Urbina 9.3
2005 Jeremy Bonderman 6.9
2006 Joel Zumaya 10.5
2007 Justin Verlander 8.2
2008 Bobby Seay 9.3
2009 Justin Verlander 10.1
2010 Jose Valverde 9.0
2011 Joaquin Benoit 9.3
2012 Max Scherzer 11.1
2013 Max Scherzer 10.1
2014 Max Scherzer 10.3
2015 Al Alburquerque 8.4
2016 J. Verlander, J. Wilson 10.0
2017 Justin Wilson 12.3
2018 Joe Jimenez 11.2
2019 Joe Jimenez 12.4
2020 Gregory Soto 11.3
2021 Joe Jimenez 11.3

Year	Pitcher	SO/BB
1901	**Jack Cronin**	**1.48**
1902	Ed Siever	1.13
1903	**Frank Kitson**	**2.68**
1904	Frank Kitson	1.82
1905	Frank Kitson	1.37
1906	Ed Siever	1.58
1907	Ed Siever	1.69
1908	Bill Donovan	2.66
1909	Ed Summers	2.06
1910	Bill Donovan	1.75
1911	George Mullin	1.43
1912	Joe Lake	2.21
1913	Hooks Dauss	1.30
1914	Hooks Dauss	1.72
1915	Harry Coveleski	1.72
1916	Harry Coveleski	1.71
1917	Willie Mitchell	1.74
1918	Hooks Dauss	1.26
1919	Dutch Leonard	1.57
1920	Doc Ayers	1.66
1921	Dutch Leonard	1.90
1922	Hooks Dauss	1.32
1923	Syl Johnson	1.98
1924	Rip Collins	1.19
1925	Earl Whitehill	0.94
1926	Earl Whitehill	1.38
1927	Earl Whitehill	0.90
1928	Earl Whitehill	1.19
1929	George Uhle	1.72
1930	George Uhle	1.56
1931	George Uhle	1.29
1932	Vic Sorrell	1.09
1933	Firpo Marberry	1.38
1934	Schoolboy Rowe	1.84
1935	Schoolboy Rowe	2.06
1936	Schoolboy Rowe	1.80
1937	Tommy Bridges	1.52
1938	Elden Auker	0.82
1939	Tommy Bridges	2.11
1940	Bobo Newsom	1.64
1941	Bobo Newsom	1.48
1942	Tommy Bridges	1.59
1943	Virgil Trucks	2.27
1944	Hal Newhouser	1.83
1945	Hal Newhouser	1.93
1946	**Hal Newhouser**	**2.81**
1947	Fred Hutchinson	1.85
1948	Fred Hutchinson	1.92
1949	Art Houtteman	1.44
1950	Fred Hutchinson	1.48
1951	Fred Hutchinson	1.96
1952	Art Houtteman	1.68
1953	Billy Hoeft	1.55
1954	Billy Hoeft	1.93
1955	Steve Gromek	1.97
1956	Billy Hoeft	1.65
1957	Jim Bunning	2.53
1958	Jim Bunning	2.24
1959	**Frank Lary**	**2.98**
1960	**Jim Bunning**	**3.14**

Jordan Zimmermann

Year	Pitcher	SO/BB
1961	Don Mossi	2.91
1962	**Don Mossi**	**3.36**
1963	Jim Bunning	2.84
1964	Mickey Lolich	3.00
1965	Mickey Lolich	3.14
1966	**Earl Wilson**	**3.50**
1967	Mickey Lolich	3.11
1968	**Denny McLain**	**4.44**
1969	Denny McLain	2.70
1970	Mickey Lolich	2.11
1971	Mickey Lolich	3.35
1972	Mickey Lolich	3.38
1973	John Hiller	3.18
1974	Mickey Lolich	2.59
1975	Mickey Lolich	2.17
1976	Mark Fidrych	1.83
1977	Dave Rozema	2.71
1978	Milt Wilcox	1.94
1979	Aurelio Lopez	2.08
1980	Aurelio Lopez	2.16
1981	Milt Wilcox	1.52
1982	Jack Morris	1.41
1983	Jack Morris	2.80
1984	Willie Hernandez	3.11
1985	**Willie Hernandez**	**5.43**
1986	Willie Hernandez	3.67
1987	Frank Tanana	2.61
1988	Doyle Alexander	2.74
1989	Frank Tanana	1.99
1990	Jerry Don Gleaton	2.24
1991	Bill Gullickson	2.07
1992	Mike Henneman	2.90
1993	David Wells	3.31
1994	Bill Gullickson	2.60
1995	Joe Boever	1.61
1996	Mike Myers	2.03
1997	Justin Thompson	2.29
1998	Doug Brocail	3.06
1999	Doug Brocail	3.12
2000	Todd Jones	2.68
2001	Matt Anderson	2.89
2002	Jamie Walker	4.44
2003	Jamie Walker	2.65
2004	Jamie Walker	4.42
2005	Jeremy Bonderman	2.54
2006	Jamie Walker	4.63
2007	Jeremy Bonderman	3.02
2008	Bobby Seay	2.32
2009	Justin Verlander	4.27
2010	Justin Verlander	3.08
2011	Justin Verlander	4.39
2012	Octavio Dotel	5.17
2013	Drew Smyly	4.76
2014	Max Scherzer	4.00
2015	Alex Wilson	3.45
2016	Justin Verlander	4.46
2017	Justin Wilson	3.44
2018	Jordan Zimmermann	4.27
2019	Matt Boyd	4.76
2020	Joe Jimenez	3.67
2021	Michael Fulmer	3.65

Year	Pitcher	Runs/9
1901	**Roscoe Miller**	**4.6**
1902	**Ed Siever**	**3.5**
1903	**Bill Donovan**	**3.0**
1904	Ed Killian	3.2
1905	Ed Killian	3.1
1906	Red Donahue	3.6
1907	**Ed Siever**	**2.9**
1908	**Bill Donovan**	**2.9**
1909	**Ed Killian**	**2.3**
1910	Bill Donovan	3.2
1911	George Mullin	3.8
1912	Jean Dubuc	3.8
1913	Hooks Dauss	4.0
1914	Harry Coveleski	3.2
1915	Hooks Dauss	3.3
1916	Harry Coveleski	2.9
1917	B. James, Willie Mitchell	3.2
1918	Bernie Boland	3.0
1919	Bernie Boland	3.4
1920	Howard Ehmke	4.5
1921	Dutch Leonard	4.6
1922	Herman Pillette	3.6
1923	Hooks Dauss	4.0
1924	Rip Collins	4.1
1925	Hooks Dauss	4.3
1926	Rip Collins	3.9
1927	Earl Whitehill	4.2
1928	Ownie Carroll	3.9
1929	George Uhle	5.1
1930	George Uhle	4.1
1931	George Uhle	4.1
1932	Tommy Bridges	4.3
1933	Firpo Marberry	3.7
1934	Schoolboy Rowe	3.7
1935	Elden Auker, S. Rowe	4.0
1936	Tommy Bridges	4.3
1937	Elden Auker	4.5
1938	George Gill	4.5
1939	Bobo Newsom	3.7
1940	Schoolboy Rowe	3.6
1941	Al Benton	3.6
1942	Hal White	3.3
1943	Tommy Bridges	2.7
1944	Hal Newhouser	2.7
	Dizzy Trout	2.7
1945	**Hal Newhouser**	**2.1**
1946	Hal Newhouser	2.4
1947	Hal Newhouser	3.3
1948	Hal Newhouser	3.6
1949	Virgil Trucks	3.1
1950	Art Houtteman	3.7
1951	Fred Hutchinson	4.0
1952	Hal Newhouser	4.2
1953	Ned Garver	4.9
1954	Steve Gromek	3.0
1955	Billy Hoeft	3.1
1956	Frank Lary	3.6
1957	Jim Bunning	3.1
1958	Frank Lary	3.1
1959	Don Mossi	3.6
1960	Jim Bunning	3.3

Jean Dubuc

Year	Pitcher	Runs/9
1961	Don Mossi	3.6
1962	Hank Aguirre	2.8
1963	Hank Aguirre	3.8
1964	Mickey Lolich	3.4
1965	Denny McLain	3.0
1966	Earl Wilson	2.7
1967	Mickey Lolich	3.1
1968	Denny McLain	2.3
1969	Denny McLain	2.9
1970	Mickey Lolich	4.1
1971	Mickey Lolich	3.2
1972	Mickey Lolich	2.7
1973	Joe Coleman	3.9
1974	Mickey Lolich	4.5
1975	Mickey Lolich	4.5
1976	Mark Fidrych	2.7
1977	Dave Rozema	3.6
1978	Dave Rozema	3.6
1979	Jack Morris	3.5
1980	Dan Schatzeder	4.1
1981	Jack Morris	3.1
1982	Dan Petry	3.6
1983	Juan Berenguer	3.3
1984	Dan Petry	3.6
1985	Jack Morris	3.6
1986	Jack Morris	3.5
1987	Jack Morris	3.8
1988	Jeff Robinson	3.2
1989	Frank Tanana	4.2
1990	Dan Petry	4.7
1991	Frank Tanana	4.1
1992	Bill Gullickson	4.4
1993	David Wells	4.5
1994	David Wells	4.4
1995	David Wells	3.7
1996	Omar Olivares	5.1
1997	Justin Thompson	3.3
1998	Brian Moehler	4.2
1999	Dave Mlicki	5.1
2000	Jeff Weaver	4.6
2001	Steve Sparks	4.3
2002	Jeff Weaver	3.7
2003	Nate Cornejo	5.1
2004	Mike Maroth	4.6
2005	Jeremy Bonderman	4.8
2006	Justin Verlander	3.8
2007	Justin Verlander	3.9
2008	Armando Galarraga	4.2
2009	Justin Verlander	3.7
2010	Justin Verlander	3.6
2011	Justin Verlander	2.6
2012	Justin Verlander	3.1
2013	Anibal Sanchez	2.8
2014	Max Scherzer	3.3
2015	David Price	3.1
2016	Michael Fulmer	3.2
	Justin Verlander	3.2
2017	Michael Fulmer	4.0
2018	Alex Wilson	3.5
2019	Buck Farmer	4.3
2020	Bryan Garcia	2.5
2021	Michael Fulmer	3.5

Year	Pitcher	GS
1901	**Roscoe Miller**	**36**
1902	Win Mercer	33
1903	**George Mullin**	**36**
1904	**George Mullin**	**44**
1905	George Mullin	41
1906	George Mullin	40
1907	George Mullin	42
1908	Ed Summers	32
1909	George Mullin	35
1910	George Mullin	32
1911	George Mullin	29
1912	Ed Willett	31
1913	Ed Willett	30
1914	Harry Coveleski	36
1915	Harry Coveleski	38
1916	Harry Coveleski	39
1917	Hooks Dauss	31
1918	Hooks Dauss	26
1919	Hooks Dauss	32
1920	Howard Ehmke	33
1921	Dutch Leonard	32
1922	Herman Pillette	37
1923	Hooks Dauss	39
1924	Earl Whitehill	32
1925	Earl Whitehill	33
1926	Earl Whitehill	34
1927	Earl Whitehill	31
1928	Earl Whitehill	30
1929	Vic Sorrell	31
1930	Earl Whitehill	31
1931	Earl Whitehill	34
1932	Vic Sorrell, Earl Whitehill	31
1933	Firpo Marberry	32
1934	Tommy Bridges	35
1935	Tommy Bridges, S. Rowe	34
1936	Tommy Bridges	38
1937	Elden Auker	32
1938	Vern Kennedy	26
1939	Bobo Newsom	31
1940	Bobo Newsom	34
1941	Bobo Newsom	36
1942	Al Benton	30
1943	Dizzy Trout	30
1944	Dizzy Trout	40

Year	Pitcher	GS
1945	Hal Newhouser	36
1946	Hal Newhouser	34
1947	Hal Newhouser	36
1948	Hal Newhouser	35
1949	Hal Newhouser	35
1950	Art Houtteman	34
1951	Ted Gray	28
1952	Ted Gray	32
1953	Ted Gray	28
1954	Ned Garver, S. Gromek	32
1955	Ned Garver	32
1956	Frank Lary	38
1957	Frank Lary	35
1958	Jim Bunning, Frank Lary	34
1959	Paul Foytack	37
1960	Frank Lary	36

Fernando Arroyo

Year	Pitcher	GS
1961	Jim Bunning	37
1962	Jim Bunning	35
1963	Jim Bunning	35
1964	Dave Wickersham	36
1965	Mickey Lolich	37
1966	Denny McLain	38
1967	Earl Wilson	38
1968	Denny McLain	41
1969	Denny McLain	41
1970	Mickey Lolich	39
1971	**Mickey Lolich**	**45**
1972	Mickey Lolich	41
1973	Mickey Lolich	42
1974	J. Coleman, Mickey Lolich	41
1975	Mickey Lolich	32
1976	Dave Roberts	36

Year	Pitcher	GS
1977	F. Arroyo, Dave Rozema	28
1978	Jim Slaton	34
1979	Milt Wilcox	29
1980	Jack Morris	36
1981	Jack Morris	25
1982	Jack Morris	37
1983	Dan Petry	38
1984	Jack Morris, Dan Petry	35
1985	Jack Morris	35
1986	Jack Morris	35
1987	Walt Terrell	35
1988	D. Alexander, Jack Morris	34
1989	D. Alexander, F. Tanana	33
1990	Jack Morris	36
1991	Bill Gullickson	35
1992	Bill Gullickson	34
1993	Mike Moore	36
1994	Tim Belcher, Mike Moore	25
1995	Sean Bergman	28
1996	Felipe Lira	32
1997	Justin Thompson	32
1998	Justin Thompson	34
1999	Brian Moehler	32
2000	Hideo Nomo	31
2001	Steve Sparks, Jeff Weaver	33
2002	Steve Sparks	31
2003	Mike Maroth	33
2004	J. Johnson, Mike Maroth	33
2005	Mike Maroth	34
2006	Jeremy Bonderman	34
2007	Justin Verlander	32
2008	Justin Verlander	33
2009	Justin Verlander	35
2010	Justin Verlander	33
2011	Justin Verlander	34
2012	Justin Verlander	33
2013	Justin Verlander	34
2014	Max Scherzer	33
2015	Alfredo Simon	31
2016	Justin Verlander	34
2017	Jordan Zimmermann	29
2018	Matt Boyd	31
2019	Matt Boyd	32
2020	Matt Boyd	12
2021	Casey Mize	30

YEARLY TIGER PITCHING LEADERS – COMPLETE GAMES

Year	Pitcher	CG
1901	**Roscoe Miller**	**35**
1902	Win Mercer	28
1903	Bill Donovan	34
1904	**George Mullin**	**42**
1905	George Mullin	35
1906	George Mullin	35
1907	George Mullin	35
1908	George Mullin	26
1909	George Mullin	29
1910	George Mullin	27
1911	George Mullin	25
1912	Ed Willett	28
1913	Hooks Dauss, Jean Dubuc	22
1914	Harry Coveleski	23
1915	Hooks Dauss	27
1916	Harry Coveleski	22
1917	Hooks Dauss	22
1918	Hooks Dauss	21
1919	Hooks Dauss	22
1920	Howard Ehmke	23
1921	H. Dauss, Dutch Leonard	16
1922	Herman Pillette	18
1923	Hooks Dauss	22
1924	Earl Whitehill	16
1925	Hooks Dauss	16
1926	Sam Gibson	16
1927	Earl Whitehill	17
1928	Ownie Carroll	19
1929	George Uhle	23
1930	George Uhle	18
1931	Earl Whitehill	22
1932	Earl Whitehill	17
1933	Tommy Bridges	17
1934	Tommy Bridges	23
1935	Tommy Bridges	23
1936	Tommy Bridges	26
1937	Elden Auker	19
1938	T. Bridges, George Gill	13
1939	Bobo Newsom	21
1940	Bobo Newsom	20
1941	Bobo Newsom	12
1942	Dizzy Trout	13
1943	Dizzy Trout	18
1944	Dizzy Trout	33
1945	Hal Newhouser	29
1946	Hal Newhouser	29
1947	Hal Newhouser	24
1948	Hal Newhouser	19
1949	Hal Newhouser	22
1950	Art Houtteman	21
1951	T. Gray, Fred Hutchinson	9
1952	Ted Gray	13
1953	Ned Garver	13
1954	Steve Gromek	17
1955	Billy Hoeft	17
1956	Frank Lary	20
1957	Jim Bunning	14
1958	Frank Lary	19
1959	Don Mossi	15
1960	Frank Lary	15
1961	Frank Lary	22
1962	Jim Bunning	12
1963	Hank Aguirre	14
1964	Mickey Lolich	12
1965	Denny McLain	13
1966	Denny McLain	14
1967	Earl Wilson	12
1968	Denny McLain	28
1969	Denny McLain	23
1970	Mickey Lolich	13
1971	Mickey Lolich	29
1972	Mickey Lolich	23
1973	Mickey Lolich	17
1974	Mickey Lolich	27
1975	Mickey Lolich	19
1976	Mark Fidrych	24
1977	Dave Rozema	16
1978	Milt Wilcox	16
1979	Jack Morris	9
1980	Milt Wilcox	13
1981	Jack Morris	15
1982	Jack Morris	17
1983	Jack Morris	20
1984	Jack Morris	9
1985	Jack Morris	13
1986	Jack Morris	15
1987	Jack Morris	13
1988	Walt Terrell	11
1989	Jack Morris	10
1990	Jack Morris	11
1991	Walt Terrell	8
1992	Bill Gullickson	4
1993	Mike Moore	4
1994	David Wells	5
1995	David Wells	3
1996	Omar Olivares	4
1997	Justin Thompson	4
1998	Justin Thompson	5
1999	Dave Mlicki, Brian Moehler	2
2000	B. Moehler, Jeff Weaver	2
2001	Steve Sparks	8
2002	Redman, Sparks, Weaver	3
2003	Nate Cornejo	2
2004	J. Johnson, M. Maroth	2
	Jeremy Bonderman	2
2005	Jeremy Bonderman	4
2006	Z. Miner, N. Robertson,	1
	Justin Verlander	1
2007	Justin Verlander	1
2008	Justin Verlander	1
2009	Justin Verlander	3
2010	Justin Verlander	4
2011	Justin Verlander	4
2012	Justin Verlander	6
2013	Fister, Porcello, Sanchez	1
2014	Rick Porcello	3
2015	David Price	3
2016	Justin Verlander	2
2017	M. Boyd, Michael Fulmer	1
2018	13 Starting Pitchers	0
2019	13 Starting Pitchers	0
2020	Matt Boyd	1
2021	Casey Mize	1

Zach Miner

Year	Pitcher	SHO
1901	**Roscoe Miller**	**3**
1902	**Win Mercer, Ed Siever**	**4**
1903	**George Mullin**	**6**
1904	**George Mullin**	**7**
1905	**Ed Killian**	**8**
1906	Red Donahue	3
1907	George Mullin	5
1908	Bill Donovan	6
1909	Bill Donovan	4
1910	George Mullin	5
1911	Ralph Works	3
1912	J. Dubuc, George Mullin	2
1913	Hooks Dauss	2
1914	Harry Coveleski	5
1915	Jean Dubuc	5
1916	Harry Coveleski	3
1917	Hooks Dauss	6
1918	Bernie Boland	4
1919	Dutch Leonard	4
1920	Doc Ayers, Dutch Leonard	3
1921	Four Pitchers	1
1922	Herman Pillette	4
1923	Hooks Dauss	4
1924	Earl Whitehill	2
1925	Hooks Dauss, E. Whitehill	1
1926	Ed Wells	4
1927	Earl Whitehill	3
1928	Ownie Carroll	2
1929	Five Pitchers	1
1930	Vic Sorrell	2
1931	Tommy Bridges, G. Uhle	2
1932	Tommy Bridges	4
1933	Tommy Bridges	2
1934	Tommy Bridges, S. Rowe	3
1935	Schoolboy Rowe	6
1936	Tommy Bridges	5
1937	Tommy Bridges	3
1938	Three Pitchers	1
1939	Bobo Newsom	3
1940	Bobo Newsom	3
1941	Bobo Newsom	2
1942	Hal White	4
1943	Dizzy Trout	5
1944	Dizzy Trout	7
1945	**Hal Newhouser**	**8**
1946	Hal Newhouser	6
1947	Three Pitchers	3
1948	Hal Newhouser, D. Trout	2
1949	Virgil Trucks	6
1950	Art Houtteman	4
1951	Fred Hutchinson	2
1952	Virgil Trucks, Bill Wight	3
1953	S. Gromek, A. Houtteman	1
1954	Steve Gromek, Billy Hoeft	4
1955	Billy Hoeft	7
1956	Billy Hoeft	4
1957	Frank Lary, Duke Maas	2
1958	Jim Bunning, Frank Lary	3
1959	Frank Lary, Don Mossi	3
1960	Jim Bunning	3
1961	Jim Bunning, Frank Lary	4

Jack Billingham

Year	Pitcher	SHO
1962	Hank Aguirre, Jim Bunning	2
1963	Hank Aguirre	3
1964	Mickey Lolich	6
1965	Denny McLain	4
1966	Denny McLain	4
1967	Mickey Lolich	6
1968	Denny McLain	6
1969	**Denny McLain**	**9**
1970	Mickey Lolich	3
1971	Mickey Lolich	4
1972	Mickey Lolich	4
1973	Mickey Lolich	3
1974	Mickey Lolich	3
1975	Vern Ruhle	3
1976	Mark Fidrych, D. Roberts	4
1977	Three Pitchers	1
1978	Jack Billingham	4
1979	Jack Morris, Dave Rozema	1
1980	Dan Petry	3
1981	Dan Petry, Dave Rozema	2
1982	Jack Morris	3
1983	Dan Petry, Milt Wilcox	2
1984	Dan Petry	2
1985	Jack Morris	4
1986	Jack Morris	6
1987	D. Alexander, F. Tanana	3
1988	Jack Morris, Jeff Robinson	2
1989	Three Players	1
1990	Jack Morris	3
1991	Frank Tanana, Walt Terrell	2
1992	Bill Gullickson, Dave Haas	1
1993	Mike Moore	3
1994	David Wells	1
1995	Sean Bergman	1
1996	Felipe Lira	2
1997	Omar Olivares	2
1998	Brian Moehler	3
1999	Brian Moehler	2
2000	Steve Sparks	1
2001	Steve Sparks	1
2002	Jeff Weaver	3
2003	10 Starting Pitchers	0
2004	Jeremy Bonderman	2
2005	10 Starting Pitchers	0
2006	Justin Verlander	1
2007	Justin Verlander	1
2008	10 Starting Pitchers	0
2009	Justin Verlander	1
2010	Armando Galarraga	1
2011	Justin Verlander	2
2012	Three Starting Pitchers	1
2013	Anibal Sanchez	1
2014	Rick Porcello	3
2015	Four starting Pitchers	1
2016	Michael Fulmer	1
2017	Matt Boyd	1
2018	13 Starting Pitchers	0
2019	13 Starting Pitchers	0
2020	10 Starting Pitchers	0
2021	Spencer Turnbull	1

Year	Pitcher	Wins
1901	**Roscoe Miller**	**22**
1902	Win Mercer	15
1903	George Mullin	18
1904	Bill Donovan, G. Mullin	16
1905	Ed Killian	21
1906	George Mullin	21
1907	**Bill Donavan**	**23**
1908	Ed Summers	19
1909	**George Mullin**	**25**
1910	George Mullin	19
1911	George Mullin	18
1912	Jean Dubuc	16
1913	Jean Dubuc	15
1914	Harry Coveleski	20
1915	Hooks Dauss	21
1916	Harry Coveleski	20
1917	Hooks Dauss	16
1918	Bernie Boland	13
1919	Hooks Dauss	20
1920	Howard Ehmke	15
1921	Dutch Leonard	11
1922	Herman Pillette	18
1923	Hooks Dauss	20
1924	Rip Collins	14
1925	D. Leonard, Earl Whitehill	11
1926	Earl Whitehill	14
1927	Earl Whitehill	14
1928	Ownie Carroll	14
1929	George Uhle	14
1930	Earl Whitehill	17
1931	Vic Sorrell, Earl Whitehill	13
1932	Earl Whitehill	15
1933	Firpo Marberry	14
1934	Tommy Bridges	22
1935	Tommy Bridges	21
1936	Tommy Bridges	23
1937	Elden Auker	17
1938	T. Bridges, George Gill	12
1939	T. Bridges, Bobo Newsom	17
1940	Bobo Newsom	20
1941	Bobo Newsom	11
1942	Hal White	11
1943	Dizzy Trout	17
1944	**Hal Newhouser**	**25**
1945	Hal Newhouser	24
1946	**Hal Newhouser**	**26**
1947	Hal Newhouser	17
1948	Hal Newhouser	20
1949	H. Newhouser, V. Trucks	17
1950	Art Houtteman	17
1951	Bob Cain, Virgil Trucks	9
1952	Ted Gray	12
1953	Ned Garver, Ted Gray	10
1954	Steve Gromek	16
1955	Billy Hoeft	16
1956	Frank Lary	21
1957	Jim Bunning	18
1958	Frank Lary	16
1959	Jim Bunning, Frank Lary,	17
	Don Mossi	17
1960	Frank Lary	15

Hal Newhouser

Year	Pitcher	Wins
1961	Frank Lary	23
1962	Jim Bunning	19
1963	Hank Aguirre	14
1964	Dave Wickersham	19
1965	Denny McLain	15
1966	Denny McLain	20
1967	Earl Wilson	22
1968	**Denny McLain**	**31**
1969	Denny McLain	24
1970	Mickey Lolich	14
1971	Mickey Lolich	25
1972	Mickey Lolich	22
1973	Joe Coleman	23
1974	Mickey Lolich	16
1975	Mickey Lolich	12
1976	Mark Fidrych	19
1977	Dave Rozema	15
1978	Jim Slaton	17
1979	Jack Morris	17
1980	Jack Morris	16
1981	Jack Morris	14
1982	Jack Morris	17
1983	Jack Morris	20
1984	Jack Morris	19
1985	Jack Morris	16
1986	Jack Morris	21
1987	Jack Morris	18
1988	Jack Morris	15
1989	Frank Tanana	10
1990	Jack Morris	15
1991	Bill Gullickson	20
1992	Bill Gullickson	14
1993	John Doherty	14
1994	Mike Moore	11
1995	Sean Bergman, Felipe Lira	7
1996	Omar Olivares	7
1997	Justin Thompson	15
1998	Brian Moehler	14
1999	Dave Mlicki	14
2000	Brian Moehler	12
2001	Steve Sparks	14
2002	Mark Redman, S. Sparks	8
2003	Mike Maroth	9
2004	Nate Robertson	12
2005	J. Bonderman, M. Maroth	14
2006	K. Rogers, J. Verlander	17
2007	Justin Verlander	18
2008	Armando Galarraga	13
2009	Justin Verlander	19
2010	Justin Verlander	18
2011	Justin Verlander	24
2012	Justin Verlander	17
2013	Max Scherzer	21
2014	Max Scherzer	18
2015	Anibal Sanchez	10
2016	Justin Verlander	16
2017	M. Fulmer, J. Verlander	10
2018	Matt Boyd	9
2019	Matt Boyd	9
2020	Spencer Turnbull	4
2021	Tarik Skubal	8

Year	Pitcher	Losses
1901	**Jack Cronin**	**16**
1902	**Win Mercer**	**18**
1903	Bill Donovan	16
1904	**George Mullin**	**23**
1905	George Mullin	20
1906	George Mullin	18
1907	George Mullin	20
1908	George Mullin	13
1909	Ed Killian, Ed Summers	9
1910	George Mullin	12
1911	Ed Willett	11
1912	George Mullin	16
1913	Jean Dubuc	12
1914	Jean Dubuc	14
1915	Harry Coveleski, H. Dauss	11
1916	Hooks Dauss, Bill James	12
1917	Hooks Dauss	14
1918	Hooks Dauss	13
1919	Bernie Boland	15
1920	Hooks Dauss	18
1921	Hooks Dauss	14
1922	Howard Ehmke	15
1923	Herman Pillette	17
1924	Lil Stoner	8
1925	Rip Collins, Earl Whitehill	11
1926	Earl Whitehill	13
1927	Earl Whitehill	13
1928	Earl Whitehill	16
1929	Vic Sorrell	15
1930	G. Uhle, Earl Whitehill	12
1931	Earl Whitehill	16
1932	Vic Sorrell	14
1933	Carl Fischer, Vic Sorrell	14
1934	Tommy Bridges	11
1935	Schoolboy Rowe	13
1936	Elden Auker	16
1937	Tommy Bridges	12
1938	Elden Auker, George Gill,	9
	Vern Kennedy, R. Lawson	9
1939	Schoolboy Rowe	11
1940	T. Bridges, H. Newhouser	9
1941	Bobo Newsom	19
1942	Dizzy Trout	17
1943	Hal Newhouser	16
1944	Rufe Gentry, Dizzy Trout	14
1945	Dizzy Trout	14
1946	Dizzy Trout	13
1947	Hal Newhouser	16
1948	Art Houtteman	14
1949	H. Newhouser, V. Trucks	11
1950	Hal Newhouser	13
1951	Ted Gray, Dizzy Trout	13
1952	A. Houtteman, V. Trucks	18
1953	Ted Gray	15
1954	Steve Gromek	16
1955	Ned Garver	16
1956	Billy Hoeft	14
1957	Frank Lary	15
1958	Paul Foytack, Frank Lary	13
1959	Paul Foytack	14
1960	Frank Lary	15

Dave Wickersham

Year	Pitcher	Losses
1961	Jim Bunning	11
1962	Don Mossi	11
1963	H. Aguirre, Jim Bunning	13
1964	Dave Wickersham	11
1965	Dave Wickersham	14
1966	Denny McLain	14
1967	Denny McLain	16
1968	Earl Wilson	12
1969	Mickey Lolich	11
1970	Mickey Lolich	19
1971	Mickey Lolich	14
1972	Joe Coleman, M. Lolich	14
1973	Joe Coleman, M. Lolich	15
1974	Mickey Lolich	21
1975	Joe Coleman, M. Lolich	18
1976	Dave Roberts	17
1977	Fernando Arroyo	16
1978	Dave Rozema	12
1979	Milt Wilcox	10
1980	Jack Morris	15
1981	Dan Petry, Milt Wilcox	9
1982	Jack Morris	16
1983	Jack Morris	13
1984	Jac Morris	11
1985	Dan Petry	13
1986	Walt Terrell	12
1987	Jack Morris	11
1988	Walt Terrell	16
1989	Doyle Alexander	18
1990	Jack Morris	18
1991	Walt Terrell	14
1992	Bill Gullickson	13
1993	John Doherty	13
1994	Tim Belcher	15
1995	Mike Moore	15
1996	Felipe Lira	14
1997	Brian Moehler	12
1998	Justin Thompson	15
1999	Brian Moehler	16
2000	Jeff Weaver	15
2001	Jeff Weaver	16
2002	Steve Sparks	16
2003	Mike Maroth	21
2004	Jason Johnson	15
2005	Nate Robertson	16
2006	Nate Robertson	13
2007	Nate Robertson	13
2008	Justin Verlander	17
2009	Armando Galarraga	10
2010	Rick Porcello	12
2011	Brad Penny	11
2012	Rick Porcello	12
2013	Justin Verlander	12
2014	R. Porcello, J. Verlander	12
2015	Alfredo Simon	12
2016	Anibal Sanchez	12
2017	Jordan Zimmermann	13
2018	Matt Boyd	13
2019	Spencer Turnbull	17
2020	Matt Boyd	7
2021	Tarik Skubal	11

Year	Pitcher	Pct	W-L
1901	**Roscoe Miller**	**.629**	**22-13**
1902	Win Mercer	.455	15-18
1903	George Mullin	.563	18-14
1904	Bill Donovan	.500	16-16
1905	Ed Killian	.600	21-14
1906	Ed Killian	.600	9-6
1907	**Bill Donovan**	**.852**	**23-4**
1908	Bill Donovan	.720	18-7
1909	George Mullin	.758	25-8
1910	Bill Donovan	.696	16-7
1911	George Mullin	.667	18-9
1912	Jean Dubuc	.640	16-9
1913	Jean Dubuc	.555	15-12
1914	Harry Coveleski	.645	20-11
1915	Hooks Dauss	.656	21-11
1916	Harry Coveleski	.667	20-10
1917	Bernie Boland	.609	14-9
1918	Bernie Boland	.591	13-9
1919	Hooks Dauss	.690	20-9
1920	Howard Ehmke	.469	15-17
1921	Red Oldham	.550	11-9
1922	Herman Pillette	.600	18-12
1923	Hooks Dauss	.625	20-12
1924	Earl Whitehill	.708	17-7
1925	Don Holloway	.692	9-4
1926	Ed Wells	.556	10-8
1927	Rip Collins	.632	12-7
1928	Ownie Carroll	.583	14-10
1929	George Uhle	.560	14-11
1930	Earl Whitehill	.586	17-12
1931	Vic Sorrell	.500	13-13
1932	Earl Whitehill	.556	15-12
1933	Schoolboy Rowe	.600	6-4
1934	Elden Auker	.750	9-3
1935	Tommy Bridges	.700	21-9
1936	Tommy Bridges	.676	23-11
1937	Roxie Lawson	.714	15-6
1938	Tommy Bridges	.667	12-6
1939	Tommy Bridges	.708	17-7
1940	Bobo Newsom	.833	20-4
	Schoolboy Rowe	.833	15-3
1941	Al Benton	.692	9-4
1942	Tommy Bridges	.563	9-7
1943	Tommy Bridges	.667	12-6
1944	Hal Newhouser	.781	25-7
1945	Hal Newhouser	.727	24-9
1946	Hal Newhouser	.765	26-8
1947	Fred Hutchinson	.625	15-9
1948	Hal Newhouser	.645	20-11
1949	Fred Hutchinson	.706	12-5
1950	Dizzy Trout	.706	12-5
1951	Virgil Trucks	.600	9-6
1952	Ted Gray	.414	12-17
1953	Ned Garver	.476	10-11
1954	Ned Garver	.560	14-11
1955	Billy Hoeft	.727	16-6
1956	Frank Lary	.618	21-13
1957	Jim Bunning	.720	18-7
1958	Billy Hoeft	.563	9-7
1959	Don Mossi	.680	17-8
1960	Frank Lary	.500	15-15
	Don Mossi	.500	8-8

Roxie Lawson

Year	Pitcher	Pct	W-L
1961	Frank Lary	.719	23-9
1962	Hank Aguirre	.667	12-6
1963	Phil Regan	.619	13-8
1964	Mickey Lolich	.667	16-8
1965	Denny McLain	.714	15-6
1966	Earl Wilson	.684	13-6
1967	Earl Wilson	.667	22-11
1968	Denny McLain	.838	31-6
1969	Denny McLain	.727	24-9
1970	Les Cain	.632	12-7
1971	Joe Coleman	.690	20-9
1972	Woodie Fryman	.769	10-3
1973	Joe Coleman	.605	23-15
1974	Joe Coleman	.538	14-12
1975	Vern Ruhle	.478	11-12
1976	Mark Fidrych	.679	19-9
1977	Dave Rozema	.682	15-7
1978	Jack Billingham	.652	15-8
1979	Jack Morris	.708	17-7
1980	Milt Wilcox	.522	12-11
1981	Jack Morris	.667	14-7
1982	Dan Petry	.625	15-9
1983	Dave Rozema	.700	7-3
1984	Dan Petry	.692	18-8
1985	Jack Morris	.593	16-11
1986	Jack Morris	.724	21-8
1987	Walt Terrell	.630	17-10
1988	Jeff Robinson	.684	13-6
1989	Frank Tanana	.417	10-14
1990	Walt Terrell	.600	6-4
1991	Bill Gullickson	.690	20-9
1992	Frank Tanana	.522	12-11
1993	Gullickson, Moore	.591	13-9
1994	Mike Moore	.524	11-10
1995	Bergman, Lira	.412	7-10
1996	Omar Olivares	.389	7-11
1997	Willie Blair	.636	14-8
1998	Brian Moehler	.519	14-13
1999	Dave Mlicki	.538	14-12
2000	Willie Blair	.727	8-3
2001	Steve Sparks	.609	14-9
2002	Jeff Weaver	.429	6-8
2003	Mike Maroth	.300	9-21
2004	Nate Robertson	.545	12-10
2005	Jeremy Bonderman	.519	14-13
2006	Kenny Rogers	.708	17-7
2007	Justin Verlander	.750	18-6
2008	Armando Galarraga	.684	13-6
2009	Justin Verlander	.679	19-9
2010	Justin Verlander	.667	18-9
2011	Justin Verlander	.828	24-5
2012	Justin Verlander	.680	17-8
2013	**Max Scherzer**	**.875**	**21-3**
2014	Max Scherzer	.783	18-5
2015	David Price	.692	9-4
2016	Justin Verlander	.640	16-9
2017	Justin Verlander	.556	10-8
2018	Mike Fiers	.538	7-7
2019	Matt Boyd	.429	9-12
2020	Matt Boyd	.300	3-7
2021	Casey Mize	.438	7-9

Year	Pitcher	QS
1901	**Roscoe Miller**	**26**
1902	Win Mercer	23
1903	**George Mullin**	**27**
1904	**George Mullin**	**33**
1905	George Mullin	26
1906	George Mullin	20
1907	George Mullin	24
1908	Ed Summers	19
1909	George Mullin	23
1910	George Mullin	18
1911	George Mullin	15
1912	Jean Dubuc, Ed Willett	12
1913	Hooks Dauss	22
1914	Harry Coveleski	26
1915	H. Coveleski, Hooks Dauss	27
1916	Harry Coveleski	28
1917	Hooks Dauss	22
1918	Bernie Boland	18
1919	Hooks Dauss	19
1920	Hooks Dauss, H. Ehmke	19
1921	Dutch Leonard	22
1922	Herman Pillette	22
1923	H. Dauss, Herman Pillette	20
1924	Rip Collins	17
1925	Hooks Dauss	16
1926	Earl Whitehill	17
1927	Earl Whitehill	17
1928	Ownie Carroll	18
1929	George Uhle	15
1930	Earl Whitehill	17
1931	Earl Whitehill	16
1932	Vic Sorrell	16
1933	Tommy Bridges	18
1934	Tommy Bridges	19
1935	Tommy Bridges	21
1936	Tommy Bridges	20
1937	Eldon Auker	18
1938	George Gill	12
1939	Bobo Newsom	19
1940	Bobo Newsom	21
1941	Bobo Newsom	17
1942	Al Benton	20
1943	Dizzy Trout	21
1944	Dizzy Trout	31
1945	Hal Newhouser	31
1946	Hal Newhouser	26
1947	Hal Newhouser	26
1948	Hal Newhouser	22
1949	Hal Newhouser	21
1950	Art Houtteman	17
	Hal Newhouser	17
1951	Ted Gray	14
1952	Ted Gray	19
1953	Ted Gray	13
1954	Steve Gromek	24
1955	Frank Lary	22
1956	Frank Lary	24
1957	Jim Bunning	19
1958	Frank Lary	21
1959	Don Mossi	20
1960	Jim Bunning	23

Jason Johnson

Year	Pitcher	QS
1961	Frank Lary	25
1962	Hank Aguirre, J. Bunning	18
1963	Hank Aguirre, J. Bunning	21
1964	Dave Wickersham	24
1965	Aguirre, Lolich, McLain	20
1966	Denny McLain	23
1967	Earl Wilson	25
1968	**Denny McLain**	**35**
1969	Denny McLain	28
1970	Mickey Lolich	24
1971	Mickey Lolich	31
1972	Mickey Lolich	32
1973	J. Coleman, Mickey Lolich	23
1974	Joe Coleman	20
1975	Mickey Lolich	19
1976	Mark Fidrych	23
1977	Dave Rozema	18
1978	J. Billingham, D. Rozema,	16
	Jim Slaton	16
1979	Jack Morris	18
1980	Jack Morris	16
1981	Jack Morris	17
1982	Dan Petry	22
1983	Jack Morris	26
1984	Jack Morris	23
1985	Jack Morris	26
1986	Jack Morris	20
1987	Jack Morris, Walt Terrell	21
1988	Jack Morris	20
1989	Frank Tanana	21
1990	Jack Morris	18
1991	Bill Gullickson	20
1992	Frank Tanana	18
1993	David Wells	17
1994	Mike Moore	10
1995	David Wells	14
1996	Felipe Lira	15
1997	Justin Thompson	25
1998	Brian Moehler	20
1999	D. Mlicki, Brian Moehler	16
2000	Hideo Nomo	17
2001	Jeff Weaver	21
2002	Steve Sparks	16
2003	Nate Cornejo	17
2004	M. Maroth, N. Robertson	17
2005	Jason Johnson	19
2006	Nate Robertson	20
2007	Justin Verlander	21
2008	Armando Galarraga	16
2009	Justin Verlander	22
2010	Justin Verlander	22
2011	Justin Verlander	28
2012	Justin Verlander	25
2013	Max Scherzer	25
2014	Max Scherzer	22
2015	David Price	15
2016	Justin Verlander	27
2017	M. Fulmer, J. Verlander	18
2018	Matt Boyd	14
2019	Matt Boyd	14
2020	Spencer Turnbull	4
2021	Casey Mize	12

Year	Pitcher	HQS
1901	**Roscoe Miller**	**26**
1902	Win Mercer	23
1903	**George Mullin**	**27**
1904	**George Mullin**	**31**
1905	George Mullin	24
1906	George Mullin	20
1907	George Mullin	22
1908	Ed Summers	17
1909	George Mullin	22
1910	George Mullin	17
1911	George Mullin	15
1912	Jean Dubuc, Ed Willett	12
1913	Hooks Dauss	22
1914	Harry Coveleski	22
	Hooks Dauss	22
1915	Hooks Dauss	26
1916	Harry Coveleski	26
1917	Hooks Dauss	22
1918	Bernie Boland	17
1919	Hooks Dauss	18
1920	Hooks Dauss, H. Ehmke	19
1921	Dutch Leonard	20
1922	Herman Pillette	22
1923	Herman Pillette	18
1924	Rip Collins	14
1925	Hooks Dauss	15
1926	Hal White	15
1927	Earl Whitehill	18
1928	Ownie Carroll	18
1929	George Uhle	14
1930	Earl Whitehill	16
1931	Vic Sorrell, Hal White	14
1932	Vic Sorrell	16
1933	Tommy Bridges	18
1934	Tommy Bridges	19
1935	Tommy Bridges	19
1936	Tommy Bridges	19
1937	Elden Auker	18
1938	George Gill	11
1939	Bobo Newsom	19
1940	Bobo Newsom	20
1941	Bobo Newsom	15
1942	Al Benton	17
1943	Dizzy Trout	19
1944	Dizzy Trout	30
1945	Hal Newhouser	30
1946	Hal Newhouser	26
1947	Hal Newhouser	24
1948	Hal Newhouser	22
1949	Hal Newhouser	20
1950	Art Houtteman	16
1951	Ted Gray	12
1952	Ted Gray	17
1953	Ted Gray	12
1954	Steve Gromek	23
1955	Frank Lary	20
1956	Frank Lary	20
1957	Jim Bunning	19
1958	Frank Lary	20
1959	Don Mossi	20
1960	Jim Bunning	22

Doyle Alexander

Year	Pitcher	HQS
1961	Frank Lary	24
1962	Hank Aguirre	15
1963	Jim Bunning	20
1964	Dave Wickersham	22
1965	Denny McLain	19
1966	Denny McLain	21
1967	Earl Wilson	22
1968	**Denny McLain**	**34**
1969	Denny McLain	27
1970	Mickey Lolich	23
1971	Mickey Lolich	31
1972	Mickey Lolich	28
1973	Mickey Lolich	22
1974	Mickey Lolich	19
1975	Mickey Lolich	17
1976	Mark Fidrych	24
1977	Dave Rozema	15
1978	Jim Slaton	15
1979	Jack Morris	17
1980	Jack Morris	15
1981	Jack Morris	16
1982	Jack Morris	19
1983	Jack Morris	26
1984	Jack Morris	19
1985	Jack Morris	23
1986	Jack Morris	20
1987	Jack Morris, Walt Terrell	19
1988	Doyle Alexander	19
1989	Frank Tanana	18
1990	Jack Morris	14
1991	Bill Gullickson	17
1992	Bill Gullickson	14
1993	Doherty, Moore, Wells	13
1994	Mike Moore	8
1995	David Wells	12
1996	Felipe Lira	8
1997	Justin Thompson	20
1998	Brian Moehler	14
1999	Brian Moehler	10
2000	Jeff Weaver	13
2001	Jeff Weaver	17
2002	Mark Redman	13
2003	Nate Cornejo	11
2004	Mike Maroth	12
2005	Jeremy Bonderman	12
2006	Kenny Rogers	15
2007	Justin Verlander	13
2008	Armando Galarraga	8
2009	Justin Verlander	17
2010	Justin Verlander	17
2011	Justin Verlander	24
2012	Justin Verlander	19
2013	Max Scherzer	17
2014	Rick Porcello	15
2015	David Price	11
2016	Justin Verlander	19
2017	Justin Verlander	13
2018	Michael Fulmer	5
2019	Matt Boyd	5
2020	Spencer Turnbull	1
2021	Casey Mize, Jose Urena	4

Year	Pitcher	Starts
1901	**Roscoe Miller, Ed Siever**	**5**
1902	**Ed Siever**	**8**
1903	**Bill Donovan**	**15**
1904	Ed Killian, George Mullin	10
1905	Ed Killian	11
1906	Red Donahue	9
1907	Ed Killian	10
1908	Ed Willett	9
1909	Ed Summers	14
1910	Bill Donovan, G. Mullin	8
1911	George Mullin	7
1912	Jean Dubuc	5
1913	Hooks Dauss	7
1914	Harry Coveleski	11
1915	H. Coveleski, Hooks Dauss	8
1916	Harry Coveleski	11
1917	Hooks Dauss	11
1918	Bernie Boland	9
1919	Bernie Boland, D. Leonard	8
1920	Howard Ehmke	7
1921	Dutch Leonard	5
1922	Herman Pillette	9
1923	Hooks Dauss	8
1924	Earl Whitehill	4
1925	Hooks Dauss	6
1926	Ed Wells	5
1927	Earl Whitehill	5
1928	Ownie Carroll	8
1929	Uhle, Whitehill, Carroll	3
1930	Vic Sorrell	5
1931	George Uhle	3
1932	Vic Sorrell	6
1933	Tommy Bridges	8
1934	Tommy Bridges	7
1935	Schoolboy Rowe	10
1936	Schoolboy Rowe	10
1937	Elden Auker	6
1938	Bridges, Gill, Poffenberger	3
1939	Al Benton	6
1940	Bobo Newsom	10
1941	Bobo Newsom	5
1942	Hal White	7
1943	Dizzy Trout	11
1944	Hal Newhouser	11
1945	**Hal Newhouser**	**15**
1946	**Hal Newhouser**	**16**
1947	Hal Newhouser	9
1948	Hal Newhouser	9
1949	Virgil Trucks	10
1950	Art Houtteman	9
1951	Gray, Stuart, Trucks	4
1952	Virgil Trucks	5
1953	Ned Garver	3
1954	Ned Garver	11
1955	Billy Hoeft	8
1956	Frank Lary	10
1957	Jim Bunning	10
1958	Frank Lary	10
1959	Don Mossi	6
1960	Jim Bunning	7
1961	Jim Bunning, Frank Lary	8

Felipe Lira

Year	Pitcher	Starts
1962	Jim Bunning, Don Mossi	6
1963	Hank Aguirre	10
1964	Mickey Lolich	8
1965	Denny McLain	7
1966	Earl Wilson	8
1967	Joe Sparma	8
1968	Denny McLain	14
1969	Denny McLain	12
1970	Mickey Lolich	8
1971	Mickey Lolich	11
1972	Mickey Lolich	13
1973	Joe Coleman	8
1974	Mickey Lolich	6
1975	Mickey Lolich	6
1976	Mark Fidrych	11
1977	Dave Rozema	3
1978	Jack Billingham	5
1979	Jack Morris, Milt Wilcox	3
1980	Jack Morris, Milt Wilcox	4
1981	Jack Morris	7
1982	Dan Petry	8
1983	Milt Wilcox	6
1984	Jack Morris, Dan Petry	5
1985	Jack Morris	6
1986	Jack Morris	12
1987	Walt Terrell	6
1988	Jack Morris, Jeff Robinson	7
1989	Frank Tanana	4
1990	Jack Morris	4
1991	Frank Tanana	4
1992	Bill Gullickson	3
1993	John Doherty	5
1994	Belcher, Moore, Wells	2
1995	David Wells	2
1996	Felipe Lira	4
1997	Justin Thompson	4
1998	Brian Moehler	5
1999	Dave Mlicki	3
2000	Jeff Weaver	3
2001	Steve Sparks	6
2002	Mark Redman	5
2003	J. Bonderman, N. Cornejo	2
2004	J. Bonderman, J. Johnson,	3
	M. Maroth, N. Robertson	3
2005	Jason Johnson	12
2006	Jeremy Bonderman	12
2007	Jeremy Bonderman,	8
	N. Robertson, J. Verlander	8
2008	Nate Robertson	10
2009	Edwin Jackson	11
2010	Bonderman, Galarraga	11
2011	Brad Penny, Max Scherzer	9
2012	Drew Smyly	11
2013	Doug Fister, J. Verlander	9
2014	Max Scherzer	10
2015	David Price	8
2016	Justin Verlander	3
2017	Justin Verlander	2
2018	M. Boyd, J. Zimmermann	1
2019	13 Starting Pitchers	0
2020	10 Starting Pitchers	0
2021	Spencer Turnbull	1

Year	Pitcher	Pct
1901	**Roscoe Miller**	**.722**
1902	Win Mercer	.697
1903	**Frank Kitson**	**.750**
	George Mullin	**.750**
1904	**George Mullin**	**.750**
1905	George Mullin	.634
1906	Red Donahue	.607
1907	Ed Killian	.618
1908	Ed Willett	.696
1909	**Ed Killian**	**.789**
1910	**Bill Donovan**	**.824**
1911	George Mullin	.517
1912	Jean Dubuc	.462
1913	Hooks Dauss	.759
1914	Harry Coveleski	.722
1915	Hooks Dauss	.771
1916	Harry Coveleski	.718
1917	Bill James	.782
1918	Bernie Boland	.720
1919	Dutch Leonard	.643
1920	Doc Ayers	.636
1921	Dutch Leonard	.688
1922	Herman Pillette	.595
1923	Syl Johnson	.667
1924	Rip Collins	.567
1925	Hooks Dauss	.533
1926	Earl Whitehill	.500
1927	Earl Whitehill	.548
1928	Ownie Carroll	.643
1929	George Uhle	.500
1930	Waite Hoyt	.600
1931	Art Herring	.750
1932	Tommy Bridges	.538
1933	Tommy Bridges	.643
1934	Eldon Auker	.611
1935	Tommy Bridges	.618
1936	Tommy Bridges	.526
1937	Eldon Auker	.563
1938	George Gill	.522
1939	Dizzy Trout	.636
1940	Bobo Newsom	.618
1941	Tommy Bridges	.591
1942	Tommy Bridges	.682
1943	Tommy Bridges	.773
1944	Hal Newhouser	.794
1945	**Hal Newhouser**	**.861**
1946	Hal Newhouser	.765
1947	Hal Newhouser	.722
1948	Hal Newhouser	.629
1949	Fred Hutchinson	.667
1950	Hal Newhouser	.567
1951	Virgil Trucks	.556
1952	Ted Gray	.594
1953	Steve Gromek	.471
1954	Steve Gromek	.750
1955	Frank Lary	.710
1956	Frank Lary	.632
1957	Jim Bunning	.633
1958	Frank Lary	.618
1959	Don Mossi	.667
1960	Jim Bunning	.676

Syl Johnson

Year	Pitcher	Pct
1961	Frank Lary	.694
1962	Hank Aguirre	.818
1963	Mickey Lolich	.667
1964	Dave Wickersham	.667
1965	Denny McLain	.690
1966	Earl Wilson	.696
1967	Mickey Lolich	.667
1968	Denny McLain	.854
1969	Mickey Lolich	.694
1970	Mickey Lolich	.615
1971	Mickey Lolich	.689
1972	Mickey Lolich	.780
1973	Joe Coleman	.575
1974	Lerrin LaGrow	.529
1975	Ray Bare	.619
1976	Mark Fidrych	.793
1977	Dave Rozema	.643
1978	Dave Rozema	.571
1979	Jack Morris	.667
1980	Dan Petry	.600
1981	Jack Morris	.680
1982	Jerry Ujdur	.680
1983	Jack Morris	.703
1984	Jack Morris	.657
1985	Frank Tanana	.800
1986	Jack Morris	.571
1987	Jack Morris	.618
1988	Jeff Robinson	.652
1989	Frank Tanana	.636
1990	Jack Morris	.500
1991	Bill Gullickson	.571
1992	Frank Tanana	.581
1993	David Wells	.567
1994	David Wells	.500
1995	David Wells	.778
1996	Felipe Lira	.469
1997	Justin Thompson	.781
1998	Brian Moehler	.606
1999	Justin Thompson	.542
2000	Brian Moehler	.552
2001	Jeff Weaver	.636
2002	Jeff Weaver	.647
2003	Nate Cornejo	.531
2004	Nate Robertson	.531
2005	Jeremy Bonderman	.586
2006	Nate Robertson	.625
2007	Justin Verlander	.656
2008	Armando Galarraga	.571
2009	Edwin Jackson	.636
2010	Justin Verlander	.667
2011	Justin Verlander	.824
2012	Justin Verlander	.758
2013	Max Scherzer	.781
2014	Rick Porcello	.677
2015	David Price	.714
2016	Justin Verlander	.794
2017	Michael Fulmer	.720
2018	Mike Fiers	.476
2019	Matt Boyd	.438
2020	Spencer Turnbull	.364
2021	Matt Boyd, Casey Mize	.400

Year	Pitcher	Pct.
1901	**Roscoe Miller**	**.722**
1902	Win Mercer	.697
1903	**Frank Kitson**	**.750**
	George Mullin	**.750**
1904	Bill Donovan	.735
1905	Ed Killian	.622
1906	Red Donahue	.607
1907	Ed Killian	.588
1908	Ed Willett	.696
1909	Ed Killian	.737
1910	**Bill Donovan**	**.824**
1911	George Mullin	.517
1912	Jean Dubuc	.462
1913	Hooks Dauss	.759
1914	Hooks Dauss	.629
1915	Hooks Dauss	.686
1916	Harry Coveleski	.667
1917	Hooks Dauss	.710
1918	Bernie Boland	.680
1919	Hooks Dauss	.563
1920	Hooks Dauss	.594
1921	Dutch Leonard	.625
1922	Herman Pillette	.595
1923	Bert Cole	.538
1924	Ken Holloway	.538
1925	Hooks Dauss	.500
1926	Rip Collins	.539
1927	Earl Whitehill	.581
1928	Ownie Carroll	.643
1929	George Uhle	.467
1930	Earl Whitehill	.516
1931	Vic Sorrell	.438
1932	Vic Sorrell	.516
1933	Tommy Bridges	.643
1934	Elden Auker	.667
1935	Tommy Bridges	.618
1936	Tommy Bridges	.500
1937	Elden Auker	.563
1938	Al Benton	.700
1939	Bobo Newsom	.613
1940	Bobo Newsom	.588
1941	Tommy Bridges	.636
1942	Hal White	.640
1943	Tommy Bridges	.818
1944	Dizzy Trout	.750
1945	**Hal Newhouser**	**.833**
1946	Hal Newhouser	.765
1947	Hal Newhouser	.667
1948	Hal Newhouser	.629
1949	Fred Hutchinson	.667
1950	Fred Hutchinson	.577
1951	Fred Hutchinson	.550
1952	Hal Newhouser	.579
1953	Steve Gromek	.471
1954	Steve Gromek	.719
1955	Frank Lary	.645
1956	Frank Lary	.526
1957	Jim Bunning	.633
1958	Frank Lary	.588
1959	Don Mossi	.667
1960	Jim Bunning	.647
1961	Frank Lary	.667
1962	Hank Aguirre	.682
1963	Hank Aguirre	.576
1964	Dave Wickersham	.611
1965	Denny McLain	.655
1966	Earl Wilson	.609
1967	Mickey Lolich	.600
1968	Denny McLain	.829
1969	Mickey Lolich	.667
1970	Mickey Lolich	.590
1971	Mickey Lolich	.689
1972	Woodie Fryman	.714
1973	Mickey Lolich	.524
1974	Mickey Lolich	.463
1975	Mickey Lolich	.531
1976	Mark Fidrych	.828
1977	Dave Rozema	.536
1978	Dave Rozema	.500
1979	Jack Morris	.630
1980	Dan Schatzeder	.538
1981	Jack Morris	.640
1982	Jerry Ujdur	.600
1983	Jack Morris	.703
1984	Jack Morris	.543
1985	Jack Morris	.657
1986	Jack Morris	.571
1987	Jack Morris	.559
1988	Doyle Alexander	.559
1989	Frank Tanana	.545
1990	Jack Morris	.389
1991	Bill Gullickson	.486
1992	Frank Tanana	.419
1993	David Wells	.433
1994	David Wells	.438
1995	David Wells	.667
1996	Omar Olivares	.280
1997	Justin Thompson	.625
1998	Brian Moehler	.424
1999	Justin Thompson	.375
2000	Jeff Weaver	.433
2001	Jeff Weaver	.515
2002	Jeff Weaver	.588
2003	Nate Cornejo	.344
2004	Mike Maroth	.364
2005	Jeremy Bonderman	.414
2006	Kenny Rogers	.455
2007	Justin Verlander	.406
2008	Armando Galarraga	.286
2009	Justin Verlander	.486
2010	Justin Verlander	.515
2011	Justin Verlander	.706
2012	Justin Verlander	.576
2013	Max Scherzer	.531
2014	Rick Porcello	.484
2015	David Price	.524
2016	Justin Verlander	.559
2017	Michael Fulmer	.480
2018	Michael Fulmer	.208
2019	Matt Boyd	.156
2020	Spencer Turnbull	.091
2021	Jose Urena	.222

Woodie Fryman

Year	Pitcher	Pct.
1901	**Ed Siever**	**.152**
1902	**Ed Siever**	**.348**
1903	**Bill Donovan**	**.441**
1904	Ed Killian	.294
1905	Bill Donovan	.313
1906	Red Donahue	.321
1907	Ed Killian	.294
1908	Ed Willett	.391
1909	Ed Summers	.438
1910	**Bill Donovan**	**.471**
1911	George Mullin	.241
1912	Joe Lake	.214
1913	Hooks Dauss	.241
1914	Harry Coveleski	.306
1915	Hooks Dauss	.314
1916	Harry Coveleski	.282
1917	Hooks Dauss	.355
1918	Bernie Boland	.360
1919	Dutch Leonard	.286
1920	Howard Ehmke	.212
1921	Dutch Leonard	.156
1922	Herman Pillette	.243
1923	Hooks Dauss	.205
1924	Ken Holloway	.154
1925	Hooks Dauss	.200
1926	Rip Collins	.231
1927	Earl Whitehill	.161
1928	Ownie Carroll	.286
1929	Ownie Carroll	.115
1930	Vic Sorrell	.167
1931	George Uhle	.167
1932	Vic Sorrell	.194
1933	Tommy Bridges	.286
1934	Elden Auker	.333
1935	Elden Auker	.320
1936	Schoolboy Rowe	.286
1937	Elden Auker	.188
1938	Boots Poffenberger	.200
1939	Tommy Bridges	.269
1940	Tommy Bridges	.286
1941	Dizzy Trout	.222
1942	Virgil Trucks	.300
1943	Dizzy Trout	.367
1944	Dizzy Trout	.375
1945	Hal Newhouser	.417
1946	**Hal Newhouser**	**.471**
1947	Fred Hutchinson	.280
1948	Hal Newhouser	.257
1949	Virgil Trucks	.313
1950	Art Houtteman	.265
1951	Marlin Stuart	.267
1952	Virgil Trucks	.172
1953	Steve Gromek	.118
1954	Ned Garver	.344
1955	Billy Hoeft	.276
1956	Frank Lary	.263
1957	Jim Bunning	.333
1958	Frank Lary	.294
1959	Don Mossi	.200
1960	Don Mossi	.227
1961	Frank Lary	.222
1962	Paul Foytack	.238
1963	Hank Aguirre	.303
1964	Mickey Lolich	.242
1965	Denny McLain	.241
1966	Earl Wilson	.348
1967	Mickey Lolich	.233
1968	Denny McLain	.341
1969	Denny McLain	.293
1970	Mickey Lolich	.205
1971	Mickey Lolich	.244
1972	Mickey Lolich	.317
1973	Joe Coleman	.200
1974	Mickey Lolich	.146
1975	Mickey Lolich	.188
1976	Mark Fidrych	.379
1977	Dave Rozema	.107
1978	Jack Billingham	.167
1979	Dan Petry	.133
1980	Earl Wilson	.129
1981	Jack Morris	.280
1982	Dan Petry	.229
1983	Milt Wilcox	.231
1984	Jack Morris, Dan Petry	.143
1985	Jack Morris	.171
1986	Jack Morris	.343
1987	Walt Terrell	.171
1988	Jeff Robinson	.304
1989	Jeff Robinson	.125
1990	Jack Morris	.111
1991	Frank Tanana	.121
1992	Bill Gullickson	.088
1993	John Doherty	.161
1994	David Wells	.125
1995	David Wells	.111
1996	Felipe Lira	.125
1997	Omar Olivares	.158
1998	Brian Moehler	.152
1999	Dave Mlicki	.097
2000	Steve Sparks	.133
2001	Steve Sparks	.182
2002	Jeff Weaver	.235
2003	Jeremy Bonderman	.071
2004	Jeremy Bonderman	.094
	Nate Robertson	.094
2005	Jeremy Bonderman	.103
2006	Kenny Rogers	.121
2007	Jeremy Bonderman	.107
2008	Justin Verlander	.060
2009	Justin Verlander	.171
2010	Justin Verlander	.121
2011	Justin Verlander	.235
2012	Justin Verlander	.152
2013	Doug Fister	.094
	Max Scherzer	.094
2014	Max Scherzer	.182
2015	David Price	.286
2016	Justin Verlander	.088
2017	Justin Verlander	.071
2018	Jordan Zimmermann	.040
2019	13 Starting Pitchers	.000
2020	10 Starting Pitchers	.000
2021	Spencer Turnbull	.111

Marlin Stuart

1901	**Ed Siever, Joe Yeager**	**2**
1902	**Ed Siever**	**4**
1903	**George Mullin**	**4**
1904	**George Mullin**	**5**
1905	Frank Kitson	3
1906	R. Donahue, B. Donovan,	1
	Killian, Mullin, Siever	1
1907	**Ed Siever**	**5**
1908	B. Donovan, George Mullin	3
1909	**Ed Willett**	**5**
1910	Ed Killian	3
1911	**Ed Willett**	**5**
1912	Covington, Willett, Works	2
1913	**Hooks Dauss, Ed Willett**	**5**
1914	**Harry Coveleski, H. Dauss**	**5**
1915	**Harry Coveleski**	**9**
1916	**Harry Coveleski**	**10**
1917	Bernie Boland	5
1918	Rudy Kallio	4
1919	Howard Ehmke	5
1920	Doc Ayers	4
1921	**Dutch Leonard**	**10**
1922	Red Oldham	9
1923	Ken Holloway, H. Pillette	8
1924	Rip Collins	9
1925	**Earl Whitehill**	**11**
1926	Lil Stoner, Ed Wells	8
1927	Rip Collins	6
1928	Sam Gibson, Vic Sorrell	5
1929	Ownie Carroll	5
1930	Vic Sorrell	6
1931	Vic Sorrell	6
1932	George Uhle	6
1933	Firpo Marberry	7
1934	Carl Fischer	7
1935	General Crowder	6
1936	Schoolboy Rowe	7
1937	Jake Wade	9
1938	Vern Kennedy	6
1939	Al Benton	6
1940	Bobo Newsom	10
1941	Hal Newhouser	8
1942	**Al Benton**	**11**
1943	Hal White	7
1944	R. Gentry, S. Overmire	6
1945	Al Benton	7
1946	Virgil Trucks	8
1947	Virgil Trucks	6
1948	A. Houtteman, V. Trucks	5
1949	Lou Kretlow	8
1950	Ted Gray	6
1951	Ted Gray	8
1952	Virgil Trucks	6
1953	Al Aber, Ned Garver	5
1954	Ned Garver	7
1955	Billy Hoeft	7
1956	P. Foytack, Virgil Trucks	6
1957	Frank Lary	9
1958	Jim Bunning	8
1959	Paul Foytack	9
1960	Jim Bunning	9

Johnny Podres

1961	**Don Mossi**	**12**
1962	Frank Lary	7
1963	Jim Bunning	10
1964	**Hank Aguirre**	**12**
1965	**Mickey Lolich**	**14**
1966	J. Podres, D. Wickersham	7
1967	Joe Sparma	12
1968	Joe Sparma	12
1969	Earl Wilson	13
1970	Les Cain, Joe Niekro	10
1971	Joe Coleman	9
1972	Tom Timmermann	7
1973	Mickey Lolich	11
1974	**Joe Coleman**	**15**
1975	Vern Ruhle	8
1976	Vern Ruhle	11
1977	Bob Sykes	9
1978	Billingham, Rozema, Slaton	7
1979	Dave Rozema, Milt Wilcox	8
1980	Milt Wilcox	8
1981	Jack Morris, Jerry Ujdur	4
1982	Dan Petry	11
1983	Dan Petry	8
1984	Dan Petry	9
1985	Walt Terrell	9
1986	Frank Tanana	10
1987	Frank Tanana	9
1988	Doyle Alexander	9
1989	D. Alexander, F. Tanana	9
1990	Frank Tanana	12
1991	Frank Tanana, W. Terrell	8
1992	Frank Tanana	8
1993	Mike Moore	14
1994	Bill Gullickson	10
1995	Sean Bergman	11
1996	Felipe Lira	12
1997	B. Moehler, O. Olivares	8
1998	Justin Thompson	8
1999	Jeff Weaver	8
2000	Hideo Nomo	11
2001	Steve Sparks	10
2002	Mark Redman	7
2003	Nate Cornejo	9
2004	J. Johnson, N. Robertson	10
2005	Jason Johnson	12
2006	Jeremy Bonderman	12
2007	Jeremy Bonderman	8
	N. Robertson, J. Verlander	8
2008	Nate Robertson	10
2009	Edwin Jackson	11
2010	Bonderman, Galarraga	11
2011	Brad Penny, M. Scherzer	9
2012	Drew Smyly	11
2013	Doug Fister, J. Verlander	9
2014	Max Scherzer	10
2015	David Price	8
2016	A. Sanchez, J. Verlander	9
2017	Justin Verlander	10
2018	Jordan Zimmermann	10
2019	Daniel Norris	13
2020	Michael Fulmer	8
2021	Casey Mize	14

Year	Pitcher(s)	Wins
1901	Roscoe Miller	4
1902	George Mullin, Joe Yeager	2
1903	Donovan, Mullin	3
1904	**Frank Kitson**	**4**
1905	**Bill Donovan, Ed Killian**	**4**
1906	**Donahue, Killian, Mullin**	**4**
1907	**Bill Donovan**	**8**
1908	Bill Donovan	4
1909	Ed Willett	6
1910	Bill Donovan, Ed Willett	3
1911	Ed Willett	5
1912	Jean Dubuc, Ed Willett	6
1913	Jean Dubuc	3
1914	Harry Coveleski, H. Dauss	3
1915	Hooks Dauss	3
1916	Hooks Dauss	3
1917	H. Ehmke, Willie Mitchell	1
1918	Bernie Boland	3
1919	Hooks Dauss, H. Ehmke	5
1920	Dauss, Ehmke, Leonard	2
1921	H. Ehmke, Red Oldham	3
1922	Dauss, Ehmke, Oldham	3
1923	Hooks Dauss	7
1924	Lil Stoner	5
1925	Earl Whitehill	5
1926	Earl Whitehill	4
1927	Carroll, Collins, Stoner	3
1928	Carroll, Sorrell, Whitehill	2
1929	Earl Whitehill	5
1930	Chief Hogsett, Vic Sorrell	4
1931	Sorrell, Whitehill	3
1932	Earl Whitehill	7
1933	Vic Frazier	3
1934	Tommy Bridges	6
1935	T. Bridges, G. Crowder	4
1936	Tommy Bridges	6
1937	Lawson, Poffenberger	5
1938	Auker, Bridges, Kennedy	3
1939	Tommy Bridges, S. Rowe	4
1940	Schoolboy Rowe	3
1941	Hal Newhouser	2
1942	H. Newhouser, V. Trucks	2
1943	Virgil Trucks	5
1944	Hal Newhouser	3
1945	Dizzy Trout	2
1946	Virgil Trucks	4
1947	Fred Hutchinson	4
1948	F. Hutchinson, Dizzy Trout	2
1949	Hal Newhouser	4
1950	Fred Hutchinson	5
1951	Hal Newhouser	4
1952	Ted Gray, Hal Newhouser	1
1953	Ned Garver, Ted Gray	3
1954	Billy Hoeft	2
1955	Billy Hoeft, Frank Lary	3
1956	Billy Hoeft	5
1957	Duke Maas	3
1958	Hoeft, Foytack, Lary	1
1959	Jim Bunning	6
1960	Jim Bunning, Frank Lary	3

Duke Maas

Year	Pitcher(s)	Wins
1961	Don Mossi	3
1962	Jim Bunning	4
1963	Phil Regan	3
1964	M. Lolich, D. Wickersham	3
1965	Four Pitchers	2
1966	Mickey Lolich	5
1967	Joe Sparma	3
1968	Denny McLain	3
1969	Denny McLain	3
1970	Les Cain	3
1971	Joe Coleman	5
1972	Mickey Lolich	3
1973	Jim Perry	3
1974	Joe Coleman	6
1975	Joe Coleman	3
1976	Ray Bare, Dave Roberts	3
1977	Dave Rozema	4
1978	Billingham, Slaton, Wilcox	4
1979	Jack Morris	4
1980	Jack Morris	6
1981	Jack Morris, Milt Wilcox	2
1982	Jack Morris	3
1983	Dan Petry	7
1984	Dan Petry	3
1985	Dan Petry	4
1986	Jack Morris	7
1987	Dan Petry	3
1988	Frank Tanana	4
1989	Frank Tanana	2
1990	Jack Morris	6
1991	Bill Gullickson	6
1992	Mark Leiter, Frank Tanana	2
1993	Bill Gullickson, Moore	4
1994	Tim Belcher, Mike Moore	3
1995	Felipe Lira, Clint Sadowsky	2
1996	Omar Olivares	3
1997	Willie Blair	5
1998	Seth Greisinger	3
1999	Dave Mlicki	4
2000	Jeff Weaver	4
2001	Cornejo, Holt, Sparks	2
2002	Steve Sparks	3
2003	Mike Maroth	4
2004	Jeremy Bonderman	4
2005	Mike Maroth	5
2006	Nate Robertson	5
2007	Jeremy Bonderman	5
2008	Armando Galarraga	5
2009	Rick Porcello	6
2010	Porcello, Verlander	3
2011	Max Scherzer	6
2012	Rick Porcello	3
2013	Max Scherzer	3
2014	Justin Verlander	5
2015	Alfredo Simon	4
2016	Jordan Zimmermann	4
2017	Jordan Zimmermann	4
2018	M. Fiers, J. Zimmermann	3
2019	Matt Boyd	3
2020	Four Starting Pitchers	1
2021	Tarik Skubal	4

1901 Jack Cronin 9
1902 Win Mercer 9
1903 Bill Donovan, Mullin 10
1904 George Mullin 15
1905 George Mullin 7
1906 Donahue, Donovan, Mullin 4
1907 George Mullin 9
1908 George Mullin 3
1909 Ed Killian 7
1910 Ed Summers 6
1911 Bill Donovan, Ed Willett 3
1912 Ed Willett 3
1913 Hooks Dauss 8
1914 Harry Coveleski 7
1915 Harry Coveleski 9
1916 Hooks Dauss 7
1917 Howard Ehmke 7
1918 Boland, Dauss, Kallio 5
1919 B. Boland, Dutch Leonard 6
1920 Hooks Dauss 9
1921 Dutch Leonard 7
1922 Dauss, Oldham, Pillette 4
1923 Hooks Dauss 7
1924 Collins, Stoner, Whitehill 3
1925 Rip Collins 5
1926 Earl Whitehill 5
1927 Earl Whitehill 5
1928 O. Carroll, E. Whitehill 4
1929 Earl Whitehill 5
1930 George Uhle 6
1931 Art Herring 6
1932 Vic Sorrell 6
1933 Tommy Bridges 7
1934 Tommy Bridges 3
1935 Joe Sullivan 4
1936 Elden Auker 5
1937 Tommy Bridges 2
1938 Al Benton, George Gill 2
1939 Bobo Newsom, Trout 4
1940 Tommy Bridges 3
1941 Bridges, Bobo Newsom 5
1942 Al Benton 9
1943 Hal Newhouser 9
1944 Dizzy Trout 7
1945 Hal Newhouser 6

1946 Dizzy Trout 7
1947 Hal Newhouser 9
1948 Dizzy Trout 5
1949 Ted Gray 5
1950 Fred Hutchinson 4
1951 Ted Gray 6
1952 Art Houtteman, V. Trucks 7
1953 Ted Gray 6
1954 Steve Gromek 8
1955 Frank Lary 10
1956 Frank Lary 5
1957 Frank Lary, Duke Maas 5
1958 Jim Bunning 5
1959 Bunning, Foytack, Mossi 4
1960 Jim Bunning 8
1961 Jim Bunning, Don Mossi 4

Lerrin LaGrow

1962 Don Mossi 6
1963 Jim Bunning 6
1964 Phil Regan 5
1965 H. Aguirre, D. Wickersham 5
1966 Denny McLain 4
1967 Mickey Lolich 6
1968 Pat Dobson, Mickey Lolich, 3
Denny McLain, Joe Sparma, 3
Earl Wilson 3
1969 Lolich, McLain, Wilson 4
1970 Mickey Lolich 7
1971 Mickey Lolich 6
1972 J. Coleman, Mickey Lolich 9
1973 Mickey Lolich 6
1974 Lerrin LaGrow 7
1975 Ray Bare, Mickey Lolich 6

1976 Mark Fidrych 5
1977 Fernando Arroyo 5
1978 Dave Rozema, Kip Young 5
1979 Milt Wilcox 4
1980 Morris, Schatzeder, Wilcox 4
1981 Jack Morris 4
1982 Jack Morris, Jerry Ujdur 4
1983 Jack Morris 6
1984 Jack Morris 3
1985 Jack Morris 8
1986 Jack Morris, Dan Petry 3
1987 Jack Morris, Walt Terrell 3
1988 Walt Terrell 7
1989 D. Alexander, F. Tanana 7
1990 Jack Morris 7
1991 Walt Terrell 4
1992 Walt Terrell 3
1993 David Wells 3
1994 Belcher, Moore, Wells 2
1995 Jose Lima 4
1996 Felipe Lira 6
1997 Justin Thompson 8
1998 Justin Thompson 4
1999 Brian Moehler 4
2000 Jeff Weaver 7
2001 Jeff Weaver 6
2002 Steve Sparks 6
2003 J. Bonderman, M. Maroth 8
2004 J. Bonderman, J. Johnson, 4
Mike Maroth 4
2005 Mike Maroth 5
2006 Nate Robertson 7
2007 Nate Robertson 3
2008 K. Rogers, J. Verlander 2
2009 E. Jackson, J. Verlander 3
2010 Rick Porcello, J. Verlander 3
2011 Justin Verlander 4
2012 Doug Fister 4
2013 Justin Verlander 5
2014 Rick Porcello, J. Verlander 4
2015 Verlander, Randy Wolf 3
2016 Justin Verlander 4
2017 Michael Fulmer 7
2018 Francisco Liriano 5
2019 Spencer Turnbull 3
2020 Matt Boyd, Tarik Skubal 1
2021 Casey Mize 3

Year	Pitcher	Games
1901	**Ed Siever**	**5**
1902	**George Mullin**	**5**
1903	**George Mullin**	**5**
1904	**Ed Killian**	**6**
1905	**Gene Ford, Frank Kitson**	**6**
1906	**John Eubank**	**12**
1907	John Eubank, Ed Killian	7
1908	George Mullin	9
1909	**Ralph Works**	**12**
1910	**Ed Willett**	**12**
1911	**Ralph Works**	**15**
1912	Joe Lake	12
1913	**Fred House**	**17**
1914	**Alex Main**	**20**
1915	**Bernie Boland**	**27**
1916	**Bernie Boland**	**37**
1917	George Cunningham	36
1918	Deacon Jones	17
1919	Doc Ayers	19
1920	Doc Ayers	23
1921	Jim Middleton	28
1922	Ole Olsen	22
1923	**Bert Cole**	**39**
1924	Ken Holloway	35
1925	**Jess Doyle**	**42**
1926	Hooks Dauss	30
1927	George Smith	29
1928	George Smith	37
1929	Augie Prudhomme	28
1930	Charlie Sullivan	37
1931	Charlie Sullivan	27
1932	Chief Hogsett	32
1933	**Chief Hogsett**	**43**
1934	Chief Hogsett	26
1935	Chief Hogsett	40
1936	Roxie Lawson	33
1937	Jack Russell	25
1938	Slick Coffman	33
1939	Bud Thomas	27
1940	Al Benton	42
1941	Bud Thomas	25
1942	Johnny Gorsica	28
1943	Johnny Gorsica	31
1944	Boom-Boom Beck	26
1945	George Caster	22
1946	George Caster	26
1947	Johnny Gorsica	31
1948	Stubby Overmire	33
1949	Dizzy Trout	33
1950	Hal White	34
1951	Hal White	34
1952	Hal White	41
1953	Ray Herbert	40
1954	Ray Herbert	38
1955	Al Aber	38
1956	Al Aber	42
1957	Lou Sleater	41
1958	Hank Aguirre	41
1959	**Tom Morgan**	**45**
1960	Dave Sisler	41

Tom Morgan

Year	Pitcher	Games
1961	**Hank Aguirre**	**45**
1962	**Ron Nischwitz**	**48**
1963	Terry Fox	46
1964	Fred Gladding	42
1965	Fred Gladding	46
1966	**Larry Sherry**	**55**
1967	Fred Gladding	41
1968	P. Dobson, D. Patterson	37
1969	Pat Dobson	40
1970	**Tom Timmermann**	**61**
1971	**Fred Scherman**	**68**
1972	Chuck Seelbach	58
1973	John Hiller	65
1974	John Hiller	59
1975	John Hiller	36
1976	John Hiller	55
1977	Steve Foucault	44
1978	John Hiller	51
1979	Aurelio Lopez	61
1980	Aurelio Lopez	66
1981	Kevin Saucier	38
1982	Dave Tobik	50
1983	Aurelio Lopez	57
1984	**Willie Hernandez**	**80**
1985	Willie Hernandez	74
1986	Willie Hernandez	64
1987	Mike Henneman	55
1988	Mike Henneman	65
1989	Mike Henneman	60
1990	Mike Henneman	69
1991	Paul Gibson	68
1992	Mike Munoz	65
1993	Bob MacDonald	68
1994	Joe Boever	46
1995	Joe Boever	60
1996	**Mike Myers**	**83**
1997	**Mike Myers**	**88**
1998	**Sean Runyan**	**88**
1999	Doug Brocail	70
2000	Matt Anderson	69
2001	Matt Anderson	62
2002	Juan Acevedo	65
2003	Jamie Walker	78
2004	Jamie Walker	70
2005	Jamie Walker	66
2006	Fernando Rodney	63
2007	Todd Jones	63
2008	Bobby Seay	60
2009	Fernando Rodney	73
2010	Phil Coke	73
2011	Jose Valverde	75
2012	Joaquin Benoit	73
2013	Joaquin Benoit	66
2014	Al Alburquerque	72
2015	Blaine Hardy	70
2016	Justin Wilson	66
2017	Shane Greene	71
2018	Joe Jimenez	68
2019	Buck Farmer	72
2020	Jose Cisnero	29
2021	Jose Cisnero	67

YEARLY TIGER PITCHING LEADERS – WINS IN RELIEF

1901	**Emil Frisk**	**2**
1902	Arch McCarthy, J. Yeager	1
1903	**Rube Kisinger, F. Kitson**	**2**
1904	Killian, Kitson, Mullin	1
1905	**Ed Killian, Frank Kitson**	**2**
1906	Eubank, Killian, Siever	1
1907	**Ed Killian**	**5**
1908	**Ed Summers**	**5**
1909	George Mullin	4
1910	George Mullin	2
1911	Ralph Works	4
1912	**Joe Lake**	**5**
1913	Marc Hall	2
1914	Coveleski, Dauss, Dubuc	2
1915	Harry Coveleski	4
1916	Hooks Dauss	4
1917	Bernie Boland, Bill James	2
1918	George Cunningham	2
1919	Slim Love	3
1920	J. Bogart, A. Conkwright	2
1921	Jim Middleton	4
1922	**Howard Ehmke**	**7**
1923	**Bert Cole**	**7**
1924	**Ken Holloway**	**9**
1925	Jess Doyle, Ken Holloway	4
1926	**Hooks Dauss**	**11**
1927	George Smith	4
1928	Elam Vangilder	6
1929	Earl Whitehill	4
1930	Chief Hogsett	3
1931	George Uhle	4
1932	Chief Hogsett	6
1933	Chief Hogsett	6
1934	Firpo Marberry	7
1935	Chief Hogsett	6
1936	Roxie Lawson	5
1937	George Gill	7
1938	Harry Eisenstat	6
1939	Bud Thomas	7
1940	Al Benton	6
1941	Al Benton	6
1942	Virgil Trucks	4
1943	Johnny Gorsica	4
1944	Hal Newhouser	4
1945	George Caster	5
1946	George Caster	2

1947	Hal White	4
1948	Virgil Trucks	4
1949	Art Houtteman	3
	F. Hutchinson, D. Trout	3
1950	Hal White	6
1951	Ray Herbert,	4
	F. Hutchinson, V. Trucks	4
1952	Hal Newhouser	3
1953	Ray Herbert	4
1954	Dick Marlowe	5
1955	Al Aber	6
1956	Al Aber, Jim Bunning	4
1957	Harry Byrd	4
1958	Hank Aguirre, Al Cicotte,	2
	Bill Fischer, Tom Morgan	2
1959	Ray Narleski	2

Buck Farmer

1960	Dave Sisler	7
1961	Terry Fox	5
1962	H. Aguirre, Ron Nischwitz	4
1963	Terry Fox	8
1964	F. Gladding, Larry Sherry	7
1965	Terry Fox, Fred Gladding	6
1966	Larry Sherry	8
1967	Fred Gladding	6
1968	Fred Lasher	5
1969	Pat Dobson, John Hiller,	3
	McMahon, Timmermann	3
1970	Daryl Patterson	7
1971	Fred Scherman	10
1972	Chuck Seelbach	9
1973	John Hiller	10
1974	**John Hiller**	**17**
1975	J. Hiller, Dave Lemanczyk	2
1976	John Hiller	11
1977	Steve Foucault	7
1978	John Hiller	9
1979	Aurelio Lopez	10
1980	Aurelio Lopez	13
1981	Kevin Saucier	4
1982	Dave Rucker, Dave Tobik	4
1983	Aurelio Lopez	9
1984	Aurelio Lopez	10
1985	Willie Hernandez	8
1986	Willie Hernandez	8
1987	Mike Henneman	11
1988	Mike Henneman	9
1989	Mike Henneman	11
1990	Mike Henneman	8
1991	Mike Henneman	10
1992	John Kiely, Walt Terrell	4
1993	Mike Henneman	5
1994	Joe Boever	9
1995	Joe Boever, John Doherty	5
1996	Jose Lima	5
1997	Todd Jones	5
1998	M. Anderson, D. Brocail	5
1999	Doug Brocail, Todd Jones	4
2000	Brocail, Cruz, Patterson	5
2001	Danny Patterson	5
2002	Julio Santana	3
2003	Jamie Walker	4
2004	Ugueth Urbina	4
2005	F. German, Jamie Walker	4
2006	Fernando Rodney	7
2007	Jason Grilli	5
2008	T. Jones, Aquilina Lopez	4
2009	Brandon Lyon, Bobby Seay	6
2010	Phil Coke	7
2011	Al Alburquerque	6
2012	J. Benoit, Octavio Dotel	5
2013	Drew Smyly	6
2014	Phil Coke, Joe Nathan	5
2015	Blaine Hardy	5
2016	Bruce Rondon	5
2017	Shane Greene	4
2018	Joe Jimenez	5
2019	Buck Farmer	6
2020	Jose Cisnero, Daniel Norris	3
2021	Kyle Funkhouser	7

YEARLY TIGER PITCHING LEADERS – LOSSES IN RELIEF

1901	Seven Pitchers	0
1902	**Joe Yeager**	**2**
1903	Eason, Kitson, Mullin	1
1904	**Ed Killian**	**2**
1905	E. Cicotte, George Disch	1
	B. Donovan, George Mullin	1
1906	John Eubank	1
1907	Seven Pitchers	0
1908	Siever, Suggs, Ed Willett	1
1909	**Ed Willett**	**2**
1910	**Hub Pernoll, Ed Willett**	**2**
1911	**Ed Willett**	**3**
1912	Joe Lake	2
1913	**Marc Hall**	**3**
1914	**Marc Hall**	**3**
1915	Coveleski, Dauss, Dubuc	2
1916	Jean Dubuc	2
1917	B. Boland, Deacon Jones	2
1918	**Hooks Dauss**	**3**
1919	Doc Ayers	2
1920	**Hooks Dauss**	**3**
1921	**Jim Middleton**	**8**
1922	Red Oldham, Lil Stoner	3
1923	Ray Francis	4
1924	Hooks Dauss	5
1925	Jess Doyle	5
1926	Collins, Dauss, Holloway	3
1927	Lil Stoner	3
1928	Elam Vangilder	4
1929	Ownie Carroll	3
1930	Guy Cantrell, Whit Wyatt	3
1931	Art Herring	4
1932	Chief Hogsett	3
1933	**Chief Hogsett**	**9**
1934	Elden Auker	4
1935	Chief Hogsett	6
1936	Roxie Lawson	5
1937	Jack Russell	5
1938	T. Bridges, Slick Coffman	3
1939	Al Benton	3
1940	**Al Benton**	**10**
1941	Benton, Thomas, Trout	2
1942	Roy Henshaw, Hal White	3
1943	Johnny Gorsica	3
1944	J. Gorsica, Hal Newhouser	2
1945	Art Houtteman	2
1946	A. Benton, S. Overmire	3
1947	Virgil Trucks, Hal White	2
1948	Stubby Overmire	3
1949	Dizzy Trout	6
1950	Hal White	3
1951	Gene Bearden	3
1952	Hal White	8
1953	Ray Herbert	4
1954	Ralph Branca, Ray Herbert	3
1955	George Zuverink	4
1956	Al Aber	4
1957	A. Aber, H. Byrd, L. Sleater	3
1958	Tom Morgan	5
1959	Ray Narleski	6
1960	Dave Sisler	5

Joe Yeager

1961	Hank Aguirre	4
1962	Ron Nischwitz	5
1963	Terry Fox	6
1964	Larry Sherry	5
1965	Orlando Pena, Larry Sherry	6
1966	Larry Sherry	5
1967	Fred Gladding	4
1968	P. Dobson, Daryl Patterson	3
1969	Pat Dobson	6
1970	Tom Timmermann	7
1971	Scherman, Timmermann	6
1972	Chuck Seelbach	5
1973	John Hiller	5
1974	**John Hiller**	**14**
1975	Gene Pentz	4
1976	John Hiller	8
1977	John Hiller	9
1978	Foucault, Hiller, Morris	4
1979	John Hiller	7
1980	Aurelio Lopez	5
1981	Kevin Saucier, Dave Tobik	2
1982	Dave Tobik	8
1983	Aurelio Lopez	8
1984	Willie Hernandez	3
1985	Willie Hernandez	10
1986	Willie Hernandez	7
1987	Eric King	7
1988	Mike Henneman	6
1989	Mike Henneman, Ed Nunez	4
1990	Mike Henneman	6
1991	Paul Gibson	7
1992	Mike Henneman	6
1993	Tom Bolton	4
1994	Storm Davis	4
1995	Joe Boever, John Doherty	7
1996	Richie Lewis	6
1997	Todd Jones, Mike Myers	4
1998	Todd Jones, Sean Runyan	4
1999	Doug Brocail, Todd Jones	4
2000	Doug Brocail, Todd Jones	4
2001	Todd Jones	5
2002	Juan Acevedo, J. Santana	5
2003	Steve Sparks	6
2004	U. Urbina, Esteban Yan	6
2005	Chris Spurling	4
2006	Todd Jones	6
2007	Fernando Rodney	6
2008	Fernando Rodney	6
2009	B. Lyon, Fernando Rodney	5
2010	Phil Coke, Ryan Perry	5
2011	Jose Valverde	4
2012	Brayan Villarreal	5
2013	Phil Coke	5
2014	Joba Chamberlain	5
2015	B. Hardy, I. Krol, A. Wilson	3
2016	Justin Wilson	5
2017	Fr. Rodriguez, Alex Wilson	5
2018	Shane Greene	6
2019	Joe Jimenez	7
2020	Jose Cisnero, Joe Jimenez	3
2021	J. Cisnero, M. Fulmer	4
	Kyle Funkhouser	4

YEARLY TIGER PITCHING LEADERS – RELIEF WIN PERCENTAGE (MINIMUM 4 DECISIONS)

Year	Pitcher	Pct.	W-L
1901	No Qualified Pitchers		
1902	No Qualified Pitchers		
1903	No Qualified Pitchers		
1904	No Qualified Pitchers		
1905	No Qualified Pitchers		
1906	No Qualified Pitchers		
1907	**Ed Killian**	**1.000**	**5-0**
1908	**Ed Summers**	**1.000**	**5-0**
	George Mullin	**1.000**	**3-0**
1909	**George Mullin**	**1.000**	**4-0**
1910	Ed Willett	.333	1-2
1911	**Ralph Works**	**1.000**	**4-0**
1912	Joe Lake	.714	5-2
1913	Joe Lake	.800	4-1
1914	Hooks Dauss	.500	2-2
1915	Boland, Coveleski	.667	4-2
1916	**Bernie Boland**	**1.000**	**5-0**
	Hooks Dauss	**1.000**	**4-0**
1917	B. Boland, D. Jones	.500	2-2
1918	Hooks Dauss	.250	1-3
1919	Slim Love	.750	3-1
1920	Hooks Dauss	.250	1-3
1921	H. Ehmke, S. Parks	.600	3-2
1922	Syl Johnson	.750	3-1
1923	Bert Cole	.700	7-3
1924	Ken Holloway	.900	9-1
1925	**Ken Holloway**	**1.000**	**4-0**
1926	Hooks Dauss	.786	1-3
1927	George Smith	.800	4-1
1928	Elam Vangilder	.600	6-4
1929	Earl Whitehill	.800	4-1
1930	Chief Hogsett	.750	3-1
1931	George Uhle	.571	4-3
1932	Chief Hogsett	.667	6-3
1933	Carl Fischer	.833	5-1
1934	**Firpo Marberry**	**1.000**	**7-0**
1935	Chief Hogsett	.500	5-5
1936	Roxie Lawson	.500	5-5
1937	George Gill	.875	7-1
1938	Harry Eisenstat	.750	6-2
1939	**Bud Thomas**	**1.000**	**7-0**
1940	**Archie McKain**	**1.000**	**5-0**
1941	J. Gorsica, S. Rowe	.800	4-1
1942	Al Benton	.500	2-2
1943	Prince Oana	.600	3-2
1944	Hal Newhouser	.667	4-2
1945	George Caster	.833	5-1

Year	Pitcher	Pct.	W-L
1946	Stubby Overmire	.250	1-3
1947	Fred Hutchinson	.750	3-1
1948	Virgil Trucks	.667	4-2
1949	Art Houtteman	.600	3-2
	Fred Hutchinson	.600	3-2
1950	**Fred Hutchinson**	**1.000**	**4-0**
1951	**Ray Herbert**	**1.000**	**4-0**
1952	Dizzy Trout	.250	1-3
1953	Dick Marlowe	.750	3-1
1954	Dick Marlowe	.714	5-2
1955	Babe Birrer	.750	3-1
1956	**Jim Bunning**	**1.000**	**4-0**
1957	Paul Foytack	.600	3-2
1958	Hank Aguirre	.500	2-2
1959	Burnside, Morgan,	.250	1-3
	Ray Narleski	.250	2-6
	Dave Sisler	.250	1-3

Drew Smyly

Year	Pitcher	Pct.	W-L
1960	Pete Burnside	.750	3-1
1961	Terry Fox	.714	5-2
1962	Terry Fox	.750	3-1
1963	Terry Fox	.571	8-6
1964	Ed Rakow	.833	5-1
1965	Fred Gladding	.750	6-2
1966	**Fred Gladding**	**1.000**	**5-0**
1967	Dave Wickersham	.800	4-1
1968	**Mickey Lolich**	**1.000**	**4-0**
1969	John Hiller	.750	3-1
1970	Daryl Patterson	.875	7-1
1971	Fred Scherman	.625	10-6
1972	Fred Scherman	.875	7-1
1973	John Hiller	.667	10-5
	Bob Miller	.667	4-2
1974	John Hiller	.548	17-14
1975	John Hiller	.400	2-3

Year	Pitcher	Pct.	W-L
1976	Steve Grilli	.750	3-1
1977	Jim Crawford	.556	5-4
1978	Bob Sykes	.750	3-1
1979	Aurelio Lopez	.667	10-5
1980	Aurelio Lopez	.722	13-5
1981	Aurelio Lopez	.750	3-1
1982	A. Lopez, K. Saucier	.750	3-1
1983	Doug Bair	.667	6-3
1984	Aurelio Lopez	.909	10-1
1985	Bill Scherrer	.600	3-2
1986	Willie Hernandez	.533	8-7
1987	Mike Henneman	.786	11-3
1988	Mike Henneman	.600	9-6
	Paul Gibson	.600	3-2
1989	Mike Henneman	.733	11-4
1990	Ed Nunez	.750	3-1
1991	Mike Henneman	.833	10-2
1992	John Kiely	.667	4-2
1993	Mike Henneman	.625	5-3
1994	Joe Boever	.818	9-2
1995	**Mike Christopher**	**1.000**	**4-0**
1996	Jose Lima	.714	5-2
1997	Dan Miceli	.600	3-2
1998	Matt Anderson	.833	5-1
1999	D. Brocail, T. Jones	.500	4-4
2000	Danny Patterson	.833	5-1
2001	Matt Anderson	.750	3-1
2002	Kyle Farnsworth	.400	2-3
2003	Jamie Walker	.571	4-3
2004	Craig Dingman	.500	2-2
2005	**Franklyn German**	**1.000**	**4-0**
2006	Joel Zumaya	.667	6-3
2007	Wilfredo Ledezma	.750	3-1
2008	T. Jones, Aq. Lopez	.800	4-1
2009	Bobby Seay	.667	6-3
2010	**Eddie Bonine**	**1.000**	**4-0**
2011	Al Alburquerque	.857	6-1
2012	J. Benoit, O. Dotel	.625	5-3
2013	**Drew Smyly**	**1.000**	**6-0**
2014	Al Alburquerque	.750	3-1
2015	Al Alburquerque	.800	4-1
2016	**Alex Wilson**	**1.000**	**4-0**
2017	Warwick Saupold	.600	3-2
2018	Coleman, Saupold	.800	4-1
2019	Victor Alcantara	.600	3-2
2020	Tyler Alexander	.500	2-2
	Jose Cisnero	.500	3-3
2021	Joe Jimenez	.857	6-1

Year	Pitcher(s)	Holds
1916	**13 Pitchers**	**0**
1917	**Nine Pitchers**	**0**
1918	**16 Pitchers**	**0**
1919	**Hooks Dauss**	**1**
1920	**Red Oldham**	**1**
1921	**Holling, Perritt, Sutherland**	**1**
1922	**Red Oldham**	**1**
1923	**Bert Cole, Herman Pillette**	**1**
1924	**B. Cole, H. Dauss, E. Wells**	**1**
1925	**Bert Cole, Ed Wells**	**1**
1926	**Rip Collins, Lil Stoner**	**1**
1927	**George Smith**	**1**
1928	**Elam Vangilder**	**1**
1929	**Augie Prudhomme**	**1**
1930	**Chief Hogsett**	**1**
1931	**Tommy Bridges**	**1**
1932	10 Pitchers	0
1933	**Carl Fischer**	**1**
1934	**Red Phillips**	**1**
1935	**Elden Auker, Chief Hogsett**	**1**
1936	**Chad Kimsey**	**2**
1937	13 Pitchers	0
1938	14 Pitchers	0
1939	19 Pitchers	0
1940	17 Pitchers	0
1941	15 Pitchers	0
1942	Hal Manders, S. Rowe	1
1943	Hal White	1
1944	Dizzy Trout	1
1945	T. Bridges, George Caster,	1
	Zeb Eaton, Les Mueller	1
1946	S. Overmire, Hal White	1
1947	10 Pitchers	0
1948	**Al Benton**	**2**
1949	Dizzy Trout	1
1950	Calvert, Hutchinson, Trout	1
1951	Virgil Trucks, Hal White	1
1952	**Billy Hoeft**	**2**
1953	**Dave Madison**	**2**
1954	**Al Aber, Ray Herbert**	**2**

Year	Pitcher(s)	Holds
1955	Al Aber, Babe Birrer,	1
	Leo Cristante, Paul Foytack	1
1956	**Al Aber**	**4**
1957	Al Aber, Lou Sleater	2
1958	Hank Aguirre	3
1959	**Pete Burnside, Dave Sisler**	**4**
1960	Burnside, Labine, Sisler	1
1961	Terry Fox	3
1962	Ron Nischwitz	3
1963	F. Gladding, Willie Smith	2
1964	Julio Navarro	2
1965	F. Gladding, Larry Sherry	3
1966	**Larry Sherry**	**5**
1967	Hank Aguirre, Fred Lasher	2

Larry Sherry

Year	Pitcher(s)	Holds
1968	John Hiller	3
1969	**John Hiller**	**5**
1970	Fred Scherman	3
1971	B. Denehy, T. Timmermann	3
1972	Fred Scherman	2
1973	Lerrin LaGrow, Bob Miller,	1
	F. Scherman, C. Seelbach	1
1974	John Hiller	4
1975	Hiller, Reynolds, T. Walker	1
1976	Crawford, Grilli, Hiller	1
1977	S. Foucault, Bruce Taylor	3
1978	17 Pitchers	0
1979	Lopez, Tobik, Underwood	1
1980	**Pat Underwood**	**6**
1981	Kevin Saucier	5
1982	Larry Pashnick, D. Rucker	3
1983	John Martin	3
1984	Doug Bair, Bill Scherrer	5
1985	Aurelio Lopez	5
1986	Bill Campbell	3
1987	**Mike Henneman, E. King**	**6**
1988	**Willie Hernandez**	**8**
1989	M. Henneman, Fr. Williams	5
1990	**Paul Gibson**	**9**
1991	**Paul Gibson**	**10**
1992	**Mike Munoz**	**16**
1993	**Bob Macdonald**	**16**
1994	Buddy Groom	11
1995	Brian Bohanon	9
1996	**Mike Myers**	**17**
1997	**Mike Myers**	**18**
1998	D. Brocail, Sean Runyan	11
1999	**Doug Brocail**	**23**
2000	Doug Brocail	19
2001	Danny Patterson	16
2002	Oscar Henriquez	9
2003	Jamie Walker	12
2004	Jamie Walker	17
2005	Kyle Farnsworth	15
2006	**Joel Zumaya**	**30**
2007	Fernando Rodney	12
2008	Bobby Seay	13
2009	Bobby Seay	28
2010	Ryan Perry	19
2011	Joaquin Benoit	29
2012	**Joaquin Benoit**	**30**
2013	Drew Smyly	21
2014	Joba Chamberlain	29
2015	Blaine Hardy	13
2016	Justin Wilson	25
2017	Alex Wilson	17
2018	Joe Jimenez	23
2019	Buck Farmer, Joe Jimenez	15
2020	Jose Cisnero, Buck Farmer	7
2021	Jose Cisnero	18

YEARLY TIGER PITCHING LEADERS – GAMES FINISHED

Year	Pitcher	GF
1901	**Ed Siever**	**5**
1902	Cronin, Mullin, Yeager	4
1903	**George Mullin**	**5**
1904	**Ed Killian**	**6**
1905	**Gene Ford**	**6**
1906	**John Eubank**	**12**
1907	Ed Killian	8
1908	G. Mullin, E. Summers	8
1909	Ralph Works	10
1910	Ed Willett	10
1911	Ralph Works	10
1912	Dubuc, Lake, Works	11
1913	**Joe Lake**	**13**
1914	**Pug Cavet**	**13**
1915	**Bernie Boland**	**16**
1916	**Jean Dubuc**	**16**
1917	**George Cunningham**	**25**
1918	George Cunningham	12
1919	George Cunningham	15
1920	Doc Ayers	16
1921	Jim Middleton	20
1922	Dauss, Johnson, Olsen	13
1923	**Bert Cole**	**26**
1924	Ken Holloway	22
1925	**Jess Doyle**	**34**
1926	Hooks Dauss	23
1927	O. Carroll, George Smith	13
1928	G. Smith. Elam Vangilder	21
1929	Emil Yde	16
1930	Charlie Sullivan	18
1931	Charlie Sullivan	19
1932	Chief Hogsett	28
1933	**Chief Hogsett**	**34**
1934	Chief Hogsett	16
1935	Chief Hogsett	30
1936	Chad Kimsey	17
1937	George Gill	18
1938	Harry Eisenstat	17
1939	Al Benton	18
1940	**Al Benton**	**35**
1941	Al Benton	19
1942	Johnny Gorsica	19
1943	Johnny Gorsica	18
1944	Boom-Boom Beck	15
1945	George Caster	10
1946	George Caster	19
1947	Johnny Gorsica	16
1948	Stubby Overmire	16
1949	Dizzy Trout	24
1950	Paul Calvert	19
1951	Hal White	19
1952	Hal White	31
1953	Ray Herbert	22
1954	Bob Miller	22
1955	Al Aber	22
1956	Al Aber	28
1957	Lou Sleater	19
1958	Hank Aguirre	16
1959	Tom Morgan	22
1960	Dave Sisler	19
1961	Terry Fox	25
1962	Terry Fox	28
1963	Terry Fox	29
1964	Larry Sherry	24
1965	Terry Fox, Fred Gladding	25
1966	**Larry Sherry**	**39**
1967	Fred Gladding	25
1968	Daryl Patterson	22
1969	Pat Dobson	22
1970	**Tom Timmermann**	**43**
1971	Fred Scherman	40
1972	Chuck Seelbach	34
1973	**John Hiller**	**60**
1974	John Hiller	52
1975	John Hiller	34
1976	John Hiller	46
1977	Steve Foucault	34
1978	John Hiller	46
1979	Aurelio Lopez	49
1980	Aurelio Lopez	59
1981	Kevin Saucier	23
1982	Dave Tobik	31
1983	Aurelio Lopez	46
1984	**Willie Hernandez**	**68**
1985	Willie Hernandez	64
1986	Willie Hernandez	53
1987	Willie Hernandez	31
1988	Mike Henneman	51
1989	Mike Henneman	35
1990	Mike Henneman	53
1991	Mike Henneman	50
1992	Mike Henneman	53
1993	Mike Henneman	50
1994	Joe Boever	27
1995	Joe Boever	27
1996	Gregg Olson	28
1997	Todd Jones	51
1998	Todd Jones	53
1999	Todd Jones	62
2000	Todd Jones	60
2001	Matt Anderson	41
2002	Juan Acevedo	48
2003	Steve Sparks	24
2004	Ugueth Urbina	46
2005	Fernando Rodney	26
2006	Todd Jones	56
2007	Todd Jones	54
2008	Todd Jones	37
2009	Fernando Rodney	65
2010	Jose Valverde	55
2011	**Jose Valverde**	**70**
2012	Jose Valverde	67
2013	Joaquin Benoit	43
2014	Joe Nathan	54
2015	Joakim Soria	35
2016	Francisco Rodriguez	55
2017	Shane Greene, J. Wilson	26
2018	Shane Greene	58
2019	Shane Greene	32
2020	Bryan Garcia	12
2021	Gregory Soto	38

Chuck Seelbach

Year	Pitcher	Saves
1901	**Roscoe Miller, Joe Yeager**	**1**
1902	**Mercer, Miller, Siever**	**1**
1903	**George Mullin**	**2**
1904	Ed Killian, Frank Kitson	1
1905	Frank Kitson	1
1906	**John Eubank, Ed Killian**	**2**
1907	**George Mullin**	**3**
1908	Five Players	1
1909	Bill Donovan, Ralph Works	2
1910	**Frank Browning**	**3**
1911	Ed Lafitte, Ed Summers	1
	Ed Willett	1
1912	**Jean Dubuc**	**3**
1913	Jean Dubuc	2
1914	**Hooks Dauss**	**4**
1915	**Coveleski, Oldham, Steen**	**4**
1916	**Hooks Dauss**	**4**
1917	**Bernie Boland**	**6**
1918	Hooks Dauss	3
1919	Four Players	1
1920	Howard Ehmke	3
1921	**Jim Middleton**	**7**
1922	Hooks Dauss	4
1923	Bert Cole	5
1924	Hooks Dauss	6
1925	**Jess Doyle**	**8**
1926	**Hooks Dauss**	**9**
1927	Ken Holloway	6
1928	Elam Vangilder	5
1929	Lil Stoner	4
1930	Charlie Sullivan	5
1931	C. Hogsett, George Uhle	2
1932	Chief Hogsett	7
1933	**Chief Hogsett**	**9**
1934	Chief Hogsett, F. Marberry	3
1935	Chief Hogsett	5
1936	Kimsey, Lawson, Rowe	3
1937	Jack Russell	4
1938	Harry Eisenstat	4
1939	Al Benton	5
1940	**Al Benton**	**17**
1941	Al Benton	7
1942	Hal Newhouser	5
1943	Dizzy Trout	6
1944	Johnny Gorsica	4

Year	Pitcher	Saves
1945	Stubby Overmire	4
1946	George Caster	4
1947	Al Benton	7
1948	Art Houtteman	10
1949	Virgil Trucks	4
1950	Calvert, Houtteman, Trout	4
1951	Dizzy Trout	5
1952	Hal White	5
1953	Ray Herbert	6
1954	George Zuverink	4
1955	Al Aber, Babe Birrer,	3
	Joe Coleman	3
1956	Al Aber	7
1957	Duke Maas	6
1958	Hank Aguirre	5
1959	Tom Morgan	9

Jim Middleton

Year	Pitcher	Saves
1960	Hank Aguirre	10
1961	Terry Fox	12
1962	Terry Fox	16
1963	Terry Fox	11
1964	Larry Sherry	11
1965	Terry Fox	10
1966	**Larry Sherry**	**20**
1967	Fred Gladding	12
1968	Pat Dobson, D. Patterson	7
1969	Don McMahon	11
1970	**Tom Timmermann**	**27**
1971	Fred Scherman	20
1972	Chuck Seelbach	14
1973	**John Hiller**	**38**
1974	John Hiller	13
1975	John Hiller	14

Year	Pitcher	Saves
1976	John Hiller	13
1977	Steve Foucault	13
1978	John Hiller	15
1979	Aurelio Lopez	21
1980	Aurelio Lopez	21
1981	Kevin Saucier	13
1982	Dave Tobik	9
1983	Aurelio Lopez	18
1984	Willie Hernandez	32
1985	Willie Hernandez	31
1986	Willie Hernandez	24
1987	Eric King	9
1988	Mike Henneman	22
1989	Willie Hernandez	15
1990	Mike Henneman	22
1991	Mike Henneman	21
1992	Mike Henneman	24
1993	Mike Henneman	24
1994	Mike Henneman	8
1995	Mike Henneman	18
1996	Gregg Olson	8
1997	Todd Jones	31
1998	Todd Jones	28
1999	Todd Jones	30
2000	**Todd Jones**	**42**
2001	Matt Anderson	22
2002	Juan Acevedo	28
2003	F. German, Chris Mears	5
2004	Ugueth Urbina	21
2005	F. Rodney, Ugueth Urbina	9
2006	Todd Jones	37
2007	Todd Jones	38
2008	Todd Jones	18
2009	Fernando Rodney	37
2010	Jose Valverde	26
2011	**Jose Valverde**	**49**
2012	Jose Valverde	35
2013	Joaquin Benoit	24
2014	Joe Nathan	35
2015	Joaquim Soria	23
2016	Francisco Rodriguez	44
2017	Justin Wilson	13
2018	Shane Greene	32
2019	Shane Greene	22
2020	Joe Jimenez	5
2021	Gregory Soto	18

DECADE TIGER HITTING LEADERS

PLAYER OF THE DECADE

1900s	Ty Cobb
1910s	Ty Cobb
1920s	Ty Cobb
1930s	Hank Greenberg
1940s	Hank Greenberg
1950s	Al Kaline
1960s	Al Kaline
1970s	Steve Kemp
1980s	Kirk Gibson
1990s	Lou Whitaker
2000s	Miguel Cabrera
2010s	Miguel Cabrera

AT-BATS

1900s	Sam Crawford	4,012
1910s	Donie Bush	5,462
1920s	Harry Heilmann	5,285
1930s	Charlie Gehringer	5,629
1940s	Rudy York	3,504
1950s	Harvey Kuenn	4,372
1960s	Norm Cash	4,819
1970s	Aurelio Rodriguez	4,352
1980s	Lou Whitaker	5,282
1990s	Travis Fryman	4,297
2000s	Brandon Inge	3,823
2010s	Miguel Cabrera	5,028

HITS

1900s	Sam Crawford	1,221
1910s	Ty Cobb	1,948
1920s	Harry Heilmann	1,924
1930s	Charlie Gehringer	1,865
1940s	Rudy York	962
1950s	Harvey Kuenn	1,372
1960s	Al Kaline	1,399
1970s	Aurelio Rodriguez	1,040
1980s	Alan Trammell	1,504
1990s	Travis Fryman	1,176
2000s	Brandon Inge	901
2010s	Miguel Cabrera	1,595

GAMES

1900s	Sam Crawford	1,038
1910s	Donie Bush	1,450
1920s	Harry Heilmann	1,417
1930s	Charlie Gehringer	1,434
1940s	Rudy York	924
1950s	Harvey Kuenn	1,049
1960s	Norm Cash	1,442
1970s	Aurelio Rodriguez	1,241
1980s	Lou Whitaker	1,418
1990s	Travis Fryman	1,096
2000s	Brandon Inge	1,153
2010s	Miguel Cabrera	1,360

Placido Polanco

SINGLES

1900s	Sam Crawford	866
1910s	Ty Cobb	1,427
1920s	Harry Heilmann	1,284
1930s	Charlie Gehringer	1,243
1940s	Doc Cramer	631
1950s	Harvey Kuenn	1,032
1960s	Al Kaline	911
1970s	Ron LeFlore	755
1980s	Alan Trammell	1,068
1990s	Travis Fryman	769
2000s	Placido Polanco	617
2010s	Miguel Cabrera	998

PLATE APPEARANCES

1900s	Sam Crawford	4,408
1910s	Donie Bush	6,580
1920s	Harry Heilmann	6,115
1930s	Charlie Gehringer	6,492
1940s	Rudy York	3,993
1950s	Harvey Kuenn	4,750
1960s	Norm Cash	5,704
1970s	Aurelio Rodriguez	4,646
1980s	Lou Whitaker	6,042
1990s	Travis Fryman	4,792
2000s	Brandon Inge	4,293
2010s	Miguel Cabrera	5,795

RUNS

1900s	Sam Crawford	562
1910s	Ty Cobb	1,051
1920s	Harry Heilmann	962
1930s	Charlie Gehringer	1,179
1940s	Rudy York	515
1950s	Harvey Kuenn	620
1960s	Al Kaline	811
1970s	Ron LeFlore	532
1980s	Alan Trammell	815
1990s	Travis Fryman	607
2000s	Brandon Inge	449
2010s	Miguel Cabrera	799

DOUBLES

1900s	Sam Crawford	210
1910s	Ty Cobb	313
1920s	Harry Heilmann	397
1930s	Charlie Gehringer	400
1940s	Rudy York	175
1950s	Harvey Kuenn	244
1960s	Al Kaline	247
1970s	Aurelio Rodriguez	193
1980s	Alan Trammell	267
1990s	Travis Fryman	229
2000s	Brandon Inge	173
2010s	Miguel Cabrera	324

DECADE TIGER HITTING LEADERS

TRIPLES

1900s	Sam Crawford	114
1910s	Ty Cobb	161
1920s	Harry Heilmann	101
1930s	Charlie Gehringer	76
1940s	Barney McCosky	38
1950s	Harvey Kuenn	43
1960s	Dick McAuliffe	59
1970s	Ron LeFlore	38
1980s	Lou Whitaker	43
1990s	Travis Fryman	29
2000s	Curtis Granderson	57
2010s	Austin Jackson	43

HIT BY PITCH

1900s	Bill Coughlin	30
1910s	Ty Cobb	46
1920s	Heinie Manush	45
1930s	Charlie Gehringer	29
1940s	Hoot Evers	14
1950s	Fred Hatfield	18
1960s	Bill Freehan	72
1970s	Bill Freehan	42
1980s	Chet Lemon	83
1990s	Damion Easley	52
2000s	Brandon Inge	59
2010s	Miguel Cabrera	30

ON-BASE PERCENTAGE

1900s	Jimmy Barrett	.382
1910s	Ty Cobb	.457
1920s	Ty Cobb	.435
1930s	Hank Greenberg	.415
1940s	Roy Cullenbine	.419
1950s	George Kell	.391
1960s	Al Kaline	.381
1970s	S. Kemp, Lou Whitaker	.376
1980s	D. Evans, A. Trammell	.357
1990s	Tony Phillips	.395
2000s	Magglio Ordonez	.382
2010s	Miguel Cabrera	.399

HOME RUNS

1900s	Sam Crawford	31
1910s	Ty Cobb	47
1920s	Harry Heilmann	142
1930s	Hank Greenberg	206
1940s	Rudy York	151
1950s	Al Kaline	125
1960s	Norm Cash	278
1970s	Willie Horton	121
1980s	Lance Parrish	176
1990s	Cecil Fielder	245
2000s	Brandon Inge	123
2010s	Miguel Cabrera	268

Fred Hatfield

SLUGGING PERCENTAGE

1900s	Ty Cobb	.459
1910s	Ty Cobb	.541
1920s	Harry Heilmann	.558
1930s	Hank Greenberg	.617
1940s	Hank Greenberg	.613
1950s	Vic Wertz	.517
1960s	Rocky Colavito	.501
1970s	Norm Cash	.469
1980s	Lance Parrish	.505
1990s	Tony Clark	.503
2000s	Magglio Ordonez	.495
2010s	J.D. Martinez	.551

RUNS BATTED IN

1900s	Sam Crawford	567
1910s	Ty Cobb	828
1920s	Harry Heilmann	1,133
1930s	Charlie Gehringer	1,003
1940s	Rudy York	638
1950s	Al Kaline	544
1960s	Norm Cash	830
1970s	Willie Horton	425
1980s	Alan Trammell	637
1990s	Cecil Fielder	758
2000s	Brandon Inge	494
2010s	Miguel Cabrera	941

REACHED ON ERROR

1920s	Harry Heilmann	57
1930s	Pete Fox	85
1940s	Rudy York	54
1950s	Harvey Kuenn	70
1960s	Al Kaline	88
1970s	Mickey Stanley	75
1980s	Alan Trammell	79
1990s	Travis Fryman	59
2000s	Brandon Inge	43
2010s	Austin Jackson	35

ON BASE PLUS SLUGGING

1900s	Ty Cobb	.839
1910s	Ty Cobb	.998
1920s	Harry Heilmann	.991
1930s	Hank Greenberg	1.032
1940s	Hank Greenberg	1.018
1950s	Vic Wertz	.904
1960s	Norm Cash	.878
1970s	Norm Cash	.831
1980s	Kirk Gibson	.838
1990s	Mickey Tettleton	.867
2000s	Magglio Ordonez	.876
2010s	Miguel Cabrera	.943

DECADE TIGER HITTING LEADERS

ON BASE PLUS SLUGGING PLUS

1900s	Ty Cobb	163
1910s	Ty Cobb	192
1920s	Harry Heilmann	156
1930s	Hank Greenberg	159
1940s	Hank Greenberg	165
1950s	Vic Wertz	140
1960s	Norm Cash	142
1970s	Norm Cash	132
1980s	Kirk Gibson	129
1990s	Mickey Tettleton	135
2000s	Carlos Guillen	124
2010s	Miguel Cabrera	153

WINS ABOVE REPLACEMENT

1900s	Sam Crawford	33.4
1910s	Ty Cobb	84.3
1920s	Harry Heilmann	56.8
1930s	Charlie Gehringer	61.1
1940s	Hal Newhouser	54.6
1950s	Al Kaline	33.3
1960s	Al Kaline	48.6
1970s	Mickey Lolich	33.2
1980s	Alan Trammell	52.7
1990s	Travis Fryman	27.3
2000s	Curtis Granderson	21.2
2010s	Miguel Cabrera	43.5

DEFENSIVE WAR

1900s	Boss Schmidt	5.6
1910s	Ossie Vitt	4.5
1920s	Johnny Bassler	5.0
1930s	Billy Rogell	13.0
1940s	Eddie Mayo	5.0
1950s	Al Kaline	5.9
1960s	Bill Freehan	6.4
1970s	Aurelio Rodriguez	8.6
1980s	Alan Trammell	17.3
1990s	Travis Fryman	6.8
2000s	Brandon Inge	12.1
2010s	Ian Kinsler	6.4

TOTAL AVERAGE

1900s	Ty Cobb	.922
1910s	Ty Cobb	1.279
1920s	Harry Heilmann	1.054
1930s	Hank Greenberg	1.140
1940s	Hank Greenberg	1.079
1950s	Vic Wertz	.918
1960s	Norm Cash	.898
1970s	Norm Cash	.820
1980s	Kirk Gibson	.865
1990s	Mickey Tettleton	.912
2000s	Carlos Guillen	.835
2010s	Miguel Cabrera	.954

Steve Kemp

BATTERS RUN AVERAGE

1900s	Ty Cobb	.174
1910s	Ty Cobb	.247
1920s	Harry Heilmann	.241
1930s	Hank Greenberg	.256
1940s	Hank Greenberg	.248
1950s	Vic Wertz	.200
1960s	Norm Cash	.189
1970s	Norm Cash	.169
1980s	Kirk Gibson, Steve Kemp	.172
1990s	Mickey Tettleton	.186
2000s	Miguel Cabrera	.202
2010s	Miguel Cabrera	.217

GROSS PRODUCTION AVERAGE

1900s	Ty Cobb	.286
1910s	Ty Cobb	.341
1920s	Harry Heilmann	.334
1930s	Hank Greenberg	.341
1940s	Hank Greenberg	.335
1950s	Vic Wertz	.304
1960s	Norm Cash, Al Kaline	.295
1970s	Steve Kemp	.280
1980s	Kirk Gibson	.281
1990s	Mickey Tettleton	.294
2000s	Magglio Ordonez	.295
2010s	Miguel Cabrera	.316

OFFENSIVE WAR

1900s	Sam Crawford	34.8
1910s	Ty Cobb	84.4
1920s	Harry Heilmann	60.1
1930s	Charlie Gehringer	58.3
1940s	Rudy York	16.9
1950s	Harvey Kuenn	25.5
1960s	Al Kaline	43.6
1970s	Ron LeFlore	21.4
1980s	Alan Trammell	45.1
1990s	Travis Fryman	24.8
2000s	Carlos Guillen	22.2
2010s	Miguel Cabrera	47.9

BATTING AVERAGE

1900s	Ty Cobb	.337
1910s	Ty Cobb	.387
1920s	Harry Heilmann	.364
1930s	Charlie Gehringer	.331
1940s	George Kell	.325
1950s	George Kell	.326
1960s	Al Kaline	.296
1970s	Ron LeFlore	.296
1980s	Alan Trammell	.290
1990s	Alan Trammell	.282
2000s	Magglio Ordonez	.320
2010s	Miguel Cabrera	.317

DECADE TIGER HITTING LEADERS

BATTING AVERAGE BALLS IN PLAY

1900s	Ty Cobb	.332
1910s	Ty Cobb	.381
1920s	Harry Heilmann	.370
1930s	Hank Greenberg	.339
1940s	George Kell	.330
1950s	George Kell	.333
1960s	Jake Wood	.293
1970s	Ron LeFlore	.353
1980s	Kirk Gibson	.310
1990s	Tony Phillips	.319
2000s	Magglio Ordonez	.340
2010s	J.D. Martinez	.363

TIMES ON BASE

1900s	Sam Crawford	1,511
1910s	Ty Cobb	2,596
1920s	Harry Heilmann	2,564
1930s	Charlie Gehringer	2,608
1940s	Rudy York	1,435
1950s	Harvey Kuenn	1,702
1960s	Norm Cash	2,162
1970s	Aurelio Rodriguez	1,261
1980s	Lou Whitaker	2,119
1990s	Travis Fryman	1,597
2000s	Brandon Inge	1,299
2010s	Miguel Cabrera	2,314

AT-BATS PER RUN BATTED IN

1900s	Ty Cobb	5.8
1910s	Sam Crawford	5.7
1920s	Harry Heilmann	4.7
1930s	Hank Greenberg	3.9
1940s	Hank Greenberg	4.1
1950s	Vic Wertz	5.0
1960s	Rocky Colavito	5.4
1970s	Rusty Staub	5.9
1980s	D. Evans, Richie Hebner	5.8
1990s	Cecil Fielder	4.8
2000s	Miguel Cabrera	5.3
2010s	Miguel Cabrera	5.3

SECONDARY AVERAGE

1900s	Ty Cobb	.265
1910s	Ty Cobb	.388
1920s	Harry Heilmann	.313
1930s	Hank Greenberg	.454
1940s	Hank Greenberg	.472
1950s	Vic Wertz	.389
1960s	Norm Cash	.387
1970s	Norm Cash	.344
1980s	Darrell Evans	.395
1990s	Mickey Tettleton	.453
2000s	Curtis Granderson	.337
2010s	Miguel Cabrera	.365

Scott Livingstone

AT-BATS PER STRIKEOUT

1900s	Kid Elberfeld	31.9
1910s	Ossie Vitt	25.3
1920s	Johnny Bassler	30.7
1930s	Charlie Gehringer	26.9
1940s	George Kell	33.0
1950s	George Kell	28.4
1960s	Jerry Lumpe	10.8
1970s	Dan Meyer	17.0
1980s	Alan Trammell	9.7
1990s	Alan Trammell	9.9
2000s	Placido Polanco	16.0
2010s	Victor Martinez	8.7

IN-PLAY PERCENTAGE

1900s	Kid Gleason	87%
1910s	Sam Crawford	83%
1920s	Bob Fothergill	85%
1930s	Gee Walker	84%
1940s	Doc Cramer	88%
1950s	Harvey Kuenn	87%
1960s	Jerry Lumpe	81%
1970s	Dan Meyer	87%
1980s	Enos Cabell	85%
1990s	D. Cruz, S. Livingstone	82%
2000s	Placido Polanco	85%
2010s	Jose Iglesias	81%

AT-BATS PER HOME RUN

1900s	Ty Cobb	113.4
1910s	Harry Heilmann	91.5
1920s	Harry Heilmann	37.2
1930s	Rudy York	13.3
1940s	Hank Greenberg	14.3
1950s	Vic Wertz	18.9
1960s	Rocky Colavito	16.8
1970s	Norm Cash	18.7
1980s	Darrell Evans	16.7
1990s	Cecil Fielder	15.0
2000s	Marcus Thames	14.8
2010s	J.D. Martinez	17.1

PITCHES

1980s	Lou Whitaker	4,036
1990s	Travis Fryman	18,299
2000s	Brandon Inge	17,498
2010s	Miguel Cabrera	21,716

PITCHES PER PLATE APPEARANCE

1980s	Larry Herndon	3.92
1990s	Mickey Tettleton	4.32
2000s	Chris Shelton	4.19
2010s	Jeimer Candelario	4.22

DECADE TIGER HITTING LEADERS

BASE RUNS

1900s	Sam Crawford	567
1910s	Ty Cobb	1,165
1920s	Harry Heilmann	1,169
1930s	Charlie Gehringer	1,100
1940s	Rudy York	581
1950s	Harvey Kuenn	627
1960s	Norm Cash	883
1970s	Ron LeFlore	433
1980s	Lou Whitaker	775
1990s	Cecil Fielder	618
2000s	Carlos Guillen	455
2010s	Miguel Cabrera	1,021

RUNS CREATED

1900s	Sam Crawford	615
1910s	Ty Cobb	1,245
1920s	Harry Heilmann	1,277
1930s	Charlie Gehringer	1,168
1940s	Rudy York	600
1950s	Harvey Kuenn	670
1960s	Al Kaline	891
1970s	Ron LeFlore	464
1980s	Alan Trammell	800
1990s	Travis Fryman	639
2000s	Carlos Guillen	482
2010s	Miguel Cabrera	1,092

HOME RUN PERCENTAGE

1900s	Ty Cobb	0.8
1910s	Harry Heilmann	1.0
1920s	Harry Heilmann	2.3
1930s	Hank Greenberg	6.5
1940s	Hank Greenberg	6.0
1950s	Bud Souchock	4.6
1960s	Rocky Colavito	5.1
1970s	Norm Cash	4.6
1980s	Darrell Evans	5.0
1990s	Cecil Fielder	5.8
2000s	Marcus Thames	6.1
2010s	J.D. Martinez	5.2

RUNS PRODUCED

1900s	Sam Crawford	1,098
1910s	Ty Cobb	1,832
1920s	Harry Heilmann	1,953
1930s	Charlie Gehringer	2,036
1940s	Rudy York	1,002
1950s	Harvey Kuenn	990
1960s	Al Kaline	1,374
1970s	Aurelio Rodriguez	755
1980s	Alan Trammell	1,322
1990s	Travis Fryman	1,137
2000s	Brandon Inge	820
2010s	Miguel Cabrera	1,472

Dick Tracewski

HOME RUNS AT HOME

1900s	Sam Crawford	9
1910s	Sam Crawford	20
1920s	Harry Heilmann	75
1930s	Hank Greenberg	122
1940s	Rudy York	92
1950s	Al Kaline	67
1960s	Norm Cash	167
1970s	Willie Horton	53
1980s	Lou Whitaker	83
1990s	Cecil Fielder	127
2000s	Brandon Inge	69
2010s	Miguel Cabrera	135

RUN SCORING PERCENTAGE

1900s	Davey Jones	45%
1910s	Davey Jones	49%
1920s	Fred Haney	44%
1930s	Jo-Jo White	46%
1940s	Joe Hoover	43%
1950s	Johnny Lipon	36%
1960s	Dick Tracewski	46%
1970s	Ron LeFlore	41%
1980s	Enos Cabell	37%
1990s	Milt Cuyler	47%
2000s	Ryan Raburn	40%
2010s	R. Davis, A. Jackson	41%

HOME RUN AVERAGE

1900s	Ty Cobb	5.29
1910s	Harry Heilmann	6.56
1920s	Harry Heilmann	16.12
1930s	Rudy York	45.01
1940s	Hank Greenberg	41.87
1950s	Vic Wertz	31.67
1960s	Rocky Colavito	35.70
1970s	Norm Cash	32.13
1980s	Darrell Evans	36.02
1990s	Cecil Fielder	40.01
2000s	Marcus Thames	40.60
2010s	J.D. Martinez	35.00

HOME RUNS ON THE ROAD

1900s	Sam Crawford	22
1910s	Ty Cobb	32
1920s	Harry Heilmann	67
1930s	Hank Greenberg	84
1940s	Rudy York	59
1950s	Al Kaline	58
1960s	Norm Cash	111
1970s	Willie Horton	68
1980s	Lance Parrish	95
1990s	Cecil Fielder	118
2000s	Curtis Granderson	59
2010s	Miguel Cabrera	133

HOME RUNS VERSUS LH PITCHERS

1900s	Ty Cobb, Sam Crawford	7
1910s	Sam Crawford	13
1920s	Harry Heilmann	44
1930s	Hank Greenberg	45
1940s	Rudy York	24
1950s	Ray Boone	30
1960s	Al Kaline	74
1970s	W. Horton, M. Stanley	43
1980s	Lance Parrish	71
1990s	Cecil Fielder	74
2000s	Brandon Inge	40
2010s	Miguel Cabrera	56

HOME RUNS BY RIGHT-HANDERS

1900s	Germany Schaefer	8
1910s	Harry Heilmann	22
1920s	Harry Heilmann	142
1930s	Hank Greenberg	206
1940s	Rudy York	151
1950s	Al Kaline	125
1960s	Al Kaline	210
1970s	Willie Horton	121
1980s	Lance Parrish	176
1990s	Cecil Fielder	235
2000s	Brandon Inge	123
2010s	Miguel Cabrera	268

ISOLATED POWER

1900s	Sam Crawford	.132
1910s	Ty Cobb	.154
1920s	Harry Heilmann	.194
1930s	Hank Greenberg	.294
1940s	Hank Greenberg	.304
1950s	Vic Wertz	.231
1960s	Rocky Colavito	.230
1970s	Norm Cash	.206
1980s	Lance Parrish	.239
1990s	Mickey Tettleton	.232
2000s	Curtis Granderson	.211
2010s	J.D. Martinez	.251

HOME RUNS VERSUS RH PITCHERS

1900s	Sam Crawford	24
1910s	Ty Cobb	35
1920s	Harry Heilmann	98
1930s	Hank Greenberg	161
1940s	Rudy York	82
1950s	Al Kaline	101
1960s	Norm Cash	228
1970s	Norm Cash	84
1980s	Lou Whitaker	118
1990s	Cecil Fielder	171
2000s	Curtis Granderson	86
2010s	Miguel Cabrera	212

Howard Johnson

POWER-SPEED NUMBER

1900s	Sam Crawford	51.2
1910s	Ty Cobb	86.9
1920s	Ty Cobb	61.1
1930s	Charlie Gehringer	119.4
1940s	Rudy York	42.9
1950s	Al Kaline	72.4
1960s	Al Kaline	108.3
1970s	Ron LeFlore	86.9
1980s	Lou Whitaker	326.1
1990s	Travis Fryman	83.5
2000s	Curtis Granderson	80.9
2010s	Ian Kinsler	63.1

HOME RUNS BY LEFT-HANDERS

1900s	Sam Crawford	12
1910s	Ty Cobb	47
1920s	Ty Cobb	44
1930s	Charlie Gehringer	146
1940s	Pat Mullin	58
1950s	Charlie Maxwell	103
1960s	Norm Cash	278
1970s	Norm Cash	95
1980s	Kirk Gibson	149
1990s	Bobby Higginson	104
2000s	Curtis Granderson	102
2010s	Alex Avila	72

HOME RUNS BY SWITCH HITTERS

1900s	Doc Casey	5
1910s	Donie Bush	8
1920s	Lu Blue	19
1930s	Billy Rogell	39
1940s	Roy Cullenbine	57
1950s	Dave Philley	2
1960s	Tom Tresh	13
1970s	Tito Fuentes	5
1980s	Howard Johnson	19
1990s	Tony Clark	127
2000s	Carlos Guillen	86
2010s	Victor Martinez	115

EXTRA BASE HITS

1900s	Sam Crawford	355
1910s	Ty Cobb	521
1920s	Harry Heilmann	640
1930s	Charlie Gehringer	622
1940s	Rudy York	362
1950s	Harvey Kuenn	340
1960s	Al Kaline	488
1970s	Aurelio Rodriguez	309
1980s	Lou Whitaker	438
1990s	Travis Fryman	407
2000s	Brandon Inge	327
2010s	Miguel Cabrera	597

DECADE TIGER HITTING LEADERS

EXTRA BASES ON LONG HITS

1900s	Sam Crawford	531
1910s	Ty Cobb	776
1920s	Harry Heilmann	1,025
1930s	Charlie Gehringer	990
1940s	Rudy York	700
1950s	Al Kaline	599
1960s	Norm Cash	1,075
1970s	Aurelio Rodriguez	510
1980s	Lou Whitaker	767
1990s	Cecil Fielder	884
2000s	Brandon Inge	604
2010s	Miguel Cabrera	1,138

TOTAL BASE AVERAGE

1900s	Sam Crawford, Ty Cobb	1.7
1910s	Ty Cobb	2.0
1920s	Harry Heilmann	2.1
1930s	Hank Greenberg	2.3
1940s	Hank Greenberg	2.3
1950s	Vic Wertz	1.9
1960s	Rocky Colavito	1.9
1970s	W. Horton, R. LeFlore	1.7
1980s	Lance Parrish	1.9
1990s	Tony Clark	1.9
2000s	Granderson, Ordonez	1.9
2010s	Miguel Cabrera	2.0

BASES PRODUCED

1900s	Sam Crawford	2,177
1910s	Ty Cobb	3,902
1920s	Harry Heilmann	3,634
1930s	Charlie Gehringer	3,722
1940s	Rudy York	2,153
1950s	Harvey Kuenn	2,234
1960s	Norm Cash	3,218
1970s	Ron LeFlore	1,870
1980s	Lou Whitaker	2,965
1990s	Travis Fryman	2,358
2000s	Brandon Inge	1,884
2010s	Miguel Cabrera	3,436

EXTRA BASE HIT PERCENTAGE

1900s	Sam Crawford	29.1
1910s	Marty Kavanagh	30.0
1920s	Marty McManus	34.8
1930s	Hank Greenberg	48.0
1940s	Hank Greenberg	49.8
1950s	Bud Souchock	43.1
1960s	Rocky Colavito	40.0
1970s	Lance Parrish	38.9
1980s	Lance Parrish	38.8
1990s	Rob Deer	48.2
2000s	Marcus Thames	48.6
2010s	Justin Upton	47.0

Curtis Granderson

BASES PRODUCED AVERAGE

1900s	Ty Cobb	2.3
1910s	Ty Cobb	2.9
1920s	Harry Heilmann	2.6
1930s	Hank Greenberg	3.0
1940s	Hank Greenberg	2.9
1950s	Vic Wertz	2.5
1960s	Rocky Colavito	2.4
1970s	Ron LeFlore	2.4
1980s	Kirk Gibson	2.4
1990s	C. Fielder, T. Phillips,	2.4
	Mickey Tettleton	2.4
2000s	Miguel Cabrera	2.5
2010s	Miguel Cabrera	2.5

TOTAL BASES

1900s	Sam Crawford	1,752
1910s	Ty Cobb	2,724
1920s	Harry Heilmann	2,949
1930s	Charlie Gehringer	2,855
1940s	Rudy York	1,662
1950s	Harvey Kuenn	1,861
1960s	Norm Cash	2,401
1970s	Aurelio Rodriguez	1,550
1980s	Alan Trammell	2,239
1990s	Travis Fryman	1,910
2000s	Brandon Inge	1,505
2010s	Miguel Cabrera	2,733

TOTAL BASE PERCENTAGE

1900s	Ty Cobb	1.75
1910s	Ty Cobb	2.04
1920s	Harry Heilmann	2.08
1930s	Hank Greenberg	2.35
1940s	Hank Greenberg	2.27
1950s	Vic Wertz	1.87
1960s	Rocky Colavito	1.86
1970s	Ron LeFlore	1.68
1980s	Lance Parrish	1.81
1990s	Tony Clark	1.89
2000s	Miguel Cabrera	2.08
2010s	J.D. Martinez	2.04

STOLEN BASES

1900s	Ty Cobb	189
1910s	Ty Cobb	576
1920s	Ty Cobb	100
1930s	Gee Walker	132
1940s	Barney McCosky	32
1950s	Al Kaline, Harvey Kuenn	51
1960s	Jake Wood	79
1970s	Ron LeFlore	214
1980s	Alan Trammell	167
1990s	Brian Hunter	116
2000s	Curtis Granderson	67
2010s	Austin Jackson	78

CAUGHT STEALING

Decade	Player	CS
1910s	Ty Cobb	113
1920s	Ty Cobb	75
1930s	Charlie Gehringer	52
	Billy Rogell	52
1940s	Eddie Mayo	38
1950s	Harvey Kuenn	43
1960s	Dick McAuliffe	48
1970s	Ron LeFlore	98
1980s	Alan Trammell	71
1990s	Tony Phillips	40
2000s	Brandon Inge	35
2010s	Austin Jackson	28

STOLEN BASE RUNS CREATED

Decade	Player	Runs
1900s	Sam Crawford	963
1910s	Ty Cobb	2,072
1920s	Harry Heilmann	2,019
1930s	Charlie Gehringer	2,100
1940s	Rudy York	1,139
1950s	Harvey Kuenn	1,035
1960s	Norm Cash	1,823
1970s	Ron LeFlore	762
1980s	Lou Whitaker	1,546
1990s	Cecil Fielder	1,249
2000s	Carlos Guillen	834
2010s	Miguel Cabrera	1,930

BASE ON BALLS PERCENTAGE

1900s	Jimmy Barrett	11.7
1910s	Donie Bush	13.8
1920s	Johnny Bassler	15.2
1930s	Mickey Cochrane	18.2
1940s	Eddie Lake	17.0
1950s	Vic Wertz	13.7
1960s	Norm Cash	13.6
1970s	Dick McAuliffe	12.8
1980s	Darrell Evans	15.6
1990s	Mickey Tettleton	18.3
2000s	Gary Sheffield	13.2
2010s	Alex Avila	13.6

STOLEN BASE PERCENTAGE

1910s	Davey Jones	90.4
1920s	Larry Woodall	80.0
1930s	Gee Walker	72.5
1940s	Charlie Gehringer	84.6
1950s	Red Wilson	69.0
1960s	Gates Brown	81.5
1970s	Dan Meyer	86.4
1980s	Steve Kemp	77.8
1990s	Brian Hunter	77.9
2000s	Gary Sheffield	81.6
2010s	Mikie Mahtook	90.9

Jake Wood

WALKS TO STRIKEOUTS

1900s	Kid Elberfeld	3.7
1910s	Ossie Vitt	3.0
1920s	Johnny Bassler	5.8
1930s	Mickey Cochrane	4.1
1940s	Charlie Gehringer	4.3
1950s	George Kell	2.9
1960s	Al Kaline	1.3
1970s	Rusty Staub	1.7
1980s	Steve Kemp	1.2
1990s	Lou Whitaker	1.3
2000s	Higginson, Polanco,	0.9
	Gary Sheffield	0.9
2010s	P. Fielder, V. Martinez	0.8

STOLEN BASE RUNS

Decade	Player	Runs
1900s	Ty Cobb	57.9
1910s	Ty Cobb	105.0
1920s	Larry Woodall	2.4
1930s	Gee Walker	9.6
1940s	Paul Richards	2.7
1950s	Red Wilson	0.6
1960s	Jake Wood	9.9
1970s	Ron LeFlore	29.4
1980s	Kirk Gibson	20.1
1990s	Brian Hunter	15.0
2000s	Curtis Granderson	9.9
2010s	Austin Jackson	6.6

BASE ON BALLS

Decade	Player	BB
1900s	Jimmy Barrett	309
1910s	Donie Bush	912
1920s	Harry Heilmann	615
1930s	Charlie Gehringer	714
1940s	Rudy York	466
1950s	Al Kaline	344
1960s	Norm Cash	778
1970s	Jason Thompson	285
1980s	Lou Whitaker	659
1990s	C. Fielder, T. Phillips	519
2000s	Brandon Inge	339
2010s	Miguel Cabrera	689

INTENTIONAL WALKS

Decade	Player	IBB
1950s	Al Kaline	41
1960s	Norm Cash	74
1970s	Willie Horton	45
1980s	Lou Whitaker	47
1990s	Cecil Fielder	66
2000s	Dmitri Young	32
2010s	Miguel Cabrera	144

BUNT HITS

Decade	Player	Hits
1980s	Lou Whitaker	14
1990s	Milt Cuyler	32
2000s	Ramon Santiago	22
2010s	Ramon Santiago	14

SACRIFICE HITS

1900s	Germany Schaefer	123
1910s	Donie Bush	183
1920s	Harry Heilmann	190
1930s	Charlie Gehringer	68
	Billy Rogell	68
1940s	Eddie Mayo	75
1950s	Frank Lary	37
1960s	Don Wert	50
1970s	Aurelio Rodriguez	52
1980s	Alan Trammell	86
1990s	Deivi Cruz	33
2000s	Ramon Santiago	44
2010s	Ramon Santiago	30

STRIKEOUT RATIO

1900s	Elberfeld, Gleason	0.03
1910s	Ossie Vitt	0.03
1920s	Johnny Bassler, Ty Cobb	0.03
1930s	Charlie Gehringer	0.03
1940s	D. Cramer, George Kell	0.03
1950s	George Kell	0.03
1960s	Jerry Lumpe	0.08
1970s	D. Meyer, R. Staub	0.06
1980s	Alan Trammell	0.09
1990s	Alan Trammell	0.09
2000s	Placido Polanco	0.06
2010s	Victor Martinez	0.10

AT-BATS PER STRIKEOUT

1900s	Kid Elberfeld	31.9
1910s	Ossie Vitt	25.3
1920s	Johnny Bassler	30.7
1930s	Charlie Gehringer	26.9
1940s	George Kell	33.0
1950s	George Kell	28.4
1960s	Jerry Lumpe	10.8
1970s	Dan Meyer	17.0
1980s	Alan Trammell	9.7
1990s	Alan Trammell	9.9
2000s	Placido Polanco	16.0
2010s	Victor Martinez	8.7

TOTAL SACRIFICES

1900s	Germany Schaefer	123
1910s	Donie Bush	183
1920s	Harry Heilmann	190
1930s	Charlie Gehringer	68
	Billy Rogell	68
1940s	Eddie Mayo	75
1950s	Frank Bolling	52
1960s	Don Wert	77
1970s	Aurelio Rodriguez	73
1980s	Alan Trammell	139
1990s	Travis Fryman	74
2000s	Brandon Inge	72
2010s	Miguel Cabrera	48

Deivi Cruz

HITTING STREAK

1900s	Gleason (01), Cobb (06)	25
1910s	Ty Cobb (1911)	40
1920s	Harry Heilmann (1921)	23
1930s	Goose Goslin (1934)	30
1940s	Dick Wakefield (1943)	21
1950s	Harvey Kuenn (1959)	22
1960s	Al Kaline (1961)	22
1970s	Ron LeFlore (1976)	30
1980s	Alan Trammell (1987)	21
1990s	Easley (98), Clark (99)	19
2000s	Ordonez (05), White (05)	20
2010s	Miguel Cabrera (2010)	20

STRIKEOUTS

1900s	Germany Schaefer	305
1910s	Donie Bush	478
1920	Harry Heilmann	324
1930s	Hank Greenberg	556
1940s	Rudy York	493
1950s	Charlie Maxwell	323
1960s	Norm Cash	770
1970s	Ron LeFlore	628
1980s	Kirk Gibson	710
1990s	Travis Fryman	931
2000s	Brandon Inge	975
2010s	Miguel Cabrera	936

STRIKEOUT PERCENTAGE

1900s	Kid Elberfeld	2.7
1910s	Ossie Vitt	3.3
1920s	Johnny Bassler	2.6
1930s	Charlie Gehringer	3.2
1940s	George Kell	2.7
1950s	George Kell	3.1
1960s	Jerry Lumpe	8.4
1970s	Dan Meyer	5.5
1980s	Alan Trammell	9.0
1990s	Alan Trammell	9.0
2000s	Placido Polanco	5.7
2010s	Victor Martinez	10.4

INFIELD HITS

1980s	Chet Lemon	31
1990s	Travis Fryman	113
2000s	Placido Polanco	87
2010s	Jose Iglesias	101

SACRIFICE FLIES

1950s	Al Kaline	30
1960s	Al Kaline	46
1970s	Rusty Staub	36
1980s	Alan Trammell	53
1990s	Travis Fryman	59
2000s	Brandon Inge	34
2010s	Miguel Cabrera	48

DECADE TIGER HITTING LEADERS

PINCH HIT AT-BATS

1900s	Davy Jones	31
1910s	Marty Kavanagh	68
1920s	Bob Fothergill	136
1930s	Jo-Jo White	120
1940s	Don Ross	49
1950s	Pat Mullin	137
1960s	Gates Brown	226
1970s	Gates Brown	197
1980s	Dave Bergman	133
1990s	Lou Whitaker	81
2000s	Marcus Thames	52
2010s	Don Kelly	48

PINCH HITS

1900s	Davy Jones	4
1910s	Marty Kavanagh	17
1920s	Bob Fothergill	47
1930s	Jo-Jo White	38
1940s	Dick Wakefield	13
1950s	Pat Mullin	29
1960s	Gates Brown	61
1970s	Gates Brown	45
1980s	Larry Herndon	29
1990s	Lou Whitaker	17
2000s	Marcus Thames	16
2010s	Victor Martinez	10

PINCH HIT BATTING AVERAGE

1900s	Davy Jones	.129
1910s	Harry Heilmann	.321
1920s	Marty McManus	.385
1930s	Jo-Jo White	.317
1940s	Bruce Campbell	.318
1950s	Charlie Maxwell	.346
1960s	Al Kaline	.386
1970s	Mickey Stanley	.323
1980s	C. Lemon, A. Trammell	.333
1990s	Chad Kreuter	.583
2000s	Ramon Santiago	.353
2010s	James McCann	.381

PINCH HIT HOME RUNS

1930s	Goose Goslin	2
1940s	Dick Wakefield	3
1950s	Ned Harris, Fred Hatfield,	2
	Frank House, Pat Mullin,	2
	Charlie Maxwell	2
1960s	Gates Brown	8
1970s	Gates Brown	8
1980s	Johnny Grubb	7
1990s	Kirk Gibson	3
	Bobby Higginson	3
2000s	Marcus Thames	5
2010s	Tyler Collins	3
	Victor Martinez	3

PINCH HIT RUNS BATTED IN

1920s	Lu Blue	7
	Fred Haney	7
1930s	Jo-Jo White	18
1940s	Dick Wakefield	11
1950s	Pat Mullin	21
1960s	Gates Brown	37
1970s	Gates Brown	36
1980s	Larry Herndon	31
1990s	Kirk Gibson	18
	Lou Whitaker	18
2000s	Marcus Thames	14
2010s	Andy Dirks	9

OUTS

1900s	Sam Crawford	2,897
1910s	Donie Bush	4,382
1920s	Harry Heilmann	3,607
1930s	Charlie Gehringer	3,891
1940s	Rudy York	2,685
1950s	Harvey Kuenn	3,175
1960s	Norm Cash	3,669
1970s	Aurelio Rodriguez	3,511
1980s	Lou Whitaker	4,051
1990s	Travis Fryman	3,315
2000s	Brandon Inge	3,100
2010s	Miguel Cabrera	3,682

GROUNDED INTO DOUBLE PLAY

1940s	Rudy York	107
1950s	Al Kaline	84
	Harvey Kuenn	84
1960s	Al Kaline	122
1970s	Aurelio Rodriguez	107
1980s	Chet Lemon	102
1990s	Cecil Fielder	113
2000s	Magglio Ordonez	87
2010s	Miguel Cabrera	193

DOUBLE PLAY OPPORTUNITIES

1930s	Rudy York	239
1940s	Rudy York	619
1950s	Al Kaline	873
1960s	Norm Cash	1,195
1970s	Aurelio Rodriguez	860
1980s	Alan Trammell	1,152
1990s	Travis Fryman	1,146
2000s	Brandon Inge	774
2010s	Miguel Cabrera	1,219

DOUBLE PLAY PERCENTAGE

1940s	Pat Mullin	6.2
1950s	Charlie Maxwell	5.3
1960s	Charlie Maxwell	3.8
1970s	Dick McAuliffe	4.7
1980s	Kirk Gibson	4.6
1990s	Kirk Gibson	4.3
2000s	Curtis Granderson	4.4
2010s	Jeimer Candelario	4.7

DECADE TIGER PITCHING LEADERS

PITCHER OF THE DECADE

1900s	Ed Summers
1910s	Harry Coveleski
1920s	Herman Pillette
1930s	Firpo Marberry
1940s	Hal Newhouser
1950s	Frank Lary
1960s	Denny McLain
1970s	Mickey Lolich
1980s	Jack Morris
1990s	David Wells
2000s	Justin Verlander
2010s	Justin Verlander

LOSSES

Decade	Pitcher	Losses
1900s	George Mullin	134
1910s	Hooks Dauss	92
1920s	Hooks Dauss	90
1930s	Tommy Bridges	102
1940s	Dizzy Trout	119
1950s	Billy Hoeft	78
1960s	Mickey Lolich	74
1970s	Mickey Lolich	101
1980s	Jack Morris	119
1990s	Justin Thompson	43
2000s	Nate Robertson	68
2010s	Justin Verlander	71

INNINGS

Decade	Pitcher	Innings
1900s	George Mullin	2,592.1
1910s	Hooks Dauss	1,869.0
1920s	Hooks Dauss	1,521.2
1930s	Tommy Bridges	2,083.0
1940s	Hal Newhouser	2,453.1
1950s	Billy Hoeft	1,324.2
1960s	Mickey Lolich	1,528.1
1970s	Mickey Lolich	1,833.1
1980s	Jack Morris	2,443.2
1990s	Bill Gullickson	722.2
2000s	Nate Robertson	1,042.2
2010s	Justin Verlander	1,671.0

GAMES

Decade	Pitcher	Games
1900s	George Mullin	330
1910s	Hooke Dauss	269
1920s	Hooks Dauss	269
1930s	Tommy Bridges	309
1940s	Hal Newhouser	377
1950s	Billy Hoeft	239
1960s	Hank Aguirre	287
1970s	Mickey Lolich	241
1980s	Willie Hernandez	358
1990s	Mike Henneman	311
2000s	Jamie Walker	327
2010s	Phil Coke	299

Nate Robertson

HITS

Decade	Pitcher	Hits
1900s	George Mullin	2,434
1910s	Hooks Dauss	1,714
1920s	Hooks Dauss	1,693
1930s	Tommy Bridges	2,015
1940s	Hal Newhouser	2,127
1950s	Billy Hoeft	1,331
1960s	Mickey Lolich	1,318
1970s	Mickey Lolich	1,775
1980s	Jack Morris	2,212
1990s	Bill Gullickson	826
2000s	Nate Robertson	1,149
2010s	Justin Verlander	1,428

WINS

Decade	Pitcher	Wins
1900s	George Mullin	157
1910s	Hooks Dauss	126
1920s	Hooks Dauss	97
1930s	Tommy Bridges	150
1940s	Hal Newhouser	170
1950s	Frank Lary	79
1960s	Denny McLain	114
1970s	Mickey Lolich	105
1980s	Jack Morris	162
1990s	Bill Gullickson	51
2000s	Justin Verlander	65
2010s	Justin Verlander	118

WIN PERCENTAGE

Decade	Pitcher	Pct.
1900s	Ed Summers	.672
1910s	Bill Donovan	.644
1920s	Syl Johnson, G. Smith	.600
1930s	Bobo Newsom	.630
1940s	Schoolboy Rowe	.735
1950s	Don Mossi	.654
1960s	Fred Gladding	.703
1970s	Aurelio Lopez	.667
1980s	Mike Henneman	.705
1990s	Joe Boever	.615
2000s	F. German, Bobby Seay	.667
2010s	Al Alburquerque	.739

HOME RUNS

Decade	Pitcher	HR
1900s	B. Donovan, G. Mullin	19
1910s	Hooks Dauss	25
1920s	Hooks Dauss	62
1930s	Tommy Bridges	138
1940s	Fred Hutchinson	84
	Hal Newhouser	84
1950s	Billy Hoeft	129
1960s	Denny McLain	176
1970s	Mickey Lolich	184
1980s	Jack Morris	264
1990s	Bill Gullickson	109
2000s	Nate Robertson	145
2010s	Justin Verlander	160

WALKS

1900s	George Mullin	833
1910s	Hooks Dauss	591
1920s	Earl Whitehill	540
1930s	Tommy Bridges	902
1940s	Hal Newhouser	1,068
1950s	Billy Hoeft	481
1960s	Mickey Lolich	518
1970s	Joe Coleman	576
1980s	Jack Morris	858
1990s	Mike Moore	246
2000s	Nate Robertson	374
2010s	Justin Verlander	484

EARNED RUNS

1900s	George Mullin	765
1910s	Hooks Dauss	592
1920s	Earl Whitehill	654
1930s	Tommy Bridges	870
1940s	Hal Newhouser	774
1950s	Billy Hoeft	591
1960s	Mickey Lolich	587
1970s	Mickey Lolich	702
1980s	Jack Morris	995
1990s	Bill Gullickson	376
2000s	Nate Robertson	564
2010s	Justin Verlander	609

RUNS

1900s	George Mullin	1,116
1910s	Hooks Dauss	781
1920s	Hooks Dauss	813
1930s	Tommy Bridges	1,021
1940s	Hal Newhouser	927
1950s	Billy Hoeft	634
1960s	Mickey Lolich	640
1970s	Mickey Lolich	775
1980s	Jack Morris	1,085
1990s	Bill Gullickson	403
2000s	Nate Robertson	609
2010s	Justin Verlander	664

STRIKEOUTS

1900s	George Mullin	1,091
1910s	Hooks Dauss	739
1920s	Earl Whitehill	567
1930s	Tommy Bridges	1,207
1940s	Hal Newhouser	1,579
1950s	Billy Hoeft	783
1960s	Mickey Lolich	1,336
1970s	Mickey Lolich	1,343
1980s	Jack Morris	1,629
1990s	Justin Thompson	427
2000s	Justin Verlander	746
2010s	Justin Verlander	1,627

Phil Coke

BALKS

1900s	Ed Summers	2
1910s	Red Oldham	4
1920s	Rip Collins	4
	Howard Ehmke	4
	Earl Whitehill	4
1930s	Tommy Bridges	7
1940s	Hal Newhouser	6
	Dizzy Trout	6
1950s	Jim Bunning	5
1960s	Hank Aguirre	7
1970s	Jim Crawford	3
	Daryl Patterson	3
1980s	Jack Morris	20
1990s	C.J. Nitkowski	3
	Frank Tanana	3
2000s	Justin Verlander	10
2010s	Al Alburquerque	8

HIT BY PITCH

1900s	George Mullin	78
1910s	Hooks Dauss	82
1920s	Howard Ehmke	49
1930s	T. Bridges, C. Hogsett	29
1940s	Dizzy Trout	21
1950s	Frank Lary	53
1960s	Mickey Lolich	60
1970s	Joe Coleman	52
1980s	Dan Petry	33
1990s	Felipe Lira	20
2000s	Justin Verlander	46
2010s	Justin Verlander	37

WILD PITCHES

1900s	George Mullin	67
1910s	Jean Dubuc	48
1920s	Dutch Leonard	25
1930s	Tommy Bridges	41
1940s	Hal Newhouser	52
1950s	Paul Foytack	25
1960s	Mickey Lolich	53
1970s	J. Coleman, M. Lolich	56
1980s	Jack Morris	124
1990s	Mike Henneman	26
2000s	Jeremy Bonderman	40
2010s	Justin Verlander	41

INTENTIONAL WALKS

1950s	Frank Lary	24
1960s	Mickey Lolich	27
1970s	John Hiller	60
1980s	Jack Morris	66
1990s	Mike Henneman	46
2000s	Jeremy Bonderman	22
2010s	Phil Coke	22

DECADE TIGER PITCHING LEADERS

BATTERS FACED

1900s	George Mullin	10,636
1910s	Hooks Dauss	7,558
1920s	Earl Whitehill	6,299
1930s	Tommy Bridges	9,033
1940s	Hal Newhouser	10,360
1950s	Billy Hoeft	5,693
1960s	Mickey Lolich	6,375
1970s	Mickey Lolich	7,605
1980s	Jack Morris	10,208
1990s	Bill Gullickson	3,093
2000s	Nate Robertson	4,558
2010s	Justin Verlander	6,835

EARNED RUN AVERAGE

1900s	Ed Summers	1.93
1910s	Harry Coveleski	2.34
1920s	Herman Pillette	3.42
1930s	Bobo Newsom	3.37
1940s	Hal Newhouser	2.84
1950s	Frank Lary	3.32
1960s	Fred Gladding	2.70
1970s	Aurelio Lopez	2.41
1980s	Kevin Saucier	2.32
1990s	Doug Brocail	2.83
2000s	Juan Acevedo	2.65
2010s	Joaquin Benoit	2.89

FIELDING INDEPENDENT PITCHING

1900s	Ed Summers	2.30
1910s	Harry Coveleski	2.67
1920s	George Uhle	3.55
1930s	Bobo Newsom	3.67
1940s	Hal Newhouser	3.01
1950s	Don Mossi	3.27
1960s	Mickey Lolich	3.13
1970s	Mark Fidrych	3.14
1980s	Mike Henneman	3.48
1990s	Mike Henneman	3.41
2000s	Kyle Farnsworth	3.00
2010s	Octavio Dotel	2.42

TECHNICAL RUNS

1900s	Ed Summers	3.14
1910s	Harry Coveleski	3.39
1920s	George Smith	4.00
1930s	Tommy Bridges	3.66
1940s	Hal Newhouser	3.40
1950s	Don Mossi	3.63
1960s	Fred Gladding	2.96
1970s	Aurelio Lopez	2.62
1980s	Kevin Saucier	2.62
1990s	Doug Brocail	3.11
2000s	Brandon Lyon	2.86
2010s	Joaquin Benoit	3.08

Mark Thurmond

DICE

1900s	Ed Summers	3.14
1910s	Harry Coveleski	3.29
1920s	George Uhle	3.39
1930s	Bobo Newsom	3.70
1940s	Hal Newhouser	3.48
1950s	Don Mossi	3.73
1960s	Mickey Lolich	3.62
1970s	Mark Fidrych	3.48
1980s	Mike Henneman	3.68
1990s	Mike Henneman	3.44
2000s	Kyle Farnsworth	2.95
2010s	Octavio Dotel	2.33

LEFT ON BASE PERCENTAGE

1900s	Ed Killian	71.7
1910s	Willie Mitchell	71.0
1920s	Syl Johnson	67.7
1930s	Bobo Newsom	73.9
1940s	Hal Newhouser	73.8
1950s	Jim Bunning	77.4
1960s	Fred Gladding	81.2
1970s	Aurelio Lopez	84.7
1980s	Mark Thurmond	81.3
1990s	Sean Runyan	81.4
2000s	Brandon Lyon	80.8
2010s	Joaquin Benoit	81.3

EARNED RUN AVERAGE PLUS

1900s	Ed Summers	127
1910s	Harry Coveleski	123
1920s	Herman Pillette	114
1930s	Bobo Newsom	144
1940s	Hal Newhouser	138
1950s	Frank Lary, Don Mossi	121
1960s	Terry Fox	137
1970s	Aurelio Lopez	181
1980s	Kevin Saucier	170
1990s	Doug Brocail	168
2000s	Juan Acevedo	161
2010s	Joaquin Benoit	145

WHIP

1900s	Ed Summers	1.066
1910s	Harry Coveleski	1.131
1920s	George Uhle	1.369
1930s	George Uhle	1.293
1940s	Fred Hutchinson	1.231
1950s	Don Mossi	1.136
1960s	Denny McLain	1.094
1970s	Mark Fidrych	1.136
1980s	Willie Hernandez	1.121
1990s	Doug Brocail	1.168
2000s	Brandon Lyon	1.106
2010s	Joaquin Benoit	1.075

DECADE TIGER PITCHING LEADERS

PITCHER WAR

1900s	Bill Donovan	28.8
1910s	Hooks Dauss	21.3
1920s	Hooks Dauss	15.6
1930s	Tommy Bridges	35.4
1940s	Hal Newhouser	54.1
1950s	Frank Lary	20.0
1960s	Denny McLain	22.1
1970s	Mickey Lolich	32.6
1980s	Jack Morris	30.3
1990s	Justin Thompson	13.1
2000s	Justin Verlander	15.2
2010s	Justin Verlander	40.8

WALKS PER NINE INNINGS

1900s	Ed Summers	1.65
1910s	Harry Coveleski	2.37
1920s	George Uhle	2.10
1930s	George Uhle	2.58
1940s	Schoolboy Rowe	2.21
1950s	Tom Morgan	1.27
1960s	Don Mossi	1.69
1970s	Dave Rozema	1.80
1980s	Dave Rozema	2.39
1990s	Bill Gullickson	2.03
2000s	Brian Moehler	1.88
2010s	Doug Fister	1.76

STRIKEOUTS TO WALKS

1900s	Ed Summers	1.96
1910s	Bill Donovan	1.52
1920s	George Uhle	1.72
1930s	Schoolboy Rowe	1.66
1940s	Fred Hutchinson	1.70
1950s	Tom Morgan	3.23
1960s	Don Mossi	2.99
1970s	Mickey Lolich	2.71
1980s	Willie Hernandez	2.78
1990s	David Wells	2.84
2000s	Jamie Walker	3.47
2010s	Octavio Dotel	4.13

HITS PER NINE INNINGS

1900s	Bill Donovan	7.77
1910s	Bernie Boland	7.68
1920s	George Smith	9.18
1930s	Bobo Newsom	8.12
1940s	T. Gray, H. Newhouser	7.80
1950s	Jim Bunning	7.88
1960s	Fred Lasher	7.25
1970s	Aurelio Lopez	6.73
1980s	Kevin Saucier	6.15
1990s	Doug Brocail	7.32
2000s	Brandon Lyon	6.41
2010s	Jose Valverde	6.84

Dave Rozema

RUNS PER NINE INNINGS

1900s	Ed Summers	3.14
1910s	Harry Coveleski	3.39
1920s	Herman Pillette	4.45
1930s	Bobo Newsom	3.66
1940s	Hal Newhouser	3.40
1950s	Don Mossi	3.63
1960s	Fred Gladding	2.96
1970s	Aurelio Lopez	2.62
1980s	Kevin Saucier	2.62
1990s	Doug Brocail	3.11
2000s	Brandon Lyon	2.86
2010s	Joaquin Benoit	3.08

HOME RUNS PER NINE INNINGS

1900s	Ed Killian	0.04
1910s	George Cunningham	0.04
1920s	Herman Pillette	0.22
1930s	Waite Hoyt	0.36
1940s	Roy Henshaw	0.31
	Hal Newhouser	0.31
1950s	Ray Herbert	0.52
1960s	Fred Gladding	0.72
1970s	Mark Fidrych	0.44
1980s	Kevin Saucier	0.10
1990s	Mike Henneman	0.48
2000s	Juan Acevedo	0.48
2010s	Octavio Dotel	0.43

STRIKEOUTS PER NINE INNINGS

1900s	Bill Donovan	4.56
1910s	Bill Donovan	4.49
1920s	Dutch Leonard	4.21
1930s	Bobo Newsom	6.00
1940s	Bobo Newsom	5.93
1950s	Jim Bunning	6.75
1960s	Mickey Lolich	7.87
1970s	John Hiller	8.06
1980s	Willie Hernandez	7.15
1990s	Mike Myers	8.88
2000s	Kyle Farnsworth	11.20
2010s	Joe Jimenez	11.27

GAMES STARTED

1900s	George Mullin	298
1910s	Hooks Dauss	219
1920s	Earl Whitehill	191
1930s	Tommy Bridges	266
1940s	Hal Newhouser	305
1950s	Billy Hoeft	176
1960s	Mickey Lolich	219
1970s	Mickey Lolich	240
1980s	Jack Morris	332
1990s	Bill Gullickson	116
2000s	Nate Robertson	168
2010s	Justin Verlander	248

DECADE TIGER PITCHING LEADERS

COMPLETE GAMES

1900s	George Mullin	258
1910s	Hooks Dauss	156
1920s	Hooks Dauss	89
1930s	Tommy Bridges	156
1940s	Hal Newhouser	181
1950s	Frank Lary	78
1960s	Denny McLain	93
1970s	Mickey Lolich	128
1980s	Jack Morris	133
1990s	Bill Gullickson	11
	Jack Morris	11
2000s	Steve Sparks	12
2010s	Justin Verlander	17

HIGH QUALITY STARTS

1900s	George Mullin	133
1910s	Hooks Dauss	145
1920s	Earl Whitehill	79
1930s	Tommy Bridges	130
1940s	Hal Newhouser	189
1950s	Frank Lary	91
1960s	Denny McLain	123
1970s	Mickey Lolich	140
1980s	Jack Morris	183
1990s	Bill Gullickson	46
2000s	Mike Maroth	57
2010s	Justin Verlander	131

QUALITY START PERCENTAGE

1900s	Ed Killian	.613
1910s	Harry Coveleski	.704
1920s	Rip Collins	.824
1930s	Bobo Newsom	.613
1940s	Hal Newhouser	.659
1950s	Don Mossi	.667
1960s	Denny McLain	.654
1970s	Mark Fidrych	.681
1980s	Doyle Alexander	.615
1990s	David Wells	.609
2000s	Edwin Jackson	.636
2010s	Justin Verlander	.702

COMPLETE GAME PERCENTAGE

1900s	Roscoe Miller	.926
1910s	George Mullin	.804
1920s	George Uhle	.733
1930s	Bobo Newsom	.677
1940s	Hal Newhouser	.593
1950s	Ned Garver, Don Mossi	.500
1960s	Denny McLain	.454
1970s	Mark Fidrych	.702
1980s	Jack Morris	.401
1990s	Jack Morris	.306
2000s	Steve Sparks	.154
2010s	Justin Verlander	.069

Don Mossi

HIGH QUALITY START PERCENTAGE

1900s	Ed Killian	.583
1910s	Hooks Dauss	.662
1920s	Herman Pillette	.539
1930s	Bobo Newsom	.613
1940s	Hal Newhouser	.620
1950s	Don Mossi	.667
1960s	Denny McLain	.600
1970s	Mark Fidrych	.702
1980s	Doyle Alexander	.577
1990s	David Wells	.500
2000s	Jeff Weaver	.500
2010s	Justin Verlander	.528

SHUTOUTS

1900s	Bill Donovan	25
	George Mullin	25
1910s	Hooks Dauss	16
1920s	Earl Whitehill	8
1930s	Tommy Bridges	25
1940s	Hal Newhouser	31
1950s	Billy Hoeft	16
1960s	Denny McLain	26
1970s	Mickey Lolich	18
1980s	Jack Morris	20
1990s	Brian Moehler	6
2000s	Justin Verlander	3
2010s	Justin Verlander	4

DOMINATE STARTS

1900s	George Mullin	46
1910s	Hooks Dauss	49
1920s	Hooks Dauss	23
1930s	Tommy Bridges	48
1940s	Hal Newhouser	79
1950s	Frank Lary	36
1960s	Denny McLain	49
1970s	Mickey Lolich	51
1980s	Jack Morris	60
1990s	Brian Moehler	10
2000s	Jeremy Bonderman	15
2010s	Justin Verlander	27

DOMINATE START PERCENTAGE

1900s	Ed Summers	.344
1910s	Bernie Boland	.273
1920s	Herman Pillette	.184
1930s	Bobo Newsom	.226
1940s	Hal Newhouser	.259
1950s	Frank Lary	.212
1960s	Denny McLain	.239
1970s	Mark Fidrych	.319
1980s	Jeff Robinson	.183
1990s	Jack Morris	.111
2000s	Steve Sparks	.115
2010s	Doug Fister	.132

DECADE TIGER PITCHING LEADERS

STARTER WINS

1900s	George Mullin	147
1910s	Hooks Dauss	114
1920s	Earl Whitehill	77
1930s	Tommy Bridges	144
1940s	Hal Newhouser	161
1950s	Frank Lary	78
1960s	Denny McLain	113
1970s	Mickey Lolich	105
1980s	Jack Morris	162
1990s	Bill Gullickson	51
2000s	Justin Verlander	65
2010s	Justin Verlander	183

NO DECISIONS

1900s	George Mullin	15
1910s	Harry Coveleski	25
1920s	Earl Whitehill	40
1930s	Vic Sorrell	34
1940s	Hal Newhouser	35
1950s	Billy Hoeft	34
1960s	Mickey Lolich	54
1970s	Joe Coleman	35
1980s	Dan Petry	56
1990s	Bill Gullickson	29
2000s	Nate Robertson	50
2010s	Justin Verlander	59

CHEAP WINS

1900s	George Mullin	17
1910s	Ed Willett	16
1920s	Earl Whitehill	25
1930s	Tommy Bridges	36
1940s	Hal Newhouser	21
1950s	Billy Hoeft	13
1960s	M. Lolich, D. McLain	14
1970s	Joe Coleman	18
1980s	Jack Morris	28
1990s	Bill Gullickson	12
2000s	Nate Robertson	16
2010s	Justin Verlander	14

STARTER LOSSES

1900s	George Mullin	133
1910s	Hooks Dauss	84
1920s	Hooks Dauss	76
1930s	Tommy Bridges	94
1940s	Hal Newhouser	109
1950s	Billy Hoeft	72
1960s	Mickey Lolich	70
1970s	Mickey Lolich	101
1980s	Jack Morris	119
1990s	Justin Thompson	43
2000s	Nate Robertson	68
2010s	Justin Verlander	114

Al Aber

TOUGH LOSSES

1900s	George Mullin	39
1910s	Hooks Dauss	43
1920s	Hooks Dauss	27
1930s	Tommy Bridges	24
1940s	Hal Newhouser	44
1950s	Frank Lary	27
1960s	Mickey Lolich	24
1970s	Mickey Lolich	38
1980s	Jack Morris	43
1990s	Justin Thompson	15
2000s	Mike Maroth	20
2010s	Justin Verlander	27

STARTER WIN PERCENTAGE

1900s	Ed Summers	.644
1910s	Bill Donovan	.628
1920s	Syl Johnson	.600
1930s	Bobo Newsom	.630
1940s	Schoolboy Rowe	.714
1950s	Don Mossi	.577
1960s	Denny McLain	.669
1970s	Jack Morris	.667
1980s	Jeff Robinson	.610
1990s	Bill Gullickson	.586
2000s	Rick Porcello	.609
2010s	Max Scherzer	.701

PITCHES

1980s	Doyle Alexander	7,072
1990s	Bill Gullickson	10,368
2000s	Nate Robertson	16,305
2010s	Justin Verlander	27,381

PITCHES PER PLATE APPEARANCE

Decade	Pitcher	P/PA
1980s	Walt Terrell	3.49
1990s	Bill Gullickson	3.35
2000s	Danny Patterson	3.39
2010s	Phil Coke	3.66

GAMES IN RELIEF

Decade	Pitcher	Games
1900s	Ed Killian	30
1910s	Bernie Boland	88
1920s	Ken Holloway	135
1930s	Chief Hogsett	170
1940s	Al Benton, J. Gorsica	140
1950s	Al Aber	129
1960s	Fred Gladding	216
1970s	John Hiller	409
1980s	Willie Hernandez	358
1990s	Mike Henneman	311
2000s	Jamie Walker	327
2010s	Phil Coke	284

DECADE TIGER PITCHING LEADERS

WINS IN RELIEF

1900s	Ed Killian, George Mullin	10
1910s	Bernie Boland	13
1920s	Hooks Dauss	29
1930s	Chief Hogsett	24
1940s	Dizzy Trout	19
1950s	Al Aber	15
1960s	Terry Fox, Fred Gladding	26
1970s	John Hiller	63
1980s	Willie Hernandez	36
1990s	Mike Henneman	26
2000s	Fernando Rodney	15
2010s	Al Alburquerque	17

RELIEF WIN PERCENTAGE

1900s	George Mullin	.909
1910s	George Cunningham	.700
1920s	K. Holloway, E. Whitehill	.714
1930s	Schoolboy Rowe	.750
1940s	Virgil Trucks	.650
1950s	Fred Hutchinson	.909
1960s	Dave Wickersham	.727
1970s	Aurelio Lopez	.667
1980s	Doug Bair	.706
1990s	Joe Boever	.615
2000s	F. German, Bobby Seay	.667
2010s	Al Alburquerque	.739

SAVES

1900s	George Mullin	6
1910s	Hooks Dauss	15
1920s	Hooks Dauss	26
1930s	Chief Hogsett	27
1940s	Al Benton	40
1950s	Al Aber	14
1960s	Terry Fox	55
1970s	John Hiller	112
1980s	Willie Hernandez	120
1990s	Mike Henneman	117
2000s	Todd Jones	146
2010s	Jose Valverde	119

Fred Hutchinson

HOLDS

1910s	H. Dauss, D. Leonard	1
1920s	Bert Cole	3
1930s	Chief Hogsett	3
1940s	Four Pitchers	2
1950s	Al Aber	9
1960s	Larry Sherry	9
1970s	John Hiller	15
1980s	Mike Henneman,	13
	Willie Hernandez	13
1990s	Doug Brocail	50
2000s	Jamie Walker	59
2010s	Joaquin Benoit	68

Fernando Rodney

LOSSES IN RELIEF

1900s	Ed Willett	3
1910s	Hooks Dauss	8
1920s	Lil Stoner	15
1930s	Chief Hogsett	24
1940s	Al Benton	19
1950s	Hal White	12
1960s	Terry Fox, Larry Sherry	17
1970s	John Hiller	53
1980s	Willie Hernandez	31
1990s	Mike Henneman	21
2000s	Fernando Rodney	30
2010s	Phil Coke	17

GAMES FINISHED

Decade	Pitcher	Games
1900s	George Mullin	30
1910s	George Cunningham	66
1920s	Ken Holloway	82
1930s	Chief Hogsett	129
1940s	Dizzy Trout	93
1950s	Al Aber	74
1960s	Terry Fox	128
1970s	John Hiller	303
1980s	Willie Hernandez	279
1990s	Mike Henneman	255
2000s	Todd Jones	235
2010s	Jose Valverde	219

PICK OFFS

Decade	Pitcher	Pick Offs
1910s	Howard Ehmke	4
1920s	Rip Collins, K. Holloway,	6
	Earl Whitehill	6
1930s	Vic Sorrell	8
1940s	Hal Newhouser	15
1950s	Frank Lary	7
1960s	Mickey Lolich	19
1970s	Mickey Lolich	33
1980s	D. Petry, Frank Tanana	16
1990s	Justin Thompson	18
2000s	Mike Maroth	28
2010s	Justin Verlander	14

Rank	Player	Games
001	Al Kaline	2,834
002	Ty Cobb	2,806
003	Lou Whitaker	2,390
004	Charlie Gehringer	2,323
005	Alan Trammell	2,293
006	Sam Crawford	2,114
007	Norm Cash	2,018
008	Harry Heilmann	1,990
009	Donie Bush	1,871
010	Miguel Cabrera	1,867
011	Bill Freehan	1,774
012	Dick McAuliffe	1,656
013	Bobby Veach	1,604
014	Mickey Stanley	1,516
015	Willie Horton	1,515
016	Brandon Inge	1,408
017	Bobby Higginson	1,362
018	Jim Northrup	1,279
019	Hank Greenberg	1,269
020	Rudy York	1,268
021	Aurelio Rodriguez	1,241
022	Billy Rogell	1,207
023	Tom Brookens	1,206
024	Chet Lemon	1,203
025	Kirk Gibson	1,177
026	Lance Parrish	1,146
027	Travis Fryman	1,096
028	Oscar Stanage	1,095
029	Don Wert	1,090
030	Gates Brown	1,051
031	Harvey Kuenn	1,049
032	Pete Fox	997
033	Cecil Fielder	982
034	Victor Martinez	969
035	Lu Blue	925
036	Ralph Young	890
037	Dave Bergman	871
038	Pat Mullin	864
039	Pinky Higgins	857
040	Bob Jones	853
	Charlie Maxwell	853
042	Magglio Ordonez	847
043	Larry Herndon	843
044	Damion Easley	841
045	Nicholas Castellanos	837
046	Vic Wertz	836
047	Charley O'Leary	833
048	George Kell	826
049	Ramon Santiago	818
050	Carlos Guillen	817

Al Kaline

Rank	Player	Games
051	Bob Fothergill	802
052	Matty McIntyre	795
053	Gee Walker	794
054	Marv Owen	792
055	Ron LeFlore	787
056	Frank Bolling	785
057	Tony Clark	772
058	George Moriarty	771
059	Hoot Evers	769
060	Johnny Bassler	767
	Ossie Vitt	767
062	Alex Avila	760
063	Johnny Groth	737
064	Darrell Evans	727
065	Tony Phillips	722
066	Doc Cramer	720
067	Deivi Cruz	703
068	Steve Kemp	684
069	Ray Boone	683
070	John Wockenfuss	677
071	Omar Infante	676
072	Curtis Granderson	674
073	Craig Monroe	672
074	Austin Jackson	670
075	Ray Hayworth	658
076	Davy Jones	646
	Birdie Tebbetts	646
078	John Stone	644
079	Bob Swift	642
080	Marty McManus	640
081	Placido Polanco	632
	Dick Wakefield	632
083	Eddie Brinkman	630
	Jo-Jo White	630
085	Rocky Colavito	629
086	Germany Schaefer	626
087	Heinie Manush	615
	Jason Thompson	615
089	Johnny Lipon	611
	Ivan Rodriguez	611
091	Ian Kinsler	607
092	Barney McCosky	596
093	Bill Coughlin	593
094	Jake Wood	592
095	Jimmy Barrett	589
096	Eddie Mayo	587
097	Bill Tuttle	581
098	Mickey Tettleton	570
099	Ryan Raburn	566
100	Mike Henneman	561

ALL TIME TIGER HITTING LEADERS – PLATE APPEARANCES

Rank	Player	PA
001	Ty Cobb	12,132
002	Al Kaline	11,596
003	Charlie Gehringer	10,244
004	Lou Whitaker	9,967
005	Alan Trammell	9,376
006	Sam Crawford	8,885
007	Donie Bush	8,466
008	Harry Heilmann	8,395
009	Miguel Cabrera	7,921
010	Norm Cash	7,776
011	Bill Freehan	6,900
012	Dick McAuliffe	6,828
013	Bobby Veach	6,796
014	Willie Horton	5,978
015	Bobby Higginson	5,664
016	Hank Greenberg	5,588
017	Mickey Stanley	5,477
018	Rudy York	5,352
019	Brandon Inge	5,196
020	Billy Rogell	5,093
021	Jim Northrup	4,926
022	Travis Fryman	4,792
023	Kirk Gibson	4,773
024	Harvey Kuenn	4,749
025	Chet Lemon	4,676
026	Lance Parrish	4,674
027	Aurelio Rodriguez	4,649
028	Don Wert	4,300
029	Pete Fox	4,282
030	Cecil Fielder	4,252
031	Lu Blue	4,133
032	Victor Martinez	3,942
033	Tom Brookens	3,903
034	Oscar Stanage	3,847
035	Ralph Young	3,786
036	George Kell	3,735
037	Pinky Higgins	3,609
038	Ron LeFlore	3,559
039	Magglio Ordonez	3,531
040	Damion Easley	3,512
041	Matty McIntyre	3,424
042	Nicholas Castellanos	3,421
043	Carlos Guillen	3,384
044	Bob Jones	3,369
045	Tony Phillips	3,320
046	Marv Owen	3,310
047	Ossie Vitt	3,275
048	Frank Bolling	3,265
049	Gee Walker	3,240
050	Vic Wertz	3,221

Oscar Stanage

Rank	Player	PA
051	Tony Clark	3,212
052	Charlie Maxwell	3,150
053	Charley O'Leary	3,136
054	Hoot Evers	3,100
055	Larry Herndon	3,013
056	George Moriarty	3,012
057	Austin Jackson	2,994
058	Doc Cramer	2,963
059	Steve Kemp	2,930
060	Curtis Granderson	2,896
061	Ray Boone	2,854
062	Pat Mullin	2,848
063	Placido Polanco	2,819
064	Darrell Evans	2,809
065	Johnny Bassler	2,769
066	Rocky Colavito	2,723
067	Alex Avila	2,709
068	Barney McCosky	2,707
069	Bob Fothergill	2,693
	Ian Kinsler	2,693
071	John Stone	2,673
072	Marty McManus	2,636
073	Johnny Lipon	2,634
074	Jimmy Barrett	2,628
075	Johnny Groth	2,573
076	Deivi Cruz	2,550
077	Craig Monroe	2,545
078	Gates Brown	2,544
079	Jason Thompson	2,534
080	Davy Jones	2,529
081	Ivan Rodriguez	2,523
082	Ramon Santiago	2,522
083	Germany Schaefer	2,520
084	Dick Wakefield	2,500
085	Eddie Mayo	2,494
086	Omar Infante	2,449
087	Bill Tuttle	2,420
088	Rusty Staub	2,407
089	Heinie Manush	2,378
090	Bill Coughlin	2,374
091	Mickey Tettleton	2,343
092	Birdie Tebbetts	2,287
093	Dave Bergman	2,276
094	Eddie Brinkman	2,272
095	Ray Hayworth	2,239
096	Billy Bruton	2,228
097	Goose Goslin	2,216
098	Jackie Tavener	2,141
099	Roy Johnson	2,134
100	John Wockenfuss	2,117

Rank	Player	At Bats
001	Ty Cobb	10,596
002	Al Kaline	10,116
003	Charlie Gehringer	8,860
004	Lou Whitaker	8,570
005	Alan Trammell	8,288
006	Sam Crawford	7,984
007	Harry Heilmann	7,297
008	Donie Bush	6,970
009	Miguel Cabrera	6,931
010	Norm Cash	6,593
011	Bill Freehan	6,073
012	Bobby Veach	5,979
013	Dick McAuliffe	5,898
014	Willie Horton	5,405
015	Mickey Stanley	5,022
016	Bobby Higginson	4,910
017	Hank Greenberg	4,791
018	Rudy York	4,677
019	Brandon Inge	4,626
020	Jim Northrup	4,437
021	Billy Rogell	4,418
022	Harvey Kuenn	4,372
023	Aurelio Rodriguez	4,352
024	Travis Fryman	4,297
025	Lance Parrish	4,273
026	Kirk Gibson	4,170
027	Chet Lemon	4,074
028	Pete Fox	3,919
029	Don Wert	3,800
030	Cecil Fielder	3,674
031	Victor Martinez	3,558
032	Tom Brookens	3,543
033	Oscar Stanage	3,502
034	Lu Blue	3,394
035	George Kell	3,303
036	Ron LeFlore	3,266
037	Magglio Ordonez	3,171
038	Ralph Young	3,158
039	Nicholas Castellanos	3,148
040	Pinky Higgins	3,134
041	Damion Easley	3,090
042	Gee Walker	3,046
043	Carlos Guillen	3,008
044	Matty McIntyre	2,997
045	Bob Jones	2,990
046	Marv Owen	2,954
047	Frank Bolling	2,915
048	Tony Clark	2,831
049	Charley O'Leary	2,825
050	Vic Wertz	2,793

Willie Horton

Rank	Player	At Bats
051	Ossie Vitt	2,763
052	Larry Herndon	2,748
053	Tony Phillips	2,747
054	Doc Cramer	2,720
055	Hoot Evers	2,718
056	Charlie Maxwell	2,696
057	Austin Jackson	2,678
058	George Moriarty	2,666
059	Placido Polanco	2,589
060	Curtis Granderson	2,579
061	Steve Kemp	2,504
062	Pat Mullin	2,493
063	Ray Boone	2,485
064	Ian Kinsler	2,477
065	Bob Fothergill	2,444
066	John Stone	2,428
067	Deivi Cruz	2,405
068	Barney McCosky	2,385
069	Ivan Rodriguez	2,382
070	Darrell Evans	2,349
071	Craig Monroe	2,348
072	Rocky Colavito	2,336
073	Marty McManus	2,314
074	Alex Avila	2,303
075	Johnny Lipon	2,272
076	Omar Infante	2,271
077	Johnny Groth	2,266
078	Gates Brown	2,262
079	John Barrett	2,259
080	Johnny Bassler	2,240
081	Germany Schaeffer	2,236
082	Eddie Mayo	2,215
083	Ramon Santiago	2,210
084	Jason Thompson	2,204
085	Davy Jones	2,175
086	Bill Tuttle	2,155
087	Dick Wakefield	2,128
088	Bill Coughlin	2,117
089	Rusty Staub	2,100
090	Heinie Manush	2,099
091	Eddie Brinkman	2,060
092	Birdie Tebbetts	2,058
093	Ray Hayworth	2,006
094	Billy Bruton	1,977
095	Dave Bergman	1,967
096	Goose Goslin	1,957
097	Roy Johnson	1,918
098	Jose Iglesias	1,913
099	Mickey Tettleton	1,887
100	Jackie Tavener	1,881

ALL TIME TIGER HITTING LEADERS – RUNS

Rank	Player	Runs
001	Ty Cobb	2,085
002	Charlie Gehringer	1,775
003	Al Kaline	1,622
004	Lou Whitaker	1,386
005	Donie Bush	1,243
006	Alan Trammell	1,231
007	Harry Heilmann	1,209
008	Sam Crawford	1,115
009	Miguel Cabrera	1,056
010	Norm Cash	1,027
011	Hank Greenberg	975
012	Bobby Veach	863
013	Dick McAuliffe	856
014	Rudy York	738
015	Bobby Higginson	736
016	Bill Freehan	706
017	Kirk Gibson	698
018	Willie Horton	671
019	Lu Blue	670
	Pete Fox	670
	Billy Rogell	670
022	Mickey Stanley	641
023	Harvey Kuenn	619
024	Travis Fryman	607
025	Lance Parrish	577
026	Jim Northrup	571
027	Chet Lemon	570
028	Cecil Fielder	558
029	Ron LeFlore	532
030	Brandon Inge	527
031	George Kell	502
	Tony Phillips	502
033	Gee Walker	476
034	Carlos Guillen	469
035	Damion Easley	456
036	Magglio Ordonez	452
037	Austin Jackson	447

Rank	Player	Runs
038	Tom Brookens	445
039	Vic Wertz	443
040	Curtis Granderson	435
041	Tony Clark	428
042	Ossie Vitt	418
043	Aurelio Rodriguez	417
044	Pinky Higgins	415
	Charley Maxwell	415
	Ralph Young	415
	Don Wert	415
048	Davy Jones	412
	Matty McIntyre	412
050	Hoot Evers	409

Lou Whitaker

Rank	Player	Runs
	Barney McCosky	409
052	Victor Martinez	405
053	Ian Kinsler	401
054	Bob Jones	400
055	Placido Polanco	393
056	Heinie Manush	386
057	Jimmy Barrett	383
	Pat Mullin	383
059	Frank Bolling	382
060	Bob Fothergill	380
	John Stone	380
062	Steve Kemp	378
063	Rocky Colavito	377

Rank	Player	Runs
064	Nicholas Castellanos	365
065	Marv Owen	364
066	Larry Herndon	358
067	Darrell Evans	357
068	Ray Boone	351
	Roy Johnson	351
070	Marty McManus	350
071	Jo-Jo White	348
072	Goose Goslin	345
073	Dick Wakefield	334
074	Gates Brown	330
075	Doc Cramer	329
076	Craig Monroe	324
077	Billy Bruton	315
078	Johnny Groth	307
	Johnny Lipon	307
080	Mickey Tettleton	303
081	Ivan Rodriguez	300
082	Eddie Lake	296
083	Charley O'Leary	284
084	Jason Thompson	279
085	Germany Schaefer	278
	Bill Tuttle	278
	Jake Wood	278
088	Alex Avila	276
089	Omar Infante	273
090	Eddie Mayo	272
	George Moriarty	272
092	Dale Alexander	271
093	Roy Cullenbine	268
094	Ramon Santiago	265
095	Rusty Staub	264
096	Fred Haney	263
097	Deivi Cruz	258
098	J.D. Martinez	257
099	Dmitri Young	255
100	Oscar Stanage	248

Rank	Player	Hits
001	Ty Cobb	3,900
002	Al Kaline	3,007
003	Charlie Gehringer	2,839
004	Harry Heilmann	2,499
005	Sam Crawford	2,466
006	Lou Whitaker	2,369
007	Alan Trammell	2,365
008	Miguel Cabrera	2,145
009	Bobby Veach	1,859
010	Norm Cash	1,793
011	Donie Bush	1,745
012	Bill Freehan	1,591
013	Hank Greenberg	1,528
014	Willie Horton	1,490
015	Dick McAuliffe	1,471
016	Harvey Kuenn	1,372
017	Bobby Higginson	1,336
018	Rudy York	1,317
019	Mickey Stanley	1,243
020	Billy Rogell	1,210
021	Jim Northrup	1,184
022	Pete Fox	1,182
023	Travis Fryman	1,176
024	Kirk Gibson	1,140
025	Lance Parrish	1,123
026	Brandon Inge	1,083
027	George Kell	1,075
028	Chet Lemon	1,071
029	Aurelio Rodriguez	1,040
030	Victor Martinez	1,033
031	Lu Blue	1,002
032	Magglio Ordonez	989
033	Ron LeFlore	970
034	Gee Walker	966
035	Cecil Fielder	947
036	Don Wert	927
037	Carlos Guillen	892
038	Pinky Higgins	878
039	Tom Brookens	871
040	Nicholas Castellanos	862
041	Bob Fothergill	823
042	Marv Owen	820
043	Oscar Stanage	819
044	Placido Polanco	806
045	Damion Easley	803
046	Vic Wertz	798
047	Ralph Young	792
048	Bob Jones	791
049	Hoot Evers	787
050	Tony Clark	783

George Moriarty

Rank	Player	Hits
	Matty McIntyre	783
052	Tony Phillips	771
053	Doc Cramer	768
054	Larry Herndon	765
055	Frank Bolling	761
056	Barney McCosky	744
057	Austin Jackson	743
058	John Stone	736
059	Ray Boone	723
	Charlie Maxwell	723
061	Steve Kemp	711
062	Ivan Rodriguez	709
063	Curtis Granderson	702
064	Johnny Bassler	690
065	Ian Kinsler	681
066	Pat Mullin	676
067	Heinie Manush	674
068	Ossie Vitt	671
069	George Moriarty	670
070	Marty McManus	664
071	Johnny Groth	663
072	Jimmy Barrett	660
073	Deivi Cruz	652
074	Charley O'Leary	642
075	Rocky Colavito	633
076	Dick Wakefield	624
077	Johnny Lipon	609
078	Craig Monroe	607
079	Omar Infante	605
080	Davy Jones	586
	Eddie Mayo	586
082	Dale Alexander	583
083	Gates Brown	582
	Goose Goslin	582
	Rusty Staub	582
086	Bill Tuttle	566
087	Jason Thompson	565
088	Alex Avila	564
089	Darrell Evans	559
090	Germany Schaefer	558
091	Roy Johnson	550
092	Ramon Santiago	540
093	Ray Hayworth	538
094	Birdie Tebbetts	535
095	Billy Bruton	525
096	Jose Iglesias	513
097	Dave Bergman	509
	J.D. Martinez	509
099	Bill Coughlin	500
	Dmitri Young	500

ALL TIME TIGER HITTING LEADERS – SINGLES

Rank	Player	Singles
001	Ty Cobb	2,840
002	Al Kaline	2,035
003	Charlie Gehringer	1,935
004	Sam Crawford	1,745
005	Alan Trammell	1,713
006	Harry Heilmann	1,693
007	Lou Whitaker	1,640
008	Donie Bush	1,482
009	Miguel Cabrera	1,360
010	Bobby Veach	1,319
011	Norm Cash	1,139
012	Bill Freehan	1,115
013	Harvey Kuenn	1,032
014	Dick McAuliffe	991
015	Willie Horton	986
016	Billy Rogell	880
017	Mickey Stanley	877
018	Pete Fox	849
019	Bobby Higginson	846
020	George Kell	805
021	Rudy York	800
022	Jim Northrup	793
023	Hank Greenberg	787
024	Travis Fryman	769
025	Ron LeFlore	755
026	Lu Blue	741
027	Aurelio Rodriguez	731
028	Victor Martinez	730
029	Kirk Gibson	713
030	Don Wert	707
031	Brandon Inge	693
032	Magglio Ordonez	690
033	Lance Parrish	687
034	Chet Lemon	679
035	Ralph Young	672
036	Gee Walker	657
037	Oscar Stanage	654
038	Pinky Higgins	638
039	Doc Cramer	631
040	Bob Jones	626
041	Marv Owen	622
042	Matty McIntyre	617
	Placido Polanco	617
044	Tom Brookens	605
045	Johnny Bassler	576
	Carlos Guillen	576
047	Bob Fothergill	568
048	Tony Phillips	566
049	Jimmy Barrett	561
050	Cecil Fielder	557
051	Ossie Vitt	553

Harvey Kuenn

Rank	Player	Singles
052	Hoot Evers	550
053	Frank Bolling	545
054	Barney McCosky	543
055	Charlie O'Leary	537
056	Larry Herndon	535
057	George Moriarty	534
058	Davy Jones	520
059	Nicholas Castellanos	518
060	Austin Jackson	514
	Vic Wertz	514
062	Damion Easley	509
063	Johnny Lipon	496
064	John Stone	495
065	Steve Kemp	490
	Ivan Rodriguez	490
067	Ray Boone	488
068	Johnny Groth	484
069	Charlie Maxwell	478
070	Heinie Manush	470
071	Tony Clark	464
072	Ian Kinsler	456
073	Eddie Mayo	451
074	Germany Schaefer	450
075	Deivi Cruz	449
076	Marty McManus	445
077	Pat Mullin	440
078	Dick Wakefield	437
079	Bill Tuttle	431
080	Bill Coughlin	428
081	Ray Hayworth	427
082	Omar Infante	422
083	Curtis Granderson	418
	Ramon Santiago	418
085	Gates Brown	401
	Birdie Tebbetts	401
087	Rusty Staub	400
088	Goose Goslin	394
089	Dale Alexander	386
090	Dave Bergman	385
091	Billy Bruton	382
092	Rocky Colavito	380
093	Topper Rigney	376
	Jo-Jo White	376
095	Jason Thompson	375
096	Jose Iglesias	374
097	Craig Monroe	367
098	Jimmy Outlaw	359
099	Alex Avila	358
100	Roy Johnson	353
	Jake Wood	353

001	Ty Cobb	665
002	Charlie Gehringer	574
003	Al Kaline	498
004	Harry Heilmann	497
005	Lou Whitaker	420
006	Miguel Cabrera	414
007	Alan Trammell	412
008	Sam Crawford	402
009	Hank Greenberg	366
010	Bobby Veach	345
011	Bobby Higginson	270
012	Harvey Kuenn	244
013	Norm Cash	241
	Bill Freehan	241
015	Rudy York	236
016	Travis Fryman	229
017	Billy Rogell	227
018	Pete Fox	222
019	Chet Lemon	218
	Dick McAuliffe	218
021	Gee Walker	216
022	Brandon Inge	212
023	Willie Horton	211
024	George Kell	210
025	Nicholas Castellanos	208
026	Jim Northrup	204
027	Lance Parrish	201
	Mickey Stanley	201
029	Aurelio Rodriguez	193
030	Victor Martinez	188
031	Kirk Gibson	187
032	Carlos Guillen	186
	Magglio Ordonez	186
034	Bob Fothergill	182
035	Donie Bush	181
036	Lu Blue	176
037	Damion Easley	174
038	Pinky Higgins	164
039	Tom Brookens	162
040	Deivi Cruz	157
041	Tony Clark	156
042	John Stone	146
043	Marty McManus	145
	Vic Wertz	145
045	Cecil Fielder	141
046	Hoot Evers	140
	Austin Jackson	140
	Ivan Rodriguez	140
049	Placido Polanco	139
050	Marv Owen	135

Nicholas Castellanos

051	Barney McCosky	130
	Craig Monroe	130
053	Ian Kinsler	129
	Tony Phillips	129
055	Don Wert	128
056	Frank Bolling	126
	Johnny Groth	126
	Roy Johnson	126
	Ron LeFlore	126
	Curtis Granderson	125
061	Heinie Manush	124
062	Dale Alexander	123
	Oscar Stanage	123

064	Alex Avila	122
065	Bob Jones	120
066	Goose Goslin	116
067	Steve Kemp	114
068	Jose Iglesias	113
069	Omar Infante	112
	George Moriarty	112
071	J.D. Martinez	111
072	Larry Herndon	110
073	Matty McIntyre	109
074	Rocky Colavito	107
075	Pat Mullin	106
076	Jeimer Candelario	105
077	Rusty Staub	104
078	Dick Wakefield	102
079	Ray Boone	100
	Dmitri Young	100
081	Eddie Mayo	99
	Birdie Tebbetts	99
083	Johnny Bassler	98
084	Doc Cramer	96
085	Ryan Raburn	95
086	Jhonny Peralta	94
087	Charlie Maxwell	92
088	Ray Hayworth	90
089	Charlie O'Leary	89
	Ralph Young	89
091	Al Wingo	86
092	Mickey Tettleton	85
093	Juan Encarnacion	84
094	Mickey Cochrane	83
095	Jason Thompson	82
096	Johnny Lipon	80
097	Jackie Tavener	79
098	Gates Brown	78
099	Jerry Priddy	77
	Bill Tuttle	77

Rank	Player	Triples
001	Ty Cobb	284
002	Sam Crawford	249
003	Charlie Gehringer	146
004	Harry Heilmann	145
005	Bobby Veach	136
006	Al Kaline	75
007	Donie Bush	73
008	Dick McAuliffe	70
009	Hank Greenberg	69
010	Lu Blue	66
011	Lou Whitaker	65
012	Billy Rogell	64
013	Curtis Granderson	57
014	Alan Trammell	55
015	Matty McIntyre	54
016	Pete Fox	52
	Barney McCosky	52
018	John Stone	50
019	Jackie Tavener	49
020	Roy Johnson	48
	Mickey Stanley	48
022	Bob Fothergill	47
023	Kirk Gibson	45
024	Austin Jackson	43
	Harvey Kuenn	43
	Pat Mullin	43
027	Heinie Manush	42
	Jim Northrup	42
	Rudy York	42
030	Norm Cash	40
	Ossie Vitt	40
032	Tom Brookens	38
	Brandon Inge	38
	Bob Jones	38
	Ron LeFlore	38
	Marv Owen	38
037	Larry Herndon	37
038	Bill Freehan	35
	Carlos Guillen	35
	George Kell	35
041	Hoot Evers	34
	Oscar Stanage	34
043	Bobby Higginson	33
	Jo-Jo White	33
045	Nicholas Castellanos	32
	Chet Lemon	32
	Gee Walker	32
048	Willie Horton	31
	Aurelio Rodriguez	31
050	Jimmy Barrett	30

Marv Owen

Rank	Player	Triples
	Ray Boone	30
	Vic Wertz	30
053	Doc Cramer	29
	Travis Fryman	29
	Topper Rigney	29
	Dick Wakefield	29
057	Ralph Young	28
058	Marty McManus	27
059	Dale Alexander	26
	Frank Bolling	26
	Jake Wood	26
062	Omar Infante	25
	Germany Schaefer	25
064	George Burns	24
	Juan Encarnacion	24
	Claude Rossman	24
067	Billy Bruton	23
	Johnny Lipon	23
	Lance Parrish	23
	Bill Tuttle	23
071	Goose Goslin	22
	Boss Schmidt	22
073	Milt Cuyler	21
074	Kid Elberfeld	20
	Charlie Maxwell	20
	George Mullin	20
077	Gates Brown	19
	Jim Delahanty	19
	Johnny Groth	19
	Davy Jones	19
	Marty Kavanagh	19
	George Moriarty	19
	Harry Rice	19
	Birdie Tebbetts	19
	Jack Warner	19
086	Jim Delahanty	18
	Del Gainer	18
	Steve Kemp	18
	Ian Kinsler	18
	Ramon Santiago	18
091	Eddie Ainsmith	17
	Shane Halter	17
	Jerry Priddy	17
	Ivan Rodriguez	17
095	Doc Casey	16
	Damion Easley	16
	Kid Gleason	16
	Ray Hayworth	16
	Pinky Higgins	16
	Al Wingo	16

Rank	Player	HR
001	Al Kaline	399
002	Norm Cash	373
003	Miguel Cabrera	364
004	Hank Greenberg	306
005	Willie Horton	262
006	Cecil Fielder	245
007	Lou Whitaker	244
008	Rudy York	239
009	Lance Parrish	212
010	Bill Freehan	200
011	Kirk Gibson	195
012	Dick McAuliffe	192
013	Bobby Higginson	187
014	Alan Trammell	185
015	Charlie Gehringer	184
016	Harry Heilmann	164
017	Tony Clark	156
018	Travis Fryman	149
019	Jim Northrup	145
020	Chet Lemon	142
021	Darrell Evans	141
022	Brandon Inge	140
023	Rocky Colavito	139
024	Charlie Maxwell	133
025	Mickey Stanley	117
026	Victor Martinez	115
027	Mickey Tettleton	112
028	Ty Cobb	111
029	Vic Wertz	109
030	Magglio Ordonez	107
031	Ray Boone	105
032	Nicholas Castellanos	104
	Damion Easley	104
034	Curtis Granderson	102
035	Craig Monroe	101
036	J.D. Martinez	99
	Marcus Thames	99
038	Jason Thompson	98
039	Carlos Guillen	95
040	Steve Kemp	89
041	Pat Mullin	87
042	Aurelio Rodriguez	85
043	Gates Brown	84
044	Larry Herndon	83
045	Dmitri Young	82
046	John Wockenfuss	80
047	Ian Kinsler	78
	Dean Palmer	78
049	Alex Avila	77
	Don Wert	77

Brandon Inge

Rank	Player	HR
051	Carlos Pena	75
052	Rob Deer	71
053	Sam Crawford	70
	Rusty Staub	70
055	Tom Brookens	66
056	Frank Bolling	64
057	Roy Cullenbine	63
	Hoot Evers	63
059	Ivan Rodriguez	62
060	Matt Nokes	61
	Tony Phillips	61
	Gee Walker	61
063	Pinky Higgins	60
064	Pete Fox	59
	Justin Upton	59
	Bobby Veach	59
067	Dick Wakefield	56
068	Prince Fielder	55
069	Ryan Raburn	54
070	Juan Encarnacion	53
	Harvey Kuenn	53
	Jhonny Peralta	53
073	Jeimer Candelario	52
074	Ron LeFlore	51
075	Goose Goslin	50
076	Ben Oglivie	49
077	Dale Alexander	48
078	Marty McManus	47
079	Billy Bruton	46
	Omar Infante	46
	Austin Jackson	46
082	Robert Fick	45
	John Stone	45
084	Melvin Nieves	44
	Gary Sheffield	44
086	Don Demeter	43
087	Brennan Boesch	42
	Niko Goodrum	42
	Frank House	42
090	Walt Dropo	40
	James McCann	40
	Eric Munson	40
	Champ Summers	40
094	Dave Bergman	39
	Billy Rogell	39
096	Heinie Manush	38
	Steve Souchock	38
098	Deivi Cruz	37
	Shane Halter	37
	Placido Polanco	37

ALL TIME TIGER HITTING LEADERS – RUNS BATTED IN

Rank	Player	RBI
001	Ty Cobb	1,811
002	Al Kaline	1,582
003	Harry Heilmann	1,446
004	Charlie Gehringer	1,427
005	Miguel Cabrera	1,281
006	Sam Crawford	1,262
007	Hank Greenberg	1,200
008	Norm Cash	1,088
009	Lou Whitaker	1,084
010	Bobby Veach	1,049
011	Alan Trammell	1,003
012	Rudy York	933
013	Willie Horton	886
014	Cecil Fielder	758
	Bill Freehan	758
016	Bobby Higginson	709
017	Lance Parrish	700
018	Travis Fryman	679
019	Dick McAuliffe	671
020	Kirk Gibson	668
021	Brandon Inge	589
022	Jim Northrup	570
023	Victor Martinez	540
024	Chet Lemon	536
025	Magglio Ordonez	533
	Billy Rogell	533
027	Vic Wertz	531
028	Tony Clark	514
029	Mickey Stanley	500
030	Pete Fox	492
031	Pinky Higgins	472
032	Gee Walker	469
033	Ray Boone	460
034	Charlie Maxwell	455
035	Carlos Guillen	449
036	Bob Fothergill	447
037	Donie Bush	436
038	Rocky Colavito	430
039	Hoot Evers	429
040	Nicholas Castellanos	424
041	Harvey Kuenn	423
	Marv Owen	423
	Aurelio Rodriguez	423
044	Steve Kemp	422
045	George Kell	414
046	Lu Blue	407
047	Darrell Evans	405
048	Damion Easley	400
049	Tom Brookens	397
050	Pat Mullin	385

Heinie Manush

Rank	Player	RBI
051	Craig Monroe	379
052	Marty McManus	374
053	Goose Goslin	371
054	Larry Herndon	364
055	Dale Alexander	363
	Don Wert	363
057	John Stone	359
058	Rusty Staub	358
059	Justin Thompson	354
060	Heinie Manush	345
061	Mickey Tettleton	333
062	Oscar Stanage	323
063	Gates Brown	322
064	Alex Avila	314
	Dick Wakefield	314
066	Johnny Bassler	313
067	Frank Bolling	312
068	Bob Jones	310
069	Tony Phillips	309
070	Johnny Groth	302
071	Ian Kinsler	300
	Ivan Rodriguez	300
073	Curtis Granderson	299
074	J.D. Martinez	285
	Placido Polanco	285
076	John Wockenfuss	284
077	George Moriarty	283
078	Deivi Cruz	277
079	Dmitri Young	267
080	Ron LeFlore	265
081	Roy Cullenbine	259
082	Marcus Thames	255
083	Birdie Tebbetts	254
084	Bob Tuttle	250
085	Topper Rigney	249
086	Dean Palmer	248
087	Doc Cramer	243
088	Jhonny Peralta	242
089	Ray Hayworth	239
090	Austin Jackson	234
	Johnny Lipon	234
092	Barney McCosky	231
093	Eddie Mayo	229
094	Omar Infante	225
095	Juan Encarnacion	224
096	George Burns	222
097	Ralph Young	220
098	Dave Bergman	219
099	Billy Bruton	218
100	Ryan Raburn	216
	Jackie Tavener	216

ALL TIME TIGER HITTING LEADERS – HIT BY PITCH

Rank	Player	HBP
001	Bill Freehan	114
002	Damion Easley	87
	Chet Lemon	87
004	Norm Cash	85
	Ty Cobb	85
006	Brandon Inge	66
007	Al Kaline	55
008	Bobby Veach	53
009	Charlie Gehringer	50
010	Willie Horton	49
011	Ramon Santiago	48
012	Heinie Manush	45
013	Miguel Cabrera	44
014	Kirk Gibson	43
015	Placido Polanco	41
016	Harry Heilmann	39
017	Bobby Higginson	37
	Alan Trammell	37
019	Jim Delahanty	35
	George Moriarty	35
021	Dick McAuliffe	32
022	Travis Fryman	31
023	George Burns	30
	Bill Coughlin	30
	Don Wert	30
026	Donie Bush	29
027	Jose Iglesias	28
	Ian Kinsler	28
	Jim Northrup	28
	Charley O'Leary	28
	Dmitri Young	28
032	Lu Blue	27
	Cecil Fielder	27
034	Prince Fielder	26
035	Juan Encarnacion	25
	Victor Martinez	25
	Oscar Stanage	25
038	JaCoby Jones	24
039	Kid Elberfeld	23
040	Brad Ausmus	22
	Charlie Maxwell	22
042	Jimmy Barrett	21
	Jeimer Candelario	21
	Nicholas Castellanos	21
	Frank O'Rourke	21
	Marv Owen	21
047	Hoot Evers	20
	Gee Walker	20
	Lou Whitaker	20
	Eddie Yost	20
051	Pete Fox	19
	Dean Palmer	19
	Lance Parrish	19
054	Fred Hatfield	18
	Matty McIntyre	18
	Boss Schmidt	18
	Joe Yeager	18
058	Frank Bolling	17
	Doc Casey	17
	Carlos Guillen	17
	Baldy Louden	17
	Billy Rogell	17
063	Sam Crawford	16
	Ira Flagstead	16
	Austin Jackson	16
	George Kell	16
	James McCann	16
	Rusty Staub	16
069	Brennan Boesch	15
	Ray Boone	15
	Gates Brown	15
	Deivi Cruz	15
	Bob Fothergill	15
	Pinky Higgins	15
	Davy Jones	15
	Ron LeFlore	15
	Carlos Pena	15
	Ryan Raburn	15
079	Eddie Brinkman	14
	Tom Brookens	14
	Del Gainer	14
	Curtis Granderson	14
	Torii Hunter	14
	Gerald Laird	14
	Tony Phillips	14
	Aurelio Rodriguez	14
	Gary Sheffield	14
	Jake Wood	14
089	Wayne Belardi	13
	Frank Catalanotto	13
	Tony Clark	13
	Milt Cuyler	13
	Tom Jones	13
	Steve Kemp	13
	Rondell White	13
096	Alex Avila	12
	Robert Fick	12
	Hank Greenberg	12
	Shane Halter	12
	Dick Harley	12
	Mike Heath	12
	Tubby Spencer	12
	Jack R. Warner	12
	Ralph Young	12

Doc Casey

Rank	Player	ROE
001	Al Kaline	173
002	Mickey Stanley	118
003	Alan Trammell	117
004	Charlie Gehringer	106
	Lou Whitaker	106
006	Bill Freehan	86
007	Willie Horton	85
008	Norm Cash	73
	Dick McAuliffe	73
010	Harvey Kuenn	70
	Aurelio Rodriguez	70
012	Ron LeFlore	64
013	Rudy York	62
014	Tom Brookens	59
	Travis Fryman	59
016	Lance Parrish	58
017	Kirk Gibson	57
	Don Wert	57
019	Chet Lemon	55
	Jim Northrup	55
021	Frank Bolling	52
022	Miguel Cabrera	50
023	Pete Fox	49
	Brandon Inge	49
025	Cecil Fielder	48
026	Billy Rogell	46
027	Ray Boone	44
028	Hank Greenberg	43
	George Kell	43
030	Hoot Evers	42
031	Doc Cramer	39
	Bobby Higginson	39
	Eddie Lake	39
	Tony Phillips	39
035	Deivi Cruz	38
	Marv Owen	38
037	Barney McCosky	37
	Gee Walker	37
039	Eddie Brinkman	35
	Nicholas Castellanos	35
	Damion Easley	35
	Pinky Higgins	35
	Austin Jackson	35
	Charlie Maxwell	35
045	Placido Polanco	34
046	Steve Kemp	33
047	Billy Bruton	32
	Carlos Guillen	32
	Johnny Lipon	32
050	Harry Heilmann	31
	Marty McManus	31

Tom Brookens

Rank	Player	ROE
	Craig Monroe	31
	John Stone	31
	Bill Tuttle	31
055	Larry Herndon	30
	Jerry Lumpe	30
	Victor Martinez	30
	Vic Wertz	30
059	Rocky Colavito	29
	Jim Delsing	29
	Jerry Groth	29
	Eddie Mayo	29
	Jimmy Outlaw	29
	Jerry Priddy	29
	Jackie Tavener	29
	Birdie Tebbetts	29
067	Gates Brown	28
	Ray Hayworth	28
	Roy Johnson	28
	Jason Thompson	28
071	Jimmy Bloodworth	27
	Milt Cuyler	27
	Bob Fothergill	27
074	Dave Bergman	26
	Darrell Evans	26
	Juan Encarnacion	26
	Ramon Santiago	26
	Jake Wood	26
079	Fred Hatfield	25
	John Wockenfuss	25
081	Mike Heath	24
	Jose Iglesias	24
	Bob Swift	24
	Red Wilson	24
085	Dale Alexander	23
	Tony Clark	23
	Pat Mullin	23
088	Chico Fernandez	22
	Shane Halter	22
	Joe Hoover	22
	Omar Infante	22
	Rusty Staub	22
	Dick Wakefield	22
094	Ivan Rodriguez	21
	Tom Veryzer	21
096	Don Kolloway	19
	Heinie Manush	19
	Magglio Ordonez	19
099	Curtis Granderson	18
	Ian Kinsler	18
	Gary Sutherland	18
	Jo-Jo White	18

ALL TIME TIGER HITTING LEADERS – ON-BASE PERCENTAGE

Rank	Player	OBP
001	Ty Cobb	.434
002	Johnny Bassler	.420
003	Roy Cullenbine	.412
	Hank Greenberg	.412
005	Harry Heilmann	.410
006	Al Wingo	.406
007	Charlie Gehringer	.404
008	Lu Blue	.403
009	Dick Wakefield	.396
010	Tony Phillips	.395
011	Jim Delahanty	.394
012	Dale Alexander	.391
	George Kell	.391
014	Topper Rigney	.389
015	Miguel Cabrera	.387
	Prince Fielder	.387
	Mickey Tettleton	.387
018	Barney McCosky	.386
019	Fred Haney	.383
020	Jimmy Barrett	.382
021	Bob Fothergill	.379
	Heinie Manush	.379
023	Goose Goslin	.376
	Al Kaline	.376
	Steve Kemp	.376
	Vic Wertz	.376
027	Norm Cash	.374
028	Magglio Ordonez	.373
029	Ray Boone	.372
030	Johnny Groth	.370
	Bobby Veach	.370
032	Rudy York	.369
033	Hoot Evers	.368
034	Carlos Guillen	.366
035	Rocky Colavito	.364
	Pinky Higgins	.364
	Eddie Lake	.364
038	Charlie Maxwell	.363
	Lou Whitaker	.363
	Jo-Jo White	.363
041	Sam Crawford	.362
	Billy Rogell	.362
	John Stone	.362
044	J.D. Martinez	.361
045	Harvey Kuenn	.360
046	Marty McManus	.359
047	Bobby Higginson	.358
	Pat Mullin	.358
049	Donie Bush	.357
	Darrell Evans	.357

Roy Cullenbine

Rank	Player	OBP
051	Tony Clark	.355
	Roy Johnson	.355
	Davy Jones	.355
	Johnny Lipon	.355
	Placido Polanco	.355
	Jerry Priddy	.355
057	Kirk Gibson	.354
058	Rusty Staub	.353
059	Alan Trammell	.352
060	Gee Walker	.351
	Cecil Fielder	.351
	Pete Fox	.351
063	Alex Avila	.350
064	Jim Delsing	.349
	Chet Lemon	.349
	Victor Martinez	.349
067	Ron LeFlore	.348
068	Larry Woodall	.347
069	Dave Bergman	.346
	John Wockenfuss	.346
071	Dick McAuliffe	.345
072	Ralph Young	.344
	Curtis Granderson	.344
074	Jason Thompson	.343
	Red Wilson	.343
076	Marv Owen	.342
	Austin Jackson	.342
078	Bill Freehan	.340
	Dmitri Young	.340
080	Damion Easley	.339
	Jimmy Outlaw	.339
082	Matty McIntyre	.338
083	Willie Horton	.337
084	Billy Bruton	.336
	Jeimer Candelario	.336
086	Fred Hatfield	.335
087	Travis Fryman	.334
088	Ray Hayworth	.333
089	Don Kolloway	.332
	Jim Northrup	.332
	Jhonny Peralta	.332
092	Larry Herndon	.331
	Carlos Pena	.331
094	Gates Brown	.330
	Bill Tuttle	.330
	Doc Cramer	.330
097	Ian Kinsler	.328
	Ivan Rodriguez	.328
099	Dean Palmer	.327
100	Frank Bolling	.326
	Eddie Mayo	.326
	Pat Sheridan	.326
	Birdie Tebbetts	.326

Rank	Player	SLG
001	Hank Greenberg	.616
002	J.D. Martinez	.551
003	Miguel Cabrera	.529
004	Harry Heilmann	.518
005	Ty Cobb	.516
006	Dale Alexander	.512
007	Rudy York	.503
008	Tony Clark	.502
009	Rocky Colavito	.501
	Marcus Thames	.501
011	Cecil Fielder	.498
012	Prince Fielder	.491
013	Norm Cash	.490
014	Dmitri Young	.486
015	Curtis Granderson	.484
016	Ray Boone	.482
	Bob Fothergill	.482
018	Charlie Gehringer	.480
	Kirk Gibson	.480
	Al Kaline	.480
	Mickey Tettleton	.480
022	Carlos Guillen	.476
	Vic Wertz	.476
	Magglio Ordonez	.476
025	Heinie Manush	.475
026	Willie Horton	.472
027	Lance Parrish	.469
	Gee Walker	.469
029	Charlie Maxwell	.465
030	Carlos Pena	.461
031	Dean Palmer	.460
	John Stone	.460
033	Nicholas Castellanos	.459
034	Goose Goslin	.456
035	Bobby Higginson	.455
036	Roy Cullenbine	.454
037	Pat Mullin	.453
038	Craig Monroe	.451
039	Steve Kemp	.450
	Darrell Evans	.450
041	Ivan Rodriguez	.449
042	Sam Crawford	.448
043	Dick Wakefield	.447
044	Juan Encarnacion	.444
	Travis Fryman	.444
	Ben Oglivie	.444
	Bobby Veach	.444
048	Victor Martinez	.440
049	John Wockenfuss	.439
050	Roy Johnson	.438
051	Chet Lemon	.437
052	Jason Thompson	.436
	Larry Herndon	.436
	Hoot Evers	.436
	Ian Kinsler	.436
056	Rusty Staub	.434
	Barney McCosky	.434
	Marty McManus	.434
059	George Kell	.433
	Jhonny Peralta	.433
061	Pete Fox	.430
	Jim Northrup	.430
	Ryan Raburn	.430
064	Damion Easley	.428
065	Lou Whitaker	.426
	Harvey Kuenn	.426
067	Al Wingo	.423
068	Gates Brown	.420
069	Placido Polanco	.418
070	Jeimer Candelario	.415
	Alan Trammell	.415
072	Brennan Boesch	.414
073	Austin Jackson	.413
074	Bill Freehan	.412
075	Johnny Groth	.410
076	Walt Dropo	.408
	Dick McAuliffe	.408
078	Ron LeFlore	.406
079	Tony Phillips	.405
080	Alex Avila	.404
081	Lu Blue	.403
082	Niko Goodrum	.401
083	Pinky Higgins	.400
084	Jim Delahanty	.399
	Shane Halter	.399
	Omar Infante	.399
087	Billy Bruton	.396
088	Mike Heath	.395
089	Jim Delsing	.394
090	Topper Rigney	.393
091	Deivi Cruz	.390
092	Frank Bolling	.388
093	Brandon Inge	.387
094	Billy Rogell	.381
095	Jerry Priddy	.380
096	Frank House	.377
	Mickey Stanley	.377
098	Marv Owen	.374
099	Pat Sheridan	.372
	Jackie Tavener	.372

Ray Boone

Rank	Player	OPS
001	Hank Greenberg	1.028
002	Ty Cobb	.950
003	Harry Heilmann	.927
004	Miguel Cabrera	.916
005	J.D. Martinez	.912
006	Dale Alexander	.903
007	Charlie Gehringer	.884
008	Prince Fielder	.878
009	Rudy York	.873
010	Mickey Tettleton	.867
011	Rocky Colavito	.865
	Norm Cash	.865
	Roy Cullenbine	.865
014	Bob Fothergill	.861
015	Tony Clark	.857
016	Al Kaline	.855
017	Ray Boone	.854
018	Heinie Manush	.853
019	Vic Wertz	.852
020	Cecil Fielder	.849
	Magglio Ordonez	.849
022	Dick Wakefield	.843
023	Carlos Guillen	.842
024	Kirk Gibson	.834
025	Goose Goslin	.832
026	Al Wingo	.829
027	Curtis Granderson	.828
	Charlie Maxwell	.828
029	Steve Kemp	.826
	Dmitri Young	.826
031	George Kell	.824
032	John Stone	.822
033	Barney McCosky	.820
	Gee Walker	.820
035	Bobby Veach	.814
036	Bobby Higginson	.813
037	Pat Mullin	.811
038	Sam Crawford	.810
039	Willie Horton	.808
	Marcus Thames	.808
041	Darrell Evans	.806
	Lu Blue	.806
043	Hoot Evers	.803
044	Tony Phillips	.800
045	Jim Delahanty	.793
	Darrell Evans	.793
	Roy Johnson	.793
	Marty McManus	.793
049	Carlos Pena	.792
050	Victor Martinez	.789
	Lou Whitaker	.789

Prince Fielder

Rank	Player	OPS
052	Dean Palmer	.787
	Rusty Staub	.787
054	Johnny Bassler	.786
	Lance Parrish	.786
	Chet Lemon	.786
	Harvey Kuenn	.786
058	John Wockenfuss	.785
059	Nicholas Castellanos	.783
060	Topper Rigney	.782
061	Pete Fox	.781
062	Johnny Groth	.780
063	Travis Fryman	.779
	Jason Thompson	.779
065	Ivan Rodriguez	.777
066	Placido Polanco	.773
067	Ben Oglivie	.770
068	Larry Herndon	.767
	Damion Easley	.767
	Alan Trammell	.767
071	Pinky Higgins	.764
	Ian Kinsler	.764
	Jhonny Peralta	.764
074	Jim Northrup	.762
075	Austin Jackson	.755
076	Alex Avila	.754
	Ron LeFlore	.754
	Craig Monroe	.754
079	Juan Encarnacion	.753
	Dick McAuliffe	.753
081	Bill Freehan	.752
082	Jeimer Candelario	.751
083	Gates Brown	.750
084	Jim Delsing	.744
085	Fred Haney	.742
	Billy Rogell	.742
087	Jimmy Barrett	.741
088	Ryan Raburn	.740
089	Jerry Priddy	.735
090	Billy Bruton	.732
091	Brennan Boesch	.729
092	Marv Owen	.717
093	Walt Dropo	.716
094	Dave Bergman	.714
	Frank Bolling	.714
096	Red Wilson	.709
097	Shane Halter	.708
	Mike Heath	.708
099	Niko Goodrum	.707
	Jo-Jo White	.707

001	Ty Cobb	171
002	Hank Greenberg	161
003	Harry Heilmann	149
004	J.D. Martinez	147
005	Miguel Cabrera	145
	Sam Crawford	145
007	Norm Cash	139
008	Prince Fielder	136
009	Mickey Tettleton	135
010	Roy Cullenbine	134
	Al Kaline	134
012	Dick Wakefield	131
013	Ray Boone	130
	Rocky Colavito	130
	Bobby Veach	130
016	Dale Alexander	129
	Jim Delahanty	129
018	Rudy York	128
019	Willie Horton	127
020	Cecil Fielder	126
021	Kirk Gibson	125
	Steve Kemp	125
	Vic Wertz	125
024	Charlie Gehringer	124
025	Magglio Ordonez	123
026	Bob Fothergill	122
027	Tony Clark	121
	Darrell Evans	121
	Carlos Guillen	121
030	Heinie Manush	120
	Charlie Maxwell	120
	Tony Phillips	120
	Dmitri Young	120
034	George Kell	119
035	Jimmy Barrett	117
	Chet Lemon	117
	Rusty Staub	117
	Lou Whitaker	117
039	John Wockenfuss	116
040	Victor Martinez	115
	Pat Mullin	115
	Jim Northrup	115
	Claude Rossman	115
044	Curtis Granderson	114
	Lance Parrish	114
	Al Wingo	114
047	Bobby Higginson	113
	Ben Oglivie	113
	Jason Thompson	113
050	Hoot Evers	112
	Bill Freehan	112
	Harvey Kuenn	112
	Matty McIntyre	112
	Carlos Pena	112
055	Goose Goslin	111
	Dick McAuliffe	111
057	Lu Blue	110
	Gates Brown	110
	Nicholas Castellanos	110
	Larry Herndon	110
	Barney McCosky	110
	John Stone	110
	Alan Trammell	110
064	Ian Kinsler	108
	Ron LeFlore	108
	Marcus Thames	108
	Gee Walker	108
068	Johnny Groth	107
069	Alex Avila	106
	Johnny Bassler	106
	Travis Fryman	106
	Jhonny Peralta	106
073	Austin Jackson	105
	Topper Rigney	105
075	Jeimer Candelario	104
076	Jim Delsing	103
	Marty McManus	103
	Dean Palmer	103
	Placido Polanco	103
	Ivan Rodriguez	103
081	Pinky Higgins	102
	Roy Johnson	102
083	George Burns	101
	Damion Easley	101
085	Dave Bergman	100
	Davy Jones	100
087	George Mullin	99
088	Billy Bruton	97
	Pete Fox	97
	Mike Heath	97
	Craig Monroe	97
092	Brennan Boesch	96
	Walt Dropo	96
	Ryan Raburn	96
095	Juan Encarnacion	95
	Jerry Priddy	95
097	Fred Haney	94
	Germany Schaefer	94
099	Pat Sheridan	93
100	Donie Bush	92

J.D. Martinez

001	Ty Cobb	9.20
002	Charlie Gehringer	13.67
003	Harry Heilmann	13.93
004	Hank Greenberg	14.40
005	Dale Alexander	17.87
006	Heinie Manush	22.80
007	Miguel Cabrera	22.93
008	J.D. Martinez	24.27
009	Goose Goslin	25.40
010	Bob Fothergill	25.93
011	Al Kaline	26.53
012	Gee Walker	26.60
013	Rudy York	26.87
014	Sam Crawford	26.93
015	Barney McCosky	27.20
016	Carlos Guillen (121 OPS+)	28.60
017	John Stone (110 OPS+)	28.60
018	Prince Fielder	29.00
019	Bobby Veach	29.20
020	Kirk Gibson	29.20
021	Curtis Granderson	29.33
022	Roy Johnson	29.47
023	George Kell	29.87
024	Rocky Colavito	30.07
025	Vic Wertz	30.67
026	Ray Boone	31.07
027	Magglio Ordonez	31.13
028	Lu Blue	31.40
029	Dick Wakefield	31.93
030	R. Cullenbine (134 OPS+)	32.67
031	Tony Clark (121 OPS+)	32.67
032	Norm Cash	32.80
033	Mickey Tettleton	34.00
034	Al Wingo	34.27
035	Steve Kemp	35.20
036	Pete Fox	35.60
037	Tony Phillips	35.93
038	Jim Delahanty	36.07
039	Marty McManus	36.13
040	Cecil Fielder	36.40
041	Harvey Kuenn	37.60
042	Bobby Higginson	38.13
043	Dmitri Young	38.20
044	Hoot Evers	38.67
045	Lou Whitaker	39.07
046	Charlie Maxwell	39.33
047	Ron LeFlore	39.60
048	Pat Mullin	41.33
049	Placido Polanco	41.60
050	Ian Kinsler	42.13
051	Alan Trammell	43.73

Dale Alexander

052	Austin Jackson	44.13
053	Rusty Staub	44.47
054	Willie Horton	44.53
055	Travis Fryman	44.80
056	Topper Rigney	45.13
057	Jimmy Barrett	45.33
058	Darrell Evans	46.47
059	Carlos Pena	46.80
060	Ivan Rodriguez	46.93
061	Lance Parrish	47.40
062	Victor Martinez	47.60
063	Chet Lemon	47.87
064	Damion Easley	47.93
065	Dean Palmer	48.00
066	Billy Rogell	48.33
067	N. Castellanos (110 OPS+)	48.40
068	M. Thames (108 OPS+)	48.40
069	Johnny Groth (107 OPS+)	48.40
070	Fred Haney	49.00
071	Juan Encarnacion	49.13
072	Johnny Bassler	50.27
073	Pinky Higgins	50.53
074	Ben Oglivie	51.53
075	Jason Thompson	51.60
076	Billy Bruton	51.87
077	D. McAuliffe (111 OPS+)	52.27
078	L. Herndon (110 OPS+)	52.27
079	J. Wockenfuss (116 OPS+)	52.67
080	Jim Northrup (115 OPS+)	52.67
081	Craig Monroe	53.40
082	Jeimer Candelario	53.67
083	Jhonny Peralta	54.67
084	Jim Delsing	55.20
085	Jo-Jo White	56.53
086	Alex Avila	57.73
087	Gates Brown	57.87
088	Bill Freehan (112 OPS+)	58.47
089	Jerry Priddy (95 OPS+)	58.47
090	Marv Owen	58.60
091	Ryan Raburn	58.80
092	Johnny Lipon	59.13
093	Brennan Boesch	59.67
094	Davy Jones	60.00
095	Eddie Lake	60.53
096	Frank Bolling	60.60
097	Matty McIntyre	61.20
098	Niko Goodrum	61.33
099	Donie Bush	62.27
100	Brian Hunter	62.53

Rank	Player	Avg
001	Hank Greenberg	1.128
002	Ty Cobb	1.099
003	Harry Heilmann	.971
004	Roy Cullenbine	.935
005	Charlie Gehringer	.924
006	Mickey Tettleton	.923
007	Miguel Cabrera	.912
008	Dale Alexander	.908
009	J.D. Martinez	.905
010	Norm Cash	.883
011	Prince Fielder	.877
012	Kirk Gibson	.872
013	Rudy York	.869
014	Rocky Colavito	.862
015	Al Wingo	.854
016	Heinie Manush	.853
017	Al Kaline	.849
018	Lu Blue	.845
019	Dick Wakefield	.842
020	Vic Wertz	.841
021	Curtis Granderson	.838
	Goose Goslin	.838
023	Tony Clark	.837
	Cecil Fielder	.837
	Charlie Maxwell	.837
026	Ray Boone	.835
027	Tony Phillips	.831
028	Jim Delahanty	.829
029	Bob Fothergill	.828
	Carlos Guillen	.822
	Steve Kemp	.820
	Darrell Evans	.820
033	Sam Crawford	.819
034	Johnny Bassler	.811
	Bobby Higginson	.811
	Barney McCosky	.811
	Bobby Veach	.811
038	Gee Walker	.808
039	Magglio Ordonez	.802
040	John Stone	.792
041	Roy Johnson	.790
042	Pat Mullin	.789
043	Topper Rigney	.788
044	Marty McManus	.785
045	Lou Whitaker	.781
046	Dmitri Young	.776
047	George Kell	.775
048	Carlos Pena	.774
049	Jimmy Barrett	.770
	Marcus Thames	.770

Brennan Boesch

Rank	Player	Avg
051	Ron LeFlore	.769
052	Dean Palmer	.764
053	Hoot Evers	.760
054	Willie Horton	.754
055	Damion Easley	.748
056	Chet Lemon	.747
	John Wockenfuss	.747
058	Jason Thompson	.746
059	Pete Fox	.744
060	Rusty Staub	.739
061	Alan Trammell	.738
062	Travis Fryman	.737
063	Dick McAuliffe	.733
064	Alex Avila	.730
	Fred Haney	.730
066	Austin Jackson	.726
067	Billy Rogell	.725
068	Nicholas Castellanos	.722
	Lance Parrish	.722
070	Ben Oglivie	.721
071	Jeimer Candelario	.720
	Victor Martinez	.720
073	Johnny Groth	.717
	Harvey Kuenn	.717
075	Ian Kinsler	.715
076	Jo-Jo White	.714
077	Gates Brown	.710
	Jim Delsing	.710
	Juan Encarnacion	.710
080	Pinky Higgins	.709
	Dick McAuliffe	.709
082	Billy Bruton	.704
	Bill Freehan	.704
084	Jim Northrup	.703
085	Larry Herndon	.702
086	Placido Polanco	.697
087	Jhonny Peralta	.691
088	Ivan Rodriguez	.689
089	Donie Bush	.688
	Davy Jones	.688
091	Niko Goodrum	.683
092	Craig Monroe	.682
093	Eddie Lake	.679
094	Ryan Raburn	.676
095	Jerry Priddy	.673
096	Brennan Boesch	.672
097	Dave Bergman	.666
	Pat Sheridan	.666
099	Brian Hunter	.660
100	Marv Owen	.657

001	Hank Greenberg	1.127
002	Ty Cobb	1.096
003	Harry Heilmann	.972
004	Roy Cullenbine	.936
005	Charlie Gehringer	.926
006	Mickey Tettleton	.924
007	Miguel Cabrera	.913
008	Dale Alexander	.911
009	J.D. Martinez	.906
010	Norm Cash	.884
011	Prince Fielder	.879
012	Kirk Gibson	.875
013	Rudy York	.870
014	Rocky Colavito	.864
015	Heinie Manush	.861
016	Al Wingo	.860
017	Lu Blue	.852
	Al Kaline	.852
019	Dick Wakefield	.843
020	Vic Wertz	.842
021	Curtis Granderson	.840
	Charlie Maxwell	.840
023	Ray Boone	.839
	Tony Clark	.839
	Cecil Fielder	.839
	Goose Goslin	.839
027	Bob Fothergill	.836
028	Tony Phillips	.834
029	Sam Crawford	.826
030	Carlos Guillen	.825
	Barney McCosky	.825
032	Steve Kemp	.823
033	Johnny Bassler	.822
	Darrell Evans	.822
	Bobby Veach	.822
036	Bobby Higginson	.815
037	Gee Walker	.811
038	Magglio Ordonez	.805
	Topper Rigney	.805
040	John Stone	.795
041	Marty McManus	.793
042	Roy Johnson	.792
	Pat Mullin	.792
044	Lou Whitaker	.787
045	George Kell	.782
046	Dmitri Young	.778
047	Carlos Pena	.777
048	Jimmy Barrett	.775
049	Ron LeFlore	.772
	Marcus Thames	.772

Jhonny Peralta

051	Dean Palmer	.767
052	Hoot Evers	.765
053	Willie Horton	.757
054	Damion Easley	.752
055	Chet Lemon	.751
056	Jason Thompson	.750
	John Wockenfuss	.750
058	Pete Fox	.749
059	Fred Haney	.747
060	Rusty Staub	.746
	Alan Trammell	.746
062	Travis Fryman	.743
063	Dick McAuliffe	.737
064	Alex Avila	.734
065	Austin Jackson	.731
	Billy Rogell	.731
067	Ben Oglivie	.726
	Lance Parrish	.726
069	Nicholas Castellanos	.725
070	Victor Martinez	.724
071	Bill Coughlin	.723
072	Jeimer Candelario	.721
	Harvey Kuenn	.721
	Johnny Groth	.721
075	Jo-Jo White	.719
076	Ian Kinsler	.718
077	Pinky Higgins	.716
078	Juan Encarnacion	.715
079	Gates Brown	.714
080	Jim Delsing	.713
081	Billy Bruton	.710
082	Bill Freehan	.709
083	Larry Herndon	.707
084	Donie Bush	.706
	Jim Northrup	.706
086	Placido Polanco	.703
087	Davy Jones	.698
088	Jhonny Peralta	.696
089	Ivan Rodriguez	.694
090	Craig Monroe	.688
091	Eddie Lake	.687
092	Niko Goodrum	.685
093	Ryan Raburn	.681
094	Jerry Priddy	.679
095	Brennan Boesch	.675
096	Dave Bergman	.674
	Pat Sheridan	.674
098	Red Wilson	.669
099	Marv Owen	.667
100	Brian Hunter	.666
	Jackie Tavener	.666

Rank	Player	GPA
001	Hank Greenberg	.339
002	Ty Cobb	.324
003	Harry Heilmann	.314
004	Miguel Cabrera	.306
005	Dale Alexander	.304
006	Charlie Gehringer	.302
007	J.D. Martinez	.300
008	Roy Cullenbine	.299
009	Prince Fielder	.297
010	Mickey Tettleton	.294
011	Rudy York	.292
012	Norm Cash	.291
	Bob Fothergill	.291
014	Dick Wakefield	.290
015	Rocky Colavito	.289
	Al Kaline	.289
	Heinie Manush	.289
	Al Wingo	.289
019	Vic Wertz	.288
	Ray Boone	.288
021	Magglio Ordonez	.287
022	Tony Clark	.285
023	Carlos Guillen	.284
	George Kell	.284
025	Cecil Fielder	.283
	Goose Goslin	.283
027	Lu Blue	.282
	Barney McCosky	.282
	Steve Kemp	.282
030	Johnny Bassler	.280
	Charlie Maxwell	.280
032	Kirk Gibson	.279
	Tony Phillips	.279
034	John Stone	.278
	Bobby Veach	.278
036	Jim Delahanty	.277
037	Curtis Granderson	.276
038	Sam Crawford	.275
	Bobby Higginson	.275
	Gee Walker	.275
041	Hoot Evers	.274
	Pat Mullin	.274
	Dmitri Young	.274
044	Darrell Evans	.273
	Topper Rigney	.273
046	Marty McManus	.270
	Lou Whitaker	.270
048	Johnny Groth	.269
	Willie Horton	.269
	Roy Johnson	.269
051	Harvey Kuenn	.268
052	Victor Martinez	.267
	Rusty Staub	.267

Rudy York

Rank	Player	GPA
054	Chet Lemon	.266
	John Wockenfuss	.266
056	Pete Fox	.265
057	Pinky Higgins	.264
	Carlos Pena	.264
	Placido Polanco	.264
060	Marcus Thames	.263
	Jason Thompson	.263
062	Jimmy Barrett	.262
	Travis Fryman	.262
	Fred Haney	.262
	Dean Palmer	.262
	Alan Trammell	.262
067	Nicholas Castellanos	.260
	Damion Easley	.260
	Lance Parrish	.260
	Ivan Rodriguez	.260
071	Alex Avila	.258
	Larry Herndon	.258
	Ron LeFlore	.258
	Ben Oglivie	.258
	Billy Rogell	.258
076	Austin Jackson	.257
	Dick McAuliffe	.257
	Jim Northrup	.257
	Jhonny Peralta	.257
080	Jim Delsing	.256
	Bill Freehan	.256
	Ian Kinsler	.256
083	Jeimer Candelario	.255
	Jerry Priddy	.255
085	Gates Brown	.254
086	Billy Bruton	.250
	Juan Encarnacion	.250
088	Craig Monroe	.249
	Jo-Jo White	.249
090	Dave Bergman	.248
	Marv Owen	.248
092	Ryan Raburn	.247
093	Red Wilson	.246
094	Brennan Boesch	.245
095	Johnny Lipon	.244
	Frank Bolling	.244
097	Eddie Lake	.243
098	Walt Dropo	.241
	Bill Tuttle	.241
100	Mike Heath	.240
	Pat Sheridan	.240

Rank	Player	WAR
001	Ty Cobb	144.7
002	Al Kaline	92.8
003	Charlie Gehringer	80.7
004	Lou Whitaker	75.1
005	Alan Trammell	70.7
006	Harry Heilmann	67.7
007	Sam Crawford	63.5
008	Hank Greenberg	54.2
009	Norm Cash	51.7
010	Miguel Cabrera	50.5
011	Bobby Veach	45.8
012	Bill Freehan	44.8
013	Donie Bush	38.5
014	Dick McAuliffe	37.5
015	Rudy York	32.0
016	Chet Lemon	30.7
017	Lance Parrish	30.1
018	Kirk Gibson	27.7
019	Travis Fryman	27.5
020	Willie Horton	25.9
021	Tony Phillips	25.3
022	Billy Rogell	24.9
023	Bobby Higginson	23.1
024	George Kell	22.9
025	Jim Northrup	21.4
026	Curtis Granderson	21.2
027	Johnny Bassler	21.1
028	Harvey Kuenn	21.0
029	Lu Blue	20.9
030	Austin Jackson	20.5
031	Ian Kinsler	20.0
032	Charlie Maxwell	19.2
	Placido Polanco	19.2
034	Carlos Guillen	18.6
	Brandon Inge	18.6
036	Damion Easley	17.8
037	Rocky Colavito	17.3
	Mickey Stanley	17.3
039	Cecil Fielder	16.9
040	Matty McIntyre	16.8
041	Ray Boone	16.4
042	Steve Kemp	16.0
	Vic Wertz	16.0
044	Roy Cullenbine	14.9
045	Mickey Tettleton	14.8
046	Darrell Evans	14.5
047	Ron LeFlore	14.2
	Ivan Rodriguez	14.2
049	Jimmy Barrett	13.8
050	Magglio Ordonez	13.4

Bobby Veach

Rank	Player	WAR
051	Marty McManus	13.2
	Dick Wakefield	13.2
053	Barney McCosky	13.1
	George Moriarty	13.1
055	Alex Avila	12.9
	Bob Fothergill	12.9
057	J.D. Martinez	12.8
	Ossie Vitt	12.8
059	Tom Brookens	12.4
	Heinie Manush	12.4
061	Tony Clark	12.2
062	Hoot Evers	12.1
063	Jason Thompson	11.9
064	Gee Walker	11.7
065	Mickey Cochrane	11.4
066	Pinky Higgins	11.3
	Larry Herndon	11.3
	George Mullin	11.3
069	Frank Bolling	11.2
070	Topper Rigney	10.9
071	Dale Alexander	10.7
	John Stone	10.7
073	Pete Fox	10.6
074	Don Wert	10.3
075	Gates Brown	9.9
076	Pat Mullin	9.8
077	Aurelio Rodriguez	9.2
078	Goose Goslin	9.1
	Jhonny Peralta	9.1
080	Davy Jones	9.0
081	Billy Bruton	8.3
082	Victor Martinez	8.2
083	Kid Elberfeld	8.1
084	Fred Haney	8.0
085	Jim Delahanty	7.9
086	Brad Ausmus	7.6
087	Ramon Santiago	7.3
	Boss Schmidt	7.3
089	Jose Iglesias	7.2
	Eddie Mayo	7.2
091	Omar Infante	7.1
	Justin Upton	7.1
	Eddie Yost	7.1
094	Jeimer Candelario	6.9
	Shane Halter	6.9
096	Jerry Priddy	6.8
	John Wockenfuss	6.8
	Dmitri Young	6.8
099	Prince Fielder	6.6
	Johnny Groth	6.6
	Al Wingo	6.6

Rank	Player	oWAR
001	Ty Cobb	145.2
002	Al Kaline	78.3
003	Charlie Gehringer	77.7
004	Harry Heilmann	72.9
005	Sam Crawford	68.8
006	Lou Whitaker	67.7
007	Alan Trammell	63.0
008	Miguel Cabrera	56.8
009	Hank Greenberg	52.4
010	Norm Cash	49.7
011	Bill Freehan	43.3
012	Donie Bush	43.1
013	Bobby Veach	42.4
014	Dick McAuliffe	41.8
015	Rudy York	30.0
016	Kirk Gibson	28.9
017	Willie Horton	28.8
018	Lance Parrish	26.1
019	Harvey Kuenn	25.6
020	Travis Fryman	24.8
	Chet Lemon	24.8
022	Bobby Higginson	24.4
023	Carlos Guillen	22.9
024	Ron LeFlore	21.4
	Tony Phillips	21.4
026	George Kell	21.2
027	Jim Northrup	19.6
028	Billy Rogell	19.4
029	Lu Blue	19.0
	Cecil Fielder	19.0
031	Johnny Bassler	18.5
032	Ray Boone	18.2
033	Curtis Granderson	18.1
034	Mickey Tettleton	17.5
035	Magglio Ordonez	17.4
036	Steve Kemp	16.9
037	Damion Easley	16.5
038	Austin Jackson	16.0
039	Mickey Stanley	15.4
040	Charlie Maxwell	15.3
	Vic Wertz	15.3
042	Nicholas Castellanos	15.2
043	J.D. Martinez	15.1
044	Placido Polanco	14.1
045	Dick Wakefield	13.9
046	Alex Avila	13.8
	Bob Fothergill	13.8
	Ian Kinsler	13.8
049	Heinie Manush	13.6

Lu Blue

Rank	Player	oWAR
050	Roy Cullenbine	13.3
	Pinky Higgins	13.3
052	Rocky Colavito	13.2
053	Jimmy Barrett	13.1
	Tony Clark	13.1
055	Topper Rigney	13.0
	Ivan Rodriguez	13.0
057	Matty McIntyre	12.7
058	Marty McManus	12.1
059	Dale Alexander	12.0
	George Mullin	11.3
061	Gee Walker	11.9
062	Mickey Cochrane	11.5
	Jim Delahanty	11.5
	Barney McCosky	11.5
065	Darrell Evans	11.0
066	Hoot Evers	10.8
067	Pat Mullin	10.6
	Ossie Vitt	10.6
069	Brandon Inge	10.2
070	John Wockenfuss	10.1
071	John Stone	9.9
072	Frank Bolling	9.8
	George Moriarty	9.8
074	Don Wert	9.5
	Ralph Young	9.3
076	Goose Goslin	9.2
	Jhonny Peralta	9.2
	Eddie Yost	9.2
079	Jason Thompson	9.0
080	Gates Brown	8.9
081	Pete Fox	8.8
	Germany Schaefer	8.8
083	Jeimer Candelario	8.6
	Larry Herndon	8.6
085	Victor Martinez	8.5
086	Prince Fielder	8.4
087	Davy Jones	8.1
088	Kid Elberfeld	8.0
089	Tom Brookens	7.9
	Johnny Groth	7.9
091	Billy Bruton	7.8
092	Fred Haney	7.6
	Dmitri Young	7.6
094	Omar Infante	7.4
095	Mike Heath	7.3
	Al Wingo	7.3
097	Rusty Staub	7.2
098	Shane Halter	6.9
	Oscar Stanage	6.9
100	Matt Nokes	6.8

Rank	Player	dWAR
001	Alan Trammell	22.7
002	Lou Whitaker	16.3
003	Brandon Inge	13.3
004	Billy Rogell	13.0
005	Bill Freehan	12.0
006	Lance Parrish	10.9
007	Charlie Gehringer	10.7
008	Donie Bush	9.9
009	Aurelio Rodriguez	8.6
010	Ian Kinsler	8.3
011	Tom Brookens	7.7
012	Placido Polanco	7.1
013	Travis Fryman	6.8
014	Austin Jackson	6.7
015	Eddie Brinkman	6.2
016	George Moriarty	5.6
017	Ramon Santiago	5.5
018	Boss Schmidt	5.4
019	Chet Lemon	5.3
020	Ray Oyler	5.2
021	Johnny Bassler	5.0
	Eddie Mayo	5.0
	Ivan Rodriguez	5.0
024	Curtis Granderson	4.9
025	Deivi Cruz	4.7
026	Brad Ausmus	4.5
	Bob Jones	4.5
	Ossie Vitt	4.5
029	Frank Bolling	4.2
	Damion Easley	4.2
	Dick McAuliffe	4.2
	Oscar Stanage	4.2
033	Paul Richards	4.1
034	Don Wert	4.0
035	Alex Avila	3.8
	Jose Iglesias	3.8

Rank	Player	dWAR
037	Tony Phillips	3.7
	Birdie Tebbetts	3.7
039	James McCann	3.3
	Johnny Lipon	3.3
041	Frank House	3.1
042	Shane Halter	3.0
	Bob Swift	3.0
044	Ray Hayworth	2.9
045	Al Kaline	2.8
046	Skeeter Webb	2.7
047	Milt Cuyler	2.6
	Chico Fernandez	2.6
	Gary Pettis	2.6

Aurelio Rodriguez

Rank	Player	dWAR
050	Jimmy Bloodworth	2.5
	Jhonny Peralta	2.5
052	Marty McManus	2.4
	Jackie Tavener	2.4
054	Jerry Priddy	2.2
055	Fritz Buelow	2.1
	Kid Elberfeld	2.1
	Phil Mankowski	2.1
	Milt May	2.1
059	Kimera Bartee	2.0
	Red Berberet	2.0
	Omar Infante	2.0
	Chad Kreuter	2.0
	Nook Logan	2.0
	Dick Tracewski	2.0

Rank	Player	dWAR
065	Dick Brown	1.9
	Brian Hunter	1.9
067	Adam Everett	1.7
	Red Wilson	1.7
069	Doc Casey	1.6
	Mike Heath	1.6
	Fred Haney	1.6
	George Kell	1.6
	Jerry Lumpe	1.6
	Joe Randa	1.6
075	Joe Hoover	1.5
	Gerald Laird	1.5
077	Tommy Matchick	1.4
	Mickey Cochrane	1.4
079	Vance Wilson	1.3
	Mickey Stanley	1.3
	Glenn Wilson	1.3
082	Lew Drill	1.2
	Aaron Robinson	1.2
	Jack J. Warner	1.2
	Jack R. Warner	1.2
086	Rocky Colavito	1.1
	Fred Hatfield	1.1
	JaCoby Jones	1.1
	Topper Rigney	1.1
	Mike Roarke	1.1
	Ozzie Virgil Sr.	1.1
092	Matt Nokes	1.0
	Andrew Romine	1.0
094	Enos Cabell	0.9
	Bruce Kimm	0.9
	Warren Morris	0.9
	Charley O'Leary	0.9
	Leon Roberts	0.9
	Coot Veal	0.9
	Bob Wood	0.9

ALL TIME TIGER HITTING LEADERS – BATTERS RUN AVERAGE

001	Hank Greenberg	.254
002	Ty Cobb	.224
003	Harry Heilmann	.212
004	Miguel Cabrera	.205
005	Dale Alexander	.200
006	J.D. Martinez	.199
007	Charlie Gehringer	.194
008	Prince Fielder	.190
009	Roy Cullenbine	.187
010	Mickey Tettleton	.186
	Rudy York	.186
012	Norm Cash	.184
013	Bob Fothergill	.183
014	Rocky Colavito	.182
015	Al Kaline	.180
	Heinie Manush	.180
017	Ray Boone	.179
	Vic Wertz	.179
019	Tony Clark	.178
	Magglio Ordonez	.178
021	Dick Wakefield	.177
022	Cecil Fielder	.175
023	Carlos Guillen	.174
024	Al Wingo	.172
025	Goose Goslin	.171
026	Kirk Gibson	.170
027	George Kell	.169
	Steve Kemp	.169
	Charlie Maxwell	.169
030	Barney McCosky	.168
031	Curtis Granderson	.166
	John Stone	.166
033	Gee Walker	.165
	Dmitri Young	.165
035	Bobby Veach	.164
036	Lu Blue	.163
	Bobby Higginson	.163
038	Sam Crawford	.162
	Pat Mullin	.162
040	Darrell Evans	.160
	Hoot Evers	.160
	Tony Phillips	.160
043	Willie Horton	.159
044	Jim Delahanty	.157
045	Roy Johnson	.156
	Marty McManus	.156
047	Lou Whitaker	.155
048	Johnny Bassler	.154
	Victor Martinez	.154
	Marcus Thames	.154

Jim Northrup

051	Harvey Kuenn	.153
	Carlos Pena	.153
	Topper Rigney	.153
	Rusty Staub	.153
055	Johnny Groth	.152
	Chet Lemon	.152
	John Wockenfuss	.152
058	Pete Fox	.151
059	Dean Palmer	.150
060	Nicholas Castellanos	.149
	Travis Fryman	.149
	Lance Parrish	.149
	Jason Thompson	.149
064	Placido Polanco	.148
065	Ivan Rodriguez	.147
066	Pinky Higgins	.146
	Alan Trammell	.146
068	Damion Easley	.145
	Ben Oglivie	.145
070	Larry Herndon	.144
071	Ian Kinsler	.143
	Jim Northrup	.143
	Jhonny Peralta	.143
074	Alex Avila	.141
	Austin Jackson	.141
	Ron LeFlore	.141
	Dick McAuliffe	.141
078	Bill Freehan	.140
079	Gates Brown	.139
	Jeimer Candelario	.139
081	Jim Delsing	.138
	Billy Rogell	.138
083	Jimmy Barrett	.137
	Juan Encarnacion	.137
	Fred Haney	.137
	Craig Monroe	.137
087	Jerry Priddy	.135
088	Billy Bruton	.133
	Ryan Raburn	.133
090	Brennan Boesch	.131
091	Marv Owen	.128
092	Dave Bergman	.127
	Frank Bolling	.127
094	Walt Dropo	.126
	Red Wilson	.126
096	Jo-Jo White	.125
097	Mike Heath	.124
098	Niko Goodrum	.123
	Shane Halter	.123
100	Omar Infante	.122
	Bill Tuttle	.122

001	Ty Cobb	.368
002	Harry Heilmann	.342
003	Bob Fothergill	.337
004	Dale Alexander	.331
005	George Kell	.325
006	Heinie Manush	.321
007	Charlie Gehringer	.320
008	Hank Greenberg	.319
009	Gee Walker	.317
010	Harvey Kuenn	.314
011	Barney McCosky	.312
	Magglio Ordonez	.312
013	Placido Polanco	.311
	Bobby Veach	.311
015	Miguel Cabrera	.309
	Sam Crawford	.309
	Al Wingo	.309
018	Johnny Bassler	.308
019	Jim Delahanty	.306
020	John Stone	.303
021	Pete Fox	.302
022	J.D. Martinez	.300
023	Ivan Rodriguez	.298
024	Goose Goslin	.297
	Carlos Guillen	.297
	Fred Haney	.297
	Al Kaline	.297
	Ron LeFlore	.297
029	Topper Rigney	.296
030	Lu Blue	.295
	Prince Fielder	.295
032	Johnny Groth	.293
	Dick Wakefield	.293
034	Jimmy Barrett	.292
035	Ray Boone	.291
036	Hoot Evers	.290
	Victor Martinez	.290
038	Roy Johnson	.287
	Marty McManus	.287
040	Vic Wertz	.286
041	Alan Trammell	.285
042	Steve Kemp	.284
043	Doc Cramer	.282
	Rudy York	.282
045	Tony Phillips	.281
046	Pinky Higgins	.280
	Claude Rossman	.280
048	Don Kolloway	.279
	Dmitri Young	.279

Johnny Lipon

050	Larry Herndon	.278
	Marv Owen	.278
052	Tony Clark	.277
	Austin Jackson	.277
	Rusty Staub	.277
055	Willie Horton	.276
	Lou Whitaker	.276
057	Ian Kinsler	.275
	Ben Oglivie	.275
	Jhonny Peralta	.275
060	Nicholas Castellanos	.274
	Travis Fryman	.274
	Billy Rogell	.274
063	Kirk Gibson	.273
064	Norm Cash	.272
	Curtis Granderson	.272
	Bobby Higginson	.272
067	Rocky Colavito	.271
	Deivi Cruz	.271
	Pat Mullin	.271
070	Roy Cullenbine	.270
071	Juan Encarnacion	.269
	Davy Jones	.269
073	Ray Hayworth	.268
	Jose Iglesias	.268
	Johnny Lipon	.268
	Charlie Maxwell	.268
	Jimmy Outlaw	.268
	Larry Woodall	.268
079	Jim Northrup	.267
	Jerry Priddy	.267
081	Billy Bruton	.266
	George Burns	.266
	Walt Dropo	.266
	Mike Heath	.266
	Omar Infante	.266
086	Bob Jones	.265
	Eddie Mayo	.265
088	Jo-Jo White	.264
089	Chet Lemon	.263
	Lance Parrish	.263
	Bill Tuttle	.263
092	Bill Freehan	.262
	Red Wilson	.262
094	Frank Bolling	.261
	Brian Hunter	.261
	Matty McIntyre	.261
	George Mullin	.261
	John Wockenfuss	.261
099	Jim Delsing	.260
	Damion Easley	.260
	Jackie Tavener	.260
	Birdie Tebbetts	.260

Rank	Player	BABIP
001	Ty Cobb	.385
002	J.D. Martinez	.363
003	Austin Jackson	.357
004	Ron LeFlore	.353
005	Harry Heilmann	.352
006	Bob Fothergill	.350
007	Dale Alexander	.344
008	Ivan Rodriguez	.337
009	Miguel Cabrera	.336
010	Nicholas Castellanos	.333
011	Jimmy Barrett	.332
	Jim Delahanty	.332
	Al Wingo	.332
014	George Kell	.331
	Gee Walker	.331
016	Magglio Ordonez	.330
017	Hank Greenberg	.329
	Heinie Manush	.329
	Barney McCosky	.329
020	Carlos Guillen	.326
021	Alex Avila	.323
	Bobby Veach	.323
023	Sam Crawford	.321
	Curtis Granderson	.321
025	Charlie Gehringer	.320
026	Harvey Kuenn	.319
	Tony Phillips	.319
	Placido Polanco	.319
	John Stone	.319
030	Johnny Bassler	.318
	Topper Rigney	.318
032	Tony Clark	.317
	Pete Fox	.317
034	Niko Goodrum	.315
	Dick Wakefield	.315
036	Prince Fielder	.314
	Ryan Raburn	.314
038	Lu Blue	.313
	Travis Fryman	.313
	Fred Haney	.313
041	Jhonny Peralta	.312
042	Jeimer Candelario	.311
	Dmitri Young	.311
044	Juan Encarnacion	.308
	Brian Hunter	.308
	Roy Johnson	.308
	Claude Rossman	.308
048	Kirk Gibson	.306
049	Johnny Groth	.305
050	George Mullin	.304
051	Larry Herndon	.303
052	Hoot Evers	.302
053	Goose Goslin	.301
054	Omar Infante	.299
	Victor Martinez	.299
056	Brennan Boesch	.298
	Mike Heath	.298
	Steve Kemp	.298
	James McCann	.298
	Alan Trammell	.298
	Vic Wertz	.298
062	Jose Iglesias	.296
	Al Kaline	.296
064	Marty McManus	.295
	Ben Oglivie	.295
	Marv Owen	.295
	Andrew Romine	.295
068	Shane Halter	.294
	Davy Jones	.294
	Ian Kinsler	.294
	Carlos Pena	.294
	Jerry Priddy	.294
073	Milt Cuyler	.293
	Jo-Jo White	.293
	Jake Wood	.293
076	Ray Hayworth	.292
	Don Kolloway	.292
	Pat Sheridan	.292
079	Matty McIntyre	.291
080	Lou Whitaker	.290
081	Deivi Cruz	.289
	Bobby Higginson	.289
	Willie Horton	.289
084	Ray Boone	.288
	George Burns	.288
	Doc Cramer	.288
	Jimmy Outlaw	.288
	Billy Rogell	.288
089	Jackie Tavener	.287
090	Damion Easley	.286
	Pinky Higgins	.286
	Germany Schaefer	.286
	Rudy York	.286
094	Billy Bruton	.285
095	Craig Monroe	.283
096	Brandon Inge	.282
	Larry Woodall	.282
098	Pat Mullin	.281
	Ramon Santiago	.281
100	Chet Lemon	.280
	Jim Northrup	.280
	Lance Parrish	.280

Jimmy Barrett

Rank	Player	Avg
001	Hank Greenberg	.460
002	Mickey Tettleton	.453
003	Roy Cullenbine	.427
004	Darrell Evans	.395
005	Cecil Fielder	.382
006	Rocky Colavito	.378
007	Norm Cash	.376
008	Rudy York	.361
009	Kirk Gibson	.358
010	J.D. Martinez	.349
011	Miguel Cabrera	.348
012	Charlie Maxwell	.346
013	Tony Clark	.345
014	Carlos Pena	.342
015	Marcus Thames	.340
016	Curtis Granderson	.337
017	Dean Palmer	.334
018	Vic Wertz	.331
019	Prince Fielder	.329
020	Tony Phillips	.324
021	Bobby Higginson	.323
022	Ty Cobb	.320
023	Alex Avila	.319
	Ray Boone	.319
025	Steve Kemp	.319
	Dick Wakefield	.319
027	Al Kaline	.316
028	Jason Thompson	.314
029	Pat Mullin	.311
030	Charlie Gehringer	.304
031	John Wockenfuss	.303
032	Dick McAuliffe	.301
033	Carlos Guillen	.297
	Eddie Lake	.297
	Lou Whitaker	.297
036	Niko Goodrum	.296
037	Lu Blue	.290
	Harry Heilmann	.290
039	Dmitri Young	.289
040	Jeimer Candelario	.288
041	Goose Goslin	.287
042	Chet Lemon	.285
043	Lance Parrish	.283
044	Willie Horton	.280
045	Gates Brown	.279
	Damion Easley	.279
	Rusty Staub	.279
	Al Wingo	.279
049	Dale Alexander	.273
050	Roy Johnson	.270
051	Travis Fryman	.269

Billy Bruton

Rank	Player	Avg
052	Jim Delsing	.268
053	Marty McManus	.266
054	Hoot Evers	.264
	Magglio Ordonez	.264
056	Craig Monroe	.258
	Jim Northrup	.258
058	Donie Bush	.257
	Ben Oglivie	.257
060	Nicholas Castellanos	.256
061	Billy Bruton	.255
062	Sam Crawford	.254
	Bill Freehan	.254
	Barney McCosky	.254
065	Topper Rigney	.253
066	Jo-Jo White	.252
067	Austin Jackson	.251
068	Ryan Raburn	.250
069	Johnny Bassler	.249
	Pat Sheridan	.249
071	Alan Trammell	.248
072	Pinky Higgins	.247
073	Juan Encarnacion	.246
	Ron LeFlore	.246
	Topper Rigney	.246
	Billy Rogell	.246
077	Larry Herndon	.244
	Brandon Inge	.244
	John Stone	.244
080	Jimmy Barrett	.243
	Dave Bergman	.243
	Ian Kinsler	.243
083	Jim Delahanty	.242
	Jhonny Peralta	.242
085	Victor Martinez	.239
	Jerry Priddy	.239
087	Brennan Boesch	.237
	Bobby Veach	.237
089	Red Wilson	.236
090	Heinie Manush	.235
091	Johnny Groth	.230
092	Jake Wood	.228
093	Shane Halter	.227
094	Brian Hunter	.226
095	Davy Jones	.225
	Gee Walker	.225
097	Frank Bolling	.222
098	Matty McIntyre	.216
099	George Kell	.212
	Pete Fox	.212

Rank	Player	Pct
001	Doc Cramer	88.49
002	Harvey Kuenn	87.20
003	Boss Schmidt	85.66
004	Placido Polanco	85.46
005	Don Kolloway	84.93
006	George Kell	84.90
007	Bob Fothergill	84.66
008	Gee Walker	84.32
009	Sam Crawford	84.01
010	Bob Jones	83.91
011	Deivi Cruz	83.57
012	Eddie Mayo	83.44
013	Birdie Tebbetts	83.38
014	Charley O'Leary	83.20
015	Pete Fox	82.70
016	Claude Rossman	82.16
017	Jimmy Outlaw	82.08
018	Bobby Veach	81.99
019	Larry Woodall	81.96
020	Frank House	81.71
021	Johnny Lipon	81.51
022	Marv Owen	81.45
023	Jerry Lumpe	81.43
024	Ray Hayworth	81.42
025	Barney McCosky	81.31
026	Heinie Manush	81.24
027	Charlie Gehringer	81.06
028	Ty Cobb	81.04
029	John Stone	80.96
030	Ossie Vitt	80.95
031	Jose Iglesias	80.61
032	George Burns	80.32
033	Roy Johnson	80.22
034	Johnny Groth	80.14
035	George Moriarty	80.11
036	Mickey Stanley	79.88
037	Goose Goslin	79.87
038	Bill Tuttle	79.79
039	Billy Rogell	79.78
040	Rusty Staub	79.64
041	Aurelio Rodriguez	79.57
042	Marty McManus	79.48
043	Pinky Higgins	79.38
044	Dale Alexander	79.20
045	Harry Heilmann	79.04
046	Walt Dropo	79.03
047	Eddie Brinkman	78.96
048	Bill Coughlin	78.85
	Davy Jones	78.85
050	Oscar Stanage	78.76

Doc Cramer

Rank	Player	Pct
051	Frank Bolling	78.59
052	Fred Haney	78.56
053	Bob Swift	78.25
054	Matty McIntyre	78.24
055	Johnny Bassler	78.22
056	Victor Martinez	77.98
057	Alan Trammell	77.91
058	Jackie Tavener	77.86
059	Red Wilson	77.85
060	George Mullin	77.77
061	Ralph Young	77.76
062	Hoot Evers	77.32
063	Chico Fernandez	77.22
064	Jim Delsing	77.06
065	Jim Delahanty	76.69
066	Omar Infante	76.32
067	Germany Schaefer	76.31
068	Jo-Jo White	76.26
069	Ian Kinsler	76.20
070	Ivan Rodriguez	76.06
071	Lu Blue	75.95
072	Al Wingo	75.92
073	Al Kaline	75.90
074	Tom Brookens	75.81
075	Fred Hatfield	75.77
076	Magglio Ordonez	75.70
077	Gates Brown	75.63
078	Billy Bruton	75.49
079	Jim Northrup	75.42
080	Ray Boone	75.23
081	Topper Rigney	75.22
082	Brian Hunter	75.21
	Don Wert	75.21
084	Donie Bush	74.92
085	Bill Freehan	74.90
086	Dave Bergman	74.78
087	Larry Herndon	74.74
088	Don Kelly	74.68
089	Mike Heath	74.59
090	Jimmy Barrett	74.54
091	Jerry Priddy	74.24
092	Ben Oglivie	73.57
093	Pat Mullin	73.53
094	Lou Whitaker	73.42
095	Ron LeFlore	73.14
096	Hal Newhouser	72.84
097	John Wockenfuss	72.74
098	Carlos Guillen	72.34
099	Ramon Santiago	72.16
	Dick Wakefield	72.16

Rank	Player	Times on Base
001	Ty Cobb	5,133
002	Al Kaline	4,339
003	Charlie Gehringer	4,075
004	Lou Whitaker	3,586
005	Harry Heilmann	3,330
006	Alan Trammell	3,252
007	Sam Crawford	3,128
008	Miguel Cabrera	3,066
009	Norm Cash	2,903
010	Donie Bush	2,899
011	Bobby Veach	2,424
012	Dick McAuliffe	2,345
013	Bill Freehan	2,331
014	Hank Greenberg	2,288
015	Bobby Higginson	2,022
016	Willie Horton	2,008
017	Rudy York	1,969
018	Billy Rogell	1,817
019	Harvey Kuenn	1,702
020	Kirk Gibson	1,682
021	Jim Northrup	1,632
022	Chet Lemon	1,626
023	Mickey Stanley	1,622
024	Lu Blue	1,618
025	Travis Fryman	1,597
026	Brandon Inge	1,566
027	Cecil Fielder	1,493
028	Pete Fox	1,480
029	Lance Parrish	1,476
030	George Kell	1,428
031	Victor Martinez	1,377
032	Don Wert	1,342
033	Magglio Ordonez	1,318
034	Tony Phillips	1,304
035	Pinky Higgins	1,292
036	Aurelio Rodriguez	1,261
037	Ralph Young	1,241
038	Carlos Guillen	1,236
	Ron LeFlore	1,236
040	Vic Wertz	1,203
041	Damion Easley	1,186
042	Tom Brookens	1,141
043	Tony Clark	1,139
	Charlie Maxwell	1,139
045	Matty McIntyre	1,132
046	Gee Walker	1,126
047	Hoot Evers	1,123
048	Johnny Bassler	1,121
049	Marv Owen	1,110

Chet Lemon

Rank	Player	Times on Base
050	Nicholas Castellanos	1,107
051	Steve Kemp	1,099
052	Oscar Stanage	1,063
053	Ray Boone	1,055
054	Frank Bolling	1,052
055	Barney McCosky	1,033
056	Austin Jackson	1,016
057	Pat Mullin	1,012
058	Bob Jones	1,007
059	Ossie Vitt	1,004
060	Darrell Evans	1,001
061	Larry Herndon	996
062	Placido Polanco	993
063	Jimmy Barrett	990
	Bob Fothergill	990
	Curtis Granderson	990
066	Rocky Colavito	988
067	Dick Wakefield	985
068	Doc Cramer	962
069	John Stone	958
070	Alex Avila	944
	Johnny Groth	944
072	Marty McManus	924
073	Johnny Lipon	917
074	Mickey Tettleton	906
075	George Moriarty	883
076	Ian Kinsler	881
077	Davy Jones	873
078	Heinie Manush	868
079	Jason Thompson	867
080	Rusty Staub	848
081	Gates Brown	839
082	Goose Goslin	829
083	Ivan Rodriguez	824
084	Charley O'Leary	814
085	Roy Cullenbine	798
086	Bill Tuttle	791
087	Edie Mayo	789
088	Dave Bergman	783
089	Craig Monroe	771
090	Ramon Santiago	763
091	Jo-Jo White	756
092	Dale Alexander	755
093	Roy Johnson	752
094	Billy Bruton	740
	Omar Infante	740
096	Topper Rigney	739
097	Deivi Cruz	736
	Birdie Tebbetts	736
099	Ray Hayworth	734
100	John Wockenfuss	731

ALL TIME TIGER HITTING LEADERS – AT-BATS PER HOME RUN

001	Marcus Thames	14.78
002	Cecil Fielder	15.00
003	Hank Greenberg	15.66
004	Darrell Evans	16.66
005	Rocky Colavito	16.81
006	Mickey Tettleton	16.85
007	J.D. Martinez	17.14
008	Norm Cash	17.68
009	Dean Palmer	17.92
010	Tony Clark	18.15
011	Miguel Cabrera	19.00
012	Carlos Pena	19.55
013	Rudy York	19.57
014	Lance Parrish	20.16
015	Charlie Maxwell	20.27
016	Willie Horton	20.63
017	Kirk Gibson	21.38
018	Dmitri Young	21.87
019	Prince Fielder	21.91
020	Jason Thompson	22.49
021	John Wockenfuss	23.19
022	Craig Monroe	23.25
023	Ray Boone	23.67
024	Roy Cullenbine	24.78
025	Curtis Granderson	25.28
026	Al Kaline	25.35
027	Vic Wertz	25.62
028	Bobby Higginson	26.26
029	Gates Brown	26.93
030	Ben Oglivie	27.33
031	Steve Kemp	28.13
032	Pat Mullin	28.66
033	Chet Lemon	28.69
034	Travis Fryman	28.84
035	Ryan Raburn	29.13
036	Magglio Ordonez	29.64
037	Damion Easley	29.71
038	Alex Avila	29.91
039	Rusty Staub	30.00
040	Nicholas Castellanos	30.27
041	Bill Freehan	30.37
042	Jim Northrup	30.60
043	Dick McAuliffe	30.72
044	Victor Martinez	30.94
045	Niko Goodrum	31.31
046	Juan Encarnacion	31.51
047	Carlos Guillen	31.66
048	Jhonny Peralta	31.74
049	Ian Kinsler	31.76
050	Brennan Boesch	32.43

Lance Parrish

051	Jeimer Candelario	32.88
052	Brandon Inge	33.04
053	Larry Herndon	33.11
054	Frank House	33.74
055	Mike Heath	33.79
056	Walt Dropo	34.63
057	Lou Whitaker	35.12
058	Dale Alexander	36.69
059	Dick Wakefield	38.00
060	James McCann	38.40
061	Ivan Rodriguez	38.42
062	Goose Goslin	39.14
063	Shane Halter	39.41
064	Mickey Stanley	42.92
065	Billy Bruton	42.98
066	Hoot Evers	43.14
067	Pat Sheridan	43.23
068	Jim Delsing	44.37
069	Harry Heilmann	44.49
070	Alan Trammell	44.80
071	Tony Phillips	45.03
072	Don Kelly	45.35
073	Frank Bolling	45.55
074	Charlie Gehringer	48.15
075	Dizzy Trout	48.26
076	Don Wert	49.35
077	Omar Infante	49.37
078	Gee Walker	49.93
079	Marty McManus	49.23
080	Dave Bergman	50.44
081	Aurelio Rodriguez	51.20
082	Pinky Higgins	52.23
083	Chico Fernandez	52.67
084	Jake Wood	53.14
085	Tom Brookens	53.68
086	John Stone	53.96
087	Heinie Manush	55.24
088	Austin Jackson	58.22
089	Bill Tuttle	61.57
090	Ron LeFlore	64.04
091	Jerry Priddy	64.50
092	Deivi Cruz	65.00
093	Pete Fox	66.42
094	Johnny Groth	66.65
095	Red Wilson	67.23
096	Placido Polanco	69.97
097	Eddie Lake	71.04
098	Eddie Brinkman	73.57
099	Ramon Santiago	78.93
100	Harvey Kuenn	82.49

001	Hank Greenberg	4.0
002	Cecil Fielder	4.8
003	Dale Alexander	4.9
004	Harry Heilmann	5.0
	Rudy York	5.0
006	Goose Goslin	5.3
	Vic Wertz	5.3
008	Ray Boone	5.4
	Miguel Cabrera	5.4
	Rocky Colavito	5.4
011	Tony Clark	5.5
	Bob Fothergill	5.5
013	Prince Fielder	5.6
	Dean Palmer	5.6
015	Mickey Tettleton	5.7
	Marcus Thames	5.7
	Bobby Veach	5.7
018	Darrell Evans	5.8
019	Ty Cobb	5.9
	Steve Kemp	5.9
	Charlie Maxwell	5.9
	Magglio Ordonez	5.9
	Rusty Staub	5.9
024	Roy Cullenbine	6.0
	J.D. Martinez	6.0
026	Norm Cash	6.1
	Willie Horton	6.1
	Heinie Manush	6.1
	Lance Parrish	6.1
030	Charlie Gehringer	6.2
	Kirk Gibson	6.2
	Marty McManus	6.2
	Craig Monroe	6.2
	Jason Thompson	6.2
035	Sam Crawford	6.3
	Hoot Evers	6.3
	Travis Fryman	6.3
038	Al Kaline	6.4
039	Pat Mullin	6.5
	Gee Walker	6.5
	John Wockenfuss	6.5
042	Walt Dropo	6.6
	Pinky Higgins	6.6
	Victor Martinez	6.6
	Topper Rigney	6.6
046	Jim Delahanty	6.7
	Carlos Guillen	6.7
	Al Wingo	6.7
	Dmitri Young	6.7
050	John Stone	6.8

Rusty Staub

	Dick Wakefield	6.8
052	Bobby Higginson	6.9
	Carlos Pena	6.9
054	Gates Brown	7.0
	Marv Owen	7.0
	Jhonny Peralta	7.0
057	Johnny Bassler	7.2
058	Alex Avila	7.3
	Ryan Raburn	7.3
060	Nicholas Castellanos	7.4
061	Juan Encarnacion	7.5
	Johnny Groth	7.5
	Larry Herndon	7.5
064	Jim Delsing	7.6
	Chet Lemon	7.6
066	Damion Easley	7.7
	Ben Oglivie	7.7
	Claude Rossman	7.7
069	Brennan Boesch	7.8
	Jim Northrup	7.8
071	George Burns	7.9
	Brandon Inge	7.9
	Ivan Rodriguez	7.9
	Lou Whitaker	7.9
075	Pete Fox	8.0
	Bill Freehan	8.0
	Frank House	8.0
	George Kell	8.0
079	Birdie Tebbetts	8.1
080	Larry Woodall	8.2
081	Lu Blue	8.3
	Ian Kinsler	8.3
	Billy Rogell	8.3
	Alan Trammell	8.3
085	Ray Hayworth	8.4
086	Fred Haney	8.5
087	Curtis Granderson	8.6
	Pat Sheridan	8.6
	Dizzy Trout	8.6
	Bill Tuttle	8.6
091	Deivi Cruz	8.7
	Niko Goodrum	8.7
	James McCann	8.7
	Jackie Tavener	8.7
095	Jeimer Candelario	8.8
	Dick McAuliffe	8.8
	Red Wilson	8.8
098	Tom Brookens	8.9
	Tony Phillips	8.9
100	Dave Bergman	9.0

Rank	Player	AB/SO
001	Doc Cramer	31.6
002	George Kell	30.9
003	Johnny Bassler	30.7
004	Ossie Vitt	25.3
005	Charlie Gehringer	23.8
006	Harvey Kuenn	21.3
007	Eddie Mayo	20.0
008	Johnny Lipon	19.8
009	Larry Woodall	19.7
010	Bob Jones	19.2
011	Sam Crawford	17.7
	Bob Fothergill	17.7
013	Fred Haney	17.3
014	Bobby Veach	17.2
015	Heinie Manush	16.3
016	Ty Cobb	16.2
017	Placido Polanco	16.0
018	Don Kolloway	15.9
019	Birdie Tebbetts	15.2
020	Pinky Higgins	15.0
	Ralph Young	15.0
022	Harry Heilmann	14.7
023	Barney McCosky	14.5
024	Lu Blue	14.4
025	Goose Goslin	14.3
026	Rusty Staub	14.1
027	Billy Rogell	14.0
028	Boss Schmidt	13.6
029	Marty McManus	13.5
030	Johnny Groth	13.3
	Charley O'Leary	13.3
032	Frank House	13.0
033	Jimmy Outlaw	12.8
034	Marv Owen	12.7
035	Topper Rigney	12.4
036	Pete Fox	12.3
037	Davy Jones	12.0
	Gee Walker	12.0
039	Al Wingo	11.8
040	Bob Swift	11.7
041	Jim Delahanty	11.5
042	Dale Alexander	11.3
	Donie Bush	11.3
	Ray Hayworth	11.3
045	John Stone	11.1
046	Jerry Lumpe	10.8
	George Moriarty	10.8
048	Bill Tuttle	10.6
	Red Wilson	10.6
050	Hoot Evers	10.5
	Roy Johnson	10.5
	Claude Rossman	10.5
053	Jim Delsing	10.4
054	George Burns	10.3
055	Al Kaline	9.9
056	Ray Boone	9.7
057	Frank Bolling	9.6
058	Roy Cullenbine	9.5
	Matty McIntyre	9.5
	Alan Trammell	9.5
061	Deivi Cruz	9.4
	Jo-Jo White	9.4
063	Jackie Tavener	9.3
064	Eddie Lake	9.1
065	Mickey Stanley	8.9
066	Bill Coughlin	8.7
	Fred Hatfield	8.7
	Victor Martinez	8.7
069	Gates Brown	8.2
070	Eddie Brinkman	8.1
	Chico Fernandez	8.1
	Bill Freehan	8.1
	Jose Iglesias	8.1
074	Walt Dropo	8.0
	Pat Mullin	8.0
076	Dave Bergman	7.9
	Dick Wakefield	7.9
078	Jimmy Barrett	7.8
	Rocky Colavito	7.8
	Jerry Priddy	7.8
	Lou Whitaker	7.8
082	Billy Bruton	7.7
083	Magglio Ordonez	7.5
	Oscar Stanage	7.5
	Vic Wertz	7.5
	John Wockenfuss	7.5
087	Jim Northrup	7.4
	Aurelio Rodriguez	7.4
089	Germany Schaefer	7.3
	Don Wert	7.3
091	Rudy York	7.0
092	Steve Kemp	6.9
	Ian Kinsler	6.9
	George Mullin	6.9
095	Hal Newhouser	6.6
096	Tom Brookens	6.4
	Don Kelly	6.4
098	Chet Lemon	6.3
	Dick McAuliffe	6.3
100	Hank Greenberg	6.2
	Larry Herndon	6.2
	Bobby Higginson	6.2
	Charlie Maxwell	6.2

Ossie Vitt

001	Miguel Cabrera	29,689
002	Bobby Higginson	21,997
003	Brandon Inge	21,132
004	Travis Fryman	18,299
005	Cecil Fielder	16,716
006	Victor Martinez	15,276
007	Lou Whitaker	14,774
008	Tony Phillips	13,416
009	Nicholas Castellanos	13,055
010	Damion Easley	12,864
011	Carlos Guillen	12,717
012	Magglio Ordonez	12,627
013	Tony Clark	12,405
014	Alan Trammell	12,153
015	Austin Jackson	12,068
016	Curtis Granderson	11,791
017	Alex Avila	11,185
018	Mickey Tettleton	10,107
019	Ian Kinsler	10,064
020	Placido Polanco	9,743
021	Craig Monroe	9,498
022	Ramon Santiago	8,844
023	Omar Infante	8,745
024	Ivan Rodriguez	8,709
025	Jeimer Candelario	8,088
026	Deivi Cruz	8,056
027	Jose Iglesias	7,726
028	J.D. Martinez	7,390
029	Jhonny Peralta	7,158
030	Dmitri Young	7,109
031	Ryan Raburn	6,666
032	Carlos Pena	6,586
033	Juan Encarnacion	6,362
034	Marcus Thames	6,310
035	James McCann	6,289
036	Dean Palmer	6,286
037	Shane Halter	6,106
038	Niko Goodrum	6,045
038	Rob Deer	5,717
039	Dave Bergman	5,504
040	Chet Lemon	5,405
041	Brad Ausmus	5,381
042	Brennan Boesch	5,325
043	Robert Fick	5,288
044	Brian Hunter	5,221
045	Milt Cuyler	5,182
046	Prince Fielder	5,176
047	Justin Upton	4,795
049	Gary Pettis	4,666
050	JaCoby Jones	4,641

Christin Stewart

051	Don Kelly	4,471
052	Gary Sheffield	4,408
053	Chad Curtis	4,406
054	Torii Hunter	4,363
055	Chris Gomez	4,320
056	Kirk Gibson	4,263
057	Andrew Romine	3,864
058	Andy Dirks	3,821
059	Chris Shelton	3,777
060	Mike Heath	3,762
061	Victor Reyes	3,709
062	Gerald Laird	3,453
063	Chad Kreuter	3,437
064	Melvin Nieves	3,424
065	Eric Munson	3,253
066	Rondell White	3,222
067	Jonathan Schoop	3,212
068	John Hicks	3,147
069	Rajai Davis	3,124
070	Jose Macias	2,993
071	Dan Gladden	2,984
072	Wendell Magee Jr.	2,962
073	Lloyd Moseby	2,900
074	Scott Livingstone	2,880
075	Matt Nokes	2,845
076	Robbie Grossman	2,827
077	Mikie Mahtook	2,738
078	Harold Castro	2,732
079	Delmon Young	2,696
080	Willi Castro	2,591
081	Anthony Gose	2,561
082	Johnny Damon	2,517
083	Alex Sanchez	2,409
084	Sean Casey	2,389
085	Christian Stewart	2,345
086	Gary Ward	2,307
087	Luis Polonia	2,272
088	Mark Lewis	2,248
089	Luis Gonzalez	2,245
090	Randall Simon	2,243
091	Tyler Collins	2,135
092	Darrell Evans	2,089
093	Frank Catalanotto	2,065
094	Roger Cedeno	2,048
095	Phil Nevin	2,033
096	Edgar Renteria	2,030
097	Pat Sheridan	2,003
098	John Flaherty	1,997
099	Dixon Machado	1,961
100	Skeeter Barnes	1,947

Rank	Player	P/PA
001	Mickey Tettleton	4.32
002	Rob Deer	4.23
003	Chris Shelton	4.19
004	Mikie Mahtook	4.17
	Justin Upton	4.17
006	Jeimer Candelario	4.16
007	Alex Avila	4.13
008	Niko Goodrum	4.11
009	Johnny Damon	4.10
	Gary Sheffield	4.10
011	Tony Phillips	4.08
012	Brandon Inge	4.06
013	Curtis Granderson	4.05
014	Darrell Evans	4.03
	Chad Kreuter	4.03
016	Darnell Coles	4.02
	Austin Jackson	4.02
	Curtis Pride	4.02
019	Phil Nevin	4.01
020	Cecil Fielder	4.00
	Anthony Gose	4.00
022	Chad Curtis	3.99
	Christin Stewart	3.99
024	Robert Fick	3.98
025	Chris Gomez	3.96
	Clete Thomas	3.96
027	Kirk Gibson	3.93
	Melvin Nieves	3.93
	Dean Palmer	3.93
030	Larry Herndon	3.92
	Carlos Pena	3.92
	Victor Reyes	3.92
033	Bobby Higginson	3.91
	J.D. Martinez	3.91
	Marcus Thames	3.91
036	Dave Bergman	3.89
037	Brad Ausmus	3.88
	JaCoby Jones	3.88
	Mark Lewis	3.88
040	Tyler Collins	3.87
	Travis Fryman	3.87
	Dixon Machado	3.87
	Victor Martinez	3.87
	Lloyd Moseby	3.87
	Gary Pettis	3.87
046	Tony Clark	3.86
047	Don Kelly	3.86
	Chet Lemon	3.86
	Jhonny Peralta	3.86

Mickey Tettleton

Rank	Player	P/PA
	Ryan Raburn	3.86
	Lou Whitaker	3.86
052	Nicholas Castellanos	3.82
053	Eric Munson	3.80
054	Tom Brookens	3.78
	James McCann	3.78
	Andrew Romine	3.78
	Pat Sheridan	3.78
058	Kimera Bartee	3.76
	John Hicks	3.76
060	Carlos Guillen	3.75
061	Miguel Cabrera	3.74
	Shane Halter	3.74
063	Jose Iglesias	3.73
064	Ian Kinsler	3.72
	Craig Monroe	3.72
066	Wendell Magee Jr.	3.71
067	Brian Hunter	3.69
	Prince Fielder	3.69
069	Will Rhymes	3.68
070	Ronny Rodriguez	3.67
071	Damion Easley	3.66
	Gary Ward	3.66
073	Luis Gonzalez	3.64
074	Milt Cuyler	3.63
075	Adam Everett	3.61
	Alan Trammell	3.61
	Kenny Williams	3.61
078	Frank Catalanotto	3.59
	Rajai Davis	3.59
	Andy Dirks	3.59
081	Rondell White	3.58
	Dmitri Young	3.58
083	Brennan Boesch	3.57
	Gerald Laird	3.57
	Magglio Ordonez	3.57
086	Omar Infante	3.56
087	Dan Gladden	3.55
088	Juan Encarnacion	3.54
089	Torii Hunter	3.52
090	Skeeter Barnes	3.51
091	Ramon Santiago	3.50
092	Jose Macias	3.49
093	Matt Nokes	3.48
	Luis Polonia	3.48
095	Danny Bautista	3.47
096	John Flaherty	3.46
097	Sean Casey	3.45
	Placido Polanco	3.45
	Ivan Rodriguez	3.45
100	Nook Logan	3.43

Rank	Player	Base Runs
001	Ty Cobb	2,245
002	Al Kaline	1,780
003	Charlie Gehringer	1,676
004	Harry Heilmann	1,456
005	Lou Whitaker	1,346
006	Miguel Cabrera	1,328
007	Sam Crawford	1,226
008	Norm Cash	1,196
009	Alan Trammell	1,188
010	Hank Greenberg	1,135
011	Bobby Veach	926
012	Dick McAuliffe	851
013	Rudy York	850
014	Bill Freehan	825
015	Willie Horton	824
016	Bobby Higginson	796
017	Donie Bush	795
018	Kirk Gibson	691
019	Cecil Fielder	642
020	Harvey Kuenn	637
021	Travis Fryman	621
022	Jim Northrup	619
	Lance Parrish	619
024	Billy Rogell	618
025	Chet Lemon	601
026	Lu Blue	577
027	Mickey Stanley	560
028	Pete Fox	556
029	Brandon Inge	541
030	George Kell	540
031	Magglio Ordonez	539
032	Victor Martinez	527
033	Carlos Guillen	506
034	Vic Wertz	493
035	Tony Clark	492
036	Tony Phillips	464
037	Pinky Higgins	456
	Charlie Maxwell	456
039	Gee Walker	454
040	Nicholas Castellanos	445
041	Ron LeFlore	440
042	Ray Boone	435
043	Steve Kemp	428
044	Rocky Colavito	425
045	Damion Easley	424
	Hoot Evers	424
047	Don Wert	418
048	Curtis Granderson	415
	Aurelio Rodriguez	415
050	Bob Fothergill	408
051	Pat Mullin	402

Victor Martinez

Rank	Player	Base Runs
052	Darrell Evans	397
053	Barney McCosky	395
054	Dick Wakefield	385
055	Larry Herndon	384
	John Stone	384
057	Tom Brookens	382
058	Johnny Bassler	371
059	Mickey Tettleton	370
060	Austin Jackson	369
061	Marv Owen	367
062	Frank Bolling	364
063	Marty McManus	352
	Placido Polanco	352

Rank	Player	Base Runs
065	Johnny Groth	342
066	Matty McIntyre	341
067	Alex Avila	340
	Heinie Manush	340
069	Jason Thompson	337
	Ralph Young	337
071	Ian Kinsler	334
072	Dale Alexander	329
073	Goose Goslin	328
074	Ivan Rodriguez	325
075	Rusty Staub	320
076	J.D. Martinez	315
077	Craig Monroe	314
078	Jimmy Barrett	313
	Gates Brown	313
080	Roy Cullenbine	312
081	Bob Jones	303
082	Doc Cramer	301
083	Roy Johnson	291
084	John Wockenfuss	284
085	Johnny Lipon	278
	Oscar Stanage	278
087	Dmitri Young	277
088	Ossie Vitt	275
089	Omar Infante	265
090	Bill Tuttle	262
091	Billy Bruton	261
092	Topper Rigney	260
093	Dave Bergman	258
094	Deivi Cruz	255
095	Eddie Mayo	249
096	Davy Jones	240
	George Moriarty	240
098	Jo-Jo White	236
099	Jhonny Peralta	235
100	Jeimer Candelario	232
	Birdie Tebbetts	232

Rank	Player	Runs Produced
001	Ty Cobb	3,785
002	Charlie Gehringer	3,018
003	Al Kaline	2,805
004	Harry Heilmann	2,491
005	Sam Crawford	2,307
006	Lou Whitaker	2,226
007	Alan Trammell	2,049
008	Miguel Cabrera	1,973
009	Hank Greenberg	1,869
010	Bobby Veach	1,853
011	Norm Cash	1,742
012	Donie Bush	1,670
013	Rudy York	1,432
014	Dick McAuliffe	1,335
015	Willie Horton	1,295
016	Bill Freehan	1,264
017	Bobby Higginson	1,258
018	Kirk Gibson	1,171
019	Billy Rogell	1,164
020	Travis Fryman	1,137
021	Pete Fox	1,103
022	Cecil Fielder	1,071
023	Lance Parrish	1,065
024	Lu Blue	1,058
025	Mickey Stanley	1,024
026	Jim Northrup	996
027	Harvey Kuenn	989
028	Brandon Inge	976
029	Chet Lemon	964
030	George Kell	891
031	Gee Walker	884
032	Magglio Ordonez	878
033	Vic Wertz	865
034	Victor Martinez	830
035	Pinky Higgins	827
036	Carlos Guillen	823
037	Bob Fothergill	801
038	Tony Clark	786
039	Tom Brookens	776
040	Hoot Evers	775
041	Marv Owen	762
042	Aurelio Rodriguez	755
043	Damion Easley	752
044	Tony Phillips	750
045	Ron LeFlore	746
046	Charlie Maxwell	737
047	Steve Kemp	711
048	Ray Boone	705
049	Bob Jones	703
050	Don Wert	701

Kirk Gibson

Rank	Player	Runs Produced
051	John Stone	694
052	Heinie Manush	693
053	Nicholas Castellanos	685
054	Pat Mullin	681
055	Marty McManus	677
056	Rocky Colavito	668
057	Goose Goslin	666
058	Placido Polanco	641
059	Larry Herndon	639
060	Austin Jackson	635
061	Curtis Granderson	632
	Ralph Young	632
063	Frank Bolling	630
064	Ossie Vitt	627
065	Ian Kinsler	623
066	Darrell Evans	621
	Barney McCosky	621
068	Matty McIntyre	620
069	Craig Monroe	602
070	Dick Wakefield	592
071	Dale Alexander	586
072	Johnny Groth	575
073	Gates Brown	568
074	Oscar Stanage	563
075	Doc Cramer	560
076	Johnny Bassler	557
077	Rusty Staub	552
078	George Moriarty	550
079	Davy Jones	549
080	Jimmy Barrett	547
081	Ivan Rodriguez	538
082	Jason Thompson	535
083	Johnny Lipon	531
084	Mickey Tettleton	524
085	Jo-Jo White	518
086	Alex Avila	513
087	Roy Johnson	508
088	Deivi Cruz	498
089	Bill Tuttle	493
090	Billy Bruton	487
091	Eddie Mayo	478
092	Topper Rigney	474
093	Charley O'Leary	470
094	Germany Schaefer	466
095	Roy Cullenbine	464
096	Ray Hayworth	452
	Omar Infante	452
098	John Wockenfuss	450
099	J.D. Martinez	443
100	Dmitri Young	440

Rank	Player	Pct
001	Milt Cuyler	47.48
002	Davy Jones	47.19
003	Jo-Jo White	45.60
004	Roy Johnson	44.99
005	Fred Haney	43.58
006	Pete Fox	43.00
007	Donie Bush	42.70
008	Heinie Manush	41.93
009	Ossie Vitt	41.46
010	Austin Jackson	41.34
011	Charlie Gehringer	40.89
012	Lu Blue	40.71
013	Ron LeFlore	40.59
014	Brian Hunter	40.32
015	Jake Wood	40.23
016	Ian Kinsler	40.22
017	Ty Cobb	39.31
018	Bob Jones	39.30
019	Andrew Romine	39.08
020	Eddie Lake	39.06
021	Gee Walker	38.97
022	Billy Bruton	38.76
023	Barney McCosky	38.46
024	Don Kelly	38.17
025	Jimmy Barrett	38.06
026	Germany Schaefer	37.97
027	Goose Goslin	37.87
028	Curtis Granderson	37.50
029	Placido Polanco	37.24
030	Bob Fothergill	36.72
031	John Stone	36.69
032	Matt McIntyre	36.23
033	Billy Rogell	35.49
034	Tony Phillips	35.48
035	Ryan Raburn	35.43
036	Bill Coughlin	35.40
037	Tom Brookens	35.26
038	Al Wingo	35.08
039	Pat Sheridan	34.97
040	Jimmy Outlaw	34.89
041	Mickey Stanley	34.82
042	Jim Delahanty	34.73
043	Don Kolloway	34.69
044	Charley O'Leary	34.65
045	Marty McManus	34.55
046	Harvey Kuenn	34.32
047	Sam Crawford	34.17
	Lou Whitaker	34.17
049	Alan Trammell	34.10
050	George Kell	34.00

Jo-Jo White

Rank	Player	Pct
	Bobby Veach	34.00
052	Kirk Gibson	33.83
053	Juan Encarnacion	33.80
054	Hank Greenberg	33.75
055	Jackie Tavener	33.64
056	Doc Cramer	33.37
057	George Burns	33.33
058	Craig Monroe	33.28
	Ralph Young	33.28
060	Harry Heilmann	33.01
061	Tommy Bridges	32.94
062	Carlos Guillen	32.78
063	Johnny Lipon	32.75
064	Omar Infante	32.71
065	Hoot Evers	32.64
066	Jerry Lumpe	32.61
067	Boss Schmidt	32.60
068	Gates Brown	32.58
069	Damion Easley	32.53
070	Eddie Mayo	32.51
071	Ramon Santiago	32.24
072	Dizzy Trout	32.22
073	Frank Bolling	32.19
074	Bill Tuttle	32.14
075	Pat Mullin	32.00
076	Travis Fryman	31.63
077	Deivi Cruz	31.62
078	Dale Alexander	31.54
079	Niko Goodrum	31.45
080	Brennan Boesch	31.38
081	Larry Woodall	31.25
082	Marv Owen	31.24
083	Ivan Rodriguez	31.23
084	Jose Iglesias	31.18
	Mickey Lolich	31.18
086	Jerry Priddy	31.08
087	Al Kaline	31.04
088	Dick McAuliffe	30.84
089	Topper Rigney	30.82
090	Vic Wertz	30.53
091	George Moriarty	30.41
092	George Mullin	30.15
093	Larry Herndon	30.12
094	Johnny Groth	30.00
095	Jeimer Candelario	29.95
096	Bobby Higginson	29.92
	Dick Wakefield	29.92
098	Fred Hatfield	29.71
099	Jim Delsing	29.68
100	Marcus Thames	29.55

ALL TIME TIGER HITTING LEADERS – ESTIMATED RUNS PRODUCED

001	Ty Cobb	2,240
002	Al Kaline	1,761
003	Charlie Gehringer	1,647
004	Harry Heilmann	1,422
005	Lou Whitaker	1,338
006	Miguel Cabrera	1,325
007	Sam Crawford	1,263
008	Norm Cash	1,202
	Alan Trammell	1,202
010	Hank Greenberg	1,118
011	Bobby Veach	951
012	Donie Bush	870
013	Dick McAuliffe	853
014	Bill Freehan	847
015	Rudy York	839
016	Willie Horton	827
017	Bobby Higginson	803
018	Kirk Gibson	724
019	Cecil Fielder	637
020	Travis Fryman	630
021	Harvey Kuenn	626
022	Billy Rogell	622
023	Jim Northrup	619
	Lance Parrish	619
025	Chet Lemon	616
026	Lu Blue	572
027	Pete Fox	569
028	Brandon Inge	553
029	Mickey Stanley	551
030	Magglio Ordonez	525
031	George Kell	521
032	Victor Martinez	520
033	Carlos Guillen	505
034	Tony Clark	489
035	Vic Wertz	483
036	Gee Walker	478
037	Ron LeFlore	474
038	Tony Phillips	461
039	Charlie Maxwell	458
040	Damion Easley	456
041	Nicholas Castellanos	453
042	Pinky Higgins	447
043	Curtis Granderson	429
044	Ray Boone	428
045	Steve Kemp	421
046	Hoot Evers	420
047	Rocky Colavito	418
048	Don Wert	415
049	Bob Fothergill	406
050	Aurelio Rodriguez	402

Sam Crawford

051	Pat Mullin	398
052	Darrell Evans	393
053	Tom Brookens	388
054	Barney McCosky	387
055	John Stone	384
056	Larry Herndon	383
057	Austin Jackson	378
058	Marv Owen	373
059	Dick Wakefield	369
060	Frank Bolling	366
061	Mickey Tettleton	364
062	Johnny Bassler	362
063	Matty McIntyre	360
064	Placido Polanco	359
065	Marty McManus	357
066	Heinie Manush	356
067	Ralph Young	352
068	Ian Kinsler	347
069	Alex Avila	336
070	Jason Thompson	331
071	Jimmy Barrett	330
	Johnny Groth	330
073	Goose Goslin	327
	Ivan Rodriguez	327
075	Dale Alexander	323
076	J.D. Martinez	318
077	Gates Brown	316
	Rusty Staub	316
079	Craig Monroe	315
080	Bob Jones	310
081	Roy Cullenbine	303
082	Doc Cramer	298
083	Roy Johnson	297
084	Ossie Vitt	291
085	Oscar Stanage	285
086	Dmitri Young	284
087	John Wockenfuss	280
088	George Moriarty	278
089	Johnny Lipon	276
090	Omar Infante	271
091	Billy Bruton	268
	Davy Jones	268
093	Topper Rigney	257
	Bill Tuttle	257
095	Dave Bergman	256
096	Deivi Cruz	255
097	Eddie Mayo	246
098	Jo-Jo White	244
099	Jeimer Candelario	242
100	Jhonny Peralta	232

Rank	Player	Runs Created
001	Ty Cobb	2,349
002	Al Kaline	1,824
003	Charlie Gehringer	1,706
004	Harry Heilmann	1,537
005	Miguel Cabrera	1,418
006	Lou Whitaker	1,333
007	Sam Crawford	1,290
008	Hank Greenberg	1,212
009	Alan Trammell	1,211
010	Norm Cash	1,196
011	Bobby Veach	969
012	Rudy York	867
013	Willie Horton	850
014	Bill Freehan	828
015	Dick McAuliffe	825
016	Bobby Higginson	797
017	Lance Parrish	748
018	Donie Bush	744
019	Kirk Gibson	703
020	Harvey Kuenn	672
021	Cecil Fielder	640
022	Travis Fryman	638
023	Jim Northrup	630
024	Billy Rogell	605
025	Chet Lemon	603
026	Pete Fox	586
027	Mickey Stanley	566
028	Magglio Ordonez	565
029	George Kell	555
030	Lu Blue	546
	Victor Martinez	546
032	Brandon Inge	533
033	Carlos Guillen	524
034	Tony Clark	504
035	Vic Wertz	498
036	Gee Walker	496
037	Nicholas Castellanos	466
038	Ron LeFlore	460
039	Pinky Higgins	453
	Charlie Maxwell	453
041	Ray Boone	445
042	Bob Fothergill	442
043	Tony Phillips	440
044	Hoot Evers	430
045	Damion Easley	429
046	Rocky Colavito	427
	Curtis Granderson	427
048	Steve Kemp	425
049	Aurelio Rodriguez	424
050	Don Wert	413
051	Pat Mullin	402
	John Stone	402
053	Larry Herndon	398
	Barney McCosky	398
055	Tom Brookens	388
056	Darrell Evans	378
057	Austin Jackson	377
	Placido Polanco	377
059	Dick Wakefield	376
060	Marv Owen	374
061	Frank Bolling	367
062	Heinie Manush	365
063	Marty McManus	359
064	Dale Alexander	351
	Mickey Tettleton	351
066	Ivan Rodriguez	350
067	Ian Kinsler	348
068	Johnny Bassler	343
	Johnny Groth	343
070	Matty McIntyre	338
071	J.D. Martinez	337
072	Goose Goslin	334
073	Jason Thompson	331
074	Alex Avila	325
075	Rusty Staub	323
	Ralph Young	323
077	Craig Monroe	322
078	Bob Jones	315
079	Doc Cramer	314
080	Gates Brown	313
081	Jimmy Barrett	305
082	Roy Johnson	298
083	Roy Cullenbine	291
084	Dmitri Young	290
085	Oscar Stanage	288
086	John Wockenfuss	282
087	Omar Infante	277
088	Deivi Cruz	273
089	Johnny Lipon	271
090	Ossie Vitt	269
091	Bill Tuttle	263
092	Billy Bruton	262
093	Eddie Mayo	253
094	Dave Bergman	251
	Topper Rigney	251
096	George Moriarty	249
097	Jhonny Peralta	242
098	Davy Jones	235
099	Jeimer Candelario	234
100	Birdie Tebbetts	233

Bobby Higginson

ALL TIME TIGER HITTING LEADERS – RUNS CREATED PER 27 OUTS

Rank	Player	RC/27
001	Ty Cobb	87.02
002	Al Kaline	67.57
003	Charlie Gehringer	63.17
004	Harry Heilmann	56.93
005	Miguel Cabrera	52.54
006	Lou Whitaker	49.37
007	Sam Crawford	47.76
008	Hank Greenberg	44.90
009	Alan Trammell	44.85
010	Norm Cash	44.29
011	Bobby Veach	35.89
012	Rudy York	32.10
013	Willie Horton	31.49
014	Bill Freehan	30.67
015	Dick McAuliffe	30.57
016	Bobby Higginson	29.53
017	Donie Bush	27.56
018	Kirk Gibson	26.03
019	Harvey Kuenn	24.87
020	Cecil Fielder	23.71
021	Travis Fryman	23.64
022	Lance Parrish	23.50
023	Jim Northrup	23.33
024	Billy Rogell	22.39
025	Chet Lemon	22.33
026	Pete Fox	21.72
027	Mickey Stanley	20.96
028	Magglio Ordonez	20.92
029	George Kell	20.54
030	Victor Martinez	20.23
031	Lu Blue	20.22
032	Brandon Inge	19.73
033	Carlos Guillen	19.40
034	Tony Clark	18.67
035	Vic Wertz	18.43
036	Gee Walker	18.37
037	Nicholas Castellanos	17.25
038	Ron LeFlore	17.04
039	Pinky Higgins	16.79
	Charlie Maxwell	16.79
041	Ray Boone	16.47
042	Bob Fothergill	16.37
043	Tony Phillips	16.28
044	Hoot Evers	15.94
045	Damion Easley	15.88
046	Rocky Colavito	15.83
047	Curtis Granderson	15.80
048	Steve Kemp	15.76
049	Aurelio Rodriguez	15.70
050	Don Wert	15.28

Travis Fryman

Rank	Player	RC/27
051	Pat Mullin	14.90
	John Stone	14.90
053	Barney McCosky	14.76
054	Larry Herndon	14.75
055	Tom Brookens	14.36
056	Darrell Evans	13.98
057	Austin Jackson	13.97
058	Placido Polanco	13.95
059	Dick Wakefield	13.93
060	Marv Owen	13.84
061	Frank Bolling	13.60
062	Heinie Manush	13.51
063	Marty McManus	13.28
064	Dale Alexander	13.01
	Mickey Tettleton	13.01
066	Ivan Rodriguez	12.97
067	Ian Kinsler	12.88
068	Johnny Bassler	12.70
069	Johnny Groth	12.69
070	Matty McIntyre	12.51
071	J.D. Martinez	12.49
072	Goose Goslin	12.37
073	Jason Thompson	12.28
074	Alex Avila	12.03
075	Ralph Young	11.98
076	Rusty Staub	11.96
077	Craig Monroe	11.91
078	Bob Jones	11.66
079	Doc Cramer	11.64
080	Gates Brown	11.58
081	Jimmy Barrett	11.31
082	Roy Johnson	11.02
083	Roy Cullenbine	10.77
084	Dmitri Young	10.73
085	Oscar Stanage	10.68
086	John Wockenfuss	10.44
087	Omar Infante	10.25
088	Deivi Cruz	10.12
089	Johnny Lipon	10.02
090	Ossie Vitt	9.96
091	Bill Tuttle	9.73
092	Billy Bruton	9.72
093	Eddie Mayo	9.37
094	Dave Bergman	9.31
	Topper Rigney	9.31
096	George Moriarty	9.22
097	Jhonny Peralta	8.97
098	Davy Jones	8.71
099	Jeimer Candelario	8.66
100	Birdie Tebbetts	8.64

001	Ty Cobb	2,363.7
002	Al Kaline	1,782.6
003	Charlie Gehringer	1,769.7
004	Harry Heilmann	1,554.8
005	Miguel Cabrera	1,365.5
006	Lou Whitaker	1,333.7
007	Sam Crawford	1,303.8
008	Hank Greenberg	1,244.9
009	Norm Cash	1,229.3
010	Alan Trammell	1,166.2
011	Bobby Veach	968.1
012	Rudy York	860.3
013	Dick McAuliffe	850.0
014	Bill Freehan	842.8
015	Willie Horton	818.9
016	Bobby Higginson	800.4
017	Donie Bush	797.7
018	Kirk Gibson	702.0
019	Harvey Kuenn	643.4
020	Billy Rogell	636.9
021	Cecil Fielder	633.4
022	Travis Fryman	621.3
023	Chet Lemon	609.6
024	Jim Northrup	603.5
025	Lance Parrish	594.2
026	Pete Fox	578.9
027	Lu Blue	578.4
028	Magglio Ordonez	538.1
029	George Kell	533.5
030	Mickey Stanley	530.3
031	Brandon Inge	528.2
032	Victor Martinez	516.1
033	Carlos Guillen	500.6
034	Vic Wertz	500.4
035	Tony Clark	494.4
036	Gee Walker	488.3
037	Charlie Maxwell	473.3
038	Tony Phillips	456.2
039	Nicholas Castellanos	455.9
040	Damion Easley	438.2
041	Ray Boone	436.8
042	Pinky Higgins	436.7
043	Curtis Granderson	435.2
044	Bob Fothergill	427.8
045	Steve Kemp	423.7
046	Ron LeFlore	422.9
047	Rocky Colavito	421.7
048	Hoot Evers	411.4
049	John Stone	408.9
050	Pat Mullin	403.7

Mickey Stanley

051	Barney McCosky	400.4
052	Don Wert	398.4
053	Darrell Evans	392.6
054	Aurelio Rodriguez	391.6
055	Marv Owen	388.7
056	Dick Wakefield	381.8
057	Johnny Bassler	376.6
058	Larry Herndon	374.6
059	Mickey Tettleton	370.9
060	Heinie Manush	370.7
061	Austin Jackson	370.1
062	Placido Polanco	367.3
063	Matty McIntyre	364.7
064	Frank Bolling	360.5
065	Tom Brookens	360.3
066	Marty McManus	358.7
067	Dale Alexander	353.2
068	Goose Goslin	352.1
069	Ian Kinsler	341.5
070	Jimmy Barrett	337.1
071	Ralph Young	334.0
072	Alex Avila	332.6
073	Johnny Groth	330.5
074	Jason Thompson	329.8
075	J.D. Martinez	326.7
076	Ivan Rodriguez	319.5
077	Roy Cullenbine	315.4
078	Gates Brown	309.0
079	Bob Jones	308.9
	Rusty Staub	308.9
081	Oscar Stanage	301.8
082	Doc Cramer	300.4
083	Craig Monroe	300.3
084	Roy Johnson	294.8
085	Dmitri Young	281.9
086	John Wockenfuss	279.3
087	Ossie Vitt	273.5
088	Johnny Lipon	268.0
089	Omar Infante	264.6
090	Billy Bruton	257.1
091	Davy Jones	257.0
092	George Moriarty	254.7
093	Topper Rigney	253.9
094	Dave Bergman	253.7
095	Jeimer Candelario	247.6
096	Deivi Cruz	244.2
	Bill Tuttle	244.2
098	Ray Hayworth	236.4
099	Jo-Jo White	235.8
100	Eddie Mayo	232.2

Rank	Player	Batting Runs
001	Ty Cobb	1,147
002	Al Kaline	1,005
003	Charlie Gehringer	978
004	Harry Heilmann	881
005	Miguel Cabrera	827
006	Hank Greenberg	759
007	Norm Cash	691
008	Sam Crawford	688
009	Lou Whitaker	670
010	Alan Trammell	559
011	Bobby Veach	492
012	Rudy York	479
013	Bobby Higginson	413
014	Willie Horton	403
015	Kirk Gibson	396
016	Bill Freehan	373
017	Dick McAuliffe	367
018	Cecil Fielder	353
019	Donie Bush	333
020	Lu Blue	301
021	Travis Fryman	297
022	Harvey Kuenn	295
023	Magglio Ordonez	294
024	Chet Lemon	293
025	George Kell	280
026	Lance Parrish	277
027	Carlos Guillen	275
028	Vic Wertz	272
029	Tony Clark	270
030	Jim Northrup	267
031	Billy Rogell	265
032	Pete Fox	260
033	Victor Martinez	258
034	Charlie Maxwell	248
035	Tony Phillips	246
036	Gee Walker	244
037	Ray Boone	242
038	Rocky Colavito	238
039	Steve Kemp	230
040	Curtis Granderson	228
041	Ron LeFlore	224
042	Damion Easley	211
	Bob Fothergill	211
044	Hoot Evers	210
	Barney McCosky	210
046	Mickey Tettleton	208
047	Pinky Higgins	206
	Dick Wakefield	206
049	Nicholas Castellanos	205
050	Darrell Evans	198

Juan Encarnacion

Rank	Player	Batting Runs
051	Johnny Bassler	197
052	Pat Mullin	195
053	Heinie Manush	194
054	J.D. Martinez	190
055	John Stone	189
056	Roy Cullenbine	184
057	Goose Goslin	176
058	Jimmy Barrett	173
	Larry Herndon	173
060	Austin Jackson	172
061	Placido Polanco	171
062	Brandon Inge	169
063	Marty McManus	168
064	Rusty Staub	161
065	Jason Thompson	158
066	Alex Avila	154
	Ian Kinsler	154
	Mickey Stanley	154
069	Johnny Groth	153
070	Ivan Rodriguez	149
071	Dmitri Young	148
072	Gates Brown	141
073	Matty McIntyre	137
074	Marv Owen	136
075	Roy Johnson	135
076	Prince Fielder	132
	John Wockenfuss	132
078	Frank Bolling	130
079	Craig Monroe	127
080	Topper Rigney	125
081	Jim Delahanty	119
082	Dale Alexander	117
083	Davy Jones	116
	Al Wingo	116
085	Billy Bruton	111
	Don Wert	111
087	Carlos Pena	108
088	Jeimer Candelario	106
089	Marcus Thames	105
090	Jhonny Peralta	102
091	Dean Palmer	101
092	Dave Bergman	99
093	Johnny Lipon	97
094	Juan Encarnacion	96
095	Jo-Jo White	94
096	Omar Infante	92
097	Tom Brookens	91
098	Jerry Priddy	90
099	Ralph Young	88
100	Fred Haney	87

Rank	Player	XR
001	Ty Cobb	2,198
002	Al Kaline	1,829
003	Charlie Gehringer	1,628
004	Miguel Cabrera	1,405
005	Harry Heilmann	1,399
006	Lou Whitaker	1,382
007	Sam Crawford	1,255
008	Norm Cash	1,245
009	Alan Trammell	1,221
010	Hank Greenberg	1,118
011	Bobby Veach	922
012	Donie Bush	885
013	Dick McAuliffe	873
014	Rudy York	862
015	Bill Freehan	858
	Willie Horton	858
017	Bobby Higginson	810
018	Kirk Gibson	729
019	Cecil Fielder	673
020	Harvey Kuenn	638
	Jim Northrup	638
022	Lance Parrish	636
023	Travis Fryman	634
024	Billy Rogell	616
025	Chet Lemon	609
026	Mickey Stanley	576
027	Lu Blue	561
028	Pete Fox	557
029	Victor Martinez	554
030	Brandon Inge	543
031	Magglio Ordonez	542
032	George Kell	529
033	Carlos Guillen	514
034	Tony Clark	507
035	Vic Wertz	501
036	Ron LeFlore	472
	Charlie Maxwell	472
038	Tony Phillips	471
039	Pinky Higgins	461
	Gee Walker	461
041	Nicholas Castellanos	450
042	Ray Boone	444
043	Damion Easley	436
	Don Wert	436
045	Rocky Colavito	435
046	Steve Kemp	433
047	Curtis Granderson	427
048	Hoot Evers	426
049	Darrell Evans	415
050	Aurelio Rodriguez	414

Pete Fox

Rank	Player	XR
051	Pat Mullin	403
052	Larry Herndon	395
053	Barney McCosky	391
054	Bob Fothergill	389
055	Tom Brookens	385
	Mickey Tettleton	385
057	Dick Wakefield	384
058	Austin Jackson	378
059	John Stone	376
060	Johnny Bassler	370
061	Frank Bolling	369
062	Marv Owen	367
063	Matty McIntyre	363
064	Placido Polanco	357
065	Ralph Young	353
066	Marty McManus	349
067	Jason Thompson	348
068	Alex Avila	347
069	Ian Kinsler	342
070	Jimmy Barrett	337
	Heinie Manush	337
072	Johnny Groth	334
	Ivan Rodriguez	334
074	Rusty Staub	331
075	Gates Brown	327
076	Goose Goslin	326
077	J.D. Martinez	324
078	Dale Alexander	318
	Craig Monroe	318
080	Roy Cullenbine	315
081	Bob Jones	308
082	Doc Cramer	303
083	Ossie Vitt	292
	Dmitri Young	292
085	John Wockenfuss	290
086	Roy Johnson	285
	Johnny Lipon	285
088	Oscar Stanage	283
089	Davy Jones	276
090	Omar Infante	272
091	Billy Bruton	270
	George Moriarty	270
093	Dave Bergman	268
	Bill Tuttle	268
095	Topper Rigney	256
096	Deivi Cruz	252
097	Eddie Mayo	249
098	Jo-Jo White	241
099	Jeimer Candelario	239
	Jhonny Peralta	239

ALL TIME TIGER HITTING LEADERS – HOME RUN AVERAGE

Rank	Player	Average
001	Marcus Thames	40.60
002	Cecil Fielder	40.01
003	Hank Greenberg	38.32
004	Darrell Evans	36.02
005	Rocky Colavito	35.70
006	Mickey Tettleton	35.61
007	J.D. Martinez	35.00
008	Norm Cash	33.95
009	Dean Palmer	33.48
010	Tony Clark	33.06
011	Miguel Cabrera	31.51
012	Carlos Pena	30.70
013	Rudy York	30.66
014	Lance Parrish	29.77
015	Charlie Maxwell	29.60
016	Willie Horton	29.08
017	Kirk Gibson	28.06
018	Dmitri Young	27.44
019	Prince Fielder	27.39
020	Jason Thompson	26.68
021	John Wockenfuss	25.88
022	Craig Monroe	25.81
023	Ray Boone	25.35
024	Roy Cullenbine	24.22
025	Curtis Granderson	23.73
026	Al Kaline	23.67
027	Vic Wertz	23.42
028	Bobby Higginson	22.85
029	Gates Brown	22.28
030	Ben Oglivie	21.96
031	Steve Kemp	21.33
032	Pat Mullin	20.94
033	Chet Lemon	20.91
034	Travis Fryman	20.81
035	Ryan Raburn	20.60
036	Magglio Ordonez	20.25
037	Damion Easley	20.19
038	Alex Avila	20.06
039	Rusty Staub	20.00
040	Nicholas Castellanos	19.82
041	Bill Freehan	19.76
042	Jim Northrup	19.61
043	Dick McAuliffe	19.53
044	Victor Martinez	19.39
045	Niko Goodrum	19.16
046	Juan Encarnacion	19.04
047	Carlos Guillen	18.95
048	Jhonny Peralta	18.91
049	Ian Kinsler	18.89
050	Brennan Boesch	18.50
051	Jeimer Candelario	18.25
052	Brandon Inge	18.16
053	Larry Herndon	18.12
054	Frank House	17.78
055	Walt Dropo	17.33
056	Lou Whitaker	17.08
057	Dale Alexander	16.35
058	Dick Wakefield	15.79
059	James McCann	15.63
060	Ivan Rodriguez	15.62
061	Goose Goslin	15.33
062	Shane Halter	15.23
063	Mike Heath	15.08
064	Mickey Stanley	13.98
065	Billy Bruton	13.96
066	Hoot Evers	13.91
067	Pat Sheridan	13.88
068	Jim Delsing	13.52
069	Harry Heilmann	13.48
070	Alan Trammell	13.39
071	Tony Phillips	13.32
072	Don Kelly	13.23
073	Frank Bolling	13.17
074	Charlie Gehringer	12.46
075	Dizzy Trout	12.43
076	Marty McManus	12.19
077	Don Wert	12.16
078	Omar Infante	12.15
079	Gee Walker	12.02
080	Dave Bergman	11.90
081	Aurelio Rodriguez	11.72
082	Pinky Higgins	11.49
083	Chico Fernandez	11.39
084	Jake Wood	11.29
085	Tom Brookens	11.18
086	John Stone	11.12
087	Heinie Manush	10.86
088	Austin Jackson	10.31
089	Bill Tuttle	9.74
090	Ron LeFlore	9.37
091	Jerry Priddy	9.30
092	Deivi Cruz	9.23
093	Pete Fox	9.03
094	Johnny Groth	9.00
095	Red Wilson	8.92
096	Placido Polanco	8.57
097	Eddie Lake	8.45
098	Eddie Brinkman	8.16
099	Ramon Santiago	7.60
100	Harvey Kuenn	7.27

Marcus Thames

001	Cecil Fielder	0.07
	Marcus Thames	0.07
003	Norm Cash	0.06
	Tony Clark	0.06
	Rocky Colavito	0.06
	Darrell Evans	0.06
	Hank Greenberg	0.06
	J.D. Martinez	0.06
	Dean Palmer	0.06
	Mickey Tettleton	0.06
011	Miguel Cabrera	0.05
	Prince Fielder	0.05
	Kirk Gibson	0.05
	Willie Horton	0.05

Chico Fernandez

	Charlie Maxwell	0.05
	Lance Parrish	0.05
	Carlos Pena	0.05
	Rudy York	0.05
	Dmitri Young	0.05
020	Ray Boone	0.04
	Gates Brown	0.04
	Roy Cullenbine	0.04
	Curtis Granderson	0.04
	Bobby Higginson	0.04
	Al Kaline	0.04
	Steve Kemp	0.04
	Craig Monroe	0.04
	Ben Oglivie	0.04
	Jason Thompson	0.04
	Vic Wertz	0.04
	John Wockenfuss	0.04
032	Dale Alexander	0.03
	Alex Avila	0.03
	Brennan Boesch	0.03
	Jeimer Candelario	0.03
	Nicholas Castellanos	0.03
	Walt Dropo	0.03
	Damion Easley	0.03
	Juan Encarnacion	0.03
	Bill Freehan	0.03
	Travis Fryman	0.03
	Niko Goodrum	0.03
	Goose Goslin	0.03
	Carlos Guillen	0.03
	Shane Halter	0.03
	Mike Heath	0.03
	Larry Herndon	0.03
	Frank House	0.03
	Brandon Inge	0.03
	Ian Kinsler	0.03
	Chet Lemon	0.03
	Victor Martinez	0.03
	Dick McAuliffe	0.03
	James McCann	0.03
	Pat Mullin	0.03
	Jim Northrup	0.03
	Magglio Ordonez	0.03
	Jhonny Peralta	0.03
	Ryan Raburn	0.03
	Ivan Rodriguez	0.03
	Rusty Staub	0.03
	Dick Wakefield	0.03
	Lou Whitaker	0.03
063	Frank Bolling	0.02
	Billy Bruton	0.02
	Dave Bergman	0.02
	Tom Brookens	0.02
	Deivi Cruz	0.02
	Jim Delsing	0.02
	Hoot Evers	0.02
	Pete Fox	0.02
	Chico Fernandez	0.02
	Charlie Gehringer	0.02
	Johnny Groth	0.02
	Harry Heilmann	0.02
	Pinky Higgins	0.02
	Omar Infante	0.02
	Austin Jackson	0.02
	Don Kelly	0.02
	Ron LeFlore	0.02

Don Kelly

	Heinie Manush	0.02
	Marty McManus	0.02
	Jerry Priddy	0.02
	Tony Phillips	0.02
	Aurelio Rodriguez	0.02
	John Stone	0.02
	Mickey Stanley	0.02
	Pat Sheridan	0.02
	Dizzy Trout	0.02
	Bill Tuttle	0.02
	Alan Trammell	0.02
	Gee Walker	0.02
	Don Wert	0.02
	Jake Wood	0.02

Rank	Player	HR
001	Al Kaline	226
002	Norm Cash	211
003	Hank Greenberg	187
004	Miguel Cabrera	183
005	Lou Whitaker	146
006	Rudy York	139
007	Cecil Fielder	127
008	Willie Horton	124
009	Dick McAuliffe	107
010	Bill Freehan	100
011	Lance Parrish	98
012	Alan Trammell	97
013	Kirk Gibson	95
014	Bobby Higginson	94
015	Charlie Gehringer	92
016	Jim Northrup	87
017	Harry Heilmann	84
018	Charlie Maxwell	83
019	Chet Lemon	82
020	Tony Clark	78
021	Travis Fryman	77
022	Brandon Inge	76
023	Darrell Evans	75
024	Rocky Colavito	67
025	Mickey Stanley	62
026	Jason Thompson	61
027	Mickey Tettleton	58
	Vic Wertz	58
029	J.D. Martinez	57
030	Damion Easley	56
	Magglio Ordonez	56
032	Ray Boone	55
033	Steve Kemp	54
034	Carlos Guillen	52
	Pat Mullin	52
	Victor Martinez	52
037	Gates Brown	50
038	Marcus Thames	49
039	Don Wert	47
040	Craig Monroe	45
	Aurelio Rodriguez	45
042	Nicholas Castellanos	44
	Dean Palmer	44
044	Alex Avila	43
	Curtis Granderson	43
046	John Wockenfuss	42
047	Tom Brookens	41
048	Roy Cullenbine	40
	Pinky Higgins	40
	Ian Kinsler	40

Ben Oglivie

Rank	Player	HR
	Rusty Staub	40
052	Larry Herndon	39
053	Carlos Pena	37
054	Hoot Evers	35
	Dmitri Young	35
056	Rob Deer	34
	Dick Wakefield	34
058	Ty Cobb	32
059	Prince Fielder	31
	Matt Nokes	31
	Tony Phillips	31
	Gee Walker	31
063	Frank Bolling	30
	Marty McManus	30
065	Sam Crawford	29
	Harvey Kuenn	29
067	Ron LeFlore	27
	Jhonny Peralta	27
	Ivan Rodriguez	27
	Gary Sheffield	27
	Champ Summers	27
	Justin Upton	27
073	Brennan Boesch	25
	Jeimer Candelario	25
	Pete Fox	25
	James McCann	25
	Ben Oglivie	25
	Ryan Raburn	25
079	Dave Bergman	24
	Billy Bruton	24
	Frank House	24
082	Mike Heath	23
083	Don Demeter	22
	Jake Wood	22
085	Dale Alexander	21
	Robert Fick	21
	JaCoby Jones	21
	Eric Munson	21
	Bud Souchock	21
090	Jim Delsing	20
	Goose Goslin	20
	Johnny Groth	20
	Richie Hebner	20
	Omar Infante	20
	Placido Polanco	20
	Ramon Santiago	20
097	Juan Encarnacion	19
	Bill Tuttle	19
	Bobby Veach	19
	Eddie Yost	19

Rank	Player	HR
001	Miguel Cabrera	181
002	Al Kaline	173
003	Norm Cash	162
004	Willie Horton	138
005	Hank Greenberg	119
006	Cecil Fielder	118
007	Lance Parrish	114
008	Bill Freehan	100
	Kirk Gibson	100
	Rudy York	100
011	Lou Whitaker	98
012	Bobby Higginson	93
013	Charlie Gehringer	92
014	Alan Trammell	88
015	Dick McAuliffe	85
016	Harry Heilmann	80
017	Ty Cobb	79
018	Tony Clark	78
019	Rocky Colavito	72
	Travis Fryman	72
021	Darrell Evans	66
022	Brandon Inge	64
023	Victor Martinez	63
024	Nicholas Castellanos	60
	Chet Lemon	60
026	Curtis Granderson	59
027	Jim Northrup	58
	Jason Thompson	58
029	Craig Monroe	57
030	Mickey Stanley	55
031	Mickey Tettleton	54
032	Magglio Ordonez	51
033	Ray Boone	50
	Charlie Maxwell	50
	Marcus Thames	50
036	Damion Easley	48
037	Dmitri Young	47
038	Vic Wertz	46
038	Larry Herndon	44
040	Carlos Guillen	43
041	J.D. Martinez	42
042	Sam Crawford	41
043	Aurelio Rodriguez	40
	Bobby Veach	40
045	Ian Kinsler	38
	Carlos Pena	38
	John Wockenfuss	38
048	Rob Deer	37
049	Steve Kemp	35
	Pat Mullin	35
	Ivan Rodriguez	35

Rocky Colavito

Rank	Player	HR
052	Alex Avila	34
	Frank Bolling	34
	Gates Brown	34
	Juan Encarnacion	34
	Pete Fox	34
	Dean Palmer	34
058	Justin Upton	32
059	Goose Goslin	30
	Austin Jackson	30
	Matt Nokes	30
	Tony Phillips	30
	Rusty Staub	30
	Gee Walker	30
	Don Wert	30
066	Ryan Raburn	29
	John Stone	29
068	Hoot Evers	28
069	Dale Alexander	27
	Jeimer Candelario	27
	Niko Goodrum	27
	Melvin Nieves	27
073	Jhonny Peralta	26
074	Tom Brookens	25
	Omar Infante	25
076	Prince Fielder	24
	Robert Fick	24
	Harvey Kuenn	24
	Ron LeFlore	24
	Ben Oglivie	24
	Billy Rogell	24
082	Roy Cullenbine	23
	Walt Dropo	23
	Shane Halter	23
	Heinie Manush	23
086	Billy Bruton	22
	Dick Wakefield	22
088	Don Demeter	21
089	Deivi Cruz	20
	Pinky Higgins	20
091	Eric Munson	19
	Chris Shelton	19
	Rondell White	19
094	Chad Curtis	18
	Frank House	18
	Torii Hunter	18
097	Brennan Boesch	17
	John Hicks	17
	Marty McManus	17
	Placido Polanco	17
	Gary Sheffield	17
	Bud Souchock	17

Rank	Player	HR
001	Al Kaline	129
002	Lance Parrish	98
003	Willie Horton	97
004	Miguel Cabrera	77
005	Bill Freehan	75
006	Cecil Fielder	74
007	Alan Trammell	73
008	Hank Greenberg	70
009	John Wockenfuss	69
010	Mickey Stanley	65
011	Norm Cash	61
	Chet Lemon	61
013	Rudy York	53
014	Brandon Inge	51
015	Harry Heilmann	50
016	Larry Herndon	46
017	Tony Clark	43
018	Travis Fryman	42
019	Kirk Gibson	41
	Aurelio Rodriguez	41
021	Marcus Thames	38
022	Magglio Ordonez	36
	Lou Whitaker	36
024	Victor Martinez	35
025	Nicholas Castellanos	34
	Bobby Higginson	34
	Craig Monroe	34
	Don Wert	34
029	Tom Brookens	32
	Dick McAuliffe	32
031	Rocky Colavito	31
032	Ray Boone	30
	J.D. Martinez	30
	Jim Northrup	30
	Ryan Raburn	30
036	Rob Deer	29
	Ron LeFlore	29
038	Ty Cobb	28
	Hoot Evers	28
040	Charlie Gehringer	27
	Rusty Staub	27
	Mickey Tettleton	27
043	Damion Easley	26
	Steve Kemp	26
045	Jason Thompson	25
046	Darrell Evans	24
047	Carlos Guillen	23
	James McCann	23
	Tony Phillips	23
	Vic Wertz	23
051	Dean Palmer	22
	Carlos Pena	22
	Dmitri Young	22
054	Jhonny Peralta	21
055	Sam Crawford	20
	Mike Heath	20
	Omar Infante	20
	Steve Souchock	20
059	Ian Kinsler	19
060	Justin Upton	18
061	Ike Brown	17
	Don Demeter	17
	Juan Encarnacion	17
064	Pete Fox	16
	Curtis Granderson	16
	Harvey Kuenn	16
	Bobby Veach	16
068	Walt Dropo	15
	Prince Fielder	15
	Austin Jackson	15
	Placido Polanco	15
	Ivan Rodriguez	15
	Gee Walker	15
074	Shane Halter	14
	Billy Rogell	14
	John Stone	14
	Bill Tuttle	14
	Gary Ward	14
079	Eddie Brinkman	13
	Frank Howard	13
	Charlie Maxwell	13
	Jerry Morales	13
083	Jeimer Candelario	12
	Bob Fothergill	12
	Dan Gladden	12
	Torii Hunter	12
	Jim Price	12
	Gary Sheffield	12
089	Frank Bolling	11
	Steve Boros	11
	Eric Haase	11
092	Deivi Cruz	10
	Pinky Higgins	10
	Jose Iglesias	10
	Marty McManus	10
	Jerry Priddy	10
	Jonathan Schoop	10
098	Gates Brown	9
	Rajai Davis	9
	Barbaro Garbey	9
	Johnny Groth	9
	Mike Ivie	9
	George Kell	9
	Pat Mullin	9
	Eric Munson	9
	George Thomas	9
	Jake Wood	9

George Thomas

Rank	Player	HR
001	Norm Cash	312
002	Miguel Cabrera	287
003	Al Kaline	270
004	Hank Greenberg	236
005	Lou Whitaker	208
006	Rudy York	186
007	Cecil Fielder	171
008	Willie Horton	165
009	Dick McAuliffe	160
010	Charlie Gehringer	157
011	Kirk Gibson	154
012	Bobby Higginson	153
013	Bill Freehan	125
014	Charlie Maxwell	120
015	Darrell Evans	117
016	Jim Northrup	115
017	Harry Heilmann	114
	Lance Parrish	114
019	Tony Clark	113
020	Alan Trammell	112
021	Rocky Colavito	108
022	Travis Fryman	107
023	Jason Thompson	94
024	Brandon Inge	89
025	Curtis Granderson	86
026	Mickey Tettleton	85
027	Ty Cobb	83
028	Chet Lemon	81
	Vic Wertz	81
030	Victor Martinez	80
031	Damion Easley	78
	Pat Mullin	78
033	Ray Boone	75
	Gates Brown	75
035	Carlos Guillen	72
036	Magglio Ordonez	71
037	Alex Avila	70
	Nicholas Castellanos	70
039	J.D. Martinez	69
040	Craig Monroe	68
041	Steve Kemp	63
042	Marcus Thames	61
043	Dmitri Young	60
044	Ian Kinsler	59
045	Dean Palmer	56
046	Roy Cullenbine	55
047	Frank Bolling	53
	Matt Nokes	53
	Carlos Pena	53
050	Mickey Stanley	52
051	Sam Crawford	50

Pinky Higgins

Rank	Player	HR
	Pinky Higgins	50
053	Dick Wakefield	48
054	Goose Goslin	47
	Ivan Rodriguez	47
056	Gee Walker	46
057	Aurelio Rodriguez	44
058	Pete Fox	43
	Rusty Staub	43
	Bobby Veach	43
	Don Wert	43
062	Billy Bruton	42
	Rob Deer	42
	Ben Oglivie	42
065	Justin Upton	41
066	Dale Alexander	40
	Jeimer Candelario	40
	Prince Fielder	40
	Frank House	40
070	Dave Bergman	39
071	Robert Fick	38
	Tony Phillips	38
073	Larry Herndon	37
	Harvey Kuenn	37
	Marty McManus	37
	Champ Summers	37
077	Brennan Boesch	36
	Juan Encarnacion	36
	Niko Goodrum	36
	Melvin Nieves	36
081	Hoot Evers	35
082	Tom Brookens	34
083	Johnny Grubb	32
	Heinie Manush	32
	Jhonny Peralta	32
	Gary Sheffield	32
087	Austin Jackson	31
	Eric Munson	31
	John Stone	31
090	Eddie Yost	30
091	Deivi Cruz	27
	Jim Delsing	27
	Chris Shelton	27
094	Dick Brown	26
	Don Demeter	26
	Omar Infante	26
	JaCoby Jones	26
	Jake Wood	26
099	Walt Dropo	25
	Johnny Groth	25
	Billy Rogell	25
	Pat Sheridan	25

Rank	Player	HR
001	Norm Cash	373
002	Lou Whitaker	244
003	Kirk Gibson	195
004	Dick McAuliffe	192
005	Bobby Higginson	187
006	Charlie Gehringer	184
007	Jim Northrup	145
008	Darrell Evans	141
009	Charlie Maxwell	133
010	Jason Thompson	119
011	Ty Cobb	111
012	Vic Wertz	104
013	Curtis Granderson	102
014	Steve Kemp	89
015	Pat Mullin	87
016	Gates Brown	84
017	Alex Avila	77
018	Carlos Pena	75
019	Sam Crawford	70
	Rusty Staub	70
021	Matt Nokes	61
022	Bobby Veach	59
023	Dick Wakefield	56
024	Prince Fielder	55
025	Goose Goslin	50
026	Ben Oglivie	49
027	Billy Bruton	46
028	Robert Fick	45
	John Stone	45
030	Brennan Boesch	42
	Frank House	42
032	Eric Munson	40
	Champ Summers	40
034	Dave Bergman	39
035	Heinie Manush	38
036	Johnny Grubb	32
037	Jim Delsing	30
038	Gail Harris	29
039	Pat Sheridan	26
040	Richie Hebner	25
	Randall Simon	25
042	Andy Dirks	24
043	Bruce Campbell	23
	Luis Gonzalez	23
	Roy Johnson	23
	Don Kelly	23
	Eddie Mayo	23
048	Milt May	22
	Aaron Robinson	22

Gates Brown

Rank	Player	HR
	Earl Torgeson	22
051	Lloyd Moseby	20
052	Barney McCosky	19
053	Lou Berberet	18
	Bob Hamelin	18
	Fred Lynn	18
056	Wayne Belardi	17
	Frank Catalanotto	17
058	Ned Harris	16
	Dick Kryhoski	16
	Luis Polonia	16
061	Fred Hatfield	15
	Jerry Lumpe	15
	Christin Stewart	15
064	Tyler Collins	14
	Karim Garcia	14
	Joe Ginsberg	14
	Harry Rice	14
068	Akil Baddoo	13
	Dan Meyer	13
070	Earl Averill	12
	Doc Cramer	12
	Ruppert Jones	12
	Matthew Joyce	12
	Curtis Pride	12
	Duke Sims	12
	George Vico	12
077	Neil Chrisley	11
	Mickey Cochrane	11
	Dalton Jones	11
	Jackie Tavener	11
081	Jimmy Barrett	10
	Mark Salas	10
	Larry Sheets	10
	Dixie Walker	10
	Kevin Witt	10
086	Sean Casey	9
	Cliff Mapes	9
	Leonys Martin	9
	Eddie Mathews	9
	Al Wingo	9
091	Harold Castro	8
	Johnny Damon	8
	Mike Laga	8
	Scott Livingstone	8
	Phil Mankowski	8
	Jack Pierce	8
	Clete Thomas	8
	Jerry Turner	8
099	Rich Becker	7
	Tim Corcoran	7
	Anthony Gose	7
	Bob Jones	7
	Rick Leach	7

Rank	Player	HR
001	Al Kaline	399
002	Miguel Cabrera	364
003	Hank Greenberg	306
004	Willie Horton	262
005	Cecil Fielder	245
006	Rudy York	239
007	Lance Parrish	212
008	Bill Freehan	200
009	Alan Trammell	185
010	Harry Heilmann	164
011	Travis Fryman	149
012	Chet Lemon	142
013	Brandon Inge	140
014	Rocky Colavito	139
015	Mickey Stanley	117
016	Magglio Ordonez	107
017	Ray Boone	105
018	Nicholas Castellanos	104
	Damion Easley	104
020	Craig Monroe	102
021	J.D. Martinez	99
	Marcus Thames	99
023	Aurelio Rodriguez	85
024	Larry Herndon	83
025	John Wockenfuss	80
026	Ian Kinsler	78
	Dean Palmer	78
028	Don Wert	77
029	Rob Deer	71
030	Tom Brookens	66
031	Frank Bolling	64
032	Hoot Evers	63
033	Ivan Rodriguez	62
034	Gee Walker	61
035	Pinky Higgins	60
036	Pete Fox	59
	Justin Upton	59
038	Ryan Raburn	54

Rank	Player	HR
039	Juan Encarnacion	53
	Harvey Kuenn	53
	Jhonny Peralta	53
042	Ron LeFlore	51
043	Dale Alexander	48
044	Marty McManus	47
045	Austin Jackson	46
046	Omar Infante	45
047	Gary Sheffield	44
048	Don Demeter	43
049	Walt Dropo	40
	James McCann	40
051	Steve Souchock	38

Dick Brown

Rank	Player	HR
052	Deivi Cruz	37
	Shane Halter	37
	Placido Polanco	37
055	Chris Shelton	35
	Bill Tuttle	35
	Jake Wood	35
	Eddie Yost	35
059	Johnny Groth	34
	Mike Heath	34
	Torii Hunter	34
062	JaCoby Jones	32
063	Chad Curtis	31
	Rondell White	31

Rank	Player	HR
065	Jonathan Schoop	30
066	Eddie Brinkman	28
	Dick Brown	28
	John Hicks	28
069	Chico Fernandez	27
070	Bob Fothergill	26
	Jerry Priddy	26
	Delmon Young	26
073	Darnell Coles	25
	George Kell	25
	Marv Owen	25
076	Jimmy Bloodworth	24
077	Eddie Lake	23
	Bob Nieman	23
	Glenn Wilson	23
080	Juan Gonzalez	22
	Eric Haase	22
	Red Wilson	22
083	Steve Boros	21
	Mikie Mahtook	21
085	Brad Ausmus	20
	Ike Brown	20
	Dan Gladden	20
	Chris Gomez	20
089	Jose Iglesias	19
	Phil Nevin	19
	Ronny Rodriguez	19
	Dizzy Trout	19
093	Yoenis Cespedes	18
	Gabe Kapler	18
	Wendell Magee Jr.	18
	Jim Price	18
	Gary Ward	18
098	Earl Wilson	17
099	Rajai Davis	16
	Birdie Tebbetts	16
	George Thomas	16

Rank	Player	HR
001	Tony Clark	156
002	Victor Martinez	115
003	Mickey Tettleton	112
004	Carlos Guillen	95
005	Dmitri Young	82
006	Roy Cullenbine	63
007	Tony Phillips	61
008	Jeimer Candelario	52
009	Melvin Nieves	44
010	Niko Goodrum	42
011	Billy Rogell	39
012	Ramon Santiago	28
013	Robbie Grossman	23

Robbie Grossman

Rank	Player	HR
014	Lu Blue	19
	Howard Johnson	19
016	Pinky Hargrave	18
	Chad Kreuter	18
018	Willi Castro	16
019	Junior Felix	13
	Victor Reyes	13
	Tom Tresh	13
022	Jarrod Saltalamacchia	12
023	Jose Macias	11
024	Raul Casanova	10
	Andrew Romine	10
	Nelson Simmons	10

Victor Reyes

Rank	Player	HR
027	Donie Bush	9
028	Gregg Jefferies	8
029	Milt Cuyler	7
	John Shelby	7
031	Roger Cedeno	6
032	Wilson Betemit	5
	Doc Casey	5
	Tito Fuentes	5
	Gary Pettis	5
036	Kimera Bartee	4
	Kid Gleason	4
	Sport McAllister	4
	Brayan Pena	4
	Matt Walbeck	4
041	Gene Michael	3
	Boss Schmidt	3
	Ralph Young	3

Jarrod Saltalamacchia

Rank	Player	HR
044	Bill Donovan	2
	Mark Koenig	2
	Torey Lovullo	2
	Archie McKain	2
	Greg Norton	2
	Red Oldham	2
	Rick Peters	2
	Dave Philley	2
	Ed Summers	2
	Casey Wise	2
054	Sergio Alcantara	1
	Eric Aybar	1
	Mike Brumley	1

Brayan Pena

Rank	Player	HR
	Dave Collins	1
	Tony Giarratano	1
	Michael Hollimon	1
	Gene Kingsale	1
	George Lerchen	1
	Nook Logan	1
	Billy Lush	1
	Neifi Perez	1
	Mike Rabelo	1
	Ruben Sierra	1
	Doug Strange	1
	Andres Torres	1
	Jim Walewander	1

ALL TIME TIGER HITTING LEADERS – INSIDE THE PARK HOME RUNS

Rank	Player	HR
001	Ty Cobb	46
002	Sam Crawford	30
006	Charlie Gehringer	6
003	Harry Heilmann	6
008	Donie Bush	5
	Bob Jones	4
	John Stone	4
013	Lu Blue	3
	Kid Gleason	3
	Heinie Manush	3
	Bobby Veach	3
	Lou Whitaker	3
019	George Burns	2
	Norm Cash	2
	Doc Cramer	2
	Bill Donovan	2
	Red Downs	2
	Hoot Evers	2
	Bob Fothergill	2
	Curtis Granderson	2
	Shane Halter	2
	Fred Haney	2
	Ducky Holmes	2
	Willie Horton	2
	Roy Johnson	2
	Al Kaline	2
	Marty Kavanagh	2
	Ron LeFlore	2
	Dick McAuliffe	2
	Barney McCosky	2
	George Mullin	2
	Pat Mullin	2
	Germany Schaefer	2
	Jake Wood	2

Kid Gleason

ALL TIME TIGER HITTING LEADERS – GRAND SLAM HOME RUNS

Rank	Player	GS
001	Cecil Fielder	10
002	Norm Cash	8
	Dick McAuliffe	8
	Jim Northrup	8
005	Hank Greenberg	6
	Willie Horton	6
	Marcus Thames	6
008	Ray Boone	5
	Miguel Cabrera	5
	Darrell Evans	5
	Pete Fox	5
	Bill Freehan	5
	Brandon Inge	5
	Lance Parrish	5
	Mickey Tettleton	5
	Alan Trammell	5
017	Nicholas Castellanos	4
	Ty Cobb	4
	Travis Fryman	4
	Bobby Higginson	4
	Victor Martinez	4
	Lou Whitaker	4
	Rudy York	4
024	Charlie Gehringer	3
	Dan Gladden	3
	Johnny Groth	3
	Al Kaline	3
	Steve Kemp	3
	Charlie Maxwell	3
	James McCann	3
	Marty McManus	3
	Craig Monroe	3
	Matt Nokes	3
	Carlos Pena	3
	Ryan Raburn	3
	Jason Thompson	3
	Justin Upton	3
	Dmitri Young	3
039	Tom Brookens	2
	Tony Clark	2
	Sam Crawford	2
	Milt Cuyler	2
	Kirk Gibson	2
	Carlos Guillen	2
	Harry Heilmann	2
	George Kell	2
	Chet Laabs	2
	Heinie Manush	2
	J.D. Martinez	2
	Pat Mullin	2
	Dean Palmer	2
	Jhonny Peralta	2
	Edgar Renteria	2
	Jonathan Schoop	2
	Gary Sheffield	2
	Pat Sheridan	2
	Randall Simon	2
	Mickey Stanley	2
	Rusty Staub	2
	Birdie Tebbetts	2
	Dizzy Trout	2
	Bobby Veach	2
	Vic Wertz	2
	John Wockenfuss	2
	Eddie Yost	2

Dan Gladden

ALL TIME TIGER HITTING LEADERS – ISOLATED POWER

Rank	Player	ISO
001	Hank Greenberg	.297
002	Marcus Thames	.256
003	J.D. Martinez	.251
004	Cecil Fielder	.241
005	Mickey Tettleton	.232
006	Rocky Colavito	.230
007	Tony Clark	.225
008	Rudy York	.222
009	Miguel Cabrera	.219
010	Norm Cash	.218
011	Carlos Pena	.217
012	Dean Palmer	.216
013	Darrell Evans	.212
014	Curtis Granderson	.211
016	Kirk Gibson	.207
	Lance Parrish	.207
	Dmitri Young	.207
019	Charlie Maxwell	.197
020	Prince Fielder	.196
	Willie Horton	.196
022	Craig Monroe	.192
023	Ray Boone	.191
024	Vic Wertz	.190
025	Nicholas Castellanos	.186
026	Roy Cullenbine	.184
027	Bobby Higginson	.183
028	Al Kaline	.182
	Pat Mullin	.182
030	Dale Alexander	.181
031	Carlos Guillen	.180
	Jason Thompson	.180
033	John Wockenfuss	.178
034	Harry Heilmann	.175
035	Juan Encarnacion	.174
	Chet Lemon	.174
	Ryan Raburn	.174
038	Travis Fryman	.171
039	Niko Goodrum	.169
	Ben Oglivie	.169
040	Damion Easley	.168
041	Steve Kemp	.167
042	Jeimer Candelario	.165
043	Magglio Ordonez	.164
044	Gates Brown	.163
	Jim Northrup	.163
046	Ian Kinsler	.161
047	Charlie Gehringer	.160
048	Alex Avila	.159
049	Goose Goslin	.158
	Larry Herndon	.158
	Dick McAuliffe	.158
	Jhonny Peralta	.158
053	Rusty Staub	.157
	John Stone	.157
055	Brennan Boesch	.155
056	Dick Wakefield	.154
057	Brandon Inge	.153
	Heinie Manush	.153
059	Roy Johnson	.152
	Gee Walker	.152
061	Ivan Rodriguez	.151
062	Bill Freehan	.150
	Victor Martinez	.150
	Lou Whitaker	.150
065	Ty Cobb	.148
	Shane Halter	.148
067	Marty McManus	.147
068	Hoot Evers	.146
069	Bob Fothergill	.145
070	Walt Dropo	.142
071	Sam Crawford	.139
072	Austin Jackson	.136
073	Jim Delsing	.134
074	Bobby Veach	.133
075	Omar Infante	.132
076	Billy Bruton	.131
077	Alan Trammell	.130
078	Mike Heath	.129
	Mickey Stanley	.129
080	Pete Fox	.128
081	Frank Bolling	.127
082	Frank House	.126
	James McCann	.126
084	Tony Phillips	.124
085	Tom Brookens	.123
086	Barney McCosky	.122
087	Pat Sheridan	.121
088	Pinky Higgins	.120
089	Deivi Cruz	.119
090	Johnny Groth	.117
	Aurelio Rodriguez	.117
092	Al Wingo	.114
093	Jerry Priddy	.113
	Jake Wood	.113
095	Harvey Kuenn	.112
	Jackie Tavener	.112
097	Dave Bergman	.109
	Ron LeFlore	.109
099	Lu Blue	.108
	Dizzy Trout	.108

Bill Freehan

Rank	Player	PSN
001	Alan Trammell	207.4
002	Al Kaline	204.0
003	Ty Cobb	196.9
004	Kirk Gibson	194.5
005	Charlie Gehringer	182.5
006	Lou Whitaker	180.3
007	Harry Heilmann	132.4
008	Bobby Higginson	122.4
009	Sam Crawford	114.7
010	Hank Greenberg	97.5
011	Dick McAuliffe	92.6
012	Damion Easley	91.1
013	Bobby Veach	89.9
014	Ron LeFlore	86.9
015	Travis Fryman	83.5
016	Gee Walker	83.4
017	Curtis Granderson	80.9
018	Pete Fox	76.1
019	Norm Cash	75.5
020	Tom Brookens	74.3
021	Carlos Guillen	72.8
022	Brandon Inge	68.1
023	Tony Phillips	65.2
024	Mickey Stanley	64.0
025	Ian Kinsler	63.1
026	Jim Northrup	61.5
027	Juan Encarnacion	59.6
028	Rudy York	59.5
029	Austin Jackson	57.9
030	Marty McManus	54.6
031	Billy Bruton	53.5
032	Harvey Kuenn	52.0
033	Billy Rogell	51.5
034	Jake Wood	48.5
035	Larry Herndon	46.2
036	Omar Infante	46.0
037	Hoot Evers	45.0
038	Ben Oglivie	44.6
039	Gates Brown	44.2
040	Niko Goodrum	43.4
041	Bill Freehan	42.9
042	Heinie Manush	42.4
043	Miguel Cabrera	41.5
044	Ivan Rodriguez	40.4
045	Lance Parrish	39.9
046	Frank Bolling	39.0
047	Steve Kemp	37.8
048	Gary Sheffield	36.4
049	Chad Curtis	36.0
050	Roy Johnson	35.4

Alan Trammell

Rank	Player	PSN
051	Pinky Higgins	35.3
052	Don Wert	34.2
053	Pat Mullin	32.5
054	Goose Goslin	32.4
055	John Stone	31.3
056	Pat Sheridan	31.2
057	Lu Blue	31.1
058	Placido Polanco	30.5
059	JaCoby Jones	30.4
060	Bob Fothergill	30.2
061	Craig Monroe	29.1
062	Chico Fernandez	28.9
063	George Kell	28.8
064	Justin Upton	28.7
065	Ramon Santiago	28.0
066	Barney McCosky	27.8
067	Charlie Maxwell	27.0
068	Willie Horton	26.6
069	Eddie Lake	26.4
070	Jose Iglesias	26.2
071	Brennan Boesch	25.2
	Mike Heath	25.2
073	Rajai Davis	24.7
	Ryan Raburn	24.7
075	Eddie Mayo	24.4
076	Dale Alexander	24.0
077	Chet Lemon	23.8
	Bill Tuttle	23.8
079	George Burns	22.7
080	Brad Ausmus	22.6
	Aurelio Rodriguez	22.6
082	Red Wilson	22.5
083	Lloyd Moseby	22.2
	Marv Owen	22.2
	Carlos Pena	22.2
086	Darrell Evans	22.1
087	Magglio Ordonez	21.6
088	Robbie Grossman	21.4
	J.D. Martinez	21.4
090	Eddie Yost	20.0
091	Nicholas Castellanos	19.9
092	Luis Polonia	19.5
093	Dean Palmer	19.3
094	Don Kelly	18.9
095	Champ Summers	18.5
096	Victor Reyes	18.3
097	Harry Rice	18.2
098	Deivi Cruz	18.1
099	Jimmy Barrett	18.0
100	Howard Johnson	17.9

Rank	Player	Extra Base Hits
001	Ty Cobb	1,060
002	Al Kaline	972
003	Charlie Gehringer	904
004	Harry Heilmann	806
005	Miguel Cabrera	785
006	Hank Greenberg	741
007	Lou Whitaker	729
008	Sam Crawford	721
009	Norm Cash	654
010	Alan Trammell	652
011	Bobby Veach	540
012	Rudy York	517
013	Willie Horton	504
014	Bobby Higginson	490
015	Dick McAuliffe	480
016	Bill Freehan	476
017	Lance Parrish	436
018	Kirk Gibson	427
019	Travis Fryman	407
020	Chet Lemon	392
021	Jim Northrup	391
022	Cecil Fielder	390
	Brandon Inge	390
024	Mickey Stanley	366
025	Nicholas Castellanos	344
026	Harvey Kuenn	340
027	Pete Fox	333
028	Billy Rogell	330
029	Tony Clark	319
030	Carlos Guillen	316
031	Aurelio Rodriguez	309
	Gee Walker	309
033	Victor Martinez	303
034	Magglio Ordonez	299
035	Damion Easley	294
036	Curtis Granderson	284
	Vic Wertz	284
038	George Kell	270
039	Tom Brookens	266
040	Donie Bush	263
041	Lu Blue	261
042	Bob Fothergill	255
043	Rocky Colavito	253
044	Charlie Maxwell	245
045	John Stone	241
046	Pinky Higgins	240
	Craig Monroe	240
048	Hoot Evers	237
049	Pat Mullin	236
050	Ray Boone	235
051	Larry Herndon	230

Dick McAuliffe

Rank	Player	Extra Base Hits
052	Austin Jackson	229
053	Ian Kinsler	225
054	Steve Kemp	221
055	Don Wert	220
056	J.D. Martinez	219
	Marty McManus	219
	Ivan Rodriguez	219
059	Frank Bolling	216
060	Ron LeFlore	215
061	Darrell Evans	214
062	Alex Avila	206
063	Tony Phillips	205
	Mickey Tettleton	205
065	Heinie Manush	204
066	Deivi Cruz	203
067	Barney McCosky	201
068	Marv Owen	198
069	Dale Alexander	197
	Roy Johnson	197
071	Dmitri Young	195
072	Jason Thompson	190
073	Placido Polanco	189
074	Goose Goslin	188
075	Dick Wakefield	187
076	Omar Infante	183
077	Rusty Staub	182
078	Gates Brown	181
079	Johnny Groth	179
080	Marcus Thames	174
081	Jeimer Candelario	168
082	Matty McIntyre	166
083	Bob Jones	165
	Oscar Stanage	165
085	Juan Encarnacion	161
086	John Wockenfuss	160
087	Ryan Raburn	157
088	Carlos Pena	154
089	Johnny Peralta	153
090	Roy Cullenbine	150
091	Billy Bruton	143
092	Dean Palmer	142
093	Jose Iglesias	139
	Jackie Tavener	139
095	Doc Cramer	137
096	George Moriarty	136
097	Eddie Mayo	135
	Bill Tuttle	135
099	Birdie Tebbetts	134
100	Niko Goodrum	127

ALL TIME TIGER HITTING LEADERS – EXTRA BASES ON LONG HITS

Rank	Player	Extra Bases
001	Al Kaline	1,845
002	Ty Cobb	1,566
003	Miguel Cabrera	1,520
004	Norm Cash	1,440
005	Hank Greenberg	1,422
006	Charlie Gehringer	1,418
007	Lou Whitaker	1,282
008	Harry Heilmann	1,279
009	Sam Crawford	1,110
010	Alan Trammell	1,077
011	Willie Horton	1,059
012	Rudy York	1,037
013	Dick McAuliffe	934
014	Bill Freehan	911
015	Bobby Higginson	897
016	Cecil Fielder	884
017	Lance Parrish	883
018	Kirk Gibson	862
019	Bobby Veach	794
020	Travis Fryman	734
021	Jim Northrup	723
022	Brandon Inge	708
	Chet Lemon	708
024	Mickey Stanley	648
025	Tony Clark	638
026	Nicholas Castellanos	584
027	Curtis Granderson	545
028	Carlos Guillen	541
029	Rocky Colavito	538
030	Victor Martinez	533
031	Vic Wertz	532
032	Charlie Maxwell	531
033	Magglio Ordonez	519
034	Damion Easley	518
035	Aurelio Rodriguez	510
036	Pete Fox	503
037	Darrell Evans	497
038	Harvey Kuenn	489
039	Ray Boone	475
040	Billy Rogell	472
041	Gee Walker	463
042	Pat Mullin	453
043	Craig Monroe	451
044	Mickey Tettleton	437
045	Tom Brookens	436
046	Larry Herndon	433
047	J.D. Martinez	426
048	Steve Kemp	417
049	Ian Kinsler	399

Rob Deer

Rank	Player	Extra Bases
050	Hoot Evers	397
051	Jason Thompson	396
052	Don Wert	389
053	John Stone	381
054	Pinky Higgins	376
055	Marcus Thames	375
056	Dmitri Young	372
057	Frank Bolling	370
058	Gates Brown	368
059	Alex Avila	367
060	Lu Blue	365
061	Austin Jackson	364
062	Ivan Rodriguez	360
063	George Kell	355
	Ron LeFlore	355
065	Donie Bush	354
	Bob Fothergill	354
067	Tony Phillips	342
068	Marty McManus	340
069	Rusty Staub	330
	John Wockenfuss	330
071	Dick Wakefield	328
072	Heinie Manush	322
073	Dale Alexander	319
074	Carlos Pena	318
075	Goose Goslin	310
076	Dean Palmer	302
077	Omar Infante	300
078	Juan Encarnacion	291
	Roy Johnson	291
	Barney McCosky	291
081	Roy Cullenbine	287
082	Deivi Cruz	286
	Marv Owen	286
084	Jeimer Candelario	283
085	Placido Polanco	276
086	Ryan Raburn	273
087	Johnny Groth	266
088	Jhonny Peralta	265
089	Rob Deer	264
090	Billy Bruton	258
091	Justin Upton	246
092	Matt Nokes	237
093	Prince Fielder	236
094	Bill Tuttle	228
095	Matty McIntyre	226
	Ben Oglivie	226
097	Niko Goodrum	222
098	Bob Jones	217
099	Shane Halter	216
100	Oscar Stanage	215

Rank	Player	Pct
001	Hank Greenberg	13.26
002	J.D. Martinez	11.61
003	Marcus Thames	10.79
004	Nicholas Castellanos	10.06
005	Dale Alexander	10.02
006	Tony Clark	9.93
007	Miguel Cabrera	9.91
008	Dmitri Young	9.87
009	Curtis Granderson	9.81
010	Rudy York	9.66
011	Harry Heilmann	9.60
012	Gee Walker	9.54
013	Bob Fothergill	9.47
014	Craig Monroe	9.43
015	Carlos Guillen	9.34
016	Lance Parrish	9.33
017	Rocky Colavito	9.29
018	Roy Johnson	9.23
019	Carlos Pena	9.19
020	Cecil Fielder	9.17
021	Ryan Raburn	9.13
022	John Stone	9.02
023	Juan Encarnacion	8.95
	Kirk Gibson	8.95
025	Prince Fielder	8.92
	Dean Palmer	8.92
027	Charlie Gehringer	8.82
	Vic Wertz	8.82
029	Mickey Tettleton	8.75
030	Ty Cobb	8.74
031	Ivan Rodriguez	8.68
032	Jeimer Candelario	8.65
	Niko Goodrum	8.65
	Bobby Higginson	8.65
035	Heinie Manush	8.58
036	Travis Fryman	8.49
037	Goose Goslin	8.48
038	Magglio Ordonez	8.47
039	Willie Horton	8.43
040	Norm Cash	8.41
041	Al Kaline	8.38
	Chet Lemon	8.38
043	Damion Easley	8.37
044	Ian Kinsler	8.35
045	Marty McManus	8.31
046	Pat Mullin	8.29
047	Jhonny Peralta	8.27
048	Ray Boone	8.23
049	Brennan Boesch	8.14
050	Sam Crawford	8.11

Carlos Guillen

Rank	Player	Pct
	Ben Oglivie	8.11
052	Deivi Cruz	7.96
053	Bobby Veach	7.95
054	Jim Northrup	7.94
055	Pete Fox	7.78
	Charlie Maxwell	7.78
057	Shane Halter	7.70
058	Victor Martinez	7.69
059	Roy Cullenbine	7.68
060	Hoot Evers	7.65
	Austin Jackson	7.65
062	Larry Herndon	7.63
063	Darrell Evans	7.62
064	Alex Avila	7.60
065	Rusty Staub	7.56
	John Wockenfuss	7.56
067	Steve Kemp	7.54
068	Brandon Inge	7.51
069	Jason Thompson	7.50
070	Dick Wakefield	7.48
071	Omar Infante	7.47
072	Barney McCosky	7.43
073	Walt Dropo	7.33
074	Al Wingo	7.32
075	Lou Whitaker	7.31
076	George Kell	7.23
077	Harvey Kuenn	7.16
078	Gates Brown	7.11
079	Jim Delsing	7.06
080	Dick McAuliffe	7.03
081	Johnny Groth	6.96
082	Alan Trammell	6.95
083	Bill Freehan	6.90
084	Tom Brookens	6.82
085	Mike Heath	6.81
086	Jose Iglesias	6.72
087	Placido Polanco	6.70
088	Mickey Stanley	6.68
089	Pinky Higgins	6.65
	Aurelio Rodriguez	6.65
091	Frank Bolling	6.62
092	Jackie Tavener	6.49
093	Billy Rogell	6.48
094	Billy Bruton	6.42
095	James McCann	6.39
096	Lu Blue	6.32
097	Jerry Priddy	6.21
098	Tony Phillips	6.17
099	Ron LeFlore	6.04
100	Red Wilson	6.02

ALL TIME TIGER HITTING LEADERS – PERCENTAGE OF HITS THAT ARE FOR EXTRA BASES

Rank	Player	Pct
001	Marcus Thames	48.60
002	Hank Greenberg	48.49
003	Mickey Tettleton	43.71
004	J.D. Martinez	43.03
005	Carlos Pena	43.02
006	Niko Goodrum	41.64
	Dean Palmer	41.64
008	Cecil Fielder	41.18
009	Tony Clark	40.74
010	Curtis Granderson	40.46
011	Rocky Colavito	39.97
012	Nicholas Castellanos	39.91
013	Craig Monroe	39.54
014	Jeimer Candelario	39.44
015	Rudy York	39.26
016	Dmitri Young	39.00
017	Ryan Raburn	38.96
018	Lance Parrish	38.82
019	Darrell Evans	38.28
020	Kirk Gibson	37.46
021	Bobby Higginson	36.68
022	Damion Easley	36.61
023	Miguel Cabrera	36.60
	Chet Lemon	36.60
025	Alex Avila	36.52
026	Norm Cash	36.48
027	Brandon Inge	36.01
028	Roy Johnson	35.82
029	Juan Encarnacion	35.78
030	Roy Cullenbine	35.63
031	Vic Wertz	35.59
032	Carlos Guillen	35.43
033	Prince Fielder	35.11
034	Pat Mullin	34.91
035	Travis Fryman	34.61
036	Brennan Boesch	34.28
037	Shane Halter	34.15
038	Charlie Maxwell	33.89
039	Willie Horton	33.83
040	Dale Alexander	33.79
041	Jason Thompson	33.63
042	Jhonny Peralta	33.05
043	Ian Kinsler	33.04
044	Jim Northrup	33.02
045	John Wockenfuss	32.99
046	Marty McManus	32.98
047	John Stone	32.74
048	Dick McAuliffe	32.63
049	Ray Boone	32.50
050	Ben Oglivie	32.34
051	Al Kaline	32.32
052	Goose Goslin	32.30
053	Harry Heilmann	32.25
054	Gee Walker	31.99
055	Charlie Gehringer	31.84
056	Rusty Staub	31.27
057	Jim Delsing	31.21
058	Deivi Cruz	31.13
059	Gates Brown	31.10
060	Steve Kemp	31.08
061	Bob Fothergill	30.98
062	Ivan Rodriguez	30.89
063	Austin Jackson	30.82
064	Lou Whitaker	30.77
065	Tom Brookens	30.54
066	Heinie Manush	30.27
067	Omar Infante	30.25
068	Magglio Ordonez	30.23
069	Hoot Evers	30.11
070	Larry Herndon	30.07
071	Dick Wakefield	29.97
072	Bill Freehan	29.92
073	Aurelio Rodriguez	29.71
074	Walt Dropo	29.62
075	Mickey Stanley	29.44
076	Victor Martinez	29.33
077	Sam Crawford	29.24
078	Bobby Veach	29.05
079	James McCann	28.80
080	Hooks Dauss	28.77
081	Al Wingo	28.39
082	Frank Bolling	28.38
083	Jackie Tavener	28.37
084	Pete Fox	28.17
085	Mike Heath	27.78
086	Alan Trammell	27.57
087	Pinky Higgins	27.33
088	Billy Rogell	27.27
089	Billy Bruton	27.24
090	Ty Cobb	27.18
091	Dizzy Trout	27.14
092	Ray Oyler	27.12
093	Jose Iglesias	27.10
094	Barney McCosky	27.02
095	Johnny Groth	27.00
096	Jerry Priddy	26.79
097	Pat Sheridan	26.60
098	Tony Phillips	26.59
099	Red Wilson	26.55
100	Lu Blue	26.05

Damion Easley

ALL TIME TIGER HITTING LEADERS – TOTAL BASES

001	Ty Cobb	5,466
002	Al Kaline	4,852
003	Charlie Gehringer	4,257
004	Harry Heilmann	3,778
005	Miguel Cabrera	3,665
006	Lou Whitaker	3,651
007	Sam Crawford	3,576
008	Alan Trammell	3,442
009	Norm Cash	3,233
010	Hank Greenberg	2,950
011	Bobby Veach	2,653
012	Willie Horton	2,549
013	Bill Freehan	2,502
014	Dick McAuliffe	2,405
015	Rudy York	2,354
016	Bobby Higginson	2,233
017	Donie Bush	2,099
018	Lance Parrish	2,006
019	Kirk Gibson	2,002
020	Travis Fryman	1,910
021	Jim Northrup	1,907
022	Mickey Stanley	1,891
023	Harvey Kuenn	1,861
024	Cecil Fielder	1,831
025	Brandon Inge	1,791
026	Chet Lemon	1,779
027	Pete Fox	1,685
028	Billy Rogell	1,682
029	Victor Martinez	1,566
030	Aurelio Rodriguez	1,550
031	Magglio Ordonez	1,508
032	Nicholas Castellanos	1,446
033	Carlos Guillen	1,433
034	George Kell	1,430
035	Gee Walker	1,429
036	Tony Clark	1,421
037	Lu Blue	1,367
038	Vic Wertz	1,330
039	Ron LeFlore	1,325
040	Damion Easley	1,321
041	Don Wert	1,316
042	Tom Brookens	1,307
043	Pinky Higgins	1,254
	Charlie Maxwell	1,254
045	Curtis Granderson	1,247
046	Ray Boone	1,198
	Larry Herndon	1,198
048	Hoot Evers	1,184
049	Bob Fothergill	1,177
050	Rocky Colavito	1,171
051	Frank Bolling	1,131
052	Pat Mullin	1,129
053	Steve Kemp	1,128
054	John Stone	1,117
055	Tony Phillips	1,113
056	Austin Jackson	1,107
057	Marv Owen	1,106
058	Placido Polanco	1,082
059	Ian Kinsler	1,080
060	Ivan Rodriguez	1,069
061	Craig Monroe	1,058
062	Darrell Evans	1,056
063	Barney McCosky	1,035
064	Oscar Stanage	1,034
065	Marty McIntyre	1,009
066	Bobby Jones	1,008
067	Marty McManus	1,004
068	Heinie Manush	996
069	Jason Thompson	961
070	Doc Cramer	958
071	Dick Wakefield	952
072	Gates Brown	950
073	Ralph Young	946
074	Deivi Cruz	938
075	J.D. Martinez	935
076	Alex Avila	931
077	Johnny Groth	929
078	Rusty Staub	912
079	Mickey Tettleton	906
080	Omar Infante	905
081	Dale Alexander	902
082	Goose Goslin	892
083	Dmitri Young	872
084	Roy Johnson	841
085	George Moriarty	835
	Ossie Vitt	835
087	Johnny Bassler	821
088	John Wockenfuss	815
089	Jimmy Barrett	809
090	Bill Tuttle	794
091	Billy Bruton	783
092	Eddie Mayo	780
093	Charley O'Leary	766
094	Johnny Lipon	765
095	Juan Encarnacion	741
096	Ramon Santiago	736
097	Marcus Thames	733
098	Jhonny Peralta	728
099	Dave Bergman	723
100	Birdie Tebbetts	720

Frank Bolling

ALL TIME TIGER HITTING LEADERS – TOTAL BASE AVERAGE

001	Hank Greenberg	2.32
002	J.D. Martinez	2.04
003	Miguel Cabrera	1.96
004	Ty Cobb	1.95
005	Dale Alexander	1.93
006	Harry Heilmann	1.90
007	Rocky Colavito	1.86
	Cecil Fielder	1.86
	Rudy York	1.86
010	Curtis Granderson	1.85
011	Tony Clark	1.84
012	Prince Fielder	1.83
	Charlie Gehringer	1.83
014	Gee Walker	1.80
015	Dmitri Young	1.79
016	Roy Johnson	1.78
	Ian Kinsler	1.78
	Magglio Ordonez	1.78
019	Harvey Kuenn	1.77
020	Ray Boone	1.75
	Carlos Guillen	1.75
	Lance Parrish	1.75
	Ivan Rodriguez	1.75
024	Travis Fryman	1.74
	Barney McCosky	1.74
026	Nicholas Castellanos	1.73
	George Kell	1.73
	John Stone	1.73
029	Al Kaline	1.71
	Placido Polanco	1.71
031	Kirk Gibson	1.70
	Goose Goslin	1.70
033	Sam Crawford	1.69
	Pete Fox	1.69
035	Willie Horton	1.68
	Ron LeFlore	1.68
	Dean Palmer	1.68
038	Juan Encarnacion	1.67
039	Rusty Staub	1.66
040	Austin Jackson	1.65
	Steve Kemp	1.65
	Bobby Veach	1.65
043	Bobby Higginson	1.64
044	Heinie Manush	1.62
	Victor Martinez	1.62
046	Norm Cash	1.60
047	Mickey Tettleton	1.59
	Vic Wertz	1.59
049	Carlos Pena	1.58
	Jhonny Peralta	1.58

Claude Rossman

051	Damion Easley	1.57
	Marty McManus	1.57
	Craig Monroe	1.57
054	Jason Thompson	1.56
055	Hoot Evers	1.54
	Tony Phillips	1.54
057	Lou Whitaker	1.53
058	Jeimer Candelario	1.52
059	Walt Dropo	1.51
	Marcus Thames	1.51
	Dick Wakefield	1.51
062	Alan Trammell	1.50
063	Jim Northrup	1.49
064	Lu Blue	1.48
	Brennan Boesch	1.48
	Chet Lemon	1.48
067	Bob Fothergill	1.47
	Charlie Maxwell	1.47
069	Pinky Higgins	1.46
070	Darrell Evans	1.45
	Dick McAuliffe	1.45
072	Frank Bolling	1.44
073	Jim Delahanty	1.42
	Larry Herndon	1.42
075	Roy Cullenbine	1.41
	Bill Freehan	1.41
	Jerry Priddy	1.41
078	Billy Bruton	1.40
	Niko Goodrum	1.40
	Marv Owen	1.40
081	Brian Hunter	1.39
	Billy Rogell	1.39
083	Jimmy Barrett	1.37
	Bill Tuttle	1.37
085	Ben Oglivie	1.35
	Claude Rossman	1.35
087	Omar Infante	1.34
088	Doc Cramer	1.33
	Deivi Cruz	1.33
	Eddie Mayo	1.33
091	Topper Rigney	1.32
092	Pat Mullin	1.31
093	Jackie Tavener	1.30
094	George Burns	1.28
095	Brandon Inge	1.27
	Matty McIntyre	1.27
097	Jim Delsing	1.26
	Johnny Groth	1.26
099	Jose Iglesias	1.25
	Johnny Lipon	1.25
	Aurelio Rodriguez	1.25
	Mickey Stanley	1.25

ALL TIME TIGER HITTING LEADERS – TOTAL BASE PERCENTAGE

001	Ty Cobb	0.43
002	Johnny Bassler	0.42
003	Roy Cullenbine	0.41
	Hank Greenberg	0.41
	Harry Heilmann	0.41
	Al Wingo	0.41
007	Lu Blue	0.40
	Charlie Gehringer	0.40
	Tony Phillips	0.40
	Dick Wakefield	0.40
011	Dale Alexander	0.39
	Miguel Cabrera	0.39
	Jim Delahanty	0.39
	Prince Fielder	0.39
	George Kell	0.39
	Barney McCosky	0.39
	Topper Rigney	0.39
	Mickey Tettleton	0.39
019	Jimmy Barrett	0.38
	Norm Cash	0.38
	Bob Fothergill	0.38
	Goose Goslin	0.38
	Fred Haney	0.38
	Al Kaline	0.38
	Steve Kemp	0.38
	Heinie Manush	0.38
	Magglio Ordonez	0.38
	Vic Wertz	0.38
029	Ray Boone	0.37
	Rocky Colavito	0.37
	Hoot Evers	0.37
	Johnny Groth	0.37
	Carlos Guillen	0.37
	Charlie Maxwell	0.37
	Bobby Veach	0.37
	Lou Whitaker	0.37
	Rudy York	0.37
038	Donie Bush	0.36
	Sam Crawford	0.36
	Tony Clark	0.36
	Darrell Evans	0.36
	Kirk Gibson	0.36
	Pinky Higgins	0.36
	Bobby Higginson	0.36
	Harvey Kuenn	0.36
	Eddie Lake	0.36
	Johnny Lipon	0.36
	Marty McManus	0.36
	Pat Mullin	0.36
	J.D. Martinez	0.36
	Placido Polanco	0.36

Davy Jones

	Billy Rogell	0.36
	John Stone	0.36
	Rusty Staub	0.36
	Jo-Jo White	0.36
056	Alex Avila	0.35
	Dave Bergman	0.35
	Jim Delsing	0.35
	Cecil Fielder	0.35
	Pete Fox	0.35
	Curtis Granderson	0.35
	Davy Jones	0.35
	Roy Johnson	0.35
	Ron LeFlore	0.35
	Chet Lemon	0.35
	Victor Martinez	0.35
	Dick McAuliffe	0.35
	Jerry Priddy	0.35
	Jason Thompson	0.35
	Alan Trammell	0.35
	Gee Walker	0.35
	Red Wilson	0.35
	John Wockenfuss	0.35
	Larry Woodall	0.35
075	Billy Bruton	0.34
	Jeimer Candelario	0.34
	Damion Easley	0.34
	Bill Freehan	0.34
	Travis Fryman	0.34
	Fred Hatfield	0.34
	Willie Horton	0.34
	Austin Jackson	0.34
	Matty McIntyre	0.34
	Marv Owen	0.34
	Jimmy Outlaw	0.34
	Dmitri Young	0.34
	Ralph Young	0.34
087	Frank Bolling	0.33
	Gates Brown	0.33
	Nicholas Castellanos	0.33
	Doc Cramer	0.33
	Ray Hayworth	0.33
	Larry Herndon	0.33
	Ian Kinsler	0.33
	Don Kolloway	0.33
	Eddie Mayo	0.33
	Jim Northrup	0.33
	Ben Oglivie	0.33
	Dean Palmer	0.33
	Carlos Pena	0.33
	Johnny Peralta	0.33
	Ivan Rodriguez	0.33
	Pat Sheridan	0.33
	Birdie Tebbetts	0.33
	Bill Tuttle	0.33

Rank	Player	Bases Produced
001	Ty Cobb	7,483
002	Al Kaline	6,266
003	Charlie Gehringer	5,624
004	Lou Whitaker	4,991
005	Harry Heilmann	4,681
006	Miguel Cabrera	4,564
007	Sam Crawford	4,540
008	Alan Trammell	4,528
009	Norm Cash	4,300
010	Hank Greenberg	3,756
011	Donie Bush	3,626
012	Bobby Veach	3,354
013	Dick McAuliffe	3,308
014	Bill Freehan	3,152
015	Willie Horton	3,032
016	Rudy York	3,029
017	Bobby Higginson	2,973
018	Kirk Gibson	2,695
019	Jim Northrup	2,366
020	Lance Parrish	2,362
021	Travis Fryman	2,358
022	Cecil Fielder	2,352
023	Billy Rogell	2,348
024	Mickey Stanley	2,306
025	Chet Lemon	2,260
026	Brandon Inge	2,253
027	Harvey Kuenn	2,234
028	Pete Fox	2,071
029	Lu Blue	2,041
030	Victor Martinez	1,889
031	Ron LeFlore	1,870
032	Magglio Ordonez	1,838
033	Carlos Guillen	1,819
034	George Kell	1,801
035	Tony Clark	1,770
	Aurelio Rodriguez	1,770
037	Vic Wertz	1,730
038	Don Wert	1,723
039	Tony Phillips	1,702
040	Gee Walker	1,701
041	Damion Easley	1,698
042	Nicholas Castellanos	1,681
043	Pinky Higgins	1,678
044	Charlie Maxwell	1,663
045	Tom Brookens	1,648
046	Curtis Granderson	1,588
047	Hoot Evers	1,535
048	Steve Kemp	1,527
049	Ray Boone	1,523
	Rocky Colavito	1,523

Charlie Maxwell

Rank	Player	Bases Produced
051	Darrell Evans	1,505
052	Pat Mullin	1,479
053	Ralph Young	1,465
054	Larry Herndon	1,452
055	Austin Jackson	1,442
056	Frank Bolling	1,433
057	Matty McIntyre	1,429
058	Marv Owen	1,395
059	Barney McCosky	1,370
060	Bob Fothergill	1,365
061	John Stone	1,357
062	Mickey Tettleton	1,341
063	Marty McManus	1,322
064	Dick Wakefield	1,320
065	Alex Avila	1,306
066	Ian Kinsler	1,305
067	Oscar Stanage	1,283
068	Bob Jones	1,265
069	Jason Thompson	1,263
070	Ossie Vitt	1,257
071	Placido Polanco	1,254
072	Johnny Bassler	1,253
073	Craig Monroe	1,228
074	Gates Brown	1,222
075	Jimmy Barrett	1,210
	Johnny Groth	1,210
077	George Moriarty	1,206
078	Ivan Rodriguez	1,205
079	Heinie Manush	1,193
080	Rusty Staub	1,170
081	Doc Cramer	1,162
082	Goose Goslin	1,157
083	Roy Johnson	1,117
084	J.D. Martinez	1,108
085	Johnny Lipon	1,092
086	Roy Cullenbine	1,091
087	Dale Alexander	1,086
088	Davy Jones	1,083
089	Omar Infante	1,080
090	John Wockenfuss	1,058
091	Billy Bruton	1,054
092	Bill Tuttle	1,032
093	Dmitri Young	1,021
094	Deivi Cruz	1,019
095	Eddie Mayo	1,002
096	Dave Bergman	1,000
097	Germany Schaefer	988
098	Charley O'Leary	981
099	Jo-Jo White	969
100	Ramon Santiago	939

001	Hank Greenberg	2.96
002	Ty Cobb	2.67
003	Miguel Cabrera	2.44
004	Rocky Colavito	2.42
	Charlie Gehringer	2.42
006	Cecil Fielder	2.40
007	J.D. Martinez	2.42
008	Rudy York	2.39
009	Ron LeFlore	2.38
010	Curtis Granderson	2.36
	Roy Johnson	2.36
	Tony Phillips	2.36
013	Harry Heilmann	2.35
	Mickey Tettleton	2.35
015	Dale Alexander	2.33
	Prince Fielder	2.33
017	Barney McCosky	2.30
018	Tony Clark	2.29
	Kirk Gibson	2.29
020	Ray Boone	2.23
	Carlos Guillen	2.23
	Steve Kemp	2.23
023	Lu Blue	2.21
	Goose Goslin	2.21
	Al Kaline	2.21
026	Roy Cullenbine	2.18
	Bobby Higginson	2.18
	George Kell	2.18
029	Magglio Ordonez	2.17
030	Sam Crawford	2.15
	Travis Fryman	2.15
	Austin Jackson	2.15
	Ian Kinsler	2.15
034	Gee Walker	2.14
035	Norm Cash	2.13
	Harvey Kuenn	2.13
	Dean Palmer	2.13
	Rusty Staub	2.13
039	John Stone	2.11
040	Dmitri Young	2.10
041	Bobby Veach	2.09
	Dick Wakefield	2.09
	Lou Whitaker	2.09
044	Pete Fox	2.08
	Brian Hunter	2.08
046	Darrell Evans	2.07
	Marty McManus	2.07
	Vic Wertz	2.07
049	Lance Parrish	2.06
050	Jimmy Barrett	2.05
	Jason Thompson	2.05

Tony Phillips

052	Carlos Pena	2.04
053	Damion Easley	2.02
054	Nicholas Castellanos	2.01
055	Juan Encarnacion	2.00
	Hoot Evers	2.00
	Willie Horton	2.00
	Dick McAuliffe	2.00
059	Jeimer Candelario	1.98
	Placido Polanco	1.98
061	Jim Delahanty	1.97
	Ivan Rodriguez	1.97
	Alan Trammell	1.97
064	Pinky Higgins	1.96
065	Victor Martinez	1.95
	Charlie Maxwell	1.95
	Billy Rogell	1.95
068	Donie Bush	1.94
	Heinie Manush	1.94
070	Jerry Priddy	1.92
071	Jhonny Peralta	1.91
072	Billy Bruton	1.89
	Topper Rigney	1.89
074	Niko Goodrum	1.88
	Chet Lemon	1.88
076	Jim Northrup	1.85
077	Frank Bolling	1.83
	Craig Monroe	1.83
079	Eddie Lake	1.81
080	Brennan Boesch	1.80
	Matty McIntyre	1.80
082	Johnny Lipon	1.79
083	Bill Freehan	1.78
	Marcus Thames	1.78
	Bill Tuttle	1.78
086	Marv Owen	1.76
087	Walt Dropo	1.73
088	Alex Avila	1.72
	Larry Herndon	1.72
090	Eddie Mayo	1.71
	Pat Mullin	1.71
092	Jim Delsing	1.70
	Bob Fothergill	1.70
094	Davy Jones	1.68
	Ben Oglivie	1.68
	Jackie Tavener	1.68
097	Fred Haney	1.67
098	Claude Rossman	1.65
	Ralph Young	1.65
100	Johnny Groth	1.64
	Ossie Vitt	1.64

Rank	Player	SB
001	Ty Cobb	869
002	Donie Bush	402
003	Sam Crawford	318
004	Ron LeFlore	294
005	Alan Trammell	236
006	Kirk Gibson	194
007	George Moriarty	193
008	Bobby Veach	189
009	Charlie Gehringer	181
010	Lou Whitaker	143
011	Davy Jones	140
012	Al Kaline	137
013	Gee Walker	132
014	Germany Schaefer	123
015	Brian Hunter	116
016	Harry Heilmann	111
017	Pete Fox	107
018	Gary Pettis	100
019	Ossie Vitt	99
020	Jimmy Barrett	92
021	Bobby Higginson	91
022	Matty McIntyre	89
023	Lu Blue	85
	Tom Brookens	85
025	Ralph Young	82
026	Damion Easley	81
027	Jake Wood	79
028	Austin Jackson	78
029	Roy Johnson	77
030	Billy Rogell	76
031	Jo-Jo White	75
032	Bill Coughlin	73
033	Charley O'Leary	71
034	Milt Cuyler	70
	Tony Phillips	70
036	Juan Encarnacion	68
037	Curtis Granderson	67
038	Marty McManus	65
039	Billy Bruton	64
040	Alex Sanchez	63
041	Dick McAuliffe	61
042	Carlos Guillen	59
043	Travis Fryman	58
	Hank Greenberg	58
045	Doc Casey	56
046	Roger Cedeno	55
047	Rajai Davis	54
048	Ian Kinsler	53
049	Barney McCosky	52
050	Ducky Holmes	51
	Harvey Kuenn	51

Niko Goodrum

Rank	Player	SB
052	Kid Gleason	49
	Bob Jones	49
054	Jim Delahanty	48
	Kid Elberfeld	48
	Heinie Manush	48
057	George Burns	47
058	Omar Infante	46
059	Niko Goodrum	45
	Brandon Inge	45
	Jackie Tavener	45
062	Mickey Stanley	44
063	Chad Curtis	43
064	Norm Cash	42
	Jose Iglesias	42
066	Ben Oglivie	41
067	Jim Northrup	39
	Pat Sheridan	39
069	Claude Rossman	38
070	Topper Rigney	37
071	Bob Fothergill	36
	Andrew Romine	36
073	Kimera Bartee	35
	Hoot Evers	35
	Del Gainer	35
076	Fred Haney	34
	George Kell	34
	Rudy York	34
079	Baldy Louden	33
080	Larry Herndon	32
081	Chico Fernandez	31
	Tom Jones	31
	Eddie Lake	31
	Nook Logan	31
	Victor Reyes	31
	Gary Sheffield	31
087	Gates Brown	30
	Johnny Neun	30
	Ivan Rodriguez	30
	Oscar Stanage	30
091	JaCoby Jones	29
092	Frank Bolling	28
	Chris Lindsay	28
	Ramon Santiago	28
095	Dave Collins	27
096	Brad Ausmus	26
	Bill Donovan	26
	JaCoby Jones	26
	Johnny Lipon	26
	Jose Macias	26
	Eddie Mayo	26
	Placido Polanco	26
	Harry Rice	26
	Jack R. Warner	26

Rank	Player	CS
001	Ty Cobb	188
002	Alan Trammell	109
003	Ron LeFlore	98
004	Charlie Gehringer	90
005	Donie Bush	89
006	Bobby Veach	79
007	Lou Whitaker	75
008	Al Kaline	65
009	Kirk Gibson	64
	Harry Heilmann	64
011	Dick McAuliffe	59
012	Tom Brookens	57
	Pete Fox	57
014	Lu Blue	56
015	Bobby Higginson	53
	Ralph Young	53
017	Billy Rogell	52
018	Gee Walker	50
019	Roy Johnson	49
020	Bob Fothergill	46
021	Sam Crawford	43
	Harvey Kuenn	43
023	Marty McManus	42
024	Tony Phillips	40
	Jo-Jo White	40
026	Brandon Inge	39
027	Eddie Mayo	38
028	Jim Northrup	37
029	Damion Easley	34
	Carlos Guillen	34
	Ossie Vitt	34
032	Brian Hunter	33
033	Hoot Evers	31
	Alex Sanchez	31
035	Bob Jones	30
	Eddie Lake	30
	Lance Parrish	30
038	Norm Cash	29
	Willie Horton	29
	Gary Pettis	29
041	Austin Jackson	28
	Chet Lemon	28
	John Stone	28
044	Pinky Higgins	27
	George Kell	27
	Pat Mullin	27
	Jackie Tavener	27
048	Frank Bolling	26
	Juan Encarnacion	26
	Travis Fryman	26
	Hank Greenberg	26
	Heinie Manush	26
	Harry Rice	26
	Topper Rigney	26
055	Billy Bruton	25
	Doc Cramer	25
	Chad Curtis	25
	Johnny Groth	25
	George Moriarty	25
060	Johnny Lipon	24
	Ben Oglivie	24
	Don Wert	24
	Rudy York	24
064	Milt Cuyler	23
	Jose Iglesias	23
	Mickey Stanley	23
	Jake Wood	23
068	Dale Alexander	22
	Marty Kavanagh	22
	Al Wingo	22
071	Bill Freehan	21
	Ian Kinsler	21
	Barney McCosky	21
	Jimmy Outlaw	21
	Marv Owen	21
	Pat Sheridan	21
	Bill Tuttle	21
078	Baldy Louden	20
079	Kimera Bartee	19
	Deivi Cruz	19
	Rajai Davis	19
	Johnny Neun	19
	Jerry Priddy	19
	Aurelio Rodriguez	19
085	Brad Ausmus	18
	Jimmy Bloodworth	18
	Fred Haney	18
	Omar Infante	18
	Frank O'Rourke	18
090	Darrell Evans	17
	Curtis Granderson	17
	Larry Herndon	17
	Joe Hoover	17
	Mickey Tettleton	17
	Dick Wakefield	17
096	George Burns	16
	Steve Kemp	16
	Craig Monroe	16
099	Roger Cedeno	15
	Don Kolloway	15

Ron LeFlore

Rank	Player	Pct
001	Quintin Berry	100.00
002	Dan Meyer	86.36
003	Akil Baddoo	81.81
004	Victor Reyes	81.58
	Gary Sheffield	81.58
006	Lloyd Moseby	80.65
007	Robbie Grossman	80.00
	Larry Woodall	80.00
009	Curtis Granderson	79.76
010	Nook Logan	79.49
011	Gates Brown	78.95
012	Roger Cedeno	78.57
013	Brian Hunter	77.85
014	Niko Goodrum	77.59
015	Gary Pettis	77.52
016	Jake Wood	77.45
017	Cameron Maybin	76.92
018	Andrew Romine	76.60
019	Jose Macias	76.47
020	Milt Cuyler	75.27
021	Kirk Gibson	75.19
022	Ron LeFlore	75.00
023	Rajai Davis	73.97
024	Austin Jackson	73.58
025	Heinie Schuble	73.08
	Tony Taylor	73.08
027	Gee Walker	72.53
028	Juan Encarnacion	72.34
029	George Moriarty	72.22
030	Brennan Boesch	72.00
031	Billy Bruton	71.91
032	Omar Infante	71.88
	Red Wilson	71.88
034	Ian Kinsler	71.62
035	Charlie Maxwell	71.43
036	Barney McCosky	71.23
037	JaCoby Jones	70.73
038	Chico Fernandez	70.45
039	Damion Easley	70.43
040	Placido Polanco	70.27
041	Eddie Yost	70.00
042	Ivan Rodriguez	69.77
043	Davy Jones	69.57
044	Dave Collins	69.23
045	Travis Fryman	69.05
	Hank Greenberg	69.05
047	Miguel Cabrera	68.75
048	Alan Trammell	68.41
049	Sam Crawford	67.91
050	Justin Upton	67.86

Akil Baddoo

Rank	Player	Pct
051	Al Kaline	67.82
052	Alex Sanchez	67.02
053	Charlie Gehringer	66.79
054	George Burns	66.67
	Ramon Santiago	66.67
	Jack R. Warner	66.67
057	Anthony Gose	65.71
058	Ty Cobb	65.69
059	Mickey Stanley	65.67
060	Lou Whitaker	65.60
061	Fred Haney	65.38
062	Larry Herndon	65.31
063	Pete Fox	65.24
064	Jo-Jo White	65.22
065	Pat Sheridan	65.00
066	Goose Goslin	64.86
	Heinie Manush	64.86
068	Kimera Bartee	64.81
069	Jose Iglesias	64.62
070	Luis Polonia	64.10
071	Ryan Raburn	64.00
072	Tony Phillips	63.64
073	Carlos Guillen	63.44
074	Chad Curtis	63.24
075	Bobby Higginson	63.19
076	Ben Oglivie	63.08
077	Howard Johnson	62.96
	Curtis Pride	62.96
079	Jackie Tavener	62.50
080	Johnny Neun	61.22
081	Roy Johnson	61.11
082	Ossie Vitt	60.92
083	Marty McManus	60.75
084	Mike Heath	60.61
085	Lu Blue	60.28
086	Steve Kemp	60.00
	Bill Sweeney	60.00
088	Tom Brookens	59.86
089	Billy Rogell	59.38
090	Donie Bush	59.36
091	Norm Cash	59.15
092	Brad Ausmus	59.09
	Carlos Pena	59.09
094	Topper Rigney	58.73
095	Rudy York	58.62
096	Harry Davis	58.33
	Alex Johnson	58.33
	Skeeter Webb	58.33
099	Enos Cabell	57.58
100	Baldy Louden	57.44

Rank	Player	SBR
001	Ron LeFlore	29.4
002	Kirk Gibson	19.8
003	Brian Hunter	15.0
004	Gary Pettis	12.6
005	Curtis Granderson	9.9
	Jake Wood	9.9
007	Gee Walker	9.6
008	Roger Cedeno	7.5
009	Milt Cuyler	7.2
010	Austin Jackson	6.6
011	Quintin Berry	6.3
012	Niko Goodrum	5.7
013	Alan Trammell	5.4
014	Victor Reyes	5.1
	Gary Sheffield	5.1
016	Rajai Davis	4.8
	Juan Encarnacion	4.8
018	Nook Logan	4.5
	George Moriarty	4.5
020	Gates Brown	4.2
	Billy Bruton	4.2
	Andrew Romine	4.2
023	Damion Easley	3.9
	Dan Meyer	3.9
	Lloyd Moseby	3.9
026	Don Kelly	3.6
027	Ian Kinsler	3.3
028	Akil Baddoo	3.0
	Robbie Grossman	3.0
	Omar Infante	3.0
	Jose Macias	3.0
	Barney McCosky	3.0
033	Josh Anderson	2.7
	Johnny Damon	2.7
	George Lombard	2.7
	Paul Richards	2.7
	Hub Walker	2.7
038	Mikie Mahtook	2.4
	Cameron Maybin	2.4
	Larry Woodall	2.4
041	Daz Cameron	2.1
	Al Kaline	2.1
	Earl Torgeson	2.1
044	Dick Bartell	1.8
	Travis Fryman	1.8
	Hank Greenberg	1.8
	Damian Jackson	1.8
	Mark Koenig	1.8
049	Sam Crawford	1.5
	Andy Dirks	1.5

Heinie Schuble

Rank	Player	SBR
	Chico Fernandez	1.5
	JaCoby Jones	1.5
	Don Ross	1.5
	Heinie Schuble	1.5
	Tony Taylor	1.5
	Red Wilson	1.5
057	Brennan Boesch	1.2
	Roy Cullenbine	1.2
	Placido Polanco	1.2
	Ivan Rodriguez	1.2
	Dick Tracewski	1.2
062	Paddy Baumann	0.9
	Dave Collins	0.9
	Don Demeter	0.9
	Gabe Kapler	0.9
	Charlie Maxwell	0.9
	Jim Walewander	0.9
068	Miguel Cabrera	0.6
	Eric Haase	0.6
	Pinky Hargrave	0.6
	Davy Jones	0.6
	Jerry Morales	0.6
	Jonathan Schoop	0.6
	Rusty Staub	0.6
	Ned Yost	0.6
076	Steve Boros	0.3
	George Cutshaw	0.3
	Adam Everett	0.3
	Chick Galloway	0.3
	Charlie Gehringer	0.3
	Chet Laabs	0.3
	Jerry Lumpe	0.3
	Leonys Martin	0.3
	Alex Sanchez	0.3
	Justin Upton	0.3
086	Reno Bertoia	0.0
	Mike Brumley	0.0
	George Burns	0.0
	Harold Castro	0.0
	Liz Funk	0.0
	Nolen Richardson	0.0
	Ramon Santiago	0.0
	Jack R. Warner	0.0
094	Jeimer Candelario	-0.3
	Ira Flagstead	-0.3
	Anthony Gose	-0.3
	Dean Palmer	-0.3
	Bubba Phillips	-0.3
	Bud Souchock	-0.3
	Dixie Walker	-0.3
	Kenny Williams	-0.3

Rank	Player	Runs
001	Al Kaline	1,825
002	Charlie Gehringer	1,706
003	Miguel Cabrera	1,418
004	Lou Whitaker	1,333
005	Harry Heilmann	1,266
006	Alan Trammell	1,214
007	Hank Greenberg	1,211
008	Ty Cobb	1,209
009	Norm Cash	1,192
010	Rudy York	863
011	Willie Horton	840
012	Bill Freehan	825
013	Dick McAuliffe	816
014	Bobby Higginson	793
015	Kirk Gibson	711
016	Harvey Kuenn	664
017	Cecil Fielder	639
018	Travis Fryman	638
019	Bobby Veach	629
020	Lance Parrish	625
021	Jim Northrup	622
022	Billy Rogell	602
023	Chet Lemon	594
024	Pete Fox	583
025	Mickey Stanley	565
026	Magglio Ordonez	562
027	George Kell	551
028	Lu Blue	545
	Victor Martinez	545
030	Brandon Inge	526
031	Carlos Guillen	521
032	Tony Clark	501
033	Gee Walker	498
034	Vic Wertz	496
035	Ron LeFlore	475
036	Jeimer Candelario	468
037	Nicholas Castellanos	462
038	Charlie Maxwell	454
039	Pinky Higgins	449
040	Ray Boone	443
041	Tony Phillips	441
042	Curtis Granderson	432
043	Damion Easley	430
044	Bob Fothergill	428
045	Rocky Colavito	425
	Hoot Evers	425
047	Steve Kemp	424
048	Aurelio Rodriguez	419
049	Don Wert	409
050	Barney McCosky	401
051	Larry Herndon	397

Ramon Santiago

Rank	Player	Runs
052	Pat Mullin	395
	John Stone	395
054	Austin Jackson	381
	Tom Brookens	381
056	Placido Polanco	377
057	Darrell Evans	373
058	Dick Wakefield	372
059	Marv Owen	370
060	Frank Bolling	363
061	Heinie Manush	362
062	Marty McManus	354
063	Ivan Rodriguez	350
064	Ian Kinsler	348
065	Mickey Tettleton	346
066	Dale Alexander	344
067	Johnny Bassler	343
068	J.D. Martinez	336
069	Johnny Groth	335
070	Goose Goslin	334
071	Jason Thompson	330
072	Alex Avila	323
	Rusty Staub	323
074	Craig Monroe	318
075	Gates Brown	315
076	Niko Goodrum	314
077	Doc Cramer	309
078	Sam Crawford	306
079	Roy Cullenbine	292
	Roy Johnson	292
081	Dmitri Young	289
082	Donie Bush	286
083	Omar Infante	278
	John Wockenfuss	278
085	Deivi Cruz	268
	Johnny Lipon	268
087	Billy Bruton	265
088	Bill Tuttle	259
089	Topper Rigney	250
090	Dave Bergman	249
091	Eddie Mayo	245
092	Jhonny Peralta	240
093	Birdie Tebbetts	231
094	Bob Jones	230
095	Jo-Jo White	226
096	Juan Encarnacion	224
	Prince Fielder	224
098	Ray Hayworth	222
099	Ramon Santiago	221
	Jackie Tavener	221
	Marcus Thames	221
	Ralph Young	221

Rank	Player	Walks
001	Al Kaline	1,277
002	Lou Whitaker	1,197
003	Charlie Gehringer	1,186
004	Ty Cobb	1,148
005	Donie Bush	1,125
006	Norm Cash	1,025
007	Miguel Cabrera	877
008	Alan Trammell	850
009	Dick McAuliffe	842
010	Harry Heilmann	792
011	Hank Greenberg	748
012	Bobby Higginson	649
013	Sam Crawford	646
014	Rudy York	641
015	Bill Freehan	626
016	Billy Rogell	590
017	Lu Blue	589
018	Cecil Fielder	519
	Tony Phillips	519
020	Bobby Veach	512
021	Kirk Gibson	499
022	Willie Horton	469
023	Chet Lemon	468
024	Darrell Evans	437
	Ralph Young	437
026	Mickey Tettleton	429
027	Johnny Bassler	422
028	Jim Northrup	420
029	Brandon Inge	417
030	Pinky Higgins	399
031	Vic Wertz	395
032	Charlie Maxwell	394
033	Travis Fryman	390
034	Don Wert	385
035	Steve Kemp	375
036	Roy Cullenbine	373
037	Mickey Stanley	371
038	Alex Avila	368
039	Dick Wakefield	358
040	Rocky Colavito	346
041	Tony Clark	343
042	Eddie Lake	342
043	George Kell	337
044	Lance Parrish	334
045	Matty McIntyre	331
046	Pat Mullin	330
047	Carlos Guillen	327
048	Ossie Vitt	323
049	Harvey Kuenn	322
050	Victor Martinez	319
051	Magglio Ordonez	318
052	Ray Boone	317
053	Hoot Evers	316
054	Jimmy Barrett	309
055	Johnny Lipon	301
056	Jason Thompson	298
057	Damion Easley	296
058	Barney McCosky	283
059	Pete Fox	279
060	Jo-Jo White	275
061	Frank Bolling	274
	Curtis Granderson	274
	Johnny Groth	274
064	Davy Jones	272
065	Marv Owen	269
066	Dave Bergman	268
067	Eddie Yost	260
068	Austin Jackson	257
069	Tom Brookens	256
070	Marty McManus	253
071	Ron LeFlore	251
072	Rusty Staub	250
073	Topper Rigney	246
074	Mickey Cochrane	245
075	Gates Brown	242
076	Goose Goslin	241
077	John Wockenfuss	239
078	Nicholas Castellanos	224
079	Jerry Priddy	223
	Bob Swift	223
081	Larry Herndon	222
082	Bill Tuttle	220
083	Oscar Stanage	219
084	John Stone	216
085	Bob Jones	208
086	Billy Bruton	207
	Aurelio Rodriguez	207
	Al Wingo	207
089	Jeimer Candelario	206
090	Roy Johnson	199
091	Eddie Mayo	196
092	Birdie Tebbetts	195
093	Ray Hayworth	190
094	Doc Cramer	185
095	Fred Haney	182
096	Red Wilson	181
097	Carlos Pena	180
098	Rob Deer	178
	George Moriarty	178
100	Jim Delsing	177

Carlos Pena

Rank	Player	IBB
001	Miguel Cabrera	165
002	Al Kaline	131
003	Norm Cash	109
004	Lou Whitaker	79
005	Willie Horton	78
006	Bill Freehan	67
	Victor Martinez	67
008	Cecil Fielder	66
009	Dick McAuliffe	54
010	Kirk Gibson	50
011	Mickey Tettleton	49
012	Alan Trammell	48
013	Jim Northrup	47
014	Darrell Evans	39
015	Tony Clark	38
016	Lance Parrish	37
017	Bobby Higginson	36
	Don Wert	36
019	Carlos Guillen	33
020	Mickey Stanley	32
	Rudy York	32
	Dmitri Young	32
023	Chet Lemon	31
024	Vic Wertz	30
025	Charlie Maxwell	26
026	Harvey Kuenn	25
027	Ray Boone	24
028	Prince Fielder	23
	Bob Swift	23
030	Rocky Colavito	22
031	Rusty Staub	21
	Dick Wakefield	21
	Red Wilson	21
034	Jason Thompson	20
035	J.D. Martinez	19
036	Gates Brown	18
	Pinky Higgins	18
	Aurelio Rodriguez	18
039	Dave Bergman	17
	Eddie Brinkman	17
	Hoot Evers	17
	Frank House	17
044	Magglio Ordonez	16
045	Sean Casey	15
	Hank Greenberg	15
	Brandon Inge	15
	Tony Phillips	15
	Paul Richards	15
	Aaron Robinson	15
051	Alex Avila	14

Miguel Cabrera

Rank	Player	IBB
	Damion Easley	14
	Travis Fryman	14
	Ivan Rodriguez	14
	Birdie Tebbetts	14
056	Roy Cullenbine	13
	Larry Herndon	13
	George Kell	13
	Steve Kemp	13
	Ron LeFlore	13
	Jimmy Outlaw	13
	Champ Summers	13
	Bill Tuttle	13
064	Pat Mullin	12
	Pat Sheridan	12
	John Wockenfuss	12
067	Nicholas Castellanos	11
	Ned Harris	11
	Phil Mankowski	11
	Ben Oglivie	11
071	Tom Brookens	10
	Chico Fernandez	10
	Richie Hebner	10
	Craig Monroe	10
	Matt Nokes	10
	Ray Oyler	10
077	Frank Bolling	9
	Dick Brown	9
	Don Demeter	9
	Robert Fick	9
	Eddie Mayo	9
	Barney McCosky	9
	Jerry Priddy	9
084	Jimmy Bloodworth	8
	Brennan Boesch	8
	Curtis Granderson	8
	Fred Hatfield	8
	Bob Nieman	8
	Melvin Nieves	8
	Jhonny Peralta	8
091	Matt Batts	7
	Ike Brown	7
	Al Cowens	7
	Walt Dropo	7
	Luis Gonzalez	7
	Gail Harris	7
	Whitey Herzog	7
	Austin Jackson	7
	Don Kolloway	7
	Jerry Lumpe	7
	Placido Polanco	7
	Randall Simon	7

Rank	Player	Pct
001	Roy Cullenbine	19.11
002	Mickey Tettleton	18.31
003	Eddie Lake	16.98
004	Tony Phillips	15.63
005	Darrell Evans	15.56
006	Johnny Bassler	15.24
007	Dick Wakefield	14.32
008	Lu Blue	14.25
009	Al Wingo	13.65
010	Alex Avila	13.58
011	Hank Greenberg	13.39
012	Donie Bush	13.29
013	Norm Cash	13.18
014	Jo-Jo White	13.08
015	Steve Kemp	12.80
016	Rocky Colavito	12.71
017	Charlie Maxwell	12.51
018	Dick McAuliffe	12.33
019	Topper Rigney	12.26
	Vic Wertz	12.26
021	Cecil Fielder	12.21
022	Lou Whitaker	12.01
023	Rudy York	11.98
024	Dave Bergman	11.78
025	Jimmy Barrett	11.76
	Jason Thompson	11.76
027	Pat Mullin	11.59
028	Charlie Gehringer	11.58
	Billy Rogell	11.58
030	Jim Delsing	11.57
031	Jerry Priddy	11.54
	Ralph Young	11.54
033	Bobby Higginson	11.46
034	Johnny Lipon	11.43
035	Prince Fielder	11.41
036	Bob Swift	11.38
037	John Wockenfuss	11.29
038	Fred Haney	11.12
039	Ray Boone	11.11
040	Miguel Cabrera	11.07
041	Pinky Higgins	11.06
042	Al Kaline	11.01
043	Goose Goslin	10.88
044	Davy Jones	10.76
045	Carlos Pena	10.75
046	Tony Clark	10.68
047	Hooks Dauss	10.66
048	Johnny Groth	10.65
049	Jeimer Candelario	10.60
050	Mickey Lolich	10.59

Frank House

Rank	Player	Pct
051	Red Wilson	10.58
052	Kirk Gibson	10.45
	Barney McCosky	10.45
054	Larry Woodall	10.43
055	Rusty Staub	10.39
056	Fred Hatfield	10.29
057	Hoot Evers	10.19
058	Dean Palmer	10.05
059	Chet Lemon	10.01
060	Jim Delahanty	9.98
061	Pat Sheridan	9.87
062	Ossie Vitt	9.86
063	Matty McIntyre	9.67
064	Carlos Guillen	9.66
065	Marty McManus	9.60
066	Gates Brown	9.51
067	Ty Cobb	9.46
	Curtis Granderson	9.46
069	Harry Heilmann	9.43
070	Roy Johnson	9.33
	Jimmy Outlaw	9.33
072	Billy Bruton	9.29
073	Niko Goodrum	9.20
074	Bill Tuttle	9.09
075	Bill Freehan	9.07
	Alan Trammell	9.07
077	George Kell	9.02
078	Magglio Ordonez	9.01
079	Ray Oyler	8.98
080	Don Wert	8.95
081	Austin Jackson	8.58
082	Dale Alexander	8.55
083	J.D. Martinez	8.54
084	Jim Northrup	8.53
	Birdie Tebbetts	8.53
086	Ray Hayworth	8.49
087	Damion Easley	8.43
088	Frank Bolling	8.39
089	Travis Fryman	8.14
090	Marv Owen	8.13
091	Victor Martinez	8.09
092	John Stone	8.08
093	Brandon Inge	8.03
094	Marcus Thames	7.94
095	Eddie Mayo	7.86
096	Willie Horton	7.85
097	Jhonny Peralta	7.83
098	Jerry Lumpe	7.79
099	Hal Newhouser	7.77
100	Chico Fernandez	7.74

Rank	Player	Ratio
001	Johnny Bassler	5.78
002	Charlie Gehringer	3.19
003	George Kell	3.15
004	Ossie Vitt	2.96
005	Johnny Lipon	2.62
006	Lu Blue	2.50
007	Larry Woodall	2.37
008	Fred Haney	2.30
009	Roy Cullenbine	2.27
010	Doc Cramer	2.15
011	Ralph Young	2.07
012	Al Wingo	1.93
013	Pinky Higgins	1.91
	Eddie Lake	1.91
015	Billy Rogell	1.87
016	Topper Rigney	1.85
017	Donie Bush	1.82
018	Eddie Mayo	1.77
019	Ty Cobb	1.76
	Goose Goslin	1.76
021	Barney McCosky	1.72
022	Rusty Staub	1.68
023	Johnny Groth	1.60
024	Harry Heilmann	1.59
025	Harvey Kuenn	1.57
026	Bob Swift	1.54
027	Davy Jones	1.50
028	Marty McManus	1.47
	Bobby Veach	1.47
030	Sam Crawford	1.44
	Birdie Tebbetts	1.44
	Jo-Jo White	1.44
033	Jim Delsing	1.38
034	Jim Delahanty	1.36
035	Jimmy Outlaw	1.34
	Dick Wakefield	1.34

Rank	Player	Ratio
037	Bob Jones	1.33
038	Red Wilson	1.30
039	Al Kaline	1.25
040	Ray Boone	1.24
041	Hoot Evers	1.22
042	Don Kolloway	1.19
043	Heinie Manush	1.16
044	Rocky Colavito	1.15
	Marv Owen	1.15
046	Bob Fothergill	1.10
047	Frank House	1.09
	Roy Johnson	1.09
	Lou Whitaker	1.09

Larry Woodall

Rank	Player	Ratio
050	Dale Alexander	1.08
	Dave Bergman	1.08
	Tony Phillips	1.08
	Bill Tuttle	1.08
055	Jimmy Barrett	1.07
	Ray Hayworth	1.07
057	Pat Mullin	1.06
	Vic Wertz	1.06
059	Matty McIntyre	1.05
060	Fred Hatfield	1.04
	Steve Kemp	1.04
062	Jerry Priddy	1.03
063	Darrell Evans	1.01

Rank	Player	Ratio
064	John Stone	0.99
065	Hank Greenberg	0.97
	Alan Trammell	0.97
	John Wockenfuss	0.97
068	Norm Cash	0.95
	Rudy York	0.95
070	Jerry Lumpe	0.93
071	Charlie Maxwell	0.91
072	Frank Bolling	0.90
	Dick McAuliffe	0.90
	Placido Polanco	0.90
075	Gates Brown	0.88
076	Pete Fox	0.87
077	Mickey Tettleton	0.85
078	Bill Freehan	0.83
079	Bobby Higginson	0.82
080	Billy Bruton	0.81
081	Prince Fielder	0.80
082	Jackie Tavener	0.79
	Jason Thompson	0.79
084	Victor Martinez	0.78
085	Magglio Ordonez	0.76
086	Don Wert	0.74
087	Chet Lemon	0.72
	George Moriarty	0.72
089	Chico Fernandez	0.70
	Jim Northrup	0.70
091	Charley O'Leary	0.68
092	Miguel Cabrera	0.66
	Carlos Guillen	0.66
	Mickey Stanley	0.66
095	Hal Newhouser	0.59
096	Eddie Brinkman	0.57
097	Cecil Fielder	0.56
098	Bill Coughlin	0.55
	Claude Rossman	0.55
	Gee Walker	0.55

Rank	Player	SF
001	Al Kaline	104
002	Lou Whitaker	91
003	Alan Trammell	76
004	Miguel Cabrera	69
005	Travis Fryman	59
006	Norm Cash	53
007	Bobby Higginson	52
008	Bill Freehan	48
009	Willie Horton	44
	Brandon Inge	44
011	Kirk Gibson	43
012	Victor Martinez	40
013	Rusty Staub	36
014	Tom Brookens	35
	Lance Parrish	35
016	Mickey Stanley	34
017	Cecil Fielder	32
018	Steve Kemp	31
019	Craig Monroe	30
	Magglio Ordonez	30
	Don Wert	30
022	Dick McAuliffe	29
023	Nicholas Castellanos	28
	Larry Herndon	28
	Chet Lemon	28
026	Carlos Guillen	27
	Harvey Kuenn	27
028	Rocky Colavito	26
	Jim Northrup	26
030	Tony Clark	25
	Jason Thompson	25
032	Charlie Maxwell	24
033	Dave Bergman	22
	Ray Boone	22
	Damion Easley	22
	Tony Phillips	22
037	Gates Brown	21
	Aurelio Rodriguez	21
039	Frank Bolling	20
	Austin Jackson	20
041	Deivi Cruz	19
	Placido Polanco	19
	Mickey Tettleton	19
044	Alex Avila	17
	Eddie Brinkman	17
	Torii Hunter	17
	Omar Infante	17
	J.D. Martinez	17
	Jhonny Peralta	17
	Ivan Rodriguez	17
051	Frank House	16
	Ron LeFlore	16

Whitey Herzog

Rank	Player	SF
053	Shane Halter	15
	Dean Palmer	15
	Bubba Phillips	15
	Ramon Santiago	15
	Bill Tuttle	15
058	Darrell Evans	14
	Ben Oglivie	14
	Red Wilson	14
061	Chad Curtis	13
	Juan Encarnacion	13
	Ian Kinsler	13
064	Robert Fick	12
	Marcus Thames	12
	John Wockenfuss	12
067	Lou Berberet	11
	Prince Fielder	11
	Curtis Granderson	11
	John Grubb	11
	Scott Livingstone	11
	Tom Veryzer	11
	Dmitri Young	11
074	Reno Bertoia	10
	Frank Catalanotto	10
	Darnell Coles	10
	Jerry Lumpe	10
	Carlos Pena	10
	Jonathan Schoop	10
	Pat Sheridan	10
	Earl Torgeson	10
	Delmon Young	10
083	Brennan Boesch	9
	Steve Boros	9
	Harold Castro	9
	Niko Goodrum	9
	Mike Heath	9
	Jose Iglesias	9
	Chad Kreuter	9
	Milt May	9
	James McCann	9
	Ryan Raburn	9
	Randall Simon	9
094	Skeeter Barnes	8
	Billy Bruton	8
	Enos Cabell	8
	Tim Corcoran	8
	Luis Gonzalez	8
	Gail Harris	8
	Richie Hebner	8
	Whitey Herzog	8
	Jerry Morales	8
	Eric Munson	8
	Matt Nokes	8
	Gary Sutherland	8
	George Thomas	8

Rank	Player	SH
001	Donie Bush	327
002	Ty Cobb	277
003	Harry Heilmann	262
004	Bobby Veach	238
005	Sam Crawford	223
006	Ossie Vitt	173
	Ralph Young	173
008	Bob Jones	160
009	Charlie Gehringer	141
010	Charley O'Leary	138
011	Alan Trammell	124
012	Germany Schaefer	122
013	George Moriarty	121
014	Lu Blue	114
015	Topper Rigney	104
016	Oscar Stanage	98
017	Bill Coughlin	94
018	Johnny Bassler	92
019	Jackie Tavener	90
020	Lou Whitaker	89
021	Heinie Manush	84
022	Bob Fothergill	82
023	George Kell	78
024	Eddie Mayo	75
025	Ramon Santiago	74
026	Mickey Lolich	73
027	George Burns	72
028	Hal Newhouser	71
029	Matty McIntyre	68
	Billy Rogell	68
031	Fred Haney	67
032	Marv Owen	66
033	Tommy Bridges	65
034	Pete Fox	64
035	Marty McManus	61
036	Pinky Higgins	60
037	Boss Schmidt	58
038	Claude Rossman	57
039	Frank O'Rourke	56
040	Tom Brookens	55
	Johnny Lipon	55
	Don Wert	55
043	Aurelio Rodriguez	52
044	George Cutshaw	51
	Davy Jones	51
	Denny McLain	51
047	Doc Cramer	50
	Jim Delahanty	50
	Frank Lary	50
050	Al Benton	49
051	Hoot Evers	47

Fritz Buelow

Rank	Player	SH
052	Joe Hoover	46
053	Hooks Dauss	45
	Al Kaline	45
	Chick Shorten	45
056	Bill Donovan	44
	Tom Jones	44
	Bob Swift	44
059	Jim Bunning	43
	Brandon Inge	43
061	Deivi Cruz	42
	Mickey Stanley	42
	Larry Woodall	42
064	Paul Foytack	41
065	Del Pratt	40
066	Jimmy Barrett	39
	Jack R. Warner	39
068	Frank Bolling	38
	Bill Freehan	38
070	Ira Flagstead	37
	Al Wingo	37
072	Eddie Brinkman	36
	Chico Fernandez	36
074	Hank Greenberg	35
	Chris Lindsay	35
	Vic Sorrell	35
	Gee Walker	35
078	Ray Hayworth	34
	Billy Lush	34
080	Eddie Lake	33
	Harry Rice	33
082	Dale Alexander	32
	Fritz Buelow	32
	Charlie Carr	32
	Barney McCosky	32
086	Bobby Lowe	31
	Earl Whitehill	31
088	Milt Cuyler	30
089	Red Wilson	29
090	Elden Auker	28
	Fred Hatfield	28
	Marty Kavanagh	28
	Dick McAuliffe	28
	Jerry Priddy	28
	Joe Sparma	28
096	Baldy Louden	27
	Birdie Tebbetts	27
098	Jimmy Bloodworth	26
	Billy Bruton	26
	Kid Gleason	26
	Johnny Groth	26
	Omar Infante	26
	Dizzy Trout	26

ALL TIME TIGER HITTING LEADERS – TOTAL SACRIFICES

Rank	Player	Sacrifices
001	Donie Bush	327
002	Ty Cobb	277
003	Harry Heilmann	262
004	Bobby Veach	238
005	Sam Crawford	223
006	Alan Trammell	200
007	Lou Whitaker	180
008	Ossie Vitt	173
009	Ralph Young	173
010	Bob Jones	160
011	Al Kaline	149
012	Charlie Gehringer	141
013	Charley O'Leary	138
014	Germany Schaefer	122
015	George Moriarty	121
016	Lu Blue	114
017	Topper Rigney	104
018	Oscar Stanage	98
019	Bill Coughlin	94
020	Johnny Bassler	92
021	Tom Brookens	90
	Jackie Tavener	90
023	Ramon Santiago	89
024	Brandon Inge	87
025	Bill Freehan	86
026	Don Wert	85
027	Heinie Manush	84
028	Bob Fothergill	82
029	George Kell	78
030	Mickey Stanley	76
031	Eddie Mayo	75
032	Travis Fryman	74
	Mickey Lolich	74
034	Aurelio Rodriguez	73
035	George Burns	72
036	Hal Newhouser	71
037	Miguel Cabrera	69
	Norm Cash	69
039	Matty McIntyre	68
	Billy Rogell	68
041	Fred Haney	67
042	Marv Owen	66
043	Tommy Bridges	65
044	Pete Fox	64
	Bobby Higginson	64
046	Deivi Cruz	61
	Kirk Gibson	61
	Marty McManus	61
049	Pinky Higgins	60
050	Frank Bolling	58
	Boss Schmidt	58
052	Dick McAuliffe	57
	Claude Rossman	57
054	Frank O'Rourke	56
055	Willie Horton	55
	Johnny Lipon	55
	Denny McLain	55
058	Eddie Brinkman	53
059	Frank Lary	52
060	George Cutshaw	51
	Davy Jones	51
062	Doc Cramer	50
	Jim Delahanty	50
064	Al Benton	49
065	Harvey Kuenn	48
	Lance Parrish	48
067	Hoot Evers	47
068	Joe Hoover	46
	Chet Lemon	46
070	Jim Bunning	45
	Hooks Dauss	45
	Chick Shorten	45
073	Bill Donovan	44
	Tom Jones	44
	Bob Swift	44
076	Chico Fernandez	43
	Omar Infante	43
	Austin Jackson	43
	Red Wilson	43
080	Placido Polanco	42
	Larry Woodall	42
082	Paul Foytack	41
	Jim Northrup	41
	Rusty Staub	41
085	Victor Martinez	40
	Tony Phillips	40
	Del Pratt	40
	Bill Tuttle	40
089	Jimmy Barrett	39
	Ray Boone	39
	Damion Easley	39
	Jack R. Warner	39
093	Steve Kemp	38
	Charlie Maxwell	38
095	Ira Flagstead	37
	Al Wingo	37
097	Milt Cuyler	36
	Shane Halter	36
099	Dave Bergman	35
	Hank Greenberg	35
	Chris Lindsay	35
	Jerry Lumpe	35
	Vic Sorrell	35
	Gee Walker	35

Tom Jones

001	Miguel Cabrera	1,338
002	Brandon Inge	1,189
003	Lou Whitaker	1,099
004	Norm Cash	1,081
005	Al Kaline	1,020
006	Willie Horton	945
007	Dick McAuliffe	932
008	Travis Fryman	931
009	Kirk Gibson	930
010	Cecil Fielder	926
011	Alan Trammell	874
012	Lance Parrish	847
013	Bobby Higginson	796
014	Nicholas Castellanos	793
015	Hank Greenberg	771
016	Bill Freehan	753
017	Alex Avila	733
018	Tony Clark	721
019	Austin Jackson	699
020	Rudy York	672
021	Ty Cobb	653
022	Chet Lemon	647
023	Ron LeFlore	628
024	Donie Bush	618
	Curtis Granderson	618
026	Jim Northrup	603
027	Aurelio Rodriguez	589
028	Mickey Stanley	564
029	Damion Easley	563
030	Tom Brookens	553
031	Don Wert	519
032	Mickey Tettleton	505
033	Harry Heilmann	498
034	Carlos Guillen	492
035	Craig Monroe	488
036	J.D. Martinez	486
037	Tony Phillips	480
038	Oscar Stanage	464
039	Jeimer Candelario	461
040	Sam Crawford	450
041	Niko Goodrum	446
042	Larry Herndon	441
043	Carlos Pena	437
044	Darrell Evans	433
045	Charlie Maxwell	432
046	Rob Deer	426
047	Magglio Ordonez	421
048	Ivan Rodriguez	418
049	Ryan Raburn	416
050	Marcus Thames	411

Alex Avila

051	Victor Martinez	409
052	James McCann	406
053	Dean Palmer	391
054	JaCoby Jones	389
055	Dmitri Young	379
056	Ramon Santiago	377
057	Jason Thomson	375
058	Omar Infante	373
059	Charlie Gehringer	372
	Vic Wertz	372
061	Steve Kemp	362
062	Ian Kinsler	360
063	Jake Wood	359
064	Bobby Veach	348
065	Juan Encarnacion	339
066	Donie Bush	334
067	Jhonny Peralta	332
068	Mickey Lolich	331
069	Ty Cobb	329
070	Justin Upton	326
071	Pete Fox	319
072	Shane Halter	318
073	Billy Rogell	316
074	Matty McIntyre	315
	Melvin Nieves	315
076	Pat Mullin	312
077	Frank Bolling	305
	Germany Schaefer	305
079	Rocky Colavito	301
080	Jimmy Barrett	290
081	Hooks Dauss	289
082	Brennan Boesch	286
083	Gates Brown	275
084	Ray Oyler	273
085	Tommy Bridges	271
086	Dick Wakefield	268
087	Hoot Evers	258
088	Billy Bruton	257
089	Deivi Cruz	256
090	Ray Boone	255
	Eddie Brinkman	255
092	Milt Cuyler	254
093	Gee Walker	253
094	Bill Donovan	249
095	Dave Bergman	248
	George Moriarty	248
097	John Wockenfuss	247
098	John Hicks	244
099	Bill Coughlin	243
100	Lu Blue	236
	Jose Iglesias	236

Rank	Player	Ratio
001	Doc Cramer	0.032
	George Kell	0.032
003	Johnny Bassler	0.033
004	Ossie Vitt	0.039
005	Charlie Gehringer	0.042
006	Harvey Kuenn	0.047
007	Eddie Mayo	0.050
008	Johnny Lipon	0.051
	Larry Woodall	0.051
010	Bob Jones	0.052
011	Sam Crawford	0.056
	Bob Fothergill	0.056
013	Fred Haney	0.058
	Bobby Veach	0.058
015	Heinie Manush	0.061
016	Ty Cobb	0.062
017	Don Kolloway	0.063
	Placido Polanco	0.063
019	Birdie Tebbetts	0.066
020	Pinky Higgins	0.067
	Ralph Young	0.067
022	Harry Heilmann	0.068
023	Barney McCosky	0.069
024	Lu Blue	0.070
	Goose Goslin	0.070
026	Rusty Staub	0.071
027	Billy Rogell	0.072
028	Marty McManus	0.074
	Boss Schmidt	0.074
030	Johnny Groth	0.075
	Charley O'Leary	0.075
032	Frank House	0.077
033	Jimmy Outlaw	0.078
034	Marv Owen	0.079
035	Pete Fox	0.081
	Topper Rigney	0.081
037	Davy Jones	0.083
	Gee Walker	0.083
039	Al Wingo	0.084
040	Bob Swift	0.086
041	Jim Delahanty	0.087
042	Dale Alexander	0.089
	Donie Bush	0.089
	Ray Hayworth	0.089
045	John Stone	0.090
046	Jerry Lumpe	0.093
	George Moriarty	0.093
048	Red Wilson	0.094
049	Hoot Evers	0.095
	Roy Johnson	0.095
	Bill Tuttle	0.095
052	Jim Delsing	0.096
	Claude Rossman	0.096
054	George Burns	0.097
055	Al Kaline	0.101
056	Ray Boone	0.103
057	Frank Bolling	0.105
	Roy Cullenbine	0.105
	Matty McIntyre	0.105
	Alan Trammell	0.105
061	Deivi Cruz	0.106
	Jo-Jo White	0.106
063	Jackie Tavener	0.108
064	Eddie Lake	0.110
065	Mickey Stanley	0.112
066	Bill Coughlin	0.115
	Fred Hatfield	0.115
	Victor Martinez	0.115
069	Gates Brown	0.122
070	Chico Fernandez	0.123
	Jose Iglesias	0.123
072	Eddie Brinkman	0.124
	Bill Freehan	0.124
074	Walt Dropo	0.125
	Pat Mullin	0.125
076	Dave Bergman	0.126
	Dick Wakefield	0.126
078	Jimmy Barrett	0.128
	Lou Whitaker	0.128
080	Rocky Colavito	0.129
	Jerry Priddy	0.129
082	Billy Bruton	0.130
083	Oscar Stanage	0.132
084	Magglio Ordonez	0.133
	Vic Wertz	0.133
	John Wockenfuss	0.133
087	Aurelio Rodriguez	0.135
088	Jim Northrup	0.136
	Germany Schaefer	0.136
090	Don Wert	0.137
091	Rudy York	0.144
092	Steve Kemp	0.145
	Ian Kinsler	0.145
	George Mullin	0.145
095	Hal Newhouser	0.152
096	Tom Brookens	0.156
	Don Kelly	0.156
098	Dick McAuliffe	0.158
099	Chet Lemon	0.159
100	Larry Herndon	0.160

George Kell

Rank	Player	Pct
001	Johnny Bassler	2.64
002	George Kell	2.86
003	Doc Cramer	2.90
004	Ossie Vitt	3.33
005	Charlie Gehringer	3.63
006	Harvey Kuenn	4.32
007	Johnny Lipon	4.37
008	Larry Woodall	4.40
009	Eddie Mayo	4.45
010	Bob Jones	4.63
011	Fred Haney	4.83
012	Sam Crawford	5.06
013	Bob Fothergill	5.12
	Bobby Veach	5.12
015	Ty Cobb	5.38
016	Heinie Manush	5.42
017	Ralph Young	5.57
018	Lu Blue	5.71
019	Don Kolloway	5.75
	Placido Polanco	5.75
021	Pinky Higgins	5.79
022	Birdie Tebbetts	5.90
023	Harry Heilmann	5.93
024	Barney McCosky	6.10
025	Goose Goslin	6.18
026	Rusty Staub	6.19
027	Billy Rogell	6.20
028	Marty McManus	6.53
029	Topper Rigney	6.63
030	Johnny Groth	6.65
031	Charley O'Leary	6.79
032	Boss Schmidt	6.83
033	Frank House	6.95
034	Jimmy Outlaw	6.99
035	Marv Owen	7.04
036	Al Wingo	7.06
037	Davy Jones	7.16
038	Donie Bush	7.30
039	Jim Delahanty	7.33
040	Bob Swift	7.40
041	Pete Fox	7.45
042	Gee Walker	7.81
043	Dale Alexander	7.93
044	Ray Hayworth	7.95
045	Red Wilson	8.12
046	John Stone	8.19
047	George Moriarty	8.23
048	Hoot Evers	8.32
049	Jim Delsing	8.37
050	Jerry Lumpe	8.38
051	Roy Cullenbine	8.40
052	Bill Tuttle	8.43

Johnny Bassler

Rank	Player	Pct
053	Roy Johnson	8.58
054	George Burns	8.69
	Claude Rossman	8.69
056	Al Kaline	8.80
057	Eddie Lake	8.89
058	Ray Boone	8.93
059	Jo-Jo White	9.09
060	Matty McIntyre	9.20
061	Alan Trammell	9.32
062	Frank Bolling	9.34
063	Jackie Tavener	9.48
064	Fred Hatfield	9.91
065	Deivi Cruz	10.04
066	Bill Coughlin	10.24
067	Mickey Stanley	10.30
068	Victor Martinez	10.38
069	Dick Wakefield	10.72
070	Gates Brown	10.81
071	Dave Bergman	10.90
072	Bill Freehan	10.91
073	Pat Mullin	10.96
074	Chico Fernandez	11.01
075	Lou Whitaker	11.03
076	Jimmy Barrett	11.04
077	Rocky Colavito	11.05
078	Jerry Priddy	11.17
079	Eddie Brinkman	11.22
080	Jose Iglesias	11.41
081	Billy Bruton	11.54
082	Vic Wertz	11.55
083	Walt Dropo	11.63
084	John Wockenfuss	11.67
085	Magglio Ordonez	11.92
086	Oscar Stanage	12.06
087	Don Wert	12.07
088	Germany Schaefer	12.10
089	Jim Northrup	12.24
090	Steve Kemp	12.35
091	Rudy York	12.56
092	Aurelio Rodriguez	12.67
093	Hal Newhouser	13.10
094	George Mullin	13.20
095	Ian Kinsler	13.37
096	Dick McAuliffe	13.65
097	Charlie Maxwell	13.71
098	Hank Greenberg	13.80
099	Chet Lemon	13.84
100	Norm Cash	13.90

Rank	Player	GIDP
001	Al Kaline	271
002	Miguel Cabrera	255
003	Alan Trammell	156
004	Lou Whitaker	143
005	Willie Horton	141
006	Norm Cash	139
007	Bill Freehan	138
008	Mickey Stanley	133
009	Victor Martinez	131
010	Jim Northrup	117
011	Lance Parrish	116
012	Rudy York	115
013	Cecil Fielder	113
014	Magglio Ordonez	111
015	Chet Lemon	110
016	Aurelio Rodriguez	107
	Don Wert	107
018	Pinky Higgins	104
019	Travis Fryman	94
020	Brandon Inge	92
021	George Kell	89
022	Hoot Evers	85
023	Harvey Kuenn	84
024	Carlos Guillen	83
	Bobby Higginson	83
	Rusty Staub	83
027	Larry Herndon	80
028	Ivan Rodriguez	75
029	Tony Clark	74
	Bill Tuttle	74
031	Ray Boone	72
032	Johnny Groth	70
	Steve Kemp	70
034	Dick McAuliffe	69
035	Deivi Cruz	68
	Vic Wertz	68
037	Rocky Colavito	67
038	Damion Easley	66
039	Placido Polanco	65
040	Eddie Brinkman	62
041	Tom Brookens	61
042	Nicholas Castellanos	59
043	Craig Monroe	59
044	Alex Avila	58
045	Ron LeFlore	56
	Johnny Lipon	56
047	Dmitri Young	55
048	Gates Brown	54
	Doc Cramer	54
	Eddie Mayo	54
051	Jason Thompson	53
052	Jimmy Bloodworth	52

Torii Hunter

Rank	Player	GIDP
	Walt Dropo	52
054	Bob Swift	51
	Dick Wakefield	51
056	Hank Greenberg	50
	Jerry Priddy	50
	Jhonny Peralta	50
	Tony Phillips	50
060	Frank Bolling	49
061	Ian Kinsler	47
	Red Wilson	47
063	Chico Fernandez	46
	Austin Jackson	46
	James McCann	46
066	Kirk Gibson	45
	Birdie Tebbetts	45
	John Wockenfuss	45
069	Don Kolloway	44
070	Shane Halter	42
	Mike Heath	42
	Frank House	42
	Jose Iglesias	42
	J.D. Martinez	42
075	Jimmy Outlaw	40
076	Dave Bergman	39
	Juan Encarnacion	39
	Prince Fielder	39
079	Pat Mullin	37
	Matt Nokes	37
	Ben Oglivie	37
082	Ramon Santiago	36
	Steve Souchock	36
084	Gary Sutherland	35
085	Brad Ausmus	34
	Darrell Evans	34
	Barney McCosky	34
	Ryan Raburn	34
089	Robert Fick	33
	Charlie Maxwell	33
	Ray Oyler	33
092	Billy Bruton	32
	Fred Hatfield	32
	Omar Infante	32
095	Eddie Lake	31
096	Jake Wood	30
097	Torii Hunter	29
	Jerry Lumpe	29
	Gary Sheffield	29
100	Roy Cullenbine	28
	Chris Gomez	28
	Milt May	28
	Dan Meyer	28
	Paul Richards	28

Rank	Player	Outs
001	Al Kaline	7,594
002	Ty Cobb	7,156
003	Lou Whitaker	6,599
004	Alan Trammell	6,388
005	Charlie Gehringer	6,279
006	Sam Crawford	5,784
007	Donie Bush	5,641
008	Harry Heilmann	5,124
009	Miguel Cabrera	5,120
010	Norm Cash	5,037
011	Bill Freehan	4,727
012	Dick McAuliffe	4,612
013	Bobby Veach	4,437
014	Willie Horton	4,140
015	Mickey Stanley	4,011
016	Bobby Higginson	3,774
017	Brandon Inge	3,761
018	Rudy York	3,520
019	Aurelio Rodriguez	3,511
020	Jim Northrup	3,448
021	Hank Greenberg	3,374
022	Lance Parrish	3,344
023	Billy Rogell	3,330
024	Travis Fryman	3,315
025	Kirk Gibson	3,200
026	Chet Lemon	3,187
027	Harvey Kuenn	3,175
028	Don Wert	3,089
029	Tom Brookens	2,880
030	Cecil Fielder	2,875
	Pete Fox	2,875
032	Oscar Stanage	2,787
033	Victor Martinez	2,700
034	Ralph Young	2,592
035	Lu Blue	2,562
036	Ron LeFlore	2,477
037	Pinky Higgins	2,447
038	Damion Easley	2,426
039	George Kell	2,422
040	Bob Jones	2,389
041	Nicholas Castellanos	2,386
042	Magglio Ordonez	2,335
043	Charley O'Leary	2,321
044	Ossie Vitt	2,299
045	Frank Bolling	2,287
046	Matty McIntyre	2,282
047	Carlos Guillen	2,265
048	Marv Owen	2,221
049	Gee Walker	2,165
050	Tony Clark	2,156
051	George Moriarty	2,142
052	Larry Herndon	2,112
053	Tony Phillips	2,106
054	Hoot Evers	2,094
055	Vic Wertz	2,090
056	Doc Cramer	2,081
057	Austin Jackson	2,052
058	Charlie Maxwell	2,050
059	Curtis Granderson	1,941
060	Steve Kemp	1,917
061	Deivi Cruz	1,901
	Pat Mullin	1,901
	Placido Polanco	1,901
064	Ray Boone	1,880
	Ian Kinsler	1,880
066	Darrell Evans	1,859
067	Craig Monroe	1,849
068	Alex Avila	1,831
069	Rocky Colavito	1,810
070	Ramon Santiago	1,809
071	Germany Schaefer	1,800
072	Johnny Lipon	1,798
073	Eddie Mayo	1,796
074	Ivan Rodriguez	1,787
075	Gates Brown	1,768
076	Omar Infante	1,759
077	Marty McManus	1,753
078	Bob Fothergill	1,749
079	John Stone	1,742
080	Barney McCosky	1,728
081	Jason Thompson	1,726
082	Johnny Groth	1,725
083	Bill Tuttle	1,724
084	Eddie Brinkman	1,722
085	Johnny Bassler	1,648
086	Davy Jones	1,647
087	Rusty Staub	1,645
088	Jimmy Barrett	1,638
089	Birdie Tebbetts	1,609
090	Dick Wakefield	1,582
091	Dave Bergman	1,545
092	Billy Bruton	1,543
093	Heinie Manush	1,535
094	Ray Hayworth	1,508
	Jackie Tavener	1,508
096	Jose Iglesias	1,495
097	Mickey Tettleton	1,480
098	Jake Wood	1,464
099	John Wockenfuss	1,442
100	Roy Johnson	1,428

Vic Wertz

Rank	Games	Player	Year
001	40	Ty Cobb	1911
002	35	Ty Cobb	1917
003	30	Goose Goslin	1934
	30	Ron LeFlore	1976
005	29	Dale Alexander	1930
	29	Pete Fox	1935
007	28	Sam Crawford	1911
008	27	Gee Walker	1937
	27	Ron LeFlore	1978
010	26	John Stone	1930
011	25	Kid Gleason	1901
	25	Ty Cobb	1906
	25	John Stone	1931
014	23	Sam Crawford	1909
	23	Ty Cobb	1912
	23	Harry Heilmann	1921
017	22	Ty Cobb	1907
	22	Harvey Kuenn	1959
	22	Al Kaline	1961
019	21	Ty Cobb	1918
	21	Harry Heilmann	1919
	21	Harry Heilmann	1923
	21	Ty Cobb	1926
	21	Charlie Gehringer	1927
	21	Harry Heilmann	1928
	21	Dick Wakefield	1943
	21	Alan Trammell	1987
027	20	Sam Crawford	1903
	20	Sam Crawford	1913-14
	20	Ty Cobb	1920
	20	Charlie Gehringer	1937
	20	Rip Radcliff	1941
	20	Eddie Mayo	1947
	20	George Kell	1949
	20	George Kell	1950
	20	Alan Trammell	1984
	20	Magglio Ordonez	2005
	20	Rondell White	2005
	20	Miguel Cabrera	2010
039	19	Sam Crawford	1915
	19	Hoot Evers	1950
	19	Johnny Lipon	1950
	19	Glenn Wilson	1982
	19	D. Easley (May)	1998
	19	D. Easley (July)	1998
	19	Tony Clark	1999
	19	Juan Encarnacion	2000
047	18	Jimmy Barrett	1902
	18	Jim Delahanty	1910
	18	Ty Cobb	1910-11
	18	Roy Johnson	1931
	18	Pete Fox	1933

Gee Walker

Rank	Games	Player	Year
	18	Hank Greenberg	1934
	18	Hank Greenberg	1940
	18	Doc Cramer	1944
	18	Johnny Groth	1950
	18	Frank Bolling	1957
	18	Al Kaline	1958
	18	Lou Whitaker	1983
	18	Alan Trammell	1984
	18	Alan Trammell	1987
	18	Chad Curtis	1995
	18	Robert Fick	2002
062	17	Dick Harley	1902
	17	Matty McIntyre	1904
	17	Ty Cobb	1915
	17	Pete Fox	1935
	17	Billy Rogell	1935
	17	Hank Greenberg	1937
	17	Jo-Jo White	1937
	17	Rudy York	1940
	17	Barney McCosky	1941
	17	Harvey Kuenn	1958
	17	Leon Roberts	1975
	17	Ron LeFlore	1977
	17	Champ Summers	1980
	17	Larry Herndon	1982
	17	Junior Felix	1994
	17	Nicholas Castellanos	2017
076	16	Ty Cobb	1911
	16	Ty Cobb	1922
	16	Hank Greenberg	1933
	16	Billy Rogell	1934
	16	Goose Goslin	1935
	16	Al Simmons	1936
	16	Gee Walker	1936
	16	Charlie Gehringer	1937
	16	Hank Greenberg	1940
	16	Pinky Higgins	1943
	16	Doc Cramer	1944
	16	Wakefield (Aug-Sep)	1944
	16	Dick Wakefield (Sep)	1944
	16	Neil Berry	1949
	16	Harvey Kuenn	1952
	16	Ray Boone	1956
	16	Al Kaline	1963
	16	Willie Horton	1970
	16	Jason Thompson	1978
	16	Lou Whitaker	1986
	16	Alan Trammell	1993
	16	Lou Whitaker	1994
	16	Austin Jackson	2012
	16	Jonathan Schoop	2021

Rank	Player	Hits
001	Jose Iglesias	124
002	Travis Fryman	113
003	Tony Phillips	112
004	Miguel Cabrera	111
005	Alan Trammell	107
006	Austin Jackson	96
007	Brandon Inge	94
008	Lou Whitaker	92
009	Ramon Santiago	90
010	Brian Hunter	89
011	Placido Polanco	87
012	Omar Infante	79
013	Alex Sanchez	77
014	Damion Easley	73
	Bobby Higginson	73
016	Magglio Ordonez	71
017	Nicholas Castellanos	67
	Ian Kinsler	67
019	Deivi Cruz	66
020	Curtis Granderson	61
	Carlos Guillen	61
022	Cecil Fielder	60
023	Milt Cuyler	58
024	Tony Clark	57
025	Ivan Rodriguez	52
026	Craig Monroe	49
027	Mickey Tettleton	47
028	Victor Martinez	45
029	Rajai Davis	44
	J.D. Martinez	44
031	Chet Lemon	42
032	Ryan Raburn	41
033	Brennan Boesch	40
	Jeimer Candelario	40
035	Dave Bergman	39
	Juan Encarnacion	39
	Gerald Laird	39
038	Gary Pettis	38
039	Nook Logan	37
040	Jhonny Peralta	36
041	Niko Goodrum	34
042	Andy Dirks	33
	Scott Livingstone	33
044	Joe Randa	31
045	Rob Deer	30
	JaCoby Jones	30
	Victor Reyes	30
048	Chad Curtis	29
	Dan Gladden	29
	Jonathan Schoop	29

Skeeter Barnes

Rank	Player	Hits
	Rondell White	29
052	Skeeter Barnes	28
	Kimera Bartee	28
	Marcus Thames	28
055	Torii Hunter	27
	Andrew Romine	27
057	Prince Fielder	26
	Kirk Gibson	26
	Luis Polonia	26
	Gary Sheffield	26
061	Brad Ausmus	25
	Frank Catalanotto	25
	Don Kelly	25
064	Chad Kreuter	24
	James McCann	24
066	Alex Avila	23
	Mike Heath	23
	Luis Salazar	23
069	Paul Bako	22
	Mikie Mahtook	22
071	Anthony Gose	21
	Shane Halter	21
	Delmon Young	21
074	Willi Castro	20
	Edgar Renteria	20
076	Johnny Damon	19
	Luis Gonzalez	19
	Ronny Rodriguez	19
079	Danny Bautista	18
	Adam Everett	18
	Lloyd Moseby	18
082	Harold Castro	17
	Chris Gomez	17
	Carlos Pena	17
	Dmitri Young	17
086	Yoenis Cespedes	16
	John Hicks	16
	Cameron Maybin	16
089	Akil Baddoo	15
	Leonys Martin	15
	Will Rhymes	15
	Justin Upton	15
	Gary Ward	15
094	Tom Brookens	14
	Roger Cedeno	14
	Bryan Holaday	14
097	Junior Felix	13
	Jose Macias	13
	Juan Samuel	13
	Pat Sheridan	13

Rank	Player	Bunt Hits
001	Alex Sanchez	59
002	Ramon Santiago	36
003	Milt Cuyler	32
004	Lou Whitaker	28
005	Luis Polonia	19
006	Tony Phillips	17
007	Omar Infante	16
008	Nook Logan	15
009	Shane Halter	14
	Jose Iglesias	14
	Gerald Laird	14
	Luis Salazar	14
013	Alan Trammell	13
014	Roger Cedeno	12

Omar Infante

Rank	Player	Bunt Hits
	Austin Jackson	12
016	Kimera Bartee	11
	Damion Easley	11
	Gary Pettis	11
019	Brian Hunter	10
020	Juan Encarnacion	9
	Ian Kinsler	9
	Jose Macias	9
023	Ryan Raburn	8
	Victor Reyes	8
	Andres Torres	8
025	Andy Dirks	7
	Anthony Gose	7
	Curtis Granderson	7

Rank	Player	Bunt Hits
	Chad Kreuter	7
	Wendell Magee	7
	Leonys Martin	7
	Placido Polanco	7
033	Quintin Berry	6
	Carlos Guillen	6
	Bryan Holaday	6
036	Brad Ausmus	5
	Skeeter Barnes	5
	Deivi Cruz	5
	Mike Heath	5
	Brandon Inge	5
	Jim Walewander	5
042	Danny Bautista	4

Gerald Laird

Rank	Player	Bunt Hits
	Dave Bergman	4
	Rajai Davis	4
	Junior Felix	4
	James McCann	4
	Johnny Paredes	4
	Curtis Pride	4
	Will Rhymes	4
	Ronny Rodriguez	4
051	Josh Anderson	3
	Mike Brumley	3
	Chad Curtis	3
	Alexis Gomez	3
	Bobby Higginson	3
	Torii Hunter	3

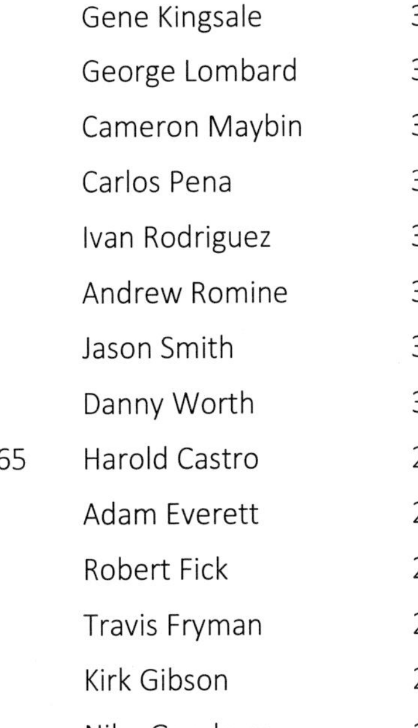

Rank	Player	Bunt Hits
	Gene Kingsale	3
	George Lombard	3
	Cameron Maybin	3
	Carlos Pena	3
	Ivan Rodriguez	3
	Andrew Romine	3
	Jason Smith	3
	Danny Worth	3
065	Harold Castro	2
	Adam Everett	2
	Robert Fick	2
	Travis Fryman	2
	Kirk Gibson	2
	Niko Goodrum	2

Roger Cedeno

Rank	Player	Bunt Hits
	John Hicks	2
	Tracy Jones	2
	Don Kelly	2
	Dan Klassen	2
	Chet Lemon	2
	Victor Martinez	2
	John McDonald	2
	Warren Morris	2
	Lloyd Moseby	2
	Edgar Renteria	2
	Pat Sheridan	2
	Clete Thomas	2
83	33 Hitters	1

Rank	Player	At Bats
001	Gates Brown	423
002	Dave Bergman	213
003	Pat Mullin	181
004	Lou Whitaker	148
005	Norm Cash	140
006	Bob Fothergill	131
007	Charlie Maxwell	122
008	Jo-Jo White	121
009	Al Kaline	119
010	Al Wingo	116
011	Jake Wood	115
012	John Wockenfuss	112
013	Vic Wertz	103
014	Larry Herndon	101
015	Mickey Stanley	100
016	John Grubb	97
	Bobo Osborne	97
018	George Mullin	94
019	Jim Northrup	92
020	Neil Chrisley	87
021	Dalton Jones	81
022	Kirk Gibson	79
023	Jim Price	78
	Larry Woodall	78
025	Charlie Gehringer	76
026	Pinky Hargrave	75
	Bud Souchock	75
028	Ike Brown	74
029	Chick Shorten	73
030	Ben Oglivie	72
031	Willie Horton	71
032	Darrell Evans	70
	Fred Hutchinson	70
034	Ryan Raburn	67
035	Ira Flagstead	66
036	Johnny Neun	65
	Gus Zernial	65
038	Tim Corcoran	64
039	Frank Catalanotto	61
	Charlie Keller	61
041	Bill Freehan	60
	Jerry Lumpe	60
	Dick McAuliffe	60
044	Davy Jones	59
	Bubba Morton	59
	Johnny Pesky	59
047	Harry Heilmann	57
048	Sam Crawford	56
	Rip Radcliff	56
	Alan Trammell	56
051	George Uhle	55

Dave Bergman

Rank	Player	At Bats
052	Sammy Hale	54
053	Heinie Manush	53
	Matt Nokes	53
	Ramon Santiago	53
	Champ Summers	53
057	Wayne Belardi	52
	Don Kelly	52
	Marcus Thames	52
060	Ty Cobb	51
	Kevin Collins	51
	Pete Fox	51
	Johnny Groth	51
	Chet Lemon	51
065	Billy Bruton	50
	Lynn Jones	50
	Don Kolloway	50
	Don Ross	50
069	Skeeter Barnes	49
070	George Thomas	48
071	Don Demeter	47
	Earl Torgeson	47
073	Alex Avila	46
	Gary Ward	46
075	Barbaro Garbey	45
	Pat Sheridan	45
	Dick Wakefield	45
078	Sandy Amoros	44
	George Harper	44
	Bobby Higginson	44
	Gee Walker	44
082	Johnny Bassler	43
	Rick Leach	43
084	Tom Brookens	42
	Bubba Phillips	42
	Curtis Pride	42
087	Doc Cramer	40
	Fred Hatfield	40
	Frank House	40
090	Roy Cullenbine	39
	Jim Delsing	39
	Gail Harris	39
	Hugh High	39
	Wendell Magee	39
	Dan Meyer	39
	Tony Taylor	39
097	Earl Averill	38
098	Mike Heath	37
099	Danny Clark	36
	Ned Harris	36
	Richie Hebner	36
	Aurelio Rodriguez	36

Rank	Player	Pinch Hits
001	Gates Brown	106
002	Dave Bergman	41
003	Jo-Jo White	38
004	Bob Fothergill	37
	Al Kaline	37
006	Lou Whitaker	36
	Pat Mullin	36
008	Charlie Maxwell	33
009	Norm Cash	29
	Larry Herndon	29
	John Wockenfuss	29
012	Al Wingo	28
013	Mickey Stanley	27
014	Vic Wertz	26
015	John Grubb	25
	Larry Woodall	25
017	Dalton Jones	24
018	Jake Wood	23
019	Chick Shorten	21
	Gus Zernial	21
021	Harry Heilmann	20
	Heinie Manush	20
023	Charlie Gehringer	19
	Kirk Gibson	19
	Pinky Hargrave	19
	George Mullin	19
	Jim Northrup	19
	Bud Souchock	19
029	Darrell Evans	18
	Sammy Hale	18
	Charlie Keller	18
	Johnny Neun	18
	Ben Oglivie	18
	Johnny Pesky	18
035	Willie Horton	17
	Fred Hutchinson	17
037	Tim Corcoran	16
	Johnny Groth	16
	Chet Lemon	16
	Bubba Morton	16
	Bobo Osborne	16
	Marcus Thames	16
	Earl Torgeson	16
044	Ike Brown	15
	Frank Catalanotto	15
	Sam Crawford	15
	Neil Chrisley	15
	Bill Freehan	15
	Dick McAuliffe	15
	Ramon Santiago	15
051	Billy Bruton	14
	Tommy Matchick	14
	Champ Summers	14

Charlie Keller

Rank	Player	Pinch Hits
	Alan Trammell	14
055	Kevin Collins	13
	Don Kolloway	13
	Jim Price	13
	Bobby Veach	13
	Dick Wakefield	13
060	Ty Cobb	12
	Don Demeter	12
	Ira Flagstead	12
	Fred Hatfield	12
	Lynn Jones	12
	Wendell Magee	12
066	Roy Cullenbine	11
	Earl Averill	11
	Alex Avila	11
	Les Burke	11
	Barbaro Garbey	11
	Ned Harris	11
	Bobby Higginson	11
	Jack Phillips	11
	Ryan Raburn	11
	Gee Walker	11
	Gary Ward	11
077	Skeeter Barnes	10
	Wayne Belardi	10
	Doc Cramer	10
	Jim Delsing	10
	Fred Haney	10
	Richie Hebner	10
	Don Kelly	10
	Victor Martinez	10
	Matt Nokes	10
	Dave Philley	10
	Rip Radcliff	10
	Boss Schmidt	10
	Jim Small	10
	Tony Taylor	10
	George Uhle	10
092	Sandy Amoros	9
	Tom Brookens	9
	Andy Dirks	9
	Pete Fox	9
	George Harper	9
	Gail Harris	9
	Mike Heath	9
	Frank House	9
	Davy Jones	9
	Rick Leach	9
	Dan Meyer	9
	Bob Nieman	9
	Billy Rhiel	9
	Aurelio Rodriguez	9
	George Thomas	9

ALL TIME TIGER HITTING LEADERS – PINCH HIT BATTING AVERAGE (MINIMUM 10 AT-BATS)

Rank	Player	Avg
001	Red Kress	.700
002	Chad Kreuter	.583
003	Bill Taylor	.500
004	Fred Payne	.462
005	Johnny Damon	.455
	Aaron Robinson	.455
007	Bobby Veach	.433
008	Ryan Jackson	.429
	Dick Kryhoski	.429
010	Mike Laga	.417
	Tony Phillips	.417
	Del Pratt	.417
013	Les Burke	.407
014	Ruppert Jones	.400
	Tommy Matchick	.400
	Phil Nevin	.400
	Dave Philley	.400
018	Jack Phillips	.393
019	James McCann	.381
020	Heinie Manush	.377
021	Sean Casey	.375
	Billy Rhiel	.375
023	Boss Schmidt	.370
024	Danny Bautista	.364
	Lu Blue	.364
	Tito Francona	.364
	Schoolboy Rowe	.364
	Ira Thomas	.364
	Vance Wilson	.364
030	Paul Campbell	.353
	Andrew Romine	.353
032	Harry Heilmann	.351
033	Earl Torgeson	.340
034	Bob Adams	.333
	Miguel Cabrera	.333
	Frank Carswell	.333
	Jack Dittmer	.333
	Sammy Hale	.333
	Brandon Inge	.333
	Paul Jata	.333
	Mark Koenig	.333
	Alejandro Sanchez	.333
	Joe Small	.333
044	Victor Martinez	.323
	Gus Zernial	.323
046	Larry Woodall	.321
047	Harold Castro	.320
048	Bruce Campbell	.318
049	Marty McManus	.316
	Dmitri Young	.316

Red Kress

Rank	Player	Avg
051	Johnny Groth	.314
	Chet Lemon	.314
	Jo-Jo White	.314
054	Kimera Bartee	.313
	Alex Johnson	.313
	Jeff Larish	.313
	Rusty Kuntz	.313
058	Al Kaline	.311
059	Alexis Gomez	.308
	Wendell Magee Jr.	.308
	Marcus Thames	.308
	Bill Tuttle	.308
063	Ned Harris	.306
064	Johnny Pesky	.305
065	Mickey Tettleton	.304
066	Matt Batts	.300
	Walt Dropo	.300
	Avisail Garcia	.300
	Cesar Gutierrez	.300
	Fred Hatfield	.300
	Warren Morris	.300
	Harry Spilman	.300
	Casper Wells	.300
	Glenn Wilson	.300
075	Dalton Jones	.296
076	Charlie Keller	.295
077	Victor Reyes	.294
078	Jose Macias	.292
079	Earl Averill	.289
	Dick Wakefield	.289
081	Chick Shorten	.288
082	Larry Herndon	.287
083	Fred Haney	.286
	Ted Lepcio	.286
	Matt Tuiasosopo	.286
086	Ramon Santiago	.283
087	Roy Cullenbine	.282
	Bob Fothergill	.282
089	Billy Bruton	.280
090	Curtis Granderson	.278
	Richie Hebner	.278
	Steve Kemp	.278
	Chick Lathers	.278
	Billy McMillon	.278
	Luis Polonia	.278
	Chris Shelton	.278
097	Johnny Neun	.277
098	Juan Samuel	.276
099	Andy Dirks	.273
	Purnal Goldy	.273
	Aubrey Huff	.273
	Bob Nieman	.273

001	Gates Brown	16
002	Norm Cash	8
003	John Grubb	7
004	John Wockenfuss	6
005	Charlie Maxwell	5
	Marcus Thames	5
007	Larry Herndon	4
	Ryan Raburn	4
	Vic Wertz	4
	Gus Zernial	4
011	Tyler Collins	3
	Kirk Gibson	3
	Bobby Higginson	3
	Frank Howard	3
	Heinie Manush	3
	Victor Martinez	3
	Dick McAuliffe	3
	Ben Oglivie	3
	Champ Summers	3
	Dick Wakefield	3
020	Dave Bergman	2
	Ike Brown	2
	Frank Catalanotto	2
	Kevin Collins	2
	Andy Dirks	2
	Zeb Eaton	2
	Darrell Evans	2
	Gail Harris	2
	Ned Harris	2
	Fred Hatfield	2
	Bob Hazle	2
	Richie Hebner	2
	John Hicks	2
	Willie Horton	2
	Frank House	2
	Al Kaline	2
	Don Kolloway	2
	Chet Laabs	2
	Jose Macias	2
	J.D. Martinez	2
	Dan Meyer	2
	Pat Mullin	2
	Phil Nevin	2
	Jim Northrup	2
	Jim Price	2
	Alejandro Sanchez	2
	John Shelby	2
	Mickey Stanley	2
	George Thomas	2
	Earl Torgeson	2
	Lou Whitaker	2
	Earl Wilson	2
052	Bob Adams	1
	Sandy Amoros	1
	Alex Avila	1
	Kimera Bartee	1
	Matt Batts	1
	Danny Bautista	1
	Rich Becker	1
	Wayne Belardi	1
	Ray Boone	1
	Tom Brookens	1
	Bruce Campbell	1
	Paul Campbell	1
	Danny Clark	1
	Wayne Comer	1
	Tim Corcoran	1

Kevin Collins

	Sam Crawford	1
	Rob Deer	1
	Jim Delsing	1
	Don Demeter	1
	Brandon Dixon	1
	Walt Dropo	1
	Ira Flagstead	1
	Barbaro Garbey	1
	Charlie Gehringer	1
	Goose Goslin	1
	Robbie Grossman	1
	Johnny Groth	1
	Eric Haase	1
	Sammy Hale	1
	Pinky Hargrave	1
	Aubrey Huff	1
	Howard Johnson	1
	Dalton Jones	1
	Lynn Jones	1
	Ruppert Jones	1
	Don Kelly	1
	Red Kress	1
	Chad Kreuter	1
	Jim Landis	1
	Rick Leach	1
	Ron LeFlore	1
	Dawel Lugo	1
	Fred Lynn	1
	Wendell Magee	1
	Phil Mankowski	1
	Cliff Mapes	1
	Milt May	1
	James McCann	1
	Dutch Meyer	1
	Orlando Miller	1
	Craig Monroe	1
	Eric Munson	1
	Bob Nieman	1
	Melvin Nieves	1
	Lance Parrish	1
	Jhonny Peralta	1
	Johnny Pesky	1
	Bubba Phillips	1
	Tony Phillips	1
	Luis Polonia	1
	Curtis Pride	1
	Victor Reyes	1
	Aaron Robinson	1
	Aurelio Rodriguez	1
	Bill Roman	1
	Mark Salas	1
	Jarrod Saltalamacchia	1
	Ramon Santiago	1
	Larry Sheets	1
	Pat Sheridan	1
	Scott Sizemore	1
	Nelson Simmons	1
	Bud Souchock	1
	Billy Sullivan	1
	Mickey Tettleton	1
	Justin Thompson	1
	Andy Tomberlin	1
	Alan Trammell	1
	Matt Tuiasosopo	1
	Jerry Turner	1
	Al Unser	1
	Ozzie Virgil	1
	Al Wingo	1

Rank	Player	RBI
001	Gates Brown	73
002	Larry Herndon	31
003	Bob Fothergill	30
	Pat Mullin	30
	John Wockenfuss	30
006	Norm Cash	29
007	Kirk Gibson	28
	Lou Whitaker	28
	Al Wingo	28
010	Dave Bergman	27
	John Grubb	27
012	Charlie Maxwell	26
013	Charlie Keller	24
014	Al Kaline	23
015	Vic Wertz	20
016	Gus Zernial	19
017	Jo-Jo White	18
018	Jim Northrup	16
019	Pinky Hargrave	15
	Heinie Manush	15
	Bud Souchock	15
022	Darrell Evans	14
	Ben Oglivie	14
	Marcus Thames	14
	Larry Woodall	14
026	Ty Cobb	13
	Barbaro Garbey	13
	Johnny Groth	13
	Willie Horton	13
	Dick McAuliffe	13
	Bubba Morton	13
	Bobo Osborne	13
	George Uhle	13
034	Skeeter Barnes	12
	Harry Heilmann	12
	Don Kolloway	12
	Chet Lemon	12
	Gary Ward	12
039	Billy Bruton	11
	Charlie Gehringer	11
	Mickey Stanley	11
	Earl Torgeson	11
	Dick Wakefield	11
044	Ike Brown	10
	Jim Delsing	10
	Goose Goslin	10
	Howard Johnson	10
	Dalton Jones	10
	Marty McManus	10
	Jim Price	10
	Champ Summers	10

Larry Herndon

Rank	Player	RBI
	Jake Wood	10
053	Alex Avila	9
	Ray Boone	9
	Frank Catalanotto	9
	Tim Corcoran	9
	Andy Dirks	9
	Frank House	9
	Fred Hutchinson	9
	Ryan Raburn	9
	Pat Sheridan	9
	Alan Trammell	9
063	Earl Averill	8
	Tom Brookens	8
	Danny Clark	8
	Tyler Collins	8
	Don Demeter	8
	Richie Hebner	8
	Lynn Jones	8
	Chad Kreuter	8
	Fred Lynn	8
	Tommy Matchick	8
	Matt Nokes	8
	Schoolboy Rowe	8
	Chick Shorten	8
	Bobby Veach	8
077	Sandy Amoros	7
	Lu Blue	7
	Neil Chrisley	7
	Kevin Collins	7
	Doc Cramer	7
	Robert Fick	7
	Pete Fox	7
	Sammy Hale	7
	Fred Haney	7
	Bobby Higginson	7
	Wendell Magee Jr.	7
	Victor Martinez	7
	Jay Porter	7
	Franklin Stubbs	7
	Tony Taylor	7
	Mickey Tettleton	7
	Matt Tuiasosopo	7
094	Johnny Bassler	6
	Bruce Campbell	6
	Mickey Cochrane	6
	Roy Cullenbine	6
	Zeb Eaton	6
	Gail Harris	6
	Jose Macias	6
	Clyde Manion	6
	Phil Mankowski	6
	Dan Meyer	6
	Lance Parrish	6

Rank	Pitcher	Games
001	John Hiller	545
002	Hooks Dauss	538
003	Mickey Lolich	508
004	Dizzy Trout	493
005	Mike Henneman	491
006	Todd Jones	480
007	Hal Newhouser	460
008	George Mullin	435
009	Jack Morris	430
010	Tommy Bridges	424
011	Justin Verlander	380
012	Willie Hernandez	358
013	Aurelio Lopez	355
014	Hank Aguirre	334
015	Jamie Walker	327
016	Earl Whitehill	325
017	Virgil Trucks	316
018	Fernando Rodney	308
019	Dan Petry	306
020	Jim Bunning	304
	Frank Lary	304
022	Phil Coke	299
023	Al Benton	296
024	Paul Foytack	285
025	Vic Sorrell	280
026	Hal White	273
027	Bill Donovan	261
028	Frank Tanana	250
029	Alex Wilson	246
030	Matt Anderson	245
	Schoolboy Rowe	245
032	Shane Greene	243
033	Fred Hutchinson	242
034	Al Alburquerque	241
	Buck Farmer	241
036	Doug Brocail	240
037	Billy Hoeft	239
038	Joe Jimenez	235
039	Milt Wilcox	234
040	Blaine Hardy	233
041	Ken Holloway	232
042	Ed Willett	230
043	Denny McLain	227
044	Jose Valverde	226
045	Chief Hogsett	223
046	Jeremy Bonderman	218
047	Fred Gladding	217
	Lil Stoner	217
049	Walt Terrell	216
050	Paul Gibson	214

C.J. Nitkowski

Rank	Pitcher	Games
051	C.J. Nitkowski	213
052	Fred Scherman	212
053	Ted Gray	208
	Dave Rozema	208
055	Terry Fox	207
056	Art Houtteman	206
057	Joaquin Benoit	205
	Ed Killian	205
059	Johnny Gorsica	204
060	Joe Coleman	203
061	Bernie Boland	202
062	Bobby Seay	199
063	Nate Robertson	196
064	Elden Auker	195
	Stubby Overmire	195
	Tom Timmerman	195
067	Howard Ehmke	186
068	Jean Dubuc	184
	Rick Porcello	184
070	Mike Myers	182
071	Danny Patterson	180
072	Joe Sparma	174
073	Joel Zumaya	171
074	Phil Regan	170
075	Max Scherzer	161
076	Daniel Stumpf	159
077	Al Aber	158
078	Harry Coveleski	157
	Zach Miner	157
080	Larry Sherry	152
081	Don Mossi	151
	Anibal Sanchez	151
083	Ryan Perry	149
	Earl Wilson	149
085	Red Oldham	148
	Dave Wickersham	148
087	Matt Boyd	147
	Mike Maroth	147
089	John Doherty	145
090	Ed Siever	143
091	Steve Gromek	138
	Ed Summers	138
093	Bert Cole	137
	Rip Collins	137
	Michael Fulmer	137
	Dave Tobik	137
097	Jose Cisnero	131
	Brian Moehler	131
	Chris Spurling	131
100	Steve Sparks	129

Rank	Pitcher	Wins
001	Hooks Dauss	223
002	George Mullin	209
003	Mickey Lolich	207
004	Hal Newhouser	200
005	Jack Morris	198
006	Tommy Bridges	194
007	Justin Verlander	183
008	Dizzy Trout	161
009	Bill Donovan	140
010	Earl Whitehill	133
011	Frank Lary	123
012	Dan Petry	119
013	Jim Bunning	118
014	Denny McLain	117
015	Virgil Trucks	114
016	Schoolboy Rowe	105
017	Ed Killian	100
018	Milt Wilcox	97
019	Frank Tanana	96
	Ed Willett	96
021	Fred Hutchinson	95
022	Vic Sorrell	92
023	Joe Coleman	88
024	John Hiller	87
025	Max Scherzer	82
026	Paul Foytack	81
027	Walt Terrell	79
028	Elden Auker	77
029	Rick Porcello	76
030	Howard Ehmke	75
031	Billy Hoeft	74
032	Jean Dubuc	72
033	Al Benton	71
034	Harry Coveleski	69
035	Jeremy Bonderman	68
	Ed Summers	68
037	Bernie Boland	67
038	Hank Aguirre	64
	Earl Wilson	64
040	Ed Siever	60
041	Don Mossi	59
042	Ted Gray	58
043	Mike Henneman	57
	Ken Holloway	57
	Dave Rozema	57
046	Art Houtteman	53
	Aurelio Lopez	53
048	Joe Sparma	52
049	Bill Gullickson	51
	Nate Robertson	51

Hooks Dauss

Rank	Pitcher	Wins
051	Mike Maroth	50
	Bobo Newsom	50
	Lil Stoner	50
054	Dutch Leonard	49
055	Brian Moehler	48
056	Stubby Overmire	47
057	Anibal Sanchez	46
058	Steve Gromek	45
059	Rip Collins	44
	George Uhle	44
061	Phil Regan	42
062	Hal White	40
	Dave Wickersham	40
064	Chief Hogsett	39
	Jeff Weaver	39
066	Ned Garver	38
	Roxie Lawson	38
068	Matt Boyd	37
	Ownie Carroll	37
070	Willie Hernandez	36
	Frank Kitson	36
	Jeff Robinson	36
	Justin Thompson	36
074	Bill James	35
075	Red Oldham	34
	Herman Pillette	34
077	John Doherty	32
	Doug Fister	32
079	Johnny Gorsica	31
	Firpo Marberry	31
081	Willie Blair	30
082	Doyle Alexander	29
	Mark Fidrych	29
	Michael Fulmer	29
	Roscoe Miller	29
	Mike Moore	29
	Kenny Rogers	29
	Steve Sparks	29
089	Sam Gibson	28
090	Bert Cole	26
	Terry Fox	26
	Fred Gladding	26
	Tom Timmermann	26
	David Wells	26
095	Juan Berenguer	25
	Jack Billingham	25
	General Crowder	25
	Eric King	25
	Zach Miner	25
	Vern Ruhle	25
	Fred Scherman	25
	Jordan Zimmermann	25

001	Hooks Dauss	182
002	George Mullin	179
003	Mickey Lolich	175
004	Dizzy Trout	153
005	Jack Morris	150
006	Hal Newhouser	148
007	Tommy Bridges	138
008	Earl Whitehill	119
009	Justin Verlander	114
010	Frank Lary	110
011	Vic Sorrell	101
012	Bill Donovan	96
	Virgil Trucks	96
014	Dan Petry	93
015	Jim Bunning	87
016	Frank Tanana	82
017	Paul Foytack	81
018	Ed Willett	80
019	Jeremy Bonderman	78
	Billy Hoeft	78
021	John Hiller	76
	Walt Terrell	76
023	Howard Ehmke	75
	Milt Wilcox	75
025	Ed Killian	74
026	Joe Coleman	73
027	Ted Gray	72
028	Fred Hutchinson	71
029	Art Houtteman	69
030	Nate Robertson	68
031	Hank Aguirre	64
	Al Benton	64
033	Rick Porcello	63
034	Mike Maroth	62
	Denny McLain	62
	Schoolboy Rowe	62
037	Matt Boyd	60
	Jean Dubuc	60
038	Lil Stoner	57
039	Ed Siever	53
040	Elden Auker	52
	Brian Moehler	52
043	Jeff Weaver	51
044	Dutch Leonard	50
045	Bernie Boland	49
	Anibal Sanchez	49
	Hal White	49
048	Joe Sparma	48
049	Chief Hogsett	47
050	Ken Holloway	46
	Dave Rozema	46

Johnny Gorsica

052	Stubby Overmire	45
	Ed Summers	45
	Earl Wilson	45
055	Don Mossi	44
	Red Oldham	44
	Phil Regan	44
058	Harry Coveleski	43
	Frank Kitson	43
	Justin Thompson	43
061	Ownie Carroll	42
062	Steve Gromek	41
	George Uhle	41
	Jordan Zimmermann	41
065	Rip Collins	40
	Ned Garver	40
	Lerrin LaGrow	40
068	Michael Fulmer	39
	Johnny Gorsica	39
069	Bill Gullickson	36
	Bill James	36
	Steve Sparks	36
072	Bobo Newsom	35
	Max Scherzer	35
074	Mike Henneman	34
	Felipe Lira	34
	Mike Moore	34
	Dave Wickersham	34
078	Daniel Norris	33
079	Todd Jones	32
	Jose Lima	32
	Herman Pillette	32
082	John Doherty	31
	Willie Hernandez	31
	Dave Mlicki	31
085	Aurelio Lopez	30
	Fernando Rodney	30
088	Doyle Alexander	29
	Willie Blair	29
	Nate Cornejo	29
	Sam Gibson	29
	Vern Ruhle	29
093	Jason Johnson	28
	Ed Wells	28
095	Bert Cole	27
	Duke Maas	27
	Dave Roberts	27
	Tom Timmermann	27
099	Armando Galarraga	26
	Jeff Robinson	26

Rank	Pitcher	Pct
001	Max Scherzer	.701
002	Denny McLain	.654
003	Firpo Marberry	.646
004	Aurelio Lopez	.639
005	Schoolboy Rowe	.629
006	Mike Henneman	.626
007	Jack Billingham	.625
	Fred Scherman	.625
009	Harry Coveleski	.616
	Justin Verlander	.616
011	Doug Fister	.615
012	Terry Fox	.605
013	Mark Fidrych	.604
014	Roxie Lawson	.603
015	Ed Summers	.602
016	Syl Johnson	.600
017	Elden Auker	.597
018	Bill Donovan	.593
019	Bobo Newsom	.588
020	Earl Wilson	.587
021	Bill Gullickson	.586
022	Tommy Bridges	.584
023	Jeff Robinson	.581
024	Bernie Boland	.578
	David Wells	.578
026	Jim Bunning	.576
027	Ed Killian	.575
	Hal Newhouser	.575
029	Don Mossi	.573
030	Fred Hutchinson	.572
031	Jack Morris	.569
032	Milt Wilcox	.564
033	Mark Leiter	.561
	Dan Petry	.561
035	Eric King	.556
	Zach Miner	.556
037	Ken Holloway	.553
	Dave Rozema	.553
039	Hooks Dauss	.551
040	Les Cain	.548
041	Joe Coleman	.547
	Rick Porcello	.547
043	Jean Dubuc	.545
	Ed Willett	.545
045	Juan Berenguer	.543
	Virgil Trucks	.543
	Mickey Lolich	.542
048	Dave Wickersham	.541
049	George Mullin	.539
	Frank Tanana	.539
051	Willie Hernandez	.537
	Roscoe Miller	.537
	Kenny Rogers	.537
054	John Hiller	.534
055	Ed Siever	.531
056	Frank Lary	.528
	Earl Whitehill	.528
058	Al Benton	.526
059	Rip Collins	.524
060	Steve Gromek	.523
061	Joe Sparma	.520
062	George Uhle	.518
063	Herman Pillette	.515
064	Dizzy Trout	.513
065	Stubby Overmire	.511
	Ralph Works	.511
067	Walt Terrell	.510
068	Willie Blair	.508
	John Doherty	.508
070	Hank Aguirre	.500
	Doyle Alexander	.500
	Howard Ehmke	.500
	Paul Foytack	.500
074	Dutch Leonard	.495
075	Bill James	.493
076	Bert Cole	.491
	Sam Gibson	.491
	Tom Timmermann	.491
079	Joe Niekro	.488
	Phil Regan	.488
081	Ned Garver	.487
	Billy Hoeft	.487
083	Anibal Sanchez	.484
084	Brian Moehler	.480
085	Al Aber	.478
086	Vic Sorrell	.477
087	Armando Galarraga	.469
088	Ownie Carroll	.468
	Woodie Fryman	.468
090	Lil Stoner	.467
091	Jeremy Bonderman	.466
092	Vern Ruhle	.463
093	Ed Wells	.462
094	Mike Moore	.460
095	Frank Kitson	.456
	Justin Thompson	.456
097	Chief Hogsett	.453
098	Hal White	.449
099	Ted Gray	.446
	Mike Maroth	.446
	Steve Sparks	.446

Max Scherzer

Rank	Name	Innings
001	George Mullin	3,394.0
002	Hooks Dauss	3,390.2
003	Mickey Lolich	3,361.2
004	Jack Morris	3,042.2
005	Hal Newhouser	2,944.0
006	Tommy Bridges	2,826.1
007	Dizzy Trout	2,591.2
008	Justin Verlander	2,511.0
009	Earl Whitehill	2,171.1
010	Bill Donovan	2,137.1
011	Frank Lary	2,008.2
012	Jim Bunning	1,867.1
013	Dan Petry	1,843.0
014	Virgil Trucks	1,800.2
015	Vic Sorrell	1,671.2
016	Denny McLain	1,593.0
017	Frank Tanana	1,551.1
018	Ed Willett	1,545.2
019	Ed Killian	1,536.2
020	Milt Wilcox	1,495.1
021	Fred Hutchinson	1,464.0
022	Schoolboy Rowe	1,445.0
023	Paul Foytack	1,425.1
024	Joe Coleman	1,407.2
025	Walt Terrell	1,328.0
026	Billy Hoeft	1,324.2
027	John Hiller	1,242.0
028	Howard Ehmke	1,236.1
029	Al Benton	1,218.2
030	Jeremy Bonderman	1,192.2
031	Hank Aguirre	1,179.0
032	Jean Dubuc	1,145.0
033	Ted Gray	1,110.2
034	Elden Auker	1,083.2
035	Art Houtteman	1,076.1
036	Rick Porcello	1,073.1
037	Nate Robertson	1,042.2
038	Ed Siever	1,036.0
039	Bernie Boland	1,035.0
040	Harry Coveleski	1,023.1
041	Max Scherzer	1,013.0
042	Dave Rozema	1,007.1
043	Ed Summers	999.0
044	Lil Stoner	984.1
045	Ken Holloway	976.2
046	Earl Wilson	962.1
047	Don Mossi	929.2
048	Mike Maroth	880.0
049	Joe Sparma	835.1
050	Dutch Leonard	830.2
	Stubby Overmire	830.2

Mike Maroth

Rank	Name	Innings
052	George Uhle	828.1
053	Hal White	820.1
054	Brian Moehler	809.0
055	Anibal Sanchez	798.1
056	Matt Boyd	777.2
057	Bobo Newsom	760.1
058	Red Oldham	759.2
059	Phil Regan	746.2
060	Rip Collins	742.0
061	Chief Hogsett	738.1
062	Steve Gromek	724.0
063	Johnny Gorsica	723.2
064	Bill Gullickson	722.2
065	Jeff Weaver	714.2
066	Aurelio Lopez	713.0
067	Ned Garver	702.0
068	Frank Kitson	683.0
069	Dave Wickersham	675.1
070	Mike Henneman	669.2
071	Ownie Carroll	666.0
072	Justin Thompson	647.0
073	Steve Sparks	614.2
074	Herman Pillette	562.2
075	Michael Fulmer	553.1
076	Bill James	548.0
077	Doyle Alexander	540.1
078	Roxie Lawson	539.2
079	Jeff Robinson	522.1
080	John Doherty	515.0
081	Jordan Zimmermann	514.1
082	Sam Gibson	500.2
	Mike Moore	500.2
084	Bert Cole	495.0
085	Willie Blair	489.2
086	Vern Ruhle	489.0
087	Willie Hernandez	483.2
088	Roscoe Miller	480.2
089	Todd Jones	479.1
090	George Cunningham	477.0
091	Lerrin LaGrow	474.1
092	Ralph Works	474.0
093	Armando Galarraga	466.2
094	Daniel Norris	460.2
095	Ed Wells	445.1
096	Doug Fister	440.2
	Kenny Rogers	440.2
098	Felipe Lira	436.1
099	David Wells	428.2
100	Juan Berenguer	427.2

ALL TIME TIGER PITCHING LEADERS – HITS ALLOWED

001	Hooks Dauss	3,407
002	George Mullin	3,206
003	Mickey Lolich	3,093
004	Jack Morris	2,767
005	Tommy Bridges	2,675
006	Hal Newhouser	2,639
007	Dizzy Trout	2,504
008	Earl Whitehill	2,329
009	Justin Verlander	2,225
010	Frank Lary	1,975
011	Bill Donovan	1,862
012	Vic Sorrell	1,820
013	Dan Petry	1,742
014	Jim Bunning	1,692
015	Virgil Trucks	1,618
016	Frank Tanana	1,578
017	Schoolboy Rowe	1,521
018	Fred Hutchinson	1,487
019	Ed Willett	1,450
020	Milt Wilcox	1,443
021	Ed Killian	1,402
022	Walt Terrell	1,379
023	Billy Hoeft	1,331
024	Joe Coleman	1,326
025	Denny McLain	1,321
026	Paul Foytack	1,309
027	Jeremy Bonderman	1,263
028	Howard Ehmke	1,232
029	Elden Auker	1,207
	Al Benton	1,207
031	Rick Porcello	1,196
032	Ken Holloway	1,151
	Lil Stoner	1,151
034	Nate Robertson	1,149
035	Art Houtteman	1,123
036	Ed Siever	1,070
037	John Hiller	1,040
038	Ted Gray	1,034
039	Hank Aguirre	1,031
040	Jean Dubuc	1,026
041	Mike Maroth	1,007
042	Dave Rozema	1,006
043	Ed Summers	930
044	Don Mossi	910
045	Max Scherzer	908
046	Stubby Overmire	904
047	Brian Moehler	903
048	Bernie Boland	891
049	Dutch Leonard	888
050	Harry Coveleski	887
051	Chief Hogsett	881
052	George Uhle	866
053	Red Oldham	856
054	Earl Wilson	830
055	Bill Gullickson	826
056	Anibal Sanchez	807
057	Rip Collins	787
058	Matt Boyd	778
	Johnny Gorsica	778
060	Hal White	772
061	Phil Regan	771
062	Joe Sparma	740
063	Steve Gromek	731
064	Ownie Carroll	730
065	Jeff Weaver	728
066	Bobo Newsom	722
067	Ned Garver	719
068	Frank Kitson	718
069	Steve Sparks	685
070	Justin Thompson	629
071	Mike Henneman	624
072	Jordan Zimmermann	618
073	Dave Wickersham	614
074	Aurelio Lopez	609
075	John Doherty	605
076	Bert Cole	601
077	Herman Pillette	596
078	Roxie Lawson	587
079	Willie Blair	578
080	Doyle Alexander	568
081	Mike Moore	558
082	Sam Gibson	555
083	Ed Wells	547
084	Vern Ruhle	544
085	Michael Fulmer	528
086	Lerrin LaGrow	520
087	Bill James	500
088	Roscoe Miller	497
089	Todd Jones	493
	Ralph Works	493
091	Daniel Norris	488
092	Kenny Rogers	472
093	Dave Mlicki	470
	Jeff Robinson	470
095	Felipe Lira	463
096	Jason Johnson	455
097	Armando Galarraga	453
098	George Cunningham	444
099	Doug Fister	439
100	Firpo Marberry	428

Vic Sorrell

ALL TIME TIGER PITCHING LEADERS – HOME RUNS ALLOWED

Rank	Name	HR
001	Mickey Lolich	329
002	Jack Morris	321
003	Justin Verlander	240
004	Jim Bunning	223
005	Denny McLain	195
006	Dan Petry	187
007	Frank Tanana	182
008	Tommy Bridges	181
009	Frank Lary	180
010	Paul Foytack	165
011	Jeremy Bonderman	150
012	Nate Robertson	145
013	Milt Wilcox	143
014	Matt Boyd	137
015	Hal Newhouser	133
016	Joe Coleman	130
017	Billy Hoeft	129
018	Fred Hutchinson	127
019	Walt Terrell	126
020	Virgil Trucks	123
021	Mike Maroth	122
	Phil Regan	113
023	Hank Aguirre	111
	Rick Porcello	111
025	Ted Gray	110
	John Hiller	110
	Don Mossi	110
028	Bill Gullickson	109
	Dizzy Trout	109
030	Max Scherzer	108
	Earl Wilson	108
032	Anibal Sanchez	106
033	Earl Whitehill	105
034	Dave Rozema	102
035	Vic Sorrell	101
036	Brian Moehler	98
037	Steve Gromek	97
	Art Houtteman	97
039	Schoolboy Rowe	91
040	Jordan Zimmermann	90
041	Hooks Dauss	87
042	Aurelio Lopez	86
	Mike Moore	86
044	Al Benton	77
045	Jeff Weaver	76
046	Armando Galarraga	73
047	Justin Thompson	71
048	Willie Blair	70
	Joe Sparma	70
050	Jeff Robinson	68
051	Daniel Norris	67

Mark Leiter

Rank	Name	HR
052	Felipe Lira	64
053	Elden Auker	63
	Michael Fulmer	63
	Steve Sparks	63
056	Doyle Alexander	61
057	Ned Garver	60
	Jose Lima	60
	Dave Mlicki	60
	Lil Stoner	60
	Dave Wickersham	60
062	David Wells	56
063	Kenny Rogers	53
	George Uhle	53
065	Willie Hernandez	52
066	Buck Farmer	51
067	Roxie Lawson	49
068	Bobo Newsom	48
069	Pat Underwood	47
070	John Doherty	46
	Lerrin LaGrow	46
	Vern Ruhle	46
073	Juan Berenguer	45
	Woodie Fryman	45
	Jason Johnson	45
	C.J. Nitkowski	45
077	Johnny Gorsica	44
	Joe Niekro	44
	Tarik Skubal	44
080	Howard Ehmke	43
	Eric King	43
082	Mark Leiter	42
	Jerry Ujdur	42
084	Todd Jones	41
085	Mike Henneman	40
	Ken Holloway	40
087	Shane Greene	39
	Chief Hogsett	39
	Duke Maas	39
	Jamie Walker	39
	Hal White	39
092	Adam Bernero	38
	Nate Cornejo	38
	Dutch Leonard	38
095	Paul Gibson	37
	George Mullin	37
097	Dave Roberts	36
	Dan Schatzeder	36
099	Joe Jimenez	35
	Zach Miner	35
	Stubby Overmire	35
	Dave Tobik	35

Rank	Pitcher	Walks
001	Hal Newhouser	1,227
002	Tommy Bridges	1,192
003	George Mullin	1,106
004	Jack Morris	1,086
005	Hooks Dauss	1,067
006	Mickey Lolich	1,014
007	Dizzy Trout	978
008	Earl Whitehill	831
009	Justin Verlander	766
010	Dan Petry	744
011	Virgil Trucks	732
012	Vic Sorrell	706
013	Bill Donovan	685
014	Paul Foytack	631
015	Ted Gray	580
016	Frank Lary	579
017	Joe Coleman	576
018	Jim Bunning	564
019	Milt Wilcox	537
020	John Hiller	535
021	Frank Tanana	527
022	Howard Ehmke	516
	Walt Terrell	516
024	Al Benton	500
025	Ed Willett	491
026	Billy Hoeft	481
027	Ed Killian	469
028	Denny McLain	450
029	Jean Dubuc	448
030	Jeremy Bonderman	414
031	Joe Sparma	411
032	Bernie Boland	404
	Hal White	404
034	Schoolboy Rowe	403
035	Hank Aguirre	393
036	Fred Hutchinson	388
037	Elden Auker	378
038	Nate Robertson	374
039	Lil Stoner	366
040	Art Houtteman	351
041	Ken Holloway	338
042	Bobo Newsom	322
043	Roxie Lawson	316
044	Max Scherzer	305
045	Chief Hogsett	300
046	Earl Wilson	296
047	Aurelio Lopez	288
048	Ownie Carroll	283
	Bill James	283
050	Harry Coveleski	270

Tommy Bridges

Rank	Pitcher	Walks
051	Rick Porcello	263
052	Jeff Robinson	260
053	Phil Regan	258
054	Red Oldham	256
055	Dutch Leonard	252
056	Mike Henneman	250
057	Matt Boyd	247
	Johnny Gorsica	247
059	Mike Moore	246
060	Mike Maroth	245
061	Rip Collins	239
062	Justin Thompson	235
063	Stubby Overmire	234
064	Dave Rozema	233
065	Anibal Sanchez	230
066	Dave Wickersham	229
067	Brian Moehler	227
068	Les Cain	225
069	George Uhle	224
070	Ed Summers	221
071	Sam Gibson	213
072	Ned Garver	211
073	Jeff Weaver	209
074	Juan Berenguer	207
	Ed Siever	207
	Jake Wade	207
077	Todd Jones	205
078	Steve Sparks	194
079	Herman Pillette	192
	Ed Wells	192
081	Steve Gromek	190
082	Ralph Works	189
083	Bert Cole	186
084	Eric King	185
085	Paul Gibson	183
	C.J. Nitkowski	183
087	Lerrin LaGrow	181
	Don Mossi	181
089	Armando Galarraga	179
090	George Cunningham	178
091	Mike Kilkenny	177
092	Marlin Stuart	176
	Whit Wyatt	176
094	Fernando Rodney	170
095	Felipe Lira	169
	George Smith	169
097	Bill Gullickson	163
098	Woodie Fryman	162
099	Michael Fulmer	160
	Fred Scherman	160

Rank	Pitcher	Strikeouts
001	Mickey Lolich	2,679
002	Justin Verlander	2,373
003	Jack Morris	1,980
004	Hal Newhouser	1,770
005	Tommy Bridges	1,674
006	Jim Bunning	1,406
007	George Mullin	1,380
008	Hooks Dauss	1,201
009	Dizzy Trout	1,199
010	Denny McLain	1,150
011	Max Scherzer	1,081
012	Bill Donovan	1,079
013	Virgil Trucks	1,046
014	John Hiller	1,036
015	Frank Lary	1,031
016	Joe Coleman	1,000
017	Frank Tanana	958
018	Dan Petry	957
019	Jeremy Bonderman	945
020	Milt Wilcox	851
021	Earl Whitehill	838
022	Paul Foytack	789
023	Billy Hoeft	783
024	Hank Aguirre	755
028	Matt Boyd	752
025	Anibal Sanchez	738
026	Nate Robertson	709
	Earl Wilson	709
029	Ted Gray	676
030	Schoolboy Rowe	662
031	Rick Porcello	655
032	Walt Terrell	621
033	Vic Sorrell	619
034	Fred Hutchinson	591
035	Joe Sparma	563
036	Don Mossi	520
037	Aurelio Lopez	519

Rank	Pitcher	Strikeouts
038	Al Benton	510
039	Ed Willett	508
040	Bobo Newsom	503
041	Ed Killian	498
042	Mike Henneman	480
043	Jeff Weaver	477
044	Howard Ehmke	458
045	Art Houtteman	453
046	Michael Fulmer	449
046	Brian Moehler	446
047	Daniel Norris	428
047	Justin Thompson	427
048	Mike Maroth	420

Earl Whitehill

Rank	Pitcher	Strikeouts
049	Phil Regan	414
050	Dave Wickersham	410
051	Dave Rozema	403
052	Harry Coveleski	400
053	Dutch Leonard	389
055	Willie Hernandez	384
057	Todd Jones	372
058	Jordan Zimmermann	368
059	Ed Summers	362
060	Bernie Boland	358
061	Jean Dubuc	354
062	Doug Fister	353
063	Elden Auker	351
064	Juan Berenguer	337
065	George Uhle	332
066	Jeff Robinson	328
067	Steve Sparks	316
068	Fernando Rodney	314
069	Hal White	313
070	Steve Gromek	309
071	Les Cain	303
	Ed Siever	303
073	Lil Stoner	296
074	Armando Galarraga	295
075	David Wells	293
088	Buck Farmer	292
076	Shane Greene	290
	Bill Gullickson	290
078	Woodie Fryman	283
079	Al Alburquerque	276
080	Chief Hogsett	273
081	Johnny Gorsica	272
082	Felipe Lira	269
083	Doyle Alexander	265
084	Drew Smyly	264
085	Fred Gladding	262
086	Willie Blair	261
087	Eric King	258
088	Joe Jimenez	256
	Spencer Turnbull	256
089	Ned Garver	254
090	Tom Timmermann	251
091	Mike Kilkenny	249
	Frank Kitson	249
093	Mark Leiter	248
094	Phil Coke	244
095	Ken Holloway	242
096	Red Oldham	241
097	Paul Gibson	235
098	Doug Brocail	234
	C.J. Nitkowski	234

Rank	Pitcher	Balks
001	Jack Morris	23
002	Justin Verlander	17
003	Al Alburquerque	8
	Tommy Bridges	8
005	Hank Aguirre	7
	Paul Foytack	7
	Hal Newhouser	7
	Dizzy Trout	7
009	Matt Boyd	6
	Eric King	6
	Frank Lary	6
	Denny McLain	6
	Dave Rozema	6
	Anibal Sanchez	6
	Milt Wilcox	6
016	Jeremy Bonderman	5
	Jim Bunning	5
	Don Heinkel	5
	Willie Hernandez	5
	Wil Ledezma	5
	Mickey Lolich	5
	Red Oldham	5
	Daryl Patterson	5
	Dan Petry	5
	Rick Porcello	5
	Jeff Robinson	5
	Frank Tanana	5
	Virgil Trucks	5
029	Juan Berenguer	4
	Rip Collins	4
	Hooks Dauss	4
	Howard Ehmke	4
	Johnny Gorsica	4
	Aurelio Lopez	4
	Don Mossi	4
	C.J. Nitkowski	4
	Schoolboy Rowe	4
	Steve Sparks	4
	Earl Whitehill	4
040	Doc Ayers	3
	Jim Crawford	3
	Bill Faul	3
	Vic Frazier	3
	Armando Galarraga	3
	Paul Gibson	3
	Ken Holloway	3
	Nate Robertson	3
	Bruce Rondon	3
	Max Scherzer	3
	Ed Wells	3

Hank Aguirre

Rank	Pitcher	Balks
	Dave Wickersham	3
	Bill Wight	3
053	Scott Aldred	2
	Doyle Alexander	2
	Steve Baker	2
	Willie Blair	2
	Doug Brocail	2
	Pete Burnside	2
	Bob Cain	2
	Les Cain	2
	Ryan Carpenter	2
	Slick Coffman	2
	Bert Cole	2
	Joe Coleman	2
	Harry Coveleski	2
	Brian Dubois	2
	Woodie Fryman	2
	Michael Fulmer	2
	Ned Garver	2
	Franklyn German	2
	Jerry Don Gleaton	2
	Ted Gray	2
	Steve Grilli	2
	Buddy Groom	2
	Mike Henneman	2
	Fred Hutchinson	2
	Vern Kennedy	2
	Mike Kilkenny	2
	Ian Krol	2
	Roxie Lawson	2
	Bill Laxton	2
	Richie Lewis	2
	Brian Maxcy	2
	Bobo Newsom	2
	Orlando Pena	2
	Ryan Perry	2
	Herman Pillette	2
	Phil Regan	2
	Matt Roney	2
	Fred Scherman	2
	George Smith	2
	Joe Sparma	2
	Marlin Stuart	2
	Ed Summers	2
	Bob Sykes	2
	Walt Terrell	2
	George Uhle	2
	Jerry Ujdur	2
	Brayan Villarreal	2
	Jeff Weaver	2
	Earl Wilson	2

Rank	Pitcher	HBP
001	Hooks Dauss	121
002	George Mullin	115
003	Ed Willett	92
004	Mickey Lolich	91
005	Frank Lary	90
006	Justin Verlander	83
007	Jim Bunning	73
008	Ed Killian	66
009	Earl Whitehill	65
010	Bill Donovan	64
011	Howard Ehmke	60
012	Jeff Weaver	54
013	Joe Coleman	52
014	Milt Wilcox	51
015	Ed Summers	46
016	Harry Coveleski	45
017	Hank Aguirre	40
	Frank Tanana	40
019	Jeremy Bonderman	39
	Matt Boyd	39
	Steve Gromek	39
022	Dan Petry	38
023	Jean Dubuc	36
	Jack Morris	36
025	Tommy Bridges	35
	Rip Collins	35
	Ken Holloway	35
	Dave Wickersham	35
029	Virgil Trucks	33
030	Chief Hogsett	32
031	Billy Hoeft	31
	Rick Porcello	31
	Ed Siever	31
	Dizzy Trout	31
035	Mike Maroth	30
	Red Oldham	30
037	Max Scherzer	29
038	Elden Auker	28
	Michael Fulmer	28
	Ted Gray	28
	Bill James	28
	Lil Stoner	28
043	Bernie Boland	27
	Dutch Leonard	27
	Dave Rozema	27
046	Doug Fister	26
	Art Houtteman	26
	Nate Robertson	26
049	Steve Sparks	25
	Joe Sparma	25
	Walt Terrell	25
052	Herman Pillette	24
053	Ownie Carroll	23
	Frank Kitson	23
	Spencer Turnbull	23
056	Joe Jimenez	22
	Denny McLain	22
	Roscoe Miller	22
	C.J. Nitkowski	22
060	Buck Farmer	21
	Sam Gibson	21
	Dave Mlicki	21
063	Felipe Lira	20
	Vic Sorrell	20
065	Willie Mitchell	19
	Hal Newhouser	19
	Ole Olsen	19
	Fernando Rodney	19
	Kenny Rogers	19
070	John Doherty	18
	Shane Greene	18
	Greg Keagle	18
	Eric King	18
	Omar Olivares	18
	Anibal Sanchez	18
	Ralph Works	18
077	George Cunningham	17
	Johnny Gorsica	17
	Mike Henneman	17
	Jeff Robinson	17
	Jordan Zimmermann	17
082	Armando Galarraga	16
	Casey Mize	16
	Brian Moehler	16
	Phil Regan	16
	Jesse Stovall	16
087	Adam Bernero	15
	Jack Billingham	15
	George Boehler	15
	Bert Cole	15
	Paul Foytack	15
	Willie Hernandez	15
	Jose Lima	15
	Vern Ruhle	15
	George Uhle	15
096	Jack Cronin	14
	Woodie Fryman	14
	Art Herring	14
	Fred Hutchinson	14
	Fred Scherman	14

Red Oldham

Rank	Pitcher	IBB
001	Jack Morris	88
002	Mike Henneman	76
003	John Hiller	71
004	Dan Petry	66
005	Dizzy Trout	61
006	Mickey Lolich	60
	Frank Tanana	60
008	Walt Terrell	48
009	Hal Newhouser	45
010	Paul Gibson	40
	Virgil Trucks	40
012	Dave Rozema	39
013	Milt Wilcox	37
014	Billy Hoeft	36
	Aurelio Lopez	36
016	Tommy Bridges	35
017	Vic Sorrell	33
018	Jim Bunning	31
	Joe Coleman	31
	Ted Gray	31
	Frank Lary	31
022	John Doherty	28
	Paul Foytack	28
	Steve Gromek	28
025	Joe Boever	27
	Schoolboy Rowe	27
	Justin Verlander	27
028	Hank Aguirre	26
	Willie Hernandez	26
030	Fred Hutchinson	25
031	Jeremy Bonderman	24
	Hal White	24
033	Bill Gullickson	23
	Art Houtteman	23
	Fred Scherman	23
036	Phil Coke	22
	Johnny Gorsica	22
038	Todd Jones	21
	Mike Moore	21
040	Tom Timmermann	20
	Dave Tobik	20
042	Edwin Nunez	19
	Nate Robertson	19
	Fernando Rodney	19
045	Bobo Newsom	18
	Jeff Robinson	18
	Bill Scherrer	18

Walt Terrell

Rank	Pitcher	IBB
048	Ned Garver	17
	Fred Gladding	17
	Lerrin LaGrow	17
	David Wells	17
	Earl Wilson	17
053	Eric King	16
	Denny McLain	16
	C.J. Nitkowski	16
	Stubby Overmire	16
057	Matt Anderson	15
	Terry Fox	15
	Buddy Groom	15
	Bobby Seay	15
	Earl Whitehill	15
	Dave Wickersham	15
063	Jack Billingham	14
	Chief Hogsett	14
	Mark Leiter	14
	Rick Porcello	14
	Larry Sherry	14
068	Al Alburquerque	13
	Nate Cornejo	13
	Ray Herbert	13
	Duke Maas	13
	Alex Wilson	13
073	Al Aber	12
	Ray Bare	12
	Jim Crawford	12
	Pat Dobson	12
	Kurt Knudsen	12
	Les Lancaster	12
	Randy O'Neal	12
	Phil Regan	12
	Kevin Ritz	12
	A.J. Sager	12
	Joe Sparma	12
084	Elden Auker	11
	Doug Bair	11
	Sean Bergman	11
	Storm Davis	11
	Shane Greene	11
	Roxie Lawson	11
	Dave Lemanczyk	11
	Jose Lima	11
	Felipe Lira	11
	Orlando Pena	11
	Jamie Walker	11
	Joel Zumaya	11
096	15 Pitchers	10

Rank	Pitcher	WP
001	Jack Morris	155
002	Mickey Lolich	109
003	George Mullin	80
004	Justin Verlander	78
005	Dan Petry	68
006	Hal Newhouser	64
007	Tommy Bridges	59
008	Joe Coleman	56
009	Ed Willett	55
010	Jeremy Bonderman	49
011	Hooks Dauss	48
	Jean Dubuc	48
	Frank Tanana	48
014	Dizzy Trout	47
015	Virgil Trucks	42
016	Mike Henneman	41
	Frank Lary	41
	Rick Porcello	41
019	Milt Wilcox	40
020	John Hiller	39
021	Bill Donovan	38
	Max Scherzer	38
	Joe Sparma	38
024	Walt Terrell	36
025	Paul Foytack	33
	Jeff Robinson	33
027	Nate Robertson	32
	Anibal Sanchez	32
029	Dutch Leonard	29
030	Todd Jones	28
031	Aurelio Lopez	27
	Mike Maroth	27
	Mike Moore	27
034	Matt Boyd	26
	Jim Bunning	26
	Ted Gray	26
037	Al Benton	25
	Vic Sorrell	25
	Steve Sparks	25
	Earl Wilson	25
041	Billy Hoeft	24
	Jason Johnson	24
	David Wells	24
044	Lil Stoner	23
045	Ed Killian	22
	Lerrin LaGrow	22
	Denny McLain	22
	Dave Rozema	22
049	Hank Aguirre	21
050	Al Alburquerque	20
	Matt Anderson	20
	Jim Crawford	20
053	Rip Collins	19
	Fred Gladding	19
	Felipe Lira	19
	Larry Sherry	19

Dan Petry

Rank	Pitcher	WP
	Gregory Soto	19
	Ralph Works	19
059	Hal White	18
060	Sean Bergman	17
	Doug Brocail	17
	Les Cain	17
	Harry Coveleski	17
	Fernando Rodney	17
	Schoolboy Rowe	17
	Tom Timmermann	17
	Dave Wickersham	17
068	Bill Gullickson	16
	Fred Hutchinson	16
	Eric King	16
	Hideo Nomo	16
	Red Oldham	16
	Phil Regan	16
	Kevin Ritz	16
	George Uhle	16
	Joel Zumaya	16
077	Ownie Carroll	15
	George Cunningham	15
	Gary Knotts	15
	Ed Summers	15
	Drew VerHagen	15
082	Juan Berenguer	14
	Franklyn German	14
	Richie Lewis	14
	Brian Moehler	14
	Randy O'Neal	14
	Alfredo Simon	14
	Earl Whitehill	14
089	Steve Baker	13
	Willie Blair	13
	John Doherty	13
	Buck Farmer	13
	Bryce Florie	13
	Blaine Hardy	13
	Roxie Lawson	13
	Daniel Norris	13
	Daryl Patterson	13
098	Jack Billingham	12
	Phil Coke	12
	Ned Garver	12
	Paul Gibson	12
	Ray Herbert	12
	Art Houtteman	12
	Bill James	12
	Wil Ledezma	12
	Jose Lima	12
	Ryan Perry	12
	Herman Pillette	12
	Fred Scherman	12
	Dave Sisler	12
	Drew Smyly	12
	Whit Wyatt	12

001	Mickey Lolich	1,289
002	Jack Morris	1,262
003	Hooks Dauss	1,245
004	Tommy Bridges	1,122
005	George Mullin	1,042
006	Earl Whitehill	1,004
007	Hal Newhouser	1,003
008	Justin Verlander	975
009	Dizzy Trout	922
010	Vic Sorrell	823
011	Dan Petry	787
012	Frank Lary	772
013	Jim Bunning	715
014	Frank Tanana	703
015	Virgil Trucks	700
016	Paul Foytack	656
017	Jeremy Bonderman	651
018	Milt Wilcox	650
019	Schoolboy Rowe	644
020	Walt Terrell	629
021	Fred Hutchinson	606
022	Joe Coleman	597
023	Bill Donovan	591
024	Billy Hoeft	591
025	Nate Robertson	564
026	Denny McLain	554
027	Ted Gray	525
028	Lil Stoner	518
029	Elden Auker	513
	Rick Porcello	513
031	Ed Willett	497
032	Howard Ehmke	496
033	Art Houtteman	494
034	Ken Holloway	479
035	Mike Maroth	470
036	Al Benton	468
037	Hank Aguirre	431
038	Matt Boyd	421
039	Ed Killian	406
040	Brian Moehler	399
041	Max Scherzer	396
042	Anibal Sanchez	393
043	John Hiller	391
044	Jean Dubuc	389
045	Dave Rozema	378
046	Bill Gullickson	376
047	Phil Regan	373
048	Chief Hogsett	365
049	Stubby Overmire	362
050	Don Mossi	360
	George Uhle	360

Joe Sparma

052	Joe Sparma	356
053	Bernie Boland	355
054	Dutch Leonard	350
055	Red Oldham	345
	Hal White	345
057	Jeff Weaver	344
058	Earl Wilson	340
059	Johnny Gorsica	336
060	Mike Moore	328
061	Rip Collins	325
062	Jordan Zimmermann	322
063	Roxie Lawson	308
064	Ownie Carroll	305
065	Steve Sparks	304
066	Steve Gromek	303
	Bobo Newsom	303
068	Ed Siever	301
069	Willie Blair	296
070	Ned Garver	287
071	Justin Thompson	286
072	John Doherty	278
073	Aurelio Lopez	270
	Jeff Robinson	270
075	Ed Summers	269
076	Harry Coveleski	266
077	Dave Wickersham	255
078	Bert Cole	249
079	Felipe Lira	246
080	Michael Fulmer	243
081	Ed Wells	242
082	Dave Mlicki	238
083	Armando Galarraga	236
084	Doyle Alexander	235
	Daniel Norris	235
086	Lerrin LaGrow	232
087	Frank Kitson	229
088	Kenny Rogers	228
089	Mike Henneman	227
090	Sam Gibson	226
091	Jose Lima	224
	Vern Ruhle	224
093	Jason Johnson	218
094	Todd Jones	217
095	Herman Pillette	214
096	C.J. Nitkowski	203
097	Jake Wade	196
	Whit Wyatt	196
099	Woodie Fryman	195
100	Ralph Works	194

ALL TIME TIGER PITCHING LEADERS – RUNS ALLOWED

Rank	Pitcher	Runs
001	Hooks Dauss	1,594
002	George Mullin	1,480
003	Mickey Lolich	1,415
004	Jack Morris	1,382
005	Tommy Bridges	1,321
006	Earl Whitehill	1,225
007	Hal Newhouser	1,181
008	Dizzy Trout	1,101
009	Justin Verlander	1,057
010	Vic Sorrell	949
011	Dan Petry	889
012	Frank Lary	884
013	Bill Donovan	802
014	Jim Bunning	796
015	Virgil Trucks	786
016	Frank Tanana	774
017	Schoolboy Rowe	721
	Milt Wilcox	721
019	Paul Foytack	718
020	Jeremy Bonderman	704
	Ed Willett	704
022	Walt Terrell	687
023	Fred Hutchinson	681
024	Joe Coleman	671
025	Billy Hoeft	634
026	Howard Ehmke	615
027	Nate Robertson	609
028	Lil Stoner	607
029	Denny McLain	605
030	Ted Gray	594
031	Elden Auker	587
032	Ken Holloway	577
033	Al Benton	576
034	Ed Killian	561
035	Rick Porcello	557
036	Art Houtteman	556
037	Jean Dubuc	526
038	Mike Maroth	507
039	Hank Aguirre	478
040	Ed Siever	460
041	Chief Hogsett	459
042	Matt Boyd	445
043	John Hiller	438
044	Dave Rozema	436
045	Red Oldham	435
046	Brian Moehler	433
047	Dutch Leonard	426
048	Anibal Sanchez	425
	George Uhle	425
050	Bernie Boland	424
051	Max Scherzer	420

Jeremy Bonderman

Rank	Pitcher	Runs
052	Rip Collins	415
053	Phil Regan	411
054	Don Mossi	407
055	Stubby Overmire	406
056	Ed Summers	404
057	Bill Gullickson	403
058	Joe Sparma	398
059	Hal White	397
060	Ownie Carroll	386
061	Harry Coveleski	385
	Johnny Gorsica	385
063	Earl Wilson	375
064	Jeff Weaver	372
065	Steve Sparks	356
066	Mike Moore	350
	Bobo Newsom	350
068	Roxie Lawson	347
069	Jordan Zimmermann	345
070	Steve Gromek	334
071	Frank Kitson	332
072	Ned Garver	327
073	Bert Cole	317
074	Justin Thompson	316
075	Willie Blair	311
076	John Doherty	306
077	Jeff Robinson	295
078	Dave Wickersham	293
079	Aurelio Lopez	291
080	Sam Gibson	290
081	Ed Wells	287
082	Lerrin LaGrow	278
	Herman Pillette	278
084	Michael Fulmer	266
	Mike Henneman	266
086	Felipe Lira	263
087	Vern Ruhle	260
	Ralph Works	260
089	Doyle Alexander	256
	Dave Mlicki	256
091	Roscoe Miller	253
092	Daniel Norris	252
093	Armando Galarraga	251
	Kenny Rogers	251
095	George Cunningham	247
	Bill James	247
097	Todd Jones	246
098	Jason Johnson	238
099	Jose Lima	236
100	Whit Wyatt	231

ALL TIME TIGER PITCHING LEADERS – BATTERS FACED

Rank	Pitcher	Batters Faced
001	Hooks Dauss	14,192
002	Mickey Lolich	13,980
003	George Mullin	13,902
004	Jack Morris	12,745
005	Hal Newhouser	12,449
006	Tommy Bridges	12,165
007	Dizzy Trout	11,019
008	Justin Verlander	10,393
009	Earl Whitehill	9,543
010	Bill Donovan	8,649
011	Frank Lary	8,472
012	Dan Petry	7,819
013	Jim Bunning	7,815
014	Virgil Trucks	7,653
015	Vic Sorrell	7,403
016	Frank Tanana	6,635
017	Denny McLain	6,443
019	Ed Willett	6,348
018	Milt Wilcox	6,341
020	Ed Killian	6,254
021	Schoolboy Rowe	6,151
022	Fred Hutchinson	6,142
023	Paul Foytack	6,093
024	Joe Coleman	6,024
025	Walt Terrell	5,726
026	Billy Hoeft	5,693
027	Al Benton	5,297
028	Howard Ehmke	5,245
029	John Hiller	5,206
030	Jeremy Bonderman	5,179
031	Hank Aguirre	4,937
032	Ted Gray	4,866
033	Elden Auker	4,741
034	Jean Dubuc	4,681
035	Art Houtteman	4,626
036	Rick Porcello	4,563
037	Nate Robertson	4,558
038	Lil Stoner	4,375
039	Ken Holloway	4,344
040	Ed Siever	4,240
041	Bernie Boland	4,175
042	Dave Rozema	4,174
043	Max Scherzer	4,160
044	Harry Coveleski	4,076
045	Ed Summers	4,040
046	Earl Wilson	3,940
047	Don Mossi	3,838
048	Mike Maroth	3,782
049	Joe Sparma	3,609
050	Stubby Overmire	3,575

Schoolboy Rowe

Rank	Pitcher	Batters Faced
051	Hal White	3,553
052	Dutch Leonard	3,532
	George Uhle	3,532
054	Brian Moehler	3,475
055	Anibal Sanchez	3,386
056	Chief Hogsett	3,345
057	Matt Boyd	3,338
058	Red Oldham	3,287
059	Bobo Newsom	3,281
060	Phil Regan	3,242
061	Rip Collins	3,207
062	Johnny Gorsica	3,136
063	Bill Gullickson	3,093
064	Steve Gromek	3,081
065	Jeff Weaver	3,060
066	Ned Garver	2,981
067	Aurelio Lopez	2,978
068	Ownie Carroll	2,944
069	Dave Wickersham	2,844
070	Mike Henneman	2,843
071	Frank Kitson	2,810
072	Justin Thompson	2,730
073	Steve Sparks	2,682
074	Roxie Lawson	2,485
075	Herman Pillette	2,451
076	Bill James	2,321
077	Michael Fulmer	2,314
078	Doyle Alexander	2,302
079	Jeff Robinson	2,268
080	Bert Cole	2,253
	Mike Moore	2,253
082	Jordan Zimmermann	2,251
083	Sam Gibson	2,237
084	John Doherty	2,224
085	Willie Blair	2,135
086	Vern Ruhle	2,127
087	Todd Jones	2,093
088	Lerrin LaGrow	2,083
089	Roscoe Miller	2,053
090	Ed Wells	2,020
091	Armando Galarraga	2,005
092	Ralph Works	2,003
093	Daniel Norris	1,993
094	Willie Hernandez	1,981
095	George Cunningham	1,955
096	Felipe Lira	1,920
097	Kenny Rogers	1,906
098	Juan Berenguer	1,828
099	Doug Fister	1,827
100	Woodie Fryman	1,819

ALL TIME TIGER PITCHING LEADERS – TECHINCAL RUNS ALLOWED

Rank	Pitcher	Runs
001	Fred Gladding	2.96
002	Joaquin Benoit	3.08
003	John Hiller	3.17
004	Terry Fox	3.19
005	Al Alburquerque	3.20
006	Willie Hernandez	3.26
007	Ed Killian	3.29
008	Doug Brocail	3.36
009	Bill Donovan	3.38
010	Harry Coveleski	3.39
011	Denny McLain	3.42
012	Alex Wilson	3.50
013	Earl Wilson	3.51
014	Mark Fidrych	3.56
015	Mike Henneman	3.57
016	Hal Newhouser	3.61
017	Ed Summers	3.64
018	Hank Aguirre	3.65
019	Jose Valverde	3.66
020	Aurelio Lopez	3.67
021	Bernie Boland	3.69
022	Fred Scherman	3.73
	Max Scherzer	3.73
024	Doug Fister	3.74
025	Mickey Lolich	3.79
	Justin Verlander	3.79
027	Jamie Walker	3.80
028	Dizzy Trout	3.82
029	Tom Timmermann	3.83
030	Jim Bunning	3.84
031	Dave Rozema	3.90
	Dave Wickersham	3.90
033	George Mullin	3.92
034	Virgil Trucks	3.93
035	Don Mossi	3.94
036	Frank Lary	3.96
037	Bobby Seay	4.00
	Ed Siever	4.00
039	Bill James	4.06
040	Blaine Hardy	4.07
041	Jack Morris	4.09
042	Ed Willett	4.10
043	Paul Gibson	4.12
044	Jean Dubuc	4.13
045	Bobo Newsom	4.14
046	Steve Gromek	4.15
047	Ned Garver	4.19
	Fred Hutchinson	4.19
049	Tommy Bridges	4.21
050	David Wells	4.22

Fred Gladding

Rank	Pitcher	Runs
051	Hooks Dauss	4.23
052	Al Benton	4.25
053	Doyle Alexander	4.26
054	Joe Coleman	4.29
	Joe Sparma	4.29
056	Juan Berenguer	4.31
	Billy Hoeft	4.31
058	Michael Fulmer	4.33
059	Dan Petry	4.34
	Milt Wilcox	4.34
061	Hal White	4.36
062	Frank Kitson	4.37
063	Eric King	4.38
	Firpo Marberry	4.38
065	Stubby Overmire	4.40
	Justin Thompson	4.40
067	Woodie Fryman	4.45
	Herman Pillette	4.45
069	Howard Ehmke	4.48
070	Schoolboy Rowe	4.49
	Frank Tanana	4.49
072	Paul Foytack	4.53
073	Todd Jones	4.62
	Dutch Leonard	4.62
	George Uhle	4.62
076	Art Houtteman	4.65
077	Spencer Turnbull	4.64
078	George Cunningham	4.66
	Walt Terrell	4.66
080	Rick Porcello	4.67
081	Jeff Weaver	4.68
082	Fernando Rodney	4.69
083	Roscoe Miller	4.74
084	Johnny Gorsica	4.79
	Vern Ruhle	4.79
	Anibal Sanchez	4.79
087	Phil Coke	4.81
	Ted Gray	4.81
089	Brian Moehler	4.82
090	Armando Galarraga	4.84
091	Elden Auker	4.88
092	Daniel Norris	4.92
093	Ralph Works	4.94
094	Phil Regan	4.95
095	Bill Gullickson	5.02
096	Rip Collins	5.03
097	Jeff Robinson	5.08
	Earl Whitehill	5.08
099	Shane Greene	5.09
100	Vic Sorrell	5.11

001	Joaquin Benoit	81.34
002	Fred Gladding	81.24
003	John Hiller	80.18
004	Al Alburquerque	79.83
005	Terry Fox	79.51
006	Willie Hernandez	78.89
007	Aurelio Lopez	78.39
008	Denny McLain	78.16
009	Jamie Walker	78.11
010	Doug Brocail	77.68
011	Earl Wilson	77.34
012	Fred Scherman	77.03
013	Jim Bunning	76.01
014	Steve Gromek	75.95
015	Alex Wilson	75.80
016	Paul Gibson	75.42
017	Max Scherzer	75.36
018	Hank Aguirre	75.35
019	Blaine Hardy	74.96
020	Mike Henneman	74.85
021	Jose Valverde	74.69
022	Mickey Lolich	74.46
023	Dave Rozema	73.90
024	Dave Wickersham	73.68
025	Justin Verlander	73.67
026	Frank Lary	73.58
027	Eric King	73.47
028	Doyle Alexander	73.37
029	Don Mossi	73.26
030	Hal Newhouser	73.10
031	Doug Fister	72.90
032	Jack Morris	72.89
033	David Wells	72.85
034	Armando Galarraga	72.74
035	Billy Hoeft	72.73
036	Frank Tanana	72.53
037	Tom Timmermann	72.44
038	Joe Coleman	72.40
039	Juan Berenguer	72.32
040	Dan Petry	72.27
041	Virgil Trucks	72.24
042	Joe Sparma	72.17
043	Mark Fidrych	72.16
044	Bobby Seay	72.14
045	Woodie Fryman	72.05
046	Justin Thompson	72.04
047	Dizzy Trout	71.78
048	Paul Foytack	71.75
049	Michael Fulmer	71.68
	Ned Garver	71.68
051	Daniel Norris	71.61
052	Milt Wilcox	71.55
053	Phil Regan	71.49
054	Ed Killian	71.45
055	Bobo Newsom	71.28
056	Fernando Rodney	71.14
057	Todd Jones	71.10
058	Matt Boyd	70.97
059	Al Benton	70.90
060	Tommy Bridges	70.74
061	Walt Terrell	70.72
062	Brian Moehler	70.68
063	Fred Hutchinson	70.59
064	Buck Farmer	70.55
065	Bill Gullickson	70.45
066	Ted Gray	70.43
067	Bill James	70.39
068	Bill Donovan	70.30
069	Jeff Weaver	69.98
070	Rick Porcello	69.91
071	Nate Robertson	69.84
072	Hal White	69.79
073	Mike Maroth	69.74
074	Phil Coke	69.54
075	Anibal Sanchez	69.49
076	Vern Ruhle	69.42
077	Jeff Robinson	69.35
078	Kenny Rogers	69.24
079	Art Houtteman	69.20
080	Felipe Lira	69.17
081	Harry Coveleski	68.93
082	Bernie Boland	68.73
083	Howard Ehmke	68.26
084	Spencer Turnbull	68.09
085	Firpo Marberry	67.95
086	Ed Summers	67.75
087	Matt Anderson	67.68
088	Shane Greene	67.57
089	Stubby Overmire	67.46
090	Herman Pillette	67.39
091	George Mullin	67.36
092	Elden Auker	67.29
093	Jeremy Bonderman	67.20
094	Steve Sparks	67.17
095	Hooks Dauss	67.09
	Schoolboy Rowe	67.09
097	Johnny Gorsica	67.01
098	Roxie Lawson	66.83
099	Mike Moore	66.80
100	Lerrin LaGrow	66.76

Joaquin Benoit

001	Harry Coveleski	2.34
002	Ed Killian	2.38
003	Ed Summers	2.42
004	Bill Donovan	2.49
005	Ed Siever	2.61
006	Fred Gladding	2.70
007	George Mullin	2.76
008	Terry Fox	2.77
009	John Hiller	2.83
010	Joaquin Benoit	2.89
	Ed Willett	2.89
012	Willie Hernandez	2.98
013	Bill James	3.01
014	Frank Kitson	3.02
015	Mike Henneman	3.05
016	Doug Brocail	3.06
	Jean Dubuc	3.06
018	Hal Newhouser	3.07
019	Bernie Boland	3.09
020	Mark Fidrych	3.10
021	George Cunningham	3.13
	Denny McLain	3.13
023	Roscoe Miller	3.18
	Earl Wilson	3.18
025	Al Alburquerque	3.20
	Dizzy Trout	3.20
	Alex Wilson	3.20
028	Jose Valverde	3.22
029	Hank Aguirre	3.29
	Doug Fister	3.29
031	Hooks Dauss	3.30
032	Jamie Walker	3.33
033	Dave Rozema	3.38
034	Fred Scherman	3.39
	Tom Timmermann	3.39
036	Dave Wickersham	3.40
037	Aurelio Lopez	3.41
038	Herman Pillette	3.42
039	Jim Bunning	3.45
	Mickey Lolich	3.45
041	Al Benton	3.46
	Frank Lary	3.46
043	Don Mossi	3.49
	Justin Verlander	3.49
045	Virgil Trucks	3.50
046	Max Scherzer	3.52
047	Tommy Bridges	3.57
048	Bobo Newsom	3.59
049	Howard Ehmke	3.61
050	Ned Garver	3.68

Harry Coveleski

	Ralph Works	3.68
052	Blaine Hardy	3.73
	Fred Hutchinson	3.73
	Jack Morris	3.73
055	Steve Gromek	3.77
056	David Wells	3.78
057	Dutch Leonard	3.79
	Hal White	3.79
059	Firpo Marberry	3.81
060	Joe Coleman	3.82
061	Dan Petry	3.84
	Joe Sparma	3.84
063	Juan Berenguer	3.87
064	Paul Gibson	3.88
065	Doyle Alexander	3.91
	George Uhle	3.91
	Milt Wilcox	3.91
068	Stubby Overmire	3.92
069	Rip Collins	3.94
070	Michael Fulmer	3.95
071	Justin Thompson	3.98
072	Bobby Seay	4.00
073	Schoolboy Rowe	4.01
074	Billy Hoeft	4.02
075	Sam Gibson	4.06
076	Todd Jones	4.07
077	Frank Tanana	4.08
078	Red Oldham	4.09
079	Ownie Carroll	4.12
	Vern Ruhle	4.12
081	Woodie Fryman	4.13
	Art Houtteman	4.13
083	Paul Foytack	4.14
084	Earl Whitehill	4.16
085	Johnny Gorsica	4.18
086	Eric King	4.23
087	Phil Coke	4.25
	Ted Gray	4.25
	Spencer Turnbull	4.25
090	Elden Auker	4.26
	Walt Terrell	4.26
092	Fernando Rodney	4.28
093	Rick Porcello	4.30
094	Jeff Weaver	4.33
095	Lerrin LaGrow	4.40
096	Ken Holloway	4.41
097	Anibal Sanchez	4.43
	Vic Sorrell	4.43
099	Brian Moehler	4.44
100	Chief Hogsett	4.45
	Steve Sparks	4.45

Rank	Pitcher	ERA+
001	Doug Brocail	155
002	Joaquin Benoit	145
003	Terry Fox	137
004	Mike Henneman	136
005	Willie Hernandez	135
	Alex Wilson	135
007	John Hiller	134
008	Fred Gladding	132
009	Bobo Newsom	131
	Jose Valverde	131
	Jamie Walker	131
012	Hal Newhouser	130
013	Doug Fister	128
014	Al Alburquerque	127
015	Tommy Bridges	126
	Mark Fidrych	126
017	Dizzy Trout	125
018	Harry Coveleski	123
	Justin Verlander	123
020	David Wells	122
021	Al Benton	121
	Ed Siever	121
024	Roscoe Miller	120
	Dave Rozema	120
026	Aurelio Lopez	119
	Justin Thompson	119
028	Blaine Hardy	117
	Max Scherzer	117
	George Uhle	117
031	Jim Bunning	116
	Frank Lary	116
	Don Mossi	116
034	Hank Aguirre	115
035	Herman Pillette	114
	Bobby Seay	114
037	Fred Hutchinson	113
	Todd Jones	113
	Firpo Marberry	113
	Schoolboy Rowe	113
	Virgil Trucks	113
042	Michael Fulmer	111
	Ed Summers	111
044	Denny McLain	110
045	Bill Donovan	109
	Ed Killian	109
	Spencer Turnbull	109
048	Elden Auker	108
	Jack Morris	108
050	Fred Scherman	107
	Earl Wilson	107
052	Ned Garver	106
	Brian Moehler	106
054	Rip Collins	105
	Mickey Lolich	105
	Dan Petry	105
	Tom Timmermann	105
	Hal White	105
059	Steve Gromek	104
	Fernando Rodney	104
	Jeff Weaver	104
	Earl Whitehill	104
	Dave Wickersham	104
064	Ownie Carroll	103
	Milt Wilcox	103
066	Juan Berenguer	102
	Hooks Dauss	102
	Paul Gibson	102
	Chief Hogsett	102
	Dutch Leonard	102
	George Mullin	102
	Vic Sorrell	102
073	Sam Gibson	101
	Art Houtteman	101
075	Doyle Alexander	100
076	Frank Tanana	99
	Ed Willett	99
078	Jean Dubuc	98
	Howard Ehmke	98
	Paul Foytack	98
	Johnny Gorsica	98
	Billy Hoeft	98
	Daniel Norris	98
	Steve Sparks	98
085	Phil Coke	97
	Joe Coleman	97
	Armando Galarraga	97
	Ted Gray	97
	Eric King	97
	Felipe Lira	97
	Rick Porcello	97
	Kenny Rogers	97
093	Walt Terrell	96
094	Vern Ruhle	95
095	Matt Anderson	94
	Bernie Boland	94
	Red Oldham	94
	Stubby Overmire	94
	Anibal Sanchez	94
100	Ken Holloway	93
	Roxie Lawson	93

Bobo Newsom

ALL TIME TIGER PITCHING LEADERS – FIELDING INDEPENDENT PITCHING

Rank	Pitcher	FIP
001	Bill Donovan	2.62
002	Ed Summers	2.64
003	Harry Coveleski	2.67
004	Ed Killian	2.78
005	Ed Siever	2.80
006	George Mullin	2.86
007	George Cunningham	2.87
008	Frank Kitson	2.88
009	Bernie Boland	3.05
010	Ed Willett	3.09
011	Hal Newhouser	3.18
012	Mickey Lolich	3.19
013	Doug Fister	3.20
014	Ralph Works	3.25
015	Tom Timmermann	3.26
016	Jean Dubuc	3.31
017	Fred Gladding	3.32
	Max Scherzer	3.32
019	Hooks Dauss	3.33
	Mark Fidrych	3.33
021	Al Alburquerque	3.34
	Dizzy Trout	3.34
023	Stubby Overmire	3.38
024	Joaquin Benoit	3.39
	John Hiller	3.39
026	Mike Henneman	3.40
027	Bill James	3.46
	Earl Wilson	3.46
029	Virgil Trucks	3.47
030	Bobby Seay	3.48
	Justin Verlander	3.48
032	Willie Hernandez	3.52
	Dutch Leonard	3.52
034	Denny McLain	3.55
035	Roscoe Miller	3.57
036	Hank Aguirre	3.59
	Jim Bunning	3.59
	Don Mossi	3.59
039	Frank Lary	3.62
	Bobo Newsom	3.62
041	Phil Coke	3.63
	Spencer Turnbull	3.63
043	Joe Coleman	3.64
044	Dave Wickersham	3.67
045	Doug Brocail	3.68
	Billy Hoeft	3.68
047	Fred Hutchinson	3.71
048	Johnny Gorsica	3.73
049	Schoolboy Rowe	3.75
050	Terry Fox	3.77
051	Ned Garver	3.78

Bill Donovan

Rank	Pitcher	FIP
052	Woodie Fryman	3.81
	Joe Sparma	3.81
054	Howard Ehmke	3.83
055	Hal White	3.84
056	Al Benton	3.86
057	Alex Wilson	3.87
058	Tommy Bridges	3.88
	Jose Valverde	3.88
060	Firpo Marberry	3.89
061	Art Houtteman	3.91
062	Jack Morris	3.92
063	Red Oldham	3.93
	Herman Pillette	3.93
	Anibal Sanchez	3.93
067	Rip Collins	3.99
	Dave Rozema	3.99
	Milt Wilcox	3.99
070	Fred Scherman	4.02
071	Michael Fulmer	4.03
	Rick Porcello	4.03
073	Vern Ruhle	4.05
074	Todd Jones	4.06
075	Juan Berenguer	4.07
076	Aurelio Lopez	4.10
077	Blaine Hardy	4.11
078	George Uhle	4.12
079	Lerrin LaGrow	4.13
080	Doyle Alexander	4.15
	Fernando Rodney	4.15
082	Jamie Walker	4.16
083	Ken Holloway	4.18
	Frank Tanana	4.18
	Earl Whitehill	4.18
086	Sam Gibson	4.19
	Shane Greene	4.19
	David Wells	4.19
089	Paul Gibson	4.22
	Ted Gray	4.22
091	Jeff Weaver	4.23
092	Paul Foytack	4.25
093	Steve Gromek	4.26
	Ed Wells	4.26
095	Daniel Norris	4.27
096	Jeremy Bonderman	4.29
	Jason Johnson	4.29
098	Dan Petry	4.30
099	Elden Auker	4.31
	Walt Terrell	4.31

Rank	Pitcher	ERA
001	Doug Fister	3.13
002	Bill Donovan	3.21
003	Al Alburquerque	3.24
	Max Scherzer	3.24
005	Harry Coveleski	3.29
	Ed Siever	3.29
007	Frank Kitson	3.30
008	Ed Summers	3.32
009	Bobby Seay	3.33
010	Joaquin Benoit	3.34
011	Justin Verlander	3.37
012	George Mullin	3.41
013	Spencer Turnbull	3.43
014	Ed Killian	3.46
015	Mike Henneman	3.54
016	Doug Brocail	3.55
017	Phil Coke	3.56
018	George Cunningham	3.58
019	Ralph Works	3.61
020	Ed Willett	3.62
021	Hal Newhouser	3.65
022	Mark Fidrych	3.66
	Mickey Lolich	3.66
024	Dutch Leonard	3.67
025	Hooks Dauss	3.68
026	Bernie Boland	3.70
027	Roscoe Miller	3.72
	Alex Wilson	3.72
030	Schoolboy Rowe	3.75
031	Willie Hernandez	3.76
032	Fred Gladding	3.77
	Tom Timmermann	3.77
034	Jean Dubuc	3.79
	Dizzy Trout	3.79
036	John Hiller	3.80
	Bobo Newsom	3.80
038	Anibal Sanchez	3.81
	Jose Valverde	3.81
040	Michael Fulmer	3.88
	Stubby Overmire	3.88
042	George Uhle	3.90
043	Todd Jones	3.92
044	Tommy Bridges	3.95
	Blaine Hardy	3.95
	Herman Pillette	3.95
	Rick Porcello	3.95
	Earl Wilson	3.95
049	Firpo Marberry	3.96
050	Rip Collins	3.97
051	Virgil Trucks	4.00
052	Shane Greene	4.03

Doug Fister

Rank	Pitcher	ERA
	Don Mossi	4.03
054	Hank Aguirre	4.04
	Denny McLain	4.04
	Red Oldham	4.04
	Fernando Rodney	4.04
058	Jim Bunning	4.07
059	Daniel Norris	4.09
	Earl Whitehill	4.09
061	Howard Ehmke	4.11
	Jamie Walker	4.11
	Dave Wickersham	4.11
064	Joe Coleman	4.12
065	Johnny Gorsica	4.13
	David Wells	4.13
067	Fred Hutchinson	4.14
	Frank Lary	4.14
069	Jeff Weaver	4.15
070	Bill James	4.17
071	Ken Holloway	4.18
	Jack Morris	4.18
073	Jeremy Bonderman	4.19
074	Terry Fox	4.22
075	Elden Auker	4.23
	Sam Gibson	4.23
077	Al Benton	4.24
	Billy Hoeft	4.24
	Justin Thompson	4.24
080	Jason Johnson	4.25
	Ed Wells	4.25
082	Milt Wilcox	4.28
083	Woodie Fryman	4.29
	Dave Rozema	4.29
085	Chief Hogsett	4.31
	Joe Sparma	4.31
087	Juan Berenguer	4.33
088	Ned Garver	4.34
	Vic Sorrell	4.34
090	Doyle Alexander	4.36
091	Brian Moehler	4.37
	Steve Sparks	4.37
093	Ownie Carroll	4.38
	Art Houtteman	4.38
	Aurelio Lopez	4.38
	Hal White	4.38
097	Lil Stoner	4.39
	Frank Tanana	4.39
099	Bert Cole	4.40
	Joe Jimenez	4.40

Rank	Pitcher	WHIP
001	Joaquin Benoit	1.075
002	Denny McLain	1.112
003	Willie Hernandez	1.121
004	Harry Coveleski	1.131
005	Ed Summers	1.152
006	Alex Wilson	1.164
007	Earl Wilson	1.170
008	Don Mossi	1.174
	Jamie Walker	1.174
010	Doug Fister	1.191
	Justin Verlander	1.191
012	Bill Donovan	1.192
013	Max Scherzer	1.197
014	Mark Fidrych	1.203
	Jose Valverde	1.203
016	Hank Aguirre	1.208
	Jim Bunning	1.208
018	Doug Brocail	1.211
	Terry Fox	1.211
	David Wells	1.211
021	Ed Killian	1.218
022	Mickey Lolich	1.222
023	Dave Rozema	1.230
024	Fred Gladding	1.231
025	Ed Siever	1.233
026	Michael Fulmer	1.243
027	Frank Kitson	1.246
028	Dave Wickersham	1.248
029	Bernie Boland	1.251
030	Ed Willett	1.256
031	Aurelio Lopez	1.258
032	Jack Morris	1.266
033	John Hiller	1.268
034	George Mullin	1.270
035	Frank Lary	1.271
036	Steve Gromek	1.272
037	Fred Hutchinson	1.281
038	Tom Timmermann	1.284
039	Jean Dubuc	1.287
040	Anibal Sanchez	1.299
041	George Cunningham	1.304
042	Mike Henneman	1.305
	Virgil Trucks	1.305
044	Jeff Weaver	1.311
045	Hal Newhouser	1.313
046	George Uhle	1.316
047	Matt Boyd	1.318
048	Juan Berenguer	1.319
049	Hooks Dauss	1.320
050	Firpo Marberry	1.322

Denny McLain

Rank	Pitcher	WHIP
051	Shane Greene	1.323
	Spencer Turnbull	1.323
053	Milt Wilcox	1.324
054	Doyle Alexander	1.325
	Ned Garver	1.325
056	Blaine Hardy	1.329
057	Schoolboy Rowe	1.331
058	Al Alburquerque	1.333
059	Justin Thompson	1.335
060	Bobby Seay	1.338
061	Dizzy Trout	1.344
062	Dan Petry	1.349
063	Joe Coleman	1.351
064	Woodie Fryman	1.353
065	Armando Galarraga	1.354
066	Roscoe Miller	1.356
067	Frank Tanana	1.357
068	Rick Porcello	1.359
069	Paul Foytack	1.361
070	Fred Scherman	1.367
071	Tommy Bridges	1.368
	Billy Hoeft	1.368
073	Bill Gullickson	1.369
	Art Houtteman	1.369
075	Stubby Overmire	1.370
076	Dutch Leonard	1.372
077	Bobo Newsom	1.373
078	Eric King	1.377
079	Phil Regan	1.378
	Joe Sparma	1.378
081	Rip Collins	1.383
082	Jason Johnson	1.387
083	Daniel Norris	1.389
084	Brian Moehler	1.397
085	Jeff Robinson	1.398
086	Herman Pillette	1.400
087	Al Benton	1.401
088	Joe Jimenez	1.404
089	Jeremy Bonderman	1.406
090	Vern Ruhle	1.409
091	Howard Ehmke	1.414
092	Johnny Gorsica	1.416
093	Mike Maroth	1.423
094	Fernando Rodney	1.424
095	Walt Terrell	1.427
096	Bill James	1.429
097	Kenny Rogers	1.430
	Steve Sparks	1.430
099	Hal White	1.434
100	John Doherty	1.439
	Ralph Works	1.439

Rank	Pitcher	WAR
001	Hal Newhouser	58.7
002	Justin Verlander	56.1
003	Tommy Bridges	51.6
004	Mickey Lolich	46.7
005	Dizzy Trout	44.3
006	Jack Morris	37.7
007	Bill Donovan	35.7
008	Hooks Dauss	36.8
009	George Mullin	34.8
010	John Hiller	31.0
011	Jim Bunning	29.6
012	Frank Lary	28.7
013	Virgil Trucks	27.2
014	Earl Whitehill	25.0
015	Ed Killian	23.5
016	Schoolboy Rowe	23.4
017	Denny McLain	22.7
018	Max Scherzer	21.4
019	Fred Hutchinson	20.7
020	Vic Sorrell	20.3
021	Al Benton	18.9
022	Hank Aguirre	18.1
023	Bobo Newsom	17.7
024	Dan Petry	17.3
025	Ed Siever	17.0
026	George Uhle	16.6
027	Harry Coveleski	15.7
028	Joe Coleman	15.6
029	Dave Rozema	15.1
030	Milt Wilcox	14.1
031	Billy Hoeft	14.0
032	Don Mossi	13.5
033	Howard Ehmke	13.4
034	Frank Tanana	13.1
	Bernie Boland	13.1
	Justin Thompson	13.1
	Ed Willett	13.1
038	Mike Henneman	12.8
039	Brian Moehler	12.2
040	Earl Wilson	12.0
041	Elden Auker	11.7
042	Ed Summers	11.6
043	Mark Fidrych	11.4
044	Paul Foytack	11.1
045	Michael Fulmer	10.9
046	Art Houtteman	10.6
	Rick Porcello	10.6
048	David Wells	10.3
049	Jeff Weaver	10.2
050	Doug Fister	9.9

Ed Summers

Rank	Pitcher	WAR
051	Aurelio Lopez	9.6
052	Dutch Leonard	9.5
053	Jean Dubuc	9.2
054	Ted Gray	8.9
055	Hal White	8.8
056	Willie Hernandez	8.5
057	Roscoe Miller	8.4
058	Steve Gromek	8.3
	Anibal Sanchez	8.3
060	Ned Garver	8.1
061	Matt Boyd	8.0
	Terry Fox	8.0
063	Walt Terrell	7.7
064	Doug Brocail	7.3
065	Ownie Carroll	6.7
066	Fred Gladding	6.5
	Felipe Lira	6.5
068	Doyle Alexander	6.3
069	Herman Pillette	6.3
070	Mike Maroth	6.2
071	Win Mercer	6.1
072	Rip Collins	5.9
	Johnny Gorsica	5.9
	Drew Smyly	5.9
075	Nate Robertson	5.8
076	Firpo Marberry	5.7
077	Daniel Norris	5.4
	David Price	5.4
079	Jeremy Bonderman	5.3
	Dave Wickersham	5.3
	Alex Wilson	5.3
082	Steve Sparks	5.2
083	Omar Olivares	5.1
	Tom Timmermann	5.1
085	Joaquin Benoit	5.0
	Archie McKain	5.0
087	George Gill	4.9
	Vern Ruhle	4.9
089	Red Oldham	4.8
	Fred Scherman	4.8
091	Al Alburquerque	4.7
092	Jack Billingham	4.6
	Armando Galarraga	4.6
	Chief Hogsett	4.6
095	Bill Gullickson	4.5
	Blaine Hardy	4.5
	Spencer Turnbull	4.5
	Jamie Walker	4.5
099	Red Donahue	4.4
100	Joel Zumaya	4.2

001	Jose Valverde	6.84
002	Joaquin Benoit	6.92
003	Al Alburquerque	7.00
004	Denny McLain	7.46
005	Juan Berenguer	7.51
006	Willie Hernandez	7.52
007	John Hiller	7.54
008	Fred Gladding	7.58
009	Aurelio Lopez	7.69
010	Bernie Boland	7.75
011	Earl Wilson	7.76
012	Harry Coveleski	7.80
013	Doug Brocail	7.84
	Bill Donovan	7.84
015	Hank Aguirre	7.87
016	Joe Sparma	7.97
	Justin Verlander	7.97
018	Jean Dubuc	8.06
019	Hal Newhouser	8.07
	Max Scherzer	8.07
021	Virgil Trucks	8.09
022	Jeff Robinson	8.10
	Fred Scherman	8.10
024	Jim Bunning	8.15
025	Jack Morris	8.18
	Fernando Rodney	8.18
	Dave Wickersham	8.18
028	Bill James	8.21
	Ed Killian	8.21
030	Eric King	8.25
031	Terry Fox	8.26
032	Paul Foytack	8.27
033	Mickey Lolich	8.28
034	Tom Timmermann	8.31
035	Alex Wilson	8.37
036	George Cunningham	8.38
	Ted Gray	8.38
	Ed Summers	8.38
039	Matt Anderson	8.39
	Mike Henneman	8.39
041	Ed Willett	8.44
042	Spencer Turnbull	8.46
043	Hal White	8.47
044	Joe Coleman	8.48
	Bobby Seay	8.48
046	George Mullin	8.50
047	Dan Petry	8.51
048	Tommy Bridges	8.52
049	Bobo Newsom	8.55
050	Joe Jimenez	8.56
051	Michael Fulmer	8.59

Jose Valverde

052	Jamie Walker	8.60
053	Shane Greene	8.63
054	Mark Fidrych	8.67
055	Milt Wilcox	8.69
056	Dizzy Trout	8.70
057	David Wells	8.73
058	Armando Galarraga	8.74
059	Woodie Fryman	8.75
	Justin Thompson	8.75
061	Blaine Hardy	8.79
062	Don Mossi	8.81
063	Frank Lary	8.85
064	Al Benton	8.91
065	Howard Ehmke	8.97
	Doug Fister	8.97
067	Dave Rozema	8.99
068	Matt Boyd	9.00
069	Billy Hoeft	9.04
	Hooks Dauss	9.04
071	Steve Gromek	9.09
072	Anibal Sanchez	9.10
073	Paul Gibson	9.12
074	Fred Hutchinson	9.14
075	Frank Tanana	9.15
076	Jeff Weaver	9.17
077	Ned Garver	9.22
078	Todd Jones	9.26
079	Phil Regan	9.29
080	Ed Siever	9.30
081	Roscoe Miller	9.31
082	Firpo Marberry	9.33
083	Walt Terrell	9.35
084	Ralph Works	9.36
085	Buck Farmer	9.37
086	Art Houtteman	9.39
087	George Uhle	9.41
088	Doyle Alexander	9.46
	Frank Kitson	9.46
090	Schoolboy Rowe	9.47
091	Jeremy Bonderman	9.53
	Daniel Norris	9.53
	Herman Pillette	9.53
094	Rip Collins	9.55
	Felipe Lira	9.55
096	Dutch Leonard	9.62
097	Kenny Rogers	9.64
098	Earl Whitehill	9.65
099	Johnny Gorsica	9.68
100	Roxie Lawson	9.79
	Stubby Overmire	9.79

Rank	Name	HR/9
001	George Cunningham	0.04
002	Ed Killian	0.05
003	Roscoe Miller	0.07
004	Jean Dubuc	0.09
	Ralph Works	0.09
006	Bernie Boland	0.10
	George Mullin	0.10
	Ed Willett	0.10
009	Harry Coveleski	0.11
	Bill Donovan	0.11
	Bill James	0.11
012	Ed Siever	0.13
013	Ed Summers	0.17
014	Herman Pillette	0.22
015	Hooks Dauss	0.23
016	Frank Kitson	0.24
017	Rip Collins	0.30
018	Howard Ehmke	0.31
019	Ownie Carroll	0.34
	Sam Gibson	0.34
021	Ken Holloway	0.37
022	Red Oldham	0.38
	Stubby Overmire	0.38
	Dizzy Trout	0.38
025	Bert Cole	0.40
	Ed Wells	0.40
027	Dutch Leonard	0.41
	Hal Newhouser	0.41
029	Hal White	0.43
030	Earl Whitehill	0.44
031	Chief Hogsett	0.49
	Bobby Seay	0.49
033	Mark Fidrych	0.50
034	Elden Auker	0.52
035	Mike Henneman	0.54
	Vic Sorrell	0.54
037	Johnny Gorsica	0.55
	Lil Stoner	0.55
039	Phil Coke	0.56
	Schoolboy Rowe	0.56
041	Al Benton	0.57
	Bobo Newsom	0.57
	Tom Timmermann	0.57
044	Tommy Bridges	0.58
	George Uhle	0.58
046	Firpo Marberry	0.59
047	Virgil Trucks	0.61
048	Spencer Turnbull	0.63
049	Al Alburquerque	0.64
050	Doug Fister	0.67
051	Fred Gladding	0.72

Ralph Works

Rank	Name	HR/9
052	Joe Sparma	0.75
053	Fred Scherman	0.76
	Jose Valverde	0.76
055	Ned Garver	0.77
	Todd Jones	0.77
057	Fred Hutchinson	0.78
058	Doug Brocail	0.79
059	Paul Gibson	0.80
	John Hiller	0.80
	Dave Wickersham	0.80
062	Terry Fox	0.81
	John Doherty	0.81
	Art Houtteman	0.81
	Frank Lary	0.81
066	Roxie Lawson	0.82
067	Joe Coleman	0.83
068	Hank Aguirre	0.85
	Fernando Rodney	0.85
	Vern Ruhle	0.85
	Walt Terrell	0.85
	Alex Wilson	0.85
073	Justin Verlander	0.86
	Milt Wilcox	0.86
075	Lerrin LaGrow	0.87
076	Billy Hoeft	0.88
	Mickey Lolich	0.88
078	Ted Gray	0.89
079	Dan Petry	0.91
	Dave Rozema	0.91
081	Steve Sparks	0.92
082	Rick Porcello	0.93
083	Juan Berenguer	0.95
	Woodie Fryman	0.95
	Jack Morris	0.95
086	Eric King	0.96
	Max Scherzer	0.96
	Jeff Weaver	0.96
089	Willie Hernandez	0.97
090	Matt Anderson	0.99
	Blaine Hardy	0.99
	Justin Thompson	0.99
093	Jason Johnson	1.00
094	Earl Wilson	1.01
095	Doyle Alexander	1.02
	Michael Fulmer	1.02
097	Paul Foytack	1.04
098	Don Mossi	1.06
	Frank Tanana	1.06
100	Jim Bunning	1.07

ALL TIME TIGER PITCHING LEADERS – WALKS PER NINE INNINGS

Rank	Name	BB/9
001	Frank Kitson	1.75
	Don Mossi	1.75
003	Doug Fister	1.76
004	Ed Siever	1.80
005	Jamie Walker	1.97
006	Ed Summers	1.99
007	Bill Gullickson	2.03
008	Dave Rozema	2.08
009	Alex Wilson	2.11
010	Jordan Zimmermann	2.15
011	Mark Fidrych	2.16
	David Wells	2.16
013	Rick Porcello	2.21
014	Steve Gromek	2.36
015	Harry Coveleski	2.37
016	Fred Hutchinson	2.39
017	Jason Johnson	2.41
018	John Doherty	2.42
019	George Uhle	2.43
020	Doyle Alexander	2.47
021	Willie Blair	2.50
022	Mike Maroth	2.51
	Schoolboy Rowe	2.51
024	Brian Moehler	2.53
025	Denny McLain	2.54
	Stubby Overmire	2.54
027	Willie Hernandez	2.57
	Firpo Marberry	2.57
029	Frank Lary	2.59
	Anibal Sanchez	2.59
031	Michael Fulmer	2.60
032	Jeff Weaver	2.63
033	Terry Fox	2.64
034	Vern Ruhle	2.67
035	Ned Garver	2.71
	Mickey Lolich	2.71
	Max Scherzer	2.71
038	Jim Bunning	2.72
039	Dutch Leonard	2.73
040	Ed Killian	2.75
	Justin Verlander	2.75
042	Joaquin Benoit	2.76
043	Earl Wilson	2.77
044	Hooks Dauss	2.83
045	Steve Sparks	2.84
046	Matt Boyd	2.86
	Ed Willett	2.86
048	Bill Donovan	2.88
049	Rip Collins	2.90
	Roscoe Miller	2.90

Don Mossi

Rank	Name	BB/9
051	Art Houtteman	2.93
	George Mullin	2.93
053	Daniel Norris	2.97
054	Hank Aguirre	3.00
055	Red Oldham	3.03
056	Dave Wickersham	3.05
057	Doug Brocail	3.06
	Frank Tanana	3.06
059	Johnny Gorsica	3.07
	Herman Pillette	3.07
061	Ken Holloway	3.11
	Phil Regan	3.11
063	Jeremy Bonderman	3.12
064	Elden Auker	3.14
065	Blaine Hardy	3.17
066	Jack Morris	3.21
067	Nate Robertson	3.23
	Kenny Rogers	3.23
	Milt Wilcox	3.23
070	Tom Timmermann	3.24
071	Billy Hoeft	3.27
	Justin Thompson	3.27
073	Shane Greene	3.28
074	Lil Stoner	3.35
075	George Cunningham	3.36
	Mike Henneman	3.36
077	Bert Cole	3.38
078	Dizzy Trout	3.40
079	Woodie Fryman	3.43
	Lerrin LaGrow	3.43
081	Earl Whitehill	3.44
082	Armando Galarraga	3.45
	Spencer Turnbull	3.45
084	Phil Coke	3.48
085	Felipe Lira	3.49
086	Fred Gladding	3.50
	Walt Terrell	3.50
088	Bernie Boland	3.51
089	Jean Dubuc	3.52
090	Bobby Seay	3.56
091	Ralph Works	3.59
092	Dan Petry	3.63
093	Aurelio Lopez	3.64
094	Chief Hogsett	3.66
	Virgil Trucks	3.66
096	Joe Coleman	3.68
097	Al Benton	3.69
098	Hal Newhouser	3.75
099	Howard Ehmke	3.76
100	Tommy Bridges	3.80
	Vic Sorrell	3.80

ALL TIME TIGER PITCHING LEADERS – STRIKEOUTS PER NINE INNINGS

Rank	Pitcher	SO/9
001	Al Alburquerque	11.04
002	Joe Jimenez	11.01
003	Joaquin Benoit	9.95
005	Max Scherzer	9.60
006	Matt Boyd	8.70
007	Fernando Rodney	8.56
008	Justin Verlander	8.51
009	Spencer Turnbull	8.49
010	Daniel Norris	8.36
011	Shane Greene	8.34
012	Anibal Sanchez	8.32
013	Buck Farmer	8.20
014	Matt Anderson	8.03
015	Jose Valverde	8.01
016	Bobby Seay	7.83
017	Doug Brocail	7.70
018	John Hiller	7.51
019	Michael Fulmer	7.30
020	Doug Fister	7.21
021	Mickey Lolich	7.17
022	Willie Hernandez	7.15
023	Jeremy Bonderman	7.13
024	Blaine Hardy	7.12
025	Juan Berenguer	7.09
026	Fred Gladding	7.00
027	Todd Jones	6.98
028	Jamie Walker	6.83
029	Jim Bunning	6.78
	Phil Coke	6.78
031	Earl Wilson	6.63
032	Aurelio Lopez	6.55
	C.J. Nitkowski	6.55
034	Denny McLain	6.50
035	Mike Henneman	6.45
036	Jordan Zimmermann	6.44
037	Joe Coleman	6.39
038	David Wells	6.15
039	Nate Robertson	6.12
040	Joe Sparma	6.07
041	Jeff Weaver	6.01
042	Woodie Fryman	5.99
043	Bobo Newsom	5.95
044	Justin Thompson	5.94
045	Jack Morris	5.86
046	Alex Wilson	5.85
047	Eric King	5.77
048	Hank Aguirre	5.76
049	Armando Galarraga	5.69
050	Jeff Robinson	5.65
051	Frank Tanana	5.56
052	Felipe Lira	5.55
053	Rick Porcello	5.49
054	Ted Gray	5.48
055	Tom Timmermann	5.46
	Dave Wickersham	5.46
057	Hal Newhouser	5.41
058	Tommy Bridges	5.33
059	Billy Hoeft	5.32
060	Virgil Trucks	5.23
061	Milt Wilcox	5.12
062	Paul Gibson	5.07
063	Don Mossi	5.03
064	Phil Regan	4.99
065	Paul Foytack	4.98
066	Brian Moehler	4.96
067	Fred Scherman	4.94
068	Jason Johnson	4.82
069	Willie Blair	4.80
070	Dan Petry	4.67
071	Steve Sparks	4.63
072	Frank Lary	4.62
073	Bill Donovan	4.54
074	Kenny Rogers	4.43
075	Doyle Alexander	4.41
076	Mike Maroth	4.30
077	Dutch Leonard	4.21
	Walt Terrell	4.21
079	Dizzy Trout	4.16
080	Terry Fox	4.13
081	Schoolboy Rowe	4.12
082	Lerrin LaGrow	3.97
083	Mike Moore	3.86
084	Steve Gromek	3.84
085	Art Houtteman	3.79
086	Ralph Works	3.78
087	Al Benton	3.77
088	Mark Fidrych	3.71
089	George Mullin	3.66
090	Fred Hutchinson	3.63
091	Bill Gullickson	3.61
	George Uhle	3.61
093	Dave Rozema	3.60
094	Vern Ruhle	3.53
095	Harry Coveleski	3.52
096	Earl Whitehill	3.47
097	Hal White	3.43
098	Johnny Gorsica	3.38
	Firpo Marberry	3.38
100	Howard Ehmke	3.33
	Chief Hogsett	3.33
	Vic Sorrell	3.33

Al Alburquerque

001	Doug Fister	4.10
002	Joaquin Benoit	3.61
003	Max Scherzer	3.54
004	Jamie Walker	3.47
005	Anibal Sanchez	3.21
006	Justin Verlander	3.10
007	Matt Boyd	3.04
008	Jordan Zimmermann	2.99
009	Don Mossi	2.87
010	David Wells	2.84
011	Daniel Norris	2.82
012	Michael Fulmer	2.81
013	Willie Hernandez	2.78
014	Alex Wilson	2.77
015	Joe Jimenez	2.69
016	Mickey Lolich	2.64
017	Denny McLain	2.56
018	Shane Greene	2.54
019	Doug Brocail	2.52
020	Jim Bunning	2.49
	Rick Porcello	2.49
022	Spencer Turnbull	2.46
023	Earl Wilson	2.40
024	Jeremy Bonderman	2.28
	Jeff Weaver	2.28
026	Blaine Hardy	2.25
027	Al Alburquerque	2.21
028	Bobby Seay	2.20
029	Jose Valverde	2.01
030	Fred Gladding	2.00
	Jason Johnson	2.00
032	Brian Moehler	1.96
033	Phil Coke	1.95
034	John Hiller	1.94
035	Hank Aguirre	1.92
	Willie Blair	1.92
	Mike Henneman	1.92
038	Buck Farmer	1.91
039	Nate Robertson	1.90
040	Frank Kitson	1.87
041	Fernando Rodney	1.85
042	Jack Morris	1.82
	Frank Tanana	1.82
	Justin Thompson	1.82
045	Todd Jones	1.81
046	Aurelio Lopez	1.80
047	Doyle Alexander	1.79
	Dave Wickersham	1.79
049	Bill Gullickson	1.78
	Frank Lary	1.78

Willie Blair

051	Woodie Fryman	1.75
052	Joe Coleman	1.74
053	Dave Rozema	1.73
054	Mark Fidrych	1.72
055	Mike Maroth	1.71
056	Tom Timmermann	1.68
057	Armando Galarraga	1.65
058	Schoolboy Rowe	1.64
	Ed Summers	1.64
060	Juan Berenguer	1.63
	Steve Gromek	1.63
	Billy Hoeft	1.63
	Steve Sparks	1.63
064	Phil Regan	1.60
065	Felipe Lira	1.59
066	Bill Donovan	1.58
	Milt Wilcox	1.58
068	Terry Fox	1.56
	Bobo Newsom	1.56
070	Dutch Leonard	1.54
071	Fred Hutchinson	1.52
072	Matt Anderson	1.51
073	Harry Coveleski	1.48
	George Uhle	1.48
075	Ed Siever	1.46
076	Hal Newhouser	1.44
077	Virgil Trucks	1.43
078	Tommy Bridges	1.40
079	Eric King	1.39
080	Kenny Rogers	1.37
	Joe Sparma	1.37
082	Vern Ruhle	1.32
083	Firpo Marberry	1.31
084	Art Houtteman	1.29
	Dan Petry	1.29
086	Paul Gibson	1.28
	C.J. Nitkowski	1.28
088	Jeff Robinson	1.26
	John Doherty	1.26
090	Paul Foytack	1.25
	George Mullin	1.25
092	Dizzy Trout	1.23
093	Ned Garver	1.20
	Walt Terrell	1.20
095	Fred Scherman	1.18
096	Ted Gray	1.17
097	Lerrin LaGrow	1.15
098	Hooks Dauss	1.13
099	Johnny Gorsica	1.10
100	Ed Killian	1.06

Rank	Pitcher	R/9
001	Fred Gladding	2.96
002	Joaquin Benoit	3.08
003	John Hiller	3.17
004	Terry Fox	3.19
005	Al Alburquerque	3.20
006	Willie Hernandez	3.26
007	Ed Killian	3.29
008	Doug Brocail	3.36
009	Bill Donovan	3.38
010	Harry Coveleski	3.39
011	Denny McLain	3.42
012	Alex Wilson	3.50
013	Earl Wilson	3.51
014	Mark Fidrych	3.56
015	Mike Henneman	3.57
016	Hal Newhouser	3.61
017	Ed Summers	3.64
018	Hank Aguirre	3.65
019	Jose Valverde	3.66
020	Aurelio Lopez	3.67
021	Bernie Boland	3.69
022	Fred Scherman	3.73
	Max Scherzer	3.73
024	Doug Fister	3.74
025	Mickey Lolich	3.79
	Justin Verlander	3.79
027	Jamie Walker	3.80
028	Dizzy Trout	3.82
029	Tom Timmermann	3.83
030	Jim Bunning	3.84
031	Dave Rozema	3.90
	Dave Wickersham	3.90
033	George Mullin	3.92
034	Virgil Trucks	3.93
035	Don Mossi	3.94
036	Frank Lary	3.96
037	Bobby Seay	4.00
	Ed Siever	4.00
039	Bill James	4.06
040	Blaine Hardy	4.07
041	Jack Morris	4.09
042	Ed Willett	4.10
043	Paul Gibson	4.12
044	Jean Dubuc	4.13
045	Bobo Newsom	4.14
046	Steve Gromek	4.15
047	Ned Garver	4.19
	Fred Hutchinson	4.19
049	Tommy Bridges	4.21
050	David Wells	4.22
051	Hooks Dauss	4.23
052	Al Benton	4.25
053	Doyle Alexander	4.26
054	Joe Coleman	4.29
	Joe Sparma	4.29
056	Juan Berenguer	4.31
	Billy Hoeft	4.31
058	Michael Fulmer	4.33
059	Dan Petry	4.34
	Milt Wilcox	4.34
061	Hal White	4.36
062	Frank Kitson	4.37
063	Eric King	4.38
	Firpo Marberry	4.38
065	Stubby Overmire	4.40
	Justin Thompson	4.40
067	Woodie Fryman	4.45
	Herman Pillette	4.45
069	Howard Ehmke	4.48
070	Schoolboy Rowe	4.49
	Frank Tanana	4.49
072	Paul Foytack	4.53
073	Todd Jones	4.62
	Dutch Leonard	4.62
	George Uhle	4.62
076	Spencer Turnbull	4.64
077	Art Houtteman	4.65
078	George Cunningham	4.66
	Walt Terrell	4.66
080	Rick Porcello	4.67
081	Jeff Weaver	4.68
082	Fernando Rodney	4.69
083	Roscoe Miller	4.74
084	Johnny Gorsica	4.79
	Vern Ruhle	4.79
	Anibal Sanchez	4.79
087	Phi Coke	4.81
	Ted Gray	4.81
089	Brian Moehler	4.82
090	Armando Galarraga	4.84
091	Elden Auker	4.88
092	Daniel Norris	4.92
093	Ralph Works	4.94
094	Phi Regan	4.95
095	Bill Gullickson	5.02
096	Rip Collins	5.03
097	Jeff Robinson	5.08
	Earl Whitehill	5.08
099	Shane Greene	5.09
100	Vic Sorrell	5.11

Earl Wilson

Rank	Name	GS
001	Mickey Lolich	459
002	Jack Morris	408
003	George Mullin	395
004	Hooks Dauss	388
005	Justin Verlander	380
006	Hal Newhouser	373
007	Tommy Bridges	362
008	Dizzy Trout	305
009	Earl Whitehill	287
010	Frank Lary	274
	Dan Petry	274
012	Jim Bunning	251
013	Frank Tanana	243
014	Bill Donovan	242
015	Virgil Trucks	229
016	Milt Wilcox	220
017	Denny McLain	219
018	Vic Sorrell	216
019	Joe Coleman	201
020	Jeremy Bonderman	193
021	Walt Terrell	190
022	Paul Foytack	185
023	Schoolboy Rowe	181
024	Rick Porcello	180
025	Ed Willett	179
026	Billy Hoeft	176
027	Ed Killian	172
028	Fred Hutchinson	169
029	Nate Robertson	168
030	Max Scherzer	161
031	Ted Gray	159
032	Earl Wilson	145
033	Howard Ehmke	144
034	Matt Boyd	143
	Mike Maroth	143
036	Hank Aguirre	138
037	Elden Auker	136
	Joe Sparma	136
039	Brian Moehler	131
040	Jean Dubuc	130
	Anibal Sanchez	130
042	Don Mossi	129
043	Dave Rozema	128
044	Al Benton	126
	Art Houtteman	126
046	Harry Coveleski	125
047	Ed Siever	123
048	Bill Gullickson	116
049	Bernie Boland	113
050	Dutch Leonard	112

Virgil Trucks

Rank	Name	GS
	Ed Summers	112
052	Lil Stoner	110
053	Jeff Weaver	109
054	Stubby Overmire	103
055	Rip Collins	102
056	Bobo Newsom	101
	Phil Regan	101
	Justin Thompson	101
059	Ken Holloway	97
	Jordan Zimmermann	97
061	Ned Garver	94
062	George Uhle	92
063	Michael Fulmer	89
064	Steve Gromek	88
065	Red Oldham	87
	Jeff Robinson	87
067	Mike Moore	86
068	Dave Wickersham	81
069	Frank Kitson	79
070	Doyle Alexander	78
	Steve Sparks	78
072	Armando Galarraga	77
	Daniel Norris	77
074	Ownie Carroll	76
	Herman Pillette	76
	Vern Ruhle	76
077	Kenny Rogers	74
078	Bill James	71
079	Felipe Lira	69
080	Doug Fister	68
	Sam Gibson	68
082	Dave Mlicki	67
	Hal White	67
084	Jason Johnson	66
085	Woodie Fryman	65
086	Willie Blair	64
	Les Cain	64
	Johnny Gorsica	64
	David Wells	64
090	Lerrin LaGrow	63
091	John Doherty	61
092	Juan Berenguer	60
	Roxie Lawson	60
094	Dave Roberts	58
095	Nate Cornejo	56
	Mark Fidrych	56
	Joe Niekro	56
	Ed Wells	56
099	Roscoe Miller	54
100	Firpo Marberry	53
	Spencer Turnbull	53

Rank	Pitcher	CG
001	George Mullin	336
002	Hooks Dauss	245
003	Bill Donovan	213
004	Hal Newhouser	212
005	Tommy Bridges	200
006	Mickey Lolich	190
007	Dizzy Trout	156
008	Jack Morris	154
009	Earl Whitehill	147
010	Ed Killian	142
011	Ed Willett	127
012	Frank Lary	123
013	Vic Sorrell	95
014	Denny McLain	94
015	Ed Siever	93
016	Schoolboy Rowe	92
017	Jean Dubuc	90
018	Howard Ehmke	89
019	Virgil Trucks	84
020	Fred Hutchinson	81
021	Ed Summers	79
022	Jim Bunning	78
023	Billy Hoeft	71
024	Elden Auker	70
025	Harry Coveleski	68
	Frank Kitson	68
027	Paul Foytack	63
	Milt Wilcox	63
029	George Uhle	61
030	Bernie Boland	59
031	Art Houtteman	58
032	Joe Coleman	56
033	Dutch Leonard	55
034	Bobo Newsom	53
035	Ted Gray	50
	Roscoe Miller	50
037	Dan Petry	48
038	Al Benton	47
	Ned Garver	47
	Don Mossi	47
041	Lil Stoner	45
042	Walt Terrell	44
043	Hank Aguirre	41
044	Ownie Carroll	40
045	Earl Wilson	39
046	Stubby Overmire	38
047	Ken Holloway	37
	Joe Yeager	37
049	Dave Rozema	36
050	Steve Gromek	35
	Red Oldham	35

Dizzy Trout

Rank	Pitcher	CG
052	Mark Fidrych	34
053	Rip Collins	33
	Herman Pillette	33
055	Sam Gibson	32
056	Joe Sparma	30
057	Bill James	29
058	Win Mercer	28
059	Roxie Lawson	27
	Frank Tanana	27
	Ralph Works	27
062	Red Donahue	26
063	Dave Roberts	23
	Justin Verlander	23
	Hal White	23
066	Johnny Gorsica	22
	Firpo Marberry	22
	Dave Wickersham	22
069	Jack Cronin	21
070	General Crowder	20
	Phil Regan	20
072	George Cunningham	19
	Willie Mitchell	19
	Ed Wells	19
075	Bert Cole	18
	Chief Hogsett	18
	Rube Kisinger	18
	Lerrin LaGrow	18
079	George Gill	17
	Joe Lake	17
081	Ed Lafitte	16
082	Vern Ruhle	14
	Whit Wyatt	14
084	Doyle Alexander	13
	Carl Fischer	13
	Art Herring	13
	John Hiller	13
	Waite Hoyt	13
	Duke Maas	13
	Boots Poffenberger	13
	Jesse Stovall	13
092	Jack Billingham	12
	Rufe Gentry	12
	Syl Johnson	12
	Vern Kennedy	12
	Steve Sparks	12
097	Doc Ayers	11
	John Eubank	11
	Woodie Fryman	11
	Bill Gullickson	11
	Mike Kilkenny	11
	Jim Slaton	11
	Jake Wade	11

ALL TIME TIGER PITCHING LEADERS – SHUTOUTS

Rank	Pitcher	SHO
001	Mickey Lolich	39
002	George Mullin	34
003	Tommy Bridges	33
	Hal Newhouser	33
005	Bill Donovan	29
006	Dizzy Trout	28
007	Deny McLain	26
008	Jack Morris	24
009	Hooks Dauss	22
010	Frank Lary	20
	Virgil Trucks	20
012	Ed Killian	19
013	Jim Bunning	16
	Billy Hoeft	16
	Schoolboy Rowe	16
016	Fred Hutchinson	13
017	Ed Willette	12
018	Joe Coleman	11
	Jean Dubuc	11
	Art Houtteman	11
	Ed Siever	11
	Earl Whitehill	11
023	Bernie Boland	10
	Howard Ehmke	10
	Dan Petry	10
	Joe Sparma	10
027	Elden Auker	9
	Harry Coveleski	9
	Stubby Overmire	9
	Ed Summers	9
	Walt Terrell	9
032	Al Benton	8
	Dutch Leonard	8
	Bobo Newsom	8
	Vic Sorrell	8
036	Hank Aguirre	7
	Paul Foytack	7
	Ted Gray	7
	Steve Gromek	7
	Willie Mitchell	7
	Don Mossi	7
	Dave Rozema	7
	Frank Tanana	7
	Justin Verlander	7
	Hal White	7
	Milt Wilcox	7
	Earl Wilson	7
048	Rip Collins	6
	John Hiller	6
	Brian Moehler	6
051	Doyle Alexander	5
	Mark Fidrych	5
	Frank Kitson	5
	Jeff Robinson	5
	George Uhle	5

Frank Tanana

Rank	Pitcher	SHO
056	Doc Ayers	4
	Jack Billingham	4
	Bert Cole	4
	Ned Garver	4
	Johnny Gorsica	4
	Bill James	4
	Mike Kilkenny	4
	Duke Maas	4
	Win Mercer	4
	Roscoe Miller	4
	Herman Pillette	4
	Dave Roberts	4
	Vern Ruhle	4
	Ed Wells	4
	Dave Wickersham	4
	Ralph Works	4
072	Ray Bare	3
	General Crowder	3
	Red Donahue	3
	Rufe Gentry	3
	Sam Gibson	3
	Felipe Lira	3
	Mike Moore	3
	Rick Porcello	3
	Sailor Stroud	3
	Jeff Weaver	3
	Bill Wight	3
083	Juan Berenguer	2
	Jeremy Bonderman	2
	Ownie Carroll	2
	John Doherty	2
	John Eubank	2
	Woodie Fryman	2
	George Gill	2
	Ken Holloway	2
	Rudy Kallio	2
	Rube Kisinger	2
	Lerrin LaGrow	2
	Roxie Lawson	2
	Firpo Marberry	2
	Les Mueller	2
	Joe Niekro	2
	Red Oldham	2
	Omar Olivares	2
	Anibal Sanchez	2
	Dan Schatzeder	2
	Jim Slaton	2
	Steve Sparks	2
	Bob Sykes	2
	Tom Timmermann	2
	Jake Wade	2
	Joe Yeager	2
	George Zuverink	2

Rank	Pitcher	Wins
001	Mickey Lolich	200
002	Jack Morris	195
003	Hal Newhouser	187
004	Tommy Bridges	186
005	Justin Verlander	183
006	Hooks Dauss	181
007	Dizzy Trout	137
008	Frank Lary	122
	Earl Whitehill	122
010	Denny McLain	116
011	Dan Petry	114
012	Jim Bunning	110
013	Virgil Trucks	97
014	Frank Tanana	95
015	Milt Wilcox	94
016	Joe Coleman	88
	Schoolboy Rowe	88
018	Vic Sorrell	83
019	Max Scherzer	82
020	Fred Hutchinson	78
021	Rick Porcello	76
022	Walt Terrell	74
023	Paul Foytack	72
024	Billy Hoeft	70
025	Elden Auker	68
026	Jeremy Bonderman	67
027	Howard Ehmke	64
	Earl Wilson	64
029	Harry Coveleski	61
030	Ted Gray	56
	Don Mossi	56
032	Bernie Boland	55
033	Al Benton	54
034	Hank Aguirre	52
035	Bill Gullickson	51
036	Mike Maroth	50
	Nate Robertson	50
038	Dutch Leonard	49
	Dave Rozema	49
	Joe Sparma	49
041	Brian Moehler	48
	Bobo Newsom	48
043	Jean Dubuc	47
044	Art Houtteman	45
045	Anibal Sanchez	44
046	Rip Collins	41
047	Lil Stoner	40
048	Stubby Overmire	39
	Jeff Weaver	39
050	Steve Gromek	38
	George Uhle	38

Milt Wilcox

Rank	Pitcher	Wins
052	Matt Boyd	37
	Ned Garver	37
	Ken Holloway	37
055	Phil Regan	36
	Justin Thompson	36
057	Jeff Robinson	35
058	Dave Wickersham	32
059	Doug Fister	31
060	Red Oldham	30
	Herman Pillette	30
062	Doyle Alexander	29
	Ownie Carroll	29
	Mark Fidrych	29
	Mike Moore	29
	Kenny Rogers	29
	Steve Sparks	29
068	Bill James	28
069	Sam Gibson	27
070	Roxie Lawson	26
	David Wells	26
072	Willie Blair	25
	Michael Fulmer	25
	John Doherty	25
	Vern Ruhle	25
076	General Crowder	24
	Dave Mlicki	24
078	Les Cain	23
	Armando Galarraga	23
	Hal White	23
081	Jack Billingham	22
	Woodie Fryman	22
	Firpo Marberry	22
084	Willie Mitchell	20
	Dave Roberts	20
086	Ed Wells	19
087	Mark Leiter	18
	Felipe Lira	18
	Joe Niekro	18
090	Johnny Gorsica	17
	Mike Kilkenny	17
	Jim Slaton	17
	Jordan Zimmermann	17
094	Bert Cole	16
	George Gill	16
	Jason Johnson	16
	Lerrin LaGrow	16
	Jordan Zimmermann	16
099	John Hiller	15
	Chief Hogsett	15
	Syl Johnson	15
	Eric King	15
	Daniel Norris	15

Rank	Pitcher	Losses
001	Mickey Lolich	171
002	Hooks Dauss	159
003	Jack Morris	146
004	Hal Newhouser	139
005	Dizzy Trout	135
006	Justin Verlander	114
007	Frank Lary	105
008	Dan Petry	93
009	Vic Sorrell	91
010	Jim Bunning	85
	Virgil Trucks	85
012	Frank Tanana	82
013	Jeremy Bonderman	77
014	Milt Wilcox	74
015	Joe Coleman	73
016	Paul Foytack	72
	Billy Hoeft	72
	Walt Terrell	72
019	Ted Gray	71
020	Howard Ehmke	69
021	Nate Robertson	68
022	Fred Hutchinson	65
023	Mike Maroth	62
	Rick Porcello	62
025	Denny McLain	61
026	Matt Boyd	60
	Art Houtteman	60
028	Schoolboy Rowe	57
029	Brian Moehler	52
030	Jeff Weaver	51
031	Hank Aguirre	49
032	Anibal Sanchez	48
033	Bernie Boland	47
034	Joe Sparma	46
035	Elden Auker	45
	Dutch Leonard	45
	Earl Wilson	45
038	Jean Dubuc	44
039	Justin Thompson	43
040	Al Benton	42
	Lil Stoner	42
042	Don Mossi	41
	Dave Rozema	41
	Jordan Zimmermann	41
045	Ned Garver	40
	Steve Gromek	40
047	Harry Coveleski	39
	Phil Regan	39
049	Ken Holloway	38
050	Rip Collins	37
	Stubby Overmire	37
052	Bill Gullickson	36
	George Uhle	36
054	Ownie Carroll	35
	Michael Fulmer	35
	Bill James	35
	Lerrin LaGrow	35
	Red Oldham	35
	Max Scherzer	35
060	Mike Moore	34
061	Bobo Newsom	33
062	Johnny Gorsica	31
	Dave Mlicki	31
	Dave Wickersham	31
065	Felipe Lira	30
	Daniel Norris	30
	Herman Pillette	30
	Steve Sparks	30
069	Doyle Alexander	29
	Nate Cornejo	29
071	Jason Johnson	28
	Jose Lima	28
	Vern Ruhle	28
	Hal White	28
075	Sam Gibson	27
	Dave Roberts	27
077	Woodie Fryman	25
	Armando Galarraga	25
	Jeff Robinson	25
	Spencer Turnbull	25
081	Duke Maas	24
	Kenny Rogers	24
083	Willie Blair	23
	Chief Hogsett	23
085	Ray Bare	22
	George Cunningham	22
	John Doherty	22
	Ed Wells	22
089	Joe Niekro	21
	Dan Schatzeder	21
091	Doug Fister	20
092	Adam Bernero	19
	Les Cain	19
	Mark Fidrych	19
	John Hiller	19
	Roxie Lawson	19
	C.J. Nitkowski	19
	David Wells	19
099	Kevin Ritz	18
	Scott Aldred	18

Frank Lary

001	Max Scherzer	.701	82-35
002	Denny McLain	.655	116-61
003	General Crowder	.632	24-14
004	Jack Billingham	.629	22-13
005	Justin Verlander	.616	183-114
006	Harry Coveleski	.610	61-39
007	Doug Fister	.608	31-20
008	Schoolboy Rowe	.607	88-57
009	Mark Fidrych	.604	29-19
010	Elden Auker	.602	68-45
011	Bobo Newsom	.593	48-33
012	Tommy Bridges	.592	186-128
013	Earl Wilson	.587	64-45
014	Bill Gullickson	.586	51-36
015	Jeff Robinson	.583	35-25
016	Mark Leiter	.581	18-13
017	Roxie Lawson	.578	26-19
	David Wells	.578	26-19
019	Don Mossi	.577	56-41
020	Hal Newhouser	.574	187-139
021	Jack Morris	.572	195-146
022	Willie Mitchell	.571	20-15
023	Jim Bunning	.564	110-85
	Firpo Marberry	.564	22-17
025	Al Benton	.563	54-42
026	Milt Wilcox	.560	94-74
027	Bernie Boland	.557	54-43
028	Dan Petry	.551	114-93
	Rick Porcello	.551	76-62
030	Les Cain	.548	23-19
031	Joe Coleman	.547	88-73
	Kenny Rogers	.547	29-24
033	Fred Hutchinson	.545	78-65
034	Dave Rozema	.544	49-41
035	Jean Dubuc	.543	63-53
036	Mickey Lolich	.539	200-171
037	Frank Lary	.537	122-105
	Frank Tanana	.537	95-82
039	Virgil Trucks	.533	97-85
040	Hooks Dauss	.532	182-160
	John Doherty	.532	25-22
042	Rip Collins	.526	41-37
043	Juan Berenguer	.524	22-20
044	Willie Blair	.521	25-23
	Dutch Leonard	.521	49-45
046	Earl Whitehill	.517	122-114
047	Joe Sparma	.516	49-46
048	Hank Aguirre	.515	52-49
	Mike Kilkenny	.515	17-16
050	George Uhle	.514	38-36
051	Stubby Overmire	.513	39-37

General Crowder

052	D. Wickersham	.508	32-31
053	Walt Terrell	.507	74-72
054	Dizzy Trout	.504	137-135
055	Doyle Alexander	.500	29-29
	Paul Foytack	.500	72-72
	Sam Gibson	.500	27-27
	Herman Pillette	.500	30-30
059	Billy Hoeft	.493	70-72
	Ken Holloway	.493	37-38
061	Steve Sparks	.492	29-30
062	Lil Stoner	.488	40-42
063	Steve Gromek	.487	38-40
064	Bert Cole	.485	16-17
065	Howard Ehmke	.481	64-69
	Ned Garver	.481	37-40
067	Brian Moehler	.480	48-52
	Phil Regan	.480	36-39
069	A. Galarraga	.479	23-25
070	Anibal Sanchez	.478	44-48
071	Vic Sorrell	.477	83-91
072	Vern Ruhle	.472	25-28
073	Woodie Fryman	.468	22-25
074	J. Bonderman	.465	67-77
075	Ed Wells	.463	19-22
076	Joe Niekro	.462	18-21
	Red Oldham	.462	30-35
078	Mike Moore	.460	29-34
079	Justin Thompson	.456	36-43
080	Ownie Carroll	.453	29-35
081	Hal White	.451	23-28
082	Mike Maroth	.446	50-62
083	Bill James	.444	28-35
084	Ted Gray	.441	56-71
	John Hiller	.441	15-19
086	Dave Mlicki	.436	24-31
087	Jeff Weaver	.433	39-51
088	Art Houtteman	.429	45-60
089	Dave Roberts	.426	20-27
090	Nate Robertson	.424	50-68
091	Michael Fulmer	.417	25-35
092	Chief Hogsett	.395	15-23
093	Ray Bare	.389	14-22
094	Dan Schatzeder	.382	13-21
095	Matt Boyd	.381	37-60
096	J. Zimmermann	.379	25-41
097	Felipe Lira	.375	18-30
098	Duke Maas	.368	14-24
099	Jason Johnson	.364	16-28
100	Johnny Gorsica	.354	17-31

Rank	Pitcher	QS
001	Mickey Lolich	274
002	Justin Verlander	248
003	Jack Morris	240
004	Hal Newhouser	234
005	George Mullin	232
006	Hooks Dauss	230
007	Tommy Bridges	200
008	Dizzy Trout	187
009	Frank Lary	163
010	Jim Bunning	145
	Bill Donovan	145
	Dan Petry	145
013	Denny McLain	141
014	Frank Tanana	139
015	Earl Whitehill	131
016	Virgil Trucks	129
017	Joe Coleman	113
018	Milt Wilcox	110
019	Ed Killian	105
020	Max Scherzer	101
	Walt Terrell	101
022	Ed Summers	98
023	Vic Sorrell	97
024	Jeremy Bonderman	95
	Rick Porcello	95
026	Ed Willett	91
027	Paul Foytack	90
028	Harry Coveleski	88
029	Billy Hoeft	86
	Fred Hutchinson	86
031	Schoolboy Rowe	85
	Earl Wilson	85
033	Hank Aguirre	84
034	Nate Robertson	81
035	Al Benton	77
	Don Mossi	77
037	Ted Gray	76
038	Howard Ehmke	74
039	Jean Dubuc	72
040	Bernie Boland	69
041	Elden Auker	68
	Mike Maroth	68
043	Brian Moehler	67
044	Dave Rozema	65
	Ed Siever	65
046	Dutch Leonard	64
047	Anibal Sanchez	62
	Joe Sparma	62
049	Jeff Weaver	61
050	Justin Thompson	60
051	Art Houtteman	58
052	Matt Boyd	57

Joe Coleman

Rank	Pitcher	QS
	Bobo Newsom	57
054	Bill Gullickson	54
	Stubby Overmire	54
056	Ned Garver	52
	Phil Regan	52
058	Rip Collins	50
	Steve Gromek	50
	George Uhle	50
061	Doyle Alexander	48
	Frank Kitson	48
063	Doug Fister	47
064	Bill James	45
	Herman Pillette	45
066	Ken Holloway	44
	Steve Sparks	44
	Dave Wickersham	44
069	Michael Fulmer	43
	Lil Stoner	43
071	Red Oldham	42
072	David Wells	39
073	Jeff Robinson	38
	Kenny Rogers	38
075	Ownie Carroll	37
	Roscoe Miller	37
	Vern Ruhle	37
	Hal White	37
079	Mark Fidrych	36
080	Armando Galarraga	35
081	Les Cain	34
	Jason Johnson	34
083	Woodie Fryman	32
	Felipe Lira	32
	Jordan Zimmermann	32
086	Lerrin LaGrow	31
	Mike Moore	31
088	Juan Berenguer	30
	Sam Gibson	30
090	Johnny Gorsica	29
	Dave Mlicki	29
092	Willie Mitchell	28
	Joe Niekro	28
	Dave Roberts	28
095	Jack Billingham	27
	John Doherty	27
	Firpo Marberry	27
098	John Hiller	26
099	Nate Cornejo	23
	Carl Fischer	23
	Duke Maas	23
	Win Mercer	23
	Joe Yeager	23

001	Mickey Lolich	249
002	George Mullin	223
003	Hooks Dauss	221
004	Hal Newhouser	220
005	Jack Morris	217
006	Justin Verlander	180
007	Tommy Bridges	176
008	Dizzy Trout	167
009	Frank Lary	148
010	Jim Bunning	132
011	Denny McLain	128
012	Earl Whitehill	121
013	Dan Petry	116
	Virgil Trucks	116
015	Frank Tanana	109
016	Ed Killian	100
017	Joe Coleman	93
018	Vic Sorrell	87
	Milt Wilcox	87
020	Walt Terrell	86
	Ed Willett	86
022	Fred Hutchinson	83
023	Paul Foytack	82
	Billy Hoeft	82
025	Harry Coveleski	78
026	Schoolboy Rowe	76
027	Hank Aguirre	74
028	Earl Wilson	73
029	Don Mossi	71
030	Jean Dubuc	70
	Howard Ehmke	70
032	Ted Gray	69
033	Al Benton	68
034	Bernie Boland	67
035	Max Scherzer	65
036	Elden Auker	64
	Bill Donovan	64
038	Ed Summers	60
039	Jeremy Bonderman	57
	Jean Dubuc	57
	Dutch Leonard	57
042	Art Houtteman	56
043	Bobo Newsom	54
044	Ned Garver	51
045	Nate Robertson	50
046	Stubby Overmire	49
	Rick Porcello	49
	George Uhle	49
049	Frank Kitson	48
	Dave Rozema	48
	Jeff Weaver	48

Mickey Lolich

052	Steve Gromek	47
053	Bill Gullickson	46
054	Doyle Alexander	45
	Justin Thompson	45
056	Rip Collins	44
	Phil Regan	44
058	Ken Holloway	43
059	Joe Sparma	42
060	Dave Wickersham	41
061	Mike Maroth	40
	Brian Moehler	40
	Herman Pillette	40
064	Lil Stoner	39
065	Bill James	37
	Roscoe Miller	37
	Red Oldham	37
068	Mark Fidrych	36
069	Ownie Carroll	35
070	Doug Fister	34
	Hal White	34
072	Anibal Sanchez	32
	David Wells	32
074	Steve Sparks	31
075	Jeff Robinson	28
	Vern Ruhle	28
077	Michael Fulmer	27
	Sam Gibson	27
079	Willie Mitchell	26
080	Johnny Gorsica	25
081	Les Cain	23
	Woodie Fryman	23
	Jason Johnson	23
	Lerrin LaGrow	23
	Win Mercer	23
	Mike Moore	23
	Joe Niekro	23
	Dave Roberts	23
	Kenny Rogers	23
090	John Hiller	22
	Joe Yeager	22
092	Firpo Marberry	21
093	Jack Billingham	20
	John Doherty	20
	Carl Fischer	20
	Mike Kilkenny	20
	Roxie Lawson	20
098	Matt Boyd	19
	Armando Galarraga	19
100	Ray Bare	18
	Bert Cole	18
	General Crowder	18
	Dave Mlicki	18

ALL TIME TIGER PITCHING LEADERS – DOMINANT STARTS

Rank	Pitcher	Dominant Starts
001	Mickey Lolich	92
002	Hal Newhouser	89
003	George Mullin	78
004	Hooks Dauss	72
005	Dizzy Trout	70
006	Tommy Bridges	69
007	Jack Morris	67
008	Bill Donovan	64
009	Frank Lary	50
010	Denny McLain	49
011	Jim Bunning	48
	Virgil Trucks	48
013	Ed Killian	43
014	Justin Verlander	40
015	Schoolboy Rowe	35
	Ed Willett	35
017	Dan Petry	33
018	Harry Coveleski	31
019	Bernie Boland	30
	Milt Wilcox	30
021	Ed Summers	29
	Walt Terrell	29
	Earl Whitehill	29
024	Hank Aguirre	27
	Elden Auker	27
	Joe Coleman	27
	Paul Foytack	27
	Billy Hoeft	27
	Earl Wilson	27
030	Fred Hutchinson	26
	Don Mossi	26
	Frank Tanana	26
033	Jean Dubuc	24
	Art Houtteman	24
035	Al Benton	22
	Howard Ehmke	22
	Vic Sorrell	22
038	Stubby Overmire	20
039	Jean Dubuc	19
	Ned Garver	19
	Dutch Leonard	19
	Bobo Newsom	19
043	Joe Sparma	18
044	Ted Gray	17
045	Jeremy Bonderman	16
	Steve Gromek	16
	Max Scherzer	16
048	Mark Fidrych	15
	Dave Rozema	15
	Dave Wickersham	15
051	Bill James	14
	Herman Pillette	14
053	Jeff Robinson	13
054	Ownie Carroll	12
	Ken Holloway	12
	Mike Kilkenny	12
	Phil Regan	12
	George Uhle	12
	Hal White	12
060	John Hiller	11
	Brian Moehler	11
	Rick Porcello	11
	Dave Roberts	11
	Jeff Weaver	11
065	Rip Collins	10
	Frank Kitson	10
	Nate Robertson	10
068	Red Donahue	9
	Roscoe Miller	9
	Steve Sparks	9
070	General Crowder	8
	Doug Fister	8
	Sam Gibson	8
	Johnny Gorsica	8
	Red Oldham	8
	Vern Ruhle	8
	Lil Stoner	8
	Justin Thompson	8
078	Doyle Alexander	7
	Jack Billingham	7
	Bert Cole	7
	Woodie Fryman	7
	Bill Gullickson	7
	Lerrin LaGrow	7
	Mike Maroth	7
	Willie Mitchell	7
	David Price	7
	Anibal Sanchez	7
088	Carl Fischer	6
	George Gill	6
	Felipe Lira	6
	Duke Maas	6
	Firpo Marberry	6
	Mike Moore	6
	David Wells	6
	Ed Wells	6
096	Doc Ayers	5
	John Doherty	5
	Art Herring	5
	Eric King	5
	Win Mercer	5
	Joe Niekro	5
	Omar Olivares	5
	Jim Perry	5
	Mark Redman	5
	Kenny Rogers	5

Elden Auker

ALL TIME TIGER PITCHING LEADERS – QUALITY START PERCENTAGE (MINIMUM 15 QUALITY STARTS)

Rank	Pitcher	Pct
001	Harry Coveleski	.704
002	Doug Fister	.691
003	David Price	.688
004	Roscoe Miller	.685
005	Willie Mitchell	.667
006	Justin Verlander	.653
007	Denny McLain	.644
008	Mark Fidrych	.643
009	Bill James	.634
010	Hal Newhouser	.627
	Max Scherzer	.627
012	Rufe Gentry	.618
013	Doyle Alexander	.615
014	Dizzy Trout	.613
015	Al Benton	.611
	Bernie Boland	.611
017	Ed Killian	.610
018	Hank Aguirre	.609
	David Wells	.609
020	Red Donahue	.607
021	Carl Fischer	.605
	John Hiller	.605
023	Bill Donovan	.599
024	Mickey Lolich	.597
	Don Mossi	.597
026	Frank Lary	.595
027	Justin Thompson	.594
028	Hooks Dauss	.593
029	Herman Pillette	.592
030	Jack Morris	.588
031	George Mullin	.587
032	Doc Ayers	.586
	Earl Wilson	.586
034	George Cunningham	.583
035	Jim Bunning	.578
036	Frank Tanana	.572
037	Dutch Leonard	.571
	Ed Summers	.571
039	Steve Gromek	.568
040	Bobo Newsom	.564
	Steve Sparks	.564
042	Virgil Trucks	.563
043	Joe Coleman	.562
044	Ed Siever	.561
045	Jeff Weaver	.560
046	Jean Dubuc	.554
047	Ned Garver	.553
048	Tommy Bridges	.552
	Art Herring	.552
	Hal White	.552
051	Jack Billingham	.551
052	Hideo Nomo	.548
053	George Uhle	.543
	Dave Wickersham	.543
055	Edwin Jackson	.537
056	Walt Terrell	.532
057	Les Cain	.531
058	Dan Petry	.529
059	Rick Porcello	.528
060	Stubby Overmire	.524
061	Marc Hall	.517
	Tom Timmermann	.517
063	Jason Johnson	.515
	Phil Regan	.515
065	Howard Ehmke	.514
	Syl Johnson	.514
	Kenny Rogers	.514
068	Brian Moehler	.511
069	Fred Hutchinson	.509
	Firpo Marberry	.509
071	Dave Rozema	.508
	Ed Willett	.508
073	Elden Auker	.500
	Waite Hoyt	.500
	Joe Niekro	.500
	Jim Perry	.500
	Milt Wilcox	.500
078	Jeremy Bonderman	.492
	Woodie Fryman	.492
	Lerrin LaGrow	.492
081	Rip Collins	.490
082	Billy Hoeft	.489
083	Bert Cole	.488
084	Ownie Carroll	.487
	Vern Ruhle	.487
086	Paul Foytack	.486
	Jerry Ujdur	.486
088	Michael Fulmer	.483
	Dave Roberts	.483
090	Nate Robertson	.482
091	Ted Gray	.478
092	Anibal Sanchez	.477
093	Mike Maroth	.476
094	Dan Schatzeder	.475
095	George Gill	.471
	Red Oldham	.471
	Jim Slaton	.471
098	Schoolboy Rowe	.470
099	Duke Maas	.469
	Mark Redman	.469

David Price

ALL TIME TIGER PITCHING LEADERS – HIGH QUALITY START PERCENTAGE (10 HIGH QUALITY STARTS)

Rank	Pitcher	Pct
001	Mark Fidrych	.643
002	Harry Coveleski	.624
003	Willie Mitchell	.619
004	Red Donahue	.607
005	Bernie Boland	.593
006	Hal Newhouser	.590
007	Denny McLain	.584
008	Doyle Alexander	.577
009	Hooks Dauss	.570
010	David Price	.563
011	Doc Ayers	.552
012	Don Mossi	.550
	Kip Young	.550
014	Dizzy Trout	.548
015	Ned Garver	.543
016	Mickey Lolich	.542
017	Al Benton	.540
	Frank Lary	.540
019	Jean Dubuc	.538
020	Hank Aguirre	.536
	Ed Summers	.536
022	Bobo Newsom	.535
023	Steve Gromek	.534
024	George Uhle	.533
025	Jack Morris	.532
026	Jim Bunning	.526
	Carl Fischer	.526
	Herman Pillette	.526
029	Bill James	.521
030	Art Herring	.517
031	John Hiller	.512
032	George Uhle	.511
033	Dutch Leonard	.509
034	Virgil Trucks	.507
	Hal White	.507
036	Dave Wickersham	.506
037	Earl Wilson	.503
038	George Cunningham	.500
	Doug Fister	.500
	Rufe Gentry	.500
	David Wells	.500
042	Fred Hutchinson	.491
043	Tommy Bridges	.486
	Howard Ehmke	.486
045	Marc Hall	.483
046	Rudy Kallio	.478
047	Stubby Overmire	.476
048	Justin Verlander	.474
049	Elden Auker	.471

Mark Fidrych

Rank	Pitcher	Pct
050	Duke Maas	.469
051	Billy Hoeft	.466
052	Joe Coleman	.463
053	Ownie Carroll	.461
054	Walt Terrell	.453
055	Frank Tanana	.449
056	Justin Thompson	.446
057	Art Houtteman	.444
058	Paul Foytack	.443
	Ken Holloway	.443
060	George Gill	.441
	Jim Perry	.441
062	Jeff Weaver	.440
063	Phil Regan	.436
064	Ted Gray	.434
065	Rip Collins	.431
066	Mike Kilkenny	.426
067	Red Oldham	.425
	Dan Schatzeder	.425
069	Dan Petry	.423
	George Zuverink	.423
071	Earl Whitehill	.422
072	Schoolboy Rowe	.420
073	Bert Cole	.419
074	Jim Slaton	.412
075	Joe Niekro	.411
076	Jack Billingham	.408
077	Mark Redman	.406
078	Jerry Ujdur	.405
079	Max Scherzer	.404
080	Vic Sorrell	.403
081	Sam Gibson	.397
	Bill Gullickson	.397
	Dave Roberts	.397
	Steve Sparks	.397
085	Firpo Marberry	.396
086	Milt Wilcox	.395
087	Ray Bare	.391
	Johnny Gorsica	.391
089	General Crowder	.375
	Dave Rozema	.375
	Waite Hoyt	.375
092	Marlin Stuart	.370
093	Vern Ruhle	.368
094	Edwin Jackson	.366
095	Lerrin LaGrow	.365
096	Michael Fulmer	.360
097	Les Cain	.359
098	Lil Stoner	.355
099	Woodie Fryman	.354
100	Jason Johnson	.348

Rank	Pitcher	Pct
001	Red Donahue	.321
002	Mark Fidrych	.268
003	Bernie Boland	.265
004	Bill Donovan	.264
005	Ed Summers	.259
006	John Hiller	.256
007	Mike Kilkenny	.255
008	Ed Killian	.250
009	Harry Coveleski	.248
010	Hal Newhouser	.239
011	Dizzy Trout	.230
012	Denny McLain	.224
013	David Price	.219
014	Virgil Trucks	.210
015	Ned Garver	.202
	Don Mossi	.202
017	Mickey Lolich	.200
018	Elden Auker	.199
019	Bill James	.197
	George Mullin	.197
021	Hank Aguirre	.196
	Ed Willett	.196
023	Stubby Overmire	.194
024	Schoolboy Rowe	.193
025	Tommy Bridges	.191
	Jim Bunning	.191
027	Art Houtteman	.190
	Dave Roberts	.190
029	Bobo Newsom	.188
030	Hooks Dauss	.186
	Earl Wilson	.186
032	Jean Dubuc	.185
	Dave Wickersham	.185
034	Herman Pillette	.184
035	Steve Gromek	.182
	Frank Lary	.182
037	Hal White	.179
038	George Gill	.176
039	Al Benton	.175
040	Doc Ayers	.172
	Art Herring	.172
042	Dutch Leonard	.170
043	General Crowder	.167
	Roscoe Miller	.167
	Willie Mitchell	.167
046	Jack Morris	.164
047	Bert Cole	.163
048	Ownie Carroll	.158
049	Mark Redman	.156
050	Fred Hutchinson	.154

Mike Kilkenny

Rank	Pitcher	Pct
051	Howard Ehmke	.153
	Billy Hoeft	.153
	Walt Terrell	.153
054	Jeff Robinson	.149
055	Jim Perry	.147
056	Jean Dubuc	.146
	Paul Foytack	.146
058	Jack Billingham	.143
059	Milt Wilcox	.136
060	Joe Coleman	.134
061	Carl Fischer	.132
	Joe Sparma	.132
063	George Uhle	.130
064	Eric King	.128
065	Frank Kitson	.127
066	Johnny Gorsica	.125
067	Ken Holloway	.124
068	Duke Maas	.122
069	Dan Petry	.120
070	Phil Regan	.119
071	Doug Fister	.118
	Sam Gibson	.118
073	Dave Rozema	.117
074	Steve Sparks	.115
075	Omar Olivares	.114
076	Firpo Marberry	.113
077	Lerrin LaGrow	.111
078	Woodie Fryman	.108
079	Ted Gray	.107
	Frank Tanana	.107
	Ed Wells	.107
082	Vern Ruhle	.105
	Justin Verlander	.105
084	Vic Sorrell	.102
085	Jeff Weaver	.101
	Earl Whitehill	.101
087	Max Scherzer	.099
088	Rip Collins	.098
089	David Wells	.094
090	Red Oldham	.092
091	Doyle Alexander	.090
092	Joe Niekro	.089
093	Felipe Lira	.087
094	Brian Moehler	.084
095	Jeremy Bonderman	.083
096	John Doherty	.082
097	Justin Thompson	.079
098	Lil Stoner	.073
099	Mike Moore	.070
100	Kenny Rogers	.068

Rank	Name	No Decisions
001	Mickey Lolich	88
002	Justin Verlander	83
003	Jack Morris	67
	Dan Petry	67
005	Frank Tanana	66
006	Jim Bunning	56
007	Milt Wilcox	52
008	Earl Whitehill	51
009	Nate Robertson	50
010	Jeremy Bonderman	49
011	Tommy Bridges	48
012	Frank Lary	47
	Hal Newhouser	47
	Virgil Trucks	47
015	Matt Boyd	46
	Hooks Dauss	46
017	Max Scherzer	44
	Walt Terrell	44
019	Rick Porcello	42
	Vic Sorrell	42
021	Paul Foytack	41
	Denny McLain	41
	Joe Sparma	41
024	Joe Coleman	40
025	Dave Rozema	38
	Anibal Sanchez	38
027	Hank Aguirre	37
	Daniel Norris	37
029	Schoolboy Rowe	36
	Earl Wilson	36
031	Billy Hoeft	34
032	Dizzy Trout	33
033	Ted Gray	32
	Don Mossi	32
035	Mike Maroth	31
	Brian Moehler	31
	Jordan Zimmermann	31
038	Al Benton	30
039	Michael Fulmer	29
	Armando Galarraga	29
	Bill Gullickson	29
042	Lil Stoner	28
043	Stubby Overmire	27
044	Fred Hutchinson	26
	George Mullin	26
	Phil Regan	26
	Jeff Robinson	26
048	Harry Coveleski	25
049	Rip Collins	24
050	Elden Auker	23
	Mike Moore	23
	Vern Ruhle	23

Nate Robertson

Rank	Name	No Decisions
053	Les Cain	22
	Ken Holloway	22
	Jason Johnson	22
	Red Oldham	22
	Justin Thompson	22
058	Art Houtteman	21
	Felipe Lira	21
	Kenny Rogers	21
061	Doyle Alexander	20
	Bobo Newsom	20
063	Steve Sparks	19
	Jeff Weaver	19
	David Wells	19
	Ed Willett	19
067	Woodie Fryman	18
	Dutch Leonard	18
	Casey Mize	18
	George Uhle	18
	Dave Wickersham	18
072	Bernie Boland	17
	Ned Garver	17
	Joe Niekro	17
	Spencer Turnbull	17
076	Willie Blair	16
	Doug Fister	16
	Johnny Gorsica	16
	Herman Pillette	16
	Hal White	16
081	Tyler Alexander	15
	Nate Cornejo	15
	Roxie Lawson	15
	Omar Olivares	15
	Drew Smyly	15
	Ed Wells	15
087	Jack Billingham	14
	John Doherty	14
	Jean Dubuc	14
	Sam Gibson	14
	Mike Kilkenny	14
	Firpo Marberry	14
	C.J. Nitkowski	14
094	Scott Aldred	13
	Gary Knotts	13
	Tarik Skubal	13
097	Ownie Carroll	12
	Bill Donovan	12
	Lerrin LaGrow	12
	Wil Ledezma	12
	Mark Leiter	12
	Dave Mlicki	12
	Johnny Podres	12
	Dontrelle Willis	12

Rank	Pitcher	Wins
001	Jack Morris	39
002	Tommy Bridges	36
003	Earl Whitehill	32
004	Bill Donovan	29
005	George Mullin	28
	Justin Verlander	28
007	Hal Newhouser	27
008	Vic Sorrell	21
009	Jeremy Bonderman	18
	Joe Coleman	18
	Rick Porcello	18
012	Mike Maroth	17
	Nate Robertson	17
	Schoolboy Rowe	17

Rick Porcello

Rank	Pitcher	Wins
015	Ed Killian	16
	Frank Lary	16
	Mickey Lolich	16
	Dan Petry	16
	Frank Tanana	16
020	Jim Bunning	15
	Howard Ehmke	15
	Fred Hutchinson	15
	Lil Stoner	15
024	Paul Foytack	13
	Max Scherzer	13
026	Elden Auker	12
	Jean Dubuc	12
	Bill Gullickson	12
	Denny McLain	12
	Ed Summers	12
	Milt Wilcox	12
	Jordan Zimmermann	12
033	Willie Blair	11
	Billy Hoeft	11
	Anibal Sanchez	11
	Walt Terrell	11
	Virgil Trucks	11
038	Ted Gray	10
	Brian Moehler	10
	Don Mossi	10
041	Armando Galarraga	9
	Art Houtteman	9
	Roxie Lawson	9
	Dutch Leonard	9
	Jeff Robinson	9
	Ed Siever	9
	Dizzy Trout	9
048	Matt Boyd	8
	General Crowder	8
	Daniel Norris	8
	Kenny Rogers	8
	Jeff Weaver	8
053	Ownie Carroll	7
	Dave Mlicki	7
	Mike Moore	7
	Steve Sparks	7
	Justin Thompson	7
058	Al Benton	6
	Michael Fulmer	6
	Steve Gromek	6
	Chief Hogsett	6
	Ken Holloway	6
	Frank Kitson	6
	Stubby Overmire	6
	Boots Poffenberger	6
	Dave Rozema	6
	Earl Wilson	6
068	Jack Billingham	5
	Rip Collins	5
	John Doherty	5
	Mark Leiter	5
	Zach Miner	5
	Bobo Newsom	5
	Brad Penny	5
	Phil Regan	5
	Tarik Skubal	5
	George Uhle	5
078	Nate Cornejo	4
	Ned Garver	4

Ed Siever

Rank	Pitcher	Wins
	Jason Johnson	4
	Wil Ledezma	4
	Felipe Lira	4
	Firpo Marberry	4
	Roscoe Miller	4
	C.J. Nitkowski	4
	Alfredo Simon	4
	Joe Sparma	4
	Spencer Turnbull	4
	David Wells	4
	Ed Wells	4
	Dave Wickersham	4
	Whit Wyatt	4
093	26 Pitchers	3

Rank	Pitcher	Tough Losses
001	George Mullin	64
002	Mickey Lolich	62
003	Jack Morris	54
	Hal Newhouser	54
005	Dizzy Trout	49
006	Frank Lary	43
007	Tommy Bridges	39
008	Bill Donovan	38
009	Justin Verlander	34
010	Earl Whitehill	33
011	Jim Bunning	30
012	Ed Killian	28
	Virgil Trucks	28
014	Vic Sorrell	25
015	Ted Gray	24
016	Joe Coleman	23
	Howard Ehmke	23
	Frank Tanana	23
019	Jeremy Bonderman	21
	Frank Kitson	21
	Denny McLain	21
	Dan Petry	21
	Walt Terrell	21
024	Mike Maroth	20
	Ed Siever	20
026	Hank Aguirre	19
	Al Benton	19
	Art Houtteman	19
	Fred Hutchinson	19
	Milt Wilcox	19
031	Paul Foytack	18
	Don Mossi	18
	Jeff Weaver	18
034	Billy Hoeft	17
	Dutch Leonard	17
036	Steve Gromek	16
037	Rick Porcello	15
	Phil Regan	15
	Justin Thompson	15
040	Rip Collins	14
	Nate Robertson	14
	Dave Rozema	14
	George Uhle	14
	Earl Wilson	14
045	Ned Garver	13
	Brian Moehler	13
	Anibal Sanchez	13
	Ed Summers	13
049	Michael Fulmer	12
	Ken Holloway	12
	Rube Kisinger	12
	Lerrin LaGrow	12
	Lil Stoner	12

Phil Regan

Rank	Pitcher	Tough Losses
054	Les Cain	11
	Bobo Newsom	11
	Schoolboy Rowe	11
057	George Cunningham	10
	Stubby Overmire	10
	Joe Sparma	10
	Hal White	10
	Dave Wickersham	10
062	Doyle Alexander	9
	Matt Boyd	9
	Ownie Carroll	9
	Johnny Gorsica	9
	Felipe Lira	9
	Herman Pillette	9
	Steve Sparks	9
068	Elden Auker	8
	Mark Fidrych	8
	Doug Fister	8
	Jason Johnson	8
	Jose Lima	8
	Duke Maas	8
	Win Mercer	8
	Willie Mitchell	8
	Dave Roberts	8
	Max Scherzer	8
	Joe Yeager	8
079	Ray Bare	7
	Jack Cronin	7
	Bill Gullickson	7
	Vern Ruhle	7
084	Adam Bernero	6
	Matt Boyd	6
	Eric Erickson	6
	Carl Fischer	6
	Rufe Gentry	6
	Art Herring	6
	Dick Marlowe	6
	Dave Mlicki	6
	Joe Niekro	6
	David Wells	6
	Whit Wyatt	6
	Kip Young	6
	Jordan Zimmermann	6
097	Fernando Arroyo	5
	Nate Cornejo	5
	Sam Gibson	5
	John Hiller	5
	Chief Hogsett	5
	Rudy Kallio	5
	Francisco Liriano	5
	Firpo Marberry	5
	Kenny Rogers	5
	Dan Schatzeder	5
	Ed Wells	5

001	John Hiller	502
002	Mike Henneman	491
003	Todd Jones	480
004	Willie Hernandez	358
005	Aurelio Lopez	351
006	Jamie Walker	327
007	Fernando Rodney	308
008	Phil Coke	284
009	Matt Anderson	245
010	Alex Wilson	245
011	Al Alburquerque	241
012	Doug Brocail	236
013	Joe Jimenez	235
014	Jose Valverde	226
015	Shane Greene	224
016	Buck Farmer	220
	Blaine Hardy	220
018	Fred Gladding	216
019	Fred Scherman	208
020	Terry Fox	207
021	Hal White	206
022	Joaquin Benoit	205
023	Paul Gibson	200
024	Bobby Seay	199
025	Hank Aguirre	196
026	Dizzy Trout	188
027	Mike Myers	182
028	Danny Patterson	180
029	C.J. Nitkowski	176
030	Chief Hogsett	173
031	Joel Zumaya	171
032	Al Benton	170
033	Tom Timmermann	166
034	Daniel Stumph	159
035	Larry Sherry	152
036	Hooks Dauss	150
037	Ryan Perry	149
038	Johnny Gorsica	140
039	Ken Holloway	135
	Dave Tobik	135
041	Jose Cisnero	131
	Chris Spurling	131
043	Al Aber	129
044	Franklyn German	126
045	Joe Boever	125
046	Bruce Rondon	123
047	Zach Miner	122
048	Drew VerHagen	119
049	Jason Grilli	118
050	Gregory Soto	115

Willie Hernandez

051	Daryl Patterson	111
052	Justin Wilson	108
053	Lil Stoner	107
054	Tom Morgan	105
055	Pat Dobson	104
	Jerry Don Gleaton	104
057	Sean Runyan	103
058	Paul Foytack	100
	George Smith	100
060	Joba Chamberlain	99
061	Ian Krol	96
062	Fred Lasher	95
063	Bert Cole	94
064	Stubby Overmire	92
065	Doug Bair	90
066	Bernie Boland	89
	Eric King	89
	Francisco Rodriguez	89
069	Ray Herbert	88
070	George Cunningham	87
	Hal Newhouser	87
	Virgil Trucks	87
073	Orlando Pena	86
074	John Doherty	84
075	Warwick Saupold	82
076	Kurt Knudsen	81
077	Buddy Groom	80
	Art Houtteman	80
	Dick Marlowe	80
	Dave Rozema	80
081	Victor Alcantara	79
	Mike Munoz	79
	Kyle Ryan	79
	Bill Scherrer	79
	Pat Underwood	79
	Ugueth Urbina	79
087	Slick Coffman	78
	A.J. Sager	78
089	Jim Crawford	77
090	Fred Hutchinson	73
	Wil Ledezma	73
	Ron Nischwitz	73
	Daniel Schlereth	73
	Dave Sisler	73
	Brayan Villarreal	73
096	Bryan Garcia	72
	Richie Lewis	72
	Chuck Seelbach	72
099	Dan Miceli	71
	Drew Smyly	71

Rank	Name	Wins
001	John Hiller	72
002	Mike Henneman	57
003	Aurelio Lopez	51
004	Hooks Dauss	41
005	Willie Hernandez	36
006	Terry Fox	26
	Fred Gladding	26
008	Chief Hogsett	24
	Fred Scherman	24
	Dizzy Trout	24
011	Todd Jones	23
012	Ken Holloway	20
013	Larry Sherry	18
014	Al Alburquerque	17
	Al Benton	17
	Doug Brocail	17
	Schoolboy Rowe	17
	Virgil Trucks	17
	Hal White	17
020	Joe Boever	16
	Phil Coke	16
	Paul Gibson	16
	Fred Hutchinson	16
	Joe Jimenez	16
	Tom Timmermann	16
026	Al Aber	15
	Matt Anderson	15
	Fernando Rodney	15
029	Johnny Gorsica	14
	Shane Greene	14
031	Joaquin Benoit	13
	Bernie Boland	13
	Hal Newhouser	13
	Alex Wilson	13
	Joel Zumaya	13
036	Hank Aguirre	12
	Doug Bair	12
	Ray Herbert	12
	Roxie Lawson	12
	Jamie Walker	12
	Alex Wilson	12
042	Howard Ehmke	11
	Blaine Hardy	11
	Earl Whitehill	11
045	Buck Farmer	10
	Blaine Hardy	10
	Eric King	10
	Fred Lasher	10
	Zach Miner	10

Aurelio Lopez

Rank	Name	Wins
	Danny Patterson	10
	Bobby Seay	10
	Chuck Seelbach	10
	Lil Stoner	10
054	Elden Auker	9
	Bert Cole	9
	Steve Foucault	9
	Paul Foytack	9
	Syl Johnson	9
	Firpo Marberry	9
	Dick Marlowe	9
	Archie McKain	9
	Daryl Patterson	9
	Vic Sorrell	9
	Dave Tobik	9
065	Tommy Bridges	8
	Jim Bunning	8
	Ownie Carroll	8
	Slick Coffman	8
	Harry Coveleski	8
	Kyle Funkhouser	8
	Franklyn German	8
	Art Houtteman	8
	Stubby Overmire	8
	Orlando Pena	8
	Bruce Rondon	8
	Dave Rozema	8
	Warwick Saupold	8
	Dave Sisler	8
	George Smith	8
	Bud Thomas	8
	Dave Wickersham	8
082	George Caster	7
	Jose Cisnero	7
	Jim Crawford	7
	George Cunningham	7
	Pat Dobson	7
	John Doherty	7
	Jean Dubuc	7
	George Gill	7
	Jason Grilli	7
	Steve Gromek	7
	Bill James	7
	Wil Ledezma	7
	Mickey Lolich	7
	Kyle Ryan	7
	A.J. Sager	7
	Kevin Saucier	7
	Drew Smyly	7
	Jose Valverde	7
	Drew VerHagen	7
	Justin Wilson	7

Rank	Pitcher	Losses
001	John Hiller	57
002	Mike Henneman	34
003	Todd Jones	32
004	Willie Hernandez	31
005	Fernando Rodney	30
006	Aurelio Lopez	28
007	Chief Hogsett	24
008	Al Benton	22
	Hooks Dauss	22
010	Hal White	21
011	Dizzy Trout	18
012	Phil Coke	17
	Terry Fox	17
	Joe Jimenez	17
	Larry Sherry	17
016	Paul Gibson	16
	Tom Timmermann	16
018	Hank Aguirre	15
	Lil Stoner	15
	Dave Tobik	15
021	Doug Brocail	13
	Shane Greene	13
	Fred Scherman	13
	Jose Valverde	13
025	Jim Crawford	12
	Jamie Walker	12
	Alex Wilson	12
	Joel Zumaya	12
029	Al Aber	11
	Jose Cisnero	11
	Buck Farmer	11
	Steve Foucault	11
	Fred Gladding	11
	Danny Patterson	11
	Virgil Trucks	11
036	Joe Boever	10
	Tommy Bridges	10
	Bert Cole	10
	Pat Dobson	10
	Tom Morgan	10
	Vic Sorrell	10
042	John Doherty	9
	Paul Foytack	9
	Art Houtteman	9
	Zach Miner	9
	Mike Myers	9
	Hal Newhouser	9
	Red Oldham	9
	Orlando Pena	9
	Francisco Rodriguez	9
	Ugueth Urbina	9
	Justin Wilson	9
053	Johnny Gorsica	8
	Art Herring	8
	Ken Holloway	8
	Jim Middleton	8
	Stubby Overmire	8
	Dave Sisler	8
	Brayan Villarreal	8
060	Matt Anderson	7
	Elden Auker	7
	Joaquin Benoit	7
	Joba Chamberlain	7
	Slick Coffman	7
	Jason Grilli	7
	Ray Herbert	7
	Eric King	7
	C.J. Nitkowski	7
	Daryl Patterson	7
	Bruce Rondon	7
	A.J. Sager	7
	Chris Spurling	7
	Daniel Stumph	7
	Whit Wyatt	7
075	Al Alburquerque	6
	Willie Blair	6
	Bernie Boland	6
	Bill Campbell	6
	Storm Davis	6
	Jean Dubuc	6
	Howard Ehmke	6
	Bill Fischer	6
	Marc Hall	6
	Blaine Hardy	6
	Billy Hoeft	6
	Fred Hutchinson	6
	Syl Johnson	6
	Fred Lasher	6
	Roxie Lawson	6
	Richie Lewis	6
	Don McMahon	6
	Ray Narleski	6
	Ryan Perry	6
	Gregory Soto	6
	Ed Wells	6
	Esteban Yan	6
097	32 Pitchers	5

Dave Tobik

Rank	Pitcher	Pct	W-L
001	Jim Bunning	.800	8-2
002	Schoolboy Rowe	.773	17-5
003	Archie McKain	.750	9-3
004	Al Alburquerque	.739	17-6
005	Fred Hutchinson	.727	16-6
	Dave Wickersham	.727	8-3
007	Ken Holloway	.714	20-8
008	Doug Bair	.706	12-5
009	Fred Gladding	.703	26-11
010	G. Cunningham	.700	7-3
	Kyle Ryan	.700	7-3
	Kevin Saucier	.700	7-3
013	Dick Marlowe	.692	9-4
014	Earl Whitehill	.688	11-5
015	Bernie Boland	.684	13-6
016	Matt Anderson	.682	15-7
017	Franklyn German	.667	8-4
	Roxie Lawson	.667	12-6
	Bobby Seay	.667	10-5
	Chuck Seelbach	.667	10-5
	George Smith	.667	8-4
	Bud Thomas	.667	8-4
023	Hooks Dauss	.651	41-22
024	Joaquin Benoit	.650	13-7
025	Fred Scherman	.649	24-13
026	Howard Ehmke	.647	11-6
027	Aurelio Lopez	.646	51-28
028	Johnny Gorsica	.636	14-8
	Mickey Lolich	.636	7-4
030	Ray Herbert	.632	12-7
031	Mike Henneman	.626	57-34
032	Blaine Hardy	.625	10-6
	Fred Lasher	.625	10-6
034	Joe Boever	.615	16-10
	Ownie Carroll	.615	8-5
	Harry Coveleski	.615	8-5
	Kyle Funkhouser	.615	8-5
	Dave Rozema	.615	8-5
	Drew VerHagen	.615	8-5
040	Virgil Trucks	.607	17-11
041	Terry Fox	.605	26-17
042	Syl Johnson	.600	9-6
	Kurt Knudsen	.600	6-4
	Elam Vangilder	.600	6-4
045	Hal Newhouser	.591	13-9
046	Eric King	.588	10-7
047	Wil Ledezma	.583	7-5
048	Al Aber	.577	15-11
049	Dizzy Trout	.571	24-18

Jim Bunning

Rank	Pitcher	Pct	W-L
050	Doug Brocail	.567	17-13
051	Elden Auker	.563	9-7
	Daryl Patterson	.563	9-7
053	John Hiller	.558	72-57
054	Brandon Lyon	.545	6-5
	Ed Nunez	.545	6-5
	Phil Regan	.545	6-5
	George Uhle	.545	6-5
058	Jean Dubuc	.538	7-6
059	Willie Hernandez	.537	36-31
060	Slick Coffman	.533	8-7
	Bruce Rondon	.533	8-7
062	Zach Miner	.526	10-9
063	Joel Zumaya	.520	13-12
064	Larry Sherry	.514	18-17
065	Bill Fischer	.500	6-6
	Paul Foytack	.500	9-9
	Paul Gibson	.500	16-16
	Jason Grilli	.500	7-7
	Chief Hogsett	.500	24-24
	Mark Leiter	.500	5-5
	Don McMahon	.500	6-6
	Ron Nischwitz	.500	5-5
	Stubby Overmire	.500	8-8
	A.J. Sager	.500	7-7
	Dave Sisler	.500	8-8
	Gregory Soto	.500	6-6
	Tom Timmermann	.500	16-16
	Jamie Walker	.500	12-12
079	Phil Coke	.485	16-17
	Joe Jimenez	.485	16-17
081	Shane Greene	.480	12-13
	Alex Wilson	.480	12-13
083	Buck Farmer	.476	10-11
	Danny Patterson	.476	10-11
085	Bert Cole	.474	9-10
	Vic Sorrell	.474	9-10
087	Art Houtteman	.471	8-9
	Orlando Pena	.471	8-9
089	Willie Blair	.455	5-6
	Ryan Perry	.455	5-6
	Ed Wells	.455	5-6
092	Steve Foucault	.450	9-11
093	Hal White	.447	17-21
094	Hank Aguirre	.444	12-15
	Tommy Bridges	.444	8-10
096	John Doherty	.438	7-9
	Justin Wilson	.438	7-9
098	Al Benton	.436	17-22
099	Todd Jones	.418	23-32
100	Pat Dobson	.412	7-10

Rank	Pitcher	Holds
001	Joaquin Benoit	68
002	Joel Zumaya	60
003	Jamie Walker	59
004	Phil Coke	53
005	Alex Wilson	52
006	Bobby Seay	51
007	Joe Jimenez	47
008	Doug Brocail	42
	Joe Jimenez	42
010	Al Alburquerque	41
	Fernando Rodney	41
012	Joba Chamberlain	37
013	Mike Myers	36
014	C.J. Nitkowski	33
	Justin Wilson	33
016	Buck Farmer	32
	Blaine Hardy	32
	Danny Patterson	32
019	Matt Anderson	31
	Danny Patterson	31
021	Shane Greene	30
	Ryan Perry	30
023	Jose Cisnero	29
024	Daniel Stumpf	25
025	Zach Miner	24
026	Buck Farmer	23
	Drew Smyly	23
028	Paul Gibson	22
029	Jason Grilli	21
	Bruce Rondon	21
031	Mike Henneman	20
032	Kyle Farnsworth	18
033	Mike Munoz	17
034	Al Levine	16
	Bob MacDonald	16
036	John Doherty	15
	John Hiller	15
	Kurt Knudsen	15
	Brandon Lyon	15
	Chris Spurling	15
041	Drew VerHagen	14
042	Victor Alcantara	13
	Buddy Groom	13
	Willie Hernandez	13
	Gregory Soto	13
046	Jerry Don Gleaton	12
	Sean Runyan	12
	A.J. Sager	12
	Brayan Villarreal	12
050	Joe Boever	11
	Octavio Dotel	11
	Ian Krol	11
	Aurelio Lopez	11
	Dan Miceli	11
	Bill Scherrer	11
	Esteban Yan	11
057	Franklyn German	10
058	Al Aber	9
	Brian Bohanon	9
	Michael Fulmer	9
	Kyle Funkhouser	9
	Mike Gardiner	9
	Oscar Henriquez	9
	Eric King	9
	Bill Krueger	9
	Daniel Schlereth	9
	Larry Sherry	9
	Pat Underwood	9
	Jose Veras	9
070	Tim Byrdak	8
	Storm Davis	8
	Bryan Garcia	8
	Fred Gladding	8
	Todd Jones	8
	Mark Lowe	8
	Kyle Ryan	8
	Fred Scherman	8
078	Doug Bair	7
	Freddy Dolsi	7
	John Kiely	7
	Fred Lasher	7
	Edwin Nunez	7
	Jose Paniagua	7
	Julio Santana	7
085	Hank Aguirre	6
	Louis Coleman	6
	Francisco Cordero	6
	Nelson Cruz	6
	Bryce Florie	6
	Casey Fossum	6
	Mark Leiter	6
	Alex Lange	6
	Richie Lewis	6
	Jose Lima	6
	Daniel Norris	6
	Matt Roney	6
	Kevin Saucier	6
	Tom Timmermann	6
	Dave Tobik	6
100	10 Pitchers	5

Joel Zumaya

Rank	Name	GF
001	Todd Jones	401
002	Mike Henneman	369
003	John Hiller	363
004	Willie Hernandez	279
005	Aurelio Lopez	245
006	Jose Valverde	210
007	Fernando Rodney	179
008	Chief Hogsett	131
009	Terry Fox	128
010	Dizzy Trout	126
011	Shane Greene	121
012	Hooks Dauss	120
013	Hal White	116
014	Fred Gladding	115
015	Al Benton	111
016	Fred Scherman	106
017	Matt Anderson	105
018	Larry Sherry	90
	Tom Timmermann	90
020	Hank Aguirre	88
021	Ken Holloway	82
022	Johnny Gorsica	80
023	Paul Gibson	79
024	Jamie Walker	78
025	Doug Brocail	76
026	Francisco Rodriguez	75
027	Al Aber	74
	Joaquin Benoit	74
029	Phil Coke	73
	Joe Jimenez	73
031	Dave Tobik	69
032	Lil Stoner	67
033	George Cunningham	66
034	Bert Cole	64
	Hal Newhouser	64
036	Ugueth Urbina	60
037	Art Houtteman	58
038	Joe Boever	57
039	Joe Nathan	55
040	Danny Patterson	54
	George Smith	54
042	Gregory Soto	53
	Virgil Trucks	53
044	Joe Jimenez	52
	Stubby Overmire	52
046	Mike Myers	51
047	Al Alburquerque	50
	Jerry Don Gleaton	50
049	Bernie Boland	49
	Steve Foucault	49
	Tom Morgan	49
052	Juan Acevedo	48
	Fred Hutchinson	48
054	Tommy Bridges	47
	Paul Foytack	47
	Schoolboy Rowe	47
057	Jean Dubuc	46
	Daryl Patterson	46
	Bobby Seay	46
	Alex Wilson	46
061	Buck Farmer	45
	Blaine Hardy	45
	Eric King	45
	Dave Rozema	45
065	Ray Herbert	44
066	Pat Dobson	41
	Vic Sorrell	41
068	Slick Coffman	40
	Franklyn German	40
	Steve Grilli	40
	Art Herring	40
	Syl Johnson	40
	Joaquim Soria	40
074	Fred Lasher	39
	Red Oldham	39
	Ryan Perry	39
	Ralph Works	39
078	Archie McKain	38
	Orlando Pena	38
	Charlie Sullivan	38
081	Jess Doyle	37
	George Mullin	37
	Bruce Rondon	37
	Kevin Saucier	37
	Dave Sisler	37
	Ed Willett	37
087	Chuck Seelbach	36
	Pat Underwood	36
	Justin Wilson	36
090	Elden Auker	35
	Jason Grilli	35
	Dick Marlowe	35
	Joel Zumaya	35
094	Roxie Lawson	34
	George Uhle	34
	Ed Wells	34
097	Jim Crawford	33
	Howard Ehmke	33
	Bill Fischer	33
	Bob Miller	33

Joe Nathan

Rank	Name	Saves
001	Todd Jones	235
002	Mike Henneman	154
003	John Hiller	125
004	Willie Hernandez	120
005	Jose Valverde	119
006	Aurelio Lopez	85
007	Fernando Rodney	70
008	Shane Greene	65
009	Terry Fox	55
010	Francisco Rodriguez	51
011	Al Benton	45
012	Hooks Dauss	41
013	Larry Sherry	37
	Dizzy Trout	37
015	Joe Nathan	36
016	Fred Scherman	34
017	Fred Gladding	33
	Tom Timmermann	33
019	Ugueth Urbina	30
020	Juan Acevedo	28
	Joaquin Benoit	28
022	Hank Aguirre	27
	Chief Hogsett	27
024	Matt Anderson	26
025	Joakim Soria	24
026	Gregory Soto	20
027	Hal Newhouser	19
028	Joe Jimenez	18
	Kevin Saucier	18
	Hal White	18
031	Steve Foucault	17
	Johnny Gorsica	17
	Fred Lasher	17
034	Pat Dobson	16
	Ken Holloway	16
	Art Houtteman	16
	Eric King	16
038	Jerry Don Gleaton	15
039	Al Aber	14
	Michael Fulmer	14
	Chuck Seelbach	14
	Lil Stoner	14
	Justin Wilson	14
044	Bernie Boland	13
	Dave Tobik	13
046	Jim Bunning	12
	Don McMahon	12
	Dave Sisler	12
	Virgil Trucks	12
050	Paul Gibson	11
	Billy Hoeft	11
	Tom Morgan	11
	Orlando Pena	11
	Vic Sorrell	11
	George Uhle	11
056	Tommy Bridges	10
	Mickey Lolich	10
	Mike Marshall	10
	Red Oldham	10
	Stubby Overmire	10
	Dave Rozema	10
062	Joe Boever	9
	Bert Cole	9
	John Doherty	9
	Jess Doyle	9
	Daryl Patterson	9
067	Doug Bair	8
	Harry Coveleski	8
	George Cunningham	8
	Jean Dubuc	8
	Mike Myers	8
	Gregg Olson	8
	Troy Percival	8
	Schoolboy Rowe	8
	Mark Thurmond	8
	Pat Underwood	8
077	Howard Ehmke	7
	Franklyn German	7
	Steve Gromek	7
	Ray Herbert	7
	Fred Hutchinson	7
	Kurt Knudsen	7
	Frank Lary	7
	Roxie Lawson	7
	Archie McKain	7
	Jim Middleton	7
	Ed Nunez	7
	Bruce Rondon	7
	Ed Wells	7
	Earl Whitehill	7
	Dave Wickersham	7
	Esteban Yan	7
093	George Caster	6
	Phil Coke	6
	Kyle Farnsworth	6
	Paul Foytack	6
	Bryan Garcia	6
	Duke Maas	6
	George Mullin	6
	Danny Patterson	6

Todd Jones

TIGERS QUADRUPLE TRIPLE CROWN

	H	HR	RBI	AVG	
1903	184	4	89	.335	Sam Crawford
1905	171	6	75	.297	Sam Crawford
1907	212	5	119	.350	Ty Cobb
1909	216	9	107	.377	Ty Cobb
1911	248	8	127	.420	Ty Cobb
1921	237	19	139	.394	Harry Heilmann
1923	211	18	115	.403	Harry Heilmann
1925	225	13	134	.393	Harry Heilmann
1927	201	14	120	.398	Harry Heilmann
1933	204	12	105	.325	Charlie Gehringer
1963	172	27	101	.312	Al Kaline
1998	175	34	103	.291	Tony Clark
2003	167	29	85	.297	Dmitri Young
2007	216	28	139	.363	Magglio Ordonez
2009	198	34	103	.324	Miguel Cabrera
2011	197	30	105	.344	Miguel Cabrera
2012	205	44	139	.330	Miguel Cabrera
2013	193	44	137	.348	Miguel Cabrera
2016	188	38	108	.316	Miguel Cabrera
2018	185	23	89	.298	Nicholas Castellanos

TIGERS TRIPLE CROWN

	HR	RBI	AVG	
1903	4	89	.335	Sam Crawford
1905	6	75	.297	Sam Crawford
1907	5	119	.350	Ty Cobb
1909	9	107	.377	Ty Cobb
1911	8	127	.420	Ty Cobb
1921	19	139	.394	Harry Heilmann
1923	18	115	.403	Harry Heilmann
1924	10	114	.346	Harry Heilmann
1925	13	134	.393	Harry Heilmann
1927	14	120	.398	Harry Heilmann
1928	14	107	.328	Harry Heilmann
1933	12	105	.325	Charlie Gehringer
1938	58	146	.315	Hank Greenberg
1940	41	150	.340	Hank Greenberg
1963	27	101	.312	Al Kaline
1967	25	78	.308	Al Kaline
1979	26	105	.318	Steve Kemp
1998	34	103	.291	Tony Clark
2002	19	82	.301	Randall Simon
2003	29	85	.297	Dmitri Young
2007	28	139	.363	Magglio Ordonez
2009	34	103	.324	Miguel Cabrera
2010	38	126	.328	Miguel Cabrera
2011	30	105	.344	Miguel Cabrera
2012	44	139	.330	Miguel Cabrera
2013	44	137	.348	Miguel Cabrera
2016	38	108	.316	Miguel Cabrera
2018	23	89	.298	Nicholas Castellanos

TIGERS SABERMETRIC TRIPLE CROWN

	TB	RC	OBP	
1902	197	78	.397	Jimmy Barrett
1905	247	88	.357	Sam Crawford
1907	283	108	.380	Ty Cobb
1909	296	128	.431	Ty Cobb
1910	279	127	.456	Ty Cobb
1911	367	171	.467	Ty Cobb
1912	323	147	.456	Ty Cobb
1915	274	133	.486	Ty Cobb
1916	267	121	.452	Ty Cobb
1917	335	149	.444	Ty Cobb
1918	217	96	.440	Ty Cobb
1922	297	137	.462	Ty Cobb
1923	331	159	.481	Harry Heilmann
1927	311	148	.475	Harry Heilmann
1930	326	132	.404	Charlie Gehringer
1932	307	114	.370	Charlie Gehringer
1933	294	116	.393	Charlie Gehringer
1936	356	153	.431	Charlie Gehringer
1938	380	166	.438	Hank Greenberg
1940	384	166	.433	Hank Greenberg
1942	247	90	.365	Barney McCosky
1955	321	135	.421	Al Kaline
1958	266	100	.374	Al Kaline
1961	354	172	.487	Norm Cash
1964	246	94	.383	Al Kaline
1967	248	102	.411	Al Kaline
1976	255	98	.386	Rusty Staub
1977	310	113	.363	Ron LeFlore
1979	266	106	.398	Steve Kemp
1981	156	61	.389	Steve Kemp
1985	301	110	.364	Kirk Gibson
1987	329	132	.402	Alan Trammell
1990	339	128	.377	Cecil Fielder
1995	255	89	.349	Chad Curtis
1998	314	112	.358	Tony Clark
2000	321	121	.377	Bobby Higginson
2003	302	112	.372	Dmitri Young
2007	354	154	.434	Magglio Ordonez
2009	334	132	.396	Miguel Cabrera
2010	341	143	.420	Miguel Cabrera
2011	335	150	.448	Miguel Cabrera
2013	353	156	.442	Miguel Cabrera
2016	332	131	.393	Miguel Cabrera
2018	310	111	.354	Nicholas Castellanos
2019	196	66	.346	Miguel Cabrera

161 GAMES PLAYED

162	Jimmy Barrett	1904
163	**Rocky Colavito**	**1961**
162	Jake Wood	1961
161	Rocky Colavito	1962
162	Dick McAuliffe	1964
162	Don Wert	1965
162	Eddie Brinkman	1973
161	Rusty Staub	1976
162	Rusty Staub	1978
161	Lou Whitaker	1983
162	Cecil Fielder	1991
161	Travis Fryman	1992
162	Brian Hunter	1997
161	Brandon Inge	2009
161	Miguel Cabrera	2011
162	Prince Fielder	2012
161	Miguel Cabrera	2012
162	Prince Fielder	2013
161	Ian Kinsler	2014

123 RUNS SCORED

147	**Ty Cobb**	**1911**
126	Donie Bush	1911
144	Ty Cobb	1915
124	Ty Cobb	1921
131	Lu Blue	1922
131	Charlie Gehringer	1929
128	Roy Johnson	1929
144	Charlie Gehringer	1930
134	Charlie Gehringer	1934
123	Charlie Gehringer	1935
144	Charlie Gehringer	1936
137	Hank Greenberg	1937
133	Charlie Gehringer	1937
144	Hank Greenberg	1938
133	Charlie Gehringer	1938
129	Hank Greenberg	1940
123	Barney McCosky	1940
129	Rocky Colavito	1961
126	Ron LeFlore	1978

25-25 TIGERS

HR	SB		
27	29	Kirk Gibson	1984
29	30	Kirk Gibson	1985
28	34	Kirk Gibson	1986

20-20 TIGERS

HR	SB		
21	25	Alan Trammell	1986
24	26	Kirk Gibson	1987
28	21	Alan Trammell	1987
21	27	Chad Curtis	1995
22	28	Damion Easley	1997
23	26	Curtis Granderson	2007
25	22	Gary Sheffield	2007
30	20	Curtis Granderson	2009
23	20	Robbie Grossman	2021

.340-40-130 TIGERS

AVG	HR	RBI		
.340	41	150	Hank Greenberg	1940
.361	41	132	Norm Cash	1961
.348	44	137	Miguel Cabrera	2013

712 PLATE APPEARANCES

714	Jimmy Barrett	1904
721	Donie Bush	1914
726	Ty Cobb	1924
715	Charlie Gehringer	1929
713	Roy Johnson	1929
731	Charlie Gehringer	1936
732	Eddie Lake	1947
729	Jerry Priddy	1950
724	George Kell	1950
731	Jake Wood	1961
741	**Ron LeFlore**	**1978**
734	Rusty Staub	1978
720	Lou Whitaker	1983
712	Cecil Fielder	1991
733	Tony Phillips	1992
721	Travis Fryman	1992
712	Prince Fielder	2013
726	Ian Kinsler	2014

630 AT BATS

640	Roy Johnson	1929
634	Charlie Gehringer	1929
641	Charlie Gehringer	1936
635	Gee Walker	1937
634	Pete Fox	1938
630	Doc Cramer	1942
641	George Kell	1950
679	Harvey Kuenn	1953
656	Harvey Kuenn	1954
663	Jake Wood	1961
652	Ron LeFlore	1977
666	Ron LeFlore	1978
642	Rusty Staub	1978
643	Lou Whitaker	1983
659	Travis Fryman	1992
658	Brian Hunter	1997
631	Curtis Granderson	2009
684	**Ian Kinsler**	**2014**

210 HITS

212	Ty Cobb	1907
216	Ty Cobb	1909
248	**Ty Cobb**	**1911**
217	Sam Crawford	1911
226	Ty Cobb	1912
225	Ty Cobb	1917
237	Harry Heilmann	1921
211	Harry Heilmann	1923
211	Ty Cobb	1924
225	Harry Heilmann	1925
215	Dale Alexander	1929
215	Charlie Gehringer	1929
214	Charlie Gehringer	1934
227	Charlie Gehringer	1936
213	Gee Walker	1937
218	George Kell	1950
212	Ron LeFlore	1977
206	Lou Whitaker	1983
216	Magglio Ordonez	2007

150 SINGLES

152	Jimmy Barrett	1904
165	Ty Cobb	1907
164	Ty Cobb	1909
169	**Ty Cobb**	**1911**
160	Sam Crawford	1911
166	Ty Cobb	1912
161	Ty Cobb	1915
155	Ty Cobb	1916
151	Ty Cobb	1917
161	Harry Heilmann	1921
159	Ty Cobb	1924
161	Harry Heilmann	1925
154	Charlie Gehringer	1937
150	George Kell	1951
167	Harvey Kuenn	1953
162	Harvey Kuenn	1954
156	Tito Fuentes	1977
156	Ron LeFlore	1977
153	Ron LeFlore	1978
152	Placido Polanco	2007

17 TRIPLES

25	Sam Crawford	1903
17	Sam Crawford	1907
20	Ty Cobb	1908
19	Sam Crawford	1910
24	Ty Cobb	1911
23	Ty Cobb	1912
21	Sam Crawford	1912
23	Sam Crawford	1913
26	**Sam Crawford**	**1914**
19	Sam Crawford	1915
24	Ty Cobb	1917
17	Bobby Veach	1919
17	Charlie Gehringer	1926
18	Heinie Manush	1927
19	Charlie Gehringer	1929
19	Roy Johnson	1931
19	Barney McCosky	1940
23	Curtis Granderson	2007

12 HIT BY PITCH

12	Dick Harley	1902
12	George Burns	1914
17	Heinie Manush	1923
16	Heinie Manush	1924
13	Norm Cash	1962
20	Bill Freehan	1967
24	**Bill Freehan**	**1968**
15	Chet Lemon	1982
20	Chet Lemon	1983
16	Damion Easley	1997
16	Damion Easley	1998
19	Damion Easley	1999
14	Brad Ausmus	1999
13	Damion Easley	2001
17	Brandon Inge	2009
17	Prince Fielder	2012
13	Ian Kinsler	2016

45 DOUBLES

47	Ty Cobb	1911
45	Bobby Veach	1919
49	Harry Heilmann	1923
45	Harry Heilmann	1924
50	Harry Heilmann	1927
45	Charlie Gehringer	1929
45	Roy Johnson	1929
47	Charlie Gehringer	1930
47	Dale Alexander	1931
63	**Hank Greenberg**	**1934**
50	Charlie Gehringer	1934
46	Hank Greenberg	1935
60	Charlie Gehringer	1936
55	Gee Walker	1936
49	Hank Greenberg	1937
50	Hank Greenberg	1940
56	George Kell	1950
46	Deivi Cruz	2000
54	Magglio Ordonez	2007
48	Miguel Cabrera	2011
52	Miguel Cabrera	2014
45	Nicholas Castellanos	2018

37 HOME RUNS

36	Hank Greenberg	1935
40	Hank Greenberg	1937
58	**Hank Greenberg**	**1938**
41	Hank Greenberg	1940
44	Hank Greenberg	1946
45	Rocky Colavito	1961
41	Norm Cash	1961
39	Norm Cash	1962
37	Rocky Colavito	1962
40	Darrell Evans	1985
51	Cecil Fielder	1990
44	Cecil Fielder	1991
38	Dean Palmer	1999
37	Miguel Cabrera	2008
38	Miguel Cabrera	2010
44	Miguel Cabrera	2012
44	Miguel Cabrera	2013
38	J.D. Martinez	2015
38	Miguel Cabrera	2016

132 RUNS BATTED IN

139	Harry Heilmann	1921
128	Bobby Veach	1921
134	Harry Heilmann	1925
137	Dale Alexander	1929
135	Dale Alexander	1930
139	Hank Greenberg	1934
170	Hank Greenberg	1935
183	**Hank Greenberg**	**1937**
146	Hank Greenberg	1938
150	Hank Greenberg	1940
134	Rudy York	1940
133	Vic Wertz	1949
140	Rocky Colavito	1961
132	Norm Cash	1961
132	Cecil Fielder	1990
133	Cecil Fielder	1991
139	Magglio Ordonez	2007
139	Miguel Cabrera	2012
137	Miguel Cabrera	2013

13 REACHED BASE ON ERROR

14	Eddie Lake	1947
13	Ray Boone	1953
13	Al Kaline	1955
13	Al Kaline	1956
16	Harvey Kuenn	1957
14	Al Kaline	1957
18	**Al Kaline**	**1961**
15	Billy Bruton	1961
13	Jake Wood	1961
14	Al Kaline	1963
14	Willie Horton	1965
15	Mickey Stanley	1969
17	Mickey Stanley	1970
17	Mickey Stanley	1973
14	Ron LeFlore	1976
13	Lou Whitaker	1984
14	Deivi Cruz	1998
13	Damion Easley	2001

1.030 ON BASE PLUS SLUGGING

1.088	Ty Cobb	1911
1.040	Ty Cobb	1912
1.051	Harry Heilmann	1921
1.048	Ty Cobb	1921
1.030	Harry Heilmann	1922
1.113	Harry Heilmann	1923
1.066	Ty Cobb	1925
1.091	Harry Heilmann	1927
1.039	Hank Greenberg	1935
1.105	Hank Greenberg	1937
1.122	Hank Greenberg	1938
1.042	Hank Greenberg	1939
1.103	Hank Greenberg	1940
1.040	Dick Wakefield	1944
1.148	**Norm Cash**	**1961**
1.042	Miguel Cabrera	2010
1.033	Miguel Cabrera	2011
1.078	Miguel Cabrera	2013

175 ON-BASE PLUS SLUGGING +

193	Ty Cobb	1909
206	Ty Cobb	1910
196	Ty Cobb	1911
200	Ty Cobb	1912
196	Ty Cobb	1913
190	Ty Cobb	1914
185	Ty Cobb	1915
179	Ty Cobb	1916
209	**Ty Cobb**	**1917**
194	Ty Cobb	1918
194	Harry Heilmann	1923
180	Harry Heilmann	1927
190	Dick Wakefield	1944
175	Roy Cullenbine	1946
201	Norm Cash	1961
176	Al Kaline	1967
178	Miguel Cabrera	2010
179	Miguel Cabrera	2011
190	Miguel Cabrera	2013

.450 ON BASE PERCENTAGE

.456	Ty Cobb	1910
.467	Ty Cobb	1911
.456	Ty Cobb	1912
.467	Ty Cobb	1913
.466	Ty Cobb	1914
.486	Ty Cobb	1915
.452	Ty Cobb	1916
.452	Ty Cobb	1921
.462	Ty Cobb	1922
.481	Harry Heilmann	1923
.468	Ty Cobb	1925
.457	Harry Heilmann	1925
.456	Al Wingo	1925
.475	Harry Heilmann	1927
.450	Charlie Gehringer	1934
.452	Mickey Cochrane	1935
.458	Charlie Gehringer	1937
.464	Dick Wakefield	1944
.477	Roy Cullenbine	1946
.487	**Norm Cash**	**1961**

.595 SLUGGING PERCENTAGE

.621	Ty Cobb	1911
.606	Harry Heilmann	1921
.596	Ty Cobb	1921
.598	Harry Heilmann	1922
.632	Harry Heilmann	1923
.598	Ty Cobb	1925
.616	Harry Heilmann	1927
.600	Hank Greenberg	1934
.628	Hank Greenberg	1935
.668	Hank Greenberg	1937
.651	Rudy York	1937
.683	**Hank Greenberg**	**1938**
.622	Hank Greenberg	1939
.670	Hank Greenberg	1940
.604	Hank Greenberg	1946
.662	Norm Cash	1961
.595	Magglio Ordonez	2007
.622	Miguel Cabrera	2010
.606	Miguel Cabrera	2012
.636	Miguel Cabrera	2013

1.135 TOTAL AVERAGE

1.193	Ty Cobb	1909
1.321	Ty Cobb	1910
1.464	**Ty Cobb**	**1911**
1.310	Ty Cobb	1913
1.170	Ty Cobb	1915
1.253	Ty Cobb	1917
1.135	Harry Heilmann	1922
1.288	Harry Heilmann	1923
1.206	Ty Cobb	1925
1.265	Harry Heilmann	1927
1.138	Hank Greenberg	1935
1.277	Hank Greenberg	1937
1.306	Hank Greenberg	1938
1.152	Hank Greenberg	1939
1.215	Hank Greenberg	1940
1.162	Dick Wakefield	1944
1.202	Roy Cullenbine	1946
1.358	Norm Cash	1961
1.184	Miguel Cabrera	2013

.344 GROSS PRODUCTION AVERAGE

.365	Ty Cobb	1911
.351	Ty Cobb	1912
.352	Ty Cobb	1921
.352	Harry Heilmann	1921
.349	Ty Cobb	1922
.344	Harry Heilmann	1922
.374	Harry Heilmann	1923
.360	Ty Cobb	1925
.348	Harry Heilmann	1925
.368	Harry Heilmann	1927
.363	Hank Greenberg	1937
.368	Hank Greenberg	1938
.363	Hank Greenberg	1940
.353	Dick Wakefield	1944
.349	Roy Cullenbine	1946
.384	**Norm Cash**	**1961**
.348	Miguel Cabrera	2011
.358	Miguel Cabrera	2013

7.5 OFFENSE WAR

9.5	Ty Cobb	1909
9.6	Ty Cobb	1910
10.2	Ty Cobb	1911
8.9	Ty Cobb	1912
7.6	Ty Cobb	1913
9.9	Ty Cobb	1915
8.7	Ty Cobb	1916
10.6	**Ty Cobb**	**1917**
8.9	Harry Heilmann	1923
7.7	Harry Heilmann	1927
7.5	Charlie Gehringer	1934
7.5	Hank Greenberg	1937
8.5	Norm Cash	1961
8.2	Alan Trammell	1987
7.9	Miguel Cabrera	2011
7.7	Miguel Cabrera	2012
9.1	Miguel Cabrera	2013

.255 BATTER'S RUN AVERAGE

.285	Ty Cobb	1911
.263	Ty Cobb	1912
.263	Harry Heilmann	1921
.262	Ty Cobb	1921
.293	Harry Heilmann	1923
.277	Ty Cobb	1925
.284	Harry Heilmann	1927
.257	Hank Greenberg	1935
.291	Hank Greenberg	1937
.298	Hank Greenberg	1938
.256	Hank Greenberg	1939
.273	Hank Greenberg	1940
.255	Roy Cullenbine	1946
.321	**Norm Cash**	**1961**
.265	Miguel Cabrera	2007
.261	Miguel Cabrera	2010
.285	Miguel Cabrera	2011
.281	Miguel Cabrera	2013

7.7 WINS ABOVE REPLACEMENT

9.8	Ty Cobb	1909
10.5	Ty Cobb	1910
10.7	Ty Cobb	1911
9.2	Ty Cobb	1912
9.5	Ty Cobb	1915
8.0	Ty Cobb	1916
11.3	**Ty Cobb**	**1917**
9.3	Harry Heilmann	1923
8.4	Charlie Gehringer	1934
7.8	Charlie Gehringer	1935
7.7	Hank Greenberg	1935
7.7	Hank Greenberg	1937
8.2	Al Kaline	1955
9.2	Norm Cash	1961
8.4	Al Kaline	1961
8.2	Alan Trammell	1987

2.3 DEFENSE WAR

2.4	Donie Bush	1914
2.4	George Moriarty	1914
2.5	Ossie Vitt	1916
2.3	Charlie Gehringer	1933
2.3	Billy Rogell	1933
3.7	**Billy Rogell**	**1935**
2.4	Eddie Mayo	1944
2.7	Jerry Priddy	1950
2.7	Ray Oyler	1967
2.4	Alan Trammell	1981
2.3	Chet Lemon	1983
2.7	Brandon Inge	2006
3.4	Austin Jackson	2011
2.9	Ian Kinsler	2.14
2.6	Ian Kinsler	2015
2.3	Jacoby Jones	2018

.375 BATTING AVERAGE

.377	Ty Cobb	1909
.383	Ty Cobb	1910
.420	**Ty Cobb**	**1911**
.378	Sam Crawford	1911
.409	Ty Cobb	1912
.390	Ty Cobb	1913
.383	Ty Cobb	1917
.382	Ty Cobb	1918
.384	Ty Cobb	1919
.394	Harry Heilmann	1921
.389	Ty Cobb	1921
.401	Ty Cobb	1922
.403	Harry Heilmann	1923
.393	Harry Heilmann	1925
.378	Ty Cobb	1925
.378	Heinie Manush	1926
.398	Harry Heilmann	1927

.450 SECONDARY AVERAGE

.512	Hank Greenberg	1937
.456	Rudy York	1937
.586	**Hank Greenberg**	**1938**
.477	Rudy York	1938
.502	Hank Greenberg	1939
.497	Hank Greenberg	1940
.488	Hank Greenberg	1946
.479	Roy Cullenbine	1946
.496	Roy Cullenbine	1947
.544	Norm Cash	1961
.482	Rocky Colavito	1961
.481	Norm Cash	1962
.469	Cecil Fielder	1990
.451	Mickey Tettleton	1992
.499	Mickey Tettleton	1994
.456	Miguel Cabrera	2010
.456	Miguel Cabrera	2013

.394 BABIP

.399	Ty Cobb	1909
.411	Ty Cobb	1910
.444	Ty Cobb	1911
.395	Sam Crawford	1911
.425	Ty Cobb	1912
.415	Ty Cobb	1913
.397	Ty Cobb	1915
.394	Ty Cobb	1916
.400	Ty Cobb	1917
.398	Ty Cobb	1918
.401	Ty Cobb	1919
.399	Harry Heilmann	1921
.416	Ty Cobb	1922
.414	Harry Heilmann	1923
.398	Harry Heilmann	1925
.394	Harry Heilmann	1927
.396	Austin Jackson	2010
.448	**Willi Castro**	**2020**

14.2 AT BATS PER HOME RUN

10.7	Rudy York	1937
9.6	**Hank Greenberg**	**1938**
14.0	Rudy York	1938
14.0	Hank Greenberg	1940
11.9	Hank Greenberg	1946
13.0	Norm Cash	1961
13.0	Rocky Colavito	1961
13.0	Norm Cash	1962
13.7	Al Kaline	1962
14.1	Norm Cash	1971
12.6	Darrell Evans	1985
11.2	Cecil Fielder	1990
12.3	Robb Deer	1992
13.9	Tony Clark	1996
13.4	Marcus Thames	2006
12.6	Marcus Thames	2008
14.1	Miguel Cabrera	2012
12.6	Miguel Cabrera	2013

88% IN PLAY PERCENTAGE

88%	Sport McAllister	1901
89%	Kid Gleason	1902
88%	Charlie Carr	1903
90%	Sam Crawford	1906
89%	Bob Fothergill	1929
92%	Mark Koenig	1931
88%	Charlie Gehringer	1931
88%	Chet Morgan	1938
90%	Rip Radcliff	1941
90%	Doc Cramer	1942
91%	Doc Cramer	1943
89%	Doc Cramer	1944
88%	Harvey Kuenn	1953
92%	**Harvey Kuenn**	**1954**
89%	Harvey Kuenn	1955
89%	Gary Sutherland	1974

290 TIMES ON BASE

300	Ty Cobb	1911
336	**Ty Cobb**	**1915**
290	Ty Cobb	1917
292	Harry Heilmann	1921
290	Harry Heilmann	1923
297	Ty Cobb	1924
293	Harry Heilmann	1925
316	Charlie Gehringer	1934
290	Hank Greenberg	1935
283	Charlie Gehringer	1935
314	Charlie Gehringer	1936
305	Hank Greenberg	1937
300	Charlie Gehringer	1937
297	Hank Greenberg	1938
292	Eddie Yost	1959
326	Norm Cash	1961
313	Tony Phillips	1993
308	Miguel Cabrera	2011

4.2 AT BATS PER RUN BATTED IN

4.1	Ty Cobb	1925
4.2	Harry Heilmann	1927
3.8	Harry Heilmann	1929
3.6	Hank Greenberg	1935
3.2	**Hank Greenberg**	**1937**
3.6	Rudy York	1937
3.6	Rudy York	1938
3.8	Hank Greenberg	1938
3.8	Hank Greenberg	1940
4.1	Hank Greenberg	1946
4.1	Ray Boone	1953
4.1	Norm Cash	1961
4.2	Rocky Colavito	1961
4.2	Al Kaline	1962
4.2	Richie Hebner	1980
4.1	Miguel Cabrera	2013

34.0 AT BATS PER STRIKEOUT			135 BASE RUNS			220 RUNS PRODUCED		
34.1	Ossie Vitt	1917	148	Ty Cobb	1911	266	Ty Cobb	1911
44.5	Ossie Vitt	1918	138	Ty Cobb	1915	240	Ty Cobb	1915
38.4	George Cutshaw	1922	135	Ty Cobb	1917	234	Harry Heilmann	1921
25.3	Bob Jones	1922	143	Harry Heilmann	1921	222	Bobby Veach	1921
39.7	Ty Cobb	1923	144	Harry Heilmann	1923	224	Charlie Gehringer	1929
42.9	Del Pratt	1924	137	Harry Heilmann	1925	222	Dale Alexander	1929
34.7	Ty Cobb	1924	136	Harry Heilmann	1927	226	Charlie Gehringer	1930
57.3	**Johnny Bassler**	**1925**	137	Charlie Gehringer	1934	250	Charlie Gehringer	1934
34.6	Ty Cobb	1925	144	Hank Greenberg	1935	231	Hank Greenberg	1934
35.9	Charlie Gehringer	1930	142	Charlie Gehringer	1936	255	Hank Greenberg	1935
38.1	Charlie Gehringer	1935	155	Hank Greenberg	1937	245	Charlie Gehringer	1936
49.3	Charlie Gehringer	1936	137	Gee Walker	1937	223	Goose Goslin	1936
35.0	Doc Cramer	1942	152	Hank Greenberg	1938	**280**	**Hank Greenberg**	**1937**
46.6	Doc Cramer	1943	145	Hank Greenberg	1940	232	Hank Greenberg	1938
36.8	George Kell	1947	**159**	**Norm Cash**	**1961**	220	Charlie Gehringer	1938
40.2	George Kell	1949	140	Magglio Ordonez	2007	238	Hank Greenberg	1940
35.6	George Kell	1950	143	Miguel Cabrera	2011	224	Rocky Colavito	1961
50.5	Harvey Kuenn	1954	140	Miguel Cabrera	2013	228	Magglio Ordonez	2007

2,650 PITCHES			4.17 PITCHES PER PLATE APP			47% RUN SCORING PERCENTAGE		
2,708	Cecil Fielder	1991	4.26	Rob Deer	1991	53%	Doc Casey	1901
2,904	Tony Phillips	1992	4.20	Mickey Tettleton	1991	51%	Davy Jones	1907
2,853	Mickey Tettleton	1992	4.34	Mickey Tettleton	1992	47%	Bill Coughlin	1907
2,753	Travis Fryman	1992	4.23	Rob Deer	1992	50%	Germany Schaefer	1908
2,948	**Tony Phillips**	**1993**	4.33	Mickey Tettleton	1993	48%	Donie Bush	1909
2,731	Mickey Tettleton	1993	4.19	Rob Deer	1993	**57%**	**Davy Jones**	**1911**
2,705	Travis Fryman	1993	4.17	Tony Phillips	1993	54%	Donie Bush	1911
2,674	Cecil Fielder	1993	**4.46**	**Mickey Tettleton**	**1994**	48%	Ty Cobb	1911
2,726	Brian Hunter	1997	4.36	Tony Phillips	1994	52%	Ossie Vitt	1915
2,610	Tony Clark	1997	4.21	Brandon Inge	2002	48%	Lu Blue	1922
2,712	Bobby Higginson	2000	4.24	Chris Shelton	2005	50%	Charlie Gehringer	1927
2,781	Brandon Inge	2005	4.17	Chris Shelton	2006	50%	Roy Johnson	1930
2,778	Curtis Granderson	2006	4.23	Brandon Inge	2007	51%	Jo-Jo White	1934
2,690	Curtis Granderson	2007	4.24	Curtis Granderson	2008	50%	Pete Fox	1934
2,678	Curtis Granderson	2008	4.19	Austin Jackson	2014	50%	Pete Fox	1935
2,818	Curtis Granderson	2009	4.19	Justin Upton	2017	48%	Jo-Jo White	1935
2,704	Austin Jackson	2010	4.30	Jeimer Candelario	2018	55%	Jake Wood	1962
2,674	Jeimer Candelario	2018	4.20	Jeimer Candelario	2019			
2,827	Robbie Grossman	2021	4.21	Robbie Grossman	2021			

131 ESTIMATED RUNS PRODUCED

154	Ty Cobb	1911
139	Ty Cobb	1915
138	Ty Cobb	1917
137	Harry Heilmann	1921
135	Harry Heilmann	1923
145	Hank Greenberg	1935
139	Charlie Gehringer	1936
155	**Hank Greenberg**	**1937**
135	Gee Walker	1937
152	Hank Greenberg	1938
140	Hank Greenberg	1940
153	Norm Cash	1961
131	Rocky Colavito	1961
137	Magglio Ordonez	2007
136	Miguel Cabrera	2011
133	Miguel Cabrera	2012
138	Miguel Cabrera	2013

5.34 RUNS CREATED/27

6.34	Ty Cobb	1911
5.45	Ty Cobb	1912
5.51	Ty Cobb	1917
6.01	Harry Heilmann	1921
5.90	Harry Heilmann	1923
5.52	Harry Heilmann	1925
5.47	Harry Heilmann	1927
5.34	Dale Alexander	1929
5.92	Hank Greenberg	1935
5.69	Charlie Gehringer	1936
6.42	**Hank Greenberg**	**1937**
6.17	Hank Greenberg	1938
5.83	Hank Greenberg	1940
6.38	Norm Cash	1961
5.77	Magglio Ordonez	2007
5.55	Miguel Cabrera	2011
5.49	Miguel Cabrera	2012
5.78	Miguel Cabrera	2013

88 BATTING RUNS

95	Ty Cobb	1915
93	Harry Heilmann	1921
98	Harry Heilmann	1923
88	Harry Heilmann	1925
92	Harry Heilmann	1927
98	Hank Greenberg	1935
93	Charlie Gehringer	1936
112	Hank Greenberg	1937
90	Gee Walker	1937
109	Hank Greenberg	1938
96	Hank Greenberg	1940
114	**Norm Cash**	**1961**
88	Rocky Colavito	1961
97	Magglio Ordonez	2007
90	Miguel Cabrera	2010
97	Miguel Cabrera	2011
90	Miguel Cabrera	2012
100	Miguel Cabrera	2013

145 RUNS CREATED

171	Ty Cobb	1911
147	Ty Cobb	1912
149	Ty Cobb	1917
162	Harry Heilmann	1921
159	Harry Heilmann	1923
149	Harry Heilmann	1925
148	Harry Heilmann	1927
160	Hank Greenberg	1935
153	Hank Greenberg	1936
173	**Hank Greenberg**	**1937**
166	Hank Greenberg	1938
166	Hank Greenberg	1940
172	Norm Cash	1961
154	Magglio Ordonez	2007
150	Miguel Cabrera	2011
150	Miguel Cabrera	2012
156	Miguel Cabrera	2013

140.0 TECHNICAL RUNS CREATED

174.6	Ty Cobb	1911
152.6	Ty Cobb	1917
161.4	Harry Heilmann	1921
158.9	Harry Heilmann	1923
148.6	Harry Heilmann	1925
149.6	Harry Heilmann	1927
146.8	Charlie Gehringer	1934
145.9	Hank Greenberg	1934
166.4	Hank Greenberg	1935
162.1	Charlie Gehringer	1936
182.8	**Hank Greenberg**	**1937**
149.2	Gee Walker	1937
176.5	Hank Greenberg	1938
156.7	Hank Greenberg	1940
171.1	Norm Cash	1961
153.3	Magglio Ordonez	2007
147.3	Miguel Cabrera	2011
153.8	Miguel Cabrera	2013

42.40 HOME RUN AVERAGE

56.00	Rudy York	1937
62.59	Hank Greenberg	1938
42.76	Rudy York	1938
42.93	Hank Greenberg	1940
50.48	Hank Greenberg	1946
46.31	Rocky Colavito	1961
45.98	Norm Cash	1961
46.15	Norm Cash	1962
43.72	Al Kaline	1962
42.48	Norm Cash	1971
47.52	Darrell Evans	1985
53.40	Cecil Fielder	1990
48.85	Rob Deer	1992
43.09	Tony Clark	1996
44.83	Marcus Thames	2006
47.47	Marcus Thames	2008
42.44	Miguel Cabrera	2012
47.57	Miguel Cabrera	2013

128 EXTRAPOLATED RUNS BASIC

135	Harry Heilmann	1921
133	Harry Heilmann	1923
128	Harry Heilmann	1925
128	Charlie Gehringer	1934
144	Hank Greenberg	1935
136	Charlie Gehringer	1936
153	Hank Greenberg	1937
135	Gee Walker	1937
153	Hank Greenberg	1938
136	Hank Greenberg	1940
129	Rudy York	1940
154	**Norm Cash**	**1961**
133	Rocky Colavito	1961
136	Magglio Ordonez	2007
131	Miguel Cabrera	2010
138	Miguel Cabrera	2011
135	Miguel Cabrera	2012
141	Miguel Cabrera	2013

.08 HOME RUN RATIO

.09	Rudy York	1937
.10	**Hank Greenberg**	**1938**
.08	Hank Greenberg	1946
.08	Norm Cash	1961
.08	Rocky Colavito	1961
.08	Norm Cash	1962
.08	Darrell Evans	1985
.09	Cecil Fielder	1990
.08	Rob Deer	1992
.08	Miguel Cabrera	2013

TIGERS HITTING FOR THE CYCLE

09-17-1920	B. Veach	vs BOS
09-26-1926	B. Fothergill	vs BOS
04-20-1937	G. Walker	vs CLE
05-27-1939	C. Gehringer	vs SLB
09-14-1947	V. Wertz	at WSH
06-02-1950	G. Kell	at PHA
09-07-1950	H. Evers	vs CLE
07-28-1993	T. Fryman	vs NYY
06-08-2001	D. Easley	vs MIL
08-01-2006	C. Guillen	at TBD

6.0% HOME RUN PERCENTAGE

8.4	Rudy York	1937
8.5	**Hank Greenberg**	**1938**
6.1	Hank Greenberg	1940
7.3	Hank Greenberg	1946
6.4	Rocky Colavito	1961
6.1	Norm Cash	1961
6.4	Al Kaline	1962
6.2	Norm Cash	1962
6.2	Willie Horton	1968
6.1	Norm Cash	1971
6.0	Lance Parrish	1982
6.7	Darrell Evans	1985
6.3	Matt Nokes	1987
8.0	Cecil Fielder	1990
6.2	Cecil Fielder	1991
7.1	Rob Deer	1992
6.1	Kirk Gibson	1994
6.7	Tony Clark	1996
6.0	Dean Palmer	1999
6.7	Marcus Thames	2006
7.3	Marcus Thames	2008
6.3	Miguel Cabrera	2012
6.7	Miguel Cabrera	2013

20 HOME RUNS AT HOME

25	Hank Greenberg	1937
39	**Hank Greenberg**	**1938**
27	Hank Greenberg	1940
29	Hank Greenberg	1946
21	Charlie Maxwell	1959
21	Norm Cash	1961
25	Norm Cash	1962
22	Al Kaline	1963
20	Willie Horton	1968
22	Lance Parrish	1982
21	Darrell Evans	1985
25	Cecil Fielder	1990
27	Cecil Fielder	1991
20	Cecil Fielder	1993
24	Dean Palmer	1999
28	Miguel Cabrera	2012
20	J.D. Martinez	2015
20	Miguel Cabrera	2016

18 HOME RUNS ON THE ROAD

18	Hank Greenberg	1935
18	Rudy York	1937
19	Hank Greenberg	1938
18	Rocky Colavito	1960
27	**Rocky Colavito**	**1961**
20	Norm Cash	1961
18	Rocky Colavito	1962
18	Norm Cash	1971
19	Willie Horton	1975
20	Lance Parrish	1984
19	Darrell Evans	1985
18	Matt Nokes	1987
26	Cecil Fielder	1990
19	Rob Deer	1992
19	Tony Clark	1999
18	Bobby Higginson	2000
19	Dmitri Young	2003
18	Miguel Cabrera	2008
20	Curtis Granderson	2009
21	Miguel Cabrera	2010
27	**Miguel Cabrera**	**2013**
18	J.D. Martinez	2015
18	Miguel Cabrera	2016

27 HOME RUNS VS RHP

27	Rocky Colavito	1960
36	Norm Cash	1961
35	Rocky Colavito	1961
33	Norm Cash	1962
30	Rocky Colavito	1962
31	Darrell Evans	1985
29	Darrell Evans	1987
28	Matt Nokes	1987
31	Cecil Fielder	1991
28	Dean Palmer	1999
28	Miguel Cabrera	2008
28	Curtis Granderson	2009
27	Miguel Cabrera	2009
32	Miguel Cabrera	2010
40	**Miguel Cabrera**	**2012**
31	Miguel Cabrera	2013
28	J.D. Martinez	2015
29	Miguel Cabrera	2016

27 HR BY LEFT-HANDED HITTERS

27	Vic Wertz	1950
27	Vic Wertz	1951
28	Charlie Maxwell	1956
31	Charlie Maxwell	1959
41	**Norm Cash**	**1961**
39	Norm Cash	1962
30	Norm Cash	1965
32	Norm Cash	1966
32	Norm Cash	1971
31	Jason Thompson	1977
27	Kirk Gibson	1984
40	Darrell Evans	1985
29	Kirk Gibson	1985
29	Darrell Evans	1986
28	Kirk Gibson	1986
34	Darrell Evans	1987
32	Matt Nokes	1987
28	Lou Whitaker	1989
27	Bobby Higginson	1997
30	Bobby Higginson	2000
27	Carlos Pena	2004
30	Curtis Granderson	2009
30	Prince Fielder	2012

13 HOME RUNS VS LHP

13	Norm Cash	1966
13	Al Kaline	1966
14	Al Kaline	1967
16	Willie Horton	1968
15	Al Kaline	1969
13	Lance Parrish	1978
14	John Wockenfuss	1979
13	Jerry Morales	1979
16	Lance Parrish	1980
16	John Wockenfuss	1980
14	Lance Parrish	1984
25	**Cecil Fielder**	**1990**
13	Cecil Fielder	1991
14	Rob Deer	1992
14	Craig Monroe	2003
13	Marcus Thames	2008
13	Miguel Cabrera	2013

34 HR BY RIGHT-HANDED HITTERS

36	Hank Greenberg	1935
40	Hank Greenberg	1937
35	Rudy York	1937
58	**Hank Greenberg**	**1938**
41	Hank Greenberg	1940
34	Rudy York	1943
44	Hank Greenberg	1946
35	Rocky Colavito	1960
45	Rocky Colavito	1961
37	Rocky Colavito	1962
36	Willie Horton	1968
51	Cecil Fielder	1990
44	Cecil Fielder	1991
35	Cecil Fielder	1992
38	Dean Palmer	1999
37	Miguel Cabrera	2008
34	Miguel Cabrera	2009
38	Miguel Cabrera	2010
44	Miguel Cabrera	2012
44	Miguel Cabrera	2013
38	J.D. Martinez	2015
38	Miguel Cabrera	2016

18 HOME RUNS BY SWITCH HITTERS

18	Roy Cullenbine	1945
24	Roy Cullenbine	1947
31	Mickey Tettleton	1991
32	Mickey Tettleton	1992
32	Mickey Tettleton	1993
19	Tony Phillips	1994
27	Tony Clark	1996
24	Melvin Nieves	1996
32	Tony Clark	1997
20	Melvin Nieves	1997
34	**Tony Clark**	**1998**
31	Tony Clark	1999
29	Dmitri Young	2003
20	Carlos Guillen	2004
18	Dmitri Young	2004
21	Dmitri Young	2005
19	Carlos Guillen	2006
21	Carlos Guillen	2007
32	Victor Martinez	2014
27	Victor Martinez	2016
19	Jeimer Candelario	2018
23	Robbie Grossman	2021

INSIDE THE PARK HR (1930-2021)

1	Bill Akers	1930
1	Charlie Gehringer	1930
1	Harry Rice	1930
1	John Stone	1931
1	John Stone	1933
1	Billy Rogell	1935
1	Mickey Cochrane	1936
1	Goose Goslin	1936
1	Charlie Gehringer	1939
1	Barney McCosky	1942
1	Bob Harris	1943
1	Doc Cramer	1944
1	Dick Wakefield	1944
1	Johnny Groth	1949
2	**Hoot Evers**	**1950**
1	Don Kolloway	1950
1	Don Lund	1953
1	Bill Tuttle	1955
1	Frank Lary	1956
1	Al Kaline	1959
1	Norm Cash	1961
1	Jake Wood	1962
1	Jake Wood	1963
1	Al Kaline	1964
1	Jerry Lumpe	1964
1	Norm Cash	1965
1	Dick McAuliffe	1965
1	Willie Horton	1966
1	Dick McAuliffe	1967
1	Willie Horton	1971
1	Ron LeFlore	1975
1	Ben Oglivie	1976
1	Steve Kemp	1977
1	Ron LeFlore	1977
1	Lou Whitaker	1978
1	Kirk Gibson	1983
1	Lou Whitaker	1991
1	Bobby Higginson	1997
1	Juan Gonzalez	2000
1	Damion Easley	2001
1	Shane Halter	2001
1	Wendell Magee	2002
1	Shane Halter	2003
1	Carlos Guillen	2004
1	Curtis Granderson	2007
1	Austin Jackson	2012
1	James McCann	2015
1	Nicholas Castellanos	2017
1	Eric Haase	2021

TWO GRAND SLAM HOME RUNS

2	Hank Greenberg	1937
2	Rudy York	1937
2	Hank Greenberg	1938
2	Ray Boone	1953
2	Eddie Yost	1959
2	Norm Cash	1961
2	Jim Northrup	1967
4	**Jim Northrup**	**1968**
3	Willie Horton	1969
2	Norm Cash	1971
2	Bill Freehan	1972
2	Dick McAuliffe	1973
2	Alan Trammell	1982
2	Lance Parrish	1983
2	Darrell Evans	1985
2	Darrell Evans	1986
2	Matt Nokes	1987
2	Pat Sheridan	1988
2	Cecil Fielder	1990
2	Cecil Fielder	1992
3	Dan Gladden	1993
2	Mickey Tettleton	1993
2	Lou Whitaker	1994
2	Travis Fryman	1995
2	Cecil Fielder	1996
3	Bobby Higginson	1997
2	Brandon Inge	2004
2	Carlos Pena	2004
2	Dmitri Young	2005
2	Carlos Guillen	2007
2	Edgar Renteria	2008
2	Marcus Thames	2008
2	Brandon Inge	2009
2	Nicholas Castellanos	2015
3	Justin Upton	2017

HOME RUNS HIT IN FIRST MLB AT BAT

Hack Miller	04-23-1944	at	CLE
*George Vico	04-20-1948	at	CHI
Gates Brown	06-19-1963	at	BOS
Bill Roman	09-30-1964	at	NYY
Gene Lamont	09-02-1970	at	BOS
Reggie Sanders	09-01-1974	vs	OAK
Daniel Norris	08-19-2015	at	CHC
Sergio Alcantara	09-06-2020	at	MIN
*Akil Baddoo	04-04-2021	vs	CLE

*Homer was hit on his first MLB pitch.

.03 STRIKEOUT RATIO

.03	Sam Crawford	1916
.03	Ossie Vitt	1917
.02	**Ossie Vitt**	**1918**
.03	Harry Heilmann	1918
.03	George Cutshaw	1922
.03	Johnny Bassler	1922
.03	Johnny Bassler	1923
.03	Ty Cobb	1923
.03	Bobby Jones	1923
.02	**Del Pratt**	**1924**
.03	Johnny Bassler	1924
.03	Ty Cobb	1924
.02	**Johnny Bassler**	**1925**
.03	Ty Cobb	1925
.03	Harry Heilmann	1929
.03	Charlie Gehringer	1929
.03	Charlie Gehringer	1930
.03	Mark Koenig	1931
.03	Charlie Gehringer	1935
.02	**Charlie Gehringer**	**1936**
.03	Charlie Gehringer	1940
.03	Rip Radcliff	1941
.03	Doc Cramer	1942
.02	**Doc Cramer**	**1943**
.03	George Kell	1946
.03	George Kell	1947
.02	**George Kell**	**1949**
.03	George Kell	1950
.03	George Kell	1951
.02	**Harvey Kuenn**	**1954**

TIGERS WITH SEVEN HITS

(Extra-Inning Games)		AB	H	2B	3B	HR
07-13-63	Colavito	12	7	0	0	0
05-25-70	Gutierrez	7	7	0	0	0

TIGERS WITH SIX HITS (Nine Innings)

(Nine-Inning Games)		AB	H	2B	3B	HR
07-13-01	Nance	6	6	1	0	0
05-25-25	Cobb	6	6	1	0	3
09-20-46	Kell	7	6	1	0	0
08-08-01	Easley	6	6	0	0	1
05-27-04	Pena	6	6	1	0	2

150 STRIKEOUTS

182	**Cecil Fielder**	**1990**
175	Rob Deer	1991
151	Cecil Fielder	1991
151	Cecil Fielder	1992
158	Melvin Nieves	1996
157	Melvin Nieves	1997
153	Dean Palmer	1999
174	Curtis Granderson	2006
150	Brandon Inge	2007
170	Brandon Inge	2009
170	Austin Jackson	2010
181	Austin Jackson	2011
151	Alex Avila	2014
178	J.D. Martinez	2015
152	Nicholas Castellanos	2015
179	Justin Upton	2016
160	Jeimer Candelario	2018
151	Nicholas Castellanos	2018
155	Robbie Grossman	2021

2.6% STRIKEOUT PERCENTAGE

2.5	Ossie Vitt	1917
1.9	Ossie Vitt	1918
2.3	George Cutshaw	1922
2.6	Johnny Bassler	1922
2.2	Ty Cobb	1923
2.0	Del Pratt	1924
2.4	Johnny Bassler	1924
2.5	Ty Cobb	1924
1.4	**Johnny Bassler**	**1925**
2.4	Ty Cobb	1925
2.4	Charlie Gehringer	1930
2.3	Charlie Gehringer	1935
1.8	Charlie Gehringer	1936
2.6	Doc Cramer	1942
2.0	Doc Cramer	1943
2.4	George Kell	1947
2.1	George Kell	1949
2.5	George Kell	1950
1.9	Harvey Kuenn	1954

NORTHRUP GRAND SLAMS IN 1968

	AB	R	H	2B	3B	HR	RBI	BB
05-17-68	5	2	3	1	0	1	4	0
06-24-68	4	2	2	0	0	2	8	1
06-29-68	4	1	1	0	0	1	4	0
10-09-68	5	1	2	0	0	1	4	0

4.3 WALKS TO STRIKEOUTS

5.3	Ossie Vitt	1918
5.2	Johnny Bassler	1922
5.8	Johnny Bassler	1923
4.7	Ty Cobb	1923
5.6	Johnny Bassler	1924
4.7	Ty Cobb	1924
12.3	**Johnny Bassler**	**1925**
5.4	Ty Cobb	1925
5.0	Lu Blue	1926
4.5	Harry Heilmann	1927
6.4	Mickey Cochrane	1935
4.9	Charlie Gehringer	1935
6.4	Charlie Gehringer	1936
5.4	Charlie Gehringer	1938
4.3	Charlie Gehringer	1939
5.9	Charlie Gehringer	1940
5.5	George Kell	1949

19.5 POWER/SPEED NUMBER

20.2	Gee Walker	1937
22.7	Ron LeFlore	1977
20.4	Ron LeFlore	1978
28.0	Kirk Gibson	1984
29.5	Kirk Gibson	1985
30.7	**Kirk Gibson**	**1986**
22.8	Alan Trammell	1986
25.0	Kirk Gibson	1987
24.0	Alan Trammell	1987
23.6	Chad Curtis	1995
24.6	Damion Easley	1997
24.1	Juan Encarnacion	1999
20.0	Bobby Higginson	2000
19.5	Carlos Guillen	2006
24.4	Curtis Granderson	2007
23.4	Gary Sheffield	2007
24.0	Curtis Granderson	2009
21.4	Robbie Grossman	2021

151 EXTRA BASES ON LONG HITS

155	Hank Greenberg	1934
186	Hank Greenberg	1935
197	Hank Greenberg	1937
203	**Hank Greenberg**	**1938**
155	Hank Greenberg	1939
189	Hank Greenberg	1940
157	Rudy York	1940
171	Hank Greenberg	1946
169	Rocky Colavito	1961
161	Norm Cash	1961
180	Cecil Fielder	1990
157	Cecil Fielder	1991
153	Curtis Granderson	2007
151	Miguel Cabrera	2008
161	Miguel Cabrera	2010
172	Miguel Cabrera	2012
160	Miguel Cabrera	2013
151	J.D. Martinez	2015

.275 ISOLATED POWER

.300	Hank Greenberg	1935
.344	Rudy York	1937
.332	Hank Greenberg	1937
.369	**Hank Greenberg**	**1938**
.281	Rudy York	1938
.310	Hank Greenberg	1939
.330	Hank Greenberg	1940
.327	Hank Greenberg	1946
.301	Norm Cash	1961
.290	Rocky Colavito	1961
.289	Al Kaline	1962
.314	Cecil Fielder	1990
.300	Rob Deer	1992
.293	Marcus Thames	2006
.275	Marcus Thames	2008
.294	Miguel Cabrera	2010
.277	Miguel Cabrera	2012
.288	Miguel Cabrera	2013

78 EXTRA BASE HITS

79	Ty Cobb	1911
83	Dale Alexander	1929
78	Charlie Gehringer	1930
98	Hank Greenberg	1935
87	Charlie Gehringer	1936
103	**Hank Greenberg**	**1937**
85	Hank Greenberg	1938
82	Hank Greenberg	1939
99	Hank Greenberg	1940
85	Rudy York	1940
78	Hank Greenberg	1946
78	Bobby Higginson	2000
84	Curtis Granderson	2007
82	Magglio Ordonez	2007
84	Miguel Cabrera	2010
78	Miguel Cabrera	2011
84	Miguel Cabrera	2012
79	Miguel Cabrera	2014

12.1% XBH PERCENTAGE

12.1%	Ty Cobb	1911
12.2%	Harry Heilmann	1927
13.3%	Bob Fothergill	1929
12.1%	Harry Heilmann	1929
14.4%	Hank Greenberg	1934
13.8%	Hank Greenberg	1935
12.2%	Gee Walker	1936
14.7%	Hank Greenberg	1937
13.4%	Rudy York	1937
12.5%	Hank Greenberg	1938
13.6%	Hank Greenberg	1939
14.8%	**Hank Greenberg**	**1940**
12.4%	Rudy York	1940
12.9%	Hank Greenberg	1946
12.3%	Marcus Thames	2006
12.4%	Curtis Granderson	2007
12.1%	Magglio Ordonez	2007
13.0%	Miguel Cabrera	2010
12.1%	Miguel Cabrera	2012
13.5%	Justin Upton	2017

47% X/H PERCENTAGE

52%	Hank Greenberg	1937
49%	Rudy York	1937
49%	Hank Greenberg	1938
53%	Hank Greenberg	1939
51%	Hank Greenberg	1940
54%	Hank Greenberg	1946
48%	Pat Mullin	1947
50%	Vic Wertz	1952
48%	Cecil Fielder	1990
51%	Rob Deer	1991
55%	**Rob Deer**	**1992**
48%	Mickey Tettleton	1993
47%	Travis Fryman	1994
48%	Melvin Nieves	1996
48%	Melvin Nieves	1997
54%	Marcus Thames	2006
47%	Craig Monroe	2006
47%	Miguel Cabrera	2010
51%	Justin Upton	2017

338 TOTAL BASES

367	Ty Cobb	1911
365	Harry Heilmann	1921
363	Dale Alexander	1929
337	Charlie Gehringer	1929
356	Hank Greenberg	1934
389	Hank Greenberg	1935
356	Charlie Gehringer	1936
397	**Hank Greenberg**	**1937**
380	Hank Greenberg	1938
384	Hank Greenberg	1940
343	Rudy York	1940
354	Norm Cash	1961
338	Rocky Colavito	1961
339	Cecil Fielder	1990
354	Magglio Ordonez	2007
338	Curtis Granderson	2007
341	Miguel Cabrera	2010
377	Miguel Cabrera	2012
353	Miguel Cabrera	2013

2.9 BASES PRODUCED AVERAGE

2.9	Ty Cobb	1910
3.4	**Ty Cobb**	**1911**
3.1	Ty Cobb	1912
3.1	Ty Cobb	1915
3.0	Ty Cobb	1917
3.0	Ty Cobb	1921
2.9	Harry Heilmann	1922
2.9	Harry Heilmann	1923
3.2	Hank Greenberg	1935
2.9	Charlie Gehringer	1936
3.3	Hank Greenberg	1937
3.3	Hank Greenberg	1938
3.0	Hank Greenberg	1939
3.3	Hank Greenberg	1940
3.1	Norm Cash	1961
2.9	Al Kaline	1962
2.9	Miguel Cabrera	2010
3.0	Miguel Cabrera	2013

2.3 TOTAL BASE AVERAGE

2.5	Ty Cobb	1910
2.3	Ty Cobb	1912
2.4	Harry Heilmann	1921
2.4	Ty Cobb	1921
2.3	Harry Heilmann	1922
2.3	Harry Heilmann	1923
2.3	Dale Alexander	1929
2.3	Hank Greenberg	1934
2.6	**Hank Greenberg**	**1935**
2.3	Charlie Gehringer	1936
2.6	**Hank Greenberg**	**1937**
2.3	Rudy York	1937
2.5	Hank Greenberg	1938
2.3	Hank Greenberg	1939
2.5	Hank Greenberg	1940
2.4	Al Kaline	1962
2.3	Magglio Ordonez	2007
2.3	Miguel Cabrera	2010
2.3	Miguel Cabrera	2012
2.4	Miguel Cabrera	2013

45% TB PERCENTAGE

46%	Ty Cobb	1910
47%	Ty Cobb	1911
46%	Ty Cobb	1912
47%	Ty Cobb	1913
47%	Ty Cobb	1914
49%	**Ty Cobb**	**1915**
45%	Ty Cobb	1916
45%	Ty Cobb	1921
46%	Ty Cobb	1922
48%	Harry Heilmann	1923
47%	Ty Cobb	1925
46%	Harry Heilmann	1925
46%	Al Wingo	1925
45%	Harry Heilmann	1926
47%	Harry Heilmann	1927
45%	Charlie Gehringer	1934
45%	Mickey Cochrane	1935
46%	Charlie Gehringer	1937
48%	Roy Cullenbine	1946
45%	Tony Phillips	1993
45%	Miguel Cabrera	2011

425 BASES PRODUCED

494	Ty Cobb	1911
427	Ty Cobb	1912
488	Ty Cobb	1915
451	Ty Cobb	1917
428	Charlie Gehringer	1929
428	Hank Greenberg	1934
480	Hank Greenberg	1935
443	Charlie Gehringer	1936
507	**Hank Greenberg**	**1937**
453	Gee Walker	1937
506	Hank Greenberg	1938
462	Hank Greenberg	1940
435	Rudy York	1940
489	Norm Cash	1961
452	Rocky Colavito	1961
429	Cecil Fielder	1990
434	Magglio Ordonez	2007
433	Miguel Cabrera	2010
445	Miguel Cabrera	2011
447	Miguel Cabrera	2012
446	Miguel Cabrera	2013

44 STOLEN BASES

49	Ty Cobb	1907
76	Ty Cobb	1909
53	Donie Bush	1909
65	Ty Cobb	1910
49	Donie Bush	1910
83	Ty Cobb	1911
61	Ty Cobb	1912
51	Ty Cobb	1913
44	Donie Bush	1913
96	**Ty Cobb**	**1915**
68	Ty Cobb	1916
55	Ty Cobb	1917
58	Ron LeFlore	1976
68	Ron LeFlore	1978
78	Ron LeFlore	1979
44	Gary Pettis	1988
74	Brian Hunter	1997
55	Roger Cedeno	2001
44	Alex Sanchez	2003

80% STOLEN BASE PCT (20 ATT)

.83	30-06	Gee Walker	1932
.82	25-06	Jo-Jo White	1934
.83	20-04	Barney McCosky	1939
.82	19-04	Al Kaline	1960
.89	24-03	Jake Wood	1962
.81	68-16	Ron LeFlore	1978
.84	78-14	Ron LeFlore	1979
.88	30-04	Kirk Gibson	1985
.85	34-06	Kirk Gibson	1986
.91	21-02	Alan Trammell	1987
.88	44-10	Gary Pettis	1988
.80	41-10	Milt Cuyler	1991
.80	74-18	Brian Hunter	1997
.80	16-04	Juan Encarnacion	2000
.96	26-01	Curtis Granderson	2007
.81	22-05	Gary Sheffield	2007
.81	27-06	Austin Jackson	2010
.81	22-05	Austin Jackson	2011
1.000	**21-00**	**Quintin Berry**	**2012**
.82	18-04	Akil Baddoo	2021
.80	20-05	Robbie Grossman	2021

4.0 STOLEN BASE RUNS

6.0	Ty Cobb	1915
6.0	Ty Cobb	1916
5.7	Donie Bush	1916
5.4	Ossie Vitt	1916
5.4	Gee Walker	1932
4.8	Jo-Jo White	1934
5.4	Jake Wood	1962
5.4	Ron LeFlore	1976
10.8	Ron LeFlore	1978
15.0	**Ron LeFlore**	**1979**
6.6	Kirk Gibson	1985
6.6	Kirk Gibson	1986
5.1	Alan Trammell	1987
7.2	Gary Pettis	1988
6.3	Milt Cuyler	1991
11.4	Brian Hunter	1997
5.4	Brian Hunter	1998
4.5	Austin Jackson	2010
4.2	Rajai Davis	2014

14 CAUGHT STEALING

17	Lu Blue	1921
15	Ty Cobb	1921
14	Ty Cobb	1924
15	Bob Fothergill	1927
15	Roy Johnson	1929
15	Charlie Gehringer	1930
21	**Roy Johnson**	**1931**
20	Ron LeFlore	1975
20	Ron LeFlore	1976
19	Ron LeFlore	1977
16	Ron LeFlore	1978
14	Ron LeFlore	1979
14	Alan Trammell	1979
15	Gary Pettis	1989
15	Chad Curtis	1995
18	Brian Hunter	1997
15	Roger Cedeno	2001
18	Alex Sanchez	2003

250 STOLEN BASE RUNS CREATED

285	Ty Cobb	1915
252	Harry Heilmann	1923
260	Charlie Gehringer	1934
268	Hank Greenberg	1935
256	Charlie Gehringer	1936
304	Hank Greenberg	1937
279	Gee Walker	1937
319	Hank Greenberg	1938
256	Charlie Gehringer	1938
275	Hank Greenberg	1940
259	Eddie Yost	1959
334	**Norm Cash**	**1961**
276	Rocky Colavito	1961
255	Tony Phillips	1993
250	Magglio Ordonez	2007
255	Miguel Cabrera	2010
287	Miguel Cabrera	2011
271	Miguel Cabrera	2013

105 WALKS

117	Donie Bush	1912
112	Donie Bush	1914
118	Donie Bush	1915
118	Ty Cobb	1915
119	Hank Greenberg	1938
113	Charlie Gehringer	1938
137	Roy Cullenbine	1947
120	Eddie Lake	1947
135	**Eddie Yost**	**1959**
125	Eddie Yost	1960
124	Norm Cash	1961
113	Rocky Colavito	1961
105	Dick McAuliffe	1967
122	Mickey Tettleton	1992
114	Tony Phillips	1992
132	Tony Phillips	1993
109	Mickey Tettleton	1993
108	Miguel Cabrera	2011

17.5% BASES ON BALL PERCENTAGE

18.2	Donie Bush	1912
18.4	Mickey Cochrane	1935
17.5	Hank Greenberg	1938
17.7	Charlie Gehringer	1941
21.0	Roy Cullenbine	1946
22.6	**Roy Cullenbine**	**1947**
17.7	Dick Wakefield	1947
17.8	Dick Wakefield	1948
20.9	Aaron Robinson	1950
19.5	Earl Torgeson	1956
20.0	Eddie Yost	1959
19.7	Eddie Yost	1960
18.5	Norm Cash	1961
18.7	Mickey Tettleton	1992
18.7	Tony Phillips	1993
21.8	Mickey Tettleton	1994
17.7	Tony Phillips	1994

NINE SACRIFICE FLIES

9	Frank Bolling	1958
10	Bubba Phillips	1963
11	Rusty Staub	1976
10	Rusty Staub	1977
9	Jason Thompson	1977
11	Rusty Staub	1978
9	Steve Kemp	1980
10	Kirk Gibson	1985
9	Alana Trammell	1985
9	Lou Whitaker	1989
13	**Travis Fryman**	**1994**
10	Travis Fryman	1996
11	Travis Fryman	1997
10	Dean Palmer	2000
9	Bobby Higginson	2001
12	Craig Monroe	2005
9	Miguel Cabrera	2008
9	Jhonny Peralta	2011
10	Torii Hunter	2013
11	Miguel Cabrera	2014
9	Miguel Cabrera	2021

30 TOTAL SACRIFICES

34	Billy Lush	1903
36	Bill Coughlin	1906
43	Germany Schaefer	1908
52	**Billy Lush**	**1909**
33	Tom Jones	1910
30	Donie Bush	1910
30	Donie Bush	1911
42	Ossie Vitt	1915
32	Ossie Vitt	1916
31	Ossie Vitt	1917
31	Ralph Young	1917
46	Ralph Young	1919
48	Donie Bush	1920
40	Donie Bush	1921
37	Topper Rigney	1922
36	Bobby Veach	1922
33	George Cutshaw	1922
33	Topper Rigney	1923
31	Topper Rigney	1924
34	Lu Blue	1925

13 INTENTIONAL WALKS

13	Frank House	1957
19	Norm Cash	1961
15	Bill Freehan	1967
13	Norm Cash	1972
16	Kirk Gibson	1985
18	Mickey Tettleton	1992
15	Cecil Fielder	1993
13	Tony Clark	1997
16	Dmitri Young	2003
14	Miguel Cabrera	2009
32	**Miguel Cabrera**	**2010**
22	Miguel Cabrera	2011
18	Prince Fielder	2012
17	Miguel Cabrera	2012
19	Miguel Cabrera	2013
28	Victor Martinez	2014
15	Miguel Cabrera	2015
15	Miguel Cabrera	2016

30 SACRIFICE HITS

34	Billy Lush	1903
43	Germany Schaefer	1908
52	**Billy Lush**	**1909**
33	Tom Jones	1910
30	Donie Bush	1910
30	Donie Bush	1911
42	Ossie Vitt	1915
32	Ossie Vitt	1916
31	Ossie Vitt	1917
31	Ralph Young	1917
46	Ralph Young	1919
48	Donie Bush	1920
40	Donie Bush	1921
37	Topper Rigney	1922
36	Bobby Veach	1922
33	George Cutshaw	1922
33	Topper Rigney	1923
31	Topper Rigney	1924
34	Lu Blue	1925

23 GROUNDED INTO DOUBLE PLAY

29	**Jimmy Bloodworth**	**1943**
23	Dick Wakefield	1943
23	George Vico	1948
23	George Kell	1950
25	Bill Tuttle	1955
23	Rusty Staub	1976
27	Rusty Staub	1977
24	Rusty Staub	1978
24	Steve Kemp	1980
24	Lance Parrish	1980
25	Deivi Cruz	2000
27	Magglio Ordonez	2008
24	Miguel Cabrera	2011
28	Miguel Cabrera	2012
23	Victor Martinez	2013
26	Miguel Cabrera	2016

FIVE BUNT HITS

14	Luis Salazar	1988
11	Lou Whitaker	1988
6	Gary Pettis	1989
8	Tony Phillips	1990
15	Milt Cuyler	1991
9	Kimera Bartee	1996
5	Brian Hunter	1998
15	Luis Polonia	1999
12	Roger Cedeno	2001
20	Alex Sanchez	2003
10	Ramon Santiago	2003
29	**Alex Sanchez**	**2004**
10	Nook Logan	2005
7	Gerald Laird	2009
5	Ramon Santiago	2010
8	Austin Jackson	2011
7	Anthony Gose	2015
5	Ian Kinsler	2015
7	Leonys Martin	2018

25 INFIELD HITS

36	Tony Phillips	1992
32	Travis Fryman	1992
23	Mickey Tettleton	1992
27	Tony Phillips	1993
37	Brian Hunter	1997
48	**Brian Hunter**	**1998**
39	Damion Easley	1998
36	Bobby Higginson	1998
32	Tony Clark	1998
31	Joe Randa	1998
30	Deivi Cruz	1998
41	Alex Sanchez	2003
36	Alex Sanchez	2004
27	Nook Logan	2005
32	Austin Jackson	2010
32	Austin Jackson	2011
26	Rajai Davis	2014
30	Jose Iglesias	2015
26	Jose Iglesias	2016

TWO PINCH-HIT HOME RUNS

2	Bob Harris	1942
2	Zeb Eaton	1945
3	**Dick Wakefield**	**1948**
2	Don Kolloway	1952
2	Frank House	1956
2	Bob Hazle	1958
3	**Norm Cash**	**1960**
3	**Ben Oglivie**	**1976**
2	Richie Hebner	1980
3	**Larry Herndon**	**1986**
2	Darrell Evans	1986
2	Kirk Gibson	1994
2	Bobby Higginson	1996
3	**Victor Martinez**	**2016**

Sammy Hale

FIVE PINCH-HIT RUNS BATTED IN

6	Dick Wakefield	1948
9	**Charlie Keller**	**1950**
9	**Charlie Keller**	**1951**
5	Steve Souchock	1951
5	Steve Souchock	1952
8	Pat Mullin	1953
6	Gus Zernial	1959
6	Norm Cash	1960
7	Ben Oglivie	1976
5	Kirk Gibson	1983
7	Barbaro Garbey	1984
6	Dave Bergman	1984
6	Larry Herndon	1986
6	Gary Ward	1990
5	Dave Bergman	1990
5	Lou Whitaker	1993

27 PINCH-HIT AT BATS

31	Charlie Gehringer	1942
30	Rip Radcliff	1943
29	Charlie Keller	1950
27	Pat Mullin	1950
31	Charlie Keller	1951
30	Steve Souchock	1951
29	Johnny Hopp	1952
57	**Pat Mullin**	**1953**
31	Johnny Pesky	1953
37	Wayne Belardi	1956
27	Earl Torgeson	1956
28	Bob Hazle	1958
43	Neil Chrisley	1959
27	Gus Zernial	1959
27	Billy Bruton	1964
28	Gates Brown	1972
38	Ben Oglivie	1976
36	Dan Meyer	1976
33	Dave Bergman	1990

TWO HOME RUNS IN ONE INNING

Al Kaline	4-17-1955	6th
Magglio Ordonez	8-12-2007	2nd

11 PINCH-HITS

17	Sammy Hale	1920
12	Johnny Neun	1926
19	**Bob Fothergill**	**1929**
13	Billy Rhiel	1932
12	Earl Averill	1940
11	Charlie Gehringer	1942
11	Rip Radcliffe	1943
13	Pat Mullin	1953
12	Johnny Pesky	1953
15	Gus Zernial	1958
12	Charlie Maxwell	1961
11	Bubba Morton	1961
17	Vic Wertz	1962
13	Gates Brown	1966
18	Gates Brown	1968
11	Dalton Jones	1970
13	Dalton Jones	1971
16	Gates Brown	1974

.300 PINCH HIT AVERAGE (MIN 20 AB)

.500	**(10-20)**	**Marty Kavanagh**	**1915**
.327	(17-52)	Sammy Hale	1920
.364	(08-22)	Bobby Veach	1923
.300	(09-30)	Bob Fothergill	1923
.345	(10-29)	Al Wingo	1924
.304	(07-23)	Pinky Hargrave	1928
.387	(12-31)	Bob Fothergill	1929
.400	(08-20)	Dick Wakefield	1948
.345	(10-29)	Charlie Keller	1950
.300	(06-20)	Don Kolloway	1952
.387	(12-31)	Johnny Pesky	1953
.308	(08-26)	Bob Nieman	1954
.370	(10-27)	Earl Torgeson	1956
.400	(10-25)	Dave Philley	1957
.395	(15-38)	Gus Zernial	1958
.364	(08-22)	Tito Francona	1958
.391	(09-23)	Norm Cash	1960
.321	(17-53)	Vic Wertz	1962
.360	(09-25)	Jake Wood	1965
.325	(13-40)	Gates Brown	1966
.450	(18-40)	Gates Brown	1968
.379	(11-29)	Dalton Jones	1970
.333	(07-21)	Ike Brown	1970
.346	(09-26)	Gates Brown	1971
.300	(09-30)	Kevin Collins	1971
.417	(10-24)	Al Kaline	1972
.300	(06-20)	Tony Taylor	1972
.302	(16-53)	Gates Brown	1974
.313	(10-32)	Tim Corcoran	1977
.350	(07-20)	Aurelio Rodriguez	1978
.348	(08-23)	Johnny Grubb	1984
.320	(08-25)	Barbaro Garbey	1984
.304	(07-23)	Dave Bergman	1984
.381	(08-21)	Larry Herndon	1987
.385	(10-26)	Wendell Magee	2000

Norm Cash
June 8-13, 1961: 7 HR, 10 RBI, .650 BA.
7-22-1966: 2-for-3 (HR, 6 RBI, BB, SF).

Jim Northrup
6-24-1968: 2-for-4 (2 HR, 8 RBI, 2 R).
8-28-1969: 6-for-6 (2 HR, 3 RBI, 2 R).

Gates Brown
6-19-1963: Hit a homer in first at-bat.
1968: .370 BA, .685 SLG, 234 OPS+.
6-22-1971: 5-for-6 in double-header.

485 OUTS

494	Ossie Vitt	1916
489	Doc Cramer	1942
509	Eddie Mayo	1944
508	Eddie Lake	1947
489	Jerry Priddy	1950
486	Harvey Kuenn	1953
493	Harvey Kuenn	1954
515	Jake Wood	1961
489	Jerry Lumpe	1964
489	Gary Sutherland	1974
490	Rusty Staub	1977
505	Rusty Staub	1978
501	Ron LeFlore	1978
512	Travis Fryman	1992
525	Brian Hunter	1997
487	Brandon Inge	2005
486	Curtis Granderson	2009
528	**Ian Kinsler**	**2014**

22 GAME HITTING STREAKS

25	Kid Gleason	1901
25	Ty Cobb	1906
23	Sam Crawford	1909
40	**Ty Cobb**	**1911**
28	Sam Crawford	1911
23	Ty Cobb	1912
35	Ty Cobb	1917
23	Harry Heilmann	1921
29	Dale Alexander	1930
26	John Stone	1930
25	John Stone	1931
30	Goose Goslin	1934
29	Pete Fox	1935
27	Gee Walker	1937
22	Harvey Kuenn	1959
22	Al Kaline	1961
30	Ron LeFlore	1976
27	Ron LeFlore	1978

TIGER UNASSISTED TRIPLE PLAY

Johnny Neun 1B 5-31-1927 9th Inn

AMERICAN LEAGUE TRIPLE CROWN

	WINS	ERA	SO	
1945	25	1.81	212	Hal Newhouser
2011	24	2.40	250	Justin Verlander

TIGERS TRIPLE CROWN

	WINS	ERA	SO	
1904	17	2.40	161	George Mullin
1911	18	3.07	87	George Mullin
1912	17	2.77	97	Jean Dubuc
1916	21	1.97	108	Harry Coveleski
1923	21	3.62	105	Hooks Dauss
1927	16	3.36	95	Earl Whitehill
1935	21	3.51	163	Tommy Bridges
1936	23	3.60	175	Tommy Bridges
1939	17	3.37	164	Bobo Newsom
1940	21	2.83	164	Bobo Newsom
1945	25	1.81	212	Hal Newhouser
1946	26	1.94	275	Hal Newhouser
1948	21	3.01	143	Hal Newhouser
1949	19	2.81	153	Virgil Trucks
1955	16	2.99	133	Billy Hoeft
1957	20	2.69	182	Jim Bunning
1968	31	1.96	280	Denny McLain
1970	14	3.80	230	Mickey Lolich
1971	25	2.92	308	Mickey Lolich
1972	22	2.50	250	Mickey Lolich
1975	12	3.78	139	Mickey Lolich
1976	19	2.34	97	Mark Fidrych
1977	15	3.09	92	Dave Rozema
1979	17	3.28	113	Jack Morris
1985	16	3.33	191	Jack Morris
1986	21	3.27	223	Jack Morris
1987	18	3.38	208	Jack Morris
1999	14	4.60	119	Dave Mlicki
2002	8	4.21	109	Mark Redman
2007	18	3.66	183	Justin Verlander
2009	19	3.45	269	Justin Verlander
2010	18	3.37	219	Justin Verlander
2011	24	2.40	250	Justin Verlander
2012	17	2.64	239	Justin Verlander
2014	18	3.15	252	Max Scherzer
2016	16	3.04	254	Justin Verlander
2017	10	3.82	176	Justin Verlander
2019	9	4.56	238	Matt Boyd

Fred Hutchinson

TIGERS SABERMETRIC TRIPLE CROWN

	ERA+	FIP	DICE	
1902	195	2.83	3.16	Ed Siever
1913	117	3.10	3.55	Hooks Dauss
1915	124	2.56	3.15	Harry Coveleski
1916	145	2.57	3.26	Harry Coveleski
1919	115	2.96	3.47	Dutch Leonard
1921	114	3.81	3.71	Dutch Leonard
1923	107	3.49	3.55	Hooks Dauss
1924	128	3.64	3.60	Rip Collins
1927	125	3.89	3.86	Earl Whitehill
1929	105	3.55	3.39	George Uhle
1931	130	3.96	3.84	George Uhle
1943	146	2.68	3.27	Tommy Bridges
1945	195	2.45	2.91	Hal Newhouser
1946	190	1.97	2.58	Hal Newhouser
1947	132	2.85	3.35	Hal Newhouser
1948	145	3.19	3.53	Hal Newhouser
1951	113	3.21	3.66	Fred Hutchinson
1953	91	3.97	4.38	Ned Garver
1955	130	3.27	3.86	Billy Hoeft
1956	132	3.44	4.07	Frank Lary
1958	139	3.39	3.91	Frank Lary
1959	121	3.27	3.73	Don Mossi
1960	143	2.86	3.33	Jim Bunning
1962	185	2.99	3.37	Hank Aguirre
1963	102	3.74	4.26	Hank Aguirre
1964	113	3.30	3.69	Mickey Lolich
1966	134	2.97	3.42	Earl Wilson
1967	107	2.65	3.11	Mickey Lolich
1968	154	2.53	3.15	Denny McLain
1969	134	3.05	3.54	Denny McLain
1970	99	3.49	3.85	Mickey Lolich
1972	127	2.80	3.40	Mickey Lolich
1974	91	3.66	4.08	Mickey Lolich
1975	105	3.26	3.67	Mickey Lolich
1976	159	3.15	3.52	Mark Fidrych
1977	139	3.95	4.21	Dave Rozema
1978	123	3.71	4.13	Dave Rozema
1979	133	3.79	4.06	Jack Morris
1980	105	3.92	4.17	Dan Petry
1982	126	3.70	3.99	Dan Petry
1983	117	3.38	3.63	Jack Morris
1985	122	3.14	3.46	Frank Tanana
1986	127	3.97	4.20	Jack Morris
1989	108	3.77	4.01	Frank Tanana
1993	103	4.09	4.11	David Wells
1995	112	4.71	4.61	Felipe Lira
1996	104	5.03	4.86	Omar Olivares
1997	152	3.83	3.73	Justin Thompson
2007	125	3.99	3.75	Justin Verlander
2009	131	2.80	2.70	Justin Verlander
2010	124	2.97	2.89	Justin Verlander
2011	172	2.99	2.97	Justin Verlander
2012	161	2.94	2.85	Justin Verlander
2013	162	2.39	2.35	Anibal Sanchez
2015	158	3.06	2.92	David Price
2016	136	3.48	3.34	Justin Verlander
2017	117	3.67	3.52	Michael Fulmer
2020	118	3.49	3.30	Spencer Turnbull
2021	143	3.46	3.29	Michael Fulmer

69 GAMES

1971	Fred Scherman	69
1984	Willie Hernandez	80
1985	Willie Hernandez	74
1990	Mike Henneman	69
1996	Mike Myers	83
1997	**Mike Myers**	**88**
1998	**Sean Runyan**	**88**
1999	Doug Brocail	70
2000	Matt Anderson	69
2003	Jaime Walker	78
2004	Jaime Walker	70
2009	Fernando Rodney	73
2010	Phil Coke	74
2011	Jose Valverde	75
2012	Joaquin Benoit	73
2014	Al Alburquerque	72
2015	Blaine Hardy	70
2017	Shane Greene	71
2019	Buck Farmer	73

23 WINS

1901	Roscoe Miller	23
1905	Ed Killian	23
1907	Bill Donovan	25
	Ed Killian	25
1908	Ed Summers	24
1909	George Mullin	29
1915	Hooks Dauss	24
1934	Schoolboy Rowe	24
1936	Tommy Bridges	23
1944	Hal Newhouser	29
1945	Hal Newhouser	25
1946	Hal Newhouser	26
1961	Frank Lary	23
1968	**Denny McLain**	**31**
1969	Denny McLain	24
1971	Mickey Lolich	25
1973	Joe Coleman	23
2011	Justin Verlander	24

305 INNINGS

1901	Roscoe Miller	332.0
1902	Win Mercer	281.2
1903	George Mullin	320.2
1904	**George Mullin**	**382.1**
1905	George Mullin	347.2
1906	George Mullin	330.0
1907	George Mullin	357.1
1915	Harry Coveleski	312.2
1916	Harry Coveleski	324.1
1923	Hooks Dauss	316.0
1944	Dizzy Trout	352.1
1945	Hal Newhouser	313.1
1968	Denny McLain	336.0
1969	Denny McLain	325.0
1971	Mickey Lolich	376.0
1972	Mickey Lolich	327.1
1973	Mickey Lolich	308.2
1974	Mickey Lolich	308.0

18 LOSSES

1902	Win Mercer	18
1904	**George Mullin**	**23**
1905	George Mullin	21
1906	George Mullin	18
1907	George Mullin	20
1920	Hooks Dauss	21
1923	Herman Pillette	19
1941	Bobo Newsom	20
1942	Dizzy Trout	18
1952	Art Houtteman	20
1970	Mickey Lolich	19
1974	Mickey Lolich	21
1975	Joe Coleman	18
	Mickey Lolich	18
1977	Fernando Arroyo	18
1989	Doyle Alexander	18
1990	Jack Morris	18
2003	Mike Maroth	21
2003	Jeremy Bonderman	19

.725 WINNING PERCENTAGE (15 DEC)

1907	Bill Donovan	.862	25-4
1909	George Mullin	.784	29-8
1925	Ken Holloway	.765	13-4
1934	Firpo Marberry	.750	15-5
	Schoolboy Rowe	.750	24-8
1937	George Gill	.733	11-4
1940	Schoolboy Rowe	.842	16-3
1944	Hal Newhouser	.763	29-9
1945	Hal Newhouser	.735	25-9
1946	Hal Newhouser	.743	26-9
1965	Denny McLain	.727	16-6
1968	Denny McLain	.838	31-6
1969	Denny McLain	.727	24-9
1986	Eric King	.730	11-4
1989	Mike Henneman	.730	11-4
2007	Justin Verlander	.750	18-6
2011	Justin Verlander	.828	24-5
2013	**Max Scherzer**	**.875**	**21-3**
2014	Max Scherzer	.783	18-5

285 HITS ALLOWED

1901	Roscoe Miller	339
1904	George Mullin	345
1905	George Mullin	303
1906	George Mullin	315
1907	**George Mullin**	**346**
1908	George Mullin	301
1920	Hooks Dauss	308
1922	Howard Ehmke	299
1923	Hooks Dauss	331
1931	Earl Whitehill	287
1936	Tommy Bridges	289
1944	Dizzy Trout	314
1956	Frank Lary	289
1969	Denny McLain	288
1971	Mickey Lolich	336
1973	Mickey Lolich	315
1974	Mickey Lolich	310

31 HOME RUNS ALLOWED

1948	Fred Hutchinson	32
1957	Jim Bunning	33
1959	Jim Bunning	37
1963	Jim Bunning	38
1966	**Denny McLain**	**42**
1967	Denny McLain	35
1968	Denny McLain	31
1971	Mickey Lolich	36
1973	Mickey Lolich	35
1974	Mickey Lolich	38
1982	Jack Morris	37
1983	Dan Petry	37
1986	Jack Morris	40
1987	Jack Morris	39
1992	Bill Gullickson	35
1993	Mike Moore	35
2000	Hideo Nomo	31
2003	Mike Maroth	34
2019	Matt Boyd	39
2021	Tarik Skubal	35

210 STRIKEOUTS

1945	Hal Newhouser	212
1946	Hal Newhouser	275
1965	Mickey Lolich	226
1968	Denny McLain	280
1969	Mickey Lolich	271
1970	Mickey Lolich	230
1971	**Mickey Lolich**	**308**
1972	Mickey Lolich	250
1973	Mickey Lolich	214
1983	Jack Morris	232
1986	Jack Morris	223
2009	Justin Verlander	269
2010	Justin Verlander	219
2011	Justin Verlander	250
2012	Justin Verlander	239
2013	Max Scherzer	240
2014	Max Scherzer	252
2016	Justin Verlander	254
2019	Matt Boyd	238

THREE BALKS

1914	Red Oldham	3
1925	Ed Wells	3
1926	Rip Collins	3
1952	Bill Wight	3
1956	Paul Foytack	3
1958	Jim Bunning	3
1963	Bill Faul	3
1977	Jim Crawford	3
1983	Dave Rozema	3
1985	Jack Morris	3
1986	Eric King	3
1987	Jeff Robinson	3
1988	**Jack Morris**	**11**
1999	C.J. Nitkowski	3
2008	Justin Verlander	3
2009	Justin Verlander	4
2010	Armando Galarraga	3
	Rick Porcello	3
2015	Al Alburquerque	4
2019	Matt Boyd	4

111 WALKS

1904	George Mullin	131
1905	George Mullin	138
1915	Hooks Dauss	115
1920	Howard Ehmke	124
1931	Earl Whitehill	118
1932	Tommy Bridges	119
1935	Tommy Bridges	113
1936	Tommy Bridges	115
1937	Roxie Lawson	115
1938	Vern Kennedy	113
1941	Hal Newhouser	137
1942	Hal Newhouser	114
1943	Hal Newhouser	111
1949	Virgil Trucks	124
1956	Paul Foytack	142
1969	Mickey Lolich	122
1974	**Joe Coleman**	**158**

15 HIT BY PITCH

1904	Ed Killian	17
1906	George Mullin	15
1907	George Mullin	15
1908	Ed Summers	20
1909	Ed Willett	15
1910	Ed Willett	17
1912	Ed Willett	17
1914	Hooks Dauss	18
1915	Harry Coveleski	20
1916	Hooks Dauss	16
1922	**Howard Ehmke**	**23**
1960	Frank Lary	19
1999	Jeff Weaver	17
2000	Jeff Weaver	15
2007	Justin Verlander	19
2013	Doug Fister	16
2019	Spencer Turnbull	16

11 INTENTIONAL WALKS

1956	Billy Hoeft	12
1957	Paul Foytack	12
1970	Tom Timmermann	11
1974	**John Hiller**	**19**
1979	Jack Billingham	11
1980	Dan Petry	14
	Dave Rozema	14
1981	Jack Morris	11
1985	Bill Scherrer	13
1989	Mike Henneman	15
1990	Jack Morris	13
1991	Bill Gullickson	13
1992	Les Lancaster	12
1994	Joe Boever	12
1995	Joe Boever	12

13 WILD PITCHES

1902	George Mullin	13
1912	Jean Dubuc	16
1920	Dutch Leonard	13
1962	Jim Bunning	13
1969	Mickey Lolich	14
1970	Mickey Lolich	14
1974	Joe Coleman	13
1975	Joe Coleman	15
1983	Jack Morris	18
1984	Jack Morris	14
1985	Jack Morris	15
1987	**Jack Morris**	**24**
1990	Jack Morris	16
	Jeff Robinson	16
1993	David Wells	13
1995	Sean Bergman	13
1996	Richie Lewis	14
2000	Hideo Nomo	16
2005	Jason Johnson	17
2007	Justin Verlander	17
2015	Alfredo Simon	14

140 RUNS

1901	**Roscoe Miller**	**168**
1902	George Mullin	155
1904	George Mullin	154
1905	George Mullin	149
1907	George Mullin	153
1908	George Mullin	142
1912	Ed Willett	144
1920	Hooks Dauss	158
1921	Hooks Dauss	141
1922	Howard Ehmke	146
1923	Hooks Dauss	140
1929	Vic Sorrell	152
1931	Earl Whitehill	152
1936	Tommy Bridges	141
1937	Roxie Lawson	141
1941	Bobo Newsom	140
1973	Mickey Lolich	143
1974	Joe Coleman	160
1990	Jack Morris	144

2.68 TECHINCAL RUNS ALLOWED

1909	Ed Killian	2.34
1943	Tommy Bridges	2.68
1944	Dizzy Trout	2.66
1945	Hal Newhouser	2.10
1946	Hal Newhouser	2.37
1968	Denny McLain	2.30
1973	**John Hiller**	**1.51**
1979	Aurelio Lopez	2.62
1981	Kevin Saucier	2.02
1984	Willie Hernandez	1.92
1988	Mike Henneman	2.27
1999	Doug Brocail	2.52
2006	Joel Zumaya	2.16
2007	Bobby Seay	2.33
2011	Jose Valverde	2.61
2013	Joaquin Benoit	2.01
2014	Al Alburquerque	2.51
2015	Alex Wilson	2.44
2017	Justin Wilson	2.68

120 EARNED RUNS

1922	Howard Ehmke	131
1923	Hooks Dauss	127
1925	Earl Whitehill	124
1929	Vic Sorrell	130
1931	Earl Whitehill	123
1932	Earl Whitehill	123
1936	Schoolboy Rowe	123
1937	Roxie Lawson	127
1941	Bobo Newsom	128
1959	Paul Foytack	124
1971	Mickey Lolich	122
1973	Mickey Lolich	131
1974	**Mickey Lolich**	**142**
1975	Joe Coleman	124
1982	Jack Morris	120
1990	Jack Morris	125
1993	Mike Moore	124
2003	Mike Maroth	123

1,250 BATTERS FACED

1901	Roscoe Miller	1,408
1903	George Mullin	1,312
1904	**George Mullin**	**1,568**
1905	George Mullin	1,428
1906	George Mullin	1,361
1907	George Mullin	1,470
1915	Harry Coveleski	1,269
1923	Hooks Dauss	1,340
1936	Tommy Bridges	1,272
1944	Dizzy Trout	1,421
1945	Hal Newhouser	1,261
1956	Frank Lary	1,269
1968	Denny McLain	1,288
1969	Denny McLain	1,304
1971	Mickey Lolich	1,538
1972	Mickey Lolich	1,321
1973	Mickey Lolich	1,286
1974	Mickey Lolich	1,263

82.14 LEFT ON-BASE PERCENTAGE

1957	Jim Bunning	82.14
1968	Denny McLain	84.02
1971	Fred Scherman	82.56
1973	John Hiller	90.52
1979	Aurelio Lopez	84.72
1983	Aurelio Lopez	84.03
1984	Willie Hernandez	83.07
1986	Willie Hernandez	82.28
1988	Mike Henneman	85.03
1990	Paul Gibson	83.08
1997	Doug Brocail	82.83
1999	Doug Brocail	83.33
2005	Franklyn German	82.80
2006	**Jamie Walker**	**91.32**
2011	Jose Valverde	82.93
2013	Joaquin Benoit	87.30
2014	Al Alburquerque	89.70
2017	Shane Greene	84.17

2.24 EARNED RUN AVERAGE

1902	Ed Siever	1.91
1907	Ed Killian	1.78
1908	Ed Summers	1.64
1909	Ed Killian	1.71
1916	Harry Coveleski	1.97
1917	Bill James	2.09
1944	Dizzy Trout	2.12
1945	Hal Newhouser	1.81
1946	Hal Newhouser	1.94
1962	Hank Aguirre	2.21
1968	Denny McLain	1.96
1973	**John Hiller**	**1.44**
1981	Kevin Saucier	1.65
1984	Willie Hernandez	1.92
1988	Mike Henneman	1.87
2006	Joel Zumaya	1.94
2011	Jose Valverde	2.24
2013	Joaquin Benoit	2.01
2015	Alex Wilson	2.19
2020	Bryan Garcia	1.66

2.60 FIP

1906	Red Donahue	2.51
1907	Ed Siever	2.27
1908	**Bill Donovan**	**1.78**
1909	George Mullin	2.29
1910	Bill Donovan	2.53
1915	Harry Coveleski	2.56
1916	Harry Coveleski	2.57
1917	Willie Mitchell	2.49
1918	George Cunningham	2.60
1944	Hal Newhouser	2.58
1945	Hal Newhouser	2.45
1946	Hal Newhouser	1.97
1968	Denny McLain	2.53
1973	John Hiller	2.25
1984	Willie Hernandez	2.58
2012	Octavio Dotel	2.30
2013	Anibal Sanchez	2.39

2.96 DEFENSE-INDEPENDENT ERA

1903	Bill Donovan	2.89
1908	Bill Donovan	2.67
1912	Joe Lake	2.96
1945	Hal Newhouser	2.91
1946	Hal Newhouser	2.58
1973	John Hiller	2.68
1984	Willie Hernandez	2.81
1998	Doug Brocail	2.57
2001	Matt Anderson	2.57
2007	Bobby Seay	2.74
2009	Justin Verlander	2.70
2010	Justin Verlander	2.89
2011	Joaquin Benoit	2.93
2012	**Octavio Dotel**	**2.21**
2013	Drew Smyly	2.26
2014	Max Scherzer	2.71
2015	Blaine Hardy	2.76

165 EARNED RUN AVERAGE PLUS

1902	Ed Siever	187
1945	Hal Newhouser	186
1946	Hal Newhouser	180
1962	Hank Aguirre	180
1973	John Hiller	265
1979	Aurelio Lopez	176
1981	Kevin Saucier	222
1984	Willie Hernandez	208
1988	Mike Henneman	213
1998	Doug Brocail	171
1999	Doug Brocail	193
2002	Juan Acevedo	169
2006	Joel Zumaya	235
2007	Bobby Seay	194
2011	Jose Valverde	182
2013	Joaquin Benoit	199
2015	Alex Wilson	183
2017	Shane Greene	172
2020	**Bryan Garcia**	**284**

1.051 WALKS PLUS HITS PER INNING

1902	Ed Siever	1.051
1909	Ed Summers	1.047
1916	Harry Coveleski	1.051
1962	Hank Aguirre	1.051
1966	Earl Wilson	1.004
1968	Denny McLain	.905
1973	John Hiller	1.021
1981	Kevin Saucier	.959
1984	Willie Hernandez	.941
1985	**Willie Hernandez**	**.900**
1988	Mike Henneman	1.051
1998	Doug Brocail	1.037
1999	Doug Brocail	1.037
2002	Jamie Walker	.939
2011	Justin Verlander	.920
2013	Max Scherzer	.970
2015	Alex Wilson	1.029
2016	Justin Verlander	1.001
2017	Justin Wilson	.942

7.0 PITCHER WAR

1939	Bobo Newsom	7.2
1940	Bobo Newsom	7.4
1944	Dizzy Trout	9.3
	Hal Newhouser	7.8
1945	**Hal Newhouser**	**11.3**
1946	Hal Newhouser	9.6
	Dizzy Trout	7.6
1962	Hank Aguirre	7.4
1968	Denny McLain	7.4
1969	Denny McLain	8.1
1971	Mickey Lolich	8.5
1972	Mickey Lolich	7.4
1973	John Hiller	7.9
1976	Mark Fidrych	9.6
1997	Justin Thompson	7.7
2011	Justin Verlander	8.6
2012	Justin Verlander	8.1
2016	Justin Verlander	7.2

6.7 HITS PER NINE INNINGS

1942	Hal Newhouser	6.7
1946	Hal Newhouser	6.6
1968	Denny McLain	6.5
1973	John Hiller	6.4
1979	Aurelio Lopez	6.7
1981	**Kevin Saucier**	**4.8**
1984	Willie Hernandez	6.2
1988	Jeff Robinson	6.3
1999	Doug Brocail	6.6
2002	Jamie Walker	6.6
2004	Ugueth Urbina	6.3
2006	Joel Zumaya	6.0
2009	Brandon Lyon	6.4
2010	Jose Valverde	5.9
2011	Justin Verlander	6.2
2013	Joaquin Benoit	6.3
2020	Gregory Soto	6.3
2021	Gregory Soto	6.5

1.7 WALKS PER NINE INNINGS

1901	Jack Cronin	1.7
1902	Ed Siever	1.5
1903	Frank Kitson	1.3
1904	Frank Kitson	1.7
1907	Ed Siever	1.7
1908	Ed Summers	1.6
1909	Ed Summers	1.7
1916	Harry Coveleski	1.7
1951	Fred Hutchinson	1.3
1968	Denny McLain	1.7
1977	Dave Rozema	1.4
1985	**Willie Hernandez**	**1.2**
1991	Bill Gullickson	1.7
2001	Danny Patterson	1.7
2004	Jamie Walker	1.7
2006	Todd Jones	1.5
	Jamie Walker	1.5
2018	Jordan Zimmermann	1.7

3.50 STRIKEOUTS TO WALKS

1966	Earl Wilson	3.50
1968	Denny McLain	4.44
1985	**Willie Hernandez**	**5.43**
1986	Willie Hernandez	3.67
2002	Jamie Walker	4.44
2004	Jamie Walker	4.42
2006	Jamie Walker	4.63
2009	Justin Verlander	4.27
2011	Justin Verlander	4.39
2012	Octavio Dotel	5.17
2013	Drew Smyly	4.76
2014	Max Scherzer	4.00
2016	Justin Verlander	4.46
2018	Jordan Zimmermann	4.44
	Joe Jimenez	3.90
2019	Matt Boyd	4.76
	Joe Jimenez	3.57
2020	Joe Jimenez	3.67
2021	Michael Fulmer	3.65

9.5 STRIKEOUTS PER NINE INNINGS

1996	Mike Myers	9.6
2006	Joel Zumaya	10.5
2009	Justin Verlander	10.1
2012	Max Scherzer	11.1
2013	Max Scherzer	10.1
2014	Max Scherzer	10.3
2016	Justin Verlander	10.0
	Justin Wilson	10.0
2017	Justin Wilson	12.3
2018	Joe Jimenez	11.1
2019	**Joe Jimenez**	**12.4**
	Matt Boyd	11.6
	Buck Farmer	9.7
2020	Gregory Soto	11.3
	Tarik Skubal	10.4
	Jose Cisnero	10.3
2021	Joe Jimenez	11.3
	Gregory Soto	10.7
	Tarik Skubal	9.9

0.0 HOME RUNS PER NINE INNINGS

1901	Roscoe Miller	0.0
1902	Ed Siever	0.0
1904	Ed Killian	0.0
	George Mullin	0.0
1905	Ed Killian	0.0
1906	Red Donahue	0.0
	Ed Killian	0.0
1907	George Mullin	0.0
	Ed Siever	0.0
1908	George Mullin	0.0
1909	Bill Donovan	0.0
	George Mullin	0.0
1913	Jean Dubuc	0.0
	Ed Willett	0.0
1915	Hooks Dauss	0.0
1917	Bernie Boland	0.0
1918	Bernie Boland	0.0
	Rudy Kallio	0.0
2020	Bryan Garcia	0.0

25 COMPLETE GAMES

1901	Roscoe Miller	35
1902	Win Mercer	28
1903	Bill Donovan	34
1904	**George Mullin**	**42**
1905	George Mullin	35
1906	George Mullin	35
1907	George Mullin	35
1908	George Mullin	26
1909	George Mullin	29
1910	George Mullin	27
1911	George Mullin	25
1912	Ed Willett	28
1915	Hooks Dauss	27
1936	Tommy Bridges	26
1944	Dizzy Trout	33
1945	Hal Newhouser	29
1946	Hal Newhouser	29
1968	Denny McLain	28
1971	Mickey Lolich	29
1974	Mickey Lolich	27

2.9 RUNS PER NINE INNINGS

1907	Ed Siever	2.9
1908	Bill Donovan	2.9
1909	Ed Killian	2.3
1916	Harry Coveleski	2.9
1943	Tommy Bridges	2.7
1944	Hal Newhouser	2.7
	Dizzy Trout	2.7
1945	**Hal Newhouser**	**2.1**
1946	Hal Newhouser	2.4
1962	Hank Aguirre	2.8
1966	Earl Wilson	2.7
1968	Denny McLain	2.3
1969	Denny McLain	2.9
1972	Mickey Lolich	2.7
1976	Mark Fidrych	2.7
2011	Justin Verlander	2.6
2013	Anibal Sanchez	2.8
2020	Bryan Garcia	2.5

SIX SHUTOUTS

1903	George Mullin	6
1904	George Mullin	7
1905	Ed Killian	8
1908	Bill Donovan	6
1917	Hooks Dauss	6
1935	Schoolboy Rowe	6
1944	Dizzy Trout	7
	Hal Newhouser	6
1945	Hal Newhouser	8
1946	Hal Newhouser	6
1949	Virgil Trucks	6
1955	Billy Hoeft	7
1964	Mickey Lolich	6
1967	Mickey Lolich	6
1968	Denny McLain	6
1969	**Denny McLain**	**9**
1986	Jack Morris	6

17 STARTER LOSSES

1941	Bobo Newsom	19
1942	Dizzy Trout	17
1952	Art Houtteman	18
1952	Virgil Trucks	18
1952	Ted Gray	17
1970	Mickey Lolich	19
1974	**Mickey Lolich**	**21**
1974	Lerrin LaGrow	19
1975	Joe Coleman	18
1975	Mickey Lolich	18
1976	Dave Roberts	17
1989	Doyle Alexander	18
1990	Jack Morris	18
2003	**Mike Maroth**	**21**
2003	Jeremy Bonderman	19
2003	Nate Cornejo	17
2008	Justin Verlander	17
2019	Spencer Turnbull	17

38 GAMES STARTED

1904	George Mullin	44
1905	George Mullin	41
1906	George Mullin	40
1907	George Mullin	42
1915	Harry Coveleski	38
1916	Harry Coveleski	39
1923	Hooks Dauss	39
1936	Tommy Bridges	38
1944	Dizzy Trout	40
1956	Frank Lary	38
1966	Denny McLain	38
1967	Earl Wilson	38
1968	Denny McLain	41
1969	Denny McLain	41
1970	Mickey Lolich	39
1971	**Mickey Lolich**	**45**
1972	Mickey Lolich	41
1973	Mickey Lolich	42
1974	Joe Coleman	41
	Mickey Lolich	41
1983	Dan Petry	38

21 STARTER WINS

1909	George Mullin	25
	Ed Willett	21
1915	Hooks Dauss	21
1934	Tommy Bridges	22
1935	Tommy Bridges	21
1936	Tommy Bridges	23
1944	Hal Newhouser	25
1944	Dizzy Trout	24
1945	Hal Newhouser	24
1946	Hal Newhouser	26
1956	Frank Lary	21
1961	Frank Lary	23
1967	Earl Wilson	22
1968	**Denny McLain**	**31**
1969	Denny McLain	24
1971	Mickey Lolich	25
1972	Mickey Lolich	22
1973	Joe Coleman	23
1986	Jack Morris	21
2011	Justin Verlander	24
2013	Max Scherzer	21

.715 STARTER WIN PERCENTAGE

1934	Elden Auker	.750	9-3
1934	Schoolboy Rowe	.731	19-7
1940	Schoolboy Rowe	.833	15-3
1940	Bobo Newsom	.833	20-4
1944	Hal Newhouser	.781	25-7
1945	Hal Newhouser	.727	24-9
1946	Hal Newhouser	.765	26-8
1955	Billy Hoeft	.727	16-6
1957	Jim Bunning	.720	18-7
1961	Frank Lary	.719	23-9
1968	Denny McLain	.838	31-6
1969	Denny McLain	.727	24-9
1972	Woodie Fryman	.769	10-3
1986	Jack Morris	.724	21-8
2007	Justin Verlander	.750	18-6
2011	Justin Verlander	.828	24-5
2013	**Max Scherzer**	**.875**	**21-3**
2014	Max Scherzer	.783	18-5

26 QUALITY STARTS

Year	Pitcher	QS
1914	Harry Coveleski	26
1915	Harry Coveleski	27
	Hooks Dauss	27
1916	Harry Coveleski	28
1944	Dizzy Trout	31
1945	Hal Newhouser	31
1946	Hal Newhouser	26
1947	Hal Newhouser	26
1968	**Denny McLain**	**35**
1969	Denny McLain	28
1971	Mickey Lolich	31
1972	Mickey Lolich	32
1983	Jack Morris	26
1985	Jack Morris	26
2011	Justin Verlander	28
2016	Justin Verlander	27

23 HIGH QUALITY STARTS

Year	Pitcher	HQS
1915	Hooks Dauss	26
1916	Harry Coveleski	26
1944	Dizzy Trout	30
1945	Hal Newhouser	30
1946	Hal Newhouser	26
1947	Hal Newhouser	24
1954	Steve Gromek	23
1961	Frank Lary	24
1968	**Denny McLain**	**34**
1969	Denny McLain	27
1970	Mickey Lolich	23
1971	Mickey Lolich	31
1972	Mickey Lolich	28
1976	Mark Fidrych	24
1983	Jack Morris	26
1985	Jack Morris	23
2011	Justin Verlander	24

.310 DOMINANT START PERCENTAGE

Year	Pitcher	Pct.
1915	Hooks Dauss	.314
1917	Hooks Dauss	.355
1918	Bernie Boland	.360
1934	Elden Auker	.333
1935	Elden Auker	.320
1943	Dizzy Trout	.367
1944	Dizzy Trout	.375
1945	Hal Newhouser	.417
1946	**Hal Newhouser**	**.471**
1949	Virgil Trucks	.313
1954	Ned Garver	.344
1957	Jim Bunning	.333
1966	Earl Wilson	.348
1968	Denny McLain	.341
1972	Mickey Lolich	.317
1976	Mark Fidrych	.379
1986	Jack Morris	.343

11 DOMINANT STARTS

Year	Pitcher	DS
1914	Harry Coveleski	11
1916	Harry Coveleski	11
1917	Hooks Dauss	11
1943	Dizzy Trout	11
1944	Hal Newhouser	11
1945	Hal Newhouser	15
1946	**Hal Newhouser**	**16**
1954	Ned Garver	11
1968	Denny McLain	14
1969	Denny McLain	12
1971	Mickey Lolich	11
1972	Mickey Lolich	13
1976	Mark Fidrych	11
1986	Jack Morris	12
2005	Jason Johnson	12
2006	Jeremy Bonderman	12
2009	Edwin Jackson	11
2010	Jeremy Bonderman	11
	Armando Galarraga	11
2012	Drew Smyly	11

.725 QUALITY START PERCENTAGE

Year	Pitcher	Pct.
1915	Hooks Dauss	.771
1917	Bill James	.782
1931	Art Herring	.750
1943	Tommy Bridges	.773
1944	Hal Newhouser	.794
1945	**Hal Newhouser**	**.861**
1946	Hal Newhouser	.765
1954	Steve Gromek	.750
1962	Hank Aguirre	.818
1968	Denny McLain	.854
1972	Mickey Lolich	.780
1976	Mark Fidrych	.793
1985	Frank Tanana	.800
1995	David Wells	.778
1997	Justin Thompson	.781
2011	Justin Verlander	.824
2012	Justin Verlander	.758
2013	Max Scherzer	.781
2016	Justin Verlander	.794

.675 HIGH QUALITY START PCT.

Year	Pitcher	Pct.
1913	Hooks Dauss	.759
1915	Hooks Dauss	.686
1917	Hooks Dauss	.710
1918	Bernie Boland	.680
1938	Al Benton	.700
1943	Tommy Bridges	.818
1944	Dizzy Trout	.750
1945	**Hal Newhouser**	**.833**
1946	Hal Newhouser	.765
1954	Steve Gromek	.719
1962	Hank Aguirre	.682
1968	Denny McLain	.829
1971	Mickey Lolich	.689
1972	Woodie Fryman	.714
1976	Mark Fidrych	.828
1983	Jack Morris	.703
2011	Justin Verlander	.706

12 STARTER NO DECISIONS

1961	Don Mossi	12
1964	Hank Aguirre	12
1965	Mickey Lolich	14
1967	Joe Sparma	12
1968	Joe Sparma	12
1969	Earl Wilson	13
1974	**Joe Coleman**	**15**
1990	Frank Tanana	12
1993	Mike Moore	14
1996	Felipe Lira	12
2005	Jason Johnson	12
2006	Jeremy Bonderman	12
2019	Daniel Norris	13
2021	Casey Mize	14

SIX STARTER CHEAP WINS

1923	**Hooks Dauss**	**7**
1932	**Earl Whitehill**	**7**
1934	Tommy Bridges	6
1936	Tommy Bridges	6
1959	Jim Bunning	6
1974	Joe Coleman	6
1980	Jack Morris	6
1983	**Dan Petry**	**7**
1986	**Jack Morris**	**7**
1990	Jack Morris	6
1991	Bill Gullickson	6
2009	Rick Porcello	6
2011	Max Scherzer	6

10 WINS IN RELIEF

1926	Hooks Dauss	11
1971	Fred Scherman	10
1973	John Hiller	10
1974	**John Hiller**	**17**
1976	John Hiller	11
1979	Aurelio Lopez	10
1980	Aurelio Lopez	13
1984	Aurelio Lopez	10
1987	Mike Henneman	11
1989	Mike Henneman	11
1991	Mike Henneman	10

SEVEN STARTER TOUGH LOSSES

1915	Harry Coveleski	9
1919	Bernie Boland	6
	Dutch Leonard	6
1920	Hooks Dauss	9
1942	Al Benton	9
1943	Hal Newhouser	9
1947	Hal Newhouser	9
1954	Steve Gromek	8
1955	**Frank Lary**	**10**
1960	Jim Bunning	8
1972	Joe Coleman	9
	Mickey Lolich	9
1985	Jack Morris	8
1997	Justin Thompson	8
2003	Jeremy Bonderman	8
	Mike Maroth	8

69 GAMES IN RELIEF

1984	Willie Hernandez	80
1985	Willie Hernandez	74
1990	Mike Henneman	69
1996	Mike Myers	83
1997	**Mike Myers**	**88**
1998	**Sean Runyan**	**88**
1999	Doug Brocail	70
2000	Matt Anderson	69
2003	Jamie Walker	78
2004	Jamie Walker	70
2009	Fernando Rodney	73
2010	Phil Coke	73
2011	Jose Valverde	75
2012	Joaquin Benoit	73
2014	Al Alburquerque	72
2015	Blaine Hardy	70
2017	Shane Greene	71
2019	Buck Farmer	72

SEVEN LOSSES IN RELIEF

1921	Jim Middleton	8
1933	Chief Hogsett	9
1940	Al Benton	10
1952	Hal White	8
1970	Tom Timmermann	7
1974	**John Hiller**	**14**
1976	John Hiller	8
1977	John Hiller	9
1979	John Hiller	7
1982	Dave Tobik	8
1983	Aurelio Lopez	8
1985	Willie Hernandez	10
1986	Willie Hernandez	7
1987	Eric King	7
1991	Paul Gibson	7
1995	Joe Boever	7
	John Doherty	7
2019	Joe Jimenez	7

.667 RELIEF WIN PCT (8 DEC)

1923	Bert Cole	.700	7-3
1924	Ken Holloway	.900	9-1
1926	Hooks Dauss	.786	11-3
1932	Chief Hogsett	.667	6-3
1937	George Gill	.875	7-1
1938	Harry Eisenstat	.750	6-2
1965	Fred Gladding	.750	6-2
1970	Daryl Patterson	.875	7-1
1972	Fred Scherman	.875	7-1
1973	John Hiller	.667	10-5
1979	Aurelio Lopez	.667	10-5
1980	Aurelio Lopez	.722	13-5
1983	Doug Bair	.667	6-3
1984	**Aurelio Lopez**	**.909**	**10-1**
1987	Mike Henneman	.786	11-3
1989	Mike Henneman	.733	11-4
1991	Mike Henneman	.833	10-2
1994	Joe Boever	.818	9-2
2006	Joel Zumaya	.667	6-3
2009	Bobby Seay	.667	6-3

16 HOLDS

1992	Mike Munoz	16
1993	Bob Macdonald	16
1996	Mike Myers	17
1997	Mike Myers	18
1999	Doug Brocail	23
2000	Doug Brocail	19
2001	Danny Patterson	16
2004	Jamie Walker	17
2006	**Joel Zumaya**	**30**
2009	Bobby Seay	28
2010	Ryan Perry	19
2011	Joaquin Benoit	29
2012	**Joaquin Benoit**	**30**
2013	Drew Smyly	21
2014	Joba Chamberlain	29
2016	Justin Wilson	25
2017	Alex Wilson	17
2018	Joe Jimenez	23
2021	Jose Cisnero	18

Daryl Patterson

Mike Munoz

Drew Smyly

Jose Valverde

53 GAMES FINISHED

1973	John Hiller	60
1980	Aurelio Lopez	59
1984	Willie Hernandez	68
1985	Willie Hernandez	64
1986	Willie Hernandez	53
1990	Mike Henneman	53
1992	Mike Henneman	53
1998	Todd Jones	53
1999	Todd Jones	62
2000	Todd Jones	60
2006	Todd Jones	56
2007	Todd Jones	54
2009	Fernando Rodney	65
2010	Jose Valverde	55
2011	**Jose Valverde**	**70**
2012	Jose Valverde	67
2014	Joe Nathan	54
2016	Francisco Rodriguez	55
2018	Shane Greene	58

25 SAVES

1970	Tom Timmermann	27
1973	John Hiller	38
1984	Willie Hernandez	32
1985	Willie Hernandez	31
1997	Todd Jones	31
1998	Todd Jones	28
1999	Todd Jones	30
2000	Todd Jones	42
2002	Juan Acevedo	28
2006	Todd Jones	37
2007	Todd Jones	38
2009	Fernando Rodney	37
2010	Jose Valverde	26
2011	**Jose Valverde**	**49**
2012	Jose Valverde	35
2014	Joe Nathan	35
2016	Francisco Rodriguez	44
2018	Shane Greene	32

GAMES

1901	Jimmy Barrett	135
	Kid Gleason	135
1902	Jimmy Barrett	136
1903	Sam Crawford	137
1904	Jimmy Barrett	162
1961	Rocky Colavito	163

PLATE APPEARANCES

1901	Jimmy Barrett	630
1904	Jimmy Barrett	714
1914	Donie Bush	721
1924	Ty Cobb	726
1936	Charlie Gehringer	731
1947	Eddie Lake	732
1978	Ron LeFlore	741

AT BATS

1901	Kid Gleason	547
1903	Sam Crawford	550
1904	Jimmy Barrett	624
1924	Ty Cobb	625
1929	Roy Johnson	640
1936	Charlie Gehringer	641
1950	George Kell	641
1953	Harvey Kuenn	679
2014	Ian Kinsler	684

RUNS

1901	Jimmy Barrett	110
1909	Ty Cobb	116
1911	Ty Cobb	147

HITS

1901	Jimmy Barrett	159
1903	Sam Crawford	184
1907	Ty Cobb	212
1909	Ty Cobb	216
1911	Ty Cobb	248

SINGLES

1901	Jimmy Barrett	130
1903	Jimmy Barrett	138
1904	Jimmy Barrett	152
1907	Ty Cobb	165
1911	Ty Cobb	169

DOUBLES

1901	Ducky Holmes	28
1905	Sam Crawford	38
1911	Ty Cobb	47
1927	Harry Heilmann	50
1934	Hank Greenberg	63

TRIPLES

1901	Kid Gleason	12
1903	Sam Crawford	25
1914	Sam Crawford	26

HOME RUNS

1901	Jimmy Barrett	4
	Ducky Holmes	4
1902	Jimmy Barrett	4
1903	Sam Crawford	4
1905	Sam Crawford	6
1908	Sam Crawford	7
1909	Ty Cobb	9
1913	Sam Crawford	9
1920	Bobby Veach	11
1921	Harry Heilmann	19
1922	Harry Heilmann	21
1929	Dale Alexander	25
1934	Hank Greenberg	26
1935	Hank Greenberg	36
1937	Hank Greenberg	40
1938	Hank Greenberg	58

RUNS BATTED IN

1901	Kid Elberfeld	76
1903	Sam Crawford	89
1907	Ty Cobb	119
1910	Sam Crawford	120
1911	Ty Cobb	127
1921	Harry Heilmann	139
1934	Hank Greenberg	139
1935	Hank Greenberg	170
1937	Hank Greenberg	183

HIT BY PITCH

1901	Doc Casey	10
1902	Dick Harley	12
1914	George Burns	12
1923	Heinie Manush	17
1967	Bill Freehan	20
1968	Bill Freehan	24

REACHED ON ERROR

1930	Charlie Gehringer	9
1931	Dale Alexander	11
1933	Marv Owen	11
1935	Pete Fox	12
1937	Gee Walker	12
1947	Eddie Lake	14
1957	Harvey Kuenn	16
1961	Al Kaline	18

ON BASE PERCENTAGE

1901	Kid Elberfeld	.397
1902	Jimmy Barrett	.397
1903	Jimmy Barrett	.407
1909	Ty Cobb	.431
1910	Ty Cobb	.458
1911	Ty Cobb	.467
1913	Ty Cobb	.467
1915	Ty Cobb	.486
1961	Norm Cash	.487

SLUGGING PERCENTAGE

1901	Kid Elberfeld	.428
1903	Sam Crawford	.489
1909	Ty Cobb	.517
1910	Ty Cobb	.554
1911	Ty Cobb	.621
1923	Harry Heilmann	.632
1937	Hank Greenberg	.668
1938	Hank Greenberg	.683

ON BASE PCT PLUS SLUGGING

1901	Kid Elberfeld	.825
1903	Sam Crawford	.855
1909	Ty Cobb	.947
1910	Ty Cobb	1.012
1911	Ty Cobb	1.088
1923	Harry Heilmann	1.113
1938	Hank Greenberg	1.122
1961	Norm Cash	1.148

ON BASE PLUS SLUGGING PLUS

1901	Kid Elberfeld	124
1903	Sam Crawford	159
1907	Ty Cobb	167
1908	Ty Cobb	169
1909	Ty Cobb	193
1910	Ty Cobb	206
1917	Ty Cobb	209

MOST EFFECTIVE PLAYER

1901	Kid Elberfeld	2.00
1902	Jimmy Barrett	1.33
1903	Sam Crawford	1.25
1909	Ty Cobb	1.17
1924	Harry Heilmann	1.17
1974	Bill Freehan	1.08

TOTAL AVERAGE

1901	Kid Elberfeld	.910
1907	Ty Cobb	.919
1909	Ty Cobb	1.193
1910	Ty Cobb	1.321
1911	Ty Cobb	1.464

BASE-OUT PERCENTAGE

1901	Kid Elberfeld	.913
1907	Ty Cobb	.921
1909	Ty Cobb	1.181
1910	Ty Cobb	1.305
1911	Ty Cobb	1.449

GROSS PRODUCTION AVERAGE

1901	Kid Elberfeld	.286
1903	Sam Crawford	.287
1907	Ty Cobb	.288
1909	Ty Cobb	.323
1910	Ty Cobb	.343
1911	Ty Cobb	.365
1923	Harry Heilmann	.374
1961	Norm Cash	.384

WEIGHTED ON BASE AVERAGE

1901	Ducky Holmes	.302
1903	Sam Crawford	.349
1907	Ty Cobb	.376
1909	Ty Cobb	.387
1910	Ty Cobb	.472
1911	Ty Cobb	.497

WINS ABOVE REPLACEMENT

1901	Kid Elberfeld	3.8
1903	Sam Crawford	5.6
1907	Ty Cobb	6.8
1909	Ty Cobb	9.8
1910	Ty Cobb	10.5
1911	Ty Cobb	10.7
1917	Ty Cobb	11.3

OFFENSIVE WAR

1901	Kid Elberfeld	4.0
1903	Sam Crawford	5.3
1907	Ty Cobb	6.5
1909	Ty Cobb	9.5
1910	Ty Cobb	9.6
1911	Ty Cobb	10.2
1917	Ty Cobb	10.6

DEFENSIVE WAR

1901	Doc Casey	1.0
1902	Kid Elberfeld	1.1
1909	Donie Bush	2.2
1914	Donie Bush	2.4
	George Moriarty	2.4
1916	Ossie Vitt	2.5
1935	Billy Rogell	2.7
1950	Jerry Priddy	2.7
1967	Ray Oyler	2.7
2006	Brandon Inge	2.7
2011	Austin Jackson	3.4

BATTERS RUN AVERAGE

1901	Kid Elberfeld	.166
1903	Sam Crawford	.171
1907	Ty Cobb	.175
1909	Ty Cobb	.214
1910	Ty Cobb	.248
1911	Ty Cobb	.285
1923	Harry Heilmann	.293
1938	Hank Greenberg	.298
1961	Norm Cash	.321

BATTING AVERAGE

1901	Kid Elberfeld	.308
1903	Sam Crawford	.335
1907	Ty Cobb	.350
1909	Ty Cobb	.377
1910	Ty Cobb	.385
1911	Ty Cobb	.420

BATTING AVERAGE BALLS IN PLAY

1901	Jimmy Barrett	.327
1902	Jimmy Barrett	.338
1903	Sam Crawford	.360
1907	Ty Cobb	.380
1909	Ty Cobb	.399
1910	Ty Cobb	.413
1911	Ty Cobb	.444
2020	Willi Castro	.448

SECONDARY AVERAGE

1901	Kid Elberfeld	.306
1903	Billy Lush	.314
1909	Ty Cobb	.356
1910	Ty Cobb	.422
1915	Ty Cobb	.430
1935	Hank Greenberg	.443
1937	Hank Greenberg	.512
1938	Hank Greenberg	.586

IN PLAY PERCENTAGE

1901	Sport McAllister	88%
1902	Kid Gleason	89%
1906	Sam Crawford	89%
1929	Bob Fothergill	89%
1931	Mark Koenig	92%
1954	Harvey Kuenn	92%

TIMES ON BASE

1901	Jimmy Barrett	240
1903	Jimmy Barrett	243
1904	Jimmy Barrett	249
1908	Matty McIntyre	258
1909	Ty Cobb	270
1911	Ty Cobb	300
1915	Ty Cobb	336

AT BATS PER HOME RUN

1901	Sport McAllister	102.0
1905	Sam Crawford	95.8
1908	Sam Crawford	84.4
1909	Ty Cobb	63.7
1910	Ty Cobb	63.6
1918	Harry Heilmann	57.2
1920	Bobby Veach	55.6
1921	Harry Heilmann	31.7
1922	Harry Heilmann	21.7
1935	Hank Greenberg	17.2
1937	Rudy York	10.7
1938	Hank Greenberg	9.6

AT BATS PER RUN BATTED IN

1901	Sport McAllister	5.4
1907	Ty Cobb	5.1
1910	Sam Crawford	4.9
1911	Ty Cobb	4.7
1921	Harry Heilmann	4.3
1925	Ty Cobb	4.1
1929	Harry Heilmann	3.8
1935	Hank Greenberg	3.7
1937	Hank Greenberg	3.2

AT BATS PER STRIKEOUT

1901	Sport McAllister	43.7
1902	Kid Elberfeld	48.8
1925	Johnny Bassler	57.3

NUMBER OF PITCHES

1988	Chet Lemon	2,195
1989	Lou Whitaker	2,231
1990	Cecil Fielder	2,632
1991	Cecil Fielder	2,708
1992	Tony Phillips	2,904
1993	Tony Phillips	2,948

PITCHES PER PLATE APPEARANCE

1988	Darrell Evans	4.03
1989	Gary Pettis	4.13
1991	Rob Deer	4.26
1992	Mickey Tettleton	4.34
1994	Mickey Tettleton	4.46

BASE RUNS

1901	Jimmy Barrett	79
1903	Sam Crawford	87
1907	Ty Cobb	95
1909	Ty Cobb	115
1910	Ty Cobb	120
1911	Ty Cobb	148
1937	Hank Greenberg	155
1961	Norm Cash	159

RUNS PRODUCED

1901	Jimmy Barrett	171
1903	Sam Crawford	173
1907	Ty Cobb	211
1909	Ty Cobb	214
1911	Ty Cobb	266
1937	Hank Greenberg	281

ESTIMATED RUNS PRODUCED

1901	Jimmy Barrett	84
1903	Sam Crawford	92
1907	Ty Cobb	104
1909	Ty Cobb	124
1911	Ty Cobb	154
1937	Hank Greenberg	155

RUNS CREATED

1901	Jimmy Barrett	79
1903	Sam Crawford	98
1907	Ty Cobb	108
1909	Ty Cobb	127
1911	Ty Cobb	171
1937	Hank Greenberg	173

RUNS CREATED PER 27 OUTS

1901	Jimmy Barrett	2.92
1903	Sam Crawford	3.64
1907	Ty Cobb	3.98
1909	Ty Cobb	4.72
1910	Ty Cobb	4.78
1911	Ty Cobb	6.34
1937	Hank Greenberg	6.42

Gary Pettis

TECHNICAL RUNS CREATED

1901	Jimmy Barrett	86.1
1903	Sam Crawford	96.8
1907	Ty Cobb	108.4
1909	Ty Cobb	128.7
1910	Ty Cobb	133.5
1911	Ty Cobb	174.6
1937	Hank Greenberg	182.8
1961	Norm Cash	188.6

TOTAL SACRIFICES

1901	Doc Nance	24
1903	Billy Lush	34
1906	Bill Coughlin	36
1908	Germany Schaefer	43
1909	Donie Bush	52

BATTING RUNS

1920	Bobby Veach	48
1921	Harry Heilmann	93
1923	Harry Heilmann	98
1935	Hank Greenberg	98
1937	Hank Greenberg	112
1961	Norm Cash	116

SACRIFICE FLIES

1954	Frank House	7
1955	Ray Boone	7
	Earl Torgeson	7
1956	Harvey Kuenn	8
	Charlie Maxwell	8
1958	Frank Bolling	9
1963	Bubba Phillips	10
1976	Rusty Staub	11
1978	Rusty Staub	11
1983	Lance Parrish	13
1994	Travis Fryman	13

EXTRAPOLATED RUNS BASIC

1901	Jimmy Barrett	85
1903	Sam Crawford	91
1907	Ty Cobb	104
1909	Ty Cobb	125
1911	Ty Cobb	152
1937	Hank Greenberg	153
1938	Hank Greenberg	153
1961	Norm Cash	154

HOME RUN AVERAGE

1901	Sport McAllister	5.88
1905	Sam Crawford	6.26
1908	Sam Crawford	7.11
1909	Ty Cobb	9.42
1910	Ty Cobb	9.49
1918	Harry Heilmann	10.49
1920	Bobby Veach	10.78
1921	Harry Heilmann	18.94
1922	Harry Heilmann	27.69
1935	Hank Greenberg	34.89
1937	Rudy York	56.00
1938	Hank Greenberg	62.50

HOME RUN RATIO

1903	Sam Crawford	0.01
1905	Sam Crawford	0.01
1907	Ty Cobb	0.01
	Sam Crawford	0.01
1908	Three Batters	0.01
1909	Ty Cobb	0.02
1910	Ty Cobb	0.02
1918	Harry Heilmann	0.02
1919	Ira Flagstead	0.02
1920	Harry Heilmann	0.02
	Bobby Veach	0.02
1921	Harry Heilmann	0.03
	Bobby Veach	0.03
1922	Harry Heilmann	0.05
1935	Hank Greenberg	0.06
1937	Rudy York	0.09
1938	Hank Greenberg	0.10

HOME RUNS ON THE ROAD

1930	Dale Alexander	10
1932	Charlie Gehringer	13
1935	Hank Greenberg	18
1937	Rudy York	18
1938	Hank Greenberg	19
1961	Rocky Colavito	27
2013	Miguel Cabrera	27

HOME RUNS BY LH BATTERS

1901	Jimmy Barrett	4
	Ducky Holmes	4
1902	Jimmy Barrett	4
1903	Sam Crawford	4
1905	Sam Crawford	6
1908	Sam Crawford	7
1909	Ty Cobb	9
1913	Sam Crawford	9
1920	Bobby Veach	11
1921	Bobby Veach	16
1930	Charlie Gehringer	16
1932	Charlie Gehringer	19
1936	Goose Goslin	24
1950	Vic Wertz	27
1951	Vic Wertz	27
1956	Charlie Maxwell	28
1959	Charlie Maxwell	31
1961	Norm Cash	41

HOME RUNS VERSUS RH PITCHERS

1901	Jimmy Barrett	4
1903	Sam Crawford	4
1907	Sam Crawford	4
1908	Sam Crawford	5
1909	Ty Cobb	5
1910	Ty Cobb	5
1913	Sam Crawford	5
1914	Sam Crawford	5
1916	Ty Cobb	5
1917	Bobby Veach	7
1920	Harry Heilmann	7
1921	Harry Heilmann	14
1922	Harry Heilmann	18
1929	Dale Alexander	21
1935	Hank Greenberg	24
1937	Hank Greenberg	30
1938	Hank Greenberg	49

HOME RUNS BY RH BATTERS

1901	Kid Elberfeld	3
	Doc Nance	3
1908	Germany Schaefer	3
1910	Jim Delahanty	3
1911	Jim Delahanty	3
	Oscar Stanage	3
1914	George Burns	5
1915	George Burns	5
1917	Harry Heilmann	5
1918	Harry Heilmann	5
1919	Harry Heilmann	8
1920	Harry Heilmann	9
1921	Harry Heilmann	19
1922	Harry Heilmann	21
1929	Dale Alexander	25
1934	Hank Greenberg	26
1935	Hank Greenberg	36
1937	Hank Greenberg	40
1938	Hank Greenberg	58

HOME RUNS AT HOME

1930	Dale Alexander	10
1934	Hank Greenberg	15
1935	Hank Greenberg	18
1937	Hank Greenberg	25
1938	Hank Greenberg	39

HOME RUNS VERSUS LH PITCHERS

1901	Six Batters	1
1902	Jimmy Barrett	2
1905	Sam Crawford	3
1909	Ty Cobb	4
1911	Ty Cobb	4
1913	Sam Crawford	4
1920	Bobby Veach	5
1921	Harry Heilmann	5
	Bobby Veach	5
1923	Harry Heilmann	5
1925	Harry Heilmann	10
1935	Hank Greenberg	12
1940	Hank Greenberg	13
1966	Norm Cash	13
	Willie Horton	13
1967	Al Kaline	14
1968	Willie Horton	16
1980	Lance Parrish	16
	John Wockenfuss	16
1990	Cecil Fielder	25

INSIDE THE PARK HOME RUNS

1901	Kid Gleason	2
	Ducky Holmes	2
1903	Sam Crawford	2
1904	Sam Crawford	2
1905	Sam Crawford	4
1908	Ty Cobb	4
1909	Ty Cobb	9

HOME RUN PERCENTAGE

1901	Sport McAllister	0.9
1905	Sam Crawford	1.0
1908	Sam Crawford	1.1
1909	Ty Cobb	1.4
1910	Ty Cobb	1.4
1918	Harry Heilmann	1.5
1919	Ira Flagstead	1.5
1920	Bobby Veach	1.6
1921	Harry Heilmann	2.8
1922	Harry Heilmann	4.0
1935	Hank Greenberg	5.1
1937	Rudy York	8.4
1938	Hank Greenberg	8.5

POWER SPEED NUMBER

1901	Ducky Holmes	7.2
1905	Sam Crawford	9.4
1908	Sam Crawford	9.5
1909	Ty Cobb	16.1
1929	Charlie Gehringer	17.6
1936	Goose Goslin	17.7
1937	Gee Walker	20.2
1977	Ron LeFlore	22.7
1984	Kirk Gibson	28.0
1985	Kirk Gibson	29.5
1986	Kirk Gibson	30.7

HOME RUNS BY SWITCH HITTERS

1901	Kid Gleason	3
	Sport McAllister	3
1902	Doc Casey	3
1910	Donie Bush	3
1921	Lu Blue	5
1922	Lu Blue	6
1928	Pinky Hargrave	10
1945	Roy Cullenbine	18
1947	Roy Cullenbine	24
1991	Mickey Tettleton	31
1992	Mickey Tettleton	32
1993	Mickey Tettleton	32
1997	Tony Clark	32
1998	Tony Clark	34

GRAND SLAM HOME RUNS

1930	Bob Fothergill	1
	Charlie Gehringer	1
1932	John Stone	1
1936	Mickey Cochrane	1
	Goose Goslin	1
1937	Hank Greenberg	2
	Rudy York	2
1938	Hank Greenberg	2
1953	Ray Boone	2
1959	Eddie Yost	2
1961	Norm Cash	2
1967	Jim Northrup	2
1968	Jim Northrup	4

ISOLATED POWER

1901	Kid Elberfeld	.120
1903	Sam Crawford	.155
1910	Ty Cobb	.169
1911	Ty Cobb	.201
1921	Harry Heilmann	.213
1922	Harry Heilmann	.242
1934	Hank Greenberg	.261
1935	Hank Greenberg	.300
1937	Rudy York	.344
1938	Hank Greenberg	.369

EXTRA BASE HITS

1901	Ducky Holmes	42
1903	Sam Crawford	52
1905	Sam Crawford	54
1907	Sam Crawford	55
1908	Ty Cobb	60
1911	Ty Cobb	79
1929	Dale Alexander	83
1934	Hank Greenberg	96
1935	Hank Greenberg	98
1937	Hank Greenberg	103

PERCENTAGE OF HITS EXTRA BASES

1901	Ducky Holmes	26.6
1903	Billy Lush	28.4
1905	Sam Crawford	31.6
1908	Ty Cobb	31.9
1911	Ty Cobb	31.9
1913	Sam Crawford	33.2
1916	Harry Heilmann	33.9
1919	Bobby Veach	34.0
1920	Bobby Veach	34.6
1921	Bobby Veach	34.8
1922	Harry Heilmann	35.8
1924	Harry Heilmann	36.0
1925	Frank O'Rourke	36.9
1929	Harry Heilmann	40.4
1934	Hank Greenberg	47.8
1935	Hank Greenberg	48.3
1937	Hank Greenberg	51.5
1939	Hank Greenberg	52.6
1946	Hank Greenberg	53.8
1992	Rob Deer	54.6

EXTRA BASES ON LONG HITS

1901	Ducky Holmes	60
1903	Sam Crawford	85
1908	Ty Cobb	88
1911	Ty Cobb	119
1921	Harry Heilmann	128
1929	Dale Alexander	148
1934	Hank Greenberg	155
1935	Hank Greenberg	186
1937	Hank Greenberg	197
1938	Hank Greenberg	205

EXTRA BASE HIT PERCENTAGE

1901	Ducky Holmes	7.1
1903	Sam Crawford	8.6
1905	Sam Crawford	8.6
1907	Sam Crawford	8.7
1908	Ty Cobb	9.4
1911	Ty Cobb	12.1
1927	Harry Heilmann	12.2
1929	Bob Fothergill	13.3
1934	Hank Greenberg	14.4
1937	Hank Greenberg	14.7
1940	Hank Greenberg	14.8

TOTAL BASES

1901	Ducky Holmes	218
1903	Sam Crawford	269
1907	Ty Cobb	283
1909	Ty Cobb	296
1911	Ty Cobb	367
1935	Hank Greenberg	389
1937	Hank Greenberg	397

TOTAL BASE PERCENTAGE

1901	Kid Elberfeld	0.40
1902	Jimmy Barrett	0.40
1903	Jimmy Barrett	0.41
1909	Ty Cobb	0.43
1910	Ty Cobb	0.46
1911	Ty Cobb	0.47
1913	Ty Cobb	0.47
1914	Ty Cobb	0.47
1915	Ty Cobb	0.49
1961	Norm Cash	0.49

TOTAL BASE AVERAGE

1901	Ducky Holmes	1.7
1903	Sam Crawford	2.0
1910	Ty Cobb	2.0
1911	Ty Cobb	2.5
1935	Hank Greenberg	2.6
1937	Hank Greenberg	2.6
1940	Hank Greenberg	2.6

BASES PRODUCED

1901	Jimmy Barrett	307
1903	Sam Crawford	312
1905	Sam Crawford	319
1907	Ty Cobb	356
1909	Ty Cobb	420
1911	Ty Cobb	494
1937	Hank Greenberg	507

BASES PRODUCED AVERAGE

1901	Jimmy Barrett	2.3
1903	Sam Crawford	2.3
1907	Ty Cobb	2.4
1909	Ty Cobb	2.7
1910	Ty Cobb	2.9
1911	Ty Cobb	3.4

STOLEN BASES

1901	Ducky Holmes	35
1907	Ty Cobb	49
1909	Ty Cobb	76
1911	Ty Cobb	83
1915	Ty Cobb	96

CAUGHT STEALING

1920	Ralph Young	13
1921	Lu Blue	17
1931	Roy Johnson	21

STOLEN BASE PERCENTAGE

1920	Donie Bush	.682	15-07
1921	Ralph Young	.917	11-01
1938	C. Gehringer	.933	14-01
1940	C. Gehringer	1.000	10-00
1958	Red Wilson	1.000	10-00
1976	Dan Meyer	1.000	10-00
2012	Quintin Berry	1.000	21-00

STOLEN BASE RUNS

1901	Ducky Holmes	10.5
1907	Ty Cobb	14.7
1909	Ty Cobb	22.8
1911	Ty Cobb	24.9

STOLEN BASE RUNS CREATED

1901	Jimmy Barrett	171
1903	Jimmy Barrett	173
1908	Matty McIntyre	184
1909	Ty Cobb	204
1910	Ty Cobb	224
1911	Ty Cobb	248
1915	Ty Cobb	285
1937	Hank Greenberg	304
1938	Hank Greenberg	319
1961	Norm Cash	334

Ty Cobb

INTENTIONAL WALKS

1955	Al Kaline	12
1957	Frank House	13
1961	Norm Cash	19
2010	Miguel Cabrera	32

BASE ON BALLS PERCENTAGE

1901	Jimmy Barrett	12.1
1902	Jimmy Barrett	12.5
1903	Billy Lush	13.3
1911	Donie Bush	14.2
1912	Donie Bush	18.2
1935	Mickey Cochrane	18.4
1946	Roy Cullenbine	21.0
1947	Roy Cullenbine	22.6

STRIKEOUTS

1901	Jimmy Barrett	64
1903	Jimmy Barrett	67
1904	Jimmy Barrett	91
1905	Germany Schaefer	91
1934	Hank Greenberg	93
1937	Hank Greenberg	101
1943	Joe Hoover	101
1961	Jake Wood	141
1990	Cecil Fielder	182

STRIKEOUT PERCENTAGE

1901	Sport McAllister	02.1
1902	Kid Elberfeld	01.8
1925	Johnny Bassler	01.4

STRIKEOUT RATIO

1901	Sport McAllister	0.08
1902	Kid Elberfeld	0.08
1913	Donie Bush	0.05
	Sam Crawford	0.05
	Ossie Vitt	0.05
1914	Sam Crawford	0.05
	Bobby Veach	0.05
1915	Ossie Vitt	0.04
1916	Sam Crawford	0.03
1917	Ossie Vitt	0.03
1918	Ossie Vitt	0.02
1924	Del Pratt	0.02
1925	Johnny Bassler	0.02
1936	Charlie Gehringer	0.02
1943	Doc Cramer	0.02
1949	George Kell	0.02
1954	Harvey Kuenn	0.02

WALK TO STRIKEOUT RATIO

1901	Kid Elberfeld	03.2
1902	Kid Elberfeld	05.5
1923	Johnny Bassler	05.8
1925	Johnny Bassler	12.3

HITTING STREAKS

1901	Kid Gleason	25
1906	Ty Cobb	25
1911	Ty Cobb	40

INFIELD HITS

1988	Luis Salazar	23
1991	Tony Phillips	24
1992	Tony Phillips	36
1997	Brian Hunter	37
1998	Brian Hunter	48

BUNT HITS

1988	Luis Salazar	14
1991	Milt Cuyler	15
1999	Luis Polonia	15
2003	Alex Sanchez	30

GROUNDED INTO DOUBLE PLAY

1939	Pinky Higgins	14
1940	Hank Greenberg	15
1941	Pinky Higgins	20
1942	Pinky Higgins	21
1943	Jimmy Bloodworth	29

OUTS

1901	Kid Gleason	412
1904	Jimmy Barrett	465
1908	Germany Schaefer	476
1914	Donie Bush	482
1915	Donie Bush	482
1916	Ossie Vitt	494
1944	Eddie Mayo	509
1961	Jake Wood	515
1997	Brian Hunter	525
2014	Ian Kinsler	528

WALKS

1901	Jimmy Barrett	76
1904	Jimmy Barrett	79
1908	Matty McIntyre	83
1909	Donie Bush	88
1911	Donie Bush	98
1912	Donie Bush	117
1915	Donie Bush	118
	Ty Cobb	118
1938	Hank Greenberg	119
1947	Roy Cullenbine	137

PINCH HIT AT BATS

1901	Emil Frisk	6
1904	George Mullin	6
1906	George Mullin	8
1907	George Mullin	20
1908	Davy Jones	21
1913	Jean Dubuc	28
1914	Jean Dubuc	32
1916	Marty Kavanagh	39
1920	Sammy Hale	52
1929	Bob Fothergill	53
1953	Pat Mullin	57

PINCH HITS

1901	Emil Frisk	2
	Sport McAllister	2
1904	George Mullin	2
1906	George Mullin	3
	Fred Payne	3
1907	George Mullin	5
1911	Bill Schaller	6
	Boss Schmidt	6
1914	Jean Dubuc	6
1915	Marty Kavanagh	10
1920	Sammy Hale	17
1929	Bob Fothergill	19

PINCH HIT AVERAGE (MIN 5 PH AB)

1901	Emil Frisk	.333	2-6
1904	George Mullin	.333	2-6
1906	Fred Payne	.429	3-7
1912	Hank Perry	.500	3-6
1915	Marty Kavanagh	.500	10-20
1916	Sam Crawford	.533	8-15
1924	Les Burke	.571	4-7
1926	Bob Fothergill	.667	4-6
1939	Red Kress	.800	4-5
1950	Aaron Robinson	.800	4-5

RUN SCORING PERCENTAGE

1901	Doc Casey	53%
1911	Davy Jones	57%

PINCH HIT RUNS BATTED IN

1925	Bob Fothergill	5
1928	Pinky Hargrave	8
1950	Charlie Keller	9
1951	Charlie Keller	9
1958	Gus Zernial	10
1962	Vic Wertz	12

PINCH HIT HOME RUNS

1906	Germany Schaefer	1
1917	Sam Crawford	1
1920	Sammy Hale	1
1922	Danny Clark	1
	Ira Flagstead	1
1923	Heinie Manush	1
1924	Al Wingo	1
1925	Heinie Manush	1
1927	Heinie Manush	1
1928	Pinky Hargrave	1
1932	Gee Walker	1
1937	Goose Goslin	2
1940	Billy Sullivan	2
1942	Ned Harris	2
1945	Zeb Eaton	2
1948	Dick Wakefield	3
1958	Gus Zernial	3
1960	Norm Cash	3
1961	Charlie Maxwell	3
1962	Vic Wertz	3
1968	Gates Brown	3
1973	Frank Howard	3
1974	Gates Brown	3
1976	Ben Oglivie	3
1984	Johnny Grubb	3
1986	Larry Herndon	3
2016	Victor Martinez	3

SACRIFICE HITS

1901	Doc Nance	24
1903	Billy Lush	34
1906	Bill Coughlin	36
1908	Germany Schaefer	43
1909	Donie Bush	52

GAMES

1901	Roscoe Miller	38
	Ed Siever	38
1903	George Mullin	41
1904	George Mullin	45
1907	George Mullin	46
1915	Harry Coveleski	50
1923	Bert Cole	52
1966	Larry Sherry	55
1970	Tom Timmermann	61
1971	Fred Scherman	69
1984	Willie Hernandez	80
1996	Mike Myers	83
1997	Mike Myers	88
1998	Sean Runyan	88

WINS

1901	Roscoe Miller	23
1905	Ed Killian	23
1907	Bill Donovan	25
	Ed Killian	25
1909	George Mullin	29
1944	Hal Newhouser	29
1968	Denny McLain	31

LOSSES

1901	Jack Cronin	15
	Ed Siever	15
1902	Win Mercer	18
1904	George Mullin	23

WIN PERCENTAGE

1901	Roscoe Miller	.639	23-13
1907	Bill Donovan	.862	25-04
1984	Aurelio Lopez	.910	10-01

INNINGS

1901	Roscoe Miller	332.0
1904	George Mullin	382.1

HITS ALLOWED

1901	Roscoe Miller	339
1904	George Mullin	345
1907	George Mullin	346

HOME RUNS ALLOWED

1901	Ed Siever	9
1910	Sailor Stroud	9
1920	Hooks Dauss	11
1921	Howard Ehmke	15
	Dutch Leonard	15
1928	Lil Stoner	16
1929	Earl Whitehill	16
1930	George Uhle	18
1931	Earl Whitehill	22
1935	Tommy Bridges	22
1946	Virgil Trucks	23
1948	Fred Hutchinson	32
1957	Jim Bunning	33
1963	Jim Bunning	38
1966	Denny McLain	42

BALKS

1901	Jack Cronin	0
	Emil Frisk	0
	Ed High	0
	Roscoe Miller	0
	Frank Owen	0
	Ed Siever	0
	Joe Yeager	0
1902	Ed Siever	1
1904	Ed Killian	1
1905	George Mullin	1
1907	George Mullin	1
1908	Ed Summers	1
1909	Ed Summers	1
1911	Tex Covington	1
1912	Bill Burns	1
1914	Red Oldham	3
1925	Ed Wells	3
1926	Rip Collins	3
1952	Bill Wight	3
1956	Paul Foytack	3
1958	Jim Bunning	3
1963	Bill Faul	3
1977	Jim Crawford	3
1983	Dave Rozema	3
1985	Jack Morris	3
1986	Eric King	3
1987	Jeff Robinson	3
1988	Jack Morris	11

STRIKEOUTS

1901	Ed Siever	85
1903	Bill Donovan	187
1944	Hal Newhouser	187
1945	Hal Newhouser	212
1946	Hal Newhouser	275
1968	Denny McLain	280
1971	Mickey Lolich	308

WALKS

1901	Roscoe Miller	98
1903	George Mullin	106
1904	George Mullin	131
1905	George Mullin	138
1956	Paul Foytack	142
1974	Joe Coleman	158

HIT BY PITCH

1901	Roscoe Miller	13
1904	Ed Killian	17
1908	Ed Summers	20
1915	Harry Coveleski	20
1922	Howard Ehmke	23

INTENTIONAL WALKS

1955	Ned Garver	10
1956	Billy Hoeft	12
1957	Paul Foytack	12
1974	John Hiller	19

WILD PITCHES

1901	Jack Cronin	5
1902	George Mullin	13
1912	Jean Dubuc	16
1983	Jack Morris	18
1987	Jack Morris	24

EARNED RUNS

1901	Roscoe Miller	109
1921	Hooks Dauss	112
1922	Howard Ehmke	131
1973	Mickey Lolich	131
1974	Mickey Lolich	142

RUNS

1901	Roscoe Miller	168

TECHNICAL RUNS ALLOWED

Year	Player	Value
1901	Roscoe Miller	4.55
1902	Ed Siever	3.49
1903	Bill Donovan	3.05
1907	Ed Siever	2.92
1908	Bill Donovan	2.89
1909	Ed Killian	2.34
1945	Hal Newhouser	2.10
1973	John Hiller	1.51

WALKS PER NINE INNINGS

Year	Player	Value
1901	Jack Cronin	1.7
1902	Ed Siever	1.5
1903	Frank Kitson	1.3
1951	Fred Hutchinson	1.3
1985	Willie Hernandez	1.2

WALKS PLUS HITS PER INNING PITCHED

Year	Player	Value
1901	Joe Yeager	1.277
1902	Ed Siever	1.051
1909	Ed Summers	1.047
1966	Earl Wilson	1.004
1968	Denny McLain	0.905
1985	Willie Hernandez	0.900

EARNED RUN AVERAGE PLUS

Year	Player	Value
1901	Joe Yeager	140
1902	Ed Siever	187
1973	John Hiller	265

FIELDING INDEPENDENT PITCHING

Year	Player	Value
1901	Jack Cronin	3.44
1902	Ed Siever	2.83
1903	Bill Donovan	2.64
1906	Red Donahue	2.51
1907	Ed Siever	2.27
1908	Bill Donovan	1.78

HITS ALLOWED PER NINE INNINGS

Year	Player	Value
1901	Roscoe Miller	9.2
1902	Ed Siever	7.9
1903	Bill Donovan	7.2
1910	Ed Willett	7.0
1942	Hal Newhouser	6.7
1946	Hal Newhouser	6.6
1968	Denny McLain	6.5
1973	John Hiller	6.4
1981	Kevin Saucier	4.8

BATTERS FACED

Year	Player	Value
1901	Roscoe Miller	1408
1904	George Mullin	1568

LEFT ON-BASE PERCENTAGE

Year	Player	Value
1901	Roscoe Miller	62.86
1902	Win Mercer	66.58
1903	Bill Donovan	70.89
1907	Ed Killian	74.12
1908	Ed Willett	75.04
1909	Ed Killian	78.59
1945	Hal Newhouser	80.70
1954	Steve Gromek	81.91
1957	Jim Bunning	82.14
1968	Denny McLain	84.02
1973	John Hiller	90.52
2006	Jamie Walker	91.32

STRIKEOUTS PER NINE INNINGS

Year	Player	Value
1901	Ed Siever	2.7
1902	George Mullin	2.7
1903	Bill Donovan	5.5
1931	Tommy Bridges	5.5
1939	Bobo Newsom	6.0
1940	Tommy Bridges	6.1
1941	Bobo Newsom	6.3
1943	Hal Newhouser	6.6
1946	Hal Newhouser	8.5
1969	Mickey Lolich	8.7
1973	John Hiller	8.9
1996	Mike Myers	9.6
2006	Joel Zumaya	10.5
2012	Max Scherzer	11.1
2017	Justin Wilson	12.3
2019	Joe Jimenez	12.4

STRIKEOUTS TO WALKS

Year	Player	Value
1901	Jack Cronin	1.48
1903	Frank Kitson	2.68
1946	Hal Newhouser	2.81
1959	Frank Lary	2.98
1960	Jim Bunning	3.14
1962	Don Mossi	3.36
1966	Earl Wilson	3.50
1968	Denny McLain	4.44
1985	Willie Hernandez	5.43

DICE

Year	Player	Value
1901	Jack Cronin	3.51
1902	Ed Siever	3.16
1903	Bill Donovan	2.89
1908	Bill Donovan	2.67
1946	Hal Newhouser	2.58
1998	Doug Brocail	2.57
2001	Matt Anderson	2.57
2012	Octavio Dotel	2.21

EARNED RUN AVERAGE

Year	Player	Value
1901	Joe Yeager	2.61
1902	Ed Siever	1.91
1907	Ed Killian	1.78
1908	Ed Summers	1.64
1973	John Hiller	1.44

RUNS ALLOWED PER NINE INNINGS

Year	Player	Value
1901	Roscoe Miller	4.6
1902	Ed Siever	3.5
1903	Bill Donovan	3.0
1907	Ed Siever	2.9
1908	Bill Donovan	2.9
1909	Ed Killian	2.3
1945	Hal Newhouser	2.1

HOMERS ALLOWED PER NINE INNINGS

Year	Player	Value
1901	Roscoe Miller	0.0
1902	Ed Siever	0.0
1904	Ed Killian	0.0
	George Mullin	0.0
1905	Ed Killian	0.0
1906	Red Donahue	0.0
1907	George Mullin	0.0
	Ed Siever	0.0
1908	George Mullin	0.0
1909	George Mullin	0.0
1913	Jean Dubuc	0.0
	Ed Willett	0.0
1915	Hooks Dauss	0.0
1916	Hooks Dauss	0.0
	Jean Dubuc	0.0
1917	Bernie Boland	0.0
1918	Bernie Boland	0.0
	George Cunningham	0.0
	Rudy Kallio	0.0
2020	Bryan Garcia	0.0

PITCHER WINS ABOVE REPLACEMENT

1901	Roscoe Miller	7.1
1939	Bobo Newsom	7.4
1940	Bobo Newsom	7.6
1944	Dizzy Trout	9.6
1945	Hal Newhouser	11.2

GAMES STARTED

1901	Roscoe Miller	36
1903	George Mullin	36
1904	George Mullin	44
1971	Mickey Lolich	45

COMPLETE GAMES

1901	Roscoe Miller	35
1904	George Mullin	42

STARTER WINS

1913	Jean Dubuc	15
1914	Harry Coveleski	20
1915	Hooks Dauss	21
1934	Tommy Bridges	22
1936	Tommy Bridges	23
1944	Hal Newhouser	25
1946	Hal Newhouser	26
1968	Denny McLain	31

STARTER LOSSES

1913	Jean Dubuc	12
1914	Jean Dubuc	14
1917	Hooks Dauss	14
1920	Hooks Dauss	18
1941	Bobo Newsom	19
1970	Mickey Lolich	19
1974	Mickey Lolich	21
2003	Mike Maroth	21

STARTER WIN PERCENTAGE

1913	Jean Dubuc	.555	15-12
1914	Harry Coveleski	.645	20-11
1915	Hooks Dauss	.656	21-11
1916	Harry Coveleski	.667	20-10
1919	Hooks Dauss	.690	20-9
1924	Earl Whitehill	.708	17-7
1934	Elden Auker	.750	9-3
1940	Bobo Newsom	.833	20-4
	Schoolboy Rowe	.833	15-3
1968	Denny McLain	.838	31-6
2013	Max Scherzer	.875	21-3

SHUTOUTS

1901	Roscoe Miller	3
1902	Win Mercer	4
	Ed Siever	4
1903	George Mullin	6
1904	George Mullin	7
1905	Ed Killian	8
1945	Hal Newhouser	8
1969	Denny McLain	9

QUALITY STARTS

1914	Harry Coveleski	26
1915	Harry Coveleski	27
	Hooks Dauss	27
1916	Harry Coveleski	28
1944	Dizzy Trout	31
1945	Hal Newhouser	31
1968	Denny McLain	35

HIGH QUALITY STARTS

1913	Hooks Dauss	22
1914	Harry Coveleski	22
	Hooks Dauss	22
1915	Hooks Dauss	26
1916	Harry Coveleski	26
1944	Dizzy Trout	30
1945	Hal Newhouser	30
1968	Denny McLain	34

DOMINANT STARTS

1913	Hooks Dauss	06
1914	Harry Coveleski	11
1916	Harry Coveleski	11
1917	Hooks Dauss	11
1943	Dizzy Trout	11
1944	Hal Newhouser	11
1945	Hal Newhouser	15
1946	Hal Newhouser	16

QUALITY START PERCENTAGE

1914	Harry Coveleski	.722
1915	Hooks Dauss	.771
1917	Bill James	.782
1944	Hal Newhouser	.794
1945	Hal Newhouser	.861

HIGH QUALITY START PERCENTAGE

1913	Hooks Dauss	.759
1943	Tommy Bridges	.818
1945	Hal Newhouser	.833

DOMINANT STARTER PERCENTAGE

1913	Hooks Dauss	.241
1914	Harry Coveleski	.306
1915	Hooks Dauss	.314
1917	Hooks Dauss	.355
1918	Bernie Boland	.360
1943	Dizzy Trout	.367
1944	Dizzy Trout	.375
1945	Hal Newhouser	.417
1946	Hal Newhouser	.471

STARTER NO DECISIONS

1914	Harry Coveleski	5
	Hooks Dauss	5
1915	Harry Coveleski	9
1916	Harry Coveleski	10
1921	Dutch Leonard	10
1925	Earl Whitehill	11
1942	Al Benton	11
1961	Don Mossi	12
1964	Hank Aguirre	12
1965	Mickey Lolich	14
1974	Joe Coleman	15

WINS IN RELIEF

1908	Ed Summers	5
1912	Joe Lake	5
1922	Howard Ehmke	7
1923	Bert Cole	7
1924	Ken Holloway	9
1926	Hooks Dauss	11
1974	John Hiller	17

LOSSES IN RELIEF

1908	Ed Siever	1
	George Suggs	1
	Ed Willett	1
1909	Ed Willett	2
1910	Hub Pernoll	2
	Ed Willett	2
1911	Ed Willett	3
1913	Marc Hall	3
1914	Marc Hall	3
1918	Hooks Dauss	3
1920	Hooks Dauss	3
1921	Jim Middleton	8
1933	Chief Hogsett	9
1940	Al Benton	10
1974	John Hiller	14

GAMES IN RELIEF

Year	Pitcher	
1901	Ed Siever	5
1902	George Mullin	5
1903	George Mullin	5
1904	Ed Killian	6
1905	Gene Ford	6
	Frank Kitson	6
1906	John Eubank	12
1909	Ralph Works	12
1910	Ed Willett	12
1911	Ralph Works	15
1913	Fred House	17
1914	Alex Main	20
1915	Bernie Boland	27
1916	Bernie Boland	37
1923	Bert Cole	39
1925	Jess Doyle	42
1933	Chief Hogsett	43
1959	Tom Morgan	45
1961	Hank Aguirre	45
1962	Ron Nischwitz	48
1966	Larry Sherry	55
1970	Tom Timmermann	61
1971	Fred Scherman	68
1984	Willie Hernandez	80
1996	Mike Myers	83
1997	Mike Myers	88
1998	Sean Runyan	88

STARTER CHEAP WINS

Year	Pitcher	
1914	Harry Coveleski	3
	Hooks Dauss	3
1915	Hooks Dauss	3
1916	Hooks Dauss	3
1918	Bernie Boland	3
1919	Hooks Dauss	5
	Howard Ehmke	5
1923	Hooks Dauss	7
1932	Earl Whitehill	7
1983	Dan Petry	7
1986	Jack Morris	7

STARTER TOUGH LOSSES

Year	Pitcher	
1914	Harry Coveleski	7
1915	Harry Coveleski	9
1920	Hooks Dauss	9
1942	Al Benton	9
1943	Hal Newhouser	9
1947	Hal Newhouser	9
1955	Frank Lary	10

RELIEF WIN PERCENTAGE (5 DEC.)

Year	Pitcher		
1908	Ed Summers	1.000	5-0
1916	Bernie Boland	1.000	5-0
1934	Firpo Marberry	1.000	7-0
1939	Bud Thomas	1.000	7-0
1940	Archie McKain	1.000	5-0
1966	Fred Gladding	1.000	5-0
2013	Drew Smyly	1.000	6-0

HOLDS

Year	Pitcher	
1925	Bert Cole	1
	Ed Wells	1
1926	Rip Collins	1
	Lil Stoner	1
1927	George Smith	1
1928	Elam Vangilder	1
1929	Augie Prudhomme	1
1930	Chief Hogsett	1
1931	Tommy Bridges	1
1933	Carl Fischer	1
1934	Red Phillips	1
1935	Elden Auker	1
	Chief Hogsett	1
1936	Chad Kimsey	2
1948	Al Benton	2
1952	Billy Hoeft	2
1953	Dave Madison	2
1954	Al Aber	2
	Ray Herbert	2
1956	Al Aber	4
1959	Pete Burnside	4
	Dave Sisler	4
1966	Larry Sherry	5
1969	John Hiller	5
1980	Pat Underwood	6
1987	Mike Henneman	6
	Eric King	6
1988	Willie Hernandez	8
1990	Paul Gibson	9
1991	Paul Gibson	10
1992	Mike Munoz	16
1993	Bob Macdonald	16
1996	Mike Myers	17
1997	Mike Myers	18
1999	Doug Brocail	23
2006	Joel Zumaya	30
2012	Joaquin Benoit	30

GAMES FINISHED

Year	Pitcher	
1901	Ed Siever	5
1903	George Mullin	5
1904	Ed Killian	6
1905	Gene Ford	6
1906	John Eubank	12
1913	Joe Lake	13
1914	Pug Cavet	13
1915	Bernie Boland	16
1916	Jean Dubuc	16
1917	George Cunningham	25
1923	Bert Cole	26
1925	Jess Doyle	34
1933	Chief Hogsett	34
1940	Al Benton	35
1966	Larry Sherry	39
1970	Tom Timmermann	43
1973	John Hiller	60
1984	Willie Hernandez	68
2011	Jose Valverde	70

SAVES

Year	Pitcher	
1901	Roscoe Miller	1
	Joe Yeager	1
1902	Win Mercer	1
	Roscoe Miller	1
	Ed Siever	1
1903	George Mullin	2
1906	John Eubank	2
	Ed Killian	2
1907	George Mullin	3
1910	Frank Browning	3
1912	Jean Dubuc	3
1914	Hooks Dauss	4
1915	Harry Coveleski	4
	Red Oldham	4
	Bill Steen	4
1916	Hooks Dauss	4
1917	Bernie Boland	6
1921	Jim Middleton	7
1925	Jess Doyle	8
1926	Hooks Dauss	9
1933	Chief Hogsett	9
1940	Al Benton	17
1966	Larry Sherry	20
1970	Tom Timmermann	27
1973	John Hiller	38
2000	Todd Jones	42
2011	Jose Valverde	49

A - Assist. Credited to a player who fields or touches a ball prior to a putout by another player.
AB - At bat. Plate appearances, not including hit by pitch, interference, obstruction, or walks.
AB/HR - At bats per home run. Measures how frequently a batter hits a home run (AB ÷ HR).
AB/RBI - At bats per run batted in. Percentage of a batter's at-bats that result in a run being driven in (AB ÷ RBI).
AB/SO - At bats per strikeout. Measures the number of at bats for every strikeout. (AB ÷ SO).
AL - American League. The American League is one of two major leagues in American professional baseball.
BA - Batting average. Created to measure the success of a batter. This statistic considers only a batter's hits. (H ÷ AB).
BABIP - Batting average on balls in play. Measures how often a ball in play goes for a hit (H – HR) ÷ (AB – SO – HR + SF).
BASES - Bases. Number of bases generated by a player (TB + BB + HBP + SB + SH + SF).
BATR - Batting runs. Runs formula with linear weights adjusted for a batter's home ballpark and era.
BB - Bases on balls or walk. Batter does not swing at four pitches out of the strike zone and is awarded first base.
BB/K - Walk to strikeout ratio. A measurement of a batter's plate discipline and knowledge of the strike zone (BB ÷ SO).
BB/9 - Walks per nine innings. The number of walks issued by a pitcher per nine innings pitched (BB ÷ IP x 9).
BB% - Walk percentage. Percentage of plate appearances that result in a walk due to a batter's plate discipline (BB ÷ PA).
BF - Batters faced. The number of batters who made a plate appearance against a pitcher.
BH - Bunt hit. Bunts that result in a hit, with batter reaching first base.
BK - Balks. Pitcher commits an illegal pitching action on the pitching rubber. Existing runners are awarded the next base.
BOP - Base out percentage. The ratio of bases to outs (BASES ÷ OUTS).
BP - Bases produced. The total number of bases reached by a player (TB + SB + BB).
BPA - Bases produced average. A player's average number of bases produced per games played (BP ÷ GM).
BSR - Base runs. The number of runs a batter creates.

(H + BB - HR) x (1.4 x TB - .6 x H – 3 x HR + .1 x BB) ÷ (1.4 x TB - .6 x H – 3 x HR + .1 x BB) + (AB – H) + HR).

BRA - Batters run average. The number is a result of multiplying a batter's run scoring ability by his slugging (OBP x SLG).
BS - Blown save. Credited to a relief pitcher that enters a game in a save situation and then allows the tying run to score.
CG - Complete games. The number of games when a player is the only pitcher for their team.
CS - Caught stealing. Times a runner is tagged out while attempting to steal a base.
CW - Cheap wins. Starting pitcher is credited with a win when not having qualified for a quality start.
DH - Designated hitter. The designated hitter does not play in the field, and hits in place of a pitcher in the batting order.
DICE - Defense independent component ERA. Player's results separate of team (3 + (3 x (BB + HBP) + 13 x HR – 2 x SO) ÷ IP).
DS - Dominant start. Pitcher throws at least eight innings while allowing no more than one run.
DS% - Dominant start percentage. The percentage of starts that are dominate (DS ÷ GS).
DWAR - Defensive WAR. Wins contributed defensively to a team over a replacement-level player.
E - Error. Given to a defensive player failing to convert a play that was determined an average player would have made.
EBH - Extra base hit. A hit that allows the batter to take more than one base, a double, triple or home run (2B + 3B + HR).
EBHP - Extra base hit percentage. The percentage of a batter's hits that are for extra bases (EBH ÷ H).
EBLH - Extra bases on long hits. The number of extra bases from hitting an extra base hit. (1 x 2B + 2 x 3B + 3 x HR).
ER - Earned runs. The number of runs that did not occur with the aid of an error or passed ball.
ERA - Earned run average. The measure of pitching effectiveness (ER x 9 ÷ IP).
ERA+ - Earned run average +. The pitcher's earned run average adjusted for the ballpark and league average.
ERB - Extrapolated runs basic. A linear weights formula to estimate the number of runs a batter contributes to his team.

(.50 × 1B) + (.72 × 2B) + (1.04 × 3B) + (1.44 × HR) + (.34 × (TBB)) + (.18 × SB) + (–.32 × CS) + (–.096 × (AB – H))

ERP - Estimated runs produced. A method to determine the number of runs that a batter produces for his team.

(2 x (TB + BB + HBP) + H + SB - (.605 x (AB + CS + GIDP - H))) x .16

FA - Fielding average. The percentage of times a batted or thrown ball is handled properly. (PO + A ÷ PO + A + E).
FIP - Fielding independent pitching. Focuses primarily on events within a pitcher's control and outs which is not.
GF - Games finished. The number of games that a reliever was the last pitcher for a team.
GIDP - Ground into double play. The number of ground balls hit that result in a double play by the defense.
GIR - Games in relief. The number of games a pitcher enters the game as a reliever.
GM - Games. The number of games a player has participated in.
GPA - Gross production average. The ability to get on base and hit for power with relative weights. (OBP x 1.8 + SLG) ÷ 4.
GRSL - Grand slam home runs. Home run recorded by a batter with three runners on base.
GS - Games started. The number of games started by a pitcher.
H - Hit. Reaching base because of a batted fair ball without the aid of a defensive error.
HA - Hits allowed. The total number of hits allowed by a pitcher.
HBP - Hit by pitch. Batter is hit by a pitch and awarded first base.
HLD - Hold. Pitcher enters in a save situation, records at least one out, does not surrender lead and did not finish game.

HQS - High quality start. Pitcher throws at t seven innings while allowing no more than three earned runs.
HQS% - High quality start percentage. The number of high-quality starts divided by the number of games started.
HR - Home runs or homers. Hits on which the batter successfully touches all four bases, without the aid of a fielding error.
HRA - Home run average. The number of home runs for a player playing a full schedule with 600 at bats. (HR ÷ AB x 600).
HRHM - Home runs at home. The number of home runs hit by a player in his home ballpark.
HR% - Home run percentage. The number of home runs hit per every 100 times at bat (HR ÷ AB x 100).
HRR - Home run ratio. Measures how frequently a player hits a home run (AB ÷ HR).
HRRD - Home runs on the road. The number of home runs hit by a player during away games played on the road.
HRLHH - Home runs by lefthanded hitters. The number of home runs by a batter hitting lefthanded.
HRLHP - Home runs versus lefthanded pitchers. The number of home runs hit by a player against a lefthanded pitcher.
HRRHH - Home runs by righthanded hitters. The number of home runs hit by a batter hitting righthanded.
HRRHP - Home runs versus righthanded pitchers. The number of home runs hit by a batter facing a righthanded pitcher.
HRSH - Home runs by switch hitters. The number of home runs by a batter hitting lefthanded and righthanded.
HS - Hitting streak. The number of consecutive games in which a player appears and gets at least one base hit.
H/9 - Hits per nine innings. The average number of hits a pitcher allows for every nine innings pitched. (H ÷ IP x 9).
HR/9 - Home runs per nine. The number of home runs allowed by a pitcher for every nine innings pitched. (HR ÷ IP x 9).
HSTC - Hitting sabermetric triple crown. Player leading in total bases, runs created and on-base percentage.
HTC - Hitting triple crown. Player leading in the categories of batting average, home runs and runs batted in.
IBB - Intentional walk. The pitcher intentionally throws ball four, allowing the batter to walk and reach first base.
IH - Infield hit. The batter reaches first base safely when a ground ball does not leave the infield or shallow outfield.
IP - Innings pitched. The number of complete or partial innings thrown by a pitcher.
ISO - Isolated power. A measure of a hitter's raw power and indicates how often a player hits for extra bases (SLG – BA).
IPHR - Inside the park home run. Hits a batter touches all four bases, without the aid of an error or ball hit over the fence.
IPP - In play percentage. Percentage of plate appearances resulting in the ball being put into play. (AB - SO - HR + SF ÷ PA).
L - Losses. Charged to the pitcher that allows the winning run to score during a loss to the opposing team.
LH - Lefthanded. Batter that hits lefthanded or a pitcher that throws with their left hand.
LIR - Losses in relief. The number of losses credited to a relief pitcher.
LOB - Left on base. The number of runners that remain on a base at the end of an inning.
LOB% - Left on base percentage. Percentage of runners that a pitcher strands on base at the end of an inning. (H + BB + HBP – R) ÷ (H + BB + HBP – (1.4 x HR)).
MEH - Most effective hitter. The most proficient hitter taking into consideration OBP, SLG, OPS, OPS+, TA, BOP, GPA, BA, BABIP, SECA, IP%, RS%, TBA and BPA.
MEP - Most effective pitcher. The most proficient pitcher taking into consideration W%, TRA, ERA, ERA+, FIP, DICE, WHIP, H/9, HR/9, SO/9, SO/BB, R/9, and LOB%.
MVP - Most Valuable Player. The individual voted on to have been the best player during a season or playoff series.
ND - No decision. The starting pitcher leaves a game without recording either a win or a loss.
NL - National League. The oldest major-league professional baseball organization in the United States.
NP - Number of pitches. The number of pitches a batter faces or the number of pitches thrown by a pitcher.
OBP - On base percentage. The number of times a batter reaches base (H + BB + HBP) divided by (AB + BB + HBP + SF).
OPS - On base percentage plus slugging percentage. On-base percentage plus slugging average.
OPS+ - On base percentage plus slugging percentage +. On-base plus slugging number adjusted for park and league.
OUTS - Outs. The number of outs made by a player ((AB – H) + GIDP + SF + SH + CS)
OWAR - Offensive WAR. The number of wins a hitter contributes offensively to his team over a replacement-level player.
PA - Plate appearance. Every time a player enters the batter's box, with a result between the hitter and pitcher obtained.
PB - Passed ball. Credited to a catcher that is unable to hold onto a pitched ball.
PE - Pythagorean expectation. The team's expected winning percentage based upon runs scored and runs allowed.
PH - Pinch hits. Number of hits by a batter hitting in place for another.
PHAB - Pinch hit at bats. Number of at bats by a batter hitting in place for another.
PHBA - Pinch hit batting average. The measure of how successful a batter is when pinch-hitting. (PH ÷ PHAB).
PHEBH - Percentage of hits that are extra base hits. (EBH ÷ H).
PHHR - Pinch hit home run. Player with a home run while batting in place of another.
PHRBI - Pinch hit runs batted in. Runs batted in recorded by a batter hitting as a pinch-hitter.
PK - Pickoff. Pitcher throws to a fielder between pitches in an attempt for the fielder to tag a runner off base for an out.
PO - Putout. Credited to a defensive player who records an out.
POY - Player of the Year. Player of the Year chosen by popular vote rather than a specific performance statistical formula.
PSN - Power speed number. Combines home run and stolen base numbers. (2 x (HR x SB) ÷ (HR + SB)).
PSTC - Pitching sabermetric triple crown. Pitcher leading in the categories of ERA+, FIP and DICE).
PTC - Pitching triple crown. Pitcher who leads in the categories of wins, earned run average and strikeouts.

QS - Quality Start. Pitcher throws at least six innings while allowing three or less earned runs.
QS% - Quality Start Percentage. The percentage of games started that are quality starts (QS ÷ GS).
QTC - Quadruple Triple Crown. A player who leads all hitters in hits, batting average, home runs and runs batted in.
R - Runs. Number of times a player scores a run by crossing home plate.
RBI - Runs Batted In. Number of runners driven in by a batter, except those scoring due to a double play or error.
RC - Runs Created. Measures how many runs a player has contributed to a team (H + BB) x TB ÷ (AB + BB).
RC/27 - Runs Created Per 27 Outs. The number of runs created per a team's 27 outs in a game (RC ÷ 27).
RD - Relief Decisions. A decision earned by a relief pitcher.
RH - Righthanded. Player who either bats righthanded or throws righthanded.
ROE - Reached on Error. The batter reaches base because of an error committed by the defense.
R/9 - Runs Per Nine. The number of runs allowed multiplied by nine and divided by innings pitched.
RP - Runs Produced. Measures how many runs a player has contributed.
RS% - Run Scoring Percentage. The percentage of times a runner on base scores (R – HR) ÷ (H + HBP + BB – HR)
RW% - Relief Win Percentage. The percentage of wins for decisions earned as a reliever (RW ÷ RD).
SB - Stolen base. The runner advances a base during a pitch, pickoff attempt or when catcher throws ball back to pitcher.
SBP - Stolen Base Percentage. Measures a player's rate of success in stealing bases. (SB ÷ (SB + CS)).
SBRC - Stolen Base Runs Created. Stolen base version of runs created (H + BB – CS) x (TB + (.55 x SB)) ÷ AB + BB).
SECA - Secondary Average. The bases gained considering power, plate discipline and speed. (BB + TB – H + SB – CS ÷ AB).
SF - Sacrifice Fly. Fly ball caught for an out by the defense, with a runner at third base scoring on the play.
SH - Sacrifice Hit. Player bunts the pitch and is out on the play, with a runner advancing to the next base.
SHO - Shutout. Pitcher throws a complete game without allowing a run.
SL - Starter Losses. Losses credited to the starting pitcher.
SLG - Slugging Percentage. Measures batting productivity with an average of bases a player achieves per at bat (TB ÷ AB).
SO - Strikeout. Batter is out with a third strike either on a swing and miss or taking a pitch that is a called strike.
SO% - Strikeout Percentage. The percentage of at bats that result in a strikeout (SO ÷ PA).
SOR - Strikeout Ratio. The ratio of at bats that result in a strikeout. (SO ÷ AB)
SO/BB - Strikeout to Walk Ratio. A measurement of a pitcher's ability to control pitches (SO ÷ BB).
SV - Saves. Credited to last pitcher of winning team if he does not get the win, allows tying run, his team led by three or less runs when entering game, with potential tying run on base, at bat, on deck or pitches at least three innings.
SW - Starter Wins. The number of wins earned as a starting pitcher.
SW% - Starter Win Percentage. The pitcher's percentage of wins earned in games started (SW ÷ GS).
SO/9 - Strikeouts Per Nine Innings. The number of strikeouts a player averages for every nine innings pitched (SO ÷ IP x 9).
TA - Total average. Measures a batter's overall offensive contributions. (TB + HBP + BB + SB) ÷ (AB - H + CS + GIDP)
TB - Total bases. The number of bases a player has gained with hits. (1B + 2 x 2B + 3 x 3B + 4 x HR).
TBA - Total base average. The average of total bases produced by a hitter per game (TB ÷ GM)
TC - Total chances. The number of plays that a defensive player has participated in. (PO + A + E).
QHTC - Quadruple Hitting Triple Crown. Player leading in hits, batting average, home runs and runs batted in.
TL - Starter Tough Losses. Starter credited with a loss while having pitched a quality start.
TOB - Times on base. The cumulative total number of times a batter has reached base. (H + BB + HBP).
TP - Triple play. The act of a defense making three outs during the same continuous play.
TPL - Total plays. The number of times a defense properly handles a batted or thrown ball. (A + PO).
TRC - Technical Runs Created. Technical version of runs created that accounts for all basic offensive statistics. (H + BB – CS + HBP – GIDP) x (TB + (.26 x (BB – IBB + HBP)) + (.52 x (SH + SF + SB))) ÷ (AB + BB + HBP + SH + SF).
TS - Total Sacrifices. The players total number of sacrifice hits and sacrifice flies. (SH + SF).
W - Wins. The number of games a player was pitching when their team took the lead and went on to win.
W/SO - Walks to Strikeouts Ratio. The measure of a batter's plate discipline and knowledge of strike zone. (BB ÷ SO).
WAR - Wins Above Replacement. The number of wins a player contributes to their team over a replacement-level player.
WHIP - Walks Plus Hits Per Inning Pitched. Average number of walks and hits allowed by a pitcher per inning.
WIR - Wins in Relief. The number of wins credited to a relief pitcher.
WOBA - Weighted on Base Average. Measures a batter's offensive value, based upon pertinent offensive events. (0.73 x BB + 0.76 x HBP + 0.93 x 1B + 1.3 x 2B + 1.63 x 3B + 2.07 x HR) ÷ PA.
WP - Wild Pitch. A pitcher throws a pitch too high, low, or wide for the catcher to field, allowing any runners to advance.
WRC - Weighted runs created. Measures a player's offensive value in terms of runs.
WRC+ - Weighted runs created +. Represents a batter's offensive value by adjusting WRC for park factors.
W% - Win Percentage. The percentage of games a pitcher or teams wins of their total decisions. (W ÷ (W + L)).
1B - Single. A batter hits a fair ball and reaches first base safely, except when reaching because of a fielder's choice.
2B - Double. Batter reaches second base after hitting a pitch, without the aid of a defensive error or a fielder's choice.
3B - Triple. The batter reaches third base after hitting a ball, without the benefit of a defensive error or fielder's choice.